standard catalog of
BUICK
1903-2000

Wouldn't you really rather have a Buick?

Edited by Ron Kowalke

Published by

700 E. State Street • Iola, WI 54990-0001
Telephone: 715/445-2214

Please call or write for our free catalog.
Our toll-free number to place an order or obtain a free catalog is 800-258-0929
or please use our regular business telephone 715-445-2214
for editorial comment and further information.

Library of Congress Catalog Number: 91-61302
ISBN: 0-87341-576-0

Printed in the United States of America

CONTENTS

CATALOG STAFF

Editor: Ron Kowalke

Cover/color section artist: Jon Stein

Pagination artist: Ethel Thulien

FOREWORD

Traditionally, the concept behind Krause Publications' Standard Catalog series is to compile massive amounts of information about vehicles and present it in a standardized format that the hobbyist, collector or professional dealer can use to answer commonly asked questions.

Those questions include: What year, make and model is the vehicle? What did it sell for when new? How rare is it? What is special about it? Some answers are provided by photos while others can be found in the fact-filled text.

Chester L. Krause, retired founder of Krause Publications, is responsible for the overall concept of creating the Standard Catalog series covering American automobiles. David V. Brownell undertook preliminary work on the concept while serving as editor of *Old Cars Weekly* in the 1970s. Then editor John A. Gunnell assumed the project in 1978. The first Standard Catalog, covering postwar models (1946-1975), was published in 1982, while Beverly Rae Kimes and Henry Austin Clark, Jr. continued their work on the *Standard Catalog of American Cars 1805-1942*, which was published in 1985. In 1987, the second edition of SCAC 1946-1975 was published followed a year later by the second edition of SCAC 1805-1942. Also in 1988, James M. Flammang authored the *Standard Catalog of American Cars 1976-1986*, which went into its second edition in 1990. A third edition of SCAC 1946-1975 appeared in 1992. Ron Kowalke took over the editing of the Standard Catalog series in 1995, and a third edition of SCAC 1805-1942 was published in 1996 while a fourth edition of SCAC 1946-1975 was printed in 1997. Flammang and Kowalke co-authored SCAC 1976-1999, the third edition of that catalog, which was published in late-1999.

The Standard Catalog series devoted to American cars provides a wealth of detailed information the automobile enthusiasts will not find from any other publishing house. The data compiled encompasses a physical description, a list of known equipment and original specifications, technical data, historical footnotes and appraisal of each car's (through 1992 models) current value.

In each catalog, all compilations were made by an experienced editorial team consisting of the automotive staff of Krause Publications and numerous contributors who are recognized experts on a certain marque or specific area of automotive history. A major benefit of combining teamwork with expertise has been the gathering of many significant facts about each model.

No claims are made about the catalogs being history textbooks or encyclopedias. Nor are they repair manuals or "bibles" for motor vehicle enthusiasts. They are, rather, intended as a contribution to the pursuit of greater knowledge of the many wonderful automobiles built in the United States since 1805. They are much larger in size, broader in scope and more deluxe in format than any previously published collectors' guides, buyers' digests or pricing guides.

With this second edition of *Standard Catalog of Buick*, Krause Publications continues the venture into researching a single automotive marque that has been responsible for millions of production vehicles since the early-1900s. A special thank you goes out to the authors of and contributors to the three volumes of Standard Catalogs of American Cars for providing much of the material herein. For it is through their research and editing effort that Krause Publications produced this *Standard Catalog of Buick 1903-2000* with an assurance that the information combined herein from those three catalogs is accurate and well-researched.

Should anyone have access to expanded information that could improve this catalog, please contact the automotive books department in care of: Krause Publications, Standard Catalog of Buick, 700 E. State St., Iola, WI 54990.

INTRODUCTION

This updated, second edition of *Standard Catalog of Buick 1903-2000* is a compilation of photos, specification tables for all Buick models and current value listings for Buick models through 1992. As such, the introduction to this catalog should recognize the valued contributions of writers and historians whose work is included in its pages.

Realizing that many automotive hobbyists have a preference for a specific brand (marque) of car or various marques built by a single corporation, it seemed logical that a catalog formatted along those lines would be appealing. Therefore, the editors of Krause Publications were asked to handle the organization of such a catalog from material existing within the Krause archives.

The primary source of photographs showing the automobiles of Buick Motor Division was the *Old Cars Weekly* photo archive, a vast collection containing over 20,000 images of vehicles.

This archive includes automakers' publicity stills, photos obtained from specialized vendors such as Applegate & Applegate, photographs taken at hobby events by the *Old Cars Weekly* staff and advertisements gleaned from periodicals beginning in the early 1900s. Photos were also obtained from the Buick Motor Division of General Motors. In addition, where photographs were unavailable, illustrations from sales and technical literature and advertisements were used to show what the cars looked like when new.

The main section of this catalog is the lengthy and detailed specification tables that present, in standardized format, styling and engineering features of virtually all of Buick's models. Engine sizes, horsepower ratings, wheelbase and overall dimensions and tire sizes are a few of the measurements found in this catalog.

A special thank you for the gathering of these facts and figures go to the authors of three other catalogs previously published by Krause Publications: *Standard Catalog of American Cars 1805-1942* by Beverly Rae Kimes and Henry Austin Clark, Jr.; *Standard Catalog of American Cars 1946-1975* edited by John A. Gunnell and Ron Kowalke; and *Standard Catalog of American Cars 1976-1999* by James M. Flammang and Ron Kowalke.

The final element that comes into use in this catalog is the presentation of current values for all Buick models from 1903 to 1992. The source for these values is the *Old Cars Price Guide*, which is compiled as a bimonthly magazine edited by Ken Buttolph and Ron Kowalke. The prices are formatted according to Krause Publications' time-tested 1-6 condition scale, so that Buick enthusiasts who use this catalog can determine their cars' values in a variety of conditions.

ABBREVIATIONS

A/C .... Air conditioning
A.L.A.M. ....Assoc. of Licensed Automobile Mfgs.
Adj. .... Adjustable
Aero. .... Fastback
AM, FM, AM/FM .... Radio types
Amp. .... Amperes
Approx. .... Approximate
Auto. .... Automatic
Auxil. .... Auxiliary
Avail. .... Available
Avg. .... Average
BxS .... Bore x Stroke
Base .... Base (usually lowest-priced) model
Bbl. .... Barrel (carburetor)
B.H.P. .... Brake horsepower
BSW .... Black sidewall (tire)
Brk/Brkwd/Brkwood .... Brookwood
Brdcl. .... Broadcloth
Bus. .... Business (i.e. Business Coupe)
C-A .... Carryall
C.C. .... Close-coupled
Cabr. .... Cabriolet
Carb. .... Carburetor
Capr. .... Caprice
Cass. .... Cassette (tape player)
Cav. .... Cavalier
CB .... Citizens Band (radio)
Celeb. .... Celebrity
CEO .... Chief Executive Officer
CFI .... Cross Fire (fuel) Injection
Chvt. .... Chevette
C.I.D. .... Cubic inch displacement
Cit. .... Citation
Clb .... Club (Club Coupe)
Clth. .... Cloth-covered roof
Col. .... Colonnade (coupe body style)
Col. .... Column (shift)
Conv/Conv. .... Convertible
Conv. Sed. .... Convertible Sedan
Corp Limo .... Corporate Limousine
Cpe .... Coupe
Cpe P.U. .... Coupe Pickup
C.R. .... Compression ratio
Crsr. .... Cruiser
Cu. In. .... Cubic Inch (displacement)
Cust. .... Custom
Cyl. .... Cylinder
DeL. .... DeLuxe
DFRS .... Dual facing rear seats
Dia. .... Diameter
Disp. .... Displacement
Dr. .... Door
Ea. .... Each
E.D. .... Enclosed Drive
E.F.I. .... Electronic Fuel Injection
E.W.B. .... Extended Wheelbase
Eight. .... Eight-cylinder engine
8-tr. .... Eight-track
Encl. .... Enclosed
EPA .... Environmental Protection Agency
Equip. .... Equipment
Est. Wag. .... Estate Wagon
Exc. .... Except
Exec. .... Executive
F .... Forward (3F - 3 forward speeds)
F.W.D. .... Four-wheel drive

Fam. .... Family
Fml. .... Formal
"Four" .... Four-cylinder engine
4WD .... Four-wheel drive
4-dr. .... Four-door
4-spd. .... Four-speed (transmission)
4V .... Four-barrel carburetor
FP .... Factory Price
Frsm. .... Foursome
Frt. .... Front
FsBk .... Fastback
Ft. .... Foot/feet
FWD .... Front wheel drive
G.B. .... Greenbrier
GBR .... Glass-belted radial (tire)
Gal. .... Gallon
GM .... General Motors (Corporation)
GT .... Gran Turismo
G.R. .... Gear Ratio
H .... Height
H.B. .... Hatchback
H.D. .... Heavy Duty
HEI .... High Energy Ignition
H.O. .... High-output
H.P. .... Horsepower
HT/HT Hdtp. .... Hardtop
Hr. .... Hour
Hwg. .... Highway
I. .... Inline
I.D. .... Identification
Imp. .... Impala
In. .... Inches
Incl. .... Included or Including
Int. .... Interior
King/Kingwd. .... Kingswood
Lan .... Landau (coupe body style)
Lb. or Lbs. .... Pound-feet (torque)
LH .... Left hand
Lift. .... Liftback (body style)
Limo .... Limousine
LPO .... Limited production option
Ltd. .... Limited
Lthr. Trm. .... Leather Trim
L.W.B. .... Long Wheelbase
Mag. .... Wheel style
Mast. .... Master
Max. .... Maximum
MFI .... Multi-port Fuel Injection
M.M. .... Millimeters
Monte. .... Monte Carlo
MPG .... Miles per gallon
MPH .... Miles per hour
Mstr. .... Master
N/A .... Not available (or not applicable)
NC .... No charge
N.H.P. .... Net horsepower
No. .... Number
Notch or N.B. .... Notchback
OHC .... Overhead cam (engine)
OHV .... Overhead valve (engine)
O.L. .... Overall length
OPEC ....Organization of Petroleum Exporting Countries
Opt. .... Optional
OSRV .... Outside rear view
O.W. or O/W. .... Opera window
OWL .... Outline White Letter (tire)

Oz. .... Ounce
P .... Passenger
Park/Parkwd .... Parkwood
PFI .... Port fuel injection
Phae. .... Phaeton
Pkg. .... Package (e.g. option pkg)
Prod. .... Production
Pwr. .... Power
R .... Reverse
RBL .... Raised black letter (tire)
Rbt. .... Runabout
Rds. .... Roadster
Reg. .... Regular
Remote .... Remote control
Req. .... Requires
RH .... Right-hand drive
Roch. .... Rochester (carburetor)
R.P.M. .... Revolutions per minute
RPO .... Regular production option
R.S. or R/S .... Rumbleseat
RV .... Recreational vehicle
RVL .... Raised white letter (tire)
S .... Gm lowtrim model designation
S.A.E. .... Society of Automotive Engineers
SBR .... Steel-belted radials
Sed. .... Sedan
SFI .... Sequential fuel injection
"Six" .... Six-cylinder engine
S.M. .... Side Mount
Spd. .... Speed
Spec. .... Special
Spt. .... Sport
Sq. In. .... Square inch
SR .... Sunroof
SS .... Super Sport
Sta. Wag. .... Station wagon
Std. .... Standard
Sub. .... Suburban
S.W.B. .... Short Wheelbase
Tach. .... Tachometer
Tax. .... Taxable (horsepower)
TBI .... Throttle body (fuel) injection
Temp. .... Temperature
THM .... Turbo Hydramatic (transmission)
3S .... Three-seat
Trans. .... Transmission
Trk. .... Trunk
2-Dr. .... Two-door
2 V. .... Two-barrel (carburetor)
2WD .... Two-wheel drive
Univ. .... Universal
Utl. .... Utility
V. .... Venturi (carburetor)
V-6, V-8 .... Vee-type engine
VIN .... Vehicle Identification Number
W .... With
W/O .... Without
Wag. .... Wagon
w (2w) .... Window (two window)
W.B. .... Wheelbase
Woodie .... Wood-bodied car
WLT .... White-lettered tire
WSW .... White sidewall (tire)
W.W. .... Whitewalls
W. Whl. .... Wire wheel

PHOTO CREDITS

Whenever possible, throughout the Catalog, we have strived to picture all cars with photographs that show them in their most original form. All photos gathered from reliable outside sources have an alphabetical code following the caption which indicates the photo source. An explanation of these codes is given below. Additional photos from Krause Publications file are marked accordingly. With special thanks to the editors of the previous *Standard Catalogs of American Cars* for their original research and obtaining many of these photos of Chevrolet over the years.

(AA)   Applegate & Applegate
(CP)   Crestline Publishing
(GM)   General Motors
(HAC)   Henry Austin Clark, Jr.
(HFM)   Henry Ford Museum
(IMSC)   Indianapolis Motor Speedway Corporation

(JAC)   John A. Conde
(JG)   John Gunnell
(NAHC)   National Automotive History Collection
(OCW)   Old Cars Weekly
(PH)   Phil Hall
(WLB)   William L. Bailey

BODY STYLES

Body style designations describe the shape and character of an automobile. In earlier years automakers exhibited great imagination in coining words to name their products. This led to names that were not totally accurate. Many of those **'car words'** were taken from other fields: mythology, carriage building, architecture, railroading, and so on. Therefore, there was no 'correct' automotive meaning other than that brought about through actual use. Inconsistences have persisted into the recent period, though some of the imaginative terms of past eras have faded away. One manufacturer's 'sedan' might resemble another's 'coupe.' Some automakers have persisted in describing a model by a word different from common usage, such as Ford's label for Mustang as a 'sedan.' Following the demise of the true pillarless hardtop (two- and four-door) in the mid-1970s, various manufacturers continued to use the term 'hardtop' to describe their offerings, even though a 'B' pillar was part of the newer car's structure and the front door glass may not always have been frameless. Some took on the description 'pillared hardtop' or 'thin pillar hardtop' to define what observers might otherwise consider, essentially, a sedan. Descriptions in this catalog generally follow the manufacturers' choice of words, except when they conflict strongly with accepted usage.

One specific example of inconsistency is worth noting: the description of many hatchback models as 'three-door' and 'five-door,' even though that extra 'door' is not an entryway for people. While the 1976-1986 domestic era offered no real phaetons or roadsters in the earlier senses of the words, those designations continue to turn up now and then, too.

TWO-DOOR (CLUB) COUPE: The Club Coupe designation seems to come from club car, describing the lounge (or parlor car) in a railroad train. The early postwar club coupe combined a shorter-than-sedan body structure with the convenience of a full back seat, unlike the single-seat business coupe. That name has been used less frequently in the 1976-86 period, as most notchback two-door models (with trunk rather than hatch) have been referred to as just 'coupes.' Moreover, the distinction between two-door coupes and two-door sedans has grown fuzzy.

TWO-DOOR SEDAN: The term sedan originally described a conveyance seen only in movies today: a wheelless vehicle for one person, borne on poles by two men, one ahead and one behind. Automakers pirated the word and applied it to cars with a permanent top, seating four to seven (including driver) in a single compartment. The two-door sedan of recent times has sometimes been called a pillared coupe, or plain coupe, depending on the manufacturer's whim. On the other hand, some cars commonly referred to as coupes carry the sedan designation on factory documents.

TWO-DOOR (THREE-DOOR) HATCHBACK COUPE: Originally a small opening in the deck of a sailing ship, the term 'hatch' was later applied to airplane doors and to passenger cars with rear liftgates. Various models appeared in the early 1950s, but weather-tightness was a problem. The concept emerged again in the early 1970s, when fuel economy factors began to signal the trend toward compact cars. Technology had remedied the sealing difficulties. By the 1980s, most manufacturers produced one or more hatchback models, though the question of whether to call them 'two-door' or 'three-door' never was resolved. Their main common feature was the lack of a separate trunk. 'Liftback' coupes may have had a different rear-end shape, but the two terms often described essentially the same vehicle.

TWO-DOOR FASTBACK: By definition, a fastback is any automobile with a long, moderately curving, downward slope to the rear of the roof. This body style relates to an interest in streamlining and aerodynamics and has gone in and out of fashion at various times. Some (Mustangs for one) have grown quite popular. Others have tended to turn customers off. Certain fastbacks are, technically, two-door sedans or pillared coupes. Four-door fastbacks have also been produced. Many of these (such as Buick's late 1970s four-door Century sedan) lacked sales appeal. Fastbacks may or may not have a rear-opening hatch.

TWO-DOOR HARDTOP: The term hardtop, as used for postwar cars up to the mid-1970s, describes an automobile styled to resemble a convertible, but with a rigid metal (or fiberglass) top. In a production sense, this body style evolved after World War II, first called 'hardtop convertible.' Other generic names have included sports coupe, hardtop coupe or pillarless coupe. In the face of proposed rollover standards, nearly all automakers turned away from the pillarless design to a pillared version by 1976-77.

COLONNADE HARDTOP: In architecture, the term colonnade describes a series of columns, set at regular intervals, usually supporting an entablature, roof or series of arches. To meet Federal rollover standards in 1974 (standards that never emerged), General Motors introduced two- and four-door pillared body types with arch-like quarter windows and sandwich type roof construction. They looked like a cross between true hardtops and miniature limousines. Both styles proved popular (especially the coupe with louvered coach windows and canopy top) and the term colonnade was applied. As their 'true' hardtops disappeared, other manufacturers produced similar bodies with a variety of quarter-window shapes and sizes. These were known by such terms as hardtop coupe, pillared hardtop or opera-window coupe.

FORMAL HARDTOP: The hardtop roofline was a long-lasting fashion hit of the postwar car era. The word 'formal' can be applied to things that are stiffly conservative and follow the established rule. The limousine, being the popular choice of conservative buyers who belonged to the Establishment, was looked upon as a formal motorcar. So when designers combined the lines of these two body styles, the result was the Formal Hardtop. This style has been marketed with two or four doors, canopy and vinyl roofs (full or partial) and conventional or opera-type windows, under various trade names. The distinction between a formal hardtop and plain pillared-hardtop coupe (see above) hasn't always followed a strict rule.

CONVERTIBLE: To Depression-era buyers, a convertible was a car with a fixed-position windshield and folding top that, when raised, displayed the lines of a coupe. Buyers in the postwar period expected a convertible to have roll-up windows, too. Yet the definition of the word includes no such qualifications. It states only that such a car should have a lowerable or removable top. American convertibles became extinct by 1976, except for Cadillac's Eldorado, then in its final season. In 1982, though, Chrysler brought out a LeBaron ragtop; Dodge a 400; and several other companies followed it a year or two later.

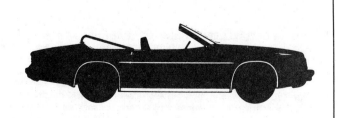

ROADSTER: This term derives from equestrian vocabulary where it was applied to a horse used for riding on the roads. Old dictionaries define the roadster as an open-type car designed for use on *ordinary* roads, with a single seat for two persons and, often, a rumbleseat as well. Hobbyists associate folding windshields and side curtains (rather than roll-up windows) with roadsters, although such qualifications stem from usage, not definition of term. Most recent roadsters are either sports cars, small alternative-type vehicles or replicas of early models.

RUNABOUT: By definition, a runabout is the equivalent of a roadster. The term was used by carriage makers and has been applied in the past to light, open cars on which a top is unavailable or totally an add-on option. None of this explains its use by Ford on certain Pinto models. Other than this inaccurate usage, recent runabouts are found mainly in the alternative vehicle field, including certain electric-powered models.

FOUR-DOOR SEDAN: If you took the wheels off a car, mounted it on poles and hired two weightlifters (one in front and one in back) to carry you around in it, you'd have a true sedan. Since this idea isn't very practical, it's better to use the term for an automobile with a permanent top (affixed by solid pillars) that seats four or more persons, including the driver, on two full-width seats.

FOUR-DOOR HARDTOP: This is a four-door car styled to resemble a convertible, but having a rigid top of metal or fiberglass. Buick introduced a totally pillarless design in 1955. A year later most automakers offered equivalent bodies. Four-door hardtops have also been labeled sports sedans and hardtop sedans. By 1976, potential rollover standards and waning popularity had taken their toll. Only a few makes still produced a four-door hardtop and those disappeared soon thereafter.

FOUR-DOOR PILLARED HARDTOP: Once the 'true' four-door hardtop began to fade away, manufacturers needed another name for their luxury four-doors. Many were styled to look almost like the former pillarless models, with thin or unobtrusive pillars between the doors. Some, in fact, were called 'thin-pillar hardtops.' The distinction between certain pillared hardtops and ordinary (presumably humdrum) sedans occasionally grew hazy.

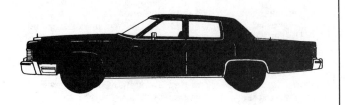

FOUR-DOOR (FIVE-DOOR) HATCHBACK: Essentially unknown among domestic models in the mid-1970s, the four-door hatchback became a popular model as cars grew smaller and front-wheel-drive versions appeared. Styling was similar to the orignal two-door hatchback, except for — obviously — two more doors. Luggage was carried in the back of the car itself, loaded through the hatch opening, not in a separate trunk.

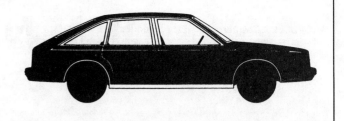

LIMOUSINE: This word's literal meaning is 'a cloak.' In France, Limousine means any passenger vehicle. An early dictionary defined limousine as an auto with a permanently enclosed compartment for 3-5, with a roof projecting over a front driver's seat. However, modern dictionaries drop the separate compartment idea and refer to limousines as large luxury autos, often chauffeur-driven. Some have a movable division window between the driver and passenger compartments, but that isn't a requirement.

TWO-DOOR STATION WAGON: Originally defined as a car with an enclosed wooden body of paneled design (with several rows of folding or removable seats behind the driver), the station wagon became a different and much more popular type of vehicle in the postwar years. A recent dictionary states that such models have a larger interior than sedans of the line and seats that can be readily lifted out, or folded down, to facilitate light trucking. In addition, there's usually a tailgate, but no separate luggage compartment. The two-door wagon often has sliding or flip-out rear side windows.

FOUR-DOOR STATION WAGON: Since functionality and adaptability are advantages of station wagons, four-door versions have traditionally been sales leaders. At least they were until cars began to grow smaller. This style usually has lowerable windows in all four doors and fixed rear side glass. The term 'suburban' was almost synonymous with station wagon at one time, but is now more commonly applied to light trucks with similar styling. Station wagons have had many trade names, such as Country Squire (Ford) and Sport Suburban (Plymouth). Quite a few have retained simulated wood paneling, keeping alive the wagon's origin as a wood-bodied vehicle.

LIFTBACK STATION WAGON: Small cars came in station wagon form too. The idea was the same as bigger versions, but the conventional tailgate was replaced by a single lift-up hatch. For obvious reasons, compact and subcompact wagons had only two seats instead of the three that had been available in many full-size models.

DIMENSIONS

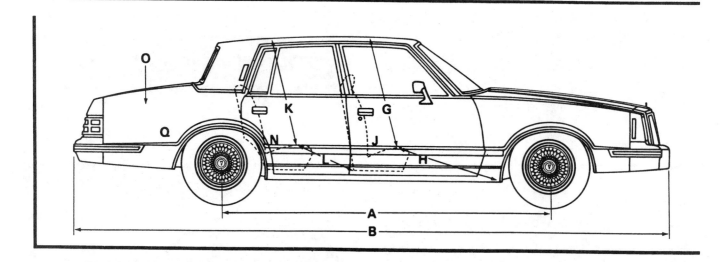

DIMENSIONS

Exterior:
A Wheelbase
B Overall length
C Width
D Overall height
E Tread, front
F Tread, rear

Interior—front:
G Headroom
H Legroom
I Shoulder room
J Hip room

Interior—rear:
K Headroom
L Legroom
M Shoulder room
N Hip room
O Trunk capacity (liters/cu. ft.)
P Cargo index volume (liters/cu. ft.)
Q Fuel tank capacity (liters/gallons)

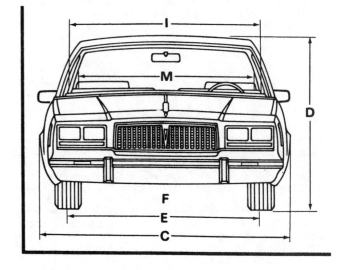

BUICK
1903-1942

Buick's chief engineer, Walter L. Marr (left) and Thomas D. Buick, son of company founder David Dunbar Buick, pictured in the first Flint, Michigan-produced Buick as it ended its successful Flint-Detroit round trip in July 1904. OCW

Buick Data Compilation
by Robert C. Ackerson

BUICK — Detroit, Michigan — (1903)/Flint, Michigan — (1904-1942 et. seq.) —That the man behind the first Buick was also the man who developed a method of affixing porcelain to cast iron and thus gave the world the white bathtub is a piece of historical trivia that has become part of the popular saga of the automobile. Beyond that, however, little is known about David Dunbar Buick.

In 1899, finding the mechanical age more challenging than bathtubs, Buick sold off his plumbing business to the Standard Sanitary Manufacturing Company and organized the Buick Auto-Vim and Power Company to produce gasoline engines for farm and marine use, this venture reorganized in 1902 to Buick Manufacturing Company. Joining Buick's venture were Walter Marr (beginning an on-again, off-again relationship with Buick) and Eugene Richard (who worked for Olds prior to its historic fire).

Among these three men, the famous Buick valve-in-head engine was developed, and the first Buick car was built and tested. Putting up the money was Detroit sheet-metal manufacturer Benjamin Briscoe, who soon tired of doing only that. Despite Briscoe's yet-again reorganization of the Buick venture into the Buick Motor Company in the spring of 1903, all he had to show thus far for his continuing infusions of cash was a factory facility and no sign that production was about to commence.

Meanwhile, he had met another Olds veteran named Jonathan D. Maxwell who did not seem quite so tentative about the production side of the automobile industry. Divesting himself of David Dunbar Buick was next on Briscoe's agenda, and he did this neatly by unloading the whole Buick business to James H. Whiting of Flint Wagon Works during the late summer of 1903. In Flint the Buick pace did not pick up appreciably, the production prototype arriving only during the summer of 1904, the first sale of a Buick following in August.

Within two months 16 Buicks had been ordered but Whiting's capital investment had been entirely expended, and David Buick's procrastination at the factory did not hold promise that the business would ever be a par-

ticularly profitable one. Thus the Buick business was again unloaded, Whiting turning over the company and its future on November 1, 1904, to a fellow Flint resident, the co-owner of the Durant-Dort Carriage Company, one William Crapo Durant.

The first experimental Buick automobile was built in 1900-01 and sold in 1901 to Walter Marr, who may have built it for David Buick. Marr and his wife Abbie are pictured in what is believed to be that first Buick. OCW

Durant was a dynamo. Within a year he increased the capital stock of the Buick Motor Company from $75,000 to $1,500,000, reportedly selling a half million dollars of it in a single day to neighbors in Flint. Joining the company engineering staff in 1905 was Enos DeWaters, who had previously worked at Thomas and Cadillac and who would take over as chief engineer upon Walter Marr's retirement during World War I.

Dr. Herbert H. Hills, first buyer of a production Buick, admiring his Model B touring in July 1904. OCW

Being lost in the shuffle somehow was David Dunbar Buick. By the end of 1908 he would leave the company, his series of financial misadventures thereafter to in-

clude carburetor manufacture and two automobiles (the Lorraine and the Dunbar); in 1928 he would be found working at the information desk at the Detroit School of Trades; in 1929 he would die impoverished at age 74. That responsibility for David Buick's tragic career largely lay with David Buick himself is unassailable; unassailable, too, is the astonishing success Billy Durant made of Buick's company.

Aside from their overhead-valve design, the early two-cylinder Buicks were conventional, with two-speed planetary transmissions and single chain final drive. But with Durant as super salesman, Buick production rose to 750 cars in 1905, 1,400 in 1906, 4,641 in 1907. For the 1907 model year, a four had joined the twin, this a T-head design featuring shaft drive and, depending upon model, either three-speed sliding gear or two-speed planetary transmission.

In 1908, as production was practically doubling (to 8,820 units), Billy Durant used Buick as his base for founding another company: General Motors, in mid-September. The most popular Buick that year was the four-cylinder Model 10 that was priced in the $1,000 range and that was a close competitor of Henry Ford's new Model T. Ford's monolithic vision of the auto industry was not Durant's, however, and though the latter's multi-dimensional approach to setting up his new corporation would ultimately bear incredible fruit, Durant's idea of a bargain in companies to buy up for General Motors during these first years frequently brought real lemons. Nineteen ten found Durant desperately in need of money, which the banks agreed to provide only if he gave up effective control of General Motors. He had no choice but to accept, and left GM to join forces with Louis Chevrolet in the establishment of another automobile company with which he ultimately planned to get GM back.

Meanwhile, among his last suggestions before relinquishing control of GM was for his Durant-Dort superintendent to take over Buick. To this the banking interests agreed, and Charles W. Nash moved into Buick's presidential chair until November 1912, when he was promoted to the same one for General Motors itself. Taking over from Nash as Buick president at that time was Walter P. Chrysler. That both Nash and Chrysler were superb managers for Buick is undeniable, but the car Durant had left them was already a success in the marketplace and in competition.

Though Durant's interest in the latter was not overwhelming, he was aware that racing could sell cars. This was of paramount importance. It was Durant who recruited Bob Burman and Louis Chevrolet as the stars of the Buick racing team, and it was Burman and Chevrolet who made the Buick stock automobile a racing star.

Though the factory seldom contested the major international events of the day, its record in middle-echelon contests was unsurpassed. In 1909 alone, Buick won 166 events, over 90 percent of those entered, and by 1913, when Buick racing ended, the company held a flurry of AAA speed records, 30 of which would still stand in the record books a decade later.

In 1914 Buick's first six arrived. Like the first Buicks, the new 48 hp unit was an overhead valve, with the cylinders cast in pairs. Unlike earlier Buicks, it was a big car, set in a 130-inch wheelbase chassis more than a

foot longer than most models that had preceded. Production for 1915 of 43,946 cars practically sextupled to 124,834 in 1916. Part of the reason for this astounding increase was the salesmanship of Richard H. Collins, who earned the nickname "Trainload" (which was how he sold Buicks) before moving over to the presidency of Cadillac in 1917 following the Lelands' departure.

The Lelands' departure from Cadillac had followed Durant's triumphant return to the helm of General Motors that soon resulted in the departure from GM and Buick of Charles Nash and Walter Chrysler. Most people liked Billy Durant; few found it possible to work for him for long. Of brief duration, too, was Durant's second incumbency at GM. Getting himself into financial trouble again, he was forced out of the company for the last time in November 1920.

As Alfred Sloan began to pick up the pieces of Durant's GM empire, he recognized Buick as its vital link. "It is far better that the rest of General Motors be scrapped than any chances be taken with Buick's earning power," he wrote Pierre du Pont. But no chances would be taken at Buick.

In charge since Chrysler's departure was Harry H. Bassett, the likeable, careful former Weston-Mott executive who would remain with Buick until his sudden death in 1926. Unlike sister GM companies, Buick had neither a long love affair nor even a brief flirtation with a V-8. Fours and sixes satisfied Buick just fine, with detachable cylinder heads and four-wheel brakes being the biggest engineering news from the company for 1924, though the new styling caused some additional comment because it looked rather like a Packard.

Packard, exercising *noblesse oblige*, did not take legal steps, but did rather cleverly plagiarize the famous Buick slogan in a few ads that year — "When prettier cars are built, Packard will build them" — with the result that Buick redefined its radiator configuration somewhat away from the Packard's for 1925. In 1925, too, after vacillating for years as to whether fours or sixes were preferred, Buick opted for sixes across the board.

Thereafter, Buick did little, except gloat. The company was riding high with one of America's most popular cars, routinely placing in the top five of the industry and, except for the 1921 recession year, with annual production in six figures (and usually over 200,000) throughout the Twenties.

Buick's Silver Anniversary was in 1929, and the company chose to celebrate it with bigger and better Buicks featuring sloping non-glare windshields (which was fine) and new styling with side panels that bulged perceptibly (which was not). The infamous pregnant Buick had arrived.

Compared to the good years of the Twenties, not many of these cars were delivered. Buick also conceived a cheaper companion car that year called the Marquette, which didn't deliver well either. The early Depression years were awful at Buick. In mid-1932, Edward T. Strong, the former Buick sales manager who had been elevated to Buick's presidency after Bassett's death, retired — and former Olds man Irving Reuter took over briefly.

Still heading engineering was the conservative Ferdinand A. ("Dutch") Bower, who had taken over from DeWaters who had retired in ill health in 1929. For 1931 the company had remained overhead valve, but went straight-eight across the board. Synchromesh came for 1932, together with Wizard Control, a combined freewheeling and automatic clutch. But Buick's real wizard entered late in 1933, when Harlow H. ("Red") Curtice, the former spark of the AC plug division, came onboard as Buick's president.

Recognizing that the cars had become literally heavy with the success of the Twenties and that complacency had resulted in a Buick look that was by now old-fashioned, Curtice first attacked the remedial, making Buicks overall lighter in both weight and price tag, and introducing the Series 40, a smaller, less expensive car that could be counted upon for volume sales while Curtice geared up for the all-new Buick line for 1936. These were the cars for which names joined designations: the Special (Series 40), Century (Series 60), Roadmaster (Series 80) and Limited (Series 90).

Harley Earl at GM Art and Colour had contributed in great measure to their styling; Buick engineering had introduced aluminum pistons and, following the earlier lead of other GM cars, hydraulic brakes and turret tops. (Independent front suspension had been a feature since 1934.) It was in a 1936 Roadmaster that Wallis Warfield Simpson made her celebrated escape to the Continent — and to worldwide headlines — during the British Abdication crisis that followed her romance with the Prince of Wales, briefly Edward VIII. Roadmasters, too, were driven for fine exposure by Joan Crawford and Bette Davis in vintage films of this period.

The Curtice-era Buicks found considerable favor among movie folk; indeed the Estate Wagon of 1940 was conceived in Hollywood. But a *cause celebre* or cinema celebrity wasn't necessary to sell Buicks now. In 1937, for the first time since 1928, Buick surpassed the 200,000 mark. And in 1938, the Buick company, having been relegated to the bottom half of the top ten for a half-decade, returned to a solid number four spot it would enjoy until the war brought a halt to all automobile production.

By now Charles A. Chayne was Buick's chief engineer and Chayne's handiwork for the 1938 Buicks included all-around coil springs. Also new for 1938 were domed high-compression pistons for the Buick engine that was now designated "Dynaflash"; a Century model was clocked by Buick at 103 mph, which was admittedly a flashy performance. Dynaflow would follow postwar, but Buick did have a tentative go with a semi-automatic Self-Shifting Transmission in 1939.

A genuine industry first was the Buick's turn signals as standard equipment in 1939, and though Harlow Curtice's attempts to go custom with Brunn and the Limited — to the consternation of Cadillac — produced only a few cars at decade's turn, he had to be pleased with what the Buick had become since he took over. Once again, it was one of America's most popular cars.

Buick's record year production of 310,955 cars in 1940 was followed in 1941 by another new record: 316,251. Soon there were Hellcats on the Buick assembly line, but with the arrival of peace in 1945, Curtice and Buick would be ready to take up where they had left off.

1904

1904 Buick, Model B, touring, JAC

BUICK — MODEL B — TWO: The Model B Buick was a four-passenger touring car with an indigo blue body and bright yellow wheels. Typical of most early designs, right-hand drive was installed and simple curved fenders were used. Doors were provided for the rear seat compartment but none were provided for the front passengers. Weather protection was nonexistent since neither a windshield or top were provided as standard equipment.

I.D. DATA: Engine number on outside rim of flywheel on all Model B and Model C cars.

Model No.	Body Type & Seating	Price	Weight	Prod. Total
B (early)	Tr.-4P	950	1675	27
B (late)	Tr.-4P	1200	1700	8

*Note: Two Model C Buicks were made during calendar 1904 making a total of 37 cars.

ENGINE: Opposite. Valve in head. Two. Cast iron block. B & S: 4.5 x 5 in. Disp.: 159 cu. in. Brake H.P.: (early) 15 @ 1200 R.P.M. (late) 22 @ 1230 R.P.M. / N.A.C.C. H.P.: 16.2. Valve lifters: mechanical. Carb.: float feed.

CHASSIS: (early) W.B.: 83 in.; (late) W.B.: 86 in. Front/Rear Tread: 56 in. Tires (early) 28 x 3; (late) 30 x 3.5.

TECHNICAL: Planetary transmission. Speeds: 2F/1R. Floor shift controls. Cone clutch. Chain drive. Mechanical brakes on two wheels. Wood spoke wheels.

OPTIONS: Top ($100.00). Windshield (20.00). Acetylene headlamps and oil side lights (75.00).

HISTORICAL: Early B in production late July 1904 to October 31, 1904; late B from November 1 to December 14, 1904; C introduced December 15, 1904. Introduced August 13, 1904 (date of first Buick sold). Calendar year production: 37. Model year production: 37. The president of Buick was James Whiting to November 1, succeeded by Charles L. Begole. A Model B won its class in hill climb held at Eagle Rock, New Jersey, on Thanksgiving Day 1904. Another Model B sans body and nonessential features won its class in the first "Race to the Clouds" up Mt. Washington, New Hampshire.

1905

BUICK — MODEL C — TWO: The Model C was virtually identical to the Model B, however, a new royal blue body, ivory wheels

color combination was used. In addition room was provided for five passengers and the service brake was now foot-operated.

1905 Buick, Model C, touring, HAC

1905 Buick, Model C, touring, OCW

I.D. DATA: Serial numbers on plate on left side of frame. Body and engine were made in Flint and final assembly took place in Jackson.

Model No.	Body Type & Seating	Price	Weight	Prod. Total
C	Tr.-5P	1200	1850	750

ENGINE: Inline. Two. Cast iron block. B & S: 4.5 x 5 in. Disp.: 159 cu. in. Brake H.P : 22 @ 1200 R.P.M./N.A.C.C. H.P.: 16.2. Valve lifters: mechanical. Carb.: float feed, Kingston adjustable.

CHASSIS: [Model C] W.B.: 87 in. Front/Rear Tread: 56 in. Tires: 30 x 3.5.

TECHNICAL: Planetary transmission. Speeds: 2F/1R. Floor and steering column controls. Cone clutch. Chain drive. Mechanical brakes on two wheels. Wood spoke wheels.

OPTIONS: Cape Cart Top.

HISTORICAL: Buick claimed three major performance records in 1905. In Boston at the Readville track a world's record for two-cylinder cars for the five mile distance was established. The Buick's time was 6 minutes, 19-3/5 seconds. At a one mile Newark, New Jersey, track a Buick set a new track record of 62 seconds. In a six-mile event held at the same location a Buick also was the overall winner. Calendar year production: 750. Model year production: 750. The president of Buick was Charles L. Begole.

1906

BUICK — MODEL G — TWO: The Model G was a two-seat roadster version of the Model F. Its running gear was identical

to the Model F. All Buicks had as standard equipment acetylene headlight and oil side and taillamps. Also included in the base price was a storage battery and vibrator horn.

1906 Buick, Model G, runabout, HAC

BUICK — MODEL F — TWO: The Model F was a revised version of the Model C. A new radiator design ran the full height of the hood and provided easy identification. The paint scheme for 1906 consisted of a purple lake body with ivory wheels and running gear.

I.D. DATA: Serial numbers on plate on left side of frame. Starting: 1 to 1207 Model F.

Model No.	Body Type & Seating	Price	Weight	Prod. Total
F	Tr.-5P	1250	1850	1207
G	Rds.-2P	1150	—	193

Note 1: Model G price reduced to $1,000.

ENGINE: Inline. Two. Cast iron block. B & S: 4.5 x 5. Disp. 159 cu. in. Brake H.P.: 22 @ 1200 R.P.M. N.A.C.C. H.P.: 16.2. Valve lifters: mechanical. Carb.: float feed, Kingston adjustable.

CHASSIS: [Model G] W.B.: 87 in. Front/Rear Tread: 56 in. Tires: 30 x 3.5. [Model F] W.B.: 87 in. Front/Rear Tread: 56 in. Tires: 30 x 3.5

TECHNICAL: Planetary transmission. Speeds: 2F/1R. Floor and steering column controls. Cone clutch. Chain drive. Mechanical brakes on two wheels. Wood spoke wheels.

OPTIONS: Cape Cart top ($100.00).

HISTORICAL: Introduced January 1906. Calendar year production: 1,400. Model year production: 1,400. The president of Buick was Charles L. Begole. Buicks set new overall records at the Eagle Rock, New Jersey, and Mt. Washington, New Hampshire, hill climbs. Race victories were attained at Yonkers, New York, and the New York City Empire City track in events of 100 mile duration. In addition a Model F Buick was the only car to complete a 1,000 mile, New York to Chicago relay run.

1907

BUICK — MODELS F TOURING & G ROADSTER — TWO: These two Buick models were given a longer, 89-inch wheelbase and a belly pan that enclosed the engine and transmission. A smaller 15 instead of 16 gallon fuel tank was installed.

BUICK — MODELS D TOURING & S ROADSTER — FOUR: These two new Buick models were powered by Buick's first four-cylinder engine linked to a three-speed, sliding gear transmission. The Model D was introduced in May 1906 as a 1907 model and featured a royal blue body with ivory wheels. The sporty Model S had a French gray body accentuated by green striping.

BUICK — MODELS H TOURING & K ROADSTER — FOUR: These two Buicks had the same finishes as the Model D and Model S models and were identical in all other areas except they used the two-speed planetary transmission.

I.D. DATA: Serial numbers on plate on left side of frame. Starting: 101 (Models D and S). Ending: 523. During 1906 construction of a new Buick plant began in Flint and thus Buicks were constructed both in Jackson and Flint, Michigan. Engine No. Starting: 101 (Models D and S). Ending: 523.

Model No.	Body Type & Seating	Price	Weight	Prod. Total
F	Tr.-5P	1250	1850	3365
G	Rds.-2P	1150	1800	535
D	Tr.-5P	2000	2250	523
S	Rds.-2P	2500	2000	69
H	Tr.-5P	1750	2250	36
K	Rds.-2P	2500	NA	13

1907 Buick, Model G, roadster, OCW

ENGINE: [Models F and G] Inline. Two. Cast iron block. B & S: 4.5 x 5 in. Disp.: 159 cu. in. Brake H.P.: 22 @ 1200 R.P.M. N.A.C.C. H.P.: 16.2. Valve lifters: mechanical. Carb.: float feed. [Models D, S, H and K] Inline. T-head. Four. Cast iron block. B & S: 4.25 x 4.5 in. Disp.: 255 cu. in. Brake H.P.: 30. Main bearings: Five. Valve lifters: mechanical.

CHASSIS: [Model F] W.B.: 89 in. Front/Rear Tread: 59 in. Tires: 30 x 3.5. [Model G] W.B.: 89 in. Front/Rear Tread: 59 in. Tires: 30 x 3.5. [Model D] W.B.: 102.5 in. Tires: 32 x 4. [Model S] W.B.: 106.5 in. Tires: 32 x 4. [Model H] W.B. 102.5 in. Tires: 32 x 4. [Model K] W.B.: 106.5 in. Tires: 32 x 4.

TECHNICAL: Models F and G planetary transmission. Speeds: 2F/1R. Floor and steering column controls. Cone clutch. Chain drive. Mechanical brakes on two wheels. Wooden spoke wheels. Models D and S sliding gear transmission. Speeds: 3F/1R. Floor shift. Multiple disc in oil bath. Shaft drive. Mechanical brakes on two wheels. Wooden spoke wheels. Models K and H planetary transmission. Speeds: 2F/1R. Floor and steering column controls. Cone clutch. Chain drive. Mechanical brakes on two wheels. Wooden spoke wheels.

OPTIONS: Top Model G (70.00).

HISTORICAL: Introduced May 1906. The Model D was Buick's first four-cylinder engine. Calendar year production: 4,641. Model year production: 4,641. The president of Buick was Charles L. Begole. The only automobile company to outproduce the Buick in 1907 was Ford. Buick introduced torque tube drive on the Model D and Model S in 1907 and continued its use until 1962.

1908

1908 Buick, Model 5, touring, HAC

BUICK — MODELS F & G — TWO: The Model F and Model G Buicks were extensively restyled with a longer wheelbase plus reshaped hoods, fenders and grille form. Both cars had wine-colored bodies with red wheels.

BUICK — MODELS D & S — FOUR: Body styles for the Model S were extended to include a rumbleseat version and a four-place tourabout as well as the original roadster. The Model D was virtually unchanged but a $100 price drop helped maintain its popularity. Even more dramatic was the Model S price reduction of $750.

1908 Buick, Model 10, touring, JAC

BUICK — MODEL 10 — FOUR: This new Buick was its most popular model in 1908 and for good reason. With brass trim, an off-white Buick gray finish and an attractive $900 price (that included acetylene headlights, oil-fired side and taillights and a bulb horn) it was bound to be a success.

BUICK — MODEL 5 — FOUR: Replacing the Model K was this big touring car available in either red or blue bodies with ivory wheels and appointments. Its engine was a new four-cylinder with its cylinders cast in pairs and fitted with an aluminum crankcase.

I.D. DATA: Serial numbers on plate on left side of frame. Starting: Models D & S 524, Model 10 1, Model 5 101. Ending: Models D & S 1692, Model 10 4002, Model 5 501. Starting: Models F & G 6301, Models D & S 524, Model 10 1, Model 5 1. Ending: Models F & G 15 010, Models D & S 1699, Model 10 4002, Model 5405.

Model No.	Body Type & Seating	Price	Weight	Prod. Total
F	Tr.-5P	1250	1850	3281
G	Rds.-2P	1150	1800	219
D	Tr.-5P	1750	2250	543
S	Rds.-2P	1750	2000	373
10	Tr.-3P	900	NA	4002
5	Tr.-5P	2500	3700	402

Note 1: Model S, four-passenger Tourabout body available for $1,800.

ENGINE: [Models F and G] Inline. Two. Cast iron block. B & S: 4.5 x 5 in. Disp.: 159 cu. in. Brake H.P. 22 @ 1200 R.P.M. SAE H.P.: 16.2. Valve lifters: mechanical. Carb.: float feed Schebler. [Models D and S] Inline. T-head. Four. Cast iron block. B & S: 4.25 x 4.5 in. Disp.: 255 cu. in. Brake H.P.: 30. Main bearings: Five. Valve lifters: mechanical. Carb.: Schebler. [Model 10] Inline. Valve in head. Four. Cast iron block. B & S: 3-3/4 x 3-3/4 in. Disp.: 165 cu. in. Brake H.P.: 22.5. Valve lifters: mechanical. Carb.: Schebler. [Model 5] Inline. T-head, cast in pairs. Four. Cast iron block. B & S: 4-5/8 x 5 in. Disp.: 336 cu. in. Brake H.P.: 40. SAE H.P.: 34.2.

CHASSIS: [Model F] W.B.: 92 in. Front/Rear Tread: 59 in. Tires: 30 x 3.5. [Model G] W.B.: 92 in. Front/Rear Tread: 59 in. Tires: 30 x 3.5. [Model D] W.B.: 102.5 in. Tires: 32 x 4. [Model S] W.B.: 106.5 in. Tires: 32 x 4. [Model 10] W.B.: 88 in. Tires: 30 x 3. [Model 5] W.B.: 108 in. Tires: 34 x 4.

TECHNICAL: Models F & G planetary transmission. Speeds: 2F/1R. Floor and steering column controls. Cone clutch. Chain drive. Mechanical brakes on two wheels. Wooden spoke wheels. Models D & S sliding gear transmission. Speeds: 3F/1R. Floor shift. Multiple disc in oil. Shaft drive. Mechanical brakes on two wheels. Wooden spoke wheels. Model 10 planetary transmission. Speeds: 2F/1R. Floor and steering column controls. Cone clutch. Shaft drive. Divided rear axle. Mechanical brakes on two wheels. Wooden spoke wheels. Model 5 sliding gear transmission. Speeds: 3F/1R. Floor shift. Cone clutch. Shaft drive. Mechanical brakes on two wheels. Wooden spoke wheels.

OPTIONS: Model F — gas headlights, horn, tool kit ($90.00). Model 10 top (50.00).

HISTORICAL: Introduced November 1907. Calendar year production: 8,820. Model year production: 8,820. The president of Buick was Charles L. Begole. Both the Model D and Model 5 Buicks served as the basis for racing ventures during 1908 that included victories in the light car class at the Vanderbilt Cup Races. Buicks also participated in the Savannah, Georgia, races as well as in a Montreal two-day affair where they won 11 of 14 races.

1909

BUICK MODELS 10 & 15 — Four: Buick remained the nation's number two auto producer with a model lineup that retained its most popular models and replaced the poor sellers with improved offerings. No longer produced were the Model D, Model S, and Model 5 styles. The Model 10 was offered in four body types all of which had a longer, 92-inch wheelbase and the new and racy Model 16 Buicks took on a modern appearance by virtue of their rounded front and rear fenders.

BUICK MODEL 6 — FOUR: Replacing the Model 5 was the Model 6A roadster with a 113-inch wheelbase.

BUICK MODELS F & G — TWO: The two-cylinder Model F and G Buick continued unchanged but remained strong sellers. Their exterior color schemes retained the same wine body finish with red wheels and running gear.

Overshadowing Buick's tremendous sales success that enabled it to hold onto second place in the industry were the machinations of William Durant that brought Buick into the fold of his newly created General Motors.

1909 Buick, Model 10, roadster, OCW

I.D. DATA: Serial numbers on plate on left side of frame. Starting: Models F and S 9950, Model 10 4003, Models 16 and 17 1, Model 6A 1. Ending: Models F and S 13900, Model 10 12152, Models 16 and 17 2500, Model 6A 6. Engine No. Starting: Models F and S 15011, Model 10 4003, Models 16 and 17 1, Model 6A 1. Ending: Models F and S 19050, Model 10 12111, Models 16 and 17 2517, Model 6A 6.

1909 Buick, Model 17, touring, HAC

Model No.	Body Type & Seating	Price	Weight	Prod. Total
F	Tr.-5P	1250	1850	3856
G	Rbt.-2P	1150	1800	144
6A	Rds.-2P	2750	3700	6
10	Rds.-3P	1000	—	Note 2
10	Tourabout-4P	1050	—	Note 2
10	Toy Tonneau-4P	—	—	Note 2
16	Rds.-2P	1750	2620	Note 3
16	Tourabout-4P	1750	2620	Note 3
17	Tr.-5P	1750	2790	2003

Note 1: There was a mid-year price reduction on the Model F touring to $1,000.
Note 2: Total production of all Model 10 styles was 8,100.
Note 3: Total production of all Model 16 styles was 497.

ENGINE: [Models F and G] Inline. Two. Cast iron block. B & S: 4.5 x 5 in. Disp.: 159 cu. in. Brake H.P.: 22 @ 1200 R.P.M. SAE H.P.: 16.2. Valve lifters: mechanical. Carb.: float feed Schebler. [Model 6A] Inline, T-head, cast in pairs. Four. Cast iron block. B & S: 4-5/8 x 5 in. Disp.: 336 cu. in. Brake H.P.: 40. N.A.C.C. H.P.: 34.2. Valve lifters: mechanical. [Model 10] Inline, valve in head. Four. Cast iron block. B & S: 3-3/4 x 3-3/4 in. Disp.: 165 cu. in. Brake H.P.: 22.5. Valve lifters: mechanical. Carb.: Sche-

bler. [Models 16 and 17] Inline. Four. Cast iron block. B & S: 4.5 x 5 in. Disp.: 318 cu. in. SAE H.P.: 32.4. Carb.: Schebler.

CHASSIS: [Model F] W.B.: 92 in. Front/Rear Tread: 59 in. Tires: 30 x 3.5. [Model G] W.B.: 92 in. Front/Rear Tread: 59 in. Tires: 30 x 3.5. [Model 6A] W.B.: 113 in. [Model 10] W.B.: 92 in. Front/Rear Tread: 56 in. Tires: 30 x 3. [Model 16] W.B.: 112 in. Tires: 34 x 4. [Model 17] W.B.: 112.5 in. Tires: 34 x 4.

TECHNICAL: Models 16 and 17 sliding gear transmission. Speeds: 3F/1R. Floor shift controls. Shaft drive. Bevel gear, torque tube. Mechanical brakes on two wheels. Wooden spoke wheels. Models F and G planetary transmission. Speeds: 2F/1R. Floor and steering column controls. Cone clutch. Chain drive. Mechanical brakes on two wheels. Wooden spoke wheels. Model 6A sliding gear transmission. Speeds: 3F/1R. Floor shift controls. Cone clutch. Shaft drive. Mechanical brakes on two wheels. Wooden spoke wheels. Model 10 planetary transmission. Speeds: 2F/1R. Floor and steering column controls. Cone clutch. Shaft drive. Divided rear axle. Mechanical brakes on two wheels. Wooden spoke wheels.

OPTIONS: Rumbleseat (Model 10) ($100). Hood straps. Windshield. Sidemounted spare.

HISTORICAL: Calendar year production: 14,606. Model year production: 14,606. The president of Buick was Charles L. Begole. Buick was an active, enthusiastic competitor in racing events during 1909. Modified Model 17s competed at the old Indianapolis raceway and at the Atlanta, Georgia, race. At both locations the Buicks set track records with ease. Louis Chevrolet drove a Model 16 to a victory in the 200 race in Atlanta and a win in a 393-mile race, the Cobe Trophy Stock Car Road Race at Crown Point, Indiana. Other Buick successes took place at Daytona Beach and Giant's Despair hill climb at Wilkes-Barre, Pennsylvania.

1910

1910 Buick, touring, OCW

BUICK — MODEL 10 — FOUR: The Model 10 was essentially unchanged for 1910 but its basic appeal and 13 different body styles boosted output to nearly 11,000 cars.

BUICK — MODEL F — TWO: No changes for 1910 except for a new vertical tube radiator.

BUICK — MODELS 16 & 17 — FOUR: No changes for 1910 except for a new vertical tube radiator.

BUICK — MODEL 7 — FOUR: This new model with a big 392.6 cid engine was Buick's prestige open vehicle for 1910.

BUICK — MODEL 19 — FOUR: The Model 19 touring car was a new model with a Buick green body and ivory wheels. Its engine was based on the Model D unit from 1907. However its wheelbase was increased from 102 to 105 inches.

BUICK — MODEL 41 — FOUR: With this limousine model Buick made its first venture into the closed car market. Among its prestige features was imported goatskin upholstery and a rear compartment speaking tube.

1910 Buick, Model 41, limousine, JAC

I.D. DATA: Serial numbers on plate on left side of frame. Starting: Model 10 12152, Model F 13951, Models 16 & 17 2501, Model 7 1, Model 19 1, Model 41 1. Ending: Model 10 23150, Model F 17901, Models 16 & 17 10754, Model 7 85, Model 19 4012, Model 41 41. Engine No. Starting: Model 10 12251, Model F 19051, Models 16 & 17 2518, Model 7 1, Model 19 1, Model 41 1. Ending: Model 10 23267, Model F 25203, Models 16 & 17 10878, Model 7 96, Model 19 4023, Model 41 40.

Model No.	Body Type & Seating	Price	Weight	Prod. Total
10	Rbt.-3P	1000	NA	Note 1
10	Tourabout-4P	1050	NA	Note 1
10	Toy Tonneau-4P	1150	1730	Note 1
F	Tr.-5P	1000	2300	4000
16	Rds.-2P	1750	2620	Note 2
16	Surrey-4P	1750	2620	Note 2
16	Toy Tonneau-4P	1750	2620	Note 2
7	Tr.-7P	2750	3700	85
17	Tr.-5P	1750	2790	6002
19	Tr.-5P	1400	2500	4000
41	Limo.-5P	2750	3400	40

Note 1: Total production of all Model 10 styles was 10,998.

Note 2: Total production of all Model 16 styles was 2,252.

ENGINE: [Model 19] Inline. T-head. Four. Cast iron block. B & S: 4.25 x 4.5 in. Disp.: 255 cu. in. Brake H.P.: 28.9. Main bearings: Five. Valve lifters: mechanical. Carb.: Schebler. [Model 7] Inline. T-head, cast in pairs. Four. Cast iron block. B & S: 4-5/8 x 5 in. Disp.: 336 cu. in. Brake H.P.: 40. SAE H.P.: 34.2. Valve lifters: mechanical. [Model 10] Inline. Valve in head. Four. Cast iron block. B & S: 3-3/4 x 3-3/4 in. Disp.: 165 cu. in. Brake H.P.: 22.5 in. Valve lifters: mechanical. Carb.: Marvel 10-501. [Model F] Inline. Two. Cast iron block. B & S: 4.5 x 5 in. Disp.: 159 cu. in. Brake H.P.: 22. SAE H.P.: 16.2. Valve lifters: mechanical. Carb.: float feed Schebler. [Models 16, 17 and 41] Inline. Four. Cast iron block. B & S: 4.5 x 5 in. Disp.: 318 cu. in. SAE H.P.: 32.4. Valve lifters: mechanical. Carb.: Marvel 10-508.

CHASSIS: [Model 10] W.B.: 92 in. Front/Rear Tread: 56 in. Tires: 30 x 3. [Model 16] W.B.: 112 in. Tires: 34 x 4. [Model 17] W.B.: 112.5 in. Tires: 34 x 4. [Model 7] W.B.: 122 in. Tires: 36 x 4. [Model 19] W.B.: 105 in. Tires: 32 x 4. [Model 41] Tires: 34 x 4.

TECHNICAL: Model 10 planetary transmission. Speeds: 2F/1R. Floor and steering column controls. Cone clutch. Shaft drive. Divided rear axle. Mechanical brakes on two wheels. Wooden spoke wheels. Model F planetary transmission. Speeds: 2F/1R. Floor and steering column controls. Cone clutch. Chain drive. Mechanical brakes on two wheels. Wooden spoke wheels. Models 16 & 17 sliding gear transmission. Speeds: 3F/1R. Floor shift controls. Shaft clutch. Bevel gear, torque tube. Mechanical brakes on two wheels. Wooden spoke wheels. Model 7 sliding gear transmission. Speeds: 3F/1R. Floor shift controls. Leather faced cone clutch. Shaft drive. Mechanical brakes on two wheels. Wooden spoke wheels. Model 19 sliding gear transmission. Speeds: 3F/1R. Floor shift controls. Cone clutch. Shaft drive. Mechanical brakes on two wheels. Wooden spoke wheels. Model 41 sliding gear transmission. Speeds: 3F/1R. Floor shift controls. Cone clutch. Shaft drive. Mechanical brakes on two wheels. Wooden spoke wheels.

OPTIONS: Model 7 — top, side curtains. Model 17 — spare tire. Model 10 — windshield, wicker picnic basket.

HISTORICAL: Calendar year sales: 29,425 (includes 2048 Model 14 Buicks generally regarded as 1911 models). Model year production: 27,377. The president of Buick was Thomas Neal. The famous Buick Bugs appeared in 1910 and in July 1910 they were driven by Bob Burman and Louis Chevrolet to an impressive array of records at the Grand Circuit Speedway Meet in Indianapolis. A total of five firsts, and three second-place marks were set including a time trial record of 105.87 mph. Other victories were achieved in races ranging from 10 to 100 miles held at Indianapolis. At a three-day meet held at Lowell, Massachusetts, Buick won 7 of 10 races in the stock chassis division as well as the Vesper Trophy for cars in the 301-450 cid engine class. Marquette Buicks competed in the Vanderbilt Cup Race and one such racer driven by Burman finished third in the 1910 Savannah, Georgia, Grand Prize race behind two Benz racers.

1911

1911 Buick, Model 38, roadster, JAC

BUICK — MODELS 14 & 14B — TWO: The Model 14 or Buggyabout (also available as the 14B with the fuel tank moved from under the seat to the rear) was a tiny, 79-inch wheelbase two-seater. It was the last Buick to be equipped with a two-cylinder engine and chain drive. It's possible that if it had been produced in 1908 when it was first developed the Model 14

could have provided the base for a Buick challenge to Ford's supremacy in the low priced field.

BUICK — MODELS 32 & 33 — FOUR: These two new Buicks used the 165 cid engine of the discontinued Model 10 and were, respectively, a roadster and tourer. Both cars were equipped with an automatic high speed clutch release.

BUICK — MODEL 21 — FOUR: This touring model was one of the most attractive Buicks with its angular body particularly pleasing in its Buick green finish and available cream-colored wheels.

BUICK — MODELS 26 & 27 — FOUR: Both of these Buicks in roadster and touring bodies were powered by a new 210 cid four-cylinder engine. The standard color for the Model 26 was battleship gray. The Model 27 was given a dark blue body with white wheels.

BUICK — MODELS 38 & 39 — FOUR: In effect these two Buicks were larger versions of the Model 26 and Model 27 Buicks. The Model 38 roadster with its large, 27-gallon, rear mounted fuel tank was finished in a dark blue body and gray wheels. The Model 39 tourer attracted attention with its four-door body. However the driver's door was inoperative. The standard color for the Model 39 was dark blue. Its wooden wheels were painted gray.

BUICK — MODEL 41 — FOUR: The Model 41 limousine was powered by a four-cylinder engine of 318 cubic inch displacement.

I.D. DATA: Serial numbers on plate on left side of frame. Starting: Model 21 1, Model 26 & 27 1, Model 32 & 33 1, Model 38 & 39 1, Model 41 41. Ending: Model 21 300, Model 26 & 27 400, Model 32 & 33 3150, Model 38 & 39 1050, Model 41 67. Engine Nos. Starting: Model 21 1, Model 26 & 27 1, Model 32 & 33 1, Model 38 & 39 1, Model 41 41. Ending: Model 21 300, Model 26 & 27 405, Model 32 & 33 3153, Model 38 & 39 1059, Model 41 67.

Model No.	Body Type & Seating	Price	Weight	Prod. Total
14	Rds.-2P	550	1500	Note 1
21	Tr.-5P	1500	2610	Note 2
21	Tr. Closed-Coupled Touring-5P	1500	2610	Note 2
21	Rds. R./S.-3P	1550	2610	Note 2
26	Rds.-2P	1050	2100	1000
27	Tr.-5P	1150	2280	3000
32	Rds.-2P	800	1695	1150
33	Tr.-5P	950	1855	2000
38	Rds.-2P	1850	2650	153
39	Tr.-5P	1850	3225	905
41	Limo.-5P	2750	3400	27

Note 1: Total production of 3,300 includes 2,048 built in late 1910.

Note 2: Total production of all Model 21 styles was 3,000.

ENGINE: [Model 14] Inline. Two. Cast iron block. B & S: 4.5 x 40 in. Disp. 127 cu. in. SAE H.P. 14.2. Valve lifters: mechanical. [Model 21] Inline. Four. Cast iron block. B & S: 4.25 x 4.5 in. Disp.: 255 cu. in. Brake H.P.: 40. SAE H.P.: 28.9. Main bearings: Five. Valve lifters: mechanical. Carb.: Schebler. [Models 32 & 33] Inline. Valve in head. Four. Cast iron block. B & S: 3-3/4 x 3-3/4 in. Disp.: 165 cu. in. SAE H.P 22.5. Valve lifters: mechanical. Carb.: Schebler. [Models 26 & 27] Inline. Four. Cast iron block. B & S: 4 x 4 in. Disp.: 201 cu. in. SAE H.P.: 25.6. Valve lifters: mechanical. Carb.: Marvel E 10501. [Models 38 and 39] Inline. Four. Cast iron block. B & S: 4.5 x 5 in. Disp. 318 cu. in. Brake H.P.: 48. SAE H.P . 32.4. Valve lifters- mechanical. Carb.: Marvel E 10-502. [Model 41] Inline Four. Cast iron block. B & S: 4.5 x 5 in. Disp.: 318 cu. in. (some sources credit Model 41 with a 338 cid engine). SAE H.P.: 32.4. Valve lifters: mechanical.

CHASSIS: [Model 14] W.B.: 79 in. Tires: 30 x 3. [Model 21] W.B.: 110 in. Tires: 34 x 4. [Model 26] W.B.: 100 in. Tires: 32 x 3.5. [Model 27] W.B.: 106 in. Tires: 32 x 3.5. [Model 32] W.B.: 89 in. Tires: 30 x 3.5. [Model 33] W.B. 100 in. Tires: 30 x 3.5.

[Models 38 & 39] W.B.: 116 in. Tires: 36 x 4. [Model 41] W.B.: 112.5 in. Tires: 36 x 4.5.

TECHNICAL: Model 14 selective sliding gear transmission. Speeds: 2F/1R. Floor & steering column controls. Disc clutch. Chain drive. Mechanical brakes on two wheels. Wooden wheels. Model 21 sliding gear transmission. Speeds: 3F/1R. Floor shift controls. Cone clutch. Shaft drive. Mechanical brakes on two wheels. Wooden wheels. Models 26 & 27 sliding gear transmission. Speeds: 3F/1R. Floor shift controls. Multiple disc clutch. Shaft drive. Mechanical brakes on two wheels. Wooden wheels. Models 32 & 33 planetary transmission. Speeds: 2F/1R. Floor and steering column controls. Cone clutch. Shaft drive. Mechanical brakes on two wheels. Wooden rim wheels. Models 38 & 39 & 41 sliding gear transmission. Speeds: 3F/1R. Floor shift controls. Multiple disc clutch. Shaft drive. Mechanical brakes on two wheels. Wooden rim wheels.

OPTIONS: Windshield. Top.

HISTORICAL: Calendar year production: 13,389. Model year production: 13,389. The president of Buick was Thomas Neal. Two Marquette-Buicks were entered in the first Indianapolis 500. However they retired after 30 and 46 laps, respectively. Similarly two Marquette-Buicks competed in the Savannah, Georgia, Grand Prize race but neither car finished.

1912 Buick, Model 28, roadster, OCW

1912 BUICK — OVERVIEW: Improvements common to all 1912 Buicks included improved lubrication arrangements for the pushrods and the addition of grease cups to the spring shackles, steering knuckles, and clutch. All models were fitted with three-speed sliding-gear transmission.

Buick eliminated a number of models for 1912 including Model 14, Model 21, Model 38, and Model 41.

BUICK — MODEL 28 — FOUR: This roadster, as all Buicks for 1912, was fitted with true doors, thus acquiring a more modern appearance. A number of color combinations were available including a two-tone wine and black body and blue-black fenders as well as a body finish of Buick gray and black body with blue-black fenders, hood and tank.

BUICK — MODEL 29 — FOUR: Customers could also order this touring model in either of two color combinations. Its hood, fenders and wheels were finished in blue-black while body color could be gray or wine.

BUICK — MODEL 34 — FOUR: This roadster was fitted on a trim, 90.7-inch wheelbase and was delivered with a gray body, matching wheels, and blue hood and fenders.

BUICK — MODEL 35 — FOUR: This most popular Buick for 1912 was updated with a three-speed selective sliding gear transmission replacing the planetary transmission used previously. Also sharing in this change-over was the Model 34. The driver's door on the Model 35 was inoperative. Standard body color was dark blue with the wheels finished in gray.

BUICK — MODEL 36 — FOUR: This model was one of three roadsters offered by Buick in 1912. It shared its 201 cid engine with both the Model 28 and Model 29 Buicks and was available in two color schemes. A blue and gray body with blue-black hood, fenders and fuel tank was standard. A second choice was a Buick-brown body with blue-black fenders.

BUICK — MODEL 43 — FOUR: This was the largest Buick offered in 1912. The Model 43 318 cid engine, like all 1912 Buick engines, had its spark plugs positioned in the cylinder head at a 45-degree angle instead of the older, horizontal location.

I.D. DATA: Serial numbers on plate on left side of frame. Starting: Model 29 1, Models 34, 35, 36 1, Model 43 1. Ending: Model 29 8500, Models 34, 35, 36 9051, Model 43 1501. Engine Nos. Starting: Model 29 1, Models 34, 35, 36 1, Model 43, 1. Ending: Model 29 8500, Models 34, 35, 36 9059, Model 43 1506.

Model No.	Body Type & Seating	Price	Weight	Prod. Total
28	2-dr. Rds.-2/4P	1025	2375	2500
29	3-dr. Tr.-5P	1180	2600	6000
34	2-dr. Rds.-2P	900	1875	1400
35	3-dr. Tr.-5P	1000	2100	6050
36	2-dr. Rds.-2P	900	1950	1600
43	3-dr. Tr.-5P	1725	3360	1501

ENGINE: [Models 28 and 29] Inline. Four. Cast iron block. B & S: 4 x 4 in. Disp.: 201 cu. in. SAE H.P.: 25.5. Valve lifters: mechanical. Carb.: Marvel E 10-543. [Models 34, 35 and 36] Inline. Four. Cast iron block. B & S: 3.75 x 3.75 in. Disp.: 165 cu. in. SAE H.P.: 22.5. Valve lifters: mechanical. Carb.: Schebler. [Model 43] Inline. Four. Cast iron block. B & S: 4.5 x 5 in. Disp.: 318 cu. in. Brake H.P.: 48. SAE H.P.: 32.4. Valve lifters: mechanical. Carb.: Schebler.

1912 Buick, touring, OCW

CHASSIS: [Model 28] W.B.: 108 in. Tires: 34 x 3.5. [Model 29] W.B.: 108 in. Tires: 34 x 3.5. [Model 34] W.B.: 90.75 in. Tires: 30 x 3.5. [Model 35] W.B.: 101.75 in. Tires: 32 x 3.5. [Model 36] W.B.: 101.75 in. Tires: 32 x 3.5. [Model 43] W.B.: 116 in. Tires: 36 x 4.

TECHNICAL: All models sliding gear transmission. Speeds: 3F/1R. Floor shift controls. Leather faced, aluminum cone clutch. Shaft drive. Mechanical brakes on two wheels. Wooden wheels.

OPTIONS: Top. Windshield.

HISTORICAL: Innovations: Buick enclosed the selective type shift lever and emergency brake in a panel attached to the non-operating front right-hand door on all models. Calendar year production: 19,051. Model year production: 19,051. The president of Buick was Walter P. Chrysler. A Marquette-Buick was entered in the 1912 Indianapolis 500 but retired after 72 laps.

1913

1913 Buick, touring, OCW

BUICK — MODEL 24 & 25 — FOUR: These two Buicks with roadster and touring bodies replaced the Models 34, 35, and 36 of 1912. Both were offered in maroon or Buick gray bodies with blue-black fenders and wheels.

BUICK — MODEL 30 & 31 — FOUR: These roadsters and touring Buicks were offered in blue-black or gray finished bodies.

BUICK — MODEL 40 — FOUR: The prestige Buick for 1913 was this touring model. An interesting design feature was the extension of its leather upholstery over the upper door surfaces.

I.D. DATA: Serial numbers on plate on left side of frame. Starting: Model 24 & 25 1, Model 30 6250 and 12751, Model 31 1 and 8000, Model 40 1. Ending: Models 24 & 25 11000, Model 30 7999 and 13501, Model 31 6250 and 12749, Model 40 1508. Engine Nos. Starting: Models 24 & 25 1, Models 30 & 31 1, Model 40 1. Ending: Models 24 & 25 11005, Models 30 & 31 13504, Model 40 1510.

Model No.	Body Type & Seating	Price	Weight	Prod. Total
24	2-dr. Rds.-2P	950	2130	2850
25	3-dr. Tr.-5P	1050	2335	8150
30	2-dr. Rds.-2P	1125	2480	3500
31	3-dr. Tr.-5P	1285	2750	10,000
40	3-dr. Tr.-5P	1650	—	1506

ENGINE: [Models 24 and 25] Inline. Ohv. Four. Cast iron block. B & S: 3.75 x 3.75 in. Disp.: 165 cu. in. N.A.C.C. H.P.: 22.5. Valve lifters: mechanical. Carb.: Marvel E 10-501. [Models 30 and 31] Inline. Ohv. Four. Cast iron block. B & S: 4 x 4 in. Disp. 201 cu. in. N.A.C.C. H.P.: 25.6. Valve lifters: mechanical. Carb.: Schebler. [Model 40] Inline. Ohv. Four. Cast iron block. B & S: 4.25 x 4.5 in. Disp.: 255 cu. in. Brake H.P.: 40. N.A.C.C. H.P.: 28.9. Main bearings: Five. Valve lifters: mechanical. Carb.: Schebler.

CHASSIS: [Model 24] W.B.: 105 in. Front/Rear Tread: 56 or 60 in. Tires: 32 x 3.5. [Model 25] W.B.: 105 in. Front/ Rear Tread: 56 or 60 in. Tires: 32 x 3.5. [Model 30] W.B.: 108 in. Tires: 34 x 3.5. [Model 31] W.B.: 108 in. Tires: 34 x 3.5. [Model 40] W.B.: 115 in. Tires: 36 x 4.

1913 Buick, touring (Louis Chevrolet at wheel), JAC

TECHNICAL: Sliding gear transmission. Speeds: 3F/1R. Floor shift control. Cone clutch. Shaft drive. Mechanical brakes on two wheels. Wooden wheels.

OPTIONS: Electric head, tail, and side lights.

HISTORICAL: Calendar year production: 26,006. Model year production: 26,006. The president of Buick was Walter P. Chrysler. A Buick won a 102-mile "Corona Race" on the West Coast in 1913. In addition, on July 17, 1913, a Model 10 Buick of 1910 vintage became the first car to climb Pike's Peak unassisted. 1913 was the last year for right-hand drive in a Buick. Nickel plating instead of brass was also introduced.

1914

1914 BUICK: Highlighting the 1914 Buicks was a six-cylinder engine, the use of a Delco electric starter and lighting system and a switch to left-hand drive with center mounted gear shift and emergency brake.

1914 Buick, Model B-24, roadster, JAC

BUICK — SERIES B — MODELS B-24 & B-25 — FOUR: These roadster and touring models retained Buick's familiar front end design with angular forms for the hood and radiator. Adding to their sales appeal were a standard top and windshield.

BUICK — SERIES B — MODELS B-36 & B-37 — FOUR: With their rounded hoods and grille outlines, these roadster and touring Buicks took on a more modern appearance that was accompanied by runningboards free from supporting the battery boxes.

BUICK — SERIES B — MODEL B-38 — FOUR: In a year of major styling and engineering changes the B-38 was a benchmark Buick since it was the first production Buick with a fully enclosed coupe body.

BUICK — SERIES B — MODEL B-55 — SIX: This touring model was the first Buick available with a six-cylinder, overhead valve engine. With the rounded hood and nose of the B-24 and B-25 models plus fenders set lower than previously, the B-55 represented a break from the styling confines of Buick's early years.

1914 Buick, Model B-25, touring, HAC

I.D. DATA: Serial numbers on plate on left side of frame. Starting: B-24 101, B-25 101, B-55 101. Ending: B-24 3226, B-25 13521, B-55 2137. Engine Nos. Starting: B-24 101, B-25 101, B-55 104. Ending: B-24 16674, B-25 16774, B-55 2103.

Model No.	Body Type & Seating	Price	Weight	Prod. Total
B-24	2-dr. Rds.-2P	950	2200	3126 (A)
B-25	4-dr. Tr.-5P	1050	2400	13446 (B)
B-36	2-dr. Rds.-2P	1375	2726	2550
B-37	4-dr. Tr.-5P	1485	2930	9050
B-38	2-dr. Cpe.-2P	1800	2930	50
B-55	4-dr. Tr.-5P	1985	3664	2045

Note 1: (A) — 239 built for export (chassis only).
Note 2: (B) — 1,544 were built for export (chassis only).

ENGINE: [Models B-24 and B-25] Inline. Ohv. Four. Cast iron block. B & S: 3.75 x 3.75 in. Disp.: 165 cu. in. SAE H.P.: 22. Main bearings: Three. Valve lifters: mechanical. Carb.: Marvel E 10-501. [Models B-36, B-37 and B-38] Inline. Ohv. Four. Cast iron block. B & S: 3.75 x 5 in. Disp.: 221 cu. in. Brake H.P.: 35. Main bearings: Three. Valve lifters: mechanical. Carb.: Marvel E 10-502. [Model B-55] Inline. Ohv. Six-cast in pairs. Cast iron block. B&S: 3.75 x 5 in. Disp.: 331 cu. in. Brake H.P.: 48. SAE H.P.: 33.75. Main bearings: Four Valve lifters: mechanical. Carb.: Marvel.

CHASSIS: [Series B-24] W.B.: 105 in. Front/Rear Tread: 56 in. or 60 in. Tires: 32 x 3.5. [Series B-25] W.B.: 105 in. Front/Rear Tread: 56 in. or 60 in. Tires: 32 x 3.5. [Series B-36] W.B.: 112 in. Front/Rear Tread: 56 in. or 60 in. Tires: 34 x4. [Series B-37] W.B.: 112 in. Front/Rear Tread: 56 in. or 60 in. Tires: 34 x 4. [Series B-38] W.B.: 112 in. Front/Rear Tread: 56 in. or 60 in. Tires: 34 x 4. [Series B-55] W.B.: 130 in. Front/Rear Tread: 56 in. Tires: 36 x 4.5.

TECHNICAL: Sliding gear transmission. Speeds: 3F/1R. Floor shift controls. Cone clutch. Shaft drive. 3/4 floating rear axle. Mechanical brakes on two wheels. Wooden wheels.

OPTIONS: Front bumper. Rear bumper. Spotlight.

HISTORICAL: Calendar year production: 21,217. Model year production: 21,217. The president of Buick was Walter P. Chrysler.

1915

1915 Buick, Model C-55, touring, HAC

1915 Buick, Model C-36, roadster, HAC

1915 BUICK: This was a record production year for Buick. Lower prices and improvements such as cantilevered rear springs on six-cylinder models, an improved electric starter on four-cylinder Buicks and the use of concealed door hinges on all models were the most important revisions.

BUICK — SERIES C — MODELS C-24 & C-25 — FOUR: The roadster body of the C-24 with its exposed gas tank was definitely dated. However the rounded front end of this Buick and the C-25 tourer helped maintain their popularity with Buick customers.

BUICK — SERIES C — MODELS C-36 & C-37 — FOUR: These Buicks were visually nearly identical to their 1914 counterparts. Both models were offered with an all-black finish or a combination of blue-black hood and body with black fenders and wheels.

BUICK — SERIES C — MODELS C-54 & C-55 — SIX: Joining the C-55 Buick that now had a seven-passenger capacity was the C-54 roadster model.

I.D. DATA: Serial numbers on plate on left side of frame. Starting: C-24 and C-25 100000, C-36 and C-37 106000, C-54 and C-55 105000. Ending: C24 and C-25 144713, C-36 and C-37 143913, C-54 and C-55 144715. Engine No. Starting: C-24 and C-25 100000, C-36 and C-37 100000, C-54 and C-55 100000. Ending: C-24 and C-25 144723, C-36 and C-37 144723, C-54 and C-55 144723.

Model No.	Body Type & Seating	Price	Weight	Prod. Total
C-24	2-dr. Rds.-2P	900	2200	3256 (A)
C-25	4-dr. Tourer-5P	950	2334	19080 (B)
C-36	2-dr. Rds.-2P	1185	2795	2849
C-37	4-dr. Tourer-5P	1235	2980	12450
C-54	2-dr. Rds.-2P	1635	3400	352
C-55	4-dr. Tourer-7P	1650	3680	3449

Note 1: (A) — 186 CX-24 export models were also produced.
Note 2: (B) — 931 CX-25 export models were also produced.

ENGINE: [Models C-24 and C-25] Inline. Ohv. Four. Cast iron block. B & S: 3.75 x 3.75. in Disp.: 165 cu. in. N.A.C.C. H.P.: 22.5. Main bearings: Three. Valve lifters: mechanical. Carb.: Marvel E 10-501. [Models C-36 and C-37] Inline. Ohv. Four. Cast iron block. B & S: 3.75 x 5 in. Disp.: 221 cu. in. Brake H.P.: 37. N.A.C.C. H.P.: 22.5. Main bearings: Three. Valve lifters: mechanical. Carb.: Marvel 10-502. [Models C-54 and C-55] Inline. Ohv. Six. Cast iron block. B & S: 3.75 x 5 in. Disp.: 331 cu. in. Brake H.P.: 55. N.A.C.C. H.P.: 33.75. Main bearings: Four. Valve lifters: mechanical. Carb.: Marvel.

CHASSIS: [Model C-24] W.B.: 106 in. Front/Rear Tread: 56 or 60 in. Tires: 32 x 3.5. [Model C-25] W.B.: 106 in. Front/Rear Tread: 56 or 60 in. Tires. 32 x 3.5. [Model C-36] W. B.: 112 in. Front/Rear Tread: 56 or 60 in. Tires: 34 x 4. [Model C-37] W.B.: 112 in. Front/Rear Tread: 56 or 60 in. Tires: 34 x 4. [Model C-54] W.B.: 130 in. Front/Rear Tread: 56 in. Tires: 36 x 4.5. [Model C-55] W.B.: 130 in. Front/RearTread: 56 in. Tires: 36 x 4.5.

TECHNICAL: All models sliding gear transmission. Speeds: 3F/1R. Floor shift controls. Cone clutch. Shaft drive. 3/4 floating rear axle. Mechanical brakes on two wheels. Wooden wheels.

OPTIONS: Speedometer (C-24, C-25). Bumpers. Spotlight.

HISTORICAL: The C-36 was the first Buick to carry its spare tire enclosed in the body. Calendar year production: 42,553. Model year production: 42,553. The president of Buick was Walter P. Chrysler.

1916

1916 Buick, funeral car, JAC

BUICK — SERIES D — MODELS D-44 & D-45 — SIX: These Buicks were powered by a new six-cylinder engine with a single block casting and a displacement of 224 cubic inches. The D-44 roadster had trim new lines including a squared off rear deck while the D-45 was to become the most popular Buick of 1916.

BUICK — SERIES D — MODELS D-46 & D-47 — SIX: The D-46 coupe was the first true Buick convertible and was equipped with plate glass windows. The D-47 was the first Buick with a sedan body style.

BUICK — SERIES D — MODELS D-54 & D-55 — SIX: Both of these Buicks, unchanged from 1915, were discontinued at the end of the 1916 model year.

This was Buick's greatest production year to date with an output of 124,834 cars.

I.D. DATA: Serial numbers on plate on left side of frame. Starting: D-44 & D-45 144717, D-54 59217, D-55 156717. Ending: D-44 & D-45 254501, D-54 213022, D-55 214822. Engine Nos. Starting: All models — 144729 & up.

Model No.	Body Type & Seating	Price	Weight	Prod. Total
D-44	2-dr. Rds.-2P	985	2660	12,978 (A)
D-45	4-dr. Tourer-5P	1020	2760	73,827 (B)
D-46	2-dr. Cpe.-2P	1425	2900	1443
D-47	2-dr. Sed.-5P	1800	3130	881
D-54	2-dr. Rds.-2P	1450	3400	1194
D-55	4-dr. Tourer-5P	1485	3670	9866

Note 1: (A) — 541 were produced for export. Note 2: (B) — 4,741 were produced for export.

ENGINE: [Models D-44, D-45, D-46, and D-47] Inline. Ohv. Six. Cast iron block. B & S: 3.25 x 4.5 in. Disp.: 225 cu. in. Brake H.P.: 45. N.A.C.C. H.P.: 25.35. Main bearings: Four. Valve lifters: mechanical. Carb.: Marvel E 10-543. [Models D-54 and D-55] Inline. Ohv. Six. Cast iron block. B & S: 3.75 x 5 in. Disp.: 331 cu. in. Main bearings: Four. Valve lifters: mechanical. Carb.: Marvel.

CHASSIS: [Model D-44] W.B.: 115 in. Front/Rear Tread: 56 in. Tires: 34 x 4. [Model D-45] W.B.: 115 in. Front/Rear Tread: 56 in. Tires: 34 x 4. [Model D-46] W.B.: 115 in. Front/Rear Tread: 56. Tires: 34 x 4. [Model D-47] W.B.: 115 in. Front/Rear Tread: 56. Tires: 34 x 4. [Model D-54] W.B.: 130 in. Front/Rear Tread: 56 in. Tires: 36 x 4-1/2. [Model D-55] W.B.: 130 in. Front/Rear Tread: 56 in. Tires: 36 x 4-1/2.

TECHNICAL: Sliding gear transmission. Speeds: 3F/1R. Floor shift controls. Cone clutch. Shaft drive. Full floating rear axle. Mechanical brakes on two wheels. Wooden spoke wheels.

OPTIONS: Front bumper. Cowl spot lights.

HISTORICAL: Introduced August 1916. Calendar year production: 122,315. Model year production: 105,471. The president of Buick was Walter P. Chrysler. Calendar year production included Model D-34 and D-35 four-cylinder models that, while most Buick histories regard as 1916 models, Buick tended to almost totally ignore. Because of this inconsistency they will be examined in the 1917 model year section.

I.D. DATA: Serial numbers on plate on left side of frame. Starting: Model D-34, D-35 215,823, D-44 154717. Ending: Model D-34, D-35 331774, D-44 28985 1. * Engine No. Starting: all models 144729 & up.

*Includes some D-54, D-55 models built in 1916.

Model No.	Body Type & Seating	Price	Weight	Prod. Total
D-34	2-dr. Rds.-2P	660	1900	2292 (A)
D-35	4-dr. Tr.-5P	675	2100	20,126 (B)
D-44	2-dr. Rds.-2P	1040	2660	4366 (C)
D-45	4-dr. Tr.-5P	1070	—	25,371 (D)
D-46	2-dr. Cpe.-3P	1440	2900	485
D-47	2-dr. Sed.-5P	1835	3130	132

Note 1: (A) — 238 more were built for export. Note 2: (B) — 1,097 more were built for export. Note 3: (C) — 100 more were built for export. Note 4: (D) — 1,371 more were built for export.

ENGINE: [Model D-34 and D-35] Inline. Ohv. Four. Cast iron block. B & S: 3-3/8 x 4-3/4 in. Disp.: 170 cu. in. Brake H.P.: 35. N.A.C.C. H.P.: 18.2. Main bearings: Three. Valve lifters: mechanical. Carb.: Marvel E 10-502. [Model D44, D-45, D-46, D-47] Inline. Ohv. Six. Cast iron block. B & S: 3-1/4 x 4-1/2 in. Disp.: 225 cu. in. Brake H.P.: 45. N.A.C.C. H.P.: 25.3. Main bearings: Four. Valve lifters: mechanical. Carb.: Marvel.

CHASSIS: [Model D-34] W.B.: 106 in. Front/Rear Tread: 56 in. Tires: 31 x 4. [Model D-35] W.B.: 106 in. Front/Rear Tread: 56 in. Tires: 31 x 4. [Model D-44] W.B.: 115 in. Front/Rear Tread: 56 in. Tires: 34 x 4. [Model D-45] W.B.: 115 in. Front/Rear Tread: 56 in. Tires: 34 x 4. [Model D-46] W.B.: 115 in. Front/Rear Tread: 56 in. Tires: 34 x 4. [Model D-47] W.B.: 115 in. Front/Rear Tread: 56 in. Tires: 35 x 4-1/2.

TECHNICAL: Sliding gear transmission. Speeds: 3F/1R. Floor shift controls. Cone clutch. Shaft drive. Full floating rear axle. Mechanical brakes on two wheels. Wooden spoke wheels.

OPTIONS: Front bumper. Rear bumper. Solid top — D-34.

HISTORICAL: Introduced August 1916. Calendar year production: 115,267. Model year production: 55,578. The president of Buick was Walter P. Chrysler.

1917

1918

1917 Buick, roadster, OCW

1918 Buick, E-6-49, touring, HAC

BUICK — SERIES D — D-34 & D-35 — FOUR: Buick production, due to limited supplies of strategic materials, fell to 115,267 in 1917. The large Model D-54 and D-55 Buicks were dropped while the D-34 and D-35 models were given considerable publicity. Their four-cylinder engine developed an impressive 35 hp and displaced 170 cubic inches. A detachable cylinder head was incorporated and the chassis used semi-elliptic springs rather than cantilever units. The remaining cars in the Buick lineup remained unchanged.

BUICK — SERIES E — FOUR & SIX: Buick dropped the 225 cid six in favor of a larger 242 cid version. The four-cylinder models continued with a new gear-driven oil pump and new oil and ammeter gauges were installed on the dash. Other changes included a trimmer instrument panel, revised seats with higher backs and the substitution of linoleum in place of rubber for the floor covering.

With windshields given a slight rearward slant the open Buick models took on a racier appearance. An interesting feature of the Model E-50 sedan was its removable rear door post. This early example of "hardtop styling" was featured only in 1918.

1918 Buick, roadster, JAC

I.D. DATA: Serial numbers on plate on left side of frame. Starting: 343783. Ending: 480995.

Model No.	Body Type & Seating	Price	Weight	Prod. Total
E-34	2-dr. Rds.-2P	795	1900	3800 (A)
E-35	4-dr. Tr.-5P	795	2100	27,125 (B)
E-37	2-dr. Sed.-5P	1185	2420	700
E-44	2-dr. Rds.-2P	1265	2750	10,391 (C)
E-45	4-dr. Tr.-5P	1265	2850	58,971 (D)
E-46	2-dr. Cpe.-2P	1695	2965	2965
E-47	4-dr. Sed.-5P	1845	3230	463
E-49	4-dr. Tr.-7P	1385	3075	16,148
E-50	4-dr. Sed.-7P	2175	3620	987

Note 1: (A) — 172 were built for export. Note 2: (B) — 1,190 were built for export. Note 3: (C) — 275 were built for export. Note 4: (D) — 3,035 were built for export.

ENGINE: [Models E-34, E-35, E-37] Inline. Ohv. Four. Cast iron block. B & S: 3-3/8 x 4-3/4 in. Disp.: 170 cu. in. Brake H.P.: 35. N.A.C.C. H.P.: 18.2. Valve lifters: mechanical. Carb.: Marvel E 10-517. [Models E-44, E-45, E-46, E-47, E-49, E-50] Inline. Ohv. Six. Cast iron block. B & S: 3-3/8 x 4-1/2 in. Disp.: 242 cu. in. Brake H.P.: 60. N.A.C.C. H.P.: 27.3. Valve lifters: mechanical. Carb.: Marvel 10-520.

CHASSIS: [Models E-34, E-35, E-37] W.B.: 106 in. Tires: 31 x 4 (E-37 — 23 x 3.5). [Models E-44, E-45, E-46, E-47] W.B.: 118 in. Tires: 34 x 4. [Models E-49, E-50] W.B.: 124 in. Tires: 34 x 4.5.

TECHNICAL: Sliding gear transmission. Speeds: 3F/1R. Floor shift controls. Multiple disc clutch. Shaft drive. Full floating rear axle. Mechanical brakes on two wheels. Wooden rim wheels.

OPTIONS: Front bumper. Spotlight. Dual spare tire carrier.

HISTORICAL: Introduced August 1917. Calendar year production: 77,691. Model year production: 126,222. The president of Buick was Walter P. Chrysler.

1919

1919 Buick, H-6-46, coupe, HAC

BUICK — SERIES H — SIX: Only cosmetic changes were made in the appearance of the 1919 Buick. Thinner and more numerous hood louvers were used and the six-cylinder engine that was common to all Buicks had new valve, push rod, and spark plug covers.

The instrument panel was not illuminated and the pull-type switches for the ignition and lights gave way to a lever-action Delco combined ignition and light switch.

I.D. DATA: Serial numbers on left side of frame by gas tank and again behind left front wheel. Starting: 480996. Ending: 547523.

Model No.	Body Type & Seating	Price	Weight	Prod. Total
H-44	2-dr. Rds.-2P	1595	2813	7839 (A)
H-45	4-dr. Tr.-5P	1595	2950	44,589 (B)
H-46	2-dr. Cpe.-4P	2085	3100	3971
H-47	4-dr. Sed.-5P	2195	3296	501
H-49	4-dr. Tr.-7P	1985	3175	6795
H-50	4-dr. Sed. 7P	2585	3736	531

Note 1: (A) — 176 were also exported. Note 2: (B) — 2,595 were also exported.

ENGINE: Inline. Ohv. Six. Cast iron block. B & S: 3-3/8 x 4-1/2 in. Disp.: 242 cu. in. Brake H.P.: 60. N.A.C.C. H.P.: 27.3. Valve lifters: mechanical. Carb.: Marvel E 10-526.

CHASSIS: [Models H-44, H-45, H-46, H-47] W.B.: 118 in. Front/Rear Tread: 56 in. Tires: 33 x 4. [Models H-49, H-50] W.B.: 124 in. Front/Rear Tread: 56 in. Tires: 34 x 4.5.

TECHNICAL: Sliding gear transmission. Speeds: 3F/1R. Floor shift controls. Multiple disc clutch. Shaft drive. Full floating rear axle. Mechanical brakes on two wheels. Wooden spoke wheels.

OPTIONS: Front bumper. Spotlight.

HISTORICAL: Calendar year production: 119,310. Model year production: 65,997. The president of Buick was Walter P. Chrysler.

1920

1920 Buick, K-6-44, roadster, HAC

BUICK — SERIES K — SIX: The Series K Buicks were unchanged from the 1919 Series H versions.

I.D. DATA: Serial numbers on left side of frame by gas tank and repeated behind left front wheel. Starting: 547524. Ending: 687794. Engine numbers on crankcase on left side near front of oil filler tube.

Model No.	Body Type & Seating	Price	Weight	Prod. Total
K-44	2-dr. Rds.-3P	1495	2813	19,000 (A)
K-45	2-dr. Tr.-5P	1495	2950	85,245 (B)
K-46	2-dr. Cpe.-4P	2085	3100	6503
K-47	4-dr. Sed.-5P	2255	3296	2252
K-49	4- dr. Tr.- 7P	1785	3175	16,801 (C)
K-50	4-dr. Sed.-7P	2695	3736	1499

Note 1: (A) — 200 built for export. Note 2: (B) — 7,400 built for export. Note 3: (C) — 1,100 built for export.

ENGINE: Inline. Ohv. Six. Cast iron block. B & S: 3-3/8 x 4-1/2 in. Disp.: 242 cu. in. Brake H.P.: 60. N.A.C.C. H.P.: 27.3. Main bearings: Four. Valve lifters: mechanical. Carb.: Marvel E 10-526.

CHASSIS: [Models K-44, 45, 46] W.B.: 118 in. Front/Rear Tread: 56 in. Tires: 33 x 4. [Model K-47] W.B.: 118 in. Front/Rear Tread: 56 in. Tires: 34 x 4.5. [Models K-49, 50] W.B.: 124 in. Front/Rear Tread: 56 in. Tires: 34 x 4.5.

TECHNICAL: Sliding gear transmission. Speeds: 3F/1R. Floor shift controls. Multiple disc clutch. Shaft drive. Full floating rear axle. Mechanical brakes on two wheels. Wooden spoke wheels with detachable rims.

OPTIONS: Front bumper. Spotlight.

HISTORICAL: Calendar year production: 115,176. Model year production 140,000. The president of Buick was Harry H. Bassett.

1921

1921 Buick, Model 48, coupe, HAC

1921 Buick, Model 50, sedan, JAC

BUICK — SERIES 21 — SIX: Buick's styling was moderately changed for 1921 with its higher hood and radiator now forming a straight horizontal line to the windshield base. Technical improvements included cord tires on all models produced after January 1, 1921.

I.D. DATA: Serial numbers on brass plate left side of frame by gas tank and repeated behind left front wheel. Starting: 687795. Ending: 760555. Engine numbers on brassplate next to timing gear inspection hole. Starting: 687795. Ending: 760555.

Model No.	Body Type & Seating	Price	Weight	Prod. Total
44	2-dr. Rds.-3P	1795	2845	7236 (A)
45	2-dr. Tr.-5P	1795	2972	31,877 (B)
46	2-dr. Cpe.-4P	2585	3137	4063
47	4-dr. Sed.-5P	2895	3397	2252
48	2-dr. Cpe.-4P	2985	3397	2606
49	4-dr. Tr.-7P	2060	3272	6424 (C)
50	4-dr. Sed.-7P	3295	3612	1460

Note 1: (A) — 56 produced for export
Note 2: (B) — 1,192 produced for export
Note 3: (C) — 366 produced for export
Note 4: All models carry a 21 prefix, i.e. 21-44.

ENGINE: Inline. Ohv. Six. Cast iron block. B & S: 3-3/8 x 4-1/2 in. Disp.: 242 cu. in. Brake H.P.: 60. N.A.C.C. H.P.: 27.3. Main bearings: Four. Valve lifters: mechanical. Carb.: Marvel E 10-526.

CHASSIS: [Models 44, 45, 46, and 47] W.B.: 118 in. Front/Rear Tread: 56 in. Tires: 34 x 4.5. [Models 48, 49, and 50] W.B.: 124 in. Front/Rear Tread: 56 in. Tires: 34 x 4.5.

TECHNICAL: Sliding gear transmission. Speeds: 3F/1R. Floor shift controls. Multiple disc clutch. Shaft drive. Full floating rear axle. Mechanical brakes on two wheels. Wooden spoke wheels with detachable rims.

OPTIONS: Toolbox. Bumper. Spotlight. Step plates. Two tops (Touring car)

HISTORICAL: A Buick Model 46 completed the 750 mile route between San Francisco and Portland in 29 hours, which was 44 minutes less than the Southern Pacific's crack Shasta Limited train. Calendar year production: 82,930. Model year production: 55,337. The president of Buick was Harry H. Bassett.

1922

1922 Buick, Model 22-44, roadster, OCW

BUICK — SERIES 22-FOUR — FOUR: Buick's big news for 1922 was the reintroduction of a four-cylinder model in August 1921. Retained from 1921 were the smoother and higher radiators and hoods.

BUICK — SERIES 22-SIX — SIX: Highlighting the six-cylinder Buick line were new Sport Roadster and Sport Touring models with standard Houk wire wheels, red interior and dash-installed clock and speedometer manufactured by Van Sicklen.

I.D. DATA: Serial numbers on left side of frame by gas tank and repeated behind left front wheel. Starting: Models 34, 35, 36, 37 — 688795 & up. Models 44, 45, 46, 47, 48, 49, 50 —

753000 & up. Model 55 — 852537. Ending: Model 55 — 857599. Engine numbers on crankcase.

Model No.	Body Type & Seating	Price	Weight	Prod. Total
34	2-dr. Rds.-2P	935	2310	5583 (A)
35	4-dr. Tr.-5P	975	2380	22,521 (B)
36	2-dr. Cpe.-3P	1475	2560	2225
37	4-dr. Sed.-5P	1650	2780	3118
44	2-dr. Rds.-3P	1495	2285	7666 (C)
45	4-dr. Tr.-5P	1525	3005	34,433 (D)
46	2-dr. Cpe.-4P	2135	3235	2293
47	4-dr. Sed.-5P	2435	3425	4878
48	2-dr. Cpe.-4P	2325	3430	8903
49	4-dr. Tr.-7P	1735	3280	6714 (E)
50	4-dr. Sed.-7P	2635	3615	4201
50L	4-dr. Limo.-7P	2735	—	178
54	2-dr. Spt. Rds.-3P	1785	3180	2562
55	2-dr. Spt. Tr.-4P	1785	3270	900

Note 1: (A) — 5 built for export.
Note 2: (B) — 29 built for export.
Note 3: (C) — 9 built for export.
Note 4: (D) — 499 built for export.
Note 5: (E) — 71 built for export.
Note 6: All models carry a 22 prefix, i.e. 22-34.

1922 Buick, Model 22-36, coupe, JAC

ENGINE: [Models 34, 35, 36, 37 Series 22-4] Inline. Ohv. Four. Cast iron block. B & S: 3-3/8 x 4-3/4 in. Disp.: 170 cu. in. Brake H.P.: 35-40. N.A.C.C. H.P.: 18.23. Main bearings: Three. Valve lifters: mechanical. Carb.: Marvel H 10-502. [Models 44, 45, 46, 47, 48, 49, 50, 50L, 54, 55 Series 22-Six] Inline. Ohv. Six. Cast iron block. B & S: 3-3/8 x 4-1/2 in. Disp.: 242 cu. in. Brake H.P.: 60. N.A.C.C. H.P.: 27.3. Main bearings: Four. Valve lifters: mechanical. Carb.: Marvel H 10-54.

CHASSIS: [Models 34, 35, 36, 37] W.B.: 109 in. Tires: 31 x 4. [Models 44, 45, 46, 47] W.B.: 118 in. Front/Rear Tread: 56 in. Tires: 33 x 4. [Models 48, 49, 50, 50L] W.B.: 124 in. Front/Rear Tread: 56 in. Tires: 34 x 4.5. [Models 54, 55] W.B.: 124 in. Front/Rear Tread: 56 in. Tires: 32 x 4.5.

TECHNICAL: Sliding gear transmission. Speeds: 3F/1R. Floor shift controls. Multiple disc clutch. Shaft drive. Full floating rear axle. Mechanical brakes on two wheels. Wooden spoke wheels with detachable rims. (Models 54, 55 have Houk wire wheels).

OPTIONS: Dual Sidemount (124-inch wheelbase cars only). Cowl lamps (open models).

HISTORICAL: Introduced August 1921. Calendar year production: 123,152 (including truck models). Model year production: 106,788. The president of Buick was Harry H. Bassett.

1923

BUICK — SERIES 23-FOUR — FOUR: Buick styling was substantially improved with crowned fenders, cowl lights, new drum-shaped headlights and rounded window edges. Also providing the Buick with a fresh appearance was its new grille form that would remain virtually unchanged through 1927. Technical improvements included repositioned rear spring hangers, a lower suspension system and a transmission lock. Increased engine life was achieved through a harder cylinder casting, a larger crankshaft, and stronger connecting rods, pistons and main bearings.

BUICK — SERIES 23-SIX — SIX: The six-cylinder Buicks although sharing the styling of the Series 23-Four were identified by their longer 118- and 124-inch wheelbases. In addition open bodied six-cylinder Buicks had rectangular rear windows while those of the four-cylinder models were oval-shaped.

I.D. DATA: Serial numbers on left side of frame by gas tank and repeated behind left front wheel. Starting: four-cylinder models 34, 35, 36, 37, 38, 39 — 832673, six-cylinder models 44, 45, 47, 48, 49, 50, 54, 55 — 871321. Ending: four-cylinder models — 1051558, Six-cylinder models — 1060176. Engine numbers on left side of crankcase near front of oil filler tube.

Model No.	Body Type & Seating	Price	Weight	Prod. Total
34	2-dr. Rds.-2P	865	2415	5768 (A)
35	4-dr. Tr.-5P	885	2520	36,935 (B)
36	2-dr. Cpe.-3P	1175	2745	7004
37	4-dr. Sed.-5P	1395	2875	8885 (C)
38	2-dr. Tr. Sed.-5P	1325	2750	6025
39	2-dr. Spt. Rds.-2P	1025	2445	1971
41	2-dr. Tr. Sed.-5P	1935	3380	8719
44	2-dr. Rds.-3P	1175	2940	6488 (D)
45	4-dr. Tr.-5P	1195	3085	45,227 (E)
47	4-dr. Sed.-5P	1985	3475	7358
48	2-dr. Cpe.-4P	1895	3440	10,847
49	4-dr. Tr.-7P	1435	3290	5906 (F)
50	4-dr. Sed.-7P	2195	3670	10,279 (G)
54	2-dr. Spt. Rds.-3P	1625	—	4501
55	4-dr. Spt. Tr.-4P	1675	3330	12,857

Note 1: (A) — 8 built for export.
Note 2: (B) — 7,004 built for export.
Note 3: (C) — 1 built for export.
Note 4: (D) — 3 built for export.
Note 5: (E) — 47 built for export.
Note 6: (F) — 25 built for export.
Note 7: (G) — 1 built for export.
Note 8: All models carry a 23 prefix, i.e. 23-34.

1923 Buick, coupe, OCW

ENGINE: [Series 23-Four] Inline. Ohv. Four. Cast iron block. B & S: 3-3/8 x 4-3/4 in. Disp.: 170 cu. in. Brake H.P.: 35. N.A.C.C. H.P.: 18.23. Main bearings: Three. Valve lifters: mechanical. Carb.: Marvel K 10-514. [Series 23-Six] Inline. Ohv. Six. Cast iron block. B & S: 3-3/8 x 4-1/2 in. Disp.: 242 cu. in. Brake H.P.: 60. N.A.C.C. H.P.: 27.3. Main bearings: Four. Valve lifters: mechanical. Carb.: Marvel K 10-511.

CHASSIS: [Models 34-39] W.B.: 109 in. Tires: 31 x 4. [Models 44, 45] W.B.: 118 in. Front/Rear Tread: 56 in. Tires: 32 x 4. [Models 48, 49, 50] W.B.: 124 in. Tires: 33 x 4.5. [Models 54, 55] W.B.: 124 in. Tires: 32 x 4.5.

TECHNICAL: Sliding gear transmission. Speeds: 3F/1R. Floor shift controls. Multiple disc clutch. Shaft drive. Full floating rear axle. Mechanical brakes on two wheels. Wooden spoke wheels with detachable rims.

Note 1: Models 39 & 50 Sport Roadster and Model 55 Sport Touring were offered with either Houk wire or Tuare steel disc wheels as well as wooden.

OPTIONS: Disc wheels. Front bumper. Spotlight. Wind wings. White sidewall tires. Taillights (diamond-shaped). Spare tire cover. Heater (Perfection types AB, GB).

HISTORICAL: Introduced January 1923. Calendar year production: 210,572. Model year production: 181,657. The president of Buick was Harry H. Bassett. A modified Model 54 Series 23-Six was timed at 108.24 mph in a run at the Muroc dry lake in California. Buick built its one-millionth car on March 21, 1923.

1924

1924 Buick, Model 24-Six-55, sport touring, HAC

BUICK — SERIES 24-FOUR — FOUR: The Buicks for 1924 were, with the exception of the engine in its four-cylinder line, new automobiles. With a gently sloping hood and smoothly molded fenders the Buick attracted plenty of attention. The radiator shell that was extremely close to Packard's familiar pattern also became a center of controversy that Packard responded to with its "When prettier automobiles are built, Packard will build them."

BUICK — SERIES 24-SIX — SIX: Giving the six-cylinder models added distinction was their nickel-plated trim and longer 128-inch wheelbase for some models.

Mechanically, Buick's 1924 models were noted for their four-wheel mechanical brakes, stronger frames and axles. The six-cylinder engine had a larger displacement and was equipped with a removable cylinder head and aluminum crankcase. Nineteen twenty-four was the last year Buick's closed cars had horizontally divided windshields.

I.D. DATA: Serial numbers on left side of frame by gas tank and repeated behind left front wheel. Starting: Series 24-Four 1060178 & up, Series 24-Six 1064324. Ending: Series 24-Six 1239258. Engine numbers on left side of crankcase near front of oil filler tube.

Model No.	Body Type & Seating	Price	Weight	Prod. Total
33	2-dr. Cpe.-4P	1395	2845	5479 (A)
34	2-dr. Rds.-2P	935	2576	4296
35	4-dr. Tr.-5P	965	2680	21,857
37	4-dr. Sed.-5P	1495	2955	6563
41	4-dr. Dbl. Service Sed.-5P	1695	3675	14,094
44	2-dr. Rds.-2P	1275	3300	9700
45	4-dr. Tr.-5P	1295	3455	48,912
47	4-dr. Sed.-5P	2095	3845	10,377
48	2-dr. Cpe.-4P	1995	3770	13,009
49	4-dr. Tr.-7P	1565	3645	7224
50	4-dr. Sed.-7P	2285	4020	9561
50L	4-dr. Limo. Sed.-7P	2385	—	713
51	4-dr. Brgm. Tr. Sed.-5P	2235	3940	4991
54	2-dr. Spt. Rds.-3P	1675	3470	1938
54C	2-dr. Ctry. Clb. Cpe.-3P	1945	3765	1107
55	4-dr. Spt. Tr.-4P	1725	3605	4111
57	4-dr. Twn. Car-7P	2795	3860	25

Note 1: (A) A total of 6,087 Buicks of various models and body styles were built for export.

Note 2: All models carry a 24 prefix, i.e.: 24-33.

1924 Buick, Model 24-Four-33, coupe, HAC

ENGINE: [Models 24-Four] Inline. Ohv. Four. Cast iron block. B & S: 3-3/8 x 4-3/4 in. Disp.: 170 cu. in. Brake H.P.: 35. N.A.C.C. H.P.: 18.23. Main bearings: Three. Valve lifters: mechanical. Carb.: Marvel K 10-514. [Models 24-Six] Inline. Ohv. Four. Cast iron block. B & S: 3-3/8 x 4-3/4 in. Disp.: 255 cu. in. Brake H.P.: 70. N.A.C.C. H.P.: 27.3. Main bearings: Four. Valve lifters: mechanical. Carb.: Marvel R 10-578.

CHASSIS: [24-Four] W.B.: 109 in. Tires: 31 x 4. [24-Six Models 41, 44, 45, 46, 47] W.B.: 120 in. Tires: 32 x 4. [24-Six Models 48, 49, 50, 51, 54, 55] W.B.: 128 in. Tires: 32 x 4-1/2.

TECHNICAL: Series 24-Four. Sliding gear transmission. Speeds: 3F/1R. Floor shift controls. Multiple disc clutch. Shaft drive. 3/4 floating rear axle. Mechanical brakes on four wheels. Wooden spoke wheels with detachable rim. Series 24-Six. Sliding gear transmission. Speeds: 3F/1R. Floor shift controls. Multiple disc clutch. Shaft drive. Full floating rear axle. Mechanical brakes on four wheels. Wooden spoke wheels with detachable rims.

OPTIONS: Front bumper. Rear bumper. Wind wings. Motometer.

HISTORICAL: Introduced August 1, 1923. Four-wheel mechanical brakes. Calendar year production: 160,411. Model year production: 171,561. The president of Buick was Harry H. Bassett.

1925

BUICK — STANDARD SIX — SIX: Buick adopted a new series designation for 1925 and Standard Six models replaced the 24-Fours as the lower priced Buicks. A new six-cylinder engine powered nine models of this series all of which were higher priced than their predecessors. A longer 114.3-inch wheelbase was used.

BUICK — MASTER SIX — SIX: The Master Six was powered by the same engine used in 1924 by the 24-Six of 1924. Styling changes were extremely modest but several new body styles kept public interest in Buick high. The age of the open tourer as the dominant product of any manufacturer was passing and

for the first time Buick's best selling body styles were closed models. An interesting response to the tourer's decline was Buick's introduction of "Enclosed Touring" models in both the Standard and Master series. These cars used normal touring bodies fitted with permanently fixed tops.

1925 Buick, roadster, OCW

1925 Buick, Model 25-Six-51, brougham sedan, HAC

I.D. DATA: Serial numbers on left side of frame by gas tank and repeated behind left front wheel. Starting: Standard — 1239259 & up, Master — 1211720 & up. Engine numbers on crankcase on left side near front of oil filler tube.

Standard Six Series

Model No.	Body Type & Seating	Price	Weight	Prod. Total
20	4-dr. C'ch.-5P	1295	3050	21,900
21	4-dr. Dbl. Serivce Sed.- 5P	1475	3185	9252
24	2-dr. Rds.-2P	1150	2750	3315
24A	2-dr. Encl. Rds.-2P	1190	2800	1725
24S	2-dr. Spt. Rds.-5P	1250	—	501
25	4-dr. Tr.-5P	1175	2920	16,040
25A	4-dr. Encl. Tr.-5P	1250	2970	4450
25S	4-dr. Spt. Tr.-5P	—	—	651
26	2-dr. Cpe.-2P	1375	2960	4398
26S	2-dr. Spt. Cpe.-4P	—	—	550
27	4-dr. Sed.-5P	1665	3245	10,772
28	2-dr. Cpe.-4P	1565	3075	7743

Master Six Series

Model No.	Body Type & Seating	Price	Weight	Prod. Total
40	2-dr. C'ch.-5P	1495	3560	30,600
44	2-dr. Rds.-2P	1365	3285	2975
44A	2-dr. Encl. Rds.-2P	1400	3335	850
45	4-dr. Tr.-5P	1395	3465	5203
45A	4-dr. Encl. Tr.-5P	1475	3540	1900
47	4-dr. Sed.-5P	2225	3850	4200
47A	4-dr. Encl. Tr.-7P	1475	3540	500
50	4-dr. Sed.-7P	2425	3995	4606
50L	4-dr. Limo.-7P	2525	4030	768
51	4-dr. Brgm. Sed.-5P	2350	3905	6850
54	2-dr. Spt. Rds.-3P	1750	3485	1917
54C	2-dr. Ctry. Clb. Cpe.-3P	2075	3745	2751
55S	2-dr. Spt. Tr.-4P	1800	3550	2774
57	4-dr. Twn. Car-7P	2925	3850	92

Note 1: All models had a 25 prefix, i.e.: 25-20.
In addition a total of 9,412 Buicks of all models were exported.

ENGINE: [Standard Six] Inline. Ohv. Six. Cast iron block. B & S: 3 x 4-1/2 in. Disp.: 191 cu. in. Brake H.P.: 50 at 2800 R.P.M. N.A.C.C. H.P.: 21.6. Main bearings: Four. Valve lifters: mechanical. Carb.: Marvel T38. Torque: 120 lb. ft. at 1600 R.P.M. [Master Six] Inline. Ohv. Four. Cast iron block. B & S: 3-3/8 x 4-3/4 in. Disp.: 255 cu. in. Brake H.P.: 70. N.A.C.C. H.P.: 27.3. Main bearings: Four. Valve lifters: mechanical. Carb.: Marvel T4S.

CHASSIS: [Standard Six] W.B.: 114.3 in. Tires: 5.00 x 22. [Master Six] W.B.: 120/128 in. Tires: 32 x 5.77 (6.00 x 22 opt.)

TECHNICAL: Sliding gear transmission. Speeds: 3F/1R. Floor shift controls. Multiple disc clutch. Shaft drive. 3/4 floating-Standard Six, full floating-Master Six. Mechanical brakes on four wheels. Wooden spoke wheels with detachable rims.

OPTIONS: White sidewall tires. Bumpers. Spotlight. Wind wings. Moto-meter.

HISTORICAL: Introduced August 1924. Vacuum-operated windshield wipers replaced hand-powered versions. Nineteen twenty-five was the first model year Buick equipped its car with balloon tires. Calendar year production: 192,100. Model year production: 157,071 plus 9,412 for export. The president of Buick was Harry H. Bassett. Buick sent a touring model around the world via a dealer-to-dealer route. Each dealer was responsible for driving the car to the next and having its log book signed. Nineteen twenty-five was the first year Buick used a nitrocellulose lacquer in place of a varnish-color finish process.

1926

1926 Buick, Standard Six, two-door coupe, HAC

BUICK STANDARD SIX, MASTER SIX — SIX: Both Buick series were restyled for 1926 with smoother radiator edges and on those cars with Fisher bodies, double belt moldings. Hubcaps and the gas filler caps were now constructed of aluminum and a straight tie rod running vertically across the grille supported the headlights.

Technical improvements included new air, oil and gas filters, a stronger clutch, and one-piece brake linings. The Buick's new dual-beam headlights were mounted in interchangeable shells. The dimming switch for these lights was mounted in the steering wheel center. Components such as the chassis, driveshaft, and rear axle were now of a heavier construction. In addition the Buick chassis had Zerk lubrication fittings.

BUICK MASTER SIX — SIX: Engine displacement and power was increased in both series. In addition to their longer wheelbase the Master series models were distinguished from their Standard runningmates by such features as a Motometer, scuff

plates, clock, cigarette lighter, and heater that were included in their base price.

1926 Buick, Master Six, sedan, JAC

I.D. DATA: Serial numbers on right side of frame behind front wheel position. Starting: Standard — 1398244, Master — 1426599. Ending: Standard 1638576, Master — 1638773. Engine numbers on left side of crankcase near front of oil filler tube.

Standard Six Series

Model No.	Body Type & Seating	Price	Weight	Prod. Total
20	2-dr. Sed.-5P	1195	3140	40,113
24	2-dr. Rds.-2P	1125	2865	1891
25	4-dr. Tr.-5P	1150	2920	4859
26	2-dr. Cpe.-2P	1195	3030	10,531
27	4-dr. Sed.-5P	1295	3210	43,375
28	2-dr. Cpe.-4P	1275	3110	8271

Master Six Series

Model No.	Body Type & Seating	Price	Weight	Prod. Total
40	2-dr. Sed.-5P	1395	3655	21,861
44	2-dr. Rds.-2P	1250	3380	2654
45	4-dr. Tr.-5P	1295	3535	2630
47	4-dr. Sed.-5P	1495	3790	53,490
48	2-dr. Cpe.-4P	1795	3845	10,028
49	4-dr. Sed.-7P	1995	—	1
50	4-dr. Sed.-7P	1995	4040	12,690
50T	4-dr. Taxi Cab-7P	—	4040	220
51	4-dr. Brgm. Tr. Sed.-5P	1925	3945	10,873
54	2-dr. Spt. Rds.-3P	1495	3580	2501
54C	2-dr. C.C. Spt. Cpe.-3P	1765	3820	4436
55	4-dr. Spt. Tr.-4P	1525	3650	2051
58	2-dr. Cpe.-4P	1275	—	1

Note 1: All models carry a 26 prefix, i.e. 26-20.

ENGINE: [Standard Six] Inline. Ohv. Six. Cast iron block. B & S: 3-1/8 x 4-1/2 in. Disp.: 207 cu. in. Brake H.P.: 60. N.A.C.C. H.P.: 23.4. Main bearings Four. Valve lifters: mechanical. Carb.: Marvel T3. [Master Six] Inline. Ohv. Six. Cast iron block. B & S: 3-1/2 x 4-3/4 in. Disp.: 274 cu. in. Brake H.P.: 75. N.A.C.C. H.P.: 29.4. Main bearings: Four. Valve lifters: mechanical. Carb.: Marvel T-4.

CHASSIS: [Standard Six] W.B.: 114.5 in. Tires: 6.00 x 21. [Master Six] W. B.: 120/128 in. Tires: 6.00 x 21.

TECHNICAL: Sliding gear transmission. Speeds: 3F/1R. Floor shift controls. Multiple disc clutch. Shaft drive. 3/4 floating-Standard Six, full floating-Master Six. Mechanical brakes on four wheels. Wooden spoke wheels with detachable rims.

OPTIONS: Bumpers. Fog lights. Moto-meter (Standard Six). Runningboard step plates (Standard Six). Instrument panel light. Cadmium rims. White sidewall tires.

HISTORICAL: Introduced August 1, 1925. The old combination starter-generator was replaced by separate Delco starter and generator units. Calendar year production: 266,753. Model year production: 240,533 (including 7,480 for export and 1 experimental model). On October 17, 1926, Harry Bassett (president of Buick) died of pneumonia. His successor was Edward Thomas Strong.

1927

1927 Buick, Model 25, Deluxe touring, OCW

BUICK — STANDARD SIX — SIX: The appearance of both Buick lines was left almost unaltered for 1927. All open models in both series had one-piece windshields and a reorganized dash that placed the speedometer directly before the driver and provided dashboard lighting on all models.

Technical advancements were headlined by new motor mounts, a counterbalanced crankshaft, a "vacuum ventilation" for the crankcase, and a torsional balancer that enabled Buick to describe its engines as "Vibrationless Beyond Belief." The Standard Six models continued to have gas tank mounted fuel gauges.

1927 Buick, Standard Six, sport roadster, HAC

BUICK MASTER SIX — SIX: Master Six models on the 128-inch wheelbase chassis had a Gothic Goddess radiator cap replete with wings. This ornament was also fitted to Models 24 and 25 of the Standard Six series. Master Six closed car interiors were finished in walnut, satin and broadcloth. With the exception of the three lowest priced Models 40, 47, and 48, the Master Six Buicks featured new dash-mounted fuel gauges.

I.D. DATA: Serial numbers on right side of frame behind front wheel position. Starting: Standard Six Serial-1638800, Master Six Serial-1661435. Engine numbers on crankcase on left side near front of oil filler tube.

Standard Six Series

Model No.	Body Type & Seating	Price	Weight	Prod. Total
20	2-dr. Sed.-5P	1195	3215	33,190
24	2-dr. Spt. Rds.-4P	1195	2990	4985
25	4-dr. DeL. Spt. Tr.-5P	1225	3040	3272
26	2-dr. Cpe.-2P	1195	3110	10,512
26S	2-dr. Ctry. Clb. Cpe.-4P	1275	3190	11,688
26CC	2-dr. Clp. Top. Cpe.-4P	—	—	1
27	4-dr. Sed.-5P	1295	3300	40,272
28	2-dr. Cpe.-4P	1275	3190	7178
29	4-dr. Twn. Brgm. Sed.-5P	1375	3305	11,032

Master Six Series

Model No.	Body Type & Seating	Price	Weight	Prod. Total
40	2-dr. Sed.-5P	1395	3750	12,130
47	4-dr. Sed.-5P	1495	3870	49,105
48	2-dr. Cpe.-4P	1465	3800	9350
50	4-dr. Sed.-7P	1995	4115	11,259
50T	4-dr. Taxi Cab.-7P	—	—	60
51	4-dr. Brgm. Sed.-5P	1925	4050	13,862
54	2-dr. DeL. Spt. Rds.-4P	1495	3655	4310
54C	2-dr. Ctry. Clb. Cpe.-4P	1765	3905	7095
54CC	2-dr. Conv. Cpe.-4P	1925	3915	2354
55	4-dr. DeL. Spt. Tr.-4P	1525	3735	2092
58	2-dr. Cpe.-5P	1850	3940	7655

ENGINE: [Standard Six] Inline. Ohv. Six. Cast iron block. B & S: 3-1/8 x 4-1/2 in. Disp.: 207 cu. in. Brake H.P.: 63 @ 2800 R.P.M. N.A.C.C. H.P.: 23.4. Main bearings: Four. Valve lifters: mechanical. Carb.: Marvel T3. [Master Six] Inline. Ohv. Six. Cast iron block. B & S: 3-1/2 x 4-3/4 in. Disp.: 274 cu. in. Brake H.P.: 75. N.A.C.C. H.P.: 29.4. Main bearings; Four. Valve lifters: mechanical. Carb.: Marvel T4.

CHASSIS: [Standard Six] W.B.: 114.5 in. Tires: 33 x 6. [Master Six] W.B.: 120/128 in. Tires: 33 x 6.

TECHNICAL: Sliding gear transmission. Speeds: 3F/1R. Floor shift controls. Multiple disc clutch. Shaft drive. 3/4 floating rear axle — Standard Six, full floating rear axle — Master Six. Mechanical brakes on four wheels. Wooden spoke wheels with detachable rims.

OPTIONS: Bumpers. Trunk.

HISTORICAL: Introduced August 1926. Calendar year production: 255,160. Model year production: 250,116 (includes 8,109 for export). The president of Buick was Edward Thomas Strong. The two-millionth Buick was produced on November 1, 1927.

1928

1928 Buick, opera coupe, DM

BUICK STANDARD SIX — SERIES 115 — SIX:

Buick's styling for 1928 featured thinner windshield and corner posts (on closed models), standard hood emblems and smooth-surfaced fenders. The older, barrel-shaped headlight cases gave way to bullet-shaped versions that, along with the radiator, windshield molding and hood fasteners, were nickel-plated. Giving the Buick a new face was a smoother radiator shell that shed almost all that had remained of its Packard-look.

A new stronger, double-drop frame with deeper side channels allowed body height to be reduced by three inches. A noteworthy improvement in handling and roadability was attained by the use of four-wheel Lovejoy hydraulic shock absorbers on all models. Engine changes for 1928 were highlighted by reshaped hemispherical combustion chambers.

Interior improvements were led by Buick's adoption of the standard H-shift pattern, an adjustable steering column and dash-mounted engine temperature and fuel level gauges. Plush mohair was used for the upholstery.

Also added to the Buick's standard equipment list for 1928 were Wolverine bumpers. All Standard Six models had dash-mounted gas gauges and painted headlight shells. The exceptions to the latter were Models 24 and 25 that had chromed shells.

BUICK MASTER SIX — SERIES 120 — SIX: A new DeLuxe four-door sedan was added to the Master Six line while Models 54CC (convertible coupe) and 40 (two-door sedan) were eliminated. The four-door sport touring Master Six was the only Buick offered with standard side mounts. All Master Six models had chromed headlight shells. A new model on the 120-inch wheelbase chassis was the 47S, five-passenger DeLuxe sedan. Its back was leather trimmed and was fitted with side landau hinges. Interiors were finished in taupe and green figured-design mohair plush. All closed models in both series had wide doors, new outside door handles and rear compartment carpets. The Master Six Buicks on the 128-inch wheelbase has a 128 Series designation.

1928 Buick, roadster, OCW

I.D. DATA: Serial numbers on right side of frame behind front wheel opening. Starting: Standard Six 1901476, Master Six — 1911026. Ending: Standard Six -- 2137872, Master Six — 2169650. Engine numbers on crankcase.

Standard Series

Model No.	Body Type & Seating	Price	Weight	Prod. Total
20	2-dr. Sed.-5P	1195	3310	32,481
24	2-dr. Spt. Rds.-4P	1195	3090	4513
25	4-dr. Spt. Tr.-5P	1225	3140	3134
26	2-dr. Cpe.-2P	1195	3215	12,417
26S	2-dr. Ctry. Clb. Cpe.-4P	1275	3300	13,211
27	4-dr. Sed.-5P	1295	3370	50,224
29	4-dr. Twn. Brgm.-5P	1375	3400	10,840

Master Six Series

Model No.	Body Type & Seating	Price	Weight	Prod. Total
47	4-dr. Sed.-5P	1495	3920	34,197
47S	4-dr. DeL. Sed.-5P	1575	3930	16,398
48	2-dr. Cpe.-4P	1465	3835	9002
49	4-dr. Tr.-7P	NA	NA	2
50	4-dr. Sed.-7P	1995	4085	10,827
51	4-dr. Brgm. Sed.-5P	1925	3980	10,258
54	2-dr. Spt. Rds.-4P	1495	3655	3853
54C	2-dr. Ctry. Clb. Cpe.-4P	1765	3890	6555
55	4-dr. Spt. Tr.-5P	1525	3735	1333
58	2-dr. Cpe.-5P	1850	3925	9984

Note 1: All models carry a 28 prefix, i.e. 28-20.

ENGINE: [Standard Six] Inline. Ohv. Six. Cast iron block. B & S: 3-1/8 x 4-1/2 in. Disp.: 207 cu. in. Brake H.P.: 63 @ 2800 R.P.M. N.A.C.C. H.P.: 23.44. Main bearings: four. Valve lifters: mechanical. Carb.: Marvel T3. Torque: 140. [Master Six] Inline. Ohv. Six. Cast iron block. B & S: 3-1/2 x 4-3/4 in. Disp.: 274 cu. in. Brake H.P.: 77@ 2800 R.P.M. N.A.C.C. H.P.: 29.4. Main bearings: four. Valve lifters: mechanical. Carb.: Marvel T4. Torque: 178.

CHASSIS: [Standard Six] W.B.: 114.5 in. Tires: 31 x 5.25. [Master Six] W.B: 120 in. (Models 47 and 47S only). Tires: 33 x 6. [Master Six] (Models 50, 51, 54, 54C, 55 and 58): W. B.: 128 in. Tires: 33 x 6.

TECHNICAL: Sliding gear transmission. Speeds: 3F/1R. Floor shift controls. Multiple disc clutch. Shaft drive. 3/4 floating rear axle — (Standard Six); full floating rear axle — (Master Six). Overall ratio: Models 20, 27, 29 — 5.1:1. Models 48, 54, 54C, 55, 58 — 4.72:1. Models 24, 25, 26, 26S, 47, 47S, 50, 51 — 4.9:1. Mechanical brakes on four wheels. Wooden spoke wheels with detachable rims.

OPTIONS: Buffalo wire wheels (Standard Six Models 24 & 25 and 128-inch wheelbase Master Six models only). Dual tire carrier. Moto-meter.

HISTORICAL: Introduced July 28, 1927. Calendar year production: 221,758. Model year production: 235,009 (including 5,194 for export). The president of Buick was Edward Thomas Strong. A 1928 model coupe produced in November 1927 was the two-millionth Buick built.

1929

1929 Buick, Series 129, Model 58, coupe, JAC

BUICK — SERIES 116 — SIX: The 1929 Buicks were the first cars styled in their entirety by General Motors' Art and Colour department. Three new series — the 116, 121 and 129 (which represented wheelbase measurements) — replaced the older Standard and Master Six designations and all carried the body styling that earned them the sobriquet, Pregnant Buicks. This non-complimentary designation was due to the 1-1/2-inch bulge below the beltline.

Aside from this feature, which lasted only for one year, the 1929 Buicks had slightly slanted windshields on closed body models and a radiator bearing the Buick nameplate in its center rather than on the shell. Major technical improvements included (on closed models) dual electric windshield wipers and side cowl ventilators.

Buick was also celebrating its silver anniversary with a total of 43 exterior color options. Standard in all models was a mechanical fuel pump in place of the vacuum tank.

The chassis design of all three series was, with the exception of the external mechanical brakes, virtually all new. The frame was constructed of thicker steel with deeper cross sections and key suspension components were strengthened. Lovejoy shock absorbers were also installed. All engines were increased both in terms of displacement and power and steel-backed main bearings were also used by Buick for the first time.

The 116-inch wheelbase chassis Buick now featured interiors with ashtrays and cigarette lighters as standard equipment.

1929 Buick, Series 121, Model 47, sedan, LD

1929 Buick, Series 121, Model 44, sport roadster, JAC

BUICK — SERIES 121 — SIX: Offered in six styles, the 121 Series Buick shared its walnut interior trim with all 1929 Buicks. Also common to all Buicks was a new molded rubber steering wheel.

1929 Buick, Series 129, Model 51, sport sedan, JAC

1929 Buick, Series 129, Model 57, sedan, JAC

BUICK — SERIES 129 — SIX: Eight body styles, all on the 129-inch wheelbase, were available in this series. The optional bumpers now consisted of three rather than two horizontal bars.

I.D. DATA: Serial numbers on right side of frame behind front fender opening. Starting: 2123926. Ending: 2313805. Engine numbers on crankcase. Starting: Ser. 116-22225361, Ser. 121,129-2340300.

Series 116

Model No.	Body Type & Seating	Price	Weight	Prod. Total
20	2-dr. Sed.-5P	1220	3525	17,783
25	4-dr. Tr.-5P	1225	3330	2938
26	2-dr. Bus. Cpe.-2P	1195	3465	8745
26S	2-dr. Spt. Cpe. R/S-4P	1250	3520	10,308
27	4-dr. Sed.-5P	1320	3630	44,345

Series 121

41	4-dr. Cl. C. Sed.-5P	1450	4180	10,110
44	2-dr. Spt. Rds.-4P	1325	3795	6195
46	2-dr. Bus. Cpe.-2P	1395	3990	4339
46S	2-dr. Spt. Cpe. R./S.-4P	1450	4055	6638
47	4 dr. Sed.-5P	1520	4175	30,356
48	2-dr. Cpe.-4P	1445	4010	4255

Series 129

49	4-dr. Tr.-7P	1550	3990	1530
50	4-dr. Sed.-7P	2045	4360	8058
50L	4-dr. Imp. Sed. Limo.-7P	2145	4405	736
51	4-dr. Spt. Sed.	1875	4230	7014
54CC	2-dr. DeL. Conv. Cpe.-4P	1875	4085	2021
55	4-dr. Spt. Tr.-5P	1525	3905	1122
57	4-dr. Sed.-5P	1935	4260	5175
58	2-dr. Cpe.-5P	1865	4145	734

Note 1: All models carry a 29 prefix, i.e.: 29-20

ENGINE: [Series 116] Inline. Ohv. Six. Cast iron block. B & S: 3-5/16 x 4-5/8 in. Disp.: 239.1 cu. in. C.R.: 4.3:1. Brake H.P.: 94 @ 2800 R.P.M. Taxable H.P.: 26.3. Main bearings: four. Valve lifters: mechanical. Carb.: Marvel three-jet, updraft T3-10-704. Torque: 172-lb.-ft. @ 1200 R.P.M. [Series 121, 129] Inline. Ohv. Six. Cast iron block. B & S: 3-5/8 x 5 in. Disp.: 309.6 cu. in. C.R.: 4.3:1. N.A.C.C. H.P.: 31.5. Main bearings: four. Valve lifters: mechanical. Carb.: Marvel three-jet updraft T4-10-706.

CHASSIS: [Series 116] W.B.: 116 in. O.L.: 167-3/4 in. Height: 74-7/8 in. Front/Rear Tread: 56-7/16 in./58 in. Tires: 30 x 5.50. [Series 121] W.B.: 121 in. Front/Rear Tread: 56-1/16 in./58 in. Tires: 30 x 6.5. [Series 129] W.B.: 129 in. Front/Rear Tread: 56-7/16 in./58 in. Tires: 32 x 6.50.

TECHNICAL: Sliding gear transmission. Speeds: 3F/1R. Floor shift controls. Multiple disc clutch. Shaft drive. Series 116 — 3/4 floating rear axle, all others — full floating rear axle. Overall ratio: 4.9:1. Mechanical external contracting brakes on four wheels. Wooden spoke wheels with detachable rims. Rim size: 20 in.

OPTIONS: Front bumper. Rear bumper. Clock. Welled fenders, side mounts. Wide-spoke artillery. Wire wheels. Step plates. Spare tire, tube. Spare tire cover. Spare tire lock. Disc wheels.

HISTORICAL: Introduced July 29, 1928. Calendar year production: 196,104. Model year production: 187,861 (includes 8,932 cars built for export). The president of Buick was Edward Thomas Strong.

1930

BUICK — SERIES 40 — SIX: The Buicks for 1930 appeared as handsome and graceful as the 1929 models had been bulbous. As one observer noted, "the cars retain the Buick individuality without ... the bulge." A new vertically mounted, thermostatically controlled shutter system gave the Buick's radiator a long racy appearance. More importantly a height reduction of two inches and a new around the body belt line worked visual wonders in the Buick's appearance. Also contributing to the Buick's more modern styling were flatter hubcaps for the increasingly popular wire wheel option.

1930 Buick, Series 40, Model 46S, sport coupe, JAC

The Series 40 Buicks replaced the Series 116 and were mounted on a longer 118-inch wheelbase. Interiors carried rubber floor mats.

1930 Buick, Series 50, Model 57, sedan, JAC

BUICK — SERIES 50 — SIX: Series 50 models that replaced the Series 121 had wheelbases of 124-inches plus fully carpeted interiors as did the Series 60 Buicks.

1930 Buick, Series 60, Model 64, sport roadster, JAC

BUICK — SERIES 60 — SIX: Both the 132-inch wheelbase Series 60 and the Series 50 shared a 331.5 cid engine for 1931. All Buicks had a new dash panel with the instruments both directly and indirectly lighted. Beginning on January 1, 1930, a new sport roadster with rumbleseat, Model 30-64, was added to Series 60.

I.D. DATA: Serial numbers on right side of frame behind front fender opening. Starting: Series 40 — 2313806, Series 50, 60 — 2334956. Ending: Series 40 — 2459715, Series 50, 60 — 2460543. Engine numbers on crankcase. Starting: Series 40 — 2439593, Series 50, 60 — 2489593. Ending: Series 40 — 2568138, Series 50, 60 — 2613337.

Series 40

Model No.	Body Type & Seating	Price	Weight	Prod. Total
40	2-dr. Sed.-5P	1270	3600	6101
44	2-dr. Spt. Rds.-4P	1310	3420	3476
45	4-dr. Phae.-5P	1310	3410	972
46	2-dr. Bus. Cpe.-2P	1260	3540	5695
46S	2-dr. Sp. Cpe.-4P	1300	3600	10,719
47	4-dr. Sed.-5P	1330	3700	47,294

Series 50

Model No.	Body Type & Seating	Price	Weight	Prod. Total
57	4-dr. Sed.-5P	1540	4235	22,929
58	2-dr. Cpe.-4P	1510	4120	5275

Series 60

Model No.	Body Type & Seating	Price	Weight	Prod. Total
60	4-dr. Sed.-7P	1910	4415	6583
60L	4-dr. Limo.-7P	2070	4475	690
61	4-dr. Sp. Sed.-5P	1760	4330	12,508
64	2-dr. Spt. Rds.-4P	1585	4015	2006
64C	2-dr. DeL. Cpe.-4P	1695	4225	5370
68	2-dr. Cpe.-4P	1740	4200	10,216
69	4-dr. Phae.-7P	1595	4100	807

Note 1: All models carry a 30 prefix, i.e. 30-40.

ENGINE: [Series 40] Inline. Ohv. Six. Cast iron block. B & S: 3-7/16 x 4-5/8 in. Disp.: 257.5 cu. in. Brake H.P.: 80.5 @ 2800 R.P.M. N.A.C.C. H.P.: 28.39. Main bearings: four. Valve lifters: mechanical. Carb.: Marvel T3S-10-758. [Series 50, 60] Inline. Ohv. Six. Cast iron block. B & S: 3-3/4 x 5 in. Disp.: 331.4 cu. in. Brake H.P.: 99 @ 2800 R.P.M. N.A.C.C. H.P.: 33.75. Main bearings: four. Valve lifters: mechanical. Carb.: Marvel T4-10-754.

CHASSIS: [Series 40] W.B.: 118 in. Tires: 29 x 5.50. [Series 50] W.B.: 124 in. Front/Rear Tread: 56-7/8 in./58 in. Tires: 31 x 6.50. [Series 60] W.B.: 132 in. Front/Rear Tread: 56-7/8 in./58 in. Tires: 19 x 6.50.

TECHNICAL: Sliding gear transmission. Speeds: 3F/1R. Floor shift controls. Multiple disc clutch. Shaft drive. 3/4 floating rear axle. Mechanical, internal expanding brakes on four wheels. Wooden spoke wheels with detachable rims.

OPTIONS: Wire wheels. Chrome grille guard. Side mounts. White sidewall tires. Luggage rack. Fog lights. Wind wings.

HISTORICAL: Introduced July 28, 1929. Calendar year production: 119,265. Model year production: 181,743 (including 6,098 stripped chassis and cars for export.) The president of Buick was Edward Thomas Strong. Entered at Indianapolis was a Buick powered car, the Butchers Brothers Special, which was credited with a 14th place finish.

1930 Marquette, touring, OCW

1930 MARQUETTE — SIX: The Marquette, which was offered only for the 1930 model year represented a combination of Oldsmobile styling and engineering with a number of traditional Buick features. For several years Buick production had been declining. With the impact of the Depression becoming more severe Buick decided to produce an economy car to shore up its position.

The Marquette's appearance was contemporary with thin vertical hood louvers and a radiator shell similar to Buick's but with angled "herringbone" bars. However its L-head six-cylinder engine was definitely out of step with Buick design philosophy. Nonetheless the Marquette could make a good account of itself

under acceleration, having the ability to travel from 5 to 25 mph in 8.8 seconds and from 10 to 60 mph in 31 seconds.

However with Buick planning an all-eight-cylinder line for 1931 the Marquette really didn't have a future as a Buick product and thus it was manufactured only as a 1930 model.

I.D. DATA: Serial numbers on frame beneath left front fender. Starting: 10000. Ending: 52998. Engine numbers on crankcase. Starting: 10000. Ending: 48450.

Model No.	Body Type & Seating	Price	Weight	Prod. Total
30	2-dr. Sed.-5P	1000	2850	4630
34	2-dr. Spt. Rds.-4P	1020	2640	2397
35	4-dr. Phae.-5P	1020	2670	889
36	2-dr. Bus. Cpe.-2P	990	2760	2475
36S	2-dr. Sp. Cpe.-4P	1020	2760	4384
37	4-dr. Sed.-5P	1060	2925	15,795

Note 1: All models carried a 30 prefix, i.e. 30-30

ENGINE: Inline. L head. Six. Cast iron block. B & S: 3-1/8 x 4-5/8 in. Disp.: 212.8 cu. in. Brake H.P.: 67.5 @ 3000 R.P.M. N.A.C.C. H.P.: 23.4. Main bearings: four. Valve lifters: mechanical. Carb.: Marvel.

CHASSIS: W.B. 114 in. Tires: 28 x 5.25.

TECHNICAL: Sliding gear transmission. Speeds: 3F/1R. Floor shift controls. Single plate clutch. Shaft drive. Semi-floating rear axle. Overall ratio: 4.5:1. Mechanical brakes on four wheels. Wooden spoke wheels.

OPTIONS: Wire wheels. Side mounts. Demountable wood wheels. Trunk rack.

HISTORICAL: Calendar year production: 35,007. Model year production: 35,007 (including 4,437 stripped chassis and cars for export). The president of Buick was Edward Thomas Strong. The Marquette took part in a number of performance trials including a 778 mile run from Death Valley to Pikes Peak in 40 hours, 45 minutes.

1931

1931 Buick, Series 90, Model 96, coupe, OCW

BUICK — SERIES 50 — EIGHT: Buick's styling was all but unchanged (the only observeable difference was a radiator cap bearing a figure 8) but that hardly mattered since three new straight-eight engines were introduced for 1931. None of these engines shared any interchangeable parts and the smallest, displacing 220 cubic inches, was used for the Series 40 that had the same 114-inch wheelbase of the discontinued Marquette.

The Series 50 interior was equipped with either mohair or cloth upholstery, carpeting for the rear seat floor area, dome lights, and armrests. A rear foot rail was provided as was an adjustable driver's seat. Midway through the model year the Series 50 received the synchromesh transmission previously

available only on the more costly Buicks. Also appearing as a mid-season offering was a new convertible coupe model.

BUICK — SERIES 60 — EIGHT: In Buick's new lineup the Series 60 corresponded to the old Series 40 models with a 118-inch wheelbase and a 272 cid engine. Their interior of either mohair plush or cloth was of higher quality than that of the Series 50. Open models were finished in a leather interior. All Series 60, 80 and 90 Buicks closed cars had a standard equipment passenger-side windshield wiper.

BUICK — SERIES 80 — EIGHT: Only two models were offered in this series with a 124-inch wheelbase and 344 cid engine. As were all 1930 Buicks, the Series 80s had a revamped instrument panel, lower front seats with deeper cushions and a new cooling system with thermostatically controlled shutters.

1931 Buick, Series 90, Model 94, sport roadster, JAC

BUICK — SERIES 90 — EIGHT: The Series 90 Buick was powered by the 344 cid engine and had a wheelbase of 132 inches. Closed car interiors had mohair plush interiors with silk roller shades for the rear side and back windows; full floor carpeting was provided. The convertible coupe that had a mid-season introduction had a leather interior as did the other open-model Series 90 Buicks.

I.D. DATA: Serial numbers on right side of frame behind front fender opening. Starting: 2460544. Ending: 2602731. Engine numbers on crankcase. Starting: 2624638. Ending: 2751921.

Model No.	Body Type & Seating	Price	Weight	Prod. Total
Series 50				
50	2-dr. Sed.-5P	1035	3145	3616
54	2-dr. Spt. Rds.-4P	1055	2935	907
55	4-dr. Phae.-5P	1055	2970	358
56	2-dr. Bus. Cpe.	1025	3055	2782
56C	2-dr. Conv. Cpe.-4P	1095	3095	1531
56S	2-dr. Sp. Cpe.-4P	1055	3155	5733
57	4-dr. Sed.-5P	1095	3265	33,184
Series 60				
64	2-dr. Spt. Rds.-4P	1335	3465	1050
65	4-dr. Phae.-5P	1335	3525	463
66	2-dr. Bus. Cpe.-2P	1285	3615	2732
66S	2-dr. Sp. Cpe.-4P	1325	3695	6489
67	4-dr. Sed.-5P	1355	3795	30,665
Series 80				
86	2-dr. Cpe.-4P	1535	4120	3579
87	4-dr. Sed.-5P	1565	4255	14,731
Series 90				
90	4-dr. Sed.-7P	1935	4435	4159
90L	4-dr. Limo.-7P	2035	4505	514
91	4-dr. Sp. Sed.-5P	1785	4340	7853
94	2-dr. Spt. Rds.-4P	1610	4010	824
95	4-dr. Phae.-7P	1620	4125	392
96	2-dr. Cpe.-5P	1765	4260	7705
96C	2-dr. Conv. Cpe.-4P	1785	4195	1066
96S	2-dr. Ctry. Club. Cpe.-4P	1720	4250	2990

ENGINE: [Series 50] Inline. Ohv. Eight. Cast iron block. B & S: 2-7/8 x 4-1/4 in. Disp.: 220.7 cu. in. C.R.: 4.75:1. Brake H.P.: 77 @ 3200 R.P.M. N.A.C.C. H.P.: 26.45. Main bearings: five. Valve lifters: mechanical. Carb.: two-barrel Marvel updraft T-3-10-894. Torque (Compression): 156 lb.-ft. @ 1600 R.P.M. [Se-

ries 60] Inline. Ohv. Eight. Cast iron block. B & S: 3-1/16 x 5 in. Disp.: 272.6 cu. in. C.R.: 4.63:1. Brake H.P.: 90 @ 3000 R.P.M. N.A.C.C. H.P.: 30.02. Main bearings: five. Valve lifters: mechanical. Carb.: Marvel TD25-10-795, late 1931 TD-25-10-983. Torque: 200 lb.-ft. 43.5 @ 1600 R.P.M. [Series 80, 90] Inline. Ohv. Eight. Cast iron block. B & S: 3-5/16 x 5 in. Disp.: 344.8 cu. in. C.R.: 4.5:1. Brake H.P.: 104 @ 2800 R.P.M. N.A.C.C. H.P.: 35.12. Main bearings: five. Valve lifters: mechanical. Carb.: Marvel TD-3 10-796, late 1931 TD-3 10-984. Torque: 250 lb.-ft. @ 1400 R.P.M.

CHASSIS: [Series 50] W.B.: 114 in. Front/Rear Tread: 56-1/2 in./57 in. Tires: 18 x 5.25. [Series 60] W.B.: 118 in. Length: 175. in. Height: 72. in. Front/Rear Tread: 56-3/4 in./58 in. Tires: 19 x 6.50. [Series 80] W.B.: 124 in. Front/Rear Tread: 56-7/8 in./58 in. Tires: 19 x 6.50. [Series 90] W.B.: 132 in. Front/Rear Tread: 56-7/8 in./58 in. Tires: 19 x 6.50.

1931 Buick, Series 50, Model 56S, special coupe, OCW

TECHNICAL: Sliding gear, synchromesh transmission (Series 60, 80, 90). Speeds: 3F/1R. Floor shift controls. Series 50, 60 — single dry plate, Series 80, 90 — double dry plate clutch. Shaft drive. 3/4 floating rear axle, Series 50 — semi-floating rear axle. Overall ratio: Series 60 — 4.5:1, Series 80, 90 — 4.5:1. 4.18:1. Mechanical brakes on four wheels. Wooden spoke wheels on demountable rims. Series 50 — 18 x 4, Series 60 — 19 x 4, Series 80, 90 — 19 x 4-1/2.

OPTIONS: Front bumper. Rear bumper. Dual sidemount. Heater (two types, hot water and exhaust pipe types). Clock. Side mounts. Side mount covers (metal and wood). Trunk cover. Demountable wire wheels. Grille guard. Luggage rack. White sidewalls. Wind wings. Gravel deflectors.

HISTORICAL: Introduced July 26, 1930. The Buick eight-cylinder engines were equipped with an oil temperature regulator that cooled the oil at high speeds and warmed it in cold weather. Calendar year production: 88,417. Model year production: 138,965 (including 5,642 stripped chassis and cars for export). The president of Buick was Edward Thomas Strong. The Butcher Brothers Special with a Buick 8 crashed at Indianapolis after six laps of racing. The Shafer 8 powered by a 272-cid Buick engine qualified for the 500 at a speed of 105.103 mph and finished in 12th place.

1932

BUICK — SERIES 50 — EIGHT: The 1932 Buicks were easily identified by their new hood doors that replaced the long-used louvers, the elimination of external sun visors and a more pronounced 10 degree rearward windshield slope. The radiator grille was given a new tapered shape with a narrower base. All Buicks also were equipped with dual taillights and longer and more streamlined fenders. The Series 60 and 80 models were available with a thinner head gasket and different spark plugs

at no extra cost, which raised their compression ratio and boosted top speed by 3 mph.

The Series 50 Buick that continued to use the 114-inch wheelbase chassis was available, as was the rest of the Buick line, with Wizard Control, which provided owners both free wheeling and no clutch shifting between second and third gears. New styles for the Series 50 consisted of a two-door five-passenger victoria coupe, and an attractive five-passenger convertible phaeton with a choice of either leather or whipcord upholstery.

Distinguishing the Series 50 from other Buicks was the lack of chrome beaded radiator shutters and chrome plated hood handles. Their headlight shells were painted rather than chromed. Only a single taillight was fitted.

1932 Buick, club sedan & convertible coupe, JAC

BUICK — SERIES 60 — EIGHT: The larger 118-inch wheelbase Series 60 line also added the victoria coupe and convertible phaeton models to its offerings. The interior of the latter model featured leather upholstery and dual rear ashtrays.

BUICK — SERIES 80 — EIGHT: Only two models were offered in this series on a new 126-inch wheelbase. The victoria coupe version had a unit-type rear trunk.

1932 Buick, Series 90, Model 96, victoria coupe, JAC

BUICK — SERIES 90 — EIGHT: The top of the line Series 90 Buick used a new 134-inch wheelbase chassis and among its various models were two new body styles, the four-door club sedan and two-door victoria coupe. Standard on all Series 90 Buicks were wire wheels and dual side mounts.

I.D. DATA: Serial numbers on right side of frame behind front fender opening. Starting: 2602732. Ending: 2659522. Engine numbers on crankcase. Starting: 2751922.

Series 50

Model No.	Body Type & Seating	Price	Weight	Prod. Total
55	4-dr. Spt. Phae.-5P	1155	3270	69
56	2-dr. Bus. Cpe.-2P	935	3275	1726
56C	2-dr. Conv. Cpe.-4P	1080	3335	630
56S	2-dr. Spe. Cpe.-4P	1040	3395	1905
57	4-dr. Sed.-5P	995	3450	10,803
57S	4-dr. Spe. Sed.-5P	1080	3510	9766
58	2-dr. Vic. Cpe.	1060	3420	2194
58C	2-dr. Conv. Phae.-5P	1080	3425	380

Series 60

Model No.	Body Type & Seating	Price	Weight	Prod. Total
65	4-dr. Spt. Phae.-5P	1390	3795	79
66	2-dr. Bus. Cpe.-2P	1250	3796	636
66C	2-dr. Conv. Cpe.-4P	1310	3795	450

Model No.	Body Type & Seating	Price	Weight	Prod. Total
66S	2-dr. Spe. Cpe.-4P	1270	3860	1678
67	4-dr. Sed.-5P	1310	3980	9013
68	2-dr. Vic. Cpe.-5P	1290	3875	1514
68C	2-dr. Conv. Phae.-5P	1310	3880	366

Series 80

Model No.	Body Type & Seating	Price	Weight	Prod. Total
86	2-dr. Vic. Trav. Cpe.-5P	1540	4335	1800
87	4-dr. Sed.-5P	1570	4450	4089

Series 90

Model No.	Body Type & Seating	Price	Weight	Prod. Total
90	4-dr. Sed.-7P	1955	4695	1368
90L	4-dr. Limo.-7P	2055	4810	164
91	2-dr. Clb. Sed.-5P	1820	4620	2237
95	4-dr. Spt. Phae.-7P	1675	4470	131
96	2-dr. Vic. Cpe.-5P	1785	4460	1460
96C	2-dr. Conv. Cpe.-4P	1805	4460	289
96S	2-dr. Ctry. Clb. Cpe.-4P	1740	4470	586
97	4-dr. Sed.-5P	1805	4565	1485
98	2-dr. Conv. Phae.-5P	1830	4550	268

ENGINE: [Series 50] Inline. Ohv. Eight. Cast iron block. B & S: 2-15/16 x 4-1/4 in. Disp.: 230.4 cu. in. C.R.: 4.75:1. Brake H.P.: 82.5 @ 3200 R.P.M. N.A.C.C. H.P.: 27.61. Main bearings: five. Valve lifters: mechanical. Carb.: two barrel Marvel updraft TD-15 10 982. Torque: 200 lb.-ft. @ 1600 R.P.M. [Series 60] Inline. Ohv. Eight. Cast iron block. B & S: 3-1/16 x 5 in. Disp.: 272.6 cu. in. C.R.: 4.63:1. Brake H.P.: 90 (high compression 96) @ 3000 R.P.M. N.A.C.C. H.P.: 30.02. Main bearings: five. Valve lifters: mechanical. Carb.: two barrel Marvel updraft TD-25 10-1501. Torque: 200 lb.-ft. @ 1600 R.P.M. [Series 80, 90] Inline. Ohv. Eight. Cast iron block. B & S: 3-5/16 x 5 in. Disp.: 344.8 cu. in. C.R.: 4.5:1. Brake H.P.: High compression 113, 104 @ 2800 R.P.M. N.A.C.C. H.P.: 35.12. Main bearings: five. Valve lifters: mechanical. Carb.: Two-barrel Marvel updraft TD-3 10-1503. Torque: 250 lb.-ft. @ 1400 R.P.M.

CHASSIS: [Series 50] W.B.: 114 in. Front/Rear Tread: 56-1/2 in./57 in. Tires: 18 x 5.50. [Series 60] W.B.: 118 in. Front/Rear Tread: 56-3/4 in./58 in. Tires: 18 x 6.00. [Series 80] W.B.: 126 in. Tires: 18 x 7.00. [Series 90] W.B.: 134 in. Tires: 18 x 7.00.

TECHNICAL: Sliding gear, synchromesh transmission. Speeds: 3F/1R. Floor shift controls. Series 50, 60 — single dry plate, Series 80, 90 — double dry plate. Shaft drive. 3/4 floating rear axle. Series 50 — 4.6:1, Series 60 — 4.27, 4.54:1, Series 80 — 4.27:1, Series 90 — 4.18, 4.27:1. Mechanical brakes on four wheels. Painted wire wheels or 12 wood spoke wheels with demountable rims. Wizard Control. Automatic clutch (Series 80, 90).

OPTIONS: Heater. Clock. Chrome grille guard. Dual side mounts. Single bar bumpers. Tire locks. Tire covers. Cigarette lighter. Wheel trim rings. Trunk. Trunk rack. Vacuum windshield pump (Series 50 only, standard on all others). 12 spoke wood wheel (Series 50, DeLuxe models).

HISTORICAL: Introduced November 14, 1931. A Buick powered racer entered and driven by Phil Shafer finished 11th in the Indy 500. Shafer also won an Elgin, Illinois, race with the same car. Innovations: Adjustable shock absorbers, Wizard Control free wheeling and automatic clutch. Calendar year production: 41,522. Model year production: 55,086 (another 1,704 stripped chassis and cars for export were produced). The president of Buick was Irving J. Reuter. Buick discontinued the use of wood spoke wheels at the end of the 1932 model year.

1933

BUICK — SERIES 50 EIGHT: This was a year of major styling changes for Buick. New front and rear fenders with deeper valances and more sweeping curves plus a 2-1/4-inch height reduction gave all models a fresh appearance. Adding to this sense of newness was the Buick's vee-shaped grille and the discontinuation of wood spoke wheels throughout all series. Customers could now select either wire or steel spoke artillery wheels.

1933 Buick, Series 50, Model 57, sedan, JAC

Technical improvements were headlined by a new X-cross-member frame and the Fisher No-Draft ventilation. In addition the free-wheeling unit now allowed the driver to switch back and forth from direct drive to freewheeling as desired. The adjustable shock absorber system wasn't offered in 1933. A new type of headlight whose passing beam brightly illuminated the pavement edge while shedding a far dimmer light on the traffic side was common to all Buicks.

The Series 50 Buicks continued to use a 114-inch wheelbase chassis. Body styles were trimmed to five from the 1932 level of eight as the sport phaeton, special sedan and convertible phaeton were dropped. Twin taillights were fitted to all models.

1933 Buick, Series 60, Model 66C, convertible coupe, OCW

BUICK — SERIES 60 — EIGHT: A 127-inch wheelbase was used for the Series 60 that also consisted of five models for 1933. Eliminated for the 1933 model year were the sport phaeton and business coupe models.

BUICK — SERIES 80 — EIGHT: The Series 80 wheelbase for 1933 was an impressive 130 inches. Whereas only two models were offered in this series in 1932, three new models, the convertible coupe, sport coupe and convertible phaeton were added for the new model year.

BUICK — SERIES 90 — EIGHT: 1933 was the poorest sales year for Buick since 1915 but in terms of prestige the Series 90 models with an ultra-long 138-inch wheelbase took Buick to a new status level. However only five body styles were offered as Buick eliminated the sport phaeton, country club coupe, five-passenger sedan, convertible coupe roadster and convertible phaeton from the Series 90 line. Closed car interiors were available in mohair plush, whipcord or cloth.

I.D. DATA: Serial numbers on right side of frame behind front fender opening, on plate on firewall. Starting: 2659523. Ending: 2706452. Engine numbers on right side of crankcase. Starting: 2751922. Ending: 2798851.

Series 50

Model No.	Body Type & Seating	Price	Weight	Prod. Total
56	2-dr. Bus. Cpe.-2P	995	3520	1321
56C	2-dr. Conv. Cpe.-2P	1115	3525	346
56S	2-dr. Spt. Cpe.-2P	1030	3585	1643
57	4-dr. Sed.-5P	1045	3705	19,109
58	2-dr. Vic. Cpe.-5P	1065	3605	4118

Series 60

Model No.	Body Type & Seating	Price	Weight	Prod. Total
66C	2-dr. Conv. Cpe.-2P	1365	3940	1 52
66S	2-dr. Spt. Cpe.	1270	3975	1000
67	4-dr. Sed.-5P	1310	4115	7450
68	2-dr. Vic. Cpe.-5P	1310	4005	2887
68C	4-dr. Conv. Phae.-5P	1585	4110	183

Series 80

Model No.	Body Type & Seating	Price	Weight	Prod. Total
86	2-dr. Vic. Cpe.-5P	1540	4420	758
86C	2-dr. Conv. Cpe.-2P	1575	4325	90
86S	2-dr. Spt. Cpe.-2P	1495	4355	401
87	4-dr. Sed.-5P	1570	4505	1545
88C	4-dr. Conv. Phae.-5P	1845	4525	124

Series 90

Model No.	Body Type & Seating	Price	Weight	Prod. Total
90	4-dr. Sed.-7P	1955	4705	890
90L	4-dr. Limo.-7P	2055	4780	299
91	2-dr. Clb. Sed.-5P	1820	4520	1637
96	2-dr. Vic. Cpe.-5P	1785	4520	556
97	4-dr. Sed.-5P	1805	4595	641

ENGINE: [Series 50] Inline. Ohv. Eight. Cast iron block. B & S: 2-15/16 x 4-1/4 in. Disp.: 230.4 cu. in. C.R.: 4.63:1. Brake H.P.: 86 @ 3200 R.P.M. N.A.C.C. H.P.: 27.61. Main bearings: five. Valve lifters: mechanical. Carb.: two-barrel Marvel updraft ED-18 10-1515. [Series 60] Inline. Ohv. Eight. Cast iron block. B & S: 3-1/16 x 5 in. Disp.: 272.6 cu in. C.R.: 4.63:1. Brake H.P.: 97 @ 3200 R.P.M. N.A.C.C. H.P.: 30.02. Main bearings: five. Valve lifters: mechanical. Carb.: two barrel Marvel updraft ED-28 10-1518. [Series 80, 90] Inline. Ohv. Eight. Cast iron block. B & S: 3-5/16 x 5 in. Disp.: 344.8 cu. in. C.R.: 4.63:1. Brake H.P.: 104 @ 2800 R.P.M. Main bearings: five. Valve lifters: mechanical. Carb.: two-barrel Marvel updraft ED-3 10-1514.

CHASSIS: [Series 50] W.B.: 119 in. Front/Rear Tread: 59/60-1/2 in. Tires: 17 x 6. [Series 60] W.B.: 127 in. Front/Rear Tread: 59/60-1/2 in. Tires: 17 x 6.50. [Series 80] W.B.: 130 in. Front/Rear Tread: 58-1/2 in./60-1/2 in. Tires: 17 x 7. [Series 90] W.B.: 138 in. Front/Rear Tread: 58-1/2 in./60-1/2 in. Tires: 17 x 7.

TECHNICAL: Sliding gear, synchromesh transmission. Speeds: 3F/1R. Floor shift controls. Single dry plate clutch — Series 50, 60. Double dry plate clutch — Series 80, 90. Shaft drive. 3/4 floating rear axle. Overall ratio: Series 50 — 4.7:1, Series 60 — 4.6:1, Series 80 — 4.273:1, Series. 90 — 4.27, 4.36:1. Mechanical brakes on four wheels. Wire on steel spoke artillery wheels. Wizard control.

OPTIONS: Side mounts. Luggage rack. Trunk. Fog lights. Wire wheels. Artillery-type all steel wheels.

HISTORICAL: Introduced December 3, 1932. The Shafer 8 Special powered by a 284-cid Buick engine was driven by H.W. "Stubby" Stubblefield to a fifth place Indy 500 finish at an average speed of 100.762 mph. The top four cars were powered by Miller racing engines. Innovations: Dash mounted starter button. Calendar year production: 40,620. Model year sales: 43,247. Model year production: 45,150 (1,774 stripped chassis and cars for export were also produced). Harlow Herbert Curtice became Buick president on October 23, 1933.

1934

1934 BUICK: Buick's year-old synchromesh transmission was improved by the adoption of helical gears. The actual gear shifting procedure was made more convenient by the shift lever's shorter movement. Also noteworthy was the mid-year revision made in the automatic starting mechanism that prevented the starter from being used to move the car when the ignition was locked.

An interesting feature of the Buick instrument panel was its octane selector handle that altered the spark timing to allow the use of either standard or premium fuel.

The headlights used on the 1934 models produced 20 percent more illumination and provided four different light patterns: city and country driving beams, a passing beam and a parking light. Series 40 Buicks had three horizontal hood louvers while models in the remaining series had four. Also not included as standard equipment on the Series 40 were the dual chrome horns of the Series 50 through 90.

1934 Buick, Series 40, Model 41, sedan, AA

BUICK — SERIES 40 — EIGHT: In terms of Buick's recent past the introduction of this low-priced series on May 12, 1934, was nothing short of revolutionary. But it came at a time when business as usual patterns could spell disaster. Although its wheelbase of 117 inches was longer than the 1933 Series 50 Buick, the Series 40 was both considerably lighter in weight and less expensive. These models were the only Buicks not equipped with dual exterior mounted horns. Closed models in the Series 40 had either whipcord or mohair velvet upholstery with leather used for open models. All models in all series had their radiator filler cap placed under the hood.

BUICK — SERIES 50 — EIGHT: Body choices in this Buick line remained unchanged but a longer 119-inch wheelbase was used. As was the case with all Buicks, the new Series 50 had narrow horizontal hood louvers and safety glass in their windshields and vent windows. Interiors featured (on closed models) wide walnut grained metal window trim.

1934 Buick, Series 50, Model 56S, sport coupe, JAC

BUICK — SERIES 60 — EIGHT: Series 60 Buicks had a longer, by one inch, wheelbase for 1934. A new club sedan model was added to its lineup. A more powerful 100 hp, 278-cid engine was also introduced. Common to all Buicks for 1934 was General Motors "Knee Action" independent front suspension and a "Ride Stabilizer" rear anti-roll bar.

BUICK — SERIES 90 — EIGHT: With the Series 80 dropped for 1934, the Series 90 received new convertible coupe, sport coupe, and convertible phaeton models. The Series 90 was equipped both with safety glass in all windows and a Bendix vacuum power brake booster. The Series 90 models shared their combination accelerator-starter with the rest of the 1934

Buicks. Interiors of closed models featured mohair velvet plush upholstery.

I.D. DATA: Serial numbers on right side of frame, behind front fender opening. Starting: 2706453. Ending: 2777649. Engine numbers on crankcase. Starting. Series 40 — 2984900, Series 50, 60, 90 — 2861223.

Series 40

Model No.	Body Type & Seating	Price	Weight	Prod. Total
41	4-dr. Sed. Built-in Trunk-5P	925	3175	10,953
46	2-dr. Bus. Cpe.-2P	795	2995	1806
46S	2-dr. Spt. Cpe. R/S-4P	855	3085	1232
47	4-dr. Sed.-5P	895	3155	7425
48	4-dr. Tr. Sed. Built-in Trunk-5P	865	3120	4779

Series 50

Model No.	Body Type & Seating	Price	Weight	Prod. Total
56C	2-dr. Bus. Cpe.-2P	1110	3682	1078
56C	2-dr. Conv. Cpe.-2P	1230	3692	506
56S	2-dr. Sp. Cpe. R/S-4P	1145	3712	1150
57	4-dr. Sed.-5P	1190	3852	12,094
58	2-dr. Vic. Cpe.Built-in Trunk-5P	1160	4316	4405

Series 60

Model No.	Body Type & Seating	Price	Weight	Prod. Total
61	2-dr. Clb. Sed. Built-in Trunk-5P	1465	4318	5395
66C	2-dr. Conv. Cpe. R/S-4P	1495	NA	253
66S	2-dr. Sp. Cpe.-2P	1375	4193	816
67	4-dr. Sed.-5P	1425	4303	5171
68	2-dr. Vic. Cpe.Built-in Trunk-5P	1395	4213	1935
68C	4-dr. Conv. Phae. Built-in Trunk-5P	1675	4353	444

Series 90

Model No.	Body Type & Seating	Price	Weight	Prod. Total
90	4-dr. Sed.-7P	2055	4906	1151
90L	4-dr. Limo.-7P	2175	4876	262
91	2-dr. Clb. Sed. Built-in Trunk-5P	1965	4696	1477
96C	2-dr. Conv. Cpe. R/S-4P	1945	4511	68
96S	2-dr. Spt. Cpe. R/S-4P	1875	4546	137
97	4-dr. Sed.-4P	1945	4691	635
98	2-dr. Vic. Cpe.-5P	1895	4571	347
98C	4-dr. Conv. Phae. Built-in Trunk-5P	2145	4691	119

ENGINE: [Series 40] Inline. Ohv. Eight. Cast iron block. B & S: 3-3/32 x 3-7/8 in. Disp.: 233 cu. in. Brake H.P.: 93 @ 3200 R.P.M. N.A.C.C. H.P.: 30.63. Main bearings: five. Valve lifters: mechanical. Carb.: two- barrel Marvel downdraft BB-1, 10-1633. [Series 50] Inline. Ohv. Eight. Cast iron block. B & S: 2-31/32 x 4-1/4 in. Disp.: 235 cu. in. Brake H.P.: 88 @ 3200 R.P.M. N.A.C.C. H.P.: 28.2. Main bearings: five. Valve lifters: mechanical. Carb.: two barrel Marvel updraft ED-IS, 10-1577. [Series 60] Inline. Ohv. Eight. Cast iron block. B & S: 3-3/32 x 4-5/8 in. Disp.: 278 cu. in. Brake H.P.: 100 @ 3200 R.P.M. N.A.C.C. H.P.: 30.63. Main bearings: 5. Valve lifters: mechanical. Carb.: two barrel Marvel ED-2S, 10-1579. [Series 90] Inline. Ohv. Eight. Cast iron block. B & S: 3-5/16 x 5. Disp.: 344.8 cu. in. Brake H.P.: 116 @ 3200 R.P.M. N.A.C.C. H.P.: 35.12. Main bearings: five. Valve lifters: mechanical. Carb.: Marvel ED3S 10-1581.

CHASSIS: [Series 40] W.B.: 117 in. Tires: 16 x 6.25. [Series 50] W.B.: 119 in. Front/Rear Tread: 59/60-1/2 in. Tires: 16 x 7.00. [Series 60] W.B.: 128 in. Tires: 16 x 7.50. [Series 90] W.B.: 136 in. Tires: 16 x 7.50.

TECHNICAL: Sliding gear, synchromesh transmission. Speeds: 3F/1R. Floor shift controls. Single dry plate clutch. Shaft drive. 3/4 floating rear axle. Overall ratio: Series 40 — 4.33:1, Series 50 — 4.89:1, Series 60 — 4.7:1, Series 90 — 4.36:1. Mechanical brakes on four wheels. Steel spoke artillery wheels.

OPTIONS: White sidewalls. Two-tone paint. Safety glass (Series 50 & 60) ($9.75-$20.00). Radio (dealer installed). Metal spare tire cover. Luggage rack. Side mounts. Passenger side windshield wipers (Series 40).

HISTORICAL: Introduced December 27, 1933. Calendar year production 78,757. Model year production: 63,647 (plus 7,362 stripped chassis and cars for export). The president of Buick was Harlow Curtice. Two Buickpowered Rigling cars were qualified in sixth and eighth starting positions in the Indy 500. One car retired with a broken cam drive after 130 laps. The second entry, the Shafer Special with a 286 cid Buick 8, finished in sixth position

with an average speed of 98.26 mph. The cars in front at the race's end were powered by either Duesenberg or Miller engines.

1934 Buick, Series 90, Model 91, club sedan, JAC

1934 Buick, Series 90, Model 96C, convertible coupe, OCW

1935

1935 Buick, convertible coupe, OCW

BUICK — SERIES 40 — EIGHT: Visual changes in the Buick's appearance for 1935 were extremely modest consisting mainly of new colors and exterior trim revisions. The Series 40 models received a glovebox lock and dual windshield wipers along with numerous design improvements intended to remedy complaints of poor clutch and timing chain durability. A convertible coupe was also added to the Series 40 model line. Whereas the more costly Buicks were fitted with chrome headlight shells, those on the Series 40 were painted. All models received automatic chokes and a girder-type frame was used on all Buick convertibles.

BUICK — SERIES 50 — EIGHT: Changes to the Series 50 were limited to the installation of center rear armrests on closed models.

1935 Buick, Series 60, Model 61, club sedan, JAC

BUICK — SERIES 60 — EIGHT: All body styles were continued unchanged for 1935. Series 60 sedans shared the folding center rear seat armrest with Series 90 models.

BUICK — SERIES 90 — EIGHT: Series 90 models were equipped with shatterproof glass in all windows.

I.D. DATA: Serial numbers on right side of frame, behind front fender opening. Starting: 2777650. Ending: 2830898. Engine numbers on crankcase. Starting: Series 40 — 42937408, Series 50, 60, 90 — 2922072. Ending: Series 40 — 42995237, Series 50, 60, 90 — 2984413.

Series 40

Model No.	Body Type & Seating	Price	Weight	Prod. Total
41	4-dr. Sed.-5P	925	3210	18,638
46	2-dr. Bus. Cpe.-2P	795	3020	2850
46C	2-dr. Conv. Cpe.-4P	925	3140	933
46S	2-dr. Spt. Cpe.-4P	855	NA	1136
47	4-dr. Sed.-5P	895	3180	6250
48	2-dr. Tr. Sed.-5P	865	3160	4957

Series 50

Model No.	Body Type & Seating	Price	Weight	Prod. Total
56	2-dr. Bus. Cpe.-2P	1110	3652	257
56C	2-dr. Conv. Cpe.-2P	1230	3662	170
56S	2-dr. Sp. Cpe.-4P	1145	3682	268
57	4-dr. Sed.-5P	1190	3822	3778
58	2-dr. Vic. Cpe.	1160	3737	1589

Series 60

Model No.	Body Type & Seating	Price	Weight	Prod. Total
61	2-dr. Clb. Sed.-5P	1462	4288	2762
66C	2-dr. Conv. Cpe.-4P	1375	4163	111
66S	2-dr. Sp. Cpe.-4P	NA	NA	257
67	4-dr. Sed.-5P	1425	4273	1716
68	2-dr. Vic. Cpe.-5P	1395	4183	597
68C	4-dr. Conv. Phae.-5P	1675	4323	256

Series 90

Model No.	Body Type & Seating	Price	Weight	Prod. Total
90	4-dr. Sed.-7P	2055	4766	609
90L	4-dr. Limo.-7P	2175	4846	191
91	4-dr. Clb. Sed.-5P	1965	4606	573
96C	2-dr. Conv. Cpe.-4P	1945	4481	10
96S	2-dr. Spt. Cpe.-4P	1875	4516	41
97	4-dr. Sed.-5P	1945	4661	117
98	2-dr. Vic. Cpe.-5P	1895	4541	32
98C	4-dr. Conv. Phae.-5P	2145	4661	38

1935 Buick, Series 90, Model 98C, convertible phaeton, JAC

ENGINE: [Series 40] Inline. Ohv. Eight. Cast iron block. B & S: 3-3/12 x 3-7/8 in. Disp.: 233 cu. in. Brake H.P.: 93 @ 3200

R.P.M. N.A.C.C. H.P. 30.63. Main bearings: five. Valve lifters: mechanical. Carb.: two-barrel, Stromberg downdraft EE-1 or Marvel ED-15. [Series 50] Inline. Ohv. Eight. Cast iron block. B & S: 2-31/32 x 4-1/4 in. Disp.: 235 cu. in. Brake H.P.: 88 @ 3200 R.P.M. N.A.C.C. H.P.: 28.2. Main bearings: five. Valve lifters: mechanical. Carb.: Marvel ED-15, 10-157. [Series 60] Inline. Ohv. Eight. Cast iron block. B & S: 3-3/32 x 4-5/8 in. Disp. 278 cu. in. Brake H.P.: 100 @ 3200 R.P.M. N.A.C.C. H.P.: 30.63. Main bearings: five. Valve lifters: mechanical. Carb.: Marvel ED-25, 10-1579. [Series 90] Inline. Ohv. Eight. Cast iron block. B & S: 3-5/16 x 5 in. Disp.: 344.8 cu. in. C.R.: 4.63:1. Brake H.P.: 116 @ 3200 R.P.M. N.A.C.C. H.P.: 35.12. Main bearings: five. Valve lifters: mechanical. Carb. Marvel ED-3, 10-1581.

1935 Buick, Series 50, Model 57 sedan, OCW

CHASSIS: [Series 40] W.B.: 117 in. Tires: 16 x 6.25. [Series 50] W.B.: 119 in. Front/Rear Tread: 59/60-1/2 in. Tires: 16 x 7.00. [Series 60] W.B.: 128 in. Tires: 16 x 7.50. [Series 90] W.B.: 136 in. Tires: 16 x 7.50.

TECHNICAL: Sliding gear, synchromesh transmission. Speeds: 3F/1R. Floor shift controls. Single dry plate clutch. Shaft drive. 3/4 floating rear axle. Overall ratio: Series 40 — 4.33:1, Series 50 — 4.88:1, Series 60 — 4.7:1, Series 90 — 4.36:1. Mechanical brakes on four wheels. Steel spoke artillery wheels.

OPTIONS: Sidemount (standard on Model 98C). Wire wheels. Luggage rack. Steel side mount tire covers. Two-tone paint.

HISTORICAL: Introduced October 18, 1934. Calendar year production: 107,611. Model year production: 48,256 (4,993 stripped chassis and cars for export were also produced). The president of Buick was Harlow Curtice. A Shafer Special with a Buick eight-cylinder engine was qualified by Cliff Bergere at 114.1 mph at Indy. After starting in 16th position it ran out of gas just four laps from the finish.

1936

1936 Buick, Special, Model 46C, convertible coupe, JAC

1936 Buick, Special, Model 41, sedan, OCW

BUICK SPECIAL — SERIES 40 — EIGHT: Buick historians are unanimous in regarding the 1936 models as the cars that marked the start of the Buick renaissance. Across the board were turret top bodies, hydraulic brakes and dramatic new styling with sharply slanted vee-type windshields, high, wedged-shaped radiators, twin taillamps and bullet-shaped headlights. Technical advancements included an improved independent front suspension, new alloy pistons, and an improved water temperature control. To celebrate the occasion Buick also assigned names to its traditional series designations. Buick wasn't the least bit bashful about touting the top speed ability of these new cars. The Special was capable of 85 mph, the Limited 87 mph, and the Roadmaster 90 mph. The hot new Century could achieve a sizzling 95 mph.

The Series 40 Special retained the 233 cid engine, which now featured Anolite aluminum pistons, as did the 320 cid Buick engine.

1936 Buick, Century, Model 61, sedan, OCW

BUICK CENTURY — SERIES 60 — EIGHT: The first of the great Century Buicks shared a new 320.2 cid straight eight with the Series 80 (Roadmaster) and Series 90 (Limited) models that were destined to remain in production through 1952. On a relatively short, 118-inch wheelbase the Century's styling with its rearward sweeping lines and rounded grille with vertical bars was particularly appealing.

1936 Buick, Roadmaster, Model 80C, convertible phaeton, AA

BUICK ROADMASTER — SERIES 80 — EIGHT: Only two body styles, a four-door trunk sedan, and an elegant convertible phaeton were offered in this Roadmaster Series. Standard on the latter was a single sidemount.

1936 Buick, Limited, Model 91, sedan, JAC

BUICK LIMITED — SERIES 90 — EIGHT: The four Limited models all used the same four-door body style with glass partitions provided for the limousine and formal sedan versions. Standard on all Buick Limited models was a left side external tire mount.

I.D. DATA: Serial numbers on right side of frame, behind front fender opening. Starting: 2830899. Ending: 2999496. Engine numbers on crankcase. Starting: Series 40 — 42995239, Series 60, 80, 90 — 63001000. Ending: Series 40 — 43166224, Series 60, 80, 90 — 93166224.

Series 40 (Special)

Model No.	Body Type & Seating	Price	Weight	Prod. Total
41	4-dr. Sed.-5P	885	3360	77,007
46	2-dr. Bus. Cpe.-2P	765	3150	10,912
46C	2-dr. Conv. Cpe.-4P	820	3190	1488
46S	2-dr. Spt. Cpe.-4P	820	3190	1086
46Sr	2-dr. Spt. Cpe.-4P	820	3190	1390
48	2-dr. Vic. Cpe.-5P	835	3305	21,214

Series 60 (Century)

Model No.	Body Type & Seating	Price	Weight	Prod. Total
61	4-dr. Sed.-5P	1090	—	17,806
66C	2-dr. Conv. Cpe.-4P	1135	3775	717
66So	2-dr. Spt. Cpe.-4P	1035	3625	1078
66Sr	2-dr. Spt. Cpe.-4P	1035	3635	1001
68	2-dr. Vic. Cpe.-5P	1055	3730	3762

Series 80 (Roadmaster)

Model No.	Body Type & Seating	Price	Weight	Prod. Total
80C	4-dr. Conv. Phae.-6P	1565	4228	1064
81	4-dr. Sed.-6P	1255	4098	14,985

Series 90 (Limited)

Model No.	Body Type & Seating	Price	Weight	Prod. Total
90	4-dr. Sed.-8P	1845	4517	1590
90	4-dr. Limo.-8P	1945	4577	709
91	4-dr. Sed.-6P	1695	4477	1713
91F	4-dr. Formal Sed.-6P	1795	4487	74

1936 Buick, Century, Model 66R, sport coupe, OCW

ENGINE: [Series 40] Inline. Ohv. Eight. Cast iron block. B & S: 3-3/32 x 3-7/8 in. Disp.: 233 cu. in. Brake H.P.: 93 @ 3200 R.P.M. N.A.C.C. H.P.: 30.63. Main bearings: five. Valve lifters: mechanical. Carb.: two-barrel Stromberg downdraft EEl. [Series 60, 80, 90] Inline. Ohv. Eight. Cast iron block. B & S: 3-7/16 x 4-5/16 in. Disp. 320.2 cu. in. Brake H.P.: 120 @ 3200 R.P.M. N.A.C.C. H.P.: 37.81. Main bearings: five. Valve lifters: mechan-

ical. Carb.: two-barrel Stromberg downdraft EE22. Torque: 238 lb.-ft. @ 1600 R.P.M.

CHASSIS: [Series 40] W.B.: 118 in. Tires: 16 x 6.50. [Series 60] W.B. 122 in. O.L.: 197 in. Height: 68 in. Front/Rear Tread: 58.1 in./57.5 in. Tires: 15 x 7.00. [Series 80] W.B.: 131 in. Tires: 16 x 7.00. [Series 90] W.B.: 138 in. Tires: 16 x 7.50.

TECHNICAL: Sliding gear transmission. Speeds: 3F/1R. Floor shift control. Single dry plate clutch. Shaft drive. Semi-floating rear axle. Overall ratio: Series 40 — 4.44:1, Series 60 — 3.90:1, Series 80 — 4.22:1, Series 90 — 4.55:1. Hydraulic brakes on four wheels. Pressed steel wheels. 16 inch. (Series 60 — 15 inch).

OPTIONS: Heater, Master and DeLuxe. Dual sidemounts. Fog lights. White sidewalls. Grille guard. Electric watch. Buick Master five-tube radio. Buick Ranger six-tube radio. Trim rings.

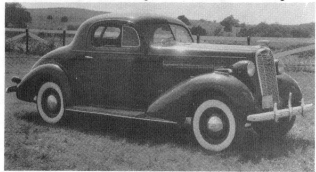

1936 Buick, Special, Model 46, coupe, OCW

HISTORICAL: Introduced September 28, 1935. Hydraulic brakes. Turret top. Calendar year sales: 164,861. Calendar year production: 179,533. Model year production: 157,623 (in addition 10,973 stripped chassis and cars for export were produced). The president of Buick was Harlow Curtice. The three millionth Buick, a Series 40 Special four-door sedan, was built on May 28, 1936.

1937

1937 Buick, Special, Model 46C, convertible coupe, AA

BUICK SPECIAL — SERIES 40 — EIGHT: Buick's art deco styling of 1937 was substantially revised with a divided grille with horizontal bars, fenders with squared-off ends and extremely graceful streamlined headlight shells. The center section of the die-cast grille was painted to match the body color. While overall height was reduced by 1-1/2 inches the floors were lowered 2-1/2 inches to maintain interior head room.

Among Buick's technical improvements for 1937 was a quieter overhead valve mechanism, "streamlined" intake valves, a new oil pump and a cooling system with seven percent greater capacity.

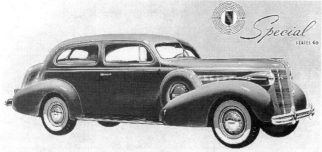

1937 Buick, Special, Model 48, two-door trunkback sedan, OCW

The Buick Special received both a longer 122 inch wheelbase chassis and a new 248 cid engine. Particularly attractive was the four-door Model 47 with its swept-back rear deck. Another addition to the Special line was the five-passenger convertible phaeton. Buick claimed the Series 40 Sedan could accelerate from 10 to 60 mph in 19.2 seconds.

1937 Buick, Century, Model 66C, convertible coupe, JAC

1937 Buick, Century, Model 61, trunkback sedan, OCW

BUICK CENTURY — SERIES 60 — EIGHT: The Century series with a 126-inch wheelbase was highlighted by two swept-back body styles, the Model 64 two-door sedan and Model 67 four-door sedan. With an official top speed of 101 mph the Century was one of the most impressive automobiles of 1937. The coupe bodies in both the Series 40 and Series 60 Buicks were lengthened to provide space for two passengers behind the front seat. These "opera" seats could also be folded flush into the body when not in use.

BUICK ROADMASTER — SERIES 80 — EIGHT: The Roadmaster, on the same 131-inch wheelbase of 1936, was available in three body styles, including a new six-passenger formal sedan.

BUICK LIMITED — SERIES 90 — EIGHT: The seven Limited models along with all other Buicks were available with a windshield defroster and a radio antenna installed in the running-board. Unlike the Special and Century models that used all-steel body construction, the Limited and Roadmaster retained composite wood and steel bodies.

I.D. DATA: Serial numbers on right side of frame, behind front fender opening. Starting: 2999497. Ending: 3219847. Engine numbers on crankcase. Starting: Series — 43166225, all others — 63176225. Ending: Series 40 — 43396936, all others 43388399.

1937 Buick, Century, Model 41, trunkback sedan, OCW

Series 40 (Special)

Model No.	Body Type & Seating	Price	Weight	Prod. Total
40C	4-dr. Conv. Phae.-5P	1302	3630	1689
41	4-dr. Trunk Back Sed.-5P	1021	3490	82,440
44	2-dr. Tr. Sed.-5P	959	3490	9330
46	2-dr. Bus. Cpe.-2P	913	3380	13,742
46C	2-dr. Conv. Cpe.-4P	1056	3480	2265
46S	2-dr. Spt. Cpe.-4P	975	3445	5059
47	4-dr. Tr. Sed.	995	3510	22,312
48	2-dr. Trunk Back Sed.-5P	895	3480	15,936

Series 60 (Century)

Model No.	Body Type & Seating	Price	Weight	Prod. Total
60C	4-dr. Conv. Phae.-5P	1524	3840	410
61	4-dr. Trunk Back Sed.-5P	1233	3720	20,679
64	2-dr. Tr. Sed.-5P	1172	3720	1117
66C	2-dr. Conv. Cpe.-4P	1269	3715	787
66S	2-dr. Spt. Cpe.-4P	1187	3660	2840
67	4-dr. Tr. Sed.-5P	1207	3750	4750
68	2-dr. Trunk Back Sed.-5P	1197	3750	2874

Series 80 (Roadmaster)

Model No.	Body Type & Seating	Price	Weight	Prod. Total
80C	4-dr. Phae.-6P	1856	4214	1040
81	4-dr. Trunk Back Sed.-6P	1518	4159	14,637
81C	4-dr. Formal Sed.-6P	1641	4299	452

Series 90 (Limited)

Model No.	Body Type & Seating	Price	Weight	Prod. Total
90	4-dr. Trunk Back Sed.-8P	2240	4549	1592
90L	4-dr. Limo.-8P	2342	4599	720
91	4-dr. Trunk Back Sed.-6P	2066	4469	1229
91F	4-dr. Formal Sed.-6P	2240	4409	156

ENGINE: [Series 40] Inline. Ohv. Eight. Cast iron block. B & S: 3-3/32 x 11-1/8 in. Disp.: 248 cu. in. C.R.: 5.7:1. Brake H.P.: 100 @ 3200 R.P.M. N.A.C.C. H.P.: 30.6. Main bearings: five. Valve lifters: mechanical. Carb.: Stromberg AA1. [Series 60, 80, 90] Inline. Ohv. Eight. Cast iron block. B & S: 3-7/16 x 4-5/16 in. Disp.: 320.2 cu. in. C.R.: 5.9:1. Brake H.P.: 130 @ 3400 R.P.M. N.A.C.C. H.P.: 37.81. Main bearings: five. Valve lifters: mechanical. Carb.: Stromberg AA2.

CHASSIS: [Series 40] W.B.: 122 in. O.L.: 200-1/16 in. Front/Rear Tread: 58-7/16 in./59-5/32 in. Tires: 16 x 6.50. [Series 60] W.B.: 126 in. O.L.: 203-9/16 in. Front/Rear Tread: 58-5/16 in./59-1/4 in. Tires: 15 x 7.00. [Series 80] W.B.: 131 in. O.L.: 210-1/4 in. Front/Rear Tread: 59-19/32 in./62-1/2 in. Tires: 16 x 7.00. [Series 90] W.B.: 138 in. O.L.: 216-1/2 in. Front/Rear Tread: 59-7/16 in./62-1/2 in. Tires: 16 x 7.50.

TECHNICAL: Sliding gear transmission. Speeds: 3F/1R. Floor shift controls. Single dry plate clutch. Shaft drive. Semi-floating rear axle (Series 40 & 60 — hypoid gears, Series 80 & 90 continued to use spiral bevel gears.) Overall ratio: Series 40 — 4.44:1, Series 60 — 3.90:1, Series 80 — 4.22:1, Series 90 — 4.55:1. Hydraulic brakes on four wheels. Pressed steel wheels. Rim: 16 in. (Series 60 — 15 in.)

OPTIONS: Heater. Dual sidemounts. Fog lights. White sidewall tires. Grille guard. Defroster in combination with heater. Heater. Dash installed radio with built-in speaker grille.

HISTORICAL: Introduced October 18, 1936. Cowl-mounted windshield wipers on all models. Calendar year sales: 203,739. Calendar year production: 227,038. Model year production: 220,346 (including 14,290 stripped chassis and cars for export). The president of Buick was Harlow Curtice. The three millionth Buick, a 1937 Model 81 Roadmaster six-passenger sedan, was presented to Arthur L. Newton on October 25, 1936. Mr. Newton was president of Glidden Buick Corporation of New York City, which had been Buick's largest dealer for 20 years.

1938

1938 BUICK: The major changes in the Buick line for 1938 consisted of the adoption of coil springs for its rear suspension and the availability of a semi-automatic transmission for the Series 40 models.

Styling changes were minor. The front line of the grille was now nearly vertical, which enabled a longer hood to be used. The graceful form of the headlights was mirrored in the shape of the front fender-mounted parking lights and the front bumper guards were taller than previously.

Other engineering changes included a redesigned frame X-member of channel section rather than I-beam construction. Although not the first to move its battery to a location under the hood, this Buick feature for 1938 was a welcomed development.

1938 Buick, Special, Model 41, trunkback sedan, OCW

BUICK SPECIAL — SERIES 40 — EIGHT: The Automatic Safety Transmission semi-automatic transmission option (which Oldsmobile had introduced in June 1937) required use of the clutch only when the car was started or stopped. A steering column-mounted lever with reverse, neutral, low-range and high-range forward position controlled the operation of the transmission. Low range provided first and second gears with an automatic upshift. High range encompassed first, third and fourth gears. Above 20 mph in high range the car was in fourth gear with a downshift to third possible by fully depressing the accelerator. The use of crowned head pistons raised the Series 40 engine's compression ratio to 6.15:1 and increased maximum horsepower to 107 at 3400 rpm.

BUICK CENTURY — SERIES 60 — EIGHT: The wheelbase of the Buick Century remained unchanged at 126 inches. The two-door touring sedan was dropped for 1938. Its engine, identical to that used in the Series 80 and 90, developed 141 hp.

1938 Buick, Roadmaster, Model 81, four-door sedan, JAC

1938 Buick, Roadmaster, Model 80C, sport phaeton, PH

1938 Buick, Limited, Model 91, sedan, AA

BUICK ROADMASTER & LIMITED — SERIES 80 & 90 — EIGHT: Wheelbases of the 80 and 90 Buick were increased two inches to 133 and 140 inches, respectively. The use of the crowned "turbulator" pistons raised the engine's compression ratio to 6.5:1. Horsepower was boosted to 141 at 3600 rpm. The Series 90 formal sedan was not offered while the four-door sedan was added to the Series 80 line.

I.D. DATA: Serial numbers on riveted plate on right side cowling under hood, right frame rail at cowl. Starting: 13219848 (Flint), 23238767 (South Gate), 33245765 (Linden). Ending: 13388546 (Flint), 23386843 (South Gate), 33376283 (Linden). Identification of different numbers used at other factories: Prefix 1 — Flint, Michigan, assembly. Prefix 2 — South Gate, California, assembly. Prefix 3 — Linden, New Jersey, assembly. Engine numbers on low right rear side of crankcase adjacent to dipstick. Starting: 43396937 — Series 40, 63396937 — Series 60, 83396937 — Series 80, 93396937 — Series 90. Ending: 93544292 — Series 90.

1938 Buick, Century, Model 68, two-door sedan, OCW

Series 40 (Special)

Model No.	Body Type & Seating	Price	Weight	Prod. Total
40C	2-dr. Conv. Phae.-5P	1406	3705	776
41	4-dr. Tr. Sed.-5P	1047	3560	79,510
44	2-dr. Spt. Sed.-5P	981	3515	5943
46	2-dr. Bus. Cpe.-2P	945	3385	11,337
46C	2-dr. Conv. Cpe.-4P	1103	3575	2473
46S	2-dr. Spt. Cpe.-4P	1001	3425	5381
47	4-dr. Spt. Sed.-5P	1022	3535	11,265
48	2-dr. Tr. Sed.	1006	3520	14,153

Series 60 (Century)

Model No.	Body Type & Seating	Price	Weight	Prod. Total
60C	4-dr. Conv. Phae.-5P	1713	3950	208
61	4-dr. Tr. Sed.-5P	1297	3780	12,364
66C	2-dr. Conv. Cpe.-4P	1359	3815	642
66S	2-dr. Spt. Cpe.-4P	1226	3690	1991
67	4-dr. Spt. Sed.-5P	1272	3785	1515
68	2-dr. Tr. Sed.-5P	1256	3760	1380

Series 80 (Roadmaster)

Model No.	Body Type & Seating	Price	Weight	Prod. Total
80C	4-dr. Spt. Phae.-6P	1983	4325	350
81	4-dr. Tr. Sed.-6P	1645	4245	4505
81F	4-dr. Fml. Sed.-6P	1759	4305	247
87	4-dr. Spt. Sed.-6P	1645	4245	466

Series 90 (Limited)

Model No.	Body Type & Seating	Price	Weight	Prod. Total
90	4-dr. Tr. Sed.-8P	2350	4608	644
90L	4-dr. Limo.-8P	2453	4653	410
91	4-dr. Tr. Sed.-6P	2077	4568	437

ENGINE: [Series 40] Inline. Ohv. Eight. Cast iron block. B & S: 3-3/32 x 4-1/8 in. Disp.: 248 cu. in. C.R.: 6.15:1. Brake H.P.: 107 @ 3400 R.P.M. Taxable H.P.: 30.63. Main bearings: five. Valve lifters: mechanical. Carb.: Marvel CDI or Stromberg AAV-1 dual downdraft. Torque: 203 lb.-ft. @ 2000 R.P.M. [Series 60, 80, 90] Inline. Ohv. Eight. Cast iron block. B & S: 3-7/16 x 4-5/16 in. Disp.: 320.2 cu. in. C.R.: 6.35:1. Brake H.P.: 141 @ 3600 R.P.M. Taxable H.P. 37.81. Main bearings: five. Valve lifters: mechanical. Carb.: Marvel CD-2 or Stromberg AAV-2 dual downdraft (1-1/4 inch). Torque: 269 lb.-ft. @ 2000 R.P.M.

CHASSIS: [Series 40] W.B.: 122 in. O.L.: 200-1/16 in. Front/Rear Tread: 58-7/16 in./59-5/32 in. Tires: 15 x 6.50. [Series 60] W.B.: 126 in. O.L.: 203-9/16 in. Front/Rear Tread: 58-5/16 in./59-1/4 in. Tires: 15 x 7.00. [Series 80] W.B.: 133 in. O.L.: 213-1/4in. Front/RearTread: 59-19/32 in./62-1/2 in. Tires: 16 x 7.00. [Series 90] W.B.: 140 in. O.L.: 219-1/2 in. Front/RearTread: 59-7/16 in./62-1/2 in. Tires: 16 x 7.50.

TECHNICAL: Sliding gear transmission. Speeds: 3F/1R. Floor shift controls. Single dry plate clutch. Shaft drive. Semi-floating rear axle. Overall ratio: 4.40:1 — Series 40, 3.90:1 — Series 60, 4.18:1 — Series 80, 4.56:1 Series 90. Hydraulic brakes on four wheels. Pressed steel wheels. Automatic Safety Transmission ($80.00). No Rol Hill-Holder (Series 60, 80, 90).

OPTIONS: Single sidemount. Dual sidemount. Electric clock (Special only). DeLuxe modern seat covers ($6.55-9.35). Master heater (13.95). DeLuxe heater (18.95). Grille guard (1.85). Ivory plastic steering wheel with full horn ring (Special Model 48 only). Fog lamps (5.50). Grille covers (1.35). Centerline radio (59.75). Centerline dual radio (67.50). Electric windshield defroster (3.00). Dual heater defroster (8.85).

HISTORICAL: Introduced October 1937. A Shafer Special powered by a Buick engine was bumped from the starting lineup after initially qualifying at 112.7 mph at Indy. The 1938 Series 80 and 90 models were the last Buicks using wood in the construction of their bodies. Innovations: Although Buick offered the Automatic Safety Transmission only for the 1938 model year it still represented an important step in the development of the modern automatic transmission. The use of coil springs at the rear was also an industry first. Calendar year production: 173,905. Model year production: 168,689 (including 12,692 stripped chassis and cars for export). The president of Buick was Harlow Curtice.

1939

1939 BUICK: Buick's styling for 1939 was highlighted by a new two-piece "waterfall" grille with thin vertical bars and a substantial increase in window area. On the Series 40 and 60 bodies the windshield area was 26 percent larger, their front door windows were 16 percent larger and a 21 percent increase in area was claimed for their rear windows, which were on all models of a one-piece design. Other key design changes included a narrower hood, thinner front door pillars, and larger hubcaps.

A new dash arrangement and "Handi-shift" column-mounted gearshifts were key interior changes. All major gauges except for the clock that was mounted on the passenger's side were positioned directly in front of the driver.

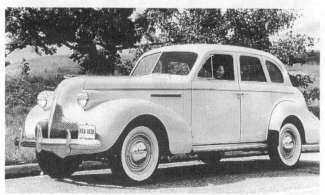

1939 Buick, Special, Model 41, sedan, PH

BUICK SPECIAL — SERIES 40 — EIGHT: The Series 40 wheelbase was reduced two inches to 120 inches. Both a new clutch with only nine parts as compared to 41 in 1938 and a new lighter and stronger transmission were introduced. In place of the normal runningboards, optional narrow trim strips could be installed. The Series 40 interior was finished in walnut finish garnish moldings.

The sport sedan Model 47 was dropped from the Special and Century lines and the convertible coupe now was fitted with rear opera seats rather than the rumbleseat that was no longer offered for any Buick. The convertible phaeton model was also dropped for 1939. Its successor was the convertible sport phaeton with a trunk-back body style in both the Special and Century lines.

1939 Buick, Century, Model 61, sedan, AA

BUICK CENTURY — SERIES 60 — EIGHT: The Series 60 shared the new clutch assembly with the Series 40 and was also available with the optional rocker panel trim strip. Its interior garnish molding was mahogany.

1939 Buick, Roadmaster, Model 81C, (trunkback) phaeton, OCW

BUICK ROADMASTER — SERIES 80 — EIGHT: The Roadmaster shared stainless steel windshield and rear window trim plus mahogany interior trim panels with the Limited models. The Series 80 sport phaeton could be ordered with either the fastback or rear trunk style.

BUICK LIMITED — SERIES 90 — EIGHT: The three Series 90 Buicks continued to use a 140-inch wheelbase and the limousine model featured a movable glass partition in back of the chauffeur's compartment. Standard equipment for Models 90 and 90L included rear compartment cigarette lighter and vanity case.

I.D. DATA: Serial numbers on riveted plate on right side cowling under hood. Starting: 13388547 (Flint), 23395088 (South Gate), 33405088 (Linden). Ending: 13596806 (Flint), 23592131 (South Gate), 33593652 (Linden). Same factory build identification as 1938. Engine numbers on low right rear side of crankcase adjacent to dipstick. Starting: 43572652 (Series 40), 63576652 (Series 60, 80, 90). Ending: 43786213 (Series 40), 93755912 (Series 60, 80, 90).

Note 1: Some cars were fitted with 0.010-inch oversize pistons. These engines are identified by a dash (—) following the engine number.

Series 40

Model No.	Body Type & Seating	Price	Weight	Prod. Total
41	4-dr. Tr. Sed.-5P	996	3547	109,213
41C	4-dr. Spt. Phae.-5P	1406	3707	724
46	2-dr. Bus. Cpe.-2P	849	3387	14,582
46C	2-dr. Conv. Cpe.-4P	1077	3517	4569
46S	2-dr. Spt. Cpe.-4P	950	3437	10,043
48	2-dr. Tr. Sed.-5P	955	3482	27,218

Series 60

Model No.	Body Type & Seating	Price	Weight	Prod. Total
61	4-dr. Tr. Sed.-5P	1246	3832	18,462
61C	4-dr. Spt. Phae.-5P	1713	3967	249
66C	2-dr. Conv. Cpe.-4P	1343	3762	790
66S	2-dr. Spt. Cpe.-4P	1175	3687	3408
68	2-dr. Tr. Sed.-5P	1205	3557	521

Series 80

Model No.	Body Type & Seating	Price	Weight	Prod. Total
80C	4-dr. Spt. Phae.-6P	1938	4932	3
81	4-dr. Tr. Sed.-6P	1543	4247	5460
81C	4-dr. Phae.-6P	1983	4362	311
81F	4-dr. Fml. Sed.-6P	1758	4312	303
87	4-dr. Spt. Sed.-6P	1543	4247	20

Series 90

Model No.	Body Type & Seating	Price	Weight	Prod. Total
90	4-dr. Tr. Sed.-8P	2350	4608	650
90L	4-dr. Limo.-8P	2453	4653	423
91	4-dr. Tr. Sed.-6P	2074	4568	378

ENGINE: [Series 40] Inline. Ohv. Eight. Cast iron block. B & S: 3-3/32 x 4-1/8 in. Disp.: 248 cu. in. C.R.: 6.15:1. Brake H.P.: 107 @ 3400 R.P.M. Taxable H.P.: 30.63. Main bearings: five. Valve lifters: mechanical. Carb.: Carter 4195. Torque: 126 lb.-ft. @ 1000 R.P.M. [Series 60, 80, 90] Inline. Ohv. Eight. Cast iron block. B & S: 3-7/16 x 4-5/16 in. Disp.: 320.2 cu. in. C.R. 6.35:1. Brake H.P. 141 @ 3600 R.P.M. Taxable H.P.: 37.81. Main bearings: five. Valve lifters: mechanical. Carb.: Stromberg AAV26. Torque: 130 lb.-ft. @ 1000 R.P.M.

CHASSIS: [Series 40] W.B.: 120 in. O.L.: 198-1/16 in. Front/Rear Tread: 58-1/4- in./59-3/32 in. Tires: 15 x 6.50 four ply. [Series 60] W.B.: 126 in. O.L.: 203-9/16 in. Front/Rear Tread: 58-23/32 in./59-21/32 in. Tires: 15 x 7.00 four ply. [Series 80] W.B.: 133 in O.L.: 213-1/4 in. Front/Rear Tread: 59-19/32 in./62-1/2 in. Tires: 16 x 7.00 four ply. [Series 90] W.B.: 140 in. O.L.: 219-1/2 in. Front/Rear Tread: 59-7/16 in./62-1/2 in. Tires: 16 x 7.50 six ply.

TECHNICAL: Sliding gear transmission. Speeds: 3F/1R. Column controls. Single dry plate clutch. Shaft drive. Semi-floating rear axle. Overall ratio: 4.40, 3.9, 3.6 — Series 40; 3.9. 3.6. 3.4 — Series 60; 4.18 — Series 80; 4.56 — Series 90. Hydraulic brakes on four wheels. Pressed steel wheels. No Rol Hill-Holder (Series 60, 80, 90).

OPTIONS: Dual sidemounts. Fender skirts. Leather interior. Sonomatic push-button radio. White sidewalls. Sunshine turret roof. Fender-mounted parking lights.

HISTORICAL: Introduced October 9, 1938. Standard equipment directional signals (rear only), push-button "Sonomatic" radio, "Sunshine Turret Roof" (sun roof) optional for Series 40 and 60 two-door and four-door. Calendar year production: 231,219. Model year production: 208,256 (including 10,932 stripped chassis and cars for export). The president of Buick was Harlow Curtice.

1940

1940 Buick, Special, Model 41, sedan, OCW

1940 Buick, Century, Model 46S, sport coupe, JAC

BUICK SPECIAL — SERIES 40 — EIGHT: A one-inch wheelbase increase to 121 inches enabled the sidemount option and front doors that fully opened to coexist. A full-width rear seat was installed in the sport coupe model and a dual diaphragm fuel pump was used to improve windshield wiper operation. Interior features included white trim panels and combination Bedford cloth and mohair upholstery.

1940 Buick, Super, Model 59, estate wagon, JAC

BUICK SUPER — SERIES 50 — EIGHT: The new Series 50 Buick shared the 121-inch wheelbase chassis with the Specials. Five body styles were offered, all of which were devoid of run-

ningboards. Bedford cord upholstery in a two-tone tan was standard. A mid-year estate wagon model was exclusive to the Super Series.

1940 Buick, Century, Model 61C, convertible phaeton, OCW

BUICK CENTURY — SERIES 60 — EIGHT: Five body styles were offered in the Century line.

1940 Buick, Roadmaster, Model 71, sedan, PH

1940 Buick, Roadmaster, Model 76C, convertible coupe, OCW

1940 Buick, Roadmaster, Model 76S, sport coupe, OCW

BUICK ROADMASTER — SERIES 70 — EIGHT: To make room for the new Series 80 Limited models the Roadmaster was given a new Series 70 designation. It shared its body shell with the new Super line and was available in four body styles. Interiors of either gray or tan Bedford cord were offered.

1940 Buick, Limited, Model 81, sedan, PH

BUICK LIMITED — SERIES 80 — EIGHT: These Limited models, mounted on 133-inch wheelbase chassis previously used for the Roadmasters, had standard equipment heaters and defrosters. All body styles were of a six-passenger capacity. Interior appointments included a choice of Bedford cloth (either tan or gray), broadcloth or cloth (tan or gray) or leather.

BUICK LIMITED — SERIES 90 — EIGHT: Although all Buicks had the same front end design the 140-inch wheelbase and eight-passenger capacity set the Series 90 models apart. Three body styles were offered.

I.D. DATA: Serial numbers on riveted plate on right side cowling under hood, right side of frame top near cowling. Starting: 13596807 (Flint), 23601856 (South Gate), 33611856 (Linden). Ending: 13880011 (Flint), 23871217 (South Gate), 33874783 (Linden). Same factory build identification as 1939. Engine numbers on right side of crankcase below pushrod cover toward front (Series 40-50) same location except near rear of engine (Series 60, 70, 80). Starting: 43786214 (Series 40), 53786214 (Series 50, 60, 70, 80, 90). Ending: 44074857 (Series 40), 94074858 (Series 50, 60, 70, 80, 90).

Series 40

Model No.	Body Type & Seating	Price	Weight	Prod. Total
41	4-dr. Tr. Sed.-5P	996	3660	67,308
41C	4-dr. Conv. Phae.	1355	3755	552
41T	4-dr. Taxi-5P	NA	NA	48
46	2-dr. Bus. Cpe.-2P	895	3505	12,372
46C	2-dr. Conv. Cpe.-4P	1077	3665	3664
46S	2-dr. Spt. Cpe.-4P	950	3540	8291
48	2-dr. Tr. Sed.-5P	955	3605	20,739

Series 50

51	4-dr. Tr. Sed.-6P	1109	3790	95,875
51C	4-dr. Conv. Phae.-6P	1549	3895	1351
56C	2-dr. Conv. Cpe.-6P	1211	3785	4764
56S	2-dr. Spt. Cpe.-5P	1058	3735	26,251
59	4-dr. Est. Wag.-6P	1242	3870	495

Series 60

61	4-dr. Tr. Sed.-5P	1211	3935	8597
61C	4-dr. Conv. Phae.-5P	1620	4050	194
66	2-dr. Bus. Cpe.-2P	1128	3800	44
66C	2-dr. Conv. Cpe.-4P	1343	3915	542
66S	2-dr. Spt. Cpe.-5P	1175	3765	96

Series 70

71	4-dr. Tr. Sed.-6P	1359	4045	13,583
71C	4-dr. Conv. Phae.-6P	1768	4195	235
76C	4-dr. Conv. Cpe.-6P	1431	4055	606
76S	2-dr. Spt. Cpe.-5P	1277	3990	3921

Series 80

80C	4-dr. Conv. Phae.-6P	1952	4550	7
81	4-dr. Tr. Sed.-6P	1553	4400	3810
81C	4-dr. Fsbk. Conv. Phae.-6P	1952	4540	230
81F	4-dr. Fml. Sed.-6P	1727	4455	248
87	4-dr. Spt. Sed.-6P	1553	4380	14
87F	4-dr. Fml. Spt. Sed.-6P	1727	4435	7

Series 90

90	4-dr. Tr. Sed.-8P	2096	4645	796
90L	4-dr. Limo.-8P	2199	4705	526
91	4-dr. Tr. Sed.-6P	1942	4590	417

ENGINE: [Series 40, 50] Inline. Ohv. Eight. Cast iron block. B & S: 3-3/32 x 4-1/8 in. Disp.: 248 cu. in. C.R.: 6.15:1. Brake H.P.: 107 @ 3400 R.P.M. Taxable H.P.: 30.63. Main bearings: five. Valve lifters: mechanical. Carb.: Carter Model 440S, 474S

or Stromberg AAV-16, A-19181. Torque: 126 lb.-ft. @ 1000 R.P.M. [Series 60, 70, 80, 90] Inline. Ohv. Eight. Cast iron block. B & S: 3-7/16 x 4-5/16 in. Disp.: 320.2 cu. in. C.R.: 6.35:1. Brake H.P.: 141 @ 3600 R.P.M. Taxable H.P.: 37.81. Main bearings: five. Valve lifters: mechanical. Carb.: Carter No. 4485 or Stromberg AAV-25 A-19182. Torque: 130 lb.-ft. @ 1000 R.P.M.

combustion chambers. All series were available with a choice of rear axle ratios at no extra cost. All cars were offered in two-tone color combinations with 19 selections at no extra charge.

1941 Buick, Special, Model 44C, convertible coupe, PH

1940 Buick, Super, Model 56C, convertible coupe, OCW

CHASSIS: [Series 40] W.B.: 121 in. O.L.: 204 in. Front/Rear Tread: 58-7/16 in./59-5/32 in. Tires: 16 x 6.50. [Series 50] W.B.: 121 in. O.L.: 204 in. Front/Rear Tread: 58-7/16 in./59-5/32 in. Tires: 16 x 6.50. [Series 60] W.B.: 126 in. O.L.: 209 in. Front/Rear Tread: 58-5/16 in./59-1/4 in. Tires: 15 x 7.00. [Series 70] W.B.: 126 in. O.L.: 214 in. Front/Rear Tread: 58-5/16 in./59-1/4 in. Tires: 15 x 7.00. [Series 80] W.B.: 133 in. O.L.: 213-1/4 in. Front/Rear Tread: 59-19/32 in./62-1/2 in. Tires: 16 x 7.50. [Series 90] W.B.: 140 in. O.L.: 219-1/2 in. Front/Rear Tread: 59-7/16 in./62-1/2 in. Tires: 16 x 7.50.

TECHNICAL: Sliding gear transmission. Speeds: 3F/1R. Column controls. Single dry plate clutch. Shaft drive. Semi-floating rear axle. Overall ratio: 3.9 (Series 40). Hydraulic brakes on four wheels. Pressed steel wheels. No Rol Hill-Holder.

OPTIONS: Seat covers. Front bumper guard. Fog lights. Roof mounted radio antenna (closed cars). Telescoping vacuum-powered mounted on left front fender (open cars). Sonomatic radio ($63.00). Fender skirts. Dual white sidewall tires. Fresh Aire underseat heater/defroster. DeLuxe steering wheel (12.50). Rear seat radio (Model 90-L). Outside mirrors. Grille guard. Electric clock (Standard Series 60, 70, 80, 90). Folding rear center guard. Winter grille cover. Radiator insect screen. Twin comfort cushions. Front door scuff pads. Visor vanity mirrors.

HISTORICAL: Introduced September 22, 1939. Innovations: All Buick engines were equipped with oil filters and sealed beam headlights were used on all models. A new feature was Fore-N-Aft Flash-Way directionals. Calendar year production: 310,995. Model year production: 283,404 (including 8,288 stripped chassis and cars for export). The president of Buick was Harlow Curtice. Buick had its best production year in history in 1940. On November 18, 1940, the four millionth Buick was produced. 1940 was the last year Buicks were available with sidemounts.

1941 Buick, Special, Model 46S, two-door sedanette, OCW

1941 Buick, Special, Model 47, sedan, OCW

BUICK SPECIAL — SERIES 40 — EIGHT: Both the Special and Century lines received new bodies for 1941. As with all 1941 Buicks they featured front fenders that extended nearly to the front door, headlights that were almost totally integrated into the front fender line, and a broader front grille. The estate model moved into the Series 40 line for 1941. On February 3, 1941, four new Special Series 40A models were introduced with a 118-inch wheelbase. These carried a 40-A designation that brought a new 40-B identification for the original Series 40.

1941

1941 BUICK: For the 1941 model year that was destined to set new records Buick introduced twin carburetion, new bodies, and, on a limited (five cars in all) basis, custom body work by Brunn on Roadmaster and Limited Series chassis. Buick's "Fireball" engine for 1941 was fitted with dome-shaped pistons and

1941 Buick, Super, Model 51C, convertible phaeton, OCW

1941 Buick, Super, Model 56, business coupe, OCW

BUICK SUPER — SERIES 50 — EIGHT: The Super Buicks as all other Buicks above Series 40 were equipped with standard compound carburetion. Bodies were carried over from 1940 but all Buicks had overall heights lowered from 9/10 to 2-3/4 inches.

BUICK CENTURY — SERIES 60 — EIGHT: With its new body and 165 hp the Century ranked both as America's most powerful automobile and one of its most attractive. It shared thin chrome strips on the front fenders with all production Buicks except the 40-B Specials. Introduced into both the Century and Special lines was the new Sedanet body style.

1941 Buick, Roadmaster, Model 71C, convertible phaeton, OCW

BUICK ROADMASTER — SERIES 70 — EIGHT: Four Roadmaster body styles were available, all with the 165 hp carburetion engine.

1941 Buick, Limited, Model 90, sedan, PH

BUICK LIMITED — SERIES 90 — EIGHT: The 133-inch wheelbase Limited Series was not offered in 1941. Standard equipment on the 139-inch Limited included rear fender skirts.

I.D. DATA: Serial numbers underhood, on right side of firewall. Starting: Series 40A-14034052 (Flint), 23994170 (South Gate), 34007924 (Linden). All others — 13880012 (Flint), 23892008 (South Gate), 33897008 (Linden). Ending: Series 40A — 14257441 (Flint). Engine numbers on crankcase as in 1940. Starting: Series 40 — 44074859, Series 40-A — A4074859, Series 50, 60, 70, 90 — 54074859. Ending: Series 40-A — A4457940, Series 50, 60, 70, 80, 90 — 94453893.

Series 40-A

Model No.	Body Type & Seating	Price	Weight	Prod. Total
44	2-dr. Bus. Cpe.-3P	915	3530	3258
44C	2-dr. Conv. Cpe.-6P	1138	3780	4282
44S	2-dr. Spt. Cpe.-6P	980	3590	5269
47	4-dr. Tr. Sed.-6P	1021	3670	13,992

Series 40-B

Model No.	Body Type & Seating	Price	Weight	Prod. Total
41	4-dr. Tr. Sed.-6P	1052	3730	91,138
44SE	4-dr. Sed. Sup. Equipment	NA	NA	13,378
46	2-dr. Bus. Cpe.-3P	735	3630	9185
46S	2-dr. S'net.	1006	3700	87,687
46SSE	2-dr. S'net. Sup. Equipment-6P	1063	NA	9591
49	4-dr. Est. Wag.-6P	1463	3980	838

Series 50

51	4-dr. Tr. Sed.-6P	1185	3770	57,367
51C	4-dr. Conv. Phae.-6P	1555	4015	467
56	2-dr. Bus. Cpe.-3P	1031	3620	2449
56C	2-dr. Conv. Cpe.-6P	1267	3810	12,181
56S	2-dr. Spt. Cpe.-6P	1113	3670	19,603

Series 60

61	4-dr. Tr. Sed.-6P	1288	4239	15,027
66	2-dr. Bus. Cpe.-3P	1195	4093	220
66S	2-dr. S'net.-6P	1241	4157	5521

Series 70

71	4-dr. Tr. Sed.-6P	1364	4204	10,431
71C	4-dr. Conv. Phae.-6P	1457	4285	312
76C	2-dr. Conv. Cpe.-6P	1775	4451	1845
76S	2-dr. Spt. Cpe.-6P	1282	4109	2784

Series 90

90	4-dr. Tr. Sed.-8P	2360	4680	885
90L	4-dr. Limo.-8P	2465	4760	605
91	4-dr. Tr. Sed.-6P	2155	4575	1223
90F	4-dr. Fml. Sed.-6P	2310	4665	293

ENGINE: [Series 40A, 40B] Inline. Ohv. Eight. Cast iron block. B & S: 3-3/32 x 4-1/8 in. Disp.: 248 cu. in. C.R.: 6.15:1. Brake H.P.: 115 @ 3500 R.P.M. Optional compound carburetion for Series 40A & 40B boosts H.P. to 125 @ 3800 R.P.M.: Main bearings: five. Valve lifters: mechanical. Carb.: Carter 487-S or Stromberg AAV-16. Torque: 210 lb.-ft. @ 2000 R.P.M. [Series 50] Inline. Ohv. Eight. Cast iron block. B & S: 3-3/32 x 4-1/8 in. Disp.: 248 cu. in. C.R.: 7:0. Brake H.P. 125 @ 3800 R.P.M. Main bearings: five. Valve lifters: mechanical. Carb.: Carter 509S, 510S or Stromberg AAV-16, AA-1. Torque: 278 lb.-ft. @ 2200 R.P.M. [Series 60, 70, 90] Inline. Ohv. Eight. Cast iron block. B & S: 3-7/16 x 4-5/16 in. Disp.: 320.2 cu. in. C.R.: 7.0:1. Brake H.P.: 165 @ 3800 R.P.M. Main bearings: five. Valve lifters: mechanical. Carb.: Carter 509S, 510S or Stromberg AAV-16, AA1. Torque: 278 lb.-ft. @ 2200 R.P.M.

CHASSIS: [Series 40-A] W.B.: 118 in. O.L.: 202-17/32 in. Height: 67-13/32 in. Front/Rear Tread: 59-1/8 in./62-3/16 in. Tires: 15 x 6.50. [Series 40B] W.B.: 121 in. O.L.: 208-3/4 in. Height 66-11/16 in. Front/Rear Tread: 58-7/16 in./59-5/32 in. Tires: 16 x 6.50. [Series 50] W.B.: 121 in. O.L.: 210-3/8 in. Height: 66 in. Front/Rear Tread: 58-7/16 in./59-5/32 in. Tires: 16 x 6.50. [Series 60] W.B.: 126 in. O.L.: 213-1/2 in. Height: 66-13/16 in. Front/Rear Tread: 58-5/16 in./59-1/4 in. Tires: 15 x 7.00. [Series 70] W.B.: 126 in. O.L.: 215 in. Height: 66-1/8 in. Front/Rear Tread: 59-1/8 in./62-1/4 in. Tires: 15 x 7.00. [Series 90] W.B.: 139 in. O.L.: 228-5/8 in. Height: 68-7/8 in. Front/Rear Tread: 58-11/32 in./62-1/2 in. Tires: 16 x 7.50.

1941 Buick, Super, Model 51C, convertible phaeton, OCW

TECHNICAL: Sliding gear transmission. Speeds: 3F/1R. Column controls. Single dry plate clutch. Shaft drive. Semi-floating rear axle. Overall ratio: Series 40 — single carburetor, 4.4:1, compound carburetor 4.1:1. Series 50, 4.4:1, Series 60, 70 — 3.9: 1. Series 90 4.2:1. Hydraulic brakes on four wheels.

Pressed steel wheels. Drivetrain options: No Rol Hill-Holder ($9.00). Compound carburetion (Series 40 except Models 41SE & 46SSE) (15.39).

OPTIONS: Clock electric (Special only). Super Sonomatic (shortwave & regular band). Underseat heater & defroster (standard on models 51C, 71C, & Series 90) ($33.00). Rear stainless steel footrest molding (sedan). Vacuum pump windshield washer (standard on Series 90) (3.85). EZI, no glare mirrors. Fender skirts (standard on Series 90) (10.00). Fog lights (10.75). Sonomatic push-button radio and antenna (65.00). Special paint (41.05). DeLuxe dash heater (15.50). Dual defroster (7.50).

HISTORICAL: Introduced October 13, 1940. Buick introduced its two-way hood that could be opened from either side for 1941. Calendar year sales: 297,381. Calendar year production: 316,251. Model year production: 377,428 (including 7,597 stripped chassis & cars for export.) The president of Buick was Harlow Curtice.

1942

1942 BUICK: The 1942 Buicks offered the appealing sedanet fastback style that had been the sensation of 1941 in all series except the Limited line. New wider and lower bodies were offered for the Series 50 and Series 70 and "Airfoil" front fenders that flowed into the lines of the rear fenders were introduced on convertibles and sedanet models in Series 50 and Series 70. All models had new front fender trim featuring parallel chrome strips. Also featured for 1942 was a handsome new grille with a lower outline and thin vertical bars.

After the government prohibited the use of chrome trim on January 1, 1942, Buick began production of the H models. A number of body styles were dropped and most trim was now painted. Cast iron pistons were used in the 248 cid engine and the Series 90 cars were dropped. The last of the 1942 Buicks was completed on February 4, 1942.

1942 Buick, Special, Model 41, sedan, AA

BUICK SPECIAL — SERIES 40-A, 40-B — EIGHT: All Series 40 Buicks had new front fenders that extended well into the front door region. Models 41 SE and 46SSE were fitted with Century interiors.

BUICK SUPER — SERIES 50 — EIGHT: The swept-back fenders of the convertible and sedanet Supers made them styling leaders. A feature the Supers shared with other Buicks was a new interior air intake positioned near the front grille that eliminated the old cowl-level ventilator.

BUICK CENTURY — SERIES 60 — EIGHT: The Century four-door models, along with those in the Special and Limited series, had six side windows. All Century models had, prior to January 1942, added side trim in their rear fenders. This feature was also common to all Buicks except the Series 40A and the Series 50 and Series 70 models with "Airfoil" front fenders. Those cars had twin side bars that ran unbroken the full length of the body.

1942 Buick, Roadmaster, Model 71, sedan, JAC

BUICK ROADMASTER — SERIES 70 — EIGHT: The new Roadmaster bodies were lower and wider than in 1941 and along with the Series 50 models featured small reflector lenses on their rear fenders.

BUICK LIMITED — SERIES 90 — EIGHT: The three Series 90 models combined the older notchback styling with the extended length front fender format of the Series 40, 50, and 60 Buicks. With standard rear fender skirts the Limited also carried twin chrome trim strips on their front and rear fenders.

1942 Buick, Super, Model 65S, two-door sedanette, PH

I.D. DATA: Serial numbers under hood, on right side of firewall. Starting: 14257442 — Flint, 24273684 — South Gate, 3426384 — Linden. The same factory-built identification of 1941 was continued. Engine numbers on crankcase as in 1941. Starting: Series 40A 4457941A, Series 40B 44579714, Series 50 4457941-5, Series 60 4457941-6, Series 70 4457941-7, Series 90 4457941-9. Ending: Series 40A 4556599A, Series 40B 4556599-4.

Series 40A

Model No.	Body Type & Seating	Price	Weight	Prod. Total
44	2-dr. Util. Cpe.-3P	990	3510	461
44C	2-dr. Conv. Cpe.-6P	1260	3790	1776
47	4-dr. Tr. Sed.	1080	3650	1611
48	2-dr. Bus. S'dnt.-3P	1010	3555	559
48S	2-dr. Family S'dnt.-6P	1045	3610	5981

Special 40-B

41	4-dr. Tr. Sed. 6P	1203	NA	17,187
41SE	Sed. Sup. Equipment-4P	1287	NA	2286
46	2-dr. Bus. S'dnt.-3P	1020	3650	1406
46S	2-dr. Family S'dnt.-6P	1075	3705	11,856
46SSE	8-dr. S'dnt. Sup. Equipment	NA	NA	1809
49	4-dr. Est. Wag.	1450	3925	326

Series 50

Model No.	Body Type & Seating	Price	Weight	Prod. Total
51	4-dr. Tr. Sed.-6P	1280	3890	16,001
56C	2-dr. Conv. Cpe.-6P	1450	4025	2454
56S	2-dr. S'dnt.-6P	1230	3800	14,579

Series 60

Model No.	Body Type & Seating	Price	Weight	Prod. Total
61	4-dr. Sed.-6P	1350	4065	3342
66S	2-dr. S'dnt.-6P	1300	3985	1229

Series 70

Model No.	Body Type & Seating	Price	Weight	Prod. Total
71	4-dr. Tr. Sed.-6P	1465	4150	5418
76C	2-dr. Conv. Cpe.-6P	1675	4300	509
76S	2-dr. S'dnt.-6P	1365	4075	2471

Series 90

Model No.	Body Type & Seating	Price	Weight	Prod. Total
90	4-dr. Tr. Sed.-8P	2455	4710	144
90L	4-dr. Limo.-8P	2716	NA	192
91	4-dr. Tr. Sed.-6P	2245	4665	215
90F	Formal Sed.-6P	2395	4695	85

ENGINE: [Series 40A, 40B] Inline. Ohv. Eight. Cast iron block. B & S: 3-3/32 x 4-1/8 in. Disp.: 248 cu. in. Brake H.P.: 110 @ 3400 R.P.M., 118 H.P. @ 3600 R.P.M. with compound combustion. Main bearings: five. Valve lifters: mechanical. Carb.: Carter 487-S or Stromberg AAV-16. [Series 50] Inline. Ohv. Eight. Cast iron block. B & S: 3-3/32 x 4-1/8 in. Disp.: 248 cu. in. Brake H.P.: 118 @ 3600 R.P.M. Main bearings: five. Valve lifters: mechanical. Carb.: Carter 509S, 510S, or Stromberg AAV-16, AA1. [Series 60, 70, 90] Inline. Ohv. Eight. Cast iron block. B & S: 3-7/16 x 4-5/16 in. Disp.: 320.2 cu. in. C.R.: 6.7:1. Brake H.P.: 165 @ 3800 R.P.M. Main bearings: five. Valve lift-ers: mechanical. Carb.: Carter 509S, 510S or Stromberg AAV-16, AA-1. Torque: 278 lb.-ft. @ 2200 R.P.M.

CHASSIS: [Series 40A, 40B] W.B.: 118 in. O.L.: 202-17/32 in. Height: 67-13/32 in. Front/Rear Tread: 59-1/8 in./62-3/16 in. Tires: 15 x 6.50. [Series 50] W.B.: 124 in. O.L.: 210 in. Height: 66-11/16 in. Front/Rear Tread: 58-7/16 in./59-5/32 in. Tires: 16 x 6.5. [Series 60] W.B.: 126 in. O.L.: 213-1/2 in. Height: 66-13/16 in. [Series 70] W.B.: 129 in. O.L.: 217 in. Height: 66-1/8 in. Front/Rear Tread: 59-1/8 in./62-1/4 in. Tires: 15 x 7.00. [Series 90] W.B.: 139 in. O.L.: 228-5/8 in. Height: 68-7/8 in. Tires: 15 x 7.00. [Series 40B] W.B.: 121 in. O.L.: 208-3/4 in.

TECHNICAL: Sliding gear transmission. Speeds: 3F/1R. Column controls. Single dry plate clutch. Shaft drive. Semi-floating rear axle. Overall ratio: 3.90 — Series 70, 3.6 or 3.9 — Series 60. Hydraulic brakes on four wheels. Pressed steel wheels. No Rol Hill-holder.

OPTIONS: Fender skirts on Series 40 & 50. Electric clock (Special only). Super Sonomatic radio. Under seat heater & defroster. Windshield washer. EZI mirrors. Fog lamps.

HISTORICAL: Introduced October 3, 1941. Calendar year production: 16,601. Model year production: 94,442 (including 2,575 stripped chassis and cars for export). The president of Buick was Harlow Curtice. Production of 1942 model Buicks ended on February 2, 1942.

BUICK
1946-1975

1972 Buick GS-350 hardtop.

By Terry V. Boyce

Buick entered the post-World War II market with a product for which there was enormous pent-up demand. During the years just prior to the war, Buick had become one of America's favorite cars. Large, but fast, and with sporting lines, the prewar Buick symbolized upward mobility. In 1946, many veterans came home with a dream of a family, a home in suburbia — and a Buick in the driveway. "So nice to come home to," a 1943 ad had proclaimed — using a yellow 1942 Roadmaster convertible for the illustration.

The Buick's role as part of the postwar dream was more than an ad man's pitch. This was born out by public acceptance of Buick's 1946-1948 models, although they were little more than warmed-over 1942s. Indeed, Buick's convertible styles, in Roadmaster and Super trim, were extremely popular. They are, today, treasured collector cars.

Though the styling hadn't changed for 1948, there was an important innovation — Dynaflow automatic drive. Optional on the 1948 Roadmaster, it would soon power all Roadmasters and become a popular option for other series.

New styling, still drawing on traditional design elements, appeared in 1949. Ventiports made their initial appearance on Buick front fenders. Mid-1949 saw the unveiling of a new Riviera hardtop, which led the way towards acceptance of this design. The two-door hardtop coupe was destined to be one of the most popular models of the '50s.

Then came 1950. According to many marque enthusiasts, Buick went a step too far. It was the year of the "bucktooth Buick," with a grille cavity full of large bumper guards. Actually, this new design had appeared during mid-calendar 1949, in a new "1950" Special line. There had been Specials from 1946 on, but they had been largely ignored by Buick's sales staff, which concentrated on the more expensive Supers and Roadmasters. As late as the beginning of 1949, the Buick Special had been almost identical to 1942 models. The time had come for a new push into the low-priced field, so the Special got the new styling first.

The 1950-'52 Buicks were solidly built and heavily trimmed. Yet, they were somehow a bit lacking in excitement and, even today, are not ranked among the most popular models. The straight eight era ended for the larger cars in 1952, when a four-barrel carbureted, 170-hp Roadmaster version made a fitting farewell.

Whatever excitement had been missing from Buick was back in 1953. The big news was under the hood — a 322-cid overhead valve V-8 for Super and Roadmaster models. For the first time ever (except two sedans), all

Buicks shared a common wheelbase. Celebrating its 50th anniversary, the Buick Division of General Motors offered an Anniversary Convertible, also known as the Skylark, for a cool $5,000. Just 1,690 were sold. Today, many still survive and are in great demand by collectors.

Buick chassis engineering began to catch up with the new V-8 in 1954. The updated cars were lower and wider, with greatly improved handling. Even the Special now had V-8 power. The Skylark returned for an unsuccessful encore, but the year was otherwise a smashing performance saleswise. The next year, 1955, was even better. Buick broke all the old records. A popular model line was the Century, which had returned in 1954. A new four-door Riviera pillarless hardtop debuted midyear.

By 1957, Buick styling had begun to lag. Sales started to slump. An over-chromed, overweight 1958 edition proved even less palatable to consumer tastes. It was a time of rapid change. The year 1959 brought new Buicks, with new series designations replacing those used since 1936. Wildly finned, and lacking almost any sort of continuity with Buick's past, the 1959 Buicks continued to get a cool reception in the showrooms. Buick was committed to the same basic body for 1960, but completely changed its look by blunting edges everywhere.

For 1961, Buicks looked lighter and cleaner. A new compact, the Special, was introduced and would soon be joined by a fancier Skylark Sport Coupe version. There was little real news for 1962, but the season's offerings were attractive and well-executed. A Buick highpoint, in the '60s, came the next year, with the introduction of the 1963 Riviera. It was a four-passenger sporting car that was immediately, and correctly, termed a timeless design.

By 1965, the Special/Skylark had grown to intermediate proportions and was wrapped in a handsome package. The larger Buicks, too, were restyled. Increasingly distinctive was the mid-range, Buick performance line — offering the Wildcat. Continuing through 1970, the Wildcat series provided extra performance and style. Beginning in 1963, the largest Buicks (Electras and Electra 225s) were given styling touches of their own, including unique rear fenders with skirts, distinctive bright trim and even specific grillework. They obtained a following that lasted for two decades.

A new Riviera, with some of the smoothest lines ever rendered by GM stylists, came in 1966. A GS or Gran Sport equipment option was continued, from 1965, and would be a rare option for the rest of the decade. The GS badge also appeared on a high-performance Skylark late in 1965, and evolved into a series designation by 1966.

By the end of the '60s, Buick had strong followings in many segments of the market. Never a large part of the sales picture, but still catered to with great care, were Buick's performance buyers. A 1970-'71 GSX option for the GS 455 coupe featured special paint colors, wild stripes and performance touches. The GSX would become one of the most sought after Buicks from the '70s. Buick lovers also said goodbye to the prestige Buick convertible in 1970, with the discontinuation of the Electra 225 edition that year.

Buick Division shocked the automotive world, in 1971, with a new tapered-deck 'boattail' Riviera. This design, built through 1973, will always stand out on the road. A new Centurion line also replaced the Wildcat, as Buick's full-size luxury performance line. The Centurion convertible became Buick's plushest, most expensive open car and is sure to be increasingly appreciated by collectors.

Skylark/GS models continued with little change from 1970 to 1972, although the potent GS 455s, with their Stage I engine option topping most performance cars in sheer acceleration, were detuned for 1971 to run on regular gas and decrease emissions. The Skylark/GS Sport Coupes and Convertibles, when optioned with desirable accessories, are sure bets for enthusiast attention.

An interesting series of Buick station wagons were issued throughout the post-World War II era. The Roadmaster Estates of 1947-'53 are among the most sought after of all wood-bodied cars. The 1953 model's combination of V-8 power and traditional wood sportiness presents a stunning combination. The all-steel wagons of 1954-'56 are rare. A four-door hardtop Caballero version followed in 1957. Innovative styling continued on Buick wagons into the '60s. The famous Skyroof Sport Wagons featured raised, glass-paneled roof sections, making them true specialty cars.

Buicks from any postwar year abound with the fine touches that make the cars interesting and collectible. From the showboats of the late '40s to the compact, but well-trimmed and gutsy Skylarks of the early '60s, to the boattail Riviera of the '70s, plenty of appreciation for restoration, or conservator's efforts are assured. For thousands of collector car enthusiasts, the question, "Wouldn't you really rather have a Buick?" is still answered with a resounding, "Yes."

1954 Buick, Century two-door convertible, V-8

1961 Buick, Electra 225 two-door convertible, V-8

1964 Buick, Riviera two-door hardtop, V-8

1968 Buick, Wildcat Custom two-door hardtop, V-8

The 1970 Buick lineup included the (l-to-r) Wildcat convertible, Le Sabre hardtop and Electra 225 sedan.

The 1973 Apollo line.

Something new for the 1973 summer selling season was a pair of Buick coupes with brougham-like roof treatment. At left is a Regal and right is an Electra 225. The unique styling was achieved via a short vinyl top covering the portion of the roof rear of the door. The custom treatment was done by a Detroit-area body shop. PH

1946

1946 Buick, Super two-door sedanette, 8-cyl

NOTE: Through 1950 Buick provided separate production totals for cars built for export These are given in brackets on the charts.

SPECIAL — SERIES 40 — The Special was Buick's lowest priced line. It was the only Buick line continuing the Fisher B-body fastback styles from 1941-'42 into the postwar era. Standard equipment included an automatic choke, ash receiver and turn signals. Exterior bright trim echoed 1942 models with twin strips of stainless steel flowing from the front wheelhouse to the rear edge of the standard rear wheelhouse skirts. Bright rocker moldings were also standard. Interiors featured rubber floor mats and painted instrument panels with round gauges. Series identification was found between the bumper guards, front and rear, on the crossbar. A cloisonne emblem carried the Special signature.

SPECIAL I.D. NUMBERS: The serial numbers for the 1946 Special series were the same as for other 1946 Buick series, which were mixed in production. They were: (Flint) 1436445 to 14524130, (Calif.) 24380001 to 24511494, (N.J.) 34390001 to 34429256, (Kans.) 44415001 to 44419786. Engine numbers began at 4558037-4 and up, the suffix '4' denoting a Series 40 engine.

Series No.	Body/Style No.	Body Type & Seating	Factory Price	Shipping Weight	Prod. Total
41	46-4409	4-dr Sed-6P	1580	3720	1,649 (1)
46S	46-4407	2-dr S'dn't-6P	1522	3670	1,350

ENGINE: Eight-cylinder. Inline. Overhead valve. Cast iron block. Displacement: 248.0 cid. Bore and stroke: 3-3/32 x 4-1/8 inches. Compression ratio: 6.3:1. Brake horsepower: 110 at 3600 rpm. Five main bearings. Mechanical valve lifters. Carburetor: Stromberg AAV-16 number 380106 two-barrel or Carter 608 or 663 two-barrel.

1946 Buick, Super two-door convertible coupe, 8-cyl

SUPER — SERIES 50 — Buick combined the large Series 70 body with the economical Series 40 powerplant to create the Super Series 50 line. Basic styling was continued from 1942, but now sedans had the front fender sweep across the doors to the rear fenders as did sedanettes and convertible styles. A stamped grille with vertical bars dominated the frontal ensemble. Single stainless body trim lines began on the front fenders and ended at the rear edge of the standard rear wheelhouse shields. Standard equipment was the same as the Series 40, but Series 50 Buicks had two-tone, woodgrained, instrument panels. Exterior series identification was found on the crossbar between the bumper guards, front and rear. Cloisonne emblems carried the Super signature.

SUPER I.D. NUMBERS: The serial number sequence was the same for all series (see Special — Series 40). Engine numbers began at 4558037-5 and up. The suffix '5' denoting a Series 50 engine.

Series No.	Body/Style No.	Body Type & Seating	Factory Price	Shipping Weight	Prod. Total
51	46-4569	4-dr Sed-6P	1822	3935	74,045 (3,679)
56S	46-4507	2-dr S'dn't-6P	1741	3795	34,235 (190)
56C	46-4567	2-dr Conv Cpe-6P	2046	4050	5,931 (456)
59	(Ionia)	4-dr Sta Wag-6P	2594	4170	786 (12)

ENGINE: Specifications were the same as previously listed for the 1946 Special - Series 40.

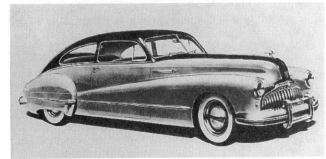

1946 Buick, Roadmaster two-door sedanette, 8-cyl

ROADMASTER — SERIES 70 — The Roadmaster was Buick's biggest and fastest car. Its larger and longer straight eight required five inches more wheelbase and longer front fenders and hood. Exterior trim was identical to the Super, except for the longer stainless moldings on the frontal sheet metal. Standard equipment was the same as for the Super, but richer interior fabrics were used. The instrument panel was two-toned with woodgrains except on convertibles, which used body-colored panels. Series identification was found on cloisonne emblems centered in the bumper guard crossbars front and rear.

ROADMASTER I.D. NUMBERS: The serial number sequence was the same for all series (see Special - Series 40). Engine numbers began at 455829-7 and up.

Series No.	Body/Style No.	Body Type & Seating	Factory Price	Shipping Weight	Prod. Total
71	46-4769	4-dr Sed-6P	2110	4165	20,597 (267)
76S	46-4707	2-dr S'dn't-6P	2014	4095	8,226 (66)
76C	46-4767	2-dr Conv Cpe-6P	2347	4345	2,576 (11)

ENGINE: Eight-cylinder. Inline. Overhead valve. Cast iron block. Displacement: 320.2 cid. Bore and stroke: 3-7/16 x 4-5/16 inches. Compression ratio: 6.6:1. Brake horsepower: 144 at 3600 rpm. Five main bearings. Mechanical valve lifters. Carburetor: Stromberg AAV-26 number 380097 two-barrel or Carter 609 or 664 two-barrel.

CHASSIS FEATURES: Wheelbase: Series 40 - 121 inches; Series 50 — 124 inches; Series 70 — 129 inches. Overall length: Series 40 — 207-1/2 inches; Series 50 — 212-3/8 inches; Series 70 — 217-1/8 inches. Front tread: Series 40 — 58-7/8 inches; Series 50 and 70 — 59-1/8 inches. Rear tread: Series 40 — 61-15/16 inches; Series 50 and 70 — 62-3/16 inches Tires: Series 40 and 50 — 6 50 x 16; Series 70 — 7.00 x 15.

POWERTRAIN OPTIONS: A three-speed manual transmission with steering column mounted shift lever was standard on all series. There were no optional gearboxes.

CONVENIENCE OPTIONS: Spotlite Sonomatic radio. Weather-Warden heater/defroster Sideview mirror. E-Z-I non-glare rearview mirror. Prismatic inside rearview mirror. Vanity visor mirror. Seat covers. Auxiliary driving lights. Multipurpose trouble lamp. "Breeze-Ease" draft deflectors.

HISTORICAL FOOTNOTES: Calendar year production of 156,080 units gave Buick a 7.2 percent market share and fifth place in sales. Model year output stood at 158,728 cars.

1947

NOTE: Through 1950 Buick provided separate production totals for cars built for export. These are given In brackets on the charts.

SPECIAL—SERIES 40—Buick's lowest-priced line continued to use the Fisher B-body design from before World War II this year. A new stamped grille with a separate upper bar distinguished 1947 Buicks from their 1946 predecessors. Standard equipment included an automatic choke, ash receiver and turn signals. Front and rear bumper guards were standard and the series designation was found, filled in red, on the chrome buttons centered in the guards' crossbars. Twin stainless moldings continued to be a Special hallmark, along the body and onto the standard rear fender wheelhouse skirts. Interiors featured round gauges with control switches flanking a center grille on the instrument panel. Rubber floor mats were standard.

SPECIAL I.D. NUMBERS: The serial numbers for the 1947 Special Series 40 were the same as for other 1947 Buick series, which were mixed in production. They were: Flint — 14524131 to 14801264, Calif. — 24530001 to 24775798, N.J. — 3454001 to 34776843, and Kans. — 44536001 to 44774870. Special Series 40 engine numbers were continued from 1946, ending at 4999880-4, the suffix 4 denoting a Series 40 engine.

Series No.	Body/Style No.	Body Type & Seating	Factory Price	Shipping Weight	Prod. Total
41	47-4409	4-dr Sed-6P	1673	3720	1,136 (1,295)
46	47-4407	2-dr S dn t-6P	1611	3670	14,278 (325)

ENGINE: Eight-cylinder. Inline. Overhead valve. Cast iron block. Displacement: 248.0 cid. Bore and stroke: 3-3/32 x 4-1/8 inches. Compression ratio: 6.3:1. Brake horsepower: 110 at 3600 rpm. Five main bearings. Mechanical valve lifters. Carburetor: Stromberg AAV-16 number 380106 two-barrel or Carter 608 or 663 two-barrel.

1947 Buick, Super two-door convertible coupe, 8-cyl (AA)

SUPER I.D. NUMBERS: The serial number sequence was the same for all series (see Special — Series 40). Engine numbers

continued from 1946, ending at 4999880-5 and up, the suffix 5 denoting a Series 50 engine.

1947 Buick, Super four-door Estate Wagon, 8-cyl

SUPER — SERIES 50—Combining big Buick room and ride with an economical Special engine continued to make an American favorite. The 1947 Super was little changed from its 1946 counterpart, except for a new stamped grille that had a separate upper bar and a new emblem. Stainless lower body moldings made a single line along the body and continued onto the standard rear wheelhouse shields. A white Tenite steering wheel was standard while the instruments were round and set in a two-toned dash panel. Exterior series identification was found on the crossbars between the standard bumper guards. A chrome emblem was used with the series script embossed and filled with red.

Series No.	Body/Style No.	Body Type & Seating	Factory Price	Shipping Weight	Prod. Total
51	47-4569	4-dr Sed-6P	1929	3920	76,866 (6,710)
56S	47-4507	2-dr S'dn't-6P	1843	3795	46,311 (606)
56C	47-4567	2-dr Conv Cpe-6P	2333	4050	27,796 (501)
59	Ionia	4-dr Sta Wag-6P	2594	4170	786 (12)

ENGINE: Specifications were the same as previously listed for the 1947 Special Series 40.

1947 Buick, Roadmaster two-door convertible coupe, 8-cyl (OCW)

ROADMASTER—SERIES 70—Buick's master of the road was a large car that continued basically unchanged from 1946. A new grille, shared with other series, was used. Exterior trim continued to be the same as used on the Super, except that the Roadmaster's longer wheelbase and front dog house required longer moldings ahead of the doors. Standard equipment was the same as found on the Super, but richer interior fabrics were used. Two-tone neutral colored instrument panels were employed, except on convertibles, which had body colored panels. The Roadmaster name appeared in red-filled script on a chrome button within the bumper guard crossbars, front and rear.

ROADMASTER I.D. NUMBERS: The serial number sequence was the same for all series (see Special - Series 40). Engine numbers continued from 1946, ending at 499980-7. The suffix 7 denoting a Series 70 engine.

1947 Buick, Roadmaster two-door sedanette, 8-cyl

Series No.	Body/Style No.	Body Type & Seating	Factory Price	Shipping Weight	Prod. Total
71	47-4769	4-dr Sed-6P	2232	4190	46,531 (621)
76S	47-4707	2-dr S'd'nt-6P	2131	4095	18,983 (229)
76C	47-4767	2-dr Conv Cpe-6P	2651	4345	11,947 (127)
79	(Ionia)	4-dr Sta Wag-6P	3249	4445	300

ENGINE: Eight-cylinder. Inline. Overhead valve. Cast iron block. Displacement: 320.2 cid. Bore and stroke: 3-7/16 x 4-5/16 inches. Compression ratio: 6.6:1. Brake horsepower: 144 at 3600 rpm. Five main bearings. Mechanical valve lifters. Carburetor: Stromberg AAV-26 number 380097 or Carter 609 or 664 two-barrel.

CHASSIS FEATURES: Wheelbase: Series 40 — 121 inches, Series 50 — 124 inches, Series 70 — 129 inches. Overall length: Series 40 — 207-1/2 inches, Series 50 — 212-3/8 inches, Series 70 — 217-1/8 inches. Front tread: Series 40 — 58-7/8 inches, Series 50 and 70 — 59-1/8 inches. Rear tread: Series 40 — 61-15/16 inches, Series 50 and 70 — 63-3/16 inches. Tires: Series 40 and 50 — 6.50 x 16, Series 70 — 7.00 x 15.

POWERTRAIN OPTIONS: A three-speed manual transmission with steering column mounted shift lever was standard on all series. There were no optional gearboxes.

CONVENIENCE OPTIONS: Spotlite. Sonomatic radio. Weather-Warden heater/defroster. Sideview mirror. E-Z-I non-glare rearview mirror. Prismatic inside rearview mirror. Vanity visor mirror. Seat covers. Auxiliary driving lights. Multi-purpose trouble lamp. "Breeze-Ease" draft deflectors.

HISTORICAL FOOTNOTES: Calendar year production was 267,830 units, earning Buick 7.5 percent of the total domestic market. Model year production stood at 277,134 cars. Models 59 and 79 were Estate Wagons, with wooden upper bodies by Ionia.

1948

NOTE: Through 1950 Buick provided separate production totals for cars built for export. These are given in brackets on the charts.

SPECIAL — SERIES 40 — Even more bright metal trim adorned the 1948 Special, as a full length upper body molding was added. Dual stainless bands along the lower body, fenders and rear skirts were continued. Inside, new nickel gray garnish moldings and a black Tenite steering wheel were featured. Sedans were carpeted in the rear, while front compartment mats had a simulated carpet insert. Leatherette seat risers and scuff pads were standard. Equipment included an automatic choke, turn signals and an ash receiver. Series identification was found within a round emblem in the bumper guard crossbars, front and rear.

1948 Buick, Special two-door sedanette, 8-cyl (AA)

SPECIAL I.D. NUMBERS: The serial numbers for the 1948 Special Series 40 were the same as for other 1948 Buick series, which were mixed in production. They were: (Flint) 14801266 to 15020983, (Calif.) 2482001 to 25003031, (N.J.) 34824001 to 5004975, (Kans.) 44830001 to 45008155, (Ga.) 64834001 to 64987817. Series 40 engine numbers were 4999881-4 to 52220971-4, the suffix 4 denoting a Series 40 engine.

Series No.	Body/Style No.	Body Type & Seating	Factory Price	Shipping Weight	Prod. Total
41	48-4409	4-dr Sed-6P	1809	3705	13,326 (815)
46S	48-4407	2-dr S'd'nt-6P	1735	3635	10,775 (401)

ENGINE: Eight-cylinder. Inline. Overhead valve. Cast iron block. Displacement: 248.0 cid. Bore and stroke: 3-3/32 x 4-1/8 inches. Compression ratio: 6.3:1. Brake horsepower: 110 at 3600 rpm. Five main bearings. Mechanical valve lifters. Carburetor: Stromberg AAV-167 number 380225 or Carter 608 or 663 two-barrel.

1948 Buick, Super four-door sedan, 8-cyl

1948 Buick, Super two-door convertible coupe, 8-cyl

SUPER — SERIES 50 — The main external change to the 1948 Super from its 1947 counterpart was the Super script on each front fender. Other series identification continued to be earned on the bumper guard crossbar. The car was a bit lower than in 1947, rolling on new 7.60 x 15 tires mounted on wheels with trim rings and small hubcaps. Super identification was also found on the center crest of the new black Tenite steering wheel. New cloth interiors featured leatherette scuff pads and trim risers. The instrument panel was redone, using silver-tone instruments on a two-tone gray panel. The sedan was carpeted in the rear with a carpet insert also found in the front rubber mat.

The Model 56C featured cloth and leather interior trim, with power top, seat and front windows standard.

SUPER I.D. NUMBERS: The serial number sequence was the same for all 1948 series (see Special - Series 40). Engine numbers continued from 1947, running from 4999881-5 to 5220971-5, the suffix (5) denoting a Series 50 engine.

Series No.	Body/Style No.	Body Type & Seating	Factory Price	Shipping Weight	Prod. Total
51	48-4569	4-dr Sed-6P	2087	3855	47,991 (5,456)
56S	48-4507	2-dr S'dn't-6P	1987	3770	32,860 (959)
56C	48-4567	2-dr Conv Cpe-6P	2518	4020	18,311 (906)
59	(Ionia)	4-dr Sta Wag-6P	3124	4170	1,955 (63)

ENGINE: Specifications were the same as previously listed for the 1948 Special Series 40, except that compression ratio was 6.6:1, brake horsepower was 115 at 3600 rpm.

1948 Buick, Roadmaster two-door convertible, 8-cyl (AA)

ROADMASTER — SERIES 70 — Exterior appearance of the 1948 Roadmaster was changed only by the addition of series script to the front fenders. Other series identification continued to be found on the bumper guards' crossbars and within the steering wheel center medallion. The steering wheel was black Tenite, coordinated with the new two-tone gray instrument panel with silver-tone instruments. Chrome full wheel discs were standard, along with features found on lesser Buicks. Interiors were cloth, with plusher grades of material available. A new optional Custom Trim was offered, consisting of cloth upholstery with leather bolsters; the robe cord cover, and lower door panels were done in leatherette. The Model 76C convertible coupe included power windows, seat and top in its standard equipment.

1948 Buick, Roadmaster four-door Estate Wagon, 8-cyl

ROADMASTER I.D. NUMBERS: The serial number sequence was the same for all 1948 series (see Special - Series 40). Series 70 engine numbers were 4999881-7 to 5220971-7, the suffix (7) denoting a Series 70 engine.

Series No.	Body/Style No.	Body Type & Seating	Factory Price	Shipping Weight	Prod. Total
71	48-4769	4-dr Sed-6P	2418	4160	47,042 (527)
76S	48-4707	2-dr S'dn't-6P	2297	4065	20,542 (107)
76C	48-4767	2-dr Conv Cpe-6P	2837	4315	11,367 (136)
79	(Ionia)	4-dr Sta Wag-6P	3433	4460	344 (6)

ENGINE: Eight-cylinder. Inline. Overhead valve. Cast iron block. Displacement: 320.2 cid. Bore and stroke: 3-7/16 x 4-5/16 inches. Compression ratio: 6.6:1. Brake horsepower: 144 at 3600 rpm. Five main bearings. Mechanical valve lifters. Carburetor: Stromberg AAV-267 #380226 or Carter 609 or 664 two-barrel.

CHASSIS FEATURES: Wheelbase: Series 40 - 121 inches; Series 50 - 124 inches; Series 70 - 129 inches. Overall length: Series 40 - 207-1/2 inches; Series 50 - 212-1/2 inches; Series 70 - 217-1/2 inches. Front tread: Series 40 - 58-7/8 inches; Series 50 and 70 - 59-1/8 inches. Rear tread: Series 40 - 61-15/16 inches; Series 50 and 70 - 62-3/16 inches. Tires: Series 40 - 6.50 x 16; Series 50 - 7.60 x 15; Series 70 - 8.20 x 15.

POWERTRAIN OPTIONS: A three-speed manual transmission with column-mounted shift lever was standard on all series. Dynaflow automatic transmission was optional on Series 70. Cars so equipped also had 6.9:1 compression ratio, 150 brake horsepower engines.

CONVENIENCE OPTIONS: Spotlite. Sonomatic radio. Weather-Warden heater/defroster. Sideview mirror. Tissue dispenser. Vanity visor mirror. E-Z-I non-glare rearview mirror. Prismatic inside rearview mirror. Seat covers. Auxiliary driving lights. Multi-purpose trouble lamp. "Breeze-Ease" draft deflectors. NoRol assembly. Automatic windshield washer. Back-up lights. Polaroid visor. Rear window wiper. Power Pak fire extinguisher/tire inflator.

HISTORICAL FOOTNOTES: Calendar year production of 275,503 units gave Buick a seven percent market share and fourth place in sales. Model year output stood at 229,718 cars. Harlow Curtice became a General Motors executive vice-president. His job as Buick general manager was filled by Ivan Wiles. Dynaflow Drive was introduced. Model 59 was the Estate Wagon, with upper wooden body by Ionia.

1949

NOTE: Through 1950 Buick provided separate production totals for cars built for export. These are given in brackets on the charts.

SPECIAL — SERIES 40 — The Special was continued from 1948 production without change, until midyear. Data plates, however, have a '49' prefix. The second series 1949 Special was continued into 1950 and its specifications may be found under that year.

SPECIAL I.D. NUMBERS: The serial numbers for the 1949 Special Series 40 were mixed in production with other 1949 series. They were: (Flint) 15020984 to 15348304, (Calif.) 25030001 to 25332419, (N.J.) 35036001 to 35333911, (Kans.) 45043001 to 45335606, (Del.) 55050001 to 5517948 and 55417001 to 55417948, (Mass.) 75057001 to 75338786, (Ga.) 65054001 to 65337687. Series 40 engine numbers were 5220972-4 to 5259136-4, the suffix 4 denoting a Series 40 engine.

Series No.	Body/Style No.	Body Type & Seating	Factory Price	Shipping Weight	Prod. Total
41	49-4409	4-dr Sed-6P	1861	3695	5,777 (163)
46S	49-4407	2-dr S'dn't-6P	1787	3625	4,631 (56)

ENGINE: Eight-cylinder. Inline. Overhead valve. Cast iron block. Displacement: 248.0 cid. Bore and stroke: 3-3/32 x 4-1/8 inches. Compression ratio: 6.3:1. Brake horsepower: 110 at 3600 rpm. Five main bearings. Mechanical valve lifters. Carburetor: Stromberg AAV-167 number 380225 or Carter 608 or 663 two-barrel.

SUPER — SERIES 50 — The Super shared a new General Motors C-body with the Roadmaster, but on a shorter wheelbase. It featured three chromed ventiports on each front fender. Super script was found just above the full-length body/fender molding on the front fenders. New fender edge taillamps were featured, while rear fender skins remained a Buick standard. New fender top parking lamps, harking back to 1941 styling, appeared. Full wheel trim discs were standard, along with such features as a cigar lighter, ashtray and automatic choke. Cloth interiors were standard, except for the Model 56C which was trimmed in leather and leatherette and had a power top, seat and windows as standard equipment.

1949 Buick, Super four-door Estate Wagon, 8-cyl (AA)

1949 Buick, Super two-door convertible coupe, 8-cyl

SUPER I.D. NUMBERS: The serial number sequence was the same for all series (see Special — Series 40). Engine numbers were 5220972-5 to 5659598-5, the suffix '5' denoting a Series 50 engine.

Series No.	Body/Style No.	Body Type & Seating	Factory Price	Shipping Weight	Prod. Total
51	49-4569	4-dr Sed-6P	2157	3835	131,514 (4,909)
56S	49-4507	2-dr S'dn't-6P	2059	3735	65,395 (865)
56C	49-4567	2-dr Conv Cpe-6P	2583	3985	21,426 (684)
59	(Ionia)	4-dr Sta Wag-6P	3178	4100	1,830 (17)

ENGINE: Specifications were the same as listed for the 1949 Special Series 40, except the compression ratio was 6.6:1 and brake horsepower was 115 at 3600 rpm.

1949 Buick, Roadmaster two-door convertible coupe, 8-cyl

ROADMASTER — SERIES 70 — The Roadmaster shared the new General Motors C-body, which used closed quarters in sedan roofs and fastback sedanette styling for coupes. Roadmasters had longer front fenders and four ventiports per side, with series script below, and also within bumper guard crossbar centers. Skirted rear wheelhouse openings were standard, as were all features found on the Super Series 50. Interior fabrics were plusher, with a Custom trim option again offered. A new instrument panel was used that continued Buick's centered radio grille flanked by operational switches. Windshield panels were curved, but still had a division bar. The Model 79R Estate Wagon had mahogany veneer panels inside, with leather upholstery and carpeted floors and cargo area, while the Model 76C was upholstered in leather and had standard power windows, seat and top. The midyear Model 76R Riviera was upholstered in leather and cloth and also had standard power windows.

1949 Buick, Roadmaster Riviera two-door hardtop, 8-cyl (AA)

1949 Buick, Roadmaster Riviera two-door hardtop (initial release with different side trim), (OCW)

ROADMASTER I.D. NUMBERS: The serial number sequence was the same for all 1949 Series (see Special — Series 40). Series 70 engine numbers were 5220972-7 to 5548366-7, the suffix '7' denoting a Series 70 engine.

Series No.	Body/Style No.	Body Type & Seating	Factory Price	Shipping Weight	Prod. Total
71	49-4769	4-dr Sed-6P	2735	4205	54,674 (568)
76S	49-4707	2-dr S'dn't-6P	2618	4115	18,415 (122)
76R	49-4737	2-dr HT Cpe-6P	3203	4420	4,314 (29)
76C	49-4767	2-dr Conv Cpe-6P	3150	4370	8,095 (149)
79	(Ionia)	4-dr Sta Wag-6P	3734	4490	632 (21)

ENGINE: Eight cylinder. Inline. Overhead valve. Cast iron block. Displacement: 320.2 cid. Bore and stroke: 3-7/16 x 4-4/16. Compression ratio: 6.9:1. Brake horsepower: 150 at 3600 rpm. Five main bearings. Mechanical valve lifters. Carburetor: Stromberg AAV-267 #380226 and Carter 609 or 664.

CHASSIS FEATURES: Wheelbase: Series 40 and 50 — 121 inches; Series 70 — 126 inches. Overall length: Series 40 — 207-1/2 inches; Series 50 — 209-1/2 inches; Series 70 — 214-1/8 inches. Front tread: Series 40 — 58-7/8 inches; Series 50 and 70 — 59-1/8 inches. Rear Tread: Series 40 — 61-15/16 inches; Series 50 and 70 — 62-3/16 inches. Tires: Series 40 — 6.50 x 15; Series 50 — 7.60 x 15; Series 70 — 8.20 x 15.

POWERTRAIN OPTIONS: Three-speed manual transmission standard on Series 40 and 50. Dynaflow drive standard on Series 70. Column-mounted shift levers. Dynaflow drive optional on Series 50; cars so equipped have 6.9:1 compression ratio, 120 brake horsepower engines.

CONVENIENCE OPTIONS: Spotlite (Series 40). Spotlamp with mirror. Sonomatic radio. Weather-Warden heater/defroster. Seat covers. NoRol assembly. Windshield washer. E-Z-I or Prismatic rearview mirrors. Vanity visor mirror. Tissue dispenser. Auxiliary driving lamps. Multi-purpose trouble lamp. All-rubber floor mats.

HISTORICAL FOOTNOTES: This all-time record production year saw 398,482 vehicles built in the calendar year. This gave Buick a 7.7 percent market share. Model year assemblies came to 409,138. Models 59 and 79 were Estate Wagons. Model 76R was the Riviera, a midyear model.

1950

NOTE: Through 1950 Buick provided separate production totals for cars built for export. These are given in brackets on the charts.

1950 Buick, Special Deluxe four-door sedan, 8-cyl

1950 Buick, Special four-door sedan, 8-cyl

SPECIAL — SERIES 40 — (Introduced as a late-1949 style.) The first Special with postwar styling previewed the basic styling for 1950. Most prominent and memorable was the car's "bucktooth" grille, consisting of bumper guards. Specials had three rectangular ventiports on each hoodside. A unique feature of the late-1949 cars was that the hood was opened through a ventiport key and slot system; 1950 production cars had inside hood releases. Specials had no side body moldings. Special Deluxe models had plusher interiors a full-length bodyside molding, bright window outlines and Special script on the front fenders. They were identified by the code 'D' in the model number.

SPECIAL I.D. NUMBERS: The serial numbers for the 1950 Special Series 40 were mixed in production with other 1950 Series. They were: (Flint) 15360001-up, (N.J.) 35374001-up, (Kans.) 45380001-up, (Del.) 55388001-up (except 55417001 to 55417948), (Ga.) 65393001-up, (Mass.) 7539001-up. Series

40 engine numbers were 5568000-up, the suffix 4 denoting a Series 40 engine.

Series No.	Body/Style No.	Body Type & Seating	Factory Price	Shipping Weight	Prod. Total
43	50-4408	4-dr Sed-6P	1909	3715	58,700
41	50-4469	4-dr Sed-6P	1941	3710	1,141
46S	50-4407	2-dr S'dn't-6P	1856	3655	42,935
46	50-4407B	2-dr Cpe-6P	1803	3615	2,500
43D	50-4408D	4-dr Sed-6P	1952	3720	14,335
41D	50-4469D	4-dr Sed-6P	1983	3735	141,396
46D	50-4407D	2-dr S'dn't-6P	1899	3665	76,902

ENGINE: Eight cylinder. Inline. Overhead valve. Cast iron block. Displacement: 248.0 cid. Bore and stroke: 3-3/32 x 3-1/8 inches. Compression ratio: 6.3:1. Brake horsepower: 110 at 3600 rpm. Five main bearings. Mechanical valve lifters. Carburetor: Stromberg AA UVB 267 #380309 or Carter 725 and 782.

1950 Buick, Super Riviera two-door hardtop, 8-cyl

SUPER — SERIES 50 — Supers shared other series' totally new, all-bumper guard grille and more rounded styling. Super script appeared on front fenders, just above the full-length lower bodyside moldings. A new, long wheelbase sedan featured a plusher interior than most Supers, which normally had cloth interiors of finer material than the Special. Supers had three ventiports on each hoodside. The Model 56C convertible had leather power seats, plus power windows and top.

1950 Buick, Super four-door sedan, 8-cyl (AA)

SUPER I.D. NUMBERS: The serial number sequence was the same for all 1950 series (see Special — Series 40). Engine numbers began at 5628758-5 (manual transmission) and 5624743-5 (Dynaflow), the suffix '5' denoting a Series 50 engine.

Series No.	Body/Style No.	Body Type & Seating	Factory Price	Shipping Weight	Prod. Total
51	50-4569	4-dr Sed-6P	2139	3745	55,672
56S	50-4507	2-dr S'dn't-6P	2041	3645	10,697
56R	50-4537	2-dr HT Cpe-6P	2139	3790	56,030
56C	50-4567	2-dr Conv Cpe	2476	3965	12,259
59	(Ionia)	4-dr Sta Wag-6P	2844	4115	2,480
52	50-4519	4-dr Sed-6P	2212	3870	114,745

ENGINE: Eight cylinder. Inline. Overhead valve. Cast iron block. Displacement: 263.3 cid. Bore and stroke: 3-3/16 x 4-1/8 inches. Compression ratio: 6.6:1. Brake horsepower: 124 at 3600 rpm. Five main bearings. Carburetor: Stromberg AA UVB #380309 or Carter 725 and 782.

ROADMASTER — SERIES 70 — Buick's finest cars had larger engines and plusher interior trims than comparable Super models. They were readily identified by the four ventiports on the hoodsides. A Roadmaster script was found above the full-length bodyside molding on cars so equipped. Cars with sweepspear

moldings had Roadmaster script engraved in the upper body trim step, behind the door trim, except on the Model 79 and 72R (which received the sweepspear at midyear). Deluxe models had plusher interiors and hydraulic window and seat controls. They were identified by an 'X' suffix in their style numbers.

ROADMASTER I.D. NUMBERS: The serial number sequence was the same for all 1950 series (see Special — Series 40). Series 70 engine numbers began at 5635021-up.

1950 Buick, Roadmaster two-door convertible, 8-cyl (AA)

Series No.	Body/Style No.	Body Type & Seating	Factory Price	Shipping Weight	Prod. Total
71	50-4769	4-dr Sed-6P	2633	4135	6,738
76S	50-4707	2-dr S'dn't-6P	2528	4025	2,968
75R	50-4737	2-dr HT Cpe-6P	2633	4135	2,300
76C	50-4767	2-dr Conv Cpe-6P	2981	4345	2,964
79	(Ionia)	4-dr Sta Wag-6P	3407	4470	420
72	50-4719	4-dr Sed-6P	2738	4220	51,212*
72R	50-4737X	4-dr Sed-6P	2854	4245	*(incl. 72R)
76R	50-4737X	2-dr HT Cpe-6P	2764	4215	8,432

ENGINE: Eight cylinder. Inline. Overhead valve. Cast iron block. Displacement: 320.2 cid. Bore and stroke: 3-7/16 x 4-5/16. Compression ratio: 6.9:1. Brake horsepower: 152 at 3600 rpm. Hydraulic valve lifters. Carburetor: Stromberg AA VG-267 #380258 or Carter 726.

1950 Buick, Super two-door convertible, 8-cyl

CHASSIS FEATURES: Wheelbase: Series 40 — 121-1/2 inches, Series 50 — 121-1/2 inches (except Model 52, which was 125.5 inches), Series 70 — 126-1/4 inches (except Models 72 and 72R, which were 130-1/4 inches). Overall length: Series 40 — 204 inches, Series 50 — 209-1/2 inches (except Model 52, 213-1/2 inches), Series 70 — 214-7/8 inches (except Models 72 and 72R, 217-1/2 inches). Front tread: Series 40 — 59.1 inches. Series 50 and 70 — 59-1/8 inches. Rear tread: Series 40 — 62.2 inches. Series 50 and 70 — 62-2/3 inches. Tires: Series 40 and 50 — 7.60 x 15; Series 70 — 8.00 x 15.

POWERTRAIN OPTIONS: Three-speed manual transmission standard on Series 40 and 50. Dynaflow drive standard on Series 70, optional on Series 40 and 50. Series 40 cars so equipped had 6.9:1 compression ratio, 120 brake horsepower engines. Series 50 cars with Dynaflow had 6.9:1 compression ratio and 128 brake horsepower.

CONVENIENCE OPTIONS: Parking brake release warning light. Cushion toppers. License frames. Handy-Mats. Visor vanity mirror. Tool kit. Full wheelcovers (standard on Series 70). "Breeze-Ease" draft deflectors. Outside rearview mirror. Safety Spotlite with mirror. Multi-purpose trouble lamp. Tissue dispenser. Glare-proof inside rearview mirror. Seat covers. All rubber floor mat. Auxiliary driving lamps. Exhaust pipe trim. Polish cloth kit.

HISTORICAL FOOTNOTES: Calendar year production was 552,827 cars, keeping Buick at fourth place in the sales charts. Model year production totaled a record 558,439 units. Body Styles 50-4408 and 50-4408D were Jetback sedans. Body styles 50-4537 and 50-4747 were Riviera hardtops. Body styles 50-4519 and 50-4719 were Riviera sedans. Models 59 and 79 were Estate Wagons.

1951

1951 Buick, Special Deluxe four-door sedan, 8-cyl (AA)

1951 Buick, Special Deluxe two-door convertible, 8-cyl

SPECIAL — SERIES 40 — Standard and Deluxe trims were offered on the Special Series. The low-priced models had only bright rear fender trim moldings and three ventiports on each fender. Deluxe models had a full-length sweepspear molding leading into the rear fender trim. A new, vertical bar grille with a more conventional bumper was used on all 1951 Buicks. Interiors were cloth, with a plusher grade used on Deluxe models. Specials had a unique instrument panel, with speedometer and gauges housed in two large round units flanking the steering column notch. Controls were centered vertically, flanking the radio speaker grille. The standard Specials were the only 1951 Buicks to have a two-piece windshield. Deluxe and other lines had a new one-piece type.

SPECIAL I.D. NUMBERS: Serial numbers were located on the front side of dash, under the hood on the right and on the left

front hinge pillar post. The first symbol was a number indicating assembly plant as follows: 1 = Flint, Mich.; 2 = Southgate, Calif.; 3 = Linden, N.J.; 4 = Kansas City, Mo.; 5 = Wilmington, Del.; 6 = Atlanta, Ga.; 7 = Framingham, Mass. The next seven symbols were numbers indicating sequential production number. Serial numbers were mixed in production with other 1951 Series. Numbers were: (Flint) 16740001 to 17214106; (Calif.) 26765001 to 27214776; (N.J.) 36774001 to 37217064; (Kans.) 46783001 to 47224950; (Del.) 56799001 to 57226180; (Ga.) 66808001 to 67228458; (Mass.) 76815001 to 77228805. Engine numbers were stamped in various locations on the crankcase, usually, or on the cylinder block. All 1951 engine numbers start at 62400100. Series 40 engines have suffix 4.

Series No.	Body/Style No.	Body Type & Seating	Factory Price	Shipping Weight	Prod. Total
41	51-4367	4-dr Sed-6P	2139	3605	999
46S	51-4327	2-dr Spt Cpe-6P	2046	3600	2,700

Deluxe Models

41D	51-4369	4-dr Sed-6P	2185	3680	87,848
48D	51-4311D	2-dr Sed-6P	2127	3615	54,311
45R	51-4337	2-dr HT Cpe-6P	2225	3645	16,491
46C	51-4367X	2-dr Conv Cpe-6P	2561	3830	2,099

ENGINE: Eight cylinder. Inline. Overhead valve. Cast iron block. Displacement: 263.3 cid. Bore and stroke: 3-3/16 x 4-1/8 inches. Compression ratio: 6.6:1. Brake horsepower 120 at 3600 rpm. Five main bearings. Hydraulic valve lifters. Carburetor: Stromberg AA UVB 267 or Carter two-barrel 725 and 882 two-barrel.

1951 Buick, Super four-door sedan, 8-cyl

1951 Buick, Super four-door Estate Wagon, 8-cyl (AA)

1951 Buick, Super two-door convertible, 8-cyl

SUPER — SERIES 50 — Supers had larger bodies than Specials, but looked similar with three round ventiports per front

fender, a full-length sweepspear molding and broad, bright rear fender shields. Series script was found on the deck lid and within the steering wheel center. Supers were trimmed in materials similar to Special Deluxes, except for in the plush Model 52 Super Riviera sedan. Front turn signals were within the bumper guard "bombs," while rear signals shared the stop lamps' housing on the rear fender edges. The Model 56C and Model 59 were trimmed in leather.

1951 Buick, Super Riviera two-door hardtop, 8-cyl (PH)

SUPER I.D. NUMBERS: Serial numbers were mixed with other 1951 series (see 1951 Special I.D. Numbers above). Engine numbers were mixed in production, but Super engines have suffix 5.

Series No.	Body/Style No.	Body Type & Seating	Factory Price	Shipping Weight	Prod. Total
51	51-4569	4-dr Sed-6P	2356	3755	92,886
56S	51-4507	2-dr S'dn't-6P	2248	2685	1,500
56R	51-4537	2-dr HT Cpe-6P	2356	3765	54,512
56C	51-4567X	2-dr Conv Cpe-6P	2728	3965	8,116
59	(Ionia)	4-dr Sta Wag-6P	3133	4100	2,212
52	51-4519	4-dr Sed-6P	2563	3825	10,000

ENGINE: Specifications were the same as those listed for the 1951 Special Series 40, except manual transmission cars had 6.9:1 compression ratio and 124 brake horsepower.

1951 Buick, Roadmaster Riviera two-door hardtop, 8-cyl (AA)

ROADMASTER — SERIES 70 — Buick's longest and most Deluxe models featured a new grille ensemble for 1951. Roadmasters had the series' designation script on the rear deck, with additional identification coming from four ventiports on each front fender. Full-length wide rocker panel moldings were used with the sweepspear molding found on cheaper models. Cloth interiors in closed models were plusher than lower priced series, with carpeting used on the floors. The Model 76C and Model 79 used leather seats. Standard equipment on the Model 76C convertible included power top, windows and seat. A Custom interior option for the Roadmaster included leatherette door panel trim. Full wheelcovers were standard.

ROADMASTER I.D. NUMBERS: Serial numbers were mixed with other 1951 series (see 1951 Special I.D. Numbers above). Engine numbers were mixed in production, but Roadmaster engines have suffix 7.

Series No.	Body/Style No.	Body Type & Seating	Factory Price	Shipping Weight	Prod. Total
76R	51-4737X	2-dr HT Cpe-6P	3143	4235	12,901
76MR	51-4737	2-dr Del HT Cpe-6P	3051	4185	809
76C	51-4767X	2-dr Conv Cpe-6P	3453	4395	2,911
79R	(Ionia)	4-dr Sta Wag-6P	3977	4505	679
72R	51-4719X	4-dr Sed-6P	3200	4285	48,758

1951 Buick, Roadmaster four-door sedan, 8-cyl

ENGINE: Eight cylinder. Inline. Overhead valve. Cast iron block. Displacement: 320.2 cid. Bore and stroke: 3-7/16 x 4-5/16 inches. Compression ratio: 7.2:1. Brake horsepower: 152 at 3600 rpm. Five main bearings. Hydraulic valve lifters. Carburetor: Stromberg AAVB 267 or Carter 726 two-barrel.

CHASSIS FEATURES: Wheelbase: Series 40 and 50 — 121-1/2 inches (except Model 52, which was 125-1/2 inches); Series 70 — 126-1/4 inches (except Model 72R, which was 130-1/4 inches). Overall length: Series 40 and 50 — 206.2 inches (except Model 52, which was 210.2 inches); Series 70 — 211 inches (except Model 72R, which was 215 inches). Front tread: Series 40 — 59 inches; Series 50 and 70 — 59 inches. Rear tread: Series 40 — 59 inches; Series 50 and 70 — 62 inches. Tires: Series 40 and 50 — 7.60 x 15; Series 70 — 8.00 x 15.

1951 Buick, Roadmaster two-door convertible, 8-cyl

POWERTRAIN OPTIONS: A three-speed manual transmission was standard on Series 40 and 50. Dynaflow drive was standard on Series 70, optional on Series 40 and 50. Cars equipped with optional Dynaflow had 7.2:1 compression ratio and 128 horsepower engines.

CONVENIENCE OPTIONS: Parking brake release signal light. Tool kit. Cushion topper. Electric clock (Series 50 and 70). License frames. Remote control outside rearview mirror. Visor vanity mirror. Handy-mats. Full wheelcovers (standard on Series 70).

HISTORICAL FOOTNOTES: Calendar year production was 404,695 units, the second highest in Buick history up to this point. This represented 7.5 percent of total industry output and made Buick America's fourth largest automaker. Model year output was 404,657. Convertibles represented 9.4 percent of Buick's business. Body Styles 51-4337, 51-4537, 51-4737 and 51-4737X are Riviera hardtops. Styles 51-4519 and 51-4719X are Riviera four-door sedans (pillared). An X in the style number indicates hydraulic control of the seat, windows and (convertibles) top. Models 59 and 79R are Estate Wagons.

1952

SPECIAL — SERIES 40 — Buick Special styling changed little from 1951. A new sweepspear molding, now incorporating the rear fender gravel guard, was used. Three round chrome ventiports on each front fender continued to be a Series 40 hallmark and were also found on Series 50 models. Specials were again divided into standard and Deluxe categories. The standard models (41 and 46S) had a windshield center division bar and lacked the bright rocker panel molding of Deluxe models. Interiors were spartan on the standard models, while Deluxe models were trimmed in a plusher cloth. The Special continued to use a distinctive instrument panel with two large dials containing the indicators. Special script was now found on rear fenders and Deluxe models had bright fender fins.

SPECIAL I.D. NUMBERS: Serial numbers were located on the front side of dash, under the hood on the right and on the left front hinge pillar post. The first symbol was a number indicating assembly plant as follows: 1 = Flint, Mich.; 2 = Southgate, Calif.; 3 = Linden, N.J.; 4 = Kansas City, Mo.; 5 = Wilmington, Del.; 6 = Atlanta, Ga.; 7 = Framingham, Mass. The next seven symbols were numbers indicating sequential production number. Serial numbers were mixed in production with other 1952 Series. Numbers were: (Flint) 1643001 to 16739745, (Calif.) 26456001 to 26714109; (N.J.) 36464001 to 36717383; (Kans.) 46471001 to 46722742; (Del.) 56483001 to 56726449; (Ga.) 66490001 to 66729512; (Mass.) 76496001 to 76730564. Engine numbers were stamped in various locations on the crankcase, usually, or on the cylinder block. All 1952 engine numbers start at 6646230, Series 40 engines have suffix 4.

Series No.	Body/Style No.	Body Type & Seating	Factory Price	Shipping Weight	Prod. Total
41	52-4369	4-dr Sed-6P	2209	3650	317
46S	52-4327	2-dr Spt Cpe-6P	2115	3605	2,206
Deluxe Models					
41D	52-4369D	4-dr Sed-6P	2255	3665	63,346
48D	52-4311D	2-dr Sed-6P	2197	3620	32,684
45R	52-4337	2-dr HT Cpe-6P	2295	3665	21,180
46C	52-4367X	2-dr Conv Cpe-6P	2634	3850	600

ENGINE: Eight cylinder. Inline. Overhead valve. Cast iron block. Displacement: 263.3 cid. Bore and stroke: 3-3/16 x 4-1/8 inches. Compression ratio: 6.6:1. Brake horsepower 120 at 3600 rpm. Five main bearings. Hydraulic valve lifters. Carburetor: Stromberg AA UVB 267 or Carter 882 two-barrel.

1952 Buick, Super two-door convertible, 8-cyl

1952 Buick, Super four-door Estate Wagon, 8-cyl

SUPER — SERIES 50 — Buick's mid-sized line resembled the Series 40 with three ventiports per fender and new sweepspear rocker panel trim. Super script on the rear fenders aided identification. The Super was built with the larger General Motors C-body, however. The full-flowing fenderline dipped deeper on this body and rear fenders had a crease line absent on the B-body Specials. A new deck lid gave a more squared-off appear-

ance. Like other Buick series, it was a near carbon copy year for 1952. Chromed rear fender fins gave distinction to 1952 Supers. Interiors were cloth, except on the Models 56C and 59, which were trimmed with leather. The Super used a different instrument panel then the Special. It was distinguished by a large center speedometer housing flanked by smaller gauge housings. Series identification was found within the steering wheel center.

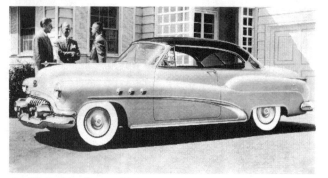

1952 Buick, Super Riviera two-door hardtop, 8-cyl (AA)

SUPER I.D. NUMBERS: Serial numbers were mixed with other 1952 series (see 1952 Special I.D. Numbers above). Engine numbers were mixed in production, but Super engines have suffix 5.

Series No.	Body/Style No.	Body Type & Seating	Factory Price	Shipping Weight	Prod. Total
56R	52-4537	2-dr HT Cpe-6P	2478	3775	55,400
56C	52-4567X	2-dr Conv Cpe-6P	2869	3970	6,904
59	(Ionia)	4-dr Sta Wag-6P	3296	4105	1,641
52	52-4519	4-dr Sed-6P	2563	3825	71,387

ENGINE: Specifications were the same as those listed for the 1952 Special Series 40, except manual transmission cars had 6.9:1 compression ratio and 124 brake horsepower.

1952 Buick, Roadmaster four-door sedan, 8-cyl (AA)

1952 Buick, Roadmaster two-door convertible, 8-cyl

ROADMASTER — SERIES 70 — Roadmasters are easy to spot by their longer front fenders and hood, and four ventiports on each side. A rehash of 1951 styling, with new sweepspear moldings and bright rocker trim provided distinction. Series identification appeared on rear fenders. New deck lids gave a higher, more substantial rear end appearance, while the frontal view was unchanged from 1951. Roadmasters continued to be the plushest Buicks. Custom trim options were available for even more richness. Quality cloth was used in sedans, while the Models 76C

and 79R were trimmed in leather. The specially-lengthened, extra-posh Model 72R Riviera sedan continued to be the most popular Roadmaster style. All Roadmasters had the popular 1952 Buick "sombrero" wheel disc as standard equipment.

ROADMASTER I.D. NUMBERS: Serial numbers were mixed with the other 1952 series (see 1952 Special I.D. numbers above). Engine numbers were mixed in production, but Roadmaster engines have suffix 7.

Series No.	Body/Style No.	Body Type & Seating	Factory Price	Shipping Weight	Prod. Total
76R	52-4737X	2-dr HT Cpe-6P	3306	4235	11,387
76C	52-4767X	2-dr Conv Cpe-6P	3453	4395	2,402
79R	(Ionia)	4-dr Sta Wag-6P	3977	4505	359
72R	52-4719X	4-dr Sed-6P	3200	4285	32,069

ENGINE: Eight cylinder. Inline. Overhead valve. Cast iron block. Displacement: 320.2 cid. Bore and stroke: 3-7/16 x 4-5/16 inches. Compression ratio: 7.5:1. Brake horsepower: 170 at 3800 rpm. Five main bearings. Hydraulic valve lifters. Carburetor: Stromberg 4AUV267 or Carter 894S-5A four-barrel.

POWERTRAIN OPTIONS: A three-speed manual transmission was standard on Series 40 and 50. Dynaflow drive was standard on Series 70. Series 40 and 50 cars equipped with the $193 Dynaflow option had 7.2:1 compression ratio and 128 brake horsepower engines.

CONVENIENCE OPTIONS: Power steering, Series 70, ($199). Parking brake release signal light. Cushion toppers. Electric clock (Series 50 and 70). License plate frames. Remote control rearview mirror. Visor vanity mirror. Full wheelcovers (standard on Series 70). Handy-Spot. Seat covers. Auto-Jack case.

HISTORICAL FOOTNOTES: A steel strike, Korean War production quotas and a long model changeover combined to hold Buick's calendar year production to 321,048 units in 1952. This kept the company in fourth spot on the sales charts with a 7.4 percent market share. Model year output was 303,745 cars. Buick was the largest builder of hardtops and the third largest convertible maker. Body Styles 52-4337, 52-4537 and 52-4737X are Riviera hardtop coupes. Styles 52-4519 and 52-4719 are Riviera four-door sedans (pillared). An 'X' suffix to the style number indicates hydraulic control of the seat, windows and (convertibles) top. Models 59 and 79R are Estate Wagons.

1953

SPECIAL — SERIES 40 — The Series 40 was Buick's only line carrying a straight eight in 1953. The small series Buick had its own version of the 1953 frontal look. Since it was a narrower car, the grilles, bumpers and sheet metal parts did not interchange with larger models. On the fenders were new teardrop-shaped ventiports, three to a side. The hood bombsight ornament had no vee on the Special. All 1953 Specials were Deluxe models, with bright sweepspears and rocker panel moldings. Interiors were cloth, with the unique Special instrument panel continuing for another year. Model 46C, the convertible, was trimmed in leather. Series call-outs were on the rear deck emblem.

SPECIAL I.D. NUMBERS: Serial numbers were located on the hinge pillar post and on the dash under the hood. The first symbol was a number indicating assembly plant as follows: 1 = Flint, Mich.; 2 = Southgate, Calif.; 3 = Linden, N.J.; 4 = Kansas City, Mo.; 5 = Wilmington, Del.; 6 = Atlanta, Ga.; 7 = Framingham, Mass. The next seven symbols were numbers indicating sequential production number. Serial numbers were mixed in production with other 1953 series. Numbers were: (Flint) 1674001 to 17214106; (Calif.) 26765001 to 27214776; (N.J.) 36774001 to 37127064; (Kans.) 46783001 to 47224950; (Del.) 56799001 to

57226180; (Ga.) 66808001 to 67228458; (Mass.) 76815001 to 77228805. Engine numbers were stamped in various locations on the crankcase, usually, or on the cylinder block. All 1953 engines start at 6950620, Series 40 engine numbers have suffix 4.

Series No.	Body/Style No.	Body Type & Seating	Factory Price	Shipping Weight	Prod. Total
41D	53-4369D	4-dr Sed-6P	2255	3710	100,312
48D	53-4311D	2-dr Sed-6P	2197	3675	53,796
45R	53-4337	2-dr HT Cpe-6P	2295	3705	58,780
46C	53-4367X	2-dr Conv Cpe-6P	2553	3815	4,282

1953 Buick, Special two-door convertible, 8-cyl (AA)

ENGINE: Eight cylinder. Inline. Overhead valve. Cast iron block. Displacement: 263.3 cid. Bore and stroke: 3-3/16 x 4-1/8 inches. Compression ratio: 6.6:1. Brake horsepower: 125 at 3600 rpm. Five main bearings. Hydraulic valve lifters. Carburetor: Stromberg AAUVB267 or Carter 882S.

1953 Buick, Super Riviera two-door hardtop, V-8

SUPER — SERIES 50 — Buick's middle-priced line shared the Roadmaster's new V-8 and, for this year, the Roadmaster shared the Super and Special's 121.5-inch wheelbase. The Super earned a horizontal trim bar on its rear fenders, which distinguished it from Series 70 Roadmasters. Otherwise, its side trim was identical, although the Super had only three ventiports on each front fender. Series identification was found on the deck emblem. Full wheelcovers were now standard. The vee in the bombsight ornament signified the V-8 power under the hood. Interiors of most models were in nylon and silky broadcloth. The Model 56C and Model 59 were trimmed in leather. Model 56C, the convertible, had power windows, seat and top as standard equipment.

1953 Buick, Super four-door Estate Wagon, V-8

SUPER I.D. NUMBERS: Serial numbers were mixed with other 1953 series (see 1953 Special I.D. Numbers above). Engine numbers began with V-2415-5.

Series No.	Body/Style No.	Body Type & Seating	Factory Price	Shipping Weight	Prod. Total
56R	53-4537	2-dr HT Cpe-6P	2611	3845	91,298
56C	53-4567X	2-dr Conv Cpe-6P	3002	4035	6,701
59	(Ionia)	4-dr Sta Wag-6P	3430	4150	1,830
52	53-4519	4-dr Sed-6P	2696	3905	90,685

ENGINE: V-8. Overhead valve. Cast iron block. Displacement: 322 cid. Bore and stroke: 4.0 x 3.2 inches. Compression ratio: 8.0:1. Brake horsepower: 164 at 4000 rpm. Five main bearings. Hydraulic valve lifters. Carburetor: Stromberg AAVB267 or Carter 2017S two-barrel.

1953 Buick, Roadmaster four-door sedan, V-8 (AA)

ROADMASTER — SERIES 70 — Buick's finest had a fore-shortened nose in 1953, to emphasize the compact power of the new V-8 under the hood. Roadmasters had chrome rear fender gravel shields between the rear wheelhouse and the bumper, in addition to the same sweepspear used on the Super. However, the upper horizontal trim strip on Super rear fenders was absent. Series call-outs were found within the deck emblem and on the steering wheel hub. Full wheelcovers were standard. Interiors were nylon, broadcloth or leather, depending on the model. Foam-backed Roxpoint nylon carpeting was standard, as were power steering, power brakes and Dynaflow drive. Color-keyed instrument panels with damascene-patterned lower panels were used. A special 1953 Roadmaster model was the Model 76X Skylark Anniversary Convertible. It was on the Roadmaster chassis, but had its own fenders with open wheelhouses painted white or red. It did not have any ventiports. A lowered top, 40-spoke Kelsey-Hayes wire wheels and a full complement of luxury accessories were included. The Skylark had its own slim, cast sweepspear moldings and special bodyside emblems on the rear quarters. Interiors were in leather.

ROADMASTER I.D. NUMBERS: Serial numbers were mixed with the other 1953 series (see 1953 Special I.D. numbers above). Engine numbers began with V-2001-7.

1953 Buick, Roadmaster Skylark sport convertible, V-8 (AA)

Series No.	Body/Style No.	Body Type & Seating	Factory Price	Shipping Weight	Prod. Total
76R	53-4737	2-dr HT Cpe-6P	3358	4125	22,927
76C	53-4767X	2-dr Conv Cpe-6P	3506	4250	3,318
79R	(Ionia)	4-dr Sta Wag-6P	3254	4100	670
72R	53-4719	4-dr Sed-6P	4031	4315	50,523
76X	53-4767SX	2-dr Sky Conv Cpe-6P	5000	4315	1,690

ENGINE: Specifications were the same as those listed for the 1953 Super, except compression ratio was 8.5:1 and brake horsepower was 188 at 4000 rpm. Carburetors were Stromberg 4AUV267 or Carter 996 or 2082S four-barrel.

CHASSIS FEATURES: Wheelbase: Series 40, 50 and 70 — 121-1/2 inches (except Models 52 and 72R, which were 125-1/2 inches). Overall length: Series 40 — 205.8 inches. Series 50 and 70 — 207.6 inches (except Model 52 and 72R, which were 211.6 inches). Front tread: Series 40 — 59 inches; Series

50 and 70 — 60 inches. Rear tread: Series 40 — 59 inches; Series 50 and 70 — 62 inches. Tires: Series 40 and 50 — 6.70 x 15; Series 70 — 8.00 x 15.

POWERTRAIN OPTIONS: Three-speed manual transmission was standard on Series 40 Specials and Series 50 Supers. Dynaflow drive was an option on Specials and Supers at $193 extra, but was standard in the Roadmaster. Specials equipped with Dynaflow had 7.2:1 compression powerplants with 130 brake horsepower. Supers equipped with Dynaflow had 8.1:1 compression powerplants with 170 brake horsepower.

CONVENIENCE OPTIONS: Power steering ($177) [standard on Series 70]. Power brakes (standard on Series 70). Simulated wire wheelcovers (Buick shield center type on Series 40; bright vee with black background type on Series 50 and 70). Full wheelcovers (standard on Series 50 and 70). Eight-inch rear seat speaker. Tool kit. Handy spot. Dor-Gard. Cushion toppers. Selectronic radio (optional Series 50 and 70 and standard Model 76X). Electric clock. License frames. Right-hand outside rearview mirror. Left-hand remote control outside mirror. Handy-mats. Air conditioning (Series 50 and 70). Fold-down tissue dispenser.

1953 Buick, Roadmaster Riviera two-door hardtop, V-8

HISTORICAL FOOTNOTES: This was Buick's 50th anniversary. The company retained fourth rank with a 7.9 percent market share. Calendar year production was 485,353 units. Model year production was 488,755 units. The seven-millionth Buick was built June 13, 1953. Dynaflow was used in 80 percent of the Buicks of 1953. The new V-8 engine went into 55 percent of the cars made, even though it wasn't available in the Specials. Styles 53-4337, 53-4537 and 53-4737X were Riviera hardtop coupes. Style 53-4767SX was the Skylark Anniversary Convertible. Models 59 and 79R were Estate Wagons. An X suffix to the style number indicates hydraulic control of the seat, windows and (convertibles) top.

1954

1954 Buick, Special four-door Estate Wagon, V-8 (AA)

SPECIAL — SERIES 40 — The Special had a new body for 1954, lower and wider, on a new V-8-powered chassis. Series identification was found on the rear quarters and within the deck ornament. Three oval ventiports adorned each front fender. Stainless

(sweepspears) on the bodysides arched over the rectangular rear wheelhouses of the sedans or station wagons and the rounded rear wheel opening of the Riviera hardtop and convertible. Rear fenders had a blunted fin at their rear edge, with dual 'bullet' taillamps below. A new Panoramic windshield, with slanting side pillars, was used. Specials were upholstered in nylon (two-tones in the Riviera hardtop), except for the Model 46C, which had leather trim and an outside rearview mirror as standard equipment, along with a power top, windows and front seat.

1954 Buick, Special two-door convertible, V-8

1954 Buick, Special four-door sedan, V-8

SPECIAL I.D. NUMBERS: Serial numbers were located on the hinge pillar post and on dash under the hood. The first symbol was a number indicating series, as follows: 4 = Series 40 Special; 6 = Series 60 Century; 5 = Series 50 Super; 7 = Series 70 Roadmaster and 8 = Series 80 Limited/Electra or 4 = 4400 (Special); 6 = 4600 (Century); 7 = 4700 (Roadmaster). The second symbol was a letter indicating year as follows: A = 1954. The third symbol was a number indicating assembly plant: 1 = Flint, Mich.; 2 = Southgate, Calif.; 3 = Linden, N.J.; 4 = Kansas City, Kans.; 5 = Wilmington, Del.; 6 = Atlanta, Ga.; 7 = Framingham, Mass.; 8 = Arlington, Tex. The remaining symbols represented the sequential production number. Buick Special serial numbers were mixed in production with other 1954 Series. Numbers used at the beginning of the season were as follows: (Flint)-A-1001001-up; (Calif.)-A-2001001-up; (N.J.)-A-3001001-up; (Kans.)-A-4001001-up; (Del.)-A-5001001-up; (Ga.)-A-6001001-up; (Mass.)-A-7001001-up and (Tex.)-A-8001001-up. Effective April 1, 1954, beginning numbers changed as follows: (Flint)-4AI-056800-up; (Calif.)-4A2-014905-up; (N.J.)-6A3-020700-up; (Kans.)-7A4-021783-up; (Del.)-7A5-013983-up; (Ga.)-7A6-012742-up; (Mass.)-6A7-010471-up and (Tex.)-7A8-002765-up. Engine numbers were stamped in various locations on the crankcase, usually, or on the cylinder block. Engine numbers were also mixed in production, beginning with number Y-273956.

Series No.	Body/Style No.	Body Type & Seating	Factory Price	Shipping Weight	Prod. Total
41D	54-4469D	4-dr Sed-6P	2265	3735	70,356
48D	54-4411D	2-dr Sed-6P	2207	3690	41,557
46R	54-4437	2-dr HT Cpe-6P	2305	3740	71,186
46C	54-4467X	2-dr Conv Cpe-6P	2563	3810	6,135
49	54-4481	4-dr Sta Wag-6P	3163	3905	1,650

ENGINE: V-8. Overhead valve. Cast iron block. Displacement: 264 cid. Bore and stroke: 3.625 x 3.2 inches. Compression ratio: 7.2:1. Brake horsepower: 143 at 4200 rpm. (150 with automatic transmission). Five main bearings. Hydraulic valve lifters. Carburetor: Stromberg AAVB267 or Carter 2081 or 2179 two-barrel.

CENTURY — SERIES 60 — Revived for the first time since 1942, the new Century shared the Series 40 Special body and basic chassis, but carried the Roadmaster engine. The new

performance car carried three ventiports per fender and was identical to the Special in most other exterior trim, except for the Century scripts on the quarter panels and the series designation within the deck ornament. It shared the Special's instrument panel, with gauges set into twin round housings. Nylon cloth upholstery, with foam cushions (two-tones in Riviera hardtops), were standard. The Model 66C convertible was trimmed in leather and had an outside rearview mirror and power-operated windows, seat and top as part of its base equipment.

1954 Buick, Century two-door convertible, V-8 (OCW)

1954 Buick, Century four-door Estate Wagon, V-8

CENTURY I.D. NUMBERS: Serial numbers were mixed with other 1954 Series (see 1954 Special I.D. Numbers above). Engine numbers were mixed in production.

Series No.	Body/Style No.	Body Type & Seating	Factory Price	Shipping Weight	Prod. Total
61	54-4669	4-dr Sed-6P	2520	3805	31,919
66R	54-4637	2-dr HT Cpe-6P	2534	3795	45,710
66C	54-4667X	2-dr Conv Cpe-6P	2963	3950	2,790
69	54-4681	4-dr Sta Wag-6P	3470	3975	1,563

ENGINE: V-8. Overhead valve. Cast iron block. Displacement: 322 cid. Bore and stroke: 4.0 x 3.2 inches. Compression ratio: 7.2:1. Brake horsepower: 195 at 4100 rpm. Five main bearings. Hydraulic valve lifters. Carburetor: Stromberg 4AUV267 or Carter 2082S four-barrel.

1954 Buick, Super four-door sedan, V-8

SUPER — SERIES 50 — Using the new, larger General Motors C-body, with vertical windshield pillars and the new Panoramic windshield, the Super for 1954 was a big Buick for the budget-minded buyer. Identified by its three ventiports per fender, the Super script on quarters and the series designation within the deck ornament, the Super shared other brightwork with the Roadmaster. Interiors were nylon and were plainer than in the Roadmasters. The Super did have the expensive car's horizon-

tal speedometer instrument panel. Model 56C, the line's convertible, was upholstered in leather and had power-operated windows, seat and top, along with an outside rearview mirror on the left, as standard equipment.

1954 Buick, Super four-door convertible, V-8 (OCW)

1954 Buick, Super Riviera two-door hardtop, V-8

SUPER I.D. NUMBERS: Serial numbers were mixed in 1954 production (see 1954 Special I.D. Numbers above). Engine numbers were also mixed in production.

Series No.	Body/Style No.	Body Type & Seating	Factory Price	Shipping Weight	Prod. Total
52	54-4519	4-dr Sed-6P	2711	4105	41,756
56R	54-4537	2-dr HT Cpe-6P	2626	4035	73,531
56C	54-4537X	2-dr Conv Cpe-6P	2964	4145	3,343

ENGINE: Specifications were the same as listed for the 1954 Century except a 7.2:1 compression ratio was used. Brake horsepower was 177 at 4100 rpm. Carburetors: Stromberg AAVB267 or Carter 2081 or 2179 two-barrel.

1954 Buick, Roadmaster four-door sedan, V-8

1954 Buick, Roadmaster two-door convertible, V-8 (OCW)

ROADMASTER — SERIES 70 — The top-of-the-line Buick looked like the cheaper Super from the outside, with the exception of a fourth ventiport on each front fender, Roadmaster script on the rear quarters and series identification within the deck ornament. Inside, though, the upholstery was much posher, with various nylon, broadcloth and leather combinations available depending on the model. Seats had chrome bands on the two-door models and all cars were fully carpeted. Power steering, brakes and Dynaflow were standard features, as was a rear seat armrest on the sedan. All had the new instrument panel with horizontal speedometer. Models 76C and 76R had an outside rearview mirror on the left and the 76C convertible was additionally equipped with power-operated windows, (vertical) seat adjustment and top.

ROADMASTER I.D. NUMBERS: Serial and engine numbers were mixed with other 1954 Series (see 1954 Special I.D. Numbers above).

Series No.	Body/Style No.	Body Type & Seating	Factory Price	Shipping Weight	Prod. Total
72R	54-4719	4-dr Sed-6P	3269	4250	26,862
76RX	54-4737X	2-dr HT Cpe-6P	3373	4215	20,404
76CX	54-4767X	2-dr Conv Cpe-6P	3521	4355	3,305

ENGINE: Specifications were the same as those listed for the 1954 Century, except compression ratio was 8.0:1 and brake horsepower was 200 at 4100 rpm.

1954 Buick, Skylark Sport two-door convertible, V-8 (AA)

SKYLARK — SERIES 100 — Buick's wild prestige convertible was the only model in this series. A new tapered deck with big chrome fins was grafted onto the 1954 Century body to create the 1954 Skylark. Specific front fenders, with wide-open wheelhouse, echoed at the rear wheelhouse, had no ventiports. Forty-spoke Kelsey-Hayes wire wheels were standard along with leather trim, special emblems, power brakes, power steering, Dynaflow, four-way powered seat, power top, power windows, Selectronic radio with power antenna, Easy-Eye glass, heater-defroster and whitewall tires.

Series No.	Body/Style No.	Body Type & Seating	Factory Price	Shipping Weight	Prod. Total
100	54-4667SX	2-dr Spt Conv	4355	4260	836

ENGINE: Specifications were the same as those listed for the 1954 Century, except compression ratio was 8.0:1 and brake horsepower was 200 at 4100 rpm.

CHASSIS FEATURES: Wheelbase: Series 40, 60 and 100 — 122 inches; Series 50 and 70 — 127 inches. Overall length: Series 40, 60 and 100 — 206.3 inches; Series 50 and 70 — 216-4/5 inches. Front tread: Series 40, 60 and 100 — 59 inches; Series 50 and 70 — 59 inches. Rear tread: Series 40, 60 and 100 — 59 inches; Series 50 and 70 — 62-1/5 inches. Tires: Series 40, 50, 60 and 100 — 6.70 x 15; Series 70 — 8.00 x 15.

POWERTRAIN OPTIONS: Three-speed manual transmission standard on Series 40, 50 and 60. Dynaflow drive standard on Series 70 and 100. Series 40 cars equipped with Dynaflow option had 8.0:1 compression ratio and 150 brake horsepower. Series 50 cars equipped with Dynaflow option had 8.0:1 compression ratio and 182 brake horsepower. Series 60 cars equipped with Dynaflow had 8.0:1 compression ratio and 200 brake horsepower.

CONVENIENCE OPTIONS: Full wheelcovers (standard Series 70). Set of five genuine 40-spoke wire wheels for Series 50, 60 and 70 (standard for Model 100). Power brakes (standard Series 70 and Model 100). Power steering (standard Series 70 and Model 100). Dor-Gard. Rear fender gas door guard. Windshield washer. Tool kit. Handy-Spot. Cushion toppers. Electric radio antenna (standard Model 100). Sonomatic radio. Selectronic radio (standard Model 100). Rear seat speaker (except convertibles, station wagons). Vent shades. Electric clock. License frames. Inside optional rearview mirror. Glare-proof outside rearview mirrors, right- and left-hand. Visor vanity mirror. Handy-mats. Air conditioning (except convertibles, Model 48). Hydraulic-electric windows (standard on Models 76RX, 76CX, 100). Horizontal front seat adjustment (standard, Model 100).

HISTORICAL FOOTNOTES: Calendar year production was 531,463. This represented a 9.6 percent market share and gave Buick third place in the industry. Model year production was 444,609 units. During 1954, Buick became the first automaker to build one-half million hardtops. The two-millionth Dynaflow was built on May 3. Style numbers 54-4437, 54-4537, 54-4637 and 54-4737X were Riviera hardtop coupes. Style numbers 54-4481 and 55-4681 were all-steel Estate Wagons. An X suffix to the Style Number indicates hydraulic control of the seat, windows, and convertible top.

1955

1955 Buick, Special Riviera two-door hardtop, V-8 (AA)

1955 Buick, Special two-door convertible, V-8

1955 Buick, Special two-door sedan, V-8

SPECIAL — SERIES 40

A major face lift, with new rear fenders housing 'tower' taillights, new front fenders and a new oval grille opening (housing a textured grille panel and a large horizontal emblem bar) distinguished the 1955 Buicks. Sweeps-pear moldings on the Special were the same as in 1954, but new round ventiports were grouped by threes on each front fender. Series script was found on the rear quarters and within the grille emblem. Cordaveen upholstery was used. The distinctive Series 40 and 60 instrument panel with twin round gauge pods was continued. Tubeless tires were now standard, as were directional signals, front and rear side armrests, sliding sunshades, a Step-On parking brake and heavy insulation.

SPECIAL I.D. NUMBERS: Serial numbers were located on the hinge pillar post and on dash under the hood. The first symbol was a number indicating series, as follows: 4 = Series 40 Special; 6 = Series 60 Century; 5 = Series 50 Super; 7 = Series 70 Roadmaster or 4 = 4400 (Special); 6 = 4600 (Century); 7 = 4700 (Roadmaster). The second symbol was a letter indicating year as follows: B = 1955. The third symbol was a number indicating assembly plant: 1 = Flint, Mich., 2 = Southgate, Calif., 3 = Linden, N.J., 4 = Kansas City, Kans., 5 = Wilmington, Del., 6 = Atlanta, Ga., 7 = Framingham, Mass., 8 = Arlington, Tex. The remaining symbols represented the sequential production number. Serial numbers were mixed in production with other 1955 series. Beginning numbers were: (Flint) 581001001-up; (Calif.) 582001001-up; (N.J.) 483001001-up; (Kans.) 484001001-up; (Del.) 485001001-up; (Ga.) 586001001-up; (Mass.) 587001001-up and (Texas) 488001001-up. Engine numbers were in various locations on the crankcase, usually, or on the cylinder block. Engine numbers were mixed in production.

Series No.	Body/Style No.	Body Type & Seating	Factory Price	Shipping Weight	Prod. Total
41	55-4469	4-dr Sed-6P	2291	3745	84,182
43	55-4439	4-dr HT-6P	2409	3820	66,409
48	55-4411	2-dr Sed-6P	2233	3715	61,879
46R	55-4437	2-dr HT Cpe-6P	2332	3720	155,818
46C	55-4467	2-dr Conv Cpe-6P	2590	3825	10,009
49	55-4481	4-dr Sta Wag-6P	2974	3940	2,952

ENGINE: V-8. Overhead valve. Cast iron block. Displacement: 264 cid. Bore and stroke: 3.625 x 3.2 inches. Compression ratio: 8.4:1. Brake horsepower: 188 at 4800 rpm. Five main bearings. Hydraulic valve lifters. Carburetor: Stromberg AAVB267, AA7-102 or Carter 2179 or 2292 two-barrel.

1955 Buick, Century Riviera four-door hardtop, V-8 (M)

1955 Buick, Century two-door convertible, V-8

CENTURY — SERIES 60

Buick's new performance car combining Roadmaster power and the Special's lighter weight, the Century had a more agile body and shared in the face lift given other 1955 Buicks. Century models were easily identified by their four ventiports per fender, the Century script on rear quarters and the series designation within the deck emblem. Inside, damascene panels were inset on the instrument panel and a quilted metallic door panel section was featured. The Century had a round Red Liner speedometer with a trip mileage indicator. An electric clock was also standard, along with features found on the Special. Interiors were cloth and Cordaveen, except for the Model 66C convertible, which was trimmed in leather and had power windows and a power horizontal seat adjuster as standard equipment. During 1955, Buick made 268 unique police cars for the California Highway Patrol. They were based on the Special two-door sedan body, but from the firewall forward they were Centurys and Buick listed them with Century production. All had the 322 cid/236 hp V-8 used in Century and Roadmaster models. About half had three-speed manual transmission and the others were equipped with Dynaflow drive.

1955 Buick, Century four-door Estate Wagon, V-8

1955 Buick, Century Riviera two-door hardtop, V-8 (PH)

CENTURY I.D. NUMBERS: Serial numbers were mixed with other 1955 series (see 1955 Special I.D. Numbers above). Engine numbers were mixed in production.

Series No.	Body/Style No.	Body Type & Seating	Factory Price	Shipping Weight	Prod. Total
61	55-4669	4-dr Sed-6P	2548	3825	13,629
63D	55-4639	4-dr HT-6P	2733	3900	55,088
66R	55-4637	2-dr HT Cpe-6P	2601	3805	80,338
66C	55-4667X	2-dr Conv Cpe-6P	2991	3950	5,588
69	55-4681	4-dr Sta Wag-6P	3175	3995	4,243
68	55-4611	2-dr Sed-6P	—	—	268

ENGINE: V-8. Overhead valve. Cast iron block. Displacement: 322 cid. Bore and stroke: 4 x 3.2 inches. Compression ratio: 9.1:1. Brake horsepower: 236 at 4600 rpm. Five main bearings. Hydraulic valve lifters. Carburetor: Carter 2197 or 2358 four-barrel.

1955 Buick, Super Riviera two-door hardtop, V-8

SUPER — SERIES 50 — Buick's popular Super combined the large C-body interior expanse with medium-bracket interiors and performance. Supers had four of the new round ventiports per fender this year, with additional series script found on rear quarters and within the deck emblem. The side sweepspear was unchanged from 1954. The larger-bodied Buicks were readily identifiable by their more rounded contours, straight up windshield pillars and sedan rear quarter windows. Series 50 and 70 headlamp bezels also housed parking lights. Inside, a new Red Liner speedometer lay horizontally across the instrument panel. Interiors were trimmed in nylon/Cordaveen combinations, except for the Model 56C convertible, which featured leather seats. Standard Super equipment included trip mileage indicator, electric clock and, on the Model 56C convertible, a power horizontal seat adjuster.

1955 Buick, Super two-door convertible, V-8 (OCW)

SUPER I.D. NUMBERS: Serial numbers were mixed in 1955 production (see 1955 Special I.D. Numbers above). Engine numbers were also mixed in production.

Series No.	Body/Style No.	Body Type & Seating	Factory Price	Shipping Weight	Prod. Total
52	55-4569	4-dr Sed-6P	2876	4140	43,280
56R	55-4537	2-dr HT Cpe-6P	2831	4075	85,656
56C	55-4567X	2-dr Conv Cpe-6P	3225	4280	3,527

ENGINE: Specifications were the same as listed for the 1955 Century.

1955 Buick, Roadmaster four-door sedan, V-8 (AA)

1955 Buick, Roadmaster two-door convertible, V-8

ROADMASTER — SERIES 70 — Buick's prestige car was given more distinction for 1955. Broad, bright lower rear fender bands, gold-colored Roadmaster deck script and hood ornament, bars on the wheelcovers and a gold-accented grille set the car apart. Four round ventiports were found on each front fender of the C-bodied Buicks, which were distinguished by vertical windshield posts and headlamp rims containing the parking lamp units as well. Interiors were plusher with 10 choices, including brocaded fabrics. The Model 76C convertible had a standard leather interior. Standard features of all Roadmasters included Variable-pitch Dynaflow, power steering, back-up lights, brake warning signal light, electric clock, windshield washer, Custom wheelcovers, double-depth foam seat cushions, plus features found on other Buick Series.

ROADMASTER I.D. NUMBERS: Serial numbers were mixed with other 1955 Series (see 1955 Special I.D. Numbers above). Engine numbers were mixed in production.

Series No.	Body/Style No.	Body Type & Seating	Factory Price	Shipping Weight	Prod. Total
72	55-4769	4-dr Sed-6P	3349	4300	31,717
76R	55-4737	2-dr HT Cpe-6P	3453	4270	28,071
76C	55-4767X	2-dr Conv Cpe-6P	3552	4415	4,730

ENGINE: Specifications were the same as listed for the 1955 Century.

CHASSIS FEATURES: Wheelbase: Series 40 and 60 — 122 inches; Series 50 and 70 — 127 inches. Overall length: Series 40 and 60 — 206.7 inches; Series 50 and 70 — 216 inches. Front tread: Series 40 and 60 — 59 inches; Series 50 and 70 — 59 inches. Rear tread: Series 40 and 60 — 59 inches; Series 50 and 70 — 62.2 inches. Tires: Series 40 — 7.10 x 15; Series 50 and 60 — 7.60 x 15; Series 70 — 8.00 x 15.

POWERTRAIN OPTIONS: A three-speed manual transmission was standard on the Special, Series 40; Century, Series 60; and Super, Series 50. Dynaflow drive was standard on the Roadmaster, Series 70; optional on other series ($193). Every 1955 Dynaflow unit contained 20 variable pitch stator blades that opened wide for quick acceleration and resumed to normal position for cruising. This new feature also gave greater gasoline economy.

CONVENIENCE OPTIONS: Two-tone and tri-tone paint. Windshield washer. Whitewall tubeless tires. Easy-Eye glass. Outside rearview mirrors. Deluxe Handy-mats. Sonomatic radio. Selectronic radio. Electric antenna. Full wheelcovers (standard on 70). Genuine 40-spoke wire wheels (except Series 40). Spotlite. Tissue dispenser. Dor-Gard gas door guard. Visor vanity mirror. Red Liner speedometer with trip mileage indicator (for Series 40 — standard other series). Power steering ($108 — standard Series 50 and 70). Air conditioning. Safety group (back-up lights, brake warning light, windshield washer — standard Series 70). Accessory group (for Series 40) — electric clock, rear license frame, full wheelcovers, truck light.

HISTORICAL FOOTNOTES: Calendar year production of 781,296 cars was an all-time record, putting Buick in third place. Model year output was 738,814. On March 16, the one-millionth Buick V-8 was built. On April 5, the eighth-millionth Buick was built (it was also the three-and-a-half millionth Buick since World War II). On Aug. 3, the one-millionth Buick hardtop was made.

During 1955, Buick took the only two wins in NASCAR Grand National stock car racing that it would see for many years. Buick Roadmasters were capable of going 0-to-60 mph in 11.2 seconds. The Century could do the same in 9.8 seconds and cover the quarter-mile in 17.5 seconds. A Century hit 110.425 mph in the Flying Mile competition at Daytona SpeedWeeks. Buick had a new X-braced frame, but continued to use torque tube drive. Body styles 55-4437, 55-4637, 55-4537 and 55-4737 are Riviera hardtop coupes. Styles 55-4439 and 55-4639 are Riviera hardtop sedans (pillarless) introduced midyear. Body styles 55-4481 and 55-4681 are Estate Wagons with all-steel bodies. An 'X' suffix to the Style Number indicates power-operated windows.

1956

1956 Buick, Special two-door convertible, V-8 (OCW)

1956 Buick, Special four-door Estate Wagon, V-8 (AA)

SPECIAL — SERIES 40 — The Special continued to use the popular sweepspear side motif in 1956. But, now all models, including sedans and wagons, had round rear wheelhouse cutouts. Face lifting included new taillights and a new, slightly forward thrusting grille. Series script continued to appear on rear quarters and within the deck and grille emblems. Specials had three oval ventiports per front fender this year, as was traditional. Closed car interiors were vinyl/Cordaveen combinations, while the Model 46C convertible was upholstered in all Cordaveen. Standard Special equipment included directional signals, front and rear armrests, sliding sunshades, cigarette lighter, glove compartment light, map light, dual horns, Step-On parking brake, a new horizontal Red Liner speedometer and a trip mileage indicator.

SPECIAL I.D. NUMBERS: Serial numbers were located on the hinge pillar post and on dash under the hood. The first symbol was a number indicating series, as follows: 4 = Series 40 Special; 6 = Series 60 Century; 5 = Series 50 Super; 7 = Series 70 Roadmaster or 4 = 4400 (Special); 6 = 4600 (Century); 7 = 4700 (Roadmaster). The second symbol was a letter indicating year as follows: C = 1956. The third symbol was a number indicating assembly plant: 1 = Flint, Mich.; 2 = Southgate, Calif.; 3 = Linden, N.J.; 4 = Kansas City, Kans.; 5 = Wilmington, Del.; 6 = Atlanta, Ga.; 7 = Framingham, Mass.; 8 = Arlington, Tex. The remaining symbols represented the sequential production number. Serial numbers were mixed in production with other 1956 Series. Num-

bers were: (Flint) 4C1001001 to 4C1207895; (Calif.) 4C2001001 to 4C2064441; (N.J.) 4C3001001 to 4C3068989; (Kans.) 4C4001001 to 4C4060680; (Del.) 4C5001001 to 4C5053478; (Ga.) 4C6001001 to 4C6055767; (Mass.) 4C7001001 to 4C7028493; (Texas) 4C8001001 to 4C8040281. Engine numbers were stamped on various locations on the crankcase or on the cylinder block.

Series No.	Body/Style No.	Body Type & Seating	Factory Price	Shipping Weight	Prod. Total
41	56-4469	4-dr Sed-6P	2416	3790	66,977
43	56-4439	4-dr HT-6P	2528	3860	91,025
48	56-4411	2-dr Sed-6P	2537	2750	38,672
46R	56-4437	2-dr HT Cpe-6P	2457	3775	113,861
46C	56-4467	2-dr Conv Cpe-6P	2740	3880	9,712
49	56-4481	4-dr Sta Wag-6P	2775	3945	13,770

1956 Buick, Special Riviera four-door hardtop, V-8

ENGINE: V-8. Overhead valve. Cast iron block. Displacement: 322 cid. Bore and stroke: 4 x 3.2 inches. Compression ratio: 8.9:1. Brake horsepower: 220 at 4400 rpm. Five main bearings. Hydraulic valve lifters. Carburetor: Stromberg 7-104 (manual transmission), 7-105 (Dynaflow); Carter 2378 (manual transmission), 2400 (Dynaflow).

1956 Buick, Century two-door convertible, V-8

1956 Buick, Century Riviera two-door hardtop, V-8

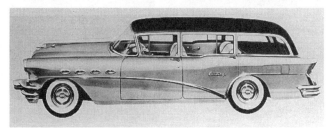

1956 Buick, Century four-door Estate Wagon, V-8

CENTURY — SERIES 60 — The Century relied chiefly on a fourth oval ventiport on each front fender, its series script on the rear quarters, and the series designations within the deck and grille emblems for its exterior identity. It shared the General Motors B-body, recognizable by its reverse slanting windshield pillars, with the Series 40 Special. All bright moldings interchanged. Colorful nylon/Cordaveen interior combinations were used in duo- and tri-tones. The convertible, Model 66C, was once more trimmed in leather. Standard features, in addition to those found on the Special, included foam seat cushions, a trunk light, electric clock and rear license frame. Model 66C, the convertible, had a power top, windows and horizontal seat adjuster included in its equipment.

CENTURY I.D. NUMBERS: Serial numbers were mixed with other 1956 Series (see 1956 Special I.D. Numbers above). Engine numbers were mixed in production.

Series No.	Body/Style No.	Body Type & Seating	Factory Price	Shipping Weight	Prod. Total
63	56-4639	4-dr HT-6P	3025	4000	20,891
63D	56-4639D	4-dr Del HT-6P	3041	4000	35,082
66R	56-4637	2-dr HT Cpe-6P	2963	3890	33,334
66C	56-4667X	2-dr Conv Cpe-6P	3306	4045	4,721
69	56-4681	4-dr Sta Wag-6P	3256	4080	8,160

ENGINE: Specifications were the same as listed for the 1956 Special, except compression ratio was 9.5:1, brake horsepower was 255 at 4400 rpm and the carburetor was a Carter 2347 or Rochester 7009200-9900 four-barrel.

1956 Buick, Super Riviera four-door hardtop, V-8 (AA)

SUPER — SERIES 50 — Although the Super was a larger Buick, with vertical windshield posts and four ventiports per fender, it had a deep sweepspear similar to the smaller Series 40 and 60 cars. Series script was found on rear quarters and within the deck and grille emblems. Interiors were Cordaveen and patterned nylon, except for the Model 56C which was all-Cordaveen trimmed and had power windows, horizontal seat adjustment, and a power top in its standard form. Dynaflow was now standard on all Supers, along with foam seat cushions, a trunk light and electric clock, plus features found on the lower-priced Special.

1956 Buick, Super four-door sedan, V-8

SUPER I.D. NUMBERS: Serial numbers were mixed in 1956 production (see 1956 Special I.D. Numbers). Engine numbers were also mixed in production.

SUPER SERIES 50

Series No.	Body/Style No.	Body Type & Seating	Factory Price	Shipping Weight	Prod. Total
52	56-4569	4-dr Sed-6P	3250	4200	14,940
53	56-4539	4-dr HT-6P	3340	4265	34,029
56R	56-4537	2-dr HT Cpe-6P	3204	4140	29,540
56C	56-4567	2-dr Conv Cpe-6P	3544	4340	2,489

ENGINE: Specifications are the same as listed for the 1956 Century.

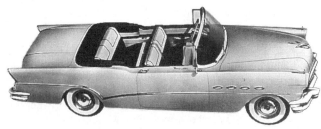

1956 Buick, Roadmaster two-door convertible, V-8 (OCW)

ROADMASTER — SERIES 70 — An effort was made to further distinguish the first class Buick for 1956. Roadmasters had a shallow sweepspear that didn't dip to the rockerpanel, as on other series. Twin chrome strips graced the deck lid, with Roadmaster spelled out in block letters between the strips. Roadmaster script was found on the front doors and beneath the vent windows. Fendertop dual bombsights were standard and the grille emblem carried flashier series identification. Standard Roadmaster equipment included a perimeter heating system, Variable-Pitch Dynaflow, power steering, power brakes, backup lights, windshield washers, glare-proof rearview mirror, parking brake signal release light, electric clock, Deluxe wheelcovers, foam-cushioned seats, foam-backed carpets and dash pad. Interiors included Custom Nylon and cord combinations and leather in the convertible, Model 76C. Two-door models had bright front seat cushion bands and Models 76R and 76C had power windows and seat adjuster as standard equipment.

1956 Buick, Roadmaster four-door sedan, V-8 (AA)

1956 Buick, Roadmaster Riviera four-door hardtop, V-8

ROADMASTER I.D. NUMBERS: Serial numbers were mixed in production with other 1956 series (see 1956 Special I.D. Numbers above). Engine numbers were mixed in production.

Series No.	Body/Style No.	Body Type & Seating	Factory Price	Shipping Weight	Prod. Total
72	56-4769	4-dr Sed-6P	3503	4280	11,804
73	56-4739	4-dr HT-6P	3692	4355	24,770
76R	56-4737	2-dr HT Cpe-6P	3591	4235	12,490
76C	56-4767	2-dr Conv Cpe-6P	3704	4395	4,354

ENGINE: Specifications were the same as listed for the 1956 Century.

CHASSIS FEATURES: Wheelbase: (Series 40 and 60) 122 inches; (Series 50 and 70) 127 inches. Overall length: (Series

40 and 60) 205 inches; (Series 50 and 70) 213.6 inches. Front tread: (All) 59 inches. Rear tread: (All) 59 inches. Tires: (Series 40) 7.10 x 15; (Series 60 and 50) 7.60 x 15; (Series 70) 8.00 x 15.

POWERTRAIN OPTIONS: Three-speed manual transmission standard on Series 40 and 60. Dynaflow drive standard on Series 50 and 70, optional ($204) on Series 40 and 60.

CONVENIENCE OPTIONS: Power steering ($108 — standard on Series 50 and 70). Air conditioning ($403). Spotlite. Carpet cover. Cushion topper. Exhaust pipe trim. DorGard. Gas door guard. Rear seat speaker. Tissue dispenser. Visor vanity mirror. License frame (open top). Seat belts. Custom Cordaveen interior on Series 40, 60 and 50. Power windows (standard on Models 66C, 56C, 76C, 76R, available all others except Model 48). Wire wheels (set of five) on Series 60, 50 and 70. Padded instrument panel (standard Series 70, available for Series 50). Six-way power seat. Sonomatic radio. Selectronic radio. Electric antenna. 30/70 rear seat (Model 49 and 69 wagons).

HISTORICAL FOOTNOTES: Buick captured third place in industry popularity with production of 535,364 units for the calendar year. That equated to a 8.9 percent market share. Model year output was 572,024 units or 9.1 percent of industry production. For the first time, all Buicks used the same engine. Dynaflow transmission was found in 96.7 percent of the cars. A new feature was a foot-operated side-lift jack. The Roadmaster was good for 0-to-60 mph in 11.7 seconds. The 1956 Century could do 0-to-60 mph in 9.6 seconds and cover the quarter-mile in 17.1 seconds. It was the fastest Century ever. All 1956 Buicks were capable of 110 mph. Ivan Wiles was named to replace Edward T. Ragsdale as Buick's general manager. Ragsdale (the "father of the hardtop") was promoted to a GM executive position. The Centuriam Motorama show car was seen in 1956. Body styles 56-4437, 56-4537, 56-4637 and 56-4737X are Riviera hardtop coupes. Styles 56-4439, 56-4539, 56-4639 and 56-4739 are Riviera hardtop sedans (pillarless). Body styles 56-4481 and 56-4681 are Estate wagons. The symbol 'X' after Body Style Number indicates power windows.

1957

1957 Buick, Special four-door sedan, V-8

SPECIAL — SERIES 40 — A new, wider and lower body graced the 1957 Special. A red-filled bright sweepspear lined the bodysides and a chromed rear fender lower panel filled the area between wheelhouse and bumper end. A new centered fuel filler door was found in the rear bumper, the ends of which the single or optional dual exhaust passed through. Three ventiports were found on each front fender. Series script was found within the deck and grille emblems. Closed models were upholstered in nylon/Cordaveen combinations except for the Model 49D Estate Wagon, which had cloth and Cordaveen upholstery. The Model 46C convertible was trimmed in two-tone Cordav-

een. Standard Special equipment included a Red Liner speedometer, glovebox lamp, dual horns, trip mileage indicator, directional signals, dual sunshades, color-coordinated dash panel, and, on Model 46C only, an outside left-hand rearview mirror.

1957 Buick, Special four-door Estate Wagon, V-8

SPECIAL I.D. NUMBERS: Serial numbers were located on the hinge pillar post and on dash under the hood. The first symbol was a number indicating series, as follows: 4 = Series 40 Special, 6 = Series 60 Century, 5 = Series 50 Super, 7 = Series 70 Roadmaster, and 8 = Series 75 Roadmaster 75, or 4 = 4400 (Special); 6 = 4600 (Century); 7 = 4700 (Roadmaster/Electra); and 8 = (4800 Roadmaster 75). The second symbol was a letter indicating year as follows: D = 1957. The third symbol was a number indicating assembly plant: 1 = Flint, Mich.; 2 = Southgate, Calif.; 3 = Linden, N.J.; 4 = Kansas City, Kans.; 5 = Wilmington, Del.; 6 = Atlanta, Ga.; 7 = Framingham, Mass.; 8 = Arlington, Tex. The remaining symbols represented the sequential production number. Serial numbers were mixed in production with other 1957 Series. Numbers were: (Flint) 4DI000989 to 4DI149460; (Calif.) 4D2001001 to 4D2038462; (N.J.) 4D3001001 to 4D3047645; (Kans.) 4D4001001 to 4D4046155; (Del.) 4D5001001 to 4D5039991; (Ga.) 4D6001001 to 4D6042248; (Mass.) 4D7001001 to 4D7018900; (Tex.) 4D8001001 to 4D8030225.

SPECIAL SERIES 40

Series No.	Body/Style No.	Body Type & Seating	Factory Price	Shipping Weight	Prod. Total
41	57-4469	4-dr Sed-6P	2660	4012	59,739
43	57-4439	4-dr HT-6P	2780	4041	50,563
48	57-4411	2-dr Sed-6P	2596	3955	23,180
46R	57-4437	2-dr HT Cpe-6P	2704	3956	64,425
46C	57-4467	2-dr Conv Cpe-6P	2987	4082	8,505
49D	57-4481	4-dr Riv Sta Wag-6P	3167	4309	6,817
49	57-4482	4-dr Sta Wag-6P	3047	4292	7,013

ENGINE: V-8. Overhead valve. Cast iron block. Displacement: 364 cid. Bore and stroke: 4.125 x 3.4 inches. Compression ratio: 9.5:1. Brake horsepower: 250 at 4400 rpm. Five main bearings. Hydraulic valve lifters. Carburetor: Stromberg two-barrel Model 7-106 or Carter 2529 or 2536.

1957 Buick, Century Cabellero four-door hardtop station wagon, V-8 (OCW)

1957 Buick, Century two-door convertible, V-8

1957 Buick, Century Riviera two-door hardtop, V-8 (AA)

CENTURY — SERIES 60 — Buick's performance star was similar to the Special in exterior trim, except for an identifying fourth ventiport on each front fender. Series designation was also found on the rear quarters or doors and within front and rear emblems. Interiors were plusher, with Rivieras upholstered in nylon/Cordaveen combinations and the Model 66C convertible being trimmed in Cordaveen and leather (power windows and seats were standard on this model). Regular features, in addition to those found on the Special, included foam rubber seat cushions and an automatic trunk lamp.

CENTURY I.D. NUMBERS: Serial numbers were mixed with other 1957 series (See 1957 Special I.D. Numbers above). Engine numbers were mixed in production.

CENTURY SERIES 60

Series No.	Body/Style No.	Body Type & Seating	Factory Price	Shipping Weight	Prod. Total
61	57-4669	4-dr Sed-6P	3316	4241	8,075
63	57-4639	4-dr HT-6P	3436	4267	26,589
66R	57-4637	2-dr HT Cpe-6P	3368	4182	17,029
66C	57-4667X	2-dr Conv Cpe-6P	3680	4302	4,085
69	57-4682	4-dr Sta Wag-6P	3831	4498	10,186

ENGINE: Specifications were the same as listed for the 1957 Special, except compression ratio was 10.0:1, brake horsepower was 300 at 4600 rpm (330 hp with high performance kit) and the four-barrel carburetor was a Carter 2507 or Rochester 7010070 (late — 7011570).

1957 Buick, Super Riviera four-door hardtop, V-8

1957 Buick, Super Riviera two-door hardtop, V-8 (OCW)

SUPER — SERIES 50 — The Super used a new C-Body treatment for 1957. Larger than the Series 40 and 60 bodies, the Riviera styles had different roof treatments as well. Supers had a group of three Chevrons on each rear quarter or door for series identification, in addition to the normal wording within the grille and deck emblems. Four ventiports were used on each front

fender. Closed models were upholstered in Nylon/Cordaveen combinations, while the Model 56C convertible had an all-Cordaveen interior and featured power windows and seat controls as part of its equipment. Standard Super equipment approximated that of the Century.

1957 Buick, Super two-door convertible, V-8

SUPER I.D. NUMBERS: Serial numbers were mixed in 1957 production (see 1957 Special I.D. numbers above). Engine numbers were also mixed in production.

SUPER SERIES 50

Series No.	Body/Style No.	Body Type & Seating	Factory Price	Shipping Weight	Prod. Total
53	57-4539	4-dr HT-6P	3681	4356	41,665
56R	57-4537	2-dr HT Cpe-6P	3536	4271	26,529
56C	57-4567	2-dr Conv Cpe-6P	3981	4414	2,056

ENGINE: Specifications are the same as listed for the 1957 Century.

1957 Buick, Roadmaster two-door convertible, V-8 (AA)

ROADMASTER — SERIES 70 — The Roadmaster Rivieras featured a new body and revised rooflines, with chrome bands sweeping over the top and down division bars on the three-piece rear windows. Consumer resistance led to the optional deletion of these bars and substitution of a one-piece rear window (Models 73A and 76A). Roadmasters had four ventiports per fender. Two-door models had the trio of Chevrons on the rear quarters such as the Super, but the four-door styles had a Roadmaster emblem nestled within the sweepspear's dip. Interiors were broadcloth and nylon in the four-door, nylon in the Rivieras and leather in the Model 76C convertible. A padded instrument panel was among the extra touches of luxury found in the Roadmaster.

ROADMASTER I.D. NUMBERS: Serial numbers were mixed in production with other 1957 series (see 1957 Special I.D. Numbers above). Engine numbers were mixed in production.

ROADMASTER SERIES 70

Series No.	Body/Style No.	Body Type & Seating	Factory Price	Shipping Weight	Prod. Total
73	57-4739	4-dr HT-6P	4053	4469	11,401
73A	57-4739A	4-dr HT-6P	4053	4455	10,526
76A	57-4737A	2-dr HT Cpe-6P	3944	4370	2,812
76R	57-4737	2-dr HT Cpe-6P	3944	4374	3,826
76C	57-4767X	2-dr Conv Cpe-6P	4066	4500	4,364

ENGINE: Specifications were the same as listed for the 1957 Century.

ROADMASTER 75 — SERIES 75 — The 75 was a new line for 1957, introduced to cap the prestigious Roadmaster line. Both models used one-piece rear windows and differed from the Roadmaster only by the use of Roadmaster 75 script on the rear quarters or doors on the exterior. Inside, a plusher custom design interior was found. Roadmaster 75s included almost every power assist in their standard price, except for air conditioning.

ROADMASTER 75 I.D. NUMBERS: Serial numbers were mixed in production (see 1957 Special I.D. Numbers above). Engine numbers were mixed in production.

ROADMASTER SERIES

Series No.	Body/Style No.	Body Type & Seating	Factory Price	Shipping Weight	Prod. Total
75	57-4839	4-dr HT Sed-6P	4483	4539	12,250
75R	57-4847	2-dr HT Cpe-6P	4373	4427	2,404

ENGINE: Specifications were the same as listed for the 1957 Century.

1957 Buick, Roadmaster Riviera two-door hardtop, V-8

CHASSIS FEATURES: Wheelbase: (Series 40 and 60)122 inches; (Series 50, 70 and 75) 127.5 inches. Overall length: (Series 40 and 60) 208.4 inches; (Series 50, 70 and 75) 215.3 inches. Front tread: (All) 59.5 inches. Rear tread: (Series 40 and 60) 59.5 inches; (Series 50, 70 and 75) 61.0 inches. Tires: (Series 40) 7.10 x 15; (Series 60 and 50) 7.60 x 15; (Series 70 and 75) 8.00 x 15.

POWERTRAIN OPTIONS: Three-speed manual standard on Series 40, Dynaflow optional at $220. Dynaflow standard on Series 50, 60, 70 and 75.

CONVENIENCE OPTIONS: Power steering ($107 — standard on Series 50 and 70). Air conditioning ($430). Spotlite. Carpet cover. Cushion topper. DorGard. Rear seat speaker. Front bumper guards. Rear seat speaker. Sonomatic radio. Selectronic radio. Electric antenna. Seat belts. Tissue dispenser. Visor vanity mirror. License frames. Padded instrument panel (standard Series 70). Six-way power seat.

HISTORICAL FOOTNOTES: Calendar year production was 407,271 units, a 24 percent decline. Buick dropped to fourth place in the industry, being passed in sales by Plymouth. Model year production was 405,086 units. Of all Buicks, 61.9 percent had power steering and 56.1 percent had power brakes. On July 7, 1957, the nine-millionth Buick was built. The 1957 Century was a bit slower then the '56. It did 0-to-60 mph in 10.1 seconds and covered the quarter-mile in 17.6 seconds. Body styles 57-4437, 57-4637, 57-4537 and 57-4737 are Riviera hardtop coupes. Styles 57-4439, 57-4539, 57-4639 and 57-4739 are Riviera hardtop sedans. Styles 57-4481 and 57-4482 are Estate wagons. Style 57-4682 is the Caballero station wagon.

1958

SPECIAL — SERIES 40 — Bulkier, more heavily chromed styling adorned the 1958 Special chassis. New Lucite paints in many colors were used. For the first time since 1948, there were no distinguishing ventiports on Buick's front fenders. At the front a new "drawer-pull" grille was used, made up of rectangular chrome squares. The Special name was spelled out across the deck lid, while a bright sweepspear and a large rear fender bright flash was similar to other models. All 1958 Buicks had four headlamps. Standard features on the Special included an

ignition key light, glovebox, cigar lighter, trip mileage indicator, geared vent panes, bumper guards, variable-speed wipers, Step-On parking brake, and, on the Model 46C convertible, an outside left-hand rearview mirror. Special interiors were trimmed with gray cloth and vinyl or Cordaveen and vinyl, or all Cordaveen in the convertible. A plusher Custom interior was available at extra cost.

1958 Buick, Special two-door convertible, V-8 (AA)

SPECIAL I.D. NUMBERS: Serial numbers were located on the hinge pillar post and on dash under the hood. The first symbol was a number indicating series, as follows: 4 = Series 40 Special; 6 = Series 60 Century; 5 = Series 50 Super; 7 = Series 70 Roadmaster; and 8 = Series 80 Limited; or 4 = 4400 (Special); 6 = 4600 (Century); 7 = 4700 (Roadmaster); and 8 = (4800 Limited). The second symbol was a letter indicating year as follows: E = 1958. The third symbol was a number indicating assembly plant: 1 = Flint, Mich.; 2 = Southgate, Calif.; 3 = Linden, N.J.; 4 = Kansas City, Kans.; 5 = Wilmington, Del.; 6 = Atlanta, Ga.; 7 = Framingham, Mass.; 8 = Arlington, Tex. The remaining symbols represented the sequential production number. Serial numbers were mixed in production with other 1958 series. Numbers were: (Flint) 4E1000985 to 4E1091650, (Calif.) 4E2001001 to 4E2020239, (N.J.) 4E3001001 to 4E3026555, (Kans.) 4E4001001 to 4E4031146, (Del.) 4E5001001 to 4E5022304, (Ga.) 4E6001001 to 4E6027283, (Mass.) 4E7001001 to 4E7011105, and (Tex.) 4E8001001 to 4E8019510.

1958 Buick, Special Riviera two-door hardtop, V-8

SPECIAL SERIES

Series No.	Body/Style No.	Body Type & Seating	Factory Price	Shipping Weight	Prod. Total
41	584469	4-dr Sed-6P	2700	4115	48,238
43	584439	4-dr HT-6P	2820	4180	31,921
48	584411	2-dr Sed-6P	2636	4063	11,566
46R	584437	2-dr HT Cpe-6P	2744	4058	34,903
46C	584467	2-dr Conv Cpe-6P	3041	4165	5,502
49D	584482	4-dr Riv Sta Wag-6P	3265	4408	3,420
49	584481	4-dr Sta Wag-6P	3145	4396	3,663

ENGINE: V-8. Overhead valve. Cast iron block. Displacement: 364 cid. Bore and stroke: 4.25 x 3.4 inches. Compression ratio: 9.5:1. Brake horsepower: 250 at 4400 rpm. Five main bearings. Hydraulic valve lifters. Carburetors: Stromberg two-barrel Model WW7-109B — also Carter two-barrel (with Synchro) Model 2674: (with Dynaflow) Model 2675.

CENTURY — SERIES 60 — The Century shared the Special's bulky new sheetmetal and had as much plated brightwork. In

addition to the Century name spelled out in block lettering on the deck lid, the 60 Series had Century script within the rear fender flashes. Standard equipment, in addition to features found on the Special, included Variable-Pitch Dynaflow, full wheelcovers, carpeting, padded dash, foam rubber cushions, electric clock and dual horns. Custom interiors were trimmed in nylon, except for the Model 69 Estate Wagon, which was upholstered in Cordaveen. The Model 46C convertible had electric windows and two-way seat controls.

1958 Buick, Century Caballero four-door hardtop station wagon, V-8 (AA)

1958 Buick, Century Riviera four-door hardtop, V-8

1958 Buick, Century two-door convertible, V-8

CENTURY I.D. NUMBERS: Serial numbers were mixed with other 1958 series (see 1958 Special I.D. Numbers above). Engine numbers were mixed in production.

CENTURY SERIES

Series No.	Body/Style No.	Body Type & Seating	Factory Price	Shipping Weight	Prod. Total
61	584669	4-dr Sed-6P	3316	4241	7,421
63	584639	4-dr HT-6P	3436	4267	15,171
66R	584637	2-dr HT-6P	3368	4182	8,110
66C	584667X	2-dr Conv Cpe-6P	3680	4302	2,588
69	584682	4-dr Sta Wag-6P	3831	4498	4,456

ENGINE: Specifications were the same as listed for the 1958 Special, except compression ratio was 10.0:1, brake horsepower was 300 at 4600 rpm and the four-barrel carburetor was a Carter Model 2800 or Rochester Models 7011600 or (late) 7013100.

SUPER — SERIES 50 — The once most popular Buick line was reduced to two models for 1958. Side trim was similar to lesser series, except for the Super lettering on the rear fender flashes, but Supers were longer than the Series 40 and 60 models. The Super name was also lettered across the deck lid. Standard equipment included Variable-Pitch Dynaflow, power steering, power brakes, a safety-cushion instrument panel, fully carpeted floor, courtesy lights and other items found on lesser models.

1958 Buick, Super Riviera four-door hardtop, V-8

SUPER I.D. NUMBERS: Serial numbers were mixed in 1958 production (see 1958 Special I.D. Numbers above). Engine numbers were also mixed in production.

SUPER SERIES

Series No.	Body/Style No.	Body Type & Seating	Factory Price	Shipping Weight	Prod. Total
53	584539	4-dr HT-6P	3789	4500	28,460
56R	584537	2-dr HT-6P	3644	4392	13,928

ENGINE: Specifications were the same as listed for the 1958 Century.

1958 Buick, Roadmaster Riviera four-door hardtop, V-8

1958 Buick, Roadmaster two-door convertible, V-8 (OCW)

ROADMASTER — SERIES 75 — The Roadmaster earned all the brightwork of the Super and added bright wheelhouse moldings, an ebbed rocker panel molding and ribbed inserts to the rear fender flashes. All 1958 Roadmasters were in the 75 Series, as attested by the script and numerals on the fender flashes. On the rear deck Roadmaster was spelled out in block lettering beneath a Buick emblem housing the trunk lock keyway. Standard Roadmaster features, in addition to those found on lesser Buicks, included power windows, a power six-way front seat, safety cushion dash, carpeted floors and lower doors, Glareproof rearview mirror, safety buzzer, brake warning light and Deluxe wheelcovers. Interiors were cloth or cloth and leather except for the convertible, trimmed in all leather.

ROADMASTER I.D. NUMBERS: Serial numbers were mixed in production with other 1958 series (see 1958 Special I.D. Numbers above). Engine numbers were mixed in production.

ROADMASTER SERIES

Series No.	Body/Style No.	Body Type & Seating	Factory Price	Shipping Weight	Prod. Total
75	584739X	4-dr HT-6P	4667	4668	10,505
75R	584737X	2-dr HT-6P	4557	4568	2,368
75C	584767X	2-dr Conv Cpe-6P	4680	4676	1,181

ENGINE: Specifications were the same as listed for the 1958 Century.

LIMITED — 700 SERIES — Buick resurrected a grand old nameplate for a new extra-long luxury line in 1958. Twelve vertical louvers, set within the rear fenders' rocket-like trim motif distinguished the Limited. All the chrome associated with other 1958 Buicks was present as well. The Limited had its own mas-

sive, louvered taillamps. Limited script was found on the rear doors or quarters, and a Buick badge flanked by four chrome bars was found on the Limited, which featured ultra-plush cloth, cloth and leather, and in the case of the Model 756 convertible all-leather upholstery.

1958 Buick, Limited four-door hardtop, V-8 (AA)

LIMITED I.D. NUMBERS: Serial numbers were mixed in production with other 1958 series (see 1958 Special I.D. Numbers above). Engine numbers were mixed in production.

LIMITED SERIES

Series No.	Body/Style No.	Body Type & Seating	Factory Price	Shipping Weight	Prod. Total
750	584839X	4-dr HT-6P	5112	4710	5,571
755	584837X	2-dr HT-6P	5002	4691	1,026
756	584867X	2-dr Conv Cpe-6P	5125	4603	839

ENGINE: Specifications were the same as listed for the 1958 Century.

CHASSIS FEATURES: Wheelbase: (Series 40 and 60) 122 inches; (Series 50, 75 and 700) 127.5 inches. Overall length: (Series 40 and 60) 211.8 inches; (Series 50 and 75) 219.1 inches; (Series 700) 227.1 inches. Front tread: (Series 40, 60 and 50) 59.5 inches; (Series 75 and 700) 60 inches. Rear tread: (Series 40, 60 and 50) 59 inches; (Series 75 and 700) 61 inches. Tires: (Series 40) 7.10 x 15; (Models 46C and 49) 7.60 x 15; (Series 60 and 50) 7.60 x 15; (Series 75 and 700) 8.00 x 15.

1958 Buick, Limited two-door convertible, V-8

POWERTRAIN OPTIONS: Three-speed manual standard on Series 40. Variable-Pitch Dynaflow optional ($220). Variable-Pitch Dynaflow standard on Series 60 and 50. Flight Pitch Dynaflow standard on Series 75 and 700, optional on other series ($296 Series 40, $75 Series 60 and 50). Dual exhaust optional.

CONVENIENCE OPTIONS: Power steering ($108 — standard Series 50, 75, 700). Power brakes (standard Series 50, 75, 700). Air Poise air suspension. In-dash or under-dash air conditioning. Sonomatic radio. Wonder Bar signal-seeking radio. Power windows (standard Model 66C, all Series 75 and 700). Perimeter heater/defroster. Autronic Eye. Electric radio antenna. Windshield washer (standard Series 75 and 700). E-Z Eye glass. Safety group — back-up lights, lower instrument panel pad, parking brake warning light, Glare-proof inside rearview mirror (standard on Series 75 and 700). Upper instrument panel pad (for Series 40, standard other series). Six-way power seat (standard Series 75, 700). Series 40 accessory group — electric clock, full wheelcovers, automatic trunk light, rear license frame.

HISTORICAL FOOTNOTES: Calendar year production was 257,124 units. Buick slid into fifth rank in the industry, with Oldsmobile capturing fourth. Model year production was 241,892 units, for a 5.7 percent market share. The four-millionth Dyna-

flow transmission was built and 98.5 percent of all Buicks had this feature, 97.6 percent had heaters and 87.6 percent had radios. The one-millionth Buick power brake installation was made. Buick dealers were authorized to sell the German Opel (available in the United States as of Oct. 1, 1957). A special "Tales of Wells Fargo" Buick with a western motif was built for actor Dale Robertson. Body styles 584437, 584637, 584537, 584737 and 584837X are Riviera coupes. Styles 584439, 584639, 584539, 584739, and 584839X are Riviera sedans. Styles 584482 and 584682 are Riviera Estate Wagons. An X in the style designation indicates electric controls of the windows, front seat, and (convertibles) top.

1959

1959 Buick, LeSabre four-door sedan, V-8

LESABRE — SERIES 4400 — New series names and totally new styling greeted the 1959 Buick buyer. These were the wildest Buicks yet, with blade fins sweeping from the front of the body rearward. One of the few continued hallmarks from 1958 was the grille made up of rectangular squares. On the sides, bright trim steps ran the length of the LeSabre body. Taillights were low and round. Interiors were trimmed in Barbary cloth and Cordaveen, except on Models 4467 and 4435, which were all-Cordaveen. An optional Balfour Cloth and Cordaveen Custom combination was offered on all, except the convertible and station wagon. Standard LeSabre equipment included a glovebox light, dual horns, electric wipers, horizontal Red Liner speedometer, trip mileage indicator and an outside rearview mirror on the Model 4467 convertible.

1959 Buick, LeSabre four-door hardtop, V-8 (PH)

LESABRE I.D. NUMBERS: Serial numbers were located on the hinge pillar post and on dash under the hood. The first symbol was a number indicating series, as follows: 4 = 4400 (LeSabre); 6 = 4600 (Invicta); 7 = 4700 (Electra); and 8 = 4800 (Electra 225). The second symbol was a letter indicating year as follows: F = 1959. The third symbol was a number indicating assembly plant: 1 = Flint, Mich.; 2 = Southgate, Calif.; 3 = Linden, N.J.; 4 = Kansas City, Kans.; 5 = Wilmington, Del.; 6 = Atlanta,

Ga.; 7 = Framingham, Mass.; 8 = Arlington, Tex. The remaining symbols represented the sequential production number. Serial numbers began with 4F1001001.

LESABRE SERIES

Series No.	Body/Style No.	Body Type & Seating	Factory Price	Shipping Weight	Prod. Total
4400	4419	4-dr Sed-6P	2804	4229	51,379
4400	4439	4-dr HT-6P	2925	4266	46,069
4400	4411	2-dr Sed-6P	2740	4159	13,492
4400	4437	2-dr HT-6P	2849	4188	35,189
4400	4467	2-dr Conv Cpe-6P	3129	4216	10,489
4400	4435	4-dr Sta Wag-6P	3320	4565	8,286

1959 Buick, LeSabre two-door convertible, V-8 (OCW)

ENGINE: V-8. Overhead valve. Cast iron block. Displacement: 364 cid. Bore and stroke: 4.25 x 3.4 inches. Compression ratio: 10.5:1. Brake horsepower: 250 at 4400 rpm. Five main bearings. Hydraulic lifters. Carburetor: Stromberg two-barrel Model WW7112A or Carter two-barrels (with Synchnomesh) Model 2847; (with Dynaflow) Model 2838 or Rochester two-barrel Model 7019042.

1959 Buick, Invicta two-door convertible, V-8

1959 Buick, Invicta four-door hardtop, V-8 (AA)

INVICTA — SERIES 4600 — Replacing the Century Series 60 for 1959 was this new performance line. The exterior was distinguished by a bright rocker panel molding and Invicta scripts on the front fenders. Inside, standard trim was Balfour cloth in a more intricate weave than the LeSabre and in four color combinations. The Estate Wagon was trimmed in Saran Balfour and Cordaveen, and the convertible was upholstered in all-Cordaveen. Standard equipment on the Invicta in addition to features found on the LeSabre, included Foamtex seat cushions, electric clock, Deluxe steering wheel, full wheelcovers, and an instrument panel cover.

INVICTA I.D. NUMBERS: Serial numbers were distinguished by the use of the numeral '6' as the first symbol of the number. The rest of the number was coded as explained under the 1959 LeSabre I.D. Number section above.

INVICTA SERIES

Series No.	Body/Style No.	Body Type & Seating	Factory Price	Shipping Weight	Prod. Total
4600	4619	4-dr Sed-6P	3357	4331	10,566
4600	4639	4-dr HT-6P	3515	4373	20,156
4600	4637	2-dr HT-6P	3447	4274	11,451
4600	4667	2-dr Conv Cpe-6P	3620	4317	5,447
4600	4635	4-dr Sta Wag-6P	3841	4660	5,231

ENGINE: V-8. Overhead valve. Cast iron block. Displacement: 401 cid. Bore and stroke: 4.1875 x 3.64 inches. Compression ratio: 10.5:1. Brake horsepower: 325 at 4400 rpm. Five main bearings. Hydraulic lifters. Carburetor: Carter four-barrel Model 2840 or Rochester four-barrel Model 7013044-15900.

ELECTRA — SERIES 4700 — A Roadmaster by another name, the Electra was trimmed with bright rocker moldings, wheelhouse moldings and Electra script on the front fenders, in addition to the brightwork found on other Buicks. Standard features, in addition to those found on lower-priced Buicks, included a Safety Pad dash, power steering, power brakes, two-speed electric wipers, and dual exhaust. Interiors were plusher, being trimmed in nylon Mojave cloth or Broadcloth combinations with Cordaveen.

ELECTRA I.D. NUMBERS: Serial numbers were distinguished by the use of the numeral '7' as the first symbol of the number. The rest of the number was coded as explained under the 1959 LeSabre I.D. Numbers section above.

ELECTRA SERIES

Series No.	Body/Style No.	Body Type & Seating	Factory Price	Shipping Weight	Prod. Total
4700	4719	4-dr Sed-6P	3856	4557	12,357
4700	4739	4-dr HT-6P	3963	4573	20,612
4700	4737	2-dr Conv Cpe-6P	3818	4465	11,216

ENGINE: Specifications are the same as those listed for the 1959 Invicta.

ELECTRA 225 — SERIES 4800 — The First Electra 225 (the 225 derived from the overall length of this stretched-body luxury car) was a big Buick. Exterior distinction came from extra-wide moldings, with a massive Electra emblem on the front fender extension. Electra 225 script was found on the front fenders, ahead of the wheelhouse. The four-door models had a lower bright rear fender molding as well. Standard features, in addition to those found on lesser Buicks, included plusher interiors (leather in the convertible), power windows and top for the convertible, Safety group, Super Deluxe wheelcovers and an outside rearview mirror.

ELECTRA 225 I.D. NUMBERS: Serial numbers were distinguished by the use of the number '8' as the first symbol of the number. The rest of the number was coded as explained under the 1959 LeSabre I.D. Numbers section above.

ELECTRA 225 SERIES

Series No.	Body/Style No.	Body Type & Seating	Factory Price	Shipping Weight	Prod. Total
4800	4829	4-dr Sed-6P	4300	4632	6,324
4800	4839	4-dr HT-6P	4300	4641	10,491
4800	4867	2-dr Conv Cpe-6P	4192	4562	5,493

ENGINE: Specifications were the same as those listed for the 1959 Invicta.

CHASSIS FEATURES: Wheelbase: (Series 4400 and 4600) 123 inches; (Series 4700 and 4800) 126.3 inches. Overall length: (Series 4400 and 4600) 217.4 inches; (Series 4700) 220.6 inches; (Series 4800 225.4 inches). Front tread: (All Series) 62 inches. Rear tread: (All series) 60 inches. Tires: (Series 4400 and 4600) 7.60 x 15; (Series 4700 and 4800) 8.00 x 15 tubeless.

POWERTRAIN OPTIONS: A three-speed manual transmission was standard on Series 4400, Twin Turbine Dynaflow (standard on Series 4600, 4700, 4800) was optional ($220). Triple Turbine Dynaflow was optional on all Series — $296 on Series 4400 and $75 on all others. A Positive Traction differential was offered.

CONVENIENCE OPTIONS: Power steering and power brakes were optional on Series 4400 models (with automatic transmission only) and on Series 4600 models. Both features were standard on Series 4700 and 4800 models. Air conditioning. Power seat (except Style 4411). Safety Pad dash on Series 4400. Heater/Defroster. Automatic heat fresh air control. Wonderbar sig-

nal-seeking radio. Transistor portable radio. Sonomatic radio. Electric antenna. Rear seat speaker. Speed control safety buzzer. Deluxe steering wheel on Series 4400. Deluxe wheelcovers on Series 4400. Super Deluxe wheelcovers on Series 4400, 4600 and 4700. Two-speed electric wipers on Series 4400 and 4600. E-Z-Eye glass (windshield only or all glass). Bucket seats (Electra 225 convertible only). Power windows. Power vents. Autronic Eye. Electric rear window for Estate Wagon. Junior third seat for Estate Wagon. Safety Group — safety buzzer, back-up lights, Glare-proof insider rearview mirror, parking brake warning light, and map light (standard Series 4800). Accessory group for Series 4400 — electric clock, trunk light, license frame.

HISTORICAL FOOTNOTES: The 1959 Buick was called "The Year's Most Changed Car." Calendar year output was 232,579. Model year production hit 285,089 for a 5.1 percent share of market. Of all Buicks built in 1959, 11 percent were convertibles. A 1959 Buick served as the Indianapolis 500 pace car. In the spring, Ed Ragsdale retired and Edward T. Rollert was named Buick's general manager. The two-millionth Buick hardtop was presented to Sarah Ragsdale upon her husband's retirement. The one-millionth Opel imported into the United States for sale by a Buick dealer took place in May 1959. The Wildcat III show car was seen this season. Models 4435 and 4635 are Estate Wagons. Model 4829 is the Riviera sedan.

1960

1960 Buick, LeSabre four-door sedan, V-8 (AA)

1960 Buick, LeSabre two-door convertible, V-8

LESABRE — SERIES 4400 — Buick rounded and softened the lines of its 1960 models. Clipping the wild fins of 1959 gave the car a shortened, heavier appearance. Ventiports returned for 1960, with a trio of the highly stylized ornaments on each LeSabre front fender. Series identification was further enhanced by LeSabre name bars on each front fender ahead of the wheelhouse. A bright lower body molding accented the car's other bright metal. Interiors were of Cordaveen and cloth (all-Cordaveen on the station wagon). A plusher Custom interior featuring deep-pile carpeting, padded instrument panel, Deluxe door handles, window cranks and armrests was optional. Standard features of all Specials included Mirromatic adjustable speedometer, electric windshield wipers, trip mileage indicator,

cigar lighter, dual sunshades, Step-On parking brake, dual horns and a single-key locking system.

LESABRE I.D. NUMBERS: Serial numbers were located on the hinge pillar post, left side, above the instrument panel. Serial numbers began with 4G( )001001. The first symbol identified the series, as follows: 4 = 4400; 6 = 4600; 7 = 4700 and 8 = 4800. The second symbol was a letter indicating model year: G = 1960. The third symbol was a number indicating the assembly plant code, as follows: 1 = Flint, Mich.; 2 = Southgate, Calif.; 3 = Linden, N.J.; 4 = Kansas City, Kans.; 5 = Wilmington, Del.; 6 = Atlanta, Ga.; 7 = Framingham, Mass.; 8 = Arlington, Tex. The final six symbols are the numerical sequence of the assembly at the coded plant, with series mixed in production. Engine numbers were stamped in various locations on crankcase, usually, or cylinder block. Engine production codes were stamped on the right side of engine block. Engine codes were as follows: 3G = 364 cid/210 or 250 or 300 hp; L3G = 364 cid/235 hp; 4G = 401 cid/325 hp.

LESABRE SERIES

Series No.	Body/Style No.	Body Type & Seating	Factory Price	Shipping Weight	Prod. Total
4400	4419	4-dr Sed-6P	2870	4219	54,033
4400	4439	4-dr HT-6P	2991	4269	35,999
4400	4411	2-dr Sed-6P	2756	4139	14,388
4400	4437	2-dr HT-6P	2915	4163	26,521
4400	4467	2-dr Conv Cpe-6P	3145	4233	13,588
4400	4445	4-dr Sta Wag-8P	3493	4574	2,222
4400	4435	4-dr Sta Wag-6P	3386	4568	5,331

1960 Buick, LeSabre four-door Estate Wagon, V-8 (OCW)

ENGINE: V-8. Overhead valve. Cast iron block. Displacement: 364 cid. Bore and stroke: 4.125 x 3.4 inches. Compression ratio: 10.25:1. Brake horsepower: 250 at 4400 rpm. Five main bearings. Hydraulic lifters. Carburetor: two-barrels. Stromberg Model WW7-11A; Carter Model 2979 (synchromesh) or Model 2980 (automatic) or Rochester Model 7019042.

1960 Buick, Invicta two-door hardtop, V-8

1960 Buick, Invicta two-door convertible, V-8 (OCW)

INVICTA — SERIES 4600 — "The most spirited Buick," read the sales catalog in its description of the Invicta. Wearing three ventiports per front fender, the Invicta had all of the LeSabre's brightwork plus bright metal wheelhouse moldings. The front

fender plaques earned Invicta lettering, of course. Interiors were cloth and Cordaveen with all-Cordaveen color-coordinated trim optional (standard in the convertible). Station wagon styles were trimmed in Saran cloth and Cordaveen. Standard Invicta features in addition to those found on the LeSabre included Twin Turbine automatic transmission, Foamtex seat cushions, electric clock, trunk light, Deluxe steering wheel, Deluxe wheelcovers, license plate frames and a glovebox light.

1960 Buick, Invicta four-door Estate Wagon, V-8

INVICTA I.D. NUMBERS: Serial numbers were distinguished by the use of the numeral '6' as the first symbol of the number. The rest of the number was coded as explained under the 1960 LeSabre Series 4400 I.D. Number section.

INVICTA SERIES

Series No.	Body/Style No.	Body Type & Seating	Factory Price	Shipping Weight	Prod. Total
4600	4619	4-dr Sed-6P	3357	4324	10,839
4600	4639	4-dr HT-6P	3515	4365	15,300
4600	4637	2-dr HT-6P	3447	4255	8,960
4600	4667	2-dr Conv Cpe-6P	3620	4347	5,236
4600	4645	4-dr Sta Wag-8P	3948	4679	1,605
4600	4635	4-dr Sta Wag-6P	3841	4644	3,471

ENGINE: V-8. Overhead valve. Cast iron block. Displacement: 401 cid. Bore and stroke: 4.1875 x 3.640 inches. Compression ratio: 10.25:1. Brake horsepower: 325 at 4400 rpm. Five main bearings. Hydraulic lifters. Carburetor: four-barrel Carter Model 29825 or Rochester 7015040.

1960 Buick, Electra four-door sedan, V-8 (OCW)

ELECTRA — SERIES 4700 — A larger Buick, identified by its four ventiports per front fender, had wider rocker panel bright moldings and the Electra script on the front fenders, ahead of the wheelhouse. Electras had plusher cloth and Cordaveen interiors and featured power steering, power brakes and all the features found on the Invicta and LeSabre models as standard.

ELECTRA I.D. NUMBERS: Serial numbers were distinguished by the use of the numeral '7' as the first symbol of the number. The rest of the number was coded as explained under the 1960 LeSabre 4400 I.D. Number section.

ELECTRA SERIES

Series No.	Body/Style No.	Body Type & Seating	Factory Price	Shipping Weight	Prod. Total
4700	4719	4-dr Sed-6P	3856	4544	13,794
4700	4739	4-dr HT-6P	3963	4554	14,488
4700	4737	2-dr HT-6P	3818	4453	7,416

ENGINE: Specifications were the same as those listed for the 1960 Invicta.

ELECTRA 225 — SERIES 4800 — Buick's plushest, fanciest model was outstanding this year with its broad, ribbed, lower body bright trim panels. An Electra 225 badge was circled on the deck lid. The Electra 225 name was found on the front fenders. Brisbane cloth interiors graced closed models while the convertible was trimmed in leather with bucket seats for front passenger optional. All of Buick's standard features were found on the Electra, plus back-up lights, a Glare-proof rearview mirror, parking brake signal light, safety buzzer, map light, Super Deluxe wheelcovers and a two-way power seat adjuster and power windows for the convertible.

ELECTRA 225 I.D. NUMBERS: Serial numbers were distinguished by the use of the numeral '8' as the first symbol of the number. The rest of the number was coded as explained under the 1960 LeSabre Series 4400 I.D. Number section.

1960 Buick, Electra 225 four-door hardtop, V-8 (AA)

ELECTRA 225 SERIES

Series No.	Body/Style No.	Body Type & Seating	Factory Price	Shipping Weight	Prod. Total
4800	4829	4-dr Sed-6P	4300	4653	8,029
4800	4839	4-dr HT-6P	4300	4650	4,841
4800	4867	2-dr Conv Cpe-6P	4192	4571	6,746

ENGINE: Specifications were the same as those listed for the 1960 Invicta.

CHASSIS FEATURES: Wheelbase: (4400/4600) 123 inches; (4700) 126.3 inches; (4800) 126.3 inches. Overall length: (4400/4600) 217.9 inches; (4700) 221.2 inches; (4800) 225.9 inches. Front tread: (all) 62.2 inches. Rear tread: (all) 60 inches. Tires: (4400/4600) 7.60 x 15; (4700/4800) 8.00 x 15.

POWERTRAIN OPTIONS: A regular fuel Wildcat 375E V-8 was optional on Series 4400 models. This engine featured a 9.1:1 compression ratio and produced 235 brake horsepower at 4400 rpm and cost $52 extra. A high-performance Wildcat 405 four-barrel V-8 was also optional on Series 4400 models with three-speed manual transmission. This combination featured 300 horsepower at 4400 rpm and cost $220 additional. (Buick's engine I.D. numbers were based on the torque rating, rather than the horsepower rating).

CONVENIENCE OPTIONS: Power steering was standard on Series 4700 and 4800 models and optional on Series 4400 and 4600 models ($108). Power brakes were standard on Series 4700 and 4800 models, optional on others. ($43). Air conditioning ($430). Twilight Sentinel automatic headlamp dimmer ($29). Tissue dispenser. Compass. Visor vanity mirror. Trunk mat (plastic foam-backed). Deluxe handy mats. Litter basket. Six-way power seat ($52-$103). Six/Two-Way power seat ($69). Four-way power seat ($65). Two-way power seat ($37). Bucket seats ($108). Power vent windows ($54). Power windows ($108). Sonotone radio with manual antenna ($99); with electric antenna ($121). Wonder Bar radio with manual antenna ($135); with electric antenna ($158). Rear seat speaker ($17). Guidematic ($43). Deluxe steering wheel on LeSabre ($16). Deluxe wheelcovers on LeSabre ($19). Super Deluxe wheelcovers ($17-$37). Heater and defroster ($99). E-Z-Eye glass ($29-$43). White sidewall tires. Custom exterior moldings ($13-$41). Station wagon electric rear window ($27). Station wagon luggage rack ($100). Standard two-tone finish ($16-$43). Special order two-toning ($97). Dual exhaust ($31). Turbine Drive transmission ($220). Dual-speed windshield washers/wipers ($19). Accessory group including trunk compartment light, electric clock and license plate frame for LeSabre ($22). Safety acces-

sory group including Glare-proof rearview mirror, back-up lights, parking brake warning signal and safety buzzer light for 4400-4600-4700 Series ($34).

HISTORICAL FOOTNOTES: Calendar year production was 307,804 for a 4.65 percent share of market, putting Buick in ninth place. It was the lowest industry ranking for the company since 1905! Model year production was 253,999 units or 4.2 percent of the industry total. Buick firsts for 1960 included a K-type Buick chassis, Twilight Sentinel, Mirrormagic adjustable angle instrument dials and separate heater controls for rear seat passengers. A 1960 Buick was taken to the Daytona International Speedway in Daytona Beach, Fla., and run for three-and-a-half days (10,000 miles) at an average of 120.12 mph. At times the car ran over 130 mph. After this impressive performance feat, Buick decided not to advertise or promote the results of the trial, due to the Automobile Manufacturer's Association (AMA) ban on high-performance advertising. Models 4435, 4445, 4635 and 4645 are Estate Wagons. Model 4829 is the Riviera sedan.

1961 Buick, Special Deluxe four-door sedan, V-8 (AA)

SPECIAL — SERIES 4000 STANDARD/4100 AND 4300 DELUXE — Buick's new quality car in a small package immediately found an enthusiastic following. Styling was related to the larger 1961 Buicks. Specials had three ventiport appliques per front fender. Trim was minimal on the Special. Standard features of the Special included dual sun visors, dual armrests, cigar lighter and electric windshield wipers. The base Special was trimmed in cloth and vinyl. Deluxe models had richer Custom interiors of cloth and vinyl (all-vinyl in the station wagon), plush carpeting, rear armrests, rear ashtrays and a Deluxe steering wheel. They were distinguished by Custom exterior moldings, which included a highlight bright strip on the upper body. A midyear Skylark Sport Coupe was added (Model 4317) that featured unique emblems. An even plusher all-vinyl interior, came with optional bucket front seats and unique taillamp housings, additional lower body bright moldings and Turbine wheelcovers. A vinyl top was standard.

SPECIAL I.D. NUMBERS: Serial numbers were located on the hinge pillar post, left side above instrument panel. They were also stamped on the top surface of the engine block, left side, ahead of valve cover. Serial numbers began with OH( )501001-up. The first symbol indicated series, as follows: 0 = 4000; 1 = 4100; or 3 = 4300. The second symbol was a letter indicating model year: H = 1961. The third symbol was a number indicating the plant code, as follows: 1 = Flint, Mich.; 2 = Southgate, Calif.; 3 = Linden, N.J.; 4 = Kansas City, Kans.; 5 = Wilmington, Del.; 6 = Atlanta, Ga.; 8 = Arlington, Tex. The last six symbols are the numerical sequence of assembly at the coded plant, with series mixed in production. Engine production codes stamped upside down on right front of engine block, opposite serial number. Production codes were as follows: (Special) 215 cid V-8 = H, LH; (Special Deluxe) same; (Skylark) same.

SPECIAL STANDARD MODELS

Series No.	Body/Style No.	Body Type & Seating	Factory Price	Shipping Weight	Prod. Total
4000	4019	4-dr Sed-6P	2384	2610	18,339
4000	4027	2-dr Spt Cpe-6P	2330	2579	4,230
4000	4035	4-dr Sta Wag-6P	2681	2775	6,101
4000	4045	4-dr Sta Wag-8P	2762	2844	798

SPECIAL DELUXE MODELS

Series No.	Body/Style No.	Body Type & Seating	Factory Price	Shipping Weight	Prod. Total
4100	4119	4-dr Sed-6P	2519	2632	32,986
4100	4135	4-dr Sta Wag-6P	2816	2794	11,729
4300	4317	2-dr Spt Cpe-5P	2621	2687	12,683

ENGINE: V-8. Overhead valve. Cast aluminum block. Displacement: 215 cid. Bore and stroke: 3.50 x 2.80 inches. Compression ratio: 8.8:1. Brake horsepower: 155 at 4600 rpm. Five main bearings. Hydraulic valve lifters. Carburetor: two-barrel Rochester Model 7019090 (automatic) or Model 7019093 (manual).

NOTE: Skylark was equipped with four-barrel Rochester Model 7020043 (automatic) or Model 7020045 (manual) and had 10.25:1 compression ratio, 185 brake horsepower.

1961 Buick, LeSabre four-door hardtop, V-8 (AA)

LESABRE — SERIES 4400 — A new slimmer and trimmer image was presented by Buick's sales leading series for 1961. Body sculpturing allowed for a relatively light application of exterior brightwork, with a single narrow bright molding along the upper body. LeSabre script was found on the front fenders, along with three ventiports. Turbine drive automatic transmission was standard on the 1961 LeSabre, along with a revised Mirromagic instrument panel, directional signals, full-flow oil filter, electric windshield wipers, a Deluxe steering wheel, trip mileage indicator, cigar lighter, Step-On brake, dual armrests, cloth and vinyl trim combinations and carpeting on some models. Estate station wagons had a standard all-vinyl interior, with cloth and vinyl optional. A power rear window was standard on the three-seat Estate Wagon.

LESABRE I.D. NUMBERS: Buick serial numbers were located on the hinge pillar post, left side, above instrument panel and on top surface of engine block, ahead of valve cover on left. The first symbol indicated series as follows: (LeSabre) 4 = 4400; (Invicta) 6 = 4600; (Electra) 7 = 4700; and (Electra 225) 8 = 4800. The second symbol was a letter indicating model year: H = 1961. The third symbol was a number indicating the plant code, as follows: 1 = Flint, Mich., 2 = Southgate, Calif., 3 = Linden, N.J., 4 = Kansas City, Kans., 5 = Wilmington, Del., 6 = Atlanta, Ga., 8 = Arlington, Tex. The last six symbols are the numerical sequence of assembly at the coded plant, with series mixed in production. Engine production codes stamped upside down on right front of block opposite serial number. Engine production codes were as follows: (LeSabre) 364 cid V-8 = 3H or L3H; (Invicta/Electra) 401 cid V-8 = 4H or 4LH.

LESABRE SERIES 4400

Series No.	Body/Style No.	Body Type & Seating	Factory Price	Shipping Weight	Prod. Total
4400	4469	4-dr Sed-6P	3107	4102	35,005
4400	4439	4-dr HT-6P	3228	4129	37,790
4400	4411	2-dr Sed-6P	2993	4033	5,959
4400	4437	2-dr HT-6P	3152	4054	14,474
4400	4467	2-dr Conv Cpe-6P	3382	4186	11,971
4400	4435	4-dr Sta Wag-6P	3623	4450	5,628
4400	4445	4-dr Sta Wag-9P	3730	4483	2,423

ENGINE: V-8. Overhead valve. Cast iron block. Displacement: 364 cid. Bore and stroke: 4.25 x 3.4 inches. Compression ratio: 10.25:1. Brake horsepower: 250 at 4400 rpm. Five main bearings. Hydraulic valve lifters. Carburetor: Carter Model 3089 four-barrel.

1961 Buick, Invicta two-door hardtop, V-8 (AA)

INVICTA — SERIES 4600 — Buick's slightly sportier performance line was graced with double belt moldings, in 1961, to set it apart from the LeSabre, with which it shared three ventiports per front fender. Invicta nameplates were used on each front fender, as well as the rear deck. Full wheelcovers, an electric clock, automatic trunk light and license frame were additional standard features of the Invicta over lesser models. Standard trim was cloth and vinyl, except for the convertible, which was all-vinyl. An optional Custom interior featured leather trim, while another featured vinyl with contrasting vertical stripes and front bucket seats with a storage consolex and power two-way seat adjustment.

INVICTA I.D. NUMBERS: Serial numbers were distinguished by the use of the numeral '6' as the first symbol of the number. The rest of the number was coded as explained under the 1961 LeSabre I.D. Number section.

INVICTA SERIES 4600

Series No.	Body/Style No.	Body Type & Seating	Factory Price	Shipping Weight	Prod. Total
4600	4639	4-dr HT-6P	3515	4179	18,398
4600	4637	2-dr HT-6P	3447	4090	6,382
4600	4667	2-dr Conv Cpe-6P	3620	4206	3,953

ENGINE: V-8. Overhead valve. Cast iron block. Displacement: 401 cid. Bore and stroke: 4.1875 x 3.640 inches. Compression ratio: 10.25:1. Brake horsepower: 325 at 4400 rpm. Five main bearings. Hydraulic valve lifters. Carburetor: four-barrel Carter Model 3088S.

ELECTRA — SERIES 4700 — Buick's first step up to the larger models featured bright rocker panel and wheelhouse moldings for 1961. Four ventiports per front fender were a hallmark, with identification spelled out on the front fender plaques. Interiors were trimmed in fabric. Standard Electra features included those of lower-priced Buicks, plus power steering, power brakes, a two-speed windshield wiper/washer system, glovebox light, Custom-padded seat cushions and Deluxe wheelcovers. Two-tone Electras had a color accent on the rear cove.

ELECTRA I.D. NUMBERS: Serial numbers were distinguished by the use of the numeral '7' as the first symbol of the number. The rest of the number was coded as explained under the 1961 LeSabre I.D. Number section.

ELECTRA SERIES 4700

Series No.	Body/Style No.	Body Type & Seating	Factory Price	Shipping Weight	Prod. Total
4700	4719	4-dr Sed-6P	3825	4298	13,818
4700	4739	4-dr HT-6P	3932	4333	8,978
4700	4737	2-dr HT-6P	3818	4260	4,250

ENGINE: Specifications were the same as those listed for the 1961 Invicta.

1961 Buick, Electra 225 two-door convertible, V-8 (AA)

ELECTRA 225 — SERIES 4800 — Buick's plushest model had a wide strip of bright trim along the lower body, with vertical "hash marks" interrupting behind the wheelhouse of the rear fender. Electra 225 nameplates were found on the front fenders. Calais cloth or leather trim was found inside. Standard equipment was the same as the Electra except for the addition of back-up lights, Glare-proof rearview mirror, parking brake signal light, safety buzzer, courtesy lights, two-way power seat, Super Deluxe wheelcovers with gold accents and power windows.

1961 Buick, Electra 225 Riviera four-door hardtop, V-8

ELECTRA 225 I.D. NUMBERS: Serial numbers were distinguished by the use of the numeral '8' as the first symbol of the number. The rest of the number was coded as explained under the 1961 LeSabre I.D. Number section.

ELECTRA 225 SERIES 4800

Series No.	Body/Style No.	Body Type & Seating	Factory Price	Shipping Weight	Prod. Total
4800	4829	4-dr HT Sed-6P	4350	4417	13,719
4800	4867	2-dr Conv Cpe-6P	4192	4441	7,158

ENGINE: Specifications were the same as listed for the 1961 Invicta.

CHASSIS FEATURES: Wheelbase: (4000, 4100 and 4300) 112 inches; (4400 and 4600) 123 inches; (4700 and 4800) 126 inches. Overall length: (4000, 4100 and 4300) 188.4 inches; (4400 and 4600) 213.2 inches; (4700 and 4800) 219.2 inches. Front tread: (Special) 56 inches; (Others) 62 inches. Rear tread: (Special) 56 inches; (Others) 61 inches. Tires: (4000, 4100 and 4300) 6.50 x 13; (4400 and 4600) 7.60 x 15; (4700 and 4800) 8.00 x 15.

POWERTRAIN OPTIONS: A three-speed manual transmission was standard on Series 4000, 4100 and 4300. Dual-path Turbine Drive was optional ($189). A four-speed manual transmission was also an option for the Series 4300 Skylark. A regular fuel V-8 was optional for the Series 4400 and was the same basic 364-cid engine with two-barrel carburetor, 9.0:1 compression and 235 brake horsepower at 4400 rpm. Dual exhaust were standard on the Series 4700 two-door hardtop and Series 4800 convertible, optional on all other full-size models. Positive traction differential was offered.

CONVENIENCE OPTIONS: Power steering on 4000, 4100, 4300 ($86); and 4400, 4600 ($108, standard on 4700 and 4800). Power brakes ($43, standard on 4700 and 4800). Air conditioning ($378 on 4000, 4100, 4300; $430 on full-size models). Size 7.00 x 13 tires on 4300. Power windows ($108, standard on 4800). Four-way power seat adjustment ($65). Sonotone radio

($90). Wonderbar radio ($127). Twilight Sentinel ($29). Guide-matic dimmer ($43). Heater/Defroster ($99). Deluxe Special wheelcovers ($15). Back-up lights (standard on 4800). Cool-Pak air conditioning on 4000, 4100 and 4300. Luggage rack on Estate Wagons ($100). Power rear window on six-passenger Estate Wagon ($27).

1961-1/2 Buick, Skylark two-door Sport Coupe, V-8 (PH)

HISTORICAL FOOTNOTES: The big news of 1961 was the return of the Special name. It was also the first time, since 1907, that Buicks did not have torque tube drive and the first time, since 1934, that the accelerator was not mounted on the starter. Calendar year production was 291,895 units for a 5.28 market share. Model year production was 277,422 units for a 5.1 percent share of industry output. Buick held the eighth place in popularity. Model 4829 was the Riviera sedan. Models 4435 and 4445 were Estate Wagons.

1962

1962 Buick, Special two-door sedan, V-6 (OCW)

1962 Buick, Special four-door station wagon, V-6 (OCW)

SPECIAL — SERIES 4000 — The second edition of Buick's compact Special was little changed from the 1961 version. Once again the basic Special had no bright side trim except for three ventiports per front fender and a Special script ahead of the

front wheelhouse. Small hubcaps were standard, as were dual sun visors, dual armrests, cigar lighter and electric windshield wipers, directional signals, heater and defroster and outside rearview mirror on convertible. Interiors were cloth and vinyl.

SPECIAL I.D. NUMBERS: Serial numbers were on the hinge pillar post, left side, above instrument panel and stamped on left side, top of engine block, ahead of valve cover. The first symbol was a letter or number denoting the series, as follows: (6-cyl.) A = 4000; B = 4100; C = 4300; (V-8) 0 = 4000;1 = 4100; 3 = 4300. The second symbol indicated model year: I for 1962. The third symbol () is a number indicating the assembly plant code, as follows: 1 = Flint, Mich.; 2 = Southgate, Calif.; 3 = Linden, N.J.; 4 = Kansas City, Kans.; 5 = Wilmington, Del.; 6 = Atlanta, Ga.; 8 = Arlington, Tex. The last six symbols are the numerical sequence of assembly at the coded plant, with series mixed in production. Engine numbers were located in various places on the crankcase, usually, or on the cylinder block. Along with serial number, the engines carried a production code with a prefix identifying engine and year, then a four symbol sequential production number: (V-8s) stamped front right of block opposite serial number; (V-6) on front of block below left cylinder head gasket. Special engine codes were as follows: (198 cid V-6) 6I; (215 cid V-8) = I, LI, HI.

SPECIAL SERIES 4000

Series No.	Body/Style No.	Body Type & Seating	Factory Price	Shipping Weight	Prod. Total
4000	4019	4-dr Sed-6P	2358	2666	23,249
4000	4027	2-dr Sed-6P	2304	2638	19,135
4000	4067	2-dr Conv-6P	2587	2858	7,918
4000	4045	4-dr Sta Wag-8P	2736	2896	2,814
4000	4035	4-dr Sta Wag-6P	2655	2876	7,382

ENGINE: V-6. Overhead valve. Cast iron block. Displacement: 198 cid. Bore and stroke: 3.625 x 3.2 inches. Compression ratio: 8.8:1. Brake horsepower: 135 at 4600 rpm. Four main bearings. Hydraulic valve lifters. Carburetor: Rochester 2GC two-barrel.

ENGINE: V-8. Overhead valve. Cast aluminum block. Displacement: 215 cid. Bore and stroke: 3.50 x 2.80 inches. Compression ratio: 9.0:1. Brake horsepower: 155 at 4600 rpm. Five main bearings. Hydraulic valve lifters. Carburetor: Rochester 2GC two-barrel.

1962 Buick, Special Deluxe two-door convertible, V-8 (PH)

SPECIAL DELUXE — SERIES 4100 — A slightly plusher Special, with a bright strip along the body, nicer vinyls and fabrics inside, and full carpeting. Rear armrests, rear ashtrays, a Deluxe steering wheel, foam seat cushions, cigarette lighter, oil filter and dual horns and visors were additional features found on the Deluxe.

SPECIAL DELUXE I.D. NUMBERS: Serial numbers were distinguished by the use of a B (6-cyl.) or 1 (V-8) as first symbol of the number. The rest of the number was coded as explained under the 1962 Special Series 4000 I.D. Number section.

SPECIAL DELUXE SERIES 4100

Series No.	Body/Style No.	Body Type & Seating	Factory Price	Shipping Weight	Prod. Total
4100	4119	4-dr Sed-6P	2593	2648	31,660
4100	4167	2-dr Conv-6P	2879	2820	8,332
4100	4135	4-dr Sta Wag-6P	2890	2845	10,300

ENGINE: Specifications were the same as listed for the 1962 Special Series 4000 V-8.

1962 Buick, Skylark two-door hardtop, V-8 (AA)

SKYLARK — SERIES 4300 — Buick's most refined compact featured a new convertible model and slightly changed styling for 1962. The hardtop coupe was of true "hardtop" design this year, without a side window. The Skylark had a Buick emblem centered in the grille and a Skylark badge on each front fender, along with the three ventiports. Taillamp housings wrapped around onto the rear fenders. Lower body bright rocker and wheelhouse moldings accented the Skylark, which came with Turbine wheelcovers. Interiors were all-vinyl, with front bucket seats. Standard features, in addition to those found on the lesser Specials, included a padded dash, Skylark steering wheel, heater and defroster, rear courtesy lamps and, on the convertible, a power top.

1962 Buick, Skylark two-door convertible, V-8 (PH)

SKYLARK I.D. NUMBERS: Serial numbers were distinguished by the use of a C (6-cyl.) or 3 (V-8) as first symbol of the number. The rest of the number was coded as explained under the 1962 Special Series 4000 I.D. Number section.

SKYLARK SERIES 4300

Series No.	Body/Style No.	Body Type & Seating	Factory Price	Shipping Weight	Prod. Total
4300	4347	2-dr HT-6P	2787	2707	34,060
4300	4367	2-dr Conv-5P	3012	2871	8,913

ENGINE: V-8. Specifications were the same as those listed for the 1962 Special Series 4000 V-8 except compression ratio was 11.0:1, a four-barrel Rochester 4GC carburetor was used and brake horsepower was 190 at 4800 rpm.

1962 Buick, LeSabre two-door hardtop, V-8 (AA)

LESABRE — SERIES 4400 — Refreshing new lines graced the 1962 LeSabre, although its body structure was unchanged from 1961. Still sporting a trio of ventiports on each front fender, LeSabres were identified by script on the front fenders and emblems front and rear. The two-door hardtop featured a new landau style top simulating a raised convertible top, but it was steel and fixed in position. Standard features included directional signals, full-flow oil filter, electric windshield wipers, a Deluxe steering wheel, cigar lighter, Step-On parking brake, dual armrests, Turbine drive transmission, padded dashboard, heater and defroster and glovebox light. Interiors were cloth and vinyl combinations.

LESABRE I.D. NUMBERS: Buick serial numbers were on the hinge pillar post, left side, above instrument panel and stamped on left side, top of engine block, ahead of valve cover. The first symbol was a number indicating the series, as follows: (LeSabre) 4 = 4000 Series; (Invicta) 6 = 4600 Series; (Electra) 7 = 4700 Series and (Electra 225) 8 = 4800 Series. The second symbol indicated model year, I for 1962. The third symbol ( ) is a number indicating the assembly plant code, as follows: 1 = Flint, Mich.; 2 = Southgate, Calif.; 3 = Linden, N.J.; 4 = Kansas City, Kans.; 5 = Wilmington, Del.; 6 = Atlanta, Ga.; and 8 = Arlington, Tex. The last six symbols are the numerical sequence of assembly at the coded plant, with series mixed in production. Engine numbers were located in various places on the crankcase, usually, or on the cylinder block. Along with serial number, the engines carried a production code with a prefix identifying engine and year, then a four symbol sequential production number. Numbers stamped on front right of block opposite serial number. Engine codes were as follows: (401 cid V-8) 2I, L2I, 4I, L4I.

LESABRE SERIES 4400

Series No.	Body/Style No.	Body Type & Seating	Factory Price	Shipping Weight	Prod. Total
4400	4469	4-dr Sed-6P	3227	4104	56,783
4400	4439	4-dr HT Sed-6P	3369	4156	37,518
4400	4411	2-dr Sed-6P	3091	4041	7,418
4400	4447	2-dr HT-6P	3293	4054	25,479

ENGINE: V-8. Overhead valve. Cast iron block. Displacement: 401 cid. Bore and stroke: 4.1875 x 3.64 inches. Compression ratio: 10.25:1. Brake horsepower: 280 at 4400 rpm. Five main bearings. Hydraulic valve lifters. Carburetor: Rochester two-barrel Model 2GC.

1962 Buick, Invicta four-door Estate Wagon, V-8 (AA)

INVICTA — SERIES 4600 — The Invicta models had all of LeSabre's features, plus Deluxe wheelcovers and the engine 'Power Pak' (four-barrel induction system). The four-door hardtop and two-door hardtop also had the Code 06 Accessory Group (trunk light, electric clock and license plate frames) as standard equipment, plus padded cushions. The distinctive Invicta nine-passenger station wagon offered a power tailgate as a regular feature and the convertible in the line came equipped with an outside rearview mirror. All models in this line were generally plusher than LeSabres, although both series shared the same body shell. Exterior distinction came from the use of Invicta front fender badges, with other trim items matching the LeSabre theme.

NOTE: The Wildcat Sport Coupe was part of the Invicta line, featuring Custom equipment including a Deluxe steering wheel, all-vinyl front bucket seats with a center console housing the Turbine drive transmission lever, a tachometer, and rear floor lamp. An electric clock, chrome roof bows and license frames

were other Wildcat equipment. The Wildcat Sport Coupe had a vinyl top covering, with Wildcat emblems on the roof quarter panels and special wheelcovers. Custom bright metal exterior moldings, including lower body rocker panel and wheelhouse bright trim, were used. Dual exhaust were standard. The Wildcat was included with the Invicta hardtop coupe's 13,471 production figure and shared its 4647 model number. However, Wildcat listed for $3,927 and weighed 4,150 pounds.

1962-1/2 Buick, (Invicta) Wildcat two-door hardtop, V-8 (PH)

INVICTA I.D. NUMBERS: Serial numbers were distinguished by the use of a '6' as first symbol of the number. The rest of the number was coded as explained under the 1962 LeSabre Series I.D. Number section.

INVICTA SERIES 4600

Series No.	Body/Style No.	Body Type & Seating	Factory Price	Shipping Weight	Prod. Total
4600	4639	4-dr HT Sed-6P	3667	4159	16,443
4600	4547	2-dr HT Cpe-6P	3733	4077	12,355
4600	4667	2-dr Conv-6P	3617	4217	13,471
4600	4645	4-dr Sta Wag-8P	3917	4505	4,617
4600	4635	4-dr Sta Wag-6P	3836	4471	9,131

NOTE: Wildcat — see reference in text in note above.

ENGINE: Specifications were the same as the LeSabre Series 4400 except brake horsepower was 325 and a Rochester 4GC or Carter AFB four-barrel carburetor was used.

1962 Buick, Electra 225 two-door hardtop, V-8 (AA)

ELECTRA 225 — SERIES 4800 — The big Buick for 1962 carried four ventiports per front fender and featured a rakish, sculptured restyle of its 1961 guise. The hardtop coupe and new Model 4839 hardtop sedan featured a convertible-inspired semi-formal roofline, while the Model 4829 Riviera sedan continued to use a six-window pillarless configuration. Electra 225 rear fenders had a group of vertical hashmarks, with Electra 225 spelled out in block letters just above. A full-length bright strip crowned the upper body ridge, while the tower rocker moldings and wheelhouses were accented with bright trim. Wheelcovers had a gold accent ring. Interiors were of the finest cloth and, on the convertible, leather was used. Standard features, in addition to those found on the less expensive Buicks, included back-up lights, power steering, Glare-proof rearview mirror, power brakes, parking brake signal light, safety buzzer, courtesy lights, two-way power seats, power windows, dual speed washer/wipers, Super Deluxe wheelcovers, Safety option group, custom padded cushions, Accessory Group options and custom moldings.

ELECTRA 225 I.D. NUMBERS: Serial numbers were distinguished by the use of the numeral '8' as the first symbol of the number. The rest of the number was coded as explained under the 1962 LeSabre I.D. Number section.

ELECTRA 225 SERIES 4800

Series No.	Body/Style No.	Body Type & Seating	Factory Price	Shipping Weight	Prod. Total
4800	4819	4-dr Sed-6P	4051	4304	13,523
4800	4829	4-dr Riv Sed-6P	4448	4390	15,395
4800	4839	4-dr HT Sed-6P	4186	4309	16,734
4800	4847	2-dr HT Cpe-6P	4062	4235	8,922
4800	4867	2-dr Conv-6P	4366	4396	7,894

ENGINE: Specifications were the same as those listed for the 1962 Invicta Series 4600.

CHASSIS FEATURES: Wheelbase: (Series 4000, 4100 and 4300) 112.1 inches; (Series 4400 and 4600) 123 inches; (Series 4800) 126 inches. Overall length: (Series 4000, 4100 and 4300) 188.4 inches; (Series 4400 and 4600) 214.1 inches; (Series 4800) 220.1 inches; (Estate wagons) 213.6 inches. Front tread: (Series 4000, 4100 and 4300) 56 inches; (Series 4400, 4600 and 4800) 62.1 inches. Rear Tread: (Series 4000, 4100 and 4300) 56 inches; (Series 4400, 4600 and 4800) 61 inches. Tires: (Series 4000, 4100 and 4300) 6.50 x 13; (Series 4400 and 4600) 7.60 x 15; (Series 4800) 8.00 x 15.

POWERTRAIN OPTIONS: A three-speed manual transmission was standard on Series 4000, 4100 and 4300. Turbine drive was optional ($189). A four-speed was optional for V-8s ($200). The 190 brake horsepower Skylark V-8 was optional on the Special ($145) and on the Special Deluxe ($39). A regular fuel V-8 was optional on the LeSabre Series 4400; it was the same basic 401-cid engine with 9.0:1 compression ratio and 265 brake horsepower. The Wildcat 401 cid/325 hp V-8 was optional on the LeSabre. Also available was a 401 cid/280 hp engine. Turbine drive was standard on Series 4400, 4600 and 4800.

BUICK CONVENIENCE OPTIONS: Air conditioning ($430). Air conditioning modification ($24). PCV system ($5). Custom padded cushions as option ($23). Divided rear seat on station wagons ($38). Chrome door guards two-door/four-door ($5/$9). Posi Traction ($48). Dual exhaust as option ($31). Tinted glass, all windows/windshield only ($43/$29). GuideMatic ($29). Luggage locker for station wagon ($22). Station wagon luggage rack ($100). Outside remote control rearview mirror ($12). Power brakes ($43). Power door locks ($70). Four-barrel Power-Pack ($22). Six-way power seat ($97). Six/Two-way power seat ($69). Four-way power seat ($65). Four/Two-way power seat ($37). Power steering ($108). Power trunk release ($10). Sonotone radio with manual/electric antennas ($90/$116). Wonder Bar radio with manual/electric antennas ($127/$153). Rear seat speaker ($17). Convertible bucket seats w/console ($229). Coupe bucket seats w/console ($296). Power bucket seat option ($129 extra). Twilight Sentinel ($29). Code 06 Accessory Group ($22). Safety Options Group: Glare-proof mirror, back-up lamps, parking brake warning signal, safety buzzer light, courtesy lights ($40).

BUICK SPECIAL CONVENIENCE OPTIONS: Air conditioning ($351). Code W1 185-horsepower engine, Series 4000 ($145)/Series 4100 ($39). Back-up lights ($11). Padded dash ($13-$26). Two-tone finish ($16). Power brakes ($43). Power steering ($86). Power windows ($102). Bucket seats, Series 4000/4100 ($96/$70). Turbine drive ($189). Four-speed manual transmission ($200). Deluxe wheelcovers ($15).

HISTORICAL FOOTNOTES: Not since 1956 had Buick built and sold as many cars as delivered in 1962. Calendar year deliveries were 415,892 while model year production stood at 400,150 for six percent of industry. The company captured 6.1 percent of U.S. sales and the Special Series gained 65 percent over the previous year. The new V-6 gave the Special a price edge in the growing domestic small car market. It was the first production V-6 in an American car and was available only in base Series Specials. It was developed in just six months. *Motor Trend* named the 1962 Buick V-6 the "Car of the Year." Tooling for the V-6 was later sold to American Motors for use in the Jeep. It was then repurchased, by Buick, in 1974 to use in more energy efficient

cars. In 1962, Dan Gurney drove a Buick V-8-powered race car, built by Mickey Thompson, in the Indianapolis 500. The car qualified at 147.88 mph and completed 92 laps before being forced out with mechanical difficulties to the rear axle. The Buick-powered Apollo sports car (See "Minor Makes" section) bowed in 1962. It was first built in Italy. On standard Buicks the engines were moved four inches forward, decreasing the size of floor humps. Style Numbers 4645 and 4635 were called Estate Wagons. Style Number 4829 was known as the Riviera sedan.

1963

1963 Buick, Special Skylark two-door hardtop, V-8 (AA)

SPECIAL — SERIES 4000 — An almost complete lack of brightwork on the bodysides of a new, slightly larger and much more square-cut bodyshell was a 1963 Special hallmark. There were three bright metal ventiports on each front fender. A vertical bar grille was spread across the car's flat face. Special series script appeared high on the rear fender. Interiors were done in cloth and vinyl, except for the convertible, which had all-vinyl upholstery.

SPECIAL I.D. NUMBERS: Serial numbers were on the hinge pillar post, left side, above instrument panel and stamped on left side, top of engine block, ahead of valve cover. The first symbol was a letter or number denoting the series, as follows: (6-cyl.) A = 4000; B = 4100; C = 4300, (V-8) 0 = 4000, 1 = 4100, 3 = 4300. The second symbol indicated model year: J for 1963. The third symbol ( ) is a number indicating the assembly plant code, as follows: 1 = Flint, Mich., 2 = Southgate, Calif., 3 = Linden, N.J., 4 = Kansas City, Kans., 5 = Wilmington, Del., 6 = Atlanta, Ga., and 8 = Arlington, Tex. The last six symbols are the numerical sequence of assembly at the coded plant, with series mixed in production. Engine numbers were located in various places on the crankcase, usually, or on the cylinder block. Along with serial number, the engines carried a production code with a prefix identifying engine and year, then a four symbol sequential production number: (V-8s) stamped front right of block opposite serial number, (V-6) on front of block below left cylinder head gasket. Special engine codes were as follows: (198 cid V-6) JL, JZ; (215 cid V-8) JM, JN, JP.

SPECIAL SERIES 4000

Series No.	Body/Style No.	Body Type & Seating	Factory Price	Shipping Weight	Prod. Total
4000	4019	4-dr Sed-6P	2363	2696	21,733
4000	4027	2-dr Sed-6P	2309	2661	21,866
4000	4067	2-dr Conv-6P	2591	2768	8,082
4000	4045	4-dr Sta Wag-8P	2740	2903	2,415
4000	4035	4-dr Sta Wag-6P	2659	2866	5,867

ENGINE: V-6. Overhead valves. Cast iron block. Displacement: 198 cid. Bore and stroke: 3.625 x 3.2 inches. Compression ratio: 8.8:1. Brake horsepower: 135 at 4600 rpm. Four main bearings. Hydraulic valve lifters. Rochester 2GC two-barrel carburetor.

ENGINE: V-8. Overhead valves. Cast aluminum block. Displacement: 215 cid. Bore and stroke: 3.5 x 2.8 inches. Compression ratio: 8.8:1. Brake horsepower: 155 at 4600 rpm. Five main bearings. Hydraulic valve lifters. Rochester 2GC two-barrel carburetor.

1963 Buick, Special Deluxe four-door sedan, V-6

SPECIAL DELUXE — SERIES 4100 — Exterior distinction for Deluxe models came from a narrow, full-length bodyside molding. Otherwise the trim was identical to the base line, except on the interior where upholstery combinations were richer.

SPECIAL DELUXE SERIES 4100 I.D. NUMBERS: Serial numbers for cars equipped with the V-6 began with BJ ( ) 501001. Serial numbers for cars equipped with the V-8 began with 1J ( ) 501001. The number coded as explained under the 1963 Special Series 4000 I.D. Number section.

SPECIAL DELUXE SERIES 4100

Series No.	Body/Style No.	Body Type & Seating	Factory Price	Shipping Weight	Prod. Total
4100	4119	4-dr Sed-6P	2592	2684	37,695
4100	4135	4-dr Sta Wag-6P	2889	2858	8,771

ENGINE: See 1963 Buick Series 4000 engine data.

SKYLARK — SERIES 4300 — Full-length bodyside moldings graced the 1963 Skylark, which was further identified on the coupe by rear quarter roof pillar emblems. A Buick insignia was centered in the grille and another was found in the bright rear cove insert. All-vinyl interior trim was standard in the convertible and optional in the coupe. Front bucket seats were optional.

SKYLARK SERIES 4300 I.D. NUMBERS: Serial numbers began with 3J ( ) 501001 and were otherwise coded as explained under the 1963 Special Series 4000 I.D. Number section.

SKYLARK SERIES 4300

Series No.	Body/Style No.	Body Type & Seating	Factory Price	Shipping Weight	Prod. Total
4300	4347	2-dr HT Cpe-5P	2857	2757	32,109
4300	4367	2-dr Conv-5P	3011	2810	10,212

ENGINE: Powerplant specifications were the same as those listed for the 1963 Special Series 4000 V-8, except the compression ratio was raised to 11.0:1 providing 200 horsepower at 5000 rpm in combination with the use of a four-barrel Rochester 4GC carburetor.

LESABRE — SERIES 4400 — A revised styling theme was featured for 1963 with vertical taillights capping the rear fenders. A new stamped grille was seen up front. Side trim was minimal, with a narrow bright strip running horizontally along the rear body and triple ventiports on each front fender. The word LeSabre was spelled out in script on the rear fenders. Standard features included directional signals, electric windshield wipers, cigar lighter, Step-On parking brake, dual armrests, and carpeting. Bayonne cloth with vinyl bolsters was used for the interior except for the convertible, which was trimmed in all-vinyl. LeSabre identification was found on the glovebox door. Station wagons had all-vinyl trim and full carpeting.

LESABRE I.D. NUMBERS: Buick serial numbers were on the hinge pillar post, left side, above instrument panel and stamped on left side, top of engine block, ahead of valve cover. The first symbol was a number indicating the series, as follows: (LeSabre) 4 = 4000 Series; (Invicta) 6 = 4600 Series; (Electra) 7 = 4700 Series and (Electra 225) 8 = 4800 Series. The second symbol indicated model year: J for 1963. The third symbol ( ) is a number indicating the assembly plant code, as follows: 1 = Flint, Mich.; 2 = Southgate, Calif.; 3 = Linden, N.J.; 4 = Kansas City, Kans.; 5 = Wilmington, Del.; 6 = Atlanta, Ga.; and 8 = Arlington, Tex. The last six symbols are the numerical sequence

of assembly at the coded plant, with series mixed in production. Engine numbers were located in various places on the crankcase, usually, or on the cylinder block. Along with serial number, the engines carried a production code with a prefix identifying engine and year, then a four symbol sequential production number. Numbers stamped on front right of block opposite serial number. Engine codes were as follows: (LeSabre 401 V-8) JR, JS, JT, JU; (Wildcat/Invicta 401 V-8) JT, JU; (Electra 225 401 V-8) JT, JU; (Riviera 401 V-8) JT, JU; (Riviera 425 V-8) JW.

1963 Buick, LeSabre four-door hardtop, V-8

LESABRE SERIES 4400

Series No.	Body/Style No.	Body Type & Seating	Factory Price	Shipping Weight	Prod. Total
4400	4469	4-dr Sed-6P	3004	3970	64,995
4400	4439	4-dr HT Sed-6P	3146	4007	50,420
4400	4411	2-dr Sed-6P	2869	3905	8,328
4400	4447	2-dr Spt Cpe-6P	3070	3924	27,977
4400	4467	2-dr Conv-6P	3339	4052	9,975
4400	4445	4-dr Sta Wag-8P	3606	4340	3,922
4400	4435	4-dr Sta Wag-6P	3526	4320	5,566

ENGINE: V-8. Overhead valves. Cast iron block. Displacement: 401 cid. Bore and stroke: 4.1875 x 3.64 inches. Compression ratio: 10.25:1. Brake horsepower: 280 at 4400 rpm. Five main bearings. Hydraulic valve lifters. Carburetor: Rochester 2GC two-barrel.

1963 Buick, Wildcat four-door hardtop, V-8 (PH)

WILDCAT — SERIES 4600 — A plusher, more sporting Buick line for 1963 grew from success of the 1962 Wildcat Sport Coupe. Standard Wildcat features for 1963 included an electric clock, Deluxe steering wheel, trunk light, license frames, padded instrument panel, foam-rubber headliner, tachometer (except on hardtops with bench seats), bucket seats (optional on four-door hardtop, standard other models), and a center console. Wildcat script was found on rear fenders and within the rear cove, while the name was lettered across the hood. A brushed finish bright insert began on the front fenders and contained the three ventiports on each fender. Bright wheelhouse and rocker moldings were used. A special grille, with distinct horizontal heavy bars and a center emblem, further distinguished the Wildcat. Sport Coupes had roof rear quarter emblems with the Wildcat logo, while the same badge was placed on the rear flanks of convertibles. Bucket seat interiors were all-vinyl. Specific full wheelcovers were used.

NOTE: Also in the 4600 series was the Invicta Estate Wagon, Model 4635. This station wagon had a plusher interior than the 4400 wagons and was available in two-seat form only. A full-length narrow bodyside molding was used, along with bright wheelhouse and rocker moldings and chromed roof team. All standard Wildcat features were included.

WILDCAT AND INVICTA — SERIES 4600 — I.D. NUMBERS: Serial numbers began with 6J () 001001. The number was coded as explained under the 1963 LeSabre I.D. Number section.

WILDCAT/INVICTA SERIES 4600

Series No.	Body/Style No.	Body Type & Seating	Factory Price	Shipping Weight	Prod. Total
4600	4639	4-dr HT Cpe-6P	3871	4222	17,519
4600	4647	2-dr Spt Cpe-6P	3849	4123	12,185
4600	4667	2-dr Conv-6P	3961	4228	6,021
4600	4635	4-dr Sta Wag-6P	3969	3897	3,495

ENGINE: Specifications were the same as those listed for the 1963 LeSabre Series 4400, except compression ratio was 10.25:1. Brake horsepower was 325 at 4400 rpm and a four-barrel Rochester 4GC or Carter AFB carburetor was used.

1963 Buick, Electra 225 two-door convertible, V-8 (PH)

ELECTRA 225 — SERIES 4800 — Buick's largest, plushest and most expensive models were redesigned for 1963, with distinctive rear fenders culminating in a sharp vertical edge housing narrow back-up lights. The taillights were horizontally placed in the vertical deck cove. A unique cast grille was used at the front. Bright wheelhouse and lower body moldings, with ribbed rear fender panels, were used. Red-filled Electra 225 badges were found on the rear fenders, while four ventiports lent status to the front fenders. Interiors were cloth and vinyl combinations, while a Custom interior in vinyl and leather, with front bucket seats and a storage console, was available for the convertible and sport coupe. Standard equipment, in addition to items found on lower-priced Buicks, included power steering; power brakes; back-up lights; power brake signal light; map light; safety buzzer; Custom padded seat cushions; Super Deluxe wheelcovers; power windows and two-way seat adjustment on the convertibles (these two features were included with the Custom interior on closed models).

1963 Buick, Electra 225 four-door sedan, V-8

ELECTRA 225 SERIES I.D. NUMBERS: Serial numbers began with 8J () 1001001. The number was coded as explained under the 1963 LeSabre I.D. Number section.

ELECTRA 225 SERIES 4800

Series No.	Body/Style No.	Body Type & Seating	Factory Price	Shipping Weight	Prod. Total
4800	4819	4-dr Sed-6P	4051	4241	14,628
4800	4829	4-dr HT Sed-6P	4254	4284	11,468
4800	4839	4-dr HT Sed-6P	4186	4272	19,714
4800	4847	2-dr Spt Cpe-6P	4062	4153	6,848
4800	4867	2-dr Conv-6P	4365	4297	6,367

ENGINE: Specifications were the same as those listed for the 1963 LeSabre Series 4400 except compression ratio was 10.25:1, brake horsepower was 325 at 4400 rpm and a four-barrel Rochester 4GC or Carter AFB carburetor was used.

1963 Buick, Riviera two-door hardtop, V-8

RIVIERA — SERIES 4700 — The Riviera was a new sports/luxury model for 1963, issued only in a stunning sport coupe body style. From the front fenders, whose leading edges were vertical grilles, to the razor-edged rear contours, the Riviera looked both elegant and fast. A car for Buick's most affluent customers, the Riviera was delivered with a host of standard features, including two-speed wipers with washers; back-up lights; Glare-proof inside mirror; parking brake signal light; safety buzzer; Riviera wheelcovers; electric clock; license frame; padded instrument panel; trip mileage odometer; smoking set; front and rear bucket seats; courtesy lamps; deep-pile carpet; foam-padded seat cushions; center console; heater and defroster; and frameless side windows.

RIVIERA SERIES 4700 I.D. NUMBERS: Serial numbers began with 7J () 001001. The number was coded as explained under the 1963 LeSabre I.D. Number section.

RIVIERA SERIES 4700

Series No.	Body/Style No.	Body Type & Seating	Factory Price	Shipping Weight	Prod. Total
4700	4747	2-dr Spt Cpe-4P	4333	3998	40,000

ENGINE: Specifications were the same as listed for the 1963 Electra 225 Series 4800.

CHASSIS FEATURES: Wheelbase: (Series 4000, 4100 and 4300) 112.1 inches; (Series 4400 and 4600) 123 inches; (Series 4800) 126 inches; (Series 4700) 117 inches. Overall length: (Series 4000, 4100 and 4300) 192.1 inches; (Series 4400 and 4600) 215.7 inches; (Series 4800) 221.7 inches; (Series 4700) 208 inches. Front tread: (Series 4000, 4100 and 4300) 56 inches; (Series 4400, 4600, 4800 and 4700) 62 inches. Rear tread: (Series 4000, 4100 and 4300) 56 inches; (Series 4400, 4600, 4800 and 4700) 61 inches. Tires: (Series 4000, 4100 and 4300) 6.50 x 13; (Series 4400 and 4600) 7.60 x 15; (Series 4800) 8.00 x 15; (Series 4700) 7.10 x 15.

POWERTRAIN OPTIONS: A three-speed manual transmission was standard on Series 4000, 4100, 4300, 4400 and 4600. Turbine drive was standard on Series 4800 and 4700 and optional on other series ($231). A four-speed manual transmission was optional on Series 4300, 4400 and 4600 models ($200-$263). The Series 4300 200-hp V-8 was optional on Series 4000 and 4100 models. A 9.0:1 compression 265 horsepower regular fuel engine was a no-cost option in all Series 4400 models. A 425 cid/340 bhp V-8 was optional on Series 4700. Positive traction differential was optional on all models.

CONVENIENCE OPTIONS: Power steering (standard on Series 4800 and 4700). Power brakes (standard on Series 4700 and 4800). Air conditioning. Cruise control on Model 4747. Wire wheelcovers. Cloth/vinyl or leather/vinyl trim on Model 4747. Seven-position tilt steering wheel on Series 4400, 4600 and 4800. Electro-Cruise. Cornering lights. Power door locks. Auto trunk release. Seat belts. Sonomatic radio. Wonderbar radio. Rear seat speaker. Soft-Ray glass. Rear window defroster. Chrome door guards. Remote control outside rearview mirror. Whitewall tires. Power windows (standard on Electra 225 convertible and Custom interior). GuideMatic dimmer. Twilight Sentinel. Gas door guard. Compass. Litter basket. Tissue dispenser. Seat covers. Spotlite. Carpet covers. Carpet savers. Trunk mat. Ski rack. Heater/Defroster delete. Divided rear seat, luggage rack and luggage locker for station wagons.

HISTORICAL FOOTNOTES: Calendar year production was 479,399, putting Buick in seventh rank in the auto industry. Model year production stood at 458,606 units or 6.3 percent share of market. The big news was the introduction of the Thunderbird-fighting Riviera sports/personal car. A Skylark SR200 show car with racing stripes and braking cooling ducts represented one of the first signs of a forthcoming high-performance series. Two Riviera "Silver Arrow" show cars were also seen, both being slightly different. *Car Life* magazine tested a 425 cid/340 hp Riviera for a 0-to-60 mph time of 7.7 seconds. The 401 cid/325 hp Riviera could do the same in about 8.1 seconds and cover the quarter-mile in 16 01 seconds. Due to production costs, the 1961-1963 aluminum V-8 was dropped for 1964 models. The engine tooling was sold to Rover in England. Models 4445, 4435 and 4635 are Estate Wagons.

1964

SPECIAL—SERIES 4000—V-6 AND V-8 — A new larger and more flowing body was used for the 1964 Special, now classed as an intermediate in the General Motors' family. Except for the Special script on rear fenders and trio of ventiports on front fenders, the Special was devoid of bright ornamentation. Interiors were in Brigade cloth. Standard features included electric windshield wipers, ashtrays, directional signals, Step-On parking brake, dome lights and, on the convertible only, carpeting.

SPECIAL I.D. NUMBERS: Serial numbers were on the hinge pillar post, left side, above instrument panel and stamped on left side, top of engine block, ahead of valve cover. On base Buick Specials equipped with the V-6, the numbers began with AK () 501001-up. On base Buick Specials equipped with a V-8, the numbers began with OK () 501001-up. The first symbol was a letter or number denoting the series, as follows: (6-cyl.) A = 4000; B = 4100; C = 4300; (V-8) 0 = 4000; 1 = 4100; 3 = 4300. The second symbol indicated model year: K for 1964. The third symbol () is a number indicating the assembly plant code, as follows: 1 = Flint, Mich.; 2 = Southgate, Calif.; 3 = Fremont, Calif.; 4 = Kansas City, Kans.; 5 = Wilmington, Del.; 6 = Atlanta, Ga.; 7 = Baltimore, Md.; and 8 = Kansas City, Mo. The last six symbols are the numerical sequence of assembly at the coded plant, with series mixed in production. Engine numbers were located in various places on the crankcase, usually, or on the cylinder block. Along with serial number, the engines carried a production code with a prefix identifying engine and year, then a four symbol sequential production number: (V-8s) stamped front right of block opposite serial number; (V-6) on front of block below left cylinder head gasket. Special engine codes were as follows: (225 cid V-6) KH, KJ; (300 cid V-8) KL, KM, KP and KR.

SPECIAL SERIES 4000

Series No.	Body/Style No.	Body Type & Seating	Factory Price	Shipping Weight	Prod. Total
4000	4069	4-dr Sed-6P	2397	3000	17,983
4000	4027	2-dr Sed-6P	2343	2983	15,030
4000	4067	2-dr Conv-6P	2605	3099	6,308
4000	4035	4-dr Sta Wag-6P	2689	3258	6,270

NOTE: The V-8 line was considered a sub-series, not an option. Factory prices were $71 higher for V-8s than the prices listed above for the V-6. Shipping weights were 16 pounds heavier for the V-8 than those listed above for the V-6. Production figures include both V-6 and V-8.

ENGINE: V-6. Cast iron block. Displacement: 225 cid. Bore and stroke: 3.75 x 3.4 inches. Compression ratio: 9.0:1. Brake horsepower: 155 at 4400 rpm. Four main bearings. Hydraulic valve lifters. Carburetor: Rochester BC two-barrel.

ENGINE: V-8. Cast iron block. Displacement: 300 cid. Bore and stroke: 3.75 x 3.4 inches. Compression ratio: 9.0:1. Brake horsepower: 210 at 4600 rpm. Five main bearings. Hydraulic valve lifters. Carburetor: Rochester 2GC two-barrel.

SPECIAL DELUXE — SERIES 4100 — V-6 AND V-8 — A narrow bright bodyside molding swept the full length of the Special Deluxe models, which were plusher inside. There was carpeting, cloth and vinyl combinations over foam-padded seats, and a padded instrument panel. Other line features were a Deluxe steering wheel, dual armrests, dual horns and additional dome lights.

SPECIAL DELUXE I.D. NUMBERS: Serial numbers for cars equipped with the V-6 began with BK () 001001. Serial numbers for cars equipped with the V-8 began with 1K () 001001. The numbers were coded as explained under the 1964 Special Series 4000 I.D. Number section.

1964 Buick, Special Deluxe four-door sedan, V-8

SPECIAL DELUXE SERIES 4100

Series No.	Body/Style No.	Body Type & Seating	Factory Price	Shipping Weight	Prod. Total
4100	4169	4-dr Sed-6P	2490	3018	31,742
4100	4127	2-dr Sed-6P	2457	2998	11,962
4100	4135	4-dr Sta Wag-6P	2787	3277	9,467

NOTE: Cars equipped with V-8s listed for $71 more than the V-6 prices given above and they weighed 16 pounds more than the weights given for the V-6. Production totals include both V-6s and V-8s.

ENGINE: Specifications were the same as those listed for the 1964 Special Series 4000.

1964-1/2 Buick, Custom four-door Sport Wagon, V-8 (PH)

SPORT WAGONS — SERIES 4200 AND 4300 — A new long-wheelbase station wagon debuted for 1964. Offered in two stag-es of trim, the wagons were numbered in 4200 and 4300 (Skylark) Series. Both Standard and Custom models had tinted transparent panels above the rear passenger compartment. The Custom models were trimmed like the Skylarks in the 4300 Series (see Skylark Series 4300). Interiors were all-vinyl.

SPORT WAGON I.D. NUMBERS: Serial numbers correspond to the numbers used for the Series 4100 and 4300 cars as detailed above.

SERIES 4200/4300 SPORT WAGONS

Series No.	Body/Style No.	Body Type & Seating	Factory Price	Shipping Weight	Prod. Total
4200	4265	4-dr Cus Sta Wag-3S	3124	3689	2,586
4200	4255	4-dr Cus Sta Wag-2S	2989	3557	2,709
4300	4365	4-dr Sta Wag-3S	3286	3727	4,446
4300	4355	4-dr Sta Wag-2S	3161	3595	3,913

ENGINE: Specifications were the same as those listed for the 1964 Special Series 4000 V-8.

1964 Buick, Skylark two-door hardtop, V-6

SKYLARK — SERIES 4300 — Buick's plushest version of its sporty intermediate had considerably more pizzaz this year with its new body and flashier trim. The Skylark emblem and signature were found on roof quarters (rear fenders on the convertible), while Skylark script was on the deck. A round Buick emblem dominated the grille. Another round emblem was housed in the deck cove, which was finished with a brushed metallic insert. Bright rocker moldings and a wider bright bodyside molding, with a brushed metallic insert, gave further distinction. Sport Coupes had twin bright strips on the roof. Standard features, in addition to those found on Special and Special Deluxe Series, included instrument panel safety padding, paddle-type armrests, Skylark steering wheel, Skylark wheelcovers and full carpeting. An all-vinyl interior with bucket seats was standard for the convertible and optional for the Sport Coupe. The sedan came in a cloth and vinyl combination with all-vinyl available as a substitution.

SKYLARK I.D. NUMBERS: Serial numbers began with CK () 001001 on cars equipped with the V-6. Serial numbers began with 3K () 001001 on cars equipped with the V-8. The number was coded as explained under the 1964 Special Series 4000 I.D. Number section.

SKYLARK SERIES 4300

Series No.	Body/Style No.	Body Type & Seating	Factory Price	Shipping Weight	Prod. Total
4300	4347	2-dr Spt Cpe-6P	2680	3049	42,356
4300	4367	2-dr Conv-5P	2834	3169	10,255

NOTE: Cars equipped with V-8s listed for $71 more than the V-6 prices listed above and they weighed six pounds more than the weights given for the V-6s. Production figures combine V-6 and V-8 production.

ENGINE: Specifications were the same as those listed for the 1964 Special Series 4000.

LESABRE — SERIES 4400 — Refined body sculpturing, with fresh frontal and rear treatments, set the 1964 LeSabre apart. A unique stamped grille was used. A narrow bright bodyside molding was found on the rear one-third of the body, with the series signature residing above it, near the fender end. Standard LeSabre features included electric windshield wipers; Step-On park-

ing brake; padded instrument panel; directional signals; front and rear armrests; dual sunshades; smoking set; courtesy lights; dual horns and cloth upholstery. Cloth and vinyl trim was optional. The convertible was trimmed in all-vinyl, with front bucket seats optional. A Custom trim package option included full-length bright bodyside moldings, with a brushed metallic insert.

1964 Buick, LeSabre Custom four-door hardtop, V-8

LESABRE I.D. NUMBERS: Buick serial numbers were on the hinge pillar post, left side, above instrument panel and stamped on left side, top of engine block, ahead of valve cover. The first symbol was a number indicating the series, as follows: (LeSabre) 4 = 4000 Series; (Invicta) 6 = 4600 Series; (Electra) 7 = 4700 Series and (Electra 225) 8 = 4800 Series. The second symbol indicated model year: K for 1964. The third symbol ( ) is a number indicating the assembly plant code, as follows: 1 = Flint, Mich.; 2 = Southgate, Calif.; 3 = Fremont, Calif.; 4 = Kansas City, Kans.; 5 = Wilmington, Del.; 6 = Atlanta, Ga.; 7 = Baltimore, Md.; and Kansas City, Md. The last six symbols are the numerical sequence of assembly at the coded plant, with series mixed in production. Engine numbers were located in various places on the crankcase, usually, or on the cylinder block. Along with serial number, the engines carried a production code with a prefix identifying engine and year, then a four symbol sequential production number. Numbers stamped on front right of block opposite serial number. Engine codes were as follows: (LeSabre/Wildcat/Electra 225 401 V-8) KT, KV; (LeSabre/Wildcat/Riviera 425 V-8) KW, KX.

LESABRE SERIES 4400

Series No.	Body/Style No.	Body Type & Seating	Factory Price	Shipping Weight	Prod. Total
4400	4469	4-dr Sed-6P	2980	3693	56,729
4400	4439	4-dr HT Sed-6P	3122	3730	37,052
4400	4447	2-dr Spt Cpe-6P	3061	3629	24,177
4400	4467	2-dr Conv-6P	3314	3787	6,685

ENGINE: Specifications were the same as those listed for the Special Series 4000 V-8.

LESABRE — SERIES 4600 — Two hybrid station wagons made up this curious series. They were trimmed as LeSabres, but had the Wildcat's chassis and power. Leather grain vinyl or vinyl and cloth (two-seater only) were trim choices. A power tailgate window was standard.

LESABRE SERIES 4600 I.D. NUMBERS: Serial numbers began with 4KC ( ) 001001. The numbers were coded as explained under the 1964 LeSabre Series I.D. Number section.

LESABRE SERIES 4600

Series No.	Body/Style No.	Body Type & Seating	Factory Price	Shipping Weight	Prod. Total
4600	4645	4-dr Sta Wag-3S	3635	4362	4,003
4600	4635	4-dr Sta Wag-2S	3554	4352	6,517

ENGINE: Specifications were the same as those listed for the Wildcat Series 4600.

WILDCAT — SERIES 4600 — Sportier and plusher, the 1964 Wildcat was liberally trimmed with brightwork including a ribbed, wide lower body molding; a trio of stacked, streamlined ventiports behind each front wheelhouse; a unique grille, with heavy horizontal wing bars, and a center emblem. There was Wildcat lettering on the deck lid and another emblem centered within the deck cove, which had a bright metallic insert with bright horizontal stripes. Wildcat badges appeared on roof quarters (except on the convertible, which had them on the fenders) and within the

full wheelcovers. Standard and Custom trim choices were available, including bucket seats and a console. Carpeting was standard, in addition to all the features found on the LeSabre.

1964 Buick, Wildcat two-door hardtop, V-8

WILDCAT SERIES 4600 I.D. NUMBERS: Serial numbers began with 6K ( ) 001001. The number was coded as explained under the 1964 LeSabre I.D. Number section.

WILDCAT SERIES 4600

Series No.	Body/Style No.	Body Type & Seating	Factory Price	Shipping Weight	Prod. Total
4600	4669	4-dr Sed-6P	3164	4021	20,144
4600	4639	2-dr HT-6P	3327	4058	33,358
4600	4647	2-dr Spt Cpe-6P	3267	4003	22,893
4600	4667	2-dr Conv-6P	3455	4076	7,850

ENGINE: V-8. Overhead valves. Cast iron block. Displacement: 401 cid. Bore and stroke: 4.18 x 3.64 inches. Compression ratio: 10.25:1. Brake horsepower: 325 at 4400 rpm. Five main bearings. Hydraulic valve lifters. Carburetor: four-barrel Rochester 4GC or Carter AFB.

1964 Buick, Electra 225 two-door hardtop, V-8

ELECTRA 225 — SERIES 4800 — The large General Motors' C-Body was used to create the Electra 225, Buick's richest full-size car. Vertical, narrow taillamps were found in the nearly straight-cut rear fender ends, and the so-called "Deuce-and-a-Quarter" came with fender skirts. Four traditional ventiports were found on the front fenders, with a heavy die-cast grille accenting the frontal aspect. Wide full-length lower body moldings were used along with a bright deck cove insert. Electra 225 lettering was found on rear fenders and specific full wheelcovers were featured. Vinyl and brocade cloth interior trims were found in closed models, while leather upholstery was offered for seats in the convertible. Among the Electra's exclusive standard equipment were power steering; power brakes; two-speed electric wipers with windshield washer; foam-padded seats; electric clock; license frame; trunk light; two-way power seat and power windows for the convertible; safety buzzer; and additional courtesy lights.

ELECTRA 225 I.D. NUMBERS: Serial numbers began with 8K ( ) 001001. The numbers were coded as explained under the 1964 LeSabre I.D. Number section.

ELECTRA 225 SERIES 4800

Series No.	Body/Style No.	Body Type & Seating	Factory Price	Shipping Weight	Prod. Total
4800	4819	4-dr Sed-6P	4059	4212	15,968
4800	4829	4-dr Pillarless Sed-6P	4261	4238	11,663
4800	4839	4-dr HT Sed-6P	4194	4229	24,935
4800	4847	2-dr Spt Cpe-6P	4070	4149	9,045
4800	4867	2-dr Conv-6P	4374	4280	7,181

ENGINE: Specifications were the same as those listed for the 1964 Wildcat Series 4600.

1964 Buick, Riviera two-door hardtop, V-8

RIVIERA — SERIES 4700 — The 1963 Riviera was immediately recognized as a timeless design and Buick saw little need for change in 1964. A new, stand-up hood ornament and revised Riviera scripts on the front fenders and right-hand deck were the major changes. The simulated rear fender cooling vents were outlined in bright metal and a thin, bright highlight line continued to follow the bodyside crease, jumping over the wheelhouse in passing. The beautiful, twin grille, with eggcrate center grille frontal ensemble, continued without alteration. The stylized letter 'R' appeared in wheelcover centers. Standard features were similar to those listed for the Electra 225, but also included deep-pile carpeting, foam-padded front and rear bucket seats and a center console with transmission selector lever. Interiors were trimmed in vinyl with wood accents.

RIVIERA I.D. NUMBERS: Serial numbers began with 7K () 001001. The numbers were coded as explained under the 1964 LeSabre I.D. Number section.

RIVIERA SERIES 4700

Series No.	Body/Style No.	Body Type & Seating	Factory Price	Shipping Weight	Prod. Total
4700	4747	2-dr Spt Cpe	4385	3951	37,958

ENGINE: V-8. Overhead valve. Cast iron block. Displacement: 425 cid. Bore and stroke: 4.3125 x 3.64 inches. Compression ratio: 10.25:1. Brake horsepower: 340 at 4400 rpm. Five main bearings. Hydraulic valve lifters. Carburetor: Carter AFB four-barrel.

CHASSIS FEATURES: Wheelbase: (Series 4000, 4100, 4200, 4300) 115 inches; (Series 4300 wagon) 120 inches; (Series 4400 and 4600) 123 inches; (Series 4800) 126 inches; (Series 4700) 117 inches. Overall length: (Series 4000, 4100, 4200 and 4300) 203.5 inches; (Series 4400 and 4600) 218.5 inches; (Series 4800) 222.8 inches; (Series 4700) 208 inches. Front tread: (Series 4000, 4100, 4300, and 4200) 58 inches; (Series 4400, 4600 and 4800) 62.1 inches; (Series 4700) 60 inches. Rear tread: (Series 4000, 4100 and 4300) 58 inches; (Series 4400, 4600 and 4800) 61 inches; (Series 4700) 59 inches. Tires: (Series 4000, 4100 and 4300) 6.50 x 14; (Series 4200 wagon) 7.00 x 14; (Series 4300 wagons) 7.50 x 14; (Series 4400 and 4700) 7.10 x 15; (Series 4600) 7.60 x 15; (Series 4800) 8.00 x 15.

POWERTRAIN OPTIONS: A three-speed manual transmission was standard on Series 4000, 4100, 4200, 4300, 4400 and 4600. Turbine 300 automatic was optional on Series 4000, 4100, 4200, 4300, 4400 and 4600. Turbine 400 was optional on Series 4600, standard on Series 4700 and 4800. A four-speed manual transmission was optional for Series 4000, 4100, 4300, 4400 and 4600. A 300 cid/250 bhp V-8 was optional for Series 4000, 4100, 4200, 4300 and 4400. The 425 cid/340 bhp V-8 was optional for Series 4600, 4800 and 4600 Estate wagons. A 425 cid/360 bhp V-8 with dual four-barrel carburetors was an option for Series 4600, 4700, and 4800.

CONVENIENCE OPTIONS: Power brakes (standard 4700 and 4800). Power steering (standard 4700 and 4800). Power windows (not available on Special station wagon). Power seat control. Air conditioning. Seven-position tilt steering wheel. Carpeting (4000 Series). Bucket seats with console and storage bin on 4600. 'Formula Five' chromed steel wheels. Whitewall tires. Custom fabric roof cover. Bucket seats in Electra 225 convertible.

AM radio in 4000, 4100 and 4300. Sonomatic radio. Wonder Bar radio. AM-FM radio on 4400, 4600, 4700 and 4800. Seat belts. Remote control inside rearview mirror. Electro-cruise. Cornering lights. Power door locks. Automatic trunk release. Rear seat speaker. Rear window defroster. GuideMatic headlight dimmer. Compass. Litter basket. Tissue dispenser. Ski rack. Luggage rack for Estate Wagons. Heater-Defroster deletion.

NOTE: Power windows standard on Electra 225 convertible.

HISTORICAL FOOTNOTES: Calendar year production was 482,685 for seventh position in the auto industry. Model year output stood at 511,666 units. Models 4645 and 4635 are called Estate Wagons.

1965

1965 Buick, Special two-door pillared coupe, V-6

SPECIAL — SERIES 43300 (V-6) — A slightly face lifted car of intermediate size was marketed by Buick under the Special name for 1965. Still largely devoid of side trim, the Special did have its name in script on the rear flanks and had a trio of ventiports on each front fender. A Buick emblem was found at the rear, while the front horizontal grille bars were bare. Interiors were of cloth and vinyl. Standard equipment included electric windshield wipers, directional signals, dual sunshades, ashtray/lighter set, dual armrests on sedans, courtesy lights, Step-On parking brake and carpeting in the convertible.

1965 Buick, Special four-door sedan, V-6 (PH)

SPECIAL I.D. NUMBERS: Serial numbers were located on the hinge pillar post, left side above the instrument panel and stamped on left side, top of engine block, ahead of valve cover. The first five symbols were the model number. The first symbol was a '4' indicating Buick Motor Division products. The second through fifth symbols indicated the series and body style (see model numbers on tables below). The sixth symbol was a number indicating model year: 5 = 1965. The seventh symbol was a letter representing the plant code, as follows: B = Baltimore, Md.; C = Southgate, Calif.; D = Doraville, Ga.; H = Flint, Mich.; K = Leeds, Mo.; X = Fairfax, Kans.; Y = Wilmington, Del.; Z = Fremont, Ohio; V = Bloomfield, Mich. The last six symbols were numerals representing the plant sequential production number, with series mixed in production. Engine numbers were stamped in various positions on the crankcase, usually, or on the cylinder block. Along with serial number, the engines carried a production code with a prefix identifying engine and year, then a four symbol sequential production number: (V-8s) stamped front right of block opposite serial number; (V-6) on front of block

below left cylinder head gasket. Special engine codes were as follows: (225 cid V-6) LH, LJ; (300 cid V-8) LL, LM, LP.

SPECIAL SERIES 43300

Series No.	Body/Style No.	Body Type & Seating	Factory Price	Shipping Weight	Prod. Total
43300	43369	4-dr Sed-6P	2345	3010	12,945
43300	43327	2-dr Sed-6P	2292	2977	13,828
43300	43367	2-dr Conv-6P	2549	3087	3,357
43300	43335	4-dr Sta Wag-6P	2631	3258	2,868

ENGINE: V-6. Overhead valve. Cast iron block. Displacement: 225 cid. Bore and stroke: 3.75 x 3.4 inches. Compression ratio: 9.0:1. Brake horsepower: 155 at 4200 rpm. Four main bearings. Hydraulic valve lifters. Carburetor: Rochester BC two-barrel.

SPECIAL — SERIES 43400 (V-8) — Identical externally to the 1965 V-6 Special described above, the V-8 Specials were numbered as a separate series.

1965 Buick, Special station wagon, V-6

SPECIAL I.D. NUMBERS: Serial numbers began with 434005 () 100001. The numbers were coded as explained under the 1965 Special Series 43300 I.D. Number section.

SPECIAL SERIES 43400

Series No.	Body/Style No.	Body Type & Seating	Factory Price	Shipping Weight	Prod. Total
43400	43469	4-dr Sed-6P	2415	3117	5,309
43400	43427	2-dr Sed-6P	2362	3080	8,121
43400	43467	2-dr Conv-6P	2618	3197	3,365
43400	43435	4-dr Sta Wag-6P	2699	3365	3,676

ENGINE: V-8. Overhead valve. Cast iron block. Displacement: 300 cid. Bore and stroke: 3.75 x 3.4 inches. Compression ratio: 9.0:1. Brake horsepower: 210 at 4600 rpm. Five main bearings. Hydraulic valve lifters. Carburetor: Rochester 2GC two-barrel.

SPECIAL DELUXE — SERIES 43500 (V-6) — A Special with a little more dressing, the Special Deluxe had bright bodyside moldings, bright window surrounds and a rear cove insert panel. Interiors were plusher vinyls with some cloth combinations. Floors were carpeted and the instrument panel was padded. Dual horns added to the standard equipment list.

SPECIAL DELUXE V-6 I.D. NUMBERS: Serial numbers began with 43500 () 100001. The numbers were coded as explained under the 1965 Special Series 43300 I.D. Number section.

SPECIAL DELUXE SERIES 43500 (V-6)

Series No.	Body/Style No.	Body Type & Seating	Factory Price	Shipping Weight	Prod. Total
43500	43569	4-dr Sed-6P	2436	3016	10,961
43500	43535	4-dr Sta Wag-6P	2727	3242	1,677

ENGINE: Specifications were the same as those listed for the 1965 Special Series 43300.

SPECIAL DELUXE — SERIES 43600 (V-8) — Identical externally to the 1965 Special Deluxe V-6 described above, the V-8 Special Deluxes were numbered as a separate series.

SPECIAL DELUXE V-8 I.D. NUMBERS: Serial numbers began with 43600 () 10001. The numbers were coded as explained under the 1965 Special Series 43300 I.D. Number section.

SPECIAL DELUXE SERIES 43600 (V-8)

Series No.	Body/Style No.	Body Type & Seating	Factory Price	Shipping Weight	Prod. Total
43600	43669	4-dr Sed-6P	2506	3143	25,675
43600	43635	4-dr Sta Wag-6P	2796	3369	9,123

ENGINE: Specifications were the same as those listed for the 1965 Special V-8 Series 43400.

1965 Buick, Skylark two-door convertible, V-8 (PH)

1965 Buick, Skylark two-door pillared coupe, V-6

SKYLARK — SERIES 44300 (V-6) — This was Buick's intermediate in its plushest form. Specific full wheelcovers, bright rocker and wheelhouse moldings, a unique cove treatment with full-width taillamps and emblems centered front and rear signified Skylark-level trim on the outside. The Skylark badge appeared on front fenders, deck lid and roof quarters (rear fenders on convertible). Interiors were plusher cloth and vinyl, or leather-grain all-vinyl. Front buckets were optional. Standard equipment on Skylark in addition to that found on lesser series included: foam-padded seats, paddle-type armrests, rear passenger courtesy lights on two-doors, ashtray, glove compartment lights and full carpeting.

NOTE: A mid-1965 option was the Skylark Gran Sport, an option package offered on the two-door coupe, Sport Coupe and convertible. A 401-cid V-8 that produced 325 hp at 4400 rpm was the heart of the option. It had a 10.25:1 compression ratio and a single Carter AFB four-barrel carburetor. A heavy-duty cross-flow radiator and dual exhaust manifolds with oversized pipes were included. Exterior identification was provided by red-filled Gran Sport badges on the grille, deck and roof quarters (rear fenders on convertibles). Another badge was affixed to the instrument panel. The Skylark GS featured 7.75 x 14 tires on six-inch rims.

SKYLARK V-6 I.D. NUMBERS: Serial numbers began with 443005 () 100001. The numbers were coded as explained under the 1965 Special Series 43300 I.D. Number section.

SKYLARK SERIES 44300 (V-6)

Series No.	Body/Style No.	Body Type & Seating	Factory Price	Shipping Weight	Prod. Total
44300	44369	4-dr Sed-6P	2611	3086	3,385
44300	44327	2-dr Sed-6P	2482	3035	4,195
44300	44337	2-dr Spt Cpe-6P	2622	3057	4,501
44300	44367	2-dr Conv-6P	2773	3149	1,181

ENGINE: Specifications were the same as those listed for the 1965 Special Series 43300 V-6.

SKYLARK V-8 SERIES 44400: Externally identical to the 1965 Skylark V-6 described above, the V-8 Skylarks were numbered as a separate series.

SKYLARK V-8 I.D. NUMBERS: Serial numbers began with 44405 () 100001. Numbers were coded as explained under the 1965 Special Series 43300 I.D. Number section.

SKYLARK SERIES 44400 (V-8)

Series No.	Body/Style No.	Body Type & Seating	Factory Price	Shipping Weight	Prod. Total
44400	44469	4-dr Sed-6P	2681	3194	22,239
44400	44427	2-dr Sed-6P	2552	3146	11,877
44400	44437	2-dr Spt Cpe-6P	2692	3198	46,698
44400	44467	2-dr Conv-6P	2842	3294	10,456

ENGINE: Specifications were the same as those listed for the 1965 Special V-8 Series 43400.

1965 Buick, Custom four-door Sport Wagon, V-8

SPORT WAGON: Buick's stretched wheelbase station wagon continued to feature the unusual Skyroof with shaded glass panels in a raised area above the rear compartment. The increased headroom allowed a three-seat version to be marketed. Cargo area was 95.6 cubic feet. Interiors were all-vinyl. Models 44465 and 44455 were Custom models and featured most Skylark equipment, but had only a full-length bright metal side molding. A tailgate lamp was also standard.

SPORT WAGON I.D. NUMBERS: Serial numbers began with the model number (sample: 44265 () 10001) and were coded as explained under the 1965 Special Series I.D. Number section.

SPORT WAGON SERIES 44200/44400

Series No.	Body/Style No.	Body Type & Seating	Factory Price	Shipping Weight	Prod. Total
44200	44265	4-dr Sta Wag-9P	3056	3750	4,664
44200	44255	4-dr Sta Wag-6P	2925	3642	4,226
44400	44465	4-dr Cus Sta Wag-9P	3214	3802	11,166
44400	44455	4-dr Cus Sta Wag-9P	3092	3690	8,300

ENGINE: Specifications were the same as those listed for the 1965 Special Series 43400 V-8.

LESABRE — SERIES 45200 — Buick's full-sized price leaders featured a new body with a wider appearance and softer, bulgy lines. A bright narrow lower body molding was used, along with a trio of ventiports on each front fender. The LeSabre signature appeared on rear body quarters. An extruded aluminum grille was used at the front. Standard equipment included electric windshield wipers; instrument panel safety pad directional signals; glove compartment light; dual armrests front and rear; door-operated courtesy lights; full carpeting and a map light. Interiors were cloth or vinyl.

LESABRE I.D. NUMBERS: Buick serial numbers were located on the hinge pillar post, left side, above the instrument panel and stamped on left side, top of engine block, ahead of valve cover. The first five symbols were the model number. The first symbol was a '4' indicating Buick Motor Division products. The second through fifth symbols indicated the series and body style (see model numbers on tables below). The sixth symbol was a number indicating model year: 5 = 1965. The seventh symbol was a letter representing the plant code, as follows: B = Baltimore, Md.; C = Southgate, Calif.; D = Doraville Ga.; H = Flint, Mich.; K = Leeds, Mo.; X = Fairfax, Kans.; Y = Wilmington, Del.; Z = Fremont, Calif.; V = Bloomfield, Mich. The last six symbols were numerals representing the plant sequential production number, with series mixed in production. Engine numbers were stamped in various positions on the crankcase, usually, or on the cylinder block. Along with serial number, the engines carried a production code with a prefix identifying engine and year, then a four symbol sequential production number. Numbers stamped on front right of block opposite serial number. Engine codes were as follows (400 cid GS 400 V-8) LR, NA; (Wildcat/Electra 225/Riviera 401 cid V-8) LT, LV; (Wildcat/Electra/Riviera 425 cid V-8) LW, LX.

LESABRE SERIES 45200

Series No.	Body/Style No.	Body Type & Seating	Factory Price	Shipping Weight	Prod. Total
45200	45269	4-dr Sed-6P	2888	3788	37,788
45200	45239	4-dr HT Sed-6P	3027	3809	18,384
45200	45237	2-dr Spt Cpe-6P	2968	3753	15,786

ENGINE: Specifications were the same as those listed for the 1965 Special Series 43400 V-8.

LESABRE CUSTOM — SERIES 45400 — Custom interior fabrics of cloth and vinyl set the Custom series apart. The convertible had a standard outside rearview mirror. Exterior trim was like the LeSabre Series 45200.

LESABRE CUSTOM I.D. NUMBERS: Serial numbers began with 454005 () 10001. Numbers were coded as explained under the 1965 LeSabre Series I.D. Number section.

LESABRE CUSTOM SERIES 45400

Series No.	Body/Style No.	Body Type & Seating	Factory Price	Shipping Weight	Prod. Total
45400	45469	4-dr Sed-6P	2962	3777	20,052
45400	45439	4-dr HT Sed-6P	3101	3811	23,394
45400	45237	2-dr Spt Cpe-6P	3037	3724	21,049
45400	45467	2-dr Conv-5P	3257	3812	6,543

ENGINE: Specifications were the the same as those listed for the 1965 Special Series 43400

1965 Buick, Wildcat two-door convertible, V-8

WILDCAT — SERIES 46200 — Buick's medium-priced line, still equipped for superior performance, shared the LeSabre's new 1965 body. It was distinguished by a die-cast grille having a large center emblem, large simulated bright front fender vents and Wildcat script on the quarter panels and deck. Inside, Wildcat emblems appeared on door panels. The full wheelcovers also used the Wildcat emblem. Standard equipment in addition to that found on the LeSabre, included a smoking set and rear seat ashtrays. Interiors were cloth or vinyl.

1965 Buick, Wildcat two-door Sport Coupe, V-8 (PH)

WILDCAT I.D. NUMBERS: Serial numbers began with 462005 () 10001. Numbers were coded as explained under the 1965 LeSabre Series I.D. Number section.

WILDCAT SERIES 46200

Series No.	Body/Style No.	Body Type & Seating	Factory Price	Shipping Weight	Prod. Total
46200	46269	4-dr Sed-6P	3117	4058	10,184
46200	46239	4-dr HT Sed-6P	3278	4089	7,499
46200	46237	2-dr Spt Cpe-6P	3219	3988	6,031
46200	46267	2-dr Conv-6P	3431	3812	4,616*

NOTE: Symbol (*) indicates that convertible production total also includes Wildcat Deluxe convertibles.

ENGINE: V-8. Overhead valve. Cast iron block. Displacement: 401 cid. Bore and stroke: 4.18 x 3.64 inches. Compression ratio: 10.25:1. Brake horsepower: 325 at 4600 rpm. Five main bearings. Hydraulic valve lifters. Carburetor: Carter AFB or Rochester 4GC four-barrel.

WILDCAT DELUXE — SERIES 46400 — This was a trim variation on the Wildcat Series 46200, with slightly plusher interior combinations available.

WILDCAT DELUXE I.D. NUMBERS: Serial numbers began with 464005 () 10001. Numbers were coded as explained under the 1965 LeSabre I.D. Number section.

WILDCAT DELUXE SERIES 46400

Series No.	Body/Style No.	Body Type & Seating	Factory Price	Shipping Weight	Prod. Total
46400	46469	4-dr Sed-6P	3218	4045	9,765
46400	46439	4-dr HT Sed-6P	3338	4075	13,903
46400	46437	2-dr Spt Cpe-6P	3272	4014	11,617
46400	46467	2-dr Conv-6P	3651	4064	4,616*

NOTE: Symbol (*) indicates that convertible production total also includes Series 46200 Wildcat convertibles.

ENGINE: Specifications were the same as those listed for the 1965 Wildcat Series 46200.

WILDCAT CUSTOM — SERIES 46600 — This was the plushest of all Wildcats with interiors featuring vinyl bucket seats or notchback full-width seats in cloth. Offered only in three styles, this was essentially a trim option. Production figures are included with those given for corresponding Wildcat Deluxe figures.

WILDCAT CUSTOM I.D. NUMBERS: Serial numbers began with 466005 () 1001. Numbers were coded as explained under the 1965 LeSabre Series I.D. Number section.

WILDCAT CUSTOM SERIES 46600

Series No.	Body/Style No.	Body Type & Seating	Factory Price	Shipping Weight	Prod. Total
46600	46639	4-dr HT Sed-6P	3552	4160	—
46600	46637	2-dr Spt Cpe-6P	3493	4047	—
46600	46667	2-dr Conv-6P	3431	4069	—

ENGINE: Specifications were the same as those listed for the 1965 Wildcat Series 46200.

1965 Buick, Electra 225 two-door Sport Coupe, V-8 (PH)

ELECTRA 225 — SERIES 48200 — The largest Buick was equipped with totally new styling for 1965, although the hallmark rear wheelhouse skirts and wide, ribbed lower body moldings were retained. A distinctive cross-hatch textured cast grille was used at the front. Interiors were fabrics or vinyls, with woodgrain dash accents. Standard Electra features, in addition to those found on less costly Buicks, included Super Turbine transmission; power steering; power brakes; Deluxe steering wheel; two-speed electric wipers with washer; electric clock; license frames; trip mileage indicator; cigar lighter in rear; safety buzzer; back-up lights; and power brake signal lamp. Convertibles had two-way power seat control and outside rearview mirror.

ELECTRA 225 SERIES 48200

Series No.	Body/Style No.	Body Type & Seating	Factory Price	Shipping Weight	Prod. Total
48200	43269	4-dr Sed-6P	3989	4261	12,459
48200	48239	4-dr HT Sed-6P	4121	4284	12,842
48200	48237	2-dr Spt Cpe-6P	3999	4208	6,302

ENGINE: Specifications were the same as those listed for the 1965 Wildcat Series 45200.

ELECTRA 225 I.D. NUMBERS: Serial numbers began with 432005 () 100001. Numbers were coded as explained under the 1965 LeSabre Series I.D. Number section.

ELECTRA 225 CUSTOM: A plusher car than the Electra, the Custom featured elegant interior appointment with fine vinyls and fabrics used for trimming.

ELECTRA 225 CUSTOM I.D. NUMBERS: Serial numbers began with 484005 () 100001. Numbers were coded as explained under the 1965 LeSabre Series I.D. Number section.

ELECTRA 225 CUSTOM SERIES 48400

Series No.	Body/Style No.	Body Type & Seating	Factory Price	Shipping Weight	Prod. Total
48400	48469	4-dr Sed-6P	4168	4292	7,197
48400	48439	4-dr HT Sed-6P	4300	4344	29,932
48400	48437	2-dr Spt Cpe-6P	4179	4228	9,570
48400	48467	2-dr Conv-6P	4350	4325	8,508

ENGINE: Specifications were the same as those listed for the 1965 Wildcat Series 45200.

1965 Buick, Riviera two-door hardtop, V-8 (AA)

RIVIERA — SERIES 49447 — The last recycle of the original Riviera body was also the most distinctive. Headlamps were now stacked vertically behind the fender grilles, which opened when the lamps were turned on. Taillamps were housed in the bumper bar, giving a cleaner rear deck appearance. Riviera script appeared on the front fenders and deck lid. Standard Riviera features included: Super Turbine transmission; power steering; power brakes; two-speed electric wipers with washer; back-up lights; Glare-proof rearview mirror; parking brake signal light; safety buzzer; map light; electric clock; tilt steering wheel; automatic trunk light; license plate frames; upper and lower instrument panel safety pads; full carpeting; double door release handles; console-mounted gear selector; Walnut paneling on instrument panel and individual front bucket seats. Optional Custom interiors included carpeted lower doors.

RIVIERA I.D. NUMBERS: Serial numbers began at 494005 () 900001. Numbers were coded as explained under the 1965 LeSabre Series I.D. Number section.

RIVIERA SERIES 48400

Series No.	Body/Style No.	Body Type & Seating	Factory Price	Shipping Weight	Prod. Total
49400	49447	2-dr Spt Cpe-4P	4318	4036	34,586

ENGINE: Specifications were the same as those listed for the 1965 Wildcat Series 45200.

NOTE: A Gran Sport option was available for the 1965 Riviera. It included a 360 brake horsepower Super Wildcat V-8 with dual four-barrel carburetors, large diameter dual exhaust, positive traction differential and bright metal engine accents including a large plated air cleaner and polished ribbed valve covers. Exterior identification was provided by the use of GS full wheelcovers and Gran Sport lettering below the Riviera script on the deck lid and on the front fenders.

CHASSIS FEATURES: Wheelbase: (Series 43300, 43400, 44300, 44400) 115 inches; (Series 44200 and 44400 Sport Wagons) 120 inches; (Series 45200 and 45400) 123 inches; (Series 46200, 46400, 46600, 48200 and 48400) 126 inches; (Series 49447) 119 inches. Overall length: (Series 43300, 43400, 44300 and 44400) 203.2 inches; (Series 43400 Station Wagon) 203.4 inches; (Series 44200 and 44400 Sport Wagon) 208.2 inches; (Series 45200 and 45400) 123 inches; (Series 46200, 46400, 46600) 219.8 inches; (Series 48200 and 48400) 224.1 inches; (Series 49447) 209 inches. Front tread: (Series 43300, 43400, 44400 and 44200) 58 inches; (Series 45200 and 45400) 63 inches; (Series 46200, 46400, 46600, 48200 and 48400) 63.4 inches; (Series 49447) 60 inches. Rear tread: (Series 43300, 43400, 44400 and 44200) 58 inches; (Series 45200, 45400, 46200, 46400, 46600, 48200 and 48400) 62 inches; (Series 49447) 59 inches. Tire sizes: (Series 43300, 43400,

44300, 43400) 6.95 x 14; (Series 44400 and 44200) 7.75 x 14; (Series 45200 and 45400) 8.15 x 15; (Series 46200, 46400 and 46600) 8.45 x 15; (Series 48200 and 48400) 8.75 x 15; and (Series 49447) 8.45 x 15.

POWERTRAIN OPTIONS: A three-speed transmission was standard on Series 43300, 43400, 44300, 43400, 44200, 44400, 45200, 45400, 46200, 46400 and 46600. Super Turbine Drive was optional on the preceding series and standard on Series 48200, 48400 and 49747. A four-speed manual transmission was optional for Series 43300, 43400, 44300, 44200, 44400, 46200, 46400 and 46600. A 300 cid/250 bhp V-8 was optional for Series 43300, 43400, 44300, 44200, 44400, 45200 and 45400. The 425 cid/340 bhp V-8 was optional for the Series 46200, 46400, 46600, 48200, 48400 and 49747. A 425 cid/360 bhp V-8 equipped with dual four-barrel carburetors was a dealer option for Series 46200, 46400, 46600, 48200, 48400 and 49747. This 360 hp V-8 was included with Riviera Gran Sport option. The 401 cid/325 hp V-8 was included with the Skylark Gran Sport option.

CONVENIENCE OPTIONS: Power steering (standard on 46000, 48000 and 49747 Series). Power brakes (standard on 46000, 48000 and 49747 Series). Power windows (standard on Electra 225 Custom convertible, not offered for 44300 and 44400 Series). Power seat controls (four-way or six-way; a two-way power seat was standard on the Electra 225 convertible). Air conditioning. AM radio. AM-FM radio (full-size only). Seven-position tilt steering wheel (standard on 49747). Remote control outside rearview mirror. Tinted glass. Four-note horn. Tachometer. Automatic trunk release (full-size only). Electra cruise (full-size only). Cornering lights (full-size only). Consoles for Skylark bucket seats. Luggage rack for Sport Wagons. Front seat belt deletion. Heater/Defroster deletion.

HISTORICAL FOOTNOTES: Calendar year production was 653,838 units, allowing Buick to slip by Dodge and Oldsmobile into fourth place in the industry. Model year production was 600,787. In July, Edward T. Rollert ("father of the Skylark") moved to a GM executive position and Robert L. Kessler became Buick's general manager. The Riviera Gran Sport was advertised as "An iron fist in a velvet glove" and had a top speed of 125-130 mph. The Skylark Gran Sport was advertised as a Howitzer with windshield wipers. 44200 and 44400 Series station wagons that had a raised roof section were called Sport Wagons.

1966

SPECIAL — SERIES 43300 (V-6) — A new body, with more sheet metal sculpting, graced the 1966 Special. Each front fender had three ventiports. Rear fenders earned Special lettering. Otherwise, the car was almost completely devoid of bright metal trim on the sides. Small hubcaps were standard. Regular equipment included a heater and defroster; directional signals; ashtray; cigar lighter; dual key locking system; Step-On parking brake; front door-operated courtesy light; upper instrument panel pad; outside rearview mirror; two-speed wipers with washer; padded sun visors; front and rear seat belts and back-up lamps. Interiors were vinyl and cloth, with an all-vinyl trim optional.

SPECIAL V-6 I.D. NUMBERS: Serial numbers began with 433006 () 10001 and up. The first five symbols were numerals representing the style. The sixth symbol was a numeral '6' representing the 1966 model year. The seventh symbol was a letter representing the plant code and the last six symbols were numerals representing sequential plant production number, with series mixed in production.

SPECIAL I.D. NUMBERS: Serial numbers were located on the hinge pillar post, left side, above the instrument panel and stamped on the engine block. The first five symbols were the model number. The first symbol was a '4' indicating Buick Motor Division products. The second through fifth symbols indicated the series and body style (see model numbers on tables below). The sixth symbol was a number indicating model year: 6 = 1966. The seventh symbol was a letter representing the plant code, as follows: B = Baltimore, Md.; C = Southgate, Calif.; D = Doraville Ga.; H = Flint, Mich.; I = Oshawa, Ont., Canada; K = Leeds, Mo.; V = Bloomfield, Mich.; X = Fairfax, Kans.; Y = Wilmington, Del.; Z = Fremont, Ohio. The last six symbols were numerals representing the plant sequential production number, with series mixed in production. Engine numbers were stamped in various positions on the crankcase, usually, or on the cylinder block. Engine production codes, stamped on right-hand side of block, were as follows: (6-cyl.) MH,MK; (300 cid V-8) ML, MM; (340 cid V-8) MB, MC, MA; (GS 400/400 cid V-8) MR; (401 cid V-8) HT, MV; (425 cid V-8) MV, MW, MZ.

SPECIAL SERIES 43300

Series No.	Body/Style No.	Body Type & Seating	Factory Price	Shipping Weight	Prod. Total
43300	43369	4-dr Sed-6P	2401	3046	8,797
43300	43307	2-dr Cpe-6P	2348	3009	9,322
43300	43367	2-dr Conv-6P	2604	3092	1,357
43300	43335	4-dr Sta Wag-6P	2695	3296	1,451

ENGINE: V-6. Overhead valve. Cast iron block. Displacement: 225 cid. Bore and stroke: 3.75 x 3.4 inches. Compression ratio: 9.0:1. Brake horsepower: 160 at 4200 rpm. Four main bearings. Hydraulic valve lifters. Carburetor: Rochester 2GC two-barrel.

SPECIAL — SERIES 43400 (V-8) — Identical externally to the 1966 Special V-6 described above, the V-8 Specials were numbered as a separate series.

SPECIAL V-8 I.D. NUMBERS: Serial numbers began with 434006 () 100001. Numbers were coded as explained under the Special Series I.D. Number section.

SPECIAL SERIES 43400

Series No.	Body/Style No.	Body Type & Seating	Factory Price	Shipping Weight	Prod. Total
43400	43469	4-dr Sed-6P	2471	3148	9,355
43400	43407	2-dr Cpe-6P	2418	3091	5,719
43400	43467	2-dr Conv-6P	2671	3223	2,036
43400	43435	4-dr Sta Wag-6P	2764	3399	3,038

ENGINE: V-8. Overhead valve. Cast iron block. Displacement: 300 cid. Bore and stroke: 3.75 x 3.4 inches. Compression ratio: 9.0:1. Brake horsepower: 210 at 4600 rpm. Five main bearings. Hydraulic valve lifters. Carburetor: Rochester 2GC two-barrel.

SPECIAL DELUXE — SERIES 43500 (V-6) — The Special Deluxe had the same body as the Special, but with slightly more brightwork, including a rear quarter bright spear with Special lettering above it (over the wheelhouse), bright window reveals and a stand-up hood ornament. Special Deluxe models had additional standard features including: rear ashtray; Deluxe steering wheel; dual armrests; carpeting and dual horns. Sedan interiors were cloth and vinyl, while the other models were trimmed in all-vinyl material. A notchback all-vinyl front seat was optional for the coupe and sport coupe.

SPECIAL DELUXE I.D. NUMBERS: Serial numbers began with 435006 () 10001. Numbers were coded as explained under the 1966 Special Series 43300 I.D. Number section.

SPECIAL DELUXE SERIES 43500

Series No.	Body/Style No.	Body Type & Seating	Factory Price	Shipping Weight	Prod. Total
43500	43569	4-dr Sed-6P	2485	3045	5,501
43500	43507	2-dr Cpe-6P	2432	3009	2,359
43500	43517	2-dr Spt Cpe-6P	2504	3038	25,071
43500	43535	4-dr Sta Wag-6P	2783	3290	824

ENGINE: Specifications were the same as those listed for the 1966 Special Series 43300.

SPECIAL DELUXE — SERIES 43600 (V-8) — Identical externally to the Special Deluxe V-6 described above, the V-8 Special Deluxes were numbered as a separate series.

SPECIAL DELUXE SERIES 43600

Series No.	Body/Style No.	Body Type & Seating	Factory Price	Shipping Weight	Prod. Total
43600	43669	4-dr Sed-6P	2555	3156	26,773
43600	43607	2-dr Cpe-6P	2502	3112	4,908
43600	43617	2-dr Spt Cpe-6P	2574	3130	10,350
43600	43635	2-dr Sta Wag-6P	2853	3427	7,592

ENGINE: Specifications were the same as those listed for the 1966 Special Series 43400 V-8.

1966 Buick, Skylark four-door hardtop, V-8

SKYLARK — SERIES 44300 (V-6) — Buick's plushest intermediate was the recipient of additional exterior bright moldings. They included a lower body molding that ran full-length, with wheelhouse kick-ups, simulated vent grids on front fenders, Skylark script and emblems on rear fenders and a specific rear cove panel. A notchback front seat was standard on the four-door hardtop, optional on other models. Bucket seats, with a reclining passenger seat, were optional, as were headrests. Trim was all-vinyl or cloth and vinyl combinations. All Skylarks had the following additional standard equipment: Custom-padded seat cushions, Deluxe specific wheelcovers, ashtray and glove compartment lights and front interior courtesy lamps.

SKYLARK V-6 I.D. NUMBERS: Serial numbers began with 44300 () 10001. Serial numbers were coded as explained under the 1966 Special Series 43300 I.D. Number section.

SKYLARK SERIES 44300

Series No.	Body/Style No.	Body Type & Seating	Factory Price	Shipping Weight	Prod. Total
44300	44339	4-dr HT Sed-6P	2846	3172	1,422
44300	44307	2-dr Cpe-6P	2624	3034	1,454
44300	44317	2-dr Spt Cpe-6P	2687	3069	2,456
44300	44367	2-dr Conv-6P	2837	3158	608

ENGINE: Specifications were the same as those listed for the 1966 Special Series 43300 V-6.

SKYLARK — SERIES 44400 (V-8) — Identical externally to the 1966 Skylark V-6 described above, the V-8 Skylarks were numbered as a separate series.

SKYLARK V-8 I.D. NUMBERS: Serial numbers began with 44400 () 10001. Serial numbers were coded as explained under the 1966 Special Series 43300 I.D. Number section.

SKYLARK SERIES 44400

Series No.	Body/Style No.	Body Type & Seating	Factory Price	Shipping Weight	Prod. Total
44400	44439	4-dr HT Sed-6P	2916	3285	18,729
44400	44437	2-dr Cpe-6P	2694	3145	6,427
44400	44417	2-dr Spt Cpe-6P	2757	3152	33,086
44400	44467	2-dr Conv-6P	2904	3259	6,129

ENGINE: Specifications were the same as listed for the 1966 Special Series 43400 V-8.

SKYLARK GRAN SPORT — SERIES 44600 — Buick moved a step closer to a muscle car image with the 1966 Gran Sport. Equipped like the Skylark, the sporting image was pursued via a black matte finish rear cove panel, Skylark GS emblems on quarters and instrument panel, Gran Sport nameplates on the grille and deck, and whitewall or redline 7.75 x 14 tires. Bright simulated air scoops, side paint stripes and a blacked-out grille gave flashier identity. There was no hood ornament. Interiors were all-vinyl,

with a notchback front seat standard and bucket front seats optional. The Skylark had a 401-cid V-8 as standard equipment. However, this engine was listed as a 400-cid engine, to get around the GM restriction on over 400-cid engines in midsize bodies.

1966 Buick, Skylark Gran Sport (GS) two-door Sport Coupe, V-8 (OCW)

SKYLARK GRAN SPORT I.D. NUMBERS: Vehicle Identification Numbers began with 446006 () 100001. Numbers were coded as explained under the 1966 Special Series I.D. Number section.

SKYLARK GRAN SPORT SERIES 44600

Series No.	Body/Style No.	Body Type & Seating	Factory Price	Shipping Weight	Prod. Total
44600	44607	2-dr Cpe-6P	2956	3479	1,835
44600	44617	2-dr Spt Cpe-6P	3019	3428	9,934
44600	44667	2-dr Conv-6P	3167	3532	2,047

ENGINE: V-8. Overhead valves. Cast iron block. Displacement: 401 cid (advertised as 400 cid). Bore and stroke: 4.18 x 3.64 inches. Compression ratio: 10.25:1. Brake horsepower: 325 at 4400 rpm. Five main bearings. Hydraulic valve lifters. Carburetor: Carter AFB four-barrel.

SPORT WAGON AND SPORT WAGON CUSTOM — SERIES 44200 AND 44400 (V-8) — Buick's popular intermediate wagons continued to feature a glass skyroof and two- or three-seat configuration. The Sport Wagon had most Special Deluxe features, plus brush-finished wiper arms, Sport Wagon quarter panel script and specific taillights. Interiors were all-vinyl. The Custom versions had satin finished lower body moldings, Deluxe steering wheel and tailgate lamps. Custom padded seat cushions and Custom interior trim was used, featuring plusher upholstery and carpeting extending to the lower doors.

SPORT WAGON AND SPORT WAGON CUSTOM I.D. NUMBERS: Serial numbers began with 442006 () 100001 for the Sport Wagon and 444006 () 100001 on the Sport Wagon Custom. Numbers were coded as described under the 1966 Special Series I.D. Number section.

SPORT WAGONS SERIES 44200/44400

Series No.	Body/Style No.	Body Type & Seating	Factory Price	Shipping Weight	Prod. Total
44200	44265	4-dr Sta Wag-3S	3173	3811	2,667
44200	44255	4-dr Sta Wag-2S	3025	3713	2,469
44400	44465	4-dr Cus Sta Wag-3S	3293	3844	9,510
44400	44455	4-dr Cus Sta Wag-2S	3155	3720	6,964

ENGINE: V-8. Overhead valve. Cast iron block. Displacement: 340 cid. Bore and stroke: 3.75 x 3.85 inches. Compression ratio: 9.0:1. Brake horsepower: 220 at 4000 rpm. Five main bearings. Hydraulic valve lifters. Carburetor: Rochester 2GC two-barrel.

LESABRE — SERIES 45200 — Slightly face lifted from 1965, the lowest-priced full-sized Buick had three ventiports on each front fender and LeSabre script on the quarter panels. Narrow lower body moldings of bright metal were used. Interiors were vinyl and cloth. Standard equipment included front and rear seat belts, Step-On parking brake, door-operated courtesy lamps, dual armrests, dual horns and carpeting.

LESABRE I.D. NUMBERS: Vehicle Identification Numbers began with 45200 () 10001. Numbers were coded as explained under the 1966 Buick Special Series I.D. Number section.

LESABRE SERIES 45200

Series No.	Body/Style No.	Body Type & Seating	Factory Price	Shipping Weight	Prod. Total
45200	45269	4-dr Sed-6P	2942	3796	39,146
45200	45239	4-dr HT Sed-6P	3081	3828	17,740
45200	45237	2-dr HT Cpe-6P	3022	3751	13,843

ENGINE: Specifications were the same as listed under 1966 Sport Wagon and Sport Wagon Custom engine data.

LESABRE CUSTOM — SERIES 45400 — Custom models had plusher interiors with Deluxe steering wheel, two-speed wiper and washer equipment, and back-up lamps. Optional Custom trim included bucket seats with black accents.

LESABRE CUSTOM I.D. NUMBERS: Vehicle Identification Numbers began with 454006 () 100001. Numbers were coded as explained under the 1966 Buick Special Series I.D. Number section.

LESABRE CUSTOM SERIES 45400

Series No.	Body/Style No.	Body Type & Seating	Factory Price	Shipping Weight	Prod. Total
45400	45469	4-dr Sed-6P	3035	3788	25,932
45400	45439	4-dr HT Sed-6P	3174	3824	26,914
45400	45437	2-dr HT Cpe-6P	3109	3746	18,830
45400	45467	2-dr Conv-6P	3326	3833	4,994

ENGINE: Specifications were the same as those listed under 1966 Sport Wagon and Sport Wagon Custom engine data.

WILDCAT — SERIES 46400 — Buick's middle-priced, full-sized car again pursued a performance image. A specific grille with vertical texturing was used. There was a Wildcat hood ornament above it. Wildcat lettering appeared across the deck lid and on rear quarter panels. (Early 1966 Wildcats had "Wildcat" spelled out in script on the rear quarter panels while the later ones used individual block letters.) Simulated air intake grids appeared behind the front wheelhouses. Interiors were cloth and vinyl, or all-vinyl. Standard features included the LeSabre's accoutrements plus a glovebox light.

WILDCAT I.D. NUMBERS: Vehicle Identification Numbers began with 464006 () 900001. Numbers were coded as explained under the 1966 Special Series I.D. Number section.

WILDCAT SERIES 46400

Series No.	Body/Style No.	Body Type & Seating	Factory Price	Shipping Weight	Prod. Total
46400	46469	4-dr Sed-6P	3233	4070	14,389
46400	46439	4-dr HT Sed-6P	3391	4108	15,081
46400	46437	2-dr HT Cpe-6P	3326	4003	9,774
46400	46467	2-dr Conv-6P	3480	4065	2,690

1966 Buick, Wildcat two-door convertible, V-8 (PH)

ENGINE: V-8. Overhead valve. Cast iron block. Displacement: 401 cid. Bore and stroke: 4.18 x 3.64 inches. Compression ratio: 10.25:1. Brake horsepower: 325 at 4600 rpm. Five main bearings. Hydraulic valve lifters. Carburetor: Carter AFB four-barrel.

WILDCAT CUSTOM — SERIES 46600 — This was a plusher Wildcat, with Deluxe steering wheel, padded-type armrests, outside rearview mirror and Custom headlining (except convertible). Plusher cloth and vinyl or all-vinyl trim was used, with notchback or Strato bucket front seat (reclining passenger seat with the latter) and headrests.

WILDCAT CUSTOM I.D. NUMBERS: Vehicle Identification Numbers began with 466006 () 900001. Numbers were coded as explained under the 1966 Special Series I.D. Number section.

WILDCAT CUSTOM SERIES 46600

Series No.	Body/Style No.	Body Type & Seating	Factory Price	Shipping Weight	Prod. Total
46600	46639	4-dr HT Sed-6P	3606	4176	13,060
46600	46637	2-dr HT Cpe-6P	3547	4018	10,800
46600	46667	2-dr Conv-6P	3701	4079	2,790

ENGINE: Specifications were the same as those listed under Wildcat Series 46400 engine data.

1966 Buick, Wildcat Gran Sport two-door hardtop, V-8

WILDCAT GRAN SPORT: In 1966, a Wildcat Gran Sport option was offered for the one, and only, time. It was available for the base or Custom two-door Sport Coupe or convertible. Ingredients included a chrome-plated air cleaner; cast aluminum rocker arm covers; dual exhaust; heavy-duty front and rear suspension; positive traction rear axle and GS identification plates for the front and rear of the car.

ELECTRA 225 — SERIES 48200 — The largest Buick, with a distinctly bigger body, was similar to 1965. Fender skirts were standard, with a full-length lower body molding wider than those of other Buicks. Electra 225 script appeared on the rear fenders. The car's prestige was enhanced by the use of four ventiports per fender. Standard features, in addition to those of lower-priced Buicks, included Custom-padded seat cushions; Custom front seat belts with retractors; electric clock; parking brake signal lamp; glovebox and map lights; Glare-proof mirror; power steering; power brakes and Super Turbine automatic transmission. Interiors were cloth and vinyl combinations.

1966 Buick, Electra 225 four-door hardtop, V-8 (AA)

ELECTRA 225 I.D. NUMBERS: Vehicle Identification Numbers began with 482006 () 100001. Numbers were coded as explained under the 1966 Special Series I.D. Numbers section.

ELECTRA 225 SERIES 48200

Series No.	Body/Style No.	Body Type & Seating	Factory Price	Shipping Weight	Prod. Total
48200	48269	4-dr Sed-6P	4022	4255	11,692
48200	48239	4-dr HT Sed-6P	4153	4271	10,792
48200	42837	2-dr HT Cpe-6P	4032	4176	4,882

ENGINE: Specifications were the same as listed under 1966 Wildcat Series 46400 engine data.

ELECTRA 225 CUSTOM — SERIES 48400 — This was an even plusher Electra 225, with Custom notchback front seat, in cloth, or Strato buckets, in vinyl, for the convertible. All Custom interiors had carpeted lower door panels. Although basically a trim option, Electra 225 Customs were numbered as a separate series.

ELECTRA 225 CUSTOM I.D. NUMBERS: Vehicle Identification Numbers began with 484006 () 100001. Numbers were coded as explained under the 1966 Buick Special Series I.D. Number section.

ELECTRA 225 CUSTOM SERIES 48400

Series No.	Body/Style No.	Body Type & Seating	Factory Price	Shipping Weight	Prod. Total
48400	48469	4-dr Sed-6P	4201	4292	9,368
48400	48439	4-dr HT Sed-6P	4332	4323	34,149
48400	48437	2-dr HT Cpe-6P	4211	4230	10,119
48400	48467	2-dr Conv-6P	4378	4298	7,175

ENGINE: Specifications were the same as those listed under 1966 Wildcat Series 46400 engine data.

RIVIERA — SERIES 49487 — A sleek new body graced the first totally restyled Riviera since 1963. Headlamps were once again horizontally paired, unlike 1965. Now, they retracted above the grille when not in use. The body's clean lines were enhanced by the lack of vent windows. Inside, a new instrument panel was found, with a unique, vertical, drum-type speedometer and a full complement of gauges. Standard equipment included power steering; power brakes; Super Turbine transmission; tilt steering wheel; dual exhaust; full carpeting; padded instrument panel; dual-speed wipers and washer; back-up lamps; outside rearview mirror; shatter-resistant inside mirror and front and rear seat belts. Bucket or bench-style front seats were standard at the purchaser's choice. Strato-buckets with Custom all-vinyl trim were available, as were other Custom trim options.

NOTE: Gran Sport equipment was offered for the 1966 Riviera. This year it consisted of a chromed air cleaner and aluminum rocker covers for the standard 425 cid/340 bhp V-8 plus heavy-duty shocks front and rear, 8.45 x 15 red or whiteline tires, positive traction differential and GS emblems on front fenders and instrument panel. Also available as a "dealer kit" was a 360 hp version of the 425 cid V-8 with dual four-barrel carburetors.

1966 Buick, Riviera two-door hardtop, V-8

RIVIERA I.D. NUMBERS: Vehicle Identification Numbers began with 494876 ( ) 900001. Numbers were coded as explained under the 1966 Special Series I.D. Number section.

RIVIERA SERIES 49400

Series No.	Body/Style No.	Body Type & Seating	Factory Price	Shipping Weight	Prod. Total
49400	49487	2-dr Spt Cpe-4P	4424	4180	45,348

ENGINE: V-8. Overhead valve. Cast iron block. Displacement: 425 cid. Bore and stroke: 4.3125 x 3.64 inches. Compression ratio: 10.25:1. Brake horsepower: 340 at 4400 rpm. Five main bearings. Hydraulic valve lifters. Carburetor: Rochester 4MC four-barrel.

CHASSIS FEATURES: Wheelbase: (Series 43300, 43400, 43500, 43600, 44300, 44400, 44600) 115 inches; (Series 44200 and 44400 Sport Wagons) 120 inches; (Series 45200 and 45400) 123 inches; (Series 46400 and 46600) 126 inches; (Series 49487) 119 inches. Overall length: (Series 43300, 43400, 43500, 43600, 44300, 44400, 44600) 204 inches; (Series 44200 and

44400 Sport Wagons) 209 inches; (Series 45200 and 45400) 216.9 inches; (Series 46400 and 46600) 219.9 inches; (Series 48200 and 48400) 223.4 inches; (Series 49487) 211.2 inches. Front tread: (Special) 58 inches; (LeSabre) 63 inches; (Wildcat/Electra/Riviera) 63.4 inches. Rear tread: (Special) 59 inches; (All others) 63 inches. Tires: (Series 43300, 43500) 6.95 x 14; (Series 43400, 43600 and 44400) 7.35 x 14; (Series 44600) 7.75 x 14; (Series 44200 and 44400 Sport Wagons) 8.25 x 14; (Series 45200 and 45400) 8.45 x 15; (Series 46400 and 46600) 8.45 x 15; (Series 48200 and 48400) 8.85 x 15; (Series 49487) 8.45 x15.

POWERTRAIN OPTIONS: A three-speed manual transmission was standard on Series 43300, 43400, 43500, 44300, 44400, 44200, 44600, 45200, 45400, 46400 and 46600. Super Turbine automatic transmission was standard on Series 48200 and 49487 and optional on Series 44400 and 46400. Turbine transmission was optional for all other models. A four-speed manual transmission was optional for Series 44400 and 44600. A 340 cid/260 bhp V-8 was optional for Series 43400, 44300, 44400, 44200, 45200 and 45400. The 425 cid/340 bhp V-8 was standard on Model 49487 and optional on Series 46400, 46600, 48200 and 48400. A 425 cid/360 bhp engine with dual four-barrel carburetors could be dealer-installed on 49487.

CONVENIENCE OPTIONS: Power steering ($121, standard on 48000 and 49487). Power brakes ($42, standard on 48000 and 49487). Power windows ($105). Four-way/Six-way power seat controls ($69/$95). Air conditioning ($421). AM radio ($88). AM/FM radio ($175). Seven-position tilt steering wheel ($42). Remote control outside rearview mirror ($7). Tinted glass ($42). Tinted windshield only ($28). Four-note horn ($16). Automatic trunk release ($13). Electro cruise ($56-$63). Cornering lights, full-size only ($34). Simulated wire wheelcovers ($58). Five-spoke chromed wheels ($89). Heater/Defroster deletion ($96 credit). Luggage rack for Sport Wagons.

NOTE: Typical option prices for midsize models. Prices vary slightly for compacts and full-size models.

HISTORICAL FOOTNOTES: Calendar year production was 580,421 units. Buick fell to sixth position and Oldsmobile became the fifth largest automaker in the United States. Model year production was 558,870 units. The Riviera GS could do the quarter-mile in 16.4 seconds at 87 mph and had a top speed of 125 mph. The Skylark GS could do 0-to-60 mph in 7.6 seconds and cover the quarter-mile in 14.13 seconds at 95.13 mph. The Wildcat GS, offered only in 1966, was even faster. It did 0-to-60 mph in 7.5 seconds and had a top speed of 125 mph.

1967

1967 Buick, Special two-door pillared coupe, V-6 (OCW)

SPECIAL — SERIES 43300 (V-6) — A rehash of the 1966 style, distinguished by a new grille, the 1967 Special continued with rear quarter model name lettering and triple ventiports on front fenders. These lowest-priced Buicks were lacking in bright trim. Even the window surrounds were plain. Standard equipment

1910 Buick Model 10 Toy Tonneau. Price new was $1,150.

1920 Buick Series K (Model 44) roadster. Production of this model totaled 19,000 including 200 for export.

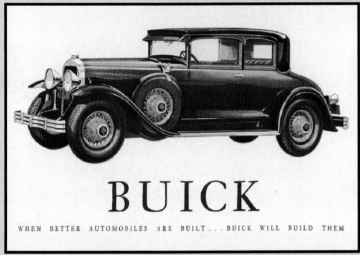

BUICK

WHEN BETTER AUTOMOBILES ARE BUILT...BUICK WILL BUILD THEM

Buick ad from the March 1929 issue of *Country Life* promoted the long-running Buick slogan: "When better automobiles are built, Buick will build them." The 1929 Buicks were the first cars styled in their entirety by General Motors Art and Colour department.

Battle Song of the Liberators

OUT of the West they have come, an army of flying men in a vast armada of planes, bent on a mission of liberation.

Conquered peoples have heard the drone of their engines, and looked up in new hope.

Oppressors have felt the weight of raining bombs, and seen inevitable doom in the endless flow of American power and wrath.

It is a fitting thing that one of our mightiest weapons in this air armada is a bomber named the Liberator.

And it is a proud though sobering task to build the engines from which such planes get their power.

To date, more than 50,000 of these engines have come from Buick plants, enough to power 12,500 bombers, whose battle song of liberation is heard over every American battle front.

But we know, here at Buick, that our task is not to be measured in terms of numbers so much as by the way our work lives up to the expectations of American flyers.

So far, we are told, they have found that work good.

And good we intend to keep it till the battle song of the Liberators is heard in triumph around the world.

BUICK

POWERS THE LIBERATOR*

*With Buick-built Pratt & Whitney air-cooled, valve-in-head aircraft engines

BUICK DIVISION of GENERAL MOTORS

Just as most automakers were involved in the war effort, Buick, too, supplied Pratt & Whitney air-cooled, valve-in-head aircraft engines to power Liberator bombers. Note the wartime alteration of the Buick slogan: "When better war goods are built, Buick will build them." A nice touch was that Buick would supply a copy of this ad to friends and family of Liberator crew members as a tribute to those men "now gallantly serving [their] country as a member of a fighting Liberator crew."

1934 Buick Series 90 (Model 96C) convertible coupe with rumbleseat. All Series 80 models were discontinued after the 1933 model year, but the convertible coupe was one of three former 80 series models "reborn" in Series 90 in 1934.

BUICK BITS 'n' PIECES

Many components of Buick automobiles through the years are memorable for one reason or another. Pictured are a few of these items that have made Buicks either fast, luxurious, styling leaders or just plain desirable.

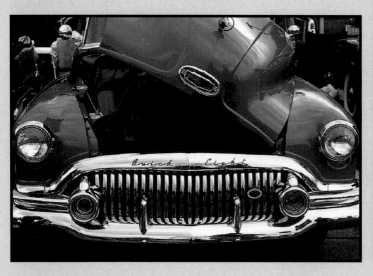

A 1951 winter maintenance reminder that Buick dealers sent to customers to "spark" service business at the dealerships. The artwork in this brochure is phenomenal for the time, reminiscent of modern-day claymation.

Current Event

1951 November							December 1951						
SUN	MON	TUE	WED	THU	FRI	SAT	SUN	MON	TUE	WED	THU	FRI	SAT
				1	2	3							1
4	5	6	7	8	9	10	2	3	4	5	6	7	8
11	12	13	14	15	16	17	9	10	11	12	13	14	15
18	19	20	21	22	23	24	16	17	18	19	20	21	22
25	26	27	28	29	30		23 30	24 31	25	26	27	28	29

QUALITY BUICK COMPANY
345 Main Street   Telephone 0000

YOUR TOWN U.S.A.

Passport to a silent world—

THE NEW "SOUND BARRIER" BODY BY FISHER

A dramatic portrayal of the Body by Fisher in the B-58 Buick Special, Two-Door Riviera.

Before you buy any new car, *listen* to how well it's built!

In a new "Sound Barrier" Body by Fisher, the absence of rattles—the freedom from road and engine noise—tells you plenty:

It tells you this body is built to shrug off the bumps, built to stay tight—for years.

The secret is Life-Span Build—a rigid,

integrally joined, bridge-type construction that provides extra body strength—more "living room" inside.

The new "Sound Barrier" body is another Fisher Body exclusive—the latest in 50 years of "firsts."

* * *

Another Fisher Body Bonus: ripple-free Safety Plate glass, front, rear *and side!*

SHAKEDOWN CRUISE FOR A TAUT SHIP. Two days on this torture rack are the equivalent of years of ruts and potholes. But even twists and jolts like these can't loosen up the tight build of a "Sound Barrier" Body by Fisher.

Only the "GM Five" give you the Bonus of BODY BY FISHER

CHEVROLET · PONTIAC · OLDSMOBILE · BUICK · CADILLAC

"Passport to a Silent World" was General Motors' 1958 ad campaign to promote Body By Fisher's new "Sound Barrier" design that was built into all GM cars, including this Buick Special Riviera coupe.

Tops in travel!

PHOTOGRAPH TAKEN AT LOS ANGELES INTERNATIONAL AIRPORT

Bob Hope, star of "Alias Jesse James" . . . makes Gulliver seem like a homebody. Naturally, he rolls on his AC-sparked Buick to start him on every trip! See him in the "Bob Hope Buick Show" on NBC-TV.

AC's symbol of lively horsepower, "Sparky," gives you "Hot Tips" for top traveling every week on the Walt Disney Studios' "Zorro" show on ABC-TV.

WHEN YOU REPLACE SPARK PLUGS . . .

ASK FOR AC . . . USED ON MORE

NEW CARS THAN ANY OTHER BRAND !

★ To maintain top horsepower, change to a new set of AC Hot Tip Spark Plugs at least every 10,000 miles.

AC SPARK PLUG · THE ELECTRONICS DIVISION OF GENERAL MOTORS

HOT TIP
SPARK PLUGS

A May 1959 ad that promoted the "Bob Hope Buick Show" on NBC-TV. The Buick convertible that Bob leaned against appears to be an Invicta.

1962 Buick Special Deluxe convertible.

1974 Buick Apollo hatchback coupe.

1996 Buick Skylark U.S. Olympic Gold Edition sedan, offered to commemorate the 100th birthday of the modern Olympic Games (1896-1996). It featured a gold USA/five-ring badge on both fenders, gold accent insert on bumper fascias and side moldings, gold Skylark nameplate, gold accented wheel covers, Gran Sport body-color grille, blacked-out rear taillamp lens, taupe fabric interior and four exterior color choices: red, white, black and (pictured) green.

1979 Buick Skyhawk Roadhawk hatchback coupe in two-tone light and dark silver. The optional Roadhawk package included wide-oval blackwall radial tires, blackout molding, Rallye ride and handling suspension, front airdam and integrated decklid spoiler, Oyster White bucket seats with hawk emblem and "Roadhawk" graphics.

1980 Buick Skylark Sport Coupe. This model was based on the new X-body shared with Chevy's Citation, Oldsmobile's Omega and Pontiac's Phoenix, which, due to safety recalls and mechanical problems resulted in one of the worst reputations among modern automobiles.

David Dunbar Buick, founder of Buick Motor Co., was commemorated in June 1994 in Arbroath, Scotland, where he was born in 1854. He moved to Detroit as a child, founded Buick Motor Co. there in 1903, and built the first production Buick automobiles in Flint, Michigan, in 1904. The Buick firm became the foundation for the creation of General Motors in 1908. David Buick left the company in 1908 and died in relative obscurity in 1929. Helping dedicate a plaque near Buick's birthplace were (l-to-r) Eric Buick—no relation—of Arbroath, who led the effort for recognition of the site; Robert E. Coletta, Buick general sales and service manager; Lawrence R. Gustin, Buick historian and news relations manager; and Brian Milne, provost of Angus District, of which Arbroath is a part. (Buick Motor Division photo).

MILESTONE CARS

1995 Buick Riviera coupe with first-year 1963 Riviera sport coupe.

Final-year 1996 Buick Roadmaster Collector's Edition sedan with first-year 1936 Roadmaster Trunk Sedan.

1999 Buick LeSabre Limited sedan with first-year 1959 LeSabre sedan.

BUICK DREAM CARS

The Buick Division of General Motors has been a prolific producer of concept cars, including the pioneering effort in 1938 called the "Y-Job" (front, left). Between 1938 and 1992, Buick exhibited many futuristic creations including the (front, middle) 1951 XP-300, (front, right) 1951 LeSabre, (second row, l-to-r) 1953 Wildcat I, 1954 Wildcat II, 1956 Centurion, 1963 Riviera Silver Arrow, and (back row, l-to-r) 1983 Questor, 1985 Wildcat, 1988 Lucerne, 1989 Park Avenue Essence, 1990 Bolero and 1992 Sceptre.

BUICK DREAM CARS

One of Buick's latest concept cars is the Cielo four-door convertible. The Cielo features roof panels that slide between two permanent rails, turning a hardtop sedan into a convertible in a few seconds.

included heater and defroster; ashtray; directional signals; cigar lighter; Step-On parking brake; front and rear seat belts; front door operated courtesy light; upper instrument panel safety pad; outside rearview mirror; dual speed wipers and washer; padded sun visors; back-up lamps and other mandated safety items. Vinyl and cloth upholstery was standard, while an all-vinyl interior was optional.

SPECIAL I.D. NUMBERS: Serial numbers were located on the hinge pillar post, left side, above the instrument panel and stamped on the engine block. The first five symbols were the model number. The first symbol was a '4' indicating Buick Motor Division products. The second through fifth symbols indicated the series and body style (see model numbers on tables below). The sixth symbol was a number indicating model year: 7 = 1967. The seventh symbol was a letter representing the plant code, as follows: B = Baltimore, Md.; C = Southgate, Calif.; D = Doraville, Ga.; H = Flint, Mich.; I = Oshawa, Ont., Canada; K = Leeds, Mo.; V = Bloomfield, Mich.; X = Fairfax, Kans.; Y = Wilmington, Del.; Z = Fremont, Ohio. The last six symbols were numerals representing the plant sequential production number, with series mixed in production. Engine numbers were stamped in various positions on the crankcase, usually, or on the cylinder block. Engine production codes, stamped on right-hand side of block, were as follows: (6-cyl.) NH; (300 cid V-8) NL, NM; (340 cid V-8) NB, NX, NA; (GS 400 400 cid V-8) NR; (430 cid V-8) ND, MD, NE.

SPECIAL SERIES 43300

Series No.	Body/Style No.	Body Type & Seating	Factory Price	Shipping Weight	Prod. Total
43300	43369	4-dr Sed-6P	2462	3077	4,711
43300	43307	2-dr Cpe-6P	2411	3071	6,989
43300	43335	4-dr Sta Wag-6P	2742	2812	908

ENGINE: V-6. Overhead valve. Cast iron block. Displacement: 225 cid. Bore and stroke: 3.75 x 3.4 inches. Compression ratio: 9.0:1. Brake horsepower: 160 at 4200 rpm. Four main bearings. Hydraulic valve lifters. Carburetor: Rochester 2GC two-barrel.

SPECIAL — SERIES 43400 V-8 — The Buick Special equipped with a V-8 engine was externally identical to the 1967 Special V-6 described above, except in regard to vehicle coding. The V-8 Specials were numbered as a separate series.

SPECIAL V-8 I.D. NUMBERS: Vehicle Identification Numbers began with 434007 () 600001. Numbers were coded as explained under the 1967 Special V-6 Series I.D. Number section.

SPECIAL SERIES 43400

Series No.	Body/Style No.	Body Type & Seating	Factory Price	Shipping Weight	Prod. Total
43400	43469	4-dr Sed-6P	2532	3196	5,793
43400	43407	2-dr Cpe-6P	2481	3173	8,937
43400	43435	4-dr Sta Wag-6P	2812	3343	1,688

ENGINE: V-8. Overhead valve. Cast iron block. Displacement: 300 cid. Bore and stroke: 3.75 x 3.4 inches. Compression ratio: 9.0:1. Brake horsepower: 210 at 4600 rpm. Five main bearings. Hydraulic valve lifters. Carburetor: Rochester 2GC two-barrel.

1967 Buick, Special Deluxe four-door sedan, V-6

SPECIAL DELUXE (V-6) — SERIES 43500 — A slightly plusher Special, with bright wheelhouse moldings, full-length bodyside bright moldings, black-accented rear cove panel and bright metal window surrounds. Special lettering appeared on the front

fenders. Standard equipment was the same as the Special, plus a rear seat ashtray, Deluxe steering wheel, dual side armrests, full carpeting and dual horns. Interiors were cloth and vinyl or all-vinyl.

SPECIAL DELUXE V-6 I.D. NUMBERS: Vehicle Identification Numbers began with 435007 () 600001. Numbers were coded as explained under the 1967 Special Series I.D. Number section.

SPECIAL DELUXE SERIES 43500

Series No.	Body/Style No.	Body Type & Seating	Factory Price	Shipping Weight	Prod. Total
43500	43569	4-dr Sed-6P	2545	3142	3,602
43500	43517	2-dr HT Cpe-6P	2566	3127	2,333

ENGINE: See 1967 Buick Special Series 43300 engine data.

SPECIAL DELUXE (V-8) — SERIES 43600 — Externally identical to the V-6-powered Special Deluxe described above, the V-8 Special Deluxes were numbered as a separate series. The Sport Wagon was available only with a 340-cid V-8.

SPECIAL DELUXE I.D. NUMBERS: Vehicle Identification Numbers began with 436007 () 100001 and up. Numbers were coded as explained under 1967 Special Series I.D. Number section.

SPECIAL DELUXE SERIES 43600

Series No.	Body/Style No.	Body Type & Seating	Factory Price	Shipping Weight	Prod. Total
43600	43669	4-dr Sed-6P	2615	3205	25,361
43600	43617	2-dr HT Cpe-6P	2636	3202	14,408
43600	43635	4-dr Sta Wag-6P	2901	3317	6,851

ENGINE: See 1967 Buick Special Series 43400 engine data.

SKYLARK — SERIES 44307 (V-6) — Only one model, the coupe, was offered with the V-6 for the 1967 Skylark. Standard equipment was the same as described for the 1967 Skylark V-8 Series 44400 below.

SKYLARK V-6 I.D. NUMBERS: Vehicle Identification Numbers began with 443077 () 600001. Numbers were coded as explained under the 1967 Special Series I.D. Number section.

SKYLARK SERIES 44307

Series No.	Body/Style No.	Body Type & Seating	Factory Price	Shipping Weight	Prod. Total
44300	44307	2-dr Cpe-6P	2665	3137	894

ENGINE: See 1967 Buick Special Series 43300 engine data.

1967-1/2 Buick, Skylark four-door sedan, V-8 (PH)

SKYLARK — SERIES 44400 (V-8) — Exterior distinction was gained by the use of rear fender skirts, a full-length lower body bright molding, simulated front fender vents, a ribbed rear cove panel and a grille with more horizontal bars. Skylark script used on the rear quarters and Skylarks had no ventiports. Cloth and vinyl trim with bench front seats was standard, except on the convertible, which was all-vinyl trimmed. All-vinyl was optional for other models and bucket seats with consoles were also offered as an option.

SKYLARK V-8 I.D. NUMBERS: Vehicle Identification Numbers began with 44407 () 600001. Numbers were coded as explained under the 1967 Special Series I.D. Number section.

SKYLARK SERIES 44400

Series No.	Body/Style No.	Body Type & Seating	Factory Price	Shipping Weight	Prod. Total
44400	44407	2-dr Cpe-6P	2735	3229	3,165
44400	44469	4-dr Sed-6P	2767	3324	9,123
44400	44439	4-dr HT Sed-6P	2950	3373	13,673
44400	44417	2-dr HT Cpe-6P	2798	3199	40,940
44400	44467	2-dr Conv-5P	2945	3335	6,319

ENGINE: Specifications for the Skylark Series 44400 models were the same as engine data listed for 1967 Buick Skylark Series 43400 models, except in the case of the four-door hardtop sedan and Sportwagon. These cars came standard with a 340 cid V-8 having 3.75 x 3.85 inch bore and stroke measurements, 9.0:1 compression and 220 horsepower at 4400 rpm with a Rochester 2GC two-barrel carburetor.

SPORTWAGON — SERIES 44200 AND 44400 — Now spelled as one word, the series name 'Sportwagon' appeared in script on station wagon rear fenders. These long-wheelbase wagons continued to feature the glass Skyroof raised roofline. They used the Skylark grille, but had ventiports and bright rocker and wheelhouse moldings. Specific taillights were used. Standard equipment was similar to that of the Special Deluxe. Interiors were vinyl. Models in the 44400 series had Custom interiors, with padded seat cushions and a tailgate lamp.

SPORTWAGON I.D. NUMBERS: Vehicle Identification Numbers began with 442007 () 600001 or 444007 () 600001. Numbers were coded as explained under the 1967 Special Series I.D. Number section.

SPORTWAGON SERIES 44200/44300

Series No.	Body/Style No.	Body Type & Seating	Factory Price	Shipping Weight	Prod. Total
44200	44255	4-dr Sta Wag-6P	3025	3713	5,440
44200	44265	4-dr Sta Wag-9P	3173	3811	5,970
44400	44455	4-dr Cus Sta Wag-6P	3202	3772	3,114
44400	44465	4-dr Cus Sta Wag-9P	3340	3876	4,559

ENGINE: V-8. Overhead valve. Cast iron block. Displacement: 340 cid. Bore and stroke: 3.75 x 3.85 inches. Compression ratio: 9.0:1. Brake horsepower: 220 at 4400 rpm. Five main bearings. Hydraulic valve lifters. Carburetor: Rochester Model 2GC two-barrel.

1967 Buick, Skylark GS 340 two-door hardtop, V-8

SKYLARK GS 340 — SERIES 43417 (V-8) — A hybrid, the GS 340 was numbered in the Special V-8 series, but was trimmed as a low-cost GS. Broad rally stripes and hood scoops were

red, as was the lower deck molding. Two body colors, white or platinum mist, were offered. An optional "Sport Pac" included specific front and rear shocks, heavy-duty springs and a large diameter stabilizer bar. Standard features included 15:1 ratio steering, 7.75 x 14 Rayon Cord tires on red 14-inch Rally-style wheels and a two-speed Super Turbine automatic or four-speed manual transmission. Interiors were similar to the Special 43400 series and black, all-vinyl upholstery was the only choice.

SKYLARK GS 340 I.D. NUMBERS: Vehicle Identification Numbers were the same as used on Skylark Series 44400 V-8 models.

SKYLARK GS 340 SERIES 43417

Series No.	Body/Style No.	Body Type & Seating	Factory Price	Shipping Weight	Prod. Total
43400	43417	2-dr HT Cpe-6P	2845	3283	(3,692)

NOTE: The production total for the GS 340 is shown in parenthesis, since these cars are also included in the Buick Special V-8 series production totals given above.

ENGINE: The GS 340 used a 340 cid/260 hp engine with 10.25:1 compression and a Rochester 4MV four-barrel carburetor.

SKYLARK GS 400 — SERIES 44600 (V-8) — The high-performance Skylark took its name from its 400-cid V-8. Three- or four-speed manual or three-speed Super Turbine automatic transmissions were offered. Exterior appearance was strengthened by the use of twin hood scoops, Rally stripes and a special grille. The GS name appeared in red letters on the grille and rear deck. F70 x 14 Wide Oval red or white stripe tires were standard. GS 400s had no fender skirts; rear wheelhouses were open, unlike other Skylark models (except GS 340). Interiors were all-vinyl and standard equipment was the same as the Skylark 44400 Series.

1967 Buick, Skylark GS 400 two-door coupe, V-8 (OCW)

1967 Buick, Skylark GS 400 two-door convertible, V-8 (OCW)

SKYLARK GS 400 I.D. NUMBERS: Vehicle Identification Numbers began with 446007 () 100001. Numbers were coded as explained under the 1967 Special Series I.D. Number section.

SKYLARK GS 400 SERIES 44600

Series No.	Body/Style No.	Body Type & Seating	Factory Price	Shipping Weight	Prod. Total
44600	44607	2-dr Cpe-6P	2956	3439	1,014
44600	44617	2-dr HT Cpe-6P	3019	3500	10,659
44600	44667	2-dr Conv-6P	3167	3505	2,140

ENGINE: V-8. Overhead valve. Cast iron block. Displacement: 401 cid (advertised as 400 cid). Bore and stroke: 4.04 x 3.90 inches. Compression ratio: 10.25:1. Brake horsepower: 340 at 5000 rpm. Five main bearings. Hydraulic valve lifters. Carburetor: Rochester 4MV four-barrel.

1967 Buick, LeSabre four-door hardtop, V-8

LESABRE — SERIES 45200 — A new body shell, with a revised sweepspear sculpted into the sheet metal, was featured for 1967. A horizontal, multiple bar grille was used. Bright lower body moldings, with rear fender extensions on some models, were used. The traditional trio of ventiports was once again found on front fenders. LeSabre script appeared on the rear fenders and deck lid. Standard equipment included heater; defroster; front and rear seatbelts; Step-On parking brake; front door operated courtesy lamps; smoking set; rear seat ashtrays; dual front and rear armrests; dual-key key locking system and other federally mandated safety features.

LESABRE I.D. NUMBERS: Vehicle Identification Numbers began with 452007 () 100001. Numbers were coded as explained under the 1967 Special Series I.D. Number section.

LESABRE SERIES 45200

Series No.	Body/Style No.	Body Type & Seating	Factory Price	Shipping Weight	Prod. Total
45200	45269	4-dr Sed-6P	3002	3847	36,220
45200	45239	4-dr HT Sed-6P	3142	3878	17,464
45200	45287	2-dr HT Cpe-6P	3084	3819	13,760

ENGINE: Specifications for the 340 cid/220 hp LeSabre engine were the same as listed for the 1967 Skylark four-door sedan and Sportwagon.

1967 Buick, LeSabre Custom two-door convertible, V-8 (OCW)

LESABRE CUSTOM — SERIES 45400 — A slightly plusher LeSabre with Custom quality cloth and vinyl interior trim. The hardtop coupe was equipped with standard all-vinyl, vinyl, front bucket seat interior. Standard equipment was the same as in the LeSabre, except for the addition of the Deluxe steering wheel, outside rearview mirror, an upper instrument panel safety pad and a cross flow radiator.

LESABRE CUSTOM I.D. NUMBERS: Vehicle Identification Numbers began with 454007 () 100001. Numbers were coded as explained under the 1967 Special Series I.D. Number section.

LESABRE CUSTOM SERIES 45400

Series No.	Body/Style No.	Body Type & Seating	Factory Price	Shipping Weight	Prod. Total
45400	45469	4-dr Sed-6P	3096	3855	27,930
45400	45439	4-dr HT Sed-6P	3236	3873	32,526
45400	45487	2-dr HTCpe-SP	3172	3853	11,871
45400	45467	2-dr Conv-6P	3388	3890	2,913

ENGINE: See 1967 Buick Sportwagon Series engine data.

1967 Buick, Wildcat two-door hardtop, V-8

WILDCAT — SERIES 46400 — A specific, more open grille set the Wildcat apart from the LeSabre at the front. Side trim used a heavier bright lower body molding, which continued across the standard rear fender skirts as a lip molding. The molding flowed out of the front fender's large simulated vent intakes. Wildcat lettering appeared on the rear quarters and deck. Interiors were vinyl and cloth, of a plusher grade than the LeSabre, which featured the same standard equipment.

WILDCAT I.D. NUMBERS: Vehicle Identification Numbers began with 464007 () 100001. Numbers were coded as explained under the 1966 Special Series I.D. Number section.

WILDCAT SERIES 46400

Series No.	Body/Style No.	Body Type & Seating	Factory Price	Shipping Weight	Prod. Total
46400	46469	4-dr Sed-6P	3277	4008	14,579
46400	46439	4-dr HT Sed-6P	3437	4069	15,510
46400	46487	2-dr HT Cpe-6P	3382	4021	10,585
46467	46467	2-dr Conv-6P	3536	4064	2,276

ENGINE: V-8. Overhead valve. Cast iron block. Displacement: 430 cid. Bore and stroke: 4.19 x 3.90 inches. Compression ratio: 10.25:1. Brake horsepower: 360 at 5000 rpm. Five main bearings. Hydraulic valve lifters. Carburetor: Rochester 4MV four-barrel.

WILDCAT CUSTOM — SERIES 46600 — A Custom interior, with plusher materials, paddle-type armrests and custom headlining (except convertible) set the Custom Wildcats apart. All-vinyl bucket seats or cloth notchback seats for front seat passengers were standard.

WILDCAT CUSTOM I.D. NUMBERS: Vehicle Identification Numbers began with 466007 () 100001. Numbers were coded as explained under the 1967 Special Series I.D. Number section.

WILDCAT CUSTOM SERIES 46600

Series No.	Body/Style No.	Body Type & Seating	Factory Price	Shipping Weight	Prod. Total
46600	46639	4-dr HT Sed-6P	3652	4119	13,547
46600	46687	2-dr HT Cpe-5P	3603	4055	11,571

ENGINE: See 1967 Buick Wildcat Series 46400 engine data.

1967 Buick, Electra 225 four-door sedan, V-8 (TVB)

ELECTRA 225 — SERIES 48200 — Buick's largest, most luxurious series was restyled for 1967, sharing with lesser, full-sized Buicks, a return to sweepspear bodyside motifs. The Electra used a larger body, however, with its own horizontal-bar grille, distinct squared-off rear fenders and four ventiports on each front fender. The lower body was lined with bright metal bumper to bumper, continuing even across the lip of the fender

skirts. Full-width taillights were used at the rear. Electra 225 script appeared on the rear fenders. Standard features included most items found on less costly Buicks plus power steering; power brakes; custom padded seat cushions; front seat belt retractors; electric clock; trunk light; license frames and mandated safety features. Interiors were cloth and vinyl.

1967 Buick, Electra 225 two-door Sport Coupe, V-8 (OCW)

ELECTRA 225 I.D. NUMBERS: Vehicle Identification Numbers began with 482007 () 100001. Numbers were coded as explained under the 1966 Special Series I.D. Number section.

ELECTRA 225 SERIES 48200

Series No.	Body/Style No.	Body Type & Seating	Factory Price	Shipping Weight	Prod. Total
48200	48269	4-dr Sed-6P	4054	4246	10,787
48200	48239	4-dr HT Sed-6P	4184	4293	12,491
48200	48287	2-dr Spt Cpe-6P	4075	4197	6,845

ENGINE: See 1967 Buick Wildcat Series 46000 engine data.

ELECTRA 225 CUSTOM — SERIES 48400 — Plusher, Custom grade interiors in cloth and vinyl set the Custom models apart. Vinyl bucket seats were an option for the Custom convertible.

NOTE: Custom Limited equipment was available for the Style Number 48439 four-door hardtop sedan. Cars so-equipped had Madrid grain or Bavere cloth and Madrid grain vinyl upholstery, with etched Electra 225 emblems; walnut door and instrument panel inserts and dual storage compartments on the front seat backrest. Limited scripts were affixed to the roof sail panels. This package retailed for $149.27, but the number of cars so-equipped was not individually recorded.

1967 Buick, Electra 225 Custom two-door convertible, V-8 (OCW)

ELECTRA 225 CUSTOM I.D. NUMBERS: Vehicle Identification Numbers began with 484007 () 100001. Numbers were coded as explained under the 1967 Special Series I.D. Number section.

ELECTRA 225 CUSTOM SERIES 48400

Series No.	Body/Style No.	Body Type & Seating	Factory Price	Shipping Weight	Prod. Total
48400	48469	4-dr Sed-6P	4270	4312	10,106
48400	48439	4-dr HT Sed-6P	4363	4336	40,978
48400	48487	2-dr Spt Cpe-6P	4254	4242	12,156
48400	48467	2-dr Conv-6P	4421	4304	6,941

ENGINE: See 1967 Buick Wildcat Series 46400 engine data.

RIVIERA — SERIES 49487 — A new grille was used with the basic 1966 body to slightly face lift the Riviera. Rocker moldings were altered and new taillamps were installed. Riviera script appeared on front fenders and the deck lid. Standard equipment included Super Turbine transmission; power steering; power brakes; tilt steering wheel; dual exhaust; heater/defroster; Cus-

tom padded seats; retractable seat belts; electric clock; trunk and glovebox lights; Glare-proof mirror; outside rearview mirror; license frames and carpeting. A bench or bucket seat all-vinyl interior was used.

1967 Buick, Riviera GS two-door hardtop, V-8 (TVB)

NOTE: Gran Sport equipment was offered for the 1967 Riviera at $138. This consisted of heavy-duty front and rear shocks, positive traction differential, Wide Oval red or white stripe tires and front fender and instrument panel GS monograms. The standard engine was used.

RIVIERA I.D. NUMBERS: Vehicle Identification Numbers began with 494877 () 90001. Numbers were coded as explained under the 1967 Special Series I.D. Number section.

RIVIERA SERIES 49400

Series No.	Body/Style No.	Body Type & Seating	Factory Price	Shipping Weight	Prod. Total
49400	49487	2-dr HT Cpe-5P	4469	4189	42,799

ENGINE: See 1967 Buick Wildcat 46400 Series engine data.

CHASSIS FEATURES: Wheelbase: (Series 43300, 43400, 43500, 43600, 44300, 44400, 44600) 115 inches; (Series 43200 and 43400 Sportwagons) 120 inches; (Series 45200 and 45400) 123 inches; (Series 46400, 46600, 48200 and 48400) 126 inches; (Series 49487) 119 inches. Overall length: (Series 43300, 43400, 43500, 43600, 44300, 44400 and 44600) 205 inches; (Station wagons) 209.3 inches; (Series 44200 and 44400 Sportwagons) 214.3 inches; (Series 45200 and 45400) 217.5 inches; (Series 46400 and 46600) 220.5 inches; (Series 48200 and 48400) 223.9 inches; (Series 49487) 211.3 inches. Tread: (Series 44300, 43400, 43500, 43600, 44300, 44400, 44600 and 44200) 58 inches front, 59 inches rear; (Series 45200, 45400, 46400 and 46600) 63 inches front and rear; (Series 48200, 48400 and 49487) 63.4 inches front, 63 inches rear. Tires: (Series 43300, 43400, 43500, 43600, 44300, 44400 and 44600) 7.75 x 14; (Series 44200 and 44400 Sportwagons) 8.25 x 14; (Series 45200, 45400, 46400 and 46600) 8.45 x 15; (Series 48200 and 48400) 8.85 x 15; (Series 49487) 8.45 x15.

POWERTRAIN OPTIONS: A three-speed manual transmission was standard on Series 43300, 43400, 43500, 43600, 44300, 44400, 44600, 44200, 45200, 45400, 46400 and 46600. Super Turbine automatic transmission was standard on Series 48200, 48400 and 49487 and was optional on Series 46400 and 46600. An automatic transmission was optional on all other models. A four-speed manual transmission was optional on the GS 340 and GS 400 at $184. A '400' package, linking the 340 cid/260 hp V-8 with four-barrel to a Super Turbine 400 transmission was offered for the Sportwagon and LeSabre models at a cost of $263. The 340 cid/260 hp V-8 was also optional with other power teams in intermediates and LeSabres. No engine options were cataloged for Wildcat, Electra 225 or Riviera models.

CONVENIENCE FEATURES: Power steering (standard Electra 225, Riviera). Power brakes (standard Electra 225, Riviera). Front power disc brakes (except Electra 225s). Automatic air conditioning (full-size only). Air conditioning. Five-spoke plated sport wheels. Wire wheelcovers. Deluxe wheelcovers. Front seat headrests. Power door locks. Tilt steering wheel (standard on Riviera). Full-length console with bucket seats (automatic

transmission equipped Skylark, GS 340, GS 400, Wildcat, Riviera). AM radio. AM/FM radio. Stereo radio, full-size only). Reclining bucket seat. Reclining Strato bench seat (Riviera only). Power seat adjustment. Electro-cruise (automatic transmission only, not available on GS 400 or Sportwagon with 400 option). Power windows. Overhead courtesy lamps (LeSabre, Wildcat). Four-note horn. Remote control mirror. Automatic trunk release (except 115-120 inch wheelbase). Rear window defroster (except convertibles and station wagons). Vinyl roof cover (specific models). Speed alert. Power tailgate for station wagons. Cornering lights (full-size models). Station wagon luggage rack.

HISTORICAL FOOTNOTES: Calendar year production was 573,866 units. Model year production was 562,507 units. The GS 340 model was introduced at midyear, during the Chicago Automobile Show. A new model sold by Buick dealers this year was the Opel Rallye Kadett coupe. The GS 400 was a true muscle car capable of going from 0-to-60 mph in 6.9 seconds with an automatic transmission or 6.6 seconds with a four-speed transmission. Its top speed was 122 mph. The Riviera GS could move to 0-to-60 mph in 7.8 seconds and 86 mph in the quarter-mile.

1968

SPECIAL DELUXE — SERIES 43300/43400 — The basic Buick was upgraded to Deluxe status this year as reflected by more brightwork on the restyled bodies, which now featured their own version of Buick's sculpted sweepspear. A trio of ventiports remained as a series hallmark, while more brightwork appeared on the window surrounds and on the lower body and wheelhouse moldings. Special Deluxe script was found on the rear fenders. Cloth and vinyl was used in the coupe and sedan. All-vinyl upholstery was used in the station wagon and was optional on the other models. Standard equipment included heater and defroster; cigar lighter; front and rear ashtrays; energy-absorbing steering column; lane change feature in directional signals; shoulder and seat belts; inside day/night mirror; side marker lamps and other mandated safety equipment. Wipers were recessed below the hood line.

BUICK I.D. NUMBERS: The serial number (VIN) was located on hinge pillar post, left side, top of instrument panel and stamped on the engine block. The first symbol was a '4' for Buick. The second and third symbols indicated series, as follows: 33 = Special Deluxe; 34 = Special Deluxe/GS 350; 35 = Skylark; 44 = Skylark Custom/Sportwagon; 46 = GS 400; 52 = LeSabre; 54 = LeSabre Custom; 64 = Wildcat; 66 = Wildcat Custom; 82 = Electra 225; 84 = Electra 225 Custom, 94 = Riviera. The fourth and fifth symbols indicated body style as follows: 27 = 2-dr cpe; 35 = 4-dr two-seat sta wag; 37 = 2-dr HT; 39 = 4-dr HT; 55 = 4-dr two-seat Sportwagon; 57 = 2-dr HT; 65 = 4-dr three-seat Sportwagon; 67 = 2-dr conv; 69 = 4-dr sed; and 87 = 2-dr Riviera HT. Combined, the first five symbols were the model number, as reflected in tables below. The sixth symbol indicated model year: 8 = 1968. The seventh symbol was a letter representing the assembly plant, as follows: B = Baltimore, Md.; C = Southgate, Calif.; D = Doraville, Ga.; H = Flint, Mich.; I = Oshawa, Ont., Canada; K = Kansas City, Mo.; V = Bloomfield, Mich.; X = Kansas City, Kans.; Y = Wilmington, Del.; Z = Fremont, Ohio. The last six digits represent the sequential assembly number at the plant with series mixed in production. In addition to the VIN, the right side of the engine block is stamped with a production code that has letters identifying the engine and numbers indicating production date codes. The letters were as follows: (250 cid six-cyl.) NA, PO; (350 cid V-8) PO, PW, PP; (GS 350 V-8) PP only; (GS 400/Sportwagon 400 cid V-8) PR; (430 cid V-8) PD or PK.

SPECIAL DELUXE SERIES 43300/43400

Series No.	Body/Style No.	Body Type & Seating	Factory Price	Shipping Weight	Prod. Total
43300	43327	2-dr Cpe-6P	2513	3125	21,988
43300	43369	4-dr Sed-6P	2564	3217	16,571
43400	43435	4-dr Sta Wag-6P	3001	3670	10,916

V-8 NOTE: Special Deluxe also offered in 43400 V-8 Series. On V-8, the third symbol in model number changes to '4.' Add $105 and 153 pounds for V-8; wagon is V-8 only.

1968 Buick, GS California two-door pillared coupe, V-8

CALIFORNIA GS NOTE: The California GS, detailed in the GS 350 section below, carried the same model number as a Special Deluxe V-8 coupe.

ENGINE: Six-cylinder. Inline. Overhead valve. Cast iron block. Displacement: 250 cid. Bore and stroke: 3.875 x 3.53 inches. Compression ratio: 8.5:1. Brake horsepower: 155 at 4200 rpm. Hydraulic valve lifters. Carburetor: Rochester MV one-barrel.

ENGINE: V-8. Overhead valve. Cast iron block. Displacement: 350 cid. Bore and stroke: 3.8 x 3.85 inches. Compression ratio: 9.0:1. Brake horsepower: 230 at 4400 rpm. Five main bearings. Hydraulic valve lifters. Carburetor: Rochester 2GV two-barrel.

SKYLARK — SERIES 43500/44500 — More similar to the Special Deluxe than previous Skylarks, the 1968 version relied on a bright metal sweepspear line, Skylark roof quarter panel emblems and Skylark script on the rear fenders for distinction. In place of the traditional ventiports there were triple-stacked horizontal bars mounted low on each fender. Inside was a Deluxe steering wheel, lighted ashtray and glovebox, and full carpeting, in addition to Special Deluxe features. Cloth and vinyl or all-vinyl upholstery was offered for the sedan. An all-vinyl front bench or notchback seat was offered for the two-door hardtop.

SKYLARK I.D. NUMBERS: On cars with V-6 power Vehicle Identification Numbers (VINs) started with 435008 () 600001. On V-8-equipped cars the VINs started with 445008 () 100001-up. An explanation of the VIN codes can be found under the 1968 Special Deluxe Series I.D. Number section.

SKYLARK SERIES 43500

Series No.	Body/Style No.	Body Type & Seating	Factory Price	Shipping Weight	Prod. Total
43500	43569	4-dr Sed-6P	2666	3282	27,384
43500	43537	2-dr HT-6P	2688	3194	32,795

V-8 NOTE: Skylark was also offered in 44500 V-8 Series. On V-8, the second symbol in model number changes to '4.' Add $105 and 153 pounds for V-8.

ENGINE: Six-cylinder and V-8 specifications were the same as those listed for the 1968 Special Deluxe Series 43300.

SKYLARK CUSTOM — SERIES 44400 — More trim and fender skirts were added to the plushest Skylark series. The sweepspear molding continued onto the skirts and a Custom signature appeared below Skylark script on the rear fenders. Full wheelcovers were featured. Interiors were refined with Custom padded seat cushions. The sedan was trimmed in plusher all-vinyl or vinyl and cloth and a notchback seat was available for the hardtop sedan. Convertibles came with all-vinyl trim and front bench seats with bucket seats optionally available. Custom

seats had brushed metallic side braces, except on the bucket type. Standard equipment was otherwise similar to the Skylark.

1968 Buick, Skylark Custom two-door hardtop, V-8 (OCW)

1968 Buick, Skylark Custom four-door hardtop, V-8 (OCW)

SKYLARK CUSTOM I.D. NUMBERS: Vehicle Identification Numbers started at 44408 () 100001. An explanation of the VIN code may be found under the 1968 Special Series I.D. Number section.

SKYLARK CUSTOM SERIES 44400

Series No.	Body/Style No.	Body Type & Seating	Factory Price	Shipping Weight	Prod. Total
44400	44469	4-dr Sed-6P	2924	3377	8,066
44400	44437	2-dr HT Cpe-6P	3108	3481	44,143
44400	44439	4-dr HT Sed-6P	2956	3344	12,984
44400	44467	2-dr Conv-6P	3098	3394	8,188

ENGINES: Specifications were the same as those listed for the 1968 Special Deluxe V-8.

GS 350 — SERIES 43400 — Trimmed like the Skylark Custom inside, the GS 350 had a more muscular outer appearance. It was coded as a Skylark Custom, although more related to the GS 400. Finned simulated air intakes were seen on the front fenders, while a lower body paint accent stripe replaced the bright molding. Bright wheelhouse moldings were used, but rear fender skirts were not. A GS 350 plaque was found on the center of the deck lid and flashier identification was seen on the grille and rear fenders with GS monograms appearing in such places, and also on the door panels. All-vinyl, foam-padded seats were standard equipment and bucket seats were optional. A specific grille with bright crossbar and textured background was used. An upper level instrument panel ventilation system was a new feature that eliminated the use of front ventipanes, or so Buick claimed. The hood had a scoop at the rear and concealed wipers.

NOTE: Another GS, the California GS two-door coupe, was similar to the GS 350 in that it was actually numbered in the Special Deluxe line (body style number 43327). Standard California GS equipment included chrome-plated "Super Sport" wheels, vinyl roof covering, Deluxe steering wheel, California script with GS emblems on the grille, roof panels and rear fenders. A GS emblem was centered in the deck lid lip. Cloth and vinyl or horizontally pleated all-vinyl seating surfaces were offered. Standard features included crank-operated vent windows, chrome exterior trim and a two-speed automatic transmission. Production figures and prices are not available.

GS 350 SERIES 43400

Series No.	Body/Style No.	Body Type & Seating	Factory Price	Shipping Weight	Prod. Total
43400	43437	2-dr HT Cpe-6P	2926	3375	8,317

ENGINE: Specifications were the same as listed for the 1968 Special Series 33300 V-8, except compression ratio was 10.25:1, brake horsepower was 280 at 4600 and a four-barrel Rochester 4MV carburetor was used.

1968 Buick, GS 400 two-door hardtop, V-8 (OCW)

GS 400 — SERIES 44600 — Yet another version of the new 1968 Buick 112-inch wheelbase intermediate coupe, the GS 400 was identified by a GS 400 plaque on each front fender, wide oval F70 x 14 white stripe tires, fake fender vents and functional hood scoops. Folding seatback latches were standard, with all-vinyl, bench front seating or optional front bucket seats.

GS 400 I.D. NUMBERS: Vehicle Identification Numbers began with 446008 () 100001. An explanation of the VIN code may be found under the 1968 Special Deluxe Series 43300 I.D. Number section.

GS 400 SERIES 44600

Series No.	Body/Style No.	Body Type & Seating	Factory Price	Shipping Weight	Prod. Total
44600	44637	2-dr HT Cpe-6P	3127	3514	10,743
44600	44667	2-dr Conv-6P	3271	3547	2,454

ENGINE: V-8. Overhead valve. Cast iron block. Displacement: 400 cid. Bore and stroke: 4.04 x 3.90 inches. Compression ratio: 10.25:1. Brake horsepower: 340 at 5000 rpm. Five main bearings. Hydraulic valve lifters. Carburetor: Rochester 4MV four-barrel with chromed air cleaner top.

1968 Buick, Custom four-door Sportwagon, V-8

SPORTWAGON CUSTOM — SERIES 44400/44800 — Still on a stretched wheelbase and using the Skyroof treatment, the intermediate station wagons followed the sweepspear theme into 1968. All were Custom trimmed. Rear fender skirts were not used. Triple ventiports replaced the lower stacked fender bars that other models used. A full-length lower body

highlight with wheelhouse moldings was seen. Sportwagon script decorated the rear quarters and tailgate. The all-vinyl interior had full-carpeting and included 100 cubic feet of cargo space. Models with woodgrain bodyside transfers had their own style numbers.

SPORTWAGON I.D. NUMBERS: Vehicle Identification Numbers began with 444008 () 100001. An explanation of the VIN code may be found under the 1968 Special Deluxe Series 43300 I.D. Number section.

SPORTWAGON SERIES 44400/44800

Series No.	Body/Style No.	Body Type & Seating	Factory Price	Shipping Weight	Prod. Total
44400	44455	4-dr Sta Wag-2S	3341	3975	5,916
44400	44465	4-dr Sta Wag-3S	3499	4118	6,063
44800	44855	4-dr Cus Sta Wag-2S	3711	3975	4,614
44800	44865	4-dr Cus Sta Wag-3S	3869	4118	6,295

ENGINE: Specifications were the same as listed under 1968 Special Deluxe Series 43300 V-8.

1968 Buick, LeSabre four-door hardtop, V-8 (OCW)

LESABRE — SERIES 45200 — Revised only slightly from 1967 the LeSabre was chiefly face lifted by the use of a new grille with a more prominent center division and a textured background. The traditional trio of front fender ventiports was again a trademark. Bright rocker panel and wheelhouse moldings were used. Series designations were found on the rear fenders and instrument panel. Cloth and vinyl upholstery was standard. Regular features included shoulder belts (except convertible); glovebox light; interior courtesy lights; smoking set; rear seat ashtrays; two-speed wipers with washer and recessed arms; outside rearview mirror; energy absorbing steering column and other federally mandated safety features.

LESABRE I.D. NUMBERS: Vehicle Identification Numbers began with 452008 () 100001. An explanation of VIN codes may be found under the 1968 Special Series 43300 I.D. Number section.

LESABRE SERIES 45200

Series No.	Body/Style No.	Body Type & Seating	Factory Price	Shipping Weight	Prod. Total
45200	45269	4-dr Sed-6P	3141	3946	37,433
45200	45287	2-dr HT Cpe-6P	3223	3923	14,922
45200	45239	4-dr HT Sed-6P	3281	3980	10,058

ENGINE: Specifications were the same as those listed for the 1968 Special Deluxe V-8.

1968 Buick, LeSabre Custom two-door convertible, V-8

LESABRE CUSTOM — SERIES 45400 — Custom interiors of plusher cloth and vinyl, with more ornate door panels, were used. All-vinyl was available and was standard in the convertible. Bucket seats were optional for the convertible and two-door hardtop. Deluxe full wheelcovers were included.

1968 Buick, LeSabre Custom two-door hardtop, V-8 (OCW)

LESABRE CUSTOM I.D. NUMBERS: Vehicle Identification Numbers started with 454008 () 100001. An explanation of VIN codes appears in the 1968 Special Deluxe Series 43300 I.D. Number section.

LESABRE CUSTOM SERIES 45400

Series No.	Body/Style No.	Body Type & Seating	Factory Price	Shipping Weight	Prod. Total
45400	45469	4-dr Sed-6P	3235	3950	34,112
45400	45487	2-dr HT-6P	3311	3932	29,596
45400	45439	4-dr HT-6P	3375	4007	40,370
45400	45467	2-dr Conv-6P	3504	3966	5,257

ENGINE: Specifications were the same as listed for the 1968 Special Deluxe V-8.

1968 Buick, Wildcat two-door Sport Coupe, V-8 (OCW)

WILDCAT — SERIES 46400 — A new grille and revised bodyside moldings helped give the 1968 Wildcat a new look. Simulated air vents continued on front fenders. Narrow lower bodyside highlights and wheelhouse moldings were used to make a full-length bright lower strip. Wildcat lettering was found on the rear fenders, on the deck lid and on the instrument panel. An outside rearview mirror and back-up lamps were additional standard equipment inherited from lower-priced Buicks. Interiors were cloth and vinyl, with all-vinyl optional. Bucket seats upholstered in vinyl were a two-door hardtop option.

WILDCAT I.D. NUMBERS: Vehicle Identification Numbers began with 464008 () 100001. An explanation of the VIN code may be found under the 1968 Special Deluxe Series I.D. 43300 Number section.

WILDCAT SERIES 46400

Series No.	Body/Style No.	Body Type & Seating	Factory Price	Shipping Weight	Prod. Total
46400	46469	4-dr Sed-6P	3416	4076	15,201
46400	46487	2-dr HT-6P	3521	4065	10,708
46400	46439	4-dr HT-6P	3576	4133	15,173

ENGINE: V-8. Overhead valve. Cast iron block. Displacement: 430 cid. Bore and stroke: 4.19 x 3.9 inches. Compression ratio: 10.25:1. Brake horsepower: 360 at 5000 rpm. Five main bearings. Hydraulic valve lifters. Carburetor: Rochester 4MV four-barrel.

1968 Buick, Wildcat Custom two-door convertible, V-8 (OCW)

WILDCAT CUSTOM — SERIES 46600 — A plusher interior was the heart of the Custom Series. Brushed metallic door panel inserts were seen with cloth and vinyl trim combinations. A notchback seat with bright side braces was used, as were paddle-type armrests and Custom headlining (except the convertible). All-vinyl trim was optional, except for the convertible, where it was standard. All-vinyl bucket seats were an option.

WILDCAT CUSTOM I.D. NUMBERS: Vehicle Identification Numbers began with 466008 () 100001. An explanation of VIN codes appears with the 1968 Special Deluxe Series 43300 I.D. listing.

WILDCAT CUSTOM SERIES 46600

Series No.	Body/Style No.	Body Type & Seating	Factory Price	Shipping Weight	Prod. Total
46600	46687	2-dr HT Cpe-6P	3742	4082	11,276
44600	44639	4-dr HT Sed-6P	3791	4162	14,059
46600	46667	2-dr Conv-6P	3896	4118	3,572

ENGINE: Specifications were the same as listed for the 1968 Wildcat Series 46400.

1968 Buick, Electra 225 two-door hardtop, V-8 (TVB)

ELECTRA 225 — SERIES 48200 — The largest Buick was mildly restyled for 1968. New eggcrate textured grilles, divided by a color-accented panel, were up front. Squared rear fenders were tied together by a bumper housing the taillamps. Four ventiports continued to crown the largest of Buick fenders. Full-length lower body moldings continued across the fender skirts. Specific full wheelcovers were used. Electra 225 script was found on rear fenders and instrument panel, while the series badge was found on the roof quarter panels (except the convertible). Standard features included power steering; power brakes; automatic transmission; custom padded seat cushions; electric clock; parking brake signal light; Deluxe steering wheel and carpeted floors and lower doors.

1968 Buick, Electra 225 four-door hardtop, V-8 (PH)

ELECTRA 225 NUMBERS: Vehicle Identification Numbers began with 482008 () 100001. An explanation of the VIN code appears with the 1968 Special Deluxe Series 43300 I.D. Number section.

ELECTRA 225 SERIES 48200

Series No.	Body/Style No.	Body Type & Seating	Factory Price	Shipping Weight	Prod. Total
48200	48269	4-dr Sed-6P	4200	4253	12,723
48200	48257	2-dr HT-6P	4330	4270	10,705
48200	48239	4-dr HT-6P	4221	4180	15,376

ENGINE: Specifications were the same as listed for the 1968 Wildcat Series 46400.

ELECTRA 225 CUSTOM — SERIES 48400 — Essentially a trim package, the Custom models were plusher inside. Cloth and vinyl combinations were used in the four-door hardtop, with an all-vinyl interior available. All-vinyl notchback seating was standard in the coupe and convertible, with all-vinyl bucket seats an option.

NOTE: Custom 'Limited' equipment was available for the Model 48439 four-door hardtop sedan and 48457 two-door hardtop. Cars so equipped had plusher cloth and vinyl upholstery with special accents. 'Limited' scripts appeared on the roof quarter panels. Production and price figures are not known.

ELECTRA 225 CUSTOM SERIES 48400

Series No.	Body/Style No.	Body Type & Seating	Factory Price	Shipping Weight	Prod. Total
48400	48469	4-dr Sed-6P	4415	4304	10,910
48400	48457	2-dr HT Cpe-6P	4400	4273	6,826
48400	48439	4-dr HT Sed-6P	4509	4314	50,846
48400	48467	2-dr Conv-6P	4541	4285	7,976

ENGINE: Specifications were the same as listed for the 1968 Wildcat Series 46400.

1968 Buick, Riviera two-door hardtop, V-8 (PH)

RIVIERA — SERIES 49487 — Once again using the same body shell, the Riviera had a new frontal appearance. Large parking lamps were housed within the bumper, which also framed the low, textured grille. Headlamps retracted above until needed. A wide full-length lower body molding with bright wheelhouse moldings was used. Specific full wheelcovers were seen. Riviera lettering appeared on front fenders and deck. Standard equipment included power steering; power brakes; tilt steering column; brake warning light; Custom-padded seat cushions; license frames and mandated safety features. Interiors were bench or bucket seats in all-vinyl trim. Plusher Custom grade interiors were offered with fancier door panels incorporating the Riviera 'R' logo and all-vinyl Strato bench or bucket seats, or cloth and vinyl Strato bench front seats.

NOTE: Gran Sport equipment was offered for the 1968 Riviera. This consisted of heavy-duty front and rear suspension, positive traction differential, H70 x 15 red or white stripe tires and front fender GS monograms. The GS signature was also found on the instrument panel.

RIVIERA I.D. NUMBERS: Vehicle Identification Numbers began with 494878 () 900001. An explanation of the VIN code may be found under the 1968 Special Deluxe Series 43300 I.D. Number section.

RIVIERA SERIES 49400

Series No.	Body/Style No.	Body Type & Seating	Factory Price	Shipping Weight	Prod. Total
49400	49487	2-dr HT Cpe-6P	5245	4222	49,284

ENGINE: Specifications were the same as listed for the 1968 Wildcat Series 46400.

CHASSIS FEATURES: Wheelbase: (Series 43300, 43500, 44400, 43400, and 44600 coupe and convertible) 112 inches; (Series 43300, 43500, 44400, 43400 and 44600 sedans and

Special Deluxe station wagon) 116 inches; (Sportwagons) 121 inches; (Series 45200 and 45400) 123 inches; (Series 46400 and 46600) 126 inches; (Series 49487) 119 inches. Overall length: (Series 43300, 43500, 44400, 43400 and 46600 coupe and convertible) 200.7 inches; (Series 43300, 43500, 44400, 43400 and 46600 sedan) 204.7 inches; (Sportwagon) 209.1 inches; (Series 45200 and 45400) 217.5 inches; (Series 46400 and 46600) 220.5 inches; (Series 48200 and 48400) 224.9 inches; (Series 49487) 215.2 inches. Tread: (Series 43300, 43500, 44400, 43400 and 44600) 59.35 inches front, 59.0 inches rear; (Series 45200 and 45400) 63 inches front and rear; (Series 46400, 46600, 48400 and 49487) 63.4 inches front, 63 inches rear. Tires: (Series 43300, 43500, 44400, 43400 and 44600) 7.75 x 14; (Sportwagon and Series 45200, 45400, 46400, 46600 and 49487) 8.45 x 15; (Series 48200 and 48400) 8.85 x 15.

POWERTRAIN FEATURES: Three-speed manual transmission was standard in all except Electra 225s and Rivieras. The GS 350 came with three-speed column shift or four-speed floor shift optional. The GS 400 came with three-speed or four-speed manual transmission on floor. Four-speed manual transmission was available in GS 350/GS 400. Super Turbine automatic transmission was standard in Electra 225 and Riviera, available in all others. Console automatic shifter was available with GS 350, GS 400, Wildcat and Riviera. The GS 350 V-8 was available in Special Deluxe, Skylark Custom, Sportwagon and LeSabre models. The GS 400 V-8 was available in Sportwagons.

CONVENIENCE FEATURES: Power steering (standard Series 48200, 48400 and 49487). Power brakes (standard on Series 48200, 48400 and 49487). Power windows (not offered for Special Deluxe six-cyl.) Four-way power seat. Six-way power seat (full-size). Air conditioning. Vinyl top (Special models). Seven-position tilt steering column. Limited trim on Electra 225 Custom hardtops. AM/FM stereo radio. Tape deck. Strato seats (Series 49487). Chrome road wheels. AM radio. AM/FM radio. Whitewall tires. Deluxe wheelcovers. Soft-Ray glass. Cruise Master. GS 350/GS 400 consolette, tachometer, for manual transmission. Full-length console (bucket seats and Super Turbine transmission required). Cornering lights (full-size only). Automatic Climate Control. Power front disc brakes. Automatic door locks. Trailer hitch. Rear window defroster. Remote control outside rearview mirror. Speed alert. Super Deluxe wheelcovers. Radial ply tires. Power tailgate window on station wagons. Luggage rack for station wagons.

HISTORICAL FOOTNOTES: Calendar year production was 652,049 units. Model year production was 651,823 units. Buick was the fifth largest automaker this year. GS production climbed 55 percent, reflecting the popularity of the sporty Skylark models. The V-6 was discontinued and replaced with an inline six built by Chevrolet. New federally mandated safety features for 1968 included larger outside rearview mirrors, side marker lights on front and rear fenders, safety armrests and improved door latches. A new Opel Kadette Sport Sedan was available from Buick dealers this year. The GS 400 had a top speed of 120 mph, down slightly from the previous year due to increased weight. The Riviera could do 0-to-60 mph in 8.1 seconds and had a top speed of 125-132 mph, depending on which car magazine you read. *Mechanix Illustrated* reported it was "Just about the best of any 1968 cars we have tested." Styles 44855 and 44865 are Sportwagons with woodgrain sides. Style 43327 was the California GS.

1969

SPECIAL DELUXE — SERIES 43300 — The basic Buick for 1969 appeared with a minimum of change from its 1968 counterpart. A trio of bright outlined ventiports and bright housings for the side marker lamps were part of the minimal bodyside

brightwork. Special Deluxe script appeared on the rear fenders. Among the standard features, many being mandated by new federal safety standards, were back-up lamps, a left-hand outside rearview mirror and seat belts.

BUICK I.D. NUMBERS: The serial number (VIN) was located on a plate, attached to top of dash on driver's side and viewable through outside of windshield. It was also stamped on the engine block. The first symbol was a '4' for Buick. The second and third symbols indicated series, as follows: 33 = Special Deluxe; 34 = Special Deluxe/GS 350; 35 = Skylark; 44 = Skylark Custom/Sportwagon; 46 = GS 400; 52 = LeSabre; 54 = LeSabre Custom; 64 = Wildcat; 66 = Wildcat Custom; 82 = Electra 225; 84 = Electra 225 Custom; 94 = Riviera. The fourth and fifth symbols indicated body style, as follows: 27 = 2-dr cpe; 35 = 4-dr two-seat sta wag; 36 = 4-dr two-seat sta wag; 37 = 2-dr HT; 39 = 4-dr HT; 56 = 4-dr two-seat Sportwagon; 57 = 2-dr HT; 66 = 4-dr three-seat Sportwagon; 67 = 2-dr conv; 69 = 4-dr sed; and 87 = 2-dr Riviera HT. Combined, the first five symbols were the model number, as reflected in tables below. The sixth symbol indicated model year: 9 = 1969. The seventh symbol was a letter representing the assembly plant, as follows: B = Baltimore, Md.; C = Southgate, Calif.; D = Doraville, Ga.; H = Flint, Mich.; I = Oshawa, Ont., Canada; K = Kansas City, Mo.; V = Bloomfield, Mich.; X = Kansas City, Kans.; Y = Wilmington, Del.; Z = Fremont, Ohio. The last six digits represent the sequential assembly number at the plant with series mixed in production. In addition to the VIN, the right side of the engine block is stamped with a production code that has letters identifying the engine and numbers indicating production date codes. The letters were as follows: (250 cid six-cyl.) N/A; (350 cid V-8) RO, RW, RP; (GS 350 V-8) RP only; (GS 400 V-8) RR, RS or Stage 1, (Sportwagon 400 cid V-8) RR; (430 cid V-8) RO or RE.

SPECIAL DELUXE SERIES 43300/43400

Series No.	Body/Style No.	Body Type & Seating	Factory Price	Shipping Weight	Prod. Total
43300	43327	2-dr Cpe	2562	3126	15,268
43300	43369	4-dr Sed	2613	3182	11,113
43400	43455	4-dr Sta Wag-2S	3092	3783	2,590
43400	43436	4-dr Sta-Wag-2S	3124	3736	6,677

V-8 NOTE: The Special Deluxe was also offered in 43400 V-8 Series. On V-8s, the third symbol in model number changes to '4.' Add $111 and 119 pounds for V-8s; wagon is V-8 only.

ENGINE: Six-cylinder. Inline. Overhead valve. Cast iron block. Displacement: 250 cid. Bore and stroke: 3.875 x 3.53 inches. Compression ratio: 8.5:1. Brake horsepower: 155 at 4200 rpm. Hydraulic valve lifters. Carburetor: Rochester MV one-barrel.

ENGINE: V-8. Overhead valve. Cast iron block. Displacement: 350 cid. Bore and stroke: 3.80 x 3.85 inches. Compression ratio: 9.0:1. Brake horsepower: 230 at 4400 rpm. Five main bearings. Hydraulic valve lifters. Carburetor: Rochester 2GV two-barrel.

NOTE: Style 43327 was also built in California GS trim, with bright wheelhouse moldings, a vinyl top with GS monograms on the roof quarters and a GS emblem on the deck lid. A functional hood scoop, with the opening near the windshield was included as well. The word California was spelled out in script on the rear fenders. The California GS coupes had vent windows. The California GS was powered by the GS 350 engine linked to a standard Turbo-Hydramatic 350 transmission. Production of this option was 4,831 units. This production number is included with the Special Deluxe coupe on table above.

SKYLARK — SERIES 43500 — Reduced to a two model line for 1969, the Skylark featured minimal side trim, with a trio of leaning vertical bright bars on each front fender. Skylark script appeared on the rear fenders. The grille had a horizontal division bar.

SKYLARK I.D. NUMBERS: Serial numbers began with 435009 () 600001 on cars equipped with the six-cylinder engine. Serial numbers began with 435009 () 100001 on V-8 cars. An expla-

nation of the VIN code may be found under the 1969 Buick I.D. Number section.

SKYLARK SERIES 43500

Series No.	Body/Style No.	Body Type & Seating	Factory Price	Shipping Weight	Prod. Total
43500	43537	2-dr HT Cpe-6P	2736	3179	38,658
43500	43569	4-dr Sed-6P	2715	3209	22,349

V-8 NOTE: Skylarks were also offered in 43500 V-8 series. On V-8, the third symbol in model number changes to a '4'. Add $111 and 119 pounds for V-8s.

ENGINES: Six-cylinder and V-8 specifications were the same as listed for the 1969 Special Deluxe Series 43300.

SKYLARK CUSTOM — SERIES 44400 — The plushest intermediate Buick had better quality vinyl and cloth or all-vinyl interiors, a bright lower body molding and wheelhouse moldings. A chrome sweepspear molding was optional and, at the front, a Buick emblem was centered in the grille.

SKYLARK CUSTOM I.D. NUMBERS: Vehicle Identification Numbers began with 444009 () 100001. VINs were coded as explained under the 1969 Buick I.D. Number section.

1969 Buick, Skylark Custom two-door convertible, V-8

SKYLARK CUSTOM SERIES 44400

Series No.	Body/Style No.	Body Type & Seating	Factory Price	Shipping Weight	Prod. Total
44440	44437	2-dr Spt Cpe-6P	3009	3341	35,639
44400	44439	4-dr HT Sed-6P	3151	3477	9,609
44400	44467	2-dr Conv-6P	3152	3398	6,552
44400	44469	4-dr Sed-6P	2978	3397	6,423

ENGINE: V-8 specifications were the same as listed for the 1969 Special Deluxe Series 43300.

GS 350 — SERIES 43437 — A one-style series for 1969 was the GS 350. Once again this car combined the Skylark Custom's interior accoutrements with a sporting car's exterior. Front fenders carried neither ventiports or vents this year, while the wheelhouse moldings were continued. A more prominent hood scoop was hooked to a special air cleaner with twin snorkels. Buick claimed this cold air induction system boosted power eight percent and increased torque 6.5 percent. However, the factory ratings did not change. A GS 350 plaque was used on the center of the deck lid, with monograms on the grille and door panels. All-vinyl, foam padded seats were standard, with the bucket versions an option. Upper level ventilation, without vent windows, was a distinctive feature.

GS 350 I.D. NUMBERS: Vehicle Identification Numbers began with 434379 () 100001. An explanation of VIN codes appears in the 1969 Buick I.D. Number section.

GS 350 SERIES 43437

Series No.	Body/Style No.	Body Type & Seating	Factory Price	Shipping Weight	Prod. Total
43400	43437	2-dr Spt Cpe-6P	2980	3406	4,933

ENGINE: Specifications were the same as listed for the 1969 Special Deluxe Series 43300 V-8, except the compression ratio was 10.25:1, brake horsepower was 280 at 4600 rpm and a four-barrel Rochester 4MV carburetor was used.

GS 400 — SERIES 44600 — Similar to the GS 350, the most potent Buick had 400 numerals on the hood scoop and rear quarters. A Deluxe steering wheel was standard, along with foam padded seats, ashtray light, glovebox light and upper in-

terior light. Interiors were all-vinyl with a bench front seat standard and buckets available optionally. There was a unique GS 400 grille and a cold air induction package. A hot, dealer-installed option was the Stage 1 package including a 400-cid V-8 with 11.0:1 compression that was rated for 345 hp at 4800 rpm and 440 lb-ft of torque at 3200 rpm. Experts said the actual output of this engine was closer to 400 hp.

1969 Buick, GS 400 two-door hardtop, V-8 (TVB)

GS 400 I.D. NUMBERS: Vehicle Identification Numbers began with 446009 () 100001. An explanation of the VIN codes appears under the 1969 Buick I.D. Number section.

GS 400 SERIES 44600

Series No.	Body/Style No.	Body Type & Seating	Factory Price	Shipping Weight	Prod. Total
44600	44637	2-dr HT Cpe-6P	3181	3549	6,356
44600	44667	2-dr Conv-6P	3325	3594	1,176

ENGINE: V-8. Overhead valve. Cast iron block. Displacement: 400 cid. Bore and stroke: 4.04 x 3.90 inches. Compression ratio: 10.25:1. Brake horsepower: 340 at 5000 rpm. Hydraulic valve lifters. Carburetor: Four-barrel.

SPORTWAGON CUSTOM — SERIES 44400 — Numbered in the Skylark Custom series, but with varied trim, these wagons had bright wheelhouse and rocker panel moldings, woodgrain side trim and Sportwagon script on the rear fenders. They were fully carpeted including the cargo areas, and used expanded vinyl trim. A Deluxe steering wheel, Custom padded seat cushions and the features of the Custom Skylark were used.

SPORTWAGON CUSTOM I.D. NUMBERS: Vehicle Identification Numbers began with 444009 () 10001. VIN numbers were coded as explained under the 1969 Buick I.D. Number section.

SPORTWAGON CUSTOM SERIES 44400

Series No.	Body/Style No.	Body Type & Seating	Factory Price	Shipping Weight	Prod. Total
44400	44456	4-dr Sta Wag-2S	3465	4106	9,157
44400	44466	4-dr Sta Wag-3S	3621	4231	11,513

ENGINE: Specifications were the same as those listed for the Special Deluxe V-8 Series 43300/43400.

LESABRE — SERIES 45200 — A new body greeted LeSabre buyers for 1969. Styling was refined and lighter than in the immediately preceding years. The LeSabre still wore its trio of front fender ventiports and a narrow argent accent strip rocker panel was used. LeSabre script appeared on the rear fenders, with further series identification found on the instrument panel. Standard equipment included upper level ventilation system (instead of ventipanes); door-operated interior lights; glove compartment light; smoking set; rear seat ashtray; front and rear armrests and full carpeting.

NOTE: The LeSabre '400' option, offered for LeSabre and LeSabre Custom models, included a 350 cid/280 hp V-8 and Turbo-Hydramatic transmission. Cars so equipped had '400' emblems on the rear fenders, below the LeSabre script.

LESABRE I.D. NUMBERS: Vehicle Identification Numbers began with 452009 () 100001. VIN numbers were coded as explained under the 1969 Buick I.D. Number section.

LESABRE SERIES 45200

Series No.	Body/Style No.	Body Type & Seating	Factory Price	Shipping Weight	Prod. Total
45200	45269	4-dr Sed-6P	3216	3966	36,664
45200	45237	2-dr HT-6P	3298	3936	16,201
45200	45239	4-dr HT-6P	3356	3983	17,235

ENGINE: Specifications were the same as listed for the 1969 Special Deluxe V-8 Series 43300/43400.

1969 Buick, LeSabre Custom four-door hardtop, V-8 (TVB)

1969 Buick, LeSabre Custom two-door convertible, V-8

LESABRE CUSTOM — SERIES 45400 — This represented a plusher edition of the popular LeSabre. A broader metal rocker panel molding, with rear fender extension, was used with bright wheelhouse moldings to accent Custom level trim. Custom script appeared on the rear fenders beneath the LeSabre signatures. Inside, plusher cloth and vinyl trim combinations were found, or an all-vinyl interior could be selected. Bucket seats were optional for the Custom Sport Coupe.

LESABRE CUSTOM I.D. NUMBERS: Vehicle Identification Numbers began with 454009 () 100001. VINs were coded as explained under the 1969 Buick I.D. Number section.

LESABRE CUSTOM SERIES 45400

Series No.	Body/Style No.	Body Type & Seating	Factory Price	Shipping Weight	Prod. Total
45400	45469	4-dr Sed-6P	3310	3941	37,136
45400	45437	2-dr HT Cpe-6P	3386	4018	38,887
45400	45439	4-dr HT Sed-6P	3450	4073	48,123
45400	45467	2-dr Conv-6P	3579	3958	3,620

ENGINE: Specifications are the same as listed for the Special Deluxe V-8 Series 43300/43400.

1969 Buick, Wildcat two-door hardtop, V-8

WILDCAT — SERIES 46400 — Sharing the LeSabre's sheet metal, but with styling touches suggesting a more powerful, sporting automobile, the Wildcat had a distinctive grille with vertical texturing. A bright, broad rocker molding with fender extensions and wheelhouse moldings was used. Wildcat script appeared above groups of five vertical bars on each front fender. Standard equipment was the same as the LeSabre except for the addition of a Deluxe steering wheel. Interiors were cloth and vinyl or all-vinyl. Bucket seats, with all-vinyl seating surfaces, were offered for the Sport Coupe.

WILDCAT I.D. NUMBERS: Vehicle Identification Numbers began with 464009 () 100001. VINs were coded as explained under the 1969 Buick I.D. Number section.

WILDCAT SERIES 46400

Series No.	Body/Style No.	Body Type & Seating	Factory Price	Shipping Weight	Prod. Total
46400	46469	4-dr Sed-6P	4448	4102	13,126
46400	46437	2-dr HT Cpe-6P	4553	3926	12,416
46400	46439	4-dr HT Sed-6P	4608	4204	13,805

ENGINE: V-8. Overhead valve. Cast iron block. Displacement: 430 cid. Bore and stroke: 4.19 x 3.9 inches. Compression ratio: 10.25:1. Brake horsepower: 360 at 5000 rpm. Five main bearings. Hydraulic valve lifters. Carburetor: Rochester 4MV four-barrel.

WILDCAT CUSTOM — SERIES 46600 — Custom quality and vinyl or all-vinyl interiors were the hallmark of the Custom series, with notchback front seats featured. Otherwise, the cars were the same as the Wildcat Series 46400 models.

WILDCAT CUSTOM I.D. NUMBERS: Vehicle Identification Numbers began with 466009 () 100001. VINs were coded as explained under the 1969 Buick I.D. Number section.

WILDCAT CUSTOM SERIES 46600

Series No.	Body/Style No.	Body Type & Seating	Factory Price	Shipping Weight	Prod. Total
46600	46637	2-dr HT-6P	3817	4134	12,136
46600	46639	4-dr HT-6P	3866	4220	13,596
46600	46667	2-dr Conv-6P	3948	4152	2,374

ENGINE: Specifications were the same as listed for the 1969 Wildcat Series 46400.

ELECTRA 225 — SERIES 48200 — A large, yet graceful body was used for Buick's biggest models in 1969. A tapering sweepspear sculpture line and rear fender skirts contributed to the smooth-flowing Electra 225 lines. A group of four ventiports were lined up on each front fender. The lower body was swathed in bright metal from the front bumper to the rear, with a kick-up over the front wheelhouse lip. A specifically designed grille texture was used. Rear taillamps were horizontal and were behind bright grids. Electra 225 emblems were on the rear fenders and deck lid. Round rear fender marker lights were exclusive to the Electra 225 styles. Standard features, in addition to those found on the Wildcat, included power steering; power brakes; automatic transmission; Custom padded seat cushions; electric clock; carpeted floors and lower doors and side coat hooks. Interiors were cloth and vinyl or all-vinyl, with front bench seats.

ELECTRA 225 I.D. NUMBERS: Vehicle Identification Numbers began with 482009 () 100001. VINs were coded as explained under the 1969 Buick I.D. Number section.

ELECTRA 225 SERIES 48200

Series No.	Body/Style No.	Body Type & Seating	Factory Price	Shipping Weight	Prod. Total
48200	42869	4-dr Sed-6P	4302	4236	14,521
48200	48257	2-dr HT Cpe-6P	4323	4203	13,128
48200	48239	4-dr HT Sed-6P	4432	4294	15,983

ENGINE: Specifications were the same as those listed for the 1969 Wildcat Series 46400.

1969 Buick, Electra 225 Custom Limited four-door hardtop, V-8 (PH)

ELECTRA 225 CUSTOM — SERIES 48400 — A more refined interior was the basis of the Custom Electra. Expanded vinyl notchback front seats were used in the two-door hardtop and four-door hardtop, while vinyl and cloth bench or notchback type front seats were found in sedans. Expanded vinyl trim, with notchback front seat, power windows and two-way power seat adjustments were standard on the Custom convertible.

NOTE: Custom Limited equipment was available for the two-door hardtop and four-door hardtop. Cars so-equipped had better quality vinyl and cloth or all-vinyl interior trims with a 60/40 front deck. Limited scripts appeared on the roof quarters.

ELECTRA 225 CUSTOM I.D. NUMBERS: Vehicle Identification Numbers began with 484009 () 100001. VINs were coded as explained under the 1969 Buick I.D. Number section.

ELECTRA 225 CUSTOM SERIES 48400

Series No.	Body/Style No.	Body Type & Seating	Factory Price	Shipping Weight	Prod. Total
48400	48469	4-dr Sed-6P	4517	4281	14,434
48400	48457	2-dr HT Cpe-6P	4502	4222	27,018
48400	48439	4-dr HT Sed-6P	4611	4328	65,240
48400	48467	2-dr Conv-6P	4643	4309	8,294

ENGINE: Specifications were the same as those listed for the 1969 Wildcat Series 46400.

1969 Buick, Riviera two-door hardtop, V-8

RIVIERA — SERIES 49487 — A slight face lift was seen for 1969 as the sleek Riviera continued to be offered only in sport coupe form. Retractable headlamps and an integral front bumper/grille continued to distinguish the front of the Riviera. New bodyside trims using bright wheelhouse moldings and bright lower body moldings with argent accents were utilized. Expanded vinyl with front bench or bucket seats was standard. Custom interiors with bench buckets or notchback front seats in plusher vinyl or vinyl and cloth combinations were available. Standard Riviera features included all items found on other Buicks, plus woodgrained dash accents and trunk lights.

NOTE: A new Riviera GS option package sold for $131.57 at retail. It included chrome covered air cleaner, front and rear heavy-duty suspension, performance axle with positive traction differential and white sidewall tires. Cars with the package installed were outwardly distinguished by special narrow rocker panel covers, the lack of gravel deflectors, and a thin side trim molding.

RIVIERA I.D. NUMBERS: Vehicle Identification Numbers began with 494879 () 900001. VINs were coded as explained under the 1969 Buick I.D. Number section.

RIVIERA SERIES 49487

Series No.	Body/Style No.	Body Type & Seating	Factory Price	Shipping Weight	Prod. Total
49400	49487	2-dr Spt Cpe-5P	4701	4199	52,872

ENGINE: Specifications were the same as those listed for the 1969 Wildcat Series 46400.

CHASSIS FEATURES: Wheelbase: (Series 43300, 43500, 44400, 43400, 44600 two-door styles) 112 inches; (four-door styles) 116 inches; (Sportwagon) 121 inches; (Series 45200, 45400, 46400 and 46600) 123.2 inches; (Series 48200 and 48400) 126.2 inches; (Series 49487) 119 inches. Overall length: (Series 43300, 43500, 44400, 43400 and 44600 two-door styles) 200.7 inches; (four-door styles) 204.7 inches; (station wagon) 209 inches; (Sportwagon) 214 inches; (Series 45200, 45400, 46400 and 46600) 218.2 inches. Tread: (Series 43300, 43500, 44400, and 43300 and 44600) 59 inches front and rear; (Series 42500, 45400, 46400 and 46600) 63.5 inches front, 63 inches rear; (Series 48200, 48400 and 49487) 63.4 inches front, 63 inches rear. Tires: (Series 43300, 43500, 44400, 43400 and 46600) 7.75 x 14; (Sportwagon) 8.55 x 14; (Series 45200, 45400, 46400, 46600, 48200, 48400 and 49487) 8.55 x 15.

POWERTRAIN OPTIONS: A three-speed manual transmission with column shift was standard on Special Deluxe, Skylark, Skylark Custom, GS 350, LeSabre and Wildcat models. A three-speed manual transmission with floor shift was standard on GS 400 models and optional on California GS and GS 350 models. A four-speed manual transmission was optional on California GS, GS 350 and GS 400 models. Super Turbine 300 automatic transmission was optional for Special Deluxe, Skylark, Skylark Custom and LeSabre models. Turbo-Hydramatic 350 automatic transmission was optional for Special Deluxe, Skylark, Skylark Custom and GS 350 models. Turbo-Hydramatic 400 automatic transmission was optional for GS 400 and Wildcat models and was standard on Electra 225, Electra 225 Custom and Riviera models. A 350 cid/280 bhp V-8 was optional for the Special Deluxe, Skylark, Skylark Custom and LeSabre. A '400' option package for the LeSabre series included the 350 cid/280 bhp V-8 and Turbo-Hydramatic 400 transmission. Cars so-equipped had '400' emblems below the rear fender LeSabre scripts. A 'Stage 1' option was offered for the GS 400. It included a high-lift camshaft, special carburetor and large diameter dual exhaust, along with a 3.64 rear axle. Cars so-equipped had 'Stage 1' emblems on the front fenders.

CONVENIENCE OPTIONS: Air conditioning ($376 on intermediate, $437 on full-size). Power windows. Vinyl top. Seven-position tilt wheel. AM radio. AM/FM radio. AM/FM radio with stereo tape. Five-spoke Sport Wheels (chrome). Strato bucket seats on specific models. Limited trim option for Electra 225 Custom ($231). Map light on rearview mirror. 60/40 seat (Electra 225 styles). Electric window defogger (Riviera). Protective bodyside moldings (full-size). Power door locks. Power steering (standard Electra 225, Electra 225 Custom and Riviera). Power brakes (standard Electra 225, Electra 225 Custom and Riviera). Climate control air (full-size). Center console with bucket seats on Skylark Custom, GS 350, GS 400 and Wildcat when equipped with THM-350 or THM-400 automatic transmission. Four-way power seat. Six-way power seat (Electra 225, Wildcat, LeSabre). Trailering packages. Dual Action tailgate on station wagons.

HISTORICAL FOOTNOTES: A record year with 713,832 units produced in the calendar year. Model year production stood at 665,422. The only bigger year for Buick, to this point, was 1955. The company went into fourth place in production. New features included Turbo-Hydramatic transmission, Accu-Drive suspension, electric fuel pump on Riviera, new anti-theft ignition lock, headrests, ventless windows (on some models) and a redesigned collapsible steering wheel. The Century Cruiser, a radical show car, was exhibited at the New York Auto Show. The California GS did 0-to-60 mph in 9.5 seconds and had a 110 mph top speed. The Riviera GS did 0-to-60 mph in 9.2 seconds and topped out at 132 mph. Model 43536 was a station wagon with dual-action tailgate and plusher interior. On April 7, 1969, Lee N. Mayes succeeded Robert L. Kessler as Buick's general manager.

1970

SKYLARK — SERIES 43300 — A new look was introduced for 1970, with crisper lines and more open wheelhouses. The sweepspear look was once again relegated to retirement, with horizontal sculpturing taking its place. The basic Buick had a vertically textured grille with a grid overlay. Narrow lower body moldings and wheelhouse bright moldings were used. Skylark emblems were on the roof sail panels and side marker lamps were rectangular. The Skylark signature appeared on rear fenders. Interiors were spartan with vinyl and cloth combinations on bench seats standard. All-vinyl was a no-cost option for the coupe and an extra-cost option for the sedan. Standard equip-

ment included a host of mandated safety features, including left-hand outside rearview mirror and back-up lights.

BUICK I.D. NUMBERS: The serial number (VIN) was located on a plate attached to top of dash on driver's side and viewable through outside of windshield. It was also stamped on the engine block. The first symbol was a '4' for Buick. The second and third symbols indicated series, as follows: 33 = Skylark; 34 = Sport Wagon/GS; 35 = Skylark 350; 44 = Skylark Custom; 46 = GS 455; 52 = LeSabre; 54 = LeSabre Custom; 60 = Estate Wagon; 64 = LeSabre Custom 455; 66 = Wildcat Custom; 82 = Electra 225; 84 = Electra 225 Custom; 94 = Riviera. The fourth and fifth symbols indicated body style, as follows: 27 = 2-dr cpe; 35 = 4-dr two-seat sta wag; 36 = 4-dr two-seat sta wag; 37 = 2-dr HT; 39 = 4-dr HT; 46 = 4-dr three-seat sta wag; 47 = 4-dr HT; 56 = 4-dr two-seat Sportwagon; 57 = 2-dr HT, 66 = 4-dr three-seat Sportwagon, 67 = 2-dr conv; 69 = 4-dr sed; and 87 = 2-dr Riviera HT. Combined, the first five symbols were the model number, as reflected in the tables below. The sixth symbol indicated model year: 0 = 1970. The seventh symbol was a letter representing the assembly plant, as follows: C = Southgate, Calif.; D = Doraville, Ga.; G = Framingham, Mass.; H = Flint, Mich.; K = Leeds, Mo.; X = Fairfax, Kans.; Y = Wilmington, Del.; Z = Fremont, Calif. The last six digits represent the sequential assembly number at the plant with series mixed in production. In addition to the VIN, the engine block is stamped with a production code. These numbers were found on different locations: (6-cyl.) right side to rear of distributor; (350 cid V-8) on front of left bank of cylinders and between front two spark plugs and left exhaust manifold; (455 cid V-8) between front two spark plugs and exhaust manifold and production code between two left rear spark plugs and exhaust manifold. The production code has letters identifying the engine and numbers indicating production date code. The letters were as follows: (250 cid six-cyl.) SA; (350 cid/285 hp V-8) SB; (350 cid/230 hp V-8) SO; (350 cid/315 hp V-8) SP; (400 cid/400 hp V-8) RR; (455 cid/370 hp V-8) SF; (455 cid/350 hp V-8) SR and (455 cid/360 hp V-8) SS.

SKYLARK SERIES 43300

Series No.	Body/Style No.	Body Type & Seating	Factory Price	Shipping Weight	Prod. Total
43300	43327	2-dr Cpe-6P	2685	3155	18,620
43300	43369	4-dr Sed-6P	2736	3214	13,420

NOTE: Add $111 and 195 pounds for V-8.

ENGINE: Six-cylinder. Overhead valve. Cast iron block. Displacement: 250 cid. Bore and stroke: 3.875 x 3.53 inches. Compression ratio: 8.5:1. Brake horsepower: 155 at 4200 rpm. Five main bearings. Hydraulic valve lifters. Carburetor: Rochester 1MV one-barrel.

ENGINE: V-8. Overhead valve. Cast iron block. Displacement: 350 cid. Bore and stroke: 3.8 x 3.85 inches. Compression ratio: 9.0:1. Brake horsepower: 260 at 4600 rpm. Five main bearings. Hydraulic valve lifters. Carburetor: Rochester 2GV two-barrel.

SKYLARK 350 — SERIES 43500 — Identical to the Skylark except for the addition of 350 emblems to the body and a Buick emblem for the center grille.

SKYLARK 350 I.D. NUMBERS: Vehicle Identification Numbers began with 43500 () 100001. VIN codes are explained under the 1970 Buick I.D. Number section.

SKYLARK SERIES 43500

Series No.	Body/Style No.	Body Type & Seating	Factory Price	Shipping Weight	Prod. Total
43500	43569	4-dr Sed-6P	2838	3223	30,281
43500	43537	2-dr HT-6P	2859	3180	70,918

NOTE: Add $111 and 195 pounds for V-8.

ENGINE: Specifications were the same as listed for the 1970 Skylark Series 43300 V-8.

SKYLARK CUSTOM — SERIES 44400 — The plushest intermediate model had a Buick emblem centered in the grille, lower body and wheelhouse moldings and Skylark signatures on the

hood, deck and rear fenders. The Custom badge appeared beneath the rear fender signatures. Interiors were done in all-vinyl or Kenora cloth and vinyl. A bench seat was standard with bucket front seats available for the convertible and coupe.

1970 Buick, Skylark Custom four-door hardtop, V-8

SKYLARK CUSTOM I.D. NUMBERS: Vehicle Numbers began with 44400 () 100001. VIN codes are explained under the 1970 Buick I.D. Number section.

SKYLARK CUSTOM SERIES 44400

Series No.	Body/Style No.	Body Type & Seating	Factory Price	Shipping Weight	Prod. Total
44400	44469	4-dr Sed-6P	3101	3499	7,113
44400	44437	2-dr HT Cpe-6P	3132	3435	36,367
44400	44439	4-dr HT Sed-6P	3220	3565	12,411
44400	44467	2-dr Conv-6P	3275	3499	4,954

ENGINES: V-8 specifications were the same as listed for the 1970 Skylark Series.

GRAN SPORT — SERIES 43437 — A one-model series constituted Buick's cosmetic muscle car for 1970. This was a mild-mannered intermediate with the trimmings of a rip-roaring charger. A textured black grille was used, with hood scoops on the panel above. GS signatures appeared on the left-hand grille, front fenders and deck. All-vinyl bench seats in sandalwood, blue or black were standard. An all-vinyl notchback seat was optional, as were individual front bucket seats. Standard equipment approximated that found on the Skylark Custom and also included dual exhaust, a full-flow oil filter, three-speed manual transmission, heavy-duty shocks and springs and a semi-enclosed cooling system.

1970 Buick, GS 455 two-door hardtop with Stage 1 option package, V-8 (OCW)

GRAN SPORT I.D. NUMBERS: Vehicle Identification Numbers began with 434370 () 100001. VINs were coded as explained under the 1970 Buick I.D. Number section.

GRAN SPORT SERIES 43400

Series No.	Body/Style No.	Body Type & Seating	Factory Price	Shipping Weight	Prod. Total
43400	43437	2-dr HT Cpe-6P	3098	3434	9,948

ENGINE: V-8. Specifications were the same as the Skylark Series 43300 V-8 except the compression ratio was 10.25:1, brake horsepower was 315 at 4800 rpm and dual exhaust were standard.

GRAN SPORT 445 — SERIES 44600 — This was the truly muscular Buick, with a new big-block V-8 and Hurst-shifted performance transmissions. Functional hood scoops dumped cold air into the big V-8's intake. Chrome red-filled lower body and wheelhouse moldings were used with five-spoke, 14 x 6-inch chrome wheels standard. A GS 455 emblem appeared on the left-hand blacked-out grille, with others showing up on the front fenders and a GS monogram appearing on the deck lid. Standard interior appointments were the same as on the GS. A number of mandated safety features were standard.

GRAN SPORT I.D. NUMBERS: Vehicle Identification Numbers began with 446000 () 100001. VINs were coded as explained under the 1970 Buick I.D. Number section.

GRAN SPORT 455 SERIES 44600

Series No.	Body/Style No.	Body Type & Seating	Factory Price	Shipping Weight	Prod. Total
44600	44637	2-dr HT-6P	3283	3562	8,732
44600	44667	2-dr Conv-6P	3469	3619	1,416
GSX SUB-SERIES					
44600	44637	2-dr HT-6P	4479	N/A	(678)
44600	44667	2-dr Conv-6P	4665	N/A	(678)

NOTE: "Production total" indicates number of option package installations.

ENGINE: V-8. Overhead valve. Cast iron block. Displacement: 455 cid. Bore and stroke: 4.3 x 3.9 inches. Compression ratio: 10.0:1. Brake horsepower: 350 at 4600 rpm. Hydraulic valve lifters. Five main bearings. Carburetor: Rochester 4MV four-barrel.

STAGE I/STAGE II NOTE: Stage I equipment, consisting of a high-lift camshaft, 10.5:1 compression pistons, positive traction rear axle, special four-barrel carburetor and low-restriction dual exhaust increased brake horsepower to 360 at 4600 rpm. Cars so equipped have Stage I badges in place of 455 emblems and a logo replacing the 455 emblem in the left-hand grille. The GS 455 produced 510 lb-ft of torque at 2800 rpm. There was also a Stage II dealer-installed package with a hotter cam, 12.0:1 forged pistons, Edelbrock B4B manifold, Holley carb, Mickey Thompson headers and 4.78 differential gears.

1970-1/2 Buick, GSX two-door hardtop, V-8 (PH)

GSX NOTE: At midyear, Buick introduced its ultra-high-performance GSX package as a $1,196 option for the GS 455. It included a hood tach with available lighting control; G60 x 15 tires on seven-inch wide chrome rims; molded plastic front/rear spoilers; twin outside rearview mirrors; four-speed Hurst shifter; front disc brakes; heavy-duty suspension and black vinyl bucket seats. It was available with both the 350 V-8 and the Stage I engine.

SPORTWAGON — SERIES 43400 — The traditional roof panel with glass inserts was missing from 1970 Sportwagons, which had flat roofs. Narrow lower body moldings were used with bright wheelhouse moldings. Sportwagon script appeared on the rear fenders. Interiors were similar to the corresponding Skylark models, with all-vinyl trimming. Fiberglass belted tires were standard.

SPORTWAGON I.D. NUMBERS: Vehicle Identification Numbers began with 434000 () 100001. VINs were coded as explained under the 1970 Buick I.D. Number section.

SPORTWAGON SERIES 43400

Series No.	Body/Style No.	Body Type & Seating	Factory Price	Shipping Weight	Prod. Total
43400	43435	4-dr Sta Wag-2S	3210	3775	2,239
43400	43436	4-dr Sta Wag-3S	3242	3898	10,002

NOTE: Prices and weights for V-8s are given. Deduct $111 for six-cylinder models.

ENGINES: Specifications for six-cylinder and V-8 were the same as listed under 1970 Skylark Series 43300.

LESABRE — SERIES 45200 — The lowest-priced full-size Buick featured a minor face lift for 1970. A new grille-bumper combination with horizontal textured grille was at the front while at the rear the taillights dropped into the bumper assembly. A lower body bright molding was used, but there were no wheelhouse moldings. The LeSabre name appeared in script on the rear fenders and triple ventiports were found on the front. Cloth and vinyl seating surfaces were standard with a front bench. The LeSabre signature was on the right-hand instrument panel. Standard equipment included Comfort-Flo ventilation; heater and defroster; front-door operated interior light; glove compartment light; smoking set; rear seat ashtray and carpeting front and rear.

LESABRE I.D. NUMBERS: Vehicle Identification Numbers began with 452000 () 100001. VINs were coded as explained under the 1970 Buick I.D. Number section.

LESABRE SERIES 45200

Series No.	Body/Style No.	Body Type & Seating	Factory Price	Shipping Weight	Prod. Total
45200	45269	4-dr Sed-6P	3337	3970	35,404
45200	45237	2-dr HT Cpe-6P	3419	3866	14,163
45200	45239	4-dr HT Sed-6P	3477	4018	14,817

ENGINE: Specifications were the same as listed for the 1970 Skylark Series 43300.

1970 Buick, LeSabre Custom 455 four-door hardtop, V-8

LESABRE CUSTOM — SERIES 45400 — A plusher LeSabre was seen this year. It had wheelhouse moldings in addition to bright lower body moldings, which now extended onto the rear fenders. Custom badges appeared below the rear fender LeSabre scripts. Richer cloth and vinyl or all-vinyl (convertible) interiors were standard.

LESABRE CUSTOM I.D. NUMBERS: Vehicle Identification Numbers began with 454000 () 100001. VINs were coded as explained under the 1970 Buick I.D. Number section.

LESABRE CUSTOM SERIES 45400

Series No.	Body/Style No.	Body Type & Seating	Factory Price	Shipping Weight	Prod. Total
45400	45469	4-dr Sed-6P	3431	3950	36,682
45400	45437	2-dr HT Cpe-6P	3507	3921	35,641
45400	45439	4-dr HT Cpe-6P	3571	3988	43,863
45400	45467	2-dr Conv-6P	3700	3947	2,487

ENGINE: Specifications were the same as listed for the 1970 Skylark Series 43300.

LESABRE CUSTOM 455 — SERIES 45600 — Identical to the LeSabre Custom externally, this model had rear fender badges signifying use of the big 455-cid V-8 and was numbered as a separate series. The convertible was not available in this series.

LESABRE CUSTOM 455 I.D. NUMBERS: Vehicle Identification Numbers began with 456000 () 100001. VINs were coded as explained under the 1970 Buick I.D. Number section.

LESABRE CUSTOM 455 SERIES 45600

Series No.	Body/Style No.	Body Type & Seating	Factory Price	Shipping Weight	Prod. Total
45600	45669	4-dr Sed-6P	3599	4107	5,555
45600	45637	2-dr HT Cpe-6P	3675	4066	5,469
45600	45639	4-dr HT Sed-6P	3739	4143	6,541

ENGINE: V-8. Overhead valve. Cast iron block. Displacement: 455 cid. Bore and stroke: 4.3 x 3.9 inches. Compression ratio: 10.0:1. Brake horsepower: 370 at 4600 rpm. Five main bearings. Hydraulic valve lifters. Carburetor: Rochester 4MV four-barrel.

1970 Buick, four-door Estate Wagon with optional woodgrain trim, V-8 (TVB)

1970 Buick, four-door Estate Wagon, V-8 (OCW)

ESTATE WAGONS — SERIES 46000 — A full-size Buick wagon was marketed for the first time since 1964. It had the basic LeSabre body, but wore four ventiports on the front fenders. The LeSabre Custom's bright rocker, wheelhouse and rear lower fender moldings were used. Woodgraining was an option for the bodysides. Interiors were all-vinyl in a Custom grade.

ESTATE WAGON I.D. NUMBERS: Vehicle Identification Numbers began with 460000 () 100001. VINs were coded as explained under the 1970 Buick I.D. Number section.

ESTATE WAGON SERIES 46000

Series No.	Body/Style No.	Body Type & Seating	Factory Price	Shipping Weight	Prod. Total
46000	46036	4-dr Sta Wag-2S	3923	4691	11,427
46000	46046	4-dr Sta Wag-3S	4068	4779	16,879

ENGINE: Specifications were the same as those listed for the 1970 LeSabre Custom 455.

1970 Buick, Wildcat Custom two-door hardtop, V-8 (OCW)

WILDCAT CUSTOM — SERIES 46600 — The Wildcat came only with trim for 1970. It shared the LeSabre body with its new integral grille and front bumper assembly, but a grid-panel bright overlay on the grille itself distinguished the Wildcat. There were no ventiports, but there was a simulated bright air intake on each front fender. There was also a wide bright molding extending along the lower body, with connecting strips over the wheelhouse, from front to rear. The Wildcat signature appeared on the grille deck and front fenders above the inlet grids. Vinyl notchback or bucket seats were standard with a cloth and vinyl combination offered for the four-door hardtop. Standard equipment was the same as on the LeSabre except for the Deluxe steering wheel. The Wildcat signature appeared on the instrument panel.

WILDCAT CUSTOM I.D. NUMBERS: Vehicle Identification Numbers began with 466000 () 100001. VINs were coded as explained under the 1970 Buick I.D. Number section.

WILDCAT CUSTOM SERIES 46600

Series No.	Body/Style No.	Body Type & Seating	Factory Price	Shipping Weight	Prod. Total
46600	46637	2-dr HT Cpe-6P	3949	4099	9,477
46600	46639	4-dr HT Sed-6P	3997	4187	12,924
46600	46667	2-dr Conv-6P	4079	4214	1,244

ENGINE: Specifications were the same as those listed for the 1970 LeSabre Custom 455.

ELECTRA 225 — SERIES 48200 — The largest Buicks were also the least changed for 1970. A new, bright grille with overlay represented the chief distinction from a 1969 edition. Once again four ventiports graced the front fenders, while a strip of bright trim ran along the lower body from front to rear and extended across the fender skirts. Standard Electra 225 features included those found on less expensive Buicks, plus Custom padded seat cushions; electric clock; trunk light; smoking set; rear seat ashtrays; carpeting on floors and lower doors and front and rear armrests. Cloth and vinyl bench seats were standard on the Electra 225.

ELECTRA 225 I.D. NUMBERS: Vehicle Identification Numbers began with 482000 () 100001. VINs were coded as explained under the 1970 Buick I.D. Number section.

ELECTRA 225 SERIES 48200

Series No.	Body/Style No.	Body Type & Seating	Factory Price	Shipping Weight	Prod. Total
48200	48269	4-dr Sed-6P	4461	4274	12,580
48200	48257	2-dr HT Cpe-6P	4482	4214	12,013
48200	48239	4-dr HT Sed-6P	4592	4296	14,338

ENGINE: Specifications were the same as listed for the 1970 LeSabre Custom 455.

ELECTRA 225 CUSTOM — SERIES 48400 — Plusher interiors with side coat hooks and additional interior lighting made up the Custom Series differences.

1970 Buick, Electra 225 Custom Limited two-door hardtop, V-8

NOTE: 'Limited' Custom trim was available on Body Styles 48457 and 48439. The finest Buick interiors, with notchback or 60/40 notchback front seats were standard. Limited script appeared on the roof sail panels when this optional package was ordered.

1970 Buick, Electra 225 Custom four-door hardtop, V-8

ELECTRA 225 CUSTOM I.D. NUMBERS: Vehicle Identification Numbers began with 484000 () 100001. VINs were coded as explained under the 1970 Buick I.D. Number section.

ELECTRA 225 CUSTOM SERIES 48400

Series No.	Body/Style No.	Body Type & Seating	Factory Price	Shipping Weight	Prod. Total
48400	48469	4-dr Sed-6P	4677	4283	14,109
48400	48457	2-dr HT Cpe-6P	4661	4297	26,002
48400	46439	4-dr HT Sed-6P	4771	4385	65,114
48400	48467	2-dr Conv-6P	4802	4341	6,045

ENGINE: Specifications were the same as those listed for the 1970 LeSabre Custom 455.

RIVIERA — SERIES 49487 — A new vertical textured grille, within the front bumper ensemble, updated the 1970 Riviera front end. At the sides, a new version of the famous Buick sweepspear was created with new bodyside moldings. Fender skirts were standard equipment for the first, and only, time on a Riviera. The headlamps were flanking the grille and did not retract. Bright metal outlined the lower body and fender skirt lip, continuing in a narrow line to the rear bumper. Riviera script

appeared on the hood, deck, roof and sail panels, while the 'R' trademark appeared within the round rear fender sidemarkers. Standard equipment included every feature found on less expensive Buicks plus padded seat cushions; full carpeting; smoking set; and an electric clock. Vinyl bench or bucket seating surfaces were standard. An optional Custom interior was available, with Strato notchback seating in all-vinyl or a vinyl and cloth combination.

NOTE: A Gran Sport option was offered for the Riviera. Cars so equipped had heavy-duty suspension, positive traction differential, H78 x 15 fiberglass belted white sidewall tires and GS monograms on the front fenders and instrument panel. The Stage I version of the 455-cid V-8 was an extra-cost option.

1970 Buick, Riviera two-door hardtop, V-8

RIVIERA I.D. NUMBERS: Vehicle Identification Numbers began with 494870 () 100001. VINs were coded as explained under the 1970 Buick I.D. Number section.

RIVIERA SERIES 49487

Series No.	Body/Style No.	Body Type & Seating	Factory Price	Shipping Weight	Prod. Total
49400	49487	2-dr HT Cpe-6P	4854	4216	37,366
49400	49487	2-dr GS HT Cpe-6P	4986	N/A	N/A

ENGINE: Specifications were the same as listed for the 1970 LeSabre Custom 455.

CHASSIS FEATURES: Wheelbase: (Series 43300, 43400, 44400, 44500 and 44600 two-door styles) 112 inches, (four-door styles) 116 inches; (Series 45300, 45400, 45600, 46000 and 46600) 124 inches; (Series 48200 and 48400) 127 inches; (Series 49487) 119 inches. Overall length: (Series 43300, 43400, 44400, 44500 and 46600 two-door styles) 202.2 inches, (four-door styles) 206.2 inches; (Series 45200, 45400, 45600, 46000 and 46600) 220.2 inches; (Series 48200 and 48400) 225.8 inches; (Series 49487) 215.5 inches. Front Tread: (Skylark) 59 inches; (LeSabre) 63 inches; (GS) 59 inches; (GS-455) 59.4 inches; (Wildcat/Electra) 63.5 inches; (Riviera) 63.4 inches. RearTread: (Skylark/GS/GS-455) 59 inches, (all others) 63 inches. Tire size: (Series 43300, 43400, 44400. 45400, 44600) G78 x 14; (Series 45200, 45400, 45600 and 49487) H78 x 15; (Series 46000) L78 x 15; (Series 48200 and 48400) J78 x 15.

POWER OPTIONS: A three-speed manual transmission with column shift was standard on Skylark, Skylark 350, Skylark Custom, Gran Sport LeSabre and Wildcat styles. A three-speed manual transmission with floor-mounted shifter was standard on GS 455. A four-speed manual transmission was optional on the GS and GS 455. Turbo-Hydramatic 350 was available with Skylark Series and the GS. Turbo-Hydramatic 400 was optional for GS 455, LeSabre Custom 455 and Wildcat and was standard on Electra 225 Series and Riviera. A 350 cid/285 bhp V-8 was optional for the Skylark Custom, as was a 315 brake horsepower version of the same engine when ordered with the "high perfor-

mance group." The 455 cid/360 hp Stage I V-8 was available in specific Skylark and Riviera models.

CONVENIENCE OPTIONS: GSX package for Gran Sport models including: hood-mounted tachometer, Rally steering wheel, front and rear spoilers, outside sport mirrors, power front disc brakes, G60 x 15 tires, 15 x 7-inch chrome spoke wheels, black bucket seat interior, GSX ornament on instrument panel and grille, GSX decals and body stripes, black-finished hood panels, heavy-duty suspension, special 455 cid/350 hp V-8 and Saturn Yellow or Apollo White exterior finish ($1,196). Air conditioning ($486 intermediate; $457 full-size). Power steering (standard on Electra 225s, Riviera). Power brakes (standard on Electra 225s, Riviera). Power windows. Vinyl top covering. AM radio. AM/FM radio. Stereo tape player. Tilt steering wheel. Limited trim for Electra 225 Custom ($318). Strato bench seats (Riviera). Five-spoke chromed wheels. Console with shifter (Riviera). Consoles (bucket seats on GS, GS 455). Automatic Climate Control (full-size). Rearview mirror map light. Cornering lights (full-size). Automatic level control (specific models). Protective bodyside moldings (except Riviera and GS/GS 455). Soft-ray tinted glass. Rim-mounted horn control. Remote control outside rearview mirror. Four-way or six-way power seat control. Electric door locks. Tow Master trailering package. Electric trunk release. Chrome luggage rack. Two-way door gate. Power rear window for Estate and station wagon styles.

HISTORICAL FOOTNOTES: Calendar year production was 459,931. Model year production was 666,501. Buick came in fourth in the production race. The five-millionth Buick was built at the Doraville, Ga., factory, near Atlanta. The GS 455 could do 0-to-60 mph in 6.5 seconds and had a 129.5 mph top speed. The Riviera GS could do 0-to-60 mph in 7.9 seconds and had a 125 mph top speed. Buick discontinued the California GS option this year. Style 43436 is the Sportwagon with dual-action tailgate. Styles 46036 and 46046 are Estate Wagons.

1971

SKYLARK — SERIES 43300 — The basic 1970 styling was continued for another year. The Skylark had its own grille and used bright metal wheelhouse and lower body moldings of a narrow width. Standard Skylark features included front and rear ashtrays, heater and defroster, Step-On parking brake, padded head restraints and other features mandated by federal safety standards. Interiors were cloth and vinyl or all-vinyl.

BUICK I.D. NUMBERS: The serial number (VIN) was located on a plate attached to top of dash on driver's side and viewable through outside of windshield. It was also stamped on the engine block. The first symbol was a '4' for Buick. The second and third symbols indicated series, as follows: 33 = Skylark; 34 = Sportwagon/GS; 44 = Skylark Custom; 52 = LeSabre; 54 = LeSabre Custom, 60 = Estate Wagon, 71 = Centurian, 82 = Electra 225, 84 = Electra 225 Custom; 94 = Riviera. The fourth and fifth symbols indicated body style, as follows: 27 = 2-dr cpe; 35 = 4-dr two-seat sta wag; 36 = 4-dr two-seat sta wag; 37 = 2-dr HT; 39 = 4-dr HT; 45 = 4-dr three-seat sta wag; 47 = 2-dr HT; 57 = 2-dr HT Spt Cpe; 67 = 2-dr conv; 69 = 4-dr sed; and 87 = 2-dr Riviera HT. Combined, the first five symbols were the model number, as reflected in tables below. The sixth symbol indicated model year: 1 = 1971. The seventh symbol was a letter representing the assembly plant, as follows: C = Southgate, Calif.; G = Framingham, Mass.; H = Flint, Mich.; I = Oshawa, Ont., Canada; X = Fairfax, Kans.; Y = Wilmington, Del.; Z = Fremont, Calif. The last six digits represent the sequential assembly number at the plant with series mixed in production. In addition to the VIN, the engine block is stamped with a production code.

These numbers were found on different locations: (6-cyl.) right side to rear of distributor (350 cid V-8) on front of left bank of cylinders and production code between front two spark plugs and left exhaust manifold; (455 cid V-8) between front two spark plugs and exhaust manifold and production code between two left rear spark plugs and exhaust manifold. The production code has letters identifying the engine and numbers indicating production date codes. The letters were as follows: (250 cid/145 hp I-6) DF; (250 cid/155 hp I-6) EA; (350 cid/230 hp V-8) TO, TC; (350 cid/260 hp V-8) TO, TB; (350 cid/315 hp V-8) TP; (455 cid/335 hp V-8) TA; (455 cid/310 hp V-8) TR; and (455 cid/345 hp V-8) TS.

SKYLARK SERIES 43300

Series No.	Body/Style No.	Body Type & Seating	Factory Price	Shipping Weight	Prod. Total
43300	43327	2-dr Cpe-6P	2847	3144	14,500
43300	43337	2-dr HT Cpe-6P	2918	3163	61,201
43300	43369	4-dr Sed-6P	2897	3216	34,037

NOTE: Add $121 and 219 pounds for V-8s.

ENGINE: Six-cylinder. Overhead valve. Cast iron block. Displacement: 250 cid. Bore and stroke: 3.875 x 3.53 inches. Compression ratio: 8.5:1. Brake horsepower: 145 at 4200 rpm. Hydraulic valve lifters. Five main bearings. Carburetor: Rochester 1MV one-barrel.

ENGINE: V-8. Overhead valve. Cast iron block. Displacement: 350 cid. Bore and stroke: 3.8 x 3.85 inches. Compression ratio: 8.5:1. Brake horsepower: 230 at 4200 rpm. Five main bearings. Hydraulic valve lifters. Carburetor: Rochester 2GV two-barrel.

1971 Buick, Skylark Custom two-door hardtop, V-8

1971 Buick, Skylark Custom four-door sedan, V-8 (OCW)

SKYLARK CUSTOM — SERIES 44400 — This was a plusher Skylark, with Comfort-Flo ventilation system, Deluxe steering wheel, glovebox light and plusher interiors with full carpeting. An additional rocker panel molding was used, along with a bright applique on the front fenders. Custom badges appeared below the Skylark rear fender scripts and on the grille. Skylark emblems were on the roof sail panels.

SKYLARK CUSTOM I.D. NUMBERS: Vehicle Identification Numbers began with 444001 () 100001. VINs were coded as explained under the 1971 Buick I.D. Number section.

SKYLARK CUSTOM SERIES 44400

Series No.	Body/Style No.	Body Type & Seating	Factory Price	Shipping Weight	Prod. Total
44400	44437	2-dr HT Cpe-6P	3317	3391	29,536
44400	44469	4-dr Sed-6P	3288	3455	8,299
44400	44439	4-dr HT Sed-6P	3397	3547	20,418
44400	44467	2-dr Conv-6P	3462	3431	3,993

NOTE: Add $121 and 219 pounds for V-8s.

ENGINE: Six-cylinder and V-8 specifications were the same as those listed for the 1971 Skylark Series 43300.

SPORTWAGON — SERIES 43436 — The Sportwagon shared the Skylark chassis and its improvements for 1971. The Sportwagon did not have bright wheelhouse moldings, using only a lower body bright molding for trim. Power front disc brakes were standard, as was an all-vinyl interior with front bench seat. The dual-action tailgate was now standard on this model only. Sportwagon script appeared on the rear fenders.

SPORTWAGON I.D. NUMBERS: Vehicle Identification Numbers began with 434361 () 100001. VINs were coded as explained under the 1971 Buick I.D. Number section.

SPORTWAGON SERIES 43436

Series No.	Body/Style No.	Body Type & Seating	Factory Price	Shipping Weight	Prod. Total
43400	43436	Sta Wag-2S	3515	3928	12,525

ENGINE: Specifications were the same as listed for the 1971 Skylark Series 43300 V-8.

1971 Buick, GS 455 two-door hardtop, V-8 (OCW)

GS AND GS 455 — SERIES 43400 — Buick combined these two series into one for 1971. These muscular Buicks had blacked-out grilles with bright trim, bright wheelhouse moldings and bright rocker panel moldings with red-filled accents. Dual, functional hood scoops were ahead of the windshield. GS monograms appeared on the front fenders, deck and hood. Cars equipped with the 455-cid or 455 Stage I options had additional emblems. Standard equipment was the same as the Skylark Custom, but bucket or notchback front seats, in all-vinyl trim were optional. A GSX appearance package was available at extra-cost. It included a painted hood, accent striping, special emblems, blacked-out grille and dual, functional hood air scoops.

GS AND GS 455 I.D. NUMBERS: Vehicle Identification Numbers began with 434001 () 100001. VINs were coded as explained under the 1971 Buick I.D. Number section.

GS/GS 455 SERIES 43400

Series No.	Body/Style No.	Body Type & Seating	Factory Price	Shipping Weight	Prod. Total
43400	43437	2-dr HT-5P	3285	3461	8,268
43400	43467	2-dr Conv-5P	3476	3497	902

NOTE: Prices and weights are for Gran Sports with 350-cid engines. Production numbers include both GS and GS 455 cars.

ENGINE: GS V-8. Specifications were the same as listed for the 1971 Skylark 350-cid V-8 except brake horsepower was 260 and a four-barrel carbureted V-8 with dual exhaust was used. The GS 455 engine produced 315 hp. The Stage I engine produced 345 hp.

ENGINE: GS 455 V-8. Overhead valve. Cast iron block. Displacement: 455 cid. Bore and stroke: 4.3 x 3.9 inches. Compression ratio: 8.5:1. Brake horsepower: 315 at 4600 rpm. Five main bearings. Hydraulic valve lifters. Carburetor: Rochester 4MV four-barrel.

LESABRE — SERIES 45200 — A new, larger body was used on the 1971 LeSabre. Full-Flo ventilation with deck lid louvers was standard. The new body, with a sweeping side sculpture, used the customary Buick ventiports in groups of three on each front fender. Bright metal lower body and wheelhouse moldings were used. The LeSabre had its own grille. Interiors were fabric and vinyl. Standard equipment included armrests; rear ashtrays; glovebox light; interior lights; front and rear carpeting; full-foam seat cushions; inside hood release; power front disc brakes; seat belts and other mandated federal safety features. LeSabre script appeared on the front fenders.

LESABRE I.D. NUMBERS: Vehicle Identification Numbers began with 45200 () 100001. VINs were coded as explained under the 1971 Buick I.D. Number section.

LESABRE SERIES 45200

Series No.	Body/Style No.	Body Type & Seating	Factory Price	Shipping Weight	Prod. Total
45200	45269	4-dr Sed-6P	3992	4078	26,348
45200	45257	2-dr HT Cpe-6P	4061	4049	13,385
45200	45239	4-dr HT Cpe-6P	4119	4109	41,098

ENGINE: Specifications were the same as listed for the 1971 Skylark Series 43300 V-8.

1971 Buick, LeSabre Custom four-door hardtop, V-8

LESABRE CUSTOM AND CUSTOM 455 — SERIES 45400 — This was a plusher Buick with more luxurious interiors. The convertible, offered only in this series, had a new top that folded inward on retracting. Custom models had a Custom badge beneath the LeSabre front fender script, unless they were equipped with the 455-cid V-8, in which case they had that engine's insignia instead.

LESABRE CUSTOM I.D. NUMBERS: Vehicle Identification Numbers began with 454001 () 100001. VINs were coded as explained under the 1971 Buick I.D. Number section.

LESABRE CUSTOM SERIES 45400

Series No.	Body/Style No.	Body Type & Seating	Factory Price	Shipping Weight	Prod. Total
45400	45469	4-dr Sed-6P	4085	4410	26,970
45400	45457	2-dr HT Cpe-6P	4149	4095	29,944
45400	45439	4-dr HT Sed-6P	4213	4147	41,098
45400	45467	2-dr Conv-6P	4342	4086	1,856

ENGINE: 350-cid V-8. Specifications were the same as listed for the 1971 Skylark Series 43300 V-8.

ENGINE: 455-cid V-8. Specifications were the same as listed for the 1971 GS 455 Series 43400 V-8.

1971 Buick, Centurion two-door hardtop, V-8 (TVB)

CENTURION — SERIES 46600 — This was the new line for Buick, replacing the Wildcat series. The Centurion was a masculine, performance image machine that went for the clean look. Side trim was minimal, with only a bright rocker panel molding and wheelhouse moldings. There were no ventiports on the Centurion. The grille was of a special texture and the taillights had bright grids over them. Centurion lettering appeared on the front fenders and the round Centurion medallion was used on closed model roof sail panels. It also appeared on the deck and hood. The Formal Coupe (two-door hardtop) included a vinyl top covering. Standard equipment was the same as on the LeSabre, plus a Deluxe steering wheel. Interiors were vinyl and fabric combinations, with bench or notchback front seats.

CENTURION I.D. NUMBERS: Vehicle Identification Numbers began with 466001 () 100001. VINs were coded as explained under the 1971 Buick I.D. Number section.

CENTURION SERIES 46600

Series No.	Body/Style No.	Body Type & Seating	Factory Price	Shipping Weight	Prod. Total
46600	46647	2-dr HT Cpe-6P	4678	4195	11,892
46600	46639	4-dr HT-6P	4564	4307	15,345
46600	46667	2-dr Conv-6P	4678	4227	2,161

ENGINE: V-8. Specifications were the same as listed for the 1971 GS 455 Series 43400.

ELECTRA 225 — SERIES 48200 — The biggest Buicks were freshly styled for 1971 with a longer, wider look predominating. Four ventiports again indicated the car's prestige in the Buick line. Series identification appeared on the deck lid and roof sail pillars. Standard equipment included Full-Flo ventilation with deck lid louvers; Custom foam seats; heater and defroster; Deluxe steering wheel; plush pile carpeting; variable ratio power steering; power brakes; remote control outside rearview mirror; windshield radio antenna and a fully-padded instrument panel. A number of mandated safety features were also included.

ELECTRA 225 I.D. NUMBERS: Vehicle Identification Numbers began with 482001 () 100001. VINs were coded as explained under the 1971 Buick I.D. Number section.

ELECTRA 225 SERIES 48200

Series No.	Body/Style No.	Body Type & Seating	Factory Price	Shipping Weight	Prod. Total
48200	48237	2-dr HT Cpe-6P	4801	4345	8,662
48200	48239	4-dr HT-6P	4915	4381	17,589

1971 Buick, Electra 225 Custom Limited four-door hardtop, V-8

ELECTRA 225 CUSTOM — SERIES 48400 — Custom models had a plusher interior than the regular Electra 225 with woodgrain inserts used liberally on door panels and the instrument panel. Exterior appearance was identical to the 48200 Series.

ELECTRA 225 CUSTOM I.D. NUMBERS: Vehicle Identification Numbers began with 484001 () 100001. Numbers were coded as explained under the 1971 Buick I.D. Number section.

ELECTRA 225 CUSTOM SERIES 48400

Series No.	Body/Style No.	Body Type & Seating	Factory Price	Shipping Weight	Prod. Total
48400	48437	2-dr HT-6P	4980	4359	26,831
48400	48439	4-dr HT-6P	5093	4421	72,954

NOTE: 'Limited' interiors were offered for both Custom Electra 225 styles. Cars so equipped had even plusher interiors, with bench seats or 60/40 notchback front seats. 'Limited' badges were applied to the roof sail panels when this option was included.

ENGINE: V-8. Specifications were the same as listed for the 1971 GS 455 Series 43400.

ESTATE WAGONS — SERIES 46000 — A new Estate Wagon was built on the 127-inch wheelbase Electra 225 chassis. Standard equipment was the same as the Electra 225, with Custom-grade all-vinyl interior trimming. Woodgrain sides were available. All wagons had the Glide-Away tailgate, Full-Flo ventilation with louvers in the tailgate, bright rocker panel and wheelhouse moldings and four ventiports on each front fender.

ESTATE WAGON I.D. NUMBERS: Vehicle Identification Numbers began with 466001 () 100001. VINs were coded as explained under the 1971 Buick I.D. Number section.

ESTATE WAGON SERIES 46000

Series No.	Body/Style No.	Body Type & Seating	Factory Price	Shipping Weight	Prod. Total
46000	46035	4-dr Sta Wag-2S	4640	4906	8,699
46000	40645	4-dr Sta Wag-3S	4786	4965	15,335

ENGINE: V-8. Specifications were the same as listed for the 1971 GS 455 Series 43400.

RIVIERA — SERIES 49487 — A sensational new Riviera debuted for 1971. A large car with a boattail rear roof and window section and sweeping side sculpture greeted 1971's Riviera customers. Wheelhouses were wide open, after a year of skirted fenders. Riviera shared Full-Flo ventilation with other 1971 Buicks and had the louvers on the deck lid. Standard features were numerous and included heater and defroster; Custom padded contoured seats; deep pile carpeting; electric clock; smoking set; head restraints; new seat belt system; inside hood lock release; variable ratio power steering; Turbo-Hydramatic; power front disc brakes and dual exhaust.

NOTE: A Gran Sport option was available for the Riviera. Cars so equipped had a 455 cid/330 hp V-8 with chrome air cleaner linked to a specially calibrated Turbo-Hydramatic 400 transmission, heavy-duty suspension, positive traction differential, H78 x 15 bias belted whitewall tires and Riviera GS monogram on front fenders and instrument panel. This model also included heavy-duty suspension.

1971 Buick, Riviera GS two-door hardtop, V-8 (TVB)

RIVIERA I.D. NUMBERS: Vehicle Identification Numbers began with 494871 () 10001. Numbers were coded as explained under the 1971 Buick I.D. Number section.

RIVIERA SERIES 49487

Series No.	Body/Style No.	Body Type & Seating	Factory Price	Shipping Weight	Prod. Total
49400	49487	2-dr Spt Cpe-5P	5253	4325	33,810

ENGINE: Specifications were the same as listed for the 1971 GS 455 Series 43400.

CHASSIS FEATURES: Wheelbase: (Series 43300, 44400 and 43400) two-door styles: 112 inches; four-door styles: 116 inches; (Series 45200, 45400, 46400) 124 inches; (Series 48200, 48400 and 46000) 127 inches; (Series 49487) 112 inches. Overall length: (Series 43300, 44400 and 43400) two-door styles: 203.3 inches; four-door styles: 207.3 inches; (Sportwagons) 213.7 inches; (Series 45200, 45400 and 46400) 221.9 inches; (Series 48200, 48400) 227.9 inches; (Series 46000) 228.3 inches; (Series 49487) 218.3 inches. Tire size: (Skylark) F78 x 14; (Skylark Custom, Sportwagon, GS and GS 455) G78 x 14; (Le-

Sabre, Centurion and Riviera) H78 x 15; (Electra 225) J78 x 15; (Estate Wagons) L78 x 15.

POWERTRAIN OPTIONS: Three-speed manual transmission was standard in Series 43300, 44400, 43400, 45200, 45400 and 46600. Four-speed manual transmission was optional in Series 43400 only. Turbo-Hydramatic 350 was optional for cars with six-cylinder or 350-cid V-8 engines. Turbo-Hydramatic 400 was optional for cars equipped with the 455-cid V-8 and was also standard in Series 48200, 48400 and 49487. A 350 cid/260 bhp V-8 was optional for Series 43300, 44400, 43400, 45200 and 45400. A 455 cid/330 bhp V-8 with four-barrel induction was optional for Series 43400, 45200, 45400, 46600, 48200 and 48400. Max-Trac all-weather traction control rear axles were optional in Series 49487 models.

CONVENIENCE AND APPEARANCE FEATURES: Air conditioning. Power windows ($116). Vinyl top. Tilt steering wheel. Strato bucket seats (Riviera $187). Chrome five-spoke wheels ($95). Limited trim (Electra 225 Custom $284). Custom trim (Estate Wagon woodgrain $199). AM radio. AM/FM radio. AM/FM stereo ($239). Speed alert control. Cornering lights (full-size). Bumper guards (except Riviera and Estate Wagon). Protective bodyside moldings (except Riviera). Console (Riviera, GS, and Skylark Custom with bucket seats). Six-way power seats. GSX equipment for GS 455 including bodyside stripes; black hood panels; GSX grille emblem; body color headlamp bezels; black rocker moldings and rear spoiler. Sport mirrors (GS and GSX). Instrument panel gauges (GS and GSX). Hood-mounted tachometer (GS and GSX). Front spoiler (GS and GSX). Automatic Climate Control. Rear window defogger. Custom interior trim (Riviera). Electric trunk release. Special sport steering wheel. Rallye steering wheel (GS and GSX). Deluxe steering wheel (LeSabre). Power door locks. Child safety seat. Chrome luggage rack (Estate Wagon). Power Glide-Away tailgate (Estate Wagon). Intermittent wipers. Auto Level Control. Remote outside rearview mirror (standard, Electra 225s).

HISTORICAL FOOTNOTES: Model year production was 551,186 units. A new "Silver Arrow" Riviera show car was exhibited. The Riviera GS could still do 0-to-60 mph in a respectable 8.1 seconds and had a 120 mph top speed. Style 46647 was the Centurion Formal Coupe. Style 46035 was the two-seat Estate Wagon. Style 46045 was the three-seat Estate Wagon.

1972

1972 Buick, Skylark 350 'Sun Coupe' two-door hardtop, V-8 (TVB)

SKYLARK AND SKYLARK 350 — SERIES 43300 — A mild face lift was done on the 1972 Skylark. The front bumper was redesigned with bumper guards now standard. At the rear, black vinyl surrounds were added to the taillamp/bumper assembly. The Skylark had a narrow lower body molding and bright wheel-

house molding. Skylark script appeared on the rear fenders, with a 350 badge added when equipment included the four-barrel carbureted 350 cid/175 bhp V-8. Standard Skylark features were front ashtray; heater and defroster; side terminal energizer battery; padded instrument panel and mandated safety features. Skylark 350 had Deluxe cloth and vinyl seats, carpeting, rear ashtrays, armrests, Deluxe steering wheel and dual horns.

BUICK I.D. NUMBERS: VIN was located on top of dash, on driver's side, visible through windshield. The first symbol was a '4' for Buick. The second symbol identified the series, as follows: D = Skylark; F = Sport Wagon; G = GS; H = Skylark Custom; L = LeSabre; N = LeSabre Custom; P = Centurion; R = Estate Wagon; U = Electra 225; V = Electra 225 Custom; Y = Riviera. The third and fourth symbols identified the body style. They appear as the last two digits of model number in tables below. The fifth symbol indicated engine type, as follows: (250-cid six) D; (350-cid V-8) G, H, J, K; (455-cid V-8) P, R, T, U, V, W. The sixth symbol indicated model year: 2 = 1972. The seventh symbol indicated assembly plant, as follows: C = Southgate, Calif.; G = Framingham, Mass.; H = Flint, Mich.; X = Fairfax, Kans.; Y = Wilmington, Del.; and Z = Fremont, Calif. The last six symbols were the sequential production number at the assembly plant.

SKYLARK/SKYLARK 350 SERIES 43300

Series No.	Body/Style No.	Body Type & Seating	Factory Price	Shipping Weight	Prod. Total
43300	43327	2-dr Cpe-6P	2925	3436	14,552
43300	43337	2-dr HT Cpe-6P	2993	3442	84,868
43300	43369	4-dr Sed-6P	2973	3491	42,206

ENGINE: Skylark V-8. Overhead valve. Cast iron block. Displacement: 350 cid. Bore and stroke: 3.8 x 3.85 inches. Compression ratio: 8.5:1. Net horsepower: 150 at 3800 rpm. Five main bearings. Hydraulic valve lifters. Carburetor: Rochester 2GV two-barrel.

ENGINE: Skylark 350 V-8. Specifications were the same as above, except a four-barrel carburetor was used and net horsepower was 175.

1972 Buick, Skylark Custom four-door hardtop, V-8

SKYLARK CUSTOM — SERIES 44400 — This was a plusher Skylark, distinguished on the exterior by a grid-textured bright grille, wider bright rocker panel moldings with rear stone guard extensions and wheelhouse moldings. Plusher Custom interiors were of cloth and viny, or all-vinyl. The Sport Wagon featured a standard dual-action tailgate.

SKYLARK CUSTOM I.D. NUMBERS: Serial numbers began with 4H002 () 100001 for Skylark Customs and 4F362 () 100001 for Sport Wagons. Numbers were coded as explained under the 1972 Buick I.D. Number section.

SKYLARK CUSTOM SERIES 44400

Series No.	Body/Style No.	Body Type & Seating	Factory Price	Shipping Weight	Prod. Total
44400	44437	2-dr HT Cpe-6P	3255	3487	34,271
44400	44469	4-dr Sed-6P	3228	3532	9,924
44400	44467	2-dr Conv-6P	3393	3550	3,608
44400	44439	4-dr HT Sed-6P	3331	3625	12,925
44400	43436	4-dr Spt Wag-6P	3443	4003	14,417

ENGINES: Specifications were the same as those listed under 1972 Skylark and Skylark 350 engine data.

GS 350 AND GS 455 — SERIES 43400

GS 350 AND GS 455 — SERIES 43400 — These sport coupe and convertible styles featured dual exhaust, functional dual hood scoops, heavy-duty springs, shocks, and stabilizer bar in conjunction with a muscular look. Appearance was enhanced by wide bright rocker moldings, wheelhouse moldings and GS monograms on the front fenders and deck. When cars had the 455-cid V-8 installed, suitable emblems were attached. Vinyl bench seats were standard (black on the convertible). Bucket seats were available at extra cost.

GS 350 AND GS 455 I.D. NUMBERS: Vehicle Identification Numbers began with 46002 () 100001. Numbers were coded as explained under the 1972 Buick I.D. Number section.

GS 350/GS 455 SERIES 43400

Series No.	Body/Style No.	Body Type & Seating	Factory Price	Shipping Weight	Prod. Total
43400	43437	2-dr HT Cpe-6P	3226	3487	7,723
43400	43467	2-dr Conv-6P	3406	3541	852

NOTE: Add $165 to above prices for 455-cid V-8.

ENGINE: GS 350 V-8. Specifications were the same as listed under 1972 Skylark 350-cid V-8 engine data, except a Rochester 4MV four-barrel carburetor was used and horsepower was rated at 190 nhp at 4000 rpm.

ENGINE: GS 455 V-8. Overhead valve. Cast iron block. Displacement: 455 cid. Bore and stroke: 4.3 x 3.9 inches. Compression ratio: 8.5:1. Net horsepower: 225 at 4000 rpm. Five main bearings. Hydraulic valve lifters. Carburetor: Rochester 4MV four-barrel. A high-performance GS 455 engine with 270 hp at 4400 rpm was optional at extra cost.

LESABRE — SERIES 45200

LESABRE — SERIES 45200 — Little changed from 1971, the LeSabre had no deck louvers for the Full-Flo ventilation this year. A trio of ventiports did continue on the front fenders. Standard exterior trim included bright rocker panel moldings, but no wheelhouse moldings. LeSabre script appeared on front fenders. Interiors were of Kalmora cloth and Madrid vinyl. Standard equipment now included power front disc brakes and variable ratio power steering, plus numerous mandated federal safety features.

LESABRE I.D. NUMBERS: Vehicle Identification Numbers began with 4L002 () 100001. Numbers were coded as explained under the 1972 Buick I.D. Number section.

LESABRE SERIES 45200

Series No.	Body/Style No.	Body Type & Seating	Factory Price	Shipping Weight	Prod. Total
45200	45257	2-dr Spt Cpe-6P	4024	4184	14,001
45200	45269	4-dr Sed-6P	3958	4219	29,505
45200	45239	4-dr HT Sed-6P	4079	4229	15,160

ENGINE: Specifications were the same as listed under 1971 Skylark 350-cid two-barrel V-8 engine data.

1972 Buick, LeSabre Custom 455 four-door hardtop, V-8

LESABRE CUSTOM — SERIES 45400

LESABRE CUSTOM — SERIES 45400 — The Custom featured a plusher interior of vinyl and fabric or all vinyl. A broader lower body molding was used with bright wheelhouse moldings. Custom plaques were used beneath the LeSabre signatures on the front fenders.

LESABRE CUSTOM I.D. NUMBERS: Vehicle Identification Numbers began with 4N002( )100001. See 1972 Buick I.D. Number section listing.

LESABRE CUSTOM SERIES 45400

Series No.	Body/Style No.	Body Type & Seating	Factory Price	Shipping Weight	Prod. Total
45400	45457	2-dr Spt Cpe-6P	4107	4199	36,510
45400	45469	4-dr Sed-6P	4047	4239	35,295
45400	45439	4-dr HT Sed-6P	4168	4244	50,804
45400	45487	2-dr Conv-6P	4291	4253	2,037

ENGINES: Specifcations were the same as listed under the 1972 Skylark 350-cid two-barrel V-8 engine data.

CENTURION — SERIES 46600

CENTURION — SERIES 46600 — A new vertical grille giving the hood more of a domed effect distinguished the 1972 Centurion. Side trim continued to be minimal with a bright metal lower body strip and wheelhouse moldings taking care of most superfluous touches. A Centurion medallion appeared on closed body roof sail panels and on all decks and hoods. Centurion lettering was used on the front fenders. There were no ventiports. Standard equipment duplicated that of the LeSabre, but interiors were of a more luxurious vinyl and fabric combination with notchback front seat standard.

1972 Buick, Centurion two-door hardtop, V-8

CENTURION I.D. NUMBERS: Vehicle Identification Numbers began with 4P002( )100001. See 1972 Buick I.D. Number section listing.

CENTURION SERIES 46600

Series No.	Body/Style No.	Body Type & Seating	Factory Price	Shipping Weight	Prod. Total
46600	46647	2-dr Spt Cpe-6P	4579	4358	14,187
46600	46639	4-dr HT Sed-6P	4508	4426	19,582
46600	46667	2-dr Conv-6P	4616	4235	2,396

ENGINE: Specifications were the same as those listed under 1972 GS 455 V-8 engine data.

ESTATE WAGON — SERIES 46000

ESTATE WAGON — SERIES 46000 — These big wagons shared the Electra body and an Electra-like grille. All-vinyl interiors with a bench front seat were standard. A notchback front seat was optional on the nine-passenger three-seat version. Standard equipment was the same as on the LeSabre, plus a four-jet windshield washer assembly.

ESTATE WAGON I.D. NUMBER: Vehicle Identification Numbers began with 4R002( )100001. See 1972 Buick I.D. Number section listing.

ESTATE WAGON SERIES 46000

Series No.	Body/Style No.	Body Type & Seating	Factory Price	Shipping Weight	Prod. Total
46000	46035	4-dr Sta Wag-2S	4589	4995	10,175
46000	46045	4-dr Sta Wag-3S	4728	5080	18,793

ENGINE: Specifications were the same as those listed under 1972 GS 455 V-8 engine data.

ELECTRA 225 — SERIES 48200

ELECTRA 225 — SERIES 48200 — A new grille was one of the face lift features of the 1972 Electra 225. Bumper guards front and rear promised better collision protection. The traditional four ventiports per fender remained. Fender skirts were again standard with their lower lip molding providing a link for

the bright metal lower body strip that ran full-length. The Electra 225 emblem appeared on the grille and deck this year. Interiors were cloth and vinyl with bench front seat. Standard features included those of lower-priced Buicks plus touches such as variable-ratio power steering, power front disc brakes and remote control outside rearview mirror.

ELECTRA 225 I.D. NUMBERS: Vehicle Identification Numbers began with 40002( )100001. Vehicle Identification Numbers were coded as explained in the 1972 Buick I.D. Numbers section listing.

ELECTRA 225 SERIES 48200

Series No.	Body/Style No.	Body Type & Seating	Factory Price	Shipping Weight	Prod. Total
48200	48237	2-dr HT Cpe-6P	4781	4465	9,961
48200	48239	4-dr HT Sed-6P	4889	4535	19,433

ENGINE: Specifications were the same as listed under 1972 GS 455 V-8 engine data.

1972 Buick, Electra 225 Custom Limited four-door hardtop, V-8

ELECTRA 225 CUSTOM LIMITED — SERIES 48400 — A plusher interior of cloth and vinyl with fold-down center armrest for front seat passengers was standard. A notchback 60/40 seat was optional. Limited script appeared on the roof sail panels of this plushest of all Buicks. Exterior trim was otherwise identical to the Electra 225 Series 48200.

ELECTRA 225 CUSTOM LIMITED I.D. NUMBERS: Vehicle Identification Numbers began with 4V002( )100001. See 1972 Buick I.D. Number section listing.

ELECTRA 225 CUSTOM LIMITED SERIES 48400

Series No.	Body/Style No.	Body Type & Seating	Factory Price	Shipping Weight	Prod. Total
48400	48437	2-dr HT Cpe-6P	4951	4475	37,974
48400	48439	4-dr HT Sed-6P	5059	4550	104,754

ENGINE: Specifications were the same as those listed under 1972 GS 455 V-8 engine data.

1972 Buick, Riviera two-door hardtop, (TVB)

RIVIERA — SERIES 49400 — A slightly restyled Riviera with the same boattail body was marketed in 1972. A new eggcrate grille thrust forward with the 'R' emblem on the left. A similar emblem was centered on the deck lid, which this year was clean, without the ill-fated Full-Flo ventilation louvers of 1971. Vinyl bodyside moldings were standard. Interiors were available with all-vinyl bench seats or in Custom trim with 60/40 notchback or bucket front seating. Standard features included all items found on the Electra 225.

NOTE: Riviera Gran Sport equipment was available at $200. Included was a 260 net horsepower 455-cid V-8 with dual exhaust, positive traction differential and GS monograms for the front fenders. An engine turned instrument panel insert was featured.

RIVIERA I.D. NUMBERS: Vehicle Identification Numbers began with 4Y002( )100001 See 1972 Buick I.D. Number section listing.

RIVIERA SERIES 49400

Series No.	Body/Style No.	Body Type & Seating	Factory Price	Shipping Weight	Prod. Total
49400	49487	2-dr Spt Cpe-6P	5149	4368	33,728

ENGINE: Specifications were the same as those listed under 1972 GS 455 except net horsepower was 250.

CHASSIS FEATURES: Wheelbase: (Series 43300, 44400 and 43400) 112 inches, two-door styles; 116 inches, four-door styles. (Series 45200, 45400 and 46600)124 inches; (Series 48200, 48400 and 46000) 127 inches; (Series 49487) 122 inches. Overall length: (Series 43300, 44400 and 43400) two-door styles, 203.3 inches; four-door styles, 207.3 inches; (Sportwagon) 213 7 inches; (Series 45200, 45400 and 46600) 2219 inches; (Series 46000) 228.3 inches; (Series 48200 and 48400) 227.9 inches; (Series 48487) 218.3 inches. Tire Sizes: (Skylark, Skylark Custom, GS 350 and GS 455) G78-14; (LeSabre, Riviera and Centurion) H78-15: (Electra 225s) J78-15; (Estate Wagons) L78-15.

POWERTRAIN OPTIONS: A three-speed manual transmission was standard in Series 43300, 44400 and 43400. A four-speed manual transmission was optional for Series 43400. Turbo-Hydramatic 350 was an automatic transmission option for Series 43300, 44400 and 43400 with 350-cid V-8. Turbo-Hydramatic 400 was optional for Series 43400 with 455-cid V-8 and Series 46200 and 45400 with 455-cid V-8 option, it was standard in Series 46600, 46000, 48200 and 49487. Turbo-Hydramatic 375B was standard with LeSabre. Max-Trac differential was offered for all full-size Buicks. A maintenance-free battery was available for Series 48200, 48400 and 49487.

CONVENIENCE AND APPEARANCE OPTIONS: Customline hard boot cover (LeSabre and Centurion convertibles). Protective impact strips. Folding vinyl sunroof (Sun Coupe on Skylark 350 Sport Coupe with roof sail panel emblems). Steel panel sunroof, electrically operated (Riviera and Electra 225). Front light monitors (full-size). AM radio. AM/FM radio. AM/FM radio with stereo and tape player ($363). Center console (Skylark, GS 350 and 455, Riviera with bucket seats). Climate Control. Automatic Climate Control (full-size). Power windows. Electric trunk release. Child safety seat. Remote control outside rearview mirror (standard on Electra 225 and Riviera). Custom seat and shoulder belts. Custom vinyl top with halo molding for Skylark Custom Sport Coupe; Sport Vinyl top for Skylark 350 Coupe and Riviera; full vinyl top for other specific styles. Soft-ray tinted glass. Rear window defroster. Mirror map light. Electric clock. Power tailgate window. Tilt steering wheel (standard on Riviera). Cornering lights (full-size). Speed alert. Luggage rack for station wagons. Five-spoke chrome sport wheels ($70 Riviera). Trailer towing packages. Automatic Level Control.

HISTORICAL FOOTNOTES: Style 43436 was the Sport Wagon. Styles 46035 and 46045 were Estate Wagons.

1973

APOLLO SERIES — (6-CYL/V-8) — Introduced as a midyear model, on April 12, 1973, the Apollo marked Buick's re-entry into the compact car market. The new car was based on the Chevrolet Nova X-body shell with Buick trim and styling motifs added. Features included unit construction from the cowl back,

with a bolted-on front stub frame. Single round headlamps in large, square bezels flanked a low, rectangular grille insert of a vertical-dash type design. Square parking lamps were set into either side of the grille and a Buick medallion was placed at the center. Buick block lettering appeared on the hood slit type cornering lamps on the front fender and three thin, rectangular ventiports on the upper rear side of front fenders. The base engine was a Chevrolet six and Apollos with the Buick 350-cid V-8 were grouped as a separate series.

1973 Buick, Apollo four-door sedan, 6-cyl

BUICK I.D. NUMBERS: Vehicle identification numbers began with 43( )100001 up. The first symbol '4' indicated Buick. The second symbol, a letter, indicated the series. The third and fourth symbols indicated the body style and correspond to the numbers in column two of the charts. The fifth symbol designated type of engine. The sixth symbol, a '3' designated the 1973 model year. The seventh symbol was the assembly plant code with Apollo production quartered at Willow Run, Michigan (W) or Los Angeles. Van Nuys (L), which were GMAD factories, not Buick. The last group of six digits indicated the sequential production number.

1973 Buick, Apollo two-door hatchback coupe, 6-cyl (TVB)

1973 Buick, Apollo two-door notchback coupe, 6-cyl (PH)

APOLLO SERIES SIX/V-8

Series No.	Body/Style No.	Body Type & Seating	Factory Price	Shipping Weight	Prod. Total
4XB	B69	4-dr Sed-5P	2628/2746	3152/3326	8,450
4XB	B27	2-dr Notch-5P	2605/2723	3108/3282	14,475
4XB	B17	2-dr Hatch-5P	2754/2872	3210/3384	9,868

NOTE: Style B27 is a two-door notchback coupe. Style B17 is a two-door hatchback coupe. Factory prices and shipping weights above slash are for sixes; below slash for V-8s

ENGINES: Inline six. Overhead valve. Cast iron block. Displacement: 250 cid. Bore and stroke: 3.87 x 3 50 inches. Compression ratio: 8.25:1. SAE net horsepower: 100 at 3600 rpm. Hydraulic valve lifters. Carburetor: one-barrel (Chevrolet manufacture). V-8. Overhead valve. Cast iron block. Displacement: 350 cid. Bore and stroke: 3 8 x 3 85 inches. Compression ratio: 8 5:1. SAE net horsepower: 150 at 3800 rpm. Hydraulic valve lifters. Carburetor: two-barrel (Buick V-8).

1973 Buick, Century two-door colonnade coupe, V-8 (PH)

CENTURY/LUXUS/REGAL SERIES — (V-8) — The Buick Century lines represented a new intermediate range of offerings on the GM A-Body platform. The cars rode on a new chassis and had disc brakes up front as standard equipment. Styling features included GM's 'colonnade' pillared hardtop look. There were single round headlights in square bezels flanking a thin crosshatch grille with three bright horizontal division bars. In between the headlamps and grille were medium size round parking lamps. The Century 350 passenger cars were in the AD series with comparable station wagons forming Series AF. These cars had '350' front fender tip nameplates. The Luxus line (Series AH passenger models and Series AK station wagons) had richer interior appointments and horizontal beltline moldings along the trailing edge of front fenders and on the front door. The Regal (Series AJ) had a distinctive grille, with a vertically segmented design and special crest emblems on the front fendersides. A Gran Sport package, with special styling and suspension features, was available as a sports/performance option. It included electric clock; wheel opening moldings; instrument gauges; glovebox, ashtray and courtesy lamps as standard extras.

1973 Buick, Century Regal two-door coupe, V-8 (TVB)

1973 Buick, Century Luxus four-door pillared hardtop, V-8

CENTURY/LUXUS/REGAL SERIES

Series No.	Body/Style No.	Body Type & Seating	Factory Price	Shipping Weight	Prod. Total
CENTURY 350					
4AD	D29	4-dr HT Sed-6P	3057	3780	38,202
4AD	D37	2-dr HT Cpe-6P	3057	3713	56,154
4AF	F45	4-dr Sta Wag-9P	3601	4192	Note 1
4AF	F35	4-dr Sta Wag-6P	3486	4156	7,760
LUXUS					
4AH	H29	4-dr HT Sed-6P	3326	3797	22,438
4AH	H57	2-dr HT Cpe-6P	3331	3718	71,712
4AK	K45	4-dr Sta Wag-9P	3767	4227	Note 1
4AK	K35	4-dr Sta Wag-6P	3652	4190	10,645
REGAL					
4AJ	J57	2-dr HT Cpe-5P	3470	3743	91,557

1973 Buick, Century Luxus two-door coupe, V-8

NOTE 1: Production totals for six- and nine-passenger station wagons are counted together, with no breakouts per seating configuration.

ENGINE: See 1973 Apollo Series V-8 engine data. Base engine for Century models was the optional Apollo 350-cid V-8.

1973 Buick, LeSabre Centurion 455 four-door hardtop, V-8

1973 Buick, LeSabre Custom four-door hardtop, V-8

LESABRE CENTURION SERIES — (V-8) —
LeSabres, LeSabre Customs and Centurions were built on the same 124-inch wheelbase platform with different levels of appointments and trims. Two Estate wagons were based on a 127-inch wheelbase version of the Electra chassis and grouped into their own separate series as well. Styling features for the entire group of cars included new energy absorbing front bumpers, dual headlamps set in square bezels, a low grille with short vertical bars and Buick medallions at the center of the hood. Standard equipment on all models included Turbo-Hydramatic transmission, power steering and brakes. LeSabres had series identification scripts behind the front wheel cutouts. Custom LeSabres included standard extras such as Custom steering wheel, Deluxe wheelcovers, vinyl notchback seats and a four-barrel carburetor. There were Custom nameplate badges placed under the LeSabre scripts on the one-step-up models. Centurions represented a slightly cleaner styled rendition of the LeSabre body, having the traditional Buick ventiports removed from the hoods. Centurion lettering was placed behind the front wheel cutout and a four-barrel V-8 was the base powerplant. An exclusive Centurion body style was the convertible. Estate Wagons came with woodgrain exterior body paneling and were trimmed comparable to Custom LeSabres, except that model identification took the form of Estate Wagons block lettering on the upper rear fender tips. They had lower rear bumper ends than other standard Buicks, with taillamps notched into the blade-shaped body edges.

LESABRE CENTURION SERIES

Series No.	Body/Style No.	Body Type & Seating	Factory Price	Shipping Weight	Prod. Total
LESABRE					
4BL	L69	4-dr Sed-6P	3998	4234	29,649
4BL	L39	4-dr HT Sed-6P	4125	4259	13,413
4BL	L57	2-dr HT Spt Cpe-6P	4067	4210	14,061

CUSTOM LESABRE

Series No.	Body/Style No.	Body Type & Seating	Factory Price	Shipping Weight	Prod. Total
4BN	N69	4-dr Sed-6P	4091	4264	42,845
4BN	N39	4-dr HT Sed-6P	4217	4284	55,879
4BN	N57	2-dr HT Spt Cpe-6P	4154	4225	41,425

ENGINE: See 1973 Apollo series V-8 engine data. Base engine for LeSabre and LeSabre Custom models was the two-barrel 350-cid V-8.

ESTATE WAGON

Series No.	Body/Style No.	Body Type & Seating	Factory Price	Shipping Weight	Prod. Total
4BR	R35	4-dr Sta Wag-6P	4645	4952	12,282
4BR	R45	4-dr Sta Wag-9P	4790	5021	23,513

CENTURION

Series No.	Body/Style No.	Body Type & Seating	Factory Price	Shipping Weight	Prod. Total
4BP	P39	4-dr HT Sed-6P	4390	4329	22,354
4BP	P57	2-dr HT Spt Cpe-6P	4336	4260	16,883
4BP	P67	2-dr Conv-SP	4534	4316	5,739

ENGINE: Base engine for Centurions was the 350-cid V-8 with four-barrel carburetor and 175 hp at 4000 rpm. V-8. Overhead valve. Cast iron block. Displacement: 455 cid. Bore and stroke: 4.3 x 3.9 inches. Compression ratio: 8.5:1. Brake horsepower: 225 at 4000 rpm. Hydraulic valve lifters. Carburetor: four-barrel.

1973 Buick, Electra 225 Custom Limited four-door hardtop, (TVB)

ELECTRA 225/ELECTRA 225 CUSTOM SERIES — (V-8) —
The Electra series was a two model line split into two sub-series: Electra 225 and Electra 225 Custom. A Limited trim package was available for the upper level. Standard equipment was the same as on Centurions plus electric clock; license frames; all courtesy and safety lights; foam seats; remote control outside rearview mirror; Super Deluxe wheelcovers; Custom safety belts and some changes in technical features. Custom models had carpeted lower door panels and special trims. The Limited had wide, bright metal body underscores.

ELECTRA 225/ELECTRA 225 CUSTOM SERIES

Series No.	Body/Style No.	Body Type & Seating	Factory Price	Shipping Weight	Prod. Total
ELECTRA 225					
4CT	T39	4-dr HT Sed-6P	4928	4581	17,189
4CT	T37	2-dr HT Spt Cpe-6P	4815	4488	9,224
ELECTRA 225 CUSTOM					
4CV	V39	4-dr HT Sed-6P	5105	4603	107,031
4CV	V37	2-dr HT Spt Cpe-6P	4993	4505	44,328

ENGINE: V-8. Overhead valve. Cast iron block. Displacement: 455 cid. Bore and stroke: 4.313 x 3.900 inches. Compression ratio: 8.5:1. SAE net horsepower: 225 at 4000 rpm. Hydraulic valve lifters. Carburetor: four-barrel.

RIVIERA SERIES — (V-8) —
Along with the other regular-size cars from Buick Division, the Riviera had a new front and rear treatment with new hood, fenders, grille and lights. Standard

equipment included new Accu Drive; variable-ratio power steering; power brakes with front discs; new, durable stamped steel rocker arms; computer selected springs; new windshield washer; radiator overflow coolant reservoirs; solenoid activated throttle stop and exhaust gas recirculation (EGR) emissions control system; integral voltage regulator and Delcotron and brake proportioning valve. The boattail body featured thicker rocker panel trim covers, which overlapped the lower door edge. New notch style front cornering lamps were seen. Riviera scripts appeared on the lower front fenders, with Riviera emblems on the roof pillar.

1973 Buick, Riviera two-door hardtop, V-8

1973 Buick, Riviera two-door with optional GS (Gran Sport) package, V-8 (PH)

RIVIERA SERIES

Series No.	Body/Style No.	Body Type & Seating	Factory Price	Shipping Weight	Prod. Total
4EY	Y87	2-dr HT Spt Cpe-6P	5221	4486	34,080

ENGINE: V-8. Overhead valve. Cast iron block. Displacement: 455 cid. Bore and stroke: 4.313 x 3.900 inches. Compression ratio: 8.5:1. SAE net horsepower: 250 at 4000 rpm. Carburetor: four-barrel.

CHASSIS FEATURES: Wheelbase: (Apollo) 111 inches; (Century, Luxus, Regal, two-door) 112 inches; (Century, Luxus, four-door) 116 inches; (LeSabre, Custom LeSabre, Centurion) 124 inches; (Estate Wagon) 127 inches; (Electra, Electra 225) 127 inches; (Riviera) 122 inches. Overall length: (Apollo) 197.5 inches; (Century, Luxus, Regal, two-door) 210.7 inches; (Century, Luxus, four-door) 212.4 inches; (LeSabre, Custom LeSabre, Centurion) 224.2 inches; (Estate Wagon) 229.5 inches; (Electra, Electra 225) 229.8 inches; (Riviera) 223.4 inches. Tires: (Apollo) E78-14; (Century) G78-14; (LeSabre) H78-14; (Centurion) L78-15; (Electra) J78-15; (Riviera) J78-15.

POWERTRAIN OPTIONS: The 150 horsepower '350' V-8 was optional in Apollo. The 175 horsepower '350' V-8 was optional in all A-Body Buicks and in LeSabre/Customs. A 190 horsepower '350' V-8 was available in Century Gran Sport. The 225 horsepower '455' V-8 was optional in Century/Luxus/Regal/LeSabre/LeSabre Custom/Centurion/Electra 225/Electra 225

Custom. A 260 horsepower '455' V-8 was optional in Riviera. A 270 horsepower '455' V-8 was optional in the Century Gran Sport.

CONVENIENCE OPTIONS: Vinyl top ($99). AM/FM stereo ($233). AM/FM stereo with tape ($363). Power seats ($103). Century Gran Sport package ($173). Power windows ($129). Vinyl top ($123). Riviera Stage I package ($139). Electra 225 Custom Limited trim ($174). 60/40 seats in Electra Custom ($77). Sunroof ($589). Riviera chrome styled wheels ($70). Apollo air-conditioning ($381). Century Stage I package ($546). Apollo Sport wagon disc brakes ($68). Disc brakes, other models ($46). Max trac wheel spin control ($89). Riviera Gran Sport package ($171).

HISTORICAL FOOTNOTES: Dealer introductions took place on September 21, 1972. Model year sales by U.S. dealers peaked at a record 726,191 cars. It was the second best season in Buick history. New 'colonnade' styling was seen on Buick Century, Century Luxus and Regals in 1973. This type of design was essentially hardtop styling with a center pillar added to better satisfy federal roll over standards. G.R. Elges was general manager of Buick Motor Division this year. The Centurion nameplate disappeared at the end of the 1973 model run.

1974

1974 Buick, Apollo two-door hatchback, V-8 (TVB)

APOLLO SERIES — (6-CYL/V-8) — Styling changes for the second year Apollo included a new, vertically segmented grille; a redesigned hood that dropped all the way to the upper grille header bar and the positioning of the front license plate bracket below the center of the bumper. A new, circular medallion was set into the center of the grille. Power for the base six-cylinder series again came from an inline Chevrolet engine. Apollos with the 350-cid Buick V-8 were considered a separate series. An Apollo GSX trim option was available for $96 extra.

BUICK I.D. NUMBERS: All Buicks continued to use the same type of serial numbers as in 1973. The sixth symbol was changed to a '4' to indicate 1974 model year.

APOLLO SERIES (SIX/V-8)

Series No.	Body/Style No.	Body Type & Seating	Factory Price	Shipping Weight	Prod. Total
4XB	B69	4-dr Sed-5P	3060/3184	3256/3469	16,779
4XB	B27	2-dr Notch-5P	3037/3161	3216/3429	28,286
4XB	B17	2-dr Hatch-5P	3160/3284	3321/3534	11,844

NOTE: Style B27 is the two-door notchback coupe; Style B17 the two-door hatchback coupe. Factory prices and shipping weights above slash are for sixes; below slash for V-8s.

ENGINES: See 1973 Apollo series engine data.

1974 Buick, Century 350 two-door colonnade coupe, V-8 (OCW)

1974 Buick, Century Luxus station wagon, V-8

1974 Buick, Regal two-door coupe, V-8 (OCW)

CENTURY/LUXUS/REGAL SERIES — (V-8) — The 'colonnade' styled A-Body Buicks were mildly face lifted. A larger grille with rectangular grid insert was seen. The front bumper guard arrangement of 1973 was replaced by a flat license plate holder. The guards became optional and, when used, were spaced wider apart. Century nameplates appeared behind the front wheel opening on Century 350 models. Luxus models had enriched trims and bright rocker moldings. Regals had a front fender crest hood and more delicately crosshatched grille insert. The A-Body station wagons were again designated Sport Wagons. Four different Gran Sport packages were optionally available on the Century Sport Coupe. The base GS group ($108) included GS styling and suspension components; instrument gauge cluster; clock; wheel opening moldings; glovebox, ashtray and courtesy lights. The GS 455 (code A5) package included all of the above plus a four-barrel 455-cid V-8 dual exhaust and power front disc brakes for $292. The GS 455 (code A9) package included all of the above plus a dual snorkel air cleaner for $338. The ultimate option was the GS Stage I package ($558) including a performance modified 455-cid V-8. All Gran Sports featured high energy ignition; dual snor-

kel air cleaner; positive traction axle; power front disc brakes and dual exhaust. The Turbo-Hydramatic 400 transmission was mandatory on Century GS Stage I models.

CENTURY/LUXUS/REGAL SERIES

Series No.	Body/Style No.	Body Type & Seating	Factory Price	Shipping Weight	Prod. Total
CENTURY 350					
4AD	D29	4-dr HT Sed-6P	3836	3890	22,856
4AD	D37	2-dr HT Cpe-6P	3790	3845	33,166
4AF	F45	4-dr Sta Wag-9P	4320	4305	Note 1
4AF	F35	4-dr Sta Wag-6P	4205	4272	4,860

1974 Buick, Century Luxus two-door coupe, V-8 (TVB)

Series No.	Body/Style No.	Body Type & Seating	Factory Price	Shipping Weight	Prod. Total
LUXUS					
4AH	H29	4-dr HT Sed-6P	4109	3910	11,159
4AH	H57	2-dr HT Cpe-6P	4089	3835	44,930
4AK	K45	4-dr Sta Wag-9P	4486	4345	Note 1
4AK	K35	4-dr Sta Wag-6P	4371	4312	6,791
REGAL					
4AJ	J57	2-dr HT Cpe-6P	4201	3900	57,512
4AJ	J29	4-dr HT Sed-6P	4221	3930	9,333

NOTE 1: Production totals for six- and nine-passenger station wagons are combined with no breakouts per seating configuration.

ENGINE: See 1973 Century/Luxus/Regal series engine data.

1974 Buick, LeSabre two-door hardtop, V-8

LESABRE/LESABRE LUXUS SERIES — (V-8) — A noticeable face lift marked the 1974 LeSabre. Round headlights were now set into individual square bezels that were separated by a body colored panel. The grille stretched across the car from end to end but ran below and in between the headlamp bezels. The front, lower gravel pan was redesigned, having twin horizontal slots on

either side of a center panel and horizontal parking lamps at the outboard ends. Cornering lamps were notched into the front fender tips. Buick lettering appeared on the upper grille shell header bar. LeSabre scripts were mounted at the trailing edge of the rear fenders. The rear end had a slanting, sweptback look and side body sculpturing was of a crisper style. Standard LeSabre features included power brakes (front disc); power steering; Turbo-Hydramatic; Accu Drive; full-flow ventilation; semi-closed cooling system; time modulated choke; EGR system; air injection reactor; front and rear ashtrays; inside hood release; full-foam seats; carpeting; Deluxe steering wheel; recessed wipers; glovebox light; automatic interior lamp; bumper guard stops and the two-barrel '350' V-8. The Luxus models also had Custom steering wheel; Deluxe wheelcovers; vinyl notchback seat (except convertible); Luxus trim and four-barrel '350' V-8.

1974 Buick, LeSabre Luxus four-door sedan, (TVB)

1974 Buick, LeSabre Luxus two-door coupe, V-8 (PH)

LESABRE/LESABRE LUXUS SERIES

Series No.	Body/Style No.	Body Type & Seating	Factory Price	Shipping Weight	Prod. Total
LESABRE					
4BN	N69	4-dr Sed-6P	4355	4337	18,572
4BN	N39	4-dr HT Sed-6P	4482	4387	11,879
4BN	N57	2-dr HT Cpe-6P	4424	4297	12,522
LESABRE LUXUS					
4BP	P69	4-dr Sed-6P	4466	4352	16,039
4BP	P39	4-dr HT Sed-6P	4629	4397	23,910
4BP	P57	2-dr HT Cpe-6P	4575	4307	27,243
4BP	P67	4-dr Conv-6P	4696	4372	3,627
ESTATE WAGON					
4BR	R45	4-dr Sta Wag-9P	5163	5182	9,831
4BR	R35	4-dr Sta Wag-6P	5019	5082	4,581

ENGINE: See 1973 LeSabre series engine data. A 455 cid/210 hp V-8 was standard equipment for Estate Wagons.

1974 Buick, Electra 225 Limited two-door hardtop with optional landau roof package, V-8 (PH)

ELECTRA 225/ELECTRA 225 CUSTOM SERIES — (V-8) — Styling changes for the big Buicks paralleled those seen on LeSabres with individual headlamp bezels and slot style front gravel pans. A wide, chrome header bar was added to the grille and had the word Buick lettered at the center. Notch style cornering lamps were set into the front corners of the body. Standard equipment was the same as on LeSabre Luxus models, plus accessory lamp group (less sunshade light); foam padded seats; remote control outside rearview mirror; Super Deluxe wheelcovers; seat belt restrainers; Custom safety belts; evaporative emissions control system; integral voltage regulator and Delcotron; Turbo-Hydramatic 400 transmission; J78-15 blackwall tires and the four-barrel '455' V-8. Custom trimmed Electra 225s had carpeted lower door panels and Custom exterior and interior trim. The Limited was now a separate series identified by wide rocker panel moldings, plus all other Custom features.

ELECTRA 225/ELECTRA 225 CUSTOM SERIES

Series No.	Body/Style No.	Body Type & Seating	Factory Price	Shipping Weight	Prod. Total
ELECTRA 225					
4CT	T39	4-dr HT Sed-6P	5373	4682	5,750
4CT	T37	2-dr HT Cpe-6P	5260	4607	3,339
ELECTRA 225 CUSTOM					
4CV	V39	4-dr HT Sed-6P	5550	4702	29,089
4CV	V37	2-dr HT Cpe-6P	5438	4682	15,099
ELECTRA 225 LIMITED					
4CX	X39	4-dr HT Sed-6P	5921	4732	30,051
4CX	X37	2-dr HT Cpe-6P	5886	4682	16,086

1974 Buick, Electra 225 Limited four-door hardtop, V-8 (OCW)

ENGINE: V-8. Overhead valve. Cast iron block. Displacement: 455 cid. Bore and stroke: 4.31 x 3.9 inches. Compression ratio: 8.0:1. SAE net horsepower: 210 at 4000 rpm. Hydraulic valve lifters. Carburetor: four-barrel.

1974 Buick, Riviera GS two-door hardtop with optional landau roof package, V-8 (PH)

RIVIERA SERIES — (V-8) — A new vertical grille with the Riviera name above it was seen as part of the 1974 restyling. An all-new notchback roofline appeared. A stand-up hood ornament was added. At the rear, the fender line sloped downward, dropping below the upper contour of the deck lid. Slanted, rectangular taillamps were horizontally mounted and decorated with a gridwork of bright metal strips. Equipment features started at the Electra 225 level, except that wire wheel hubcaps were standard and Custom safety belts were not. Standard extras included a tilt steering wheel; dual exhaust; foam contoured seats;

digital clock; courtesy and glovebox lights; dual front lighted ashtrays and H78-15 blackwall bias belted tires. The Gran Sport ride and handling package ($108) included a rear stabilizer bar; J78-15 whitewall steel belted tires; radial roadability suspension and specific body insulation and ornamentation. The Riviera Stage I option ($139) included a performance modified '455' V-8; positive traction axle and chrome plated air cleaner.

RIVIERA SERIES

Series No.	Body/Style No.	Body Type & Seating	Factory Price	Shipping Weight	Prod. Total
4EY	Y87	2-dr HT Spt Cpe-6P	5678	4572	20,129

ENGINE: V-8. Overhead valve. Cast iron block. Displacement: 455 cid. Bore and stroke: 4.31 x 3.9 inches. Compression ratio: 8.25:1. SAE net horsepower: 210 at 4000 rpm. Carburetor: four-barrel.

CHASSIS FEATURES: Wheelbase: (Apollo) 111 inches; (Century, four-door) 116 inches; (Century, two-door) 112 inches; (LeSabre) 123.5 inches; (Estate Wagon and Electra) 127 inches; (Riviera) 122 inches. Overall length: (Apollo) 200.2 inches; (Century, four-door) 212 inches; (Sport Wagon) 218.2 inches; (Century, two-door) 209.5 inches; (LeSabre) 225.9 inches; (Estate Wagon) 231.1 inches; (Electra) 231.5 inches; (Riviera) 226.4 inches. Tires: (Apollo) E78-14; (Century) G78-14; (Sport Wagon) H78-14; (LeSabre) H78-15; (Estate Wagon) L78-14; (Electra) J78-15; (Riviera) J78-15.

POWERTRAIN OPTIONS: Heavy-duty air cleaner ($9). Heavy-duty Delco energizer ($15). Dual exhaust ($30). Emission test, required for California sale ($20). Apollo '350' two-barrel V-8 ($118). Apollo '350' four-barrel V-8 ($164). Four-barrel '350' V-8 in Century or LeSabre ($46). Two-barrel '455' V-8 in LeSabre and Century ($184). Performance-modified '455' V-8 in Electras ($96), in Estate Wagons ($152), in LeSabres ($322). Four-barrel '455' V-8 in Sport Wagons ($184), in other Centurys ($230), in LeSabres ($170). Engine block heater in Apollo ($10); in other models ($5). High-energy ignition in Apollo/Century ($77), in other models ($56). Instrument gauges and clock in Centurys, except Sport Wagons ($38). Positive traction axle ($43). Max trac wheel spin control ($89). Turbo-Hydramatic 350 transmission in Apollo Six ($196), in Apollo '350' V-8 ($206). Turbo-Matic 400 transmission in Century ($21). Heavy-duty radiator in Apollo ($14); other models ($21). Heavy-duty 80-amp Delcotron ($31-$35).

CONVENIENCE OPTIONS: Air conditioning ($396-$446). Air cushion restraint system ($181-$225). Station wagon air deflector ($21). Automatic climate control ($488-$522). Custom safety belts ($11-$37). Apollo bumper impact strips ($13). Riviera bumper reinforcement ($12). Electra rear bumper reinforcement ($6). Cargo area carpeting in Sport Wagons ($19); in Estate Wagons ($51). Trunk carpet in Electras and Riviera ($41). Electric clock Apollo ($16). Century ($18). Full-length console for Century and Riviera two-doors ($61). Mini console in Century two-doors ($36). Convenience center console ($26). Custom-line convertible cover ($36). Cruise control in Century ($65). Rear window defogger ($33). Electric rear window defogger ($64). Tinted glass ($30-$50). Tinted windshield ($30-$35). Front and rear bumper guards ($31-$35). Automatic level control ($77). Buick cornering lights ($36). Front monitors ($22). Front and rear monitors ($48). Station wagon luggage rack ($64-$84). Sports mirrors, right and left ($22-$44). Special order paint ($113). Apollo body striping ($21). Riviera body striping ($31). Wide rocker moldings for LeSabre Luxus and Electra 225s, except Limited ($28). Custom bodyside trim ($24-$46). Custom door/window trim ($21-$27). Two-tone paint ($27-$43). Wide rocker panel group for LeSabre and Estate including lower rear quarter, front and rear wheel well moldings ($69). Six-way right-hand and left-hand power seats of 60/40 design or 40/40 design ($211). Other six-way seat options ($80-$106). Electric sunroof in Century ($325); in all Sport Coupes ($589). AM radio with stereo tape and dual rear speakers ($203-$216). AM/FM stereo radio with stereo tape and front and rear dual speakers ($363).

Rallye suspension ($30). Super lift shock absorbers ($41). Speed Alert ($11-$17). Manual sunroof in Century ($275); in Sport Coupes ($539). Vinyl trim with Custom bucket seats ($124); with lumbar-support reclining bucket seats ($236); vinyl bucket seats ($119), all in Century two-doors only. Vinyl roofs, Custom Apollo ($32); Custom Century ($99); Custom Century, short type ($84); Custom padded Electra ($385); Custom Landau Riviera ($385); Custom Landau Electra Sport Coupe ($525); Custom with moldings on Estate ($136); Custom Regal Landau ($310); Custom padded with moldings on Electra LeSabre/Riviera ($123-$138). Deluxe wheelcovers ($26); Wire wheelcovers ($56-$82); Super Deluxe wheelcovers ($34-$56); Deluxe wire wheelcovers ($60-$108). Chrome wheels ($66-$118). Woodgrain exterior station wagon paneling on Estate ($177); Luxus ($136); Century ($168). Code V4 accessory group ($26-$36); Code VI convenience group ($12-$27). Ride and handling package ($15). LeSabre Luxus ride and performance package ($423-$575). (Note: Prices for certain options and accessories varied by series or body style. In such cases, the low-to-high range is reflected above).

HISTORICAL FOOTNOTES: Model year introductions took place on September 27, 1974. Calendar year production peaked at 400,262 cars or 5.49 percent of industry output. Model year production hit 495,063 units. George R. Elges remained Buick's general manager.

1975

1975 Buick, Skyhawk two-door hatchback coupe, V-6 (TVB)

SKYHAWK SERIES — (V-6) — An all new car, the sub-compact Skyhawk was the smallest Buick in more than 60 years. It weighed less than 3,000 pounds and stood less than four feet high. The Skyhawk shared the GM H-Body platform — featuring torque arm rear suspension and sleek 2 + 2 styling — with the Chevrolet Monza. Under the hood, however, was a 231-cid Buick V-6. This engine had started its life as a 225-cid Buick powerplant for the Special Series in the early 1960s. In 1968, the tooling for the en-

gine was sold to American Motors Corp. Now, with a displacement increase, the engine was back in the Buick stable and many of its parts were interchangeable with a 260-cid V-8. Mounted on a 97-inch wheelbase, the Skyhawk was 179.3 inches long (21 inches shorter than the Apollo) and came with all features of larger GM cars, including the Efficiency System and a full list of options.

BUICK I.D. NUMBERS: Vehicle identification numbers and number locations followed the previous year's system. The sixth symbol was changed to a '5' for the 1975 model year.

SKYHAWK SERIES

Series No.	Body/Style No.	Body Type & Seating	Factory Price	Shipping Weight	Prod. Total
4H	HT07	2-dr 'S' Hatch-4P	3860	2851	Note 1
4H	HS07	2-dr Hatch-4P	4173	2891	Note 1

NOTE 1: Buick Skyhawks were manufactured exclusively in Canada this year. Buick reported U.S. dealer model year sales of 29,448 examples of the new 'H' car. No breakout was provided for the two trim levels.

ENGINE: V-6. Overhead valve. Cast iron block. Displacement: 231 cid. Bore and stroke: 3.80 x 3 40 inches. Compression ratio: 8.0:1. SAE net horsepower: 110 at 4000 rpm. Carburetor: two-barrel.

1975 Buick, Apollo two-door notchback sedan, V-6 (TVB)

1975 Buick, Apollo four-door sedan, V-6

APOLLO/SKYLARK SERIES — (L-6/V-6/V-8) — The Apollo lineup was the most extensively revised 1975 Buick series. Topped by the revived Skylark two-door coupe, other X-car models included a two-door hatchback coupe and a thin pillared four-door sedan. New styling gave the Apollo a European flair, with a low beltline, full-width grille, wraparound parking and directional lamps and large, horizontal taillamps. Both standard and luxury 'S/R' models were on a 111-inch wheelbase with Apollos offering the 250-cid Chevrolet L-head six as base powerplant. Cars with V-8 power were considered to be in a separate series. The 260-cid V-8 was the base V-8 and the 350-cid V-8 was optional. Base engine in the Skylark was the "new" V-6. Signature scripts below the rear fender belt moldings were helpful in identifying the various models.

ENGINES: L-6. Overhead valve. Cast iron block. Displacement: 250 cid. Bore and stroke: 3 87 x 3.5 inches. Compression ratio: 8.0:1. Brake horsepower: 105 at 4000 rpm. Carburetor: one-barrel.

V-6. See 1975 Skyhawk series engine data.

V-8. Overhead valve. Cast iron block. Displacement: 260 cid. Bore and stroke: 3.5 x 3.385 inches. Compression ratio: 8.0:1. Brake horsepower: 110 at 4000 rpm. Carburetor: two-barrel.

APOLLO/SKYLARK SERIES

Series No.	Body/Style No.	Body Type & Seating	Factory Price	Shipping Weight	Prod. Total
APOLLO SUB-SERIES					
4BX	B69	4-dr Sed-5P	3436/3514	3366/3511	21,138
SKYLARK 'S' SUB-SERIES					
4WX	W27	2-dr Notch-5P	3234/3260	3309/3502	Note 1
SKYLARK SUB-SERIES					
4BX	B27	2-dr Notch-5P	3463/3489	3341/3537	27,689
4BX	B17	2-dr Hatch-5P	3586/3612	3438/3587	6,814
APOLLO 'SR' SUB-SERIES					
4CX	C69	4-dr Sed-5P	4092/4170	3383/3574	2,241
SKYLARK 'SR' SUB-SERIES					
4CX	C27	2-dr Notch-5P	4136/4162	3309/3498	3,746
4CX	C17	2-dr Hatch-5P	4253/4279	3441/3586	1,505

1975 Buick, Skylark S/R two-door hatchback coupe, V-8 (OCW)

NOTE 1: No breakout is provided for production of the Skylark 'S' notchback coupe.

NOTE 2: A total of 504 Apollos were manufactured in Canada, late in the 1975 calendar year, to 1976 specifications. In the chart above Factory Prices and Shipping Weights above slash are for sixes below slash for V-8s. The L-6 was used in Apollos; the V-6 in Skylarks. The base V-8 was the 260 cubic inch Buick engine.

1975 Buick, Century Special two-door colonnade coupe, V-6

CENTURY/REGAL SERIES — (V-6/V-8) — The intermediate size Buick A-Body lineup offered the biggest selection of models for 1975. The Century was again the base level in terms of trim and appointments, with an equipment list comparable to similar 1974 models. A one-step-up Century Custom was comparable to the 1974 Luxus, with the same type of features and extra decorative touches. The Gran Sport was no longer a separate sub-series, but 'GS' type equipment was available as a $171 option package. Basic styling changes from a year earlier included a wider grille that varied in design from line to line. On

Century Specials it had a horizontal double-deck look, with vertical-dash type insert and vertically-mounted rectangular parking lamps housed, within the grille, at its outboard ends. On Centurys and Century Customs, the horizontal divider was deleted. On Regals, there was a shorter grille with vertical blades only and the same type of parking lamps were seen outside the grille, between the chrome surround and the headlamps. Regals had a model identification script on the left-hand side of the grille, while other models had Buick block lettering. The Century Special was marketed as a low-rung economy model with less basic equipment than other models, allowing it to be advertised at an attractive price. As in the past, the two-door A-Body cars were shorter, in wheelbase and overall length, than four-doors on this platform.

CENTURY/REGAL SERIES

Series No.	Body/Style No.	Body Type & Seating	Factory Price	Shipping Weight	Prod. Total
CENTURY/SPECIAL V-6					
4AE	E37	2-dr Cpe-6P	3815	3613	Note 1
CENTURY V-6/V-8					
4AD	D29	4-dr Sed-6P	3944/4022	3730/3906	22,075
4AD	D37	2-dr Cpe-6P	3894/3972	3674/3850	39,556
4AF	F45	4-dr Sta Wag-9P	4751	4370	Note 2
4AF	F35	4-dr Sta Wag-6P	4636	4320	4,416
CENTURY CUSTOM V-6/V-8					
4AH	H29	4-dr Sed-6P	4211/4289	3763/3939	9,995
4AH	H57	2-dr Cpe-6P	4154/4232	3671/3847	32,966
4AK	K45	4-dr Sta Wag-9P	4917	4400	Note 2
4AK	K35	4-dr Sta Wag-6P	4802	4350	7,078
REGAL V-6/V-8					
4AJ	J29	4-dr Sed-6P	4311/4389	3800/3976	10,726
4AJ	J57	2-dr Cpe-6P	4257/4335	3733/3909	56,646

NOTE 1: The Century Special came only with V-6 power and was technically an equipment deleted model and not a distinct body style. Production of this car, Style Number E37, is counted with Style Number D37.

NOTE 2: Station wagons came only with V-8 power. Production of six- and nine-passenger station wagons was counted as a single total.

ADDITIONAL NOTE: Factory Prices and Shipping Weights above slash are for sixes; below slash for V-8s. Cars with V-8 power were considered to be in a separate series.

ENGINES: V-6. See 1975 Skyhawk series engine data.

V-8. Overhead valve. Cast iron block. Displacement: 350 cid. Bore and stroke: 3.8 x 3.85 inches. Compression ratio: 8.0:1. Brake horsepower: 145 at 3800 rpm. Carburetor: two-barrel.

1975 Buick, LeSabre four-door hardtop sedan, (TVB)

LESABRE/LESABRE CUSTOM/ESTATE WAGON SERIES — (V-8) — Both LeSabre and LeSabre Custom series offered B-Body two- and four-door hardtops, plus four-door thin-pillar styles. A convertible was exclusive to the Custom level line. All LeSabres were on a 123.5-inch wheelbase with either a standard 350-cid V-8 or optional '455'. The Estate Wagons shared the 127-inch Electra wheelbase and luxury appointments. As on all Buicks, the GM Efficiency System was standard and included High-energy ignition, a catalytic convertor and steel-belted radial tires. Styling updates included a new grid-style grille with under the headlamp extensions. The square headlamp

housings returned to a side-by-side type mounting; ventiports were moved from the hood to the front fendersides and Buick block lettering was the only decoration on the lower lip of the hood. Equipment variations between the various sub-series were comparable to the previous year with Custom replacing the Luxus designation.

LESABRE/LESABRE CUSTOM/ESTATE WAGON SERIES

Series No.	Body/Style No.	Body Type & Seating	Factory Price	Shipping Weight	Prod. Total
LESABRE					
4BN	N69	4-dr Sed-6P	4771	4355	14,088
4BN	N39	4-dr HT Sed-6P	4898	4411	9,119
4BN	N57	2-dr HT Cpe-6P	4840	4294	8,647
LESABRE CUSTOM					
4BP	P69	4-dr Sed-6P	4936	4388	17,026
4BP	P39	4-dr HT Sed-6P	5061	4439	30,005
4BP	P57	2-dr HT Cpe-6P	5007	4316	25,016
4BP	P67	2-dr Conv-6P	5133	4392	5,300
ESTATE WAGON					
4BR	R45	4-dr Sta Wag-9P	5591	5135	9,612
4BR	R35	4-dr Sta Wag-6P	5447	5055	4,128

LESABRE/LESABRE CUSTOM ENGINE: The 350-cid V-8 was the standard engine in LeSabre and LeSabre Customs. General specifications were the same as for the Century '350' except that a four-barrel carburetor was used and the output was 165 hp at 4000 rpm.

ESTATE WAGON ENGINE: V-8. Overhead valve. Cast iron block. Displacement: 455 cid. Bore and stroke: 4.313 x 3.9 inches. Compression ratio: 7.9:1. Brake horsepower: 205 at 3800 rpm. Carburetor: Four-barrel.

1975 Buick, Electra 225 Limited four-door hardtop, (PH)

ELECTRA 225 CUSTOM/ELECTRA 225 LIMITED SERIES — (V-8) — Buick's most prestigious series was reduced to four models, as full-sized cars continued to be de-emphasized by General Motors. These C-Body models were built off a 127-inch wheelbase platform. The 455-cid V-8 was standard as were Efficiency System features. Rectangular headlamps were a styling change along with a Classic-looking eggcrate grille that extended below the headlamps. Also new were monogrammed hood ornaments; large opera style rear quarter windows; shag carpeting and soft velour upholstery and headliners. An especially luxurious Park Avenue option package was available for the Limited hardtop sedan, as well as an even richer Park Avenue Deluxe group.

ELECTRA 225 CUSTOM/ELECTRA 225 LIMITED

Series No.	Body/Style No.	Body Type & Seating	Factory Price	Shipping Weight	Prod. Total
CUSTOM					
4CV	V39	4-dr HT Sed-6P	6201	4706	27,357
4CV	V37	2-dr HT Cpe-6P	6041	4582	16,145
LIMITED					
4CX	X39	4-dr HT Sed-6P	6516	4762	33,778
4CX	X37	2-dr HT Cpe-6P	6352	4633	17,650

ENGINE: See 1975 Estate Wagon engine data.

RIVIERA SERIES — (V-8) — The Riviera remained as Buick's personal luxury offering. A major redesign was seen up front. Changes to the bumper, grille and trim and new rectangular headlamps were seen. Overall length was 3-1/2 inches shorter

than the previous year's model. The ultra luxurious and Sporty 'GS' option remained available and standard equipment was the same as the previous season, plus High-Energy ignition; Efficiency System features and steel-belted radial tires. Annual styling changes included closer together vertical blades in the Neo-Classic grille shell; clear cornering lamp lenses; a slotted-center bumper design and a Riviera script plate on the left-hand side of the grille.

RIVIERA SERIES

Series No.	Body/Style No.	Body Type & Seating	Factory Price	Shipping Weight	Prod. Total
4EZ	Z87	2-dr HT Spt Cpe-5P	6420	4539	17,306

ENGINE: See 1975 Estate Wagon engine data.

1975 Buick, Riviera two-door pillared hardtop, V-8 (TVB)

CHASSIS FEATURES: Wheelbase: (Skyhawk) 97 inches; (Apollo/Skylark) 111 inches; (Century, two-door) 112 inches; (Century, four-door) 116 inches; (LeSabre) 124 inches; (Electra and Estate) 127 inches; (Riviera) 122 inches. Overall length: (Skyhawk) 179.3 inches; (Apollo and Skylark) 200.3 inches; (Century, two-door) 209.5 inches; (Century, four-door) 213.5 inches; (Century, station wagon) 218.2 inches; (Regal, two-door) 212 inches; (Regal, four-door) 216 inches; (LeSabre) 226.9 inches; (Estate Wagon) 233.4 inches; (Electra) 233.4 inches; (Riviera) 223 inches. Tires: (Skyhawk) BR78-13; (Skylark and Apollo) FR78-14; (Century) GR78-15; (Estate Wagon) LR78-15; (LeSabre) HR78-15; (Electra and Riviera) JR78-15.

POWERTRAIN OPTIONS: Optional engines for Apollos included the two- and four-barrel versions of the 350-cid V-8. Optional engines for Century/Regal models were the two- and four-barrel versions of the 350-cid V-8 (145 and 165 horsepower, respectively). The four-barrel 350-cid engine was standard in Century station wagons, with no other choices available. The four-barrel 455-cid/205 hp V-8 was optional in LeSabres. There were no engine options for Electras or Rivieras. A 400 cid/185 hp engine was optional in LeSabres and was, most likely, released only for use in cars built for California sale. The horsepower rating indicates this is a Pontiac-built engine, although standard reference sources are unclear on this point.

CONVENIENCE OPTIONS: Skyhawk air conditioning ($398). Skyhawk AM/FM stereo ($214). Apollo air conditioning ($435). Apollo AM/FM stereo ($233) with tape player ($363). Century AM/FM stereo ($233) with tape player ($363). Century six-way power seat ($117). Century sunroof ($256). Gran Sport package ($171). Regal S/R package ($256). Station wagon luggage rack ($68). LeSabre six-way power seat ($117). LeSabre power windows ($149). Station wagon woodgrain applique ($182). Estate Wagon luggage rack ($89). Riviera 'GS' ride and handling package ($73). Electra and Riviera sunroof ($644). Park Avenue option group ($495). Power brakes in Apollo ($55). Rear window defroster ($60). Electra rear window defroster ($73). Bucket seats ($75). Regal sunroof ($350). Custom trim ($165). Air bags ($275). Park Avenue Deluxe package ($1,675). Electra and Riviera cornering lamps ($38). Heavy padded vinyl roof ($389).

HISTORICAL FOOTNOTES: Dealer introductions were held September 27, 1974. Calendar year production (U.S. built models only) peaked at 545,820 cars or 7.99 percent of the total industry output. Model year sales of domestically-built models peaked at 481,768 units. D.C. Collier was named general manager of Buick Division this year. A total of 49,226 Opels were also sold from Buick dealer showrooms this season. In late 1975, assemblies of Skyhawks built to 1976 specifications began at the GMAD plant in Southgate, California.

Crowds view the new 1950 Buick Roadmaster convertible at the Mid-Century Motorama, held at New York's Waldorf-Astoria hotel on Jan. 19, 1950.

BUICK
1976-2000

Production of Buick's storied Riviera luxury coupes ended in November 1998 (1999 model year); however, 200 of the 1999 Rivieras were specially painted and badged as "Silver Arrow" models, named for a 1963 concept Riviera. Pictured are the 1963 concept "Silver Arrow" (left) and the 1999 production version. The 200 1999 "Silver Arrow" Rivieras featured logos on their sides similar to the 1963 concept's logo (inset). They also used a special exterior color, Sterling Silver Metallic, as well as each having an individually numbered plaque with logo on the instrument panel and the Silver Arrow logo embroidered into the headrests. OCW

Periodic flirtations with performance aside, Buick's reputation still relied most on its long history as a well-equipped, if slightly stodgy, family car. Not ordinarily a trend-setter, Buick regularly produced the kinds of reliable cars that millions of moderately well-off families wanted. By the mid-1970s, the sprightly GS and GSX editions had become memories. So had Buick ragtops, the last of which (a LeSabre) came off the line not long before the '76 model year began. Two years earlier, the pillarless two-door hardtop had given way to a "Colonnade" coupe design with large quarter windows. Those windows got smaller in subsequent years, but the "true" two-door hardtop was gone (though four-door pillarless hardtops hung on a bit longer).

For 1975, the Skylark badge had returned on a compact Buick, and the Monza-based Skyhawk subcompact coupe arrived. Those two entered 1976 with little change, joining the midsize Century and Regal, full-size LeSabre/Electra duo, and upscale Riviera-powered by a giant 455 cubic inch, 205 horsepower V-8. Skylark was the only domestic V-6 powered compact, LeSabre the only V-6 full-size, both carrying Buick's own 231 cubic inch engine. Skyhawks could have a new Borg-Warner five-speed gearbox--a choice not common at this time. Century coupes sported a fastback roofline,

and a Hurst twin-panel Hatch Roof made the option list. The fabled "ventiports" (portholes) that had made their initial appearance in 1949 still stood on full-size Buick fenders, albeit in different form. After two years of decline, Buick sales zoomed upward by over 52 percent, approaching the model-year record set in 1973. A Buick paced the Indianapolis 500 for the second year in-a-row: this time a turbocharged Century, which prompted issuance of replica models with the pace car colors.

Both bodies and engines shrunk for 1977, in the first wave of Buick downsizing. This time the victims were LeSabre, Electra and Riviera (the latter temporarily becoming a variant of LeSabre). A 403 cubic inch V-8 took over the 455's spot as biggest Buick engine. Three different 350 cubic inch V-8s (including Chevrolet's) were available, and made standard on the shrunken Electra and Riviera. Those non-Buick engines soon would cause a lot of trouble for GM, as certain customers felt themselves cheated. Record-setting sales ended the year, though, led by popularity of the downsized full-size models.

Century and Regal got their trimming-down for 1978. Buick displayed renewed interest in performance with the arrival of an optional turbocharged V-6 under Regal and LeSabre Sport Coupe hoods. In the other direction, the 231 cubic inch V-6 had its bore slimmed to become

a 196, ready for the lighter-weight Century/Regal. Century coupes and sedans displayed a new "aeroback" profile that would not attract as many customers as hoped for in the next couple of years. Among the more collectible Buicks is Riviera's silver/black 75th anniversary ('LXXV') model, of which 1,400 were produced.

Riviera not only shrunk in size for 1979, it switched to front-wheel drive, sharing mechanical components with Eldorado and Toronado. Named *Motor Trend* Car of the Year, the revised Riviera was considered more closely related to the original '63 than to the boattail 1970s version. A sporty new S Type Riviera carried a turbo V-6. Century also added a Turbo Coupe package.

First of the 1980 Buicks was the Skylark version of the new, but ill-fated, X-car. Century continued its aero-style fastback coupe, but sedans switched to notchback bodies. That helped Century sales streak skyward. An aero restyle hit LeSabre/Electra. The 403 cubic inch V-8 disappeared, but Buicks might now have an enlarged (252 cubic inch) version of the familiar 231 V-6, a lightweight 265 V-8, or the troublesome Oldsmobile-built diesel V-8. Buick had installed its first V-8 back in 1953, but now produced no V-8 engines at all. Collectors might look for a limited-edition Regal Somerset, with tan/blue body and wire wheel covers, offered this year only. Skyhawk's Road Hawk option might also be tempting, and reasonably priced. This was the last year for Skyhawk, until it returned in front-drive form for 1982.

Regal took its turn at an aero restyle for 1981. All rear-drives now had a lockup converter clutch in their automatic transmissions. The sportiest Riviera was now called T-Type, a designation that would find its way onto a whole line of sporty Buicks a few years later. Regal continued as Buick's best seller as well as being selected to pace the Indy 500.

Either a four or V-6 powered the new '82 front-drive Skyhawk, while Century got an aerodynamic, wedge-shaped body. Regal, long offered only in coupe form, added a sedan and station wagon. Turbocharged engines had lost popularity, and production fell to a small fraction of their former level. LeSabre's F/E limited-edition might be of modest interest, but Riviera's new convertible would probably attract more collector attention. So too might the revived Riviera T-Type, which now carried improved turbo power.

All models except LeSabre/Electra came in T-Type form for 1983. Only 1,750 Riviera convertibles were built (and one paced the Indy 500). Rarer yet is the 'XX Anniversary Edition' Riviera, painted two-tone beige with true wire wheels. Model year sales rose nicely, giving Buick a new record and a fourth-place ranking.

Late in the 1984 model year came what many view as the most wanted Buick of the era: the dramatic all-black turbo-powered Regal Grand National. Even while they were still in production, boosting Buick's image among younger motorists, some brought in startling amounts at auction. Car dealers who managed to get their hands on one sometimes put astronomical price tags on their windshields—or even implied that the car was not for sale at any price. Desirable, yes, but Grand Nationals are not exactly Duesenbergs, and prices eventually stabilized. On a more modest level, Century offered an Olympia Limited sedan to mark the Olympic Games. A turbocharged four became available under Skyhawk T-Type hoods.

Front-drive moved all the way up the scale for 1985, reaching the Electra. A new Somerset Regal emerged as replacement for the Skylark X-car. Skylark actually sold fairly well through its 1980-85 lifespan, suffering less from the adverse publicity that its Citation cousin had endured as a result of recalls and lawsuits. Diesel engines finally left the lineup. Troublesome when new, they are not likely to be much better under a collectible Buick's hood.

If Regal Grand Nationals were (and are) in strong demand, imagine the interest in LeSabre's version for 1986. Buick reports that only 117 of the special-edition coupes were built, receiving little publicity. Nearly as desirable, though, might be the performance-oriented, black-bodied Century Gran Sport. Just over a thousand of those came off the line. Turbochargers under Regal Grand National hoods added an intercooler this year, and 5,512 were produced. Anti-lock braking became a Buick option for the first time in 1986, and an all-new, V-6 powered front-drive LeSabre appeared. So did a revised Riviera, which no longer came in convertible form.

Buick constructed its 26 millionth vehicle in 1986 and, for 1987, proclaimed that "traditionally Buicks have offered quality." Playing off the old "When better cars are built, Buick will build them," Buick also notes that "it is easy for someone to utter the words, "We will build better cars." "But if those words are spoken by the automotive descendants of pioneers whose first cars appeared four years after the turn of the century, they take on an added meaning.

In that historical context the latest Riviera could be regarded as an "Automotive Legend." In its second year of production the down-sized Riviera was available in both coupe and T-Type form. Both were powered by the 3.8-liter V-6, but the T-Type differed from the coupe by having among its features the firmer Gran Touring suspension.

The six passenger, front-wheel drive Electra, T-Type and Park Avenue models were depicted as epitomizing "the attention to luxury values that have, for more than 80 years, set the Buick name—and the car that proudly bears it—apart." All four Electra were powered by 3.8-liter V-6 engines updated for 1987 for quieter and more efficient operation. The Electra and Park Avenue were available with a T-Package based upon the T-Type's Gran Touring suspension.

The LeSabre was again offered as a coupe or sedan in three series: LeSabre, LeSabre Custom and LeSabre Limited. A new specialty version—the LeSabre T-Type coupe—was new for 1987. Also new for 1987 was the LeSabre T package, directed toward the driver who preferred a firm suspension package.

The rear drive Regal, reaching the end of its long production run, was still a popular Buick, available in Regal, Regal Limited and Regal Grand National.

Both the Century Custom and Limited were available in coupe or sedan body styles. Buyers could also select a Century four-door Custom or Estate Wagon. The Century standard 2.5-liter Tech IV four-cylinder engine was equipped with electronic fuel injection and mated to a three speed automatic transmission. Optional engines included a 2.8 liter V-6 with multi-port fuel injection and a 3.5-liter V-6 with sequential-port fuel injection.

The Buick Somerset was again available only as a coupe in either Custom or Limited form. A T-Package, as well as a 3.0-liter V-6, was optional. The standard 2.5-liter Tech IV engine was paired with a close ratio five-speed manual transmission.

The Skylark continued to be directed to the market located just below the Century in size. Two sedans were offered, the Skylark Custom and the Skylark Limited. Buick promised that "the T-Package, coupled with the available 3.0-liter V-6 will transform the standard Skylark Limited or Custom Sedan into a road-ready cruiser."

Buick's J-Car, the Skyhawk, was available as a Custom coupe and sedan, a Sport Hatchback, a Limited coupe and sedan, and as a Custom and Limited station wagon. The major Skyhawk development for sporting drivers was a new turbocharged engine/manual transmission combination and four new touring option packages. By selecting these touring options separately or in combination, the Skyhawk owner could create a highly individualistic automobile.

The full-size Electra and LeSabre Estate Wagons were continued into 1987 for customers needing the capacity to carry up to eight passengers.

Buick's 1988 model year lineup was highlighted by the all-new Royal coupe, two new engines and improvements throughout the line. Noting that Buick was in tune with current market demands, General Manager Edward Mertz noted that "Buick is covering the market with distinctive products, high quality workmanship, backed by what we are convinced is the finest group of dealers in the industry."

All car lines had changes in their equipment level. New standard suspension packages improved ride and handling, Optional Gran Touring packages were continued.

Buick's new front-wheel drive Regal did not share any of its exterior sheet metal with any other car. Although the new Regal was 8.4 inches shorter than the previous model (192.2 inches compared with 200.6 inches), front-seat room was within one inch of the other model's, and total interior dimensions were within two inches of the '87 Regal.

In regard to the new 2.3-liter Quad 4 and the updated 3800 V-6 engines, the Quad 4 met current emission requirements without the use of an exhaust gas recirculation system. The 3800 V-6 block was redesigned to bring all components on center. The cylinder heads were revised to fit the new block. A new one-piece intake manifold was also used.

The Skyhawk line was expanded to four models with the addition of the S/E Coupe. The new Skylark coupes had a distinctive composite front end treatment as well as new exterior colors and interior fabrics. The Skylark was available in both Custom and Limited trim levels. The Century was also offered in Custom and Limited models. Now included as standard equipment on the Century were such items as AM/FM radio with seek and scan and a clock, extended range speakers, tinted glass and white-wall tires.

All LeSabre models—the LeSabre coupe, Custom sedan, Limited coupe and sedan, and the LeSabre T-Type coupe—had new exterior colors as well as numerous interior refinements. Similarly, the rear-wheel-drive LeSabre and Electra Estate Wagons were offered in six new exterior colors as well as a number of interior refinements.

The four-door sedan Electra series again consisted of the Electra Limited, Park Avenue and T-Type. The T-Type's appearance was refined by the additional use of chrome trim for such exterior items as door frames and rear lamp bezels. The 3.8-liter 3800 V-6 was standard for the Electra as well as the Riviera which continued to be offered in coupe and T-Type coupe form.

Buick celebrated its 85th anniversary year in 1989 by enhancing its position in the GM automotive strata of offering "premium Americana motorcars" via the introduction of extensively restyled Riviera and Century models. At mid-year Buick took another major step in this direction with the introduction of its most luxurious sedan, the Park Avenue Ultra. With these new models highlighting the 1989 model year, Buick also enhanced the appeal of its entire line by adopting more powerful engines, improving Dynaride suspension and increasing the availability of anti-lock braking. Among the new equipment offered for 1989 was a compact disc player on Regal and a remote keyless entry system, standard on Reatta and optional on Riviera, Electra/Park Avenue sedans and Regal.

Dynaride, introduced on some models in 1988, was standard on all 1989 Buicks except station wagons and those cars equipped with Gran Touring suspension.

Buick's prestige luxury coupe, the Riviera, was eleven inches longer than the 1988 model. It had a "stronger" vertical grille, a new chrome bumper design, wider roof pillars and more curvaceous rear quarter panels.

New features for the subcompact Skyhawk besides Dynaride suspension on most models, included an acoustical insulation package. Its styling and model line-up were unchanged from 1988.

The compact Skylark had a new, more powerful optional V-6 engine, major acoustical insulation improvements and a number of front and rear appearance revisions. The Skylark Special Edition coupe and sedan, which were marketed only in California in 1988, was offered across the country in 1989. During the 1989 model year a Skylark Luxury Edition was also introduced.

The Regal, LeSabre and Reatta received numerous refinements for 1989. The Regal's appeal was enhanced by a new Dynaride suspension and the replacement of its 2.8-liter V-6 by a larger 3.1-liter version during the model year.

The LeSabre/Electra Estate Wagons were refined for 1989 with a new trailer towing package and several new options.

The 1990 Buick line-up was highlighted by the elimination of the Skyhawk models and the introduction of the Reatta convertible and the early launch of the 1991 Regal sedan. Along with the new Regal, another "traditional" Buick name that had been dormant since 1958—Roadmaster—returned for 1991. Initially offered as an Estate Wagon, a Roadmaster sedan, released in spring 1991 as a 1992 model, joined the station wagon. The remainder of the decade would see more familiar Buick names come and go.

At the end of the 1991 model year, the Reatta two-seater was axed from the Buick lineup. Never a sales behemoth, the Reatta suffered from being way overpriced and current value of a final-year convertible in number one condition—approximately half of the $36,000 sticker price—backs up that original sin.

Buick observed its 90th Anniversary in 1993 holding a bit better than 17 percent of total General Motors sales

for that calendar year and just under six percent of total U.S. sales. The Riviera had a short production run that year and would not return until mid-model year 1994 as a 1995 model. An upscale Limited version of the Roadmaster Estate Wagon also joined Buick's 1995 lineup, but the time for Roadmaster enthusiasts to celebrate was short-lived as the series would be dropped (again!) after 1996 model year production ended. The 1995 and 1996 versions of this well-appointed luxury station wagon—the last of GM's long-wheelbase, rear-wheel-drive wagons along with the Chevrolet Caprice—should see their stock rise in years to come as car enthusiasts with young children seek collector cars that can transport families and gear in comfort and style. While not produced in great numbers, these high-end wagons were usually not purchased for "work horse" duty in the way most wagons see service, so their survival rate should be decent. In addition, all 1996 Roadmasters received special "Collector's Edition" hood ornaments to mark their final year of availability.

In 1997, longtime Buick General Manager Edward Mertz passed the torch to Robert Coletta. This was also the final year for regular production of the long-running Skylark model. It would return the following year as a fleet-only sedan and then fade away for good. With the demise of the Skylark, the Buick lineup now was exclu-

sively powered by the V-6 engine. One of the "six-bangers" found its way under the hood of the 25th Anniversary Edition of the Regal based on the Regal LS sedan. This limited-edition Regal featured a color-keyed grille and a distinctive 25th Anniversary medallion on its taillamp, which should place it a notch higher on the collector scale than a well-appointed Regal sedan.

Closing out the decade, 1999 was Buick's 95th Anniversary as well as the 40th Anniversary of the LeSabre, with more than six million of that model sold to this point. It was also the final year of production for the venerable Riviera. With just over 10,000 produced in 1998 and probably an equal (or lesser) amount in its last run, the final coupes should maintain desirability for being sprite (supercharged V-6) and sleek as well as luxuriously appointed in leather.

Showcasing Buick's direction into the next century was the Cielo four-door convertible concept vehicle that made the auto show rounds in 1999. Borrowing ever so slightly from the prewar (World War II) convertible sedan image, the Cielo (Spanish for "sky") was a midsize, open air family car concept. Featuring permanent roof rails that spanned the A- to C-pillar locations and retractable panels, the futuristic Cielo also paid homage to past Buicks by sporting a grille reminiscent of the late-1930s Y-Job concept car.

For 1976, the Buick lineup included (l-to-r) the Special coupe, Century Custom coupe and Regal coupe.

Buick offered the option of world-class handling capability throughout its 1989 line. The available Gran Touring package for the luxury Park Avenue (left) and full-size LeSabre (right) included Gran Touring suspension, Eagle GT+4 performance tires on cast aluminum wheels, performance axle and steering ratios, leather-wrapped steering wheel and heavy-duty cooling. OCW

1976 Buick, Century Custom sedan. (OCW)

"Buick ownership," it was claimed, "is the knowledge that you have entered the House of Quality." And Buick for the Bicentennial year, according to the theme of the full-line catalog, was "Dedicated to the Free Spirit in just about everyone." No new models entered the lineup this year, but the Apollo name was dropped and replaced by Skylark. Convertibles were gone, the last LeSabre ragtop having been produced in July 1975. Depending on the Buick model ordered, though, air and sun fans could choose from four special roofs this year: an Astroroof, with sliding shade and heavily-tinted glass; electric sunroof; Hurst hatch roof; and on Skyhawk, a fixed-glass version with roof band. Rectangular headlamps that had been introduced previously on some models now appeared on Century, Regal and LeSabre. Buick's 231 cu. in. V-6, standard in Skyhawk, Skylark, Century and Regal Coupe, was the only V-6 designed and built in America. Its pistons, rings, wrist pins, rod bearings, timing gear and other parts were identical to those on the 350 V-8. But it weighed 200 pounds less and delivered a slightly better EPA rating than the inline six of 1975, due to improved fuel distribution. New carburetor calibrations for 1976 helped boost its performance. The V-6 could also squeeze into tighter engine compartments than an inline--a fact that would become more important as models were downsized. High-Energy Ignition, used on all engines, sent 35 percent more voltage to spark plugs and eliminated the old points and condenser. All Buicks needed unleaded fuel, carried a catalytic converter, and required less routine maintenance than predecessors of a few years earlier. The new "Freedom Battery," standard on Skyhawk and available on others, required no maintenance or addition of water, and had a built-in "state of charge" indicator. The Quadrajet carburetor was redesigned. Spark advance increased on the 350 and 455 cu. in. V-8 engines. A new camshaft on the 350 V-8 gave more power at low engine speeds. Riviera, LeSabre and Electra had a lower (2.56:1) rear axle ratio for improved economy. The familiar three-speed column shift remained standard on several economy-model Buicks (but not available in California). Three different Turbo Hydra-matic versions were offered. Computers were used to determine the optimum spring rates for each model, to give best height control, ride, and maneuvering characteristics. Front disc brakes were standard on all Buicks. Most models now have rubber protective strips on bumpers. All had Full-Flo ventilation and full-foam, contour-molded seats. Spray-on corrosion protection was used, along with galvanized metal and drainage panels, to improve rust-resistance. Bodies were coated with primer, sealer, and multiple applications of high-gloss acrylic lacquer. In keeping with the Bicentennial, standard Buick body colors for '76 were: Judicial Black (code A), Liberty White (C), Pewter Gray (D), Potomac Blue (G), Continental Blue (H), Concord Green (J), Constitution Green (L), Mount Vernon Cream (M), Buckskin Tan (Q), Musket Brown (R), Boston Red (V), and Independence Red (W). The list of special colors included Congressional Cream (P) and Revere Red (X), neither of which was available on Skyhawk or

Skylark; plus Colonial Yellow (N) and Firecracker Orange (U) for Skyhawk/Skylark and offered at extra cost on other models. Buick's standard safety features included seat belts with push-button buckles; seat/shoulder belts in front (with reminder light and buzzer); energy-absorbing steering column, padded instrument panel and front seatback tops; passenger guard door locks; safety door latches and hinges; soft, low-profile window control knobs, smooth contoured door and window regulator handles, lane-change feature in turn signal control; vinyl-edged wide-view inside mirror; dual master cylinder brake system with warning light; and dual-action safety latches (on front-opening hoods). Buick also announced an optional Air Cushion Restraint System for LeSabre, Electra and Riviera.

1976 Buick, Skyhawk hatchback. (OCW)

SKYHAWK - SERIES 4H - V-6 - Buick's variant of the subcompact H-special body Chevrolet Monza, descended from the Vega and directly related to Olds Starfire, was called the "smallest Buick in 60 years." As part of the attempt to capture the emerging youth market, it was also dubbed "The Free Spirit Hawk." In addition to the standard hatchback coupe, a low-budget 'S' version had been introduced halfway through the 1975 model year and continued for '76. New to the option list this year was a wide brushed aluminum band that wrapped over the roof, embossed with a Skyhawk emblem, coupled with a heavily-tinted (smoke-colored) glass Astroroof. Performance fans could also order their Skyhawk with a new Borg-Warner five-speed manual gearbox (overdrive top gear), instead of the standard fully synchronized four-speed. Three-speed Turbo Hydra-matic was also available. Sole powerplant was a V-6 engine with two-barrel carburetor that combined economy and spirited power. With the five-speed, Skyhawk turned in an impressive 30 MPG highway rating in economy tests. Skyhawk's rakish hatchback body had a "slippery, aerodynamic look" with fastback roofline and bulging hood. That hood sloped down in the middle toward the grille, but bulged upward to meet the headlamp housings. The front end carried quad rectangular headlamps. 'BUICK' letters stood above the upper corner of the minimalist rectangular grille, with a single dark horizontal bar across its small opening. Energy-absorbing bumpers had protective strips, plus front and rear guards. Large amber park/turn lamps sat below the front bumper. 'Skyhawk' and 'V6' emblems were on front fenders ahead of the door. White, gold or black accent stripes were standard; so were side-window reveal moldings. Inside were high-backed, full-foam bucket seats in a 2-2 seating arrangement (cloth/vinyl or vinyl upholstery), a center console, small "comfortably-angled" steering wheel, European-style handbrake, and floor gearshift lever. Large, bold, easy-to-read instruments included a circular 7000-rpm tachometer and KM/H-MPH speedometer, ammeter, and electric clock. In the trunk sat a stowaway spare tire. Skyhawk offered almost 28 cubic feet of storage with the rear seatback folded down. Skyhawk used unibody construction. Its radial-tuned suspension included computer-selected springs, front and rear stabilizer bars (except 'S' model), plus special suspension geometry and radial tires. Front disc brakes had vented rotors to dissipate heat for fade-resistant braking. Each pad had a brake lining wear sensor that emitted an audible squeak when replacement was needed. An oil pressure switch connected to the fuel pump shut off the fuel supply whenever oil pressure fell below the normal operating limit.

1976 Buick, Skylark S/R Landau coupe. (OCW)

1976 Buick, Skylark sedan. (OCW)

SKYLARK - SERIES 4X - V-6/V-8 - Buick's European-inspired compact sedan—the only American compact powered by a V-6—came in seven models, from low-priced 'S' to sporty S/R. Body styles included a coupe, hatchback and four-door sedan. The new horizontal-design grille was made up of thin horizontal and vertical strips forming wide segments, with a 'BUICK' badge in the lower corner. It was divided into upper and lower sections by a wider horizontal bar, with widest bar across the top. Twin round headlamps in square housings were flanked by stacked outboard park/signal lamps that wrapped around the front fenders, with amber reflectors at the rear of each unit. Skylark interiors also were new, while a thickly-padded Landau top with small side windows, accented by a brushed aluminum band, was optional. Other options included a Fuel Usage Light, Cruise-Master speed control, power windows, electric door locks, automatic trunk release, and tilt steering wheel. Skylark carried a standard 3.8-liter V-6 with High-Energy Ignition, plus front disc brakes, computer-selected springs, hefty front stabilizer bar, and large full-foam seats. That V-6 weighed 200 pounds less than the optional 350 V-8 (two- or four-barrel carburetor). The base V-8 option, though, was an economical 260 cu. in. (4.3-liter) version. A fully synchronized three-speed manual column shift was standard on V-6 powered Skylarks (except in California). The .73:1 rear axle ratio offered excellent economy. Semi-unit construction had Skylark's engine and front suspension mounted on a separate sub-frame that helped isolate vibration and road shock. Hatchbacks carried a stowaway spare tire and had 28 cubic feet of storage space. Skylark 'S' came with a vinyl bench seat; standard Skylark offered a choice of vinyl or cloth bench seats; while the S/R carried special thick, ribbed velour cloth and vinyl bucket seats (reclining on the passenger side). Roof drip moldings were standard on Skylark and S/R. The S/R instrument panel had large black dials. Its turn signal lever doubled as a headlight dimmer switch, as on European touring cars. S/R also had a rallye steering wheel; large sports console with gearshift lever and stowage bins; carpeted

door trim with map pocket and reflector; stand-up hood ornament; plus radial-tuned suspension.

CENTURY - SERIES 4A - V-6/V-8 - Buick's A-bodied Century models didn't all look alike for 1976. GM-designed rectangular headlamps were new, but two-door coupes also got new lower body sheetmetal, a fastback roofline, flared wheel openings, and a canted aerodynamic nosepiece containing a new grille with many vertical bars. The new "formal" bodies eliminated the prior "sculptured" look that had been introduced in 1973. The coupe grille was a curious six-slot design (three large horizontal cross-hatched sections on each side), set in body-colored framing. Quad rectangular headlamps stood atop quad rectangular clear park/turn lamps, with 'BUICK' emblem above the grille's upper corner. A hood ornament was standard. The 'Century' emblem sat at the trailing edge of front fenders. Small side lenses were at the front edge of front fenders, and rear of rear fenders. The Custom Coupe had the same formal roofline as Regal but with the new aerodynamic front end. Four-door sedans retained their old basic bodies, but front ends changed to hold their new vertically-stacked headlamps. Sedans had the formal Regal-style grille with 'BUICK' badge at the side, vertically-stacked headlamps, and clear vertical park/signal lamps. The Regal, which was considered a part of the Century series (see below), also had the formal-look grille. All told, the nine-model Century/Regal lineup included four different rooflines. Sedan and station wagon wheelbases were 4 in. longer than coupes. Century was described as "a leaner, smaller breed of Buick....a custom-tailored road car that rivals even the most opulent Buicks." It was the only domestic mid-size powered by a V-6. Century Special was the economy version. Custom Wagons, offering over 85 cubic feet of cargo space, came with two or three seats, standard variable-ratio power steering, power front disc brakes, Turbo Hydra-matic, and a 350 cu. in. (5.7-liter) V-8 with four-barrel carburetor. Other models had a standard 231 cu. in. (3.8-liter) V-6, with V-8 optional (except in Special). A three-speed manual transmission with column shift was standard on V-6 coupes and sedans. All models except the Special had protective bumper strips. Wagons had a "Tailgate Ajar" warning light. Base Century and Special models offered a choice of cloth or vinyl bench seat. Century Custom could have cloth or vinyl notchback seating; wagons, vinyl notchback seats. Like full-size Buicks, Century was built on a full-perimeter frame. The radial-tuned suspension used computer-selected springs, front stabilizer bar and special suspension geometry. Power front disc brakes were standard on Custom sedan and wagon; power steering on all. Disc brake pads emitted an audible squeak to warn that replacement was needed. Options included an all-metal electric sunroof, Landau vinyl roof, Cruise-Master speed control, power windows, six-way power seats, tilt steering wheel, electric door locks, automatic trunk release, and low-speed-delay wipers that could be set to operate periodically. A Hurst Hatch Roof with twin removable smoked (gray tinted) glass panels was offered on the Custom (and Regal) coupe only. Buyers could choose from two air conditioners: Climate-Control that cooled and dehumidified, or Custom-Aire (semi-automatic). There were also two economy options: a Fuel Usage Gauge that showed whether you were driving economically, and a Speed Alert that warned when you exceeded a preset speed.

1976 Buick, Century Special colonnade coupe. (OCW)

1976 Buick, Regal Landau coupe with optional wire wheel covers. (OCW)

1976 Buick, Century Custom coupe. (OCW)

CENTURY – REGAL - SERIES 4A - V-6/V-8 - Regal was considered the "high-line Century" rather than a truly separate model, but with its own styling touches. Those included a formal roofline and classic vertical crosshatch grille with 'Regal' script at the side. Like their parent Century, Regal coupes had new lower body sheet metal and flared wheel openings, plus a new formal-look grille. They also had horizontally-placed rectangular headlamps with outboard vertical amber side lenses. Regal sedans looked different, with quad stacked rectangular headlamps flanking twin vertical clear park/signal lamps that sat between headlamps and grille. Regal's crest stood at the trailing edge of front fenders; the 'Regal' script just behind opera windows on the coupe. Inside, seats were upholstered in velour, and the simulated woodgrain instrument panel held deep-set dials. Except in California, the Regal sedan came with a standard 350 cu. in. (5.7-liter) V-8, while coupes had a standard 231 cu. in. (3.8-liter) V-6. Regal sedans had Turbo Hydra-matic as standard equipment, but V-6 coupes came with three-speed manual (column) shift. Coupes could be ordered with 350 V-8 and automatic transmission. Power steering was standard. Regal's S/R package included reclining front bucket seats upholstered in ribbed velour; a large center console with gearshift lever; rallye steering wheel; headlamp dimmer in the turn signal lever; and GM-spec steel-belted radial whitewall tires.

1976 Buick, LeSabre Custom Landau hardtop coupe with optional wire wheel covers. (OCW)

LESABRE - SERIES 4B - V-8 - LeSabre for '76 received the quad rectangular headlamps that had gone on Electra in 1975,

set above clear horizontal quad park/signal lamps. The new classic-look horizontal crosshatch grille had Buick letters set into the wide upper crossbar. Clear horizontal cornering lamps (optional) at front of front fenders accompanied smaller amber lenses. Trailing ends of rear fenders displayed 'LeSabre' script. LeSabres had large three-hole horizontal "ventiport" trim strips on the upper portion of front fenders, just ahead of the door-descendants of the old Buick portholes. Front and rear bumpers carried protective strips. In a last-minute addition to the model year lineup, LeSabre added a base V-6 version--the only full-sized, six-passenger car in the world with a V-6 engine. LeSabre Custom models came with standard 350 cu. in. (5.7-liter) V-8, power steering, power front disc brakes, and Turbo Hydra-matic. Gas mileage of the optional 455 cu. in. V-8 engine improved to an 18 MPG rating Teflon inside coatings improved shock absorber operation. Ample space for six was offered with either cloth/vinyl or vinyl notchback seats. Among the many options were low-speed-delay windshield wipers, a positive-traction differential and firm suspension package.

1976 Buick, Electra Limited hardtop sedan. (OCW)

ELECTRA - SERIES 4C - V-8 - Buick's posh full-size Electra 225 and Electra Limited came in coupe or hardtop sedan form. Electra's new grille had a heavy upper bar inset with large Buick block letters, 17 vertical bars with crosshatch pattern inside each section, and 'Electra' script at the side. Unlike the 1975 version, this grille didn't extend below the headlamps. Quad rectangular headlamps sat atop four clear park/signal lights, with clear cornering lamps (optional) at front of front fenders. Horizontal "ventiport" trim strips were on upper section of front fenders, ahead of the door. They had four "holes" (actually gouge-like depressions) to distinguish Electras from the LeSabre's three. Rear fender bottoms held a small reflector lens, below the long bodyside trim molding. Front and rear bumpers had protective strips. Standard equipment included Turbo Hydra-matic, power steering, and power front disc brakes along with power windows and a digital clock. Four-link rear suspension gave a smooth, quiet ride, improved by Teflon-coated shock absorbers. A vapor return system reduced the chance of vapor lock. An altitude compensator in the Turbo Hydra-matic provided smooth shifting in various elevation. The EPA highway rating of the 455 cu. in. (7.5-liter) V-8 engine improved by 3 MPG. Increased economy came as a result of improved carburetion, new crankshaft design, increased spark advance, better axle ratio, and reduced weight. Buyers had a choice of new full-foam seat designs: cloth bench or notchback seats (or vinyl notchback in Electra 225 sedan); cloth or vinyl notchback in the Electra 225 coupe. Limited models had cloth 60/40 notchback seating (two-way power) with a fold-down center armrest. Limiteds also had wide rocker appearance moldings, and the Limited sedan included a dome reading lamp. Top-of-the-line was the Park Avenue edition of the Electra Limited hardtop sedan. That package included a formal "halo" vinyl roof, thick cut-pile carpeting, and velour upholstery that even reached the executive center console and ceiling. Two Landau tops were available: traditional, or a new type with smaller opera windows and thickly-padded vinyl with French seams on the back portion. An optional Astroroof was available on the coupe. Drivers could enjoy a glass-topped driving compartment, roll the sunshade to closed position, or retract the glass for open-air driving. Coupes could also have an electric

sunroof. Other options: variable-delay wipers, and an automatic door locking system that worked when the gear selector was put into and out of Park position. Optional Automatic Climate Control incorporated both heater and air conditioner.

ESTATE WAGON - SERIES 4BR - V-8 - Full-size station wagons came with two or three seats and 106 cubic foot cargo area. Standard powertrain was the 455 cu. in. (7.5-liter) V-8 engine and Turbo Hydra-matic transmission, plus variable-ratio power steering, power front disc brakes, and computer-selected front coil and rear leaf springs. Estates had vinyl bench seating, a hidden storage compartment, inside hood release, and a power tailgate window. The clever glide-away tailgate's lower section would glide away under the floor while the window receded up into the roof area. Three-seat models had a forward-facing third seat and divided second seat. Front and rear bumpers had protective strips. Estate Wagon's simulated woodgrain instrument panel, steering wheel, carpeting and available notchback seat were identical to LeSabre.

1976 Buick, Riviera S/R coupe. (OCW)

RIVIERA - SERIES 4E - V-8 - As it had since the first version came off the line for 1963, Riviera combined luxury with road car capabilities. As the catalog proclaimed, the personal-luxury coupe blended "performance, elegance and romance." This year it had new seat designs and interior trim, plus a more efficient engine, transmission and axle ratio combination. Riviera's 455 cu. in. (7.5-liter) V-8 offered improved gas mileage this year. Standard equipment included variable-ratio power steering and power front disc brakes; six-position tilt steering wheel; two-way power seats; electric windows; cut-pile carpeting; front bumper guards; front and rear bumper protective strips; computer-selected coil springs at all four wheels; Teflon-coated shock absorbers; JR78 steel-belted radial tires; and a digital clock. Wraparound three-section (clear/amber/clear) park/turn lamps flanked quad rectangular headlamps. Separate B-U-I-C-K letters stood above the horizontal crosshatch grille, with 'Riviera' script at the side. Similar 'Riviera' script was on the lower section of front fenders, to rear of wheel openings. A new two-tone color scheme was actually a vinyl appliqué bonded to bodysides. Silver plus a choice of four colors were available: dark red, dark blue, black, or dark gray. Options included a three-in-one Astroroof with heavily tinted glass and rollaway sunshade that permitted closed, open-air, or glass-topped motoring; Automatic Climate-Control; and an electric sunroof that came with or without a vinyl top. The popular Landau top returned for 1976.

I.D. DATA: The 13-symbol Vehicle Identification Number (VIN) was located on the upper left surface of the instrument panel, visible through the windshield. The first digit is '4', indicating the Buick division. The second symbol is a letter indicating series: 'S' Skyhawk; 'T' Skyhawk S; 'B' Skylark; 'C' Skylark S/R; 'W' Skylark S; 'D' Century; 'E' Century Special; 'H' Century Custom; 'J' Regal; 'K' Century Custom wagon; 'N' LeSabre; 'P' LeSabre Custom; 'V' Electra 225; 'X' Electra Limited; 'Z' Riviera. Next come two digits that denote body type: '07' Skyhawk hatchback coupe; '17' Skylark 2-dr hatchback coupe; '27' Skylark 2-dr. thin-pillar coupe; '37' Century 2-dr. Colonnade coupe or Electra HT coupe; '57' Century/Regal 2-dr. Colonnade coupe or LeSabre HT coupe; '87' Riviera 2-dr. HT coupe; '29' 4-dr. Colonnade sedan; '39' 4-dr. HT sedan; '69' 4-dr. thin-pillar sedan; '35' 4-dr. 2-seat wagon; '45' 4-dr. 3-seat wagon. The fifth symbol is a letter indicating engine code: 'C' V6-231 2Bbl., 'Y'

V8-301 2Bbl., 'U' V8-305 2Bbl., 'H' V8-350 2Bbl., 'L' V8-350 4Bbl. (LMI); 'R' V8-350 4Bbl. (L34); 'J' V8-350 4Bbl. (L77); 'K' V8-403 4Bbl. (L80). The sixth symbol denotes model year ('6' 1976). Next is a plant code: '2' Ste. Therese Quebec (Canada); 'K' Leeds, Missouri; 'L' Van Nuys, Calif.; 'T' Tarrytown, NY; 'G' Framingham, Mass.; 'H' Flint, Mich.; 'Z' Fremont, Calif.; 'C' Southgate, Calif.; 'X' Fairfax, Kansas; 'E' Linden, New Jersey. The final six digits are the sequential serial number, which began with 100001 except for Skyhawks (700001 up); LeSabres, Estate Wagons, Electras and Rivieras built at Flint (400001 up). Engine numbers were stamped on the front of the block. A body number plate on the shroud identified model year, car division, series, style, body assembly plant, body number, trim combination, modular seat code, paint code, and date built code.

SKYHAWK (V-6)

Model No.	Body/Style No.	Body Type & Seating	Factory Price	Shipping Weight	Prod. Total
4H	T07	2-dr 'S' Hatch-4P	3903	2857	Note 1
4H	S07	2-dr Hatch-4P	4216	2889	Note 1

Note 1: Total model year production (U.S.), 15,769 Skyhawks.

SKYLARK 'S' (V-6/V-8)

Model No.	Body/Style No.	Body Type & Seating	Factory Price	Shipping Weight	Prod. Total
4X	W27	2-dr Coupe-6P	3435/3470	3316/3515	Note 2

SKYLARK (V-6/V-8)

Model No.	Body/Style No.	Body Type & Seating	Factory Price	Shipping Weight	Prod. Total
4X	B27	2-dr Coupe-6P	3549/3584	3327/3526	Note 2
4X	B17	2-dr Hatch-6P	3687/3722	3396/3591	6,703
4X	B69	4-dr Sedan-6P	3609/3644	3283/3484	48,157

Note 2: Total U.S. model year production, 51,260 Skylark base and 'S' coupes. Of the total 106,120 Skylarks produced, 87,881 had a V-6 engine, 18,239 a V-8.

SKYLARK S/R (V-6/V-8)

Model No.	Body/Style No.	Body Type & Seating	Factory Price	Shipping Weight	Prod. Total
4X	C27	2-dr Coupe-5P	4281/4316	3319/3502	3,880
4X	C17	2-dr Hatch-5P	4398/4433	3338/3522	1,248
4X	C69	4-dr Sedan-5P	4324/4359	3312/3499	3,243

Note 3: Of the total 8,371 S/R Skylarks produced for the model year, 4,818 had a V-6 engine and 3,553 a V-8. Prices shown are for the 260 cu. in. V-8; the 350 V-8 with 2Bbl. carburetor cost $50 more.

CENTURY SPECIAL (V-6)

Model No.	Body/Style No.	Body Type & Seating	Factory Price	Shipping Weight	Prod. Total
4A	E37	2-dr Col Cpe-6P	3935	3508	Note 4

CENTURY (V-6/V-8)

Model No.	Body/Style No.	Body Type & Seating	Factory Price	Shipping Weight	Prod. Total
4A	D37	2-dr Col Cpe-6P	4070/4155	3652/3844	Note 4
4A	D29	4-dr Col Sed-6P	4105/4190	3741/3933	33,632

Note 4: Total Century and Century Special coupe production, 59,448. Of the 93,080 Century and Special models built, 66,440 had a V-6 engine and 26,640 a V-8.

CENTURY CUSTOM (V-6/V-8)

Model No.	Body/Style No.	Body Type & Seating	Factory Price	Shipping Weight	Prod. Total
4A	H57	2-dr Col Cpe-6P	4346/4431	3609/3801	34,036
4A	H29	4-dr Col Sed-6P	4424/4509	3721/3913	19,728
4A	K35	4-dr Sta Wag-6P	----/4987	----/4363	Note 5
4A	K45	4-dr Sta Wag-8P	----/5099	----/4413	Note 5

Note 5: Total Century Custom wagon production, 16,625. Of the 70,389 Century Custom models built, 21,832 had a V-6 engine and 48,557 a V-8.

REGAL (V-6/V-8)

Model No.	Body/Style No.	Body Type & Seating	Factory Price	Shipping Weight	Prod. Total
4A	J57	2-dr Col Cpe-6P	4465/4910	3710/3902	124,498
4A	J29	4-dr Col Sed-6P	----/4825	----/4104	17,118

Note 6: Total model year production, 141,616 Regals (31,907 with V-6 engine and 109,709 V-8).

LESABRE (V-6)

Model No.	Body/Style No.	Body Type & Seating	Factory Price	Shipping Weight	Prod. Total
4B	N57	2-dr HT Cpe-6P	4815	4129	3,861
4B	N69	4-dr Sedan-6P	4747	4170	4,315
4B	N39	4-dr HT Sed-6P	4871	4056	2,312

LESABRE CUSTOM (V-8)

Model No.	Body/Style No.	Body Type & Seating	Factory Price	Shipping Weight	Prod. Total
4B	P57	2-dr HT Cpe-6P	5114	4275	45,669
4B	P69	4-dr Sedan-6P	5046	4328	34,841
4B	P39	4-dr HT Sed-6P	5166	4386	46,109

ESTATE WAGON (V-8)

Model No.	Body/Style No.	Body Type & Seating	Factory Price	Shipping Weight	Prod. Total
4B	R35	4-dr Sta Wag-6P	5591	5013	5,990
4B	R45	4-dr Sta Wag-8P	5731	5139	14,384

ELECTRA 225 (V-8)

Model No.	Body/Style No.	Body Type & Seating	Factory Price	Shipping Weight	Prod. Total
4C	V37	2-dr Coupe-6P	6367	4502	18,442
4C	V39	4-dr HT Sed-6P	6527	4641	26,655

ELECTRA LIMITED (V-8)

Model No.	Body/Style No.	Body Type & Seating	Factory Price	Shipping Weight	Prod. Total
4C	X37	2-dr Coupe-6P	6689	4521	28,395
4C	X39	4-dr HT Sed-6P	6852	4709	51,067

RIVIERA (V-8)

Model No.	Body/Style No.	Body Type & Seating	Factory Price	Shipping Weight	Prod. Total
4E	Z87	2-dr Coupe-6P	6798	4531	20,082

FACTORY PRICE AND WEIGHT NOTE: Figure before the slash is for V-6 engine, after slash for V-8.

ENGINES: BASE EQUIPMENT V-6 (Skyhawk, Skylark, Century, Regal coupe, LeSabre): 90-degree overhead-valve V-6. Cast iron alloy block and head. Displacement: 231 cu. in. (3.8 liters). Bore & stroke: 3.8 x 3.4 in. Compression ratio: 8.0:1. Brake horsepower: 105 at 3400 R.P.M. Torque: 185 lb.-ft. at 2000 R.P.M. Four main bearings. Hydraulic valve lifters. Carburetor: 2Bbl. Rochester 2GC. VIN Code: C. OPTIONAL V-8 (Skylark): 90-degree overhead-valve V-8. Cast iron alloy block and head. Displacement: 260 cu. in. (4.3 liters). Bore & stroke: 3.50 x 3.385 in. Compression ratio: 8.5:1. Brake horsepower: 110 at 3400 R.P.M. Torque: 210 lb.-ft. at 1600 R.P.M. Five main bearings. Hydraulic valve lifters. Carburetor: 2Bbl. Rochester. Built by Oldsmobile. VIN Code: F. BASE V-8 (Regal sedan); OPTIONAL (Skylark, Century/Custom, Regal cpe): 90-degree, overhead valve V-8. Cast iron alloy block and head. Displacement: 350 cu. in. (5.7 liters). Bore & stroke: 3.80 x 3.85 in. Compression ratio: 8.0:1. Brake horsepower: 140 at 3200 R.P.M. Torque: 280 lb.-ft. at 1600 R.P.M. Five main bearings. Hydraulic valve lifters. Carburetor: 2Bbl. Roch. 2GC. VIN Code: H. BASE V-8 (Century wagon, LeSabre Custom); OPTIONAL (Skylark, Century/Custom, Regal): 90-degree, overhead valve V-8. Cast iron alloy block and head. Displacement: 350 cu. in. (5.7 liters). Bore & stroke: 3.80 x 3.85 in Compression ratio: 8.0:1. Brake horsepower: 155 at 3400 R.P.M. Torque: 280 lb.-ft at 1800 R.P.M. Five main bearings. Hydraulic valve lifters. Carburetor: 4Bbl. Roch. M4MC. VIN Code: J. BASE V-8 (Electra, Estate Wagon, Riviera); OPTIONAL (LeSabre Custom): 90-degree, overhead valve V-8. Cast iron alloy block and head. Displacement: 455 cu in. (7.5 liters). Bore & stroke: 4.3125 x 3.9 in. Compression ratio: 7.9:1. Brake horsepower: 205 at 3800 R.P.M. Torque: 345 lb.-ft. at 2000 R.P.M. Five main bearings. Hydraulic valve lifters. Carburetor: 4Bbl. Roch. M4MC. VIN Code: T.

CHASSIS DATA: Wheelbase: (Skyhawk) 97.0 in.; (Skylark) 111.0 in.; (Century/Regal cpe) 112.0 in.; (Century/Regal sed/wag) 116.0 in.; (LeSabre) 124.0 in.; (Electra/Estate) 127.0 in.; (Riviera) 122.0 in. Overall length: (Skyhawk) 179.3 in.; (Skylark) 200.3 in.; (Century/Regal cpe) 209.7 in.; (Century/Regal sed) 213.5 in.; (Century wag) 218.2 in.; (LeSabre) 226.8 in.; (Electra) 233.3 in.; (Estate Wagon) 231.8 in.; (Riv) 218.6 in. Height: (Skyhawk) 50.1 in.; (Skylark 2-dr.) 52.1 in.; (Skylark 4-dr.) 53.1 in.; (Century/Regal cpe) 52.6-52.8 in.; (Century/Regal sed) 53.6 in.; (Century wag) 55.3 in.; (LeSabre cpe) 53.2 in.; (LeSabre HT sed) 53.3 in.; (LeSabre 4-dr sed) 54.0 in.; (Electra cpe) 54.0 in.; (Electra sed) 54.5 in.; (Estate 2S wag) 57.8 in.; (Estate 3S wag) 57.0 in.; (Riv) 53.0 in. Width: (Skyhawk) 65.4 in.; (Skylark) 72.7 in.; (Century/Regal cpe) 77.0 in.; (Century/Regal sed/wag) 79.0 in.; (LeSabre/Electra/Estate/ Riv) 79.9 in. Front Tread: (Skyhawk) 54.7 in.; (Skylark) 59.1 in.; (Century/Regal) 61.5 in.; (LeSabre/Electra/Estate/Riv) 63.4 in. Rear Tread:(Skyhawk) 53.6 in.; (Skylark) 59.7 in.; (Century/Regal) 60.7 in.; (LeSabre/Electra/Estate/Riv) 64.0 in. Standard Tires: (Skyhawk) BR78 x 13 SBR; (Skyhawk 'S') B78 x 13; (Skylark) E78 x 14; (Skylark S/R) FR78 x 14 SBR WSW; (Century/Regal cpe) GR78 x 15 SBR; (Century Special cpe) FR78 x 15; (Century/Regal sed) FR78 x 15 SBR; (Century wagon) HR78 x 15; (LeSabre) HR78 x 15 SBR; (LeSabre w/455 V-8) JR78 x 15 SBR; (Electra/Riviera) JR78 x 15 SBR; (Estate) LR78 x 15 SBR.

TECHNICAL: Transmission: Three-speed, fully synchronized manual gearbox (column shift) standard on Skylark, Century, and Regal cpe with V-6; Turbo Hydra-matic optional. Four-speed, fully synchronized floor shift standard on Skyhawk; five-speed optional. Turbo Hydra-matic (three-speed) standard on Regal sedan, LeSabre, Electra, Estate and Riviera; also on other models with V-8 and Century sold in California. Three-speed manual transmission gear ratios: (1st) 3.11:1; (2nd) 1.84:1; (3rd) 1.00:1; (Rev) 3.22:1. Four-speed gear ratios: (1st) 3.11:1; (2nd) 2.20:1; (3rd) 1.47:1; (4th) 1.00:1; (Rev) 3.11:1.

Five-speed gear ratios: (1st) 3.10:1; (2nd) 1.89:1; (3rd) 1.27:1; (4th) 1.00:1; (5th) 0.84:1; (Rev) 3.06:1. Automatic transmission gear ratios: (1st) 2.52:1; (2nd) 1.52:1; (3rd) 1.00:1; (Rev) 1.93:1 or 2.08:1. Standard axle ratio: (Skyhawk) 2.56:1; (Skylark) 2.73:1; (Century/Regal) 3.08:1; (LeSabre/Electra/Riviera) 2.56:1. Hypoid bevel final drive. Steering: recirculating ball; variable-ratio power steering standard on Century/Regal, LeSabre, Electra, Estate and Riviera. Suspension: (Skyhawk) unequal-length front control arms w/anti-sway bar, rigid rear axle w/torque arm, Panhard rod and anti-sway bar; (Skylark) semi-elliptic rear leaf springs; (others) front/rear coil springs, independent front w/trailing links and anti-roll bar (exc. Special). Brakes: front disc, rear drum power brakes standard on LeSabre/Electra/Riviera plus Century custom sedan/wagon and Regal sedan. Body construction: (Skyhawk) unitized; (Skylark) separate front frame unit cushion mounted to unitized body; (others) separate body and perimeter box frame. Fuel tank: (Skyhawk) 18.5 gal.; (Skylark) 21 gal.; (Century/Regal/Estate) 22 gal.; (LeSabre/Electra/Riv) 26 gal. High-Energy electronic ignition (HEI) on all engines. Unleaded fuel only.

DRIVETRAIN OPTIONS: Engines: 260 cu. in. V-8, 2Bbl.: Skylark ($35). 350 cu. in. V-8, 2Bbl.: Skylark, Century/Custom, Regal cpe ($85). 350 cu. in. V-8, 4Bbl.: Skylark, Century, Custom, Regal cpe ($140); Regal sed ($55). 455 cu. in. V-8, 4Bbl.: LeSabre Cust ($159). Transmission/Differential: Five-speed manual floor shift: Skyhawk ($244). Turbo Hydra-matic: Skyhawk ($244); Skylark, Century cpe/sed, Regal cpe ($262). Positive traction differential ($48-$54). Power Accessories: Power brakes: Skyhawk ($55); Skylark/Century ($58) exc. Cust sed/wag. Power steering: Skyhawk ($120); Skylark ($136). Suspension: H5 handling pkg.: Skyhawk 'S' ($104-$124). Firm ride/handling pkg. ($17-$21) exc. Skyhawk. Rallye ride/handling pkg.: Skylark ($39); Century, except Special wagon, Regal, Riviera ($34). Automatic level control: Century/Regal ($92); LeSabre/Electra/Riviera ($93). Other: Trailer towing flasher/harness: ($16-$27) except Skyhawk. Heavy-duty 80-amp alternator: Century/Regal/LeSabre/Electra/Riviera ($35-$39). Heavy-duty Energizer battery ($15-$17) except Electra, Riviera. Freedom battery ($28-$29) except Skyhawk/Electra. Heavy-duty cooling ($25-$52) except Skyhawk. Engine block heater ($12) except Skyhawk. Heavy-duty air cleaner ($11) except Skyhawk/Skylark. Chrome air cleaner: Riviera era ($17). California emission system ($50).

SKYHAWK CONVENIENCE/APPEARANCE OPTIONS: Option Groups: Shadow light Astroroof w/roof crown molding ($550). Appearance group: 'S' ($63). Convenience group ($20). Comfort/Convenience: Air cond. ($424). Rear defogger, electric ($66). Soft Ray tinted glass ($44). Tinted windshield ($37). Rallye steering wheel: 'S' ($35). Tilt steering wheel ($48). Electric clock: 'S' ($16); clock and tach ($59). Right sport mirror ($12). Remote-control left sport mirror: 'S' ($15). Entertainment: AM radio ($71). AM/FM radio ($134). AM/FM stereo radio ($219). Rear speaker ($19). Windshield antenna ($21). Exterior Trim: Door edge guards ($8). Roof crown molding ($150). Protective bodyside moldings ($24-$39). Interior Trim/Upholstery: Full-length console: 'S' ($73). Adjustable driver's seatback ($17). Front/rear floor mats ($14). Custom seatbelts ($13). Wheels: Custom sport wheels ($74-$84). Deluxe wheel covers ($39); for radial tires only. Wheel trim rings ($33). Tires: B78 x 13 WSW: 'S' ($26-$32). BR78 x 13 SBR blackwall: 'S' ($82-$103). BR78 x 13 SBR whitewall ($26-$135). BR70 x 13 SBR WLT ($35-$148).

SKYLARK CONVENIENCE/APPEARANCE OPTIONS: Option Packages: Accessory pkg.: 'S' ($11). Convenience group ($29). Appearance group (wheel opening and roof drip moldings): 'S' ($31). Comfort/Convenience: Air cond. ($452). Cruise Master ($73). Rear defogger, blower-type ($43). Power windows ($99-$140). Electric door locks ($62-$89). Rallye steering wheel ($35); std on S/R. Tilt steering wheel ($52). Soft Ray

tinted glass ($46). Dual horns ($7). Electric clock ($18). Head-lamps-on indicator ($7). Fuel usage indicator ($16). Electric trunk release ($17). Three-speed wipers w/delay ($28). Remote-control left mirror ($14). Sport mirrors: left remote, right manual ($26); both remote ($40). Entertainment: AM radio ($75). AM/FM radio ($137). AM/FM stereo radio ($233). AM radio and stereo tape player ($209). AM/FM stereo radio w/tape ($337). Rear speaker ($20). Windshield antenna ($22). Exterior Trim: Custom vinyl roof ($91-$96). Landau top: cpe ($150-$155). Two-tone paint ($35). Special exterior paint ($107). Swing-out rear quarter vent window: two-doors ($48). Protective bodyside moldings ($37). Rocker panel moldings ($15). Wide rocker appearance group ($32). Decklid molding ($7). Custom door and window frame moldings ($23-$29). Door edge guards ($8-$12). Bodyside accent stripe ($23). Bumper guards, front ($17); front/rear ($34). Bumper strips, front/rear ($29). Interior Trim/Upholstery: Full-length console ($71). Vinyl bucket seats: base ($79). Custom trim bench seats/cushion interior: base ($138). Custom seatbelts ($13-$15). Carpet savers ($8). Carpet savers and mats ($14). Carpeted door trim w/map pocket and reflector ($35); std. on S/R. Wheels: Styled wheels ($77-$89). Chrome-plated wheels ($103-$122). Deluxe wheel covers ($31); for radial tires only. Deluxe wire wheel covers ($111); for radials only. Tires: E78 x 14 whitewall ($26-$33) exc. S/R. ER78 x 14 SBR blackwall ($69-$86) exc. S/R. ER78 x 14 SBR whitewall ($95-$119) exc. S/R. FR78 x 14 SBR WLT ($119-$149) exc. S/R ($24-$30).

CENTURY/REGAL CONVENIENCE/APPEARANCE OPTIONS:
Option Packages: Regal S/R Coupe pkg. ($379). Sunroof: cpe ($370). Hurst hatch roof: Century Custom. Regal cpe ($550). Convenience group ($5-$29). Comfort/Convenience: Air cond. ($476). Custom Aire semi-automatic air cond. ($513). Cruise Master ($73). Rear defogger: electric ($77); blower-type ($43). Soft Ray tinted glass ($50). Tinted windshield ($40). Six-way power seat ($124). Custom steering wheel ($18). Rallye steering wheel ($35). Tilt steering ($52). Power windows ($99-$140). Electric door locks ($62-$89). Electric trunk release ($17). Remote-control tailgate lock: Century wag ($20). Electric clock ($20). Headlamps-on indicator ($7). Instrument gauges and clock ($42) exc. wag. Fuel usage gauge ($25). Speed alert ($14). Dome reading lamp ($15). Three-speed wiper with delay ($28). Mirrors: Remote control mirror ($14). Sport mirrors: left remote ($26). Lighted visor vanity mirror ($39). Entertainment: AM radio ($79). AM/FM radio ($142). AM/FM stereo radio ($233). AM radio w/stereo tape player ($213). AM/FM stereo radio w/tape ($337). Rear speaker ($20). Front/rear speakers ($41). Windshield antenna ($22); incl. w/radios. Exterior Trim: Landau vinyl top: Century Cust, Regal cpe ($110); Century/Spec. ($144). Custom vinyl top: Century cpe, Regal ($106). Short custom vinyl top: Century, Special cpe ($79). Custom vinyl top w/hood ornament: Century, Custom sed ($111). Swing-out rear quarter vent windows: Century 2S wag ($48). Two-tone paint ($30-$40). Special color paint ($125). Bumper guards, front/rear ($35); rear, Century wag ($17). Bumper strips: Century Special ($28). Protective bodyside and front fender moldings ($26). Lower bodyside molding and fender moldings ($34). Door edge guards ($8-$12). Wheel opening moldings: Century/Spec. ($18). Bodyside accent stripe ($49). Woodgrain appliqué: Century wag ($146). Luggage rack: Century wag ($71). Air deflector: Century wag ($24). Interior Trim/Upholstery: Full-length console ($71). Custom notchback seat trim: Century, Special ($125-$151). Custom vinyl notchback seat trim: Century Cust cpe, Regal cpe ($99); cloth ($129). Custom vinyl 60/40 seat trim: Century Cust, Regal cpe ($185); cloth ($215). Custom reclining seat trim: Century Cust cpe ($226). Custom trim vinyl bucket seats: Century, Spec. ($132-$158). Vinyl bucket seats: Century Cust, Regal ($8). Custom seatbelts ($13-$20). Front/rear carpeting: Century Spec. ($23). Load floor mat: Century wag ($22). Carpet savers ($9); w/mats ($16). Litter pocket ($6). Wheels: Chrome-plated wheels ($106-$149); N/A wagon.

Styled wheels ($58-$89); N/A wag. Deluxe wire wheel covers: Century ($123); Regal ($91). Styled wheel covers: Century ($85); Regal ($53). Deluxe wheel covers: Century ($32). Super deluxe wheel covers: Regal ($62). Tires: FR78 x 15 SBR WSW: Century ($28-$40). GR78 x 15 SBR BSW: Century/Cust sed ($20-$25); with V-8 (NC). GR78 x 15 SBR WSW ($30-$62) exc. Century Special. White-letter tires ($22-$89) exc. Special. Space-saver spare tire (NC). Conventional spare tire: Century Spec. (NC).

LESABRE/ELECTRA/ESTATE WAGON/RIVIERA CONVENIENCE/APPEARANCE OPTIONS:
Option Packages: Electra Limited Park Avenue pkg. ($419); w/deluxe console ($525). Riviera S/R pkg. ($276). Accessory group: LeSabre, Estate ($57-$72). Electric sunroof: Electra/Riviera cpe ($725). Astroroof: Electra/Riv cpe ($891). Comfort/Convenience: Air cond. ($512). Automatic climate control air cond.: Electra/Riv ($594). Custom Aire air cond.: LeSabre/Estate ($549). Cruise Master ($79). Rear defogger, electric ($78); blower-type ($43). Soft Ray tinted glass ($64). Tinted windshield: LeSabre/Est ($41). Power windows: LeSabre/Est ($159). Electric door locks ($90). Power tailgate door: Estate ($52). Automatic door locks: Electra/Riv ($93-$120). Six-way power driver's seat ($98-$126) exc. base LeSabre. Six-way power bench seat ($126) exc. Electra Ltd. Dual six-way power seats ($220-$247) exc. base LeSabre. Custom steering wheel: LeSabre/Est ($16). Tilt steering wheel ($53); std. on Riv. Tilt/telescoping steering column ($95) exc. Riv ($42). Map light: Electra 225, Riv ($10). Low fuel indicator ($11). Fuel usage gauge ($25). Speed alert and trip odometer ($19). Electric trunk release ($17). Three-speed wipers w/delay ($28). Lighting, Horns and Mirrors: Cornering lamps ($40). Front light monitors: LeSabre/Est ($23). Front/rear monitors: Electra/Riv ($51). Door courtesy/warning lights: 2-dr ($30); 4-dr ($47). Headlamps-on indicator ($7). Dome/reading lamp ($15). Four-note horn ($17). Remote left mirror: LeSabre/Est ($14). Remote right mirror ($29). Dual remote sport mirrors ($36-$50). Remote left mirror w/thermometer ($19-$33). Lighted visor vanity mirror ($40). Entertainment: AM radio ($92). AM/FM radio ($153). AM/FM stereo radio w/four speakers ($236). AM radio and stereo tape player ($228). AM/FM stereo radio and tape ($341). Rear speaker ($20). Front/rear speakers ($41); non-stereo radio req'd. Windshield antenna ($22); incl. w/radios. Power antenna ($40). Exterior Trim: Landau top: Electra cpe ($549). Landau custom vinyl top: LeSabre/Electra cpe ($140-$159); Riviera ($399). Landau custom vinyl top w/roof crown molding: Riv ($499). Custom vinyl top: Electra Ltd. sed ($62); heavy-padded ($399). Custom vinyl top and molding ($139-$150). Custom vinyl top w/halo molding: Electra cpe ($163). Two-tone paint ($35-$60); special Riviera two-tone ($135). Special color paint ($125). Protective bodyside moldings ($37-$52). Custom wide bodyside moldings: Electra ($72). Door edge guards ($8-$12). Wide rocker panel moldings: LeSabre Cust, Estate, Electra 225 ($32). Wide rocker moldings group: base LeSabre ($93); Estate ($77). Belt reveal molding: LeSabre, Estate ($30). Custom molding: base LeSabre ($61); Estate ($46). Custom door window frame molding: base LeSabre ($30). Bodyside accent stripes ($33). Coach stripes: Electra ($52). Woodgrain appliqué: Estate ($193). Tailgate molding: Estate ($18). Bumper guards, front/rear ($37) exc. Riv; front, Riviera ($18). Front bumper reinforcement ($7-$14) exc. Riv. Luggage rack: Estate ($94). Locking luggage locker: Est. ($14). Interior Trim/Upholstery: Full-length console: Riv ($72). Custom notchback seat trim: Estate ($208); 60/40 ($295). Custom cloth notchback 60/40 seat trim: Riviera ($123); vinyl ($97); vinyl 60/40 seat ($97). Leather upholstery: Electra Ltd. ($320). Leather upholstery group: Riv ($417). Custom seatbelts: LeSabre/Est ($17-$20). Carpet savers ($10); w/mats ($17). Litter container ($6). Deluxe trunk trim: LeSabre ($40). Load floor area carpet: Estate ($61). Wheels and Tires: Chrome-plated wheels: LeSabre/Estate/Electra ($117-$151). Deluxe wheel covers: base LeSabre ($32). Super deluxe wheel covers: Riv ($40). Styled wheel covers ($32-$86).

Deluxe wire wheel covers ($70-$124). Whitewall tires ($41-$47). Wide whitewalls: Electra/Riv ($60).

HISTORY: Introduced: September 25, 1975. Model year production (U.S.): 737,467 (238,298 sixes and 499,169 V-8s) for a 9.1 percent share of the industry total. Calendar year production (U.S.): 817,669. Calendar year sales by U.S. dealers: 738,385 for an 8.6 percent market share, up from 518,032 in 1975. Model year sales by U.S. dealers: 706,249 (plus 25,007 imported Opels), up from only 463,132 in 1975.

Historical Footnotes: Since the economy was rising, Buick forecast a 40 percent jump in sales for the Bicentennial model year. Year-end results exceeded even that optimistic prediction, with sales up 52.5 percent to 706,249. That total, in fact, almost reached the model-year record set in 1973—-good news after two years of slippage. Calendar year production rose by 56 percent. Best sellers were the mid-size Century and compact Skylark, both up over 74 percent in sales. For 1976, Skylark production moved from Ste. Therese, Quebec, to Southgate, California. Skyhawk assembly continued in Canada. On the import front, a Japanese-built Opel Isuzu was introduced in mid-year. Sales amounted to less than half those of the former German-built Opel T-car, a result of dwindling import sales and a decline in the number of dealers carrying the car. Big cars, on the other hand, continued to sell strongly--a surprise to the industry. For the second year in-a-row, a Buick paced the Indianapolis 500 race. This year's pace car was a Century with turbocharged, highly modified 231 V-6. The turbo came from Rajay Industries, and the engine produced triple the normal horsepower. It was the first V-6 vehicle ever to handle the pace car duties. A total of 1,290 Century models wearing the pace car colors (orange, black and gray) and appropriate emblems were produced for the market.

1977

This year saw a total restyle for the B- and C-bodied LeSabre, Electra and Riviera. All were downsized significantly, measuring closer to mid-size dimensions—but the trimmed-down designs didn't lose their traditional spacious comfort. LeSabre and Riviera coupes offered over 2-1/2 in. more rear leg room than in 1976, as well as increased head room. Trunk space also grew on some models. Most downsized GM cars, in fact, were 1-1/2 in. taller than before. Smaller Buick models had mainly cosmetic changes. The full-line catalog continued the previous year's theme, "dedicated to the Free Spirit in just about everyone." Buick called the slimmed-down designs "trim, functional, contemporary," adding that "Suspensions are taut. Handling and maneuverability, crisp and responsive." Heralding the move to smaller engines, the mighty 455 V-8 left the lineup, replaced by a 403 cu. in. (6.6-liter) V-8 as the biggest powerplant for full-size Buicks. New 301 and 305 cu. in. V-8 engines were offered as options on Skylark and LeSabre The familiar 350 cu. in. (5.7-liter) four-barrel V-8, available on LeSabre, replaced the old 455 as standard equipment on the Electra, Riviera and Estate Wagon. Actually, three different 350 V-8s with four-barrel carburetor were offered, with two different bore/stroke dimensions, including one built by Chevrolet—a move that eventually led to serious criticism and lawsuits. The V-6 engine got redesigned cylinder heads with tapered-seat spark plugs, plus an added heat crossover hole in the head to speed warmups. Also new for 1977: an electric choke and back pressure exhaust gas recirculator. Diagnostic connections on full-size Buicks now allowed a mechanic to easily check the ignition switch, coil, starter and other critical areas by hooking up a diagnostic tester. All full-size Buicks had four-wheel coil-spring suspension, forward-mounted steering gear linkage, unequal-length front control arms, and four-link

rear suspension. Corrosion protection was improved on big Buicks, including more use of galvanized steel and rust-resistant materials: Metric dimensions saw increased use. All Buicks could have a new Citizens Band radio option; including a CB transceiver built into the AM/FM stereo system. Full-size Buicks could have an all-metal electric sunroof, or the three-in-one Astroroof. Most Skylark, Century, Regal and LeSabre models could have the Highway Economy Package, including a specially-tuned V-6 engine with vacuum spark regulator, specially calibrated Turbo Hydra-matic, lower (2.56:1) rear axle ratio, and a switch that shut off the air-conditioner compressor when the gas pedal was pushed to the floor. Various models could be ordered with special ride/handling suspension packages that included front and rear stabilizer bars, firmer springs, and stiffer shock absorber valving. LeSabre Sport Coupe and Riviera carried this suspension as standard, along with quick-ratio power steering. Standard body colors for all 1977 models were: black, white, silver, light blue, dark blue or medium green metallic, light buckskin, buckskin, brown, firethorn or orange metallic. Dark blue green metallic, red and cream gold were offered as standard on all except Skyhawk and Skylark. Dark aqua metallic, bright yellow and bright red came only on Skyhawk and Skylark. Rivieras could also have blue, amber or red firemist.

SKYHAWK - SERIES 4H - V-6 - For its third model year, the subcompact Skyhawk got a new, completely different checkerboard grille: simply two rows of eight holes each, across the body-colored grille panel. Otherwise, there was little change in appearance. Built on an H-Special body, Skyhawk was a more luxurious, perhaps even sportier version of Chevrolet's Monza. Once again, the swept-back design came in standard or 'S' hatchback form. Large, easy-to-read instruments included an 7000 R.P.M. tachometer, ammeter, and electric clock. Though similar, the 'S' edition lacked such extras as the tach and clock. As before, Skyhawk was powered by a 231 cu. in. (3.8-liter) V-6 with standard four-speed manual shift. Five-speed overdrive gearbox and automatic transmission were optional. The standard edition had front and rear stabilizer bars; the 'S' had front only. High-back bucket seats were upholstered in cloth or vinyl. The 'S' version also lacked the white, gold or black accent stripes. Skyhawks had side window reveal moldings, front and rear bumper guards, and bumper protection strips, plus a set-and-close door locking system. Options included a sliding glass sunroof, or fixed Astroroof with targa-type aluminum accent band that stretched over the car's roof.

1977 Buick, Skylark sedan. (OCW)

SKYLARK - SERIES 4X - V-6/V-8 - Buick's compact derivative of the old Chevrolet Nova (also related to Olds Omega) again came in seven models: low-priced 'S', European-inspired S/R (Sports/Rallye), and standard Skylark. Coupe, hatchback and sedan bodies were again available. The 'S' coupe lacked some details, such as a cigarette lighter, roof and wheel-opening moldings, and inside day/night mirror. Though similar to before, the front end was changed. The new Skylark grille was composed entirely of vertical bars, peaked at the nose, with a wide horizontal bar across the top. Dual round headlamps were again flanked by clear park/signal lamps that wrapped around the fender into amber lenses. As in 1976, Skylark's three-hole "ventiport" fender trim piece sat just ahead of the wide bodyside

molding that extended all the way to the tip of the rear quarter panels. A new instrument panel held large round gauges. Standard engine was the 231 cu. in. (3.8-liter) V-6, with two 5.0-liter V-8s available: 301 and 305 cu. in. Also optional was a 350 V-8 with four-barrel. All models had High-Energy ignition, front disc brakes, and front stabilizer bar. Skylark's S/R had standard Turbo Hydra-matic and full-length sports shifting console; others, three-speed manual (column shift). S/R also had a stand-up hood ornament, roof drip moldings, special cloth bucket seats with reclining right seatback, map pockets in doors, Rallye steering wheel, and console storage bins. Skylark's suspension consisted of wide-span front lower control arms with coil springs, and multiple-leaf rear springs. A new Acoustical Package to cut road noise consisted of special insulation in roof, floor and dashboard, as well as inside and under the doors, and between cowl and fenders. Also optional: a thickly-padded Landau top with small side windows, accented by brushed-aluminum band; and a V-6 Highway Economy Package.

1977 Buick, Century Special coupe with optional styled wheels. (OCW)

CENTURY - SERIES 4A - V-6/V-8 - Century's body, lowered for 1976, received a new grille and header molding this year. As in 1976, coupes displayed a different front-end treatment, with canted-back grille, than the sedans. Century and Century Special coupe rooflines swept back and framed a large rear quarter window. The Custom coupe had a formal roofline like Regal's, plus the Regal rectangular opera windows. Century sedan's front-end looked similar to the Regal sedan, while coupes repeated the 1976 design, with crosshatching behind six large grille slots framed by body-colored segments. The model lineup included three coupes, two sedans, and a two- or three-seat wagon. Sedans and wagons were four inches longer in wheelbase than coupes. Station wagons had a 350 cu. in. (5.7-liter) V-8; other models, a 231 cu. in. V-6 or optional V-8. For 1977, the V-6 engine lost some weight. Power steering was standard. So were power brakes on the Custom Sedan and wagons. Three-speed manual (column) shift remained standard, except for wagons which had Turbo Hydra-matic. All models had front and rear ashtrays, and a wide-view day/night inside mirror. All except Special had front and rear bumper protection strips. Wipers had "mist control" that gave a single pass when you touched the switch. Custom coupes could have a Hurst hatch roof that consisted of twin rectangular panels of tinted glass, which could be removed and stored in the trunk (in a special "Hatch Hutch" case). Two air conditioners were optional: Climate-Control or Custom-Aire. Joining the option list: the V-6 Highway Economy Package, consisting of specially tuned engine, specially calibrated Turbo Hydra-matic, 2.56:1 axle ratio, and wide-open-throttle air-conditioning shutoff.

REGAL - SERIES 4AJ - V-6/V-8 - Regal's coupe and sedan, like Century, received a new grille and header molding. A look more formal than Century came from the vertical, squarish grille and squared-off roofline with a small, formal opera window in the rear pillar. The coupe's grille was new but not drastically different from the 1976 version. Its small vertical segments separated into six sections by two horizontal strips and a narrow vertical bar. Quad headlamps and park/signal lamps were also

similar to the prior model. A 'V6' emblem sat in the front of front fenders. Regal's sedan again had its own front-end design featuring vertically stacked rectangular headlamps and vertical signal lamps, plus a mildly revised grille divided into four sections by dominant single horizontal and vertical bars. The subdued vertical strips sat farther apart, separating the grille into five segments on each side. 'Regal' script was at the lower corner. Instruments were recessed in simulated woodgrain paneling, with two large dials directly ahead of the driver. Power front disc brakes were standard. Turbo Hydra-matic was standard on sedan; three-speed manual shift on coupe. Options included the Hurst hatch roof (like Century Custom coupe), plus Highway Economy Package with specially tuned V-6 engine. Regal's S/R package included reclining bucket seats with new black velour fabric; large center console with aircraft-grip shift lever; rallye steering wheel; headlamp dimmer in the turn-signal lever; and whitewall steel-belted radial tires.

1977 Buick, LeSabre Custom sedan. (OCW)

LESABRE - SERIES 4B - V-6/V-8 - Downsized LeSabre was 10 in. shorter, 2.7 in. narrower, and 665 pounds lighter than before, described as "the American full-size car redefined." Wheelbase dropped from 123.4 to 115.9 in., while trunk space actually grew: from 16.8 cu. ft. in 1976 to 21.2 in the "shrunken" version. Inside, head and leg room managed to grow as well. LeSabre could still carry six adults and luggage in comfort. Aluminum reinforced bumpers cut 135 pounds from the car's weight, while a smaller frame saved 90 pounds. A 231 cu. in. V-6 was now standard. New styling included rear-canted headlamp bezels that sloped rearward from the upright grille, full-framed doors, and a pillared roof design. The airy-four door hardtop and thin-pillared variant were gone for good, replaced by sensible pillars and frames. The squared-off roof was designed to give maximum rear seat headroom. LeSabre's B-body was related to Chevrolet Caprice and Pontiac Bonneville/Parisienne, closer yet to Olds Delta 88, which received similar downsizing this year. Wraparound red/amber taillamps also served as side marker lights. Seven vertical bars divided the crosshatch grille into eight sections, slightly pointed at the front. Quad rectangular headlamps were directly above clear park/signal lamps; cornering lenses at the tip of front fenders. Farther back on the fender was the familiar three-hole "ventiport" LeSabre emblem. At the back of the rear fenders, a 'LeSabre' badge sat ahead of the wraparound taillamps. Bodyside moldings extended between front and rear wheel openings, but no farther onto the fenders. LeSabre was now powered by the 231 cu. in. (3.8-liter) V-6 or a choice of three optional V-8 engines: familiar 350 cu. in. (5.7-liter) four-barrel, new 403 cu. in. (6.6-liter) four-barrel, or new 301 cu. in. (5.0-liter) with two-barrel carburetor. Five models were offered this year: LeSabre and LeSabre Custom coupe or sedan, plus a new European-inspired LeSabre Sport Coupe. That one had a standard 301 cu. in. (5.0-liter) V-8, thin white-stripe radial tires, special steering linkage and suspension with higher-rate springs, Rallye steering wheel, chrome wheels, amber lights and, in Buick's words, "functional, downright mean-looking black accents." That meant black vertical grille bars; black anodized window frame, windshield and rear window moldings; wide black louvered rocker moldings; and wide black pillar appliqués. Styling touches also included a stand-up tri-shield hood ornament, plus 'LeSabre

Sport Coupe' nameplates on body and dash. Coupes had new inertia front seatback locks. Instrument panels were new, a maintenance-free Freedom battery and diagnostic connectors standard. Also standard: rear door (or rear quarter) armrests. Full-Flo ventilation, plus bumper protection strips front and rear. Crushed velour cloth or vinyl bench seats were standard on base LeSabre models; notchback seats on Custom and Sport Coupe. The turn signal lever doubled as a dimmer switch. An optional Highway Economy Package, intended for cruising rather than urban stop-and-go, included a specially-tuned V-6, specially calibrated automatic transmission, 2.56:1 axle ratio, and larger (24.5-gallon) gas tank.

ESTATE WAGON - SERIES 4BR - V-8 - The basic Estate Wagon's front-end appearance was just like LeSabre, but a Limited package transformed the wagon to Electra's front-end styling. Limited equipment included custom 60/40 notchback seats, power windows, power door and tailgate locks, tilt steering wheel, custom seat/shoulder belts, sunshade map light, quartz crystal clock (dial or digital), acoustic package, stand-up hood ornament, and woodgrain vinyl appliqué. The package also contained wheel openings, wide rocker panel, lower front fender and rear quarter, window frame scalp, and belt reveal moldings; plus bumper guards, luggage rack and air deflector, remote-control left mirror, and chrome-plated wheels. Base and Limited editions were available with either two or three seats; 60/40 notchback seating (cloth or vinyl) standard on Limited, vinyl bench seats on base models. Tiny lamps at the dashboard underside "floodlit" the instrument dials for night visibility. Standard equipment included a Freedom battery, power steering and brakes, 350 cu. in. (5.7-liter) V-8 with four-barrel carburetor, and Turbo Hydra-matic. Estate Wagons also had diagnostic connectors, lockable storage compartments, and rocker panel moldings. The 403 cu. in. (6.6-liter) V-8 was optional. So were five different sound systems. The standard three-way tailgate could fold down or swing open like a door, with power window up or down. Cargo area measured 87 cubic feet.

1977 Buick, Electra Limited sedan with optional wire wheel covers. (OCW)

ELECTRA - SERIES 4C - V-8 - Like the LeSabre, Electra lost 10 in. in overall length in its downsizing, but remained similar in form to the previous 225 model. Fender lines were the same as in 1976, but with a more blunt front end and shorter overhangs, both front and rear. Buick called the fresh silhouette "lean, aerodynamic....a car of today, the future, instead of a tribute to the past." Electra's C-body was similar to Olds Ninety-Eight, slightly longer than LeSabre and riding the same platform as Cadillac DeVille. Turning diameter was 4 ft. tighter than in 1976. Models included a 225 coupe and sedan, Limited coupe and sedan, and top-line Park Avenue option package for the Limited sedan. All seated six with ease. Buyers now began with a standard 350 cu. in. (5.7-liter) engine, or could opt for the 403 cu. in. (6.6-liter) V-8. The big old 7.5-liter powerplant was gone. Power steering and brakes, Turbo Hydra-matic, diagnostic connectors, and Freedom battery were standard. New interior styling featured improved rear-seat access on coupes, a result of new inertia front seatback locks. The new crosshatch grille was divided into eight sections by two horizontal bars and three vertical bars. Quad rectangular headlamps sat atop clear quad rectangular park/signal lamps; amber lenses at front of fenders,

just above the bumper. Electra's four-port trim piece was prominent at upper rear of front fenders, as in prior models. The 'Electra' nameplate stood at the back of the rear fenders, just below the long, slim bodyside molding. Wide taillamps were divided into upper and lower sections by a horizontal trim strip. Electras had bumper protective strips front and rear. Limiteds sported wide rocker panel moldings. The new instrument panel's controls and gauges were set in brushed aluminum. Six sound systems were optional, including a digital-readout stereo radio that showed station frequency, time, date, and elapsed travel time. The Park Avenue package included a thickly-padded vinyl roof with coach lamps. Tiny lamps at the dashboard underside "floodlit" the instrument dials for night visibility. Cloth or vinyl notchback seats were standard on the 225; custom cloth or vinyl 60/40 notchback seating on Limited models; 50/50 cloth seats on the Park Avenue.

1977 Buick, Riviera coupe. (OCW)

RIVIERA - SERIES 4BZ - V-8 - Buick's front-drive personal-luxury coupe received a total restyle, losing 5 in. of length and some 700 pounds. A new suspension was installed to improve roadholding and handling, while optional four-wheel disc brakes promised superior stopping power. Up front was a new vertical-bar grille. Body design included a pillared roof and full-frame door glass. Until a new downsized version emerged for 1979, Riviera was actually related to the B-body LeSabre. Its space-efficient six-passenger interior was more spacious and comfortable than before, with increased rear head/leg room. Trunk capacity grew too. Like its forerunners, the reduced Riviera was aimed at the buyer who would "like to surround himself with quality. With things that are undeniably special." Riviera's "demeanor is that of a sporty road car," Buick insisted; "Its interior rivals the most opulent luxury cars." The new upright, formal appearing, vertical-bar grille—a bit reminiscent of Rolls-Royce—curved outward at the base in a style that would soon become markedly Buick. Quad rectangular headlamps sat over quad clear park/signal lamps. Optional cornering lamps used a combination of clear, rectangular horizontal lens and smaller amber lens at the forward segment of each front fender. Standard fittings included a no-maintenance Freedom battery; lights for front ashtray, under-dash courtesy, glove compartment, trunk, and instrument flood; front and rear bumper protective strips; depressed-park windshield wipers; remote-control sport mirror on left side; custom wire wheel covers; and Rallye steering wheel. The new standard suspension included large-diameter front and rear anti-sway bars, plus special springs and shocks. New this year were inertia front seatback locks and a restyled instrument panel. Three special firemist exterior colors were available, as well as three two-tone combinations. Tiny lamps at the dashboard underside could "floodlight" the instrument dials for night visibility. Buyers could have either the 350 cu. in. (5.7-liter) engine or new 403 cu. in. (6.6-liter) V-8. Standard 50/50 notchback seat with twin armrests were upholstered in plush velour cloth or vinyl. Custom wire wheel covers were standard. Options included a leather-covered steering wheel and CB transceiver. Lighted coach lamps came with the Landau vinyl top.

I.D. DATA: The 13-symbol Vehicle Identification Number (VIN) was located on the upper left surface of the instrument panel, visible through the windshield. The first digit is '4', indicating the Buick division. The second symbol is a letter indicating series: 'S' Skyhawk; 'T' Skyhawk; 'B' Skylark; 'C'

Skylark S/R; 'W' Skylark S; 'D' Century; 'E' Century Special; 'H' Century Custom; 'J' Regal; 'K' Century Custom wagon, 'F' LeSabre Sport Coupe; 'N' LeSabre; 'P' LeSabre Custom; 'R' Estate Wagon; 'Z' Riviera; 'V' Electra 225; 'X' Electra Limited. Next come two digits that denote body type: '07' Skyhawk hatchback coupe; '17' Skylark 2-dr. hatchback coupe; '27' Skylark 2-dr. coupe; '69' 4-dr. sedan; '29' 4-dr. Colonnade sedan; '37' Century/Regal 2-dr. Colonnade coupe or full-size 2-dr. coupe; '57' 2-dr. Colonnade coupe; '35' 4-dr. 2-seat wagon. The fifth symbol is a letter indicating engine code: 'C' V6-231 2Bbl.; 'Y' V8-301 2Bbl.; 'U' V8-305 2Bbl.; 'H' V8-350 2Bbl.; 'L' V8-350 4Bbl. (LM1); 'R' V8-350 4Bbl. (L34); 'J' V8-350 4Bbl. (L77); 'K' V8-403 4Bbl. (L80). The sixth symbol denotes model year ('7' 1977). Next is a plant code: '2' Ste. Therese (Canada); 'K' Leeds, MO; 'L' Van Nuys, CA; 'T' Tarrytown, NY; 'B' Baltimore, MD; 'G' Framingham, MA; 'H' Flint, MI; 'Z' Fremont, CA; 'C' Southgate, CA; 'X' Fairfax, KS; 'E' Linden, NJ. The final six digits are the sequential serial number, which began with 100001 except for Skyhawks (700001 up); LeSabres, Estate Wagons, Electras and Rivieras built at Flint (400001 up). Engine numbers were stamped on the front right of the block, except for L34 350 cu. in. V-8 and 403 cu. in. V-8, which were stamped on the front of the left side of the block. A body number plate on the shroud identified model year, car division, series, style, body assembly plant, body number, trim combination, modular seat code, paint code, and date built code.

SKYHAWK (V-6)

Model No.	Body/Style No.	Body Type & Seating	Factory Price	Shipping Weight	Prod. Total
4H	T07	2-dr 'S' Hatch-4P	3981	2805	Note 1
4H	S07	2-dr Hatch-4P	4294	2817	Note 1

Note 1: Total model year production, 24,044 Skyhawks (built in Canada).

SKYLARK 'S' (V-6/V-8)

| 4X | W27 | 2-dr Coupe-6P | 3642/3717 | 3258/3315 | Note 2 |

SKYLARK (V-6/V-8)

4X	B27	2-dr Coupe-6P	3765/3830	3257/3314	49,858
4X	B17	2-dr Hatch-6P	3941/4006	3379/3436	5,316
4X	B69	4-dr Sedan-6P	3825/3890	3296/3353	48,121

SKYLARK S/R (V-6/V-8)

4X	C27	2-dr Coupe-5P	4527/4592	3277/3384	5,023
4X	C17	2-dr Hatch-5P	4695/4760	3304/3411	1,154
4X	C69	4-dr Sedan-5P	4587/4652	3271/3378	4,000

Note 2: Skylark 'S' is included in production total for base Skylark coupe. Of the 103,295 Skylarks built 22,098 had a V-8 engine; of the total 10,177 Skylark S/R models, 5,040 had a V-8.

CENTURY SPECIAL (V-6)

| 4A | E37 | 2-dr Coupe-6P | 4170 | 3590 | Note 3 |

CENTURY (V-6/V-8)

| 4A | D37 | 2-dr Coupe-6P | 4303/4470 | 3520/3643 | 52,864 |
| 4A | D29 | 4-dr Sedan-6P | 4363/4530 | 3692/3815 | 29,065 |

Note 3: Century Special production is included in base Century coupe total. Of the 81,629 Century models built, 25,797 had a V-8 engine.

CENTURY CUSTOM (V-6/V-8)

4A	H57	2-dr Coupe-6P	4627/4794	3549/3672	20,834
4A	H29	4-dr Sedan-6P	4687/4854	3688/3811	13,645
4A	K35	4-dr Sta Wag-6P	----/5218	----/4260	19,282
4A	(AQ4)	4-dr Sta Wag-8P	----/5371	----/N/A	Note 4

Note 4: Three-seat wagon was an option package; production total included in K35 figure. Of the 53,761 Century Custom models built, only 12,142 had a V-6 engine.

REGAL (V-6/V-8)

| 4A | J57 | 2-dr Coupe-6P | 4712/4915 | 3550/3673 | 174,560 |
| 4A | J29 | 4-dr Sedan-6P | ----/5243 | ----/3928 | 17,946 |

Note 5: Only 36,125 Regal coupes carried a V-6 engine.

LESABRE (V-6/V-8)

| 4B | N37 | 2-dr Coupe-6P | 5032/5142 | 3466/3578 | 8,455 |
| 4B | N69 | 4-dr Sedan-6P | 5092/5202 | 3504/3616 | 19,827 |

LESABRE CUSTOM (V-6/V-8)

4B	F37	2-dr Spt Cpe-6P	----/5818	----/3634	Note 6
4B	P37	2-dr Coupe-6P	5321/5431	3474/3586	Note 6
4B	P69	4-dr Sedan-6P	5381/5491	3516/3628	103,855

Note 6: Total production, 58,589 Custom coupes (including Sport Coupe). Of all LeSabres built, just 19,744 were V-6 powered.

ESTATE WAGON (V-8)

Model No.	Body/Style No.	Body Type & Seating	Factory Price	Shipping Weight	Prod. Total
4B	R35	4-dr Sta Wag-6P	5902	4015	25,075
4B	(AQ4)	4-dr Sta Wag-8P	6078	N/A	Note 7

Note 7: Three-seat Estate Wagon was an option package; production total is included in two-seat figure. Limited version was also an option package

ELECTRA 225 (V-8)

| 4C | V37 | 2-dr Coupe-6P | 6672 | 3761 | 15,762 |
| 4C | V69 | 4-dr Sedan-6P | 6865 | 3814 | 25,633 |

ELECTRA LIMITED (V-8)

| 4C | X37 | 2-dr Coupe-6P | 7032 | 3785 | 37,871 |
| 4C | X69 | 4-dr Sedan-6P | 7225 | 3839 | 82,361 |

Note 8: Electra Park Avenue was a trim option, not a separate model.

RIVIERA (V-8)

| 4E | Z37 | 2-dr Coupe-6P | 7357 | 3784 | 26,138 |

FACTORY PRICE AND WEIGHT NOTE: Figures before the slash are for V-6 engine, after the slash for V-8.

ENGINES: BUICK BASE EQUIPMENT V-6 (Skyhawk, Skylark, Century/Regal coupe, Century/Custom sedan, LeSabre): 90-degree, overhead-valve V-6. Cast iron alloy block and head. Displacement: 231 cu. in. (3.8 liters). Bore & stroke: 3.8 x 3.4 in. Compression ratio: 8.0:1. Brake horsepower: 105 at 3200 R.P.M. Torque: 185 lb.-ft. at 2000 R.P.M. Four main bearings. Hydraulic valve lifters. Carburetor: 2Bbl. Rochester 2GC. VIN Code: C. BASE V-8 (Skylark, LeSabre Sport Coupe); OPTIONAL (other LeSabres): 90-degree overhead-valve V-8. Cast iron alloy block and head. Displacement: 301 cu. in. (5.0 liters). Bore & stroke: 4.0 x 3.0 in. Compression ratio: 8.2:1. Brake horsepower: 135 at 4000 R.P.M. Torque: 245 lb.-ft. at 2000 R.P.M. Five main bearings. Hydraulic valve lifters. Carburetor: 2Bbl. Rochester M2MC. Built by Pontiac. VIN Code: Y. Ordering Code: L27. ALTERNATE 305 V-8; OPTIONAL (Skylark Century wagon): 90 degree overhead-valve V-8. Cast iron alloy block and head. Displacement: 305 cu. in. (5.0 liters). Bore & stroke: 3.736 x 3.48 in. Compression ratio: 8.5:1. Brake horsepower: 145 at 3800 R.P.M. Torque: 245 lb.-ft. at 2400 R.P.M. Five main bearings. Hydraulic valve lifters. Carburetor: 2Bbl. Roch. 2GC. VIN Code: U. BASE V-8 (Regal sedan); OPTIONAL (Century/Custom cpe/sed, Regal cpe): 90-degree, overhead valve V-8. Cast iron alloy block and head. Displacement: 350 cu. in. (5.7 liters). Bore & stroke: 3.80 x 3.85 in. Compression ratio: 8.1:1. Brake horsepower: 140 at 3200 R.P.M. Torque: 280 lb.-ft. at 1400 R.P.M. Five main bearings. Hydraulic valve lifters. Carburetor: 2Bbl. Roch. 2GC. VIN Code: H. Ordering Code: L32. BASE V-8 (Century wagon, Electra, Estate, Riviera); OPTIONAL (Skylark, Century/Regal cpe/sed, LeSabre): 90 degree, overhead valve V-8. Cast iron alloy block and head. Displacement: 350 cu. in. (5.7 liters). Bore & stroke: 3.80 x 3.85 in. Compression ratio: 8.0:1. Brake horsepower: 155 at 3400 R.P.M. Torque: 275 lb.-ft. at 1800 R.P.M. Five main bearings. Hydraulic valve lifters. Carburetor: 4Bbl. Rochester M4MC. VIN Code: J. ALTERNATE 350-4 V-8; OPTIONAL (Skylark, Century/Custom cpe/sed, Regal, LeSabre): 90-degree, overhead valve V-8. Cast iron alloy block and head. Displacement: 350 cu. in. (5.7 liters). Bore & stroke: 4.057 x 3.385 in. Compression ratio: 7.9:1. Brake horsepower: 170 at 3800 R.P.M. Torque: 275 lb.-ft. at 2000 R.P.M. Five main bearings. Hydraulic valve lifters. Carburetor: 4Bbl. Roch. M4MC. Built by Oldsmobile. VIN Code: R. Ordering Code: L34. Not available in California. ALTERNATE 350-4 V-8 (Chevrolet-built): 90 degree, overhead valve V-8. Cast iron alloy block and head. Displacement: 350 cu. in. (5.7 liters). Bore & stroke: 4.00 x 3.48 in. Compression ratio: 8.5:1. Brake horsepower: 170 at 3800 R.P.M. Torque: 270 lb.-ft. at 2400 R.P.M. Five main bearings. Hydraulic valve lifters. Carburetor: 4Bbl. Roch. M4MC. VIN Code: L. Ordering Code: LM1. OPTIONAL V-8 (Century wagon, LeSabre, Electra, Estate Wagon, Riviera): 90-degree, overhead valve V-8. Cast iron alloy block and head. Displacement: 403 cu. in. (6.6 liters). Bore & stroke: 4.351 x 3.385 in. Compression ratio: 8.5:1. Brake horsepower: 185 at 3600 R.P.M. Torque: 320 lb.-ft. at 2200 R.P.M. Five main bear-

ings. Hydraulic valve lifters. Carburetor: 4Bbl. Roch. M4MC. Built by Oldsmobile. VIN Code: K. Ordering Code: L80.

CHASSIS DATA: Wheelbase: (Skyhawk) 97.0 in.; (Skylark) 111.0 in.; (Century/Regal cpe) 112.0 in.; (Century/Regal sed/wag) 116.0 in.; (LeSabre/Estate/Riviera) 115.9 in.; (Electra) 118.9 in. Overall length: (Skyhawk) 179.3 in.; (Skylark) 200.2 in.; (Century/Regal cpe) 209.8 in.; (Century/Regal sedan) 213.6 in.; (Century wagon) 218.3 in.; (LeSabre/Riv) 218.2 in.; (Electra) 222.1 in.; (Estate) 216.7 in. Height: (Skyhawk) 50.1 in.; (Skylark 2-dr.) 52.2 in.; (Skylark 4-dr.) 53.1 in.; (Century/Regal cpe) 52.7 in.; (Century/Regal sed) 53.6 in.; (Century wag) 55.3 in.; (LeSabre cpe)54.6 in.; (LeSabre sed) 55.3 in.; (Electra cpe) 54.8 in.; (Electra sed) 55.7 in.; (Estate) 57.0 in.; (Riviera) 54.6 in. Width: (Skyhawk) 65.4 in.; (Skylark) 72.7 in.; (Century/Regal cpe) 76.5 in.; (Century/Regal sed/wag) 79.0 in.; (LeSabre/Electra/Estate/Riviera) 77.2 in. Front Tread: (Skyhawk) 54.7 in.; (Skylark) 59.1 in.; (Century/Regal) 61.5 in.; (LeSabre/Electra/Riviera) 61.8 in.; (Estate) 62.2 in. Rear Tread: (Skyhawk) 53.6 in.; (Skylark) 59.7 in.; (Estate) 64.1 in.; (others) 60.7 in. Standard Tires: (Skyhawk) BR78 x 13 SBR; (Skyhawk 'S') B78 x 13; (Skylark) E78 x 14; (Skylark S/R) ER78 x 14 SBR WSW; (Century/Regal cpe) FR78 x 15 SBR exc. V-6, GBR; (Century/Regal sed) FR78 x 15 SBR; (Century wagon) HR78 x 15 SBR; (LeSabre) FR78 x 15 GBR; (Electra/Riviera) GR78 x 15; (Estate) HR78 x 15 SBR.

TECHNICAL: Transmission: Three-speed, fully synchronized manual gearbox (column shift) standard on Skylark, Century cpe/sed, and Regal cpe; Turbo Hydra-matic optional. Four-speed, fully synchronized floor shift standard on Skyhawk; five-speed and automatic optional. Turbo Hydra-matic standard on Skylark S/R, Regal sedan, LeSabre, Electra, Estate and Riviera. Three-speed manual transmission gear ratios: (1st) 3.11:1; (2nd) 1.84:1; (3rd) 1.00:1; (Rev) 3.22:1. Four-speed gear ratios: (1st) 3.11:1; (2nd) 2.20:1; (3rd) 1.47:1; (4th) 1.00:1; (Rev) 3.11:1. Five-speed gear ratios: (1st) 3.40:1; (2nd) 2.08:1; (3rd) 1.39:1; (4th) 1.00:1; (5th) 0.80:1; (Rev) 3.36:1. Automatic trans. gear ratios: (1st) 2.52:1; (2nd) 1.52:1; (3rd) 1.00:1; (Rev) 2.08:1. Skyhawk auto. trans. gear ratios: (1st) 2.74:1; (2nd) 1.57:1; (3rd) 1.00:1; (Rev) 2.07:1. Standard axle ratio: (Skyhawk) 2.56:1; (Skylark) 3.08:1 w/manual, 2.56:1 w/automatic, 2.41:1 w/V-8; (Century/Regal) 3.08:1 w/manual, 2.73:1 w/automatic, 2.41:1 w/350 V-8; (Century wagon) 2.73:1; (LeSabre V-6) 2.73:1; (LeSabre V-8) 2.41:1; (Electra/Riviera) 2.41:1; (Estate) 2.73:1 exc. 2.56:1 w/403 V-8. Steering: recirculating ball; variable-ratio power steering standard on Century/Regal, LeSabre, Electra, Estate and Riviera. Suspension and Body Construction: same as 1976. Brakes: front disc, rear drum; power brakes standard on LeSabre/Electra/Riviera plus Century Custom sedan/wagon and Regal. Four-wheel power disc brakes optional on Riviera. High-Energy electronic ignition (HEI) on all engines. Unleaded fuel only.

DRIVETRAIN OPTIONS: Engines: 301 cu. in. V-8, 2Bbl.: Skylark ($65); LeSabre ($110). 350 cu. in. V-8, 2Bbl.: Century/Cust, Regal cpe ($167). 350 cu. in. V-8, 4Bbl.: Skylark ($155); Century/Cust. Regal cpe ($222); Regal sed. ($55); LeSabre ($200); LeSabre spt cpe ($90). 403 cu. in. V-8, 4Bbl.: LeSabre ($287); LeSabre spt cpe ($177); Century wag, Estate/Electra/Riviera ($65). V-6 economy pkg.: Skylark, 'S' ($302); Skylark S/R, LeSabre ($25). Transmission/Differential: Five-speed manual floor shift: Skyhawk ($248). Turbo Hydra-matic trans.: Skyhawk ($248); Skylark, Century cpe/sed, Regal cpe ($282); Optional rear axle ratio: Century/Regal 3.08:1 or 3.23:1 (NC); LeSabre/Electra/Riviera 3.08:1 (NC); LeSabre 3.23:1 (NC). Positive traction differential ($51-$58). Power accessories: Power brakes, Skyhawk ($58), Skylark/Century ($61). Four-wheel disc brakes: Riviera ($186). Power steering Skyhawk ($130); Skylark ($147). Suspension: WH5 handling package: Skyhawk ($11-$133). F40 Firm Ride handling package: Skylark ($22); Century/Regal/LeSabre/Electra/Riviera ($18). FE2 Rallye ride/handling package: Skylark ($42); Century, except Special wagon, Regal ($36); Riviera ($18). Automatic level control: Cen-

tury/Regal/LeSabre/Electra/Riviera ($102). Other: Trailer towing flasher/harness ($20-$32) except Skyhawk. Heavy-duty 80-amp alternator: Century/Regal/LeSabre/Electra/Riviera ($37-$42). Heavy-duty Energizer battery ($16-$18). Freedom battery: Century/Regal ($30). Heavy-duty cooling ($27-$55) except Skyhawk. Heavy-duty radiator: Skylark ($19); Engine block heater ($13) except Skyhawk. High altitude emission system ($22). California emission system ($70-$71).

SKYHAWK CONVENIENCE/APPEARANCE OPTIONS: Option Packages: Free Spirit Skyhawk pkg. ($148). Appearance group: 'S' ($67). Convenience group ($21). Shadow light Astroroof w/roof crown molding ($591). Manual glass sunroof ($210). Comfort/Convenience: Air cond. ($442). Rear defogger, electric ($71). Soft Ray tinted glass ($48). Tinted windshield ($40). Rallye steering wheel: 'S' ($37). Tilt steering ($50). Electric clock: 'S' ($18); clock and tach ($63). Right sport mirror ($13). Remote left sport mirror: 'S' ($16). Entertainment: AM radio ($71). AM/FM radio ($134). AM/FM stereo radio ($219). AM radio and tape player ($197). AM/FM stereo radio and tape ($316). Rear speaker for non-stereo radios ($20). Radio accommodation pkg. ($22). Exterior Trim: Door edge guards ($9). Roof crown molding ($162). Protective bodyside moldings ($25-$40). Hawk accent stripe ($33). Interior Trim/Upholstery: Full-length console: 'S' ($77). Adjustable driver's seatback ($18). Front/rear mats ($15). Custom seatbelts ($14). Wheels: Custom sport wheels ($79-$90). Deluxe wheel covers ($42). Wheel trim rings ($35). Tires: B78 x 13 WSW: 'S' ($30-$38). BR78 x 13 SBR blackwall: 'S' ($82-$103). BR78 x 13 SBR whitewall ($38-$141). White-letter tires ($51-$168). Conventional spare tire (NC).

SKYLARK CONVENIENCE/APPEARANCE OPTIONS: Option Packages: Accessory pkg. (day/night mirror, lighter): 'S' ($12). Acoustic insulation pkg. ($24-$36). Convenience group ($29-$31). Appearance group: 'S' ($33). Comfort/Convenience: Air cond. ($478). Cruise Master ($80). Three-speed wipers w/delay ($30). Rear defogger, blower-type ($48). Power windows ($108-$151). Electric door locks ($68-$96). Rallye steering wheel ($37) exc. S/R. Tilt steering ($57). Soft Ray tinted glass ($50). Tinted windshield ($42). Dual horns ($7). Electric clock ($21). Headlamps-on indicator ($7). Electric trunk release ($21). Remote-control mirror ($15). Sport mirrors: left remote, right manual ($28). Entertainment: AM radio ($75). AM/FM radio ($137). AM/FM stereo radio ($233). AM radio and tape player ($337). CB Transceiver ($195). Rear speaker ($21). Exterior Trim: Custom vinyl roof: S/R ($93). Custom vinyl roof w/hood ornament: base, 'S' ($98). Landau top ($162-$167). Two-tone paint ($42). Special exterior paint ($116). Swing-out rear quarter vent window: two-doors ($51). Protective bodyside moldings ($38). Rocker panel moldings ($16). Wide rocker appearance group ($34). Decklid molding ($8). Custom door and window frame moldings ($25-$31). Door edge guards ($9-$13). Bodyside accent stripes ($25). Bumper guards, front ($19); front/rear ($38). Bumper strips, front/rear ($29). Interior Trim/Upholstery: Full-length console ($75). Vinyl bucket seats: base Skylark ($84). Custom trim bench seats/interior: base ($151). Custom seatbelts ($14-$16). Front carpet savers ($9). Carpet savers and handy mats ($15). Carpeted door trim with map pocket and reflector: Skylark ($37). Wheels: Styled wheels ($82-$94). Chrome-plated wheels ($112-$132). Deluxe wheel covers ($33). Styled wheel covers ($91). Deluxe wire wheel covers ($121). Tires: E78 x 14 WSW ($31-$39) exc. S/R. ER78 x 14 SBR BSW ($69-$86) exc. S/R. ER78 x 14 SBR WSW ($100-$125) exc. S/R. FR78 x 14 SBR WLT ($29-$156). Stowaway spare tire ($17); S/R cpe (NC).

CENTURY/REGAL CONVENIENCE/APPEARANCE OPTIONS: Option Packages: Regal S/R Coupe pkg. ($432-$499). Electric sunroof: cpe ($394). Hurst hatch roof: Century Cust, Regal cpe ($587). Convenience group ($16-$31). Comfort/Convenience: Air cond. ($499). Custom Aire ($538). Cruise Master ($80). Rear defogger: electric ($82); blower-type ($48). Soft Ray

tinted glass ($54). Tinted windshield ($43). Six-way power driver's seat ($137). Custom steering wheel ($17). Rallye steering wheel ($37). Tilt steering ($57). Power windows ($108-$151). Electric door locks ($68-$96). Electric trunk release ($21). Remote-control tailgate lock: Century wag ($21). Electric clock ($21). Headlamps-on indicator ($7). Instrument gauges and electric clock ($45) exc. wag. Fuel usage gauge ($27). Speed alert ($15). Dome reading lamp ($16). Three-speed wiper with delay ($30). Lighting and Mirrors: Remote control mirror ($15). Sport mirrors: left remote ($28). Lighted visor vanity mirror ($42). Trunk light: Century Cust, Regal cpe ($5). Entertainment: AM radio ($79). AM/FM radio ($142). AM/FM stereo radio ($233). AM radio w/stereo tape player ($213). AM/FM stereo radio w/tape ($337). AM/FM stereo radio and CB ($453). CB Transceiver ($195). Rear speaker ($21). Front/rear speakers ($44). Exterior Trim: Landau vinyl top: Century Cust, Regal cpe ($120); Century/Spec. ($156). Custom vinyl top: Century cpe, Regal ($111). Custom vinyl top w/hood ornament: Century/Cust cpe ($116). Swing-out rear quarter vent windows: Century wag ($51). Two-tone paint ($42) exc. wagon. Special color paint ($134). Bumper guards, front/rear ($38); rear, Century wag ($19). Bumper strips: Century Special ($30). Protective bodyside moldings ($27). Lower bodyside molding ($36). Door edge guards ($9-$13). Wheel opening moldings: Century, Special ($19). Bodyside accent stripes ($45). Woodgrain vinyl appliqué: Century wag ($185). Luggage rack: Century wag ($76). Air deflector: Century wag ($26). Interior Trim/Upholstery: Full-length console ($75). Custom notchback seat trim: Century/Spec. ($136-$163). Custom vinyl notchback seat trim: Century Cust cpe, Regal ($108); cloth ($140). Custom vinyl 60/40 seat trim: Century Cust, Regal cpe ($199): cloth ($231). Custom reclining seat trim: Century Cust cpe ($244). Custom vinyl bucket seats: Century/Spec. cpe ($143-$168). Custom seatbelts ($14-$18). Third seat: Century wag ($152). Front/rear carpeting: Century Special ($25). Load floor area carpet: Century wag ($24). Front carpet savers ($10). Carpet savers and handy mats ($17). Litter pocket ($7). Wheels: Chrome-plated wheels ($114-$161). Styled wheels ($68-$94). Deluxe wire wheel covers: Century ($133); Regal ($99). Styled wheel covers: Century ($91); Regal ($57). Deluxe wheel covers: Century ($34). Moire wire wheel covers: Century ($102); Regal ($68). Tires: FR78 x 15 GBR WSW ($33-$41) exc. Regal sed. FR78 x 15 SBR BSW ($36-$45) exc. Regal sed. FR78 x 15 SBR WSW ($69-$86) exc. Regal sed. GR78 x 15 SBR: Century/Cust, Regal cpe ($54-$67); with V-8 (NC). GR70 x 15 SBR WLT: Century/Cust, Regal cpe ($109-$136); with V-8 ($55-$69). GR78 x 15 SBR WSW: Century/Cust, Regal cpe ($88-$110); with V-8 ($34-$43). HR78 x 15 SBR WSW: Century wag ($47). Stowaway spare tire (NC). Conventional spare: Century Spec. (NC).

LESABRE/ELECTRA/ESTATE WAGON/RIVIERA CONVENIENCE/APPEARANCE OPTIONS: Option Packages: Estate Wagon Limited pkg. ($1442). Exterior molding pkg.: LeSabre/Estate/Electra 225 ($47-$152). Accessory group: LeSabre ($46-$84). Electric sunroof ($734). Astroroof ($898). Comfort/Convenience: Air cond. ($539). Automatic climate control air cond.: Electra/Riv ($621). Custom Aire air cond.: LeSabre, Estate ($578). Cruise Master ($84). Rear defogger, electric ($83). Tinted glass ($69). Tinted windshield: LeSabre, Est ($44). Power windows: LeSabre, Est ($114-$171). Electric door locks ($70-$98). Automatic electric door locks: Electra/Riv ($124-$151). Nine-way power driver's seat ($109-$139). Six-way power seat: LeSabre, Electra 225 ($139). Six-way power passenger seat ($246-$276) exc. base LeSabre. Power passenger seatback recliner ($104); N/A on base LeSabre sedan. Custom steering wheel: LeSabre/Estate ($17). Leather steering wheel: Riviera ($36). Tilt steering ($58). Tilt/telescoping steering column ($44-$104) exc. LeSabre spt cpe. Digital clock (NC). Low fuel indicator ($12). Fuel usage light ($27). Speed alert and trip odometer ($20). Remote electric tailgate lock: Estate ($30). Electric trunk release ($21). Three-speed intermittent wipers

($30). Lighting, Horns and Mirrors: Cornering lamps ($44). Front light monitors: LeSabre/Estate ($25). Front/rear monitors: Electra/Riv ($55). Door courtesy/warning lights ($32-$50). Rear courtesy lamps: Estate ($13). Headlamps-on indicator ($7). Dome reading lamp: LeSabre/Estate/Electra 225 ($16). Sunshade map light: Electra 225 ($11). Four-note horn ($18). Remote left mirror: LeSabre, Est ($15). Remote right mirror ($26-$31) exc. Riv. Remote right sport mirror: Riv ($19). Dual remote sport mirrors ($33-$53) exc. Riv. Remote left mirror w/thermometer ($20-$35) exc. Riv. Lighted visor vanity mirror ($43). Entertainment: AM radio ($92). AM/FM radio ($153). AM/FM stereo radio w/four speakers ($236-$341). AM radio and stereo tape player ($228). AM/FM stereo radio and tape player ($341). AM/FM stereo radio and CB ($459). CB Transceiver ($197). Rear speaker ($21); front/rear ($44). Power antenna ($42). Exterior Trim: Landau vinyl top: LeSabre ($146-$164). Custom padded landau vinyl top: Electra/Riv ($196). Padded landau vinyl top ($186-$417). Long vinyl top: base LeSabre, Electra ($135-$155). Two-tone paint: LeSabre/Electra ($51-$60); Riv ($185). Special color paint ($135) exc. Riviera Firemist ($152). Protective bodyside moldings ($38-$53). Hood ornament: base LeSabre. Estate ($22). Door edge guards ($9-$13). Wheel opening moldings: base LeSabre, Estate ($24). Bodyside accent stripes ($46). Woodgrain vinyl appliqué: Estate ($198). Bumper guards, front/rear ($38); front, Estate ($19). Luggage rack w/air deflector: Estate ($127). Interior Trim/Upholstery: Custom notchback seat trim: Estate ($224) 60/40 ($318). Electra Park Ave. sedan seating ($385). Notchback 60/40 seating: LeSabre Cust/Spt Cpe, Electra 225 ($97). Third seat: Estate ($175). Custom seatbelts: LeSabre, Estate ($18-$21). Front carpet savers ($11-$12). Carpet savers and handy mats: ($18-$22). Litter pocket ($7) exc. Electra Ltd Deluxe trunk trim: LeSabre ($43). Trunk carpeting: Electra/Riv ($53). Wheels: Chrome-plated wheels: LeSabre/Estate/Electra ($116-$163); Riv ($51-$64). Styled wheels ($58-$92) exc. Riv. Deluxe wire wheels ($101-$135) exc. Riv. Custom wire wheels: Riviera (NC). Deluxe wheel covers: base LeSabre ($34). Super deluxe wheel covers: LeSabre/Electra ($24-$58). Moire wire wheel covers ($68-$102) exc. Riv. Tires: FR78 x 15 SBR: LeSabre ($36-$45). FR78 x 15 SBR WSW ($33-$86). GR78 x 15 SBR WSW ($34-$43). GR78 x 15 SBR WSW ($47-$125). GR70 x 15 SBR WLT: LeSabre ($55-$136); LeSabre spt cpe ($7); Riviera ($55-$69). Stowaway spare tire (NC).

HISTORY: Introduced: September 30, 1976. Model year production (U.S.): 845,234, for 9.3 percent of the industry total. North American production for the U.S. market was 869,277 (234,520 V-6 and 634,757 V-8). Calendar year production (U.S.): 801,202. Model year sales by U.S. dealers: 773,313 (including 28,114 imported Opels). Calendar year sales (U.S.): 746,394 for an 8.2 percent market share.

Historical Footnotes: Sales set a record for the second year in-a-row, beating the 1955 mark by nearly 35,000 cars. Full-size Buick models accounted for a healthy 44 percent of sales, with each big Buick showing an impressive sales increase for the model year. Model year production gained 15 percent over 1976. Skylark production returned to Canada for 1977—but back again to Lordstown, Ohio, in mid-year. An assembly line was added at Flint to build the popular V-6, which was also installed on other GM cars.

1978

Following up on the 1977 slimming down of big Buicks, 1978 saw a trimming of the mid-size Century and Regal. Buick's full-line catalog featured many photos and descriptions of old Buicks, with a nod to the Buick Club of America. The catalog

also admitted that Buicks were "equipped with GM-built engines produced by various divisions." That simple fact gained considerable publicity, as some buyers of a Buick or Olds that contained a "lesser" Chevrolet or Pontiac under the hood felt they'd been cheated. Five Buick series now offered the V-6 as standard equipment. For 1978, the V-6 added an "even-firing" feature. To improve smoothness, cylinder firing was changed from alternating 90- and 180-degree intervals of crankshaft rotation to even 120-degree intervals. Buick claimed that the revised V-6 idled like a V-8. A new smaller V-6, displacing just 196 cu. in. (3.2-liters), was available in the mid-size Century and Regal. This was essentially the 231 V-6 with bore reduced from 3.8 to 3.5 in. Four V-8 choices were offered: 301 cu. in. (4.9-liter), 305 (5.0-liter), 350 (5.7-liter) and 403 (6.6-liter) displacements. Of far greater interest to performance fans then and now was the new turbocharged V-6. Turbocharging wasn't a new idea, of course, having been used in the 1960s Corvair Spyder and Olds F85. But in line with its advertising slogan ("A little science. A little magic."), Buick was now pioneering the turbocharging of a small engine for a family car. The turbo arrived in both Regal and LeSabre Sport Coupes, with either two- or four-barrel carburetor. This engine was a production version of the 3.8-liter V-6 used in the Indianapolis 500 Pace Car of 1976. It was a demand-type turbocharger that didn't affect power output at normal highway speeds, but only when the accelerator was pressed. Horsepower was 150 with two-barrel, 165 with four-barrel, as opposed to the normal 105. Buick's goal: to achieve performance that matched a 350 V-8, but without losing the fuel economy of six cylinders. Turbo Buicks came with a specially calibrated automatic transmission and special rear axle ratio, Buick also introduced a new electronic spark control system on the turbo V-6 for 1978, a first in the industry. It monitored detonation (knocking) level in the engine and retarded spark to control detonation during turbo boost. To ensure reliability, each turbocharged Buick got a two-mile road test—a sensible practice that had virtually disappeared years before. Body colors available on all models were: white, silver metallic, black, medium blue metallic, light green metallic, tan, saffron metallic, dark gold metallic, brown metallic, and red metallic. Colors available only on Skyhawk/Skylark colors were bright blue metallic, dark green metallic, yellow, and bright red. Special Century/Regal, LeSabre, Estate Wagon, Electra and Riviera colors were: light blue, dark blue metallic, medium green metallic, and dark red metallic. For extra cost, Riviera buyers could have any of three Firemist metallic colors: blue, amber or red. Designers' accent colors this year were: gray accent (used with silver); or gold accent (used with tan). All Buicks had diagnostic connectors that enabled a mechanic to hook up a diagnostic test instrument to check operation of the ignition switch, coil, starter and other critical circuitry, much faster than traditional methods. All full-size Buicks (except Estate Wagon) might have a sunroof or Astroroof; cornering lights activated by the turn signal lever; or tri-color front light monitors. Other options included a new theft deterrent system that included electric door, trunk and hood locks to trigger audible and visual alarms in the event of tampering, plus an outside mirror with built-in thermometer. Electra and Riviera could have a new frequency-synthesized radio with AM/FM stereo, 8-track tape, digital clock, and push-button scanner that automatically located and locked onto strong signals in remote areas. Also on their option list: an AM/FM stereo radio with built-in 40-channel CB transceiver and a Triband power antenna that disappeared into the car fender.

SKYHAWK - SERIES 4H - V-6 - Still riding a 97 in. wheelbase in one hatchback coupe body style, the subcompact Skyhawk returned for another season powered by the even-firing 231 cu. in. (3.8-liter) V-6. Standard gearbox was a four-speed manual floor shift, with automatic or five-speed overdrive manual available. Some California Skyhawks had a new Phase II three-way catalyst system that used an oxygen sensor to adjust the air/fuel mixture. Styling touches included rectangular headlamps, a domed hood, and louvered roof pillars. Interior trim was new this year. Low-cost 'S' Skyhawks wore standard rattan vinyl upholstery. Upper models could have vinyl or sporty hobnail velour and knit fabrics. Large gauges, including a voltmeter, were recessed in a simulated wood instrument panel. The 'S' model had a new two-spoke steering wheel. On the option list, both fixed-glass Astroroof (with Targa-type aluminum band) and manual sliding-glass sunroofs were offered, as was a Hawk accent stripe package. All Skyhawks had a cigarette lighter, heater/defroster, carpeting, front/rear bumper guards with protective strips, and front stabilizer bar. The base (S07) Skyhawk added a remote-controlled left-hand sport mirror, bodyside stripes (white, black or gold), wheel opening moldings, and steel-belted radial tires.

1978 Buick, Skylark Custom Landau coupe. (OCW)

SKYLARK - SERIES 4X - V-6/V-8 - A Custom Skylark replaced the former S/R version as the luxury edition. Standard and Custom Skylarks came in coupe, sedan and hatchback form, while the low-budget 'S' was again available only as a coupe. Powerplant choices were the standard 231 cu. in. (3.8-liter) "even-firing" V-6, or two optional V-8s. Standard transmission (except in California and high-altitude areas) was the three-speed manual shift. Apart from a similarly-shaped but restyled grille that added a pair of horizontal divider bands to the vertical-bar pattern, Skylark's styling changes were modest for 1978. The wraparound parking/signal lamps were divided into three sections rather than two. Taillamps were split into two horizontal sections instead of three, with full-height backup lamps at the inner ends. Interior trim was new. The Sport Package on base and Custom models included black paint accents on the front grille and around the headlamps, back window and side window frames. The package also featured ER78 x 14 blackwall steel-belted radials, a ride/handling suspension, black sport mirrors, and choice of four body colors: silver, dark gold, yellow, and bright red. All Skylarks except 'S' had front/rear ashtrays plus wheel opening and roof drip moldings. The Custom added a stand-up hood ornament, custom rocker panel moldings, and deluxe wheel covers.

CENTURY - SERIES 4A - V-6/V-8 - A redesigned and reduced mid-size "new generation" Century (and related Regal) emerged for 1978 about 10 inches shorter than before, and some 600 pounds lighter for improved gas mileage. The new and distinctive "aeroback" sedan, with "gracefully" sloping back end, measured 18 in. shorter and 7 in. narrower than its notchback predecessor. Yet passenger space stayed just about the same as in 1977. To keep inside space ample, designers reduced the Century and Regal bodyside curvature and pushed out the roof support pillars. Instrument panels were moved closer to the windshield to add leg room. Coupe wheelbases were cut by 4 in., sedans and wagons by 8 in. The shorter 108 in. wheelbase reduced the car's turning radius. Both coupes and sedans displayed a completely new side appearance: an aerodynamic, fastback "European look." The rear roof pillar and deck lid were on the same plane. Coupes and sedans came in three series: Special, Custom, and Limited (with same lavish interior as Regal's Limited). The Century Sport Coupe came equipped with Designers' wheels and P205/70R14 steel-belted radial tires, special paint treatment and striping, body-color bumpers, and ride/handling package. The new, wide-spaced grille had a

horizontal-slat pattern separated by two horizontal bars and a vertical center bar, plus six subdued vertical bars, with 'BUICK' badge at the side. Quad headlamps were replaced by single rectangular headlamps this year, with wraparound park/signal lamps. Wraparound taillamps were divided into three horizontal sections, with clear backup lights at the inner ends of the lower segments. The new wider grille, coupled with single-headlamp front end, made the car look broader, though it was actually 7 in. narrower than before. Century was closely related to Oldsmobile's Cutlass Salon and Cutlass Supreme. The new, "even-firing" 196 cu. in. (3.2-liter) V-6 with three-speed manual shift was standard, except in California and high-altitude areas which demanded the 3.8-liter V-6 and automatic transmission. A 305 cu. in. (5.0-liter) V-8 was optional. So was a floor-mounted four-speed manual gearshift, with larger 231 cu. in. V-6 engine. All models carried a maintenance-free Delco Freedom battery. In addition to more extensive corrosion-resistant treatment, the front fender wells were made of corrosion-resistant plastic. Station wagons came in three forms: Special, Custom, and a Sport Wagon option that included Designers' Accent paint, Designers' Sport wheels, Rallye suspension similar to Sport Coupe, body-color bumpers, and wide-oval (P205/70R14) steel-belted radial tires. Wagons in California and high-altitude areas required V-8 power rather than the standard 231 cu. in. V-6. A newly-designed fold-down rear deck and lift-up window made loading easier. Also, locking storage compartments were added behind the rear wheelhousings. The six-window sedans and wagons had fixed (not roll-down) windows in the back doors, and swing-out rear vent windows. All Century models now had a turn signal lever that doubled as a headlight dimmer, windshield wipers with single-wipe mist control, space-saving compact (temporary) spare tire, and coin holder in the glove box. Power-operated sunroof and Astroroof options were offered on coupes. Designers' Accent schemes used contrasting shades of similar colors to create a distinctive appearance, offered on all models except the Century Sport Coupe. Electronic leveling was another option. New standard compact spare tires, rated for 60 psi pressure, were meant for temporary.

1978 Buick, Regal coupe with optional wire wheel covers. (OCW)

REGAL - SERIES 4A - V-6/V-8 - Regal became a separate Buick line this year, rather than a Century variant. The new version was 14 in. shorter than the '77 model, trimmed-down all around. Wheelbase cut from 112 to 108 in. permitted a smaller turning diameter. An entirely different, more formal look marked the restyled Regal. Gone were the skinny angled opera windows, replaced by upright rear windows that separated from the front windows by a bright vertical pillar. The new, slightly sloped grille, comprised of many vertical bars, angled outward at the base. Large single rectangular headlamps were recessed

and flanked by wraparound park/signal lamps. As on Century, the instrument panel was moved closer to the windshield to add front knee/leg room. Gauges and warning lights sat in a rectangular cluster, with radio, heater and air conditioner controls in a separate module. Notchback 55/45 seats (standard in Limited) were covered by crushed woven fabric, with standard folding center armrest. Door pull straps were standard. New thin-shell front seats allowed more leg room in back. Roof pillars were moved outward to add head room. Only the coupe body was offered, in three levels: base Regal, Regal Sport Coupe, and Regal Limited. Base and Limited models carried a new 196 cu. in. (3.2-liter) V-6 engine (except in California and high-altitude areas, where a 231 cu. in. V-6 was required). Standard equipment included a compact spare tire (except with positive-traction differential), Freedom battery, P195/75R14 tires, cigarette lighter, front/rear ashtrays, wide-view day/night mirror, bin-type glove box with coin holder, front and rear bumper protective strips, and deluxe wheel covers. Electronic leveling was optional. Regal's hot personal-luxury Sport Coupe came with a new 231 cu. in. (3.8-liter) turbocharged V-6 as standard. Along with LeSabre, these were the only two standard turbocharged production cars made in America. (Worldwide, only Porsche and Saab offered turbos at this time.) Buick's chief engineer Lloyd E. Reuss called Regal "the performance car of the future," since its blower cut in only when needed. Standard Sport Coupe equipment included automatic transmission, Rallye ride/handling suspension with front and rear stabilizer bars, firmer springs and shocks, distinctive domed hood with 'Turbo 3.8 Litre' insignia on the sides of the "bubble" dome, power brakes, and P205/70R145 radial tires. A dash light showed turbo "boost."

1978 Buick, LeSabre Custom sedan. (OCW)

1978 Buick, LeSabre Sport Coupe with turbocharged 3.8 Litre V-6. (OCW)

LESABRE - SERIES 4B - V-6/V-8 - Design changes were fairly modest this year, after prior downsizing. LeSabre's grille was shaped like the 1977 version but was now wider-spaced, with a dominant vertical bar at the forward peak, plus two horizontal bars dividing the grille into six segments. Grille framing bars reached all the way outward, below the headlamps, to wrap around fenders. Interior trim was new; electronic leveling optional. Standard equipment included automatic transmission,

power steering and brakes, heater/defroster, intermittent wipers, inside hood release, and front/rear protective bumper strips. LeSabre's Sport Coupe, similar to the Regal version, carried the new turbocharged 231 cu. in. V-6 engine and handling suspension. That engine replaced the 305 cu. in. V-8 in the 1977 LeSabre Sport Coupe. Instead of LeSabre's customary three-hole emblem on the front fenders, the Sport Coupe had a distinctive 'Turbo 3.8 Litre' badge at the forward end. Other distinctive touches included flat black trim around the windows and in the grille. Wide GR70 x 15 radial tires rode 7 in. chrome wheels. Other LeSabres came with a standard 231 cu. in. V-6 or optional V-8.

1978 Buick, Estate Wagon station wagon. (OCW)

ESTATE WAGON - SERIES 4BR - V-8 - Though related most closely to LeSabre, the Estate Wagon wore an Electra grille and front-end look. Its three-way tailgate could fold down or swing open, with power window up or down. The three-seat version carried up to eight passengers, or 87 cubic feet of cargo with rear seat folded down. Estate Wagon Limited option included 55/45 notchback front seating, power windows, tilt steering wheel, luggage rack with air deflector, electric door locks, remote tailgate lock, remote-control left mirror, bumper guards, map light, dial clock, exterior molding package, woodgrain vinyl appliqué, acoustic package, special ornamentation, and chrome-plated road wheels.

1978 Buick, Electra Limited sedan with optional wire wheel covers. (OCW)

1978 Buick, Electra Park Avenue Lilmited coupe. (OCW)

ELECTRA - SERIES 4C - V-8 - Electra's restyled checkerboard grille was similar to the 1977 version, but with only a single horizontal bar across the center. Wide wraparound taillamps were new, but otherwise the big Buick's design didn't change much. Coupe and sedan were offered in 225, Limited, or Park Avenue form. With vertical roofline and side-mounted coach lights, the elegant Park Avenue took on a more formal appearance. The Park Avenue coupe was new this year. Upholstery choices ranged from textured vinyl to buttoned-and-tufted crushed velour. Standard powerplant was again the 350 cu. in.

(5.7-liter) V-8 with four-barrel carburetor, as well as automatic transmission, power steering and brakes, and the customary coil springs all around. Also standard: power windows and driver's seat, wipers with mist control, quartz clock (dial or digital), and remote-control outside mirror. Limited and Park Avenue Electras added wide rocker appearance moldings.

1978 Buick, Riviera coupe with optional wire wheel covers. (OCW)

RIVIERA - SERIES 4BZ - V-8 - Riviera retained its new downsized look from 1977 with few significant changes, other than modest revisions in grille and taillamps. Spoked-look road wheels were intended to remind observers of its "classic car orientation." Optional was a new electrically-driven height control system, with sensor mounted on car frame. Powerplants included the standard 350 cu. in. V-8 with four-barrel carburetor, or an optional 403 cu. in. V-8. Standard equipment included power steering, padded three-spoke steering wheel, and power front disc brakes (four-wheel discs optional). Rich velour 50/50 seats with dual front armrests, padded Rallye steering wheel, cut-pile carpeting, and custom wire wheel covers were standard. Chrome wire wheels were optional. The padded Landau roof option included coach lamps on the roof pillars. Most interesting to collectors and enthusiasts would be the 75th anniversary Riviera, commemorating the founding of the Buick company. Introduced at the Chicago Auto Show in February 1978, only 1,400 of the LXXV Rivieras were built. Two-tone bodies were silver on the bottom, black on top. Hood, trunk lid and vinyl top were also black. 'LXXV Buick' nameplates were on front fenders and trunk lid. Inside was gray leather upholstery and dark brushed silver trim plates on the dash, plus a sport steering wheel with brushed silver accent.

I.D. DATA: The 13-symbol Vehicle Identification Number (VIN) was again on the upper left surface of the instrument panel, visible through the windshield. Coding was similar to 1977, with the first digit ('4') indicating the Buick division. The second symbol is a letter indicating series: 'S' Skyhawk; 'T' Skyhawk S; 'B' Skylark; 'C' Skylark Custom; 'W' Skylark S; 'E' Century Special; 'H' Century Custom; 'G' Century Sport Coupe; 'L' Century Ltd; 'J' Regal; 'K' Regal Sport Coupe; 'M' Regal Ltd; 'F' LeSabre Custom Sport Coupe; 'N' LeSabre; 'P' LeSabre Custom; 'R' Estate Wagon; 'V' Electra 225; 'X' Electra Limited; 'U' Electra Park Ave.; 'Z' Riviera. Next comes two digits that denote body type: '07' Skyhawk hatchback coupe; '17' Skylark 2-dr. hatchback coupe; '27' Skylark 2-dr. coupe; '69' 4-dr. sedan; '09' aero 4-dr. sedan; '37' LeSabre/Electra 2-dr. coupe; '47' Regal 2-dr. coupe; '87' aero 2-dr. coupe; '35' 4-dr. wagon. The fifth symbol is a letter indicating engine code: 'C' V6-196 2Bbl.; 'A' V6-231 2Bbl. (LD5); '2' V6-231 2Bbl. (LC6); 'G' V6-231 2Bbl. (LC5); '3' V6-231 4Bbl.; 'Y' V8-301 2Bbl,; 'U' V8-305 2Bbl.; 'H' V8-305 4Bbl.;

'L' V8-350 4Bbl. (LM1); 'R' V8-350 4Bbl. (L34); 'X' V8-350 4Bbl. (L77); 'K' V8-403 4Bbl. (L80). The sixth symbol denotes model year ('8' 1978). Next is a plant code: 'U' Lordstown, OH; 'W' Willow Run, MI; 'T' Tarrytown, NY; 'G' Framingham, MA; 'H' Flint, MI; 'Z' Fremont, CA; 'C' Southgate, CA; 'X' Fairfax, KS; 'E' Linden, NJ. The final six digits are the sequential serial number, which began with 100001 except for Skyhawks built at Lordstown and LeSabre/Electra models built at Flint, which started at 400001. Engine numbers were stamped on the front right of the block, except for L34 350 cu. in. V-8 and 403 cu. in. V-8, which were stamped on the front of the left side of the block. A body number plate on the shroud identified model year, car division, series, style, body assembly plant, body number, trim combination, modular seat code, paint code, and date built code.

SKYHAWK (V-6)

Model No.	Body/Style No.	Body Type & Seating	Factory Price	Shipping Weight	Prod. Total
4H	T07	2-dr 'S' Hatch-4P	4103	2678	Note 1
4H	S07	2-dr Hatch-4P	4367	2707	Note 1

Note 1: Total production for the model year, 24,589 Skyhawks.

SKYLARK 'S' (V-6/V-8)

4X	W27	2-dr Coupe-6P	3872/4022	3201/3369	9,050

SKYLARK (V-6/V-8)

4X	B27	2-dr Coupe-6P	3999/4149	3203/3371	33,037
4X	B17	2-dr Hatch-6P	4181/4331	3313/3481	2,642
4X	B69	4-dr Sedan-6P	4074/4224	3234/3402	40,951

SKYLARK CUSTOM (V-6/V-8)

4X	C27	2-dr Coupe-5P	4242/4392	3186/3354	12,740
4X	C17	2-dr Hatch-5P	4424/4574	3285/3453	1,277
4X	C69	4-dr Sedan-6P	4317/4467	3219/3387	14,523

Note 2: Of the 114,220 Skylarks built, 17,116 carried a V-8 engine (only 287 'S' Skylarks had a V-8).

1978 Buick, Century Limited sedan. (OCW)

CENTURY SPECIAL (V-6/V-8)

4A	E87	2-dr Coupe-6P	4389/4599	3003/3149	10,818
4A	E09	4-dr Sedan-6P	4486/4696	3014/3160	12,533
4A	E35	4-dr Sta Wag-6P	4976/5126	3148/3314	9,586

CENTURY CUSTOM (V-6/V -8)

4A	H87	2-dr Coupe-6P	4633/4843	3011/3157	12,434
4A	H09	4-dr Sedan-6P	4733/4943	3038/3184	18,361
4A	H35	4-dr Sta Wag-6P	5276/5426	3181/3349	24,014

CENTURY SPORT (V-6/V-8)

4A	G87	2-dr Coupe-6P	5019/5228	3051/3197	Note 3

CENTURY LIMITED (V-6/V-8)

4A	L87	2-dr Coupe-6P	4991/5201	3048/3294	Note 3
4A	L09	4-dr Sedan-6P	5091/5301	3075/3221	Note 3

Note 3: Production of Century Sport and Limited models is included in figures above.

REGAL (V-6/V-8)

4A	J47	2-dr Coupe-6P	4852/5042	2992/3138	236,652

REGAL SPORT (V-6)

Model No.	Body/Style No.	Body Type & Seating	Factory Price	Shipping Weight	Prod. Total
4A	K47	2-dr Coupe-6P	5853	3153	Note 4

REGAL LIMITED (V-6/V-8)

4A	M47	2-dr Coupe-6P	5233/5423	3041/3187	Note 4

Note 4: Production total listed under base Regal includes Sport and Limited models.

LESABRE (V-6/V-8)

4B	N37	2-dr Coupe-6P	5384/5582	3446/3613	8,265
4B	N69	4-dr Sedan-6P	5459/5657	3439/3606	23,354

LESABRE CUSTOM (V-6/V-8)

4B	P37	2-dr Coupe-6P	5657/5855	3413/3580	53,675
4B	P69	4-dr Sedan-6P	5757/5955	3450/3617	86,638

LESABRE SPORT (V-6)

4B	F37	2-dr Coupe-6P	6213	3559	Note 5

Note 5: Production of LeSabre Sport Coupe is included in standard LeSabre coupe total. Only 29,408 LeSabres came with a V-6.

ESTATE WAGON (V-8)

4B	R35	4-dr Sta Wag-6P	6301	4063	25,964

ELECTRA 225 (V-8)

4C	V37	2-dr Coupe-6P	7144	3682	8,259
4C	V69	4-dr Sedan-6P	7319	3730	14,590

ELECTRA LIMITED (V-8)

4C	X37	2-dr Coupe-6P	7526	3710	33,365
4C	X69	4-dr Sedan-6P	7701	3757	65,335

ELECTRA PARK AVENUE (V-8)

4C	U37	2-dr Coupe-6P	7837	3730	Note 6
4C	U69	4-dr Sedan-6P	8088	3777	Note 6

Note 6: Production totals listed under Electra Limited include the Park Avenue model. Total Limited production, 63,977.

RIVIERA (V-8)

4E	Z37	2-dr Coupe-6P	8082	3701	20,535

Note 7: Riviera had a hefty price increase during the model year, reaching $9,224.

FACTORY PRICE AND WEIGHT NOTE: Figure before the slash is for V-6 engine, after the slash for smallest (lowest-priced) V-8 engine available.

ENGINES: BASE V-6 (Century, Regal): 90-degree, overhead-valve V-6. Cast iron alloy block and head. Displacement: 196 cu. in. (3.2 liters). Bore & stroke: 3.5 x 3.4 in. Compression ratio: 8.0:1. Brake horsepower: 90 at 3600 R.P.M. (95 at 3800 w/automatic). Torque: 165 lb.-ft. at 2000 R.P.M. (155 at 2000 w/automatic). Four main bearings. Hydraulic valve lifters. Carburetor: 2Bbl. Rochester 2GE. VIN Code: C. Sales Code: LC9. BASE V-6 (Skyhawk, Skylark, Century wagon, LeSabre); OPTIONAL (Century sed/cpe, Regal): 90-degree, overhead-valve V-6. Cast iron alloy block and head. Displacement: 231 cu. in. (3.8 liters). Bore & stroke: 3.8 x 3.4 in. Compression ratio: 8.0:1. Brake horsepower: 105 at 3400 R.P.M. Torque: 185 lb.-ft. at 2000 R.P.M. Four main bearings. Hydraulic valve lifters. Carburetor: 2Bbl. Rochester 2GE. VIN Code: A. Sales Code: LD5. Note: Alternate LC6 version had VIN code 2. TURBOCHARGED V-6 (Regal and LeSabre Sport Coupes): Same as 231 V-6 above, except as follows: Brake horsepower: 150 at 3800 R.P.M. Torque: 245 lb.-ft. at 2400 R.P.M. VIN Code: G. Sales Code: LC5. TURBOCHARGED FOUR-BARREL V-6; OPTIONAL (Regal and LeSabre Sport Coupes): Same as turbocharged V-6 above, but with M4ME carburetor. Brake horsepower: 165 at 4000 R.P.M. Torque: 285 lb.-ft. at 2800 R.P.M. VIN Code: 3. Sales Code: LC8. OPTIONAL V-8 (LeSabre) 90 degree, overhead-valve V-8. Cast iron alloy block and head. Displacement: 301 cu. in. (4.9 liters). Bore & stroke: 4.0 x 3.0 in. Compression ratio: 8.2:1. Brake horsepower: 140 at 3600 R.P.M. Torque: 235 lb.-ft. at 2000 R.P.M. Five main bearings. Hydraulic valve lifters. Carburetor: 2Bbl. Rochester M2MC. Built by Pontiac. VIN Code: Y. Sales Code: L27. OPTIONAL V-8 (Skylark, Century, Regal, LeSabre): 90 degree overhead-valve V-8. Cast iron alloy block and head. Displacement: 305 cu. in. (5.0 liters). Bore & stroke: 3.736 x 3.48 in. Compression ratio: 8.5:1. Brake horsepower: 145 at 3800 R.P.M. Torque: 245 lb.-ft. at 2400 R.P.M. Five main bearings. Hydraulic valve lifters.

Carburetor: 2Bbl. Rochester 2GC. Built by Chevrolet. VIN Code: U. Sales Code: LG3. OPTIONAL V-8 (Century/Regal): 90-degree, overhead valve V-8. Cast iron alloy block and head. Displacement: 305 cu. in. (5.0 liters). Bore & stroke: 3.736 x 3.48 in. Compression ratio: 8.5:1. Brake horsepower: 160 at 4000 R.P.M. Torque: 285 lb.-ft. at 2400 R.P.M. Five main bearings. Hydraulic valve lifters. Carburetor: 4Bbl. Rochester 4GC. VIN Code: H. Sales Code: LG4. BASE V-8 (Electra, Estate, Riviera); OPTIONAL (Skylark, LeSabre): 90 degree, overhead valve V-8. Cast iron alloy block and head. Displacement: 350 cu. in. (5.7 liters). Bore & stroke: 3.80 x 3.85 in. Compression ratio: 8.0:1. Brake horsepower: 155 at 3400 R.P.M. Torque: 280 lb.-ft. at 1800 R.P.M. Five main bearings. Hydraulic valve lifters. Carburetor: 4Bbl. Rochester M4MC. VIN Code: X. Sales Code: L77. ALTERNATE 350-4 V-8 (LeSabre, Electra, Estate, Riviera): 90-degree, overhead valve V-8. Cast iron alloy block and head. Displacement: 350 cu. in. (5.7 liters). Bore & stroke: 4.057 x 3.385 in. Compression ratio: 8.0:1. Brake horsepower: 170 at 3800 R.P.M. Torque: 275 lb.-ft. at 2000 R.P.M. Five main bearings. Hydraulic valve lifters. Carburetor: 4Bbl. Rochester M4MC. VIN Code: R. Ordering Code: L34. OPTIONAL V-8 (Skylark, Century wagon): 90-degree, overhead valve V-8. Cast iron alloy block and head. Displacement: 350 cu. in. (5.7 liters). Bore & stroke: 4.00 x 3.48 in. Compression ratio: 8.2:1. Brake horsepower: 170 at 3800 R.P.M. Torque: 275 lb.-ft. at 2000 R.P.M. Five main bearings. Hydraulic valve lifters. Carburetor: 4Bbl. Rochester M4MC. Chevrolet-built. VIN Code: L. Ordering Code: LM1. OPTIONAL V-8 (LeSabre, Electra, Estate, Riviera): 90 degree, overhead valve V-8. Cast iron alloy block and head. Displacement: 403 cu. in. (6.6 liters). Bore & stroke: 4.351 x 3.385 in. Compression ratio: 8.0:1. Brake horsepower: 185 at 3600 R.P.M. Torque: 320 lb.-ft. at 2000 R.P.M. Five main bearings. Hydraulic valve lifters. Carburetor: 4Bbl. Rochester M4MC. Built by Oldsmobile. VIN Code: K. Ordering Code: L80.

CHASSIS DATA: Wheelbase: (Skyhawk) 97.0 in.; (Skylark) 111.0 in.; (Century/Regal) 108.1 in.; (LeSabre/Estate/Riviera) 115.9 in.; (Electra) 118.9 in. Overall length: (Skyhawk) 179.3 in.; (Skylark) 200.2 in.; (Century) 196.0 in.; (Regal) 200.0 in.; (LeSabre/Riviera) 218.2 in.; (Electra) 222.1 in.; (Estate Wagon) 216.7 in. Height: (Skyhawk) 50.2 in.; (Skylark 2-dr.) 52.2 in.; (Skylark 4-dr.) 53.1 in.; (Century cpe) 54.1 in.; (Century sed) 55.0 in.; (Century wagon) 55.7 in.; (Regal) 53.4 in.; (LeSabre/Electra/Riviera cpe) 55.0 in.; (LeSabre sed) 55.7 in.; (Electra sed) 55.9 in.; (Estate) 56.5 in. Width: (Skyhawk) 65.4 in.; (Skylark) 72.7 in.; (Century/Regal) 70.1 in.; (LeSabre/Electra/Riviera) 77.2 in.; (Estate) 79.9 in. Front Tread: (Skyhawk) 54.7 in.; (Skylark) 59.1 in.; (Century/Regal) 58.5 in.; (LeSabre/Electra/Riviera) 61.8 in.; (Estate) 62.2 in. Rear Tread: (Skyhawk) 53.6 in.; (Skylark) 59.7 in.; (Century/Regal) 57.8 in.; (LeSabre/Electra/Riviera) 60.7 in.; (Estate) 64.0 in. Standard Tires: (Skyhawk) BR78 x 13 SBR; (Skyhawk 'S') B78 x 13; (Skylark) E78 x 14; (Skylark Custom) ER78 x 14 SBR; (Century cpe/sed) P185/75R14 SBR; (Century wag/Regal) P195/75R14 SBR; (Century/Regal Spt Cpe) P205/70R14 SBR; (LeSabre) FR78 x 15 GBR; (LeSabre Spt Cpe) GR70 x 15 SBR; (Electra/Riviera) GR78 x 15; (Estate) HR78 x 15 SBR.

TECHNICAL: Transmission: Three-speed, fully synchronized manual gearbox (column shift) standard on Skylark, Century cpe/sed, and Regal cpe; Turbo-Hydra-matic optional. Four-speed manual gearbox available on Century/Regal. Four-speed, fully synchronized floor shift standard on Skyhawk; five-speed and automatic optional. Turbo-Hydra-matic standard on Regal sedan, LeSabre, Electra, Estate and Riviera. Three-speed manual transmission gear ratios: (1st) 3.50:1; (2nd) 1.81:1 or 1.90:1; (3rd) 1.00:1; (Rev) 3.62:1. Four-speed gear ratios: (1st) 3.50;1; (2nd) 2.48:1; (3rd) 1.66:1; (4th) 1.00:1; (Rev) 3.50:1. Five-speed gear ratios: (1st) 3.40:1; (2nd) 2.08:1; (3rd) 1.39:1; (4th) 1.00:1; (5th) 0.80:1; (Rev) 3.36:1. Automatic transmission gear ratios: (1st) 2.52:1; (2nd) 1.52:1; (3rd) 1.00:1; (Rev) 1.93:1. Standard axle ratios: (Skyhawk) 2.93:1 w/manual,

2.56:1 w/automatic, (Skylark) 3.08:1 w/manual, 2.56:1 w/automatic, 2.41:1 w/V-8; (Century/Regal) 2.93:1 w/manual, 2.56:1 w/automatic and 196 V-6, 2.73:1 w/231 V-6, 2.29:1 w/305 V-8; (Century wagon) 2.73:1 exc. 2.41:1 w/305 V-8; (Regal Sport Coupe) 2.73:1; (LeSabre V-6) 2.73:1; (LeSabre V-8) 2.41:1; (LeSabre V-6 Sport Coupe) 2.58:1; (LeSabre V-8 Sport Coupe) 3.08:1; (Electra/Riviera) 2.41:1; (Estate) 2.73:1 exc. 2.56:1 w/403 V-8. Other axle ratios were standard in California and for high-altitude operation. Hypoid bevel final drive. Steering: re-circulating ball; power assist standard on Century/Regal, LeSabre, Electra, Estate and Riviera. Suspension: front/rear coil springs, independent front except Skylark, semi-elliptic rear leaf springs. Front wishbones with lower trailing links and anti-roll bar; rigid rear axle with lower trailing radius arms, upper torque arms and transverse linkage bar. Brakes: front disc, rear drum; power brakes standard on LeSabre/Electra/Riviera plus Century wagon and Regal Sport Coupe. Four-wheel power disc brakes optional on Riviera. Body construction: (Skyhawk) unitized; (Skylark) separate front frame unit cushion-mounted to unitized body; (others) separate body and perimeter box frame. High-Energy electronic ignition (HEI) on all engines. Fuel tank: (Skyhawk) 18.5 gal.; (Skylark/LeSabre) 21 gal.; (Century/Regal) 18.1 gal.: (Electra/Estate/Riv) 22.5 gal. Unleaded fuel only.

DRIVETRAIN OPTIONS: Engines: 231 cu. in. V-6, 2Bbl.: Century cpe/sed, Regal ($40). Turbocharged 231 cu. in. V-6, 4Bbl.: Regal/LeSabre spt cpe ($50). 301 cu. in. V-8, 2Bbl.: LeSabre ($198). 305 cu. in. V-8, 2Bbl.: Skylark ($150);: Century ($150-$210); Regal ($190); LeSabre ($198). 305 cu. in. V-8, 4Bbl.: Skylark ($265); Century ($200-$260); Regal ($240). 350 cu. in. V-8, 4Bbl.: Century wagon ($265); LeSabre ($313). 403 cu. in. V-8, 4Bbl.: LeSabre ($403). Transmission/Differential: Four-speed manual floor shift: Century cpe/sed, Regal w/231 2Bbl. V-6 ($125). Five-speed manual floor shift: Skyhawk ($175). Automatic trans.: Skyhawk ($270); Skylark, Century cpe/sed, Regal ($307). Optional rear axle ratio: Skyhawk 2.93:1 (NC); Skylark 3.08:1 or 3.23:1 (NC); Century/Regal 2.73:1 or 3.23:1 (NC); LeSabre/Electra/Riv 2.73:1, 3.08:1 or 3.23:1 (NC). Positive traction differential: Skyhawk ($56); Skylark/Century/Regal ($60); LeSabre/Electra/Riviera ($64). Power Accessories: Power brakes: Skyhawk ($66); Skylark, Century cpe/sed, Regal ($69). Four-wheel disc brakes: Riviera ($199). Power steering: Skyhawk ($134); Skylark/Century/Regal ($152). Suspension: WH5 handling pkg.: Skyhawk ($101-$122). F40 Firm ride/handling pkg.: Skylark ($24); Century/Regal/LeSabre/Electra/Riv ($20). FE2 Rallye ride/handling pkg.: Skylark ($46). Century exc. wag and spt cpe, Regal ($36): Riv ($20). Automatic level control; Century/Regal/LeSabre/Electra/Riv ($116). Other: Trailer towing flasher/harness: Skylark ($21-$34) exc. Skyhawk. Heavy-duty 80-amp alternator: LeSabre/Electra/Riv ($44). H.D. battery ($17-$20). H.D. cooling; Skylark/Electra/LeSabre/Riv ($29-$56). H.D. radiator: Skylark ($21); Engine block heater ($14) exc. Skyhawk. H.D. engine/transmission cooling: Century/Regal ($29-$56). High altitude emission system ($33). California emission system ($75).

1978 Buick, Skyhawk hatchback. (OCW)

SKYHAWK CONVENIENCE/APPEARANCE OPTIONS: Option Packages: Appearance group: 'S' ($73). Convenience group ($23). Shadow light Astroroof w/roof crown molding ($615). Manual glass sunroof ($215). Comfort/Convenience: Air

cond. ($470). Rear defogger, electric ($79). Soft Ray tinted glass ($54). Tinted windshield ($42). Rally steering wheel: 'S' ($41). Tilt steering ($62). Electric clock ($19); w/tach ($69). Right sport mirror ($13). Remote left sport mirror ($18). Entertainment: AM radio ($74). AM/FM radio ($139). AM/FM stereo radio ($222). AM radio and 8-track player ($216). AM/FM stereo radio and 8-track ($320). Rear speaker ($23). Windshield antenna ($25); incl. w/radios. Exterior Trim: Door edge guards ($11). Roof crown molding ($176). Protective bodyside moldings ($28-$44). Hawk accent stripe ($36). Interior Trim/Upholstery: Full-length console ($77). Adjustable driver's seatback ($19). Front/rear mats ($18). Custom seatbelts ($16). Wheels: Custom sport wheels ($97). Deluxe wheel covers ($42). Wheel trim rings ($38). Tires: B78 x 13 WSW: 'S' ($35-$43). BR78 x 13 SBR BSW: 'S' ($84-$105). BR78 x 13 SBR WSW ($35-$148). BR70 x 13 SBR WLT ($64-$184). Conventional spare tire (NC).

SKYLARK CONVENIENCE/APPEARANCE OPTIONS: Option Packages: Sport Coupe or Sport Sedan pkg.: FE2 Rallye ride/handling suspension, ER78 x 14 SBR tires, black styling accents, sport mirrors ($182-$200); N/A on hatchback. Accessory pkg. (day/night mirror, lighter): 'S' ($14). Acoustic pkg. ($27-$40). Convenience group ($31-$34). Comfort/Convenience: Air cond. ($508). Cruise Master ($90). Two-speed wipers w/delay ($32). Rear defogger, blower-type ($51). Power windows ($118-$164). Electric door locks ($74-$103). Rallye steering wheel ($41). Tilt steering wheel ($69). Soft Ray tinted glass ($56). Tinted windshield ($44). Dual horns ($10). Electric clock ($22). Headlamps-on indicator ($10). Electric trunk release ($22). Remote left mirror ($16). Sport mirrors: left remote, right manual ($32). Entertainment: AM radio ($79). AM/FM radio ($149). AM/FM stereo radio ($236). AM radio and 8-track player ($279). AM/FM stereo radio and 8-track or cassette player ($341). Rear speaker ($23). Windshield antenna ($26); incl. w/radios. Exterior Trim: Landau vinyl top ($179-$184). Full vinyl top ($97-$102). Two-tone paint ($46). Special paint ($126). Swing-out rear quarter vent window: two-doors ($54). Protective bodyside moldings ($42). Roof drip and wheel opening moldings: 'S' ($36). Rocker panel moldings ($17); std. on Custom. Wide rocker appearance group ($43). Decklid molding ($9). Custom door and window frame moldings ($27-$34). Door edge guards ($11-$18). Bodyside stripes ($33). Bumper guards, front/rear ($40); front only ($20). Bumper strips, front/rear ($33). Interior Trim/Upholstery: Full-length console ($80). Vinyl bucket seats: base ($89). Cloth bucket seats: Custom ($109). Custom seatbelts ($16-$18). Front carpet savers ($9). Carpet savers and mats ($18). Carpeted door trim w/map pocket and reflector: base ($41). Wheels: Styled wheels ($22-$92). Chrome-plated wheels ($112-$130). Deluxe wheel covers ($38). Styled wheel covers ($63-$101). Deluxe wire wheel covers ($112-$150). Tires: E78 x 14 WSW ($35-$44). ER78 x 14 SBR BSW ($74-$92). ER78 x 14 SBR WSW ($35-$136). FR78 x 14 SBR WLT ($64-$171). Stowaway spare tire ($17).

1978 Buick, Century Special coupe. (OCW)

1978 Buick, Century Custom station wagon with Sport option package. (OCW)

1978 Buick, Century Sport Coupe. (OCW)

CENTURY/REGAL CONVENIENCE/APPEARANCE OPTIONS: Option Packages: Century Custom Sport Wagon pkg. ($430). Electric sunroof: cpe ($499). Silver electric Astroroof: cpe ($699). Hatch roof: coupe ($625). Exterior molding pkg.: Century Spec., Regal ($9-$141). Convenience group: Century Spec. ($6-$44); Regal ($6-$18). Comfort/Convenience: Air cond. ($544). Automatic climate control air cond. ($626). Cruise Master ($90). Rear defogger, electric ($92). Tinted glass ($62). Tinted windshield ($45). Six-way power driver's seat ($151). Manual seatback recliner ($59); N/A Century Spec. sed/wag. Custom steering wheel: Century ($10) exc. Ltd. Rallye steering wheel: Century ($41) exc. Ltd.; Regal ($31). Sport steering wheel: Regal spt cpe ($31). Tilt steering ($69). Power windows ($124-$172). Electric door locks ($80-$112) Electric trunk release ($22). Remote tailgate lock: Century wag ($23). Electric clock, dial-type ($22). Digital clock ($49). Headlamps-on indicator ($10). Trip odometer ($12). Instrument gauges: temp and

voltmeter ($26). Fuel usage light and instrument gauges ($55). Dome reading lamp ($18). Two-speed wiper with delay ($32). Lighting and Mirrors: Front light monitors ($28). Remote left mirror ($16). Remote right mirror ($28-$33). Sport mirrors: left remote ($27-$32). Dual remote sport mirrors ($52-$57). Lighted right visor vanity mirror ($45). Entertainment: AM radio ($83). AM/FM radio ($154). AM/FM stereo radio ($236); w/digital read-out ($392). AM radio w/8-track ($233). AM/FM stereo radio w/8-track or cassette ($341-$351); w/CB ($571). Rear speaker: each ($24). Windshield antenna ($26); incl. w/radios. Automatic power antenna ($45-$71). Triband power antenna ($83-$109). Exterior Trim: Landau vinyl top: Regal ($140-$155); heavy-padded ($168-$216). Long vinyl top ($116). Designers' accent paint ($155-$206). Solid special color paint ($146). Bumper guards, front/rear ($40). Protective bodyside moldings ($33). Rocker panel moldings: Century Spec. ($17). Door edge guards ($11-$18). Wheel opening moldings: Century Spec. wag ($21). Bodyside stripes ($72-$93). Woodgrain vinyl appliqué: Century wag ($235-$256). Luggage rack: Century wag ($85). Air deflector: Century wag ($29). Interior Trim/Upholstery: Full-length console ($90). Bucket seats: Century Custom/spt cpe, Regal ($40). 55/45 seating: Century Custom/spt cpe, Regal ($98). Custom seatbelts ($16-$20). Load floor area carpet: Century Spec. wag ($49). Front carpet savers ($10); w/mats ($18). Front/rear carpet savers with inserts ($42); front ($23). Litter pocket ($8). Trunk trim covering ($30). Lockable storage compartment: Century wag ($35-$40). Wheels: Chrome-plated wheels: Century exc. Spt ($159); Regal ($141). Designers' sport wheels: Century exc. Spt ($117); Regal ($99). Deluxe wheel covers: Century exc. Spt ($38). Styled wheel covers: Century exc. Spt ($101); Regal ($63). Designers' wheel covers: Century exc. Spt ($65). Regal ($27). Wire wheel covers: Century exc. Spt ($150); Regal ($112). Tires: P185/75R14 GBR WSW; Century V-6 cpe/sed ($37). P195/75R14 GBR BSW: Century cpe/sed ($20). P195/75R14 GBR WSW ($39-$59). P195/75R14 SBR BSW: Century ($39-$59). P195/75R14 SBR WSW: Century ($78-$97). P205/70R14 SBR wide-oval BSW: Regal ($30). P205/70R14 SBR WSW: Century Spt, Regal ($42-$72). P205/70R14 SBR WLT ($54-$143).

LESABRE/ELECTRA/ESTATE WAGON/RIVIERA CONVENIENCE/APPEARANCE OPTIONS: Option Packages: Riviera Anniversary pkg.: black/silver Designers' Accent paint, gray 50/50 leather seats, carpeting and seatbelts ($586). Estate Wagon Limited pkg. ($1568). Estate Wagon convenience group ($12-$62). Exterior molding pkg.: LeSabre/Estate/Electra 225 ($37-$167). Convenience group: LeSabre ($19-$92). Power sunroof ($695-$778). Sliding Astroroof ($895-$978). Comfort/Convenience Air cond. ($581). Automatic climate control air cond. ($669). Cruise Master ($95). Rear defogger, electric ($94). Soft Ray tinted glass ($76). Tinted windshield: LeSabre/Est ($46). Power windows: LeSabre/Est ($130-$190). Electric door locks ($82-$114). Automatic door locks: Electra/Riviera ($139-$167). Six-way power driver's seat ($120-$151). Dual power seats ($271-$302); N/A on base LeSabre. Electric seat-back recliner, passenger ($113); N/A on base LeSabre sedan. Custom steering wheel: base LeSabre ($10). Rally steering wheel: LeSabre ($31-$41). Tilt steering ($70). Tilt/telescoping steering column ($46-$126). Digital clock (NC). Low fuel indicator ($10). Fuel usage light ($16); N/A spt cpe. Speed alert and trip odometer ($22). Remote electric tailgate lock: Estate ($32). Electric trunk release ($22). Theft deterrent system ($130); N/A on Estate. Three-speed wiper w/delay ($32). Lighting, Horns and Mirrors: Front cornering monitors: LeSabre/Est ($28). Front/rear monitors: Electra/Riviera ($60). Door courtesy/warning lights ($35-$55). Rear courtesy lamps: Est ($15). Headlamps-on indicator ($10). Dome reading lamp: LeSabre/Estate/Electra 225 ($18). Sunshade map light: Electra 225 ($12). Four-note horn ($22). Remote left mirror: LeSabre/Est ($16). Remote right mirror ($28-$33) exc. Riv. Remote right sport mirror: Riviera ($33). Dual remote sport mirrors ($36-$57)

exc. Riv. Remote left mirror w/thermometer ($21-$37) exc. Riv. Lighted visor vanity mirror ($46). Entertainment: AM radio ($96); N/A on Riv. AM/FM radio ($165); N/A on Riv. AM/FM stereo radio ($239). AM/FM stereo w/digital readout: LeSabre/Est ($342-$392). AM radio and 8-track ($250): N/A on Riv. AM/FM stereo radio and 8-track or cassette player ($345-$355) exc. Riv ($106-$116). AM/FM stereo radio and CB ($577) exc. Riv ($338). Signal-seeking AM/FM stereo with 8-track: Electra ($514); Riv ($275). Rear speaker ($24) exc. Riv. Windshield antenna ($26) exc. Riv. Automatic power antenna ($45-$71). Triband power antenna ($83-$109). Exterior Trim: Landau vinyl top: LeSabre ($151). Heavy-padded landau vinyl top ($194-$405). Long vinyl top: LeSabre, Electra sed ($142-$161). Long, heavy-padded vinyl top: Electra/Riviera ($196). Two-tone paint: LeSabre ($56). Designers' accent paint: LeSabre/Riviera ($175-$201). Solid special color paint ($147) exc. Riviera Firemist ($165). Protective bodyside moldings ($42-$65). Hood ornament and windsplit: LeSabre/Est ($24). Door edge guards ($11-$18). Window frame scalp molding: LeSabre/Est ($33). Wheel opening moldings: LeSabre/Est ($26). Bodyside stripes ($50). Woodgrain vinyl appliqué: Estate ($235). Bumper guards, front/rear ($40); front, Estate ($20). Luggage rack w/air deflector: Estate ($135). Interior Trim/Upholstery: Third seat: Estate ($186). Custom seatbelts: LeSabre/Est ($20-$23). Front carpet savers ($11) exc. Riv. Carpet savers and handy mats ($21) exc. Riv. Front/rear carpet savers w/inserts: Riviera ($42); front ($23). Trunk carpeting/covering ($46-$58). Wheels: Chrome-plated wheels ($62-$161). Deluxe wheel covers: LeSabre ($38). Custom wheel covers ($28-$66) exc. Riv. Styled wheel covers ($65) exc. Riv. Wire wheel covers ($75-$113) exc. Riv. Deluxe wire wheel covers ($112-$150) exc. Riv. Custom red wire wheel covers: Riv (NC). Tires: FR78 x 15 GBR WSW: LeSabre ($37-$46). FR78 x 15 SBR: LeSabre ($39-$48). FR78 x 15 SBR WSW: LeSabre ($37-$46). GR78 x 15 SBR WSW ($39-$121). GR78 x 15 SBR wide WSW: LeSabre ($51-$136).

1978 Buick, Regal Sport Coupe with turbocharged 3.8 Litre V-6. (OCW)

HISTORY: Introduced: October 6, 1977 (Regal Sport Coupe, August 1977). Model year production (U.S.): 803,187, for 9.0 percent of the industry total. Calendar year production (U.S.): 810,350. Model year sales by U.S. dealers: 795,316 (including 18,801 imported Opels). Calendar year sales (U.S.): 781,364 for an 8.4 percent market share.

Historical Footnotes: Buick now looked toward the youth market for potential customers. Said J.D. Duffy Jr., the new general sales manager, in Ward's Auto World: "We can't live on traditional Buick buyers. They're getting older every year." A record 776,515 domestic Buicks sold through U.S. dealers, more than 30,000 over the 1977 mark. Though impressive, the figure fell short of early forecasts. Defying predictions, Skyhawk and Skylark sales rose (as did the imported Opel), while mid- and full-size Buicks didn't reach expected levels. Trimmed-down Regals grew popular, but buyers didn't take so kindly to the new fastback Century sedan styling. And Riviera sales weakened when prospective buyers heard about the new front-drive version expected for 1979. Part of the loss in full-size sales, in fact, came

because production at the Linden, New Jersey, plant was halted early to allow for changeover to the new E-body Riviera. This helped cause model year production to fall somewhat for the year. As part of the 75th anniversary festivities, an open house at Flint in June coupled with a gathering of the Buick Club of America drew 36,000 visitors. Over 600 early Buicks paraded through town. Late in 1978, Donald H. McPherson became the new general manager of Buick division.

1979

Riviera was downsized for 1979 and switched to front-wheel drive, while LeSabre and Electra were carried over except for trim changes. The free-breathing 90 degree V-6 engine, in 3.2- and 3.8-liter displacements, got a new carburetor, intake manifold, exhaust manifold, and camshaft this year. It also received an improved two-barrel carburetor (Dual Jet 210).

1979 Buick, Skyhawk "Designers' Accent Edition" hatchback. (OCW)

1979 Buick, Skyhawk "Road Hawk" (limited edition) hatchback. (OCW)

SKYHAWK - SERIES 4H - V-6 - All Skyhawks got a new hood and front-end treatment with single rectangular headlamps, meant to enhance the car's sporty image. The new body-color grille was comprised of many small openings, wider than they were high, split into 12 sections by five wider vertical bars and a single horizontal bar. A Hawk insignia sat above the grille, in the center. Buick block letters were off to the side, above the grille. Rounded-corner housings held Skyhawk's headlamps, with wide parking/signal lamps below the front bumper. The freshly styled hood had twin creases that tapered inward toward the front. Vertical louvers tapered back to the rear, from the quarter windows. Sport mirrors were standard. Sole powerplant remained the 231 cu. in. (3.8-liter) V-6, with the same choice of three transmissions as before: standard four-speed floor shift, five-speed overdrive, or automatic. Base Skyhawks (S07) had an AM radio, full-length console, sport steering wheel, twin sport mirrors (left remote-controlled), bodyside accent stripes, and bumper guards. The fewer-frills 'S' edition was again available, with rattan vinyl interior. Two special packages were offered this year, both stressing the "hawk" theme with air dam, spoiler, and hawk decal. The top level, limited-edition Road Hawk option included a Rallye ride-and-handling package with larger stabilizer bars and blackwall BR70 x 13 steel-belted radial tires. The package included 'Road Hawk' markings, Oyster White vinyl

bucket seats with hawk emblem, altered interior trim, new steering wheel, black windshield wipers, black window reveal moldings and grille, plus a front air dam and sporty decklid spoiler integrated into the rear quarter panel. Body color was light silver above the beltline darker silver below. Road Hawks also included fast-ratio power steering (when power steering was ordered). Skyhawk's "Designers' Accent Edition" came with a bright red or yellow exterior, flat black accent along and below the beltline, hawk decal on the hood, rear spoiler, deluxe wheel covers, and sporty-tone exhaust system.

SKYLARK - SERIES 4X - V-6/V-8 - Skylark entered 1979 with a totally redesigned front end, including new grille. The grille's crosshatch pattern split into four sections, peaked at the front. Single round headlamps combined with wraparound two-section park/signal lamps. Buick still promoted Skylark's tall "greenhouse" with its "generous glass." Fenders again sported triple-ventiport trim strips. Two-door, four-door and hatchback bodies were offered, in base or Custom trim. Custom Skylarks included a stand-up hood ornament, rocker panel moldings, carpeted door trim, map pockets, plus a visor vanity mirror and lights for underhood, glove box, trunk and ashtray. The low-budget Skylark 'S' lacked a day/night mirror, lighter, roof drip and wheel opening moldings. The new, improved, highly efficient "free breathing" 231 cu. in. (3.8-liter) 2Bbl. V-6 was standard, with smoother airflow adding 10 horsepower over the 1978 version. Standard powertrain was again the three-speed manual shift, with automatic transmission optional. Two V-8s were available. The Sport package (for coupe or sedan) included black paint accents on grille, around headlamps, windshield, back windows and side-window frames, plus ER78 x 14 steel-belted tires, ride/handling suspension and black sport mirrors. It came in four body colors: silver, dark gold, yellow, or bright red. Sport models could also have black painted wide rocker treatment and black protective side moldings. New individual options included sporty interiors, an AM/FM stereo radio with cassette player, and a wider range of colors and paint combinations that included a Designers' Accent treatment with darker accent color on the side body panels.

1979 Buick, Century "Turbo Coupe" (option package). (OCW)

CENTURY - SERIES 4A - V-6/V-8 - Century continued its fast-back styling, introduced for 1978, with a reworked front end. A new crosshatch grille had three rows of rectangular "holes." Three-section parking/signal lamps stood outboard of single headlamps, while tri-section taillamps wrapped around the rear fenders. Four models made up the lineup: coupe, sedan, sport

coupe, and station wagon. Engine choices were revised slightly. Base engine was again the even-firing 196 cu. in. (3.2-liter) V-6; but 3.8 V-6 in California, and on wagons. Normal and turbocharged 3.8 V-6s were available. So was a 301 cu. in. (4.9-liter) V-8. California models had an electronic fuel control system. A new Turbo Coupe package was described as an enthusiast's car, powered by the free-breathing turbocharged 231 cu. in. (3.8-liter) V-6. The performance package included automatic transmission power brakes and dual exhausts, plus a sport steering wheel, turbo hood ornament, 'Turbo Coupe' trunk decal in big and bold billboard letters on rear deck panels, and a turbo hood blister with 'Turbo 3.8 Litre' badge. In short, you couldn't help but think a turbo engine might lurk under the hood. It also included a front air dam and rear spoiler, flat black paint trim, and turbine-design polycast wheels with 7 in. rims. Many of the Turbo Coupe features were first seen on Buick's 1976 Indy 500 Pace Car, including the four-barrel turbocharged V-6, an improved-flow cylinder head, dual exhaust, front air dam, and rear spoiler. Turbo Coupes were offered in white, silver, medium blue, dark gold, and red. Century's basic Sport Coupe included flat black trim in the grille and around headlamps and moldings; black wipers; plus a hawk decal high on front fenders, ahead of the door. The package also featured Designers' Sport wheels, wide steel-belted tires, Rallye ride/handling suspension, fast-ratio power steering (optional), and a rear spoiler. Custom and Special sedans and wagons were also available, plus a Sport Wagon option with Rallye suspension, large (P205/70R14) tires on Designers' Sport wheels, hawk decal, sport mirrors, air deflector, and special paint with black accents on grille, headlamp trim, wipers, moldings and pillars. Sport Wagons had wide rocker panels and wheel opening moldings. All wagons had a split tailgate: the glass portion lifted up like a hatch, while the bottom section folded down. Limited sedans carried the same plush interior as the Regal Limited coupe, including crushed velour 55/45 seats, plus wide rocker panel and belt reveal moldings and a custom steering wheel. All three option packages were offered in a choice of five body colors. New options included different interior fabrics, reclining driver's seat, sport steering wheel, and visor vanity mirrors.

1979 Buick, Regal Limited coupe with optional wire wheel covers. (OCW)

REGAL - SERIES 4A - V-6/V-8 - Regal had been set apart from the Century line for the first time in 1978. This year, the formal roofline and full-cut wheel openings were unchanged. Subdued horizontal bars were added to the basic Regal's strong vertical-patterned grille, which again sloped outward at the base. Taillamps were newly designed as was the instrument panel. Cornering lamps were made available on all Regal models. Single rectangular headlamps were flanked by clear vertical park/signal lamps. The Buick name was inset in the top bar of the grille; 'Regal' script stood near the lower corner. Ahead of the door was an emblem denoting engine size in liters. Standard engine was the 196 cu. in. (3.2-liter) V-6, except in California. Options included the larger 231 V-6, or 301 and 305 V-8s. Standard transmission was three-speed manual (except in California,

where automatic was required). California cars added a new C-4 (Computer Controlled Catalytic Converter) system to control emissions, which included an electronically-controlled carburetor and three-way catalytic converter. As noted on its fender insignia, Regal's Sport Coupe had the turbo 231 V-6 under the hood. Also standard was a Rallye ride/handling suspension with front/rear stabilizer bars; firmer springs and shocks; fast-ratio power steering; P205/70R14 tires; and turbo boost gauge on the dash. A special Sport Coupe Decor Package included blackout trim around windshield, on rocker moldings, wipers, door pillars, around taillamps and license plate molding; plus a blacked-out grille, twin sport mirrors, and Designers' Accent paint treatment on hood, top and deck lid. Four Turbine wheels, too. Regal interiors carried handy door-pull assist straps. A simulated woodgrain instrument panel with large instruments in squares sat far forward to allow extra leg room. Regal Limited added wide chrome rocker panel moldings plus "Limited" insignia below the 'Regal' script on the roof pillar. Inside were soft velour 55/45 notchback seats, plus crushed velour door inserts and rear-seat side trim. New Regal options included cornering lamps, turbine-styled wheels, and visor vanity mirrors. Also available; a silver-tinted Astroroof, metal sunroof or Hatch roof; plus three vinyl top styles.

1979 Buick, LeSabre Limited sedan. (OCW)

LESABRE - SERIES 4B - V-6/V-8 - LeSabre's new grille had thin vertical elements separated into three sections by two horizontal bars. Quad rectangular headlamps sat over separate park/signal lamps. Buick block letters were atop the upper grille corner. Rear fenders held the LeSabre nameplates. Restyled taillamps split into two wide sections by a horizontal bar, with clear backup lamps toward the center and amber lenses wrapping around the rear quarter panels. Inside was plenty of space for six passengers. Under the hood, a standard 231 cu. in. (3.8-liter) V-6 or choice of optional V-8 engines. Standard were power steering and brakes. The new top-line LeSabre Limited coupe and sedan, replacing the former Custom model, had a special molding package. LeSabre Sport Coupe continued the turbocharged V-6 powerplant introduced for 1978, with four-barrel and automatic transmission. Grille, windows and moldings sported flat black trim, and wheels were chrome-plated. The special handling package included large front and rear stabilizer bars, firm springs and shocks, plus quick-ratio power steering and wide oval tires. Eight different sound systems were available to please audio fans. A four-page brochure announced LeSabre's Palm Beach limited edition, which featured Designers' Accent paint treatment with yellow beige accent color on door-handle inserts, center pillar appliqué (with logo), lower bodyside and fender moldings, grille bar sides, wheel covers, and bumper rub strips. Inside were 55/45 seats trimmed in yellow beige Palm Beach cloth, woodgrain door, dash and steering wheel appliqués; and Palm Beach logo on the dash. Judging by its brochure picture, the Palm Beach with gold bodyside striping was a curious and colorful beast, reminiscent of some of the pastel models of the Fifties.

ESTATE WAGON - SERIES 4BR - V-8 - Buick's full-size station wagon front end looked similar to LeSabre. As before, it seated up to eight with optional third seat. Cargo area amounted to

88.6 cubic feet with rear seat folded down. This year, Estate fender trim strips carried only three "ventiports" instead of the previous four. The Limited option package included a special grille, power windows, tilt steering column, 55/45 notchback seats, luggage rack with air deflector, chrome wheels, and simulated woodgrain vinyl appliqué. Two engine choices were offered: 350 or 403 cu. in. V-8s, both with automatic transmission.

1979 Buick, Electra Park Avenue sedan. (OCW)

ELECTRA - SERIES 4C - V-8 - The posh full-size Buick got a new front end look this year with new quad rectangular headlamps, plus new vertical-style wraparound taillamps and new body colors. The new grille ran the entire car width, encompassing the headlamps. Its tiny crosshatch pattern was divided into a dozen sections by two horizontal and five vertical bars, slightly peaked at the front. Quad rectangular headlamps stood above horizontal park/signal lamps. The slanted headlamp bezels that had become an integral part of the Buick "look" were there again for 1979. Electra still displayed the four-section "ventiport" trim strip on squared-off front fenders--a vestige of the portholes famed on Buicks through the 1950s. Full-width wraparound taillamps were accented by the Electra crest. One bright bodyside molding sat low, not far above the rocker panels. In addition to the fourteen standard Buick colors, there were three new Firemist colors (gold, gray and saffron) available on Electras. Inside was new simulated butterfly woodgrain trim on the instrument panel. A bank of lighted indicators atop the dashboard showed if high beams were on and gave information on engine operation, seat belts and parking brake position. Base engine was the 350 cu. in. (5.7-liter) V-8 with 4Bbl. carburetor; optional, the 403 (6.6-liter) V-8, which wouldn't be around much longer. Electra 225 and Limited models were offered again, plus the plush Park Avenue. That Park Avenue edition included elegantly buttoned-and-tucked velvet upholstery with an armrest for each 50/50 section—a total of seven armrests in the car. Two velvet pockets were sewn into the back of the front seat. High-intensity reading lamps illuminated from the headliner. Outside were unique new coach lamps, using electroluminiscent panels that had no bulbs to burn out. Options included a lighted vanity mirror on the underside of the driver's sun visor, and a selection of five wheel cover styles.

RIVIERA - SERIES 4BZ - V-6/V-8 - In Buick's words, the all-new Riviera was meant to be "a statement of what we think is to come, rather than simply a well-turned expression of what is already here." Freshly downsized, the new fifth-generation Riv was re-engineered to front-drive, sharing mechanical details with Cadillac Eldorado and Oldsmobile Toronado, and reclassified as a (spacious) four-passenger. Once again, it sported full-cut wheel openings and sweeping quarter panels. Underneath was a new fully independent suspension (front and rear), using front torsion bars and rear leaf springs, to improve the ride and handling. It included a standard rear stabilizer bar. Construction remained the separate body-and-frame design. Riv's raked-back front end and squared-off roofline suggested luxury. But this edition was almost a foot shorter overall than the 1978 Riviera, and two inches shorter in wheelbase. The grille was made up of vertical bars that sloped outward slightly, divided into eight sections by slightly wider bars. "Riviera" script was at the side of the grille. Quad

headlamps sat above clear parking/signal lamps. Another "Riviera" script stood just ahead of the door, not far above the rocker panel molding. Two models were now available: luxury and sport. Standard Rivieras were powered by the 350 cu. in. (5.7-liter) V-8, but the sporty new S Type carried a special version of the turbocharged 231 cu. in. (3.8-liter) V-6 with four-barrel carburetor. This was the only turbo V-6 front-drive car made in the U.S. Actually, either Riviera model could be ordered with the other engine as an option. Though hardly a lightweight, the turbocharged Riv could hit 60 MPH in about 12 seconds, while returning fairly thrifty gas mileage on the road. Riviera's lengthy standard equipment list included a Delco AM/FM stereo radio with power antenna, six-way power driver's seat, power windows, power brakes and steering, automatic transmission, digital clock, air conditioning, Soft-Ray tinted glass, side-window defrosters, cornering lights, and automatic level control. Four-wheel disc brakes were again available; front discs standard. A wide variety of fabrics and leather upholstery was available. Standard setup was 45/55 seating with velour or vinyl and a folding center armrest. S Type had new bucket seats in vinyl or cloth, with leather available. Riviera also had maintenance-free wheel bearings, front and rear. The S Type's instrument panel was trimmed in brushed black, while its chassis held ride/handling extras. Standard equipment included firmer-rate front torsion bars and rear springs; firmer shock absorbers; larger-diameter stabilizer bars (front and rear); fast-ratio power steering; bucket seats and center storage console; plus a sport steering wheel with T-shaped center section and padded rim. Outside, the S Type had flat black trim around windows, and on grille and rocker panels; streamlined sport mirrors; amber front parking lights; and Designers' Sport wheel covers. New electronically-tuned (ETR) radios were available, with digital readout and signal seeking. Other notable (if not new) options: padded Landau top with coach lamps in roof pillars; electric sunroof; and glass Astroroof. A new digital speedometer and fuel gauge—part of the optional computer-controlled Trip Monitor--was offered later in the model year. Touch the right buttons and you could learn estimated time of arrival, how far you could travel on remaining fuel, and miles remaining to destination. Plus digital readouts of engine temperature, R.P.M. and voltage; current time, average speed and elapsed trip time; and a trip odometer. This option was a harbinger of things to come in digital equipment; but the standard Riviera dash still carried a conventional speedometer and fuel gauge.

1979 Buick, Riviera S Type (turbocharged) coupe. (OCW)

I.D. DATA: The 13-symbol Vehicle Identification Number (VIN) was again on the upper left surface of the instrument panel, visible through the windshield. Coding was similar to 1978; see that listing for details. One series was added ('Y' Riviera S Type), and LeSabre (code 'P') was now called Limited rather than Custom. Engine coding (symbol five) was as follows: 'C' V6-196 2Bbl. (LD5); 'A' V6-231 2Bbl. (LD5); '2' V6-231 2Bbl. (LC6); '3' Turbo

V6-231 4Bbl. (LC8); 'Y' V8-301 2Bbl. (L27); 'W' V8-301 4Bbl. (L37); 'G' V8-305 2Bbl. (LG3); 'H' V8-305 4Bbl. (LG4); 'L' V8-350 4Bbl. (LM1); 'R' V8-350 4Bbl. (L34); 'X' V8-350 4Bbl (L77); 'K' V8-403 4Bbl. (L80). The sixth symbol (model year) changed to '9' for 1979. The code for the Lordstown plant changed to '7'.

SKYHAWK (V-6)

Model No.	Body/Style No.	Body Type & Seating	Factory Price	Shipping Weight	Prod. Total
4H	T07	2-dr 'S' Hatch-4P	4380	2724	4,766
4H	S07	2-dr. Hatch-4P	4598	2740	18,373

SKYLARK 'S' (V-6/V-8)

4X	W27	2-dr Coupe-6P	4082/4277	3105/3224	1,605

BASE SKYLARK (V-6/V-8)

4X	B27	2-dr Coupe-6P	4208/4403	3114/3233	8,596
4X	B17	2-dr Hatch-6P	4357/4552	3195/3314	608
4X	B69	4-dr Sedan-6P	4308/4503	3158/3277	10,849

SKYLARK CUSTOM (V 6/V-8)

4X	C27	2-dr Coupe-5P	4462/4657	3123/3242	3,546
4X	C69	4-dr Sedan-6P	4562/4757	3176/3295	3,822

Note 1: Of the 20,053 base Skylarks built, 2,963 had a V-8; of the 7,368 Skylark Customs, 2,497 had a V-8.

CENTURY SPECIAL (V-6/V-8)

4A	E87	2-dr Coupe-6P	4599/4855	3038/3142	3,152
4A	E09	4-dr Sedan-6P	4699/4955	3053/3157	7,364
4A	E35	4-dr Sta Wag-6P	5247/5442	3158/3286	10,413

CENTURY CUSTOM (V-6/V-8)

4A	H87	2-dr Coupe-6P	4843/5099	3051/3155	2,474
4A	H09	4-dr Sedan-6P	4968/5224	3071/3175	6,987
4A	H35	4-dr Sta Wag-6P	5561/5756	3194/3322	21,100

CENTURY SPORT (V-6/V-8)

4A	G87	2-dr Coupe-6P	5151/5386	3047/3151	1,653

1979 Buick, Century Limited sedan. (OCW)

CENTURY LIMITED (V-6/V-8)

4A	L09	4-dr Sedan-6P	5336/5592	3104/3208	2,694

Note 2: Of the total 20,929 Century Specials built, 5,053 had a V-8 engine; of the 30,561 Century Customs, 16,110 were V-8 powered.

REGAL (V-6/V-8)

4A	J47	2-dr Coupe-6P	5080/5315	3029/3133	157,228

REGAL SPORT COUPE (TURBO V-6)

4A	K47	2-dr Coupe-6P	6223	3190	21,389

REGAL LIMITED (V-6/V-8)

4A	M47	2-dr Coupe-6P	5477/5712	3071/3175	94,748

LESABRE (V-6/V-8)

4B	N37	2-dr Coupe-6P	5680/5926	3428/3556	7,542
4B	N69	4-dr Sedan-6P	5780/6026	3459/3587	25,431

LESABRE LIMITED (V-6/V-8)

4B	P37	2-dr Coupe-6P	6124/6370	3454/3582	38,290
4B	P69	4-dr Sedan-6P	6249/6495	3503/3631	75,939

LESABRE SPORT COUPE (TURBO V-6)

4B	F37	2-dr Coupe-6P	6621	3545	3,582

Note 3: Only 14,851 base and Limited LeSabres had a V-6 engine.

ESTATE WAGON (V-8)

4B	R35	4-dr Sta Wag-6P	6714	4021	21,312

ELECTRA 225 (V-8)

4C	V37	2-dr Coupe-6P	7581	3767	5,358
4C	V69	4-dr Sedan-6P	7756	3831	11,055

ELECTRA LIMITED (V-8)

4C	X37	2-dr Coupe-6P	7981	3789	28,878
4C	X69	4-dr Sedan-6P	8156	3853	76,340

ELECTRA PARK AVENUE (V-8)

Model No.	Body/Style No.	Body Type & Seating	Factory Price	Shipping Weight	Prod. Total
4C	U37	2-dr Coupe-6P	8423	3794	Note 4
4C	U69	4-dr Sedan-6P	8598	3860	Note 4

Note 4: Production totals listed under Electra Limited include Park Avenue models. A total of 61,096 Limiteds and 44,122 Park Avenue versions were produced.

Note 5: Electra had massive price increases during the model year, of more than $1,100. By mid-year, the base 225 coupe sold for $8,703 and the Park Avenue sedan for $9,959.

RIVIERA (V-8)

4E	Z57	2-dr Coupe-4P	10112	3759	37,881

RIVIERA S TYPE TURBO (V-6)

4E	Y57	2-dr Coupe-4P	10388	3774	14,300

Note 6: Total Riviera production includes 2,067 standard models with optional turbo V-6 engine, while S Type production includes 5,900 with a non-turbo V-8, which was offered with a price credit.

FACTORY PRICE AND WEIGHT NOTE: Figure before the slash is for V-6 engine, after the slash for smallest (lowest-priced) V-8 engine available.

ENGINES: BASE V-6 (Century, Regal): 90-degree, overhead-valve V-6. Cast iron alloy block and head. Displacement: 196 cu. in. (3.2 liters). Bore & stroke: 3.5 x 3.4 in. Compression ratio: 8.0:1. Brake horsepower: 105 at 4000 R.P.M. Torque; 160 lb.-ft. at 2000 R.P.M. Four main bearings. Hydraulic valve lifters. Carburetor: 2Bbl. Rochester M2ME. VIN Code: C. Sales Code: LC9. BASE V-6 (Skyhawk, Skylark, Century wagon, LeSabre); OPTIONAL (Century sed/cpe, Regal): 90 degree, overhead-valve V-6. Cast iron alloy block and head. Displacement: 231 cu. in. (3.8 liters). Bore & stroke: 3.8 x 3.4 in. Compression ratio: 8.0:1. Brake horsepower: 115 at 3800 R.P.M. Torque; 190 lb.-ft. at 2000 R.P.M. Four main bearings. Hydraulic valve lifters. Carburetor: 2Bbl. Rochester M2ME. VIN Code: A. Sales Code: LDS. Note: Alternate LC5 version (VIN code 2) with Computer Controlled Catalytic Converter (C-4) and E2ME carburetor was used on California Century and Regal models. TURBOCHARGED V-6 (Regal and LeSabre Sport Coupes, Riviera S); OPTIONAL (Century, Riviera): Same as 231 V-6 above, but with M4ME four-barrel carburetor. Brake horsepower: 170 at 4000 R.P.M. (Century, 175 at 4000; Riviera, 185 at 4200). Torque: 265 lb.-ft. at 2800 R.P.M. (Century, 275 at 2600; Riviera, 280 at 2400). VIN Code: 3. Sales Code: LC8. OPTIONAL V-8 (Century, Regal, LeSabre) 90-degree overhead-valve V-8. Cast iron alloy block and head. Displacement: 301 cu. in. (4.9 liters). Bore & stroke: 4.0 x 3.0 in. Compression ratio: 8.1:1. Brake horsepower: 140 at 3600 R.P.M. Torque: 235 lb.-ft. at 2000 R.P.M. Five main bearings. Hydraulic valve lifters. Carburetor: 2Bbl. Roch. M2MC. Built by Pontiac. VIN Code: Y. Sales Code: L27. OPTIONAL V-8 (Century, Regal): Same as above but with M4MC 4Bbl. carburetor. Brake horsepower: 150 at 4000 R.P.M. Torque: 240 lb.-ft. at 2000 R.P.M. VIN Code: W. Sales Code: L37. OPTIONAL V-8 (Skylark): 90-degree overhead-valve V-8. Cast iron alloy block and head. Displacement: 305 cu. in. (5.0 liters). Bore & stroke: 3.736 x 3.48 in. Compression ratio: 8.4:1. Brake horsepower: 130 at 3200 R.P.M. Torque: 245 lb.-ft. at 2000 R.P.M. Five main bearings. Hydraulic valve lifters. Carburetor: 2Bbl. Rochester M2MC. Built by Chevrolet. VIN Code: U. Sales Code: LG3. OPTIONAL V-8 (Century/Regal in California and for high-altitude operation): 90 degree overhead valve V-8. Cast iron alloy block and head. Displacement: 305 cu. in. (5.0 liters). Bore & stroke: 3.736 x 3.48 in. Compression ratio: 8.4:1. Brake horsepower: 115 at 4000 R.P.M. Torque: 225 lb.-ft. at 2400 R.P.M. Five main bearings. Hydraulic valve lifters. Carburetor: 4Bbl. Rochester M4MC. VIN Code: H. Sales Code: LG4. BASE V-8 (Electra, Estate); OPTIONAL (LeSabre): 90-degree, overhead valve V-8. Cast iron alloy block and head. Displacement: 350 cu. in. (5.7 liters). Bore & stroke: 3.80 x 3.85 in. Compression ratio: 8.0:1. Brake horsepower: 155 at 3400 R.P.M. Torque: 280 lb.-ft. at 1800 R.P.M. Five main bearings. Hydraulic valve lifters. Carburetor: 4Bbl. Rochester M4MC. VIN Code: X. Sales Code: L77. ALTERNATE 350-4 V-8 (Estate

in California, Riviera); OPTIONAL (Calif./high-altitude LeSabre/Electra; Riviera S): 90-degree, overhead valve V-8. Cast iron alloy block and head. Displacement: 350 cu. in. (5.7 liters). Bore & stroke: 4.057 x 3.385 in. Compression ratio: 8.0:1. Brake horsepower: 160 at 3800 R.P.M. Torque: 270 lb.-ft. at 2000 R.P.M. Five main bearings. Hydraulic valve lifters. Carburetor: 4Bbl. Rochester M4MC. Built by Buick. VIN Code: R. Ordering Code: L34. OPTIONAL V-8 (Skylark, Century wagon): 90-degree, overhead valve V-8. Cast iron alloy block and head. Displacement: 350 cu. in. (5.7 liters). Bore & stroke: 4.00 x 3.48 in. Compression ratio: 8.2:1. Brake horsepower: 165 at 3800 R.P.M. Torque: 260 lb.-ft. at 2400 R.P.M. Five main bearings. Hydraulic valve lifters. Carburetor: 4Bbl. Rochester M4MC. Chevrolet-built. VIN Code: L. Ordering Code: LM1. OPTIONAL V-8 (Electra): 90-degree, overhead valve V-8. Cast iron alloy block and head. Displacement: 403 cu. in. (6.6 liters). Bore & stroke: 4.351 x 3.385 in. Compression ratio: 8.0:1. Brake horsepower: 175 at 3600 R.P.M. Torque: 310 lb.-ft. at 2000 R.P.M. Five main bearings. Hydraulic valve lifters. Carburetor: 4Bbl. Roch, M4MC. Built by Oldsmobile. VIN Code: K. Ordering Code: L80.

CHASSIS DATA: Wheelbase: (Skyhawk) 97.0 in.; (Skylark) 111.0 in.; (Century/Regal) 108.1 in.; (LeSabre/Estate) 115.9 in.; (Electra) 118.9 in.; (Riviera) 114.0 in. Overall length: (Skyhawk) 179.3 in.; (Skylark) 200.2 in.; (Century) 196.0 in.; (Regal) 200.0 in.; (LeSabre) 218.2 in.; (Electra) 222.1 in.; (Estate) 216.7 in.; (Riv) 206.6 in. Height: (Skyhawk) 50.2 in.; (Skylark 2-dr.) 52.2 in.; (Skylark 4-dr.) 53.1 in.; (Century cpe) 54.1 in.; (Century sed) 55.0 in.; (Century wagon) 55.7 in.; (Regal) 53.4 in.; (LeSabre/Electra cpe) 55.0 in.; (LeSabre sed) 55.7 in.; (Electra sed) 55.9 in.; (Estate) 56.5 in.; (Riv) 54.3 in. Width: (Skyhawk) 65.4 in.; (Skylark) 72.7 in.; (Century/Regal cpe) 76.5 in.; (Century/Regal) 72.2 in.; (LeSabre/Electra) 77.2 in.; (Estate) 79.9 in.; (Riv) 70.4 in. Front Tread: (Skyhawk) 54.7 in.; (Skylark) 59.1 in.; (Century/Regal) 58.5 in.; (LeSabre/Electra) 61.8 in.; (Estate) 62.2 in.; (Riv) 59.3 in. Rear Tread: (Skyhawk) 53.6 in.; (Skylark) 59.7 in.; (Century/Regal) 57.8 in.; (LeSabre/Electra) 60.7 in.; (Estate) 64.0 in.; (Riv) 60.0 in. Standard Tires: (Skyhawk) BR78 x 13; (Skyhawk 'S') B78 x 13; (Skylark) E78 x 14; (Century cpe/sed) P185/75R14 GBR; (Century wag/Regal) P195/75R14 GBR; (Century/Regal Spt Cpe) P205/70R14 SBR; (LeSabre) FR78 x 15 GBR; (LeSabre Spt Cpe) GR70 x 15 SBR; (Electra) GR78 x 15; (Estate) HR78 x 15 SBR.

TECHNICAL: Transmission: Three-speed fully synchronized manual gearbox standard on Skylark (column), Century cpe/sed (floor), and Regal cpe (floor); Turbo Hydra-matic optional. Four-speed manual gearbox available on Century/Regal. Four-speed, fully synchronized floor shift standard on Skyhawk; five-speed and automatic optional. Turbo-Hydra-matic standard on Regal sedan, LeSabre, Electra, Estate and Riviera. Three-speed manual trans. gear ratios; (1st) 3.50:1; (2nd) 1.81:1; (3rd) 1.00:1; (Rev) 3.62:1. Four-speed gear ratios: (1st) 3.50:1; (2nd) 2.48:1; (3rd) 1.66:1; (4th) 1.00:1; (Rev) 3.50:1. Five-speed gear ratios: (1st) 3.40:1; (2nd) 2.08:1; (3rd) 1.39:1; (4th) 1.00:1; (5th) 0.80:1; (Rev) 3.36:1. Automatic trans. gear ratios: (1st) 2.52:1; (2nd) 1.52:1; (3rd) 1.00:1; (Rev) 1.93:1. Electra automatic: (1st) 2.48:1; (2nd) 1.48:1; (3rd) 1.00:1; (Rev) 2.08:1. Century V-8/Riviera automatic: (1st) 2.74:1; (2nd) 1.57:1; (3rd) 1.00:1; (Rev) 2.07:1 (Riviera 2.57:1). Standard axle ratios: (Skyhawk) 2.93:1; (Skylark V-6) 3.08:1; (Skylark V-8) 2.41:1; (Century V6-196) 2.93:1; (Century V6-231, V8-350) 2.73:1; (Century V8-301) 2.29:1; (Century V8-305) 2.41:1; (Century Turbo cpe) 3.08:1; (Regal) 2.93:1 exc. V-8, 2.29:1; (Regal Sport Coupe) 2.41:1; (LeSabre V-6) 2.73:1; (LeSabre V8-301) 2.29:1; (LeSabre V-8) 2.41:1; (LeSabre V-6 Sport Coupe) 2.73:1; (Electra/Riviera) 2.41:1; (Riviera turbo) 2.93:1; (Estate) 2.73:1 exc. V8-403, 2.41:1. Steering: recirculating ball; power assist standard on Century/Regal, LeSabre, Electra, Estate and Riviera. Suspension: (Riviera) front wishbones, longitudinal torsion bars and anti-roll bar; independent rear with swinging longitudinal trailing arms, transverse linkage bar and automatic leveling front-wheel drive; (others) same as 1977-78. Brakes:

front disc, rear drum; power brakes standard on LeSabre/Electra/Riviera plus Century wagon and Regal Sport Coupe. Four-wheel power disc brakes optional on Riviera. Body construction: (Skyhawk) unitized; (Skylark) separate front frame unit cushion-mounted to unitized body; (others) separate body and frame. Fuel tank: (Skyhawk) 18.5 gal.; (Skylark) 21 gal.; (Century/Regal) 18.1 gal.; (LeSabre/Electra) 25.3 gal.; (Estate) 22.5 gal.; (Riv) 20 gal. Unleaded fuel only. High-Energy electronic ignition (HEI) on all engines.

DRIVETRAIN OPTIONS: Engines: 231 cu. in. V-6, 2Bbl.: Century cpe/sed, Regal ($40); Turbocharged 231 cu. in. V-6, 4Bbl.: Century cpe/sed ($470); Riv ($110). 301 cu. in. V-8, 2Bbl.: Century/Regal ($195-$256); LeSabre ($246). 301 cu. in. V-8, 4Bbl.: Century/Regal ($255-$316). 305 cu. in. V-8, 2Bbl.: Skylark ($195). 305 cu. in. V-8, 4Bbl.: Century/Regal ($255-$316). 350 cu. in. V-8, 4Bbl.: Skylark ($320); Century wagon ($320); LeSabre ($371); Riviera S (credit ($110). 403 cu. in. V-8, 4Bbl.: Electra/Estate ($70). Transmission/Differential: Four-speed manual floor shift: Century cpe/sed, Regal with 231 V-6 ($135); Five-speed manual floor shift: Skyhawk ($175); Automatic trans.: Skyhawk ($295); Skylark, Century cpe/sed, Regal ($335); Optional rear axle ratio: Skylark 2.90:1, 3.08:1 or 3.23:1 (NC). Limited slip differential ($60-$68) exc. Riviera. Power Accessories: Power brakes: Skyhawk ($71); Skylark/Century/Regal ($76). Four-wheel disc brakes: LeSabre spt cpe, Riv ($205). Power steering: Skyhawk ($146); Skylark/Century/Regal ($163). Suspension: F40 firm ride/handling pkg.: all exc. Skyhawk ($21). FE2 Rallye ride/handling pkg.: Century/Regal ($38). FE2 Rallye ride/handling pkg. incl. rear stabilizer bar: Skylark ($48), included in Sport package. Automatic level control: Century/Regal/LeSabre/Electra ($121). Other: Trailer towing flasher/harness package: Skylark/Century/Regal/LeSabre/Electra ($22-$35). Heavy-duty alternator, 80 ampere: LeSabre/Electra/Riviera V-8 ($43-$46). Heavy-duty battery ($18-$21). Heavy-duty cooling: Skyhawk/Skylark ($30-$58). Heavy-duty radiator: Skylark V-8 ($22). Engine block heater ($15). Heavy-duty engine/transmission cooling: Century/Regal/LeSabre/Electra/Riviera ($30-$58). High altitude emission system ($35). California emission system ($83-$150).

SKYHAWK CONVENIENCE/APPEARANCE OPTIONS: Option Packages: Road Hawk pkg. (BR70 x 13 SBR wide-oval blackwall tires, specific suspension, blackout molding (N/A). Appearance group (wheel opening moldings and bodyside stripe): 'S' ($57). Acoustic pkg. ($25). Convenience group: day/night mirror, underhood light, glove box light, headlamp-on indicator ($24). Shadow light Astroroof ($641). Vista Vent roof ($180). Comfort/Convenience: Air cond. ($496). Rear defogger, electric ($87). Tinted glass ($60). Tinted windshield ($50). Tilt steering ($68). Instrument gauges, electric clock and tach ($73). Electric clock ($21). Visor vanity mirrors, pair ($10). Entertainment: AM/FM radio ($74). AM/FM stereo radio ($148). AM radio and 8-track player ($157). AM/FM stereo radio and 8-track ($250). Rear speaker ($23). Exterior Trim: Door edge guard moldings ($12). Roof crown moldings ($183). Protective bodyside moldings ($10-$45). Designer's accent paint ($175). Interior Trim/Upholstery: Adjustable driver's seatback ($20). Front/rear mats ($21). Custom seatbelts ($18). Wheels and Tires: Custom sport wheels ($58). Styled aluminum wheels ($230). B78 x 13 WSW ($36-$45) BR78 x 13 SBR BSW ($89-$111). BR78 x 13 SBR WSW ($36-$158). BR70 x 13 SBR wide-oval WLT ($49-$194). Conventional spare tire (NC).

SKYLARK CONVENIENCE/APPEARANCE OPTIONS: Option Packages: Sport Coupe or Sport Sedan pkg.: FE2 Rallye ride/handling suspension, ER78 x 14 SBR tires, sport mirrors ($202-$221); N/A on Skylark 'S'. Accessory pkg. (day/night mirror, lighter): 'S' ($15). Acoustic pkg. ($28-$42). Convenience group ($32-$43). Comfort/Convenience: Air cond. ($529). Cruise Master ($103). Two-speed wipers w/low-speed delay ($38). Rear defogger, blower-type ($55). Power windows ($126-

$178). Electric door locks ($80-$111). Sport steering wheel ($42). Tilt steering ($75). Tinted glass ($64). Tinted windshield ($50). Dual horns ($10). Electric clock ($24). Headlamps-on indicator ($11). Remote-control left mirror ($18). Sport mirrors: left remote, right manual ($45). Electric trunk release ($24). Entertainment: AM radio ($82). AM/FM radio ($158). AM/FM stereo radio ($236). AM radio and 8-track player ($244). AM/FM stereo radio and 8-track or cassette ($345). Rear speaker ($25). Windshield antenna ($29); incl. w/radios. Exterior Trim: Landau vinyl top ($190-$195). Long vinyl top ($99-$104). Two-tone painted top ($48). Designers' accent paint ($161). Swing-out rear quarter vent window: two-doors ($59). Protective bodyside moldings ($43). Roof drip and wheel opening moldings: 'S' ($38). Rocker panel moldings ($18); std. on Custom. Wide rocker appearance group ($45). Decklid molding ($10). Custom door and window frame moldings ($28-$35). Door edge guards ($13-$21). Bodyside stripes ($34). Bumper guards, front/rear ($45). Bumper strips front/rear ($37). Interior Trim/Upholstery: Full-length console ($80). Vinyl bucket trim: base Skylark ($90). Custom seatbelts ($19-$21). Front carpet savers ($15). Carpet savers and handy mats ($25). Carpeted door trim with map pocket and reflector: base ($43). Wheels: Styled wheels ($80-$99). Chrome-plated wheels ($120-$139). Deluxe wheel covers ($42). Custom wire wheel covers ($118-$160). Tires: E78 x 14 WSW ($37-$46). ER78 x 14 SBR BSW ($78-$97). ER78 x 14 SBR WSW ($37-$143). FR78 x 14 SBR WLT ($67-$180). Stowaway spare tire ($19).

CENTURY/REGAL CONVENIENCE/APPEARANCE OPTIONS: Option Packages and Groups: Regal Sport Coupe Decor ($473). Century Special Sport Wagon pkg. ($473). Century Turbo Coupe pkg.: special suspension, sporty exhaust, turbine wheels, decklid identification ($40). Electric sunroof: coupe ($529). Silver electric Astroroof: coupe ($729). Hurst hatch roof: Regal ($655). Exterior molding pkg. ($10-$147). Convenience group ($6-$58). Comfort/Convenience: Air cond. ($562). Automatic air cond. ($653). Cruise Master ($103). Rear defogger, electric ($99). Tinted glass ($70). Tinted windshield ($50). Six-way power driver's seat ($163). Manual seatback recliner ($62). Custom steering wheel: Century ($10). Sport steering wheel ($32-$42). Tilt steering ($75). Power windows ($132-$187). Electric door locks ($86-$120). Electric trunk release ($24). Remote tailgate lock: Century wag ($25). Electric dial clock ($24). Digital clock ($55). Headlamps-on indicator ($11). Trip odometer ($13). Instrument gauges ($27). Fuel usage light and instrument gauges ($57). Dome reading lamp ($19). Windshield wiper w/delay ($38). Lighting and Mirrors: Cornering lamps: Regal ($49). Front light monitors ($29). Remote left mirror ($18); right ($34-$39). Sport mirrors: left remote ($40-$45). Dual remote sport mirrors ($25-$70). Visor vanity mirrors, pair ($10). Lighted right visor vanity mirror ($46). Entertainment: AM radio ($86). AM/FM radio ($163); AM/FM stereo radio ($236). AM radio w/8-track ($248) w/digital readout ($402); w/CB ($574). AM/FM stereo radio w/8-track or cassette ($345-$351). Rear speaker ($25). Windshield antenna ($29); incl. with radios. Automatic antenna ($47-$76). Triband power antenna ($86-$115). Exterior Trim: Landau vinyl top: Regal ($146-$162); heavy-padded ($178-$228). Long vinyl top ($116). Designers' accent paint ($161-$213). Solid special color paint ($152). Bumper guards, front/rear ($45). Protective bodyside moldings ($48). Rocker panel moldings: Century Special ($18). Door edge guards ($13-$21). Belt reveal moldings ($34). Wheel opening moldings; Century Spec. wag ($22). Bodyside stripes ($34). Woodgrain vinyl appliqué: Century wag ($267-$289). Luggage rack: Century wag ($90). Air deflector: Century wag ($30). Interior Trim/Upholstery: Full-length console ($90). Bucket seats: Century Custom, Regal ($45); Century sport ($181). 55/45 seating: Century Custom; Regal ($102); Century spt ($238). Limited 55/45 seating: Regal spt cpe ($272). Notchback seating: Century spt ($136). Custom seatbelts ($19-$22). Load floor carpet area: Century Spec. wag ($51). Front carpet savers ($15-$25). Carpet

savers and mats ($25). Front/rear carpet savers with inserts ($45). Litter pocket ($9). Trunk trim covering ($31). Lockable storage compartment: Century wag ($37-$42). Wheels: Chrome-plated wheels ($44-$169). Designer's sport wheels ($106-$125). Deluxe wheel covers; Century exc. spt ($42). Designer's wheel covers: Century exc. spt ($70); Regal ($28). Custom wire wheel covers: Century exc. spt ($160); Regal ($118). Tires P185/75R14 GBR WSW: Century cpe/sed ($39). P195/75R14 GBR WSW: Century cpe/sed ($21). P195/75R14 GBR WSW ($40-$61). P195/75R14 SBR BSW: Century ($41-$61). P195/75R14 SBR WSW: Century ($81-$101). P205/70R14 SBR wide-oval BSW: Regal ($32). P205/70R14 SBR WSW: Century spt. Regal ($44-$76). P205/70R14 SBR WLT ($56-$149).

LESABRE/ELECTRA/ESTATE WAGON CONVENIENCE/APPEARANCE OPTIONS: Option Packages: LeSabre coupe Sport pkg.: cloth front bucket seats, remote sport mirror ($160); w/full-length console ($254). Estate Wagon convenience group ($13-$68). Estate Wagon Limited pkg.: 55/45 front seating, tilt steering, custom belts, power windows, electric door locks, remote tailgate lock, remote left mirror, chromed wheels, luggage rack, bumper guards, map light, dial clock, exterior molding pkg., woodgrain vinyl appliqué, acoustic pkg., special ornamentation ($1853). Exterior molding pkg. ($53-$173). Convenience group: LeSabre ($19-$99). Electric sunroof ($725-$798). Sliding Astroroof ($925-$998). Comfort/Convenience: Air cond. ($605). Automatic air cond. ($688). Cruise Master ($108). Rear defogger, electric ($101). Tinted glass ($84). Tinted windshield: LeSabre Estate ($51). Power windows LeSabre Estate ($138-$205). Electric door locks ($88-$122). Automatic door locks: Electra ($146-$175). Six-way power driver's seat ($135-$166). Dual power seats ($301-$332); N/A on base models. Manual seatback recliner, one side: LeSabre base or sport cpe ($62). Electric seatback recliner, one side ($118); N/A on base LeSabre sedan. Custom steering wheel: base LeSabre ($10). Sport steering wheel: LeSabre ($32-$42). Tilt steering ($77). Tilt/telescoping steering column ($44-$131). Digital clock: LeSabre, Estate (NC w/convenience group). Low fuel indicator ($17). Fuel usage light ($30). Speed alert and trip odometer ($23). Remote electric tailgate lock: Est ($34). Electric trunk release ($25). Electric fuel cap lock ($36). Theft deterrent system ($135); N/A on Estate. Three-speed wiper w/low-speed delay ($39). Lighting, Horns and Mirrors; Cornering lamps ($49). Front light monitors: LeSabre/Est ($29). Front/rear monitors: Electra ($62). Door courtesy/warning light ($36-$57). Rear courtesy lamps: Estate ($16). Headlamps-on indicator ($11). Dome reading lamp ($19). Sunshade map light: Electra 225 ($13). Four-note horn ($23). Remote left mirror: LeSabre/Est ($19). Remote right mirror ($34-$39). Dual remote sport mirrors ($49-$65). Dual electric remote mirrors: Electra ($97). Remote left mirror w/thermometer ($21-$38). Dual electric mirrors w/left thermometer: Electra ($118). Visor vanity mirrors, pair ($10). Lighted visor vanity mirror ($47). Entertainment: AM radio ($99); N/A on Electra. AM/FM radio ($174). AM/FM stereo radio ($239); w/CB ($581). AM/FM stereo radio w/digital readout: LeSabre, Estate ($347-$402). AM radio and 8-track ($265). AM/FM stereo radio and 8-track or cassette player ($349-$355). AM/FM stereo with 8-track and CB: Electra ($691). Signal-seeking AM/FM stereo radio with CB: Electra ($789); w/CB and 8-track ($899). Signal-seeking AM/FM stereo radio w/digital readout: Electra ($447); w/8-track ($557). Rear speaker ($26). Windshield antenna ($29); incl. w/radios. Automatic power antenna ($48-$77). Triband power antenna ($87-$116). Exterior Trim: Landau vinyl top: LeSabre ($155). Heavy-padded landau vinyl top: Electra ($200). Long vinyl top ($145-$164). Long, heavy-padded vinyl top: Electra ($206). Two-tone painted top: LeSabre ($58). Designers' accent paint: LeSabre Estate ($182-$240). Solid special color paint ($153) exc. Firemist on Electra ($172). Protective bodyside moldings: LeSabre/Est ($43). Color-coordinated bodyside moldings: Electra ($66). Hood ornament and windsplit: LeSabre/Est ($25). Door edge guards ($14-$21). Window frame scalp molding: Le-

Sabre/Est ($34). Wheel opening moldings: LeSabre/Est ($27). Belt reveal molding: LeSabre spt cpe ($34). Bodyside stripes ($52) N/A on Estate. Woodgrain vinyl appliqué: Estate ($293). Bumper guards front/rear ($45). Luggage rack w/air deflector: Est ($140). Interior Trim/Upholstery: Custom seat trim: notchback, LeSabre spt cpe or Estate ($404); 55/45 ($506); 55/45, LeSabre Ltd or Electra ($102). Third seat: Estate ($194). Custom seatbelts: LeSabre/Est ($22-$25). Full-length console: LeSabre cpe w/sport pkg. ($94). Front carpet savers ($15-$25). Front/rear carpet savers w/inserts ($45). Litter pocket ($9). Trunk carpeting/covering ($48-$60). Wheels: Deluxe wheel covers: LeSabre ($42). Custom wheel covers ($29-$71). Wire wheel covers ($87-$161). Chrome-plated wheels ($120-$171). Wire spoke wheels ($473-$625). Stowaway spare tire (N/C).

RIVIERA CONVENIENCE/APPEARANCE OPTIONS: Roof Options: Electric sunroof ($798). Electric Astroroof ($998). Comfort/Convenience: Automatic air cond. ($88). Cruise Master ($108). Rear defogger, electric ($101). Automatic door locks ($58). Six-way power seat, passenger ($166). Electric seatback recliner, one side ($118). Manual seatback recliner, one side: S ($62). Sport steering wheel ($32). Tilt steering ($77). Tilt/telescope steering wheel ($121). Electric fuel cap lock ($36). Electric trunk release ($25). Electric trunk lock ($60). Low fuel indicator, V-8 ($17). Fuel usage light, V-8 ($30). Lighting, Horns and Mirrors: Coach lamps ($85) incl. w/vinyl top. Front/rear light monitors ($62). Courtesy/reading lamp ($42). Lighted door lock and interior light control ($57). Headlamps-on indicator ($11). Four-note horn ($23). Remote left mirror w/thermometer ($21). Dual electric remote mirrors ($58); w/left thermometer ($79). Lighted visor vanity mirrors, each ($47). Entertainment: AM/FM stereo w/8-track or cassette player ($110-$116). AM/FM stereo radio w/CB ($294): w/CB and 8-track ($404). Signal seeking AM/FM stereo radio w/digital readout ($182); w/8-track ($292). Signal-seeking AM/CB/FM stereo radio w/digital clock ($524); w/8-track and clock ($634). Triband power antenna ($39). Exterior Trim: Heavy-padded landau top ($285). Long vinyl top ($285). Designers' accent paint ($193). Solid color special paint ($153) exc. Firemist ($172). Rear bumper guards ($22). Protective bodyside moldings ($59). Door edge guards ($14). Bodyside stripes ($52). Interior Trim/Upholstery: 45/55 notchback front seat, leather/vinyl ($350). Leather/vinyl bucket seats: ($350). Front/rear carpet savers w/inserts ($57). Trunk mat ($12).

HISTORY: Introduced: September 28, 1978. Model year production (U.S.): 727,275. Calendar year production (U.S.): 787,123. Model year sales by U.S. dealers: 754,619 (including 17,564 imported Opels). Calendar year sales (U.S.): 714,508 which, though down significantly, still gave Buick an increased market share of 8.6 percent.

Historical Footnotes: Buick expected to emphasize the mid-size Century lineup with the new Turbo Coupe, but buyers still liked the look of Regal better. Most models rose in price during the model year, but none so dramatically as Electra, which shot upward by over a thousand dollars. Many observers felt that the all-new Riviera, built in Linden, New Jersey, was more a descendant of the 1963 original than the 1970s boattail version. *Motor Trend* named it "Car of the Year"--the first Buick granted that title since the 1962 Special with its V-6 powerplant.

1980

First arrival for the 1980 model year was the new Skylark, continuing the old name but on an all-new front wheel drive chassis, cousin to the soon-to-be-notorious Chevrolet Citation

X-car. All the X-bodies debuted in April. Century kept the aero-style fastback coupe a little longer, but sedans took on a fresh notchback appearance for 1980. Full-size LeSabres and Electras were restyled with aerodynamics in mind. New higher-pressure tires offered less rolling resistance. Riviera, Electra and LeSabre now had match-mounted tires/wheels. Some automatic transmissions contained a torque converter clutch to reduce slippage loss. Buick fielded three new engines: a larger 252 cu. in. (4.1-liter) version of the familiar Buick 3.8-liter V-6: a lightweight 265 cu. in. (4.3-liter) 2Bbl. V-8 option for Century and Regal, intended as a middle ground between the 3.8 V-6 and 4.9 V-8: and a 5.7-liter diesel V-8 produced by Oldsmobile. Standard on Electras, the 4.1 had a larger bore than the 3.8, siamesed (no water jacket between the bores) to allow for the larger pistons. It had a new aluminum intake manifold, steel head gaskets (rather than composition), intake manifold gaskets with smaller exhaust gas crossover holes, and retuned engine mounts. The new diesel, available in Electras and Estates (later on LeSabre), differed a bit from the 5.7 diesel previously offered by other GM divisions. Its new fuel nozzle didn't require a return system to the fuel tank. For the first time, a V-6 was offered in every Buick series. The big 403 (6.6-liter) V-8 was finally gone. So were the small 3.2-liter V-6, and the 301 (4.9-liter) 2Bbl. V-8. Joining the option list was Twilight Sentinel, an automatic headlight control that would turn Electra or Riviera lights on when it grew dark, then off again as daylight emerged. The system, formerly available on Cadillacs, also kept headlights on for three minutes after you shut the engine off. Also new: tungsten-halogen high-beam headlamps that produced an intense white beam, standard on Regal/LeSabre Sport Coupes and Riviera S Type, optional elsewhere in the lineup. Electronic Touch Climate Control on Electra and LeSabre used a row of touch surfaces on a smooth panel in place of the usual protruding knobs and switches. Stereo entertainment stretched all the way up to a new six-speaker Concert Sound System available in the Electra Park Avenue sedan. Buick's Theft Deterrent System included door and trunk locks, plus a starter interrupt system to prevent the engine from firing.

1980 Buick, Skyhawk "Designers' Accent Edition" hatchback. (OCW)

SKYHAWK - SERIES 4H - V-6 - For its final year in this form, Skyhawk received only modest interior changes. In addition to standard and 'S' models, the sporty "Road Hawk" was offered again. That package included Oyster White bucket seats with hawk accents; flat black wipers, grille, headlamp trim and moldings; plus a rear spoiler and special suspension. The body featured silver/gray accent paint and striping. The Designers' Accent Edition, also available again this year, included a hawk decal, rear spoiler and special paint. Buick's subcompact was dropped early in the model year, to permit increased production of other H-Special bodied GM models. The name would return on an all-new model for 1982. Skyhawk's standard equipment included a maintenance free battery. AM radio, front/rear bumper guards, protective bumper strips deluxe wheel covers, carpeting, cigarette lighter, full-length console, high-energy ignition, day/night inside mirror, outside sport mirrors (left remote), vinyl bucket seats, sport steering wheel, rear stabilizer bar, space-saver spare tire, and four-speed floor shift. The 'S' Skyhawk lacked wheel opening moldings and bodyside stripes.

1980 Buick, Skylark Sport Coupe. (OCW)

1980 Buick, Skylark coupe. (OCW)

1980 Buick, Skylark sedan. (OCW)

1980 Buick, Skylark Limited sedan. (OCW)

SKYLARK - SERIES 4X - FOUR/V-6 - To tumultuous fanfare and glowing reviews, the new front drive unibodied Skylark, far different from its predecessor of that name, arrived in spring 1979 as an early 1980 model. Weighing much less (700-800 pounds) than prior Skylarks, it was part of the X-body family that also included Chevrolet Citation, Oldsmobile Omega, and Pontiac Phoenix. Fuel-efficient, with a roomy interior, transverse-mounted engine (four or V-6) and standard door and window frame moldings, the new Skylark came in standard, Limited or Sport trim. A compact spare tire replaced the old full-size version. The suspension used coil springs all around. The new

Skylark was 19 inches shorter than its forerunner, and far more expensive (by some $1,500). It carried five passengers (six with squeezing) and was powered by a standard "Iron Duke" 2.5-liter four-cylinder engine from Pontiac, or optional Chevrolet-built 2.8-liter V-6. The base Skylark and Limited had a slightly peaked checkerboard grille, single rectangular recessed headlamps, and vertical parking/signal lamps at the outer edge of the front-end. A Skylark nameplate was at the forward end of the front fenders; Buick lettering on the trunk lid. On the roof pillar was a round emblem. Skylark's standard AM radio could be deleted for credit. Other standard equipment included a four-speed manual transmission with floor shift lever, compact spare tire, glass-belted radial tires, rack-and-pinion steering, step-on parking brake, locking glove compartment, cigarette lighter, and cloth or vinyl notchback seating. The Limited had tan upholstery in brushed woven fabric, plus carpeted lower door panels and under-dash courtesy lamps. Other Limited extras were gas-assisted hood struts, acoustical insulation, stand-up hood ornament and windsplit molding, wheel opening moldings, wide rocker moldings that extended to front fenders and rear quarters, and deluxe wheel covers. Skylark's Sport Coupe and Sport Sedan options had an entirely different three-row, six-section blackout grille, with body-colored horizontal separators. They also had black body moldings, bright wheel opening moldings, bumper strips front and rear, smoked taillamp lenses, sport steering wheel, Designers' Sport road wheels, and amber parking/signal lamps up front. Sport Skylarks also carried a heftier Rallye suspension, larger rear stabilizer bar, black dash treatment with full instruments including a voltmeter, and P205/70R13 blackwall steel-belted radials. For extra accent, they could have wide lower body stripes with a hawk decal. One pleasant option: a flip-open glass sunroof. Before long, all the X-cars would be plagued by a long list of safety recalls and mechanical problems, which resulted in one of the worst reputations among modern American automobiles. Chevrolet's Citation got the worst publicity of the bunch, but the troubles affected all of the 980-85 X-bodied models, even though the most serious recalls applied only to the early editions.

1980 Buick, Century coupe. (OCW)

CENTURY - SERIES 4A - V-6/V-8 - After two years in slantback form, a new notchback sedan roofline replaced the fastback shape on two-door Century models. These new, dramatically styled sedans had a more formal appearance than before, resembling both Skylark and Regal. Styling features included wraparound taillamps, an angular-look decklid and sloping fenders. A horizontal grille and new signal lamps emphasized the car's angular appearance. The four-row, eight-column crosshatch grille had a tiny crosshatch pattern within each segment. Vertical rectangular parking/signal lights sat between the single recessed rectangular headlamps and the grille, with amber lenses around the fender corners. Century coupes retained the fastback design for one final attempt at luring buyers. Custom and Special designations were dropped, with their equivalents now called, simply, Century. Thus, Century came in two trim levels: base and Limited. Optional models included a Turbo coupe and Sport coupe. This year saw a larger standard engine: the 231 cu. in. (3.8-liter) V-6. Options included new 4.3-liter and 4.9-liter V-8s (5.0-liter in California), plus the turbocharged V-6. Power brakes became standard this year. Century included a dome

light; Limited added lights for front ashtray, under-dash courtesy, and glove compartment. Seats were upholstered in supple vinyl or plush crushed-knit cloth; 55/45 type in the Limited sedan. Standard Century equipment included three-speed manual transmission, fiberglass belted radial tires, compact spare tire, wide-view day/night mirror, protective bumper strips, and stand up-hood ornament. The Limited also offered wheel opening moldings and bodyside stripes. On the station wagon front, Century fielded standard and Estate (formerly Custom) Wagons, plus a Sport Wagon option. Each sat six, or held 71.8 cubic feet of cargo with second seat folded down. The Sport Wagon package contained black headlamp and grille trim, wipers, window reveal moldings, center pillar, wide rocker treatment, wheel opening moldings, air deflector and sport mirrors; plus a hawk decal, Rallye suspension and P205/70R14 steel belted radial tires on Designers' Sport wheels. Sport Coupe and Turbo Coupe options had a black treatment on grille, headlamp bezels, windshield wiper arms, pillars, moldings, decklid panel and instrument panel trim; plus twin sport mirrors and a functional rear spoiler. A hawk decal was on the front fender, just ahead of the door. Black-trimmed instrument panel, too. They also had the ride-and-handling Rallye package with firmer springs and shocks, plus larger-diameter stabilizer bars, Designers' Sport wheels, and P205/70R14 steel-belted radials. The Turbo version included a special bulged hood with 'Turbo 3.8 Litre' nameplate, Turbo Coupe identification on body side and deck lid, turbine wheels, and exhaust system with what Buick described as a "rather authoritative voice." Styled aluminum wheels were available for the first time on the Sport versions.

1980 Buick, Regal Limited Somerset coupe with optional wire wheel covers. (OCW)

REGAL - SERIES 4A - V-6/V-8 - Regal's new look included wider taillamps and quad rectangular headlamps. It came in Limited and Sport Coupe trim, as well as standard Regal. New taillamps split by horizontal lines, stretching from license plate to decklid edge, gave a wider look to the back end. A restyled grille had an undivided tight checkerboard pattern that angled outward at the base in the Buick style. Park/signal lamps set in the base of the front bumper. Regal Limited had special wide chrome rocker panel moldings, as well as standard crushed velour cloth upholstery. The Sport Coupe, still powered by a turbocharged 231 cu. in. (3.8-liter) V-6 engine, could have an optional Designers' Accent paint treatment, blacked-out grille and headlamp trim, plus sport mirrors and turbine wheels. New tungsten-halogen high beams that produced intense white light were standard on Sport Coupe, optional on other Regals. "Once in a while," declared the brochure describing the Regal Somerset limited edition, "you have an opportunity to buy a first edition.... So owning one will be a rare treat." Owning one today might be similarly pleasing. The two-tone body came only in Somerset Tan and Dark Blue Designers' Accent. The dark blue swept back over the hood and onto the top of the roof. The package (offered for the Limited coupe) included wire wheel covers, sleek sport mirrors, and special Somerset identification on front fenders. Inside, the tan and dark blue motif continued with special Somerset design plush knit velour 55/45 seat upholstery and dark blue carpeting. A color-keyed umbrella fit in a pouch on the back of the front seat. Brushed aluminum trim highlighted the instrument panel and doors. There was a roof-

mounted passenger assist strap, plus Somerset identification on the glove box door. Regal's base powerplant was the 231 cu. in. (3.8-liter) two-barrel, with other engine possibilities the new 265 (4.3-liter) two-barrel V-8, or 301 (4.9-liter) four-barrel. Power brakes and steering were standard. So were steel-belted radial tires, compact spare tire, day/night inside mirror, twin chrome outside mirrors, wipers with mist feature, an underhood light, and cigarette lighter. Regals had bumper guards and protective strips front and rear, a stand-up hood ornament, windshield and back window reveal moldings, and wheel opening moldings. Regal Limited added wide rocker moldings (extending to front fenders and rear quarter panels), belt reveal moldings, and bright pillar moldings.

1980 Buick, LeSabre sedan. (OCW)

LESABRE - SERIES 4B - V-6/V-8 - New sheet metal arrived on both LeSabre and Electra to produce a lower, longer front end appearance. The reshaped rear end was higher, with a sharper forward thrust to the decklid. A rear deck spoiler treatment, sloping hood, and reduced front-end radius improved the car's aerodynamics, cutting air drag by a claimed 14 percent. New recessed quad rectangular headlamps, set in bezels with a vertical dividing wall, highlighted the angular look. A new checkerboard grille had large holes in four rows, and the bottom row extended outward all the way to fender edges. At the side of the grille was a Buick badge. Parking/signal lamps were now set into the bumper. The familiar LeSabre "ventiport" fender trim, descended from old Buick portholes, faded away with the new restyle. LeSabres now rode on high-pressure, low-rolling-resistance tires. Match-mounted tires and wheels, plus new shock absorbers, improved ride quality. Powerplant was again the standard 3.8-liter V-6, but a new and bigger 252 cu. in. (4.1-liter) V-6 was also offered (except in California). LeSabre could also have Oldsmobile's 350 cu. in. diesel V-8. The dashboard included a blacked-out panel that showed information on headlight beam, engine conditions, brake warning, and a seat belt reminder. A new side-frame jack was standard; wheel covers were new. Optional: a theft-deterrent system with starter interrupt. LeSabre's Sport Coupe featured a blacked-out grille, black window and side moldings, plus chrome wheels. Also a ride/handling package with large stabilizer bars, firm springs and shock valving, and fast-ratio power steering. Sport Coupes were again powered by the turbocharged 231 V-6 with four-barrel carburetor. The dash held a vacuum boost light. Standard equipment included bucket seats, full-length console tungsten-halogen headlamps, sport mirrors and sport steering wheel. Four-wheel disc brakes were optional. Standard LeSabre equipment included wheel opening and roof drip scale moldings, bumper protective strips and guards, rear end panel molding notchback seating (cloth or vinyl), and a compact spare tire. To the basic list, LeSabre Limited added such styling touches as deluxe wheel covers, rocker panel moldings and black pillar appliqué.

ESTATE WAGON - SERIES 4B - V-8 - Not much was new in the Estate Wagon arena, as was usually the case. The LeSabre Estate seated six, with a third seat available, and had 86.8 cubic foot cargo volume. Standard powerplant was a 4.9-liter (301 cu. in.) gasoline V-8 this year (except in California); but the familiar 350 (5.7-liter) V-8 was available too. Electra's new Estate Wagon differed little and had the same engine choices. For the

extra price, Electra buyers got standard air conditioning, tilt steering column, digital clock, remote-control, left outside mirror, 55/45 notchback seating (cloth or vinyl), power windows, and chrome wheels. All Estates had mist wipers, dual outside mirrors, front and rear bumper guards with protective strips, power steering and brakes, and automatic transmission.

1980 Buick, Electra Limited coupe. (OCW)

ELECTRA - SERIES 4C - V-6/V-8 - Sporting a new vertical-style grille, sloping fenders and higher decklid, Electra presented a streamlined appearance and lost over 200 pounds of curb weight. Standard engine, except in California, was the new 252 cu. in. (4.1-liter) V-6, with 350 (5.7-liter) V-8 optional. For the first time, a diesel was also available. The new grille was divided into sections by nine vertical bars, tapering outward at the base, with Buick badge at the side. Quad rectangular headlamps sat in recessed housings. Park/signal lamps were inset in the bumper bottom. Electra's hood had a slight downward rake. The Electra 225 designation was dropped, replaced by Limited and Park Avenue series (those were formerly models rather than series). An Electra Estate Wagon was added (see above). Suspensions now used Pliacell-R shock absorbers, and a new compact spare tire rested in the trunk. Park Avenue coupe and sedan instrument panels and coach lamps used new electroluminescent lighting. Park Avenue also had a new standard halo-effect padded-vinyl roof, plus knit velour fabric upholstery with a draped, sheared look (leather available). Both Limited and Park Avenue had new higher-pressure tires that offered less rolling resistance. New tungsten-halogen high-beam headlamps were available. So were 14 choices of entertainment systems, including a Concert Sound System for the Park Avenue with six speakers. Park Avenue also had exclusive Touch Climate Control with no levers, buttons or switches; just a smooth touch panel. Electra kept their four-section "ventiports," which formed part of the Park Avenue's wide full-length bodyside molding.

RIVIERA - SERIES 4E - V-6/V-8 - The downsized Riviera body that had been introduced for 1979 received modest refinements this year, including revised body mounts. Rivs also got match-mounted tires and wheels, retuned shock absorbers, restyled mirrors that fit snugly against the car body for an integrated look, and a selection of new interior fabrics. Options included Twilight Sentinel, which gave automatic control of outside lights, controlled by a sensor atop the dashboard. As before, Riviera was front-drive, with fully independent suspension and 350 cu. in. (5.7-liter) V-8 engine. Pliacell-R shock absorbers were new, as was an optional theft-deterrent system with starter interrupt system. Also optional: a digital Trip Monitor that displayed a selection of travel and engine functions. Riviera standard equipment included automatic transmission, power front disc brakes, cornering lights, six-way power driver's seat, power steering, digital clock, automatic level control, air conditioning, electric door locks, remote-controlled outside mirrors and Delco AM/FM stereo radio with power antenna. One of the new interior colors, brown, was a Riviera exclusive. Four-wheel disc brakes were again available. Riviera's S Type had been chosen 1979 Car of the Year by Motor Trend. New flat black, styled outside mirrors complemented its flat black trim around windows, grille and rocker panels. Powerplant remained the turbocharged 231 cu. in. V-6 with four-barrel carb. Bucket seats were velour upholstered with ribbed inserts; the instrument panel was black-accented.

I.D. DATA: For one more year, a 13-symbol Vehicle Identification Number (VIN) was on the upper left surface of the instrument panel. visible through the windshield. Coding was similar to 1979, with the first digit ('4') indicating the Buick division. The next letter indicates series: 'S' Skyhawk; 'T' Skyhawk S; 'B' Skylark; 'C' Skylark Limited; 'E' Century wagon; 'H' Century cpe/sed and Estate wagon; 'G' Century Sport Coupe; 'L' Century Ltd.; 'J' Regal; 'K' Regal Sport Coupe; 'M' Regal Ltd.; 'F' LeSabre Sport Coupe; 'N' LeSabre; 'P' LeSabre Limited; 'R' LeSabre Estate Wagon; 'I' Electra Estate; 'X' Electra Limited; 'W' Electra Park Ave.; 'Z' Riviera; 'Y' Riviera S Type. The next two digits denote body type: '07' Skyhawk hatchback coupe; '09' aero 4-dr. sedan; '37' Skylark/LeSabre/Electra 2-dr. coupe; '47' Regal 2-dr. coupe; '57' Riviera 2-dr. coupe; '87' aero 2-dr. coupe; '69' 4-dr. sedan; '35' 4-dr. wagon. The fifth symbol indicated engine code: '5' 4-151 2Bbl.; '7' V6-173 2Bbl.; 'A' V6-231 2Bbl.; '3' Turbo V6-231 4Bbl.; 'S' V8-265 2Bbl.; 'W' V8-301 4Bbl.; 'H' V8-305 4Bbl.; 'R' V8-350 4Bbl. (L34); 'X' V8-350 4Bbl. (L77). The sixth symbol denotes model year ('A' 1980). Next is a plant code: '7' Lordstown, OH; 'W' Willow Run, MI; '6' Oklahoma City, OK; 'G' Framingham, MA; 'H' Flint, MI; 'Z' Fremont, CA; 'X' Fairfax, KS; 'E' Linden, NJ. The final six digits are the sequential serial number, which began with 100001, except 400001 for Skyhawks and for LeSabre/Electra/Estate models built at Flint. Engine numbers are stamped on the front right of the block, except for L34 and LF9 350 cu. in. V-8s, which were stamped on the front of the left side of the block; LD5, LC8 and LC6 V-6s, on left rear of block; Skylark V-6, on rear (or front) of right rocker cover; and Skylark four, on pad at left front below cylinder head. The body number plate on the shroud was the same as before.

SKYHAWK (V-6)

Model No.	Body/Style No.	Body Type & Seating	Factory Price	Shipping Weight	Prod. Total
4H	T07	2-dr 'S' Hatch-4P	4993	2754	Note 1
4H	S07	2-dr Hatch-4P	5211	2754	Note 1

Note 1: Total production for the model year 8,322 Skyhawks.

SKYLARK (FOUR/V-6)

4X	B37	2-dr Coupe-5P	5160/5385	2410/2449	55,114
4X	B69	4-dr Sedan-5P	5306/5531	2438/2477	80,940

SKYLARK LIMITED (FOUR/V-6)

4X	C37	2-dr Coupe-5P	5579/5804	2438/2477	42,652
4X	C69	4-dr Sedan-5P	5726/5951	2478/2517	86,948

SKYLARK SPORT (FOUR/V-6)

4X	D37	2-dr Coupe-5P	5774/5999	2443/2482	Note 2
4X	D69	4-dr Sedan-5P	5920/6145	2471/2510	Note 2

Note 2: Production of Skylark Sport models is included in Limited totals above. Total Limited production: 100,396.

CENTURY (V-6/V-8)

4A	H87	2-dr Aero Cpe-6P	5546/5751	3086/3190	1,074
4A	H69	4-dr Sedan-6P	5646/5851	3106/3210	129,740
4A	E35	4-dr Sta Wag-6P	5922/6102	3236/3364	6,493
4A	H35	4-dr Est Wag-6P	6220/6400	3247/3375	11,122

CENTURY SPORT (V-6/V-8)

4A	G87	2-dr Aero Cpe-6P	6063/6243	3150/3254	Note 3

CENTURY LIMITED (V-6/V-8)

4A	L69	4-dr Sedan-6P	6132/6337	3150/3254	Note 3

Note 3: Production figures shown for Century include Sport and Limited models.

REGAL (V-6/V-8)

4A	J47	2-dr Coupe-6P	6305/6485	3115/3243	Note 4

REGAL SPORT COUPE (TURBO V-6)

4A	K47	2-dr Coupe-6P	6952	3194	Note 4

REGAL LIMITED (V-6/V-8)

4A	M47	2-dr Coupe-6P	6724/6904	3142/3370	Note 4

Note 4: Total model year production, 214,735 Regals.

Note 5: Prices shown after slash for Century/Regal V-8 are for the smaller (265 cu. in.) version; larger V-8 cost $115 more.

LESABRE (V-6/V-8)

4B	N37	2-dr Coupe-6P	6674/6971	3320/3440	8,342
4B	N69	4-dr Sedan-6P	6769/7064	3369/3497	23,873

LESABRE LIMITED (V-6/V-8)

4B	P37	2-dr Coupe-6P	6929/7224	3327/3455	20,561
4B	P69	4-dr Sedan-6P	7071/7366	3375/3503	37,676

LESABRE SPORT (TURBO V-6)

Model No.	Body/Style No.	Body Type & Seating	Factory Price	Shipping Weight	Prod. Total
4B	F37	2-dr Coupe-6P	7782	3430	Note 6

Note 6: Production of Sport Turbo Coupe is included in totals for standard LeSabre coupe.

LESABRE ESTATE WAGON (V-8)

Model No.	Body/Style No.	Body Type & Seating	Factory Price	Shipping Weight	Prod. Total
4B	R35	4-dr Sta Wag-6P	7673	3898	9,318
4B	(AQ4)	4-dr 3S Wag-8P	7866	3928	Note 7

Note 7: Three-seat Estate Wagon was actually an option package (AQ4); production of all Estate Wagons is included in above figure.

ELECTRA LIMITED (V-6/V-8)

Model No.	Body/Style No.	Body Type & Seating	Factory Price	Shipping Weight	Prod. Total
4C	X37	2-dr Coupe-6P	9132/9467	3571/3756	14,058
4C	X69	4-dr Sedan-6P	9287/9622	3578/3763	54,422

ELECTRA PARK AVENUE (V-6/V-8)

Model No.	Body/Style No.	Body Type & Seating	Factory Price	Shipping Weight	Prod. Total
4C	W37	2-dr Coupe-6P	10244/10579	3600/3785	Note 8
4C	W69	4-dr Sedan-6P	10383/10718	3607/3792	Note 8

Note 8: Production figures shown for Electra Limited include Park Avenue.

ELECTRA ESTATE WAGON (V-8)

Model No.	Body/Style No.	Body Type & Seating	Factory Price	Shipping Weight	Prod. Total
4C	V35	4-dr Sta Wag-6P	10513	4105	N/A
4C	(AQ4)	4-dr 3S Wag-8P	10706	4135	N/A

RIVIERA (V-8)

Model No.	Body/Style No.	Body Type & Seating	Factory Price	Shipping Weight	Prod. Total
4E	Z57	2-dr Coupe-4P	11492	3741	41,404

RIVIERA S TYPE TURBO (V-6)

Model No.	Body/Style No.	Body Type & Seating	Factory Price	Shipping Weight	Prod. Total
4E	Y57	2-dr Coupe-4P	11823	3633	7,217

FACTORY PRICE AND WEIGHT NOTE: Figure before the slash is for V-6 engine, after the slash for smallest (lowest-priced) V-8 engine available. For Skylark, figure before the slash is for four-cylinder engine, after the slash for V-6.

ENGINES: BASE FOUR (Skylark): Inline, ohv, four-cylinder. Cast iron block and head. Displacement: 151 cu. in. (2.5 liters). Bore & stroke: 4.0 x 3.0 in. Compression ratio: 8.2:1. Brake horsepower: 90 at 4000 R.P.M. Torque: 134 lb.-ft. at 2400 R.P.M. Five main bearings. Hydraulic valve lifters. Carburetor: 2Bbl. Rochester 2SE (Varajet II). VIN Code: 5. Sales Code: LW9. OPTIONAL V-6 (Skylark): 60-degree, overhead-valve V-6. Cast iron alloy block and head. Displacement: 173 cu. in. (2.8 liters). Bore & stroke: 3.5 x 3.0 in. Compression ratio: 8.5:1. Brake horsepower: 115 at 4800 R.P.M. Torque: 145 lb.-ft. at 2400 R.P.M. Four main bearings. Hydraulic valve lifters. Carburetor: 2Bbl. Rochester 2SE. VIN Code: 7. Sales Code: LE2. BASE V-6 (Skyhawk, Century, Regal, LeSabre): 90-degree, overhead-valve V-6. Cast iron alloy block and head. Displacement: 231 cu. in. (3.8 liters). Bore & stroke: 3.8 x 3.4 in. Compression ratio: 8.0:1. Brake horsepower: 110 at 3800 R.P.M. Torque: 190 lb.-ft. at 1600 R.P.M. Four main bearings. Hydraulic valve lifters. Carburetor: 2Bbl. Rochester M2ME. Even-firing. VIN Code: A. Sales Code: LD5. TURBOCHARGED V-6 (Regal and LeSabre Sport Coupes, Riviera S); OPTIONAL (Century, Riviera): Same as 231 V-6 above, but with M4ME four-barrel carburetor. Brake horsepower: 170 at 4000 R.P.M. Torque: 265 lb.-ft. at 2400 R.P.M. VIN Code: 3. Sales Code: LC8. BASE V-6 (Electra); OPTIONAL (LeSabre): 90-degree, overhead-valve V-6. Cast iron alloy block and head. Displacement: 252 cu. in. (4.1 liters). Bore & stroke: 3.965 x 3.4 in. Compression ratio: 8.0:1. Brake horsepower: 125 at 4000 R.P.M. Torque: 205 lb.-ft. at 2000 R.P.M. Four main bearings. Hydraulic valve lifters. Carburetor: 4Bbl. Rochester M4ME. VIN Code: 4. Sales Code: LC4. OPTIONAL V-8 (Century/Regal): 90-degree, overhead-valve V-8. Cast iron alloy block and head. Displacement: 265 cu. in. (4.3 liters). Bore & stroke: 3.75 x 3.00 in. Compression ratio: 8.0:1. Brake horsepower: 120 at 3600 R.P.M. Torque: 210 lb.-ft. at 1800 R.P.M. Four main bearings. Hydraulic valve lifters. Carburetor: 2Bbl. Rochester M2ME. VIN Code: S. BASE V-8 (Estate); OPTIONAL (Century, Regal, LeSabre): 90-degree overhead-valve V-8. Cast iron alloy block and head. Displacement: 301 cu. in. (4.9 liters). Bore & stroke: 4.0 x 3.0 in. Compression ratio: 8.2:1. Brake horsepower: 140 at 4000 R.P.M. Torque: 240 lb.-ft. at 1800 R.P.M. Five main bearings. Hydraulic valve lifters. Carburetor: 4Bbl. Rochester M4ME. Built by Pontiac. VIN Code: W. Sales Code: L37. OPTIONAL V-8 (Centu-ry/Regal): 90-degree, overhead valve V-8. Cast iron alloy block and head. Displacement: 305 cu. in. (5.0 liters). Bore & stroke: 3.736 x 3.48 in. Compression ratio: 8.6:1. Brake horsepower: 155 at 4000 R.P.M. Torque: 240 lb.-ft. at 1600 R.P.M. Five main bearings. Hydraulic valve lifters. Carburetor: 4Bbl. Rochester M4MC. VIN Code: H. Sales Code: LG4. BASE V-8 (Riviera); OPTIONAL (LeSabre, Estate, Electra, Riviera S): 90-degree, overhead valve V-8. Cast iron alloy block and head. Displacement: 350 cu. in. (5.7 liters). Bore & stroke: 3.80 x 3.85 in. Compression ratio: 8.0:1. Brake horsepower: 155 at 3400 R.P.M. Torque: 280 lb.-ft. at 1600 R.P.M. Five main bearings. Hydraulic valve lifters. Carburetor: 4Bbl. Rochester M4MC. VIN Code: X. Sales Code: L77. ALTERNATE 350-4 V-8: 90-degree, over-head valve V-8. Cast iron alloy block and head. Displacement: 350 cu. in. (5.7 liters). Bore & stroke: 4.057 x 3.385 in. Compression ratio: 8.3:1. Brake horsepower: 60 at 3600 R.P.M. Torque: 270 lb.-ft. at 1600 R.P.M. Five main bearings. Hydraulic valve lifters. Carburetor: 4Bbl. Rochester M4MC. Built by Old-smobile. VIN Code: R. Sales Code: L34. OPTIONAL DIESEL V-8 (Electra, Estate): 90 degree, overhead valve V-8. Cast iron alloy block and head. Displacement: 350 cu. in. (5.7 liters). Bore & stroke: 4.057 x 3.385 in. Compression ratio: 22.5:1. Brake horsepower: 105 at 3200 R.P.M. Torque: 205 lb.-ft. at 1600 R.P.M. Five main bearings. Hydraulic valve lifters. Fuel injec-tion. Oldsmobile-built. VIN Code: N. Sales Code: LF9.

CHASSIS DATA: Wheelbase: (Skyhawk) 97.0 in.; (Skylark) 104.9 in.; (Century/Regal) 108.1 in.; (LeSabre) 116.0 in.; (Es-tate) 115.9 in.; (Electra) 118.9 in.; (Riviera) 114.0 in. Overall length: (Skyhawk) 179.3 in.; (Skylark) 181.9 in.; (Century) 196.0 in.; (Regal) 200.3 in.; (LeSabre) 217.4 in.; (Electra) 220.9 in.; (Estate) 218.8 in.; (Riv) 206.6 in. Height: (Skyhawk) 50.8 in.; (Skylark) 53.5 in.; (Century cpe) 54.6 in.; (Century sed/wag) 55.5 in.; (Regal) 54.6 in.; (LeSabre) 55.0 in.; (Electra cpe) 54.2 in.; (Electra sed) 55.6 in.; (Estate) 57.1 in.; (Riv) 54.3 in. Width: (Skyhawk) 65.4 in.; (Skylark) 67.7 in.; (Century/Regal) 71.1 in.; (LeSabre/Electra) 78.0 in.; (Estate) 80.1 in.; (Riv) 72.7 in. Front Tread: (Skyhawk) 54.7 in.; (Skylark) 58.7 in.; (Century/Regal) 58.5 in.; (LeSabre/Electra) 61.8 in.; (Estate) 62.2 in.; (Riv) 59.3 in. Rear Tread: (Skyhawk) 53.6 in.; (Skylark) 57.0 in.; (Centu-ry/Regal) 57.8 in.; (LeSabre) 60.7 in.; (Electra) 61.0 in.; (Estate) 64.1 in.; (Riv) 60.0 in. Standard Tires: (Skyhawk) BR78 x 13 SBR; (Skyhawk 'S') B78 x 13; (Skylark) P185/80R13 GBR; (Sky-lark Sport) P205/70R13 SBR; (Century cpe/sed) P185/75R14 GBR; (Century wag/Regal) P195/75R14; (Regal Spt Cpe) P205/70R14 SBR; (LeSabre) P205/75R15 SBR; (LeSabre Spt Cpe) P225/70R15 SBR; (Electra) P215/75R15 SBR; (Estate) P225/75R15 SBR; (Riviera) P205/75R15 SBR WSW; (Riviera S) GR70 x 15.

TECHNICAL: Transmission: Three-speed, fully synchronized manual gearbox standard on Century cpe/sed; Turbo Hydra-matic optional. Four-speed, fully synchronized floor shift stan-dard on Skyhawk/Skylark; automatic optional. Turbo Hydra-matic standard on Regal, LeSabre, Electra, Estate and Riviera. Three-speed manual transmission gear ratios: (1st) 3.50:1; (2nd) 1.81:1; (3rd) 1.00:1; (Rev) 3.62:1. Skyhawk four-speed gear ratios: (1st) 3.50:1; (2nd) 2.48:1; (3rd) 1.66:1; (4th) 1.00:1; (Rev) 3.50:1. Skylark four-speed gear ratios: (1st) 3.53:1; (2nd) 1.95:1; (3rd) 1.24:1; (4th) 0.81:1; (Rev) 3.42:1. Auto. trans. gear ratios: (1st) 2.52:1; (2nd) 1.52:1; (3rd) 1.00:1; (Rev) 1.93:1. Sky-lark automatic: (1st) 2.84:1; (2nd) 2.60:1; (3rd) 1.00:1; (Rev) 2.07:1. Automatic on Century V-8, Electra diesel and Riviera: (1st) 2.74:1; (2nd) 1.57:1; (3rd) 1.00:1; (Rev) 2.07:1. Standard axle ratio: (Skyhawk) 2.93:1; (Skylark) 3.34:1; (Century/Regal V6-231) 3.08:1; (Century/Regal V8-265) 2.41:1; (Century/Re-gal V8-301) 2.14:1 or 2.41:1; (Century/Regal V8-305) 2.29:1 or 2.73:1; (Century/Regal/LeSabre turbo/spt cpe) 2.73:1 or 3.08:1; (Century wag) 2.29:1, 2.41:1, 2.56:1 or 2.73:1; (LeSabre V6-231) 2.73:1 or 3.23:1; (LeSabre V6-252) 2.93:1; (LeSabre V-8) 2.41:1 or 3.23:1; (Electra V-6) 2.93:1; (Electra V8-301) 2.56:1; (Electra V8-350) 2.41:1 or 3.23:1; (Electra diesel) 2.73:1; (Es-

tate) 2.56:1, 2.73:1 or 3.08:1; (Riv) 2.41:1 exc. turbo V-6, 2.93:1. Steering: (Skylark) rack and pinion; (others) recirculating ball; power assist standard on Regal, LeSabre, Electra, Estate and Riviera. Suspension: front/rear coil springs; (Skylark) MacPherson strut front suspension, trailing arm rear with track bar; (Riviera) same as 1979; (others) same as 1976-79. Brakes: front disc. rear drum; power brakes standard on all except Skyhawk/Skylark. Four-wheel power disc brakes optional on Riviera. Body construction: (Skyhawk/Skylark) unitized; (others) separate body and frame. Fuel tank: (Skyhawk) 18.5 gal.; (Skylark) 14 gal.; (Century/Regal) 18.2 gal.; (LeSabre/Electra) 25 gal.; (Riviera) 21 gal. Unleaded fuel only.

DRIVETRAIN OPTIONS: Engines: 173 cu. in. (2.8-liter) V-6, 2Bbl.: Skylark ($225). Turbocharged 231 cu. in. V-6, 4Bbl.: Century cpe/sed ($500); Riviera ($160). 252 cu. in. (4.1-liter) V-6, 4Bbl.: LeSabre ($90). 265 cu. in. (4.3-liter) V-8, 2Bbl.: Century/Regal ($180-$205). 301 cu. in. (4.9-liter) V-8, 2Bbl.: LeSabre ($295). 301 cu. in. V-8, 4Bbl: Century/Regal ($295-$320). 305 cu. in. V-8, 4Bbl.: Century/Regal ($295-$370). 350 cu. in. (5.7-liter) V-8, 4Bbl.: LeSabre ($425); Estate ($130); Electra ($335); Riviera S (credit $160). 350 cu. in. diesel V-8: Estate ($860); Electra ($930). Transmission/Differential: Automatic trans., floor shift: Skyhawk ($320). Automatic trans., column shift: Skylark ($337); Century cpe/sed ($358). Optional rear axle ratio (NC) Limited slip differential: Skyhawk ($65); Century/Regal ($70); LeSabre/Electra ($74). Power Accessories: Power brakes: Skyhawk/Skylark ($76). Four wheel disc brakes: LeSabre spt cpe, Riv ($222). Power steering: Skyhawk ($158); Skylark ($164); Century ($174). Suspension: F40 Firm ride/handling pkg.: all exc. Skyhawk ($21-$22). F41 Rallye ride/handling pkg.: Skylark ($129); incl. in Sport. FE2 Rallye ride/handling pkg.: Century/Regal ($41); Riv ($22). Automatic level control: Century/Regal/LeSabre/Electra ($145). Superlift rear shocks: Skylark ($55). Other: Trailer towing flasher/harness ($24-$38) exc. Skyhawk. Heavy-duty alternator, 80-amp: LeSabre/Electra ($24-$61); 70-amp ($15-$52) exc. Skyhawk. H.D. battery ($19-$22); diesel ($44). H.D. cooling: Skyhawk/Skylark/Century/Regal ($32-$63). Engine block heater ($16). H.D. engine/transmission cooling: LeSabre/Electra/Riv ($32-$63). California emission system ($83-$250).

SKYHAWK CONVENIENCE/APPEARANCE OPTIONS: Option Packages: Road Hawk pkg.: Oyster white vinyl bucket seats, black wipers, grille, headlamp trim, moldings, front air dam, body-color spoiler and sport mirrors, BR70 x 13 SBR wide-oval blackwall tires, special handling suspension, silver/gray paint ($696). Appearance group (wheel opening moldings and bodyside stripes): 'S' ($62). Acoustic insulation pkg. ($27). Convenience group: underhood light, glove box light, headlamp-on indicator ($22). Shadow light Astroroof ($693). Vista Vent roof ($193). Comfort/Convenience: Air cond. ($531). Rear defogger, electric ($95). Tinted glass ($65). Tinted windshield ($54). Tilt steering ($73). Instrument gauges, electric clock and tach ($79). Electric clock ($23). Front/rear mats ($23). Tungsten-halogen high-beam headlamps ($27). Visor vanity mirrors, pair ($11). Entertainment: AM/FM radio ($64). AM/FM stereo radio ($101). AM/FM radio and cassette player ($188). AM/FM stereo radio and 8-track ($176). Rear speaker for non-stereo radios ($18). Delete AM radio ($52 credit). Exterior Trim: Bodyside stripes (NC). Door edge guards ($13). Roof crown moldings ($198). Protective bodyside moldings ($32-$49). Designer's accent paint ($189). Interior Trim/Upholstery: Adjustable driver's seatback ($21). Custom seatbelts ($19). Wheels and Tires: Custom sport wheels ($63). Styled aluminum wheels ($249). B78 x 13 WSW ($42-$52). BR78 x 13 SBR BSW ($104-$129). BR78 x 13 SBR WSW ($41-$181). BR70 x 13 SBR wide-oval WLT ($57-$226). Conventional spare tire (NC).

SKYLARK CONVENIENCE/APPEARANCE OPTIONS: Option Packages: Acoustic pkg. ($43). Lamp group: underhood, glove box, ashtray, courtesy, trunk, headlamps-on ($41-$50). Vista

Vent flip-open glass sunroof ($240). Comfort/Convenience: Air cond. ($564). Cruise Master ($105). Two-speed w/delay ($39). Rear defogger, electric ($101). Power windows ($133-$189). Electric door locks ($87-$123). Six-way power driver's seat ($165). Manual seatback recliner: each ($42). Sport steering wheel ($42). Tilt steering ($75). Tinted glass ($70). Dual horns ($11). Electric clock ($25). Digital clock ($56). Trip odometer ($13). Gauge pkg. incl. trip odometer ($40). Electric trunk release ($25). Lights and Mirrors: Tungsten-halogen high-beam headlamps ($27). Headlamps-on indicator ($11). Dome reading light ($19). Door courtesy/warning light ($39-$62). Sunshade map light ($13). Remote left mirror ($18); sport-type ($28). Sport mirrors: left remote, right manual ($43); dual ($28-$71). Visor vanity mirrors ($11). Lighted passenger visor mirror ($39). Entertainment: AM radio delete ($52 credit). AM/FM radio ($64). AM/FM stereo radio ($101); w/8-track or cassette player ($176-$188). AM/FM stereo and CB radio ($413); w/8-track or cassette ($479-$491). Rear speaker ($18); pair, for non-stereo radio ($28). Power antenna ($48), triband ($88). Exterior Trim: Landau vinyl top ($175). Long vinyl top ($116). Designers' accent paint ($174). Protective bodyside moldings ($43). Belt reveal moldings ($25). Wide rocker panel group ($54). Door edge guards ($13-$20). Hood ornament and windsplit ($25). Pillar appliqué molding ($22). Wheel opening moldings ($22). Bodyside stripes ($40). Bumper guards, front/rear ($32). Bumper strips. front/rear ($40). Roof rack ($87). Interior Trim/Upholstery: Full-length console ($80). Bucket seats ($48). Notchback bench seat: Spt ($146). Color-keyed seatbelts ($23). Front carpet savers ($15). Carpet savers and mats ($25). Trunk trim carpeting ($31). Wheels: Designers sport wheels ($82-$101); incl. On Spt. Chrome-plated wheels ($40-$141). Deluxe wheel covers ($43). Custom wire wheel covers ($151-$194). Sport wheel covers ($11-$54). Tires: P185/80R13 GBR ($45). P185/80R13 SBR ($49). P185/80R13 SBR WSW ($93). P205/70R13 SBR WSW ($51). P205/70R13 SBR WLT ($66).

1980 Buick, Century Limited sedan with optional wire wheel covers. (OCW)

1980 Buick, Century Estate Wagon station wagon with Sport option package. (OCW)

CENTURY/REGAL CONVENIENCE/APPEARANCE OPTIONS: Option Packages: Regal Somerset pkg.: blue/tan interior trim, umbrella pouch, roof assist strap, decor pkg., custom belts, brushed aluminum instrument panel, sport mirrors, wire wheel covers ($695). Regal Sport Coupe Decor pkg.: designers' accent paint, turbine wheels, sport mirrors and steering wheel, black paint accents ($511). Century Sport Wagon pkg. ($511). Century Turbo Coupe pkg.: special suspension and exhaust, 3.08:1 axle, turbine wheels ($43). Electric sunroof: cpe ($561). Silver electric sliding Astroroof: cpe ($773). Hatch roof: Regal cpe ($695). Exterior molding pkg. ($64-$178). Convenience

group ($18-$67). Comfort/Convenience: Air cond. ($601). Automatic air cond. ($700). Cruise control ($112). Rear defogger, electric ($107). Tinted glass ($75). Tinted windshield ($54). Six-way power driver's seat ($175); both ($350). Manual seatback recliner ($67). Custom steering wheel: Century ($11). Sport steering wheel ($35-$46). Tilt steering ($81). Power windows ($143-$202). Electric door locks ($93-$132). Electric trunk release ($26). Remote tailgate lock: wag ($27). Electric clock ($26). Digital clock ($59). Headlamps-on indicator ($12). Trip odometer ($14). Instrument gauges: temp, volt, trip odometer ($29-$43). Two-speed wiper w/delay ($41). Lighting and Mirrors: Cornering lamps: Regal ($53). Tungsten-halogen high-beams ($27). Coach lamps ($92). Front light monitors ($31). Dome reading lamp $20). Door/courtesy/warning lights: Ltd. sed ($39-$62). Underhood light ($5). Remote left mirror ($19); right ($37-$42). Sport mirrors: left remote ($44-$49). Dual remote sport mirrors ($27-$76). Visor vanity mirrors, pair ($11). Lighted right visor vanity mirror ($50). Entertainment: AM radio ($97). AM/FM radio ($153). AM/FM stereo radio ($192); w/8-track or cassette ($272-$285). AM/FM stereo radio and CB ($525). Rear speaker ($20); pair ($30). Automatic power antenna ($51-$80). Triband power antenna ($93-$122). Exterior Trim: Landau vinyl top: Regal ($158-$175). Heavy-padded landau vinyl top: Regal ($188-$238). Long vinyl top ($124). Long padded vinyl top: Century sed ($207). Designers' accent paint ($174-$230). Solid special color paint ($165). Bumper guards, front: Century ($25). Protective bodyside moldings ($52). Rocker panel moldings: Century ($19). Door edge guards ($14-$22). Belt reveal moldings ($37). Wheel opening moldings: Century ($24). Body accent stripes ($37). Woodgrain vinyl appliqué: Century wag ($292-$316). Luggage rack: wag ($98). Air deflector: wag ($32). Tailgate hinge cover ($13). Interior Trim/Upholstery: Full-length console ($96). Bucket seats: cpe/wag ($38-$197). 55/45 bench seating: cpe/wag ($112-$159). Limited 55/45 seating: Regal spt cpe ($294). Notchback seating: Century spt ($147). Custom seatbelts ($20-$24). Load floor carpet area: Century wag ($55). Front carpet savers ($16). Carpet savers and mats ($27). Front carpet savers w/inserts ($27); rear ($49). Litter pocket ($10). Trunk trim covering ($33). Lockable storage compartment: wag ($40-$45). Wheels: Chrome-plated wheels ($48-$183). Designers' sport wheels ($116-$135). Styled aluminum wheels ($152-$335). Turbine wheels: Regal spt cpe ($116). Deluxe wheel covers: Century exc. spt ($45). Designers' wheel covers: Century exc. spt ($76); Regal ($31). Wire wheel covers: Century exc. spt ($208); Regal ($48-$164). Tires: P185/75R14 GBR WSW: Century cpe/sed ($45). P195/75R14 GBR BSW: Century six cpe/sed ($25); V-8 (NC). P195/75R14 GBR WSW ($46-$171). P195/75R14 SBR BSW: Century ($46-$73). P195/75R14 SBR WSW: Century ($95-$119); Regal ($46). P205/70R14 SBR wide-oval BSW: Regal ($37). P205/70R14 SBR WSW: Century spt Regal ($51-$88). P205/70R14 SBR WLT ($66-$176).

LESABRE/ELECTRA/ESTATE WAGON CONVENIENCE/APPEARANCE OPTIONS:
Option packages: LeSabre coupe Sport package: front bucket seats dual remote sport mirrors ($106-$126). Exterior molding pkg.: LeSabre ($95-$114). Lamp/indicator group: LeSabre ($48-$66). Sliding Astroroof: LeSabre ($981); Electra ($1058). Accessory group (color-coordinated seatbelts, left remote mirror, rocker panel moldings, trip odometer, visor mirrors): LeSabre ($35-$95). Accessory group (trip odometer, headlamps-on, low fuel and washer fluid indicators): Electra ($25-$55). Comfort/Convenience: Air cond.: LeSabre ($647). Automatic air cond. LeSabre ($738); Electra ($91). Touch climate control air cond.: LeSabre ($834); Electra ($187). Cruise control ($118). Rear defogger, electric ($109). Tinted glass ($90). Tinted windshield: LeSabre/Est ($55). Power windows: LeSabre/Est ($149-$221). Electric door locks ($95-$135). Automatic door locks: Electra ($158-$189). Six-way power driver's seat ($148-$179); passenger ($179). Manual seatback recliner, one side: LeSabre cpe ($67). Electric seatback recliner, each side ($128).

Sport steering wheel: LeSabre ($35). Tilt steering ($83). Tilt/telescoping steering column ($121-$131). Digital clock: LeSabre ($60). Remote tailgate lock: LeSabre Est ($37). Electric trunk release ($27). Electric trunk lock: Electra ($65). Electric fuel cap lock ($39). Theft deterrent system ($146); N/A on Estate. Three-speed wiper w/delay ($42). Lighting, Horns and Mirrors: Tungsten-halogen high-beam headlamps ($27). Cornering lamps ($53). Twilight Sentinel: Electra ($51). Front light monitors: LeSabre/Est ($31). Front/rear monitors: Electra ($67). Door courtesy/warning lights ($39-$62). Lighted door lock and interior ($62). Four-note horn ($25). Remote left mirror: LeSabre/Est ($20). Remote right mirror ($22-$42). Dual remote sport mirrors ($36-$76). Remote electric right mirror: Park Ave. ($54-$74). Dual electric remote mirrors ($85-$125). Remote left mirror w/thermometer ($33-$53). Remote electric left mirror w/thermometer: Park Ave. ($33). Dual electric mirrors w/left thermometer ($118-$158). Lighted visor vanity mirror, each ($40-$51). Entertainment: AM radio: LeSabre ($99). AM/FM radio: LeSabre ($156). AM/FM stereo radio ($195) w/8-track or cassette player ($276-$289) exc. Park Ave. ($81-$94). Full-feature AM/FM stereo radio: Electra ($208-$403); w/8-track or cassette ($289-$497). AM/FM stereo radio and CB: LeSabre ($533); Electra ($338-$533). AM/FM stereo with 8-track and CB/LeSabre ($603); Electra ($408-$603). Signal-seeking AM/FM stereo radio with CB/Electra ($521-$716); w/CB and 8-track or cassette ($635-$856). Signal-seeking AM/FM stereo radio w/digital readout: Electra ($185-$380); w/8-track ($298-$493); w/cassette ($325-$520). Rear speaker: LeSabre ($21); dual ($31). Windshield antenna ($29); incl. w/radios. Automatic power antenna ($52-$81). Triband power antenna ($94-$123); w/CB (NC). Delete radio: Park Ave. ($164 credit). Exterior Trim: Heavy-padded landau vinyl top: LeSabre, Electra Ltd. cpe ($213). Long vinyl top ($155-$174). Long, heavy-padded vinyl top: Electra Ltd. ($216). Designers' accent paint: LeSabre ($197). Solid special color paint: LeSabre ($166), exc. Firemist on Electra ($186). Protective bodyside moldings: LeSabre/Est ($47). Color-coordinated bodyside moldings: Electra Ltd. ($72). Door edge guards ($15-$22). Belt reveal molding: LeSabre spt cpe ($37). Bodyside accent stripes ($56); N/A on Estate. Luggage rack w/air deflector: LeSabre Estate ($152). Interior Trim/Upholstery: Custom seat trim: notchback, LeSabre spt cpe ($152 credit); 55/45, LeSabre spt cpe ($40 credit); 55/45, LeSabre ($112). Limited notchback seating: LeSabre spt cpe ($8). Limited 55/45 seating: LeSabre spt cpe ($120); LeSabre Ltd. ($112). Leather/vinyl 50/50 seating: Park Ave. ($466). Third seat: Estate ($193). Full-length console: LeSabre cpe w/spt pkg. ($102). Front carpet savers ($27). Front/rear carpet savers w/inserts ($49). Carpet savers and mats ($27). Litter pocket: LeSabre ($10). Trunk trim carpet ($52-$65). Heels: Chrome-plated wheels ($154-$188). Custom wheel covers: Electra ($31). Wire wheel covers ($130-$164). Tires: P205/75R15 SBR WSW: LeSabre ($50). P215/75R15 SBR BSW: LeSabre ($31). P215/75R15 SBR WSW: LeSabre ($84); Electra ($53). P225/70R15 SBR WSW: LeSabre spt cpe ($56). P225/70R25 SBR WLT: LeSabre spt cpe ($72). P225/75R15 SBR WSW: Estate ($56); Electra ($87).

RIVIERA CONVENIENCE/APPEARANCE OPTIONS:
Roof Options: Electric sunroof ($848). Electric sliding Astroroof ($1058). Comfort/Convenience-Trip monitor ($859). Automatic air cond. ($95). Cruise Master ($118). Rear defogger, electric ($109). Automatic door locks ($69). Six-way power seat, passenger ($179). Electric seatback recliner, one side ($128). Manual seatback recliner, one side: 'S' ($67). Sport steering wheel ($35). Tilt steering ($83). Tilt/telescope steering wheel ($131). Electric fuel cap lock ($39). Electric trunk release ($27). Electric trunk lock ($65). Low fuel indicator ($18). Fuel usage light, V-8 ($32). Windshield washer fluid indicator ($11). Three-speed wipers w/delay ($42). Theft deterrent system ($146). Lighting, Horns and Mirrors: Tungsten-halogen high beams ($27). Coach lamps ($92); incl. w/vinyl top. Front/rear light monitors ($67). Twilight Sentinel ($51). Courtesy/reading lamps ($45). Lighted door locks and interior light control ($62). Four-note horn ($25).

Dual electric remote mirrors ($63). Lighted visor vanity mirrors, each ($51). Entertainment: AM/FM stereo w/8-track or cassette tape player ($81-$94). AM/FM stereo radio w/CB ($290); w/CB and 8-track ($360). Full-feature AM/FM stereo radio ($208); w/8-track or cassette ($289-$302). Signal-seeking AM/FM stereo radio w/digital readout ($185); w/8-track or cassette ($298-$325). Signal-seeking AM/CB/FM stereo radio w/digital clock ($461); w/8-track or cassette ($587-$661). Triband power antenna ($42); w/CB radio (NC). Delete radio ($164 credit). Exterior Trim: Heavy-padded landau top ($298). Long vinyl top w/coach lamps ($305). Designers' accent paint ($209). Solid color special Firemist paint ($186). Protective bodyside moldings ($64). Door edge guards ($15). Bodyside stripes ($56). Interior Trim/Upholstery: 45/55 notchback front seat; leather/vinyl ($60). Leather/vinyl bucket seats: 'S' ($360). Front/rear carpet savers w/inserts ($62). Trunk trim carpet ($27). Trunk mat ($13). Wheels and Tires: Chrome-plated wheels ($130). Wire wheel covers: ($166). GR70 x 15 SBR WSW tires ($33). P205/75R15 SBR WSW tires: 'S' ($33 credit).

HISTORY: Introduced: October 11, 1979 (Skylark, April 19, 1979). Model year production (U.S.): 854,011 (including early '80 Skylarks). Calendar year production (U.S.): 783,575. Model year sales by U.S. dealers: 700,083 (including just 950 imported Opels). Calendar year sales (U.S.): 720,368, which gave Buick a healthy 11.0 percent share of the market.

Historical Footnotes: Although other automakers endured weak sales for the 1980 model year, Buick did comparatively well, ending the year in third place among the GM quintet. Sales that totaled 7 percent less than 1979 still proved better than the average industry loss of 22 percent. Part of the reason may have been an upsurge of interest in the new notchback Century four-door, which proved much more popular than its Aeroback predecessor. Century sales zoomed upward by 137 percent, and the aero coupe was abandoned in February 1980. Regal continued as Buick's best seller, even though sales fell by 28 percent. Full-size Buick sales dropped by similar levels. Skyhawk never had attracted many buyers, and was dropped from the lineup in December 1979. The last imported Opels were also sold during 1980. As of April 1980, Buick no longer manufactured a V-8 engine, thus ending a long series of popular V-8s that began in 1953. The Olds-built diesel V-8 offered beginning this year on Buicks created plenty of trouble, and eventually resulted in lawsuits against GM (and settlements) because of its mechanical problems. Rather than an all-new design it was simply a modification of the standard gasoline-powered 350 cu. in. V-8 that had been popular in the 1970s, and couldn't withstand the pressures of diesel operation. Diesel popularity was short-lived, in any case, and it would be dropped after 1985. Skylarks were first built at Buick's Willow Run (Michigan) plant. Overall development of the GM X-car quartet had cost $1.5 billion. Initially priced at $4,769 and up, Skylark endured a series of increases during its first half-season and beyond. Though priced higher than the Chevrolet, Olds and Pontiac versions, Skylark enjoyed strong demand.

1981

One model was missing from the 1981 Buick lineup: the subcompact Skyhawk. The name would return the following year on an all-new model. Meanwhile, fuel economy was the focus for 1981. That included widened availability of the Olds-built 5.7 liter diesel V-8. Most Buicks had Computer Command Control, which responded to sensors around the engine and exhaust system to keep gas mileage up while meeting federal emissions regulations. All Buicks (and other GM vehicles) carried a new "Freedom

II" maintenance-free battery, whose label included more test ratings and service information. Century, Regal and Skylark wore new high-pressure tires, introduced on 1980 B-bodies. All '81 Buicks had low rolling resistance radial tires, introduced a year earlier on Skylark, LeSabre and Electra. All tires except Skylark's were now match-mounted. Self-sealing tires were now available on most Buicks. A new "fluidic" windshield washer system sprayed two fans of fluid, but had no moving parts. Buick's turbocharged V-6 got changes for cold-engine driveability this year, including an aluminum intake manifold, thermal vacuum choke valve, and Early Fuel Evaporation system to help vaporize the air/fuel mixture. New "low-drag" brake calipers arrived on Skylark, LeSabre and Electra models, with a special piston seal to pull brake pads away from the rotor. B- and C-bodied models had new quick-takeup master cylinders with a large-bore third piston for faster initial flow of brake fluid. This was especially useful for the new calipers. Cruise-Master speed controls had a new resume-speed feature. Century, Regal, LeSabre and Electra with V-6 engines could have trailer-towing packages capable of hauling a 4,000-pound load. The Turbo Hydra-matic 200-4R transmission, offered on full-size models with 5.0-liter V-8, had a new overdrive fourth-speed range to improve highway gas mileage, coupled to a higher axle ratio. It came on Electras and LeSabre Estate Wagons, and was available in LeSabre coupes and sedans. The new transmission was also standard in C-body GM cars with 4.1-liter V-6 engine. Its overdrive (0.67:1) fourth gear engaged at about 45 MPH. The converter clutch added to the standard automatic transmission on some 1980 models was now included on all rear-drive Buicks.

1981 Buick, Skylark Sport Coupe. (OCW)

SKYLARK - SERIES 4X - FOUR/V-6 - Apart from a new grille and taillamps, Skylark didn't change much for 1981. The new grille, made up of vertical bars, offered a rather formal look not unlike the 1980 Electra. Buick block letters were inset across the bar at top of grille. Vertical rectangular signal lamps sat outboard of single rectangular headlamps. Skylark's nameplate was at the forward end of fenders. Revised full-width wrap-around taillamps split into two horizontal segments, eliminating the amber turn signal lenses. Inside was new cloth upholstery. Limited models had new woven velour cloth. The standard Delco AM radio came with a new fixed-mast antenna to improve fringe-area reception. A center console with storage bin was added. and the instrument panel now had black-face gauges (as did full-size Buicks). Controls for turn signals, dimmer, wiper/washer (and optional cruise control with resume) were now on the multifunction stalk lever. Four-speed manual transmission remained standard, with automatic available. Base powerplant was again the transverse-mounted Pontiac 2.5-liter four-cylinder engine, or optional Chevrolet 2.8-liter V-6. Both engines had Computer Command Control. Rear suspension isolating/damping improved ride feel. Skylark also added higher-pressure tires with low resistance. Buick's mist wiper system continued. Skylark's Sport coupe and sedan had a new sport steering wheel to join the black-accented interior and body. Again, its grille was totally different from other Skylarks: a black-accented six-slot design. Sport models also had amber park/signal lamps, smoked taillamp lenses, bumper strips, Rallye suspension and P205/70R13 steel-belted radial tires. Optional Sport lower body stripes included a Hawk decal. Electro-luminescent coach lamps were optional on the Limited.

1981 Buick, Century sedan. (OCW)

CENTURY - SERIES 4A - V-6/V-8 - The Aeroback two-door was finally dropped, leaving only a notchback four-door to replace the prior fastback of 1978-80 (a design that wasn't universally loved). Century was described in the full-line catalog as Buick's "little limousine" for its "elegant, even formal, styling." It did indeed display a formal notchback roofline. The restyled grille contained a tiny checkerboard pattern in five rows, separated by a single vertical divider. Vertical rectangular parking lights sat between the grille and the single recessed rectangular headlamps. Amber lenses were at fender tips. Designers' Accent paint combinations were available. At the rear were new wraparound taillamps: red upper lenses, amber below. Just ahead of the taillamps was 'Century' lettering with a 'BUICK' badge on the decklid. Base engine remained the 231 cu. in. (3.8-liter) V-6, with a 265 cu. in. V-8 the sole option. Century was the last Buick to carry a three-speed manual transmission (on the base model). Century Limited had standard automatic transmission with converter clutch. All Century models had standard power steering and brakes. Two station wagons were offered: base and Estate Wagon. A fixed mast antenna improved radio reception range and interference level. A new side-lift frame jack replaced the former bumper jack. Interiors had new fabrics. Century Limited had new soft knit velour cloth upholstery in 55/45 seating. Low-rolling-resistance tires were standard; new self-sealing tires were available. Optional wraparound moldings ran the full length of the car. Also optional: electroluminescent coach lamps, and a theft-deterrent system with starter interrupt.

1981 Buick, Regal Sport Coupe with turbocharged 3.8 Litre V-6. (OCW)

REGAL - SERIES 4A - V-6/V-8 - After three years of life as a downsized coupe, Regal got a serious aerodynamic restyle for 1981, including a raked front end and taller back end, with spoiler-type cutoff. A new grille and downward-sloping hood helped

to reduce Regal's drag coefficient by eighteen percent over the 1980 model. The new vertical-bar grille angled outward sharply from a point near the top. Buick block letters were inset in the upper horizontal bar, with 'Regal' script at the lower corner. Bumper tips flush with fender edges added to the clean look. Wide horizontal turn/parking lamps were built into the bumper. At the rear sat full-width, squarish wraparound taillamps. A new rear deck was topped by an "aerodynamically correct" wedge-styled spoiler lip. Flush-set front and rear bumpers enhanced the smooth aero look. Regal Limited had a full-length, wide rocker panel molding that extended ahead of the front wheels and back of the rears for an unbroken front-to-back line. A new blue crest for '81, in stylized contemporary design, appeared on the hood, new wheel covers, and optional cornering lamps. In addition to solid colors or Designers' Accent schemes, Regals were available with a Decor Package in four colors, each with a silver lower section. The package also included sport mirrors, turbine wheels, and a sport steering wheel. The standard 231 cu. in. (3.8-liter) V-6 engine came with automatic transmission that carried a converter clutch. Options above the standard V-6 were a turbo edition and a 4.3-liter V-8. New standards included low-rolling-resistance tires and a new, lighter battery. Regal had a redesigned fiber-reinforced plastic wheelhouse panel that incorporated a battery tray, plus a new side-lift frame jack. An electronically-tuned radio with Extended Range speakers was offered for the first time on Regals. Self-sealing tires were available. Regal's Sport Coupe was easy to spot. A bulge at the rear of the hood displayed a 'Turbo 3.8-Liter' chrome emblem at its side. Sport Coupes kept their fast-ratio power steering, sport mirrors and other goodies, but added a new Gran Touring suspension for handling equivalent to LeSabre and Riviera T Type. That suspension (also available on other Century and LeSabre models) was intended to deliver a tempting combination of road feel and smooth ride. The two-tone Decor Package included a black-trimmed grille, headlamps and taillamps; wide bright center rocker molding; turbine-style wheels; sport steering wheel; and choice of four body colors over a silver lower section. Limited interiors used new soft knit velour fabric, even on the upper doors. New fur-like carpeting extended to lower door sections. Limiteds also had the option of new 45/55 seating, or standard 55/45 with fold-down center armrest.

1981 Buick, LeSabre Limited sedan with optional wire wheel covers. (OCW)

LESABRE - SERIES 4B - V-6/V-8 - Restyled for 1980, the base and Limited LeSabres enjoyed some detail changes in their second year. The rectangular grille, though similar to the 1980 version, gained an extra row of holes and a more refined look. Color-coordinated, protective bodyside moldings were now standard. Taillamps were also modified to all-red design. Base engine remained the 231 cu. in. (3.8-liter) V-6. Both the 252 cu. in. (4.1-liter) V-6 and 5.0-liter V-8 now came with the new overdrive automatic transmission; the larger diesel V-8 kept the prior three-speed automatic. All gas engines had Computer Command Control. LeSabres had bumper guards and protective strips, cut-pile carpeting, mist wipers, compact spare tire and a side-frame jack, as well as power brakes and steering. Interiors sported woven velour fabrics. Black dial faces for easier reading were set off by woodgrain vinyl trim. Optional Cruise-Master speed control had a new resume-speed feature. Also optional:

an illuminated entry system for nighttime convenience, newly-styled aluminum wheels with exposed chrome lug nuts, electroluminescent coach lamps (for Limited), and automatic door locks. An option package for the new T Type included bucket seats, console, sport steering wheel, custom seatbelts, sport mirrors, black accented pillar, and Gran Touring suspension.

ESTATE WAGON - SERIES 4B/C - V-8 - Estate Wagons came in two versions: LeSabre and Electra. Dimensions were identical, with 87.9 cubic foot cargo area; but the lower-priced edition sported LeSabre's front end. Both carried the 307 cu. in. (5.0-liter) V-8 engine with overdrive automatic transmission, or optional 5.7-liter diesel. Standard equipment included whitewall steel-belted tires, air conditioning, power windows, power steering and brakes, tilt steering column, electric door locks, load floor carpeting, two-way tailgate, and roof rack with air deflector. A wide selection of interiors included five all-cloth front-seat colors on the 55/45 notchback seats, plus two vinyl trim possibilities, and two choices of cloth up front and vinyl in back. Estates sported new colonial oak exterior vinyl woodgrain trim. A dozen Delco radio choices were available.

1981 Buick, Electra Park Avenue coupe with diesel engine. (OCW)

1981 Buick, Electra Limited sedan with optional wire wheel covers. (OCW)

ELECTRA - SERIES 4C - V-6/V-8 - Electra received few exterior changes except for its grille, which got a different paint treatment to set Electra apart from other Buick series. The basic Electra grille, a bold rectangular design, contained six separate crosshatch sections. Park Avenue's grille relied on vertical strips alone within each section, for a formal look. The new grille was created to blend with the downward-sloping hood, and with Park Avenue's brushed-finish bodyside molding. Fender "ventiports" disappeared from the Limited, but remained on the Park Avenue, incorporated into the bodyside molding. Thus, Park Avenue was the only Buick left with vestigial portholes. The standard 252 cu. in. (4.1-liter) V-6 and optional 5.0-liter V-8 were coupled to a new overdrive automatic transmission, with a fourth gear that engaged at about 45 MPH. Diesel V-8 Electras retained the old automatic. Gas engines had Computer Command Control. Low-rolling-resistance whitewall tires were standard; self-sealing tires available. Match-mounted tires were offered. Electroluminescent coach lamps, formerly only on the Park Avenue, were now offered on the Limited. Park Avenue's standard padded halo top revealed a sliver of body color above the windows. Park Avenue models had fur-like carpet as well as velour or leather seats. Aluminum wheels were newly styled. Electra also had new standard color-coordinated, protective bodyside moldings. As always, Electra carried plenty of standard equipment,

including air conditioning, power brakes and steering, single-wipe feature on the windshield wipers, remote-controlled left outside mirror, digital clock, dome reading lamp, and lights for front ashtray, trunk, underdash and glove compartment. Park Avenue added wide rocker appearance moldings, an electric left mirror, and Delco AM/FM stereo radio.

1981 Buick, Riviera coupe with optional wire wheel covers. (OCW)

RIVIERA - SERIES 4E - V-6/V-8 - Buick's full-line catalog stressed the claim that some experts had declared Riviera to be on the "leading edge of Detroit technology" by combining "interesting weight-saving materials and engineering approaches...in a way that's synergistic: the sum becomes greater than its parts." New touches this year included a revised, bolder, more distinctly detailed grille and gray bumper protective strips. The grille consisted of tiny crosshatch elements, split into eight sections by narrow vertical bars, with a 'Riviera' script at the side. Horizontal parking and signal lamps sat directly beneath the quad rectangular headlamps. The oval stand-up hood ornament carried an R insignia. Rivieras rode new low rolling-resistance radial tires, except for the T Type which carried GR70 x 15 tires. Self-sealing tires were offered as options. A new "fluidic" windshield washer used no moving parts to spray droplets in a fan pattern. Standard equipment included air conditioning, automatic transmission, six-way power driver's seat, quartz clock, electric door locks and Delco AM/FM stereo radio with power antenna. New shocks and chassis tuning allowed higher tire pressures while retaining smooth ride. Two new engines were offered: the base 252 cu. in. (4.1-liter) V-6 plus an optional 350 diesel V-8. That diesel, offered through 1985, would eventually cause more trouble than pleasure to both its owners and the company. T Type was the new designation for the sporty Riviera, replacing the S Type of 1980. Special touches included black accents and black side mirrors, plus the familiar amber turn signal lamps. The Gran Touring suspension was intended to give quicker steering and increased road feedback, without a harsh ride. Standard T Type engine continued to be the 231 cu. in. (3.8-liter) turbocharged V-6; but the 4.1-liter V-6 or 5.0-liter V-8 could also be ordered, as well as the diesel. The T Type's instrument panel was now simulated woodgrain. Seats were new, in cloth or leather. A new 45/45 seating arrangement up front featured a fold-down center armrest on the driver's side. Cloth bucket seats and a storage console were standard on the T Type. New option for stereo fans: a Concert Sound six-speaker system. Electronic climate control was also available.

I.D. DATA: All Buicks had a new 17-symbol Vehicle Identification Number (VIN), stamped on a metal tag attached to the upper left surface of the cowl, visible through the windshield. The number begins with a '1' to indicate the manufacturing country (U.S.A.), followed by 'G' for General Motors and '4' for Buick Division. The next letter indicates restraint system. The fifth symbol is a letter denoting series: 'B' Skylark; 'C' Skylark Limited; 'D' Skylark Sport; 'E' Century; 'H' Century Estate Wagon; 'L' Century Limited; 'J' Regal; 'K' Regal Sport Coupe; 'M' Regal Limited; 'N' LeSabre; 'P' LeSabre Limited; 'R' LeSabre Estate Wagon; 'V' Electra Estate Wagon; 'X' Electra Limited; 'W' Electra Park Avenue; 'Y' Riviera T Type; 'Z' Riviera. Digits six and seven indicate body type: '37' 2-dr. coupe; '47' 2-dr. coupe; '57' 2-dr. notchback coupe; '35' 4-dr. wagon; '69' 4-dr. sedan. Next is the engine code: '5' L4-151 2Bbl.; 'X' V6-173 2Bbl.; 'A' V6-231 2Bbl.;

'3' V6-231 Turbo; '4' V6-252 4Bbl.; 'S' V8-265 2Bbl.; 'Y' V8-307 4Bbl.; 'N' V8-350 diesel. Symbol nine is a check digit ('8'). Symbol ten denotes model year ('B' 1981). Symbol eleven is the plant code: 'W' Willow Run, MI; '6' Oklahoma City, OK; 'G' Framingham, MA; 'H' Flint, MI; 'Z' Fremont, CA; 'K' Leeds, MO; 'X' Fairfax, KS; 'E' Linden, NJ. The final six digits are the sequential serial number, starting with 100001 except for full-size models built in Flint and Linden, which begin with 400001. A Body Style Identification Plate on the upper horizontal surface of the shroud showed the model year, series, style number, body number, body assembly plant, trim number, paint code, modular seat code and roof option. Skylarks had their body plate on the front tie bar just behind right headlamp. The five-symbol series and body style number was identical to the combination of series and model number shown in the tables below. Example: 4XB37 indicates a Skylark two-door coupe ('4' indicates Buick; 'X' the X-body; 'B' for base Skylark; and '37' for coupe body style).

SKYLARK (FOUR/V-6)

Model No.	Body/Style No.	Body Type & Seating	Factory Price	Shipping Weight	Prod. Total
4X	B37	2-dr Coupe-5P	6405/6530	2424/2481	46,515
4X	B69	4-dr Sedan-5P	6551/6676	2453/2510	104,091

SKYLARK LIMITED (FOUR/V-6)

| 4X | C37 | 2-dr Coupe-5P | 6860/6985 | 2453/2510 | 30,080 |
| 4X | C69 | 4-dr Sedan-5P | 7007/7132 | 2484/2541 | 81,642 |

SKYLARK SPORT (FOUR/V-6)

| 4X | D37 | 2-dr Coupe-5P | 7040/7165 | 2453/2520 | Note 1 |
| 4X | D69 | 4-dr Sedan-5P | 7186/7311 | 2484/2541 | Note 1 |

Note 1: Production totals shown for Skylark include Sport models.

CENTURY (V-6/V-8)

| 4A | H69 | 4-dr Sedan-6P | 7094/7170 | 3179/3269 | 127,119 |
| 4A | E35 | 4-dr Sta Wag-6P | 7391/7441 | 3269/3384 | 5,489 |

CENTURY LIMITED (V-6/V-8)

| 4A | L69 | 4-dr Sedan-6P | 7999/8075 | 3191/3306 | Note 2 |

CENTURY ESTATE WAGON (V-6/V-8)

| 4A | H35 | 4-dr Sta Wag-6P | 7735/7785 | 3311/3426 | 11,659 |

Note 2: Century sedan production figure included Limited model. Century models had a significant price increase during the model year. The base sedan reached $7,924, though increases for other models were less dramatic.

REGAL (V-6/V-8)

| 4A | J47 | 2-dr Coupe-6P | 7555/7605 | 3188/3303 | Note 3 |

REGAL SPORT COUPE (TURBO V-6)

| 4A | K47 | 2-dr Coupe-6P | 8528 | 3261 | Note 3 |

Note 3: Total Regal coupe production for the model year, 123,848.

REGAL LIMITED (V-6/V-8)

| 4A | M47 | 2-dr Coupe-6P | 8024/8074 | 3224/3339 | 116,352 |

LESABRE (V-6/V-8)

| 4B | N37 | 2-dr Coupe-6P | 7715/7715 | 3464/3623 | 4,909 |
| 4B | N69 | 4-dr Sedan-6P | 7805/7805 | 3493/3652 | 19,166 |

LESABRE LIMITED (V-6/V-8)

| 4B | P37 | 2-dr Coupe-6P | 7966/7966 | 3482/3641 | 14,862 |
| 4B | P69 | 4-dr Sedan-6P | 8101/8101 | 3515/3674 | 39,006 |

Note 4: A V-8 engine cost $203 extra on LeSabres; but no charge for the Computer Command version. Like other Buicks, LeSabre rose in price during the model year. The base V-6 coupe reached $8,187. LeSabre Estate wagon rose even higher, reaching $9,926.

LESABRE ESTATE WAGON (V-8)

| 4B | R35 | 4-dr Sta Wag-6P | 8722 | 4002 | 4,934 |

ELECTRA LIMITED (V-6/V-8)

| 4C | X37 | 2-dr Coupe-6P | 10237/10237 | 3656/3817 | 10,151 |
| 4C | X69 | 4-dr Sedan-6P | 10368/10368 | 3722/3883 | 58,832 |

ELECTRA PARK AVENUE (V-6/V-8)

| 4C | W37 | 2-dr Coupe-6P | 11267/11267 | 3728/3889 | Note 5 |
| 4C | W69 | 4-dr Sedan-6P | 11396/11396 | 3788/3949 | Note 5 |

Note 5: Production figures for Electra Limited also include Park Avenue models. Total model year production of Limited, 27,826; Park Avenue, 41,157. Only 13,922 Electras carried a V-6 engine. Prices for Electras rose $728 to $962 during the model year, while the Electra Estate Wagon reached $12,092.

ELECTRA ESTATE WAGON (V-8)

| 4C | V35 | 4-dr Sta Wag-6P | 11291 | 4174 | 6,334 |

RIVIERA (V-6/V-8)

| 4E | Z57 | 2-dr Coupe-5P | 12147/12147 | 3563/3724 | Note 6 |

RIVIERA T TYPE TURBO (V-6)

Model No.	Body/Style No.	Body Type & Seating	Factory Price	Shipping Weight	Prod. Total
4E	Y57	2-dr Coupe-5P	13091	3651	Note 6

Note 6: Total Riviera production, 52,007 (11,793 with V-6). For the model year, 3,990 turbocharged V-6 engines were produced.

FACTORY PRICE AND WEIGHT NOTE: Figure before the slash is for V-6 engine, after the slash for smallest (lowest-priced) V-8 engine available. For Skylark, figure before the slash is for four-cylinder engine, after the slash for V-6.

1981 Buick, Century Estate Wagon station wagon. (OCW)

ENGINES: BASE FOUR (Skylark): Inline, ohv four cylinder. Cast iron block and head. Displacement: 151 cu. in. (2.5 liters). Bore & stroke: 4.0 x 3.0 in. Compression ratio: 8.2:1. Brake horsepower: 84 at 3600 R.P.M. Torque: 125 lb.-ft. at 2400 R.P.M. Five main bearings. Hydraulic valve lifters. Carburetor: 2Bbl. Rochester. Built by Pontiac. VIN Code: S. Sales Code: LW9. OPTIONAL V-6 (Skylark): 60-degree, overhead-valve V-6. Cast iron block and head. Displacement: 173 cu. in. (2.8 liters). Bore & stroke: 3.5 x 3.0 in. Compression ratio: 8.5:1. Brake horsepower: 110 at 4800 R.P.M. Torque: 145 lb.-ft. at 2400 R.P.M. Four main bearings. Hydraulic valve lifters. Carburetor: 2Bbl. Roch. 2SE. Built by Chevrolet. VIN Code: X. Sales Code: LE2. BASE V-6 (Century, Regal, LeSabre): 90-degree, overhead-valve V-6. Cast iron block and head. Displacement: 231 cu. in. (3.8 liters). Bore & stroke: 3.8 x 3.4 in. Compression ratio: 8.0:1. Brake horsepower: 110 at 3800 R.P.M. Torque: 190 lb.-ft. at 1600 R.P.M. Four main bearings. Hydraulic valve lifters. Carburetor: 2Bbl. Rochester M2ME. VIN Code: A. Sales Code: LD5. TURBOCHARGED V-6 (Regal Sport Coupe, Riviera T Type); OPTIONAL (Riviera): Same as 231 V-6 above, but with E4ME four-barrel carburetor. Brake horsepower: 170 at 4000 R.P.M. (Riviera, 180 H.P.) Torque: 275 lb.-ft. at 2400 R.P.M. (Riviera, 270 lb.-ft.) VIN Code: 3. Sales Code: LC8. BASE V-6 (Electra, Riviera); OPTIONAL (LeSabre, Riviera T Type): 90-degree, overhead-valve V-6. Cast iron block and head. Displacement: 252 cu. in. (4.1 liters). Bore & stroke: 3.965 x 3.4 in. Compression ratio: 8.0:1. Brake horsepower: 125 at 4000 R.P.M. Torque: 205 lb.-ft. at 2000 R.P.M. Four main bearings. Hydraulic valve lifters. Carburetor: 4Bbl. Rochester E4ME. VIN Code: 4. Sales Code: LC4. OPTIONAL V-8 (Century/Regal): 90 degree, overhead-valve V-8. Cast iron block and head. Displacement: 265 cu. in. (4.3 liters). Bore & stroke: 3.75 x 3.00 in. Compression ratio: 8.0:1. Brake horsepower: 119 at 4000 R.P.M. Torque: 203 lb.-ft. at 2000 R.P.M. Five main bearings. Hydraulic valve lifters. Carburetor: 2Bbl. Roch. M2ME. Built by Pontiac. VIN Code: S. Sales Code: LS5. BASE V-8 (Estate); OPTIONAL (LeSabre, Electra, Riviera): 90-degree, overhead valve V-8. Cast iron block and head. Displacement: 307 cu. in. (5.0 liters). Bore & stroke: 3.80 x 3.385 in. Compression ratio: 8.0:1. Brake horsepower: 140 at 3600 R.P.M. Torque: 240 lb.-ft. at 1600 R.P.M. Five main bearings. Hydraulic valve lifters. Carburetor: 4Bbl. Roch. M4MC. Built by Oldsmobile. VIN Code: Y. Sales Code: LV2. OPTIONAL DIESEL V-8 (Century, LeSabre, Electra, Estate, Riviera): 90 degree, overhead valve V-8. Cast iron block and head. Displacement: 350 cu. in. (5.7 liters). Bore & stroke: 4.057 x 3.385 in. Compression ratio: 22.5:1. Brake horsepower: 105 at 3200 R.P.M. Torque: 200 lb.-ft. at 1600 R.P.M. Five main bearings. Hydraulic valve lifters. Fuel injection. Oldsmobile-built. VIN Code: N. Sales Code: LF9.

CHASSIS DATA: Wheelbase: (Skylark) 104.9 in.; (Century/Regal) 108.1 in.; (LeSabre/Estate) 115.9 in.; (Electra) 118.9 in.; (Riviera) 114.0 in. Overall length: (Skylark) 181.1 in.; (Century) 196.0 in.; (Regal) 200.6 in.; (LeSabre) 218.4 in.; (Electra) 221.2 in.; (Estate Wagon) 220.5 in.; (Riviera) 206.6 in. Height: (Skylark) 53.5 in.; (Century cpe/sed) 55.5 in.; (Century wag) 55.7 in.; (Regal) 54.1 in.; (LeSabre/Electra) 55.0 in.; (Estate) 57.1 in.; (Riviera) 54.3 in. Width: (Skylark cpe) 69.1 in.; (Skylark sed) 68.9 in.; (Century/Regal) 71.5 in.; (Century wag) 71.2 in.; (LeSabre/Electra) 75.9 in.; (Estate) 79.3 in.; (Riviera) 71.5 in. Front Tread: (Skylark) 58.7 in.; (Century/Regal) 58.5 in.; (LeSabre/Electra) 61.8 in.; (Estate) 62.2 in.; (Riviera) 59.3 in. Rear Tread: (Skylark) 56.9 in.; (Century/Regal) 57.8 in.; (LeSabre/Electra) 60.7 in.; (Estate) 64.0 in.; (Riviera) 60.0 in. Standard Tires: (Skylark) P185/80R13 GBR; (Skylark Sport) P205/70R13 SBR; (Century sed) P185/75R14 GBR; (Century wag) P195/75R14 GBR; (Regal) P195/75R14 SBR (Regal Spt Cpe) P205/70R14 SBR; (LeSabre) P205/75R15 SBR; (Electra) P215/75R15 SBR WSW; (Estate) P225/75R15 SBR; (Riviera) P205/75R15 SBR WSW; (Riviera T) GR70 x 15 SBR WSW.

TECHNICAL: Transmission: Three-speed, fully synchronized manual gearbox standard on Century; Turbo Hydra-matic optional. Four-speed, fully synchronized floor shift standard on Skylark; automatic optional. Turbo Hydra-matic standard on all other models. Century three-speed manual transmission gear ratios: (1st) 3.50:1; (2nd) 1.81:1; (3rd) 1.00:1; (Rev) 3.62:1. Skylark four-speed gear ratios: (1st) 3.53:1; (2nd) 1.95:1; (3rd) 1.24:1; (4th) 0.81:1; (Rev) 3.42:1. Automatic trans. gear ratios: (1st) 2.52:1; (2nd) 1.52:1; (3rd) 1.00:1; (Rev) 1.93:1. Skylark automatic gear ratios: (1st) 2.84:1; (2nd) 1.60:1; (3rd) 1.00:1; (Rev) 2.07:1. Riviera automatic gear ratios: (1st) 2.74:1; (2nd) 1.57:1; (3rd) 1.00:1; (Rev) 2.07:1. Overdrive automatic gear ratios: (1st) 2.74:1; (2nd) 1.57:1; (3rd) 1.00:1; (4th) 0.67:1; (Rev) 2.07:1. Standard axle ratio: (Skylark) 3.32:1; (Century/Regal V-6) 3.08:1; (Century V-8) 2.41:1; (Regal V-8) 2.29:1; (Century wagon) 2.73:1; (Regal Sport Coupe) 2.73:1 or 3.08:1; (LeSabre) 2.41:1, 2.73:1 or 3.23:1; (Electra) 3.08:1 or 3.23:1; (Electra diesel) 2.41:1; (Riviera) 2.93:1 or 2.41:1. Other axle ratios were standard in California. Final drive: (Skylark) spiral bevel; (others) hypoid bevel. Steering: (Skylark) rack and pinion; (others) recirculating ball; power assist standard on all except Skylark. Suspension: same as 1980. Brakes: front disc, rear drum: power brakes standard on all except Skylark. Four-wheel power disc brakes optional on Riviera. Body construction: (Skylark) unitized; (others) separate body and frame. Fuel tank: (Skylark) 14 gal.; (Century/Regal) 18.2 gal.; (LeSabre/Electra) 25 gal.; (Riv) 23 gal. Unleaded fuel only.

DRIVETRAIN OPTIONS: Engines: 173 cu. in. (2.8-liter) V-6. 2Bbl.: Skylark ($125). Turbocharged 231 cu. in. (3.8-liter) V-6. 4Bbl.: Riviera ($750). 252 cu. in. (4.1-liter) V-6. 4Bbl.: LeSabre ($238); Riviera T Type ($750 credit). 265 cu. in. (4.3-liter) V-8: Century/Regal ($50-$76). 307 cu. in. (5.0-liter) V-8. 4Bbl.: LeSabre cpe/sed ($203) but (NC) with computer command control; Electra cpe/sed, Riviera (NC); Riviera T ($750 credit). 350 cu. in. (5.7-liter) diesel V-8: Century ($695-$721); LeSabre/Riviera ($695); Electra/Estate ($542). Transmission/Differential: Three-speed automatic trans.: Skylark ($349); LeSabre cpe/sed with 4.1- or 5.0-liter ($153 credit). Optional rear axle ratio: Century/Regal/LeSabre/Electra (NC). Limited slip differential: Century/Regal/LeSabre/Electra ($69). Suspension. Steering and Brakes: F40 Firm ride/handling pkg. ($21-$22). FE2 Gran Touring suspension: Century/Regal/LeSabre ($40); Riviera ($21). F41 Rallye ride/handling suspension incl. P205/70R13 SBR tires: Skylark ($134). Superlift rear shock absorbers: Skylark ($57). Automatic level control: Century/Regal/LeSabre/Electra ($142). Power steering: Skylark ($27). Power brakes: Skylark ($79). Four-wheel disc brakes: Riv ($215). Other: Trailer towing flasher/harness ($23-$40). Trailer towing pkg.: Century/Regal ($148-$226); LeSabre ($434); Electra exc. wag ($141). H.D. alternator, 85-amp ($27-$75). H.D. battery ($21-$22) exc. diesel ($42). H.D. cooling: Skylark ($34-

$63). Engine block heater ($16). Diesel fuel heater ($42). Heavy-duty engine/transmission cooling ($32-$61) exc. Skylark. California emission system ($46); diesel ($82).

SKYLARK CONVENIENCE/APPEARANCE OPTIONS: Option Packages: Acoustic pkg. ($45). Flip-open Vista Vent glass sunroof ($246). Lamp group ($43-$52). Comfort/Convenience: Air cond. ($385). Cruise Master w/resume ($132). Rear defogger, electric ($107). Power windows ($140-$195). Electric door locks ($93-$132). Six-way power driver's seat ($173). Manual seatback recliners, passenger ($43); both ($87). Sport steering wheel ($43); N/A on Sport. Tilt steering ($81). Tinted glass ($75). Instrument gauges incl. trip odometer ($42). Trip odometer ($14). Electric dial clock ($23). Digital clock ($55). Electric trunk release ($27). Two-speed wipers w/low-speed delay ($41). Lights, Horns and Mirrors: Tungsten-halogen high beams ($27). Coach lamps: Ltd. ($90). Headlamps-on indicator ($12). Dome reading light ($20). Dual horns ($12). Remote-control left mirror ($19); N/A on sport. Sport mirrors: left remote, right manual ($47). Dual remote sport mirrors ($28-$75). Visor vanity mirror, passenger ($12). Lighted visor vanity mirror, either side ($41). Entertainment: AM/FM radio ($64). AM/FM stereo radio ($100); w/8-track or cassette player ($174-$186). AM/FM stereo radio with CB ($398); with CB and 8-track or cassette ($463-$475). Graphic equalizer ($146). Dual rear speakers ($23-28). Windshield antenna ($10). Power antenna ($47). Triband power antenna ($77). Delete AM radio ($51 credit). Exterior Trim: Landau vinyl top; cpe ($173). Long vinyl top ($115). Designers' accent paint ($182); N/A on Sport. Protective bodyside moldings ($44). Wide rocker panel moldings ($56). Belt reveal moldings ($27). Wheel opening moldings ($25). Door edge guards ($13-$21). Pillar appliqué: sed exc. Spt ($23). Hood ornament and windsplit ($27); N/A on Sport. Bodyside or Sport stripes ($42). Bumper guards, front/rear ($34). Bumper strips, front/rear ($42). Interior Trim/Upholstery: Full-length console ($86). Bucket seats, base ($48); limited cloth/vinyl ($48-$227); limited leather/vinyl ($308-$485). Notchback bench seating: Sport ($177). Color-keyed seatbelts ($24). Front carpet savers ($15). Carpet savers and mats ($25). Trunk trim carpeting ($33). Wheels: Chrome-plated wheels ($21-$148). Designers' sport wheels ($107-$127). Sport wheel covers ($11-$56). Deluxe wheel covers ($45). Locking wire wheel covers ($157-$202). Tires: P185/80R13 GBR WSW ($51); N/A on Sport. P185/80R13 SBR BSW ($47); N/A on Spt. P185/80R13 SBR wide WSW ($105); N/A on Spt. P205/70R13 SBR WSW ($58). P205/70R13 SBR WLT ($75). Self-sealing tires ($99).

1981 Buick, Regal Limited coupe with optional Decor package. (OCW)

CENTURY/REGAL CONVENIENCE/APPEARANCE OPTIONS: Option Packages: Regal Limited Somerset II pkg.: designers paint (dark sandstone and camel), turbine wheels with camel accents, doeskin 55/45 seats with dark brown buttons/laces ($459). Regal Turbo performance pkg.: dual exhaust and 3.08:1 axle ratio ($75). Regal Sport Coupe Decor pkg. ($427). Regal Coupe Decor pkg. ($385). Sliding electric Astroroof: Regal ($773). Electric sunroof: Regal ($561). Hatch roof: Regal ($695). Convenience group ($12-$78). Exterior molding pkg. ($94-$175). Comfort/Convenience: Air cond. ($585); automatic ($677). Cruise Master with resume ($132). Rear defogger, electric ($107). Tinted glass ($75). Tinted windshield ($53). Six-way power seat, each side ($173). Manual passenger seatback recliner ($66). Custom steering wheel ($11). Sport steering wheel ($35-$46). Tilt steering ($81). Power windows ($140-$195). Electric door locks ($93-$132). Automatic door locks ($154-$183). Electric trunk release ($27). Remote electric tailgate lock: wag ($29). Electric dial clock ($23). Digital clock ($55). Headlamps-on indicator ($12). Trip odometer ($14). Instrument gauges: temp, voltage, trip odometer ($42). Two-speed wiper w/delay ($41). Theft deterrent system ($142). Lighting and Mirrors: Tungsten-halogen high-beam headlamps ($27). Cornering lamps: Regal ($52). Coach lamps: Ltd. ($90). Front lamp monitors ($31). Door courtesy/warning lights: Ltd. ($38-$60). Dome reading lamp ($20). Underhood light ($5). Remote left mirror ($19); right ($35-$41). Dual sport mirrors, left remote ($41-$47). Dual remote sport mirrors ($28-$75). Visor vanity mirrors ($11). Lighted visor vanity mirror ($49). Entertainment: AM radio ($90). AM/FM radio ($142). AM/FM stereo radio ($178); w/8-track or cassette ($252-$264). Signal-seeking AM/FM stereo radio ($379-$402). Electronic-tuning AM/FM stereo radio w/8-track or cassette ($483-$555). AM/FM stereo radio with CB ($487). Dual rear speakers ($23-$28). Fixed-mast antenna; w/radio ($10). Windshield antenna ($27); incl. w/radio. Automatic power antenna ($47-$74). Triband power antenna ($86-$113). Exterior Trim: Landau vinyl top: Regal ($146). Heavy-padded Landau vinyl top: Regal ($186). Long vinyl top ($115). Long padded vinyl top: Century ($192). Designers' accent paint ($130-$202). Solid special color paint ($162). Protective bodyside moldings ($48). Wraparound bodyside moldings: Century, Ltd. ($62-$96). Rocker panel moldings: Century sed ($19). Wheel opening moldings: Century ($25). Door edge guards ($13-$21). Belt reveal moldings: Regal spt cpe w/decor pkg. ($36). Bodyside stripes ($36). Front bumper guards: Century ($24). Woodgrain vinyl appliqué: wag ($286-$311). Luggage rack: wag ($96). Air deflector: wag ($32). Tailgate follower board: wag ($13). Interior Trim/Upholstery: Full-length console ($95). Non-shifting console: Regal ($69). Bucket seats ($72). Bench seat: Century sed ($144 credit). 55/45 seating: cloth bench ($134); leather/vinyl, Regal Ltd. ($324). Limited 55/45 cloth seating: Regal spt cpe ($358); leather/vinyl ($682). 45/55 seating, Regal Ltd.: cloth (NC); leather/vinyl ($324). Limited 45/45 Spt Cpe seating: cloth ($358); leather/vinyl ($682). Custom seat/shoulder belts ($23). Front carpet savers ($15). Carpet savers and mats ($25). Front/rear carpet savers with inserts ($45). Trunk trim covering ($44). Lockable storage compartment: wag ($45). Load floor carpet: wag ($54). Wheels: Chrome-plated wheels ($47-$180). Styled aluminum wheels ($197-$329). Turbine wheels ($114-$158). Locking wire wheel covers: Century ($205); Regal ($47-$161). Deluxe wheel covers: Century ($45). Tires: P185/75R14 GBR WSW: Century V-6 ($48). P195/75R14 GBR: Century V-6 ($26). P195/75R14 SBR BSW: Century ($53-$78). P195/75R14 GBR WSW: Century ($49-$76). P195/75R14 SBR WSW: Century ($101-$126); Regal ($49). P205/70R14 SBR wide-oval BSW: Regal ($39). P205/70R14 SBR whitewall: Regal ($54-$94). P205/70R14 SBR WLT: Century ($162-$187); Regal ($70-$109). Self-sealing tires ($99).

LESABRE/ELECTRA/ESTATE WAGON CONVENIENCE/APPEARANCE OPTIONS: Option Packages: LeSabre T Type pkg.: bucket seats, console, sport mirrors, sport steering wheel, Gran Touring suspension ($271-$295). LeSabre Coupe Sport pkg.: front bucket seats, remote sport mirrors ($103-$122). Accessory group: LeSabre ($24-$43); Electra ($30-$77). Lamp/indicator group: LeSabre ($47-$64). Comfort/Convenience: Sliding electric Astroroof ($981-$995), Air cond.: LeSabre ($625). Automatic air cond.: LeSabre ($708); Electra ($83). Air cond. with touch-climate control: LeSabre ($796); Electra ($171). Cruise Master w/resume: LeSabre ($135). Rear defogger, electric ($107). Tinted glass ($107). Power windows: LeSabre ($143-$211). Electric door locks ($93-$132). Automatic door locks ($154-$183). Six-way power seat, driver's or passenger's ($146-$173); both ($319-$346). Electric seatback recliner, one side ($124). Manual seatback recliner, one side: LeSabre ($65). Sport steering wheel: LeSabre ($34). Tilt steering ($81). Tilt/telescoping steering column ($119-$128). Dial clock: LeSabre ($55). Trip odometer: LeSabre ($14). Remote electric tailgate lock: LeSabre Estate ($43). Electric trunk lock: Electra ($63). Electric trunk release ($27). Electric fuel cap lock ($38). Theft deterrent system ($142): N/A on Estate. Three-speed wiper w/delay ($41). Lighting, Horns and Mirrors: Tungsten-halogen high-beam headlamps ($27). Twilight Sentinel headlamp control: Electra ($50). Cornering lamps ($51). Coach lamps: Electra Ltd. ($90). Light monitors, front: LeSabre, Electra Estate ($31): front/rear, Electra ($65). Door courtesy/warning lamps ($38-$60). Lighted door lock and interior light control ($60). Four-note horn ($24). Remote left mirror: LeSabre ($19). Remote right mirror: LeSabre ($40); Electra Ltd. ($21-$40), Remote electric right mirror: Park Ave. ($52-$72). Dual remote sport mirrors: LeSabre ($56-$75). Electra Ltd. Estate ($37-$55). Dual electric remote mirrors: LeSabre ($102-$121); Electra Ltd. Estate ($83-$102). Remote left mirror w/thermometer: LeSabre ($32-$52); Electra Ltd. Estate ($19-$32). Electric left mirror w/thermometer: Electra Park Ave. ($32). Dual electric mirrors w/left thermometer: LeSabre ($134-$153); Electra ($115-$134). Visor vanity mirrors: LeSabre ($11). Lighted visor vanity mirror, driver or passenger ($115-$153). Entertainment: AM radio: LeSabre ($90). AM/FM radio: LeSabre ($142). AM/FM stereo radio: LeSabre, Electra Ltd./Estate ($178). AM/FM stereo radio and 8-track or cassette player: LeSabre ($252-$264); Electra ($74-$264). Full-feature AM/FM stereo radio: LeSabre ($369), Electra ($346-$369), Park Ave. cpe ($191). Full-feature AM/FM stereo radio w/8-track or cassette: LeSabre ($420-$455); Electra ($265-$455). Signal-seeking AM/FM stereo radio: LeSabre ($379-$402); Electra ($170-$348). Signal-seeking radio and 8-track or cassette: LeSabre ($483-$555), Electra ($273-$500). AM/FM stereo radio with CB: LeSabre ($488). Signal-seeking AM/FM stereo radio with CB and 8-track or cassette player: Electra ($581-$783). Delete AM/FM stereo radio: Park Ave. ($150 credit). Concert Sound speaker system: Electra exc. wag ($91); ETR or full-feature radio req'd. Dual rear speakers ($23-$28) when ordered with radio. Windshield antenna ($27); incl. w/radio. Automatic power antenna ($48-$75). Triband power antenna ($86-$113); w/CB radio (NC). Exterior Trim: Exterior molding pkg.: LeSabre ($92). Landau vinyl top: LeSabre, Electra Ltd. cpe ($195). Long vinyl top: LeSabre, Electra Ltd. sed ($142-$159). Heavy-padded long vinyl top: Electra Ltd. sedan ($198). Designers' accent paint: LeSabre ($191). Special single-color paint: ($161): Firemist, Electra ($180). Protective bodyside moldings: Estate ($48). Wide rocker panel moldings: Electra Ltd./Estate ($56). Door edge guards ($14-$21). Bodyside stripes ($54). Woodgrain vinyl appliqué: LeSabre Estate ($279). Roof rack: LeSabre Estate ($139). Interior Trim/Upholstery: Full console: LeSabre cpe ($100). 55/45 seating: LeSabre ($108). Leather/vinyl 50/50 seating: Electra ($452). Custom seatbelts: LeSabre ($23). Third seat: Estate ($108). Front carpet savers: Electra ($25). Carpet savers and handy mats ($25). Front/rear carpet savers w/inserts ($45). Trunk trim carpet ($51-$63). Trunk mat ($13). Wheels: Chrome-plated wheels ($152-$182). Styled aluminum wheels ($253-$283). Custom wheel covers: Electra Ltd. ($30). Custom locking wire wheel covers ($129-$159). Tires: P205/75R15 SBR WSW: LeSabre ($53). P215/75R15 SBR WSW: LeSabre ($88). P225/75R15 SBR wide WSW: Electra ($36). P225/70R15 SBR wide WSW: LeSabre cpe ($139). Self-sealing tires ($99-$122).

RIVIERA CONVENIENCE/APPEARANCE OPTIONS: Comfort/Convenience: Electric sliding Astroroof ($995). Electric sunroof ($848). Automatic touch climate control air cond. ($175). Cruise control w/resume ($135). Rear defogger, electric ($107). Automatic electric door locks ($62). Six-way power seat, passenger ($173). Electric seatback recliner, one side ($124). Sport steering wheel ($34). Tilt steering ($81). Tilt/telescope steering wheel ($128). Electric fuel cap lock ($38). Electric trunk release ($27). Electric trunk lock ($63). Low fuel indicator ($17). Fuel usage light ($31). Trip monitor ($833). Three-speed wipers w/delay ($41). Windshield washer fluid indicator ($11). Theft deterrent system ($142). Lighting. Horns and Mirrors: Tungsten-halogen high-beam headlamps ($27). Twilight Sentinel ($50). Coach lamps ($90); incl. w/vinyl top. Front/rear light monitors ($65). Rear quarter courtesy/reading lamp ($43). Lighted door lock and interior light control ($60). Four-note horn ($24). Dual electric remote mirrors ($61). Lighted visor vanity mirrors, each ($50). Entertainment: Full-feature AM/FM stereo radio ($190); w/8-track or cassette ($264-$276). AM/FM stereo radio w/8-track or cassette tape player ($74-$86); with CB and 8-track or cassette ($537-$561). Signal-seeking AM/FM stereo radio ($169); w/8-track ($273), w/cassette ($322). Delete radio ($150 credit). Rear speakers ($23). Concert Sound system ($91); N/A with base radio. Triband power antenna ($42). Exterior Trim: Heavy-padded Landau vinyl top w/coach lamps ($273). Designers' accent paint ($202). Special color Firemist paint ($180). Protective bodyside moldings ($59). Door edge guards ($14). Bodyside stripes ($54). Interior Trim/Upholstery: 45/55 leather/vinyl front seat ($349). Storage console ($67). Front/rear carpet savers w/inserts ($55). Trunk trim carpeting ($27). Trunk mat ($13). Wheels and Tires: Chrome-plated wheels ($126). Custom locking wire wheel covers ($161). GR70 x 15 SBR whitewalls ($33). Self-sealing tires ($122).

HISTORY: Introduced: September 25, 1980. Model year production (U.S.): 856,996 for a 12.8 percent share of the industry total. That number included 138,058 four-cylinder Buicks, 521,837 sixes, and 197,101 V-8s--quite a drop from the days when the V-8 was king among Buick buyers. Calendar year production (U.S.): 839,960. Model year sales by U.S. dealers: 756,186 (led by Regal and Skylark). Calendar year sales (U.S.): 722,617 for a market slice of 11.6 percent.

Historical Footnotes: Buick assembled its 23 millionth car in 1981 and enjoyed a good sales year as well, beating the 1980 mark by over 56,000 cars. Such good performance came as a surprise, as other U.S. automakers endured a slump. Skylark sales rose by over 25 percent, but Regal hung on as Buick's best seller. Sales of full-size Buicks dwindled. For the fifth time, a Buick served as pace car for the Indy 500. This time it was a Regal with special 4.1-liter V-6 engine, developed by Buick along with Baker Engineering. The souped-up 4.1 produced 281 horsepower, compared with 125 for the stock version used in full-size Buicks (not yet in Regals). The same car also paced the July 4th Pike's Peak hill climb.

1982

After a year's absence, the Skylark name returned--but on an all-new front-wheel drive subcompact Buick. The new version debuted in March 1982, as a mid-year entry. Also new was a front-drive (and shrunken) Century, no longer closely related to the rear-drive Regal. Two new gas engines were offered: a high-output 2.8-liter V-6 for Skylarks (delivering 20 percent more horsepower), and a 181 cu. in. (3.0-liter) V-6 for Century, with shorter stroke than the 3.8 version from which it evolved. Flat-top pistons boosted the new 3.0's compression ratio to 8.45:1.

It developed just as much horsepower as the 3.8, but at higher engine speed. The high-output 2.8 also gained compression, from standard 8.0:1 in the base version to 8.94:1 in the high-output variant, as a result of larger intake and exhaust valves and increased valve duration and lift. A new diesel 4.3-liter V-6 became available during the model year. On existing powerplants, the biggest news was fuel injection added to the Skylark (and new Century) four. Turbo performance in the Regal Sport Coupe and Riviera T Type got a boost for 1982. The turbocharged V-6 gained a low-restriction dual exhaust system as standard on the Regal Sport Coupe, along with upgraded electronics and a larger (five-quart) oil-pan capacity. Turbo response time was reduced, and incoming air was warmed in an exhaust-heated plenum chamber. Oldsmobile's big (5.7-liter) diesel V-8 was now available on Regal, LeSabre, Electra, Riviera, and Estate Wagons. More models added the overdrive automatic transmission that had been offered on selected 1981 Buicks. Producing a claimed 10-20 percent economy boost, overdrive was standard in Electra and Riviera, optional under LeSabre hoods. Pliacell-R shock absorbers, formerly used only on big Buicks, were added to the rear of all 1982 models. They used a sealed fluid chamber and special gas rather than air. "Memory Seat" was offered as an option on Electra and Riviera, returning automatically to either of two selected positions at the touch of a button. 1982 Buick body colors were light gray, black and white, plus a selection of metallics: silver, dark gray Firemist, charcoal light sandstone, medium sandstone, dark brown Firemist, medium blue, dark blue, light or dark jadestone, light or dark redwood, and red Firemist. Not all colors were available in all models.

SKYHAWK - SERIES 4J - FOUR - Styled along Century lines on GM's J-car platform, the new Skyhawk rode a front-wheel drive chassis. According to Buick it displayed the "aerodynamic wedge shape of the fuel-efficient future." The fresh subcompact debuted at the Chicago Auto Show in February 1982. The contemporary five-passenger design featured a low hood and high rear deck to reduce drag, along with a unified front end and grille and integrated headlamp system. Backup lights sat in a black panel between the wraparound taillamps. Deluxe wheel covers carried the Buick tri-shield emblem. Buyers could eventually choose from three transverse-mounted engines. First came the base 112 cu. in. (1.8-liter) OHV four. Late arrivals were a fuel-injected 1.8-liter overhead-cam four from GM of Brazil, and a 121 cu. in. (2.0-liter) carbureted four. The 88-horsepower base engine had a cross-flow cylinder head design with intake valves on one side, exhaust on the other. GM's computer command control module controlled spark timing, and it used a fast-burn combustion chamber. The 2.0 engine was essentially the same, but with longer stroke, developing two more horsepower. Skyhawk's chassis now had MacPherson independent front suspension and semi-independent crank arm rear suspension, plus rack-and-pinion steering and Pliacell-R rear shock absorbers. Skyhawk came in Custom or Limited trim level, on coupe and sedan bodies. Limiteds carried standard soft knit velour upholstery, while Customs could have a woven cloth or vinyl interior. Coupes had swing-out rear quarter windows; sedans, roll-down rear windows. Coupes also had a standard "easy entry" passenger door. Standard Skyhawk equipment included a Delco 2000 series AM radio (which could be deleted), full console, reclining bucket seats, front and rear ashtrays, roof-mounted assist handles, Freedom II battery, two-speed wiper/washer, cigarette lighter, power brakes, power rack-and-pinion steering, side-window front defogers, compact spare tire, front stabilizer bar and black left-hand mirror. The Limited added a front-seat armrest, gauge package, trip odometer, custom steering wheel, and acoustic insulation package. Skyhawk options included electronic-tuning radios, six-way power driver's seat, remote trunk release, Vista-Vent flip-open removable glass sunroof and styled aluminum wheels. A four-speed (overdrive) manual gearbox was standard, but five-speed became available later in the model year.

1982 Buick, Skylark Sport Coupe. (OCW)

1982 Buick, Skylark Coupe. (OCW)

1982 Buick, Skylark Limited sedan with optional wire wheel covers. (OCW)

SKYLARK - SERIES 4X - FOUR/V-6 - Six models made the Skylark lineup: coupe and sedan in base, Limited or Sport trim. Not much changed except for minor revisions in grille and front-end sheetmetal. Skylark now had a "fluidic" windshield washer with single spray nozzle, plus new Pliacell-R shock absorbers in back. Major changes came under the hood and in the suspension. The base 151 cu. in. (2.5-liter) four switched from a carburetor to single-point electronic fuel injection, intended to improve cold-weather operation as well as gas mileage, and eliminate engine run-on. Two optional engines were offered: a standard 173 cu. in. (2.8-liter) V-6 or a high-output 2.8-liter V-6 with 20 percent more horsepower. That one had revised carburetion, larger valves, and an altered camshaft. Higher axle ratio boosted Skylark performance with the potent V-6 even more. Four-speed manual shift (floor lever) remained standard; automatic available. A refined interior replaced the vinyl bolsters with cloth fabric on Skylark and Sport notchback front seats. Limited and Sport again offered optional leather. There was a new steering wheel. Special lighting in glove box, under dash, in ashtray and elsewhere that was formerly optional now became standard. A Graphic Equalizer was now available with cassette tape players offering tone control in five bands. Optional speakers delivered better frequency response. For the first time, Limiteds could have back-seat reading lamps. Also optional: the Vista Vent flip-open glass sunroof.

1982 Buick, Century Limited coupe. (OCW)

1982 Buick, Century Limited sedan with optional wire wheel covers. (OCW)

CENTURY - SERIES 4A - FOUR/V-6 - Introduced after the model year began, Century underwent a total restyle for a contemporary wedge-shaped aerodynamic appearance. Bumpers and outside mirrors integrated into the basic body form added to the slick, even "slippery" look. With a transverse-mounted four-cylinder engine under the hood and a front-drive chassis, the new Century hardly seemed related to the old rear-drive that wore that name for so many years. Gas and diesel V-6 engines were available, but it was still a much different car. The modern version had MacPherson strut independent front suspension, plus trailing axle rear suspension with Pliacell-R shocks. Though almost eight inches shorter than before, it retained similar interior dimensions and trunk capacity. An integrated grille with center crest had two bright horizontal bars and a single vertical bar. Half of the lower segment extended all the way outward and around the fender tips, below the wraparound lights. Wide wraparound taillamps were split into two sections by a body-color strip. A Century script badge was at the back of the rear quarter panels, and on engine identifier at the forward end of front fenders. The rear roof pillar held a crest. Grille, front end and hood were said to "flow in an unbroken line past the windshield and side windows." Those windows were flush-mounted to cut wind resistance giving the new Century the lowest drag coefficient of any Buick. Standard engine was the 151 cu. in. (2.5-liter) four: optional, either a new 181 cu. in. (3.0-liter) V-6 or 4.3-liter diesel V-6. Standard three-speed automatic transmission included a converter clutch for added efficiency. Power rack-and-pinion steering was standard; so were power brakes and deluxe wheel covers. Custom and Limited models were offered. A new Delco AM2000 radio was standard. So were wide belt reveal moldings color-coordinated bodyside moldings, front/rear bumper guards, wheel opening moldings, black rocker panels, front and side-window defoggers, black outside mirrors, cigarette lighter, and maintenance free battery. Limiteds also carried dual horns, a stand-up hood ornament, 45/45 pillow seats (soft velour cloth or vinyl) with armrest, a custom steering wheel, and wide lower bodyside moldings. Rocker switches and thumbwheels controlled lights and other functions at the instrument panel.

1982 Buick, Regal Limited sedan. (OCW)

1982 Buick, Regal Sport coupe. (OCW)

1982 Buick, Regal Estate Wagon station wagon. (OCW)

REGAL - SERIES 4G - V-6/V-8 - After several years of success in coupe form as a top Buick seller, Regal added a four-door sedan and Estate Wagon. Now that Century had turned to front-drive, Regal remained alone as a rear-drive mid-size. Regal's formal-look grille, made up of narrow vertical bars split into eight sections and angled outward at the base, went on both coupes and new models. Both the grille and taillamp displayed Regal identification. The new sedan offered dual outside mirrors plus color-coordinated bodyside moldings, with seating for six. The Regal Estate Wagon could carry up to 71.8 cubic feet of cargo with rear seat folded down. Standard fittings included deluxe wheel covers and whitewall tires, plus bodyside moldings and bumper guards. Standard engine was the familiar 231 cu. in. (3.8-liter) V-6, hooked to automatic transmission. All but the Regal Sport Coupe could have a 252 (4.1-liter) V-6, or choice of a V-6 or V-8 diesel. Coil spring suspensions used Pliacell-R shock absorbers at the rear. Regal's Limited could be ordered with 45/45 front seating in a choice of two-tone combinations: sandstone and brown, or gray and dark charcoal. Limiteds also sported a new deluxe steering wheel. The optional resume-speed cruise control now included a tiny memory light. Other new options: Delco electronically-tuned AM/FM stereo radio with tape player; quartz analog clock; rear-seat reading lamps; Twilight Sentinel headlamp control, and Electronic Touch Climate Control air conditioning (offered on other Buicks since 1980). A trailering package was available for the 3.8 engine. Regal Limiteds could also have electroluminescent coach lamps, automatic door locks, and Gran Touring suspension. The turbocharged Regal coupe continued, with improved performance. The Sport Coupe featured a special hood, black accents styled aluminum wheels and Gran Touring suspension. Axle ratio switched to 3.08:1, and the turbo 3.8-liter V-6 now included a low-restriction dual exhaust system.

1982 Buick, LeSabre Limited sedan with optional styled wheels. (OCW)

1982 Buick, LeSabre Custom coupe with optional styled wheels. (OCW)

LESABRE - SERIES 4B - V-6/V-8 - Still (relatively) full size and rear drive, the six-passenger LeSabre entered 1982 with a new grille and more trim, including convenience lights and new color on the woodgrain-trimmed instrument panel. The vertical slat grille was divided into three rows and four columns, with Buick badge on the side of the center row. Quad headlamps were deeply recessed: parking/signal lamps set into the bumper. Taillamps were wide, but not full width. The former base LeSabre was now called LeSabre Custom. Buyers could take the standard 231 cu. in. (3.8-liter) V-6 engine for economy, or elect a 252 cu. in. (4.1-liter) V-6 for power. Other options: a 5.0-liter gas V-8 and 5.7 diesel V-8. The 4.1 V-6 had the same electronic idle speed control as the smaller version, plus electronic spark control that adjusted the spark timing when it sensed that the engine was just about to begin knocking. More carpeting was on the floor up front. Standard equipment included whitewalls, wheel opening moldings, deluxe wheel covers, and color-coordinated bodyside moldings. LeSabres also had power brakes and steering, a maintenance-free battery, front/rear bumper guards and protective strips, a compact spare tire, instrument panel courtesy lights, and lights for dome, glove compartment, trunk, front ashtray and engine compartment. The Limited carried the new woodgrain color on doors as well as dash, and also included tinted glass. New options: sail panel reading lights and programmable headlamps. Arriving later in the model year was a limited edition LeSabre F/E ("formal edition"), offered in two-tone blue and gray. The body was blue all across the top and down to the belt line molding on doors, rear quarter and front fender. Below that point, it was solid gray. Inside were gray cloth seats in a dark blue interior. F/E had light gray bodyside moldings, special 'F/E' exterior identification, a Park Avenue-type steering wheel, custom locking wire wheel covers, whitewall steel-belted radials, and remote sport mirrors.

1982 Buick, Electra Estate Wagon station wagon with diesel engine. (OCW)

ESTATE WAGON - SERIES 4B/C - V-8 - Estate Wagons were available in LeSabre and Electra dress (plus the new Regal described previously). LeSabre and Electra offered the same

87.9 cubic foot cargo area and powerteams: standard 5.0-liter gas V-8 or 5.7 diesel V-8, with automatic overdrive transmission. Electra included a standard power tailgate window with remote controlled tailgate lock plus electric door locks, power windows, chrome-plated road wheels, and woodgrain vinyl appliqué.

1982 Buick, Electra Limited coupe. (OCW)

1982 Buick, Electra Park Avenue sedan with optional wire wheel covers. (OCW)

ELECTRA - SERIES 4C - V-6/V-8 - Not much changed in the look of Electra, with its formal-style grille. Limited and Park Avenue editions were offered, in coupe or sedan form. New convenience features included optional electronic memory seats and standard Soft-Ray tinted glass. Automatic four-speed overdrive transmission, introduced the prior year, was refined. Electra's ample equipment list included standard right and left mirrors, whitewall tires, bumper guards and protective strips, digital clock, instrument panel floodlighting, two-way power driver's seat, power windows, and air conditioning. Base engine was the 252 cu. in. (4.1-liter) V-6: optional, a 307 cu. in. (5.0-liter) gasoline V-8 or the Oldsmobile 5.7-liter diesel V-8. Park Avenue again incorporated the traditional ventiport design into a bodyside molding, rather than separate as in past years. That model also featured wide, bright chrome rocker moldings and a padded halo vinyl top, plus standard Delco AM/FM stereo radio. Other Park Avenue extras: a six-way power driver's seat, remote-control trunk release, door courtesy and warning lights, and dome reading lamp. The Concert Sound Speaker introduced two years earlier was available again. The optional 'Memory Seat' returned to either of two preferred positions automatically.

RIVIERA - SERIES 4E - V/6-V-8 - Though the basic Riviera was basically a carryover for 1982, the biggest news came in mid-year with the arrival of the limited-production convertible-- the first ragtop Buick since 1975. It came in Firemist red or white with white convertible top, red leather seats, four-wheel disc brakes, and locking wire wheel covers. According to the one-page flyer, only 500 Limited Edition convertibles were planned for the year. Buick wasn't the first domestic automaker to return to the ragtop fold in the 1980s, but its arrival was a welcome sign for open-air fans. The conversion was done by American Sunroof Corp. to Buick specifications, and sold with a Buick warranty. Riviera's T Type also reappeared later in the model year, after a six-month absence from the lineup. Now it carried the new-generation turbo V-6, four-wheel power disc brakes, tungsten-halogen high-beam headlamps, Gran Touring suspension, and special aluminum wheels. T Type's exterior was gray Firemist with custom blacked-out grille, twin styled remote mirrors, amber turn signal lamps and matching gray interior with cloth bucket seats. New insignias on front fenders and deck lid highlighted the turbo V-6. Axle ratio changed to 3.36:1. Base

Riviera engine remained the 252 cu. in. (4.1-liter) V-6 with four-barrel carburetor. Options included the 305 cu. in. (5.0-liter) gas V-8 and 350 cu. in. (5.7-liter) diesel V-8. Additional standard equipment included overdrive automatic transmission and resume-speed cruise control. The optional Gran Touring suspension offered quicker steering feel and increased road feedback. Also on Riviera's standard equipment list were cornering lights, automatic level control, power brakes and steering, and automatic overdrive transmission. A new deluxe steering wheel had a padded center. Bumpers had black protective strips. On the steering column, a new multi-function lever commanded turn signal, headlamps, wiper/washer and resume-speed cruise control. The standard electronically-tuned AM/FM stereo radio with automatic power antenna could be deleted for credit.

1982 Buick, Riviera coupe. (OCW)

I.D. DATA: All Buicks again had a 17-symbol Vehicle Identification Number (VIN), introduced in 1981, stamped on a metal tag attached to the upper left surface of the cowl, visible through the windshield. The number begins with a '1' to indicate U.S.A., followed by 'G' for General Motors and '4' for Buick Division. The next letter indicates restraint system. The fifth symbol shows series: 'S' Skyhawk; 'T' Skyhawk Limited; 'B' Skylark; 'C' Skylark Limited; 'D' Skylark Sport; 'H' Century Custom; 'L' Century Limited; 'J' Regal; 'K' Regal Sport Coupe; 'M' Regal Limited; 'N' LeSabre; 'P' LeSabre Limited; 'R' LeSabre Estate Wagon; 'V' Electra Estate Wagon; 'X' Electra Limited; 'W' Electra Park Avenue; 'Y' Riviera T Type; 'Z' Riviera. Digits six and seven indicate body type: '27' 2-dr. coupe; '37' Skylark 2-dr. coupe; '47' Regal 2-dr. coupe; '57' Riviera 2-dr. coupe; '67' 2-dr. convertible coupe; '35' 4-dr. wagon; '19' Century 4-dr. sedan; '69' 4-dr. sedan. Next is the engine code: 'G' L4-112 2Bbl.; 'O' L4-112 TBI; 'B' L4-121 2Bbl.; 'R' L4-151 TBI; 'X' V6-173 2Bbl.; 'Z' H.O. V6-173 2Bbl.; 'E' V6-181 2Bbl.; 'A' V6-231 2Bbl.; '3' V6-231 Turbo; '4' V6-252 4Bbl.; 'V' V6-263 diesel; 'Y' V8-307 4Bbl.; 'N' V8-350 diesel. Symbol nine is a check digit ('8'). Symbol ten denotes model year ('C' 1982). Symbol eleven is the plant code. The final six digits are the sequential serial number. An additional identifying number can be found on the engine, showing codes for GM division, model year, assembly plant and vehicle sequence number. A body number plate shows model year, car division series, style, body assembly plant, body number, trim combination, modular seat code, paint code, and date build code.

SKYHAWK CUSTOM (FOUR)

Model No.	Body/Style No.	Body Type & Seating	Factory Price	Shipping Weight	Prod. Total
4J	S27	2-dr. Coupe-5P	7297	2327	25,378
4J	S69	4-dr. Sedan-5P	7489	2385	22,540

SKYHAWK LIMITED (FOUR)

Model No.	Body/Style No.	Body Type & Seating	Factory Price	Shipping Weight	Prod. Total
4J	T27	2-dr Coupe-5P	7739	2349	Note 1
4J	T69	4-dr Sedan-5P	7931	2411	Note 1

Note 1: Production totals listed under Skyhawk Custom also include Limited models. A total of 32,027 Customs and 15,891 Limiteds were produced for the model year.

SKYLARK (FOUR/V-6)

4X	B37	2-dr Coupe-5P	7477/7602	2462/2519	21,017
4X	B69	4-dr Sedan-5P	7647/7772	2493/2550	65,541

SKYLARK LIMITED (FOUR/V-6)

4X	C37	2-dr Coupe-5P	7917/8042	2489/2546	13,712
4X	C69	4-dr Sedan-5P	8079/8204	2519/2576	44,290

SKYLARK SPORT (FOUR/V-6)

4X	D37	2-dr Coupe-5P	8048/8173	2494/2551	Note 2
4X	D69	4-dr Sedan-5P	8219/8344	2524/2581	Note 2

Note 2: Production figures listed under base Skylark also include equivalent Sport models. Total production for the model year came to 85,263 base Skylarks, 1,295 Skylark Sports and 58,002 Limiteds.

CENTURY CUSTOM (FOUR/V-6)

4A	H27	2-dr Coupe-5P	8980/9105	2603/2684	19,715
4A	H19	4-dr Sedan-5P	9141/9266	2631/2712	83,250

CENTURY LIMITED (FOUR/V-6)

4A	L27	2-dr Coupe-5P	9417/9542	2614/2695	Note 3
4A	L19	4-dr Sedan-5P	9581/9706	2643/2724	Note 3

Note 3: Production figures for Century Custom coupe and sedan also include Century Limited models. Total production for the model year amounted to 45,036 Customs and 57,929 Limiteds.

1982 Buick, Regal Limited coupe with optional wire wheel covers. (OCW)

REGAL (V-6)

4G	J47	2-dr Coupe 6P	8712	3152	134,237
4G	J69	4-dr Sedan-6P	8862	3167	74,428
4G	J35	4-dr Sta Wag-6P	9058	3317	14,732

REGAL LIMITED (V-6)

4G	M47	2-dr Coupe-6P	9266	3192	Note 4
4G	M69	4-dr Sedan-6P	9364	3205	Note 4

Note 4: Coupe/sedan production figures listed under base Regal also include Regal Limited. A total of 105,812 base Regals and 102,850 Regal Limiteds were made; only 8,276 of those had a V-8 engine.

REGAL SPORT COUPE (TURBO V-6)

4G	K47	2-dr Coupe-6P	9738	3225	2,022

LESABRE CUSTOM (V-6/V-8)

4B	N37	2-dr Coupe-6P	8774/9016	3474/3656	5,165
4B	N69	4-dr Sedan-6P	8876/9118	3503/3685	23,220

LESABRE LIMITED (V-6/V-8)

4B	P37	2-dr Coupe-6P	9177/9419	3492/3674	16,062
4B	P69	4-dr Sedan-6P	9331/9573	3625/3707	47,224

LESABRE ESTATE WAGON (V-8)

4B	R35	4-dr Sta Wag-6P	10668	4171	7,149

ELECTRA LIMITED (V-6/V-8)

4C	X37	2-dr Coupe-6P	11713/11713	3657/3836	8,449
4C	X69	4-dr Sedan-6P	11884/11884	3717/3896	59,601

ELECTRA PARK AVENUE (V-6/V-8)

4C	W37	2-dr Coupe-6P	13408/13408	3734/3913	Note 5
4C	W69	4-dr Sedan-6P	13559/13559	3798/3977	Note 5

Note 5: Production figures listed under Electra Limited also include Park Avenue coupes and sedans. A total of 22,709 Limited and 45,346 Park Avenue editions were produced, 9,748 with a V-6 engine.

ELECTRA ESTATE WAGON (V-8)

4C	V35	4-dr Sta Wag-6P	12911	4175	8,182

RIVIERA (V-6/V-8)

4E	Z57	2-dr Coupe-5P	14272/14272	3600/3760	42,823
4E	Z67	2-dr Conv-5P	23994/24064	N/A/N/A	1,248

RIVIERA T TYPE (TURBO V-6)

4E	Y57	2-dr Coupe-5P	14940	N/A	Note 6

Note 6: T Type production is included in basic Riviera figure.

FACTORY PRICE AND WEIGHT NOTE: Figure before the slash is for four-cylinder engine, after the slash for V-6. For full-size models, figure before the slash is for V-6 engine, after slash for V-8.

ENGINES: BASE FOUR (Skyhawk): Inline, overhead-valve four cylinder. Cast iron block and head. Displacement: 112 cu. in. (1.8 liters). Bore & stroke: 3.50 x 2.91 in. Compression ratio: 9.0:1. Brake horsepower: 88 at 5100 R.P.M. Torque: 100 lb.-ft. at 2800 R.P.M. Five main bearings. Hydraulic valve lifters. Carburetor: 2Bbl. Rochester E2SE. VIN Code: G. OPTIONAL FOUR (Skyhawk): Inline, overhead-cam four-cylinder. Cast iron block and head. Displacement: 112 cu. in. (1.8 liters). Bore & stroke: 3.33 x 3.12 in. Compression ratio: 9.0:1. Brake horsepower: 80 at 5200 R.P.M. Torque: 115 lb.-ft. at 2800 R.P.M. Five main bearings. Hydraulic valve lifters. Throttle-body fuel injection. VIN Code: O. OPTIONAL FOUR (Skyhawk): Inline, overhead-cam four-cylinder. Cast iron block and head. Displacement: 121 cu. in. (2.0 liters). Bore & stroke: 3.50 x 3.14 in. Compression ratio: 9.0:1. Brake horsepower: 90 at 5100 R.P.M. Torque: 111 lb.-ft. at 2700 R.P.M. Five main bearings. Hydraulic valve lifters. Carburetor: 2Bbl. Rochester E2SE. VIN Code: B. BASE FOUR (Skylark, Century): Inline, overhead-valve four-cylinder. Cast iron block and head. Displacement: 151 cu. in. (2.5 liters). Bore & stroke: 4.0 x 3.0 in. Compression ratio: 8.2:1. Brake horsepower: 90 at 4000 R.P.M. Torque: 134 lb.-ft. at 2400 R.P.M. Five main bearings. Hydraulic valve lifters. Throttle-body fuel injection. Built by Pontiac. VIN Code: R. Sales Code: LW9. OPTIONAL V-6 (Skylark): 60-degree, overhead-valve V-6. Cast iron block and head. Displacement: 173 cu. in. (2.8 liters). Bore & stroke: 3.5 x 3.0 in. Compression ratio: 8.4.1. Brake horsepower: 112 at 5100 R.P.M. Torque: 148 lb.-ft. at 2400 R.P.M. Four main bearings. Hydraulic valve lifters. Carburetor: 2Bbl. Rochester E2SE. Built by Chevrolet. VIN Code: X. Sales Code: LE2. HIGH-OUTPUT 173 V-6; OPTIONAL (Skylark): Same as 173 cu. in. V-6 above except as follows: Compression ratio: 8.9:1. Brake horsepower: 135 at 5400 R.P.M. Torque: 142 lb.-ft. at 2400 R.P.M. VIN Code: Z. OPTIONAL V-6 (Century): 90-degree, overhead-valve V-6. Cast iron block and head. Displacement: 181 cu. in. (3.0 liters). Bore & stroke: 3.8 x 2.66 in. Compression ratio: 8.45:1. Brake horsepower: 110 at 3800 R.P.M. Torque: 145 lb.-ft. at 2600 R.P.M. Four main bearings. Hydraulic valve lifters. Carburetor: 2Bbl. Rochester E2ME. VIN Code: E. BASE V-6 (Regal, LeSabre): 90-degree, overhead-valve V-6. Cast iron alloy block and head. Displacement: 231 cu. in. (3.8 liters). Bore & stroke: 3.8 x 3.4 in. Compression ratio: 8.0:1. Brake horsepower: 110 at 3800 R.P.M. Torque: 190 lb.-ft. at 1600 R.P.M. Four main bearings. Hydraulic valve lifters. Carburetor: 2Bbl. Rochester M2ME. VIN Code: A. Sales Code: LD5. TURBOCHARGED V-6 (Regal Sport Coupe, Riviera T Type): Same as 231 V-6 above, but with E4ME four-barrel carburetor. Brake horsepower: 170 at 3800 R.P.M. (Riviera, 180 at 4000). Torque: 275 lb.-ft. at 2600 R.P.M. (Riviera, 270 at 2400). VIN Code: 3. Sales Code: LC8. BASE V-6 (Electra, Riviera) OPTIONAL (Regal LeSabre): 90-degree, overhead-valve V-6. Cast iron block and head. Displacement 252 cu. in. (4.1 liters). Bore & stroke: 3.965 x 3.4 in. Compression ratio: 8.0:1. Brake horsepower: 125 at 4000 R.P.M. Torque: 205 lb.-ft. at 2000 R.P.M. Four main bearings. Hydraulic valve lifters. Carburetor: 4Bbl. Rochester. VIN Code: 4. Sales Code: LC4. DIESEL V-6; OPTIONAL (Century, Regal cpe/sed): 90-degree. Overhead-valve V-6. Cast iron block and head. Displacement: 262.5 cu. in. (4.3 liters). Bore & stroke: 4.057 x 3.385 in. Compression ratio: 21.6:1. Brake horsepower: 85 at 3600 R.P.M. Torque: 165 lb.-ft. at 1600 R.P.M. Four main bearings. Hydraulic valve lifters. Fuel injection. VIN Code: V. BASE V-8 (Estate) OPTIONAL (LeSabre Electra Riviera): 90-degree, overhead valve V-8. Cast iron block and head. Displacement: 307 cu. in. (5.0 liters). Bore & stroke: 3.80 x 3.385 in. Compression ratio: 8.0:1. Brake horsepower: 140 at 3600 R.P.M. Torque: 240 lb.-ft. at 1600 R.P.M. Five main bearings. Hydraulic valve lifters. Carburetor: 4Bbl. Roch. M4MC. Built by Oldsmobile. VIN Code:

Y. Sales Code: LV2. OPTIONAL DIESEL V-8 (Regal, LeSabre, Electra, Estate, Riviera): 90-degree, overhead valve V-8. Cast iron block and head. Displacement: 350 cu. in. (5.7 liters). Bore & stroke: 4.057 x 3.385 in. Compression ratio: 21.6:1. Brake horsepower: 105 at 3200 R.P.M. Torque: 200 lb.-ft. at 1600 R.P.M. Five main bearings. Hydraulic valve lifters. Fuel injection. Oldsmobile-built. VIN Code: N. Sales Code: LF9.

CHASSIS DATA: Wheelbase: (Skyhawk) 101.2 in.; (Skylark/Century) 104.9 in.; (Regal) 108.1 in.; (LeSabre/Estate) 115.9 in.; (Electra) 118.9 in.; (Riviera) 114.0 in. Overall length: (Skyhawk) 175.3 in.; (Skylark) 181.1 in.; (Century) 189.1 in.; (Regal cpe) 200.6 in.; (Regal sed) 196.0 in.; (Regal wag) 196.7 in.; (LeSabre) 218.4 in.; (Electra) 221.3 in.; (Estate Wagon) 220.5 in.; (Riviera) 206.6 in. Height: (Skyhawk) 54.0 in.; (Skylark) 53.7 in.; (Century) 53.6 in.; (Regal cpe) 54.5 in.; (Regal sed) 55.4 in.; (Regal wag) 56.5 in.; (LeSabre) 56.0-56.7 in.; (Electra) 56.8-56.9 in.; (Estate) 59.1-59.4 in.; (Riviera) 54.3 in. Width: (Skyhawk) 62.0 in.; (Skylark) 69.1 in.; (Century) 66.8 in.; (Regal cpe) 71.6 in.; (Regal sed) 71.1 in.; (Regal wag) 71.2 in.; (LeSabre) 78.0 in.; (Electra cpe) 76.2 in.; (Estate) 79.3 in.; (Riviera) 72.8 in. Front Tread: (Skyhawk) 55.4 in.; (Skylark/Century) 58.7 in.; (Regal) 58.5 in.; (LeSabre/Electra) 61.8 in.; (Estate) 62.2 in.; (Riviera) 59.3 in. Rear Tread: (Skyhawk) 55.2 in.; (Skylark/Century) 57.0 in.; (Regal) 57.7 in.; (LeSabre/Electra) 60.7 in.; (Estate) 64.0 in.; (Riviera) 60.0 in. Standard Tires: (Skyhawk) P195/70R14 SBR; (Skylark/Century) P185/80R13 GBR; (Skylark Sport) P205/70R13 SBR; (Regal) P195/75R14 SBR WSW; (Regal Spt Cpe) P205/70R14 SBR; (LeSabre) P205/75R15 SBR WSW; (Electra) P215/75R15 SBR WSW; (Estate) P225/75R15 SBR WSW; (Riviera) P205/75R15 SBR WSW.

TECHNICAL: Transmission: Four-speed, fully synchronized floor shift standard on Skyhawk/Skylark; automatic optional Turbo Hydra-matic standard on all other models. Skyhawk four-speed gear ratios: (1st) 3.53:1; (2nd) 1.95:1; (3rd) 1.24:1; (4th) 0.81:1; (Rev) 3.42:1. Four-speed gear ratios: (1st) 3.53:1; (2nd) 1.95:1; (3rd) 1.24:1; (4th) 0.73:1; (Rev) 3.92:1. Skylark/Century auto trans. gear ratios: (1st) 2.84:1; (2nd) 1.60:1; (3rd) 1.00:1; (Rev) 2.07:1. Three-speed auto trans. gear ratios: (1st) 2.52:1; (2nd) 1.52:1; (3rd) 1.00:1; (Rev) 1.94:1. Four-speed automatic gear ratios: (1st) 2.74:1; (2nd) 1.57:1; (3rd) 1.00:1; (4th) 0.67:1; (Rev) 2.07:1. Steering: (Skyhawk/Skylark/Century) rack and pinion; (others) recirculating ball; power assist standard on all except Skyhawk. Suspension: front/rear coil springs; (Skyhawk/Skylark/Century) MacPherson strut front suspension trailing axle rear; front/rear stabilizer bars; (Riviera) fully independent suspension with front torsion bar, front/rear stabilizers. Brakes: power front disc, rear drum. Four-wheel power disc brakes available on Riviera. Body construction: (Skyhawk/Skylark/Century) unitized; (others) separate body and frame. Wheel size: (Skyhawk/Century) 13 x 5.5 in.; (Regal) 14 x 6 in.; (LeSabre/Riviera) 15 x 6 in.; (Estate) 15 x 7 in.

DRIVETRAIN OPTIONS: Engines: 112 cu. in. (1.8-liter) EFI four: Skyhawk ($75); 121 cu. in. (2.0-liter) four, 2Bbl.: Skyhawk ($50); 173 cu. in. (2.8-liter) V-6, 2Bbl.: Skylark ($125); High-output 173 cu. in. (2.8-liter) V-6 2Bbl.: Skylark ($250); 181 cu. in. (3.0-liter) V-6, 2Bbl.: Century ($125); 252 cu. in. (4.1-liter) V-6, 4Bbl.; Regal ($95); LeSabre exc. wag ($267) incl. overdrive automatic transmission. 263 cu. in. (4.3-liter) diesel V-6; Century ($859); Regal exc. spt cpe or wag ($874); 307 cu. in. (5.0-liter) V-8, 4Bbl.: LeSabre cpe/sed ($242) incl. overdrive automatic trans.; Electra cpe/sed (NC); Riviera (NC). 350 cu. in. (5.7-liter) diesel V-8: Regal exc. spt cpe ($924); LeSabre/Riviera ($924); LeSabre Estate, Electra ($752). Transmission/Differential: Five speed manual trans.; Skyhawk ($196). Three-speed auto trans.: Skyhawk ($370); Skylark ($396); LeSabre cpe/sed with 4.1- or 5.0-liter ($172 credit); Optional rear axle ratio: Century 2.97:1 (NC); Regal 3.23:1 (NC); Regal cpe/sed 3.08:1 (NC); LeSabre 3.08:1 or 3.23:1 (NC). Limited slip differential: Regal/LeSabre/Electra ($80). Suspension, Steering and Brakes:

F40 Firm ride/handling pkg. ($27) exc. Skyhawk. F41 Gran Touring suspension: Skyhawk ($158); Century four, Riviera ($27); Regal exc. wag, LeSabre ($49). F41 Rallye ride/handling suspension incl. P205/70R13 SBR tires: Skylark ($206). Super-lift rear shock absorbers: Skylark ($68). Automatic level control: Century/Regal/LeSabre/Electra ($165). Power steering: Skyhawk ($180). Four-wheel disc brakes: Riviera ($235). Other: Trailer towing flasher/harness ($28-$43) exc. Skyhawk. Trailer towing pkg.: Regal exc. spt cpe ($182); LeSabre exc. wagon ($459); Electra exc. wagon ($167). Heavy-duty alternator, 85-amp ($32-$85). H.D.: ($22-$50). H.D. radiator: Skyhawk ($37-$67); Skylark/Century ($38-$73). Engine block heater ($17-$18). H.D. engine/transmission cooling: Regal/LeSabre/Electra/Riviera ($38-$73). California emission system: Skyhawk ($46); Skylark ($65); Century ($65-$205). Diesel cold climate pkg. delete: Regal/LeSabre/Electra/Riviera ($99 credit).

SKYHAWK CONVENIENCE/APPEARANCE OPTIONS: Option Packages: Vista Vent flip-open sunroof ($261). Acoustic pkg. ($36). Instrument gauge pkg.: temp, oil pressure, volts, trip odometer ($60). Gauges and tachometer ($78-$138). Comfort/Convenience: Air cond. ($625). Rear defogger, electric ($115). Cruise control w/resume ($145-$155). Power windows ($152-$216). Power door locks ($99-$142). Six-way power driver's seat ($183). Tinted glass ($82). Tinted windshield ($57). Sport steering wheel ($45). Tilt steering ($88). Trip odometer ($15). Electric trunk release ($29). Two-speed wipers w/delay ($44). Lights, Horns and Mirrors: Halogen high-beam headlamps ($29). Headlamps-on indicator ($15). Dome reading lamp ($21). Rear seat reading lamps ($30). Styled left remote mirror ($21). Dual styled mirrors: left remote ($51). Dual electric styled mirrors ($130). Visor vanity mirror, passenger ($7). Lighted visor vanity mirror, either side ($45). Entertainment: AM radio w/digital clock ($55). AM/FM radio ($119). AM/FM stereo radio ($155); w/digital clock and 8-track tape player ($234): w/cassette ($272). Electronic-tuning AM/FM stereo radio ($385); w/8-track ($464); w/cassette ($497). AM radio delete ($56 credit). Power antenna ($50). Dual rear speakers ($25-$30). Exterior Trim: Door edge guards ($14-$22). Bodyside stripes ($40). Designers' accent paint ($195). Decklid luggage rack ($98). Interior Trim/Upholstery: Front carpet savers ($20); rear ($15). Trunk trim ($33). Wheels and Tires: Styled aluminum wheels ($229). Styled wheel covers ($38). Custom locking wire wheel covers ($165). P175/80R13 GBR WSW ($55). P195/70R13 SBR BSW ($133). P195/70R13 SBR WSW ($55-$188). P195/70R13 SBR WLT ($72-$205). P195/70R13 SBR wide WSW ($55-$188). Self-sealing tires ($94).

SKYLARK CONVENIENCE/APPEARANCE OPTIONS: Option Packages: Acoustic pkg. ($60). Flip-open Vista Vent glass sunroof ($275). Comfort/Convenience: Air cond. ($675). Cruise Master w/resume ($155-$165). Rear defogger, electric ($125). Power windows ($165-$235). Electric door locks ($106-$152). Six-way power driver's seat ($197). Manual seatback recliners, passenger ($50); both ($100). Sport steering wheel ($50); N/A on Sport. Tilt steering ($95). Tinted glass ($88). Instrument gauges incl. trip odometer ($48). Trip odometer ($16). Electric dial clock ($30). Digital clock ($60). Electric trunk release ($32). Two-speed wipers w/delay ($47). Lights, Horns and Mirrors: Coach lamps: Ltd. ($102). Headlamps-on indicator ($16). Dome reading light ($24). Rear seat reading lamp: Ltd. ($30). Dual horns ($15). Remote-control left mirror ($24); N/A on sport. Sport mirrors: left remote, right manual ($55); dual remote ($31-$86). Visor vanity mirror, passenger ($8). Lighted visor vanity mirror, either side ($50). Entertainment: AM/FM radio ($75). AM/FM stereo radio ($106); w/8-track or cassette player ($192-$193). AM/FM stereo radio with CB ($419); with CB and 8-track or cassette ($494-$495). Graphic equalizer ($150). Rear speakers ($25-$30). Power antenna ($55). Triband power antenna ($100). Delete AM radio ($56 credit). Exterior Trim: Landau vinyl top: cpe ($195). Long vinyl top ($140). Designers' accent paint ($210); N/A on Sport. Protective bodyside moldings ($47). Wide

rocker panel moldings ($65). Belt reveal molding ($35). Wheel opening moldings ($28). Door edge guards ($15-$25). Pillar appliqué moldings: sed exc. Spt ($27). Hood ornament and windsplit ($32); N/A on Spt Bodyside or Sport stripes ($48). Bumper guards, front/rear ($45). Bumper strips. front/rear ($49). Interior Trim/Upholstery: Full-length console ($100). 45/45 seating cloth or vinyl ($57-$252). Leather/vinyl 45/45 limited seating ($358-$553). Notchback bench seating: Spt ($195). Front carpet savers ($16); rear ($11). Carpet savers w/inserts: front ($25); rear ($20). Trunk trim carpeting ($35). Wheels: Chrome-plated wheels ($155-$175). Sport wheel covers ($20). Locking wire wheel covers ($165-$185). Tires: P185/80R13 GBR WSW ($58); N/A on Sport. P185/80R13 SBR BSW ($64); N/A on Sport. P185/80R13 SBR wide whitewall ($122); N/A on Sport. P205/70R13 SBR WSW ($66). P205/70R13 SBR WLT ($88). Self-sealing GBR whitewall tires ($106).

1982 Buick, Century Custom coupe with optional wire wheel covers. (OCW)

CENTURY/REGAL CONVENIENCE/APPEARANCE OPTIONS: Option Packages: Regal Sport Coupe Decor pkg.: designers' accent paint, wide rocker moldings, sport steering wheel, black paint treatment ($125). Regal Coupe Decor pkg. w/turbine wheels ($428). Sliding electric Astroroof: Regal cpe ($885). Flip-open Vista Vent glass sunroof: Century ($275). Hatch roof: Regal cpe ($790). Comfort/Convenience: Air cond. ($675). Automatic touch climate control air cond.: Regal ($825). Cruise Master w/resume ($155). Rear defogger, electric ($125). Tinted glass ($88). Tinted windshield: Regal ($65). Six-way power seat, each side ($197); both ($394); passenger's side N/A on Century. Manual passenger seatback recliner ($50-$75); both seats, Century only ($100). Sport steering wheel ($40). Tilt steering ($95). Power windows ($165-$235). Electric door locks ($106-$152). Automatic door locks ($180-$215). Electric trunk release ($32). Remote electric tailgate lock: Regal wag ($38). Electric dial clock ($30). Digital clock ($60). Headlamps-on indicator ($16). Trip odometer: Regal ($16). Instrument gauges: temp, voltage, trip odometer ($48). Windshield wiper w/low-speed delay ($47). Theft deterrent system ($159). Lighting and Mirrors: Tungsten-halogen high beam headlamps ($10). Twilight Sentinel headlamp control ($57). Cornering lamps: Regal ($57). Coach lamps: Ltd. ($102). Front lamp monitors ($37). Door courtesy/warning lights: Ltd. ($44-$70). Rear seat reading light: Regal ($30). Dome reading lamp ($24). Remote left mirror ($24). Remote right mirror: Regal exc. spt cpe ($48). Dual mirrors, left remote ($48-$55). Dual electric remote mirrors: Century ($137). Dual remote sport mirrors: Regal ($31-$79). Visor vanity mirror ($8). Lighted visor vanity mirror ($58); driver's N/A on Regal. Dual horns: Century ($15). Entertainment: AM radio: Regal ($99). AM/FM radio ($82-$153). AM/FM stereo radio ($118-$184). AM/FM stereo radio w/digital clock: Century ($178); w/8-track or cassette player ($277-$282). AM/FM stereo radio w/8-track or cassette: Regal ($270-$271). Electronic-tuning AM/FM stereo radio ($377-$402); w/8-track or cassette ($481-$555). AM/FM radio with CB: Regal ($497). CB radio: Century ($263). Dual rear speakers ($25-$30). Fixed-mast antenna: Regal ($39); w/radio ($12). Automatic power antenna ($55-$90). Triband power antenna ($100-$135). Exterior Trim: Landau vinyl top: cpe ($166). Heavy-padded landau vinyl top: Regal

cpe ($220). Long vinyl top ($140). Long padded vinyl top: Regal sed ($220). Designers' accent paint ($195-$235). Solid special color paint ($200). Exterior molding pkg.: Regal exc. Ltd. ($110). Protective bodyside moldings: Century, Regal spt cpe ($47-$51). Wraparound bodyside moldings: Regal sed ($104). Lower bodyside moldings: Century ($65). Hood ornament and windsplit: Century ($32): std. On Ltd. Door edge guards ($15-$25). Belt reveal moldings: Regal spt cpe w/decor pkg. ($40). Bodyside stripe ($42). Woodgrain vinyl appliqué: Regal wag ($330). Roof rack: Regal wag ($115). Air deflector: Regal wag ($37). Interior trim/Upholstery: Full length console ($100). Non-shifting console ($82). Bucket seats: Regal ($56). 55/45 seating: Regal ($133). Limited 55/45 seating: Regal spt cpe ($385). 45/45 seating: Century Cust ($133); Regal Ltd. (NC). Front carpet savers ($16); rear ($11). Front carpet savers with inserts ($25); rear ($20). Litter pocket ($9). Trunk trim covering ($47). Lockable storage compartment: Regal wag ($55). Wheels: Chrome-plated wheels ($40-$175); Regal spt cpe ($110 credit). Styled aluminum wheels: Regal exc. spt cpe ($150-$285). Turbine wheels: Regal exc. spt cpe ($135). Locking wire wheel covers: Century ($185); Regal ($50-$185): Regal spt cpe ($100 credit). Tires: P185/80R13 GBR WSW: Century four ($58). P185/80R13 SBR BSW: Century four ($64). P185/80R13 SBR WSW: Century four ($122). P185/75R14 GBR and SBR: Century V-6 ($37-$159). P195/75R14 SBR BSW: Regal exc. spt cpe (NC). P205/70R13 SBR BSW: Century four w/F41 suspension ($179). P205/70R13 SBR WSW: Century four w/F41 suspension ($245). P205/70R13 SBR WLT: Century four w/F41 ($267). P205/70R14 SBR wide-oval BSW: Regal (N/A). P205/70R14 SBR WSW: Regal spt cpe ($66). P205/70R14 SBR WLT: Regal ($84-$88). Self-sealing tires ($106).

LESABRE/ELECTRA/ESTATE WAGON CONVENIENCE/APPEARANCE OPTIONS: Comfort/Convenience: Sliding electric Astroroof ($1125). Air cond.: LeSabre ($695). Air cond. w/touch-climate control: LeSabre ($845); LeSabre, Est, Electra ($150). Cruise Master with resume ($155); std. on Park Avenue. Rear defogger, electric ($125). Tinted glass: LeSabre Cust ($102). Power windows: LeSabre ($165-$240). Electric door locks ($106-$152). Automatic door locks ($63-$215). Six way power seat, driver's or passenger's ($167-$197); both ($364-$394). Memory driver's power seat: Electra ($178-$345). Electric seatback recliner, one side ($139). Sport steering wheel: LeSabre ($40). Tilt steering: LeSabre, Electra Ltd. ($95). Tilt/telescoping steering column ($55-$150). Dial clock: LeSabre ($60). Digital clock: LeSabre, Estate (NC w/convenience group). Lamp and indicator group: LeSabre ($52-$70). Trip odometer: LeSabre ($16). Remote tailgate lock: LeSabre, Estate ($49). Electric trunk lock: Electra Ltd. ($72). Electric trunk release ($32). Electric fuel cap lock ($44). Theft deterrent system ($159); N/A on Estate. Two-speed wiper w/delay ($47). Accessory group (trip odometer, dome reading lamp, headlamps-on indicator, low fuel indicator, washer fluid indicator): Electra ($28-$86). Lighting, Horns and Mirrors: Tungsten-halogen high-beam headlamps ($10). Twilight Sentinel ($57). Cornering lamps ($57). Coach lamps: LeSabre/Electra Ltd. ($102). Light monitors, front: LeSabre, Electra, Est ($37); front/rear: Electra ($74). Door courtesy/warning lamps ($44-$70). Rear seat reading lamp: LeSabre Ltd, Electra ($30). Lighted door lock and interior light control ($72). Four-note horn ($28). Remote left mirror; LeSabre ($24). Remote right mirror; LeSabre ($48); Electra Ltd, Est ($24). Remote electric right mirror: Electra Park Ave. ($57). Dual remote sport mirrors: LeSabre ($85); Electra Ltd, Est ($38). Dual electric remote mirrors: LeSabre ($137); Electra Ltd, Est ($90). Remote left mirror w/thermometer: LeSabre ($62); Electra Ltd, Est ($38). Electric left mirror w/thermometer: Electra Park Ave. ($39). Dual electric mirrors w/left thermometer: LeSabre ($170); Electra Ltd, Est ($123). Lighted visor vanity mirror driver or passenger ($58). Entertainment: AM radio: LeSabre ($99). AM/FM radio: LeSabre ($153). AM/FM stereo radio: LeSabre, Electra Ltd/Estate ($184). AM/FM

stereo radio and 8-track or cassette player ($86-$271). Electronic-tuning AM/FM stereo radio: LeSabre ($377-$402); Electra ($170-$348). Electronic-tuning AM/FM stereo radio and 8-track or cassette ($273-$555). AM/FM stereo radio with CB ($314-$498). Electronic-tuning radio with CB and 8-track or cassette ($585-$841). Delete AM/FM stereo radio: Electra Park Ave. (credit $153). Concert Sound speaker system: Electra exc. wagon ($95); ETR radio req'd. Dual rear speakers ($25-$30) when ordered with radio. Automatic power antenna ($55-$90). Tri-band power antenna ($100-$135). Exterior Trim: Exterior molding pkg.: LeSabre ($110). Landau vinyl top: LeSabre, Electra Ltd cpe ($225). Long vinyl top: LeSabre, Electra Ltd sed ($165-$180). Heavy padded long vinyl top: Electra Ltd sed ($225). Designers' accent paint: LeSabre ($215). Special single color paint: ($200); Firemist, Electra exc. Est ($210). Protective bodyside moldings: Est ($51). Color-coordinated bodyside moldings: LeSabre Est ($51). Wide rocker panel moldings: Electra Ltd/Estate ($65). Door edge guards ($15-$25). Belt reveal molding: LeSabre ($40). Bodyside stripes ($63). Woodgrain vinyl appliqué: LeSabre Est ($320). Roof rack: LeSabre Est ($140). Interior Trim/Upholstery: 55/45 seating: LeSabre ($125). Leather-vinyl 50/50 seating: Park Ave. ($525). Third seat: Estate ($215). Front carpet savers ($16); rear ($11). Front carpet savers w/inserts ($25); rear ($20). Trunk carpeting trim ($53-$65). Trunk mat ($13). Wheels: Chrome-plated wheels ($180-$215). Styled aluminum wheels ($40-$255). Custom wheel covers: Electra Ltd ($35). Locking wire wheel covers ($150-$185); Electra Estate ($30 credit). Tires: P215/75R15 SBR wide WSW: LeSabre cpe/sed ($39). P225/75R15 SBR wide WSW: LeSabre ($106); Electra ($39). Self-sealing tires ($106-$131).

RIVIERA CONVENIENCE/APPEARANCE OPTIONS: Comfort/Convenience: Electric sliding Astroroof ($1125). Automatic touch climate control air cond. ($150). Rear defogger, electric ($125). Automatic electric door locks ($74). Six-way power seat, passenger ($197). Two-position memory power driver's seat ($178). Electric seatback recliner, one side ($139). Sport steering wheel ($40). Tilt steering ($95). Tilt/telescope steering wheel ($150). Electric fuel cap lock ($44). Electric trunk release ($32). Electric trunk lock ($72). Low fuel indicator ($18). Fuel usage light gas engine ($35). Two speed wipers w/delay ($47). Windshield washer fluid indicator ($12). Theft deterrent system ($159). Lighting, Horns and Mirrors: Tungsten-halogen high-beam headlamps ($10). Twilight Sentinel ($57). Coach lamps ($102); incl. w/vinyl top. Front/rear light monitors ($74). Rear quarter courtesy/reading lamp ($48). Lighted door lock and interior light control ($72). Four-note horn ($28). Dual electric remote mirrors ($65). Lighted visor vanity mirrors, each ($58). Entertainment: Full-feature electronic-tuning AM/FM stereo radio ($90). Electronic-tuning AM/FM stereo radio w/8-track or cassette tape player ($193-$242); w/CB and 8-track or cassette ($455-$479). Delete radio ($230 credit). Rear speakers ($25-$30). Concert Sound system ($95); N/A with base radio. Triband power antenna ($45). Exterior Trim: Heavy-padded landau vinyl top w/coach lamps ($305). Designers' accent paint ($235). Special color Firemist paint ($210). Protective bodyside moldings ($61). Door edge guards ($15). Bodyside stripes ($63). Interior Trim/Upholstery: 45/55 leather/vinyl front seat ($405). Front carpet savers w/inserts ($35); rear ($20). Trunk trim carpeting ($30). Trunk mat ($15). Wheels and Tires: Chrome-plated wheels ($145). Custom locking wire wheel covers ($185). P225/70R15 SBR BSW: conv/T ($40). P225/70R15 SBR WSW: conv/T ($106). GR70 x 15 SBR WSW ($85). Self-sealing tires ($131).

HISTORY: Introduced: September 24, 1981, except Skylark, December 12, 1981; Century, November 30, 1981; Skyhawk, March 4, 1982; and Riviera convertible, mid-April 1982. Skyhawk and Riviera convertible debuted at the Chicago Auto Show on February 25, 1982. Model year production (U.S.): 739,984 for a 14.3 percent share of the industry total. That number included 157,668 four-cylinder Buicks, 409,857 sixes, and 172,463 V-8s. The total also included 35,062 diesel engines and 2,551 turbos. Calendar year production (U.S.): 751,338. Model year sales by U.S. dealers: 694,742. Calendar year sales (U.S.): 723,011 for a market share of 12.6 percent.

Historical Footnotes: A series of mid-year introductions drew customers' attention to Buick offerings. Several Buick plants turned to employee involvement programs in an attempt to cut absenteeism and improve quality. Officials at one plant reported an impressive improvement in both areas. Turbo V-6 production fell sharply, from 25,500 in the 1979 model year to just 3,990 in 1981, in response to sluggish demand for turbocharged engines. In February 1982, a limited-edition Grand National Regal ran at Daytona. A forerunner of one of the most sought after 1980s Buicks, it sported silver-gray and charcoal-gray paint with red accent stripes, a T-top roof, blackout grille and trim, air dam and rear spoiler. Grand National's powerplant was the 4.1-liter V-6 with four-barrel carb.

1983

Buick now offered four front-drive car lines, stretching from the subcompact Skyhawk to the big Riviera. The company's full-line color catalog focused on small town America this year, including small tales and lore on locales to which one might travel by Buick. Sporty T Types, with performance packages that included sport trim, special wheels and bucket seats, were offered on every line except LeSabre and Electra. Though different, they shared a family resemblance. All except Regal's featured blacked-out sections for a striking visual appearance. And all but Regal and Riviera had charcoal accents on the car's lower body. Regal's version, powered by the 180-horsepower turbo 3.8-liter V-6, was recorded as delivering 0-50 MPH acceleration time of 7.6 seconds. Riviera used the same turbo V-6, while Skyhawk T Type's 1.8-liter engine produced 84 horsepower at 5200 R.P.M. Each T Type carried a Gran Touring suspension except for Skylark, which had a Sport suspension. On all but Riviera, quick-ratio power steering replaced the standard version. The "T" in T Type, incidentally, didn't stand for anything in particular. An electrically-heated grid in the 3.8-liter V-6 now preheated the fuel/air mixture for better response with a cold engine. On 3.0- and 3.8-liter V-6 engines, the Exhaust Gas Recirculation system was refined to regulate both timing and rate of exhaust gas flow back into the air/fuel mixture. Turbocharged engines had a new piezo sensor in the Electronic Spark Control system, plus computer-controlled EGR. Optional on some models was a new digital readout instrument cluster, which displayed numbers for miles per hour, trip odometer, and fuel level in English or metric form. Instead of the previous buzzer, a new electronic tone warned that seatbelts were not buckled or the key remained in the ignition. Riviera coupes could get ultimate sound with the new Delco GM/Bose Music System that delivered 50 watts of audio output per stereo channel.

1983 Buick, Skyhawk T Type coupe. (OCW)

1983 Buick, Skyhawk Limited sedan. (OCW)

1983 Buick, Skyhawk Limited station wagon. (OCW)

SKYHAWK - SERIES 4J - FOUR - Buick's front-drive, J bodied subcompact looked about the same as in 1982. Eight new body colors and two carryover colors were offered. Skylark Limited had standard deluxe full wheel covers and wide rocker moldings. Both Custom and Limited had a wide wraparound bodyside molding that gave the impression of running all around the car. Standard engine this year was a fuel-injected 2.0 liter four, hooked to four-speed manual gearbox and low (4.10:1) final drive (transaxle) ratio. That engine was essentially a stroked variant of the carbureted 1.8-liter four that served as base engine the year before. Powertrain options included a fuel-injected 1.8-liter overhead-cam engine and five speed manual shift, or three-speed automatic transmission with either engine. The 1.8 used a crossflow aluminum cylinder head, with intake and exhaust ports on opposite sides. Skyhawk offered a new station wagon for 1983, in both Custom and Limited trim--the first Buick front-drive wagons. Cargo volume was 64.5 cubic feet, with split folding rear seat. Engine and transmission choices were the same as other Skyhawks, except the 1.8-liter engine wasn't available with air conditioning. Limited wagons had front armrests and reclining driver and passenger seats. The new subcompact T Type was "rather authoritative looking," according to Buick's catalog. Smallest of the T Types, it was powered by the overhead-cam 1.8-liter four, producing 84 horsepower, coupled to the five-speed manual overdrive gearbox. Axle ratio of 3.83:1 helped standing start performance. So did the engine's claimed quick throttle response and strong low-end torque. When hitting the gas hard, the air conditioner compressor shut off automatically so it wouldn't drain away needed power. T Types had the usual blacked out grille--though in Skyhawk's case, even the standard grille was barely visible, consisting of a set of wide body-colored strips set below the headlamps and skinny minimal bumper. Other black accents were found on the T Type's headlamp housings, door handles, locks, and twin outside mirrors (the left one remote-controlled). Park/signal lamps had amber lenses, and foglamps were included. Lower bodies displayed charcoal accents. A Gran Touring suspension helped handling, while styled aluminum wheels held P195/70R13 blackwall tires. Skyhawk T's dash carried a voltmeter, oil pressure and temperature gauges, resettable trip odometer, and electronic tachometer. Skyhawks had standard reclining bucket seats. Both Limited and T Type had easy-entry front passenger seats. Limiteds used the same luxurious fabric as in Electras. T Types held charcoal cloth bucket seats with adjustable headrests.

SKYLARK - SERIES 4X - FOUR/V-6 - Buick continued to downplay Skylark's economy image, promoting it more as a car that "looks and feels like a Buick," which just happened to be compact in size. Styling was essentially unchanged this year, except for a new aerodynamically-designed lip above new taillamps. The left-hand mirror was also restyled. Five new interior colors were offered, plus new cloth trim on the Limited. Custom Skylarks had a new seat design with adjustable headrests. Skylark's chassis continued in the same form: MacPherson struts up front, trailing axle coil springs in the rear, with standard power rack-and-pinion steering and low-drag power front disc brakes. All Skylarks carried a new Delco Freedom II Plus battery. Base engine remained the Pontiac 2.5-liter four with electronic fuel injection; optional, two forms of Chevrolet's 2.8-liter V-6. One new Skylark appeared, however: the T Type, wearing a blacked-out grille as well as black accents at headlamp housings, door handles and locks, taillamp bezels, and styled outside mirror. Four body colors were offered (white, silver, dark red, or light sand gray), each with special charcoal lower accent paint that reached almost halfway up the doors. Taillamp lenses were smoked, parking/signal lenses amber, and 14 in. wheels of aggressive-looking styled aluminum held blackwall P215/60R14 steel-belted radials (the widest tires of any Buick T Type). Under the T's hood was the high-output (135 horsepower) 2.8-liter V-6 with specially tuned exhaust, manual four-speed gearbox, and 3.65:1 final drive ratio. Sport suspension consisted of stiffer rate springs and shocks, a stiffer front stabilizer bar, and a rear stabilizer bar. On the dash, T Types included a voltmeter and temperature gauge. Front and rear bumper rub strips and a front passenger assist strap were included, and the left-hand mirror was remote-controlled.

1983 Buick, Century Limited sedan with optional wire wheel covers. (OCW)

CENTURY - SERIES 4A - FOUR/V-6 - Buick's A-bodied five-passenger front-drive model, introduced for 1982, offered the lowest drag coefficient in the lineup. Appearance was similar to before, but Skyhawks could have ten new body colors and five new interior colors. Bodies had Plastisol-R protection in critical spots. A new electronic tone reminded drivers to fasten seat belts and remove the ignition key. The Delco 2000 AM radio included dual front speakers. A digital readout instrument cluster was also offered. Buyers could choose from the standard 2.5-liter four-cylinder engine, a 3.0-liter gasoline V-6, or 4.3-liter diesel V-6. An on-board computer added EGR monitoring to the gas V-6. Century had standard automatic transmission, power steering and brakes. At mid-year came a new overdrive automatic transmission. Limited models had integrated bumpers and a bright wide lower molding. Joining the Custom and Limited models this year was a new T Type Century sedan and coupe. Styling touches included subtle black accents on grille and moldings, around headlamps and on taillamp bezels, plus twin black mirrors (left-hand remote controlled), antenna and door handles. The 'Buick' badge went to the lower corner of the grille rather than the side, and front fenders held 'Century T Type' nameplates. Painted silver over charcoal, T Types also had special bumper detailing plus black accent stripes on the body, and rode 14 in. styled aluminum wheels with P195/75R14 blackwall steel-belted radial tires. Their Gran Touring suspension included high-rate springs, revalved shocks, and front/rear stabilizer bars. The 110-horsepower 3.0-liter V-6 drove an automatic transmission and 2.97:1 final drive ratio. A leather-covered sport steering wheel, full-length storage console and 45/45 front seats filled out the T Type goodie list. Lear Siegler cloth bucket seats with leather trim were optional.

1983 Buick, Regal Estate Wagon station wagon with optional styled wheels, roof rack and air deflector. (OCW)

1983 Buick, Regal Limited sedan with optional wire wheel covers. (OCW)

REGAL - SERIES 4G - V-6 - Rear-drive Regals, little changed since their 1978 restyle came with two personalities. Coupes were billed as having an aerodynamic, sleek look while sedans offered 'crisp', limousine-like styling. All Regals had a new grille, with Buick block letters in the center of the upper horizontal bar. Strong vertical bars angled outward from a point above the halfway mark. Regal's script sat at the side of the grille. Wide parking/signal lamps were inset in the bumper. Quad rectangular headlamps were deeply recessed. Standard wheel covers got a restyle this year and Regals came in a revised selection of body (four new choices) and interior colors. Regal's Estate Wagon was also powered by the 3.8-liter V-6 with automatic. Customers could choose a base Regal, Limited, or sporty turbo T Type. Limiteds could be ordered with leather- and vinyl-trimmed seats and cloth-trimmed doors. Standard engine was again the 231 cu. in. (3.8-liter) V-6, with automatic transmission. Larger V-6s (4.1-liter gas or 4.3-liter diesel) and a diesel V-8 were optional. A "discreet" tone told of unbuckled seatbelt with the option of a chime that warned headlamps were still turned on. T Type coupes were easily identifiable by the bulge at the rear of the hood, as well as T Type identification. They wore wide-oval P205/70R14 steel-belted radials on distinctively styled aluminum wheels. Under the hood, the turbocharged 3.8-liter V-6 fed into low-restriction dual exhaust for a "gutty exhaust growl," feeding power to a four-speed automatic overdrive transmission (with torque-converter clutching) and 3.42:1 performance axle ratio. T Type's handling was assisted by the Gran Touring suspension and fast-ratio power steering. At the dash, gauges showed turbo boost and engine temperature. A T Type Decor Package added Designers' Accent paint, blacked-out grille, black headlamp and taillamp trim, black wiper arms and blades, bright center rocker panel moldings, and a sport steering wheel. Regal T could have a hood ornament that said 'Turbo 3.8 Litre' below the Buick tri-shield emblem--words that also appeared on the hood bulge.

LESABRE - SERIES 4B - V-6/V-8 - Once again, the 231 cu. in. (3.8-liter) V-6 was standard on LeSabre. This year, it received an electric preheater grid below the carburetor to warm the fuel/air mixture when the engine was cold. On the powerplant option list: a 4.1-liter V-6 and 5.0-liter V-8, as well as the 5.7 diesel V-8. Automatic transmission was standard with all engines, and included overdrive (0.67:1 gearing) when coupled to any engine other than the base V-6. Converter clutches in third gear and overdrive, which engaged and disengaged at preset speeds, helped to eliminate slippage within the transmission. Of the dozen body colors, all but one was new for 1983.

Designers' Accent paint treatments were also available, and interior colors were new. Custom seats were covered with rich velour, Limited seats with knit fabric. Electric seatback recliners were optional. A multi-function control lever handled turn signals, high/low beams and wiper/washer. All LeSabres had front and rear armrests and a woodtone dash. LeSabre Custom included standard whitewall tires, deluxe wheel covers, bumper guards and protective strips, cigarette lighter, left-hand outside mirror, compact spare tire, and color-coordinated bodyside moldings. Limiteds added such extras as a headlamps on indicator/chime, tinted glass, simulated woodgrain door trim, 55/45 notchback seats, and custom steering wheel.

1983 Buick, LeSabre Estate Wagon station wagon with diesel engine. (OCW)

ESTATE WAGON - SERIES 4B/C - V-8 - As before, both Electra and LeSabre Estate wagons were offered (as well as a Regal version). Electra's was the most luxurious, with standard roof rack and air deflector, vinyl woodgrain trim, 55/45 seating up front with two-way power driver's seat, remote-control left-hand mirror, electric door and tailgate locks, power windows, and digital clock. The standard 307 cu. in. (5.0-liter) V-8 engine came with four-speed overdrive automatic transmission, and could be held in third-gear range when hauling a heavy load. LeSabre Estate wagons offered the same cargo capacity, but a little less luxury. They included a power tailgate window, two-way tailgate with "ajar" indicator, air conditioning, Soft Ray tinted glass, and the same standard V-8 engine. A diesel V-8 was also offered.

ELECTRA - SERIES 4C - V-6/V-8 - Apart from a dozen new body colors, the full-size Buick line didn't change much this year, either mechanically or in appearance. Measuring over 221 inches, it was still the longest regular production car made in America. A combination of slim bodyside moldings and wide rocker panel moldings accentuated Electra's long, formal lines. The upscale Park Avenue again displayed brushed aluminum bodyside moldings that contained the familiar ventiport identity badge. A padded halo vinyl top was standard again, revealing a bit of body color at the edges. Wide rocker panel moldings continued onto front and rear fenders. Soft Ray tinted glass was standard. Electras also included a headlamps-on indicator, digital clock, bumper guards and protective strips, 25-gallon fuel tank, compact spare tire, and power windows. In addition to wide color-keyed protective bodyside moldings, both models carried moldings for back and side window reveal, roof drip, window frame scalp, belt reveal, windshield, and wheel openings. Park Avenue added resume-speed Cruise Control and a tilt steering column, plus AM/FM stereo radio, six-way power driver's seat, electric door locks, and power remote left-hand mirror. Standard powertrain was the 252 cu. in. (4.1-liter V-6) and automatic transmission with overdrive (including torque converter clutch). Options included a 5.0-liter gas V-8 or the big diesel V-8, which offered excellent mileage but proved troublesome to many owners.

RIVIERA - SERIES 4E - V-6/V-8 - To mark Riviera's 20th birthday, Buick produced 502 copies of an 'XX Anniversary Edition.' To the normally ample list of Riviera equipment was added a tempting selection of extras, including true wire wheels. The body was painted two-tone beige, with Anniversary grille and front end panel. Bumper strips, front and rear, were brown with gold inserts. Rocker, belt and roof drip moldings were dark brown. Fender, decklid and grille emblems were plated in 24

carat gold. Special identification appeared on hood and wheel centers. The medium beech Anniversary interior featured English walnut wood veneer trim plates and 26-ounce wool-like carpeting. Suede inserts highlighted the glove leather seat upholstery. There was also a leather-wrapped wood steering wheel, wood horn cap, leather upper door trim, 140 MPH speedometer, and gold-plated Anniversary identification. Also standard: a rear window defogger, Gran Touring suspension and dual electric mirrors plus Uniroyal goldwall stripe steel-belted radial tires. Even the trunk trim was distinctive. Standard engine was the 4.1-liter V-6, with 5.0-liter V-8 optional. Apart from that special edition there were three "ordinary" Rivieras: a basic but luxurious coupe, sporty T Type, and recently-introduced convertible. Riviera's T Type had a blacked out grille (with fewer vertical bars), amber park/signal lenses, tungsten-halogen high/low beam headlamps, accent stripes on the body, sport steering wheel and special T Type identification inside and out. Styled aluminum wheels held self-sealing, all-season whitewall radial tires. Under the hood once again was the turbocharged 3.8-liter V-6, coupled to overdrive automatic transmission and 3.36:1 final drive axle ratio. T Type's Gran Touring suspension blended higher-rate springs with recalibrated shock absorbers and special front/rear stabilizer bars. T Types were available in any Riviera color except light green and light brown. The hood ornament carried the letter 'R'. As usual, all Rivieras were loaded with power assists and conveniences, including air conditioning and an electronically-tuned Delco 2000 AM/FM stereo radio (which could be deleted for credit). Stereo buffs could go all the way up to a premium Delco GM/Bose Music System, acoustically tailored to the Riviera interior, with 50 watt power output. Interiors had new door pull straps, and the range of colors included a tan that was a Riviera exclusive. Standard equipment included a six-way power seat. A new optional digital instrument panel cluster showed miles per hour, remaining fuel, and a trip mileage in either English or metric values. Trailer towing equipment was available for loads up to 3,000 pounds. Convertibles were produced in somewhat limited number (only 1,750 this year) in choice of white or Firemist red with white top and contrasting bodyside stripes. Interiors were upholstered in soft red Sierra grain leather and vinyl. Four-wheel disc brakes were standard. Convertibles also had custom locking wire wheel covers and heavy-duty suspension. Standard Riviera powerplant was the 4.1-liter V-6 with overdrive automatic transmission, with option of a 5.0-liter gas V-8 or 5.7-liter diesel V-8. Convertibles could not have the diesel.

1983 Buick, Riviera T Type coupe. (OCW)

I.D. DATA: Buicks again had a 17-symbol Vehicle Identification Number (VIN), introduced in 1981, stamped on a metal tag attached to the upper left surface of the cowl, visible through the windshield. The number begins with '1' to indicate U.S.A., followed by 'G' for General Motors and '4' for Buick Division. The next letter indicates restraint system. Symbol five denotes series: 'S' Skyhawk; 'T' Skyhawk Limited; 'E' Skyhawk T Type; 'B' Skylark Custom; 'C' Skylark Limited; 'D' Skylark T Type; 'H' Century Custom; 'L' Century Limited; 'G' Century T Type; 'J' Regal; 'K' Regal T Type; 'M' Regal Limited; 'N' LeSabre Custom; 'P' LeSabre Limited; 'R' LeSabre Estate Wagon; 'V' Electra Estate Wagon; 'X' Electra Limited; 'W' Electra Park Avenue; 'Y' Riviera T Type; 'Z' Riviera. Digits six and seven indicate body type: '27' 2-dr coupe; '37' Skylark 2-dr coupe; '47' Regal 2-dr coupe; '57'

Riviera 2-dr coupe; '35' 4-dr wagon; '19' 4-dr sedan; '69' 4-dr sedan. Next is the engine code: 'O' L4-112 TBI; 'P' L4-121 TBI; 'R' L4-151 TBI; 'X' V6-173 2Bbl.; 'Z' H.O. V6-173 2Bbl.; 'E' V6-181 2Bbl.; 'A' V6-231 2Bbl.; '8' V6-231 Turbo; '4' V6-252 4Bbl.; 'V' V6-263 diesel; 'Y' V8-307 4Bbl.; 'N' V8-350 diesel. Symbol nine is a check digit. Symbol ten denotes model year ('D' 1983). Symbol eleven is the plant code. The final six digits are the sequential serial number. An additional identifying number can be found on the engine, showing codes for GM division, model year, assembly plant, and vehicle sequence number. A body number plate shows model year, car division, series, style, body assembly plant, body number, trim combination, modular seat code, paint code, and date build code.

SKYHAWK CUSTOM (FOUR)

Model No.	Body/Style No.	Body Type & Seating	Factory Price	Shipping Weight	Prod. Total
4J	S27	2-dr Coupe-5P	6958	2316	27,557
4J	S69	4-dr Sedan-5P	7166	2369	19,847
4J	S35	4-dr Sta Wag-5P	7492	2439	10,653

SKYHAWK LIMITED (FOUR)

4J	T27	2-dr Coupe-5P	7457	2333	Note 1
4J	T69	4-dr Sedan-5P	7649	2411	Note 1
4J	T35	4-dr Sta Wag-5P	7934	2462	Note 1

Note 1: Production figures listed under Skyhawk Custom also include equivalent Skyhawk Limited models. For the model year, a total of 45,105 Customs and 12,952 Limiteds were manufactured.

SKYHAWK T TYPE (FOUR)

4J	E27	2-dr Coupe-5P	7961	2336	5,095

SKYLARK CUSTOM (FOUR/V-6)

4X	B37	2-dr Coupe-5P	7548/7698	2462/2523	11,671
4X	B69	4-dr Sedan-5P	7718/7868	2493/2554	51,950

1983 Buick, Skylark Limited sedan with optional vinyl top and wire wheel covers. (OCW)

SKYLARK LIMITED (FOUR/V-6)

4X	C37	2-dr Coupe-5P	7988/8138	2489/2550	7,863
4X	C69	4-dr Sedan-5P	8150/8300	2519/2580	30,674

SKYLARK T TYPE (V-6)

4X	D37	2-dr Coupe-5P	9337	2608	2,489

CENTURY CUSTOM (FOUR/V-6)

4A	H27	2-dr Coupe-5P	8841/8991	2614/2719	13,483
4A	H19	4-dr Sedan-5P	9002/9152	2662/2767	114,443

CENTURY LIMITED (FOUR/V-6)

4A	L27	2-dr Coupe-5P	9261/9411	2632/2737	Note 2
4A	L19	4-dr Sedan-5P	9425/9575	2675/2780	Note 2

CENTURY T TYPE (V-6)

4A	G27	2-dr Coupe-5P	10017	2749	Note 2
4A	G19	4-dr Sedan-5P	10178	2801	Note 2

Note 2: Production figures listed under Century Custom also include Limited and T Type models. Total production for the model year came to 50,296 Customs, 73,030 Limiteds, and 4,600 Century T Types.

REGAL (V-6)

4G	J47	2-dr Coupe-6P	9100	3123	147,935
4G	J69	4-dr Sedan-6P	9279	3139	61,285
4G	J35	4-dr Sta Wag-6P	9550	3289	15,287

REGAL LIMITED (V-6)

4G	M47	2-dr Coupe-6P	9722	3164	Note 3
4G	M69	4-dr Sedan-6P	9856	3177	Note 3

Note 3: Production figures listed under base Regal coupe and sedan also include Regal Limited models. Total coupe/sedan production was 108,458 base Regals and 100,762 Limiteds. Only 4,340 Regals had the optional diesel V-8 engine.

REGAL T TYPE (V-6)

4G	K47	2-dr Coupe-6P	10366	3194	3,732

LESABRE CUSTOM (V-6/V-8)

Model No.	Body/Style No.	Body Type & Seating	Factory Price	Shipping Weight	Prod. Total
4B	N37	2-dr Coupe-6P	9292/9517	3459/3631	6,974
4B	N69	4-dr Sedan-6P	9394/9619	3488/3660	31,196

LESABRE LIMITED (V-6/V-8)

4B	P37	2-dr Coupe-6P	9836/10061	3494/3666	22,029
4B	P69	4-dr Coupe-6P	9990/10215	3527/3699	66,547

LESABRE ESTATE WAGON (V-8)

4B	R35	4-dr Sta Wag-6P	11187	4105	9,306

ELECTRA LIMITED (V-6/V-8)

4C	X37	2-dr Coupe-6P	12415/12490	3644/3823	8,885
4C	X69	4-dr Sedan-6P	12586/12661	3704/3883	79,700

ELECTRA PARK AVENUE (V-6/V-8)

4C	W37	2-dr Coupe-6P	14094/14169	3716/3895	Note 4
4C	W69	4-dr Sedan-6P	14245/14320	3781/3960	Note 4

Note 4: Production figures listed under Electra Limited also include equivalent Park Avenue models. All told, 24,542 Limiteds and 64,043 Park Avenue Electras were built, only 4,878 with V-8 engine.

ELECTRA ESTATE WAGON (V-8)

4C	V35	4-dr Sta Wag-6P	13638	4175	9,581

RIVIERA (V-6/V-8)

4E	Z57	2-dr Coupe-5P	15238/15313	3609/3769	47,153
4E	Z67	2-dr Conv-5P	24960/24960	3795/3955	1,750

Note 5: Only 128 Riviera convertibles and 2,993 standard coupes had a V-6 engine.

RIVIERA T TYPE (V-6)

4E	Y57	2-dr Coupe-5P	15906	3593	1,331

FACTORY PRICE AND WEIGHT NOTE: Figure before the slash is for four-cylinder engine, after the slash for V-6. For full-size models, figure before the slash is for V-6 engine, after the slash for V-8.

ENGINES: BASE FOUR (Skyhawk): Inline, overhead valve four-cylinder. Cast iron cylinder block and head. Displacement: 121 cu. in. (2.0 liters). Bore & stroke: 3.50 x 3.14 in. Compression ratio: 9.0:1. Brake horsepower: 90 at 5100 R.P.M. Torque: 111 lb.-ft. at 2700 R.P.M. Five main bearings. Hydraulic valve lifters. Throttle-body fuel injection. VIN Code: P. OPTIONAL FOUR (Skyhawk): Inline, overhead-cam four-cylinder. Cast iron block and head. Displacement: 112 cu. in. (1.8 liters). Bore & stroke: 3.34 x 3.13 in. Compression ratio: 9.0:1. Brake horsepower: 84 at 5200 R.P.M. Torque: 102 lb.-ft. at 2800 R.P.M. Five main bearings. Hydraulic valve lifters. Throttle-body fuel injection. VIN Code: O. BASE FOUR (Skylark, Century): Inline, overhead-valve four-cylinder. Cast iron block and head. Displacement: 151 cu. in. (2.5 liters). Bore & stroke: 4.0 x 3.0 in. Compression ratio: 8.2:1. Brake horsepower: 90 at 4000 R.P.M. Torque: 134 lb.-ft. at 2400 R.P.M. Five main bearings. Hydraulic valve lifters. Throttle-body fuel injection. Built by Pontiac. VIN Code: R. OPTIONAL V-6 (Skylark): 60 degree, overhead-valve V-6. Cast iron alloy block and head. Displacement: 173 cu. in. (2.8 liters). Bore & stroke: 3.5 x 3.0 in. Compression ratio: 8.4:1. Brake horsepower: 112 at 5100 R.P.M. Torque: 148 lb.-ft. at 2400 R.P.M. Four main bearings. Hydraulic valve lifters. Carburetor: 2Bbl. Rochester E2SE. Built by Chevrolet. VIN Code: X. HIGH-OUTPUT 173 V-6: (Skylark T Type); OPTIONAL (Skylark): Same as 173 cu. in. V-6 above except as follows: Compression ratio: 8.94:1. Brake horsepower: 135 at 5400 R.P.M. Torque: 145 lb.-ft. at 2400 R.P.M. VIN Code: Z. OPTIONAL V-6 (Century): 90-degree overhead-valve V-6. Cast iron block and head. Displacement: 181 cu. in. (3.0 liters). Bore & stroke: 3.8 x 2.66 in. Compression ratio: 8.45:1. Brake horsepower: 110 at 4800 R.P.M. Torque: 145 lb.-ft. at 2600 R.P.M. Four main bearings. Hydraulic valve lifters. Carburetor: 2Bbl. Rochester E2ME. VIN Code: E. BASE V-6 (Regal, LeSabre): 90-degree, overhead-valve V-6. Cast iron alloy block and head. Displacement: 231 cu. in. (3.8 liters). Bore & stroke: 3.8 x 3.4 in. Compression ratio: 8.0:1. Brake horsepower: 110 at 3800 R.P.M. Torque: 190 lb.-ft. at 1600 R.P.M. Four main bearings. Hydraulic valve lifters. Carburetor: 2Bbl. Rochester. VIN Code: A. TURBOCHARGED V-6 (Regal T Type, Riviera T Type): Same as 231 V-6 above,

but with E4ME four-barrel carburetor. Brake horsepower: 180 at 4000 R.P.M. Torque: 280 lb.-ft. at 2400 R.P.M. (Riviera, 290 lb.-ft.). VIN Code: 8. BASE V-6 (Electra, Riviera); OPTIONAL (Regal, LeSabre): 90-degree, overhead-valve V-6. Cast iron alloy block and head. Displacement: 252 cu. in. (4.1 liters). Bore & stroke: 3.965 x 3.4 in. Compression ratio: 8.0:1. Brake horsepower: 125 at 4000 R.P.M. Torque: 205 lb.-ft. at 2000 R.P.M. Four main bearings. Hydraulic valve lifters. Carburetor: 4Bbl. Rochester. VIN Code: 4. DIESEL V-6; OPTIONAL (Century, Regal): 90-degree, overhead valve V-6. Cast iron block; cast iron or aluminum head. Displacement: 262.5 cu. in. (4.3 liters). Bore & stroke: 4.057 x 3.385 in. Compression ratio: 21.6:1. Brake horsepower: 85 at 3600 R.P.M. Torque: 165 lb.-ft. at 1600 R.P.M. Four main bearings. Hydraulic valve lifters. Fuel injection. VIN Code: V. BASE V-8 (Estate); OPTIONAL (LeSabre, Electra, Riviera): 90-degree, overhead valve V-8. Cast iron block and head. Displacement: 307 cu. in. (5.0 liters). Bore & stroke: 3.80 x 3.385 in. Compression ratio: 8.0:1. Brake horsepower: 140 at 3600 R.P.M. Torque: 240 lb.-ft. at 1600 R.P.M. Five main bearings. Hydraulic valve lifters. Carburetor: 4Bbl Rochester. Built by Oldsmobile. VIN Code: Y. OPTIONAL DIESEL V-8 (Regal, LeSabre, Electra, Estate, Riviera): 90-degree, overhead valve V-8. Cast iron block and head. Displacement: 350 cu. in. (5.7 liters). Bore & stroke: 4.057 x 3.385 in. Compression ratio: 21.6:1. Brake horsepower: 105 at 3200 R.P.M. Torque: 200 lb.-ft. at 1600 R.P.M. Five main bearings. Hydraulic valve lifters. Fuel injection. Oldsmobile-built. VIN Code: N.

CHASSIS DATA: Wheelbase: (Skyhawk) 101.2 in.; (Skylark/Century) 104.9 in.; (Regal) 108.1 in.; (LeSabre/Estate) 115.9 in.; (Electra) 118.9 in.; (Riviera) 114.0 in. Overall length: (Skyhawk) 175.3 in.; (Skyhawk wag) 177.1 in.; (Skylark) 181.0 in.; (Century) 189.1 in.; (Regal cpe) 200.6 in.; (Regal sed) 196.0 in.; (Regal wag) 196.7 in.; (LeSabre) 218.4 in.; (Electra) 221.3 in.; (Estate Wagon) 220.5 in.; (Riviera) 206.6 in. Height: (Skyhawk) 54.0 in.; (Skylark/Century) 53.6 in.; (Regal cpe) 54.5 in.; (Regal sed) 55.4 in.; (Regal wag) 57.1 in.; (LeSabre cpe) 56.0 in.; (Electra cpe) 56.8 in.; (LeSabre/Electra sed) 56.7-56.9 in.; (Estate) 59.1 in.; (Riv) 54.3 in. Width: (Skyhawk) 62.0 in.; (Skyhawk wag) 65.0 in.; (Skylark) 69.1 in.; (Century) 66.8 in.; (Regal cpe) 71.6 in.; (Regal sed/wag) 71.1-71.2 in.; (LeSabre) 78.0 in.; (Electra) 76.2 in.; (Estate) 79.3 in.; (Riv) 72.8 in.; Front Tread: (Skyhawk) 55.4 in.; (Skylark/Century) 58.7 in.; (Regal) 58.5 in.; (LeSabre/Electra) 61.8 in.; (Estate) 62.2 in.; (Riviera) 59.3 in. Rear Tread: (Skyhawk) 55.2 in.; (Skylark/Century) 57.0 in.; (Regal) 57.7 in.; (LeSabre/Electra) 60.7 in.; (Estate) 64.0 in.; (Riviera) 60.0 in. Standard Tires: (Skyhawk) P175/80R13 GBR; (Skylark/Century) P185/80R13 GBR; (Skylark T Type) P205/70R13 SBR; (Regal) P195/75R14 SBR WSW; (Regal T Type) P205/70R14 SBR; (LeSabre) P205/75R15 SBR WSW; (Electra) P215/75R15 SBR WSW; (Estate) P225/75R15 SBR WSW; (Riviera) P205/75R15 SBR WSW.

TECHNICAL: Transmission: Four-speed, fully synchronized floor shift standard on Skyhawk/Skylark; automatic optional (standard on all other models). Five-speed standard on Skyhawk T Type. Four-speed gear ratios: (1st) 3.53:1; (2nd) 1.95.1; (3rd) 1.24:1; (4th) 0.81:1 or 0.73:1; (Rev) 3.42:1. Five-speed gear ratios: (1st) 3.91:1; (2nd) 2.15:1; (3rd) 1.45:1; (4th) 1.03:1; (5th) 0.74:1; (Rev) 3.50:1. Three-speed auto. trans. gear ratios: (1st) 2.74:1; (2nd) 1.57:1; (3rd) 1.00:1; (Rev) 1.93:1 or 2.07:1. Skyhawk/Skylark/Century auto. trans. gear ratios: (1st) 2.84:1; (2nd) 1.60:1; (3rd) 1.00:1; (Rev) 2.07:1. Four-speed overdrive automatic gear ratios: (1st) 2.74:1; (2nd) 1.57:1; (3rd) 1.00:1; (4th) 0.67:1; (Rev) 2.07:1. T Type final drive ratios: (Skyhawk) 3.83:1; (Skylark) 3.65:1; (Century) 2.97:1; (Regal) 3.42:1; (Riviera) 3.36:1. Steering: Same as 1982. Suspension: Same as 1982. Brakes: Same as 1982. Body construction: Same as 1982. Wheel size: (Skyhawk/Century) 13 x 5.5 in.; (Regal) 14 x 6 in.; (LeSabre/Riviera) 15 x 6 in.; (Estate) 15 x 7 in. Fuel tank: (Skyhawk) 13.6 gal.; (Skylark) 15.1 gal.; (Century) 15.7 gal.;

(Regal) 18.1 gal.; (LeSabre/Electra) 25.0 gal.; (Estate) 22.0 gal.; (Riviera) 21.1 gal. Unleaded fuel only.

DRIVETRAIN OPTIONS: Engines: 112 cu. in. (1.8 liter) EFI four: Skyhawk ($50). 173 cu. in. (2.8-liter) V-6, 2Bbl; Skylark ($150). High-output 173 cu. in. (2.8 liter) V-6, 2Bbl. Skylark ($300); std. on T Type 181 cu. in. (3.0-liter) V-6. 2Bbl. Century ($150). 252 cu. in. (4.1-liter) V-6; 4Bbl. Regal ($150); LeSabre exc. wagon ($150). 263 cu. in. (4.3-liter) diesel V-6; Century Cust Ltd ($599); Regal exc. T Type or wag ($599). 307 cu. in. (5.0-liter) V-8, 4Bbl.: LeSabre cpe/sed ($225); Electra cpe/sed, Riviera ($75). 350 cu. in. (5.7-liter) diesel V-8: Regal/LeSabre/Estate/Electra/Riviera ($799). Transmission/Differential: Five-speed manual trans.: Skyhawk ($75). Automatic trans.: Skyhawk ($395); Skyhawk T Type ($320); Skylark ($425). Automatic overdrive trans.: LeSabre cpe/sed ($175); std. automatic on LeSabre (NC). Optional rear axle ratio: Regal exc. T Type 2.73:1 or 3.23:1 (NC); Regal, Ltd 3.08:1 (NC); LeSabre 2.73:1, 3.08:1 or 3.23:1 (NC); Electra 3.08:1 or 3.23:1 (NC). Limited slip differential: Regal/LeSabre/Electra ($95). Suspension, Steering and Brakes: F40 Firm ride/handling pkg.: Skylark/Century Cust/Ltd. ($27); Regal exc. T Type ($27); LeSabre/Electra ($27). F41 Gran Touring suspension: Skyhawk ($196); Century Cust/Ltd ($27); Regal/Ltd, LeSabre ($49); Riviera ($27). F41 Gran Touring ride/handling suspension incl. P205/70R13 SBR WSW tires: Skylark Cust/Ltd ($272). Superlift rear shock absorbers: Skylark Cust/Ltd ($68). Automatic level control: Century/Regal/LeSabre/Electra ($175). Power steering: Skyhawk ($199). Four-wheel disc brakes: Riviera ($235); std. on conv. Other: Trailer towing pkg.: LeSabre exc. wag ($127). Heavy-duty alternator: 85-amp ($35-$85). H.D. battery: ($25); w/diesel ($50). H.D. radiator: Skyhawk ($40-$70). H.D. cooling: Skylark ($40-$70); Cold climate pkg. Regal exc. T (NC). Engine block heater ($18). H.D. engine/transmission cooling: Century/Regal/LeSabre/Electra ($40-$70). High altitude emission pkg. (NC) except w/diesel cold climate pkg. delete ($49). California emission system ($75) exc. diesel ($215). Diesel cold climate pkg. delete ($99 credit).

SKYHAWK CONVENIENCE/APPEARANCE OPTIONS: Option Packages: Vista Vent flip open removable glass sunroof ($295). Acoustic Pkg. ($36). Instrument gauge pkg.: temp, oil pressure, volts, trip odometer: Cust ($60). Gauges and tech: Cust ($138); Ltd ($78). Comfort/Convenience: Air cond. ($625). Touch climate control air cond. ($775). Rear defogger, electric ($125). Cruise Master w/resume ($170). Power windows ($180-$255). Electric door locks ($120-$170). Six-way power driver's seat ($210). Easy entry passenger seat adjuster: Cust cpe ($16). Tinted glass ($90). Sport steering wheel ($50). Tilt steering ($99). Trip odometer: Cust ($15). Electric clock ($35). Electric trunk release ($40). Remote tailgate lock: wag ($35). Tailgate wiper/washer: wag ($120). Two-speed wipers w/delay ($49). Lights, Horns and Mirrors: Tungsten-halogen headlamps ($22). Headlamps-on indicator ($15). Dome reading lamp ($30). Dual horns: Cust cpe/sed ($15). Left remote mirror ($21). Dual mirrors: left remote ($51). Dual electric remote mirrors ($137); T Type ($86). Visor vanity mirror passenger ($7). Lighted visor vanity mirror either side ($45). Entertainment: Basic electronic-tuning AM/FM stereo radio ($138); w/clock ($177); w/cassette ($277). Electronic-tuning AM/FM stereo radio ($302); w/cassette and graphic equalizer ($505). Radio delete ($56 credit). Power antenna ($60). Dual rear speakers ($25-$30). Exterior Trim: Door edge guards ($15-$25). Rocker panel moldings: Cust cpe/sed ($26). Bodyside stripes ($42). Designers' accent paint ($195). Decklid luggage rack ($105). Roof rack: wag ($105). Interior Trim/Upholstery: Suede bucket seats: Ltd cpe/sed ($295). Front carpet savers ($17); rear ($12). Front carpet savers w/inserts ($18); rear ($15). Deluxe trunk trim ($33). Wheels and Tires: Styled aluminum wheels ($229). Styled wheel covers w/trim rings ($38). Custom locking wire wheel covers ($165). P175/80R13 GBR WSW ($54). P195/70R13 SBR BSW ($169). P195/70R13 SBR WSW ($62-

$231). P195/70R13 SBR WLT ($84-$253). P195/70R13 SBR wide WSW ($62-$231). Self-sealing tires ($106).

SKYLARK/CENTURY CONVENIENCE/APPEARANCE OPTIONS: Option Packages: Acoustic pkg.: Skylark Cust ($60). Flip-open Vista Vent glass sunroof ($295). Standard option delete (rocker panel moldings and front armrest): Century Cust ($67 credit). Comfort/Convenience: Air cond. ($725). Cruise Master w/resume ($170). Rear defogger, electric ($135). Power windows: cpe ($180); Skylark sed ($255). Electric door locks ($120-$170). Six-way power driver's seat ($210). Manual seatback recliners, passenger: Cust/Ltd ($45); both ($90). Sport steering wheel ($50). Tilt steering ($105). Tinted glass ($105). Instrument gauges incl. trip odometer ($48). Trip odometer: Skylark Cust/Ltd ($16). Digital electronic instrument cluster: Century ($299). Dial clock ($35). Electric trunk release ($40). Two-speed wipers w/delay ($49). Theft deterrent system: Century ($159). Lights, Horns and Mirrors: Tungsten-halogen headlamps: Century ($22). Twilight Sentinel: Century ($57). Front light monitors: Century ($37). Coach lamps: Ltd ($102-$129). Headlamps-on indicator ($16). Door courtesy/warning light: Century Ltd ($44). Dome reading light ($24). Rear seat reading lamp: Skylark Ltd Century ($30). Remote left mirror: Cust/Ltd ($24). Sport mirrors (left remote): Cust/Ltd ($59). Dual electric remote mirrors: Cust/Ltd ($137); T Type ($78). Visor vanity mirror, passenger ($7). Lighted visor vanity mirror, passenger: Skylark ($50); either side, Century ($58). Entertainment: (Same as Skyhawk above). Exterior Trim: Landau vinyl top: Cust/Ltd cpe ($181-$215). Long vinyl top: Cust/Ltd ($155). Designers' accent paint: Cust/Ltd ($205-$210). Special solid color paint: Century Cust/Ltd ($200). Protective bodyside moldings ($55). Lower wide bodyside moldings: Century Cust ($65). Wide rocker panel/rear quarter moldings: Skylark Cust ($65). Belt reveal molding: Skylark Cust, T ($40). Wheel opening moldings: Skylark Cust ($30). Door edge guards ($15-$25). Pillar appliqué moldings: Skylark Cust sed ($27). Hood ornament and windsplit: Cust ($22-$32). Bodyside stripe: Cust/Ltd ($42). Bumper guards front/rear: Skylark ($45). Bumper strips, front/rear: Skylark Cust ($49). Front license plate mounting: Skylark (NC). Interior Trim/Upholstery: Full length console: Skylark ($100); Century ($57). Full-length operating console: Century ($75); T Type ($18). Bucket seats: Skylark ($95). Lear Siegler bucket seats: Century T Type ($600). 45/45 seating: cloth, Century Cust ($158); leather, Century Ltd ($295). Front carpet savers ($17); rear ($12). Carpet savers w/inserts: front ($25); rear ($20). Trunk trim ($35-$47). Wheels: Styled aluminum wheels: Century Cust/Ltd ($195). Chrome-plated wheels: Skylark Cust/Ltd ($175). Locking wire wheel covers: Cust/Ltd ($185). Skylark Tires: P185/80R13 GBR WSW: Cust/Ltd ($58). P185/80R13 SBR WSW: Cust/Ltd ($123). P205/70R13 SBR WSW: Cust/Ltd ($255). P215/60R14 SBR WLT: T Type ($92). Self-sealing tires: Cust/Ltd ($106). Century Cust/Ltd Tires: P185/75R14 GBR WSW ($58). P185/75R14 SBR BSW ($64). P185/75R14 SBR WSW ($122). P195/75R14 SBR BSW ($95). P195/75R14 SBR WSW ($157). Self sealing tires ($106).

REGAL CONVENIENCE/APPEARANCE OPTIONS: Option Packages: Regal T Type Decor pkg.: designers' accent paint, wide rocker molding, black paint treatment, sport steering wheel ($365). Sliding electric Astroroof: cpe ($895). Hatch roof: cpe ($825). Standard option delete: Regal sedan w/o narrow rocker moldings, bright steering wheel bezel, passenger mirror, underhood light, bodyside moldings, brushed deck lid molding, wheel opening and window reveal moldings; with P185/75R14 GBR WSW tires ($278 credit). Comfort/Convenience: Air cond. ($725): climate control ($875). Cruise Master w/resume ($170). Rear defogger, electric ($135). Tinted glass ($105). Tinted windshield ($80). Six-way power seat, each side ($210): both ($420). Manual passenger seatback recliner ($75). Sport steering wheel ($50). Tilt steering ($105). Power windows ($180-$255). Electric door locks ($120-$170). Electric trunk release ($40). Remote electric tailgate lock: wag ($40). Electric clock ($35). Headlamps-on in-

dicator ($16). Trip odometer ($16) exc. T. Instrument gauges: temp. voltage, trip odometer ($48). Two-speed wiper w/low-speed delay ($49). Theft deterrent system ($159); N/A on wag. Lighting and Mirrors: Tungsten-halogen headlamps ($22). Twilight Sentinel headlamp control ($57). Cornering lamps ($57). Coach lamps: Ltd ($102). Door courtesy/warning lights: Ltd ($44-$70). Rear seat reading light ($30). Dome reading lamps ($24). Remote left mirror ($24) exc. T Type; right ($42). Dual sport mirrors, left remote ($51). Dual remote sport mirrors ($81); T ($30). Visor vanity mirror, passenger ($7). Lighted visor vanity mirror, passenger ($58). Entertainment: AM radio ($112). AM/FM stereo radio ($198); w/cassette ($298). Electronic-tuning AM/FM stereo radio ($402); w/cassette ($555). Dual rear speakers ($25-$30). Automatic power antenna ($95); w/radio ($60). Exterior Trim: Landau vinyl top: cpe ($181). Heavy-padded landau vinyl top: cpe ($240). Long vinyl top: sed ($155). Long padded vinyl top sed ($240). Designers' accent paint ($200-$235). Solid special color paint ($200). Exterior molding pkg. ($110): std or Ltd Protective bodyside moldings: T Type ($55). Wraparound bodyside moldings: Ltd sedan ($104). Hood ornament and windsplit: Century ($22): std on Ltd Door edge guards ($15-$25). Belt reveal moldings: T Type w/decor pkg. ($40). Bodyside stripe ($42). Woodgrain vinyl appliqué: wag ($355). Roof rack: wag ($125). Air deflector: wag ($37). Interior Trim/Upholstery: Full-length console ($82) exc. wag: operating console for bucket seats (NC). Bucket seats: cpe/sed ($195). 55/45 seating ($133). Limited 55/45 seating: T Type ($385). Limited 45/45 leather/vinyl seating: T ($680). Leather/vinyl 45/45 seating: Ltd ($295). Front carpet savers ($17); rear ($12). Front carpet savers w/inserts ($25); rear ($20). Trunk trim covering ($47). Lockable storage compartment: wag ($55). Wheels: Chrome-plated wheels ($195); T Type ($90 credit). Styled aluminum wheels ($285); std on T. Locking wire wheel covers ($185); T ($100 credit). Body color wheels ($85) exc. T. Tires: P205/70R14 SBR WSW ($62-$66). P205/70R14 SBR WLT ($88). Self-sealing tires ($106) exc. T Type.

LESABRE/ELECTRA/ESTATE WAGON CONVENIENCE/APPEARANCE OPTIONS:
Comfort/Convenience: Sliding electric Astroroof: silver, gray or gold ($1195). Air cond.: LeSabre ($725). Air cond. w/touch-climate control ($875); LeSabre Estate, Electra ($150). Cruise Master w/resume ($170); std. on Park Ave. Rear defogger, electric ($135). Tinted glass: LeSabre Cust ($105). Power windows: LeSabre ($180-$255). Electric door locks ($120-$170). Automatic door locks ($200-$250); exc. Park Ave. ($80). Six-way power seat, driver's or passenger's ($180-$210); both ($390-$420). Memory driver's seat: Electra Ltd ($358); Park Ave. ($178). Electric seatback recliner, one side ($139). Sport steering wheel: LeSabre ($50). Tilt steering: LeSabre, Electra Ltd ($105). Tilt/telescoping steering column ($160) exc. Electra Park Ave./Estate ($55). Dial clock: LeSabre ($60). Trip odometer: LeSabre ($16). Remote tailgate lock: LeSabre Est ($50). Electric trunk lock: Electra ($80). Electric trunk release ($40). Electric fuel cap lock ($44) exc. wag. Theft deterrent system ($159): N/A on Estate. Two-speed wiper w/delay ($49). Accessory group (trip odometer, dome reading lamp, low fuel indicator, washer fluid indicator): Electra ($30-$70). Lighting, Horns and Mirrors: Tungsten-halogen high-beam headlamps ($22). Twilight Sentinel ($57). Cornering lamps ($57). Coach lamps: LeSabre/Electra Ltd ($102). Light monitors, front: LeSabre, Electra Est ($37); front/rear, Electra ($74). Lamp and indicator group: LeSabre ($38-$70). Door courtesy/warning lamps ($44-$70). Lighted door lock and interior light control ($72). Four-note horn ($28). Remote left mirror: LeSabre ($24). Remote right mirror: LeSabre ($48); Electra Ltd, Est ($24). Remote electric right mirror: Electra Park Ave. ($57). Dual remote sport mirrors: LeSabre ($88); Electra Ltd, Est ($40). Dual electric remote mirrors: LeSabre ($137). Electra Ltd Est ($89). Remote left mirror w/thermometer: LeSabre ($62); Electra Ltd, Est ($38). Electric left mirror w/thermometer: Park Ave. ($38). Dual electric mirrors w/left thermometer: LeSabre ($175): Electra Ltd, Est ($127). Lighted visor vanity mirror driver or passenger ($58). Entertainment: AM radio: LeSabre

($112). AM/FM stereo radio: LeSabre, Electra Ltd/Estate ($198); w/8-track or cassette ($298) exc. Park Ave. ($100). AM/FM stereo radio with CB: Estate ($473). Electronic-tuning AM/FM stereo radio: LeSabre ($377-$402); Electra ($165-$363). Electronic-tuning radio and 8-track or cassette ($491-$555) exc. Park Ave. ($319). Electronic-tuning radio with CB and cassette player: Estate ($766-$805). Delete AM/FM stereo radio: Electra Park Ave. ($153 credit). Concert Sound speaker system: Electra exc. wag ($95); ETR radio req'd. Dual rear speakers ($25-$30). Automatic power antenna ($95); w/radio ($60). Triband power antenna: Estate ($140); w/radio ($105). Exterior Trim: Exterior molding pkg. (wide rocker panel, front/rear fender lower and belt reveal moldings): LeSabre ($110). Landau vinyl top: LeSabre, Electra Ltd cpe ($240). Long vinyl top: LeSabre, Electra Ltd sed ($180-$185). Heavy-padded long vinyl top: Electra Ltd sed ($240). Designers' accent paint: LeSabre ($215) exc. Estate. Special single-color paint: ($200): Firemist, Electra exc. Estate ($210). Protective bodyside moldings: Est ($55). Wide rocker panel moldings: Electra Ltd/Est ($65). Door edge guards ($15-$25). Belt reveal molding: LeSabre ($40). Bodyside stripes ($42). Woodgrain vinyl appliqué: LeSabre Est ($345). Roof rack w/air deflector: LeSabre Est ($150). Interior Trim/Upholstery: 55/45 seating: LeSabre Custom/Est ($125). Leather/vinyl 50/50 seating: Park Ave. ($525). Third seat: Estate ($215). Front carpet savers ($17); rear ($12). Front carpet savers w/inserts ($25); rear ($20). Trunk carpeting trim ($53-$65). Trunk mat ($14). Wheels: Chrome-plated wheels ($180-$215). Styled aluminum wheels ($220-$255) exc. Electra Est ($40). Custom wheel covers: Electra Ltd ($35). Locking wire wheel covers ($150-$185); Electra Est ($30 credit). Tires: P215/75R15 SBR wide whitewall: LeSabre cpe/sed ($38). P225/75R15 SBR wide whitewall: Electra cpe/sed ($39). Self-sealing tires ($132).

RIVIERA CONVENIENCE/APPEARANCE OPTIONS: Comfort/Convenience: Electric sliding Astroroof: silver, gray or gold ($210). Automatic touch climate-control air cond. ($150). Digital electronic instrument cluster ($238). Six-way power seat, passenger ($210). Two position memory driver's seat ($178). Electric seatback recliner, one side ($139). Sport steering wheel ($40) exc. T Type, Tilt/telescope steering wheel ($55) exc. T Type. Electric fuel cap lock ($44). Electric trunk release ($40); lock ($80). Low fuel indicator ($16). Two-speed wipers w/delay ($49). Windshield washer fluid indicator ($16). Theft deterrent system ($159). Lighting, Horns and Mirrors: Tungsten-halogen high-beam headlamps ($22); std. on T Type. Twilight Sentinel headlamp control ($57). Coach lamps ($102); incl. w/vinyl top. Front/rear light monitors: T Type ($74). Rear quarter courtesy/reading lamp ($48). Lighted door lock and interior light control ($72). Four-note horn ($28). Dual electric remote mirrors ($65). Lighted visor vanity mirrors, each ($58). Entertainment: Full-feature electronic-tuning AM/FM stereo radio ($125); w/8-track tape player ($278). Basic electronic-tuning AM/FM stereo radio w/cassette player ($100). Electronic-tuning AM/FM stereo radio with cassette and graphic equalizer ($328); w/cassette, Dolby and Bose speaker system ($895) exc. conv. CB radio ($220). Delete radio ($230 credit). Rear speakers for base radio ($25). Concert Sound system ($95) exc. conv. Triband power antenna ($45); incl. w/CB. Exterior Trim: Heavy-padded landau vinyl top w/coach lamps ($325). Designers' accent paint ($235). Special color Firemist paint ($210); std. on conv. Color-coordinated protective bodyside moldings ($55). Door edge guards ($15). Bodyside stripe ($42). Interior Trim/Upholstery: 45/45 leather/vinyl front seat ($405) exc. conv. Front carpet savers w/inserts ($35); rear ($20). Trunk trim carpeting ($30). Trunk mat ($15). Wheels and Tires: Chrome-plated wheels ($145); on conv. ($40 credit). Custom locking wire wheel covers ($185). P225/70R15 SBR wide oval tires: BSW or WSW (NC).

HISTORY: Introduced: September 23, 1982. Model year production (U.S.): 808,415 for a 14.2 percent share of the industry total. That number included 143,725 four-cylinder Buicks, 416,810 sixes, and 247,880 V-8s--an intriguing jump in V-8 pro-

duction, accounted for only, in part, by rising overall production. A total of 10,680 diesels and 5,065 turbocharged engines were installed. Calendar year production (all U.S.): 905,608 Buicks. Model year sales by U.S. dealers: 810,435. Calendar year sales (U.S.): 845,083, besting the record set in 1978.

Historical Footnotes: Sales rose markedly for the 1983 model year, edging past the record set in 1979 and giving Buick a fourth-place ranking among U.S. automakers. Skyhawk sales more than doubled but the compact Skylark didn't fare quite so well. Buick couldn't quite secure a tight grip on the sought-after youth market. Well over three-fourths of Buicks sold were mid- or full-size, and the average buyer was determined to be 52 years old. Topping the chart was the Regal coupe, which outsold the Regal sedan 2-to-1. Century upped sales by some 90 percent over 1982. Corporate plans centered around a massive $300 million project, known as Buick City, to be built at Flint, Michigan. A complex of random existing plants, now 60 years old, would be turned into a streamlined operation, consolidating the activity of a trio of separate organizations. In January 1983 came an announcement that two rear-drive assembly plants would be consolidated into one, to build front-drive Buicks for 1986. This caused 3,600 workers to be permanently laid off. Once again, a Buick paced the Indy 500. This time is was a Riviera convertible with twin turbo 4.1-liter V-6 under the hood. Churning out 450 horsepower, it used many standard Buick heavy-duty parts. A new concept car called Questor was displayed at shows. Among its futuristic features were laser key entry, a map/navigation system, video rearview mirror, and road surface traction monitor. On a more mundane level, Buick was pilot testing a high technology videotex marketing system called Electronic Product Information Center at six dealerships. A video terminal and keyboard were linked by phone to Buick's own computer. The terminal displayed information in color and graphic form, and could be used to answer specific customer or salesman inquiries. With this system, dealerships could have constant access to the Buick central computer for up-to-date information.

1984

As in the industry generally, high-tech engines got the emphasis for 1984, along with modern electronics and aero styling. T Types were now offered on five Buick models which gained a performance boost. Two new 3.8-liter V-6s were introduced: one with multi-port fuel injection (optional on Century), the other with sequential fuel injection (standard on Regal/Riviera T Types). With multi-port injection (MFI), a computer analyzed air/fuel requirements and sent a charge to all six cylinders during each engine revolution. Sequential injection gave each cylinder a precisely-metered charge, just before firing, for best performance all the way from idle to full load. Both V-6 versions had been developed at Buick Special Products Engineering. An acceleration/deceleration feature on the new electronic cruise control allowed speed change in one mile per hour increments by touching a button on the lever. Cellular phones were offered for the first time, factory-approved but installed by dealers. 1984 Buick body colors were: beige, light sand gray, bright red, white and black, plus a selection of metallics: light brown, brown, light green, green, light blue, blue, red Firemist, red, dark red, sand gray Firemist, gold Firemist, and silver. Firemists cost extra.

SKYHAWK - SERIES 4J - FOUR - New front-end panels with bigger cooling slots went on all Skyhawks this year, along with new bumper rub strips and modified turn signal lamps. The aerodynamic design used a low hood and high deck for wedge-shaped profile. Skyhawk came in Custom and Limited trim as well as the sporty T Type, which expanded its color selection

to include silver, light maple and white bodies, with charcoal accents. Newly optional: an electronic radio with five-band graphic equalizer and four speakers. All Skyhawks had an AM radio and power brakes. T Types turned to P195/70R13 tires on styled aluminum wheels and had dual mirrors (left remote-controlled), Gran Touring suspension, and a sport steering wheel. Apart from the T Type, the Chevrolet-built 121 cu. in. (2.0-liter) four remained standard, with four-speed gearbox; a 1.8 four from Brazil was again optional. Shortly after production began, a turbocharged version of the 1.8-liter overhead-cam four became available (at extra cost) on the Skyhawk T Type, with multi-port fuel injection. Horsepower shot up to 150: torque to 150 pound-feet. Included with that turbo engine was a Level III suspension system, with 205/60 series Eagle GT tires on 14 inch, forged aluminum wheels. Standard T type powerplant remained the normally-aspirated 1.8 four, with five-speed manual gearbox. Turbos came with four-speed manual. All three engines could have three-speed automatic transmission instead.

1984 Buick, Skylark T Type coupe. (OCW)

SKYLARK - SERIES 4X - FOUR/V-6 - Aside from a distinctive new (notably Buick) grille, the X-bodied Buick didn't change much for '84. One new option on either coupe or sedan: a decklid luggage rack. Electronic cruise control was also available. T Type coupes now had an electronic LED tachometer. As before, the 151 cu. in. (2.5-liter) four was standard; a 173 cu. in. (2.8-liter) V-6 optional, with a more powerful version standard in the T Type and optional on other models. Overdrive automatic transmissions were now available in the similar-size A-cars, but not in X models. Standard equipment included an AM radio, power steering, four-speed manual gearbox, notchback bench seat with adjustable headrests, roof drip and window moldings, glovebox lock, cigarette lighter, compact spare, and P185/80R13 steel belted radial tires. Skylark Limited also came with belt reveal and wheel-opening moldings, a hood ornament, wide rocker panel and rear quarter moldings, protective bumper rub strips, and a pillar appliqué on sedans. T Types added a tachometer, gauges, halogen headlamps, Rallye ride/handling suspension, specially styled sport aluminum wheels with P215/60R14 steel belted radials, black sport mirrors, and a sport steering wheel. The sporty Skylarks also had a blacked-out grille; black anodized aluminum bumpers; smoked taillamp lenses; and styled black mirrors. T bodies came in silver, light maple or white with charcoal accent.

CENTURY - SERIES 4A - FOUR/V-6 - All Century models displayed a new grille, headlamp bezels, bumper rub strips and standard wheel covers, along with new graphics at front and rear. Coupes and sedans added a new rear end and taillamps plus a modified back bumper. A new three-passenger front seat gave the Custom space for six. Century offered two new wagons for 1984: Custom and Estate, each with a unique one-piece top-hinged tailgate. Both had a split-folding back seat and separate lift-up rear window with available washer/wiper. They replaced the old Regal rear-drive wagon, which dropped out this season. Carrying six passengers in normal trim, they could have a rear-facing third seat that held two more. Wagons could hold over 74 cubic feet of cargo. Century Customs came with a standard AM radio, power brakes and steering, three-speed automatic

transmission, bumper guards and rub strips, dual horns, locking glove box, side window defogger, storage console, and full carpeting. The Limited added 55/45 cloth seating, a hood ornament, and wide lower bodyside moldings. Among other sporty extras, T Types included dual exhaust, temp/volt gauges, a blacked-out grille, styled black mirrors, black moldings, charcoal lower accent paint and striping, Gran Touring suspension, cloth bucket seats, and styled aluminum wheels. T Type dashes carried a new ribbon-type LED tachometer, and could be equipped with a special Lear Siegler bucket interior. Base Century engine remained the 2.5-liter four with throttle-body fuel injection, rated at 90 horsepower. Options included a carbureted 3.0-liter V-6 and a diesel V-6. Most notable, though, was the new fuel-injected 231 cu. in. (3.8-liter) V-6, standard in T Type and optional elsewhere, available with four-speed overdrive automatic transmission. On the special edition roster, to complement Buick's role as official car and sponsor of the games of the 23rd Olympiad in Los Angeles, there was a Century Olympia Limited sedan. Offered in white with "subtly classic" U.S. Olympic identification on front fenders, decklid and hood ornament, the sedan was accented with gold body stripes and gold aluminum wheels. It had a decklid luggage rack, and the headrest on the tan cloth interior was embroidered with the official U.S. Olympic logo in dark brown.

1984 Buick, Regal coupe with optional Grand National package. (OCW)

REGAL - SERIES 4G - V-6 - Continuing for another season in rear-drive form, Regal dropped its station wagon this year. The diesel V-8 also disappeared, but a 4.3 liter V-6 diesel remained as an option. Regals showed a new grille and front end design, along with new graphics and taillamps, and a modified instrument panel. Coupes added new headlamp bezels and park/signal lamps. Joining the option list: a digital instrument cluster similar to Riviera's, with fluorescent displays that showed speed, distance and fuel level. Standard equipment included dual mirrors and horns, automatic transmission, power brakes and steering, bumper guards and rub strips, and whitewall P195/75R14 steel-belted tires. T Type tires were P215/65R15 blackwalls, on styled aluminum wheels. Limiteds carried a 55/45 notchback seat, along with wide rocker panel and rear quarter moldings. All engines except the base 231 cu. in. (3.8-liter) V-6 could have four-speed overdrive automatic transmission (standard in T Type) for $175 more. Regal's high-performance T Type had the new 3.8-liter V-6 with turbocharger and sequential port fuel injection, which produced 200 horsepower and 300 pound-feet of torque. Distributorless ignition on the turbo used three computer-controlled ignition coils to send current to the spark plugs. T Types came with a 3.42:1 performance axle ratio, overdrive automatic transmission, Gran Touring suspension, leather-wrapped steering wheel, turbo boost gauge, trip odometer, tachometer, and air conditioning. Buick's display of turbo technology at auto shows during 1984 was highlighted later in the model year by the emergence of the '84 Regal Grand National "produced in limited numbers for those who demand a high level of performance." Its purpose: to give much of the feeling of a NASCAR race car. Though officially on the option list, carrying a relatively moderate $1,282 price tag, not many Grand National packages found their way onto T Type Regals in 1984. Grand Nationals carried the turbo 3.8 engine, P215/60R

blackwalls, sport steering wheel, tachometer and boost gauge, and 94-amp Delcotron. Distinctive bodies came only in black, with black bumpers, rub strips and guards; black front air dam and decklid spoiler; black headlamp bezels; turbo aluminum wheels with black paint; and Grand National identification on front fenders. A Lear Siegler interior held front seats embroidered with the Grand National logo.

1984 Buick, LeSabre Custom sedan with optional vinyl top and wire wheel covers. (OCW)

LESABRE - SERIES 4B - V-6/V-8 - Not much of substance changed this year on the rear-drive LeSabre, but a different grille and front-end panel gave a fresh look. Rear-end styling was also reworked, including new taillamps. New standard equipment included remote left (manual right) mirrors on all models and a redesigned steering wheel. Optional automatic touch climate control system was revised to give more precise temperature settings and control of fan speed. Standard under the hood was the familiar 231 cu. in. (3.8-liter) V-6, with 4.1-liter V-6 or 5.0-liter V-8 optional. So was the 5.7-liter diesel V-8, but not in California where it couldn't meet emissions standards. All LeSabres had color-keyed bodyside moldings, front and rear protective bumper strips, and bumper guards. Standard equipment also included dual horns, deluxe wheel covers, cut-pile carpeting, three-speed automatic transmission, power steering and brakes. LeSabre Limited added a two-way adjustable power driver's seat, headlamps-on indicator and warning chime, tinted glass, custom steering wheel, and woodgrain door trim. Limited instrument panels offered electroluminiscent floodlighting. LeSabre Custom had standard notchback seats in cloth velour with woven fabric trim; Limited cloth seats were in 55/45 arrangement.

ELECTRA ESTATE WAGON - SERIES 4D - V-8 - For '84, the LeSabre Estate Wagon was dropped, so Electra's became the last remaining Buick full-size wagon. Base engine was again the 307 cu. in. (5.0-liter) V-8, with only the 350 diesel V-8 optional. Standard 55/45 notchback seating had two-way power for the driver's side. In back, buyers could have the same cloth-covered seating as in front, or easy-to-clean vinyl. Standard equipment also included a tilt steering column, digital clock, electric door locks, power windows, remote tailgate lock, air conditioning, Soft Ray tinted glass, door edge guards, light oak woodgrain vinyl appliqué, and a luggage rack.

ELECTRA - SERIES 4D - V-6/V-8 - Since a totally new front-drive Electra was expected soon (and arrived in the spring as an early '85), the old rear-drive carried on unchanged. The new compact Electra was scheduled to arrive earlier, but mechanical and assembly difficulties held back its debut. When it finally appeared, it cut sharply into sales of its larger predecessor-- even though the rear-drive had earned some popularity lately. Base engine was the 252 cu. in. (4.1-liter) V-6, with 5.0-liter gas V-8 and 5.7 diesel available. Electra Limited carried standard equipment similar to LeSabre including a remote-controlled left outside mirror, along with 55/45 cloth notchback seating, air conditioning, digital clock, power windows, and P215/75R15 whitewalls. Park Avenue buyers got 50/50 seats (power on driver's side), a tilt steering wheel, power door locks, electronic-tuning stereo radio, reading light, remote trunk release, and power remote left mirror.

RIVIERA - SERIES 4E - V-6/V-8 - Accompanying the new turbo-charged 231 cu. in. (3.8-liter) V-6 engine on Riviera's T Type for

'84 were a new standard turbo boost gauge and LED tachometer, leather-wrapped sport steering wheel, styled black mirrors and new accent stripes. All Rivs got a new grille and front end panel, plus modified taillamp styling. Coupes (including T Type) now carried a front bench seat that held three people, while the convertible kept its bucket seats up front. Convertible tops held a new cloth headliner, while an electric defogger for the glass back window was optional. As before, the convertible was specially modified by American Sunroof Corp. Standard Riv powertrain was the 252 cu. in. (4.1-liter) four-barrel V-6 with four-speed overdrive automatic; or optional 5.0-liter carbureted V-8, GM's 5.7-liter diesel V-8 was now offered as a Riviera option for the first time (except in California). Base Rivs had whitewall tires, power brakes and steering, a notchback 55/45 front seat, power windows, tinted glass, an AM/FM electronically-tuned stereo with automatic power antenna and clock, electric door locks, power six-way driver's seat, cruise control, automatic level control, air conditioning, and P205/75R15 steel-belted radial tires. Tungsten-halogen headlamps, styled aluminum wheels, blacked-out grille and Gran Touring suspension were T Type standards. Riviera convertibles had Firemist paint and four-wheel disc brakes, plus custom locking wire wheel covers and trunk carpeting. On the option list (except for convertibles): a high end Delco/Bose music system.

I.D. DATA: Buicks again had a 17-symbol Vehicle Identification Number (VIN), stamped on a metal tag attached to the upper left surface of the cowl, visible through the windshield. Coding was similar to 1983. LeSabre Estate (series code 'R') was dropped, and the code for Electra Park Ave. changed from 'W' to 'U'. Two engine codes were added: 'J' turbo L4-110 MFI and '3' V6-231 MFI. The code for turbocharged V6-231 (now with SFI) changed to '9'. Model year symbol changed to 'E' for 1984. Symbol eleven (plant code) was as follows: 'W' Willow Run, MI; '6' Oklahoma City, OK; 'H' Flint, MI; 'K' Leeds, MO; 'X' Fairfax, KS; 'E' Linden, NJ; and 'D' Doraville. The final six digits are the sequential serial number, starting with 400001 except for LeSabres built in Flint, which began with 800001.

SKYHAWK CUSTOM (FOUR)

Model No.	Body/Style No.	Body Type & Seating	Factory Price	Shipping Weight	Prod. Total
4J	S27	2-dr Coupe-5P	7133	2316	74,760
4J	S69	4-dr Sedan-5P	7345	2369	45,648
4J	S35	4-dr Sta Wag-5P	7677	2439	13,668

SKYHAWK LIMITED (FOUR)

4J	T27	2-dr Coupe-5P	7641	2356	Note 1
4J	T69	4-dr Sedan-5P	7837	2404	Note 1
4J	T35	4-dr Sta Wag-5P	8127	2469	Note 1

Note 1: Skyhawk Custom production figures also include equivalent Limited models. Coupe/sedan production came to 97,962 Customs and 22,446 Limiteds.

SKYHAWK T TYPE (FOUR)

4J	E27	2-dr Coupe-5P	8152	2332	11,317

SKYLARK CUSTOM (FOUR/V-6)

4X	B37	2-dr Coupe-5P	7545/7795	2458/2519	12,377
4X	B69	4-dr Sedan 5P	7707/7957	2489/2550	56,495

SKYLARK LIMITED (FOUR/V-6)

4X	C37	2-dr Coupe-5P	8119/8369	2484/2545	7,621
4X	C69	4-dr Sedan-5P	8283/8533	2515/2576	33,795

SKYLARK T TYPE (V-6)

4X	D37	2-dr Coupe-5P	9557	2606	923

1984 Buick, Century sedan with optional Olympia package. (OCW)

1984 Buick, Century Estate Wagon station wagon. (OCW)

CENTURY CUSTOM (FOUR/V-6)

Model No.	Body/Style No.	Body Type & Seating	Factory Price	Shipping Weight	Prod. Total
4A	H27	2-dr Coupe-6P	9110/9360	2609/2714	15,429
4A	H19	4-dr Sedan-6P	9274/9524	2658/2763	178,454
4A	H35	4-dr Sta Wag-6P	9660/9910	2825/2930	25,975

CENTURY LIMITED (FOUR/V-6)

4A	L27	2-dr Coupe-6P	9562/9812	2631/2736	Note 2
4A	L19	4-dr Sedan-6P	9729/9979	2679/2784	Note 2
4A	L35	4-dr Sta Wag-6P	10087/10337	2843/2948	Note 2

CENTURY T TYPE (V-6)

4A	G27	2-dr Coupe-5P	10510	2775	Note 2
4A	G19	4-dr Sedan-5P	10674	2823	Note 2

Note 2: Production figures listed under Century Custom include totals for Century Limited and T Type models. In all, 71,160 Customs, 119,246 Limiteds and 3,477 Century T Types were manufactured.

REGAL (V-6)

4G	J47	2-dr Coupe-6P	9487	3079	160,638
4G	J69	4-dr Sedan-6P	9671	3125	58,715

REGAL LIMITED (V-6)

4G	M47	2-dr Coupe-6P	10125	3106	Note 3
4G	M69	4-dr Sedan-6P	10263	3125	Note 3

Note 3: Base Regal production totals also include Limited models. Total model year production, 106,306 base Regals and 113,047 Limiteds.

REGAL T TYPE (V-6)

4G	K47	2-dr Coupe-6P	12118	3249	5,401

LESABRE CUSTOM (V-6/V-8)

4B	N37	2-dr Coupe-6P	9984/10534	3472/3663	3,890
4B	N69	4-dr Sedan-6P	10129/10679	3484/3675	36,072

LESABRE LIMITED (V-6/V-8)

4B	P37	2-dr Coupe-6P	10780/11330	3497/3688	28,332
4B	P69	4-dr Sedan-6P	10940/11490	3530/3721	86,418

ELECTRA LIMITED (V-6/V-8)

4D	R37	2-dr Coupe-6P	13155/13380	3656/3835	4,075
4D	R69	4-dr Sedan-6P	13332/13557	3716/3895	52,551

ELECTRA PARK AVENUE (V-6/V-8)

4D	U37	2-dr Coupe-6P	14888/15113	3700/3879	Note 4
4D	U69	4-dr Sedan-6P	15044/15269	3766/3945	Note 4

Note 4: Park Avenue production totals are included in Electra Limited figures.

ELECTRA ESTATE WAGON (V-8)

4B	V35	4-dr Sta Wag-6P	14483	4160	17,563

RIVIERA (V-6/V-8)

4E	Z57	2-dr Coupe-5P	15967/16192	3574/3748	56,210
4E	Z67	2-dr Conv-5P	25832/26057	3680/3854	500

Note 5: Only 1,424 standard Riviera coupes and 58 convertibles had a V-6 engine this year.

RIVIERA T TYPE (V-6)

4E	Y57	2-dr Coupe-5P	17050	3660	1,153

FACTORY PRICE AND WEIGHT NOTE: Figure before the slash is for four-cylinder engine, after the slash for V-6. For full-size models, figure before slash is for V-6 engine, after slash for V-8.

ENGINES: BASE FOUR-CYLINDER (Skyhawk): Inline, overhead-valve four-cylinder. Cast iron block and head. Displacement: 121 cu. in. (2.0 liters). Bore & stroke: 3.50 x 3.15 in. Compression ratio: 9.3:1. Brake horsepower: 86 at 4900 R.P.M. Torque: 100 lb.-ft. at 3000 R.P.M. Five main bearings. Hydraulic valve lifters. Throttle-body fuel injection. VIN Code: P. OPTIONAL FOUR (Skyhawk); STANDARD (Skyhawk T Type): Inline, overhead cam four-cylinder. Cast iron block; aluminum cylinder head. Displacement: 110 cu. in. (1.8 liters). Bore & stroke: 3.34 x 3.13

in. Compression ratio: 9.0:1. Brake horsepower: 84 at 5200 R.P.M. Torque: 102 lb.-ft. at 2800 R.P.M. Five main bearings. Hydraulic valve lifters. Throttle-body fuel injection. VIN Code: 0. TURBOCHARGED FOUR (Skyhawk T Type): Same as 1.8-liter OHC four above, except--Compression ratio: 8.0:1. Brake H.P.: 150 at 5600 R.P.M. Torque: 150 lb.-ft. at 2800 R.P.M. Multi-point fuel injection. VIN Code: J. BASE FOUR (Skylark, Century): In-line, overhead-valve four-cylinder. Cast iron block and head. Displacement: 151 cu. in. (2.5-liters). Bore & stroke: 4.0 x 3.0 in. Compression ratio: 9.0:1. Brake horsepower: 92 at 4400 R.P.M. Torque: 132 lb.-ft. at 2800 R.P.M. Five main bearings. Hydraulic valve lifters. Throttle-body fuel injection. Built by Pontiac. VIN Code: R. OPTIONAL V-6 (Skylark): 60-degree, overhead-valve V-6. Cast iron block and head. Displacement: 173 cu. in. (2.8-liters). Bore & stroke: 3.50 x 2.99 in. Compression: 8.4:1. Brake horsepower: 112 at 5100 R.P.M. Torque: 148 lb.-ft. at 2400 R.P.M. Four main bearings. Hydraulic valve lifters. Carburetor: 2Bbl. Rochester. Built by Chevrolet. VIN Code: X. HIGH-OUT-PUT V-6; (Skylark T Type): OPTIONAL (Skylark); STANDARD (Skylark T): Same as 173 cu. in. V-6 above except as follows: Compression ratio: 8.94:1. Brake horsepower: 135 at 5400 R.P.M. Torque: 145 lb.-ft. at 2400 R.P.M. VIN Code: Z. OPTION-AL V-6 (Century); 90-degree, overhead-valve V-6. Cast iron block and head. Displacement: 181 cu. in. (3.0-liters). Bore & stroke: 3.8 x 2.66 in. Compression ratio: 8.45:1. Brake horsepower: 110 at 4800 R.P.M. Torque: 145 lb.-ft. at 2600 R.P.M. Four main bearings. Hydraulic valve lifters. Carburetor: 2Bbl. Rochester E2SE. VIN Code: E. BASE V-6 (Regal LeSabre): 90-degree, overhead-valve V-6. Cast iron alloy block and head. Displacement: 231 cu. in. (3.8-liters). Bore & stroke: 3.8 x 3.4 in. Compression ratio: 8.0:1. Brake horsepower: 110 at 3800 R.P.M. Torque: 190 lb.-ft. at 1600 R.P.M. Four main bearings. Hydraulic valve lifters. Carburetor: 2Bbl. Rochester 2ME. VIN Code A. Base V-6 (Century T Type): OPTIONAL (Century): Same as 231 V-6 above, but with multi-point fuel injection. Compression ratio: 8.0:1. Brake H.P.: 125 at 4400 R.P.M. Torque: 195 lb.-ft. at 2000 R.P.M. VIN Code: 3. TURBOCHARGED V-6 (Regal T Type); Same as 231 V-6 above, with turbocharger; switched from four-barrel carburetor to sequential fuel injection. Brake H.P.: 200 at 4000 R.P.M. Torque: 300 lb.-ft. at 2400 R.P.M. TURBOCHARGED V-6 (Riv-iera T Type): Same as turbo 231 V-6 above, with sequential fuel injection. Brake H.P.: 190 at 4000 R.P.M. VIN Code: 9. BASE V-6 (Electra, Riviera); OPTIONAL (Regal, LeSabre): 90-degree, overhead-valve V-6. Cast iron alloy block and head. Displace-ment: 252 cu. in. (4.1 liters). Bore & stroke: 3.965 x 3.4 in. Com-pression ratio: 8.0:1. Brake horsepower: 125 at 4000 R.P.M. Torque: 205 lb.-ft. at 2000 R.P.M. Four main bearings. Hydraulic valve lifters. Carburetor: 4Bbl. Rochester. VIN Code: 4. DIESEL V-6; OPTIONAL (Century, Regal): 90-degree, overhead-valve V-6. Cast iron block: cast iron or aluminum head. Displacement: 262.5 cu. in. (4.3-liters). Bore & stroke: 4.057 x 3.385 in. Com-pression ratio: 21.6:1. Brake horsepower: 85 at 3600 R.P.M. Torque: 165 lb.-ft. at 1600 R.P.M. Four main bearings. Hydraulic valve lifters. Fuel injection. VIN Code: V. BASE V-8 (Estate): OP-TIONAL (LeSabre, Electra, Riviera): 90-degree, overhead valve V-8. Cast iron block and head. Displacement: 307 cu. in. (5.0-liters). Bore & stroke: 3.80 x 3.385 in. Compression ratio: 8.0:1. Brake horsepower: 140 at 3600 R.P.M. Torque: 240 lb.-ft. at 1600 R.P.M. Five main bearings. Hydraulic valve lifters. Carburetor: 4Bbl. Rochester M4ME. Built by Oldsmobile. VIN Code: Y. OP-TIONAL DIESEL V-8 (LeSabre, Estate, Riviera): 90-degree, overhead valve V-8. Cast iron block and head. Displacement: 350 cu. in. (5.7-liters). Bore & stroke: 4.057 x 3.385 in. Compres-sion ratio: 21.6:1. Brake horsepower: 105 at 3200 R.P.M. Torque: 200 lb.-ft. at 1600 R.P.M. Five main bearings. Hydraulic valve lifters. Fuel injection. Oldsmobile-built. VIN Code: N.

CHASSIS DATA: Wheelbase: (Skyhawk) 101.2 in.; (Sky-lark/Century) 104.9 in.; (Regal) 108.1 in.; (LeSabre/Estate) 115.9 in.; (Electra) 118.9 in.; (Riviera) 114.0 in. Overall length: (Skyhawk cpe) 171.3 in.; (Skyhawk wag) 173.3 in.; (Skylark)

181.1 in.; (Century) 189.1 in.; (Century wag) 190.9 in.; (Regal cpe) 200.6 in.; (Regal sed) 196.0 in.; (LeSabre) 218.4 in.; (Elec-tra/Estate) 221.3 in.; (Riviera) 206.6 in. Height: (Skyhawk) 53.4-53.6 in.; (Skylark/Century) 53.6 in.; (Century wag) 54.1 in.; (Re-gal cpe) 54.6 in.; (Regal sed) 55.5 in.; (LeSabre/Electra cpe) 56.0 in.; (LeSabre/Electra sed) 56.7-56.9 in.; (Estate) 59.1 in.; (Riv) 54.3 in. Width: (Skyhawk) 65.0 in.; (Skylark) 69.1 in.; (Cen-tury) 66.8 in.; (Century wag) 69.4 in.; (Regal cpe) 71.6 in.; (Regal sed) 71.1 in.; (LeSabre) 78.0 in.; (Electra/Estate) 76.2 in.; (Riv) 72.8 in. Front Tread: (Skyhawk) 55.3 in.; (Skylark/Century) 58.7 in.; (Regal) 58.5 in.; (LeSabre/Electra/Est) 61.8 in.; (Riv) 59.3 in. Rear Tread: (Skyhawk) 55.1 in.; (Skylark) 57.0 in.; (Century) 56.7 in.; (Regal) 57.7-57.8 in.; (LeSabre/Electra/Est) 60.7 in.; (Riviera) 60.0 in. Standard Tires: (Skyhawk) P175/80R13 GBR; (Skylark/Century) P185/80R13 GBR; (Skylark T Type) P205/70R13 SBR; (Regal) P195/75R14 SBR WSW; (Regal T Type) P205/70R14 SBR; (LeSabre) P205/75R15 SBR WSW; (Electra) P215/75R15 SBR WSW; (Estate) P225/75R15 SBR WSW; (Riviera) P205/75R15 SBR WSW.

TECHNICAL: Transmission: Four-speed, fully synchronized floor shift standard on Skyhawk/Skylark; automatic optional (standard on all other models). Five-speed standard on Sky-hawk T Type. Four-speed gear ratios: (1st) 3.53:1; (2nd) 1.95:1; (3rd) 1.24:1; (4th) 0.81:1 or 0.73:1; (Rev) 3.42:1. Skylark H.O. four-speed: (1st) 3.31:1; (2nd) 1.95:1; (3rd) 1.24:1; (4th) 0.81:1; (Rev) 3.42:1. Five-speed gear ratios: (1st) 3.91:1; (2nd) 2.15:1; (3rd) 1.45:1; (4th) 1.03:1; (5th) 0.74:1; (Rev) 3.50:1. Three-speed auto. trans. gear ratios: (1st) 2.74:1; (2nd) 1.57:1; (3rd) 1.00:1; (Rev) 2.07:1. Skyhawk/Skylark auto. trans. gear ratios: (1st) 2.84:1; (2nd) 1.60:1; (3rd) 1.00:1; (Rev) 2.07:1. Four-speed overdrive automatic gear ratios: (1st) 2.74:1; (2nd) 1.57:1; (3rd) 1.00:1; (4th) 0.67:1; (Rev) 2.07:1. Century four-speed automatic: (1st) 2.92:1; (2nd) 1.57:1; (3rd) 1.00:1; (4th) 0.70:1; (Rev) 2.38:1. Standard axle ratio: (Skyhawk) 2.84:1 or 3.06:1 w/4-spd, 3.45:1 w/5-spd, 3.18:1 w/auto; (Skyhawk turbo) 3.65:1 w/4-spd, 3.33:1 w/auto.: (Skylark) 3.32:1 or 3.65:1 w/4-spd, 2.39:1 or 2.53:1 w/auto., 3.23:1 w/H.O. V-6 and auto; (Cen-tury) 2.39:1 or 2.53:1 w/3-spd, 2.84:1 or 3.06:1 w/4-spd: (Cen-tury wag) 2.84:1, 2.97:1 or 3.06:1; (Regal) 2.41:1 w/3-spd, 3.08:1 w/4-spd exc. diesel 2.93:1; (Regal T Type) 3.42:1; (Le-Sabre/Electra) 2.73:1 w/3-spd; 2.73:1, 2.93:1 or 3.23:1 w/4-spd; (Riviera) 2.73:1, 2.93:1 or 3.36:1; (Riv turbo) 3.36:1. Steering: (Skyhawk/Skylark/Century) rack and pinion; (others) recirculat-ing ball; power assist standard on all except Skyhawk. Suspen-sion: front/rear coil springs. (Skyhawk) MacPherson strut front; semi independent beam rear axle w/trailing arms; stabilizer bar on T Type. (Skylark/Century) MacPherson strut front suspen-sion; beam twist rear axle w/trailing arms and Panhard rod; front/rear stabilizer bars. (Riviera) fully independent suspension with front torsion bars, semi-trailing arms at rear, front/rear sta-bilizers and automatic level control. (Rear-drive models) front stabilizer bar; rear stabilizer bar on T Type; rigid four-link rear axle. Brakes: power front disc, rear drum. Four-wheel power disc brakes available on Riviera (std. on conv.). Body construc-tion: (Skyhawk/Skylark/Century) unitized; (others) separate body and frame. Fuel tank: (Skyhawk) 13.6 gal.; (Skylark 2-dr) 14.6 gal.; (Skylark 4-dr) 15.1 gal.; (Century) 15.7 gal.; (Regal) 18.1 gal.; (LeSabre/Electra) 26.0 gal.; (Estate) 22.0 gal.; (Rivi-era) 21.1 gal. Unleaded fuel only.

DRIVETRAIN OPTIONS: Engines: 110 cu. in. (1.8-liter) EFI four: Skyhawk ($50). Turbocharged 110 cu. in. (1.8-liter) MFI four: Sky-hawk T Type ($800). 173 cu. in. (2.8-liter) V-6 2Bbl: Skylark ($250). High-output 173 cu. in. (2.8-liter) V-6, 2Bbl. Skylark ($400): std. on T Type. 181 cu. in. (3.0-liter) V-6, 2Bbl.: Century ($250). Turbocharged 231 cu. in. (3.8-liter) V-6: Riviera conv. ($900). 252 cu. in. (4.1-liter) V-6, 4Bbl.: Regal/LeSabre ($225). 263 cu. in. (4.3-liter) diesel V-6: Century/Regal Cust/Ltd ($599). 307 cu. in. (5.0-liter) V-8, 4Bbl.: LeSabre ($375); Electra cpe/sed, Riviera ($225). 350 cu. in. (5.7-liter) diesel V-8: LeSabre/Es-tate/Riviera ($799). Transmission/Differential: Four-speed man-

ual trans.: Skyhawk T ($75 credit). Five-speed manual trans.: Skyhawk ($75). Automatic trans.: Skyhawk ($395): Skyhawk T Type ($320); Skylark ($425). Automatic overdrive trans.: Century (N/A); Regal/LeSabre ($175). Optional rear axle ratio: Skyhawk 3.43:1 (NC); Skylark 2.84:1 or 3.65:1: Century 2.84:1 or 2.97:1: Regal/LeSabre/Electra 3.08:1 or 3.23:1 (NC). Limited slip differential: Regal/LeSabre/Electra ($95). Suspension, Steering and Brakes: F40 Firm ride/handling pkg. ($27). F41 Gran Touring suspension: Skyhawk ($196); Skylark ($207); Century Cust/Ltd cpe/sed, LeSabre, Riviera ($27); Regal/Ltd, LeSabre ($49). Superlift rear shock absorbers: Skylark Cust/Ltd ($68). Automatic level control: Century/Regal/LeSabre/Electra ($175). Power steering: Skyhawk ($204). Four-wheel disc brakes: Riviera ($235). Other: Trailer towing pkg.: LeSabre ($128). Heavy-duty alternator: Skyhawk/Regal/LeSabre/Electra 85-amp ($35 or $85); 94-amp ($35 or $85) exc. Skylark: Skylark 99-amp ($35 or $85); Century/Riv 108-amp ($40). H.D. battery: ($26); diesel ($52). H.D. radiator: Skyhawk ($40-$70). H.D. cooling: Skylark ($40-$70): Engine block heater ($18). H.D. engine/transmission cooling: Century/Regal/LeSabre/Electra/Riviera ($40-$70). California emission system ($99).

1984 Buick, Skyhawk T Type coupe. (OCW)

SKYHAWK CONVENIENCE/APPEARANCE OPTIONS: Option Packages: Vista Vent flip-open removable glass sunroof ($300). Instrument gauge pkg.: temp, oil pressure, volts, trip odometer: Cust ($60). Gauges and tach: Cust ($138); Ltd ($78). Acoustic pkg. ($36); std. on Ltd Comfort/Convenience: Air cond. ($630). Touch climate control air cond. ($780). Rear defogger, electric ($130). Electronic cruise control w/resume ($175). Power windows ($185-$260). Electric door locks ($125-$175). Six-way power driver's seat ($215). Easy-entry passenger seat adjuster: Cust cpe ($16). Tinted glass ($95). Sport steering wheel: Cust/Ltd ($50). Leather-wrapped steering wheel: T Type ($40). Tilt steering ($104). Trip odometer: Cust ($15). Electric clock ($35). Electric trunk release ($40). Remote tailgate lock: wag ($40). Tailgate wiper/washer: wag ($120). Two-speed wipers w/delay ($50). Lights, Horns and Mirrors: Tungsten-halogen headlamps ($22). Headlamps-on indicator ($15). Dome reading lamp ($30). Dual horns: Cust cpe/sed ($15). Left remote mirror: Cust/Ltd ($22). Dual mirrors: left remote ($53). Dual electric remote mirrors ($139). T ($86). Visor vanity mirror, passenger ($7). Lighted visor vanity mirror, either side ($45). Entertainment: Basic electronic tuning AM/FM stereo radio ($138); w/clock ($177); w/cassette ($277). Electronic-tuning AM/FM stereo radio ($302); w/cassette and graphic equalizer ($505). Radio delete ($56 credit). Power antenna ($60). Dual rear speakers ($25-$30); incl. w/radios. Exterior Trim: Door edge guards ($15-$25); Rocker panel moldings: Cust cpe/sed ($26). Bodyside stripes ($42). Designers' accent paint ($195). Decklid luggage rack ($100). Roof rack: wag ($105). Interior Trim/Upholstery: Suede bucket seats: Ltd cpe/sed ($295). Front carpet savers ($17); rear ($12). Front carpet savers w/inserts ($18); rear ($15). Deluxe trunk trim ($33). Security cover: wag ($69). Wheels and Tires: Styled aluminum wheels ($229). Styled wheel covers w/trim rings ($38). Locking wire wheel covers ($170). P175/80R13 GBR WSW ($54). P195/70R13 SBR BSW ($169). P195/70R13 SBR WSW or wide WSW ($62-$231). P195/70R13 SBR WLT ($84-$253) P205/60R14 SBR WLT: T Type ($94-$182). Self-sealing tires ($106).

SKYLARK/CENTURY CONVENIENCE/APPEARANCE OPTIONS: Option Packages: Century Olympia Sedan pkg. (white body w/gold bodyside stripe, gold-accented aluminum wheels, decklid luggage rack, brown cloth seats with Olympic logo on headrests): Ltd sed ($406). Acoustic pkg.: Skylark Cust ($60). Flip-open Vista Vent glass sunroof ($300). Lamp group: Skylark Cust ($32-$42). Comfort/Convenience: Air cond. ($730). Cruise control ($175). Rear defogger, electric ($135-$140). Power windows ($185-$260). Electric door locks ($125-$175). Six-way power driver's seat ($215). Manual seatback recliners, passenger ($45); both ($90). Sport steering wheel ($50). Leather-wrapped steering wheel: Skylark T ($40). Tilt steering ($110). Tinted glass ($110). Instrument gauges incl. trip odometer ($48). Tachometer: Skylark Cust/Ltd ($78). Trip odometer: Skylark Cust/Ltd ($16). Digital electronic instrument cluster: Century ($205-$299). Dial clock ($35). Electric trunk release ($40). Remote tailgate lock: Century wag ($40). Tailgate washer/wiper: Century wag ($120). Two-speed wipers with delay ($49-$50). Theft deterrent system: Century ($159). Lights, Horns and Mirrors: Tungsten-halogen headlamps: Skylark Cust ($10); Century ($22). Twilight Sentinel: Century ($57). Front light monitors: Century ($37). Coach lamps: Ltd ($102-$129). Headlamps-on indicator ($16). Door courtesy/warning light: Century Ltd wag ($44). Dome reading light ($24). Rear seat reading lamp: Skylark Ltd Century Cust ($30). Dual horns: Skylark Cust ($15). Remote-control left mirror: Cust/Ltd ($25). Sport mirrors (left remote, right manual): Cust/Ltd ($61). Dual electric remote mirrors: Cust/Ltd ($39); T Type ($78). Visor vanity mirror, passenger ($7). Lighted visor vanity mirror, passenger: Skylark ($58); either side, Century ($58). Entertainment: Same as Skyhawk (above). Exterior Trim: Landau vinyl top for Cust/Ltd cpe: Skylark ($220); Century ($186). Long vinyl top: Cust/Ltd ($160). Designers' accent paint: Cust/Ltd ($205-$210). Special solid color paint: Century Cust/Ltd ($200). Protective bodyside moldings ($55); color-coordinated on Century. Lower wide bodyside moldings: Century Cust ($65). Rocker panel moldings: Skylark Cust ($26). Wide rocker panel/rear quarter moldings: Skylark Cust ($91). Belt reveal molding: Skylark Cust, T Type ($40). Wheel opening moldings: Skylark Cust ($30). Door edge guards ($15-$22). Pillar appliqué moldings: Skylark Cust sed ($27). Hood ornament and windsplit: Cust ($22-$32). Bodyside stripe: Cust/Ltd ($45). Bumper guards, front/rear: Skylark ($45). Bumper strips, front/rear: Skylark Cust ($49). Front license plate mounting: Skylark (NC). Decklid luggage rack: Century ($100). Roof rack: Century wag ($105). Swing-out rear quarter vent windows: Century wag ($75). Woodgrain vinyl appliqué: Century wag ($350). Tailgate air deflector: Century wag ($37). Interior Trim/Upholstery: Full-length console: Century ($57). Full-length operating console: Century ($80); T Type ($23). Bucket seats: Skylark Cust ($140); Skylark Ltd ($95); Century Cust ($97). 55/45 cloth seat trim: Century Cust ($133). Notchback bench seating w/armrest, cloth or vinyl: Skylark Cust ($45). Lear Siegler bucket seats: Century T type ($600). 45/45 seating: cloth, Century Ltd/Estate (NC); leather/vinyl ($295). Third seat: Century wag ($215). Front carpet savers ($17); rear ($12). Carpet savers w/inserts: front ($25); rear ($20). Trunk trim ($25-$47). Wheels: Styled aluminum wheels: Century ($195); std. on T Type. Chrome-plated wheels: Skylark Cust/Ltd ($175). Locking wire wheel covers: Cust/Ltd ($175-$190). Skylark Tires: P185/80R13 SBR WSW: Cust/Ltd ($58). P205/70R13 SBR WSW: Cust/Ltd ($180). P215/60R14 SBR WLT: T Type ($92). Self-sealing tires: Cust/Ltd ($106). Century Tires: P185/75R14 SBR WSW: Cust/Ltd ($58). P195/75R14 SBR BSW: Cust/Ltd ($31). P195/75R14 SBR WSW: Cust/Ltd ($93). P195/70R14 SBR WLT: T Type ($84). P215/60R14 SBR BSW: T ($123). P215/60R14 SBR WLT: T ($215). Self-sealing tires: Cust/Ltd ($106).

REGAL CONVENIENCE/APPEARANCE OPTIONS: Option Packages: Regal Grand National pkg. (black bumpers, lamps, moldings, spoilers, special interior trim w/console, special alum. wheels: T Type ($1282). Regal T Type Designer pkg.: designers' accent paint and rear spoiler ($403). Sliding electric silver

Astroroof: cpe ($895). Hatch roof: cpe ($825). Comfort/Convenience: Air cond. ($730); std. T Type. Touch climate control air cond. ($880); T Type ($150). Electronic cruise control w/resume ($175). Rear defogger, electric ($140). Tinted glass ($110). Tinted windshield ($90). Six-way power seat, each side ($215). Manual passenger seatback recliner ($75). Sport steering wheel ($50). Tilt steering ($110). Power windows ($185-$260). Electric door locks ($125-$175). Headlamps-on indicator ($16). Trip odometer ($16) exc. T Type. Electronic instrumentation ($299) exc. T Type ($173). Two-speed wiper w/low-speed delay ($50). Theft deterrent system ($159). Lighting and Mirrors: Tungsten-halogen headlamps ($22). Twilight Sentinel ($57). Cornering lamps ($57). Coach lamps: Ltd ($102). Door courtesy/warning lights: Ltd ($44-$70). Rear seat reading light ($30). Dome reading lamp ($24). Remote left mirror ($25) exc. T Type. Dual sport mirrors, left remote ($53) exc. T. Dual remote sport mirrors ($83); T ($30). Visor vanity mirror, passenger ($7). Lighted visor vanity mirror, passenger ($58). Entertainment: AM radio ($112). AM/FM stereo radio ($238). Electronic-tuning AM/FM stereo radio ($402); w/cassette and graphic equalizer ($605). Concert sound speaker system ($95). Dual rear speakers ($25-$30); incl. w/stereo radio. Automatic power antenna ($95); w/radio ($60). Exterior Trim: Landau vinyl top: cpe ($186) exc. T Type; heavily-padded ($245). Long vinyl top: sed ($160); padded ($245). Designers' accent paint ($200-$205). Solid special color paint ($200). Exterior molding pkg.: wide rocker panel and belt reveal ($110); std. on Ltd. Protective bodyside moldings: T Type ($55); choice of six colors. Wraparound bodyside moldings: sed ($104). Door edge guards ($15-$25). Bodyside stripe ($42); choice of nine colors. Interior Trim/Upholstery: Full-length console ($82). Bucket seats ($195) exc. Ltd. Lear Siegler bucket seats: T Type ($600). 55/45 seating ($133) exc. Ltd 45/45 leather/vinyl seating: Ltd ($295). Front carpet savers ($17); rear ($12). Front carpet savers w/inserts ($25); rear ($20). Wheels: Chrome-plated wheels ($195); T Type ($90 credit). Styled aluminum wheels ($285); std. T Type. Locking wire wheel covers ($190) exc. T. Body-color wheels ($85) exc. T. Tires: P205/70R14 SBR WSW ($62) exc. T Type. P215/65R15 SBR WLT: T Type ($92). Self-sealing tires ($106) exc. T.

LESABRE/ELECTRA/ESTATE WAGON CONVENIENCE/APPEARANCE OPTIONS: Comfort/Convenience: Sliding electric Astroroof: silver, gray or gold ($1195). Air cond.: LeSabre ($730). Air cond. w/touch-climate control: LeSabre ($880); Electra ($150). Cruise control w/resume ($175); std. Park Ave. Rear defogger, electric ($140). Tinted glass: LeSabre Cust ($110). Power windows: LeSabre ($185-$260). Electric door locks ($125-$175). Automatic door locks ($205-$255); exc. Park Ave. ($80). Six-way power seat, driver's or passenger's ($185-$215); both ($400-$430). Memory driver's seat: Electra ($363); Park Ave. ($178). Electric seatback recliner, either side ($139). Manual passenger seatback recliner: LeSabre/Estate ($75). Tilt steering: LeSabre, Electra Ltd ($110). Tilt/telescoping steering column: Electra Ltd ($165); Park Ave. ($55). Dial clock: LeSabre ($60). Digital clock: LeSabre Ltd ($60). Trip odometer ($16). Electric trunk lock: Electra ($80). Electric trunk release ($40). Electric fuel cap lock: Electra ($44) exc. wag. Theft deterrent system ($159); N/A on Estate. Two-speed wiper w/delay ($49-$50). Accessory group (trip odometer, dome reading lamp, low fuel indicator, washer fluid indicator): Electra ($46-$70). Lighting, Horns and Mirrors: Tungsten-halogen high-beam headlamps ($22). Twilight Sentinel ($60). Cornering lamps ($60). Coach lamps: LeSabre/Electra Ltd ($102). Light monitors, front: LeSabre/Est ($37); front/rear, Electra ($74). Lamp and indicator group ($38-$70). Door courtesy/warning lamps ($44-$70). Lighted door lock and interior light control ($75). Four-note horn ($28). Remote right mirror: LeSabre ($49); Electra ($25) exc. Park Ave. Remote electric right mirror: Park Ave. ($58). Dual electric remote mirrors ($91) exc. Park Ave. Dual electric mirrors w/left thermometer: Electra Ltd ($129). Lighted visor vanity mirror, driver or passenger ($58). Entertainment: AM radio: LeSabre ($112). AM/FM stereo radio: Electra ($198); std. on Park Ave. Basic ETR AM/FM stereo radio: LeSabre/Estate ($238); w/clock ($277) but std. on Park Ave.; w/cassette ($338-$402) exc. Park Ave. ($125). Electronic-tuning AM/FM stereo radio ($338-$402) exc. Park Ave. ($125). Electronic-tuning AM/FM stereo radio w/cassette and equalizer ($541-$605) exc. Park Ave ($328). CB radio: Estate ($275). Delete AM/FM stereo radio: Park Ave. ($230 credit). Concert Sound speaker system: Electra exc. wagon ($95); ETR radio req'd. Dual rear speakers ($25-$30). Automatic power antenna ($95); w/radio ($60). Triband power antenna ($140); w/radio ($105). Exterior Trim: Exterior molding pkg. (wide rocker panel, front/rear fender lower and belt reveal moldings): LeSabre ($110). Landau vinyl top: LeSabre, Electra Ltd cpe ($245). Long vinyl top: LeSabre Electra Ltd sed ($185-$190). Heavy-padded long vinyl top: Electra Ltd sedan ($245). Designers' accent paint: LeSabre ($215). Special single-color paint: ($200); Firemist, Electra exc. Estate ($210). Protective bodyside moldings: Estate ($55). Wide rocker panel moldings: Electra Ltd/Est ($65). Door edge guards ($15-$25). Belt reveal molding: LeSabre ($40). Bodyside stripes ($42-$45); choice of nine colors. Interior Trim/Upholstery: 55/45 seating: LeSabre Custom ($133). Leather/vinyl 50/50 seating: Park Ave. ($525). Third seat: Estate ($220). Front carpet savers ($17); rear ($12). Front carpet savers w/inserts ($25); rear ($20). Trunk carpeting trim ($53-$65). Trunk mat ($15). Wheels: Chrome-plated wheels ($180-$215) exc. Estate ($40 credit). Styled aluminum wheels ($220-$255). Custom wheel covers: Electra Ltd. ($35). Locking wire wheel covers ($155-$190) exc. Estate ($65 credit). Tires: P215/75R15 SBR wide WSW: LeSabre ($38). P225/75R15 SBR wide WSW: Electra cpe/sed ($39). Self-sealing tires ($107-$132).

1984 Buick, Riviera convertible with optional wire wheel covers. (OCW)

1984 Buick, Riviera T Type coupe. (OCW)

RIVIERA CONVENIENCE/APPEARANCE OPTIONS: Comfort/Convenience: Electric sliding Astroroof: silver, gray or gold ($1195). Touch climate control air cond. ($150). Electric rear defogger ($140). Digital electronic instrument cluster ($238). Six-way power seat, passenger ($215). Two position memory driver's seat ($178). Electric seatback recliner, either side ($139). Automatic door locks ($80). Leather-wrapped steering wheel ($96); std. on T Type. Tilt/telescope steering wheel ($55) exc. T Type. Electric fuel cap lock ($44). Electric trunk release ($40); lock ($80). Low fuel indicator ($16). Two-speed wipers w/delay ($49). Windshield washer fluid indicator ($16). Theft deterrent system ($159). Lighting, Horns and Mirrors: Tungsten-halogen high-beam headlamps ($22); std. on T Type. Twilight

Sentinel ($60). Coach lamps ($102); incl. w/vinyl top. Front/rear light monitors: T Type ($77). Rear quarter courtesy/reading lamp ($50). Lighted door lock and interior light control ($75). Four-note horn ($28). Dual electric remote mirrors ($66). Lighted visor vanity mirrors, each ($58). Entertainment: Full-feature electronic-tuning AM/FM stereo radio ($125). Basic electronic-tuning AM/FM stereo radio w/cassette tape player ($125). Electronic-tuning AM/FM stereo radio w/cassette and equalizer ($328); w/cassette, Dolby and Bose speaker system ($895) exc. conv. CB radio ($215). Delete radio ($230 credit). Rear speakers for base radio ($25). Concert Sound system ($95) exc. conv. Triband power antenna ($45); incl. w/CB radio. Exterior Trim: Heavy-padded landau vinyl top w/coach lamps: base ($330). Designers' accent paint: base ($235). Special color Firemist paint ($210); std. on conv. Color-coordinated protective bodyside moldings ($55); choice of eight colors but only white and dark red on conv. Door edge guards ($15). Bodyside striping ($45). Interior Trim/Upholstery: 45/45 leather/vinyl front seat ($487); std. on conv. 45/45 leather/suede seating w/storage console ($537) exc. conv. Front carpet savers w/inserts ($35); rear ($20). Trunk trim carpeting ($30); std. on conv. Trunk mat ($15). Wheels and Tires: Chrome-plated wheels ($145); exc. conv. ($45 credit). Styled aluminum wheels: conv. w/turbo V-6 ($65). Locking wire wheel covers ($190); std. on conv. P225/70R15 SBR wide oval tires: BSW or WSW (NC).

HISTORY: Introduced: October 2, 1983. Model year production (U.S.): 987,980. The yearly total included 229,934 four-cylinder Buicks and 258,422 V-8s, demonstrating that the venerable V-8 was still hanging on. Of the total production, 4,428 Buicks had a diesel engine and 15,556 a turbo. Calendar year production (U.S.): 987,833. Model year sales by U.S. dealers: 906,626 (not including front-drive Electras built during the 1984 model year). Calendar year sales (U.S.): 941,611 for a market share of 11.8 percent. When Canadian totals were added in, calendar year sales topped one million for the first time in Buick history.

Historical Footnotes: Century became Buick's best seller this year, nudging aside the Regal, which had held that title since Century sedan/wagon and Regal coupe merged under the Regal banner in 1982. Skylark sales, like those of the other GM X-cars, were slipping as a result of the lengthy recall list including a well-publicized and inconclusive recall for replacement of rear brake linings--even though those problems mainly affected 1980-81 models. Regardless, Skylark now sold almost as well as Chevrolet's Citation, which was the X-car that suffered most from bad publicity. To boost Skyhawk sales, dealers were encouraged to offer the subcompacts with extras that might appeal to young, sporty minded buyers: electronic radios, aluminum wheels, tachometers, luggage racks and the like. LeSabre and Electra gained renewed popularity in 1982-83, with an impressive sales rise this year. Riviera was especially popular among doctors, merchants and executives. As part of the preliminaries for the summer Olympics in Los Angeles, the cross-country torch passed through Flint in May, carried for a time by several Buick employees. A fleet of Rivieras and other Buick vehicles, modified for low-speed endurance running, accompanied torchbearers on their way to L.A. For off-road racing, Buick added a Stage I piston and Stage II intake manifold to the long list of heavy-duty 4.1-liter V-6 components available at dealers. Several Buick-powered vehicles had proven successful on race courses, including a record set at Bonneville this year. Bobby Allison had also driven a Regal to win the 1983 NASCAR driver's prize. At more mundane levels, a portable Diagnostic Data Analyzer could hook the electronic control module of any 1981-84 Buick into the dealer's diagnostic display--or to the computer at Flint. From there, an engineer could even alter the faraway engine's speed for evaluating problems. Buick's objective, according to retiring General Manager Lloyd Reuss, was to be "Best in Class" and rank No. 3 in sales. General Motors was divided into small car and large car groups in January 1984, with Buick falling into the latter category. Robert C. Stempel was named

head of the B-O-C (Buick-Oldsmobile-Cadillac) group, while Donald E. Hackworth took over as GM vice-president and Buick's general manager.

1985

This year marked both the beginning and end of several eras. The last rear-drive Electra had been built in April 1984, replaced by a totally different front-drive version. Though the name was the same, the contemporary Electra stood far apart from its traditional full-size predecessors. Regal's dramatic black Grand National coupe though marketed in modest numbers, was altering Buick's image among youthful motorists. Diesels went under Buick hoods for the last time this year. The final X-bodied Skylark was produced, ending Buick's connection with that sad episode in GM history. Rear-drive days were numbered. This would be LeSabre's final season in that form, but the name reappeared on an Estate Wagon for 1985, after a year's absence. A new name joined the Buick lineup: Somerset Regal.

1985 Buick, Skyhawk Custom coupe with optional sunroof. (OCW)

1985 Buick, Skyhawk Limited station wagon with optional roof rack and styled wheels. (OCW)

SKYHAWK - SERIES 4J - FOUR - After setting a sales record in 1984, Buick's J-car subcompact entered 1985 with no significant change beyond new body colors and interior trim. The lineup continued as before: Custom and Limited versions of coupe and sedan, plus a station wagon. The T Type also continued, powered by a normally-aspirated or turbocharged 1.8-liter overhead-cam four that came from GM of Brazil. Turbos added a boost gauge on the dash this year, and produced 150 horsepower as opposed to only 84 with the non-turbo 1.8 engine. That much power in a lightweight brought 0-60 acceleration times down to less than nine seconds. All-season (fourth-generation) radials were now standard on all Skyhawks. Chevrolet and Olds offered a 2.8-liter V-6 on their versions of the J-body, but Buick stuck with the fours. Standard powertrain was again the Chevrolet-made 121 cu. in. (2.0-liter) four with four-speed manual gearbox and 3.65:1 final drive ratio (three-speed

automatic available). Non-turbo T Types had a five-speed gearbox; turbos the four-speed. T Types had a blacked-out grille and headlamp housings, black door handles and locks, and blackout side mirrors. Upper bodies came in silver, red or white; lower body was charcoal. Styled aluminum wheels held P195/70R13 blackwall radial tires; fatter 60-series tires were available, either blackwall or white lettered. T Types had a leather-wrapped sport steering wheel, reclining bucket seats, foglamps, Gran Touring suspension, and full instruments. Powerplant was the 1.8-liter fuel-injected overhead-cam four. The optional turbo 1.8 with multi-port fuel injection rated 150 horsepower. On the Buick proving grounds, the turbo version reached 60 MPH in 8.5 seconds.

1985 Buick, Skylark Limited sedan. (OCW)

SKYLARK - SERIES 4X - FOUR/V-6 - Only the four-door sedan remained in Skylark's final year. The new Somerset Regal would offer buyers a coupe without the taint of the X-car's unpleasant recall and reliability history. Skylarks received a new grille that angled outward near the base, new wide taillamps split into upper/lower sections, and altered interior trim. Vertical rectangular parking lights sat between grille and single headlamps. Accentuating the revised rear-end look was a new center appliqué, and the license plate moved from the trunk lid to the bumper. The standard 2.5-liter four-cylinder engine, now dubbed "Tech IV," gained new roller bearings. The 2.8-liter carbureted V-6 was again optional, but a new addition this year was a high-output version with port fuel injection. That 2.8 used injectors mounted on a fuel rail, a design from Bosch that fed fuel from a high-pressure electric pump in the gas tank. It also had a cast aluminum intake manifold. All engines had new hydraulic engine mounts to cut vibration.

1985 Buick, Century Limited sedan. (OCW)

CENTURY - SERIES 4A - FOUR/V-6 - Once again, Century offered coupe, sedan and station wagon models, in Custom or Limited trim, along with the performance T Type. All showed a new grille and hood ornament this year, along with a new selection of body colors. Front ends held quad headlamps; rear ends, full-width taillamps. Sedans had a narrow window behind the rear door. European-look T Types now carried the advanced 3.8-liter V-6 with multi-port fuel injection, which had become available late in the 1984 model year. That engine was also offered on other Century models. Base engine, however, remained the 2.5-liter four with throttle-body fuel injection. This year, it gained roller valve lifters. Buyers could also choose a Chevrolet-built 2.8-liter V-6, Buick's own 3.0-liter V-6, or the 4.3-liter diesel V-6. The 2.8 was offered in case Buick couldn't meet

production demands of its own 3.0 V-6. Many buyers chose a gas V-6 over the low-powered 2.5 base engine. Century Customs came with three-speed automatic transmission, power brakes and steering, AM radio, notchback seating (cloth or vinyl), dual horns, bumper guards and protective strips, side-window defoggers, full carpeting, and P185/75R14 tires. Limiteds didn't add too much beyond wide lower bodyside moldings, a hood ornament and wind split moldings. In addition to the 3.8-liter engine and dual exhaust, T Types included four-speed overdrive automatic transmission, a left-hand remote-control mirror, blacked-out grille, temp/volt gauges, cloth bucket seats, Gran Touring suspension, leather-wrapped sport steering wheel, and styled aluminum road wheels with P195/70R14 tires. The F41 Gran Touring suspension, with firmer springs, recalibrated shocks and hefty stabilizer bars, was also available on other coupes and sedans.

1985 Buick, Somerset Regal coupe. (OCW)

1985 Buick, Somerset Regal Limited coupe. (OCW)

SOMERSET REGAL - SERIES 4N - FOUR/V-6 - Buick's totally new, formally styled personal-luxury sport coupe, meant to replace the X-bodied Skylark, targeted the affluent "yuppies" and baby boomers who might otherwise buy upscale imports. Oldsmobile's Calais and Pontiac's Grand Am were its close N-body front-drive relatives. Base engine was a "Tech-IV" 2.5-liter four-cylinder with throttle-body fuel injection, plus new roller bearings. Standard transaxle was a five speed manual, but three-speed automatic was optional. The optional 181 cu. in. (3.0-liter) V-6 engine with multi-port fuel injection, putting out 125 horsepower, was smaller and lighter then the same-size (lower-powered) V-6 in Buick's Century. Styled in a dramatic wedge shape, the compact coupe was accentuated by a sloping nose and raked-back windshield, plus a high roofline, large quarter windows, and vertical rear window. Somerset had body-colored bumpers with rub strips, a standard electronic-tuning AM radio, cloth or vinyl bucket seats, tachometer, trip odometer, tinted glass, full length console, and a digital clock. The Limited added chrome bumpers, front/rear

armrests, dual horns, woodgrain instrument panel, wheel opening moldings, and narrow rocker panel moldings. Options included body-color side moldings. Somersets had standard electronic digital instrumentation, including a multi-gauge which gave, at driver's command, readouts for voltage, oil pressure, engine temperature, and R.P.M. Radio controls were atop a pod remote from the radio itself. The right front seat slid forward when its seatback was tipped forward, for easy entry into the back. Controls sat in pods at each side of the steering column, and instruments were electronic. Somersets could be ordered with a high-mounted brake light (which would be required on '86 models). Somerset's chassis used a MacPherson strut front suspension, and at the rear a special trailing axle suspension patterned after the type used in the sporty Skyhawk.

1985 Buick, Regal coupe with optional Grand National package. (OCW)

REGAL - SERIES 4G - V-6 - Only the Regal coupe remained this year, as the four-door sedan left the lineup. In addition to base and Limited trim levels, buyers had a choice of two performance editions: the familiar T Type and a dramatic step-up Grand National. Regal's forward slanted front end carried a new slanted grille. Wheel covers were restyled, new body colors were offered and interiors came in an altered selection of colors. T Types had a new power brake system, with boost provided by an electric pump rather than the power steering pump. A carbureted 231 cu. in. (3.8-liter) V-6 was standard with three-speed automatic transmission. A diesel V-6 was optional. Both performance Regals came with a turbocharged version of the 3.8, with sequential port fuel injection and four-speed overdrive automatic transmission. Base Regal equipment included bumper guards and protective strips, power brakes and steering, AM radio, cigarette lighter, dual horns, dual chrome mirrors, color-keyed bodyside moldings, notchback seats (cloth or vinyl), and P195/75R14 steel-belted radial whitewalls. Regal Limited added an exterior molding package and 55/45 notchback seating. T Types included air conditioning, a performance axle ratio, temp and turbo boost gauges, 94-amp alternator leather-wrapped steering wheel, tachometer, trip odometer, and 15 in. styled aluminum wheels with wide 65-series tires. Grand National (actually a $675 T Type option package) was offered again for 1985 with its aggressive all-black exterior (even the windshield wipers), special black aluminum wheels, firm-ride Gran Touring suspension, and new two-tone cloth bucket seats. Grand Nationals carried a 200-horsepower turbo 3.8-liter V-6 with sequential fuel injection. On the test track it had hit 60 MPH in 8 seconds. Equipment also included black bumpers, rub strips and guards; black front air dam and decklid spoiler; and Grand National identification on body and instrument panel.

1985 Buick, LeSabre Limited Collector's Edition sedan. (OCW)

LESABRE - SERIES 4B - V-6/V-8 - For its final year as a rear drive Buick, LeSabre received a new grille and a few new colors (inside and out), but few other changes. The new grille was made up of thin vertical bars and stood more vertically than the sloped-back quad-headlamp section. Coupes and sedans again came in Custom or Limited dress, but to make the final season the Limited was called a Collector's Edition. Standard engine remained the 231 cu. in. (3.8-liter) V-6, but buyers could also choose the familiar four-barrel 307 (5.0-liter) V-8, or the diesel V-8. Standard Custom equipment included an AM radio, power brakes and steering, three-speed automatic transmission (four-speed overdrive required with V-8 engines), wood-tone dash appliqué, dual horns, compact spare tire, bumper guards and protective strips, and front armrest. LeSabre's Collector's Edition had plush velour upholstery on loose pillow seats. It also had a standard six-way power driver's seat, seatbelt and ignition key warning chime, headlamps-on indicator and chime, and Soft-Ray tinted glass, plus wide rocker panel moldings and accent strips. Doors carried woodgrain trim; bodies showed special identification and hood ornament. Buyers even received a booklet on Buick history and special set of keys.

1985 Buick, Electra Estate Wagon station wagon. (OCW)

ESTATE WAGON - SERIES 4B/C - V-8 - LeSabre's Estate Wagon returned to the fold for 1985, after a year's absence. As usual, Electra's version was the posher of the pair. Even though the new Electra coupe and sedan were shrunken in size with front-drive, the wagons hung on with rear-drive. Two- and three-seat versions were offered. LeSabre included air conditioning, tinted glass, dual horns, AM radio, power steering and brakes, heavy-duty suspension, styled aluminum wheels, and narrow rocker panel moldings among its many standard items. Electra's wagon added front/rear armrests, a digital clock, AM/FM seek/scan stereo radio, woodgrain vinyl appliqué, remote electric tailgate lock, power windows all around, and a roof luggage rack.

1985 Buick, Electra Park Avenue sedan. (OCW)

ELECTRA - SERIES 4C - V-6 - An entirely new Electra debuted in early spring 1984, along with the similarly downsized Cadillac DeVille/Fleetwood and Oldsmobile Ninety Eight. Dramatic cuts in exterior size and weight did not affect interior dimensions much (except for narrower width and smaller trunk volume), though Electra's six-passenger capacity tightened somewhat. The modern Electra weighed 600-900 pounds less than before, measured 2 feet shorter and 4 in. narrower, and rode a 110.8 in. wheelbase (8 in. shorter than in 1984). Electra's hood now opened from the rear. The new edition turned to contemporary front-wheel drive with a transverse-mounted engine; standard 181 cu. in. (3.0-liter) V-6, optional 231 cu. in. (3.8 liter) V-6 with multi-port fuel injection or the 4.3-liter diesel. A coupe and four-door sedan came in base or plush Park Avenue form, or the

enthusiast's T Type. The 3.8 V-6 was standard on both Park Avenue and T. (The very existence of a sporty T Type carrying the renowned Electra nameplate startled a good many traditional buyers.) Though far smaller than before, Electra hardly lacked poshness. Standard equipment on base Electras included four-speed overdrive automatic transmission, electronic climate and level controls, six-way power driver's seat, AM/FM stereo radio with seek/scan electronic tuning, power windows, side window defoggers, remote fuel filler door release, courtesy lights, headlamps-on reminder, trip odometer, velour upholstery, and P205/75R14 all-season radials. Stepping up to Park Avenue brought buyers the bigger (3.8-liter) V-6 along with power door locks, tilt steering, power decklid release, rear reading lamps, cruise control, wide bodyside moldings, accent paint striping, and luxury upholstery in cloth or leather.

1985 Buick, Riviera convertible with optional wire wheel covers. (OCW)

RIVIERA - SERIES 4E - V-6/V-8 - Since a dramatically different Riviera was expected for 1986, not much changed this year for the coupe, T Type or convertible. Late in the 1984 model year, the 5.0-liter V-8 had become the standard Riv powerplant, and that continued in 1985. The coupe could also have a 5.7-liter diesel for one more year, but T Types kept the 231 cu. in. (3.8-liter) turbocharged V-6 with sequential port fuel injection. Joining the option list was a cellular telephone--a factory-approved dealer option rather than a factory installation. A hundred or so test Rivieras carried a new optional Graphic Control Center, which had originally been planned as a regular production option. Drivers could select radio, climate control and trip functions by simply touching appropriate portions of the video screen. The convertible's hefty price tag kept sales down to a modest level, and this would be its final season. A limited edition Riviera for 1985 featured genuine wood in the form of a burled walnut veneer on dash and door panels, wood/leather steering wheel, and beige leather/suede interior trim.

I.D. DATA: All Buicks again had a 17-symbol Vehicle Identification Number (VIN), stamped on a metal tag attached to the upper left surface of the cowl, visible through the windshield. Coding was similar to 1984, starting with '1' to indicate the manufacturing country (U.S.A.), followed by 'G' for General Motors and '4' for Buick Division. The next letter indicates restraint system. Symbol five denotes series: 'S' Skyhawk Custom; 'T' Skyhawk Ltd.; 'E' Skyhawk T Type; 'B' Skylark Custom; 'C' Skylark Ltd.; 'J' Somerset Regal; 'M' Somerset Regal Ltd.; 'H' Century Custom; 'L' Century Ltd.; 'G' Century T Type (or Estate); 'J' Regal; 'K' Regal T Type; 'M' Regal Ltd.; 'N' LeSabre Custom; 'P' LeSabre Ltd.; 'R' LeSabre Estate Wagon; 'X' Electra; 'W' Electra Park Ave.; 'F' Electra T Type; 'V' Electra Estate Wagon; 'Z' Riviera. 'Y' Riviera T Type. Digits six and seven indicate body type: '27' 2-dr. coupe; '37' LeSabre 2-dr. coupe; '47' Regal 2-dr. coupe; '57' Riviera 2-dr. coupe; '11' Electra 2-dr. sedan; '19'

Electra 4-dr sedan; '69' 4-dr. sedan; '35' 4-dr. wagon; '67' 2-dr. convertible coupe. Next symbol is the engine code: 'O' L4-110 TBI; 'J' turbo L4-110 MFI; 'P' L4 121 TBI; 'U' L4-151 TBI; 'R' L4-151 TBI; 'X' V6-173 2Bbl.; 'W' V6-173 MFI; 'E' V6-181 2Bbl.; 'L' V6-181 MFI; 'A' V6-231 2Bbl.; '3' V6-231 MFI; '9' turbo V6-231 SFI; 'T' diesel V6-263; 'Y' V8-307 4Bbl.; 'N' diesel V8-350. Symbol nine is a check digit. Symbol ten denotes model year ('F' 1985). Symbol eleven is the plant code: 'M' Lansing, MI; 'T' Tarrytown, NY; 'D' Doraville, GA; 'W' Willow Run, MI; '6' Oklahoma City, OK; 'H' Flint, MI; 'K' Leeds, MO; 'X' Fairfax, KS; 'E' Linden, NJ; '1' Wentzville, MO; '2' Ste. Therese, Quebec. The final six digits are the sequential serial number starting with 400001. An additional identifying number may be found on the engine. A body number plate on upper shroud or radiator support assembly reveals model year, car division, series, style, body assembly plant, body number, trim combination, modular seat code, paint code, and date build code.

1985 Buick, Century Estate Wagon station wagon. (OCW)

SKYHAWK CUSTOM (FOUR)

Model No.	Body/Style No.	Body Type & Seating	Factory Price	Shipping Weight	Prod. Total
4J	S27	2-dr Coupe-5P	7365	2276	44,804
4J	S69	4-dr Sedan-5P	7581	2325	27,906
4J	S35	4-dr Sta Wag-5P	7919	2401	5,285

SKYHAWK LIMITED (FOUR)

4J	T27	2-dr Coupe-5P	7883	2312	Note 1
4J	T69	4-dr Sedan-5P	8083	2429	Note 1
4J	T35	4-dr Sta Wag-5P	8379	2356	Note 1

Note 1: Skyhawk Custom production totals include equivalent Skyhawk Limited models. For the model year, 63,148 Custom and 9,562 Limited coupes and sedans were built.

SKYHAWK T TYPE (FOUR)

| 4J | E27 | 2-dr Coupe-5P | 8437 | 2295 | 4,521 |

SKYLARK CUSTOM (FOUR/V-6)

| 4X | B69 | 4-dr Sedan-5P | 7707/7967 | 2478/2539 | 65,667 |

SKYLARK LIMITED (FOUR/V-6)

| 4X | C69 | 4-dr Sedan-5P | 8283/8543 | 2515/2576 | 27,490 |

CENTURY CUSTOM (FOUR/V-6)

4A	H27	2-dr Coupe-6P	9377/9637	2609/2714	13,043
4A	H19	4-dr Sedan-6P	9545/9805	2658/2763	215,928
4A	H35	4-dr Sta Wag-6P	9941/10201	2825/2930	28,221

CENTURY LIMITED (FOUR/V-6)

4A	L27	2-dr Coupe-6P	9841/10101	2632/2737	Note 2
4A	L19	4-dr Sedan-6P	10012/10272	2681/2786	Note 2
4A	L35	4-dr Sta Wag-6P	10379/10639	2845/2950	Note 2

CENTURY T TYPE (V-6)

| 4A | G27 | 2-dr Coupe-5P | 11249 | 2802 | Note 2 |
| 4A | G19 | 4-dr Sedan-5P | 11418 | 2850 | Note 2 |

Note 2: Century Custom production totals include equivalent Century Limited and T Type models. Total model year production came to 99,751 Customs, 125,177 Limiteds and 4,043 Century T Type coupes and sedans.

SOMERSET REGAL (FOUR/V-6)

| 4N | J27 | 2-dr Coupe-5P | 8857/9417 | 2472/2523 | 48,470 |

SOMERSET REGAL LIMITED (FOUR/V-6)

| 4N | M27 | 2-dr Coupe-5P | 9466/10026 | 2478/2529 | 37,601 |

REGAL (V-6)

| 4G | J47 | 2-dr Coupe-6P | 9928 | 3066 | 60,597 |

REGAL LIMITED (V-6)

| 4G | M47 | 2-dr Coupe-6P | 10585 | 3107 | 59,780 |

REGAL T TYPE (V 6)

| 4G | K47 | 2-dr Coupe-6P | 12640 | 3256 | 4,169 |

Note 3: Regal T Type total includes 2,102 Grand Nationals.

LESABRE CUSTOM (V-6/V-8)

Model No.	Body/Style No.	Body Type & Seating	Factory Price	Shipping Weight	Prod. Total
4B	N37	2-dr Coupe-6P	10453/11018	3438/3629	5,156
4B	N69	4-dr Sedan-6P	10603/10568	3447/3638	32,091

LESABRE LIMITED COLLECTOR'S EDITION (V-6/V-8)

4B	P37	2-dr Coupe-6P	11751/12316	3462/3653	22,211
4B	P69	4-dr Sedan-6P	11916/12481	3495/3686	84,432

LESABRE ESTATE WAGON (V-8)

4B	R35	4-dr Sta Wag-6P	12704	4085	5,597

ELECTRA (V-6)

4C	X11	2-dr Coupe-6P	14149	3114	5,852
4C	X69	4-dr Sedan-6P	14331	3158	131,011

ELECTRA PARK AVENUE (V-6)

4C	W11	2-dr Coupe-6P	16080	3144	Note 4
4C	W69	4-dr Sedan-6P	16240	3190	Note 4

ELECTRA T TYPE (V-6)

4C	F11	2-dr Coupe-6P	15386	3138	Note 4
4C	F69	4-dr Sedan-5P	15568	3183	Note 4

Note 4: Production figures for base Electra coupe and sedan include totals for Park Avenue and T Type models. Total T Type production, 4,644.

ELECTRA ESTATE WAGON (V-8)

4C	V35	4-dr Sta Wag-6P	15323	4148	7,769

RIVIERA (V-6/V-8)

4E	Z57	2-dr Coupe-5P	-----/16710	----/3748	63,836
4E	Z67	2-dr Conv-5P	27457/26797	3700/3873	400

Note 5: Only 49 Riviera convertibles had a turbo V-6 engine installed.

RIVIERA T TYPE (V-6)

4E	Y57	2-dr Coupe-5P	17654	3564	1,069

FACTORY PRICE AND WEIGHT NOTE: Figure before the slash is for four-cylinder engine, after the slash for V-6. For LeSabre and Riviera, figure before slash is for V-6 engine, after slash for V-8.

FACTORY PRICE NOTE: Buick announced several price increases during the model run, including some for optional engines.

ENGINES: BASE FOUR (Skyhawk): Inline, ohv, four-cylinder. Cast iron block and head. Displacement: 121 cu. in. (2.0-liters). Bore & stroke: 3.50 x 3.15. Compression ratio: 9.3:1. Brake horsepower: 86 at 4900 R.P.M. Torque: 100 lb.-ft. at 3000 R.P.M. Five main bearings. Hydraulic valve lifters. Throttle-body fuel injection. VIN Code: P. **OPTIONAL FOUR (Skyhawk); STANDARD (Skyhawk T Type):** Inline, overhead-cam four-cylinder. Cast iron block and aluminum cylinder head. Displacement: 110 cu. in. (1.8-liters). Bore & stroke: 3.34 x 3.13 in. Compression ratio: 8.8:1. Brake horsepower: 84 at 5200 R.P.M. Torque: 102 lb.-ft. at 2800 R.P.M. Five main bearings. Hydraulic valve lifters. Throttle-body fuel injection. VIN Code: O. **TURBOCHARGED FOUR (Skyhawk T Type):** Same as 1.8-liter OHC four above, except: Compression ratio: 8.0:1. Brake H.P.: 150 at 5600 R.P.M. Torque: 150 lb.-ft. at 2800 R.P.M. Multi-point fuel injection. VIN Code: J. **BASE FOUR (Skylark, Century, Somerset Regal):** Inline, overhead-valve four-cylinder. Cast iron block and head. Displacement: 151 cu. in. (2.5-liters). Bore & stroke: 4.0 x 3.0 in. Compression ratio: 9.0:1. Brake horsepower: 92 at 4400 R.P.M. Torque: 134 lb.-ft. at 2800 R.P.M. Five main bearings. Hydraulic valve lifters. Throttle-body fuel injection. Built by Pontiac. VIN Code: R. **OPTIONAL V-6 (Skylark, Century):** 60 degree, overhead valve V-6. Cast iron block and head. Displacement: 173 cu. in. (2.8 liters). Bore & stroke: 3.50 x 2.99 in. Compression ratio: 8.5:1. Brake horsepower: 112 at 4800 R.P.M. Torque: 145 lb.-ft. at 2100 R.P.M. Four main bearings. Hydraulic valve lifters. Carburetor: 2Bbl. Built by Chevrolet. VIN Code: X. **HIGH-OUTPUT V-6; OPTIONAL (Skylark):** Same as 173 cu. in. V-6 above except: Compression ratio: 8.9:1. Brake horsepower: 125 at 5400 R.P.M. Torque: 165 lb.-ft. at 3600 R.P.M. VIN Code: W. **BASE V-6 (Electra); OPTIONAL (Century):** 90-degree, overhead-valve V-6. Cast iron block and head. Displacement: 181 cu. in. (3.0-liters). Bore & stroke: 3.8 x 2.66 in. Compression ratio: 8.45:1. Brake horsepower: 110 at 3600 R.P.M. Torque: 145 lb.-ft. at 2600 R.P.M. Four main bearings. Hydraulic valve lifters. Carb.: 2Bbl. VIN Code: E. **OPTIONAL V-6 (Somerset Regal):** Same as 181 cu. in. V-6 above, with multi-point fuel injection. Compression ratio: 9.0:1. Brake horsepower: 125 at 4900 R.P.M. Torque: 150 lb.-ft. at 2400 R.P.M. VIN Code: L. **BASE V-6 (Regal, LeSabre):** 90-degree, overhead-valve V-6. Cast iron alloy block and head. Displacement: 231 cu. in. (3.8-liters). Bore & stroke: 3.8 x 3.4 in. Compression ratio: 8.0:1. Brake horsepower: 110 at 3800 R.P.M. Torque: 190 lb.-ft. at 1600 R.P.M. Four main bearings. Hydraulic valve lifters. Carb.: 2Bbl. VIN Code: A. **BASE V-6 (Century T Type Electra T/Park Ave.); OPTIONAL (Century, Electra):** Same as 231 V-6 above, but with multi-point fuel injection. Brake H.P.: 125 at 4400 R.P.M. Torque: 195 lb.-ft. at 2000 R.P.M. VIN Code: 3. **TURBOCHARGED V-6 (Regal/Riviera T Type):** Same as 231 V-6 above, but with turbocharger and sequential fuel injection. Brake horsepower: 200 at 4000 R.P.M. (Riviera, 190 H.P.). Torque: 300 lb.-ft. at 2400 R.P.M. VIN Code: 9. **DIESEL V-6; OPTIONAL (Century, Regal, Electra):** 90-degree, overhead-valve V-6. Cast iron block. Displacement: 262.5 cu. in. (4.3 liters). Bore & stroke: 4.057 x 3.385 in. Compression ratio: 21.6:1. Brake horsepower: 85 at 3600 R.P.M. Torque: 165 lb.-ft. at 1600 R.P.M. Four main bearings. Hydraulic valve lifters. Fuel injection. VIN Code: V or T. **BASE V-8 (Estate, Riviera); OPTIONAL (LeSabre):** 90-degree, overhead valve V-8. Cast iron block and head. Displacement: 307 cu. in. (5.0-liters). Bore & stroke: 3.80 x 3.385 in. Compression ratio: 8.0:1. Brake horsepower: 140 at 3200 R.P.M. (LeSabre, 140 at 3600). Torque: 255 lb.-ft. at 2000 R.P.M. (LeSabre, 240 at 1600). Five main bearings. Hydraulic valve lifters. Carburetor: 4Bbl. Built by Oldsmobile. VIN Code: Y or H. **OPTIONAL DIESEL V-8 (LeSabre, Estate, Riviera):** 90-degree, overhead valve V-8. Cast iron block and head. Displacement: 350 cu. in. (5.7-liters). Bore & stroke: 4.057 x 3.385 in. Compression ratio: 21.6:1. Brake horsepower: 105 at 3200 R.P.M. Torque: 200 lb.-ft. at 1600 R.P.M. Five main bearings. Hydraulic valve lifters. Fuel injection. Oldsmobile-built. VIN Code: N.

CHASSIS DATA: Wheelbase: (Skyhawk) 101.2 in.; (Skylark) 104.9 in.; (Somerset Regal) 103.4 in.; (Century) 104.8 in.; (Century wag) 104.9 in.; (Regal) 108.1 in.; (LeSabre/Estate) 115.9 in.; (Electra) 110.8 in.; (Riviera) 114.0 in. Overall length: (Skyhawk cpe) 175.3 in.; (Skyhawk sed/wag) 177.3 in.; (Skylark) 181.1 in.; (Somerset Regal) 180.0 in.; (Century) 189.1 in.; (Century wag) 190.9 in.; (Regal) 200.6 in.; (LeSabre) 218.4 in.; (Electra) 197.0 in.; (Estate) 221.3 in.; (Riviera) 206.6 in. Height: (Skyhawk) 54.0 in.; (Skyhawk wag) 54.4 in.; (Skylark/Century) 53.6-53.7 in.; (Century wag) 54.2 in.; (Somerset Regal) 52.1 in.; (Regal) 54.6 in.; (LeSabre cpe) 56.0 in.; (LeSabre sed) 56.7 in.; (Estate) 59.3 in.; (Electra/Riv) 54.3 in. Width: (Skyhawk) 65.0 in.; (Skylark) 69.1 in.; (Somerset Regal/Century) 67.7 in.; (Regal) 71.6 in.; (LeSabre) 78.0 in.; (Estate) 79.3 in.; (Electra) 72.4 in.; (Riv) 72.8 in. Front Tread: (Skyhawk) 55.3 in.; (Skylark/Century) 58.7 in.; (Somerset Regal) 55.5 in.; (Regal) 58.5 in.; (LeSabre) 61.8 in.; (Electra) 60.3 in.; (Estate) 62.2 in.; (Riv) 59.3 in. Rear Tread: (Skyhawk) 55.1 in.; (Skylark) 57.0 in.; (Somerset Regal) 55.2 in.; (Century) 56.7 in.; (Regal) 57.7 in.; (LeSabre) 60.7 in.; (Electra) 59.8 in.; (Estate) 64.0 in.; (Riviera) 60.0 in. Standard Tires: (Skyhawk) P175/80R13 SBR; Skyhawk T Types P195/70R13 SBR; (Skylark/Somerset Regal) P185/80R13 SBR; (Century) P185/75R14 SBR; (Century T Type) P195/70R14 SBR; (Regal) P195/75R14 SBR WSW; (Regal T Type) P215/65R15 SBR; (LeSabre) P205/75R15 SBR WSW; (Electra) P205/75R14 SBR BSW; (Estate) P225/75R15 SBR WSW; (Riviera) P205/75R15 SBR WSW.

TECHNICAL: Transmission: Four-speed, fully synchronized floor shift standard on Skyhawk/Skylark. Five-speed manual standard on Somerset Regal, available on Skyhawk. Four-speed overdrive automatic standard on Electra/Riviera, available on Century/Regal/LeSabre three-speed automatic on other models. Four-speed gear ratios: (1st) 3.53:1; (2nd) 1.95:1; (3rd) 1.24:1; (4th) 0.81:1 or 0.73:1; (Rev) 3.42:1. Skylark V-6 four-speed: (1st) 3.51:1; (2nd) 1.95:1; (3rd) 1.24:1; (4th) 0.90:1;

(Rev) 3.42:1. Skyhawk five-speed gear ratios: (1st) 3.91:1; (2nd) 2.15:1; (3rd) 1.45:1; (4th) 1.03:1; (5th) 0.74:1; (Rev) 3.50:1. Somerset Regal five-speed: (1st) 3.73:1; (2nd) 2.04:1; (3rd) 1.45:1; (4th) 1.03:1; (5th) 0.74:1; (Rev) 3.50:1. Three-speed auto. trans gear ratios: (1st) 2.74:1; (2nd) 1.57:1; (3rd) 1.00:1; (Rev) 2.07:1. Skyhawk/Skylark auto trans gear ratios: (1st) 2.84:1; (2nd) 1.60:1; (3rd) 1.00:1; (Rev) 2.07:1. Four-speed overdrive automatic gear ratios: (1st) 2.74:1; (2nd) 1.57:1; (3rd) 1.00:1; (4th) 0.67:1; (Rev) 2.07:1. Century/Electra four-speed automatic: (1st) 2.92:1; (2nd) 1.57:1; (3rd) 1.00:1; (4th) 0.70:1; (Rev) 2.38:1. Standard axle ratio: (Skyhawk) 3.65:1 w/4-spd, 3.45:1 w/5-spd, 3.18:1 w/auto.: (Skyhawk turbo) 4.10:1 w/4-spd, 3.33:1 w/auto; (Skylark) 3.32:1 or 3.65:1 w/4-spd, 2.39:1 or 2.53:1 w/auto, 2.84:1 w/H.O. V-6 and auto.; (Somerset Regal) 3.35:1 w/5-spd, 2.84:1 w/auto. (Century) 2.84:1 or 2.97:1 w/3-spd, 2.84:1 or 3.06:1 w/4-spd, 2.39:1 w/diesel; (Regal) 2.41:1; (Regal T Type) 3.42:1; (LeSabre) 2.73:1 exc. diesel, 2.93:1; (Electra) 3.08:1 exc. V6-231, 2.84:1; (Riviera) 2.73:1; (Riv diesel); (Riv turbo) 3.15:1. Steering: (Skyhawk/Skylark/Century/Somerset Regal) rack and pinion; (others) recirculating ball; power assist standard on all except Skyhawk. Suspension: front/rear coil springs. (Skyhawk/Somerset Regal) MacPherson strut front w/stabilizer; semi-independent beam rear axle w/trailing arms; rear stabilizer bar optional, std. on T Type. (Skylark/Century) MacPherson strut front suspension; beam twist rear axle w/trailing arms and Panhard rod; front/rear stabilizer bars. (Electra) MacPherson front struts, barrel springs and stabilizer bar, rear struts w/stabilizer bar and electronic level control. (Riviera) fully independent suspension with front torsion bars, semi-trailing arms at rear, front/rear stabilizers and automatic level control. (Rear-drive models) front stabilizer bar; rear stabilizer bar on T Type; rigid four-link rear axle. Brakes: power front disc, rear drum. Four-wheel power disc brakes available on Riviera (std. on conv.). Body construction: (front-drive models) unitized; (others) separate body and frame. Fuel tank: (Skyhawk/Somerset Regal) 13.6 gal.; (Skylark) 15.1 gal.; (Century) 15.7 gal.; (Regal) 18.1 gal.; (LeSabre) 25.0 gal.; (Electra) 18.0 gal.; (Estate) 22.0 gal.; (Riviera) 21.1 gal.

DRIVETRAIN OPTIONS: Engines: 110 cu. in. (1.8-liter) EFI four: Skyhawk Cust/Ltd. ($50). Turbocharged 110 cu. in. (1.8-liter) MFI four: Skyhawk T Type ($800). 173 cu. in. (2.8-liter) V-6, 2Bbl.: Skylark ($260). Century (N/A) High-output 173 cu. in. (2.8-liter) V-6, 2Bbl.: Skylark ($435). 181 cu. in. (3.0-liter) V-6, 2Bbl.: Century ($260); Somerset ($560). 231 cu. in. (3.8-liter) V-6, MFI: Century ($520); std. T Type; early base Electra ($260). Turbocharged 231 cu. in. (3.8-liter) V-6, SFI: Riviera ($660); std. on T Type. 263 cu. in. (4.3-liter) diesel V-6: Century/Regal/Electra ($359) exc. T Type, Park Ave. ($99). 307 cu. in. (5.0-liter) V-8, 4Bbl.: LeSabre ($390). 350 cu. in. (5.7-liter) diesel V-8: Regal ($589); LeSabre ($489); Estate/Electra/Riviera ($99) exc. T Type or conv. Transmission/Differential: Four-speed manual trans.: Skyhawk T Type ($75 credit). Five-speed manual trans.: Skyhawk Cust/Ltd. ($75). Auto trans.: Skyhawk/Skylark/Somerset ($425); Skyhawk T Type ($350). Automatic overdrive trans.: Century Cust/Ltd./Est, LeSabre ($175); Regal (N/A). Optional rear axle ratio: Skyhawk 3.43:1; Skylark; Century 2.84:1 or 2.97:1; Regal: LeSabre; base Electra 3.33:1, Estate; Riviera 3.15:1 (all NC). Limited slip differential: Regal/LeSabre/Est ($95). Suspension, Steering and Brakes: F40 Firm ride/handling pkg. ($27). F41 Gran Touring suspension: Skyhawk/Skylark/Somerset ($27); Century Cust/Ltd. cpe/sed ($27); Regal/LeSabre ($49); Electra/Riviera ($27). Special G.T. suspension: Skyhawk T Type (NC). Electronic control suspension: Electra (N/A); std. T Type. Superlift rear shock absorbers: Skylark ($68). Automatic level control: Century/Regal/LeSabre/Estate ($175). Power steering: Skyhawk ($215). Four-wheel disc brakes: Riviera ($235). Other: H.D. alternator: Skyhawk/Regal/LeSabre/Electra 85-amp ($35 or $85); 94-amp ($35 or $85); Century/Somerset/Electra 108 amp ($25-$40). H.D. battery ($26); diesel ($52). Power reserve Freedom battery: Electra ($145). H.D. radiator: Skyhawk ($40-$70). H.D. cooling: Skylark ($40-$70). Engine block heater ($18). H.D. engine/transmission cooling: Century/Regal/LeSabre/Electra/Riviera ($40-$70). High altitude emission package (NC). California emission system ($99).

SKYHAWK CONVENIENCE/APPEARANCE OPTIONS: Option Packages: Decor pkg.: T Type ($195). Vista Vent flip-open removable glass sunroof ($310). Instrument gauge pkg.: temp, oil pressure, volts, trip odometer: Cust ($60). Gauges and tach: Cust ($138); Ltd. ($78). Acoustic pkg. ($36); std. on Ltd. Comfort/Convenience: Air cond. ($645); touch climate control ($795). Rear defogger, electric ($135). Cruise control w/resume ($175). Power windows ($195-$270). Electric door locks ($130-$180). Six-way power driver's seat ($225). Easy-entry passenger seat adjuster: Cust cpe ($16). Tinted glass ($25). Sport steering wheel: Cust/Ltd. ($50). Leather-wrapped steering wheel: T Type ($40). Tilt steering ($115). Trip odometer: Cust ($15). Electric trunk or tailgate release ($40). Tailgate wiper/washer: wag ($125). Two-speed wipers w/delay ($50). Lights, Horns and Mirrors: Tungsten-halogen headlamps ($18). Headlamps-on indicator ($15). Front seat reading light ($30). Dual horns: Cust cpe/sed ($15). Left remote black mirror: Cust/Ltd. ($22). Dual black mirrors: left remote ($53). Dual black electric remote mirrors ($139); T Type ($86). Visor vanity mirror, passenger ($7). Lighted visor vanity mirror, either side ($45). Entertainment: Electronic-tuning AM/FM stereo radio ($138); w/clock ($177). Seek/scan AM/FM stereo ET radio w/clock ($222); w/cassette ($344). Seek/scan AM stereo/FM ET stereo radio w/clock ($242); w/cassette and equalizer ($494). Radio delete ($56 credit). Automatic power antenna ($65). Dual rear speakers ($25). Exterior Trim: Door edge guard moldings ($15-$25). Wide rocker moldings: Cust cpe/sed ($26). Bodyside stripes ($45). Designers' accent paint ($195). Decklid luggage rack ($100). Roof rack: wag ($105). Interior Trim/Upholstery: Front console armrest: T Type ($45). Front carpet mats ($17); rear ($12). Front carpet mats w/inserts ($18); rear ($15). Front/rear fiber floor mats: T Type ($65). Deluxe trunk trim ($33). Security cover: wag ($69). Wheels and Tires: Styled aluminum wheels ($229); std. T Type. Styled wheel covers w/trim rings ($38); N/A T Type. Locking wire wheel covers ($180); N/A T Type. P175/80R13 SBR WSW ($54). P195/70R13 SBR BSW ($104). P195/70R13 SBR WSW ($166). P195/70R13 SBR WLT ($188); T Type ($84). P205/60R14 SBR BSW: T Type ($94). P205/60R14 SBR WLT: T Type ($182). Self-sealing tires ($115).

SKYLARK/CENTURY CONVENIENCE/APPEARANCE OPTIONS: Comfort/Convenience: Flip-open Vista Vent glass sunroof ($300). Acoustic pkg.: Skylark Cust ($60). Lamp group: Skylark Cust ($42). Air cond. ($730). Elect. cruise control ($175). Rear defogger, electric ($140). Power windows ($185-$260). Electric door locks ($125-$175). Six-way power driver's seat ($215). Manual seatback recliners, passenger ($45); both ($90). Sport steering wheel ($50). Tilt steering ($110). Tinted glass ($110). Instrument gauges incl. trip odometer ($48); w/tachometer: Century ($126). Tachometer: Skylark ($78). Trip odometer: Skylark ($16). Digital electronic instrument cluster: Century ($225); T Type ($131). Dial clock ($35). Electric trunk release ($40). Remote tailgate lock: Century wag ($40). Tailgate washer/wiper: Century wag ($120). Two-speed wipers w/delay ($50). Theft deterrent system: Century ($159). Lights, Horns and Mirrors: Tungsten-halogen headlamps: Skylark Cust ($10); Century ($22). Twilight Sentinel: Century ($57). Front light monitors: Century ($37). Coach lamps: Ltd. ($102-$129). Center-mounted high stoplight: Century ($25). Headlamps-on indicator ($16). Door courtesy/warning light: Century Ltd./wag ($44). Front seat reading lamp ($24). Rear seat reading lamp: Skylark Ltd., Century Cust/Ltd. ($30). Dual horns: Skylark Cust ($15). Remote-control color-keyed left mirror: Cust/Ltd./Est ($25). Sport mirrors (left remote, right manual): Cust/Ltd./Est ($61). Dual electric remote mirrors ($139) exc. Century T Type ($78). Visor vanity mirror, passenger ($7). Lighted visor vanity mirror. passenger: Skylark ($50): either side, Century ($58). Entertain-

ment: Same as Skyhawk (above). Exterior Trim: Landau vinyl top: Century Cust/Ltd. cpe ($186); heavily-padded ($623). Long vinyl top: Cust/Ltd. ($160). Designers' accent paint ($205-$210); N/A T Type. Special solid color paint: Century ($200) exc. T Type. Protective bodyside moldings ($55); color-coordinated on Century. Lower wide bodyside moldings: Century Cust ($65). Rocker panel moldings: Skylark Cust ($26). Wide rocker panel/rear quarter moldings: Skylark Cust ($91). Belt reveal molding: Skylark Cust ($40). Wheel opening moldings: Skylark Cust ($30). Door edge guards ($15-$25). Pillar appliqué moldings: Skylark Cust ($27). Hood ornament and windsplit: Skylark Cust ($32). Windsplit molding: Century Cust ($22). Bodyside stripe: Cust/Ltd./Est ($45). Bumper guards, front/rear: Skylark ($45). Bumper strips, front/rear: Skylark Cust ($49). Decklid luggage rack: Century ($100). Roof rack: Century wag ($105). Cargo area vent windows: Century wag ($75). Woodgrain vinyl appliqué: Century wag ($350). Tailgate air deflector: Century wag ($37). Front license bracket (NC). Interior Trim/Upholstery: Front center armrest: Skylark Cust ($45). Full-length console: Century ($57). Full length operating console: Skylark ($105); Century ($80); T Type ($23). Bench seat: Skylark Cust ($55 credit). Cloth bucket seats: Skylark Cust ($140); Ltd. ($95): Century Cust ($97). 55/45 notchback cloth seating: Century Cust ($133). Lear Siegler bucket seats: Century T Type ($600). Cloth 45/45 seating: Century Ltd./Est (NC). Leather/vinyl 45/45 seating: Century Ltd. ($295); T ($425). Third seat: Century wag ($215). Locking storage compartment: Century wag ($44). Front carpet mats ($17); rear ($12). Carpet mats w/inserts: front ($25); rear ($20). Trunk trim ($25-$47). Wheels: Styled aluminum wheels: Century ($195); std. on T Type. Chrome wheels: Skylark ($175). Locking wire wheel covers ($190) exc. T. Skylark Tires: P185/80R13 SBR WSW ($58). P205/70R13 SBR WSW ($180). Self-sealing tires ($105). Century Tires: P185/75R14 SBR WSW: Cust/Ltd./Est ($58). P195/75R14 SBR BSW: Cust/Ltd./Est ($30). P195/75R14 SBR WSW: Cust/Ltd./Est ($92). P195/70R14 SBR WLT: T Type ($84). P215/60R14 SBR BSW: T ($122). P215/60R14 SBR WLT: T ($214). Self-sealing tires ($105).

SOMERSET REGAL CONVENIENCE/APPEARANCE OPTIONS: Comfort/Convenience: Vista Vent flip-open removable glass sunroof ($310-$329). Air cond. ($645). Electronic cruise control ($175). Rear defogger, electric ($135). Six-way power driver's seat ($225). Sport steering wheel ($50) exc. Ltd. Tilt steering ($115). Power windows ($195). Electric door locks ($130); automatic ($220). Electric trunk release ($40). Two-speed wipers w/delay ($50). Lights and Mirrors: Center high-mounted stoplight ($25). Front door courtesy/warning light: Ltd. ($44). Front-rear seat reading/courtesy lights ($40-$54). Dual mirrors, left remote ($53); std. on Ltd. Dual electric remote mirrors ($86-$139). Lighted right visor vanity mirror ($38). Entertainment: Seek/scan AM/FM stereo radio w/clock ($157); w/cassette and equalizer ($424); w/Delco GM/Bose music system and Dolby ($995). Cassette player ($142). Concert sound speakers ($100-$125). Dual extended-range speakers ($25). Automatic power antenna ($65). Exterior Trim: Designers' accent paint ($195). Bodyside stripes ($45). Rocker panel moldings ($26); std. Ltd. Wide rocker panel moldings ($50-$76). Color-keyed protective bodyside moldings ($45). Wheel opening moldings ($30); std. Ltd. Decklid luggage rack ($100). Door edge guards ($15). Interior Trim/Upholstery: Leather bucket seats: Ltd. ($275). Floor mats w/inserts: front ($18); rear ($15). Wheels and Tires: Styled aluminum wheels ($229). P185/80R13 SBR WSW ($58). P205/70R13 SBR BSW ($114). P205/70R13 SBR WSW ($180). P205/70R13 SBR WLT ($202). Self-sealing tires ($115).

REGAL CONVENIENCE/APPEARANCE OPTIONS: Option Packages: Regal Grand National pkg.: black exterior, front air dam, decklid spoiler, rub strips/guards, Gran Touring suspension, front bucket seats, aluminum wheels ($675). Regal T Type Designer pkg.: black/dark gray Designers' Accent paint and rear spoiler ($403). Base Regal exterior molding pkg.: wide rocker

panel and belt reveal moldings ($110). Sliding electric silver Astroroof ($895). Hatch roof ($825). Comfort/Convenience: Air cond. ($730); std. T Type. Touch climate control air cond. ($880); T Type ($150). Cruise control w/resume ($175). Rear defogger, electric ($140). Tinted glass ($110). Tinted windshield ($90). Six-way power seat, each side ($215). Manual passenger seatback recliner ($75). Sport steering wheel ($50); N/A T Type. Tilt steering ($110). Power windows ($185). Electric door locks ($125). Electric trunk release ($40). Digital electronic instrument cluster ($299); T Type ($173). Headlamps-on indicator ($16). Trip odometer ($16) exc. T. Two-speed wiper w/delay ($50). Theft deterrent system ($159). Lighting and Mirrors: Tungsten-halogen headlamps ($22). Twilight Sentinel ($57). Cornering lamps ($57); N/A T Type. Coach lamps: Ltd. ($102). Door courtesy/warning lights: Ltd. ($44). Front seat reading light ($24); rear ($30). Dual sport mirrors, left remote ($53); std. T Type. Dual remote sport mirrors ($83); T Type ($30). Dual chrome mirrors, left remote ($25); N/A T Type. Visor vanity mirror passenger ($7); lighted ($58). Entertainment: Same as Skyhawk (above) plus Concert sound speakers ($95). Exterior Trim: Landau vinyl top ($186) exc. T Type; heavily-padded ($245). Designers' accent paint ($205); N/A T Type. Solid special color paint ($200). Black protective bodyside moldings: T Type ($55). Door edge guards ($15). Bodyside stripe ($45). Interior Trim/Upholstery: Storage console: Ltd. ($82). Bucket seats ($195) exc. Ltd. Lear Siegler bucket seats: T Type ($600). 55/45 seating ($133) exc. Ltd. 45/45 leather/vinyl seating: Ltd. ($295); T Type ($595). Front carpet mats ($17); rear ($12). Front carpet mats w/inserts ($25); rear ($20). Trunk trim ($44). Wheels: Chrome-plated wheels ($195); N/A T Type. Styled aluminum wheels ($285); std. T Type. Locking wire wheel covers ($190) exc. T. Color-keyed wheels ($85) exc. T. Tires: P205/70R14 SBR WSW ($62) exc. T Type. P215/65R15 SBR WLT: T Type ($92). Self-sealing tires ($105) exc. T.

LESABRE/ELECTRA/ESTATE WAGON CONVENIENCE/APPEARANCE OPTIONS: Comfort/Convenience: Sliding electric Astroroof ($1195) Air cond.: LeSabre ($730); Est ($150). Air cond. with touch-climate control: LeSabre ($880); Electra ($165). Cruise control w/resume ($175); std. on Park Ave. Rear defogger, electric ($140). Tinted glass: LeSabre Custom ($110). Power windows: LeSabre ($185-$260). Keyless entry system: Electra ($185). Electric door locks ($125-$175). Automatic door locks ($205-$255) exc. Electra Est/Park Ave. ($80). Six-way power passenger seat ($215); driver's: LeSabre Cust. Est ($185-$215). Memory driver's seat: Electra ($178). Two-way power driver's seat: LeSabre Est ($60). Electric seatback recliner, either side ($139) exc. Electra Est passenger ($220). Manual passenger seatback recliner: LeSabre, Estate ($75). Tilt steering ($110); std. Park Ave. Tilt/telescoping steering column: Electra ($165); Park Ave. ($55). Dial clock: LeSabre Cust ($60). Digital clock: LeSabre Ltd. ($60). Accessory group (low fuel indicator, trip odometer, reading lights, washer fluid indicator): Electra Est ($54-$86). Trip odometer: LeSabre ($16). Remote tailgate lock: LeSabre Estate ($50). Electric trunk lock: Electra ($80). Electric trunk release ($40). Theft deterrent system ($159); N/A on Estate. Two-speed wiper w/delay ($50); std. Park Ave. Lighting, Horns and Mirrors: Tungsten-halogen headlamps ($22). Twilight Sentinel ($60). Cornering lamps: LeSabre, Electra Cust ($60). Coach lamps: LeSabre Ltd. ($102). Light monitors, front: LeSabre ($37); front/rear, Electra ($77). Lamp and indicator group: LeSabre ($38-$70). Door courtesy/warning lamps ($44-$70). Lighted door lock and interior light control ($75). Four-note horn ($28). Dual remote chrome mirrors: LeSabre ($49). Dual electric remote mirrors ($91); std. Park Ave. Dual electric remote mirrors, left heated: Electra ($126); Park Ave. ($35). Lighted visor vanity mirror, driver or passenger ($58). Entertainment: LeSabre: same selection as Skyhawk (above). Electra as follows: Seek/scan electronic-tuning AM stereo/FM stereo radio w/clock ($20) w/cassette and equalizer ($272). Seek/scan AM/FM stereo radio w/cassette ($122) w/cassette, Dolby and Delco GM/Bose music system

($895) but N/A on Estate. Delete radio ($275 credit). Concert Sound system ($95). CB radio; Estate ($275). Automatic power antenna; LeSabre/Electra/Est ($60). Triband power antenna: LeSabre, Est ($105). Exterior Trim: Exterior molding pkg. (wide rocker panel, front/rear fender lower and belt reveal moldings): LeSabre ($110). Landau padded vinyl top: LeSabre cpe ($245). Long vinyl top: LeSabre ($185). Heavy-padded long vinyl top: Electra sed ($245). Designers' accent paint: LeSabre ($215). Special single-color paint: ($200); Firemist, Electra ($200). Protective bodyside moldings: Est ($55). Wide rocker panel moldings: Electra Est ($65). Door edge guards ($15-$25). Belt reveal molding: LeSabre Cust/Est ($40). Bodyside stripes ($45); std. Ltd./Park Ave. Rear air deflector: Est ($40). Woodgrain vinyl appliqué: LeSabre Estate ($345); delete from Electra Est ($320 credit). Luggage rack: LeSabre Estate ($150). Front license bracket (NC). Interior Trim/Upholstery: Cloth 55/45 seating: LeSabre Cust ($133). Leather/vinyl 50/50 seating: LeSabre Ltd. ($525). Leather/vinyl 55/45 seating: Park Ave. ($425). Leather/vinyl 45/45 seating: Electra T Type ($175). Third seat: Estate ($220). Front carpet mats: LeSabre ($17); rear ($12). Front carpet mats w/inserts ($25); rear ($20). Trunk carpeting/trim ($53). Trunk mat ($15). Wheels: Chrome-plated wheels: LeSabre ($215); Estate ($40 credit). Styled aluminum wheels ($220-$255); Electra T Type (N/A). Locking wire wheel covers ($155-$190) exc. Estate ($65 credit). Tires: P215/75R15 SBR WSW: LeSabre ($42). P205/75R14 SBR WSW: Electra ($66); BSW, Park Ave. ($66 credit). Self-sealing tires ($105-$130).

RIVIERA CONVENIENCE/APPEARANCE OPTIONS: Comfort/Convenience: Electric sliding Astroroof: silver, gray or gold ($1195). Touch climate control air cond. ($150). Electric rear defogger ($140). Digital electronic instrument cluster ($238); T Type ($160). Six-way power seat, passenger ($215). Two-position memory power driver's seat ($178). Electric seatback recliner, either side ($139). Automatic door locks ($80). Leather-wrapped steering wheel ($96); std. on T Type. Tilt/telescope steering wheel ($55) exc. T Type. Electric trunk release ($40); pulldown ($80). Low fuel indicator ($16). Two-speed wipers w/delay ($50). Windshield washer fluid indicator ($16). Theft deterrent system ($159). Lighting, Horns and Mirrors: Tungsten-halogen high/low beam headlamps ($22); std. on T Type. Twilight Sentinel ($60). Coach lamps: base ($102); incl. w/vinyl top. Front/rear light monitors ($77) exc. conv. Rear reading lamps ($50) exc. conv. Lighted door lock and interior light control ($75). Four-note horn ($28). Automatic day/night mirror ($80). Dual electric remote mirrors ($66). Lighted visor vanity mirrors, each ($58); N/A conv. Entertainment: Seek/scan electronic-tuning AM stereo/FM stereo radio w/clock ($20); w/cassette and equalizer ($272). Seek/scan AM/FM stereo radio w/cassette ($122) w/cassette, Dolby and Delco GM/Bose music system ($895). CB radio ($215). Delete radio ($275 credit). Concert Sound system ($95). Triband power antenna ($45); incl. w/CB radio. Exterior Trim: Heavy-padded Landau vinyl top w/coach lamps: base ($330). Designers' accent paint: base ($235). Special color Firemist paint ($210); std. on conv. Color-keyed protective bodyside moldings ($55). Door edge guards ($15). Bodyside stripe: base ($45). Interior Trim/Upholstery: 45/45 leather/vinyl front seat ($487) std. on conv. Front floor mats w/inserts ($35); rear ($20). Trunk trim carpeting ($30), std. on conv. Trunk mat ($15); N/A conv. Wheels and Tires: Chrome-plated wheels: base ($145); conv. ($45 credit). Styled aluminum wheels: conv. w/turbo V-6 ($65). Locking wire wheel covers: base ($190). Credit given for BSW tires on conv.; and for P225/70R15 SBR non-self-sealing on base and conv. P225/70R15 SBR WSW: T Type ($48); BSW ($26 credit).

HISTORY: General introduction was October 2, 1984; but Electras had been introduced on April 5, 1984, and the Skyhawk didn't appear until November 8, 1984. Model year production (U.S.): 1,002,906 (including early '85 Electras); that was the first time Buick passed the one million barrier. The total included 271,423 four-cylinder Buicks, 515,995 sixes, and 215,488 V-8s. Only 1,178 diesels and 6,137 turbos were installed this year.

Calendar year production (U.S.): 1,001,461 (first time for breaking the million mark). Model year sales by U.S. dealers: 915,336, which amounted to 10.9 percent of the industry total. Calendar year sales (U.S.): 845,579 for a market share of 10.3 percent.

Historical Footnotes: The last rear-drive Electra had come off the line on April 25, 1984, a month after its rear-drive replacement emerged. It was the last of over 2.6 million old-style Electras, and would be joined by LeSabre for 1986. Clearly, front-drive and aero styling was the wave of the future, and Buick hoped to attract a new breed of buyer. Both the new Electra and the coming front-drive LeSabre were developed by the C/H Product Team ('C' for C bodies, 'H' for the H-bodied LeSabre). Part of Buick's youth-oriented promotion for the Regal Grand National included a TV commercial with a song called "Bad to the Bone" performed by George Thoroghgood and the Delaware Destroyers. Quite a change from the advertising aimed at gray flannel-suited executives in the 1950s, or even the performance promotions during the muscle-car era.

1986

Eleven new models joined Buick's list for '86, making a total of 39 (including a couple of special editions). Every line except Skylark and LeSabre fielded a T Type version. New choices included the Skyhawk Sport and T Type hatchback; Skylark Custom and Limited sedan; and Somerset T Type coupe. Most notable, though, were the all-new V-6 front-drive LeSabre (Custom and Limited coupe/sedan) and Riviera coupe and T Type. Leaving the lineup this year were Electra's T Type coupe and the Riviera convertible. On the 3.0-liter V-6 with multi-port fuel injection, introduced for 1985, a single belt drove all accessories. It also got a redesigned water pump, hardened valve seats, new air cleaner and inlet. A redesigned combustion chamber allowed more efficient combustion. This engine was 50 pounds lighter (and 5.5 inches narrower) than the carbureted 3.0 from which it evolved. Two versions of the 3.8-liter V-6 were offered: with or without roller valve lifters. A revised intake manifold improved breathing and gave more hood clearance. Spark plugs were placed in the center of the combustion chamber for added efficiency. Turbocharged 3.8s got a new intercooler between the compressor and intake manifold, to supply a denser air/fuel charge and boost horsepower output. New leading/trailing rear drum brakes on LeSabres were said to improve braking consistency and automatic adjustment. Hinged taillamps on Electra, LeSabre and Riviera allowed easier servicing of bulbs and lenses. More galvanized steel panels for rust protection were used on 1986 Buicks than on any previous models. LeSabre became the first to offer double-sided galvanized sheet metal on both sides of hood and fenders. Going a giant step further, the whole Riviera body (except the roof) would now be double-side, hot-dipped galvanized. Riviera's new Graphic Control Center, similar to the preliminary version introduced in 1984, drew considerable attention at the Chicago Auto Show. Also standard on Riviera was the Retained Accessory Power feature, which kept certain components operating after the ignition was shut off: radio, electric windows, wipers, fuel door, decklid, and glove compartment release. Most noteworthy among the new options was the anti-lock braking system (ABS), developed jointly with the West German firm of Alfred Teves GmbH, now offered on Electra. Sensors at each wheel could determine when a wheel was about to lock and relax braking pressure as needed, to prevent skidding on slippery surfaces. Pressure might be applied and released as many as 15 times per second, helping the driver to remain in control and stop in the shortest possible distance.

1986 Buick, Skyhawk T Type hatchback. (OCW)

SKYHAWK - SERIES 4J - FOUR - Buick gained a full line of subcompact models with the mid-year addition of a new Sport/Hatch and T Type hatchback. Both hatchbacks and Limited/T Type coupes had a new front-end design that featured concealed tungsten-halogen headlamps behind electrically-operated doors. They also had smoked glass taillamps. Otherwise, styling was similar to prior models. As before, the wide body-colored grille sat low on the front end, below the narrow protective strip. The sharply slanted nose held a center crest. Wide taillamps wrapped slightly around the side. In all, the modern Skyhawk offered clean, wedge-shape styling with an "aggressive" profile, highlighted by flush-mounted glass, integrated bumpers and styled mirrors. All Skyhawks were available in white, silver metallic, black, or red. All except the T Type could have bodies in metallic light blue, bright blue, dark red, gray, dark blue, light brown, or brown; or in regular cream beige. T Types could have gray metallic as the lower accent color. Hatchbacks featured a blackout treatment, and a rear spoiler was optional. Custom and Limited Skyhawks had new standard wheel covers, while hatchbacks came with turbine-design wheel covers. Hatchbacks could have an optional retractable security cover to keep valuables out of sight. Base engine remained the fuel-injected 2.0-liter four with four-speed manual gearbox. Five-speed (overdrive) manual and three-speed automatic transmissions were available. So was a 1.8-liter powerplant. Skyhawk's T Type was powered by the 1.8-liter four with overhead camshaft, either normally aspirated or (at extra cost) turbocharged. Turbos produced 150 horsepower and had multi-port fuel injection. That version delivered a claimed 0-60 MPH test time of under nine seconds. They came with a four-speed gearbox rather than the usual five. T Types also had cloth front bucket seats with console, gauges (including tachometer), sport steering wheel with T Type insignia, Gran Touring suspension, aluminum wheels, a front passenger assist strap, black antenna, foglamps, amber park/signal lamps, black door handles and locks, plus black moldings and mirrors. For looks without added performance, a low-cost SCS Coupe package came with the regular 2.0-liter engine and four-speed, riding P175/80R13 all-season blackwalls. The extras: custom cloth bucket seats and door panels, three-tone interior trim, custom steering wheel, black moldings, and styled steel wheels.

1986 Buick, Skylark Limited sedan. (OCW)

SKYLARK - SERIES 4N - FOUR/V-6 - Now that the X-bodied Skylark was gone, Buick offered a four-door replacement to match the Somerset coupe. Even through the bad publicity about X-cars, Buick's version had sold well and the company didn't want to lose the power of the Skylark name, which began with the limited edi-

tion convertible way back in 1953. The new five-passenger sedan came in Custom and Limited trim, with rakish windshield, flush-mounted glass, and rounded rear body corners. Front-end styling was just like Somerset's. The grille was comprised of tight vertical bars, flowing smoothly down from the sloping hood. Parking/signal lamps were inset low, below the bumper protective strip that wrapped around fender tips. The required high-mount stop lamp was placed on the rear shelf, flush with the back window. Bumpers were body colored on the Custom, bright on the Limited. Standard body colors were white and tan plus 10 metallics: silver, dark gray, black, light brown, brown, flame red, light blue, medium blue, light sage, and dark sage. Both Skylark and Somerset carried a new 'S' logo. Inside, brushed aluminum trim panels contained standard electronic digital instruments with vacuum-fluorescent displays that offered metric readings at the touch of a button. Readouts included voltage, engine speed, coolant temperature, oil pressure, and a trip odometer. Soft touch, low-travel controls for lights, wiper/washers and other frequently-used functions were positioned on a pod near the steering wheel. Skylark's chassis layout consisted of a transverse-mounted engine, MacPherson struts, low-drag front disc brakes, and trailing-link rear suspension. Base engine was the 2.5-liter four, with electronic fuel injection and five-speed manual gearbox. Hydraulic clutch adjustment provided easier engagement and smooth shifting. A 3.0-liter V-6 was optional, with multi-port fuel injection and three-speed automatic transmission. The 125-horsepower V-6 had a high-efficiency combustion chamber and a gerotor oil pump.

SOMERSET - SERIES 4N - FOUR/V-6 - Introduced for 1985, the Somerset Regal coupe lost the "Regal" from its name this year. Now it served as a mate to the similar N-body Skylark sedan. One difference: Somerset now offered a T Type, while Skylark did not. Manual transmission Somersets had a new hydraulic clutch. All had a new brushed-finish instrument panel. The aerodynamically-styled, rounded wedge-look coupe came with a choice of four-cylinder or V-6 power and front-wheel drive, in Custom or Limited trim (or new T Type). Styling highlights included flush windshield and backlight glass. The smooth front end carried a grille with narrow vertical strips and Buick badge on the side, with wide parking/signal lamps down in the bumper below the rub strip. A Somerset script went at the forward end of the front fenders, above the amber lenses inset into the protective bumper strip. Somerset's chassis used MacPherson struts up front, with semi-independent coil spring suspension in the back. All Somersets had power rack-and-pinion steering, plus low-drag power front disc brakes. Limiteds carried new velour cloth upholstery. Reclining bucket seats were standard with a front center armrest. Standard digital instruments included readouts for voltage, oil pressure, temperature, engine R.P.M. and trip odometer. Radio controls were housed in a pod separate from the radio, easy to reach. Standard powertrain was the 2.5-liter four-cylinder engine with electronic fuel injection, driving a close-ratio five-speed manual gearbox. Optional: an automatic transmission and 3.0-liter V-6 with multi-port fuel injection. T Types carried the 3.0-liter V-6 engine, with computer-controlled coil ignition. That meant no more distributor under the hood. A Gran Touring suspension (Level III) and low-profile P215/60R14 Eagle GT blackwall tires on new cast aluminum alloy wheels delivered a firmer ride than the standard Somerset. The minimally-trimmed body sported charcoal lower body accents all around the car, plus a new front air dam and blacked-out grille and trim items. The performance-oriented axle ratio was 3.18:1. Other T Type touches: gray instrument panel, console and door trim plates, leather-wrapped steering wheel, black pillar appliqué, wide charcoal rocker panel moldings, amber parking/signal lamp lenses, red/amber taillamps, gray protective bodyside moldings, and twin rear-view mirrors (the left one remote-controlled). T Type upper body colors were silver, black, white or red, all with dark gray lower accent. Tan and seven metallic finishes were offered on other Somersets: dark gray, light brown, brown, light blue, medium blue, light sage, and dark sage.

1986 Buick, Century Custom sedan with optional vinyl roof and wire wheel covers. (OCW)

1986 Buick, Regal T Type coupe. (OCW)

1986 Buick, Regal coupe with optional Grand National package. (OCW)

CENTURY - SERIES 4A - FOUR/V-6 - A distinctive new front-end look for Century focused on the slanted vertical element grille that extended below the low-profile quad headlamps, all the way around the edges of front fenders. A horizontal/vertical crossbar pattern divided the grille into four sections, with Buick block letters off to the side, below the center. Parking/signal lamps were inset into the bumper protective strip and amber wraparound cornering lenses stood outboard of the headlamps. A flush mounted hood ornament completed the modern look. The T Type coupe was dropped this year, but the T sedan remained. Century's lineup also included Custom and Limited sedans and coupes plus Custom or Estate Wagons. The contemporary Century was intended to compete with European sedans and coupes. Base powertrain was the 2.5-liter, 92-horsepower four with three-speed automatic transaxle. The formerly optional 3.0-liter V-6 was gone, replaced by a carbureted Chevrolet 2.8 V-6 (except in California). Also available: the 3.8-liter V-6, which gained 25 horsepower (now rated 150) by adding sequential port fuel injection and Computer Controlled Coil Ignition, along with low-friction roller valve lifters. T Type sedans ran with the 3.8-liter V-6, hooked to four-speed overdrive automatic. T Types also carried the Gran Touring suspension and low-profile (P215/60R14) steel-belted radial tires on cast aluminum wheels, and wore blackout trim. Instrument panels were gray, with LED tachometer, and the steering wheel was wrapped in leather. Blackout accents went on headlamp and taillamp bezels, radio antenna, door handles, moldings, grille and accent stripes. Optional Lear Siegler bucket seats provided improved lateral and lumbar support. Wagons had standard side-window defoggers, split folding rear seat, plus load area light and floor carpeting. Electronic cruise control and six-way power seats were optional this year. A Vista-Vent sunroof was available on all models. T Type body colors were gray, white, silver and black, with gray lower accent paint available. Other Century models came in cream beige or seven metallic shades: light brown, brown, light sage, light blue, dark blue, rosewood, or dark red. Vinyl tops came in white, black, light sage, dark red, dark gray, dark blue or tan. Century's Gran Sport was described as "a car to be reckoned with" and as "the hottest Buick this side of a race course." Just 1,029 were produced, all painted black and devoid of brightwork. The Gran Sport package for the Custom coupe included the 3.8-liter V-6 SFI engine, tough suspension, tachometer, black/gray cloth reclining bucket seats with power-6 logo, console with shift lever boot, front/rear floor mats (GS insignia up front), seek/scan AM/FM stereo radio with cassette player and clock, temp/volt gauges, and black leather-wrapped sport steering wheel. The Gran Sport body had a front air dam and spoiler plus blackout grille, black moldings and headlamp bezels, and wide aero rocker panel moldings. Black front floor mats displayed a special Gran Sport insignia. Aluminum wheels with GS identification held P205/60R15 steel-belted radial Eagle GT tires, 'Buick' decals for door and spoiler were in the trunk for installation by the dealer, and additional GS ornamentation was all over the car. To draw even more attention, the sporty exhaust emitted a "very authoritative growl," according to Buick. All told, a tempting selection of extras, but with a price tag approaching $4,000.

REGAL - SERIES 4G - V-6/V-8 - While most of Buick's lineup had switched to contemporary front-wheel drive, Regal hung on with rear-drive and little evident change. Under T Type turbo hoods, though, lay a major change: a new intercooler for the turbocharged 3.8-liter V-6. That fuel-injected engine now churned out 235 horsepower and 330 pound-feet of torque. The intercooler not only added power, but reduced the likelihood of detonation. Regal's T Type sported a blackout-trimmed grille, windows, wipers and headlamp bezels, plus a revised taillamp treatment with black moldings. It rode on low-profile P215/65R15 tires on aluminum wheels, as opposed to the P195/75R14 whitewalls on regular Regals. The Gran Touring suspension included a rear stabilizer, larger-diameter front stabilizer bar, higher-rate springs and shocks. Performance rear axle ratio was 3.42:1. Engine identification appeared on the side of the hood bulge. T Types also had body-color sport mirrors, a trip odometer, turbo boost gauge, LED tachometer, leather-wrapped steering wheel, and air conditioning. An optional T Type Designers' Package added a front air dam, rear deck spoiler, and special black and dark gray accent paint on the body. Optional, firmer Lear Siegler bucket seats had an adjustable back. Regal's Grand National, the modern-day "muscle car," strode a lengthy step beyond the "ordinary" T Type. Its all-black body, complete with air dam and spoiler, held virtually no chrome or brightwork of any kind. Rolling on four stylish chrome-plated wheels, with handling provided by a firm, performance-tuned Gran Touring suspension, the driver enjoyed the comfort of gray cloth bucket seats. The turbocharged V-6 with intercooler and sequential port fuel injection was claimed to be "the most advanced high-performance engine offered in a Buick." Rated at more than twice the horsepower of the normally-aspirated version, it fed that power to a standard four-speed overdrive automatic transmission. Grand Nationals soon brought some hefty prices at auctions, a result of their striking and stark appearance and relatively low production figures. A total of 5,512 were produced in this year. Customers could also choose a base or Limited Regal, and V-8 fanciers could order their Regals fitted with a 307 cu. in. (5.0-liter) engine, supplied by Oldsmobile. Standard powertrain was a carbureted version of the 3.8-liter V-6, with three-speed automatic transmission. Optional: four-speed overdrive automatic. The diesel V-6 was gone. Regals were sold in an even dozen colors: white, black and cream beige plus nine metallics: silver, gray, light brown, brown, light blue, dark blue, rosewood, dark red, and light sage (not available on T Types).

1986 Buick, LeSabre Limited sedan. (OCW)

1986 Buick, LeSabre Limited coupe. (OCW)

LESABRE - SERIES 4H - V-6 - Buick continued the trend toward aerodynamic design with a fully restyled LeSabre, still six-passenger but with a transverse-mounted engine and front-wheel drive. The new H-body version, sharing the same platform as Oldsmobile's Delta 88, was 400 pounds lighter and 22 inches shorter (on a 5 in. shorter wheelbase), yet didn't lose much interior space. LeSabres came in fastback coupe or notchback sedan form, Custom or Limited trim, with front-hinged hood. The new grille had a wide five-row crosshatch pattern, with familiar Buick badge near the lower corner. As on earlier LeSabres, the bottom row of the grille extended outward to the outer tip of the fenders, below deeply recessed quad headlamps. Wide, clear parking/signal lamps were inset in the bumper, directly below the protective rub strip. Outside mirrors were sleek and modern looking. Bodyside moldings stretched the full length of the car, wrapping around into the front and back bumpers. Taillamps were hinged, with a slide-in license plate holder. LeSabre used new body/frame integral construction with a separate front frame to support the powertrain. The chassis used a modified MacPherson strut front suspension with barrel springs, and fully independent rear suspension with inboard coil springs. Standard engine (except in California) was a transverse-mounted 181 cu. in. (3.0-liter) V-6 with multi-port fuel injection, coupled to four-speed automatic transmission with overdrive top gear. Capable of 125 horsepower, the 3.0 had Computer Controlled Coil Ignition, Bosch injectors, a mass air flow sensor, high-output camshaft, plus cast aluminum intake manifold and rocker covers. Performance-minded buyers could choose the optional, proven 231 cu. in. (3.8-liter) V-6, with sequential port fuel injection and roller valve lifters, rated 150 horsepower. Power rack-and-pinion steering was standard. Tires were all-season P205/75R14 blackwalls. An optional "performance package" included the Gran Touring suspension, P215/65R15 Eagle GT tires, specific transmission calibration, faster steering response, and a leather-wrapped sport steering wheel. Custom models had notchback seats covered in velour cloth with woven fabric trim. Limiteds turned to plush, reclining loose-pillow velour seats in 55/45 arrangement. LeSabre's generous standard equipment list included air conditioning and tinted glass. Body colors were: white, black and tan; plus silver, dark gray, light brown, brown, dark teal, light blue, dark blue, flame red or dark red metallic. Sedan vinyl tops came in white, black, tan, dark red, dark gray, dark blue and dark teal. Electronic instrumentation was available. Ranking among the rarest of modern Buicks is the LeSabre Grand National. "We're looking for a few good drivers," proclaimed Buick's specialty brochure: drivers who are "serious about performance." Only 117 of the special-edition coupes

were built. Powered by the turbocharged 3.8 V-6 with sequential fuel injection and roller lifters, and riding fat P215/65R15 Eagle GT tires on aluminum alloy wheels, Grand National's chassis carried a muscular, fully independent sport suspension. Bodies were finished in black or white, and the car was packed with extras including blackout moldings, a black 'B' pillar, ribbed quarter-window closeouts, leather-wrapped sport steering wheel, lay-down hood ornament, and dual-outlet exhaust. Grand National ornamentation was on front fenders; a power-6 logo on the front floor mats; interior upholstered in gray cloth.

1986 Buick, LeSabre Estate Wagon station wagon. (OCW)

1986 Buick, Electra Estate Wagon station wagon. (OCW)

ESTATE WAGON - SERIES 4B/C - V-8 - As before, the old rear-drive Estate Wagons came in both LeSabre and Electra editions. Styling and capacity remained as in prior models. Sole powertrain was the old familiar 307 cu. in. (5.0-liter) V-8, producing 140 horsepower, with four-barrel carburetor and four-speed overdrive automatic transmission. Wagon colors were white, black and cream beige; plus metallic silver, gray, light brown, brown, light sage, light blue, dark blue, rosewood, or dark red.

1986 Buick, Electra Park Avenue sedan. (OCW)

ELECTRA - SERIES 4C - V-6 - Switched to front-drive a year earlier, Electra changed little for 1986. Coupe and sedan came in base or Park Avenue trim. The T coupe was abandoned, but the T sedan stayed in the lineup. The 3.0-liter V-6 offered in 1985 was no longer available. Sole powerplant was the 231 cu. in. (3.8-liter) V-6, producing 15 more horsepower with sequential fuel injection, driving a four-speed overdrive automatic transaxle. All Electras had power rack-and-pinion steering, a modified MacPherson strut front suspension with barrel springs, and independent rear suspension with automatic level control. Added to the option list was an anti-lock braking system (ABS) that sensed wheel speed and traction, adjusting pressure to prevent lockup during a quick stop or on slippery surfaces. Other new options: an electronic instrument cluster and automatic day/night rearview mirror. A Keyless Entry System option required that a five-number sequence be entered correctly on a little keyboard before the door would open. Electra's standard AM/FM stereo radio had seek and scan tuning. Other standard equipment in-

cluded Soft-Ray tinted glass, an electric fuel filler door release, six-way power driver's seat, power windows, front-seat reading lamps, power windows, air conditioning, and the required high-mounted stop lamp. Park Avenue interiors featured rich velour upholstery in choice of five colors. Extra fittings included Electronic Cruise Control, tilt steering column, electric door locks, remote-control trunk lid, Soft-Ray back seat reading lamps, and lighted vanity mirror on the passenger's visor. Powered by the same 3.8 V-6, the T Type sedan carried a Gran Touring suspension and standard 15 in. aluminum wheels with P215/65R15 Goodyear Eagle GT tires. Also included were a leather-wrapped sport steering wheel 45/45 seats in gray or red cloth, storage console, brushed gray instrument panel and door trim, front carpet savers with T Type logo, twin-outlet exhaust, and special taillamp treatment. T Types came in five body colors: silver, white, black, flame red, or dark gray. Other Electras could be painted in standard light or dark blue metallic, dark teal metallic, tan, or medium brown metallic. Dark brown, blue and red firemist metallic paint cost extra. Vinyl tops were offered in white, dark gray, black, dark blue, dark teal, beige, flame red, and red.

1986 Buick, Riviera T Type coupe. (OCW)

RIVIERA - SERIES 4E - V-6 - In an attempt to lure both new and traditional Buick buyers, Riviera turned to a total restyle this year--the first since 1979. Still front-drive with fully independent suspension, Riv was otherwise all-new: over 19 inches shorter, with wheelbase cut by six inches (to 108). Curb weight shrunk to a mere 3,309 pounds, over 500 pounds less than before. Yet passenger space stayed close to previous dimensions. The modern versions silhouette was described as a "gentle wedge shape." Improved aerodynamically, it carried new high-intensity quad headlamps and wide taillamps. The sail panel area offered greater visibility. A new independent strut front suspension used barrel-type coil springs and a link-type control arm. Rear suspension was also a new design, using a transverse fiberglass leaf spring. Standard fittings included a front stabilizer bar, electronic level control, and four-wheel disc brakes. The new Riv was powered by the old favorite 231 cu. in. (3.8-liter) V-6, now producing 140 horsepower with sequential port fuel injection, a mass air flow sensor, and Computer Controlled Coil Ignition. Transmission was the four-speed automatic, with overdrive top gear. Rivieras contained from 7 to 10 microprocessors, depending on their option list. All of them worked with the exclusive Graphic Control Center (GCC), standard on all Rivieras. GCC, using a touch-sensitive cathode ray tube (video screen) in the center of the dash, served as the car's control center and information display. It replaced 91 controls that would otherwise be needed. When the ignition key was switched on, the display showed a summary page from the access areas: climate control, trip monitor gauges, radio and diagnostic data. Most of the time, no further effort was needed. But a touch of the screen at the appropriate spot pulled in further information. Certain electrical equipment could remain in use after the ignition was switched off. Standard equipment included electronic instrumentation and Electronic Touch Climate Control. Instrument panel, doors, glove box and pillars were cloth-covered. A console held controls for the glove box and deck lid release, fuel filler door, and cassette player. Also standard: side window defoggers (in doors), assist straps, sliding sun screen visor extensions, head-

er console with dome and reading lamps, and electroluminescent backlight control switches. A tool kit and new scissors jack fit under the trunk floor. Two new Riviera options: keyless entry and a heated outside drivers mirror. Rivieras new T Type included a Gran Touring (Level III) suspension, aluminum wheels with P215/60R15 Eagle GT blackwall tires, power comfort seats that even adjusted headrest height, reversible (leather/velour) front seat cushions and backs, leather-wrapped steering wheel and shift selector, plus gauges for washer fluid level, oil pressure, and external lamp monitors. T Types came in four two-tone body color combinations, with sporty graphics. Buick reported acceleration times of the T Type Riviera at 8.3 seconds to 50 mph, or 11.3 seconds to 60.

I.D. DATA: Buicks continued the standardized 17-symbol Vehicle Identification Number (VIN), stamped on a metal tag attached to the upper left surface of the cowl, visible through the windshield. Coding was similar to 1985, starting with '1' to indicate U.S.A., followed by 'G' for General Motors, '4' for Buick Division, and a letter to indicate restraint system. Symbol five denotes series: "S" Skyhawk; "T" Skyhawk Ltd.; "E" Skyhawk T Type; "J" Skylark/Somerset Custom; "M" Skylark/Somerset Ltd.; "K" Somerset T Type; "H" Century Custom; "L" Century Ltd.; "G" Century T Type, "J" Regal; "K" Regal T Type; "M" Regal Ltd.; "H" LeSabre; "P" LeSabre Custom; "R" LeSabre Ltd.; "L" LeSabre T Type; "X" Electra; "W" Electra Park Ave.; "F" Electra T Type; "V" Electra Estate Wagon; "Z" Riviera; and "Y" Riviera T Type; Digits six and seven indicate body type: "27" 2-dr. coupe; "37" LeSabre 2-dr. coupe; "47" Regal 2-dr. coupe; "57" Riviera 2-dr. coupe: "11" Electra 2-dr. sedan; "19" Electra 4-dr. sedan; "69" 4-dr. (4-window) sedan; "35" 4-dr. wagon. Next is the engine code: "O" L4-110 TBI; "J" turbo L4-110 MFI; "P" L4-121 TBI; "U" L4-151 TBI; "R" L4-151 TBI; "X" V6-173 2Bbl.; "L" V6-181 MFI; "A" V6-231 2Bbl.; "3" V6-231 SFI; "B" V6-231 SFI; "7" turbo V6-231 SFI; "T" diesel V6-263; "Y" V8-307 4Bbl. Symbol nine is a check digit. Symbol ten denotes model year ("G" 1986). Symbol eleven is the plant code: "M" Lansing, MI; "T" Tarrytown, NY; "D" Doraville, GA; "6" Oklahoma City, OK; "H" Flint, MI; "K" Leeds, MO; "X" Fairfax, KS; "1" Wentzville, MO. The final six digits are the sequential serial number. An additional identifying number may be found on the engine. A body number plate on upper shroud or radiator support assembly reveals model year, car division, series, style, body assembly plant, body number, trim combination, modular seat code, paint code, and date build code.

1986 Buick, Skyhawk Custom station wagon with optional styled wheels. (OCW)

SKYHAWK CUSTOM (FOUR)

Model No.	Body/Style No.	Body Type & Seating	Factory Price	Shipping Weight	Prod. Total
4J	S27	2-dr Coupe-5P	7844	2277	45,884
4J	S69	4-dr Sedan-5P	8073	2325	29,959
4J	S35	4-dr Sta Wag-5P	8426	2402	6,079

SKYHAWK LIMITED (FOUR)

Model No.	Body/Style No.	Body Type & Seating	Factory Price	Shipping Weight	Prod. Total
4J	T27	2-dr Coupe-5P	8388	2314	Note 1
4J	T69	4-dr Sedan-5P	8598	2356	Note 1
4J	T35	4-dr Sta Wag-5P	8910	2429	Note 1

SKYHAWK SPORT (FOUR)

Model No.	Body/Style No.	Body Type & Seating	Factory Price	Shipping Weight	Prod. Total
4J	S77	2-dr Hatch-5P	8184	2336	Note 2

SKYHAWK T TYPE (FOUR)

Model No.	Body/Style No.	Body Type & Seating	Factory Price	Shipping Weight	Prod. Total
4J	E77	2-dr Hatch-5P	9414	2360	Note 2
4J	E27	2-dr Coupe-5P	8971	2301	Note 1

Note 1: Production figures listed under Skyhawk Custom coupe, sedan and station wagon include totals for Limited and T Type models. For the model year, 72,687 Custom, 6,584 Limited and 6,071 T Type coupes and sedans were built.

Note 2: Total hatchback production, 9,499 units.

SKYLARK CUSTOM (FOUR/V-6)

4N	J69	4-dr Sedan-5P	9620/10230	2502/2611	Note 3

SKYLARK LIMITED (FOUR/V-6)

4N	M69	4-dr Sedan-5P	10290/10900	2519/2576	Note 3

Note 3: Total Skylark production, 62,235.

SOMERSET CUSTOM (FOUR/V-6)

4N	J27	2-dr Coupe-5P	9425/10035	2456/2561	Note 4
4N	M27	2-dr Coupe-5P	10095/10705	2473/2578	Note 4

1986 Buick, Somerset T Type coupe. (OCW)

SOMERSET T TYPE (V-6)

4N	K27	2-dr Coupe-5P	11390	2608	3,558

Note 4: Total Somerset production, 75,620. A total of 98,641 Skylark/Somerset Customs and 35,658 Limiteds were produced.

CENTURY CUSTOM (FOUR/V-6)

4A	H27	2-dr Coupe-6P	10052/10487	2616/2677	14,781
4A	H19	4-dr Sedan-6P	10228/10663	2663/2724	229,066
4A	H35	4-dr Sta Wag-6P	10648/11083	2828/2889	25,374

CENTURY LIMITED (FOUR/V-6)

4A	L27	2-dr Coupe-6P	10544/10979	2639/2700	Note 5
4A	L19	4-dr Sedan-6P	10729/11164	2685/2746	Note 5
4A	L35	4-dr Sta Wag-6P	11109/11544	2847/2908	Note 5

Note 5: Century Custom production totals include Limited models. Total model year coupe/sedan production, 116,862 Customs and 126,985 Limiteds. Coupe total includes 1,029 Gran Sport models.

CENTURY T TYPE (V-6)

4A	G19	4-dr Sedan-6P	12223	2863	5,286

REGAL (V-6/V-8)

4G	J47	2-dr Coupe-6P	10654/11194	3106/3345	39,734

REGAL LIMITED (V-6/V-8)

4G	M47	2-dr Coupe-6P	11347/11887	3132/3371	43,599

REGAL T TYPE (V-6)

4G	K47	2-dr Coupe-6P	13714	3285	7,896

Note 6: Regal production total includes 5,512 Grand Nationals.

LESABRE CUSTOM (V-6)

4H	P37	2-dr Coupe-6P	12511	3042	7,191
4H	P69	4-dr Sedan-6P	12511	3081	30,235

LESABRE LIMITED (V-6)

4H	R37	2-dr Coupe-6P	13633	3070	14,331
4H	R69	4-dr Sedan-6P	13633	3112	43,215

Note 7: Only 117 LeSabre Grand National coupes were built.

LESABRE ESTATE WAGON (V-8)

4B	R35	4-dr Sta Wag-6P	13622	4093	7,755

ELECTRA (V-6)

4C	X11	2-dr Coupe-6P	15396	3147	4,996
4C	X69	4-dr Sedan-6P	15588	3189	109,042

ELECTRA PARK AVENUE (V-6)

4C	W11	2-dr Coupe-6P	17158	3181	Note 8
4C	W69	4-dr Sedan-6P	17338	3223	Note 8

Note 8: Electra production figures include Park Avenue models. Total model year production, 23,017 base Electras and 91,021 Park Avenues.

ELECTRA T TYPE (V-6)

Model No.	Body/Style No.	Body Type & Seating	Factory Price	Shipping Weight	Prod. Total
4C	F69	4-dr Sedan-6P	16826	3234	5,816

ELECTRA ESTATE WAGON (V-8)

4C	V35	4-dr Sta Wag-6P	16402	4172	10,371

RIVIERA (V-6)

4E	Z57	2-dr Coupe-5P	19831	3203	20,096

RIVIERA T TYPE (V-6)

4E	Y57	2-dr Coupe-5P	21577	3263	2,042

FACTORY PRICE AND WEIGHT NOTE: Figure before the slash is for four cylinder engine, after the slash for V-6. For Regal, figure before the slash is for V-6 engine, after slash for V-8.

ENGINES: BASE FOUR (Skyhawk): Inline, overhead-valve four-cylinder. Cast iron block and head. Displacement: 121 cu. in. (2.0 liters). Bore & stroke: 3.50 x 3.15 in. Compression ratio: 9.0:1. Brake horsepower: 88 at 4800 R.P.M. Torque: 110 lb.-ft. at 2400 R.P.M. Five main bearings. Hydraulic valve lifters. Throttle-body fuel injection. VIN Code: P. OPTIONAL FOUR (Skyhawk); STANDARD (Skyhawk T Type): Inline, overhead-cam four-cylinder. Cast iron block; aluminum cylinder head. Displacement: 110 cu. in. (1.8 liters). Bore & stroke: 3.34 x 3.13 in. Compression ratio: 8.8:1. Brake horsepower: 88 at 4800 R.P.M. Torque: 98 lb.-ft. at 2800 R.P.M. Five main bearings. Hydraulic valve lifters. Throttle-body fuel injection. VIN code: O. TURBOCHARGED FOUR; OPTIONAL (Skyhawk): Same as 1.8-liter OHC four above, except: Compression ratio: 8.0:1. Brake H.P.: 150 at 5600 R.P.M. Torque: 150 lb.-ft. at 2800 R.P.M. Multi-point fuel injection. VIN Code: J. BASE FOUR (Skylark, Century, Somerset): Inline, overhead-valve four-cylinder. Cast iron block and head. Displacement: 151 cu. in. (2.5 liters). Bore & stroke: 4.0 x 3 0 in. Compression ratio: 9.0:1. Brake horsepower: 92 at 4400 R.P.M. Torque: 134 lb.-ft. at 2800 R.P.M. Five main bearings. Hydraulic valve lifters. Throttle-body fuel injection. Built by Pontiac. VIN Code: R. OPTIONAL V-6 (Century): 60-degree, overhead-valve V-6. Cast iron block and head. Displacement: 173 cu. in. (2.8 liters). Bore & stroke: 3.50 x 2.99 in. Compression ratio: 8.5:1. Brake horsepower: 112 at 4800 R.P.M. Torque: 145 lb.-ft. at 2100 R.P.M. Four main bearings. Hydraulic valve lifters. Carburetor: 2Bbl. Built by Chevrolet. VIN Code: X. BASE V-6 (Somerset T Type, LeSabre); OPTIONAL (Somerset/Skylark): 90-degree, overhead-valve V-6. Cast iron block and head. Displacement: 181 cu. in. (3.0 liters). Bore & stroke: 3.80 x 2.66 in. Compression ratio: 9.0:1. Brake horsepower: 125 at 4900 R.P.M. Torque: 150 lb.-ft. at 2400 R.P.M. Four main bearings. Hydraulic valve lifters. Multi-point fuel injection. VIN Code: L. BASE V-6 (Regal): 90-degree, overhead-valve V-6. Cast iron alloy block and head. Displacement: 231 cu. in. (3.8 liters). Bore & stroke: 3.8 x 3.4 in. Compression ratio: 8.0:1. Brake horsepower: 110 at 3800 R.P.M. Torque: 190 lb.-ft. at 1600 R.P.M. Four main bearings. Hydraulic valve lifters. Carb.: 2Bbl. VIN Code: A. BASE V-6 (Century T Type); OPTIONAL (Century, LeSabre): Same as 231 V-6 above, but with sequential fuel injection. Brake H.P.: 150 at 4400 R.P.M. Torque: 200 lb.-ft. at 2000 R.P.M. VIN Code: 3. BASE V-6 (Electra, Riviera): Same as 231 V-6 above, with sequential fuel injection. Compression ratio: 8.5:1. Brake H.P.: 140 at 4400 R.P.M. Torque: 200 lb.-ft. at 2000 R.P.M. VIN Code: B. TURBOCHARGED V-6 (Regal T Type): Same as 231 V-6 above, with turbocharger, intercooler and sequential fuel injection. Brake H.P.: 235 at 4400 R.P.M. Torque: 330 lb.-ft. at 2800 R.P.M. VIN Code: 7. BASE V-8 (Estate); OPTIONAL (Regal): 90-degree, overhead valve V-8. Cast iron block and head. Displacement: 307 cu. in. (5.0 liters). Bore & stroke: 3.80 x 3.385 in. Compression ratio: 8.0:1. Brake horsepower: 140 at 3200 R.P.M. Torque: 255 lb.-ft. at 2000 R.P.M. Five main bearings. Hydraulic valve lifters. Carburetor: 4Bbl. Built by Oldsmobile. VIN Code: Y or H.

CHASSIS DATA: Wheelbase: (Skyhawk) 101.2 in.; (Skylark/Somerset) 103.4 in.; (Century) 104.8 in.; (Century wag) 104.9 in.; (Regal) 108.1 in.; (Estate) 115.9 in.; (LeSabre/Electra) 110.8 in.; (Riviera) 108.0 in.; Overall length: (Skyhawk cpe) 175.3 in.; (Skyhawk sed/wag) 177.3 in.; (Skylark) 181.1 in.; (Somerset Regal) 180.0 in.; (Century) 189.1 in.; (Century wag) 190.9 in.; (Regal) 200.6 in.; (LeSabre) 196.4 in.; (Electra) 197.0 in.; (Estate) 221.3 in.; (Riviera) 187.8 in. Height: (Skyhawk) 54.0 in.; (Skyhawk hatch) 51.9 in.; (Skyhawk wag) 54.4 in.; (Skylark) 52.2 in.; (Somerset) 52.1 in.; (Century cpe) 53.7 in.; (Century sed/wag) 54.2 in.; (Regal) 54.6 in.; (LeSabre cpe) 54.7 in.; (LeSabre sed) 55.4 in.; (Estate) 59.3 in.; (Electra) 54.3 in.; (Riv) 53.5 in. Width: (Skyhawk) 65.0 in.; (Skylark) 66.6 in.; (Somerset/Century) 67.7 in.; (Regal) 71.6 in.; (Estate) 79.3 in.; (LeSabre/Electra) 72.4 in.; (Riv) 71.3 in. Front Tread: (Skyhawk cpe) 55.3 in.; (Skyhawk sed/wag) 55.4 in.; (Century) 58.7 in.; (Skylark/Somerset) 55.5 in.; (Regal) 58.5 in.; (LeSabre/Electra) 60.3 in.; (Estate) 62.2 in.; (Riv) 59.9 in. Rear Tread: (Skyhawk) 55.1-55.2 in.; (Skylark/Somerset) 55.2 in.; (Century) 56.7 in.; (Regal) 57.7 in.; (LeSabre/Electra) 59.8 in.; (Estate) 64.0 in.; (Riviera) 59.9 in. Standard Tires: (Skyhawk) P175/80R13 SBR; (Skyhawk T Type) P195/70R13 SBR; (Skylark/Somerset) P185/80R13 SBR; (Century) P185/75R14 SBR; (Somerset/Century T Type) P215/60R14 Eagle GT SBR; (Regal) P195/75R15 SBR WSW; (Regal T Type) P215/65R15 SBR (LeSabre/Electra) P205/75R14 SBR WSW; (Electra T) P215/65R15 SBR Eagle GT; (Park Ave.) P205/75R14 SBR WSW; (Estate) P225/75R15 SBR WSW; (Riviera) P205/70R14 SBR WSW; (Riviera T) P215/60R15 Eagle GT SBR.

TECHNICAL: Transmission: Four-speed, fully synchronized floor shift standard on Skyhawk. Five-speed manual standard on Skylark/Somerset, available on Skyhawk. Four-speed overdrive automatic standard on LeSabre/Electra/Estate/Riviera, available on Century/Regal, which have standard three-speed automatic. Three-speed auto. trans. gear ratios: (1st) 2.74:1; (2nd) 1.57:1; (3rd) 1.00:1; (Rev) 2.07.1. Skyhawk/Skylark/Somerset Century auto. trans. gear ratios: (1st) 2.84:1; (2nd) 1.60:1; (3rd) 1.00:1; (Rev) 2.07:1. Regal four-speed overdrive automatic gear ratios: (1st) 2.74:1; (2nd) 1.57:1; (3rd) 1.00:1; (4th) 0.67:1; (Rev) 2.07:1. Century/Electra four-speed automatic: (1st) 2.92:1; (2nd) 1.57:1; (3rd) 1.00:1; (4th) 0.70:1; (Rev) 2.38:1. Standard axle ratio: (Skyhawk) 3.65:1 w/4-spd, 3.45:1 w/5-spd, 3.18:1 w/auto.; (Skyhawk turbo) 3.65:1 w/4-spd, 3.33:1 w/auto.; (Skylark/Somerset) 2.84:1; (Century) 2.84:1 w/3-spd, 2.84:1 or 3.06:1 w/4-spd, (Regal) 2.41:1 exc. w/V-8, 2.56:1; (Regal T Type) 3.41:1; (LeSabre) 2.73:1 or 3.06:1; (Electra/Riv) 2.84:1; (Estate) 2.73:1. Steering: (Regal/Estate) recirculating ball; (others) rack and pinion; power assist standard on all except Skyhawk. Suspension: (Skyhawk/Somerset/Skylark) MacPherson strut front w/stabilizer; semi-independent beam rear axle w/trailing arms; rear stabilizer bar optional, std. on T Type. (Century) MacPherson strut front suspension; beam twist rear axle w/trailing arms and Panhard rod; front/rear stabilizer bars. (LeSabre/Electra) MacPherson front struts, barrel springs and stabilizer bar; fully independent rear suspension using struts w/stabilizer bar and electronic level control. (Riviera) four-wheel independent suspension with front struts, barrel springs, link control arms and stabilizer bar; transverse leaf rear springs w/control arms and electronic level control. (Regal/Estate) front/rear coil springs; stabilizer bars; rigid four-link rear axle. Brakes: power front disc, rear drum. Four-wheel disc brakes on Riviera. Anti-lock braking system available on Electra. Body construction: (front-drive models) unitized; (Regal/Estate) separate body and frame. Fuel tank: (Skyhawk/Somerset/Skylark) 13.6 gal.; (Century) 15.7 gal.; (Regal) 18.1 gal.; (LeSabre/Electra/Riv) 18.0 gal.; (Estate) 22.0 gal.

DRIVETRAIN OPTIONS: Engines: 110 cu. in. (1.8-liter) EFI four: Skyhawk ($50); std. on T Type. Turbocharged 110 cu. in. (1.8-liter) EFI four: Skyhawk T Type ($800 incl. boost gauge, engine block heater and Shelby aluminum wheels. 173 cu. in. (2.8-liter) V-6, 2Bbl.: Century ($435). 181 cu. in. (3.0-liter) V-6, 2Bbl.: Sky-

lark/Somerset ($610). 231 cu. in. (3.8-liter) V-6, SFI: Century ($695), std. on T Type; LeSabre ($370), std. w/Grand National pkg. 307 cu. in. (5.0-liter) V-8, 4Bbl.: Regal ($540). Transmission/Differential: Four-speed manual trans.: Skyhawk T Type ($75 credit). Five-speed manual trans.: Skyhawk ($75); std. on T. Three-speed auto. trans.: Skyhawk ($465); Skyhawk T Type ($390); Skylark/Somerset ($465), std. on T Type. Four-speed automatic overdrive trans.: Century/Regal ($175); std. on T Type. Optional rear axle ratio: Skyhawk 3.19:1 or 3.43:1; Century 2.84:1; Regal; LeSabre 2.84:1; Electra 2.73:1 or 2.97:1 (all NC). Limited slip differential: Regal/Estate ($95). Suspension, Steering and Brakes: F40 heavy-duty suspension ($27). F41 Gran Touring suspension ($27) exc. Regal ($49); N/A on Estate. Special G.T. suspension: Skyhawk T Type (NC). Automatic level control: Estate ($175). Power steering: Skyhawk ($215). Anti-lock brakes: Electra ($825). Other: H.D. alternator: 85, 94, 100, 108 and 120-amp ($20-$90). H.D. battery ($25-$26). H.D. radiator: Skyhawk ($40-$70); Century ($30). Engine block heater ($18). H.D. engine/trans. cooling: Century/Regal/LeSabre/Electra/Riviera ($40-$70). Trailer towing harness: Riviera ($30).

SKYHAWK CONVENIENCE/APPEARANCE OPTIONS: Option Packages: Performance pkg.: GT suspension, aluminum wheels, P205/60R14 SBR BSW, leather-wrapped steering wheel ($574) exc. T type/wag. SCS pkg. (P185/70R13 SBR BSW, custom seats and door trim, custom steering wheel, black moldings): Cust cpe ($51). Vista Vent flip-open removable glass sunroof ($310). Acoustic pkg. ($36). Instrument gauge pkg.: temp, oil pressure, volts, trip odometer: Cust, Spt ($60). Instrument gauges and tachometer: Cust, Spt ($138); Ltd ($78). Comfort/Convenience: Air cond. ($645). Rear defogger, electric ($135). Louvered rear window sun shield: hatch ($199). Cruise control w/resume ($175). Power windows ($195-$270). Power door locks ($130-$180). Six-way power drivers seat ($225). Easy-entry passenger seat adjuster: Cust cpe, Spt ($16). Tinted glass ($99). Sport steering wheel ($50). Leather-wrapped steering wheel: T Type ($40). Tilt steering ($115). Trip odometer: Cust, Spt ($15). Electric trunk release ($40). Remote tailgate release: wag ($40). Tailgate wiper/washer: wag, hatch ($125). Two-speed wipers w/delay ($50). Lights, Horns and Mirrors: Tungsten-halogen headlamps ($25). Headlamps-on indicator ($15). Front seat reading lamp ($30). Dual horns: Cust cpe/sed, Spt ($15). Left black remote mirror ($22) exc. T Type. Dual black mirrors: left remote ($53); std. on T Type. Visor vanity mirror, passenger ($7). Lighted visor vanity mirror ($45). Entertainment: Basic seek/scan electronic-tuning AM/FM stereo radio ($158); w/clock ($222); w/cassette ($344). Electronic-tuning AM/FM stereo radio ($242); w/cassette and graphic equalizer ($494). Radio delete ($56 credit). Power antenna ($65). Dual rear speakers ($25). Exterior Trim: Rear spoiler: Sport ($70). Door edge guards ($15-$25). Wide chrome rocker panel moldings: Cust cpe/sed ($26). Black rocker panel moldings: Spt ($76). Black wheel opening moldings: Spt ($30). Bodyside stripes ($45). Sport stripes: Cust cpe ($95). Designer's accent paint ($195). Lower gray accent paint: T Type ($195). Decklid luggage rack ($100). Roof rack: wag ($105). Front license bracket (NC). Interior Trim/Upholstery: Seat trim for SCS pkg.: Cust cpe ($291). Front armrest: Cust, T cpe ($45). Front/rear fiber doormats: Cust, T Type cpe ($66). Front carpet savers ($17); rear ($12). Front carpet savers w/inserts ($18); rear ($15). Deluxe trunk trim ($33). Rear compartment security cover ($69). Wheels and Tires: Styled aluminum wheels ($229); std. T Type. Styled alum. wheels (14 in.): Sport ($259). Locking wire wheel covers ($180). Hubcaps and trim rings: Cust/Ltd ($38). P175/80R13 SBR WSW ($54). P195/70R13 SBR BSW ($104). P195/70R13 SBR WSW ($166). P195/70R13 SBR WLT ($188); T Type ($84). P205/60R14 SBR BSW: Spt ($198); T ($94). P205/60R14 SBR WLT: Spt ($286); T ($182).

SKYLARK/SOMERSET/CENTURY CONVENIENCE/APPEARANCE OPTIONS: Option Packages: Century Gran Sport pkg.: 3.8-liter V-6, sporty exhaust, P205/60R15 SBR GT tires

on alum. wheels, tach, black leather-wrapped steering wheel, AM/FM stereo w/cassette, air dam, spoiler, gauges, black trim, wide rocker moldings: Cust cpe ($3895). Skylark/Somerset performance pkg.: Gran Touring suspension, P215/60R14 BSW tires, alum. wheels, leather-wrapped steering wheel ($592). Flip-open Vista Vent removable glass sunroof ($310-$339). Skylark/Somerset value option pkg.: tilt steering, cruise control, electric door locks, delay wiper, wire wheel covers or alum. wheels ($200 credit from list price). Century value option pkg.: tilt, cruise, lighted vanity mirror, delay wiper and AM/FM ET radio ($200 credit). Comfort/Convenience: Air cond. ($645); Century ($750). Cruise control ($175). Rear defogger, electric ($135-$145). Power windows: 2-dr. ($195); 4-dr. ($270). Electric door locks ($130-$180). Automatic door locks ($220-$270). Six-way power drivers seat ($225). Manual seatback recliner, passenger: Century ($45); both ($90). Sport steering wheel: Skylark/Somerset Cust, Century ($50). Tilt steering ($115). Tinted glass: Century ($115). Instrument gauges incl. trip odometer: Century ($48); w/tach ($126). Trip odometer: Century ($16). Digital electronic instrument cluster: Century ($225); T Type ($131). Electric trunk release ($40-$45). Remote tailgate lock: Century wag ($40). Remote fuel filler door release: Skylark/Somerset Cust, T ($11). Two-speed wipers w/delay ($50). Rear wiper/washer: Century wag ($125). Low washer fluid indicator: Skylark/Somerset ($16). Theft deterrent system: Century ($159). Lights, Horns and Mirrors: Tungsten-halogen headlamps: Century ($25). Twilight Sentinel: Century ($57). Coach lamps: Century Ltd ($129). Headlamps-on chime: Century ($16). Door courtesy/warning light: Ltd/wag ($44). Front/rear reading/courtesy lights: Skylark/Somerset ($40-$54). Rear seat reading lamp: Skylark/Somerset Ltd, Century ($30); front, Century ($24). Remote-control left mirror: Century Cust/Ltd ($25). Dual mirrors (left remote, right manual): Skylark/Somerset Cust ($53); Century ($61). Dual power remote mirrors: Cust, Century ($139); Ltd, T Type ($86). Dual black electric remote mirrors: Century ($139); T ($78). Visor vanity mirror, passenger: Century ($7). Lighted visor vanity mirror, passenger: Skylark/Somerset ($38); Century ($58). Entertainment: Electronic-tuning seek/scan AM/FM stereo radio ($157); w/cassette and equalizer ($424-$494). Somerset/Skylark AM/FM stereo w/cassette and Delco-GM/Bose music system ($995). Century ET radio w/clock ($222-$242); w/cassette ($344). Cassette tape player: Somerset/Skylark ($142); stereo radio req'd. Concert sound six-speaker system ($70-$125). Premium speakers: Century wag ($35-$60). Rear speakers ($25). Power antenna ($65). Delete radio ($56-$96 credit). Exterior Trim: Landau vinyl top: Century cpe ($186); heavy-padded ($623). Long vinyl top: Century sed ($160). Designers' accent paint: Skylark/Somerset Cust/Ltd ($195); Century ($205). Charcoal lower accent: Century T ($205). Special solid color paint: Century Cust/Ltd/Estate ($200). Color-keyed bodyside moldings: Skylark/Somerset ($45); Century T ($55). Rocker panel moldings: Skylark/Somerset Cust ($26). Wide rocker panel/rear quarter moldings: Skylark/Somerset Cust ($76); Ltd ($50); Century Cust ($65). Wheel opening moldings: Skylark/Somerset Cust ($30). Windsplit molding: Century Cust ($22). Door edge guards ($15-$25). Bodyside stripes ($45). Woodgrain appliqué: Century wag ($350). Decklid luggage rack ($100). Tailgate air deflector: Century wag ($37). Roof rack: Century wag ($105). Swing-out rear quarter vent windows: Century wag ($75). Front license bracket (NC). Interior Trim/Upholstery: Cloth 55/45 notchback seating: Century ($133). Cloth bucket seats: Century Cust ($97). Leather/vinyl 45/45 seats: Century Ltd ($295): T ($425). Cloth 45/45 seats: Century Ltd/Estate (NC). Full-length console: Century ($57). Operating console: Century ($85); T Type ($28). Leather/vinyl bucket seats: Skylark/Somerset Ltd ($275). Lear Siegler bucket seats: Somerset, Century T Type ($600). Front floor mats w/inserts: Skylark/Somerset ($18); rear ($15). Front mats: Century ($17); rear ($12). Floor mats w/inserts: Century front ($25); rear ($20). Trunk trim: Century ($25-$47). Locking storage compartment: Century wag ($44). Wheels: Cast aluminum wheels: Century ($199); std. on T.

Styled aluminum wheels: Skylark/Somerset Cust/Ltd ($229). Locking wire wheel covers ($199). Skylark/Somerset All-Season Tires: P185/80R13 SBR WSW ($58). P205/70R13 SBR BSW ($114). P205/70R13 SBR WSW ($180). P215/60R14 SBR WLT ($202). P215/60R14 SBR Eagle GT WLT: Somerset T ($92). Century All-Season Tires: P185/75R14 SBR WSW ($58). P195/75R14 SBR BSW ($30). P195/75R14 SBR WSW ($92). P215/60R14 SBR WLT T Type ($92).

REGAL CONVENIENCE/APPEARANCE OPTIONS: Option Packages: Regal Grand National pkg. (black body, front/rear bumpers, front air dam, rub strips/guards, cloth bucket seats, operating console, spoiler, performance-tuned suspension, chromed wheels): T Type ($635). Regal T Type Designer pkg.: black front air dam, rear spoilers and special black/dark gray accent paint ($403). Sliding silver electric Astroroof ($925). Hatch roof ($850). Value option pkg.: 5.0-liter V-8, cruise control, lighted visor mirror, delay wiper, tilt steering, stereo radio w/cassette, automatic power antenna ($425 credit from list prices). Comfort/Convenience: Air cond. ($750). Automatic touch climate control air cond. ($900); T ($150). Cruise control w/resume ($175). Rear defogger, electric ($145). Tinted glass ($115). Tinted windshield ($99). Six-way power driver's seat ($225). Manual passenger seatback recliner ($75). Digital electronic instrument cluster ($299); T Type ($173). Sport steering wheel ($50); N/A T Type. Tilt steering ($115). Power windows ($195). Electric door locks ($130). Electric trunk release ($40). Headlamps-on indicator ($16). Trip odometer ($16); std. T Type. Two-speed wiper w/delay ($50). Theft deterrent system ($159). Lighting and Mirrors: Tungsten-halogen headlamps ($25). Twilight Sentinel ($57). Cornering lamps ($57) exc. T Type. Coach lamps: Ltd ($102). Door courtesy/warning lights: Ltd ($44). Rear seat reading light ($30); rear ($24). Dual sport mirrors, left remote ($53); std. T Type. Dual chrome mirrors, left remote ($25) exc. T. Dual remote color-keyed mirrors ($83); T ($30). Visor vanity mirror, passenger ($7). Lighted visor vanity mirror, passenger ($58). Entertainment: Seek/scan electronic-tuning AM/FM stereo radio ($158); w/clock ($222); w/cassette ($344). Electronic-tuning AM/FM stereo radio ($242); w/cassette and equalizer ($494). Concert sound speakers ($95). Dual rear speakers ($25). Automatic power antenna ($65). Radio delete ($56 credit). Exterior Trim: Landau vinyl top ($186) exc. T Type. Heavy-padded landau vinyl top ($245) exc. T Type. Designers' accent paint ($205). Solid special color paint ($200). Exterior molding pkg. (wide rocker panel and belt reveal moldings): base ($110). Black protective bodyside moldings: T Type ($55). Door edge guards ($15). Bodyside stripes ($45). Front license bracket (NC). Interior Trim/Upholstery: Full-length console: Ltd/T ($82). Lear Siegler bucket seats: T Type ($600). Cloth bucket seats: base/T ($195). Cloth 55/45 seating ($133); std. on Ltd. Leather/vinyl 45/45 seating: Ltd ($295); T Type ($595). Front mats ($17); rear ($12). Front mats w/inserts ($25); rear ($20). Trunk trim covering ($47). Wheels: Chrome-plated wheels ($195); N/A T Type. Cast aluminum wheels ($285); std. T Type. Color-keyed wheels ($85) exc. T Type. Locking wire wheel covers ($199); N/A T Type. All-Season Tires: P205/70R14 SBR WSW ($62). P215/65R15 SBR WLT: T Type ($92).

LESABRE/ELECTRA/ESTATE WAGON CONVENIENCE & APPEARANCE OPTIONS: Option Packages: LeSabre Grand National pkg. (3.8-liter V-6, dual exhaust, white or black paint, 2.84:1 rear axle, P215/65R15 Eagle GT tires on alum. wheels, Gran Touring suspension, leather-wrapped sport steering wheel, front floor mats, side window and belt moldings, and quarter-window close-out): Cust cpe ($1237). LeSabre performance pkg.: G.T. suspension, 2.84:1 axle, P215/65R15 Eagle GT tires on alum. wheels, leather-wrapped steering wheel ($878); 3.8-liter engine incl. latter. Electra performance pkg.: G.T. suspension, P215/65R15 tires on alum. wheels, leather-wrapped steering wheel ($508); Park Ave. ($407). Sliding electric Astroroof: Electra ($1230). Vista Vent flip-open sunroof: LeSabre ($310). Comfort/Convenience: Air cond: LeSabre ($150). Automatic air

cond.: Electra ($165). Air cond. w/touch-climate control: Estate ($150). Cruise control ($175); std. on Park Ave. Rear defogger, electric ($145). Power windows: LeSabre ($195-$270). Power door locks ($130-$180). Automatic door locks: Electra ($220-$270); exc. Park Ave. ($90). Six-way power seat, passenger's: Electra ($225); either side, LeSabre ($225). Two-position memory driver's seat: Electra ($178). Power seatback recliner, one side: Electra ($145); passenger only, LeSabre Cust ($145); Ltd ($70). Manual seatback recliner, passenger: LeSabre Cust ($75). Sport steering wheel: LeSabre ($50). Tilt steering ($115); std. Park Ave. Tilt/telescoping steering column: Electra ($175) exc. Park Ave. ($60). Trip odometer: LeSabre ($16). Windshield washer fluid indicator ($16). Low fuel indicator ($16). Digital electronic instrumentation ($315). Keyless entry system: Electra ($185) exc. T Type. Electric trunk pulldown: Electra ($80). Electric trunk release ($40); std. on Park Ave. Theft deterrent system: Electra ($159); N/A on Estate. Two-speed wiper w/delay ($50); std. on Park Ave. Lighting, Horns and Mirrors: Lamp and indicator group: Estate ($70-$86). Tungsten-halogen headlamps ($25). Twilight Sentinel: Electra ($60). Cornering lamps ($60). Light monitors, front/rear: Electra ($77). Door courtesy/warning lamps ($44-$70). Lighted door lock and interior light control: Electra ($75). Four-note horn: Electra ($28). Dual chrome remote mirrors: Estate ($49). Dual electric remote mirrors: LeSabre ($91); Electra Ltd/T ($91). Dual electric remote mirrors (left heated): Electra ($126); Park Ave. ($35). Lighted visor vanity mirror ($58). Automatic day/night mirror: Electra ($80). Entertainment: Seek/scan electronic-tuning AM/FM stereo radio w/clock: LeSabre ($222). AM/FM stereo ET seek/scan radio w/clock and cassette: LeSabre ($344); Electra ($122). AM stereo/FM stereo ET seek/scan radio w/clock: LeSabre ($242); Electra ($20). AM stereo/FM stereo radio w/cassette and equalizer: LeSabre ($494); Electra ($272). AM stereo/FM stereo ET radio w/Dolby cassette and Delco GM/Bose sound system: LeSabre ($1117); Electra ($895). Radio delete: LeSabre ($56 credit); Electra ($275 credit). Concert sound speakers ($70-$100). Power antenna: Electra ($65). Exterior Trim: Exterior molding pkg. (wide rocker panel, rear fender lower and belt reveal moldings): LeSabre/Estate ($110). Landau vinyl top: LeSabre cpe ($185). Heavy-padded vinyl top: Electra ($245) exc. T Type. Special paint: Electra ($200) exc. Firemist ($210). Black lower bodyside moldings: LeSabre Cust ($55). Door edge guards ($15-$25). Bodyside stripes ($45). Woodgrain vinyl appliqué: LeSabre Estate ($345); delete from Electra Est ($320 credit). Roof rack w/air deflector: LeSabre Estate ($110). Rear air deflector: Est ($40). Decklid luggage rack ($100). Rear bumper guards: LeSabre ($24). Front license bracket (NC). Interior Trim/Upholstery: Cloth 55/45 seating: LeSabre Cust ($133). Leather/vinyl 55/45 seating: Park Ave. ($425). Leather/vinyl 45/45 seating: Electra T Type ($325). Third seat: Estate ($220). Front carpet mats w/inserts ($25); rear ($20). Trunk carpeting trim: Electra ($53). Trunk mat: Electra ($15). Wheels and Tires: Chrome-plated wheels: Estate ($40 credit). Styled aluminum wheels ($220-$285). Custom locking wire wheel covers ($164-$199); Estate ($56 credit). P205/75R14 SBR WSW ($66). P215/65R15 SBR BSW: LeSabre ($100). Self-sealing tires ($140).

RIVIERA CONVENIENCE/APPEARANCE OPTIONS: Comfort/Convenience: Performance pkg.: G.T. suspension. P215/60R15 tires on alum. wheels, leather-wrapped steering wheel ($454). Electric sliding Astroroof ($1230). Rear defogger, electric ($145). Keyless entry system ($185). Six-way power seat, passenger ($225). Electric seatback recliner, one side ($75). Automatic door locks ($90). Leather-wrapped sport steering wheel ($96); std. T Type. Electric trunk pulldown ($80). Theft deterrent system ($159). Lighting, Horns and Mirrors: Lamp and indicator group ($93). Twilight Sentinel ($60). Lighted door lock and interior light control ($75). Four-note horn ($28). Heated left mirror ($35). Lighted visor vanity mirrors, each ($58). Entertainment: Electronic-tuning AM/FM stereo radio w/cassette and clock ($342). Cassette player ($122); std. radio req'd. Electronic-tuning AM/FM

stereo radio w/Dolby cassette tape player ($895). Concert Sound II speaker system ($70). Exterior Trim: Designers' accent paint ($235). Special color Firemist paint ($210). Color-coordinated protective bodyside moldings ($55). Door edge guards ($15). Bodyside stripes ($45). Front license bracket (NC). Interior Trim/Upholstery: Cloth bucket seats ($460). Leather/suede power reclining bucket seats ($487). Leather/suede bucket seats w/lumbar support ($947). Front mats w/inserts ($35); rear ($20). Trunk mat ($50). Wheels and Tires: 14 in. aluminum wheels ($199); std. T Type. Locking wire wheel covers ($199) exc. T Type. P215/60R15 SBR WLT tires: w/performance pkg. ($70). P205/70R14 SBR BSW tires ($66 credit). Self-sealing tires ($140).

HISTORY: Buick's general introduction was October 3, 1985, but the new Somerset had debuted on August 28, 1985; and LeSabre and Riviera didn't emerge until November 14, 1985. Model year production (U.S.): 850,103 for a 10.7 percent share of the industry total. That number included 333,281 four-cylinder Buicks (up sharply from previous total), 442,699 with six cylinders, and only 74,124 V-8s—first time the V-8 total fell below 100,000. A total of 10,171 Buick engines were turbocharged this year. Calendar year production (U.S.): 775,966. Model year sales by U.S. dealers: 757,001 for a 9.4 percent share of the industry total. Calendar year sales (U.S.): 769,434 for a market share of 9.4 percent.

Historical Footnotes: Buick's sales slipped in 1986, down more than 17 percent—the lowest total since 1982. A V-6 shortage must have contributed to the slack figure. Century was the best seller by far. Starting in late September 1985, Riviera were built at the new plant in Hamtramck, Michigan. The downsized Rivieras didn't fare as well as expected, however, as big rear-drive cars began to enjoy a comeback. LeSabre production began on September 16, 1985, at the refurbished 1.5 million square-foot Buick City assembly plant in Flint, Michigan. Far fewer LeSabres than predicted were turned out. (Sales figures include the rear-drive B body LeSabre station wagons.) The Buick City operation had a number of high-tech innovations. Instead of the usual receiving dock, 22 separate docking locations put incoming materials near the areas where they would be used. "Just-in-time" scheduling meant there was no provision for storage of inventory. Robots were to be used to unload engines, seats and transaxles. Nearly 200 robots were planned for use in body assembly. At the separate Dimensional Verification Center, a car could be placed on a huge granite block, then automatically measured to make sure all fixtures and tooling were sufficiently precise. Front-drive cars with V-6 engines--especially the 3.8-liter with sequential fuel injection--were gaining in popularity. So the Buick-Oldsmobile-Cadillac (BOC) Group boosted output at the Flint plant, and initiated V-6 production at the Lansing, Michigan, facility as well. Some of the 2.8-liter V-6 engines were built in Mexico, while 1.8-liter Skyhawk fours came from Brazil. In a much different use of technology, new Consumer Information Centers were tested at shopping malls in Miami and suburban Dallas. They offered shoppers a variety of information on cars, driving, safety—and of course on the new Buicks. A futuristic Computerized Automotive Maintenance System could now let a dealer hook into a car's electronic control module to send data directly to Buick headquarters for analysis. At the design/evaluation stage, an OSCAR (On-Site Computer-Aided Research) system used sensors in a test car to send signals to a computer inside a nearby van.

1987

Buick selected Hal Holbrook to be its spokesperson for its 1987 models. Holbrook, perhaps best known for his portrayal of Mark Twain, was depicted as "the only star of super-status proportions to represent Buick in advertising in nearly two decades." Buick used such terms as "substantial," "value" and "reliability" in pro-

moting its new models. The Riviera was described as the "solid alternative to spending more for a luxurious performance automobile than you really need to." The 1987 Skylark was regarded as an automobile that "has Buick quality written all over it." The Electra, said Buick, was "the car that fits your lifestyle." The LeSabre was "the Buick that's so good at the things that really count." Buick called the Century the car that "today, as yesterday...stands for value that endures." while it considered the Regal a car with "traditional Buick comfort and ride, but decidedly performance-minded." The Somerset earned a description as "an exciting blend of sport and luxury in a personal size car." The Skylark was not left out of the receiving end of pleasing superlatives as Buick suggested: "If pure driving pleasure is the name of the game, Skyhawk is the name of the car." Throughout its product line, Buick made a strong effort to combine the virtues of a time-tested approach to building automobiles with an ample infusion of contemporary technology and performance. Its 3.8-liter SFI V-6 was standard in the Riviera, Electra and LeSabre and optional for the Century. All four Buicks were also available with a T-Package for the driver oriented toward an automobile with a firm suspension and quicker steering. The Regal, Buick's rear-drive mid-size car, was available with any of the three new Touring options, as well as the Turbo Package. The Skyhawk Custom, Limited and Sport hatchbacks were also available with a T-Package that complemented their sporty wedge profile. Similarly, the Somerset's T-Package, in conjunction with the Exterior Sport Package, made for an appealing automobile.

1987 Buick, Skyhawk Sport hatchback with optional louvered sunshield. (OCW)

1987 Buick, Skyhawk Custom sedan. (OCW)

SKYHAWK - SERIES 4J - FOUR - The big news for the 1987 Skyhawk was its new turbocharged 2.0-liter engine. Buick also offered four performance-oriented Touring options for the Skyhawk.

1987 Buick, Somerset Limited coupe. (OCW)

1987 Buick, Somerset Custom coupe with optional Sport package. (OCW)

SOMERSET - SERIES 4N - FOUR/V-6 - The Somerset was offered with a T-Package that included a Gran Touring suspension. Eagle GT tires, cast-aluminum wheels and a leather-wrapped steering wheel. The Somerset grille was redesigned for 1987. Both the Somerset Custom and Limited models had new seat and cloth trim designs. Both were also fitted with new shale gray trim plates on the dash, console and doors. Somerset coupes built after January 1987 had new automatic seat belt systems.

1987 Buick, Skylark Custom sedan with optional Sport package. (OCW)

1987 Buick, Skylark Custom sedan. (OCW)

SKYLARK - SERIES 4N - FOUR/V-6 - The 1987 Skylark could be equipped with a variety of new equipment intended to improve its road performance. The T-package consisted of a firmer Gran Touring suspension, leather-wrapped steering wheel,

cast-aluminum wheels and Eagle GT steel belted radial tires. Beginning in January 1987, all Skylark sedans were equipped with an automatic safety belt system.

1987 Buick, Century Limited coupe. (OCW)

1987 Buick, Century Limited sedan with optional wire wheel covers. (OCW)

CENTURY - SERIES 4A - FOUR/V-6 - The Century was virtually unchanged for 1987. Both the Century Custom and Limited were again offered as either coupe or sedan models. Also available was the T-Package, which included the Gran Touring suspension with firmer springs, larger diameter front and rear stabilizer bars and a quicker steering ratio. Low profile Eagle GT blackwall tires were also specified. The Century was also offered with the Exterior Sport package, which consisted of a blackout treatment for the grille, bumpers, moldings and wheel openings. As alternatives to the standard 2.5-liter Tech IV engine, either a 2.8-liter V-6 with multi-port fuel injection or a 3.8-liter V-6 with sequential fuel injection were available. The Custom interior consisted of a cloth fabric. The Limited model had 55/45 notched seats finished in velour. Optional 45/45 seats were upholstered in either cloth or leather. A new shale gray dash was used on Century coupes. The sedans had a new brushed pewter trim.

1987 Buick, Regal Limited coupe with optional wire wheel covers. (OCW)

1987 Buick, Regal with optional Sport package and Turbo package (3.8-liter turbocharged V-6). (OCW)

REGAL - SERIES 4G - V-6/V-8 - The Regal retained its rear wheel drivetrain for 1987. Three versions were offered: Regal, Limited and Grand National. Three performance packages were available. The Regal Grand National was its turbocharged and intercooled engine equipped with sequential-port fuel injection (SFI) was one of the fastest accelerating cars built in the United States. It was easily identified by its blacked-out exterior. Standard on the Grand National was a firm Gran Touring suspension. The other Regal coupes could be ordered with the T-Package as well as an Exterior Sport Package consisting of aluminum alloy wheels and Eagle GT blackwall tires. It was also possible to order the Turbo Package for any Regal coupe. The Turbo engine's SFI was developed by Buick and the Bosch firm of Germany. It injected precisely timed and metered amount of fuel directly into the cylinders. The intercooler cooled the pressurized air charge from the turbocharger to the engine. The turbocharger increased engine output by 122 percent over the normally aspirated engine. The SFI engine's 245 horsepower was linked to a four-speed automatic transmission with overdrive. The Turbo Package also included a 3.42:1 axle ratio and a turbo hood treatment. The Regal was also available with a 5.0-liter V-8 and automatic overdrive transmission. All Regals were equipped with power steering and power-assisted low-drag front disc and rear drum brakes.

1987 Buick, LeSabre T Type coupe. (OCW)

1987 Buick, LeSabre sedan. (OCW)

1987 Buick, LeSabre Limited coupe. (OCW)

1987 Buick, LeSabre Estate Wagon station wagon. (OCW)

LESABRE - SERIES 4H - V-6 - A new model of the LeSabre, the LeSabre T-Type coupe, was introduced for 1987. It featured a blackout trim treatment, Gran Touring suspension, 3.8-liter V-6,

leather-wrapped steering wheel, operating console, 45/45 seating, Eagle GT blackwall tires and aluminum alloy wheels. The T-Package was also available as a separate option. Other new options included an instrument gauge package and electronic anti-lock brakes. All LeSabre coupes had a new automatic safety belt system. After December 1986, this system was also installed on LeSabre sedans.

1987 Buick, Century Estate Wagon station wagon. (OCW)

ESTATE WAGON - SERIES 4B/C - V-8 - The LeSabre and Electra Estate Wagons were carried over in virtually unchanged form from 1986.

1987 Buick, Electra Limited sedan. (OCW)

1987 Buick, Electra Park Avenue sedan. (OCW)

1987 Buick, Electra T Type coupe. (OCW)

ELECTRA - SERIES 4C - V-6 - The Electra's V-6 engine was improved for 1987 by the use of roller valve lifters. The Electra continued to be offered in a T-Type version with the Gran Touring suspension, leather-wrapped steering wheel, operating console, 45/45 seats, aluminum wheels and Eagle GT tires. Both the Electra and Park Avenue were also available with a T-Package based upon the Gran Touring suspension.

1987 Buick, Riviera T Type coupe. (OCW)

1987 Buick, Riviera coupe. (OCW)

RIVIERA - SERIES 4E - V-6 - Although an all-new model in 1986, the 1987 Riviera was set apart from its 1986 version by many refinements and improvements. The Riviera's 3.8 liter SFI V-6 now had roller lifters. A hydraulic engine mount was also standard equipment. The Riviera's Graphic Control Center (GCC) was revised. Low travel touch switches replaced the membrane function switches on the perimeter of the screen. The GCC software was revised to include a standard oil pressure gauge and an optional windshield washer fluid level sensor. An ambient light sensor was now standard, allowing the GCC to stay on full brightness when the headlights were switched on during the day. A front seat in knit velour or leather was a new option. A standard passenger assist strap above the door was another new feature. A new, reversible, non-slip floor mat was optional. The Riviera T-Type had a unique two-tone paint theme, with a silver lower body and a selected color above. It also had Level III suspension and exclusive Power Comfort seats. In addition to six-way power adjustments, they included inflatable lumbar supports, reversible cushions, and four-way manual articulating headrests. The T-Package included Gran Touring suspension, 2.97:1 final drive ratio, Eagle GT blackwall tires on 15-inch aluminum wheels, leather-wrapped steering wheel and shift handle and exterior T-emblems. Several new exterior metallic colors were offered for the Riviera.

I.D. DATA: The 1987 Buick vehicle identification number (VIN) contained 17 characters. The first was the producing country; "1" - United States. The second character was "G" - General Motors. The third was "4" - Buick division. The fourth and fifth characters identified the car line/series: "A/G" - Century T-Type, "A/H" - Century Custom, "A/L" - Century Limited and Estate Wagon, "B/R" - LeSabre Estate wagon, "B/V" - Electra Estate Wagon, "C/F" - Electra T-Type, "C/W" - Electra Park Avenue, "C/X" - Electra 380, "E/Y" - Riviera T-Type, "E/Z" - Riviera Luxury, "G/J" - Regal, "G/K" - Regal T-Type, "G/M" - Regal T-Type, "H/H" - LeSabre, "H/P" - LeSabre Custom, "H/R" - LeSabre Limited, "J/E" - Skyhawk T-Type, "J/S" - Skyhawk Custom, "J/T" - Skyhawk Limited, "N/C" - Skylark, "N/D" - Skylark Limited, "N/J" - Somerset Custom, "N/K" - Somerset T-Type, "N/M" - Somerset Limited. The sixth digit represented the body style code as follows: "1" - two-door coupe/sedan, "2" - two-door hatchback, "3" - convertible, "5" - four-door sedan, "6" - four-door hatchback, "8" - four-door station

wagon. The seventh character identified the restraint system: "1" - manual belts, "4" - automatic belts. The eighth character represented the engine code: "1" - 2.0 liter L4-121, "K" - 2.0 liter L4-121, "M" - 2.0 liter L4-121, "U" - 2.5 liter Tech IV L4-151, "R" - 2.5 liter Tech IV L4-151 (98 hp), "W" - 2.8 liter V-6-173, "L" - 3.0 liter V-6, "A" - 3.8 liter V-6-231, "C" - 3.8 3800 V-6-231, "3" - 3.8 liter V-6-231, "7" - 3.8 liter V-6-231, "H" - 5.0 liter V-8-307, "Y" - 5.0 liter V-8-307. The ninth unit is a check digit that verifies the accuracy of the VIN. The tenth digit represents the model year (H = 1987). The eleventh entry identifies the assembly plant: "A" - Lakewood, GA, "B" - Lansing, MI, "G" - Framingham, MA, "H" - Flint, MI, "J" - Janesville, WI, "M" - Lansing, MI, "T" - Tarrytown, NY, "U" - Hamtramck, MI, "I" - Wentzville, MO, "1" - Oshawa, Ontario, Canada, "6" - Oklahoma City, OK. The characters from 12-17 are the production sequence number.

Skyhawk Custom (Four)

Model No.	Body/Style No.	Body Type & Seating	Factory Price	Shipping Weight	Prod. Total
S27	JS1	2-dr. Cpe.-5P	8522	2336	19,814
S69	JS5	4-dr. Sed.-5P	8559	2285	15,778
S35	JS8	4-dr. Sta. Wag.-5P	9249	2463	3,061

Skyhawk Limited (Four)

T27	JT1	2-dr. Cpe-5P	9445	2345	1,556
T69	JT5	4-dr. Sed-5P	9503	2423	2,200
T35	JT8	4-dr. Sta. Wag.-5P	9841	2498	498

Skyhawk Sport (Four)

S77	JS2	2-dr. Hatch-5P	8965	2396	3,757

Somerset Custom (Four/V-6)

J27	NJ1	2-dr. Cpe-5P	9957/10617	2456/2522	34,916

Somerset Limited (Four/V-6)

M27	NM1	2-dr. Cpe-5P	11003/11663	2473/2700	11,585

Skylark Custom (Four/V-6)

C69	NC5	4-dr. Sed-5P	9915/10575	2502/2568	26,173

Skylark Limited (Four/V-6)

D69	ND5	4-dr. Sed-5P	11033/11663	2519/2700	7,532

Century Custom (Four/V-6)

H27	AH1	2-dr. Cpe-6P	10844/11454	2696/2777	2,878
H19	AH5	4-dr. Sed-6P	10989/11599	2743/2824	88,445
H35	AH8	4-dr. Sta. Wag-6P	11478/12088	2824/2908	10,414

Century Limited (Four/V-6)

L27	AL1	2-dr. Cpe-6P	11297/12007	2824/2806	4,384
L19	AL5	4-dr. Sed-6P	11593/12203	2771/2852	71,340

Century Estate Station Wagon (Four/V-6)

L35	AL8	4-dr. Sta. Wag-6P	11998/12608	2847/2928	6,990

Regal (V-6)

J47	GJ1	2 dr. Cpe-6P	11562	3196	44,844

Regal (V-6 Turbocharged)

J47	GJ1	2-dr. Cpe-6P	14857	----	N/A
J47	GJ1	Grand National	15136	----	N/A

Regal Limited (V-6/V-8)

M47	GM1	2-dr. Cpe-6P	12303/12893	3225/3405	20,441

LeSabre (V-6)

H37	HH1	2-dr. Cpe-6P	13438	3105	N/A
H69	HH5	4-dr. Sed-6P	13438	3141	N/A

LeSabre Custom (V-6)

P69	HP1	2-dr. Cpe-6P	13616	3104	5,035
P37	HP5	4-dr. Sed-6P	13616	3140	60,392

LeSabre Limited (V-6)

R37	HR1	2-dr. Cpe-6P	14918	3137	7,741
R69	HR5	4-dr. Sed-6P	14918	3171	70,797

LeSabre Estate Station Wagon (V-8)

R35	BR8	4-dr. Sta. Wag.-6P	14724	4160	5,251

Electra Limited (V-6)

X69	CX5	4-dr. Sed-6P	16902	3269	7,787

Electra Park Avenue (V-6)

W11	CW1	2-dr. Cpe-6P	18577	3338	4,084
W69	CW5	4-dr. Sed-6P	18577	3236	75,600

Electra T-Type

F69	CF5	4-dr. Sed-6P	18224	3278	2,570

Electra Estate Station Wagon

Model No.	Body/Style No.	Body Type & Seating	Factory Price	Shipping Weight	Prod. Total
R35	BV8	4-dr. Sta. Wag.	17697	4239	7,508

Riviera (V-6)

Z57	EZ1	2-dr. Cpe-6P	20337	3320	15,223

ENGINES: BASE FOUR (Skyhawk) Inline, overhead valve, four-cylinder. Cast-iron block and aluminum head. Displacement: 121 cu. in. (2.0 liters). Bore & stroke: 3.50 x 3.15 in. Compression ratio: 9.0:1. Brake horsepower: 90 @ 5600 rpm. Torque: 108 lb.-ft @ 3200 rpm. Five main bearings. Hydraulic valve lifters. Throttle-body electronic fuel injection. BASE FOUR (Somerset and Skylark) Inline, overhead valve, four-cylinder. Cast iron block and head. Displacement: 151 cu. in. (2.5 liters). Bore & stroke: 4.00 x 3.00 in. Compression ratio: 9.0:1. Brake horsepower: 92 @ 4400 rpm. Torque: 134 lb.-ft @ 3400 rpm. Five main bearings. Hydraulic valve lifters. Throttle-body fuel injection. BASE FOUR (Century) Inline, overhead valve, four-cylinder. Cast iron block and head. Displacement: 151 cu. in. (2.5 liters). Bore & stroke: 4.00 x 3.00 in. Compression ratio: 9.0:1. Brake horsepower: 98 @ 4800 rpm. Torque: 135 lb.-ft. @ 3200 rpm. Five main bearings. Hydraulic valve lifters. Throttle-body electric fuel injection. BASE V-6 (Regal) 90-degree overhead valve V-6. Cast iron block and head. Displacement: 231 cu. in. (3.8 liters). Bore & stroke: 3.80 x 3.40 in. Compression ratio: 8.0:1. Brake horsepower: 110 @ 3800 rpm. Torque: 190 lb.-ft. @ 1800 rpm. Four main bearings. Hydraulic valve lifters. Carb.: 2-Bbl. BASE V-6 (LeSabre) 90-degree overhead valve V-6. Cast iron block and head. Displacement: 231 cu. in. (3.8 liters). Bore & stroke: 3.80 x 3.40 in. Compression ratio: 8.5:1. Brake horsepower: 150 @ 4400 rpm. Torque: 200 lb.-ft. @ 2000 rpm. Four main bearings. Hydraulic valve lifters. Sequential fuel injection. BASE V-8 (LeSabre Estate station wagon) 90-degree overhead valve V-8. Cast iron block and head. Displacement: 307 cu. in. (5.0 liters). Bore & stroke: 3.8 x 3.39 in. Compression ratio: 8.0:1. Brake horsepower: 140 @ 3200 rpm. Torque: 255 lb.-ft. @ 2000 rpm. Five main bearings. Hydraulic valve lifters. Carb.: 4-Bbl. BASE V-6 (Electra) 90-degree overhead valve V-6. Cast iron block and head. Displacement: 231 cu. in. (3.8 liters). Bore & stroke: 3.80 x 3.40 in. Compression ratio: 8.5:1. Brake horsepower: 150 @ 4400 rpm. Torque: 200 lb.-ft. @ 2000 rpm. Four main bearings. Hydraulic valve lifters. Sequential fuel injection. BASE V-8 (Electra Estate station wagon) 90-degree overhead valve V-8. Cast iron block and head. Displacement: 307 cu. in. (5.0 liters). Bore & stroke: 3.8 x 3.39 in. Compression ratio: 8.0:1. Brake horsepower: 140 @ 3200 rpm. Torque: 255 lb.-ft. @ 2000 rpm. Five main bearings. Hydraulic valve lifters. Carb.: 4-bbl. BASE V-6 (Riviera) 90-degree overhead valve V-6. Cast iron block and head. Displacement: 231 cu. in. (3.8 liters). Bore & stroke: 3.80 x 3.40 in. Compression ratio: 8.5:1. Brake horsepower: 150 @ 4400 rpm. Torque: 200 lb.-ft. @ 2000 rpm. Four main bearings. Hydraulic valve lifters. Sequential fuel injection. OPTIONAL (Skyhawk) Inline, overhead cam, four-cylinder. Cast iron block and aluminum head. Displacement: 121 cu. in. (2.0 liters). Bore & stroke: 3.50 x 3.14 in. Compression ratio: 8.8:1. Brake horsepower: 96 @ 4800 rpm. Torque: 118 lb.-ft. @ 3600 rpm. Five main bearings. Hydraulic valve lifters. Multi-port fuel injection. OPTIONAL (Skyhawk) Inline, overhead cam, four-cylinder. Cast iron block and aluminum head. Displacement: 121 cu. in. (2.0 liters). Bore & stroke: 3.50 x 3.14 in. Compression ratio: 8.0:1. Brake horsepower: 165 @ 5600 rpm. Torque: 175 lb.-ft. @ 4000 rpm. Five main bearings. Hydraulic valve lifters. Multi-port fuel injection, turbocharged. OPTIONAL (Skylark, Somerset) 90-degree, overhead valve, V-6. Cast iron block and cylinder head. Displacement: 181 cu. in. (3.0 liters). Bore & stroke: 3.8 x 2.66 in. Compression ratio: 9.0:1. Brake horsepower: 125 @ 4900 rpm. Torque: 150 @ 2400 rpm. Hydraulic valve lifters. OPTIONAL (Century, Century Estate Wagon) 60-degree V-6. Cast iron block and cylinder head. Displacement: 173 cu. in. (2.8 liters). Bore & stroke: 3.50 x 2.99 in. Compression ratio: 8.9:1. Brake horsepower: 125 @ 4800

rpm. Torque: 160 lb.-ft. @ 3600 rpm. Five main bearings. Hydraulic valve lifters. Multi-port fuel injection. OPTIONAL (Regal) 90-degree overhead valve V-6. Cast iron block and head. Displacement: 231 cu. in. (3.8 liters). Bore & stroke: 3.80 x 3.40 in. Compression ratio: 8.5:1. Brake horsepower: 150 @ 4400 rpm. Torque: 200 lb.-ft. @ 2000 rpm. Four main bearings. Hydraulic valve lifters. Sequential fuel injection. OPTIONAL (Regal) 90-degree overhead valve V-6. Cast iron block and head. Displacement: 231 cu. in. (3.8 liters). Bore & stroke: 3.80 in. x 3.40 in. Compression ratio: 8.0:1. Brake horsepower: 245 @ 4400 rpm. Torque: 355 lb.-ft. @ 2000 rpm. Four main bearings. Hydraulic valve lifters. Sequential fuel injection. OPTIONAL (Regal) 90-degree overhead valve V-8. Cast iron block and head. Displacement: 307 cu. in. (5.0 liters). Bore & stroke: 3.8 in. x 3.39 in. Compression ratio: 8.0:1. Brake horsepower: 140 @ 3200 rpm. Torque: 255 lb.-ft. @ 2000 rpm. Five main bearings. Hydraulic valve lifters. Carb.: 4-Bbl.

CHASSIS DATA: Wheelbase: (Skyhawk) 101.2 in.; (Skylark, Somerset) 103.4 in.; (Century) 104.9 in.; (Regal) 108.1 in.; (LeSabre) 110.8 in.; (LeSabre Estate Wagon) 115.9 in.; (Electra) 110.8 in.; (Riviera) 108.0 in. Overall length: (Skyhawk) 175.3 in.; (Skylark) 180.1 in.; (Somerset) 180.0 in.; (Century) 189.1 in.; (Century Custom/Estate station wagon) 191.0 in.; (Regal) 200.6 in.; (LeSabre) 196.2 in.; (LeSabre Estate station wagon) 220.5 in.; (Electra) 197.4 in.; (Electra Estate station wagon) 220.5 in.; (Riviera) 187.2 in. Height: (Skyhawk) 54.0 in.; (Skylark, Somerset) 52.1 in.; (Century) 53.6 in.; (Century Custom/Estate station wagon) 54.2 in.; (Regal) 54.5 in.; (LeSabre coupe) 54.7 in.; (LeSabre sedan) 55.5 in.; (LeSabre Estate station wagon) 59.3 in.; (Electra) 54.2 in.; (Riviera) 53.5 in. Width: (Skyhawk) 62.0 in.; (Skylark) 66.6 in.; (Somerset) 67.7 in.; (Century) 69.4 in.; (Century Custom/Estate station wagon) 69.4 in.; (Regal) 71.6 in.; (LeSabre sedan/coupe) 72.1 in.; (LeSabre Estate station wagon) 79.3 in.; (Electra) 72.1 in.; (Riviera) 71.7 in. Front Tread: (Skyhawk) 55.4 in.; (Skylark) 55.6 in.; (Somerset) 55.5 in.; (Century) 58.7 in.; (Century Custom/Estate station wagon) 59.7 in.; (Regal) 58.5 in.; (LeSabre coupe/sedan) 60.3 in.; (LeSabre Estate station wagon) 62.2 in.; (Electra) 60.3 in.; (Riviera) 59.9 in. Rear Tread: (Skyhawk) 55.2 in.; (Skylark) 55.2 in.; (Somerset) 55.2 in.; (Century) 56.8 in.; (Century Custom/Estate station wagon) 56.8 in.; (Regal) 57.8 in.; (LeSabre coupe/sedan) 59.8 in.; (LeSabre Estate station wagon) 64.0 in.; (Electra) 59.7 in.; (Riviera) 59.9 in. Standard Tires: (Skyhawk) P175/80R13; (Skylark) P185/80R13; (Somerset) P185/80R13; (Century) P185/75R14; (Century Custom/Estate station wagon) P185/75R14; (Regal) P195/75R14; (LeSabre coupe/sedan) P205/75R14; (LeSabre Estate station wagon) P225/75R15; (Electra) P20575/R14 (blackwall on Limited, whitewall on Park Avenue); (Electra T-Type) P215/65R15; (Riviera) P205/75R14.

TECHNICAL: Transmission: (Skyhawk) Four-speed manual; (Skylark, Somerset) Five-speed manual; (Century, Century Custom, Regal, Estate station wagon) Three-speed automatic; (LeSabre coupe/sedan) Four-speed overdrive automatic; (LeSabre Estate station wagon, Riviera) Four-speed overdrive automatic; (Electra) Three-speed automatic (four-speed overdrive automatic on Electra T-Type). Steering: (Skyhawk) Manual rack and pinion; (Skylark, Somerset, Century, Estate wag, Electra, Riviera) Power rack and pinion; (Regal) Power recirculating ball; (LeSabre coupe/sedan) Power rack and pinion; (LeSabre Estate station wagon) Power recirculating ball. Front Suspension: (Skyhawk, Skylark, Somerset, Century, Century Custom/Estate station wagon, LeSabre coupe/sedan, Electra, Electra T-Type, Riviera) MacPherson struts with coil springs, lower control arms and stabilizer bar; (Regal, LeSabre Estate station wagon) Coil springs, unequal length control arms, stabilizer bar. Rear Suspension: (Skyhawk) Semi-independent with beam axle, trailing arms, coil springs, stabilizer bar available; (Skylark, Somerset) Trailing crank bar, coil springs and stabilizer bar; (Century) Beam twist axle with integral stabilizer bar, trailing arms, Panhard arm and coil springs; (LeSabre coupe/sedan) MacPherson struts, coil springs, stabilizer bar; (LeSabre Estate station wagon) Solid axle with four links, coil springs; (Electra, Electra T-Type) Independent MacPherson struts, inboard coil springs, stabilizer bar; (Riviera) Independent tri-link, transverse fiberglass leaf spring, stabilizer bar. Brakes: (Skyhawk, Skylark, Somerset, Century, Century Custom/Estate station wagon, Regal, LeSabre coupe/sedan, LeSabre Estate station wagon, Electra, Electra T-type) Power front discs, rear drum; (Riviera) Power disc front and rear. Body Construction: Unibody except for Regal, Electra and LeSabre Estate station wagons. Fuel Tank: (Skyhawk) 13.6 gal.; (Skylark) 13.6 gal.; (Somerset) 13.6 gal.; (Century) 15.7 gal.; (Century Custom/Estate station wagon) 16.6 gal.; (Regal) 18.1 gal.; (LeSabre coupe/sedan) 18.0 gal.; (LeSabre and Electra Estate station wagon) 22.0 gal.; (Electra and Electra T-Type) 18.0 gal.; (Riviera) 18.0 gal.

DRIVETRAIN OPTIONS: Engines: (Skyhawk) 2.0 liter, overhead cam with electronic fuel injection; 2.0 liter, overhead cam with electronic fuel injection and turbocharger; (Skylark and Somerset) 3.0 liter V-6 with multi-port fuel injection; (Century, Century Custom/Estate station wagon) 2.8 liter V-6 with multi-port fuel injection; 3.8 liter V-6 with sequential-port fuel injection; (Regal) 5.0 liter V-8 with 4Bbl. carb., 3.8 liter V-6 with turbocharger, intercooler and sequential-port fuel injection. Transmission/Differential: (Skyhawk) Five-speed manual with overdrive, three-speed automatic; (Skylark) Three-speed automatic; (Century, Century Custom/Estate station wagon) Automatic transmission with overdrive; (Regal) Automatic with overdrive. Power accessories: (Skyhawk) Automatic power antenna, also with black mount, six-way power driver seat, power steering, power windows; (Skylark) Automatic power antenna, six-way power driver seat, power windows; (Somerset) Automatic power antenna, six-way power driver seat, power windows; (Century) Automatic power antenna, also with black base, six-way power driver seat, power windows; (Century Custom/Estate station wagon) Automatic power antenna, six-way power driver seat, power windows; (Regal) Automatic power antenna, also with black mount, six-way power driver seat, power windows; (LeSabre and Electra Estate station wagon) Automatic power antenna, two-way power driver seat [requires 55/45 seats-Electra only], six-way power driver seat [requires 55/45 seats], power windows [standard on Electra]; (Electra) Automatic power antenna, six-way power passenger seat; (Riviera) Six-way power passenger seat. Suspension: (Skyhawk, Skylark, Somerset) Gran Touring suspension; (Century) Gran Touring suspension, heavy-duty suspension; (Century Custom/Estate station wagon) Heavy-duty suspension; (Regal) Gran Touring suspension, heavy-duty suspension; (LeSabre coupe/sedan) P205/75R14; (LeSabre and Electra Estate station wagon) Automatic level control; (Electra) Gran Touring suspension, heavy-duty suspension; (Riviera) Gran Touring suspension.

1987 Buick, Skyhawk Custom station wagon. (OCW)

SKYHAWK CONVENIENCE/APPEARANCE OPTIONS: Air conditioning, 3.43:1 axle ratio, heavy-duty battery, electronic cruise control, electric rear window defogger, California assembly line emission equipment and testing, engine block heater, engine block heater cord delete, front carpet savers with inserts, rear carpet savers with inserts, soft-ray tinted glass, "headlamps on" warning chime, dual horns (standard on Limited), instrument gauges (includes temperature, voltmeter, oil trip odometer-standard on Limited), instrument gauges (includes temperature,

voltmeter, oil, tachometer and trip-odometer, Trip-odometer-standard on Limited), front-seat reading lamps, concealed headlamps (Custom models and Limited sedans, includes smoked tail lamp lens), electric door locks, remote electric trunk/hatch lock release, styled black remote-control, outside mirrors (left remote, right manual), lighted passenger visor vanity mirror, black rocker panel molding (Sport), black wheel opening molding (Sport), narrow, bright rocker panel molding (Custom), black door edge guards (Sport), bright door-edge guards (Custom, Limited), designers' accent paint, lower accent paint-gray (coupes/sport), ETR AM-FM stereo radio with seek and scan, ETR AM-FM stereo with seek and scan and clock, ETR AM-FM stereo with seek and scan, cassette tape, auto reverse and clock, graphic equalizer, cassette tape, ETR AM stereo-FM stereo with seek and scan with search/repeat and clock, radio delete (front speakers not deleted), rear extended-range speakers, Concert Sound II speaker system, easy-entry seat (Custom coupe/sport), four-way manual driver seat adjuster, front console-mounted armrest (standard on Limited), acoustic insulation package (standard on Limited), hatch window washer and wiper (Sport), luggage rack (black), luggage rack (bright), rear compartment security cover (Sport), rear-window louvered sunshield (Sport), front license plate mounting, tilt steering wheel, sport steering wheel, leather-wrapped sport steering wheel, body-side stripes, flip-open, Vista-Vent removable glass sunroof, styled hubcap with trim ring (not available on Sport), 13 in. aluminum wheels, custom locking wire wheel covers. Tires: Steel belted, radial-ply, all-season: P175/80R13, whitewall, P195/70R13 blackwall, P195/70R13 whitewall, P195/70R13 white letter, P205/60R14 white letter. Touring options: Interior Sport Package (coupes and sport) Includes easy-entry front seats, custom instrument panel with red backlighting and trip odometer, front and rear custom seat cushions, black and white interior with red striping and sport steering wheel, Exterior Sport Package (coupes and Sport): includes Turbo hood, blackout treatment on door handle and locks, headlamps, root drip molding, rocker panels, wheel opening molding, belt reveal, body-side and side window reveal molding mirrors, fixed-mast antenna and bumper guards, amber park and trunk lamps: fog lamps. Available in five exterior colors. "T" Package: Includes Gran Touring suspension, 14 in. aluminum wheels, steel-belted, radial-ply Eagle GT blackwall P205/60R14 tires, leather-wrapped sport steering wheel and "T" ornamentation. Turbo package: includes 2.0 liter MFI turbo engine five-speed manual transmission, Gran Touring suspension, P205/60R14 Eagle GT tires, 14 in. aluminum wheels, 3.61:1 transaxle ratio, turbo hood with turbo emblem, instrument cluster with custom instrumentation and red backlighting, leather-wrapped sport steering wheel.

SKYLARK CONVENIENCE/APPEARANCE OPTIONS: Air conditioning, 2.84:1 axle ratio, electronic cruise control, electric rear window defogger, California assembly line emission equipment and testing, engine block heater, front carpet savers with inserts, rear carpet savers with inserts, front and rear seat reading lamps, front door courtesy and warning lights (Limited), electric door locks, remote electric trunk lock release, styled black remote-control, outside mirrors (left remote, right manual-standard in Limited), lighted passenger side visor vanity mirror, electric mirrors, body color (left and right remote), wide rocker panel moldings, narrow bright rocker panel moldings (standard on Limited), color-coordinated, protective body-side moldings, wide body-side molding, bright wheel opening moldings (Custom), lower designers' accent paint, lower accent paint-available with all exterior colors, ETR AM-FM stereo radio with seek and scan, ETR AM-FM stereo with seek and scan, cassette tape, auto reverse and clock, graphic equalizer, cassette tape, ETR AM stereo-FM stereo with seek and scan with search/repeat and clock, Delco Bose Music System including Dolby, cassette and ETR AM stereo-FM stereo with seek and scan and clock, radio delete (front speakers not deleted), rear extended-

range speakers, Concert Sound II speaker system, flip-open, Vista-Vent removable glass sunroof with wind reflector, four-way manual driver seat adjuster, front seat center armrest (Custom), reclining front seat backs (Custom), remote fuel-filler door release (standard on Limited), bright deck lid luggage rack, front license plate mounting, tilt steering column, body side stripes, custom locking wire wheel covers, aluminum wheels, styled hubcap with trim ring, two-speed windshield wiper with low-speed delay feature. Tires: steel-belted, radial-ply, all-season: P185/80R13, whitewall, P205/70R13 blackwall, P205/70R13 whitewall, P205/70R13 white letter, P215/60R14 white letter.

SOMERSET CONVENIENCE/APPEARANCE OPTIONS: Air conditioning, 2.84:1 axle ratio, electronic cruise control, electric rear window defogger, California assembly line emission equipment and testing, engine block heater, front carpet savers with inserts, rear carpet savers with inserts, electric door locks, remote electric trunk lock release, styled black remote-control, outside mirrors (left remote, right manual standard on Limited), electric black mirrors (left and right remote), lighted passenger visor vanity mirror, wide rocker panel moldings, narrow, bright rocker panel moldings (standard on Limited), color-coordinated protective body-side moldings, bright door-edge guards, bright wheel opening moldings (Custom), lower designers' accent paint, ETR AM/FM stereo radio with seek and scan, ETR AM/FM stereo with seek and scan and clock, ETR AM/FM stereo with seek and scan, cassette tape, auto reverse and clock, graphic equalizer, cassette tape, ETR AM/FM stereo with seek and scan with search/repeat and clock. Radio delete (front speakers not deleted), rear dual extended-range speakers, Delco-Bose Music System including Dolby, cassette and ETR AM/FM stereo with seek and scan and clock, Concert Sound II speaker system, flip-open Vista-Vent removable glass sunroof with wind reflector, four-way manual driver seat adjuster, remote fuel-filler door release (standard on Limited), bright luggage rack, black luggage rack, front license plate mounting, tilt steering wheel, sport steering wheel, body-side stripes, 13 in. aluminum wheels, custom locking wire wheel cover. Tires: steel-belted, radial-ply, all-season: P185/80R13, whitewall, P205/70R13 blackwall, P205/70R13 whitewall, P20/70R13 white letter, P215/60R14 white letter. Touring options: "T" Package: includes Gran Touring suspension, 14 in. aluminum wheels, steel-belted radial-ply P215/60R14 Eagle GT blackwall tires, leather-wrapped sport steering wheel and "T" ornamentation. Exterior Sport Package: includes blackout treatment on door handle and locks, headlamp bezels, roof drip molding, wheel opening molding, grille, radio antenna, tail lamp bezels and trim, front and rear bumper rub strip, front air dam, hood ornament deleted, aero rocker panel molding, amber parking and taillamps. Available in five exterior colors.

CENTURY CONVENIENCE/APPEARANCE OPTIONS: Air conditioning, 3.18:1 axle ratio, electronic cruise control, electric rear defogger, California assembly line emission equipment and testing, engine block heater, 100, 105, 120-amp Delcotron, heavy-duty radiator, heavy-duty engine and transmission cooling, front carpet savers, rear carpet savers, front carpet savers with inserts, rear carpet savers with inserts, deluxe trunk trim, electric door locks, remote electric trunk lock release, styled black remote-control outside mirror (left), styled black remote-control outside mirrors (left, right manual), lighted passenger visor vanity mirror, Soft-Ray tinted glass, Twilight Sentinel headlamp control, trip odometer, electronic digital instrumentation, instrument gauges (includes temperature, voltmeter and tachometer), front-door courtesy and warning lights (Limited), front-seat reading lamps, electric door locks, remote electric trunk lock release, wide rocker panel moldings (standard on Limited), color-coordinated protective body-side moldings, bright door-edge guards, windsplit molding and stand-up hood ornament (standard on Limited), designers' accent paint, ETR AM/FM stereo radio with seek and scan, ETR AM/FM stereo with seek and scan and clock, ETR AM/FM stereo with seek

and scan, cassette tape, auto reverse and clock, graphic equalizer, cassette tape, ETR AM/FM stereo with seek and scan with search/repeat and clock, radio and front speakers delete, premium speaker system, flip-open Vista-Vent removable glass sunroof, Landau vinyl top (coupes), Landau heavily padded vinyl top (coupes), full vinyl top (sedans), manual seat back recliners (driver and passenger), manual seat back recliner (passenger), six-way power driver seat, remote fuel-filler door release, bright luggage rack, black luggage rack, front license plate mounting, tilt steering wheel, sport steering wheel, body-side stripes, custom locking wire wheel covers, styled hubcap and trim ring, 14 in. aluminum wheels, two-speed windshield wiper system with low-speed delay feature. Tires, steel-belted, radial-ply, all-season: P185/75R14, whitewall, P195/75R14 blackwall, P195/75R14 whitewall. Touring options: "T" Package (coupes/sedans): Includes Gran Touring suspension, 14 in. aluminum wheels, steel belted radial-ply P215/60R14 Eagle GT blackwall tires, leather-wrapped sport steering wheel and "T" emblem on front fender. Exterior Sport Package (sedans): Includes blackout treatment on door handle and locks, headlamp/taillamp bezels, bumpers and rub stripes, roof drip molding, belt reveal and wheel opening moldings (rocker panel moldings deleted). Available in four exterior colors. (Century Custom/Estate station wagon): Air conditioning, heavy-duty battery, full-length operating console, electronic cruise control, electric rear window defogger, California assembly line emission equipment and testing, engine block heater, 100, 105, 120-amp Delcotron, heavy-duty radiator, heavy-duty engine and transmission cooling, front carpet savers with inserts, swing-out rear-quarter vent window, electric door locks, remote-control electric tailgate lock, lockable storage compartment, styled black remote-control outside mirror (left), styled black remote-control, outside mirrors (left remote, right manual), electric black outside rearview mirrors (left and right remote), lighted passenger visor vanity mirror, Soft-Ray tinted glass, Twilight Sentinel headlamp control, trip odometer, electronic digital instrumentation, instrument gauges (includes temperature, voltmeter and trip odometer), instrument gauges (includes temperature, voltmeter, and tachometer), front-door courtesy and warning lights (Estate only), front-seat reading lamps, electric door locks, remote electric trunk lock release, wide rocker panel moldings (standard on Estate), color-coordinated protective body-side moldings, bright door-edge guards, windsplit molding (standard on Estate). designers' accent paint, ETR AM/FM stereo radio with seek and scan, ETR AM/FM stereo with seek and scan and clock. ETR AM/FM stereo with seek and scan, cassette tape, auto reverse and clock, graphic equalizer, cassette tape, ETR AM/FM stereo with seek and scan with search/repeat and clock, radio and front speakers delete, premium speaker system (not available with standard radio), flip-open Vista-Vent removable glass sunroof, manual seatback recliners (driver and passenger), manual seatback recliner (passenger), six-way power driver seat, roof rack, front license plate mounting, tailgate air deflector, tilt steering wheel, sport steering wheel, third seat (vinyl), body-side stripes, 14 in. aluminum wheels, custom locking wire wheel covers, styled hubcap and trim ring, two-speed windshield wiper system with low-speed delay feature, tailgate window wiper and washer. Tires: steel-belted, radial-ply, all-season: P185/75R14, whitewall.

1987 Buick, Regal with optional Grand National package. (OCW)

REGAL CONVENIENCE/APPEARANCE OPTIONS: Air conditioning, 2.56:1, 3.08:1, 3.23:1 axle ratios, electronic cruise control, electric rear window defogger, California assembly line emission equipment and testing, engine block heater, 85-amp, 94-amp Delcotron, heavy-duty battery, heavy-duty engine and transmission cooling, front carpet savers, rear carpet savers, front carpet savers with inserts. rear carpet savers with inserts, trunk trim covering, Soft-Ray tinted glass, Soft-Ray tinted windshield, electric door locks, remote electric trunk lock release, "Headlights On" warning chime, theft-deterrent system with starter interrupt, trip odometer, styled black remote-control outside mirror (left), body-colored sport remote-control outside mirrors (left and right remote), coach lamps (Limited), vanity visor mirror (passenger), lighted passenger visor vanity mirror, Twilight Sentinel headlamp control, trip odometer, electronic digital instrumentation, front-door courtesy and warning lights (Limited), front-seat reading lamps, tungsten-halogen headlamps, cornering lamps, electric door locks, remote electric trunk lock release, exterior molding package includes wide rocker panel moldings and belt reveal (standard on Limited), bright door-edge guards, black door edge guards, designers' accent paint, ETR AM/FM stereo with seek and scan, ETR AM/FM stereo with seek and scan and clock, ETR AM/FM stereo with seek and scan, cassette tape, auto reverse and clock, graphic equalizer, cassette tape, ETR AM/FM stereo with seek and scan with search/repeat and clock, radio and front speakers delete, rear dual extended-range speakers, Concert Sound speaker system, Silver Astroroof (electric sliding), lockable hatch roof, Landau vinyl top, Landau heavily padded vinyl top, manual seatback recliner (passenger), six-way power driver seat, remote electric trunk lock release, front license plate mounting, limited slip differential, tilt steering wheel, sport steering wheel, body-side stripes, chrome-plated wheels, color-keyed wheels with trim rings, 14 in. aluminum wheels, custom locking wire wheel covers, two-speed windshield wiper system with low-speed delay feature. Tires: steel-belted, radial-ply, all-season: P205/70R14 whitewall, P215/65R15 white letter, P195/75R14 blackwall. Touring Options: "T" Package: Includes Gran Touring suspension, fast ratio power steering, gas shock absorbers, 15 in. aluminum wheels, steel-belted radial-ply P215/65R15 Eagle GT blackwall tires, leather-wrapped sport steering wheel and "T" ornamentation. Exterior Sport Package: Includes blackout treatment on door handle and locks, grille, headlamp/taillamp bezels, antenna and door edge guards, bumpers and rub stripes, roof drip and window trim, side window reveal, belt reveal and rear window (rocker panel and body-side moldings are deleted), Regal Grand National Package: 3.8 EFI turbocharged engine with intercooler, automatic transmission with overdrive, 3.42:1 axle ratio, Gran Touring suspension, fast-ratio power steering, sport mirrors, turbo boost gauge and tachometer, trip odometer, leather-wrapped steering wheel, air conditioning, P215/85R15 Eagle GT blackwall tires, chrome-plated steel wheels, black bumpers, molding, grille, and exterior trim, deck lid spoiler, full-length operating console and reclining front bucket seats. Turbo Package: Includes 3.8 liter turbocharged SFI engine with intercooler, instrumentation panel cluster with tachometer, turbo boost gauge and trip odometer, turbo hood and ornamentation, acoustical insulation package and 3.42:1 axle ratio.

LESABRE COUPE/SEDAN CONVENIENCE/APPEARANCE OPTIONS: electronic touch climate control air conditioner, electronic cruise control, electric rear window defogger, California assembly line emission equipment and testing, engine block heater, heavy-duty battery, heavy-duty engine and transmission cooling, front carpet savers with inserts, rear carpet savers with inserts, deluxe trunk trim (Custom/Limited), electric door locks, remote electric trunk lock release, trip odometer, quartz analog gauge cluster (trip odometer, tachometer, voltmeter, oil and temperature gauge), quartz analog gauge cluster (tachometer, voltmeter, oil and temperature gauge), low fuel indicator, electronic digital instrumentation, electric body-color, outside,

rearview mirrors (left and right remote), lighted passenger visor vanity mirror, front and rear seat reading and courtesy lights, front door courtesy and warning lamps, electric door locks, remote electric trunk lock release, black protective lower body-side (standard on Limited), bright door-edge guards, rear bumper guards and bright bumper bead, designers' accent paint, ETR AM/FM stereo with seek and scan and clock, ETR AM/FM stereo with seek and scan, cassette tape, auto reverse and clock, graphic equalizer, cassette tape, ETR AM/FM stereo with seek and scan with search/repeat and clock, Delco Bose music system with ETR AM/FM stereo Dolby seek and scan, cassette tape with auto reverse, search/repeat and clock, radio delete (front speakers not deleted), Concert Sound speaker system, black power antenna base, flip-open, Vista-Vent removable glass sunroof, full vinyl top (sedans), manual passenger seatback recliner (standard on Limited), manual driver seatback recliner, electric passenger seatback recliner, six-way power driver seat, six-way power passenger seat, electric door locks, remote electric trunk lock release, front license plate mounting, bright luggage rack, anti-lock brake system, tilt steering wheel, sport steering wheel, body-side stripes, 14 in. aluminum wheels, 15 in. aluminum wheels, styled hubcap and trim ring, custom locking wire wheel covers, low windshield washer fluid indicator, two-speed windshield wiper system with low-speed delay feature. Tires: steel-belted, radial-ply, all-season: P205/70R14, whitewall, P215/65R15 Eagle GT white stripe, P215/65R15 blackwall, self-sealing tires. Special Option Packages: LeSabre T-Type: Includes special 15 in. aluminum wheels, P215/65R15 Eagle GT blackwall tires, Gran Touring suspension, 2.97:1 ratio transaxle, leather-wrapped sport steering wheel and shift handle, red and amber taillamps, dual exhaust outlets, black body-side molding treatment, lay-down hood ornament, gray-black 45/45 seats (required), front floor mats with "Power 6" logo, T-type identification blackout trim, taillamp, door handles and lock cylinder and grille, rear deck spoiler, front air dam, ETR AM/FM stereo radio with graphic equalizer, cassette tape and red backlighting, operating console with red backlighting, blacked-out instrument panel controls, special gauge package with red backlighting. Available in four exterior colors, T-Package: Includes special 15 in. aluminum wheels, P215/65R15 Eagle GT blackwall tires, Gran Touring suspension, 2.97:1 ratio transaxle, leather-wrapped sport steering wheel, "T" ornamentation.

LESABRE AND ELECTRA ESTATE STATION WAGON CONVENIENCE/APPEARANCE OPTIONS:

electronic touch climate control air conditioner, 3.08:1, 3.23:1 axle ratios, electronic cruise control, electric rear window defogger, California assembly line emission equipment and testing, engine block heater, heavy-duty battery, heavy-duty engine and transmission cooling, front carpet savers with inserts, rear carpet savers with inserts, four-note horn, electric door locks (LeSabre), automatic electric door locks, remote-control electric tailgate lock (LeSabre), trip odometer (LeSabre), chrome electric outside, rearview mirrors (left and right remote), chrome remote-control outside mirrors (left and right), lighted passenger visor vanity mirror, driver side lighted visor vanity mirror, door courtesy and warning lamps, illuminated driver door lock and interior light control, Twilight Sentinel headlamp control, cornering lamps, tungsten-halogen headlamp, front light monitors, lamp and indicator group (LeSabre - consists of "Headlamps on," low fuel and low windshield washer fluid indicators and front reading lamps), lamp and indicator group (Electra - consists of trip odometer, front seat reading lamp, low fuel and low windshield washer fluid), electric door locks (LeSabre), remote-control electric tailgate lock (LeSabre), color-coordinated protective body-side molding, belt reveal molding, bright door-edge guards (LeSabre), wide rocker, front and rear lower panel moldings (Electra), woodgrain vinyl appliqué (LeSabre), exterior molding package (consists of wide rocker panel, front and rear fender and belt reveal moldings (LeSabre), ETR AM/FM stereo with seek and scan and clock (LeSabre), ETR AM/FM stereo with seek and

scan, cassette tape, auto reverse and clock, graphic equalizer, cassette tape, ETR AM/FM stereo with seek and scan with search/repeat and clock, CB radio, radio delete (front speakers not deleted), manual passenger seatback recliner (requires 55/45 seat), electric passenger seatback recliner, two-way power driver seat (Electra - 55/45 seat required), six-way passenger and driver power seats (55/45 seats required), six-way driver power seat with 55/45 seat, third seat (vinyl), electric door locks (LeSabre), front license plate mounting, roof luggage rack (LeSabre), tilt steering column (LeSabre), automatic ride control, limited slip differential, chrome-plated wheels, custom locking wire wheel covers, two-speed windshield wiper system with low-speed delay feature, self-sealing tires.

ELECTRA/PARK AVENUE CONVENIENCE/APPEARANCE OPTIONS:

Electronic touch climate control air conditioner, 2.53:1 axle ratio, electronic cruise control (standard on Park Avenue), electric rear window defogger, California assembly line emission equipment and testing, engine block heater, heavy-duty battery, heavy-duty engine and transmission cooling, front carpet savers with inserts (standard on Park Avenue), rear carpet savers with inserts (standard on Park Avenue), trunk compartment mat, deluxe trunk trim, electric door locks (standard on Park Avenue), remote electric trunk lock release (standard on Park Avenue), electric trunk pull-down, keyless entry system, automatic electric locks, theft-deterrent system with starter interrupt, four-note horn, quartz analog gauge cluster (trip odometer, tachometer, voltmeter, oil and temperature gauge), quartz analog gauge cluster (tachometer, voltmeter, oil and temperature gauge), low fuel indicator, front and rear light monitors, electronic digital instrumentation, automatic day/light mirror, electric body-color, outside rearview mirrors (left and right remote), lighted passenger visor vanity mirror (standard on Park Avenue), lighted driver side visor vanity mirror, rear seat reading lights (standard on Park Avenue), door courtesy and warning lamps (standard on Park Avenue), illuminated driver door lock and interior light control, Twilight Sentinel headlamp control, cornering lamps, electric door locks, remote electronic trunk lock release (standard on Park Avenue), bright door-edge guards, ETR AM/FM stereo with seek and scan auto reverse and clock, graphic equalizer, cassette tape, ETR AM/FM stereo with seek and scan with search/repeat and clock, Delco Bose Music System with ETR AM/FM stereo Dolby seek and scan, cassette tape with auto reverse, search/repeat and clock, radio delete (front speakers not deleted), Concert Sound speaker system, automatic power antenna, graphic power antenna base, Astroroof, electric sliding roof, full heavily padded vinyl top, electric driver seatback recliner, electric passenger seatback recliner, two-position memory, six-way power driver seat, six-way power passenger seat, front license plate mounting, black luggage rack (T-Type), bright luggage rack (Limited and Park Avenue), anti-lock brake system, tilt and telescoping steering column, tilt steering column (standard on Park Avenue), cellular telephone accommodation package, body-side stripes (standard on Park Avenue), 14 in. aluminum wheels, custom locking wire wheel covers, low windshield washer fluid indicator and two-speed windshield wiper system with low-speed delay feature (standard on Park Avenue). Tires: steel-belted, radial-ply, all-season, P205/70R14, whitewall (standard on Park Avenue), P215/75R14 blackwall (standard on Electra), P215/65R15 blackwall, self-sealing tires. Touring Options: Electra T-Type sedan: includes 3.8 liter SFI V-6, automatic transmission with overdrive, steel-belted, radial-ply, Eagle GT blackwall P215/65R15 tires, 15 in. aluminum wheels, leather-wrapped sport steering wheel, gray, red or beige cloth 45/45 seats, rear seat head rests, operating console with leather shift handle, quartz analog gauge cluster, brushed gray instrument panel and door trim, specific front carpet savers with embroidered T-Type logo, dual-outlet exhaust, special taillamp treatment and Gran Touring suspension. Available in five exterior colors. T-Package: includes Gran Touring suspension, 2.97:1 transaxle

ratio, 15 in. aluminum wheels, steel-belted, radial-ply P215/675R15, blackwall Eagle GT tires, "T" ornamentation, leather-wrapped sport steering wheel.

RIVIERA CONVENIENCE/APPEARANCE OPTIONS: Electric rear window defogger, California assembly line emission equipment and testing, engine block heater, heavy-duty engine and transmission cooling, reversible anti-slip front carpet savers with insert, reversible anti-slip rear carpet savers with inserts, trunk compartment mat, automatic electric door locks, electric trunk pulldown, automatic Twilight Sentinel headlamp control, theft-deterrent system with starter interrupt, day/night rearview mirror, black electric outside, rearview mirrors, heated left, lighted passenger visor vanity mirror, lighted driver visor vanity mirror, rear seat reading lights, illuminated driver door lock and interior light control, door-edge guards, color-coordinated protective bodyside molding, designers' accent paint (not available on Riviera T-Type), ETR AM/FM stereo with seek and scan and clock, ETR AM/FM stereo with seek and scan, cassette tape, auto reverse and clock, graphic equalizer, cassette tape, ETR AM/FM stereo with seek and scan with search/repeat and clock, Delco Bose music system with ETR AM/FM stereo Dolby seek and scan, cassette tape with auto reverse, search/repeat and clock, Concert Sound speaker system, black power antenna base, Astroroof, electric sliding, electric driver seatback recliner, electric passenger seatback recliner, six-way power passenger seat, front license plate mounting, trailer towing harness, cellular telephone accommodation package (tri-band power antenna, wiring harness and hand-held storage), leather-wrapped sport steering wheel and shift handle, 14 in. aluminum wheels, custom locking wire wheel covers, low windshield washer fluid indicator. Tires: steel belted, radial-ply, P205/75R14, whitewall. Special Option Packages: Riviera T-Type coupe: includes 3.8 liter V-6 SFI engine, automatic transmission with overdrive, 2.97:1 performance transaxle ratio, Gran Touring suspension, amber park and turn signal lenses, 15 in. aluminum wheels, steel-belted, radial-ply P215/60R15 Eagle GT blackwall tires, fast-ratio power steering, "T"-Type ornamentation, silver lower body-side molding, black rocker panel molding, reversible leather/sheepskin power control seats in red or gray, leather-wrapped shift handle, specific paint in five colors with silver lower accent treatment. T-Package: Included "T" ornamentation, leather-wrapped sport steering wheel and shift handle, 2.97:1 performance transaxle ratio, Gran Touring suspension, 15 in. aluminum wheels, steel-belted, radial-ply P215/60R15 Eagle GT blackwall tires, fast-ratio power steering.

1987 Buick, GNX coupe (limlited edition based on Grand National). (OCW)

HISTORY: Buick's Somerset and Skylark models ranked 11th among compact cars in model year output with a combined total of 80,206 units. The Century ranked fourth in the intermediate class with a volume of 184,178. The LeSabre also held fourth place in the standard size class with a production of 154,331 cars. Riviera production totaled 15,223 cars. In a joint venture with Buick, ASC/McLaren built a limited edition model based on the Grand National and called the GNX. The GNX was powered by a turbocharged and intercooled 3.8-liter V-6 with sequential fuel injection. This engine developed 276 hp at 4400 rpm and

360 lb.-ft. of torque at 3000 rpm. Externally, the GNX was finished in gloss black paint and featured flared fenders with Vaalex fender louvers, cast aluminum wheels, a power bulge in the hood, and deck lid spoiler. Each GNX carried a badge on its instrument panel showing the car's production number. The option package was supplied by ASC/McLaren at a cost of $10,995, which priced the GNX at $29,900. In 1987, 547 GNX Buicks were produced.

1988

Buick's 1988 lineup for 1988 was highlighted by the all-new Regal coupe, the introduction of the Reatta at mid-year, two new engines and improvements in virtually all of its models. Special attention was given to improvements in ride, handling, durability and easier maintenance and service. Changes also took place in equipment levels in all lines. New suspension packages provided improved road performance. Numerous interior features that were either new or improved were introduced. Buick General Manager Edward H. Mertz noted that "Buick is covering the market with distinctive products, high quality workmanship, backed by what we are convinced is the finest group of dealers in the industry."

1988 Buick, Skyhawk coupe. (OCW)

SKYHAWK - SERIES 4J - FOUR - A new S/E coupe was added to the Skyhawk line. Among the features of the S/E were: a gauge package with tachometer, carpeted front and rear floor mats, leather-wrapped sport steering wheel, concealed headlights, blacked-out exterior trim and Gran Touring suspension. A new paint, beechwood brown, was added to the Skyhawk's color list, making a total of six exterior colors.

1988 Buick, Skylark Custom coupe. (OCW)

SKYLARK - SERIES 4N - FOUR/V-6 - The latest Skylark coupes had a composite headlamp front-end treatment, along with new exterior colors and new interior fabrics. The most noticeable interior change was a new standard analog gauge cluster, which included a trip odometer. The Limited coupe had a new combination of woven and knit fabrics, and a new door trim design. The base 2.5 liter engine was given many improvements

for 1988. They included the addition of a balance shaft and lighter pistons. The 2.3-liter Quad 4 was a new Skylark option.

1988 Buick, Century Limited sedan. (OCW)

CENTURY - SERIES 4A - FOUR/V-6 - The Century line continued to offer coupe, sedan and station wagon models. There were six new exterior colors for 1988, along with new interior colors, fabrics and other improvements. Custom models had a new seat and door design in a new knit fabric. The Limited coupe also had a new door design. All Century models had a new steering wheel. A new storage armrest was standard on Limited models, and optional for the Custom. A number of items were added to the Century's standard equipment. They included an AM/FM radio with seek and scan, rear extended range speakers, tinted glass, remote-controlled driver's mirror and whitewall tires. The base 2.5-liter engine had numerous refinements. The optional 2.8-liter V-6 was improved through more precise manufacturing methods.

1988 Buick, Regal Limited with Exterior Appearance and Gran Touring packages.

1988 Buick, Regal Custom coupe with optional styled wheels. (OCW)

1988 Buick, Regal Custom coupe with optional wire wheel covers. (OCW)

REGAL - SERIES 4W - V-6 - The all-new Regal featured front-wheel drive and the most aerodynamic design of any Buick in history. Its aerodynamics were 33 percent improved over the previous model's. The advance was made possible by the use of flush glass and "door-into-roof" construction. The Regal's front appearance, with vertical ribs in the grille, maintained a

family resemblance with the old Regal. High priority considerations in the Regal's design were performance, ride and handling. A "lubed for life" suspension was featured. All inside body metal was galvanized on both sides, and a base coat process with Plastisol was used. A stainless exhaust system was also installed. The Regal's powertrain included the 2.8-liter MFI V-6 with computer-controlled coil ignition and a self-tensioning single accessory belt. Power assisted four-wheel disc brakes were standard, as well as power rack and pinion steering. The Regal was the first General Motors car to be influenced by what Buick called the "Mona Lisa" process. This involved the identification by engineers of the best features on the best cars in the world and a systematic process to decide which ones should be incorporated into the Regal.

1988 Buick, LeSabre coupe. (OCW)

1988 Buick, LeSabre Custom sedan. (OCW)

1988 Buick, LeSabre T Type coupe. (OCW)

1988 Buick, LeSabre Limited coupe with optional vinyl top and wire wheel covers. (OCW)

LESABRE - SERIES 4H - V-6 - The LeSabre lineup for 1988 was carried over from 1987. All models were available in new exterior colors and numerous interior refinements. The T-Type was offered in four colors: black, white, red and silver. It was fitted with a rear deck spoiler. A new seat design and door trim was found on the base coupe. The Limited coupe had a new seat design in a combination woven velour and knit cloth. Also standard were new rear seat lap and shoulder belts. A new, optional leather in red, gray or tan was available for the Limited coupe. The new 3.8-liter 3800 V-6 was standard for the T-Type and optional for all other LeSabre models. It had a redesigned

cylinder block with a balanced shaft chain driven by the crankshaft. A revised standard suspension eliminated the need for heavy-duty suspension components.

1988 Buick, LeSabre Estate Wagon station wagon. (OCW)

ESTATE WAGON - SERIES 4B - V-8 - The full-size rear-wheel drive LeSabre and Electra station wagons were offered in six new exterior colors. The door design in both versions was revised to include a new armrest with the power seat controls located in a pod. A new standard steering wheel was shared by both wagons and two new interior colors, blue and saddle, were offered. New standard features included an upscale AM/FM stereo radio with dual front and rear speakers, manual reclining passenger seats, a six-way power driver's seat in the Electra, low windshield washer fluid and low fuel indicators, trip odometer, front seat reading lamps, and a third seat.

1988 Buick, Electra Park Avenue sedan. (OCW)

1988 Buick, Electra Limited sedan. (OCW)

1988 Buick, Electra T Type sedan. (OCW)

ELECTRA - SERIES 4C - V-6 - The 1988 Electra was available in Limited, Park Avenue and T-Type form. Five new exterior colors were introduced. Interior color choices now included rosewood and taupe. A new front seat storage armrest was available for the Limited and Park Avenue. The appearance of the T-Type was refined by the use of chrome door frames, belt and wheel opening moldings, rear lamp bezels and license plate frame. The T-Type could be ordered in an exclusive ruby red

finish. The T-Type package also included interior consoles, leather-wrapped steering wheel and anti-lock brakes.

1988 Buick, Riviera T Type coupe. (OCW)

1988 Buick, Riviera coupe. (OCW)

RIVIERA - SERIES 4E - V-6 - The silver anniversary Riviera had a special hood ornament and instrument panel trim plate. Other appearance changes included a front-end design with composite headlamps. Three new exterior colors were introduced along with a landau top option available in 10 colors. A new optional chrome accent stripe was also introduced. The power seat controls were changed from rocker switches to a paddle type. The Electronic Control Center featured a new 70-degree deflection CRT screen with improved visibility. Other improvements included a personal reminder feature allowing the driver to enter specific calendar events, which would later appear at a selected date. Two new functions were added to the ECC as optional items. They were an electronic compass and the integration of a cellular telephone directory into the system. Other changes for 1988 involved improved serviceability, a theft-deterrent door lock mechanism and identification on major body panels.

1988 Buick, Reatta coupe. (OCW)

REATTA - SERIES 4E - V-6 - The Reatta, Buick's luxury two-passenger car, was introduced in January 1988. It combined a sporty appearance, aerodynamic styling, a 0.34 drag coefficient, and a traditional Buick ride. The Reatta was intended to carve out a market niche that involved a combination of luxury car and sports car elements at a price well below that of cars

at the upper end of both markets. Initially offered as a coupe, the Reatta had front-wheel drive, the 3800 V-6 engine, independent suspension and fast ratio power steering. A long list of features was standard for the Reatta. A partial listing includes air conditioning, fog lamps, stereo radio with cassette player, power leather bucket seats, power windows and door locks, stainless steel exhaust and ECC. The only options were a power-operated sunroof and a 16-way power seat.

I.D. DATA: The 1988 Buick vehicle identification number (VIN) contained 17 characters. The first was the producing country; "1" - United States. The second character was "G" - General Motors. The third was "4" - Buick division. The fourth character identified the car line: "A" - Century, "B" - LeSabre and Electra Estate wagon, "C" - Electra, "D" - incomplete LeSabre wagon, "E" - Riviera and Reatta, "H" - LeSabre, "J" - Skyhawk, "N" - Skylark, "W" - Regal. The fifth character designated the series: "B" - Regal Custom/incomplete wagon, "C" - Skylark Custom/Reatta, "D" - Skylark Limited/Regal Limited, "F" - Electra T-Type, "H" - Century Custom, "J" - Skylark Custom, "L" - Century Limited/Estate wagon, "M" - Skylark Limited, "P" - LeSabre/LeSabre Custom, "R" - LeSabre Limited/Estate wagon, "S" - Skyhawk, "U" - Electra Ultra, "V" - Electra Estate Wagon, "W" - Electra Park Avenue, "Z" - Riviera. The sixth digit represented the body style code as follows: "1" - two-door coupe, "5" - four-door sedan, "8" - four-door station wagon, "9" - four-door station wagon (incomplete). The seventh character identified the restraint system: "1" - manual belts, "4" - automatic belts, "0" - incomplete vehicle. The eighth character represented the engine code: "1" - 2.0 liter L4-121, "U" - 2.5 liter Tech IV L4-151, "D" - 2.3 liter DOHC Quad L4-140, "N" - 3.3 liter 3300 V-6-204, "R" 2.5 liter Tech IV-L4-151 (98 hp), "W" - 2.8 liter V-6-173, "C" - 3.8 liter 3800 V-6-231, "Y" - 5.0 liter V-8-307. The ninth unit is a check digit that verifies the accuracy of the VIN. The next letter, "J," represents the 1988 model year. The eleventh entry identifies the assembly plant: "A" - Lakewood, GA, "B" - Lansing, MI, "G" - Framingham, MA, "H" - Flint, MI, "J" - Janesville, WI, "M" - Lansing, MI, "T" - Tarrytown, NY, "U" - Hamtramck, MI, "I" - Wentzville, MO, "1" - Oshawa, Ontario, Canada, "6" - Oklahoma City, OK. The characters from 12-17 are the production sequence number.

Skyhawk (Four)

Model No.	Body/Style No.	Body Type & Seating	Factory Price	Shipping Weight	Prod. Total
S27	JS1	2-dr. Cpe.-5P	8884	2336	13,156
S69	JS5	4-dr. Sed.-5P	8884	2336	14,271
S35	JS8	4-dr. Sta. Wag.-5P	9797	2474	1,707

Skyhawk S/E (Four)

Model No.	Body/Style No.	Body Type & Seating	Factory Price	Shipping Weight	Prod. Total
S27	JS1	2-dr. Cpe.-5P	9979	----	Note

Note: S/E production included in base coupe production.

Skylark Custom (Four/V-6)*

Model No.	Body/Style No.	Body Type & Seating	Factory Price	Shipping Weight	Prod. Total
J27	NJ1	2-dr. Cpe.-5P	10684	2522	19,590
C69	NC5	4-dr. Sed.-5P	10399	2568	24,940

Skylark Limited (Four/V-6)*

Model No.	Body/Style No.	Body Type & Seating	Factory Price	Shipping Weight	Prod. Total
M27	NM1	2-dr. Cpe.-5P	11791	2543	4,946
D69	ND5	4-dr. Sed.-5P	11721	2589	5,316

*Add $660 for V-6 engines.

Century Custom (Four/V-6)

Model No.	Body/Style No.	Body Type & Seating	Factory Price	Shipping Weight	Prod. Total
H37	AH1	2-dr. Cpe.-6P	11643/12253	2691/2760	1,322
H69	AH5	4-dr. Sed.-6P	11793/12403	2762/2831	62,214
H35	AH8	4-dr. Sta. Wag.-6P	12345/12955	2911/2980	5,312

Century Limited(Four/V-6)

Model No.	Body/Style No.	Body Type & Seating	Factory Price	Shipping Weight	Prod. Total
L69	AL5	4-dr. Sed.-6P	12613/13223	2769/2838	39,137
L37	AL1	2-dr. Cpe.-6P	12410/13020	2698/2767	1,127

Century Estate Station Wagon (Four/V-6)

Model No.	Body/Style No.	Body Type & Seating	Factory Price	Shipping Weight	Prod. Total
L35	AL8	4-dr. Sta.Wag.-6P	13077/13687	2915/2984	4,146

Regal Custom (V-6)

Model No.	Body/Style No.	Body Type & Seating	Factory Price	Shipping Weight	Prod. Total
B57	WB1	2-dr. Cpe.-6P	12449	2953	64,773

Regal Limited (V-6)

Model No.	Body/Style No.	Body Type & Seating	Factory Price	Shipping Weight	Prod. Total
D57	WD1	2-dr. Cpe.-6P	12782	2972	65,224

LeSabre (V-6)

Model No.	Body/Style No.	Body Type & Seating	Factory Price	Shipping Weight	Prod. Total
P37	HP1	2-dr. Cpe.-6P	14560	3192	8,829

LeSabre Custom (V-6)

Model No.	Body/Style No.	Body Type & Seating	Factory Price	Shipping Weight	Prod. Total
P69	HP5	4-dr. Sed.-6P	14405	3239	67,213

LeSabre Limited (V-6)

Model No.	Body/Style No.	Body Type & Seating	Factory Price	Shipping Weight	Prod. Total
R37	HR1	2-dr. Cpe.-6P	16350	3242	2,474
R69	HP5	4-dr. Sed.-6P	15745	3295	7,524

LeSabre Estate Station Wagon (V-8)

Model No.	Body/Style No.	Body Type & Seating	Factory Price	Shipping Weight	Prod. Total
R35	BR8	4-dr. Sta.Wag-6P	16040	4156	3,723

Note: Total LeSabre production: 130,104-fwd; 9,659-rwd.

Electra Limited (V-6)

Model No.	Body/Style No.	Body Type & Seating	Factory Price	Shipping Weight	Prod. Total
X69	CX5	4-dr. Sed.-6P	17479	3288	5,191

Electra T-Type (V-6)

Model No.	Body/Style No.	Body Type & Seating	Factory Price	Shipping Weight	Prod. Total
F69	CF5	4-dr. Sed.-6P	19464	3326	1,869

Electra Park Avenue (V-6)

Model No.	Body/Style No.	Body Type & Seating	Factory Price	Shipping Weight	Prod. Total
W69	CW5	4-dr. Sed.-6P	20229	3329	84,853

Electra Estate Station Wagon

Model No.	Body/Style No.	Body Type & Seating	Factory Price	Shipping Weight	Prod. Total
V35	BV8	4-dr. Sta. Wag.	18954	4217	5,901

Riviera (V-6)

Model No.	Body/Style No.	Body Type & Seating	Factory Price	Shipping Weight	Prod. Total
Z57	EZI	2-dr. Cpe.-6P	21615*	3364	8,625

* Add $1765 for T-Type option.

Reatta (V-6)

Model No.	Body/Style No.	Body Type & Seating	Factory Price	Shipping Weight	Prod. Total
C97	EC1	2-dr. Cpe.-2P	25000	3500	4,708

ENGINES: BASE FOUR (Skyhawk) Inline, overhead valve, four-cylinder. Cast iron block and aluminum head. Displacement: 121 cu. in. (2.0 liters). Bore & Stroke: 3.39 x 3.39 in. Compression ratio: 8.8:1. Brake horsepower: 96 @ 4800 rpm. Torque: 118 lb.-ft. @ 3600 rpm. Five main bearings. Hydraulic valve lifters. Throttle-body electronic fuel injection. BASE FOUR (Skylark) Inline, overhead valve, four-cylinder. Cast iron block and head. Displacement: 151 cu. in. (2.5 liters). Bore & Stroke: 4.00 x 3.00 in. Compression ratio: 9.0:1. Brake horsepower: 135 @ 5200 rpm. Torque: 135 lb.-ft. @ 3200 rpm. Five main bearings. Hydraulic valve lifters. Electronic fuel injection. BASE FOUR (Century) Inline, overhead valve, four-cylinder. Cast alloy iron block and head. Displacement: 151 cu. in. (2.5 liters). Bore & Stroke: 4.00 x 3.00 in. Compression ratio: 9.0:1. Brake horsepower: 98 @ 4800 rpm. Torque: 135 lb.-ft. @ 3200 rpm. Five main bearings. Hydraulic valve lifters. Throttle-body electric fuel injection. BASE V-6 (Regal) 60-degree overhead value V-6. Cast iron block and aluminum head. Displacement: 173 cu. in. (3.8 liters). Bore & Stroke: 3.50 x 2.99 in. Compression ratio: 8.9:1. Brake horsepower: 130 @ 4500 rpm. Torque: 160 lb.-ft. @ 3600 rpm. Hydraulic valve lifters. Multi-port fuel injection. BASE V-6 (LeSabre) 90-degree overhead valve V-6 with balance shaft. Cast iron alloy block and head. Displacement: 231 cu. in. (3.8 liters). Bore & Stroke: 3.80 x 3.40 in. Compression ratio: 8.5:1. Brake horsepower: 150 @ 4400 rpm. Torque: 200 lb.-ft. @ 2000 rpm. Four main bearings. Hydraulic valve lifters. Sequential fuel injection. BASE V-8 (LeSabre Estate wag) 90-degree overhead valve V-8. Cast iron block and head. Displacement: 307 cu. in. (5.0 liters). Bore & Stroke: 3.8 x 3.39 in. Compression ratio: 8.0:1. Brake horsepower: 140 @ 3200 rpm. Torque: 255 lb.-ft. @ 2000 rpm. Five main bearings. Hydraulic valve lifters. Carb.: 4Bbl. BASE V-6 (Electra) 90-degree overhead valve V-6 with balance shaft. Cast iron alloy block and head. Displacement: 231 cu. in. (3.8 liters). Bore & Stroke: 3.80 x 3.40 in. Compression ratio: 8.5:1. Brake horsepower: 165 @ 5200 rpm. Torque: 210 lb.-ft. @ 2000 rpm. Four main bearings. Hydraulic valve lifters. Sequential fuel injection. BASE V-8 (Electra Estate wag) 90-degree overhead valve V-8. Cast iron block and head. Displacement: 307 cu. in. (5.0 liters). Bore & Stroke: 3.8 x 3.39 in. Compression ratio: 8.0:1. Brake horsepower: 140 @ 3200 rpm. Torque: 255 lb.-ft. @ 2000 rpm. Five main bearings. Hydraulic valve lifters. Carb.: 4Bbl. BASE V-6 (Riviera) 90-degree overhead valve V-6. Cast iron alloy block and head. Displacement: 231 cu. in. (3.8 liters). Bore & Stroke: 3.80 x 3.40 in. Compression ratio: 8.5:1. Brake horsepower: 165 @ 5200 rpm. Torque: 210 lb.-ft. @ 2000 rpm. Four main bearings. Hydraulic valve lifters. Sequential fuel injection. BASE

V-6 (Reatta) 90 degree overhead valve V-6. Cast iron alloy block and head. Displacement: 231 cu. in. (3.8 liters). Bore & Stroke: 3.80 x 3.40 in. Compression ratio: 8.5:1. Brake horsepower: 165 @ 4800 rpm. Torque: 210 lb.-ft. @ 2000 rpm. Four main bearings. Hydraulic valve lifters. Sequential fuel injection. OPTIONAL (Skylark) Inline, DOHC, four-cylinder. Cast alloy iron block, cast aluminum head. Displacement: 138 cu. in. (2.3 liters). Bore & Stroke: 3.62 x 3.346 in. Compression ratio: 9.5:1. Brake horsepower: 150 @ 5200 rpm. Torque: 160 lb.-ft. @ 4000 rpm. Hydraulic valve lifters. Multi-port fuel injection. OPTIONAL (Skylark) 90-degree V-6. Cast iron block and cylinder heads. Displacement: 204 cu. in. (3.3 liters). Bore & Stroke: 3.73 x 3.16 in. Compression ratio: 9.0:1. Brake horsepower: 160 @ 5200 rpm. Torque: 185 lb.-ft. @ 2000 rpm. Four main bearings. Hydraulic valve lifters. Multi-port fuel injection. OPTIONAL (Century, Century Estate wag) 60-degree V-6. Cast iron block and cylinder head. Displacement: 204 cu. in. (3.3 liters). Bore & Stroke: 3.70 x 3.16 in. Compression ratio: 9.00:1. Brake horsepower: 160 @ 5200 rpm. Torque: 185 lb.-ft. @ 2000 rpm. Four main bearings. Hydraulic valve lifters. Multi-port fuel injection.

CHASSIS DATA: Wheelbase: (Skyhawk) 101.2 in.; (Skylark) 103.4 in.; (Century) 104.8 in.; (Regal) 107.5 in.; (LeSabre) 110.8 in.; (LeSabre Estate Wagon) 115.9 in.; (Electra) 110.8 in.; (Riviera) 108.0 in.; (Reatta) 98.5 in. Overall Length: (Skyhawk) cpe: 179.3 in.; sed and wag: 181.7 in.; (Skylark) 180.1 in.; (Century) 189.1 in.; (Century Custom/Estate wag) 190.9 in.; (Regal) 192.2 in.; (LeSabre) 196.5 in.; (LeSabre Estate wag) 220.5 in.; (Electra) 197.0 in.; (Electra Estate wag) 220.5 in.; (Riviera) 198.3 in.; (Reatta) 183.7 in. Height: (Skyhawk) cpe and sed: 54.0 in.; wag: 54.4 in.; (Skylark) 52.1 in.; (Century) cpe: 53.7 in.; sed and Century Custom/Estate wag: 54.2 in.; (Regal) 53.0 in.; (LeSabre cpe) 54.7 in.; (LeSabre sed) 55.4 in.; (LeSabre Estate wag) 59.3 in.; (Electra) 54.3 in.; (Riviera) 53.6 in.; (Reatta) 51.2 in. Width: (Skyhawk) cpe: 65.0 in.; (Skylark) 66.6 in.; (Century) 69.4 in.; (Century Custom/Estate wag) 69.4 in.; (Regal) 72.5 in.; (LeSabre sed/cpe) 72.4 in.; (LeSabre Estate wag) 79.3 in.; (Electra) 72.4 in.; (Riviera) 71.7 in.; (Reatta) 73.0 in. Front Tread: (Skyhawk) cpe and sed: 55.6 in.; wag: 55.4 in.; (Skylark) 55.6 in.; (Century) 58.7 in.; (Century Custom/Estate wag) 58.7 in.; (Regal) 59.3 in.; (LeSabre cpe/sed) 60.3 in.; (LeSabre Estate wag) 62.2 in.; (Electra) 60.3 in.; (Riviera) 59.9 in.; (Reatta) 60.3 in. Rear Tread: (Skyhawk) 55.2 in.; (Skylark) 55.2 in.; (Century) 56.7 in.; (Century Custom/Estate wag) 56.7 in.; (Regal) 58.0 in.; (LeSabre cpe/sed) 59.8 in.; (LeSabre Estate wag) 64.0 in.; (Electra) 59.8 in.; (Riviera) 59.9 in.; (Reatta) 60.3 in. Standard Tires: (Skyhawk) P175/80R13; (Skylark) P185/80R13; (Century) P185/75R14; (Century Custom/Estate wag) P185/75R14; (Regal) P205/75R14; (LeSabre cpe/sed) P205/75R14; (LeSabre Estate wag) P225/75R15; (Electra) P205/75R14, (blackwall on Limited, whitewall on Park Avenue); (Electra T-Type) P215/60R15; (Park Avenue Ultra) P205/70R15 whitewall; (Riviera) P205/75R15; (Reatta) P215/65R15 blackwall.

TECHNICAL: Transmission: (Skyhawk) Five-speed manual; (Skylark, Century, Century Custom/Estate wag) Three-speed automatic; (Regal, LeSabre, Electra, Riviera) Four-speed automatic with overdrive; (Reatta) MXO four-speed automatic. Steering: (Skyhawk, Skylark, Century, Century Custom/Estate wag, Riviera) Power rack and pinion; (LeSabre Estate wag) Power recirculating ball; (Electra) Power rack and pinion; (Reatta) Fast-Ratio power. Front Suspension: (Skyhawk, Skylark, Century, Century Custom/Estate wag, LeSabre cpe/sed, Electra, Electra T-Type, Riviera) MacPherson struts with coil springs, lower control arms and stabilizer bar; (Regal) MacPherson strut with lower control arms and unitized coil springs; (LeSabre Estate wag) Coil springs, unequal length control arms, stabilizer bar; (Reatta) Fully independent with MacPherson struts and roll bar. Rear Suspension: (Skyhawk) Semi-independent with beam axle, trailing arms, coil springs, stabilizer bar available; (Skylark) Trailing crank bar, coil springs and stabilizer bar; (Century) Beam twist axle with integral stabilizer bar, trailing

arms, Panhard arm and coil springs; (LeSabre cpe/sed) MacPherson struts, coil springs, stabilizer bar; (LeSabre Estate wag) Solid axle with four links, coil springs; (Electra, Electra T-Type) Independent MacPherson struts, inboard coil springs, stabilizer bar; (Riviera) Independent tri-link, transverse fiberglass leaf spring, stabilizer bar; (Reatta) Independent modular assembly with single traverse leaf springs. Brakes: (Skyhawk, Skylark, Century, Century Custom/Estate wag, Regal, LeSabre cpe/sed, LeSabre Estate wag, Electra, Electra T-Type) Power front disc, rear drum; (Riviera, Reatta) Power disc, front and rear. Body Construction: (Skyhawk, Skylark) Unibody, (Century/Century wag) Integral body/frame; (Regal) Integral body/frame with bolted-on powertrain cradle; (LeSabre) Unitized body/frame integral with isolated engine cradle; (Electra and LeSabre Estate wag) Welded body with full perimeter frame; (Electra) unitized body/frame construction with isolated engine cradle; (Riviera) Unitized body with isolated front frame and rear sub-frame; (Reatta) Unitized body with isolated front and rear sub-frames. Fuel Tank: (Skyhawk) 13.6 gal.; (Skylark) 13.6 gal., (Century) 15.7 gal.; (Century Custom/Estate wag) 16.6 gal.; (Regal) 16.5 gal.; (LeSabre cpe/sed): 18.0 gal.; (LeSabre and Electra Estate wag) 22.0 gal.; (Electra and Electra T-Type) 18.0 gal.; (Riviera) 18.2 gal.; (Reatta) 18.2 gal.

DRIVETRAIN OPTIONS: Engines: (Skylark) 2.3 liter Quad 4, MFI, $660; 3.3 liter V-6, MFI, $710; (Century, Century Custom/Estate wag) 3.3 liter V-6, MFI, $710. Transmission/Differential: (Skyhawk) Three-speed automatic, $440; (Century, Century Custom/Estate wag) Automatic transmission with overdrive, with 3.3 liter engine only, $200. Suspension, steering and brakes: (Skylark) Gran Touring Package (14 in. aluminum wheels, P215/60R14 Eagle GT+4 blackwall tires, Gran Touring suspension, leather-wrapped steering wheel) $603; engine block heater $18; (Century) Heavy-duty engine and transmission cooling $70 (without air conditioning); $40 with A/C: heavy-duty suspension (required with 3.3 liter engine): $27; Gran Touring Package, not available for station wagons (aluminum wheels, P15/60R Eagle GT tires, leather-wrapped steering wheel and Gran Touring suspension) $515; (Regal) Gran Touring Package consisting of Gran Touring suspension, 16 in. aluminum wheels, P215/60R16 tires and leather-wrapped steering wheel; anti-lock brake system: $925; (LeSabre cpe and sed) 2.97:1 axle (included in Y56-Gran Touring Package and WE2-T-Type; required with V-8-heavy-duty engine and transmission cooling): No additional charge; heavy-duty engine and transmission cooling (included in WE2 and Y56): $40; Gran Touring Package consisting of Gran Touring Suspension, 15 in. aluminum wheels, P215/65R15 blackwall tires, 2.97:1 axle ratio, heavy-duty cooling and leather-wrapped steering wheel; (LeSabre/Electra Estate wag) Trailer Towing Package consisting of 3.23:1 axle ratio, V-8-heavy-duty engine and transmission cooling, automatic level control: $215; Limited slip differential: $100: (Electra) heavy-duty battery, required with electronic air conditioning: $26; heavy-duty engine and transmission cooling (standard with T-Type), included in Y56-Gran Touring Package: $40; 2.97:1 axle ratio (requires V-8, included in Y56-Gran Touring Package and T-Type: No additional charge); Electronic anti-lock brake system: $925 (standard on T-Type and Ultra); Gran Touring Suspension (standard on T-Type, not available for Ultra or with fully padded vinyl top), consists of Gran Touring Suspension, 15 in. styled aluminum wheels, P215/65R15 Eagle GT blackwall tires, 2.97:1 axle ratio, heavy-duty cooling and leather-wrapped steering wheel: (Riviera) Gran Touring Package consisting of Gran Touring Suspension, 2.97:1 axle ratio, 15 in. aluminum wheels, leather-wrapped sport steering wheel and shift handle, fast ratio power steering and P215/65R15 steel belted radial ply Eagle GT+4 tires: $104.

SKYHAWK CONVENIENCE/APPEARANCE OPTIONS: automatic transmission, $440; tilt steering column, $125; two-speed windshield wipers with low speed delay, $55; electronic cruise control. $185; AM/FM ETR stereo radio with cassette tape, seek

and scan, auto reverse and clock, $122; four-way manual driver seat adjuster, front console mounted arm rest, electric rear window defogger, $150; electric door locks, $1162 (cpe), $1212 (sed), $1262 (wag), air conditioner, $695; emission equipment and testing, $100. Skyhawk S/E Package consists of front and rear carpet savers, Gran Touring Package (Gran Touring suspension, P215/60R14 Eagle GT+4 blackwall tires, 14 in. Shelby aluminum wheels, leather-wrapped steering wheel), instrument gauges and tachometer, exterior trim package (blackout moldings, concealed headlamps and fog lamps), $1095. Various Popular, Premium and Luxury Packages: $1157-$1412.

1988 Buick, Skylark Limited sedan. (OCW)

SKYLARK CONVENIENCE/APPEARANCE OPTIONS: Air conditioning, $695; tilt steering column, $125; P185/80R13 whitewall tires, $68; mirrors-remote control, left, right manual, $53; electric rear window defogger, $150: protective wide body side molding, $80; wheel opening molding, $30; plus electronic cruise control with resume, $185; two-speed windshield wipers with resume feature, $55; front and rear carpet savers, $45; AM/FM ETR stereo radio with cassette tape, seek and scan, auto reverse with search and repeat and clock, $152; custom locking wheel covers, $215; four-way manual driver seat adjuster, $35; power windows, $220 cpe; $295 sed; electric door locks, $155 cpe, $295 sed; six-way power driver seat adjuster, $250; power antenna, $70; passenger side lighted visor vanity mirror, $38; electric trunk lock release, $50; front and rear courtesy lights, $14; chrome deck lid luggage rack (not available with S/E package and exterior sport package), $115; lower body accent paint, $195; body side stripes, $145; Custom and Limited cloth bucket seats with full length operating console $180; styled 13 in. aluminum wheels, $245; styled hubcaps and trim rings, $38; custom locking wire wheel covers, $215. Special packages: Gran Touring Package, $603. Includes 14 in. aluminum wheels, P215/60R14 Eagle GT blackwall tires, Gran Touring suspension, leather-wrapped steering wheel. Exterior Sport Package, $374 Custom cpe; $318 Limited cpe. Includes blackout moldings, front air dam, aero rocker moldings, wide body side moldings.

CENTURY CONVENIENCE/APPEARANCE OPTIONS: Air conditioning, $795; tilt steering column, $150; electric rear window defogger, $150; electronic cruise control with resume, $185; two-speed windshield wipers with resume feature, $55; front carpet savers, $25; rear carpet savers, $20; AM/FM ETR stereo radio with cassette seek and scan, auto reverse and clock, $122; custom locking wire wheel covers, $215; styled steel wheels, $115; aluminum wheels, $270; body stripes, $45; six-way power driver seat adjuster, $70; power windows, $220 cpe; $295 sed; electric door locks, $155 cpe; $295 sed; six-way power driver seat adjuster. $250; power antenna, $70; passenger side lighted visor vanity mirror, $50; electric trunk lock release, $50; door edge guards, $15 cpe; $25 sed; passenger manual seat back recliner, $45; driver manual seat back recliner, $45; dual electric remote control mirrors, $70; automatic power antenna, $70; Custom only: 55/45 cloth seat with armrest, $183; Limited cloth 55/45 seat with storage armrest, $233-$416. Century Limited only: Front seat reading lights, $24. Century Estate wag only: Vinyl third seat, $215; air deflector, $47; vinyl appliqué wood grain trim, $350; rear window windshield wiper,

$125. Special Packages. Gran Touring Package. Includes aluminum wheels and P215/60R14 Eagle GT tires, leather-wrapped steering wheel and Gran Touring suspension, $515.

REGAL CONVENIENCE/APPEARANCE OPTIONS: Electric rear window defogger, $150; electronic cruise control with resume, $185; two-speed windshield wipers with resume feature, $55; front carpet savers, $25; rear carpet savers, $20; AM/FM ETR stereo radio with cassette tape, seek and scan, auto reverse and clock, $122; graphic equalizer cassette tape with auto reverse, and search/repeat and AM stereo, $150-$272; compact disc player with ETR AM/FM radio with seek/scan and clock, $274; electric glass sunroof (includes dual reading lamps and rear courtesy lamps), $650-$680; custom locking wire wheel covers, $215; styled aluminum wheels, $270; styled steel wheels, $115; 15 in. aluminum wheels with blackwall tires, $320; six-way power driver seat adjuster, $250; power windows with express down feature, $230; electric door locks, $155; six-way power driver seat adjuster, $250; automatic power antenna, $70; passenger side lighted visor vanity mirror, $50; electric trunk lock release, $50; door edge guards, $15; dual electric remote control mirrors, $91; automatic power antenna, $70; concert sound speakers, $85; redundant accessory controls-steering wheel mounted, $125; remote keyless entry (Limited and Gran Sport only), $125; electronic digital/graphic instrumentation, $299; luggage rack, $115; wide black with red striping body molding, $55-$70; lower accent paint, $205; body side stripes, $45; cloth 55/45 seat with storage armrest (Custom only), $183; cloth reclining buckets with console (Custom only), $185; leather/vinyl 55/45 with recliners (Limited only), $450.

LESABRE CONVENIENCE/APPEARANCE OPTIONS: Electric rear window defogger, $150; electronic cruise control with resume, $185; two-speed windshield wipers with low speed delay feature, $55; black protective body side molding, $60; front carpet savers, $25; rear carpet savers, $20; 55/45 split front seat with storage armrest, $183; rear bumper guards and body side molding extensions, $24; AM/FM ETR stereo radio with cassette tape, seek and scan, auto reverse and clock, $132; graphic equalizer cassette tape with auto reverse, and search/repeat and AM/FM stereo and Concert Sound speaker system, $367; Concert Sound speaker system, $85; locking wire wheel covers, $215; styled aluminum wheels, $270; styled steel wheels, $115; six-way power driver seat adjuster, $250; electric passenger seat back recliner, $70; deluxe trunk trim, $53; electronic touch climate control air conditioner, $165; power windows, cpe $220; sed $295; electric door locks, cpe $155; sed $205; six-way power drive seat adjuster, $250; six-way passenger seat adjuster, $250; front and rear courtesy and warning lights, $44; automatic power antenna, $70; passenger side lighted visor vanity mirror, $50; electric trunk lock release, $50; door edge guards, cpe $15; sed $25; dual electric remote control mirrors, $91; automatic power antenna, $70; Concert Sound speakers, $85; chrome luggage rack, $115; wide rocker panel molding package, $110. Instrumentation: tachometer, temperature, oil and volt gauges, $110; body side stripes, $45; cloth 55/45 seat with storage armrest (Custom only), $183; leather vinyl 55/45 with recliners (Limited only), $450. Special Estate Wagon options: Roof rack, $115; air deflector, $40; remote control electric tailgate lock, $60; tungsten halogen headlamps, $25; Twilight Sentinel headlamp control, $60; illuminated driver door lock and interior light control, $75; cornering lights, $60; front lights monitor, $37. Special Packages - Gran Touring Package. Includes Gran Touring suspension, 15 in. aluminum wheels, P215/65R15 Eagle GT+4 blackwall tires, 2.97:1 axle ratio, heavy-duty cooling, leather-wrapped steering wheel, $563. T-Type Package. Includes Gran Touring package (with different wheels) plus specific interior and exterior trim, cruise, gauges, 55/45 front seats and operating console, AM/FM stereo radio with cassette and graphic equalizer, rear deck spoiler and front air dam, dual exhaust outlets, blackout trim, $1958.

ELECTRA CONVENIENCE/APPEARANCE OPTIONS: Electric rear window defogger, $150; P205/75R14 whitewall tires, $76; electronic cruise control with resume, $185; two-speed windshield wipers with low speed delay feature, $55; black protective body side molding, $60; front carpet savers, $25; rear carpet savers, $20; 55/45 split front seat with storage armrest, $183; rear bumper guards and body side molding extensions, $24; AM/FM ETR stereo radio with cassette tape, seek and scan, auto reverse and clock, $132; graphic equalizer cassette tape with auto reverse, and search/repeat and AM/FM stereo and Concert Sound speaker system, $367; Concert Sound speaker system, $85; locking wire wheel covers, $215; styled aluminum wheels, $270; styled steel wheels, $115; electric passenger seat back recliner, $70; deluxe trunk trim, $53; electronic touch climate control air conditioner, $165; power windows, cpe $220; sed $295; electric door locks, $205; six-way power driver seat adjuster $250; six-way passenger seat adjuster, $250; front and rear courtesy and warning lights, $44; automatic power antenna $70; passenger side lighted visor vanity mirror, $50; Twilight Sentinel headlamp control, $60; four note horn, $28; low windshield washer fluid indicator, $16; cornering lights, $60; front and rear light monitor, $77; low fuel indicator, $16; electric trunk pulldown, $80; automatic day/night mirror, $80; dual electric remote control mirrors with heated left, $35; two-position memory driver belt adjuster, $150; deluxe trunk trim with mat, $68; rear reading lamps, $50; quartz analog gauge cluster $26; electronic instrumentation, $299; electric trunk lock release, $50; door edge guards, $25; dual electric remote control mirrors, $91; automatic power antenna, $70; remote keyless entry system, $175; Concert sound speakers, $70; chrome luggage rack, $115; firemist paint, $210; Bose music system, $553-$905; body side stripes, $45; leather/vinyl 55/45 (Park Avenue), $450; (T-Type), $395; theft deterrent system, $159; full heavily padded top, $260-$695; electric sliding Astroroof (not available with padded roof), $1230: 14 in. styled aluminum wheels, $235-$270. Special Packages: Gran Touring Package. Includes Gran Touring Suspension, 15 in. styled aluminum wheels, P215/65R15 Eagle GT blackwall tires, 2.97:1 axle ratio, heavy-duty cooling, leather-wrapped steering wheel, $462-$563.

RIVIERA CONVENIENCE/APPEARANCE OPTIONS: Graphic equalizer cassette tape with auto reverse, and search/repeat and ETR AM/FM stereo and digital clock, $120; Delco Bose music system with cassette, ETR AM/FM stereo with Dolby, seek and scan, auto reverse with search/repeat, and clock, $583-$703; six-way power passenger seat with power recliner, $325; electric trunk pull-down, $250; remote keyless entry system with automatic power door locks, $265; Twilight headlamp control, $60; theft deterrent system, $159; left and right remote mirrors with heated left, $35; automatic rearview mirror, $80; electric compass, $75; firemist paint, $210; lower accent paint, $190; electric Astroroof sliding roof, $1230; heavily padded roof, $695; leather and suede bucket seats, $550; 16-way adjustable driver leather and suede bucket seats, $1230; styled aluminum wheels, $55; cellular telephone, $1975. Special Packages: Gran Touring Package. Includes Gran Touring suspension, 2.97:1 axle ratio, 15 in. aluminum wheels, leather-wrapped steering wheel and shift handle, fast ratio power steering and P215/65R15 blackwall Eagle GT+4 tires, $104. Riviera Appearance Package: Includes platinum beige firemist lower accent paint, body side stripe and painted aluminum wheels, $205.

REATTA CONVENIENCE/APPEARANCE OPTIONS: Sliding electric steel sunroof, $895; articulated driver's seat.

HISTORY: Buick produced 484,764 vehicles in the 1988 calendar year. Its 1988 model year output was 458,768, a drop of 189,921 cars. Buick's Skylark and Skyhawk models ranked 14th and 15th in output of compact cars. The Riviera was listed last in production among 30 intermediates built in the United States. The front-wheel-drive LeSabre held fifth position among domestic standard-size cars. The Reatta outproduced Cadillac's Allante by a margin of 2,139 vehicles.

Buick celebrated its 86th anniversary by offering automobiles that it regarded as a combination of "exhilarating driving luxury without ostentation." As part of General Motors' overall strategy to regain lost market share, the Buick was depicted as the premium American motorcar." A key aspect of this philosophy was to join the best of Buick's heritage with plenty of contemporary design features and advanced technology. As a result, the 1989 Buick's Dynaride suspension was engineered to provide crisp handling without a loss of riding comfort. Similarly, the Reatta, promoted as the "premium American two-seater," was seen as a car that fused the fun of owning a two-seater sports car with the luxury surroundings typical of a Buick. The new-styled Riviera was, in Buick's view, "a classic all over again." For those Riviera owners who had been unhappy with the truncated look of the previous model, the latest Riviera was enthusiastically received. "You recognize it immediately," stated Buick. "It could only be the Riviera." Perhaps the most graphic example of Buick's resurgence came in the form of the LeSabre's ranking as the highest-placed domestic vehicle in the J.D. Powers and Associates Initial Quality Survey. As a result, LeSabre sales more than doubled.

1989 Buick, Skyhawk sedan. (OCW)

SKYHAWK - SERIES 4J - FOUR - The Buick Skyhawk had a number of new standard features for 1989 including the 2.0-liter EFI L-4 engine, an upgraded acoustical insulation package and a rear-seat lap/shoulder belt system. The door and window frames on the station wagon were now body color. A new all-leather sport steering wheel was available on the SE model.

1989 Buick, Skylark Limited sedan with optional wire wheel covers. (OCW)

SKYLARK - SERIES 4N - FOUR/V-6 - Numerous features, both standard and optional, were introduced on the 1989 Skylarks. The LE sedan was available in a Formal Appearance Luxury Edition with the following features: a formal vinyl roof with a reduced size rear window and rear side windows, tri-shield emblems on the rear deck and rear side door panel, wire wheel covers, bright "B" pillar appliqué, wide rocker panel moldings, wide lower body-side moldings, black windshield trim, wheel

opening molding and grille header appliqué. The 3.0 liter V-6 of 1988 was replaced by the 3300 V-6 engine. As in 1988, the coupes were fitted with composite headlights. These were now also installed on the sedans. A revised taillamp design was adopted. The lower body fascia was changed from black to body color. A new stand-up hood ornament with a tri-shield design was installed on all models. New standard equipment consisted of a rear-seat lap/shoulder belt system, split bench reclining seat with storage tray, champagne burl woodgrain trim plates, extended-range speakers and foot-operated parking brake. The Convenience Group Package consisting of front-seat armrest, seat recliner, trunk trim, passenger vanity mirror and remote fuel filler door release was also standard on all Skylarks. A new sew trim pattern was found in Custom and Limited models. New or revised options included restyled 13 in. aluminum wheels, an all-leather sport steering wheel and bucket seats of a new design. The Skylark package was offered for both the coupe and sedan models.

1989 Buick, Century Custom coupe with optional styled wheels. (OCW)

1989 Buick, Century Custom sedan. (OCW)

CENTURY - SERIES 4A - FOUR/V-6 - The 1989 Century models had an all-new front and rear appearance highlighted by composite headlights and wraparound park and turn signal lamps. Both coupe and sedan models had standard black wide body side moldings and dual, black, outside rearview mirrors (left remote, right manual). Additional new or revised standard equipment included a stand-up tri-shield hood ornament, rear-

seat lap/shoulder belt system, analog gauge cluster graphics, champagne burl woodgrain trim plates and a new horn pad design. The Limited sedan had the UJ5 instrument panel gauge option as standard equipment. The Limited coupe model was canceled. If 55/45 seats were ordered, a front seat storage armrest was installed. New 14 in. aluminum wheels were available.

1989 Buick, Regal coupe with optional Gran Sport package. (OCW)

1989 Buick, Regal Custom coupe with optional styled wheels. (OCW)

1989 Buick, Regal Limited coupe with optional wire wheel covers. (OCW)

REGAL - SERIES 4W - V-6 - The front-wheel drive Regal was refined both in terms of appearance and equipment for 1989. Joining the Custom and Limited model was a new Gran Sport version. The Gran Sport was marketed as a separate model but technically it was option Z13 consisting of blackout molding for the windshield, reveal moldings, grille, and antenna; a front air dam, black taillamp bezels, black front and rear bumpers, wide lower body side molding with red stripe, full aero rocker panels, fog lamps, 16 in. aluminum wheels, bucket seats with operating controls and the Y56 Gran Touring package. Standard equipment on all models now included air conditioning, a stand-up tri-shield hood ornament, rear seat lap/shoulder belt system, flash-to-pass signal, ETR AM/FM stereo radio and a tilt steering column. The Custom Regal now had standard driver and passenger seat back recliners as well as extendible sunvisors. Both the Custom and Limited models were available with 15 in. aluminum wheels. A wide, ribbed body side molding was standard on the Limited model. The instrument panel HVAC outlets were now chrome. New 16 in. wheels were included in

the Y56 Gran Touring Package. An "express down" feature was added on the driver's power window option. Anti-lock brakes were now available as was a new electric sunroof and a ETR AM/FM stereo radio with a compact disc player. All Regals could be ordered with a steering wheel that included radio controls.

1989 Buick, LeSabre T Type coupe. (OCW)

1989 Buick, LeSabre Custom coupe. (OCW)

LESABRE - SERIES 4H - V-6 - The appearance of the LeSabre models was virtually unchanged for 1989. The most apparent visual alteration was due to the elimination of the standard vinyl top previously installed on the LeSabre Limited coupe. Revisions applicable to all LeSabres consisted of a new outside rearview mirror control, a modified horn pad and the inclusion of a tilt steering column, trip odometer and a leather-wrapped sport steering wheel as standard LeSabre equipment. A replaceable-mast power antenna was now available as was a modified Concert Sound speaker system. The quartz analog gauge cluster was revised to read 10-100 mph. A new champagne burl woodgrain trim was standard on both Custom and Limited models. A front-seat storage armrest was standard on Limited models and optional for the Custom LeSabre when fitted with 55/45 seats. The LeSabre T-Type continued to be available. Although retailed as a separate model, it remained technically a special option package.

1989 Buick, Century Estate Wagon station wagon. (OCW)

1989 Buick, LeSabre Estate Wagon station wagon. (OCW)

ESTATE WAGON - SERIES 4B - V-8 - The LeSabre and Electra station wagons were, except for some minor refinements and revisions, carryover models from 1988. Both versions now had standard rear-seat lap/shoulder belt systems and a front license plate mounting. A trailer-towing package was now available, and the Electra model could be ordered with leather interior trim. The previously offered gray cloth interior for the Electra was canceled for 1989.

1989 Buick, Electra Park Avenue Ultra sedan. (OCW)

ELECTRA - SERIES 4C - V-6 - Beyond any doubt, the most significant development in the 1989 Electra lineup was the introduction of the Park Avenue Ultra sedan. This automobile was depicted as "the ultimate in Buick luxury" and was specifically targeted toward upscale sales prospects. Buick advised its sales personnel that "the Ultra appeals to many current Park Avenue owners who are ready for an upgrade." It was, continued Buick, "a most substantial motorcar, offering more of what makes a Buick a Buick." Sales strategy for the Ultras also viewed it as an automobile that enabled Buick to compete in what it described as the "premium luxury sedan market," which it said was occupied by individuals "accustomed to paying $28,000 to $30,000 for high-content luxury sedans." Its "distinctive styling," said Buick, plus a "powerful performance and premium ride are Buick Motor Division's signature characteristics carried to their highest expression." Included in its standard features were all-leather seating and trim, a 20-way power seat, anti-lock brake system, specific dark elm burl woodgrain trim, specific grille texture and taillamp array, a choice of six two-tone color treatments, smoked taillamps, specific 15 in. aluminum wheels and chrome side pillars. The Ultra was also identified by its sterling silver lower accent paint treatment and silver accent body stripe. The 1989 Electra/Park Avenue models were distinguished from the 1988 versions by their stand-up hood ornament (except for the T-Type), new outside rearview mirror control, automatic front safety belt system, analog gauge cluster modified to read from 10-100 mph, flash-to-pass signal, a new seat design for the Park Avenue and, except for the T-Type, a front-seat storage armrest. New optional equipment consisted of a replaceable-mast antenna, full vinyl top for the Park Avenue Ultra, a blue leather interior for the Park Avenue, and a remote radio Keyless

Entry System. A leather-wrapped sport steering wheel for the T-Type and Gran Touring Package (Y56) was also offered.

1989 Buick, Riviera coupe. (OCW)

RIVIERA - SERIES 4E - V-6 - The Riviera's appearance was significantly altered for 1989 to bring it more closely in line with the format established by previous models. A new roofline with a wider C or sail panel, plus handsomely contoured taillamps, were major contributors to the Riviera's return to the basics that had made the pre-1986 models sales successes. Also playing an important role in this Riviera Renaissance was the longer length of the 1989 model. The wheelbase remained at 108 inches but 11 inches were added to the Riviera's rear overhang. Additional changes for 1989 involved the following standard items: body side moldings, larger 15 in. wheels and tires, revised front end and rocker panel molding styling, two-piece body color outside mirrors, chrome windshield and backlight moldings, coach lamps and body color door-edge guards, wire wheelcovers, black rub strips, domed wheel-opening moldings, leather-wrapped sport steering wheel and shift handle, vinyl trim for the door and instrument panel dark elm burl woodgrain trim plates and flash-to-pass signal. A heavy-duty engine and transmission system was also standard as was a new engine mount system with hydraulics. A new diamond white exterior color was offered. Features added to the Riviera's option list consisted of the remote keyless entry system with automatic door locks, a new design landau roof and an electro-chromic automatic day/night mirror. The T-Type model and the 16-way optional cloth bucket seats were canceled for 1989. The trunk and fuel access buttons were moved to the glove box.

1989 Buick, Reatta coupe. (OCW)

REATTA - SERIES 4E - V-6 - A number of small changes were found in the 1989 Reatta. Like those on the Riviera, the Reatta's trunk and fuel access buttons were now located in the glove box. Similarly, the 1989 Reatta had a new hydraulic engine mount system. Additional new features included hood and steering wheel ornamentation, all leather interior trim and a standard remote keyless entry system. An electric sunroof was now optional.

I.D. DATA: The 1989 Buick vehicle identification number (VIN) contained 17 characters. The first was the producing country; "1" - United States. The second character was "G" - General Motors. The third was "4" - Buick Division. The fourth character identified the car line: "A" - Century, "B" - LeSabre and Electra Estate wagon, "C" - Electra, "D" - incomplete LeSabre wagon, "E" - Riviera and Reatta, "H" - LeSabre, "J" - Skyhawk, "N" - Skylark, "W" - Regal. The fifth character designated the series: "B" - Regal Custom/incomplete wagon, "C" - Skylark Custom/Reatta, "D" - Skylark Limited/Regal Limited, "F" - Electra T-Type, "H" - Century Custom, "J" - Skylark Custom, "L" - Century Limited/Estate wagon, "M" - Skylark Limited, "P" - LeSabre/LeSabre Custom, "R" - LeSabre Limited/Estate wagon, "S" - Skyhawk, "U" - Electra Ultra, "V" - Electra Estate Wagon, "W" - Electra Park Avenue, "Z" - Riviera. The sixth digit represented the body style code as follows: "1" - two-door coupe, "5" - four-door sedan, "8" - four-door station wagon, "9" - four-door station wagon (incomplete). The seventh character identified the restraint system: "1" - manual belts, "4" - automatic belts, "0" - incomplete vehicle. The eighth character represented the engine code: "1" - 2.0 liter L4-121, "U" - 2.5 liter Tech IV L4-151, "D" - 2.3 liter DOHC Quad L4-140, "N" - 3.3 liter 3300 V-6-204, "R" - 2.5 liter Tech IV-L4-151 (98 hp), "W" - 2.8 liter V-6-173, "C" - 3.8 liter 3800 V-6-231, "Y" - 5.0 liter V-8-307. The ninth unit is a check digit that verifies the accuracy of the VIN. The next letter, "K," represents the 1989 model year. The eleventh entry identifies the assembly plant: "A" - Lakewood, GA, "B" - Lansing, MI, "G" - Framingham, MA, "H" - Flint, MI, "J" - Janesville, WI, "M" - Lansing, MI, "T" - Tarrytown, NY, "U" - Hamtramck, MI, "I" - Wentzville, MO, "1" - Oshawa, Ontario, Canada, "6" - Oklahoma City, OK. The characters from 12-17 are the production sequence number.

Skyhawk (Four)

Model No.	Body/Style No.	Body Type & Seating	Factory Price	Shipping Weight	Prod. Total
S27	JS1	2-dr. Cpe.-5P	9285	2420	7,837
S69	JS5	4-dr. Sed.-5P	9285	2469	13,841
S35	JS8	4-dr. Sta. Wag.-5P	10230	2551	1,688

Skyhawk S/E (Four)

WN2	JS1	2-dr. Cpe.-5P	10380	2420	Note

Note: Skyhawk S/E production included in base coupe total.

Skylark Custom (Four/V-6)*

J27	NJ1	2-dr. Cpe.-5P	11115	2583	12,714
C69	NC5	4-dr. Sed.-5P	11115	2640	42,636

Skylark Limited (Four/V-6)

M27	NM1	2-dr. Cpe.-5P	12345	2600	1,416
D69	ND5	4-dr. Sed.-5P	12345	2657	4,774

* Add $660 for 2.4 liter Quad 4 and $710 for 3.3 liter V-6 engines.

Century Custom (Four/V-6)

H37	AH1	2-dr. Cpe.-6P	12199/12909	2725/2835	6,953
H69	AH5	4-dr. Sed.-6P	12429/12909	2769/2879	89,281
H35	AH8	4-dr. Sta. Wag.-6P	13156/13866	2905/3012	5,479

Century Limited (Four/V-6)

L69	AL5	4-dr. Sed.-6P	13356/14066	2785/2895	49,839

Century Estate Station Wagon (Four/V-6)

L35	AL8	4-dr. Sta. Wag.-6P	13956/14666	2924/3031	3,940

Regal Custom (V-6)

B57	WB1	2-dr. Cpe.-6P	14614	3144	41,554

Regal Limited (V-6)

D57	WB1	2-dr.Cpe.-6P	15139	3163	47,203*

* Includes 14,503 Gran Sports.

LeSabre (V-6)

P37	HP1	2-dr. Cpe.-6P	15425	3227	1,830

LeSabre Custom (V-6)

Model No.	Body/Style No.	Body Type & Seating	Factory Price	Shipping Weight	Prod. Total
P69	HP5	4-dr. Sed.-6P	15330	3267	78,738

LeSabre Limited (V-6)

Model No.	Body/Style No.	Body Type & Seating	Factory Price	Shipping Weight	Prod. Total
R37	HR1	2-dr. Cpe.-6P	16630	3262	2,287
R69	HP5	4-dr. Sed.-6P	16730	3299	61,328

LeSabre Estate Station Wagon (V-8)

Model No.	Body/Style No.	Body Type & Seating	Factory Price	Shipping Weight	Prod. Total
R35	BR8	4-dr. Sta. Wag.-6P	16770	4209	2,971

Electra Limited (V-6)

Model No.	Body/Style No.	Body Type & Seating	Factory Price	Shipping Weight	Prod. Total
X69	CX5	4-dr. Sed.-6P	18525	3289	5,814

Electra T-Type (V-6)

Model No.	Body/Style No.	Body Type & Seating	Factory Price	Shipping Weight	Prod. Total
F69	CF5	4-dr. Sed.-6P	21325	3384	1,151

Electra Park Avenue (V-6)

Model No.	Body/Style No.	Body Type & Seating	Factory Price	Shipping Weight	Prod. Total
W69	CW5	4-dr. Sed.-6P	20460	3329	71,786

Electra Park Avenue Ultra (V-6)

Model No.	Body/Style No.	Body Type & Seating	Factory Price	Shipping Weight	Prod. Total
U69	CU5	4-dr. Sed.-6P	26218	3426	4,815

Electra Estate Station Wagon

Model No.	Body/Style No.	Body Type & Seating	Factory Price	Shipping Weight	Prod. Total
V35	BV8	4-dr. Sta. Wag.	19860	4273	4,560

Riviera (V-6)

Model No.	Body/Style No.	Body Type & Seating	Factory Price	Shipping Weight	Prod. Total
Z57	EZ1	2-dr. Cpe.-6P	22540	3436	21,189

Reatta (V-6)

Model No.	Body/Style No.	Body Type & Seating	Factory Price	Shipping Weight	Prod. Total
C97	EC1	2-dr. Cpe.-2P	26700	3394	7,009

ENGINES: BASE FOUR (Skyhawk) Inline, overhead valve, four-cylinder. Cast iron block and aluminum head. Displacement: 121 cu. in. (2.0 liters). Bore & stroke: 3.50 x 3.15 in. Compression ratio: 9.0:1. Brake horsepower: 90 @ 5600 rpm. Torque: 108 lb.-ft. @ 3200 rpm. Five main bearings. Hydraulic valve lifters. Throttle-body electronic fuel injection. BASE FOUR (Skylark) Inline, overhead valve, four-cylinder. Cast iron block and head. Displacement: 151 cu. in. (2.5 liters). Bore & stroke: 4.00 x 3.00 in. Compression ratio: 9.0:1. Brake horsepower: 110 @ 5200 rpm. Torque: 135 lb.-ft. @ 3200 rpm. Five main bearings. Hydraulic valve lifters. Throttle-body fuel injection. BASE FOUR (Century) Inline, overhead valve, four-cylinder. Cast alloy iron block and head. Displacement: 151 cu. in. (2.5 liters). Bore & stroke: 4.00 x 3.00 in. Compression ratio: 9.0:1. Brake horsepower: 98 @ 4800 rpm. Torque: 135 lb.-ft. @ 3200 rpm. Five main bearings. Hydraulic valve lifters. Throttle-body electric fuel injection. BASE V-6 (Regal) 60-degree overhead valve V-6. Cast iron block and aluminum heads. Displacement: 173 cu. in. (3.8 liters). Bore & stroke: 3.50 x 2.99 in. Compression ratio: 8.9:1. Brake horsepower: 130 @ 4500 rpm. Torque: 170 lb.-ft. @ 3600 rpm. Hydraulic valve lifters. Multi-port fuel injection. BASE V-6 (LeSabre) 90-degree overhead valve V-6 with balance shaft. Cast iron alloy block and head. Displacement: 231 cu. in. (3.8 liters). Bore & stroke: 3.80 x 3.40 in. Compression ratio: 8.5:1. Brake horsepower: 165 @ 4800 rpm. Torque: 210 lb.-ft. @ 2000 rpm. Four main bearings. Hydraulic valve lifters. Sequential fuel injection. BASE V-8 (LeSabre Estate wag) 90-degree overhead valve V-8. Cast iron block and head. Displacement: 307 cu. in. (5.0 liters). Bore & stroke: 3.8 x 3.39 in. Compression ratio: 8.0:1. Brake horsepower: 140 @ 3200 rpm. Torque: 255 lb.-ft. @ 2000 rpm. Five main bearings. Hydraulic valve lifters. Carb.: 4Bbl. BASE V-6 (Electra) 90-degree overhead valve V-6 with balance shaft. Cast iron alloy block and head. Displacement: 231 cu. in. (3.8 liters). Bore & stroke: 3.80 x 3.40 in. Compression ratio: 8.5:1. Brake horsepower: 165 @ 4800 rpm. Torque: 210 lb.-ft. @ 2000 rpm. Four main bearings. Hydraulic valve lifters. Sequential fuel injection. BASE V-8 (Electra Estate wag) 90-degree overhead valve V-8. Cast iron block and head. Displacement: 307 cu. in. (5.0 liters). Bore & stroke: 3.8 x 3.39 in. Compression ratio: 8.0:1. Brake horsepower: 140 @ 3200 rpm. Torque: 255 lb.-ft. @ 2000 rpm. Five main bearings. Hydraulic valve lifters. Carb.: 4Bbl. BASE V-6 (Riviera) 90-degree overhead valve V-6. Cast iron alloy block and head. Displacement: 231 cu. in. (3.8 liters). Bore & stroke: 3.80 x 3.40 in. Compression ratio: 8.5:1. Brake horsepower: 165 @ 4800 rpm. Torque: 210 lb.-ft.

@ 2000 rpm. Four main bearings. Hydraulic valve lifters. Sequential fuel injection. BASE V-6 (Reatta) 90-degree overhead valve V-6. Cast iron alloy block and head. Displacement: 231 cu. in. (3.8 liters). Bore & stroke: 3.80 x 3.40 in. Compression ratio: 8.5:1. Brake horsepower: 165 @ 4800 rpm. Torque: 210 lb.-ft. @ 2000 rpm. Four main bearings. Hydraulic valve lifters. Sequential fuel injection. OPTIONAL (Skylark) Inline, DOHC, four-cylinder. Cast alloy iron block, cast aluminum head. Displacement: 138 cu. in. (2.3 liters). Bore & stroke: 3.62 x 3.346 in. Compression ratio: 9.5:1. Brake horsepower: 150 @ 5200 rpm. Torque: 160 lb.-ft. @ 4000 rpm. Hydraulic valve lifters. Multi-port fuel injection. OPTIONAL (Skylark): 90-degree V-6. Cast iron block and cylinder head. Displacement: 204 cu. in. (3.3 liters). Bore & stroke: 3.73 x 3.16 in. Compression ratio: 9.0:1. Brake horsepower: 160 @ 5200 rpm. Torque: 185 lb.-ft. @ 2000 rpm. Four main bearings. Hydraulic valve lifters. Multi-port fuel injection. OPTIONAL (Century, Century Estate wag): 60-degree V-6. Cast iron block and cylinder head. Displacement: 204 cu. in. (3.3 liters). Bore & stroke: 3.70 x 3.16 in. Compression ratio: 9.00:1. Brake horsepower: 160 @ 5200 rpm. Torque: 185 lb.-ft. @ 2000 rpm. Four main bearings. Hydraulic valve lifters. Multi-port fuel injection.

CHASSIS DATA: Wheelbase: (Skyhawk) 101.2 in.; (Skylark) 103.4 in.; (Century) 104.8 in.; (Regal) 107.5 in.; (LeSabre) 110.8 in.; (LeSabre Estate Wagon) 115.9 in.; (Electra) 110.8 in.; (Riviera) 108.0 in.; (Reatta) 98.5 in. Overall Length: (Skyhawk) cpe: 179.3 in., sed and wag: 181.7 in.; (Skylark) 180.1 in.; (Century) 189.1 in.; (Century Custom/Estate wag) 190.9 in.; (Regal) 192.2 in.; (LeSabre) 196.5 in.; (LeSabre Estate wag) 220.5 in.; (Electra) 197.0 in.; (Electra Estate wag) 220.5 in.; (Riviera) 198.3 in.; (Reatta) 183.7 in. Height: (Skyhawk) cpe and sed: 54.0 in., wag: 54.4 in.; (Skylark) 52.1 in.; (Century) cpe: 53.7 in., sed and Century Custom/Estate wag: 54.2 in.; (Regal) 53.0 in.; (LeSabre cpe) 54.7 in.; (LeSabre sed) 55.4 in.; (LeSabre Estate wag) 59.3 in.; (Electra) 54.3 in.; (Riviera) 53.6 in.; (Reatta) 51.2 in. Width: (Skyhawk) 65.0 in.; (Skylark) 66.6 in.; (Century) 69.4 in.; (Century Custom/Estate wag) 69.4 in.; (Regal) 72.5 in.; (LeSabre sed/cpe) 72.4 in.; (LeSabre Estate wag) 79.3 in.; (Electra) 72.4 in.; (Riviera) 71.7 in.; (Reatta) 73.0 in. Front Tread: (Skyhawk) cpe and sed: 55.6 in., wag: 55.4 in.; (Skylark) 55.6 in.; (Century) 58.7 in.; (Century) 58.7 in.; (Century Custom/Estate wag) 58.7 in.; (Regal) 59.3 in.; (LeSabre cpe/sed) 60.3 in.; (LeSabre Estate wag) 62.2 in.; (Electra) 60.3 in.; (Riviera) 59.9 in.; (Reatta) 60.3 in. Rear Tread: (Skyhawk) 55.2 in.; (Skylark) 55.2 in.; (Century) 56.7 in.; (Century Custom/Estate wag) 56.7 in.; (Regal) 58.0 in.; (LeSabre cpe/sed) 59.8 in.; (LeSabre Estate wag) 64.0 in.; (Electra) 59.8 in.; (Riviera) 59.9 in.; (Reatta) 60.3 in. Standard Tires: (Skyhawk) P175/80R13; (Skylark) P185/80R13; (Century) P185/75R14; (Century Custom/Estate wag) P185/75R14; (Regal) P205/75R14; (LeSabre cpe/sed) P205/75R14; (LeSabre Estate wag) P225/75R15; (Electra) P205/75R14 (blackwall on Limited, whitewall on Park Avenue); (Electra T-Type) P215/65R15; (Park Avenue Ultra) P205/70R15 whitewall; (Riviera) P205/75R15; (Reatta) P215/65R15.

TECHNICAL: Transmission: (Skyhawk) Five-speed manual; (Skylark, Century, Century Custom/Estate wag) Three-speed automatic; (Regal, LeSabre, Electra, Riviera, Reatta) Four-speed automatic with overdrive. Steering: (Skyhawk, Skylark, Century, Century Custom/Estate wag, Regal, LeSabre cpe/sed, Electra, Riviera) Power rack and pinion; (LeSabre Estate wag) Power recirculating ball; (Reatta) Fast ratio power steering. Front suspension: (Skyhawk, Skylark, Century, Century Custom/Estate wag, LeSabre cpe/sed, Electra, Electra T-Type, Riviera) MacPherson struts with coil springs, lower control arms and stabilizer bar; (Regal) MacPherson strut with lower control arms and unitized coil springs; (LeSabre Estate wag) Coil springs, unequal length control arms, stabilizer bar; (Reatta) Independent four-wheel Gran Touring. Rear suspension: (Skyhawk) Semi-independent with beam axle, trailing arms, coil

springs, stabilizer bar available; (Skylark) Trailing crank bar, coil springs and stabilizer bar; (Century) Beam twist axle with integral stabilizer bar, trailing arms, Panhard arm and coil springs; (LeSabre cpe/sed) MacPherson struts, coil springs, stabilizer bar; (LeSabre Estate wag) Solid axle with four links, coil springs; (Electra, Electra T-Type) Independent MacPherson struts, inboard coil springs, stabilizer bar; (Riviera) Independent tri-link. transverse fiberglass leaf spring, stabilizer bar; (Reatta) Independent modular assembly with single traverse leaf springs. Brakes: (Skyhawk, Skylark, Somerset, Century, Century Custom/Estate wag, Regal, LeSabre cpe/sed, LeSabre Estate wag, Electra, Electra T-Type) Power front disc, rear drum; (Riviera, Reatta) Power disc, front and rear. Body construction: (Skyhawk, Skylark) Unibody; (Century/Century wag) Integral body/frame; (Regal) Integral body/frame with bolted-on powertrain cradle; (LeSabre) Unitized body/frame integral with isolated engine cradle; (Electra and LeSabre Estate wag) Welded body with full perimeter frame; (Electra) Unitized body/frame construction with isolated engine cradle; (Riviera) Unitized body with isolated front frame and rear sub-frame; (Reatta) Unitized body with isolated front and rear sub-frames. Fuel tank: (Skyhawk) 13.6 gal.; (Skylark) 13.6 gal.; (Somerset) 13.6 gal.; (Century) 15.7 gal.; (Century Custom/Estate wag) 16.6 gal.; (Regal) 16.5 gal.; (LeSabre cpe/sed) 18.0 gal.; (LeSabre and Electra Estate wag) 22.0 gal.; (Electra and Electra T-Type) 18.0 gal.; (Riviera) 18.2 gal.; (Reatta) 18.2 gal.

DRIVETRAIN OPTIONS: Engines: (Skylark) 2.3 liter Quad-4, MFI, $660; 3.3 liter V-6, MFI, $710; (Century, Century Custom/Estate wag) 3.3 liter V-6, MFI, $710. Transmission/Differential: (Skyhawk) Three-speed automatic, $440; (Century, Century Custom/Estate wag) Automatic transmission with overdrive, with 3.3 liter engine only, $200. Suspension, steering and brakes: (Skylark) Gran Touring Package (14 in. aluminum wheels, P215/60R14 Eagle GT4 blackwall tires, Gran Touring suspension, leather-wrapped steering wheel) $603; engine block heater, $18; (Century) Heavy-duty engine and transmission cooling: $70 (without air conditioning); $40 with a/c; heavy duty suspension (required with 3.3 liter engine): $27; Gran Touring Package, not available for station wagons (aluminum wheels, P15/60R Eagle GT tires, leather-wrapped steering wheel and Gran Touring suspension): $515; (Regal) Gran Touring Package consisting of Gran Touring suspension, 16 in. aluminum wheels, P215/60R16 tires and leather-wrapped steering wheel: $531-$607, depending on model; anti-lock brake system: $925; (LeSabre coupe and sedan) 2.91:1 axle (included in Y56 Gran Touring package and WE2-T-Type; required with V-8-heavy-duty engine and transmission cooling): No additional charge; heavy-duty engine and transmission cooling (included in WE2 and Y56): $40; Gran Touring Package consisting of Gran Touring suspension, 15 in. aluminum wheels, P215/65R15 blackwall tires, 2.97:1 axle ratio, heavy-duty cooling and leather-wrapped steering wheel; (LeSabre/Electra Estate wag) trailer towing package consisting of 3.23:1 axle ratio, V-8-heavy-duty engine and transmission cooling, automatic level control: $215; Limited slip differential: $100; (Electra) heavy-duty battery, required with electronic air conditioning: $26; heavy-duty engine and transmission cooling (standard with T-Type, included in Y56 Gran Touring Package): $40; 2.97:1 axle ratio (requires V-8, included in Y56 Gran Touring Package and T-Type): No additional charge; Electronic anti-lock brake system: $925 (standard on T-Type and Ultra); Gran Touring Package (standard on T-Type, not available for Ultra or with fully padded vinyl top), consists of Gran Touring suspension, 15 in. styled aluminum wheels, P215/65R15 Eagle GT blackwall tires, 2.97:1 axle ratio, heavy-duty cooling and leather-wrapped steering wheel, $563 for Limited, $462 for Park Avenue; (Riviera) Gran Touring Package consisting of Gran Touring Suspension, 2.97:1 axle ratio, 15 in. aluminum wheels, leather-wrapped sport steering wheel and shift handle, fast ratio power steering and P215/65R15 steel belted radial ply Eagle GT+4 tires: $104.

1989 Buick, Skyhawk SE coupe. (OCW)

SKYHAWK CONVENIENCE/APPEARANCE OPTIONS: Automatic transmission, $440; tilt steering column, $125; two-speed windshield wipers with low speed delay, $55; electronic cruise control, $185; AM/FM ETR stereo radio with cassette tape, seek and scan, auto reverse and clock, $122; four-way manual driver seat adjuster, front console-mounted armrest, electric rear window defogger, $150; electric door locks: $1162 (cpe), $1212 (sed), $1262 (wag). Air conditioner, $695; emission equipment and testing, $100. Skyhawk S/E Package: consists of front and rear carpet savers, Gran Touring Package (Gran Touring suspension, P215/60R14 Eagle GT+4 blackwall tires, 14 in. Shelby aluminum wheels, leather-wrapped steering wheel; instrument gauges and tachometer, exterior trim package (blackout moldings, concealed headlamps and fog lamps): $1095. Various Popular, Premium and Luxury Packages: $1157-$1412.

1989 Buick, Skylark Limited coupe with optional Sport package. (OCW)

SKYLARK CONVENIENCE/APPEARANCE OPTIONS: Air conditioning, $695; tilt steering column, $125; P185/80R13 whitewall tires, $68; mirrors-remote control left, right manual, $53; electric rear window defogger, $150; protective wide body side molding, $80; wheel opening molding, $30; plus electronic cruise control with resume, $185; two-speed windshield wipers with resume feature, $55; front and rear carpet savers, $45; AM/FM ETR stereo radio with cassette tape, seek and scan, auto reverse with search and repeat and clock, $152; custom locking wheel covers, $215; four-way manual driver seat adjuster, $35; power windows, $220 cpe, $295 sed; electric door locks, $155 cpe, $295 sed; six-way power driver seat adjuster, $250; power antenna, $70; passenger side lighted visor vanity mirror, $38; electric trunk lock release, $50; front and rear courtesy lights, $14; chrome deck lid luggage rack (not available with S/E package and exterior sport package), $115; lower body accent paint, $195; body side stripes, $45; Custom and Limited cloth bucket seats with full length operating console, $180, styled 13 in. aluminum wheels, $245; styled hubcaps and trim rings, $38; custom locking wire wheel covers, $215. Special packages: Gran Touring Package, $603; includes 14 in. aluminum wheels, P215/60R14 Eagle GT blackwall tires, Gran Touring suspension, leather-wrapped steering wheel. Exterior Sport

Package, $374-Custom cpe, $318 Limited cpe; includes black-out moldings, front air dam, aero rocker moldings, wide body side moldings. Skylark S/E Package, $1134. Available for Custom models only. Includes bucket seat and console, dual mirrors with left remote, body side moldings, rocker moldings, wheel opening moldings, cassette tape radio, and Gran Touring Package. Skylark L/E Formal Appearance Luxury Edition, $1050-$1495. Includes full formal vinyl roof, wire wheel covers, wide rocker molding, body side molding, wheel opening molding, dual mirrors with left remote, and lower accent paint. Various Popular, Premium, Luxury and Prestige packages, $1201-$2994. Tires (all-steel belted radial ply): P205/70R13 blackwall, $124; P205/70R13 whitewall, $190.

CENTURY CONVENIENCE/APPEARANCE OPTIONS: Air conditioning, $795; tilt steering column, $150; electric rear window defogger, $150; electronic cruise control with resume, $185; two-speed windshield wipers with resume feature, $55; front carpet savers, $25; rear carpet savers, $20; AM/FM ETR stereo radio with cassette tape, seek and scan, auto reverse and clock, $122; custom locking wire wheel covers, $215; styled steel wheels, $115; aluminum wheels, $270; body stripes, $45; six-way power driver seat adjuster, $70; power windows, $220 cpe, $295 sed; electric door locks, $155 cpe, $295 sed; six-way power driver seat adjuster. $250; power antenna, $70; passenger side lighted visor vanity mirror, $50; electric trunk lock release, $50; door edge guards, $15 cpe, $25 sed; passenger manual seat back recliner, $45; dual electric remote control mirrors, $70; automatic power antenna, $70; (Custom only) 55/45 cloth seat with armrest, $183. Limited cloth 55/45 seat with storage armrest, $233-$416. (Century Limited only) Front seat reading lights, $24; premium rear speakers, $70. (Century Estate wag only) Vinyl third seat, $215; air deflector, $37; vinyl appliqué woodgrain trim, $350; rear window windshield wiper, $125. Special Packages: Gran Touring Package. Includes aluminum wheels and P215/60R14 Eagle GT tires, leather-wrapped steering wheel and Gran Touring suspension, $515.

REGAL CONVENIENCE/APPEARANCE OPTIONS: Electric rear window defogger, $150; electronic cruise control with resume, $185; two-speed windshield wipers with resume feature, $55; front carpet savers, $25; rear carpet savers, $20; AM/FM ETR stereo radio with cassette tape, seek and scan, auto reverse and clock, $122; graphic equalizer cassette tape with auto reverse, and search/repeat and AM stereo, $150-$272; compact disc player with ETR AM/FM radio with seek/scan and clock, $274; electric glass sunroof (includes dual reading lamps and rear courtesy lamps; $650-$680; custom locking wire wheel covers, $215; styled aluminum wheels, $270; styled steel wheels, $115; 15 in. aluminum wheel with blackwall tires. $320; six-way power driver seat adjuster, $250; power windows with express down feature, $230; electric door locks, $155; six-way power driver seat adjuster, $250; automatic power antenna, $70; passenger side lighted visor vanity mirror, $50; electric trunk lock release, $50; door edge guards, $15; dual electric remote control mirrors, $91; automatic power antenna, $70; Concert Sound speakers, $85; redundant accessory controls-steering wheel mounted, $125; remote keyless entry (Limited and Gran Sport only), $125; electronic digital/graphics instrumentation, $299; luggage rack, $115; wide black with red striping body molding, $55-$70; lower accent paint, $205: body side stripes, $45; cloth 55/45 seat with storage armrest (Custom only), $183; cloth reclining buckets with console (Custom only), $185; leather/vinyl 55/45 with recliners (Limited only), $450. Special Packages: Four Seater Package, includes front and rear bucket seats with special armrests and storage console with cassette storage, leather-wrapped steering wheel, rear headrests, $409. Gran Sport, includes Gran Touring Package, bucket seats and console, specific exterior appearance with blackout, fog lamps, aero rocker panels, wide body side molding and front spoiler, $1212.

1989 Buick, LeSabre Limited sedan with optional wire wheel covers. (OCW)

LESABRE CONVENIENCE/APPEARANCE OPTIONS: Electric rear window defogger, $150; electronic cruise control with resume, $185: two-speed windshield wipers with low speed delay feature, $55; black protective body side molding, $60: front carpet savers, $25: rear carpet savers, $20; 55/45 split front seat with storage armrest, $183; rear bumper guards and bodyside molding extensions, $24; AM/FM ETR stereo radio with cassette tape, seek and scan, auto reverse and clock, $132; graphic equalizer cassette tape with auto reverse, and search/repeat and AM/FM stereo and Concert Sound speaker system, $367; Concert Sound speaker system, $85; locking wire wheel covers, $215; styled aluminum wheels, $270: styled steel wheels, $115; six-way power driver seat adjuster, $250; electric passenger seat back recliner, $70; deluxe trunk trim, $53; electronic touch climate control air conditioner, $165; power windows, cpe $220, sed $295; electric door locks, cpe $155, sed $205; six-way power driver seat adjuster, $250; electric passenger seat back recliner, $70; deluxe trunk trim, $53; electronic touch climate control air conditioner, $165; power windows, cpe $220, sed $295; electric door locks, cpe $155, sed $205; six-way power driver seat adjuster, $250; six-way passenger seat adjuster, $250; front and rear courtesy and warning lights, $44; automatic power antenna, $70; passenger side lighted visor vanity mirror, $50; electric trunk lock release, $50; door edge guards, cpe $15, sed $25; dual electric remote control mirrors, $91; automatic power antenna, $70: Concert Sound speakers, $85; chrome luggage rack, $115; wide rocker panel molding package, $110; instrumentation-tachometer, temperature, oil and volt gauges, $110; body side stripes, $45; cloth 55/45 seat with storage armrest (Custom only), $183: leather/vinyl 55/45 with recliners (Limited only), $450. Special Estate wag options-Roof rack, $115; air deflector, $40; remote control electric tailgate lock, $60; tungsten halogen headlamps, $25; twilight sentinel headlamp control, $60; illuminated driver door lock and interior light control, $75; cornering lights, $60; front lights monitor, $37. Special Packages-Gran Touring Package, includes Gran Touring suspension, 15 in. aluminum wheels, P215/65R15 Eagle GT+4 blackwall tires, 2.97:1 axle ratio, heavy-duty cooling, leather-wrapped steering wheel, $563. T-Type Package, includes Gran Touring package (with different wheels) plus specific interior and exterior trim, cruise, gauges, 55/45 front seats and operating console, AM/FM stereo radio with cassette and graphic equalizer, rear deck spoiler and front air dam, dual exhaust outlets, blackout trim, $1927.

ELECTRA CONVENIENCE/APPEARANCE OPTIONS: Electric rear window defogger, $150; P205/75R14 whitewall tires, $76; electronic cruise control with resume, $185; two-speed windshield wipers with low speed delay feature, $55; black protective body side molding, $60; front carpet savers. $25; rear carpet savers, $20; 55/45 split front seat with storage armrest, $183; rear bumper guards and body side molding extensions, $24; AM/FM ETR stereo radio with cassette tape, seek and scan, auto reverse and clock, $132; graphic equalizer cassette tape with auto reverse, and search/repeat and AM/FM stereo and Concert Sound speaker system, $367; Concert Sound

Standard Catalog of Buick 1903-2000

speaker system, $85; locking wire wheel covers, $215; styled aluminum wheels, $270; styled steel wheels, $115; six-way power driver seat adjuster, $250; electric passenger seat back recliner, $70; deluxe trunk trim, $53; electronic touch climate control air conditioner, $165; power windows, cpe $220, sed $295; electric door locks, $205; six-way power driver seat adjuster, $250; six-way passenger seat adjuster, $250; front and rear courtesy and warning lights, $44; automatic power antenna, $70; passenger side light visor vanity mirror, $50; Twilight Sentinel headlamp control, $60; four note horn, $28; low windshield washer fluid indicator, $16; cornering lights, $60; front and rear light monitor, $77; low fuel indicator, $16; electric trunk pull-down, $80; automatic day/night mirror, $80; dual electric remote control mirrors with heated left. $35; two-position memory driver belt adjuster, $150; deluxe trunk trim with mat, $68; rear reading lamps, $50; quartz analog gauge cluster, $126; electronic instrumentation, $299; electric trunk lock release, $50; door edge guards, $25; dual electric remote control mirrors, $91; automatic power antenna, $70; remote keyless entry system, $175; concert sound speakers, $70; chrome luggage rack, $115; firemist paint, $210; Bose music system, $553-$905; body side stripes, $45; leather/vinyl 55/45 (Park Avenue), $450; (T-Type), $395; theft deterrent system, $159; full heavily padded top, $260-$895; electric sliding Astroroof (not available with padded roof), $1230; 14 in. styled aluminum wheels, $235-$270. Special Packages: Gran Touring Package, includes Gran Touring suspension, 15 in. styled aluminum wheels, P215/65R15 Eagle GT blackwall tires, 2.97:1 axle ratio, heavy-duty cooling, leather-wrapped steering wheel, $462-$563.

RIVIERA CONVENIENCE/APPEARANCE OPTIONS: Graphic equalizer cassette tape with auto reverse, and search/repeat and ETR AM/FM stereo and digital clock, $120; Delco Bose music system with cassette, ETR AM/FM stereo with Dolby, seek and scan, auto reverse with search/repeat, and clock, $583-$703; six-way power passenger seat with power recliner, $325; electric trunk pulldown, $250; remote keyless entry system with automatic power door locks, $265; Twilight Sentinel headlamp control, $60; theft deterrent system. $159; left and right remote mirrors with heated left, $35; automatic rearview mirrors, $80; electronic compass, $75: firemist paint, $210; lower accent paint, $190; electric Astroroof sliding roof, $1230; heavily padded roof, $695; leather and suede bucket seats, $550; 16-way adjustable driver leather and suede bucket seats, $1230; styled aluminum wheels, $55; cellular telephone, $1975. Special packages: Gran Touring Package, includes Gran Touring suspension, 2.97:1 axle ratio, 15 in. aluminum wheels, leather-wrapped steering wheel and shift handle, fast ratio power steering and P215/65R15 blackwall Eagle GT+4 tires, $104. Riviera Appearance Package, includes platinum beige firemist lower accent paint, body side stripe and painted aluminum wheels, $205.

REATTA CONVENIENCE/APPEARANCE OPTIONS: Sliding electric steel sunroof, $895; 16-way adjustable driver side leather bucket seats, $680.

HISTORY: Buick's general manager was Edward H. Mertz. Buick's total 1989 calendar sales totaled 542,917 vehicles. Buick's market share rose slightly to 5.5 percent from 5.49 percent in 1988. Its Century series ranked fourth among all intermediate-sized automobiles sold in the United States. The LeSabre was the third-best selling standard-sized automobile.

1990

Buick's first models of the 1990s emphasized new features, new designs, new standard and optional equipment and new technology. Buick sales material highlighted the form of Buicks of the near future by featuring the Buick Essence and Lucerne show cars. Viewed from that perspective, the 1990 Buicks were perceived as automobiles that were, in Buick's words, "powerful and mature, substantial and distinctive." After its extensive restyling in 1989, the Century received important new safety features for 1990. Numerous models, including the Electra and LeSabre, benefited from structural and engineering revisions that improved their ride and handling. The new generation 3800 V-6 engine with tuned-port fuel injection was regarded as "the smoothest, most sophisticated production V-6 ever used in a Buick."

1990 Buick, Skylark sedan. (OCW)

1990 Buick, Skylark Custom coupe with optional styled wheels. (OCW)

1990 Buick, Skylark Luxury Edition sedan. (OCW)

SKYLARK - SERIES 4N - FOUR/V-6 - The Skylark model lineup was revised for 1990. The Skylark SE Package of 1989 became the Gran Sport model while the Formal Appearance Luxury Edition Package was now listed as a Skylark model. The Limited model designation of 1989 was discontinued. Coupe and sedan base models were added. Numerous styling/design changes were apparent for 1990. They included a new vertical grille, a new gunmetal gray exterior color, and a slate color interior trim. The Custom, Gran Sport and Luxury Edition Skylarks had a standard split folding rear seat as standard equipment. Among the new or revised interior features and appointments was a bright bead added to the power window switch trim plate and the relocation of the windshield wiper controls to the multi-function lever. A new instrument panel pod was introduced for 1990 that included an integral radio and temperature controls. A new backlit cluster was also featured as was a new console with a storage bin and armrest. Both the shift and tilt levers were now chrome with black handles. Standard on the Custom coupe and sedan were P185/7R14 tires and styled hubcaps with trim rings. The Skylark coupe and sedan had standard P185/80R13 tires and deluxe wheel covers. The optional driver/passenger reading lamps were integral with the interior mirror. Fourteen inch

Shelby aluminum wheels were included in the Gran Touring Package and also offered as a separate, "free-flow" option. A higher level of interior illumination was standard as was a new 2000 Series radio and a turn signal "on" chime.

1990 Buick, Century Limited sedan with optional wire wheel covers. (OCW)

1990 Buick, Century Custom coupe. (OCW)

CENTURY - SERIES 4A - FOUR/V-6 - After the extensive revisions of 1989, changes for the 1990 model year were relatively limited. Four new exterior colors were announced and a smaller jack was found in the coupe and sedan models. Buick also reported that the ride quality of the Century's Dynaride suspension was improved. Also enhanced was the acoustical insulation package. Interior alterations included a new dark red interior, a new automatic front safety belt system and new door trim. The armrests now had reflectors and a new door-mounted map pocket was installed. New power window and door lock switches were used, and optional power seat recliners replaced the manual recliners. Air conditioning was now standard equipment. Limited models had standard four-door courtesy lamps. A new seat design was found in the Limited sedan. The steering column was revised for improved theft deterrence. The Estate Wagon was now redesignated the "Limited" wagon.

1990 Buick, Regal Limited coupe with optional wire wheel covers. (OCW)

1990 Buick, Regal Gran Sport coupe. (OCW)

REGAL - SERIES 4W - V-6 - Befitting the Regal's position in Buick's marketing strategy were the extensive changes, new

models and revisions introduced with the 1990 Regal. Three new 1991 sedan models, Custom, Limited, and Gran Sport, were added at midyear 1990. Also becoming available at midyear was the 3800 V-6 engine and a four-speed automatic transmission. A new gunmetal gray exterior color was offered. New "Regal" fender lettering was used for 1990. The following specific exterior features were found on the sedan exterior: new major body panels, black "B" and "C" pillar appliqués, clear park and turn lenses, back-up lights integrated into the rear bumper, see-through hood ornament (except Gran Sport), vertical grille with tri-shield, bright door handles and body-color mirrors. The Limited and Gran Sport versions had bright and black upper door moldings, standard bumper guards, bright finish on the front and rear bumper face bar, wraparound rear taillamp lenses and body-color flared rocker panels. The wheel opening moldings on the Custom sedan were bright and black; those on the Limited and Gran Sport were black. The Custom sedan also had body-color lower front and rear fascia with bright rub strips. Black rub strips were fitted to the Limited and Gran Sport sedans. Body-color bumpers were standard for the Custom sedan. The Limited and Gran Sport versions had chrome bumpers with bumper guards. Two-tone paint was restricted to the coupes and the Gran Sport sedan. A four-passenger package was exclusive to the Limited sedan. A new chrome luggage rack was available for the sedan with the black version continued as an option for the coupes. Other changes for 1990 consisted of the addition of a UXI radio to the SE Package on Limited models, the availability of anti-lock brakes with the SE Package on Limited models and the SF Package on the Gran Sport, two-tone paint available only on coupes (standard on the Gran Sport sedan), the replacement of 14 in. with 15 in. wire wheel covers, the addition of a new interior illumination option, three new free-flow options, electric door locks, cruise control, and power windows, new P215/60R16 blackwall touring tires and a driver lockout feature for power windows on sedans.

1990 Buick, LeSabre Custom sedan. (OCW)

1990 Buick, LeSabre coupe with optional wire wheel covers. (OCW)

1990 Buick, LeSabre Limited sedan with optional wire wheel covers. (OCW)

LESABRE - SERIES 4H - V-6 - Buick canceled the T-Type LeSabre model for 1990. The remaining models' styling was highlighted by a new front-end appearance, a new taillamp assembly that included integral back up lights and license plate pocket and a new rear-end filler panel. Custom models featured a standard lower bodyside molding and a body-color "B" pillar appliqué. Limited models also had a new standard lower bodyside molding. All models shared a new body structure package that improved ride quality. The Gran Touring Package now included electronic level control. Additional revisions included a new gunmetal gray exterior color and a matching medium slate vinyl top, a new slate gray interior and a revamped interior seat design on the Limited sedan with Primavera cloth.

1990 Buick, Estate Wagon station wagon. (OCW)

ESTATE WAGON - SERIES 4B - V-8 - Only one model, an Estate Wagon with LeSabre content, was offered for 1990. The LeSabre/Electra designations were dropped. This marketing change was accompanied by a number of interesting revisions and new features. Two new colors, light maple red and dark maple red, were introduced along with a new dark red interior color. Three new standard equipment features--delay windshield wipers, tilt steering column and tungsten-halogen headlamps--were also introduced. A new automatic front safety belt system was also included in the Estate Wagon's standard equipment. The Estate Wagon's seats, in cloth or optional leather, were carried over from the 1989 Electra wagon. Added option package content was also available. External changes were limited to the new tri-shield hood ornament and a new "Estate Wagon" emblem on the front fender. A third seat delete option was also offered.

1990 Buick, Electra Park Avenue sedan with optional sunroof and trunk lid carrier rack. (OCW)

1990 Buick, Electra T Type sedan. (OCW)

1990 Buick, Electra Park Avenue Ultra sedan. (OCW)

ELECTRA - SERIES 4C - V-6 - Key developments in the Electra and Park Avenue models were primarily oriented towards refinement of the existing format rather than startling design or styling changes. Four new exterior colors were available: dove gray, palomino brown, chestnut brown and gunmetal gray. In association with these colors were new color choices for the optional vinyl top: taupe, dark brown, dark red and medium slate. In addition, two new interior colors were offered: brown and slate. The Limited and Park Avenue now had standard 14 in. wire wheelcovers. Standard on the Limited were P205/75R14 tires. Both the limited and T-Type were fitted with a two-speed wiper system with a delay feature as well as cruise control as standard equipment. A rear-window defogger was standard on all models along with a modified windshield wiper system. A compact disc player was offered at extra cost.

1990 Buick, Riviera coupe. (OCW)

RIVIERA - SERIES 4E - V-6 - After the successful "upsizing" of the "downsized" Riviera in 1989, Buick was content to refine what was clearly a Riviera tailored to the desires of its clients. An improved body structure resulted in significantly improved ride quality. A closer look at the latest Riviera resulted in the discovery of some small external alterations. The license plate bezel was now chrome and the taillamps had a chrome bead around their perimeters. Three new exterior colors were introduced: palomino brown, chestnut brown and gunmetal gray. The Riviera's vinyl roof could be selected in six additional colors for 1990: medium slate, dark brown, light brown, black, medium blue and slate. The 1990 Riviera's lengthy list of interior revisions consisted of a new instrument panel design with analog gauges, headlamps and light control switches, push-button climate control and high-gloss woodgrain trim plates. A console with armrest, cassette storage, coin holder, ashtray and PRNDL backlighting was now standard. Additional features included as standard equipment on the 1990 Riviera were door-mounted window/mirror controls with theater lighting, door armrest with courtesy light and wraparound warning light, a steering wheel with Supplemental Inflatable Restraint System (SIRS), a 200 series cassette and ETR AM/FM stereo radio and the "passkey" anti-theft system. A new door design with a pull-strap was

also introduced along with new seat trim design. The cruise control/windshield wiper controls were now located on a multi-function control lever. If a new CD player (two versions were offered: a unit with cassette and graphic equalizer or a unit with cassette and a Delco/Bose Gold series radio) was ordered, a covered storage compartment was also installed. Replacing the older 16-way optional seat was a 14-way power seat. Two new interior colors were also offered: brown and slate.

1990 Buick, Reatta convertible. (OCW)

REATTA - SERIES 4E - V-6 - The spring 1990 introduction of the convertible model was the major development concerning the Reatta. The convertible featured a manual-operated top with a glass backlight plus a standard defogger. The hard tonneau cover was power released with a power top pull-down. The convertible top was available in two fabrics: vinyl and Sta-fast cloth. Both Reatta models were delivered with the following new items: auxiliary transmission cooler, instrument panel design with dark finish trim plates, analog gauges, integral radio and push-button climate controls, door-mounted window/mirror controls with theater lighting, console with armrest, coin holder, cassette storage and ashtray, push-button headlamp switch, steering wheel with SIRS, multi-function lever with cruise control and wiper/washer controls and "pass key" anti-theft system. Improved rear speakers were adopted for 1990 along with the 2000 series AM/FM radio with cassette and graphic equalizer. A compact disc player was also available.

I.D. DATA: The 1990 Buick vehicle identification number (VIN) contained 17 characters. The first was the producing country: "1" - United States. The second character was "G" - General Motors. The third was "4" - Buick Division. The fourth character identified the car line: "A" - Century, "B" - LeSabre and Electra Estate wagon, "C" - Electra, "E" - Riviera and Reatta, "H" - LeSabre, "N" - Skylark, "W" - Regal. The fifth character designated the series: "B" - Regal Custom/incomplete wagon, "C" - Skylark Custom/Reatta, "D" - Skylark Limited/Regal Limited, "F" - Electra T-Type, "H" - Century Custom, "J" - Skylark Custom, "L" - Century Limited/Estate wagon, "M" - Skylark Limited, "P" - LeSabre/LeSabre Custom, "R" - LeSabre Limited/Estate wagon, "U" - Electra Ultra, "V" - Electra Estate Wagon, "W" - Electra Park Avenue, "Z" - Riviera. The sixth digit represented the body style code as follows: "1" - two-door coupe, "5" - four-door sedan, "8" - four-door station wagon, "9" - four-door station wagon (incomplete). The seventh character identified the restraint system: "1" - manual belts, "3" - manual belts w/driver's side airbag, "4" - automatic belts, "0" - incomplete vehicle. The eighth character represented the engine code: "1" - 2.0 liter L4-121, "U" - 2.5 liter Tech IV L4-151, "D" - 2.3 liter DOHC Quad L4-140, "N" - 3.3 liter 3300 V-6-204, "R" - 2.5 liter Tech IV-L4-151 (98 hp),

"W" - 2.8 liter V-6-173, "C" - 3.8 liter 3800 V-6-231, "Y" - 5.0 liter V-8-307. The ninth unit is a check digit that verifies the accuracy of the VIN. The next letter, "L," represents the 1990 model year. The eleventh entry identifies the assembly plant: "A" - Lakewood, GA, "B" - Lansing, MI, "G" -Framingham, MA, "H" - Flint, MI, "J" - Janesville, WI, "M" - Lansing, MI, "T" - Tarrytown, NY, "U" - Hamtramck, MI, "I" - Wentzville, MO, "1" - Oshawa, Ontario, Canada, "6" - Oklahoma City, OK. The characters from 12-17 are the production sequence number.

Skylark (Four/V-6)

Model No.	Body/Style No.	Body Type & Seating	Factory Price	Shipping Weight	Prod. Total
V27	NV1	2-dr. Cpe.-5P	10565	2558	4,248
V69	NV5	4-dr. Sed.-5P	10465	2625	46,705

Skylark Custom (Four/V-6)*

J27	NJ1	2-dr. Cpe.-5P	11460	2570	5,490
C69	NC5	4-dr. Sed.-5P	11460	2638	24,469

Skylark Gran Sport (Four/V-6)

M27	NM1	2-dr. Cpe.-5P	12935	2603	1,637

Skylark Luxury Edition (Four/V-6)

D69	ND5	4-dr. Sed.-5P	13855	2647	3,019

* Add $660 for 2.4 liter Quad 4 and $710 for 3.3 liter V-6 engines.

Century Custom (Four/V-6)

H37	AH1	2-dr. Cpe.-6P	13250/13960	2839/2950	1,944
H69	AH5	4-dr. Sed.-6P	13150/13860	2869/2980	88,309
H35	AH8	4-dr. Sta. Wag.-6P	14570/15280	3048/3159	4,383

Century Limited (Four/V-6)

L69	AL5	4-dr. Sed.-6P	14075/14785	2870/2981	35,248
L35	AL8	4-dr. Sta. Wag.-6P	15455/16165	2870/3164	2,837

Regal Custom (V-6)

B57	WB1	2-dr. Cpe.-6P	15200	3237	26,071

1990 Buick, Regal Limited sedan with optional wire wheel covers. (OCW)

Regal Limited (V-6)

D57	WD1	2-dr. Cpe.-6P	15860	3243	31,751*

* Includes 12,965 Gran Sports.

LeSabre (V-6)

P37	HP1	2-dr. Cpe.-6P	16145	3234	2,406

LeSabre Custom (V-6)

P69	HP5	4-dr. Sed.-6P	16050	3270	96,616

LeSabre Limited (V-6)

R37	HR1	2-dr. Cpe.-6P	17300	3281	1,855
R69	HP5	4-dr. Sed.-6P	17400	3312	62,504

Estate Wagon (V-8)

R35	BR8	4-dr. Sta. Wag.-6P	17940	4339	7,999

Electra Limited (V-6)

X69	CX5	4-dr. Sed.-6P	20225	3307	2,261

Electra T-Type (V-6)

Model No.	Body/Style No.	Body Type & Seating	Factory Price	Shipping Weight	Prod. Total
F69	CF5	4-dr. Sed.-6P	23025	3390	478

Electra Park Avenue (V-6)

W69	CW5	4-dr. Sed.-6P	21750	3390	44,072

Electra Park Avenue Ultra (V-6)

U69	CU5	4-dr. Sed.-6P	27825	3437	1,967

Riviera (V-6)

Z57	EZ1	2-dr. Cpe.-6P	23040	3464	22,526

Reatta (V-6)

C97	EC1	2-dr. Cpe.-2P	28335	3373	6,383
C67	EC3	2-dr. Conv.-2P	34995	3570	2,132

ENGINES: BASE FOUR (Skylark) Inline, overhead valve, four-cylinder. Cast iron block and head. Displacement; 151 cu. in. (2.5 liters). Bore & stroke: 4.00 x 3.00 in. Compression ratio: 9.0:1. Brake horsepower: 110 @ 5200 rpm. Torque: 135 lb.-ft. @ 3200 rpm. Five main bearings. Hydraulic valve lifters. Throttle-body fuel injection. BASE FOUR (Century) Inline, overhead valve, four-cylinder. Cast alloy iron block and head. Displacement: 151 cu. in. (2.5 liters). Bore & stroke: 4.00 x 3.00 in. Compression ratio: 9.0:1. Brake horsepower: 110 @ 5200 rpm. Torque: 135 lb.-ft. @ 3200 rpm. Five main bearings. Hydraulic valve lifters, Throttle-body electric fuel injection. BASE V-6 (Regal) 60-degree overhead valve V-6. Cast iron block and aluminum heads. Displacement: 3.1 liters. Bore & stroke: 3.60 x 3.31 in. Compression ratio: 8.8:1. Brake horsepower: 135 @ 4400 rpm. Torque: 180 lb.-ft. @ 3600 rpm. Hydraulic valve lifters. Multi-port fuel injection. BASE V-6 (LeSabre) 90-degree overhead valve V-6 with balance shaft. Cast iron alloy block and head. Displacement: 231 cu. in. (3.8 liters). Bore & stroke: 3.80 x 3.40 in. Compression ratio: 8.5:1. Brake horsepower: 165 @ 4800 rpm. Torque: 210 lb.-ft. @ 2000 rpm. Four main bearings. Hydraulic valve lifters. Sequential fuel injection. BASE V-8 (Estate wag) 90-degree overhead valve V-8. Cast iron block and head. Displacement: 307 cu. in. (5.0 liters). Bore & stroke: 3.8 x 3.39 in. Compression ratio: 8.0:1. Brake horsepower: 140 @ 3200 rpm. Torque: 255 lb.-ft. @ 2000 rpm. Five main bearings. Hydraulic valve lifters. Carb.: 4Bbl. BASE V-6 (Electra) 90-degree overhead valve V-6 with balance shaft. Cast iron alloy block and head. Displacement: 231 cu. in. (3.8 liters). Bore & stroke: 3.80 x 3.40 in. Compression ratio: 8.5:1. Brake horsepower: 165 @ 4800 rpm. Torque: 210 lb.-ft. @ 2000 rpm. Four main bearings. Hydraulic valve lifters. Sequential fuel injection. BASE V-6 (Riviera) 90-degree overhead valve V-6. Cast iron alloy block and head. Displacement: 231 cu. in. (3.8 liters). Bore & stroke: 3.80 x 3.40 in. Compression ratio: 8.5:1. Brake horsepower: 165 @ 4800 rpm. Torque: 210 lb.-ft. @ 2000 rpm. Four main bearings. Hydraulic valve lifters. Sequential fuel injection. BASE V-6 (Reatta) 90-degree overhead valve V-6. Cast iron alloy block and head. Displacement: 231 cu. in. (3.8 liters). Bore & stroke: 3.80 x 3.40 in. Compression ratio: 8.5:1. Brake horsepower: 165 @ 4800 rpm. Torque: 210 lb.-ft. @ 2000 rpm. Four main bearings. Hydraulic valve lifters. Sequential fuel injection. OPTIONAL (Skylark) Inline, DOHC, four-cylinder. Cast iron alloy block, cast aluminum head. Displacement: 138 cu. in. (2.3 liters). Bore & stroke: 3.62 x 3.346 in. Compression ratio: 9.5:1. Brake horsepower: 150 @ 5200 rpm. Torque: 160 lb.-ft. @ 4000 rpm. Hydraulic valve lifters. Multi-port fuel injection. OPTIONAL (Skylark) 90-degree V-6. Cast iron block and cylinder heads. Displacement: 204 cu. in. (3.3 liters). Bore & stroke: 3.73 x 3.16 in. Compression ratio: 9.0:1. Brake horsepower: 160 @ 5200 rpm. Torque: 185 lb.-ft. @ 2000 rpm. Hydraulic valve lifters. Multi-port fuel injection. OPTIONAL (Century, Century Estate Wagon) 60-degree V-6. Cast iron block and cylinder head. Displacement: 204 cu. in. (3.3 liters). Bore & stroke: 3.70 x 3.16 in. Compression ratio: 9.00:1. Brake horsepower: 160 @ 5200 rpm. Torque: 185 lb.-ft. @ 2000 rpm. Four main bearings. Hydraulic valve lifters. Multi-port fuel injection. OPTIONAL (Regal) 90-degree overhead valve V-6 with balance shaft. Cast iron alloy block and head. Displacement: 231 cu. in. (3.8 liters). Bore & stroke: 3.80 x 3.40 in. Compression ratio: 8.5:1. Brake horsepower: 170 @ 4800 rpm. Torque: 220 lb.-ft. @ 3200 rpm. Four main bearings. Hydraulic valve lifters. Sequential fuel injection.

CHASSIS DATA: Wheelbase: (Skylark) 103.4 in.; (Century) 104.8 in.; (Regal) 107.5 in.; (LeSabre) 110.8 in.; (Estate Wagon) 115.9 in.; (Electra) 110.8 in.; (Riviera) 108.0 in.; (Reatta) 98.5 in. Overall length: (Skylark) 180.1 in.; (Century) 189.1 in.; (Century Custom/Estate wag) 190.9 in.; (Regal) 192.2 in.; (LeSabre) 196.5 in.; (Estate Wagon) 220.5 in.; (Electra) 197.0 in.; (Riviera) 198.3 in.; (Reatta) 183.7 in. Height: (Skylark) 52.1 in.; (Century) cpe: 53.7 in.; sed and Century Custom/Estate wag: 54.2 in.; (Regal) 53.0 in.; (LeSabre cpe) 54.7 in.; (LeSabre sed) 55.4 in.: (Estate Wagon) 59.3 in.; (Electra) 54.3 in.; (Riviera) 53.6 in.; (Reatta) 51.2 in. Width: (Skylark) 66.6 in.; (Century) 69.4 in.; (Century Custom/Estate wag) 69.4 in.; (Regal) 72.5 in.; (LeSabre cpe/sed) 72.5 in.; (Estate Wagon) 79.3 in.; (Electra) 72.4 in.; (Riviera) 71.7 in.; (Reatta) 73.0 in. Front Tread: (Skylark) 55.6 in.; (Century) 58.7 in.; (Century Custom/Estate wag) 58.7 in.; (Regal) 59.3 in.; (LeSabre cpe/sed) 60.3 in.; (Estate Wagon) 62.2 in.; (Electra) 60.3 in.; (Riviera) 59.9 in.; (Reatta) 60.3 in. Rear Tread: (Skylark) 55.2 in.; (Century) 56.7 in.; (Century Custom/Estate wag) 56.7 in.; (Regal) 58.0 in.; (LeSabre cpe/sed) 59.8 in.; (Estate Wagon) 64.0 in.; (Electra) 59.8 in.; (Riviera) 59.9 in.; (Reatta) 60.3 in. Standard Tires: (Skylark) P185/80R13; (Century) P185/75R14; (Century Custom/Estate Wagon) P185/75R14; (Regal) P205/75R14; (LeSabre cpe/sed) P205/75R14; (Estate Wagon) P225/75R15; (Electra) P205/75R14 (blackwall on Limited, whitewall on Park Avenue); (Electra T-Type) P215/65R15; (Park Avenue Ultra) P205/70R15 whitewall; (Riviera) P205/75R15; (Reatta) P215/65R15.

TECHNICAL: Transmission: (Skylark, Century, Century Custom) Three-speed automatic; (Regal, LeSabre cpe/sed, Estate Wagon, Electra, Riviera, Reatta) Four-speed automatic with overdrive. Steering: (Skylark, Century, Century Custom/Estate wag, Regal, LeSabre cpe/sed, Electra, Riviera) Power rack and pinion; (Estate Wagon) Power recirculating ball; (Reatta) Fast ratio power steering. Front Suspension: (Skylark, Century, Century Custom/Estate wag, LeSabre cpe/sed, Electra, Electra T-Type, Riviera) MacPherson struts with coil springs, lower control arms and stabilizer bar; (Regal) MacPherson struts with lower control arms and unitized coil springs; (Estate Wagon) Coil springs, unequal length control arms, stabilizer bar; (Reatta) Independent four-wheel Gran Touring. Rear Suspension: (Skylark) Trailing crank bar, coil springs and stabilizer bar; (Century) beam twist axle with integral stabilizer bar, trailing arms, Panhard arm and coil springs; (LeSabre cpe/sed) MacPherson struts, coil springs, stabilizer bar; (Estate Wagon) Solid axle with four links, coil springs; (Electra, Electra T-Type) Independent MacPherson struts, inboard coil springs, stabilizer bar; (Riviera) Independent tri-link, transverse fiberglass leaf spring, stabilizer bar; (Reatta) Independent modular assembly with single transverse leaf springs. Brakes: (Skylark, Century, Century Custom/Estate wag, Regal, LeSabre cpe/sed, Estate Wagon, Electra, Electra T-Type) Power front disc, rear drum; (Riviera, Reatta) Power disc, front and rear. Body Construction: (Skylark) Unibody; (Century/Century wag) Integral body/frame; (Regal) Integral body/frame with bolted-on powertrain cradle; (LeSabre) Unitized body/frame integral with isolated engine cradle; (Estate Wagon) Welded body with full perimeter frame; (Electra) Unitized body/frame construction with isolated engine cradle; (Riviera) Unitized body with isolated front frame and rear sub-frame; (Reatta) Unitized body with isolated front and rear sub-frames. Fuel Tank: (Skylark) 13.6 gal.; (Century) 15.7 gal.; (Century Custom/Estate wag) 16.6 gal.; (Regal) 16.5 gal.; (LeSabre cpe/sed) 18.0 gal.; (Estate Wagon) 22.0 gal.; (Electra and Electra T-Type) 18.0 gal.; (Riviera) 18.2 gal.; (Reatta) 18.2 gal.

DRIVETRAIN OPTIONS: Engines: (Skylark) 2.3 liter Quad-4. MFI, $660; 3.3 liter V-6, MFI, $710; (Century, Century Cus-

tom/Estate wag) 3.3 liter V-6, MFI, $710. Transmission/Differential: (Century, Century Custom/Estate wag) Automatic transmission with overdrive, with 3.3 liter engine only, $200. Suspension, steering and brakes: (Skylark) Gran Touring Package (14 in. aluminum wheels, P215/60R14 Eagle GT+4 blackwall tires, Gran Touring suspension, leather-wrapped steering wheel): $603; engine block heater: $18; (Century) heavy-duty engine and transmission cooling: $70 without air conditioning, $40 with a/c; heavy-duty suspension (required with 3.3 liter engine): $27; Gran Touring Package, not available for station wagons (aluminum wheels, P15/60R Eagle GT tires, leather-wrapped steering wheel and Gran Touring suspension): $515; (Regal): Gran Touring Package consisting of Gran Touring suspension, 16 in. aluminum wheels, P215/60R16 tires and leather-wrapped steering wheel; anti-lock brake system: $925; (LeSabre cpe and sed) 2.97:1 axle (included in Y56 Gran Touring Package and WE2-T-Type: required with V-8 heavy-duty engine and transmission cooling): no additional charge: heavy-duty engine and transmission cooling (included in WE2 and Y56): $40; Gran Touring Package consisting of Gran Touring Suspension, 15 in. aluminum wheels, P215/65R15 blackwall tires, 2.97:1 axle ratio, heavy-duty cooling and leather-wrapped steering wheel; (Estate Wagon) trailer towing package consisting of 3.23:1 axle ratio, V-8-heavy-duty engine and transmission cooling, automatic level control: $215; limited slip differential: $100; (Electra) heavy-duty battery, required with electronic air conditioning: $26; heavy-duty engine and transmission cooling (standard with T-Type, included in Y56 Gran Touring Package): $40; 2.97:1 axle ratio (requires V-8, included in Y56 Gran Touring Package and T-Type): No additional charge; electronic anti-lock brake system; $925 (standard on T-Type and Ultra); Gran Touring suspension (standard on T-Type, not available for Ultra or with fully padded vinyl top), consists of Gran Touring suspension, 15 in. styled aluminum wheels, P215/65R15 Eagle GT blackwall tires, 2.97:1 axle ratio, heavy-duty cooling and leather-wrapped steering wheel: (Riviera) Gran Touring Package consisting of Gran Touring Suspension, 2.97:1 axle ratio, 15 in. aluminum wheels, leather-wrapped sport steering wheel and shift handle, fast ratio power steering and P215/65R15 steel-belted radial ply Eagle GT+4 tires: $104.

SKYLARK CONVENIENCE/APPEARANCE OPTIONS: Air conditioning, $695; tilt steering column, $125; P185/80R13 whitewall tires, $68; mirrors-remote control left, right manual, $53; electric rear window defogger, $150; protective wide body side molding, $80: wheel opening molding, $30; plus electronic cruise control with resume, $185; two-speed windshield wipers with resume feature, $55; front and rear carpet savers, $45; AM/FM ETR stereo radio with cassette tape, seek and scan, auto reverse with search and repeat and clock, $152; custom locking wheel covers, $215; four-way manual driver seat adjuster, $35; power windows, $220 cpe, $295 sed; electric door locks, $155 cpe, $295 sed; six-way power driver seat adjuster, $250; power antenna, $70; passenger side lighted visor vanity mirror, $38; electric trunk lock release, $50; front and rear courtesy lights, $14; chrome deck lid luggage rack (not available with S/E and exterior sport package), $115; lower body accent paint, $195; body side stripes, $45; Custom and Limited cloth bucket seats with full length operation console, $180; styled 13 in. aluminum wheels, $245; styled hubcaps and trim rings, $38, custom locking wire wheel covers, $215. Special packages: Gran Touring Package, $603, includes 14 in. aluminum wheels, P215/60R14 Eagle GT blackwall tires, Gran Touring suspension, leather-wrapped steering wheel. Exterior Sport Package, $374-Custom cpe; $318-Limited cpe, includes blackout moldings, front air dam, aero rocker moldings, wide body side moldings. Skylark S/E Package, $1134; available for Custom models only, includes bucket seats and console, dual mirrors with left remote, body side moldings, rocker moldings, wheel opening moldings, cassette tape radio, and Gran Touring Package. Skylark L/E Formal Appearance Luxury Edition, $1050-$1495, in-

cludes full formal vinyl roof, wire wheel covers, wide rocker molding, body side molding, wheel opening molding, dual mirrors with left remote, and lower accent paint. Various Popular, Premium, Luxury and Prestige Packages. Tires, all steel-belted radial ply: P205/70R13 blackwall, $124; P205/70R13 whitewall, $190.

CENTURY CONVENIENCE/APPEARANCE OPTIONS: Air conditioning, $795; tilt steering column, $150; electric rear window defogger, $150; electronic cruise control with resume, $185; two-speed windshield wipers with resume feature, $55; front carpet savers, $25; rear carpet savers, $20; AM/FM ETR stereo radio with cassette tape, seek and scan, auto reverse and clock, $122; custom locking wire wheel covers. $215; styled steel wheels, $115; aluminum wheels, $270; body stripes, $45; six-way power driver seat adjuster, $70; power windows, $220 cpe; $295 sed; electric door locks, $155 cpe; $295 sed; six-way power driver seat adjuster, $250: power antenna, $70; passenger side lighted visor vanity mirror, $50; electric trunk lock release, $50; door edge guards, $15 cpe; $25 sed; passenger manual seat back recliner, $45; driver manual seat back recliner, $45; dual electric remote control mirrors, $70; automatic power antenna, $70; (Custom only) 55/45 cloth seat with armrest, $183; Limited cloth 55/45 seat with storage armrest, $233-$416; (Century Limited only) front seat reading lights, $24; Premium rear speakers, $70; (Century Estate wag only) vinyl third seat, $215; air deflector, $37; vinyl appliqué woodgrain trim, $350; rear window windshield wiper, $125. Special packages: Gran Touring Package, includes aluminum wheels and P215/60R14 Eagle GT tires, leather-wrapped steering wheel and Gran Touring suspension, $515.

1990 Buick, Regal Gran Sport sedan with optional sunroof. (OCW)

REGAL CONVENIENCE/APPEARANCE OPTIONS: Electric rear window defogger, $150; electronic cruise control with resume, $185; two-speed windshield wipers with resume feature, $55; front carpet savers, $25; rear carpet savers, $20; AM/FM ETR stereo radio with cassette tape, seek and scan, auto reverse and clock, $122; graphic equalizer cassette tape with auto reverse, and search/repeat and AM stereo, $150-$272; compact disc player with ETR AM/FM radio with seek/scan and clock, $274; electric glass sunroof (includes dual reading lamps and rear courtesy lamps), $650-$680; custom locking wire wheel covers, $215; styled aluminum wheels, $270; styled steel wheels,

$115; 15 in. aluminum wheels with blackwall tires, $320; six-way power driver seat adjuster, $250; power windows with express down feature, $230; electric door locks, $155; six-way power driver seat adjuster, $250; automatic power antenna, $70; passenger side lighted visor vanity mirror, $50; electric trunk lock release, $50; door edge guards, $15; dual electric remote control mirrors, $91; automatic power antenna, $70; Concert Sound speakers, $85; redundant accessory controls-steering wheel mounted, $125; remote keyless entry (Limited and Gran Sport only), $125; electronic digital/graphic instrumentation, $299; luggage rack, $115; wide black with red striping body molding, $55-$70; lower accent paint, $205; body side stripes, $45; cloth 55/45 seat with storage armrest (Custom only), $183; cloth reclining buckets with console (Custom only), $185; leather/vinyl 55/45 with recliners, (Limited only), $450. Special packages: Four Seater Package, includes front and rear bucket seats with rear armrests and storage console with cassette storage, leather-wrapped steering wheel, rear headrests, $409. Gran Sport, includes Gran Touring Package, bucket seats and console, specific exterior appearance with blackout, fog lamps, aero rocker panels, wide body side molding and front spoiler, $1212.

LESABRE CONVENIENCE/APPEARANCE OPTIONS: Electric rear window defogger, $150; electronic cruise control with resume, $185; two-speed windshield wipers with low speed delay feature, $55; black protective bodyside molding, $60; front carpet savers, $25; rear carpet savers, $20; 55/45 split front seat with storage armrest, $183; rear bumper guards and bodyside molding extensions, $24; AM/FM ETR stereo radio with cassette tape, seek and scan, auto reverse and clock, $132; graphic equalizer cassette tape with auto reverse, and search/repeat and AM/FM stereo and Concert Sound speaker system, $367; Concert Sound speaker system, $85; locking wire wheel covers, $215; styled aluminum wheels, $270; styled steel wheels, $115; six-way power driver seat adjuster, $250; electric passenger seat back recliner, $70; deluxe trunk trim, $53; electronic touch climate control air conditioner, $165; power windows, cpe $220, sed $295; electric door locks, cpe $155, sed $205; six-way power driver seat adjuster, $250; six-way passenger seat adjuster, $250; front and rear courtesy and warning lights, $44; automatic power antenna, $70; passenger side lighted visor vanity mirror, $50; door edge guards, cpe $15, sed $25; dual electric remote control mirrors, $91; automatic power antenna, $70; concert sound speakers, $85; chrome luggage rack, $115; wide rocker panel molding package. $110; instrumentation-tachometer, temperature, oil and volt gauges, $110; body side stripes, $45; cloth 55/45 seat with storage armrest (Custom only), $183; leather/vinyl 55/45 with recliners (limited only), $450. Special Estate wag options-roof rack, $115; air deflector, $40; remote control electric tailgate lock, $60; tungsten halogen headlamps, $25; Twilight Sentinel headlamp control, $60; illuminated driver door lock and interior light control, $75; cornering lights, $60; front lights monitor, $37. Special packages: Gran Touring Package, includes Gran Touring suspension, 15 in. aluminum wheels, P215/65R15 Eagle GT+4 blackwall tires, 2.97:1 axle ratio, heavy-duty cooling, leather-wrapped steering wheel, $563. T-Type Package, includes Gran Touring package (with different wheels) plus specific interior and exterior trim, cruise, gauges, 55/45 front seats and operating console, AM/FM stereo radio with cassette and graphic equalizer, rear deck spoiler and front air dam, dual exhaust outlets, blackout trim, $1927.

ELECTRA CONVENIENCE/APPEARANCE OPTIONS: Electric rear window defogger, $150; P205/75R14 whitewall tires, $76; electronic cruise control with resume, $185; two-speed windshield wipers with low speed delay feature, $55; black protective bodyside molding, $60; front carpet savers, $25; rear carpet savers, $20; 55/45 split front seat with storage armrest, $183; rear bumper guards and bodyside molding extensions, $183; rear bumper guards and bodyside molding extensions, $24; AM/FM ETR stereo radio with cassette tape, seek and scan, auto reverse

and clock, $132; graphic equalizer cassette tape with auto reverse, and search/repeat and AM/FM stereo and Concert Sound speaker system, $367; Concert Sound speaker system, $85; locking wire wheel covers, $215; styled aluminum wheels, $270; styled steel wheels, $115; six-way power driver seat adjuster, $250; electric passenger seat back recliner, $70; deluxe trunk trim, $53; electronic touch climate control air conditioner, $165; power windows, cpe $220, sed $295; electric door locks, $205; six-way power driver seat adjuster, $250; six-way passenger seat adjuster, $250; front and rear courtesy and warning lights, $44; automatic power antenna, $70; passenger side lighted visor vanity mirror, $50; Twilight Sentinel headlamp control, $60; four note horn. $28; low windshield washer fluid indicator, $16; cornering lights, $60; front and rear light monitor, $77; low fuel indicator, $16; electric trunk pull-down, $80; automatic day/night mirror, $80; dual electric remote control mirrors with heated left, $35; two-position memory driver belt adjuster, $150; deluxe trunk trim with mat, $68; rear reading lamps, $50; quartz analog gauge cluster, $126; electronic instrumentation, $299; electric trunk release, $50; door edge guards, $25; dual electric remote control mirrors, $91; automatic power antenna, $70; remote keyless entry system, $175; Concert Sound speakers, $70; chrome luggage rack, $115; firemist paint, $210; Bose music system, $553-$905; body side stripes, $45; leather/vinyl 55/45 (Park Avenue), $450; (T-Type), $395; theft deterrent system, $159; full heavily padded top, $260-$895; electric sliding Astroroof (not available with padded roof), $1230; 14 in. styled aluminum wheels, $235-$270. Special Packages: Gran Touring Package, includes Gran Touring suspension, 15 in. styled aluminum wheels, P215/65R15 Eagle GT blackwall tires, 2.97:1 axle ratio, heavy-duty cooling, leather-wrapped steering wheel, $462-$563.

RIVIERA CONVENIENCE/APPEARANCE OPTIONS: Graphic equalizer cassette tape with auto reverse, and search/repeat and ETR AM/FM stereo and digital clock, $120; Delco Bose music system with cassette, ETR AM/FM stereo with Dolby, seek and scan, auto reverse with search/repeat, and clock, $583-$703; six-way power passenger seat with power recliner, $325; electric trunk pull-down, $250; remote keyless entry system with automatic power door locks, $265; twilight headlamp control, $60; theft deterrent system, $159; left and right remote mirrors with heated left, $35; automatic rearview mirror, $80; electronic compass, $75; firemist paint, $210; lower accent paint, $190; electric Astroroof sliding roof, $1230; heavily padded roof, $695; leather and suede bucket seats, $550; 16-way adjustable driver leather and suede bucket seats, $1230; styled aluminum wheels, $55; cellular telephone, $1975. Special packages: Gran Touring Package, includes Gran Touring suspension, 2.97:1 axle ratio, 15 in. aluminum wheels, leather-wrapped steering wheel and shift handle, fast ratio power steering and P215/65R15 blackwall Eagle GT+4 tires, $104. Riviera Appearance Package, includes platinum beige firemist lower accent paint, body side stripe and painted aluminum wheels, $205.

REATTA CONVENIENCE/APPEARANCE OPTIONS: Sliding electric steel sunroof, $895; 16-way adjustable driver side leather bucket seats, $680.

HISTORY: Buick's efforts to strengthen its competitive position were evident by two midyear developments. The Reatta convertible arrived at along with a Regal four-door sedan. The Reatta convertible was the first Buick soft top model since the 1982-1985 Riviera model. The Buick Skyhawk was no longer offered in 1990.

1991

Big news for 1991 was the return of the Roadmaster, a name out of the Buick lineup since 1958. Offered initially only as an Estate Wagon, a 1992 Roadmaster sedan, in both base and

Limited trim levels, was also released in the spring of 1991. The Park Avenue and Park Avenue Ultra were completely redesigned with the Electra version discontinued. Also, the electronically controlled four-speed automatic transmission debuted in mid-year 1990 when the new Park Avenue line was introduced was now also standard on Reatta and Riviera. A more powerful 3800 V-6, with tuned port injection, which also debuted with the revised Park Avenue line, was now standard on Reatta, Riviera and the Regal Gran Sport coupe and sedan.

1991 Buick, Skylark sedan. (OCW)

1991 Buick, Skylark Custom coupe with optional wire wheel covers. (OCW)

SKYLARK - SERIES 4N - FOUR/V-6 - The compact Skylark underwent technical improvements that included a new dual resonator induction system to reduce noise and vibration in the standard 2.5-liter Tech 4 engine. Idle speed on the optional 3300 V-6 was reduced to also make it smoother and quieter. The three-speed automatic transmission was the only unit available. Offered in coupe and sedan in base and Custom trim levels and in Luxury Edition sedan and Gran Sport coupe, the GS model was available with the anti-lock brake option. Power door locks were standard on the base models. Fourteen-inch wheels replaced the previously offered thirteen-inch units. Standard interior equipment included analog gauges, lighting delay feature and automatic front safety belt system. Outside, composite tungsten-halogen headlamps and tinted glass became standard. All Skylarks excluding the GS were equipped with the DynaRide tuned suspension system. The GS featured Gran Touring suspension, Eagle GT+4 blackwall tires, Shelby aluminum wheels, aero rocker panel molding and leather-wrapped steering wheel.

1991 Buick, Century Custom sedan with optional wire wheel covers. (OCW)

1991 Buick, Century Limited sedan. (OCW)

1991 Buick, Century Estate Wagon station wagon. (OCW)

CENTURY - SERIES 4A - FOUR/V-6 - The midsize Century received a new grille and front end panel and new front brake rotors to lead the design enhancements. Other "cosmetic" changes included new "crystalline" park and turn signal lenses and a revised taillamp design. Century Custom came in coupe, sedan and wagon body styles while Century Limited was available in sedan and wagon models. New standard features included driver's side covered visor vanity mirror and upgraded fabric for the Custom interior. New options included remote keyless entry, steering wheel radio controls, CD player and lighted visor vanity mirrors for both driver and passenger. The DynaRide suspension was revised for a smoother ride. The 2.5-liter Tech 4 engine, rated at 110 horsepower, coupled to a three-speed automatic transmission was standard while the 3300 V-6, with electronic multiport fuel injection, mated to a four-speed automatic overdrive transmission was optional.

1991 Buick, Regal Limited sedan. (OCW)

1991 Buick, Regal Limited coupe. (OCW)

1991 Buick, Regal Gran Sport coupe. (OCW)

1991 Buick, Regal Gran Sport sedan. (OCW)

REGAL - SERIES 4W - V-6 - The three 1991 Regal sedans, Custom, Limited, and Gran Sport, were introduced midyear 1990, so it was the counterpart trio of coupes that were "freshened" for the 1991 model year. The redesign of the coupe included a new grille (body color on the Gran Sport), new front fascia with "crystalline" park and turn signal lenses and like taillamp lenses on the Limited. Bumper trim and side moldings were also revised. The Gran Sport coupe and sedan received the tuned port injection 3800 V-6 as standard engine, which remained an option for all other Regals. Inside, Regal models were upgraded with standard 55/45 front seat design, with storage armrest in Custom models and new front bucket seats with center console standard in GS models. Richer woodgrain accents and revised door panel trim complete the Regal's interior revisions. The standard 3.1-liter V-6 (multiport fuel injected) was uprated from 135 horsepower and 180 pound-feet of torque to 140 and 185, respectively. The four-speed automatic overdrive transmission was the only unit available. Other standard features of the Regal included four-wheel power disc brakes, DynaRide suspension, composite tungsten-halogen headlamps and tilt steering column.

1991 Buick, LeSabre Limited sedan with optional wire wheel covers. (OCW)

LESABRE - SERIES 4H - V-6 - The LeSabre, Buick's best-selling car, received structural revisions that included lower rail reinforcements, new steering column supports and stiffer cowl bar and dash barrier. Offered in base coupe, Custom sedan and Limited coupe and sedan versions, the LeSabre featured a new brake/transmission interlock, improved anti-lock braking

system and a maxi-fuse system that packaged all under-hood fuses in one panel for easy replacement. The sequential-port fuel injected 3.8-liter V-6 and four-speed overdrive automatic transmission were standard. An optional Gran Touring suspension package included 15-inch aluminum wheels, Eagle GT+4 blackwall tires, 2.97:1 final-drive ratio, heavy-duty cooling, leather-wrapped steering wheel and automatic level control.

1991 Buick, Roadmaster Estate Wagon station wagon. (OCW)

ROADMASTER ESTATE WAGON - SERIES 4B - V-8 - After more than three decades of dormancy, Buick dusted off the Roadmaster name and applied it to the full-size, eight-passenger Estate station wagon. Powered by a 5.0-liter V-8 delivering 170 horsepower, the Estate Wagon measured 217.7 inches, overall (Buick's largest automobile), with a wheelbase of 115.9 inches. Standard equipment included anti-lock brakes, driver's side airbag, 5,000-pound towing capacity, two-way tailgate, rear-window wiper, heavy-duty suspension, 15-inch aluminum wheels and "Vista roof," a dark-tinted glass panel positioned midway in the roof to provide an open-air look. A trailering package included automatic rear load leveling, additional radiator and engine oil cooling and a 3.23:1 axle ratio. A limited slip differential was also available.

1991 Buick, Park Avenue Ultra sedan with Gran Touring package. (OCW)

PARK AVENUE - SERIES 4C - V-6 - Gone was the Electra moniker used previously, the series now named Park Avenue and consisting of a base sedan and Ultra sedan. Launched early in 1990 as '91 models, Buick public relations termed the sedans the "most sophisticated, most advanced" six-passenger cars the automaker ever offered. Park Avenues were powered by the improved tuned port injected 3800 V-6 and 4T60-E electronically controlled four-speed automatic transmission. New features included flush-mounted solar control glass, engine oil-

life monitor and oil-level warning light, driver's side airbag, brake/transmission interlock and, standard in the Ultra, "ComforTemp" dual automatic climate controls for driver and passenger. Towing capacity increased to 3,000 pounds (up from 2,000 on the previous year's model), and trunk volume rose 3.9 cubic feet. An optional Gran Touring suspension package included 3.06:1 final-drive ratio, specific 15-inch aluminum wheels, Eagle GT+4 blackwall tires and leather-wrapped steering wheel.

1991 Buick, Riviera coupe. (OCW)

1991 Buick, Riviera coupe with Gran Touring package. (OCW)

RIVIERA - SERIES 4E - V-6 - Offered as a coupe, only, the Riviera sported the improved tuned port injected 3800 V-6 and 4T60-E electronically controlled four-speed automatic transmission as new features. Styling changes included a new vertical grille. Other revisions included new steering gear for improved "on-center" feel and additional acoustical insulation for a quieter ride. The Riviera received a new 3.06:1 final drive ratio for quicker launch from 0 to 60 mph as well as revised engine mounts to reduce vibration. Standard features included anti-lock brakes, driver's side airbag, rear-window defogger, composite tungsten-halogen headlamps and a new cupholder in the console armrest. The Gran Touring suspension package was optional.

1991 Buick, Reatta coupe. (OCW)

REATTA - SERIES 4E - V-6 - Two-passenger coupe and convertible versions remained the lineup in the Reatta's final year. The improved tuned port injected 3800 V-6 mated to a 4T60-E electronically controlled four-speed automatic transmission powered the Reatta. Gran Touring suspension was standard equipment, but included a new 3.33:1 final-drive ratio. New standard features included Twilight Sentinel, which automatically raised and turned on Reatta's retractable headlamps at dusk. Other standard equipment included a theft deterrent system, anti-lock brakes, driver's side airbag, lockable storage bins behind front seats, leather-wrapped steering wheel, foglamps, power six-way adjustable leather bucket seats and remote keyless entry.

I.D. DATA: The 1991 Buick Vehicle Identification Number (VIN) contains 17 characters. The first is the producing country: "1"—United States. The second character is "G" for General Motors.

The third is "4" for Buick Division. The fourth and fifth characters identify the car line/series: "A/H"—Century Custom; "A/L"—Century Limited; "B/R"—Roadmaster Estate Wagon; "C/U"—Park Avenue Ultra; "C/W"—Park Avenue; "E/C"—Reatta; "E/Z"—Riviera; "H/P"—LeSabre Custom; "H/R"—LeSabre Limited; "N/C"—Skylark Custom (4-dr); "N/D"—Skylark Luxury; "N/J"—Skylark Custom (2-dr); "N/M"—Skylark GS; "N/V"—Skylark; "W/B"—Regal Custom and "W/D"—Regal Limited. The sixth digit represents body style: "1"—coupe/2-dr sedan; "2"—hatch/lift back (2-dr); "3"—convertible; "4"—2-dr station wagon; "5"—4-dr sedan; "6"—hatch/lift back (4-dr) and "8"—4-dr station wagon. The seventh character represents the restraint code: "1"—active (manual) belts; "3"—active (manual) belts w/driver's side airbag and "4"—passive (automatic) belts. The eighth digit is the engine code: "C"—LN3 3.8L V-6; "D"—LD2 2.3L L4; "E"—LO3 5.0L V-8; "L"—L27 3.8L V-6; "N"—LG7 3.3L V-6; "R"—LR8 2.5L L4; "T"—LH0 3.1L V-6 and "U"—L68 2.5L L4. The ninth character is a check digit that verifies the accuracy of the VIN. The tenth character identifies the model year ("M" = 1991). The eleventh digit identifies the assembly plant. Characters twelve through seventeen are the production sequence number.

Skylark (Four/V-6)

Model No.	Body/Style No.	Body Type & Seating	Factory Price	Shipping Weight	Prod. Total
V27	NV1	2-dr. Cpe.-5P	10825/11535	2593/N/A	Note 1
V69	NV5	4-dr. Sed.-5P	10725/11435	2654/N/A	Note 2

Skylark Custom (Four/V-6)

Model No.	Body/Style No.	Body Type & Seating	Factory Price	Shipping Weight	Prod. Total
J27	NJ1	2-dr. Cpe.-5P	12020/12730	2628/2693	Note 1
C69	NC5	4-dr. Sed.-5P	12020/12730	2692/2755	Note 2

Skylark Gran Sport (Four/V-6)

Model No.	Body/Style No.	Body Type & Seating	Factory Price	Shipping Weight	Prod. Total
M27	NM1	2-dr. Cpe.-5P	13665/14375	2659/2558	Note 1

Skylark Luxury Edition (Four/V-6)

Model No.	Body/Style No.	Body Type & Seating	Factory Price	Shipping Weight	Prod. Total
D69	ND5	4-dr. Sed.-5P	13865/14575	2716/2625	Note 2

Note 1: Skylark coupe production totaled 7,100 with no further breakout available.

Note 2: Skylark sedan production totaled 68,686 with no further breakout available.

Century Special (Four/V-6)

Model No.	Body/Style No.	Body Type & Seating	Factory Price	Shipping Weight	Prod. Total
G69	AG5	4-dr. Sed.-6P	13240/13950	N/A/N/A	Note 2

Century Custom (Four/V-6)

Model No.	Body/Style No.	Body Type & Seating	Factory Price	Shipping Weight	Prod. Total
H37	AH1	2-dr. Cpe.-6P	13785/14495	2832/2915	Note 1
H69	AH5	4-dr. Sed.-6P	13685/14395	2869/2952	Note 2
H35	AH8	4-dr. Sta. Wag.-6P	15310/16020	3071/3154	Note 3

Century Limited (Four/V-6)

Model No.	Body/Style No.	Body Type & Seating	Factory Price	Shipping Weight	Prod. Total
L69	AL5	4-dr. Sed.-6P	14795/15505	2870/2953	Note 2
L35	AL8	4-dr. Sta. Wag.-6P	16230/16940	3072/3155	Note 3

Note 1: Century coupe production totaled 1,600 with no further breakout available.

Note 2: Century sedan production totaled 102,435 with no further breakout available.

Note 3: Century station wagon production totaled 6,500 with no further breakout available.

Regal Custom (V-6)

Model No.	Body/Style No.	Body Type & Seating	Factory Price	Shipping Weight	Prod. Total
B57	WB1	2-dr. Cpe.-6P	15690	3247	Note 1
B19	WB5	4-dr. Sed.-6P	15910	3321	Note 2

Regal Limited (V-6)

Model No.	Body/Style No.	Body Type & Seating	Factory Price	Shipping Weight	Prod. Total
D57	WD1	2-dr. Cpe.-6P	16455	3251	Note 1
D19	WD5	4-dr. Sed.-6P	16735	3324	Note 2

Note 1: Regal coupe production totaled 36,681 with no further breakout available.

Note 2: Regal sedan production totaled 89,879 with no further breakout available.

LeSabre (V-6)

Model No.	Body/Style No.	Body Type & Seating	Factory Price	Shipping Weight	Prod. Total
P37	HP1	2-dr. Cpe.-6P	17180	3231	Note 1

LeSabre Custom (V-6)

Model No.	Body/Style No.	Body Type & Seating	Factory Price	Shipping Weight	Prod. Total
P69	HP5	4-dr. Sed.-6P	17080	3269	Note 2

LeSabre Limited (V-6)

Model No.	Body/Style No.	Body Type & Seating	Factory Price	Shipping Weight	Prod. Total
R37	HR1	2-dr. Cpe.-6P	18330	3264	Note 1
R69	HR5	4-dr. Sed.-6P	18430	3301	Note 2

Note 1: LeSabre coupe production totaled 1,181 with no further breakout available.

Note 2: LeSabre sedan production totaled 89,575 with no further breakout available.

Roadmaster Estate Wagon (V-8)

Model No.	Body/Style No.	Body Type & Seating	Factory Price	Shipping Weight	Prod. Total
R35	BR8	4-dr. Sta. Wag.-8P	21445	4415	6,729

Park Avenue (V-6)

Model No.	Body/Style No.	Body Type & Seating	Factory Price	Shipping Weight	Prod. Total
W69	CW5	4-dr. Sed.-6P	24385	3580	Note 1

Park Avenue Ultra (V-6)

Model No.	Body/Style No.	Body Type & Seating	Factory Price	Shipping Weight	Prod. Total
U69	CU5	4-dr. Sed.-6P	27420	3662	Note 1

Note 1: Park Avenue sedan production totaled 117,075 with no further breakout available.

Riviera (V-6)

Model No.	Body/Style No.	Body Type & Seating	Factory Price	Shipping Weight	Prod. Total
Z57	EZ1	2-dr. Cpe.-5P	24560	3496	13,168

Reatta (V-6)

Model No.	Body/Style No.	Body Type & Seating	Factory Price	Shipping Weight	Prod. Total
C97	EC1	2-dr. Cpe.-2P	29300	3392	1,214
C67	EC3	2-dr. Conv.-2P	35965	3593	305

1991 Buick, LeSabre Custom sedan. (OCW)

ENGINES: BASE FOUR (Skylark, Century) Inline, overhead valve, Tech IV four-cylinder. Cast iron block and head. Displacement: 151 cu. in. (2.5 liters). Bore & stroke: 4.10 in. x 3.00 in. Compression ratio: 8.3:1. Brake horsepower: 110 @ 5200 rpm. Torque: 135 lb.-ft. @ 3200 rpm. Throttle-body fuel injection. BASE V-6 (Regal) 60-degree overhead valve V-6. Cast iron block and aluminum heads. Displacement: 191 cu. in. (3.1 liters). Bore & stroke: 4.00 in. x 3.00 in. Compression ratio: 8.9:1. Brake horsepower: 140 @ 4400 rpm. Torque: 185 lb.-ft. @ 3200 rpm. Multiport fuel injection. BASE V-6 (LeSabre, Park Avenue, Riviera, Reatta); OPTIONAL V-6 (Regal) 90-degree overhead valve V-6 with balance shaft. Cast iron block and head. Displacement: 231 cu. in. (3.8 liters). Bore & stroke: 3.80 in. x 3.40 in. Compression ratio: 8.5:1. Brake horsepower: (LeSabre) 165 @ 4800 rpm; (Park Avenue, Riviera, Reatta) 170 @ 4800 rpm. Torque: (LeSabre) 210 lb.-ft. @ 2000 rpm; (Park Avenue, Riviera, Reatta) 220 lb.-ft. @ 3200 rpm. (LeSabre) Sequential fuel injection; (Park Avenue, Riviera, Reatta) Sequential Tuned Port fuel injection. BASE V-8 (Roadmaster Estate Wagon) 90-degree overhead valve V-8. Cast iron block and head. Displacement: 305 cu. in. (5.0 liters). Bore & stroke: 3.74 in. x 3.48 in. Compression ratio: 9.3:1. Brake horsepower: 170 @ 4200 rpm. Torque: 255 lb.-ft. @ 2400 rpm. Throttle-body fuel injection. OPTIONAL FOUR (Skylark) Inline, DOHC, overhead valve, Quad 4 four-cylinder. Cast iron block and aluminum head. Displacement: 138 cu. in. (2.3 liters). Bore & stroke: 3.62 in. x 3.92 in. Compression ratio: 9.5:1. Brake horsepower: 160 @ 6200 rpm. Torque: 155 lb.-ft. @ 5200 rpm. Multiport fuel injection. OPTIONAL V-6 (Skylark, Century) 90-degree V-6. Cast iron block and cylinder heads. Displacement: 204 cu. in. (3.3 liters). Bore & stroke: 3.70 in. x 3.16 in. Compression ratio:

9.0:1. Brake horsepower: 160 @ 5200 rpm. Torque: 185 lb.-ft. @ 2000 rpm. Multi-port fuel injection.

CHASSIS DATA: Wheelbase: (Skylark) 103.4 in.; (Century) 104.9 in.; (Regal) 107.5 in.; (LeSabre) 110.8 in.; (Roadmaster Estate Wagon) 115.9 in.; (Park Avenue) 110.8 in.; (Riviera) 108.0 in.; (Reatta) 98.5 in. Overall length: (Skylark) 180.0 in.; (Century) 189.1 in.; (Century Custom) 190.9 in.; (Regal) 194.6 in.; (LeSabre) 196.5 in.; (Roadmaster Estate Wagon) 217.7 in.; (Park Avenue) 205.2 in.; (Riviera) 198.3 in.; (Reatta) 183.7 in. Height: (Skylark) 52.1 in.; (Century coupe) 53.7 in.; (Century sedan and wagon) 54.2 in.; (Regal coupe) 53.0 in.; (Regal sedan) 54.5 in.; (LeSabre coupe) 53.8 in.; (LeSabre sedan) 54.6 in.; (Roadmaster Estate Wagon) 60.1 in.; (Park Avenue) 55.7 in.; (Riviera) 53.6 in.; (Reatta) 51.2 in. Width: (Skylark) 66.6 in.; (Century) 69.4 in.; (Regal coupe) 72.5 in.; (Regal sedan) 70.9 in.; (LeSabre) 72.4 in.; (Roadmaster Estate Wagon) 79.9 in.; (Riviera) 71.7 in.; (Reatta) 73.0 in. Front Tread: (Skylark) 55.6 in.; (Century) 58.7 in.; (Regal) 59.5 in.; (LeSabre): 60.3 in.; (Roadmaster Estate Wagon) 62.1 in.; (Park Avenue) 60.5 in.; (Riviera) 59.9 in.; (Reatta) 60.3 in. Rear Tread: (Skylark) 55.2 in.; (Century) 56.7 in.; (Regal) 58.0 in.; (LeSabre) 59.8 in.; (Roadmaster Estate Wagon) 64.1 in.; (Park Avenue) 60.2 in.; (Riviera) 59.9 in.; (Reatta) 60.3 in. Standard Tires: (Skylark) P185/75R14; (Century) P185/75R14; (Regal) P205/75R14; (LeSabre) P205/75R14; (Roadmaster Estate Wagon) P225/75R15; (Park Avenue) P205/70R15; (Riviera) P205/70R15; (Reatta) P215/60R16.

TECHNICAL: Transmission: (Skylark, Century) Three-speed automatic; (Regal, LeSabre, Roadmaster Estate Wagon) Four-speed automatic w/overdrive; (Park Avenue, Riviera, Reatta) Electronically controlled four-speed automatic w/overdrive. Steering: (Skylark, Century, LeSabre, Park Avenue, Riviera, Reatta) Rack and pinion; (Roadmaster Estate Wagon) Integral. Front Suspension: (Skylark, Century, Regal, LeSabre, Riviera) MacPherson struts w/coil springs, deflected disc shock absorbers, stabilizer bar; (Roadmaster Estate Wagon) Independent short/long arm w/coil springs, tube-gas charged shock absorbers; (Park Avenue) MacPherson struts w/coil springs, double acting hydraulic shock absorbers, stabilizer bar; (Reatta) Independent strut w/lower control arms, coil springs and ball joints, deflected disc shock absorbers, stabilizer bar. Rear Suspension: (Skylark) Trailing crank arm w/twist beam, deflected disc shock absorbers, stabilizer bar (N/A on base models); (Century) Trailing arm twist axle w/track bar, double acting shock absorbers, stabilizer bar; (Regal) Tri-link independent w/transverse leaf spring, deflected disc shock absorbers, stabilizer bar; (LeSabre) MacPherson struts w/variable rate coil springs, deflected disc shock absorbers, stabilizer bar; (Roadmaster Estate Wagon) Salisbury four link w/coil springs; (Park Avenue) MacPherson struts w/coil springs, electronic level control air shock absorbers, stabilizer bar; (Riviera) Independent strut "H" arm w/transverse leaf springs, electronic level control air shock absorbers, stabilizer bar; (Reatta) Independent modular assembly w/single transverse leaf springs, deflected disc shock absorbers, stabilizer bar. Brakes: (Skylark, Century, LeSabre, Roadmaster Estate Wagon) Power front disc, rear drum; (Regal, Riviera) Power four-wheel disc; (Park Avenue) Power front disc, rear drum w/anti-lock; (Reatta) Power four-wheel disc w/anti-lock. Body Construction: (Skylark, Regal) Unibody; (Century) Integral body/frame; (LeSabre, Park Avenue) Unibody w/isolated engine cradle; (Roadmaster Estate Wagon) Welded body with full perimeter frame; (Riviera, Reatta) Unibody w/isolated front frame and rear sub-frame. Fuel Tank: (Skylark) 13.6 gal.; (Century) 15.7 gal.; (Regal) 16.5 gal.; (LeSabre) 18.0 gal.; (Roadmaster Estate Wagon) 22.0 gal.; (Park Avenue) 18.0 gal.; (Riviera) 18.8 gal.; (Reatta) 18.8 gal.

DRIVETRAIN OPTIONS: Engines: (Skylark) 2.3 liter Quad-4, $660; (Skylark, Century) 3.3 liter V-6, $710; (Regal) 3800 3.8 liter V-6, $395. Transmission/Differential: (Century) Four-speed

automatic transmission with overdrive, with 3.3 liter engine only, $200. Y56 Gran Touring Suspension Package: (Skylark) $388-$590; (Regal) $254-$679; (LeSabre) $447-$763; (Park Avenue) $17-$189; (Riviera) $134. V92 Trailer Towing Package: (Roadmaster Estate Wagon) $325; (Park Avenue) $150. (Roadmaster Estate Wagon) Limited slip differential $100.

1991 Buick, Skylark Custom sedan with optional styled wheels. (OCW)

SKYLARK CONVENIENCE/APPEARANCE OPTIONS: (Skylark cpe/sed) Popular pkg. $881/$881; Premium pkg. $1,079/$1,079; Luxury pkg. $1,225/$1,315; Prestige pkg. $2,000/$2,195. (Custom cpe/sed) Popular pkg. $1,223/$1,223; Premium pkg. $1,513/$1,513; Luxury pkg. $1,890/$1,890; Prestige pkg. $2,375/$2,480; Elite pkg. $2,922/$3,027. (Luxury sed) Popular pkg. $1,060; Premium pkg. $1,570; Luxury pkg. $2,160; Prestige pkg. $2,657. (Gran Sport cpe) Popular pkg. $1,060; Premium pkg. $1,430; Luxury pkg. $2,270; Prestige pkg. $3,855. Air conditioning, $745. Anti-lock brakes $925. Carpet savers $45. Cruise control $225. Rear window defogger (base) $170. Pwr door locks (base, Custom) 2-dr. $210/4-dr. $250. Eng. block heater $18. Deck lid luggage rack (Custom, Luxury) $115. Dual Mirrors $53. Accent paint (Custom) $195. Radio w/cassette (base, Custom) $140. Bodyside stripes $45. P185/75R14 tires (base, Custom) $68. Cloth bucket seats (Custom, Luxury) $210. Locking wire whl covers (Custom) $202. Styled alum whls (Custom) $169-$371. Styled hubcap (base) $38. Pwr windows (base, Custom) 2-dr. $275/4-dr. $340. Delay wipers (base, Custom) $65.

CENTURY CONVENIENCE/APPEARANCE OPTIONS: (Special sed) Premium pkg. $613; Luxury pkg. $863; Prestige pkg. $1,113. (Custom cpe/sed/wag) Popular pkg. $425/$425/$605; Premium pkg. $1,293/$1,333/$1,763; Luxury pkg. $2,475/$2,040/$2,475; Prestige pkg. $2,487/$2,592/$2,967. (Limited sed/wag) Premium pkg. $1,250/$1,230; Luxury pkg. $1,921/$2,365; Prestige pkg. $2,589/$2,929. Rear window defogger (Special) $170. Keyless entry (N/A Special) $135. Deck lid luggage rack $115. Door edge moldings 2-dr. $15/4-dr. $25. Cassette player (Special, Custom) $140. Cassette player w/search (Special, Custom) $170. CD player (Custom) $274; (Limited) $244. Pwr seatback recliner (Custom) $110. Strg whl radio controls (N/A Special) $125. Bodyside stripes (Custom) $45. P185/75R14 tires (Special) $68. Cloth 55/45 seat w/armrest (Special) $133; (Custom) $183. Leather/vinyl 55/45 seat (Limited sed) $500. Remote trunk release (Limited) $60. Locking wire whl covers (Custom) $240. Styled whl covers (Special, Custom) $115. Rear window wiper (wag only) $125. Woodgrain appliqué (Custom wag) $280-$325; (Limited wag) $280.

REGAL CONVENIENCE/APPEARANCE OPTIONS: (Custom cpe/sed) Popular pkg. $356/$356; Premium pkg. $931/$971; Luxury pkg. $1,605/$1,710; Prestige pkg. $2,331/$2,436. (Limited cpe/sed) Popular pkg. $836/$876; Premium pkg. $1,251/$1,356; Luxury pkg. $1,743/$1,848; Prestige pkg. $2,301/$2,406. (Gran Sport cpe/sed) Premium pkg. $2,687/$2,487; Prestige pkg. $3,373/$3,143. Anti-lock brakes $925. Cruise control w/resume (Custom) $225. Pwr door locks (Custom cpe) $210; (Custom sed) $250. Analog instrumentation (Custom) $60. Keyless entry $135. Deck lid luggage rack $115. Wide molding (Custom cpe) $70. Door edge guards: cpe

$15/sed $25. Accent paint (cpe only) $205. Cassette player $140. Graphic equalizer $290. CD player $274-$414. Pwr antenna $85. Pwr sunroof $695. Bodyside stripes (cpe only) $45. P205/70R14 tires $76. P205/70R15 tires: blackwall $20/whitewall $96. Leather/vinyl 55/45 seats (Limited) $500. Leather/vinyl bucket seats w/console (Limited, Gran Sport) $500. B1B Four Seater pkg. $409-$505. Styled steel whls $115. Locking wire whl covers $240. 14-inch alum whls $295. 15-inch alum whls $325. Pwr windows: cpe $275/sed $340.

LESABRE CONVENIENCE/APPEARANCE OPTIONS: (LeSabre cpe) Popular pkg. $764; Premium pkg. $1,354; Luxury pkg. $2,029; Prestige pkg. $2,395. (Custom sed) Popular pkg. $764; Premium pkg. $1,394; Luxury pkg. $2,144; Prestige pkg. $2,510. (Limited cpe/sed) Popular pkg. $1,501/$1,606; Premium pkg. $1,959/$2,074; Luxury pkg. $2,438/$2,553; Prestige pkg. $2,978/$3,093. Anti-lock brakes $925. H.D. cooling syst $40. Pwr door locks: cpe $210/sed $250. Tach $110. Deck lid luggage rack $115. ETR AM/FM radio w/cass $140. Graphic equalizer $150-$375. Pwr antenna $85. Bodyside stripes $45. Auto level control susp $175. Vinyl top (sed only) $200. Cloth 55/45 seats w/armrest (base, Custom) $183. Leather/vinyl 55/45 seats (Limited) $500. Styled alum whls $295. Locking wire whl covers $240. Pwr windows: cpe $265/sed $330.

ROADMASTER ESTATE WAGON CONVENIENCE/APPEARANCE OPTIONS: Premium pkg. $865; Luxury pkg. $1,620; Prestige pkg. $2,257. Coachbuilder's Wagon incl. cornering lights, V92 trailer towing pkg., woodgrain delete and locking wire whl covers $811. Rear window defogger w/heated outside mirrors $170-$205. CD player w/graphic equalizer $429. ETR AM/FM radio w/cassette $185. Six-way pwr driver's seat (Coachbuilder) $305. Leather/vinyl 55/45 seats $540.

1991 Buick, Park Avenue sedan. (OCW)

PARK AVENUE CONVENIENCE/APPEARANCE OPTIONS: (Park Avenue) Popular pkg. $654; Premium pkg. $1,054; Luxury pkg. $1,801; Prestige pkg. $2,406. (Ultra) Popular pkg. $349; Premium pkg. $539; Luxury pkg. $1,228; Prestige pkg. $1,833. Firemist paint $250. Graphic equalizer $150-$220. Bose music syst $573-$793. CD player w/graphic equalizer $224-$444. Astroroof $1,273-$1,408. P205/70R15 tires $76. Vinyl top (base) $200. Leather/vinyl 55/45 seats w/armrest $500. Heated windshield $250.

RIVIERA CONVENIENCE/APPEARANCE OPTIONS: Luxury pkg. $520; Prestige pkg. $1,069. Firemist paint $250. Pearlescent white diamond paint $250. Lower accent paint $190. Bose music syst $1,399. CD player w/graphic equalizer $516. Astroroof $1,350. Vinyl top $695. Leather/suede bucket seats $600. 14-way adjustable leather/suede bucket driver's seat $945. 15-inch alum whls $85. Riviera Appearance pkg. $235.

1991 Buick, Reatta convertible. (OCW)

REATTA CONVENIENCE/APPEARANCE OPTIONS: CD player $396. Sunroof $895. 16-way adjustable leather bucket driver's seat $680. White leather bucket seats (conv only): w/16-way adjst driver's seat $780; w/o $100. White painted whls $100.

HISTORY: Buick passed Pontiac in cars sold in 1991 to achieve second rank of GM divisions behind top-seller Chevrolet. Overall, though, it was a poor year for GM with posted losses of $4.5 billion—the worst in the automaker's history. Buick's sales for the year totaled 544,325, which was 18.71 percent of GM sales and 6.66 percent of total U.S. car sales.

1992

1992 Buick, Roadmaster sedan. (OCW)

On the heels of the previous year's return of the Roadmaster in station wagon form, Buick added a Roadmaster sedan in two trim levels (base and Limited) for 1992 (launched early in 1991). The Skylark and LeSabre were both completely redesigned inside and out. A Gran Sport sedan was added to the Skylark lineup while Regal gained both a GS coupe and sedan. The two-seater Reatta, introduced in 1988, was discontinued after its 1991 model run was completed.

1992 Buick, Skylark coupe. (OCW)

1992 Buick, Skylark sedan. (OCW)

1992 Buick, Skylark Gran Sport sedan. (OCW)

SKYLARK - SERIES 4N - FOUR/V-6 - All-new for 1992 was the motto for Buick's compact Skylark. In addition to all-new styling, the Skylark lineup was juggled with the Custom and Luxury Edition trim levels offered previously discontinued. Base and Gran Sport were the two Skylarks available, each in coupe or sedan body style. Standard Skylark engine was now the newest member of General Motors' Quad 4 engine family, the 2.3-liter overhead cam four-cylinder with port fuel injection, which replaced the 2.5-liter four-cylinder engine. GS models used the 3300 V-6 rated at 160 horsepower, which was the option engine in base Skylarks. The three-speed automatic transaxle was used in all Skylarks. The new-design Skylark vertical-bar grille was inspired by the 1939 Buick. Overall, the Skylark's new body lines achieved a 0.319 coefficient of drag, compared to 0.374 of the previous Skylark design. New standard equipment included anti-lock brakes, power door locks, split folding rear seat, rear seat headrests and overhead console storage. The GS models also featured adjustable ride control, leather/cloth bucket seats, leather-wrapped steering wheel and cast aluminum wheels as standard items.

1992 Buick, Century Limited sedan. (OCW)

1992 Buick, Century Limited station wagon with optional woodgrain appliqué and roof rack. (OCW)

CENTURY - SERIES 4A - FOUR/V-6 - Century's lineup remained unchanged from the year previous. Again, the 2.5-liter Tech 4 engine and three-speed automatic transmission was standard while the 3300 V-6 and four-speed automatic overdrive transmission was optional. New standard features included power door locks with auto feature, 55/45 seats with storage armrests on Custom models and seatback recliners for all but the Special sedan. Four new exterior colors were also available: Sterling Silver Metallic, Midnight Blue Metallic, Chamois and Dark Jadestone Metallic.

1992 Buick, Regal Limited coupe. (OCW)

1992 Buick, Regal Limited sedan. (OCW)

1992 Buick, Regal Gran Sport coupe. (OCW)

1992 Buick, Regal Gran Sport sedan. (OCW)

REGAL - SERIES 4W - V-6 - The Regal lineup consisted of coupe and sedan models in three trim levels: Custom, Limited and Gran Sport. The 3.1-liter V-6 was again the standard powerplant for Custom and Limited models while the GS versions used the 3800 V-6 (optional in 3.1 V-6-powered Regals). All Regals used the four-speed automatic transmission. New standard items in Regal models included anti-lock brakes on Limited and GS (optional on Custom) models, revised seat design, power door locks, dual covered visor vanity mirrors and two-speed windshield wipers with delay. The Gran Touring package was standard on GS models and optional on Custom and Limited models.

1992 Buick, LeSabre Custom sedan. (OCW)

1992 Buick, LaSabre Limited sedan with Gran Touring package. (OCW)

LESABRE - SERIES 4H - V-6 - The full-size LeSabre was also all-new for 1992 and offered only as a sedan in Custom and Limited trim levels. Gone were the LeSabre coupes and base trim level available previously. Under the hood, LeSabre re-

ceived the new 3800 V-6 with tuned port injection, rated at 170 horsepower, and an electronically controlled four-speed automatic transmission. Among the new standard features were 15-inch wheels (replacing the 14-inch units used previously), power seat controls located in armrests, and trunk security on/off switch. The Limited sedan added anti-lock brakes, which was an option on the Custom sedan. ComforTemp dual automatic climate controls, engine oil-life monitor and traction control were also options for the Limited sedan. A Gran Touring package was available for both sedans and included 16-inch wheels, 3.06 final-drive ratio and leather-wrapped steering wheel.

1992 Buick, Roadmaster Limited sedan. (OCW)

ROADMASTER - SERIES 4B - V-8 - In addition to the station wagon that debuted the year before, Roadmaster's 1992 lineup included a sedan in base and Limited trim levels. The full-size, rear-wheel drive trio were each powered by the 5.7-liter V-8, rated at 180 horsepower, with electronic fuel injection. Standard equipment on the sedans included analog instrument panel with gauges including tachometer, anti-lock brakes, driver's side airbag, child security locks on rear doors, power windows, and dual visor vanity mirrors. The Limited sedan added a variable-effort steering system, remote keyless entry, specific 55/45 cloth seats (leather or suede were optional), automatic power antenna and six-way front headrests. A new standard item on the Estate Wagon was a stainless steel exhaust system. New options included a solar control windshield, passenger-side power seat recliner and automatic door locks. A trailering package was again offered for the Estate Wagon, as was a limited slip differential.

1992 Buick, Park Avenue Ultra sedan with supercharged V-6. (OCW)

1992 Buick, Park Avenue sedan. (OCW)

PARK AVENUE - SERIES 4C - V-6 - Park Avenue sedans were again offered in base and Ultra trim levels, but the big news for 1992 was the Ultra's new engine—the 205-horsepower supercharged 3800 V-6. The Park Avenue sedan again used the 170-horsepower 3800 V-6 with tuned port injection. Both engines were coupled to the electronically controlled four-speed automatic transmission. New standard features included variable-effort steering and power window lockout feature. New optional equipment included traction control, automatic day/night mirror system, and programmable automatic door locks. New interior colors were graphite and beige while outside, Dark Jadestone Metallic, Alabaster Beige, Champagne Beige Metallic, Dark Mahogany Metallic and Sapphire Blue Firemist were also new. The Gran Touring package was again optional, and included a 3.06 final drive ratio on Park Avenue (2.97 on Ultra), 16-inch aluminum wheels, and leather-wrapped steering wheel.

1992 Buick, Riviera coupe. (OCW)

RIVIERA - SERIES 4E - V-6 - The Riviera coupe received solar control glass as a new standard feature. Power was again supplied by the tuned port injected 3800 V-6 mated to an electronically controlled four-speed automatic transmission. The optional Gran Touring package included 15-inch aluminum wheels and fast-ratio power steering. New Riviera exterior colors for 1992 were: Dark Jadestone Metallic, Chamois, Light Driftwood Metallic and Pewter Gray Metallic.

I.D. DATA: The 1992 Buick Vehicle Identification Number (VIN) contains 17 characters. The first is the producing country: "1"—United States. The second character is "G" for General Motors. The third is "4" for Buick Division. The fourth and fifth characters identify the car line/series: "A/G"—Century; "A/H"—Century Custom & Wagon; "A/L"—Century Limited & Wagon; "B/N"—Roadmaster; "B/R"—Roadmaster Estate Wagon; "B/T"—Roadmaster Limited; "C/U"—Park Avenue Ultra; "C/W"—Park Avenue; "E/Z"—Riviera; "H/P"—LeSabre Custom; "H/R"—LeSabre Limited; "N/J"—Skylark; "N/M"—Skylark GS; "W/B"—Regal Custom; "W/D"—Regal Limited; and "W/F"—Regal GS. The sixth digit represents body style: "1"—coupe/2-dr sedan; "2"—hatch/lift back (2-dr); "3"—convertible; "4"—2-dr station wagon; "5"—4-dr sedan; "6"—hatch/lift back (4-dr) and "8"—4-dr station wagon. The seventh character represents the restraint code:

"1"—active (manual) belts; "2"—active (manual) belts w/dual airbags; "3"—active (manual) belts w/driver's side airbag; "4"—passive (automatic) belts; and "5"—passive (automatic) belts w/driver's side airbag. The eighth digit is the engine code: "E"—L03 5.0L V-8; "L"—L27 3.8L V-6; "N"—LG7 3.3L V-6; "R"—LR8 2.5L L4; "T"—LH0 3.1L V-6; "1"—L67 3.8L V-6; "3"—L40 2.3L L4; and "7"—L05 5.7L V-8. The ninth character is a check digit that verifies the accuracy of the VIN. The tenth character identifies the model year ("N" = 1992). The eleventh digit identifies the assembly plant. Characters twelve through seventeen are the production sequence number.

Skylark (Four/V-6)

Model No.	Body/Style No.	Body Type & Seating	Factory Price	Shipping Weight	Prod. Total
J37	NJ1	2-dr. Cpe.-5P	13560/14020	2782/N/A	Note 1
J69	NJ5	4-dr. Sed.-5P	13560/14020	2846/N/A	Note 2

1992 Buick, Skylark Gran Sport coupe. (OCW)

Skylark Gran Sport (V-6)

M37	NM1	2-dr. Cpe.-5P	15555	2901	Note 1
M69	NM5	4-dr. Sed.-5P	15555	2965	Note 2

Note 1: Skylark coupe production totaled 11,639 with no further breakout available.
Note 2: Skylark sedan production totaled 44,061 with no further breakout available.

Century Special (Four/V-6)

G69	AG5	4-dr. Sed.-6P	13975/14505	2914/N/A	Note 1

Century Custom (Four/V-6)

H37	AH1	2-dr. Cpe.-6P	14550/15260	2862/N/A	627
H69	AH5	4-dr. Sed.-6P	14755/15465	2914/N/A	Note 1
H35	AH8	4-dr. Sta. Wag.-6P	15660/16370	3054/N/A	Note 2

Century Limited (Four/V-6)

L69	AL5	4-dr. Sed.-6P	15695/1640	52870/N/A	Note 1
L35	AL8	4-dr. Sta. Wag.-6P	16395/17105	3072/N/A	Note 2

Note 1: Century sedan production totaled 111,819 with no further breakout available.
Note 2: Century station wagon production totaled 6,041 with no further breakout available.

Regal Custom (V-6)

B57	WB1	2-dr. Cpe.-6P	16610	3236	Note 1
B19	WB5	4-dr. Sed.-6P	16865	3320	Note 2

Regal Limited (V-6)

D57	WD1	2-dr. Cpe.-6P	17790	3237	Note 1
D19	WD5	4-dr. Sed.-6P	18110	3336	Note 2

Regal Gran Sport (V-6)

F57	WF1	2-dr. Cpe.-6P	18600	3351	Note 1
F19	WF5	4-dr. Sed.-6P	19300	3430	Note 2

Note 1: Regal coupe production totaled 21,153 with no further breakout available.
Note 2: Regal sedan production totaled 76,561 with no further breakout available.

LeSabre Custom (V-6)

Model No.	Body/Style No.	Body Type & Seating	Factory Price	Shipping Weight	Prod. Total
P69	HP5	4-dr. Sed.-6P	18695	3417	Note 1

LeSabre Limited (V-6)

R69	HR5	4-dr. Sed.-6P	20775	3457	Note 1

Note 1: LeSabre sedan production totaled 161,736 with no further breakout available.

Roadmaster (V-8)

N69	BN5	4-dr. Sed.-6P	21865	4073	Note 1

Roadmaster Limited (V-8)

T69	BT5	4-dr. Sed-6P	24195	4113	Note 1

Roadmaster Estate Wagon (V-8)

R35	BR8	4-dr. Sta. Wag.-8P	23040	4468	11,019

Note 1: Roadmaster sedan production totaled 59,712 with no further breakout available.

Park Avenue (V-6)

W69	CW5	4-dr. Sed.-6P	25285	3536	Note 1

Park Avenue Ultra (V-6)

U69	CU5	4-dr. Sed.-6P	28780	3640	Note 1

Note 1: Park Avenue sedan production totaled 63,390 with no further breakout available.

Riviera (V-6)

Z57	EZ1	2-dr. Cpe.-5P	25415	3497	12,324

ENGINES: BASE FOUR (Skylark) Inline, overhead valve, Quad 4 four-cylinder. Cast iron block and aluminum head. Displacement: 138 cu. in. (2.3 liters). Bore & stroke: 3.63 in. x 3.35 in. Compression ratio: 9.5:1. Brake horsepower: 120 @ 5200 rpm. Torque: 140 lb.-ft. @ 3200 rpm. Electronic fuel injection. BASE FOUR (Century) Inline, overhead valve, Tech IV four-cylinder. Cast iron block and head. Displacement: 151 cu. in. (2.5 liters). Bore & stroke: 4.00 in. x 3.00 in. Compression ratio: 8.3:1. Brake horsepower: 110 @ 5200 rpm. Torque: 135 lb.-ft. @ 3200 rpm. Electronic fuel injection. BASE V-6 (Regal) 60-degree overhead valve V-6. Cast iron block and aluminum heads. Displacement: 191 cu. in. (3.1 liters). Bore & stroke: 3.50 in. x 3.31 in. Compression ratio: 8.8:1. Brake horsepower: 140 @ 4400 rpm. Torque: 185 lb.-ft. @ 3200 rpm. Multiport fuel injection. BASE V-6 (Skylark GS); OPTIONAL V-6 (Skylark, Century) 90-degree overhead valve V-6. Cast iron block and heads. Displacement: 204 cu. in. (3.3 liters). Bore & stroke: 3.70 in. x 3.16 in. Compression ratio: 9.0:1. Brake horsepower: 160 @ 5200 rpm. Torque: 185 lb.-ft. @ 2000 rpm. Multiport fuel injection. BASE V-6 (Regal Gran Sport, LeSabre, Park Avenue, Riviera); OPTIONAL V-6 (Regal) 90-degree overhead valve V-6 with balance shaft. Cast iron block and head. Displacement: 231 cu. in. (3.8 liters). Bore & stroke: 3.80 in. x 3.40 in. Compression ratio: 8.5:1. Brake horsepower: 170 @ 4800 rpm. Torque: 220 lb.-ft. @ 3200 rpm. Sequential Tuned Port fuel injection. BASE V-6 (Park Avenue Ultra) supercharged 90-degree overhead valve V-6 with balance shaft. Cast iron block and head. Displacement: 231 cu. in. (3.8 liters). Bore & stroke: 3.80 in. x 3.40 in. Compression ratio: 8.5:1. Brake horsepower: 205 @ 4400 rpm. Torque: 260 lb.-ft. @ 2800 rpm. Sequential Tuned Port fuel injection. BASE V-8 (Roadmaster) 90-degree overhead valve V-8. Cast iron block and head. Displacement: 350 cu. in. (5.7 liters). Bore & stroke: 4.00 in. x 3.48 in. Compression ratio: 9.8:1. Brake horsepower: 180 @ 4000 rpm. Torque: 300 lb.-ft. @ 2400 rpm. Throttle-body fuel injection.

CHASSIS DATA: Wheelbase: (Skylark) 103.4 in.; (Century) 104.9 in.; (Regal) 107.5 in.; (LeSabre) 110.8 in.; (Roadmaster) 115.9 in.; (Park Avenue) 110.7 in.; (Riviera) 108.0 in. Overall length: (Skylark) 189.2 in.; (Century) 189.1 in.; (Century wagon) 190.9 in.; (Regal coupe) 193.6 in.; (Regal sedan) 193.9 in.; (LeSabre) 200.0 in.; (Roadmaster sedan) 215.8 in.; (Roadmaster Estate Wagon) 217.7 in.; (Park Avenue) 205.3 in.; (Riviera) 198.3 in. Height: (Skylark) 52.2 in.; (Century coupe) 53.7 in.; (Century sedan and wagon) 54.2 in.; (Regal coupe) 53.0 in.; (Regal sedan) 54.5 in.; (LeSabre sedan) 55.7 in.; (Roadmaster) 55.9 in.; (Roadmaster Estate Wagon) 60.3 in.; (Park Avenue)

55.1 in.: (Riviera) 52.9 in. Width: (Skylark) 67.5 in.; (Century) 69.4 in.; (Regal) 72.5 in.; (LeSabre) 74.9 in.; (Roadmaster) 78.1 in.; (Roadmaster Estate Wagon) 79.9 in.; (Park Avenue) 73.6 in.; (Riviera) 73.1 in. Front Tread: (Skylark) 55.6 in.; (Century) 58.7 in.; (Regal) 59.5 in.; (LeSabre): 60.4 in.; (Roadmaster) 61.7 in.; (Roadmaster Estate Wagon) 62.1 in.; (Park Avenue) 61.5 in.; (Riviera) 59.9 in. Rear Tread: (Skylark) 55.2 in.; (Century) 56.7 in.; (Regal) 58.0 in.; (LeSabre) 60.2 in.; (Roadmaster) 60.7 in.; (Roadmaster Estate Wagon) 64.1 in.; (Park Avenue) 60.3 in.; (Riviera) 59.9 in. Standard Tires: (Skylark) P185/75R14; (Skylark GS) P205/55R16; (Century) P185/75R14; (Regal) P205/70R14; (Regal GS) P225/60R16; (LeSabre) P205/70R15; (Roadmaster) P235/70R15; (Roadmaster Estate Wagon) P225/75R15; (Park Avenue) P205/70R15; (Riviera) P205/70R15.

TECHNICAL: Transmission: (Skylark, Century) Three-speed automatic; (Regal, Roadmaster) Four-speed automatic w/overdrive; (LeSabre, Park Avenue, Riviera) Electronically controlled four-speed automatic w/overdrive. Steering: (Skylark, Century, LeSabre, Park Avenue, Riviera) Rack and pinion; (Roadmaster) Integral. Front Suspension: (Skylark) MacPherson struts w/coil springs, hydraulic shock absorbers, stabilizer bar; (Century, Regal, LeSabre, Riviera) MacPherson struts w/coil springs, deflected disc shock absorbers, stabilizer bar; (Roadmaster) Independent short/long arm w/coil springs, tube-gas charged shock absorbers, stabilizer bar; (Park Avenue) MacPherson struts w/coil springs, double acting hydraulic shock absorbers, stabilizer bar. Rear Suspension: (Skylark) Trailing crank arm w/twist beam, double acting hydraulic shock absorbers; (Century) Trailing arm twist axle w/track bar, double acting shock absorbers, stabilizer bar; (Regal) Tri-link independent w/transverse leaf spring, deflected disc shock absorbers, stabilizer bar; (LeSabre) Chapman struts w/variable rate coil springs, deflected disc shock absorbers, stabilizer bar; (Roadmaster) Salisbury four link w/coil springs, tube gas-charged shock absorbers; (Park Avenue) Chapman struts w/coil springs, electronic level control w/air shock absorbers; (Riviera) Independent strut "H" arm w/transverse leaf springs, electronic level control w/air shock absorbers. Brakes: (Skylark, Park Avenue) Power front disc, rear drum w/anti-lock; (Century, LeSabre, Roadmaster) Power front disc, rear drum; (Regal, Riviera) Power four-wheel disc. Body Construction: (Regal) Unibody; (Skylark, Century) Integral body/frame; (LeSabre, Park Avenue) Unibody w/isolated engine cradle; (Roadmaster) Welded body with full perimeter frame; (Riviera) Unibody w/isolated front frame and rear sub-frame. Fuel Tank: (Skylark) 15.2 gal.; (Century) 15.7 gal.; (Regal) 16.5 gal.; (LeSabre) 18.0 gal.; (Roadmaster) 23.0 gal.; (Roadmaster Estate Wagon) 22.0 gal.; (Park Avenue) 18.0 gal.; (Riviera) 18.8 gal.

DRIVETRAIN OPTIONS: Engines: 3.3 liter V-6, (Skylark) $460; (Century) $710. (Regal) 3800 3.8 liter V-6, $395. Transmission/Differential: (Century) Four-speed automatic transmission with overdrive, with 3.3 liter engine only, $200. FX3 Adjustable Ride Control Suspension (Skylark) $380. G67 Auto Level Control Suspension (Roadmaster Estate Wagon) $175. Y56 Gran Touring Suspension Package: (Regal) $254-$755; (LeSabre) $447-$763; (Park Avenue) $74-$300; (Riviera) $134. NW9 Traction Control System (LeSabre Limited) $175. V92 Trailer Towing Package: (LeSabre) $150-$325; (Roadmaster) $117-$325; (Park Avenue) $123-$150. (Roadmaster) Limited slip differential $100.

SKYLARK CONVENIENCE/APPEARANCE OPTIONS: (Skylark cpe/sed) Popular pkg. $1,145/$1,145; Premium pkg. $1,480/$1,480; Luxury pkg. $2,000/$2,115; Prestige pkg. $2,588/$2,703. (Gran Sport cpe/sed) Popular pkg. $1,145/$1,145; Premium pkg. $1,435/$1,435; Luxury pkg. $2,055/$2,120; Prestige pkg. $2,623/$2,688. Eng. block heater $18. Radio w/CD player $414-$624. Remote Keyless Entry $135. Two-tone paint (base only) $195. Lower accent paint (GS only) $195. P185/75R14 tires (base) $68. P195/65R15 tires (base) $131. Cloth bucket seats $160-$210. Styled hubcaps (base) $28.

CENTURY CONVENIENCE/APPEARANCE OPTIONS: (Special sed) Premium pkg. $668; Luxury pkg. $978; Prestige pkg. $1,332. (Custom cpe/sed/wag) Popular pkg. $425/$425/$480; Premium pkg. $1,030/$1,030/$790; Luxury pkg. $1,577/$1,642/$1,213; Prestige pkg. $2,237/$2,302/$1,648. (Limited sed/wag) Premium pkg. $1,030/$1,250; Luxury pkg. $1,699/$2,074; Prestige pkg. $2,364/$2,704. Rear window defogger (Special & Custom wag) $170. Keyless entry (N/A Special) $135. Deck lid luggage rack $115. Door edge moldings 2-dr. $15/4-dr. $25. ETR AM/FM radio w/Cassette player $140. ETR AM/FM radio w/Cassette player w/search $170-$274. Pwr antenna (Special & Custom wag) $75. Strg whl radio controls (Custom) $125. Bodyside stripes (Custom) $45. P185/75R14 tires (Special) $68. Empress Cloth 55/45 seat w/armrest (Custom) $368. Leather/vinyl 55/45 seat (Limited sed) $500. Remote trunk release $60. Locking wire whl covers (Custom) $240. Styled steel whls (Special, Custom) $115. Alum whl covers $55. Alum whls ($295). Rear window wiper (wag only) $125. Woodgrain appliqué (Custom wag) $305; (Limited wag) $350.

REGAL CONVENIENCE/APPEARANCE OPTIONS: (Custom cpe/sed) Popular pkg. $475/$475; Premium pkg. $935/$1,000; Luxury pkg. $1,503/$1,568; Prestige pkg. $2,070/$2,135. (Limited cpe/sed) Popular pkg. $520/$520; Premium pkg. $1,020/$1,085; Luxury pkg. $1,573/$1,628; Prestige pkg. $2,195/$2,330. (Gran Sport cpe/sed) Premium pkg. $1,228/$1,293; Prestige pkg. $1,875/$1,940. Anti-lock brakes (Custom) $450. Deck lid luggage rack $115. Wide molding (Custom cpe) $70. Door edge guards: (N/A GS) cpe $15/sed $25. Accent paint (cpe only, N/A GS) $205. Analog instrumentation w/tach (Custom) $60. Frt/Rear interior reading lights (Custom) $30; (GS sed) $70. Steering whl mounted radio controls $29-$125. Dual six-way pwr seat $305-$575. ETR AM/FM radio w/Cassette player $150-$290. ETR AM/FM radio w/CD player $124-$414. Bodyside stripes (cpe only, N/A GS) $45. Pwr sunroof $695. P205/70R14 tires $76. P205/70R15 tires: $76-$96. Leather/vinyl bucket seats w/console $500. B1B Four Seater pkg. $240-$835. Styled steel whls (Custom) $115. Locking wire whl covers $240. 14-inch alum whls (N/A GS) $295.

1992 Buick, LeSabre Limited sedan. (OCW)

LESABRE CONVENIENCE/APPEARANCE OPTIONS: (Custom sed) Premium pkg. $801; Luxury pkg. $1,271; Prestige pkg. $2,254. (Limited sed) Premium pkg. $1,201; Luxury pkg. $1,706; Prestige pkg. $2,611. Analog instrumentation w/tach (Limited) $138. Pwr six-way driver's seat (Custom) $305. ETR AM/FM radio w/cass (Custom) $140. ETR AM/FM radio w/Graphic equalizer (Custom) $220-$360. Pwr antenna $85. Bodyside stripes $45. Vinyl top $200. Leather/vinyl 55/45 seats (Limited) $500. 15-inch styled alum whls $85-$325. Locking wire whl covers $240. Heated windshield $250.

1992 Buick, Roadmaster Estate Wagon station wagon. (OCW)

ROADMASTER CONVENIENCE/APPEARANCE OPTIONS:
(Roadmaster) Luxury pkg. $727; Prestige pkg. $1,685. (Limited) Prestige pkg. $406. (Estate Wagon) Premium pkg. $565; Luxury pkg. $1,320; Prestige pkg. $2,117. Pwr antenna (N/A Limited) $85. H.D. cooling (Estate Wagon) $40. Rear window defogger w/heated outside mirrors $170-$205. ETR AM/FM radio w/CD player $394-$569. ETR AM/FM radio w/cassette $150-$325. Leather/vinyl seats (Roadmaster, Estate Wagon) $540-$760. Leather/vinyl seats (Limited) $710-$760. Vinyl landau roof (N/A wag) $695. Vista cover (N/A sed) $85. P235/70R15 tires (Roadmaster) $150. Full-size spare (N/A wag) $65. Locking wire whl covers (N/A wag) $240. 15-inch alum whls (stnd on wag) $325. Solar glass windshield (Limited) $50.

PARK AVENUE CONVENIENCE/APPEARANCE OPTIONS:
(Park Avenue) Popular pkg. $684; Premium pkg. $1,084; Luxury pkg. $1,911; Prestige pkg. $2,572. (Ultra) Popular pkg. $270; Premium pkg. $460; Luxury pkg. $1,229; Prestige pkg. $1,834. Firemist paint $250. ETR AM/FM radio w/Cassette $150-$220. Bose music syst $573-$793. CD player w/graphic equalizer $264-$484. Astroroof $1,273-$1,408. P205/70R15 tires (Park Avenue) $76. P215/70R15 (Ultra) $80. Self-sealing tires $150. Leather/vinyl 55/45 seats w/armrest (Park Avenue) $500. Heated windshield $250.

RIVIERA CONVENIENCE/APPEARANCE OPTIONS: Luxury pkg. $520; Prestige pkg. $1,069. Firemist paint $250. Riviera Appearance pkg. $235. Pearlescent white diamond paint $250. Lower accent paint $190. Bose music syst $1,399. ETR AM/FM radio w/cassette $516. Astroroof $1,350. Vinyl top $695. Leather/vinyl bucket seats $600. White leather bucket seats $700. 14-way adjustable leather/vinyl bucket driver's seat $945. 14-way white leather adjustable leather/vinyl bucket driver's seat $1,045. 15-inch alum whls $85. Painted alum whls $185.

HISTORY: It was a dismal sales year for Buick. Sales of Park Avenue alone plunged over 28 percent from the 1991 level. Offsetting this somewhat, was the 23 increase in sales (compared to the year previous) of the new LeSabre. The Riviera ended production in December 1992, with a replacement model not available until the spring of 1994 as a 1995 model.

1993

In its 90th anniversary year, aside from the realignment of the Skylark series, it was a year of little change for Buick. The base Skylark was discontinued and Custom and Limited trim levels were added. Century dropped its Limited station wagon, but added a wagon to its Special lineup. The 1993 Riviera had a short production run through December 1992 and the car was then put on hiatus until the 1995 version was issued in early 1994.

1993 Buick, Skylark Custom sedan. (OCW)

1993 Buick, Skylark Limited coupe. (OCW)

1993 Buick, Skylark Limited sedan. (OCW)

SKYLARK - SERIES 4N - FOUR/V-6 - The Skylark lineup was revised in a big way. Base models were discontinued and joining the Gran Sport were Custom and Limited trim levels, each offering a coupe and sedan. Custom models were identified by specific side molding and an analog gauge cluster. Standard engine in Custom and Limited Skylarks was the 2.3-liter Quad 4 mated to a three-speed automatic transmission. The GS models again were powered by the 3300 V-6 and three-speed automatic. New standard features on Custom and Limited models included a two-function battery rundown protection system, fixed rear seatbacks, 55/45 split bench front seats and 14-inch deluxe wheel covers. Gran Sport models received as standard the Gran Touring suspension and optional ride control system. Also optional on Limited and Gran Sports is lower accent paint treatment.

1993 Buick, Century Special station wagon with optional roof rack. (OCW)

1993 Buick, Century Limited sedan with optional wire wheel covers. (OCW)

CENTURY - SERIES 4A - FOUR/V-6 - The 2.5-liter Tech 4 that was formerly the base engine for the midsize Century was discontinued. Power was now supplied by a 2.2-liter four-cylinder engine, rated at 110 horsepower, with multi-port fuel injection. Returning as the optional powerplant was the 3300 V-6. The three-speed automatic transmission was standard with both engines while the V-6 was made available with the four-speed automatic. The Century lineup was shuffled with the previously offered Limited station wagon dropped and a wagon added to the Special lineup, joining the sedan. New standard features included driver's side airbag on Custom and Limited (optional on Special), variable-rate rear springs and body color rub strips and side moldings. Fuel tank capacity on all Centurys was increased to 16.4 gallons. Specific standard equipment to Custom and Limited models included 14-inch styled wheel covers, tilt steering column and two-speed wipers with delay. New optional items included an inside rearview mirror with map lights and P195/75R14 all-season radial tires.

1993 Buick, Regal Gran Sport coupe. (OCW)

1993 Buick, Regal Limited coupe. (OCW)

1993 Buick, Regal Limited sedan. (OCW)

1993 Buick, Regal Gran Sport sedan. (OCW)

REGAL - SERIES 4W - V-6 - The Regal lineup from the year previous was continued unchanged. Sedans sported a more "sculptured" frontal appearance with a redesigned grille and headlamps. The standard 3.1-liter V-6 for the Custom and Limited models and improved 3800 V-6 for Gran Sport models were newly mated to the 4T60-E electronically controlled four-speed automatic transmission. All Regals were equipped with the next-generation front seating, which was orthopedically contoured to provide comfort and support for almost any driver. A new four-way manual seat adjuster was standard on Limited and Gran Sport models. Other standard equipment included analog gauges, 15-inch wheels (replacing the previously offered 14-inch units). The GS's improved 3.8-liter V-6 received a new intake manifold, a higher compression ratio for improved torque and roller rocker arm pivots for reduced friction. This engine was optional for Custom and Limited Regals.

1993 Buick, LeSabre Custom sedan. (OCW)

1993 Buick, LeSabre Limited sedan. (OCW)

LESABRE - SERIES 4H - V-6 - The LeSabre retained its two sedan (Custom and Limited) lineup, with anti-lock brakes now standard equipment on both. Power door locks were also a new standard item as was variable-effort steering on Limited sedans. Optional equipment included an analog gauge cluster with tach on the Limited, 3,000-pound trailer towing package, remote keyless entry on Limited and new wire wheel covers. LeSabre sedans achieved a 0.32 coefficient of drag. The standard 3800 V-6 was "tweaked" and received five more pound-feet of torque (up from 220 to 225). The electronically controlled four-speed automatic transmission with overdrive was again used in both LeSabre sedans. A specially badged 90th Anniversary Edition LeSabre was also offered.

1993 Buick, Roadmaster Limited sedan. (OCW)

1993 Buick, Roadmaster Estate Wagon station wagon. (OCW)

ROADMASTER - SERIES 4B - V-8 - Technical enhancements were the rule for Roadmaster offerings in 1993. The two sedan, one station wagon lineup remained unchanged from the year previous, as did the powertrain. Again, the 5.7-liter V-8 and four-speed automatic transmission with overdrive supplied the power. New features included a locking system for power windows (controlled by driver), improved acoustical package, and, on the Estate Wagon, the addition of a Solar-Ray windshield to protect against sun rays. The Estate Wagon continued with its Vista Roof, a dark-tinted panel positioned midway in the roof to provide an open-air look.

1993 Buick, Park Avenue sedan. (OCW)

1993 Buick, Park Avenue Ultra sedan. (OCW)

PARK AVENUE - SERIES 4C - V-6 - Minor refinements were carried out on the Park Avenue and upscale Park Avenue Ultra for 1993. Both sedans received a redesigned grille as well as revised taillamps. Also new were the four-spoke steering wheel (introduced mid-year) and redesigned lighted visor vanity mirror. New options included an automatic ride control system and, on the Park Avenue, new 15-inch wire wheel covers. The Ultra again was powered by the supercharged 3800 V-6 while the Park Avenue's naturally aspirated, tuned port injected V-6 received an increase in torque—from 220 to 225 pound-feet. Both engines were coupled to the 4T60-E electronically controlled four-speed automatic transmission.

1993 Buick, Riviera coupe with Gran Touring package. (OCW)

RIVIERA - SERIES 4E - V-6 - Riviera's production run was minimal for the 1993 model year (ending in December 1992) due to the next generation Riviera—a 1995 model—being planned for an early-1994 release. Changes to the Riviera were minimal, centered on "cosmetic" changes. A new combination of white diamond exterior color and white leather interior was available, as was a new interior color, beige. Rivieras ordered with the optional Gran Touring suspension package had new 16-inch aluminum wheels with GA touring tires. The 3800 V-6 and electronically controlled four-speed automatic transmission were again the power source.

I.D. DATA: The 1993 Buick Vehicle Identification Number (VIN) contains 17 characters. The first is the producing country: "1"—United States. The second character is "G" for General Motors. The third is "4" for Buick Division. The fourth and fifth characters identify the car line/series: "A/G"—Century Special & Wagon; "A/H"—Century Custom & Wagon; "A/L"—Century Limited; "B/N"—Roadmaster; "B/R"—Roadmaster Estate Wagon; "B/T"—Roadmaster Limited; "C/U"—Park Avenue Ultra; "C/W"—Park Avenue; "E/Z"—Riviera; "H/P"—LeSabre Custom; "H/R"—LeSabre Limited; "N/J"—Skylark Limited; "N/M"—Skylark GS; "N/V"—Skylark Custom; "W/B"—Regal Custom; "W/D"—Regal Limited; and "W/F"—Regal GS. The sixth digit represents body style: "1"—coupe; "2"—hatch/lift back (2-dr); "3"—convertible; "4"—2-dr station wagon; "5"—4-dr sedan; "6"—hatch/lift back (4-dr) and "8"—4-dr station wagon. The seventh character represents the restraint code: "1"—active (manual) belts; "2"—active (manual) belts w/dual airbags; "3"—active (manual) belts w/driver's side airbag; "4"—passive (automatic) belts; and "5"—passive (automatic) belts w/driver's side airbag. The eighth digit is the engine code: "L"—L27 3.8L V-6; "N"—LG7 3.3L V-6; "T"—LH0 3.1L V-6; "1"—L67 3.8L V-6; "3"—L40 2.3L L4; "4"—LN2 2.2L L4; and "7"—L05 5.7L V-8. The ninth character is a check digit that verifies the accuracy of the VIN. The tenth character identifies the model year ("P" = 1993). The eleventh digit identifies the assembly plant. Characters twelve through seventeen are the production sequence number.

Skylark Custom (Four/V-6)

Model No.	Body/Style No.	Body Type & Seating	Factory Price	Shipping Weight	Prod. Total
V37	NV1	2-dr. Cpe.-5P	12955/13415	2793/2916	Note 1
V69	NV5	4-dr. Sed.-5P	12955/13415	2855/2979	Note 2

Skylark Limited (Four/V-6)

J37	NJ1	2-dr. Cpe.-5P	13875/14335	2795/2918	Note 1
J69	NJ5	4-dr. Sed.-5P	13875/14335	2857/2981	Note 2

Skylark Gran Sport (V-6)

M37	NM1	2-dr. Cpe.-5P	15760	2908	Note 1
M69	NM5	4-dr. Sed.-5P	15760	2956	Note 2

Note 1: Skylark coupe production totaled 14,498 with no further breakout available.

Note 2: Skylark sedan production totaled 41,914 with no further breakout available.

Century Special (Four/V-6)

G69	AG5	4-dr. Sed.-6P	14205/14865	2949/N/A	Note 1
G35	AG8	4-dr. Sta. Wag.-6P	14960/15620	3103/N/A	Note 2

Century Custom (Four/V-6)

H37	AH1	2-dr. Cpe.-6P	15620/16280	2903/N/A	603
H69	AH5	4-dr. Sed.-6P	15905/16565	2948/N/A	Note 1
H35	AH8	4-dr. Sta. Wag.-6P	17250/17910	3102/N/A	Note 2

Century Limited (Four/V-6)

L69	AL5	4-dr. Sed.-6P	16865/17525	2948/N/A	Note 1

Note 1: Century sedan production totaled 110,795 with no further breakout available.

Note 2: Century station wagon production totaled 9,163 with no further breakout available.

Regal Custom (V-6)

B57	WB1	2-dr. Cpe.-6P	16610	3250	Note 1
B19	WB5	4-dr. Sed.-6P	16865	3340	Note 2

Regal Limited (V-6)

D57	WD1	2-dr. Cpe.-6P	18260	3258	Note 1
D19	WD5	4-dr. Sed.-6P	18460	3362	Note 2

Regal Gran Sport (V-6)

F57	WF1	2-dr. Cpe.-6P	19095	3388	Note 1
F19	WF5	4-dr. Sed.-6P	19310	3472	Note 2

Note 1: Regal coupe production totaled 25,740 with no further breakout available.

Note 2: Regal sedan production totaled 57,563 with no further breakout available.

LeSabre Custom (V-6)

P69	HP5	4-dr. Sed.-6P	19935	3433	Note 1

LeSabre Limited (V-6)

R69	HR5	4-dr. Sed.-6P	21735	3454	Note 1

Note 1: LeSabre sedan production totaled 143,466 with no further breakout available.

Roadmaster (V-8)

Model No.	Body/Style No.	Body Type & Seating	Factory Price	Shipping Weight	Prod. Total
N69	BN5	4-dr. Sed.-6P	22555	4097	Note 1

Roadmaster Limited (V-8)

Model No.	Body/Style No.	Body Type & Seating	Factory Price	Shipping Weight	Prod. Total
T69	BT5	4-dr. Sed-6P	24920	4112	Note 1

Roadmaster Estate Wagon (V-8)

Model No.	Body/Style No.	Body Type & Seating	Factory Price	Shipping Weight	Prod. Total
R35	BR8	4-dr. Sta. Wag.-8P	23850	4508	9,525

Note 1: Roadmaster sedan production totaled 26,829 with no further breakout available.

Park Avenue (V-6)

Model No.	Body/Style No.	Body Type & Seating	Factory Price	Shipping Weight	Prod. Total
W69	CW5	4-dr. Sed.-6P	26040	3536	Note 1

Park Avenue Ultra (V-6)

Model No.	Body/Style No.	Body Type & Seating	Factory Price	Shipping Weight	Prod. Total
U69	CU5	4-dr. Sed.-6P	29395	3639	Note 1

Note 1: Park Avenue sedan production totaled 55,210 with no further breakout available.

Riviera (V-6)

Model No.	Body/Style No.	Body Type & Seating	Factory Price	Shipping Weight	Prod. Total
Z57	EZ1	2-dr. Cpe.-5P	26230	3503	4,555

ENGINES: BASE FOUR (Century) Inline, overhead valve, four-cylinder. Cast iron block and aluminum head. Displacement: 133 cu. in. (2.2 liters). Bore & stroke: 3.50 in. x 3.46 in. Compression ratio: 9.0:1. Brake horsepower: 110 @ 5200 rpm. Torque: 130 lb.-ft. @ 3200 rpm. Multi-port fuel injection. BASE FOUR (Skylark) Inline, overhead valve, Quad 4 four-cylinder. Cast iron block and aluminum head. Displacement: 138 cu. in. (2.3 liters). Bore & stroke: 3.63 in. x 3.35 in. Compression ratio: 9.5:1. Brake horsepower: 115 @ 5200 rpm. Torque: 140 lb.-ft. @ 3200 rpm. Multi-port fuel injection. BASE V-6 (Regal) 60-degree overhead valve V-6. Cast iron block and aluminum heads. Displacement: 191 cu. in. (3.1 liters). Bore & stroke: 3.50 in. x 3.31 in. Compression ratio: 8.9:1. Brake horsepower: 140 @ 4400 rpm. Torque: 185 lb.-ft. @ 3200 rpm. Multiport fuel injection. BASE V-6 (Skylark GS); OPTIONAL V-6 (Skylark, Century) 90-degree overhead valve V-6. Cast iron block and heads. Displacement: 204 cu. in. (3.3 liters). Bore & stroke: 3.70 in. x 3.16 in. Compression ratio: 9.0:1. Brake horsepower: 160 @ 5200 rpm. Torque: 185 lb.-ft. @ 2000 rpm. Multiport fuel injection. BASE V-6 (Regal Gran Sport, LeSabre, Park Avenue, Riviera); OPTIONAL V-6 (Regal) 90-degree overhead valve V-6 with balance shaft. Cast iron block and head. Displacement: 231 cu. in. (3.8 liters). Bore & stroke: 3.80 in. x 3.40 in. Compression ratio: 9.0:1. Brake horsepower: 170 @ 4800 rpm. Torque: 225 lb.-ft. @ 3200 rpm. Sequential Tuned Port fuel injection. BASE V-6 (Park Avenue Ultra) supercharged 90-degree overhead valve V-6 with balance shaft. Cast iron block and head. Displacement: 231 cu. in. (3.8 liters). Bore & stroke: 3.80 in. x 3.40 in. Compression ratio: 8.5:1. Brake horsepower: 205 @ 4400 rpm. Torque: 260 lb.-ft. @ 2600 rpm. Sequential Tuned Port fuel injection. BASE V-8 (Roadmaster) 90-degree overhead valve V-8. Cast iron block and head. Displacement: 350 cu. in. (5.7 liters). Bore & stroke: 4.00 in. x 3.48 in. Compression ratio: 9.8:1. Brake horsepower: 180 @ 4000 rpm. Torque: 300 lb.-ft. @ 2400 rpm. Throttle-body fuel injection.

CHASSIS DATA: Wheelbase: (Skylark) 103.4 in.; (Century) 104.9 in.; (Regal) 107.5 in.; (LeSabre) 110.8 in.; (Roadmaster) 115.9 in.; (Park Avenue) 110.7 in.; (Riviera) 108.0 in. Overall length: (Skylark) 189.1 in.; (Century) 189.1 in.; (Century wagon) 190.9 in.; (Regal coupe) 193.6 in.; (Regal sedan) 194.8 in.; (LeSabre) 200.0 in.; (Roadmaster sedan) 215.8 in.; (Roadmaster Estate Wagon) 217.5 in.; (Park Avenue) 205.2 in.; (Riviera) 198.2 in. Height: (Skylark) 53.2 in.; (Century coupe) 53.7 in.; (Century sedan and wagon) 54.2 in.; (Regal coupe) 53.0 in.; (Regal sedan) 54.5 in.; (LeSabre sedan) 55.7 in.; (Roadmaster) 55.9 in.; (Roadmaster Estate Wagon) 60.3 in.; (Park Avenue) 55.1 in.: (Riviera) 52.9 in. Width: (Skylark) 67.5 in.; (Century) 69.4 in.; (Regal) 72.5 in.; (LeSabre) 73.6 in.; (Roadmaster) 78.1 in.; (Roadmaster Estate Wagon) 79.9 in.; (Park Avenue) 73.6 in.; (Riviera) 73.1 in. Front Tread: (Skylark) 55.9 in.; (Century) 58.7 in.; (Regal) 59.5 in.; (LeSabre): 60.4 in.; (Roadmaster) 61.7 in.; (Roadmaster Estate Wagon) 62.1 in.; (Park Avenue) 60.4 in.; (Riviera) 59.9 in. Rear Tread: (Skylark) 54.4 in.; (Century) 56.7 in.; (Regal) 58.0 in.; (LeSabre) 60.4 in.; (Roadmaster) 60.7 in.; (Roadmaster Estate Wagon) 64.1 in.; (Park Avenue) 60.6 in.; (Riviera) 59.9 in. Standard Tires: (Skylark) P185/75R14; (Skylark GS) P205/55R16; (Century) P185/75R14; (Regal) P205/70R15; (Regal GS) P225/60R16; (LeSabre) P205/70R15; (Roadmaster) P235/70R15; (Roadmaster Estate Wagon) P225/75R15; (Park Avenue) P205/70R15; (Park Avenue Ultra) P215/70R15; (Riviera) P205/70R15.

TECHNICAL: Transmission: (Skylark, Century) Three-speed automatic; (Roadmaster) Four-speed automatic w/overdrive; (Regal, LeSabre, Park Avenue, Riviera) Electronically controlled four-speed automatic w/overdrive. Steering: (Skylark, Century, LeSabre, Park Avenue, Riviera) Rack and pinion; (Roadmaster) Integral. Front Suspension: (Skylark) MacPherson struts w/coil springs, hydraulic shock absorbers, stabilizer bar; (Century, Regal, LeSabre) MacPherson struts w/coil springs, deflected disc shock absorbers, stabilizer bar; (Roadmaster) Independent short/long arm w/coil springs, tube-gas charged shock absorbers, stabilizer bar; (Park Avenue, Riviera) MacPherson struts w/coil springs, double acting hydraulic shock absorbers, stabilizer bar. Rear Suspension: (Skylark) Trailing crank arm w/twist beam, double acting hydraulic shock absorbers; (Century) Trailing arm twist axle w/track bar, double acting shock absorbers, stabilizer bar; (Regal) Tri-link independent w/transverse leaf spring, deflected disc shock absorbers, stabilizer bar; (LeSabre) Chapman struts w/variable rate coil springs, deflected disc shock absorbers, stabilizer bar; (Roadmaster) Salisbury four link w/coil springs, tube gas-charged shock absorbers; (Park Avenue) Chapman struts w/coil springs, electronic level control w/air shock absorbers; (Riviera) Independent strut "H" arm w/transverse leaf springs, deflected disc strut shock absorbers. Brakes: (Skylark, Roadmaster Estate Wagon, Park Avenue) Power front disc, rear drum w/anti-lock; (Century, LeSabre, Roadmaster) Power front disc, rear drum; (Regal) Power four-wheel disc; (Riviera) Power four-wheel disc w/anti-lock. Body Construction: (Regal) Unibody; (Skylark, Century) Integral body/frame; (LeSabre, Park Avenue) Unibody w/isolated engine cradle; (Roadmaster) Welded body with full perimeter frame; (Riviera) Unibody w/isolated front frame and rear sub-frame. Fuel Tank: (Skylark) 15.2 gal.; (Century) 16.4 gal.; (Regal) 16.5 gal.; (LeSabre) 18.0 gal.; (Roadmaster) 23.0 gal.; (Roadmaster Estate Wagon) 22.0 gal.; (Park Avenue) 18.0 gal.; (Riviera) 18.8 gal.

DRIVETRAIN OPTIONS: Engines: 3.3 liter V-6, (Skylark) $460; (Century) $660. (Regal) 3800 3.8 liter V-6, $395. Transmission/Differential: (Century) Four-speed automatic transmission with overdrive, with 3.3 liter engine only, $200. FX3 Adjustable Ride Control Suspension (Skylark) $380; (Skylark GS) $353; (Park Avenue) $380. G67 Auto Level Control Suspension (Roadmaster Estate Wagon) $175. Y56 Gran Touring Suspension Package: (Regal) $350-$675; (LeSabre) $484-$724; (Park Avenue) $86-$300; (Riviera) $250. NW9 Traction Control System (LeSabre Limited) $175; (Park Avenue) $175. V92 Trailer Towing Package: (LeSabre) $150-$325; (Roadmaster) $117-$325; (Park Avenue) $123-$150. (Roadmaster) Limited slip differential $100.

1993 Buick, Skylark Gran Sport sedan. (OCW)

SKYLARK CONVENIENCE/APPEARANCE OPTIONS: (Skylark Custom cpe/sed) Premium pkg. $1,000/$1,000; Luxury pkg. $1,623/$1,623; Prestige pkg. $2,087/$2,152. (Skylark Limited cpe/sed) Popular pkg. $1,145/$1,145; Premium pkg. $1,515/$1,515; Luxury pkg. $1,955/$2,020; Prestige pkg. $2,543/$2,608. (Gran Sport cpe/sed) Popular pkg. $1,145/$1,145; Premium pkg. $1,435/$1,435; Luxury pkg. $2,010/$2,075; Prestige pkg. $2,578/$2,643. Eng. block heater $18. Trunk convenience net (Custom) $20. Radio w/CD player $459-$624. Remote Keyless Entry $135. Lower accent paint $195. Rear folding split seat (Limited) $150. P185/75R14 tires (Custom, Limited) $68. P195/65R15 tires (Custom, Limited) $131. Six-way pwr driver's seat (Custom) $270-$305. Bucket seats w/console $160. Styled whl covers (Custom, Limited) $28. 16-inch alum whls (Limited) $575.

CENTURY CONVENIENCE/APPEARANCE OPTIONS: (Special sed/wag) Premium pkg. $543/$763; Luxury pkg. $932/$1,221; Prestige pkg. $1,316/$1,800. (Custom cpe/sed/wag) Premium pkg. N/A/$1,019/$1,170; Luxury pkg. $913/$1,560/$1,857; Prestige pkg. $1,289/$2,168/$2,430. (Limited sed) Luxury pkg. $1,443; Prestige pkg. $2,051. Driver's side airbag $500. Gauge pkg. (Special) $48. Keyless entry $135. H.D. cooling (V-6 only) $40. Deck lid luggage rack $115. Door edge moldings: 2-dr. $15/4-dr. $25. Courtesy Lights (Custom sed) $44. ETR AM/FM radio w/Cassette player $140. ETR AM/FM radio w/CD player $274. Pwr antenna $85. Six-way pwr driver's seat $305. Strg whl radio controls (Custom) $125. Bodyside stripes (stnd on Limited) $45. P185/75R14 tires (Custom cpe) $68. P195/75R14 (Custom cpe) $40/BSW; $108/WSW. Leather 55/45 seat w/armrest (Custom) $600. Leather/vinyl 55/45 seat (Limited sed) $500. Remote trunk release $60. Locking wire whl covers (Custom) $240. Styled steel whls $115. Alum whls $55-$295. Rear window wiper (wag only) $85-$125.

REGAL CONVENIENCE/APPEARANCE OPTIONS: (Custom cpe/sed) Popular pkg. $440/$440; Premium pkg. $760/$825; Luxury pkg. $1,153/$1,218; Prestige pkg. $1,572/$1,648. (Limited cpe/sed) Premium pkg. $1,015/$1,080; Luxury pkg. $1,640/$1,705; Prestige pkg. $2,170/$2,305. (Gran Sport cpe/sed) Luxury pkg. $1,223/$1,288; Prestige pkg. $1,870/$1,935. Anti-lock brakes (Custom) $450. H.D. cooling (3800 V-6 only) $40. Deck lid luggage rack $115. Door edge guards: (N/A GS) cpe $15/sed $25. Engine block heater $18. Remote keyless entry (Custom) $135. Courtesy lights (GS sed) $70. Accent paint (cpe only, N/A GS) $205. Lighted visor vanity mirror (Custom) $92. Mirror reading lights (Custom) $30. Dual six-way pwr seat $305-$610. ETR AM/FM radio w/Cassette player $150-$290. ETR AM/FM radio w/CD player $124-$414. Bodyside stripes (cpe only, N/A GS) $45. Pwr sunroof $695. P205/70R15 tires (Custom, Limited) $76. Leather/vinyl bucket seats $500. Locking wire whl covers $240. 15-inch alum whls (N/A GS) $325.

1993 Buick, LeSabre 90th Anniversary Edition sedan with specific fender badging. (OCW)

LESABRE CONVENIENCE/APPEARANCE OPTIONS: (Custom sed) Premium pkg. $596; Luxury pkg. $1,021; Prestige pkg. $1,632. (Limited sed) Premium pkg. $1,029; Luxury pkg. $1,456; Prestige pkg. $2,361. Gauges w/tach (Limited) $163. Pwr six-way driver's seat (Custom) $305. ETR AM/FM radio w/cass $140. ETR AM/FM radio w/CD player $264-$624. Pwr antenna $85. Bodyside stripes $45. Leather/vinyl 55/45 seats $500. P205/70R15 tires $76. 15-inch styled alum whls $85-$325. Locking wire whl covers $240.

ROADMASTER CONVENIENCE/APPEARANCE OPTIONS: (Roadmaster) Luxury pkg. $727; Prestige pkg. $1,700. (Limited) Prestige pkg. $406. (Estate Wagon) Premium pkg. $565; Luxury pkg. $1,361; Prestige pkg. $2,158. Pwr antenna (N/A Limited) $85. H.D. cooling (Estate Wagon) $40. Rear window defogger w/heated outside mirrors (Estate Wagon) $170-$205. Lower accent paint (sed only) $150. ETR AM/FM radio w/CD player $394-$569. ETR AM/FM radio w/cassette $150-$325. Leather/vinyl seats (Roadmaster, Estate Wagon) $540-$760. Leather/vinyl seats (Limited) $710-$760. Vinyl landau roof (N/A wag) $695. Vista cover (N/A sed) $85. P235/70R15 tires (Roadmaster) $150. Full-size spare (N/A wag) $65. Locking wire whl covers (N/A wag) $240. 15-inch alum whls (stnd on wag) $325. Solar glass windshield (sed only) $50.

PARK AVENUE CONVENIENCE/APPEARANCE OPTIONS: (Park Avenue) Popular pkg. $684; Premium pkg. $1,084; Luxury pkg. $1,911; Prestige pkg. $2,561. (Ultra) Popular pkg. $270; Premium pkg. $460; Luxury pkg. $1,229; Prestige pkg. $1,834. Firemist paint $250. ETR AM/FM radio w/Cassette $150-$220. Bose music syst $573-$793. ETR AM/FM radio w/CD player w/graphic equalizer $244-$464. Astroroof $1,157-$1,408. P205/70R15 tires (Park Avenue) $76. P215/70R15 (Ultra) $80. Self-sealing tires $150. Leather/vinyl 55/45 seats w/armrest (Park Avenue) $500.

RIVIERA CONVENIENCE/APPEARANCE OPTIONS: Luxury pkg. $520; Prestige pkg. $1,069. Firemist paint $250. Riviera Appearance pkg. $235. Pearlescent white diamond paint $250. Lower accent paint $190. Bose music syst $1,399. ETR AM/FM radio w/cassette $516. Astroroof $1,350. Vinyl top $695. Leather/vinyl bucket seats $600. White leather bucket seats $700. 14-way adjustable leather/vinyl bucket driver's seat $945. 14-way white leather adjustable leather/vinyl bucket driver's seat $1,045. 15-inch alum whls $85. 15-inch painted alum whls $100.

HISTORY: Buick's share of the total U.S. car market was 5.88 percent (compared to 6.37 percent in 1992) on sales of 500,691 automobiles (523,569 in 1992).

1994

There was no "official" Riviera for 1994, due to the early launch (spring) of the 1995 version (see 1995 Buick listing). Besides the Riviera coupe being missing in action, the coupe body style, in general, was discontinued among most of Buick's lines. Coupes previously offered as Skylark's Limited, Century's Custom and Regal's Limited were all dropped. Also gone was Century's Custom station wagon and Limited sedan.

1994 Buick, Skylark Custom sedan. (OCW)

SKYLARK - SERIES 4N - FOUR/V-6 - Gran Sports got a new engine (also optional in Custom and Limited models) in the 3.1-

liter (191 cubic inch) V-6. This engine replaced the 3.3-liter V-6 used previously. GS models also received the electronically controlled four-speed automatic transmission (optional for Custom and Limited, both of which retained the three-speed automatic unit used previously). The 2.3-liter Quad 4 remained standard in the Custom and Limited lines. The Limited coupe was dropped, but otherwise the Skylark lineup was intact from the year previous. A driver's side airbag was now standard equipment in all Skylarks. Dark Polo Green was a new exterior color available on all Skylarks.

1994 Buick, Century Special sedan. (OCW)

1994 Buick, Century Special station wagon with optional roof rack. (OCW)

1994 Buick, Century Custom sedan with optional wire wheel covers. (OCW)

CENTURY - SERIES 4A - FOUR/V-6 - Century's ranks were thinned considerably with the discontinuation of the Custom coupe and station wagon and Limited sedan. Comprising the revised lineup were the Special sedan and station wagon and Custom sedan. This trio featured anti-lock brakes and driver's side airbag as new standard equipment. Also new was the option engine, the 3.1-liter V-6, which replaced the 3.3-liter V-6 available previously. When this option engine was selected it came with the electronically controlled four-speed automatic transmission. The 2.2-liter four-cylinder engine paired with the three-speed automatic transmission remained the standard powertrain.

1994 Buick, Regal Gran Sport sedan. (OCW)

1994 Buick, Regal Gran Sport coupe. (OCW)

REGAL - SERIES 4W - V-6 - The 3.1-liter V-6 that was standard equipment in the Regal Custom line was all-new, replacing the previously used, "old" 3.1-liter unit. With the discontinuation of the Limited coupe, Regal was available in Custom coupe and sedan, Limited sedan and Gran Sport coupe and sedan. The Limited and GS models were powered by the 3800 V-6 (optional for Custom) and all Regals used the 4T60-E electronically controlled four-speed automatic transmission with overdrive. The Limited was also previously powered by the "old" 3.1-liter V-6. A driver's side airbag was a new standard item in all Regals as was Pass-Key II theft deterrent system.

1994 Buick, LeSabre Limited sedan. (OCW)

LESABRE - SERIES 4H - V-6 - LeSabre's lineup and power source carried over from the previous year. The big change was safety related, with a passenger side airbag becoming standard equipment as well as Pass-Key II theft-deterrent system. Standard engine and transmission was again the 3800 V-6 and electronically controlled four-speed automatic with overdrive.

1994 Buick, Roadmaster Estate Wagon station wagon. (OCW)

1994 Buick, Roadmaster Limited sedan. (OCW)

ROADMASTER - SERIES 4B - V-8 - Big news in the Roadmaster camp was the base and Limited sedans and Estate Wagon received the 260 horsepower LT1 (Corvette) V-8 as the standard engine. This 5.7-liter (350 cubic inch) powerplant replaced the "old" 5.7-liter V-8 previously used. All Roadmasters used the electronically controlled four-speed automatic with overdrive. New standard features included a passenger side airbag and Pass-Key II theft deterrent system.

1994 Buick, Park Avenue sedan. (OCW)

1994 Buick, Park Avenue Ultra sedan. (OCW)

PARK AVENUE - SERIES 4C - V-6 - The supercharged version of the 3800 V-6 that powered the Park Avenue Ultra sedan received a 20 horsepower boost in 1994. The "entry level" Park Avenue sedan retained the normally aspirated 3800 V-6 as its power source. Both engines were paired with the 4T60-E electronically controlled four-speed automatic transmission with overdrive. New standard features included a passenger side airbag and Pass-Key II theft deterrent system.

I.D. DATA: The 1994 Buick Vehicle Identification Number (VIN) contains 17 characters. The first is the producing country: "1"— United States. The second character is "G" for General Motors. The third is "4" for Buick Division. The fourth and fifth characters identify the car line/series: "A/G"—Century Special & Wagon; "A/H"—Century Custom; "B/N"—Roadmaster; "B/R"—Roadmaster Estate Wagon; "B/T"—Roadmaster Limited; "C/U"—Park Avenue Ultra; "C/W"—Park Avenue; "H/P"—LeSabre Custom; "H/R"—LeSabre Limited; "N/J"—Skylark Limited; "N/M"—Skylark GS; "N/V"—Skylark Custom; "W/B"—Regal Custom; "W/D"—Regal Limited; and "W/F"—Regal GS. The sixth digit represents body style: "1"—coupe; "2"—hatch/lift back (2-dr); "3"—convertible; "4"—2-dr station wagon; "5"—4-dr sedan; "6"—hatch/lift back (4-dr) and "8"—4-dr station wagon. The seventh character represents the restraint code: "1"—active (manual) belts; "2"—active (manual) belts w/dual airbags; "3"—active (manual) belts w/driver's side airbag; "4"—passive (automatic) belts; and "5"—passive (automatic) belts w/driver's side airbag; "6"—passive (automatic) belts w/dual airbags. The eighth digit is the engine code: "L"—L27 3.8L V-6; "M"—L82 3.1L V-6; "P"—LT1 5.7L V-8; "1"—L67 3.8L V-6; "3"—L40 2.3L L4; and "4"—LN2 2.2L L4. The ninth character is a check digit that verifies the accuracy of the VIN. The tenth character identifies the model year ("R" = 1994). The eleventh digit identifies the assembly plant. Characters twelve through seventeen are the production sequence number.

Skylark Custom (Four/V-6)

Model No.	Body/Style No.	Body Type & Seating	Factory Price	Shipping Weight	Prod. Total
V37	NV1	2-dr. Cpe.-5P	13599/14009	2791/2809	Note 1
V69	NV5	4-dr. Sed.-5P	13599/14009	2855/2873	Note 2

Skylark Limited (Four/V-6)

Model No.	Body/Style No.	Body Type & Seating	Factory Price	Shipping Weight	Prod. Total
J69	NJ5	4-dr. Sed.-5P	16199/16609	2939/2957	Note 2

Skylark Gran Sport (V-6)

M37	NM1	2-dr. Cpe.-5P	18299	2985	Note 1
M69	NM5	4-dr. Sed.-5P	18299	3038	Note 2

Note 1: Skylark coupe production totaled 9,558 with no further breakout available.

Note 2: Skylark sedan production totaled 47,000 with no further breakout available.

Century Special (Four/V-6)

G69	AG5	4-dr. Sed.-6P	15495/16105	2974/2992	Note 1
G35	AG8	4-dr. Sta. Wag.-6P	16345/16955	3134/3152	8,364

Century Custom (Four/V-6)

H69	AH5	4-dr. Sed.-6P	16695/17305	2976/2994	Note 1

Note 1: Century sedan production totaled 122,326 with no further breakout available.

Regal Custom (V-6)

B57	WB1	2-dr. Cpe.-6P	17999	3240	Note 1
B19	WB5	4-dr. Sed.-6P	18299	3338	Note 2

Regal Limited (V-6)

D19	WD5	4-dr. Sed.-6P	19799	3362	Note 2

Regal Gran Sport (V-6)

F57	WF1	2-dr. Cpe.-6P	19999	3335	Note 1
F19	WF5	4-dr. Sed.-6P	20299	3429	Note 2

Note 1: Regal coupe production totaled 18,068 with no further breakout available.

Note 2: Regal sedan production totaled 60,489 with no further breakout available.

LeSabre Custom (V-6)

P69	HP5	4-dr. Sed.-6P	20860	3449	Note 1

LeSabre Limited (V-6)

R69	HR5	4-dr. Sed.-6P	24420	3449	Note 1

Note 1: LeSabre sedan production totaled 159,250 with no further breakout available.

Roadmaster (V-8)

N69	BN5	4-dr. Sed.-6P	23999	4191	Note 1

Roadmaster Limited (V-8)

T69	BT5	4-dr. Sed-6P	26399	4279	Note 1

Roadmaster Estate Wagon (V-8)

R35	BR8	4-dr. Sta. Wag.-8P	25599	4572	8,669

Note 1: Roadmaster sedan production totaled 26,429 with no further breakout available.

Park Avenue (V-6)

W69	CW5	4-dr. Sed.-6P	26999	3533	Note 1

Park Avenue Ultra (V-6)

U69	CU5	4-dr. Sed.-6P	31699	3637	Note 1

Note 1: Park Avenue sedan production totaled 64,665 with no further breakout available.

ENGINES: BASE FOUR (Century) Inline, overhead valve, four-cylinder. Cast iron block and aluminum head. Displacement: 133 cu. in. (2.2 liters). Bore & stroke: 3.50 in. x 3.46 in. Compression ratio: 9.0:1. Brake horsepower: 120 @ 5200 rpm. Torque: 130 lb.-ft. @ 4000 rpm. Multi-port fuel injection. BASE FOUR (Skylark) Inline, overhead valve, Quad 4 four-cylinder. Cast iron block and aluminum head. Displacement: 138 cu. in. (2.3 liters). Bore & stroke: 3.63 in. x 3.35 in. Compression ratio: 9.5:1. Brake horsepower: 115 @ 5200 rpm. Torque: 140 lb.-ft. @ 3200 rpm. Multi-port fuel injection. BASE V-6 (Skylark GS, Regal Custom); OPTIONAL V-6 (Skylark Limited, Century) 60-degree overhead valve V-6. Cast iron block and aluminum heads. Displacement: 191 cu. in. (3.1 liters). Bore & stroke: 3.50 in. x 3.31 in. Compression ratio: 9.5:1. Brake horsepower: 160 @ 5200 rpm (except Skylark - 155 @ 5200 rpm). Torque: 185 lb.-ft. @ 4000 rpm. Sequential Tuned Port fuel injection. BASE V-6 (Regal Limited, Regal Gran Sport, LeSabre, Park Avenue) 90-degree overhead valve V-6 with balance shaft. Cast iron block and heads. Displacement: 231 cu. in. (3.8 liters). Bore & stroke: 3.80 in. x 3.40 in. Compression ratio: 9.0:1. Brake horsepower: 170 @ 4800 rpm. Torque: 225 lb.-ft. @ 3200 rpm. Sequential Tuned Port fuel injection. BASE V-6 (Park Avenue

Ultra) supercharged 90-degree overhead valve V-6 with balance shaft. Cast iron block and head. Displacement: 231 cu. in. (3.8 liters). Bore & stroke: 3.80 in. x 3.40 in. Compression ratio: 8.5:1. Brake horsepower: 225 @ 5000 rpm. Torque: 275 lb.-ft. @ 3200 rpm. Sequential Tuned Port fuel injection. BASE V-8 (Roadmaster) 90-degree overhead valve V-8. Cast iron block and aluminum heads. Displacement: 350 cu. in. (5.7 liters). Bore & stroke: 4.00 in. x 3.48 in. Compression ratio: 10.5:1. Brake horsepower: 260 @ 5000 rpm. Torque: 335 lb.-ft. @ 3200 rpm. Sequential Tuned Port fuel injection.

CHASSIS DATA: Wheelbase: (Skylark) 103.4 in.; (Century) 104.9 in.; (Regal) 107.5 in.; (LeSabre) 110.8 in.; (Roadmaster) 115.9 in.; (Park Avenue) 110.8 in. Overall length: (Skylark) 189.1 in.; (Century) 189.1 in.; (Century wagon) 190.9 in.; (Regal coupe) 193.6 in.; (Regal sedan) 194.8 in.; (LeSabre) 200.0 in.; (Roadmaster sedan) 215.8 in.; (Roadmaster Estate Wagon) 217.5 in.; (Park Avenue) 205.2 in. Height: (Skylark) 53.2 in.; (Century) 54.2 in.; (Regal coupe) 53.0 in.; (Regal sedan) 54.5 in.; (LeSabre) 55.7 in.; (Roadmaster) 55.9 in.; (Roadmaster Estate Wagon) 60.3 in.; (Park Avenue) 55.1 in. Width: (Skylark) 67.5 in.; (Century) 69.4 in.; (Regal) 72.5 in.; (LeSabre) 73.6 in.; (Roadmaster) 78.1 in.; (Roadmaster Estate Wagon) 79.9 in.; (Park Avenue) 73.6 in. Front Tread: (Skylark) 55.8 in.; (Century) 58.7 in.; (Regal) 59.5 in.; (LeSabre): 60.4 in.; (Roadmaster) 61.7 in.; (Roadmaster Estate Wagon) 62.1 in.; (Park Avenue) 60.4 in. Rear Tread: (Skylark) 56.6 in.; (Century) 56.7 in.; (Regal) 58.0 in.; (LeSabre) 60.4 in.; (Roadmaster) 60.7 in.; (Roadmaster Estate Wagon) 64.1 in.; (Park Avenue) 60.6 in. Standard Tires: (Skylark) P185/75R14; (Skylark GS) P205/55R16; (Century) P185/75R14; (Regal) P205/70R15; (Regal GS) P225/60R16; (LeSabre) P205/70R15; (Roadmaster) P235/70R15; (Roadmaster Estate Wagon) P225/75R15; (Park Avenue) P205/70R15; (Park Avenue Ultra) P215/70R15.

TECHNICAL: Transmission: (Skylark, Century) Three-speed automatic; (Regal, LeSabre, Roadmaster, Park Avenue) Electronically controlled four-speed automatic w/overdrive. Steering: (Skylark, Century, LeSabre, Park Avenue) Rack and pinion; (Roadmaster) Integral. Front Suspension: (Skylark) MacPherson struts w/coil springs, hydraulic shock absorbers, stabilizer bar; (Century, Regal, LeSabre) MacPherson struts w/coil springs, deflected disc shock absorbers, stabilizer bar; (Roadmaster) Independent short/long arm w/coil springs, tube-gas charged shock absorbers, stabilizer bar; (Park Avenue) MacPherson struts w/coil springs, double acting hydraulic shock absorbers, stabilizer bar. Rear Suspension: (Skylark) Trailing crank arm w/twist beam, double acting hydraulic shock absorbers; (Century) Trailing arm twist axle w/track bar, double acting shock absorbers, stabilizer bar; (Regal) Tri-link independent w/transverse leaf spring, deflected disc shock absorbers, stabilizer bar; (LeSabre) Chapman struts w/variable rate coil springs, deflected disc shock absorbers, stabilizer bar; (Roadmaster) Salisbury four link w/coil springs, tube gas-charged shock absorbers; (Park Avenue) Chapman struts w/coil springs, electronic level control w/air shock absorbers. Brakes: (Skylark, Century, LeSabre, Roadmaster, Park Avenue) Power front disc, rear drum w/anti-lock; (Regal) Power four-wheel disc w/anti-lock. Body Construction: (Regal) Unibody; (Skylark, Century) Integral body/frame; (LeSabre, Park Avenue) Unibody w/isolated engine cradle; (Roadmaster) Welded body with full perimeter frame. Fuel Tank: (Skylark) 15.2 gal.; (Century) 16.5 gal.; (Regal) 16.5 gal.; (LeSabre) 18.0 gal.; (Roadmaster) 23.0 gal.; (Roadmaster Estate Wagon) 22.0 gal.; (Park Avenue) 18.0 gal.

DRIVETRAIN OPTIONS: Engines: 3.1 liter V-6, (Skylark Custom & Limited) $410; (Century) $610. (Regal Custom cpe) 3.8 liter V-6, $395. Transmission/Differential: Four-speed automatic transmission with overdrive (w/V-6 only), (Skylark Custom & Limited) $200; (Century) $200. FE2 Gran Touring suspension (Skylark GS) $27. FX3 Adjustable Ride Control Suspension (Park Avenue) $380. G67 Auto Level Control Suspension

(Roadmaster) $175. Y56 Gran Touring Suspension Package: (Regal) $675; (LeSabre) $399; (Park Avenue) $224. NW9 Traction Control System (LeSabre Limited) $175; (Park Avenue) $175. V92 Trailer Towing Package: (LeSabre) $150-$325; (Roadmaster) $225-$375; (Park Avenue) $123-$150. (Roadmaster) Limited slip differential $100.

1994 Buick, Skylark Gran Sport sedan. (OCW)

SKYLARK CONVENIENCE/APPEARANCE OPTIONS: (Skylark Custom cpe/sed) Premium pkg. Luxury pkg. $1,623/$1,623; Prestige pkg. $2,087/$2,152. (Skylark Limited sed) Prestige pkg. $1,013. (Gran Sport cpe/sed) Prestige pkg. $1,083/$1,083. Air cond. (Custom) $830. Eng. block heater $18. Trunk convenience net (Custom & Limited) $20. Pwr windows: cpe $275; sed $340. Analog gauge cluster (Custom) $126. CD player $394. Cassette player $165. Remote Keyless Entry $135. Lower accent paint $195. Rear folding split seat (Limited) $150. P185/75R14 tires (Custom, Limited) $68. P195/65R15 tires (Custom, Limited) $131. Six-way pwr driver's seat $270. Bucket seats w/console $160. 15-inch styled whl covers $28. 16-inch alum whls (Limited) $575. 14-inch styled polycast whls (Custom, Limited) $115. Dual elect. remote mirrors $78. Pwr antenna $85.

CENTURY CONVENIENCE/APPEARANCE OPTIONS: (Special sed/wag) Luxury pkg. $582/$737; Prestige pkg. $1,244/$1,593. (Custom sed) Luxury pkg. $1,254; Prestige pkg. $1,856. Remote keyless entry $135. H.D. cooling (V-6 only) $40. Deck lid luggage rack $115. Door edge moldings $25. Courtesy Lights (Special) $6. Lighted visor vanity mirrors (Special) $92. Cassette player $140. CD player $274-$414. Pwr antenna $85. Six-way pwr driver's seat $305. Bodyside stripes (Special) $45. P185/75R14 tires (Special) $68. P195/75R14 (Special) $40. Leather 55/45 seat w/armrest (Custom) $500. Remote trunk release $60. Locking wire whl covers $240. Styled steel whls $115. Alum whls $295. Rear window wiper (wag only) $85. Woodgrain appliqué (wag only) $380. Pwr windows (Special) $330.

REGAL CONVENIENCE/APPEARANCE OPTIONS: (Custom cpe/sed) Luxury pkg. $848/$848; Prestige pkg. $1,432/$1,443. (Limited sed) Luxury pkg. $918; Prestige pkg. $1,640. (Gran Sport cpe/sed) Luxury pkg. $918/$1,288; Prestige pkg. $1,570/$1,640. H.D. cooling $150. Door edge guards $25. Engine block heater $18. Remote keyless entry (Limited & GS) $135. Decklid luggage rack $115. Lighted visor vanity mirror (Custom) $92. Dual six-way pwr seat (GS cpe) $305. Six-way pwr driver's seat (Custom) $305; (Limited & GS) $270. Graphic equalizer $150. CD player $274. Steering whl mounted radio controls (GS cpe) $125. Concert sound II (Custom) $70. Pwr antenna (Custom) $85. Pwr sunroof (GS cpe) $695. P205/70R15 tires (Custom cpe) $76. Leather/vinyl 55/45 seats (Limited) $550. Leather/vinyl bucket seats (Limited, GS) $550. Locking wire whl covers (Custom cpe) $240. 15-inch alum whls (Custom cpe) $325. Chrome bodyside & fascia pkg. (Custom cpe) $150.

LESABRE CONVENIENCE/APPEARANCE OPTIONS: (Custom sed) Luxury pkg. $1,106; Prestige pkg. $1,852. (Limited sed) Prestige pkg. $670. Gauges w/tach $163. Elect. o/s rearview mirrors (Custom) $78. Pwr six-way driver's seat (Custom) $305. ETR AM/FM radio w/cass $120. ETR AM/FM radio w/CD player $244-$364. Leather/vinyl 55/45 seats (Limited) $550. P205/70R15 tires (Custom) $76. 15-inch styled alum whls (Custom) $325.

ROADMASTER CONVENIENCE/APPEARANCE OPTIONS:
(Roadmaster) Luxury pkg. $858; Prestige pkg. $1,565. (Limited) Prestige pkg. $350. (Estate Wagon) Luxury pkg. $1,467; Prestige pkg. $2,144. Programmable door locks $25. H.D. cooling, (Limited) $200; (Estate Wagon) $150. Lower accent paint (sed only) $150. ETR AM/FM radio w/CD player $394-$429. ETR AM/FM radio w/cassette $150-$185. Remote keyless entry $135. Pwr passenger seat $305. Leather/vinyl 55/45 seats $760. Vinyl landau roof (N/A wag) $695. P225/75R15 self-sealing tires (wag only) $150. P235/70R15 self-sealing tires (sed only) $150. Full-size spare (N/A wag) $65. Locking wire whl covers (sed) $240. 15-inch alum whls (stnd on wag) $325.

PARK AVENUE CONVENIENCE/APPEARANCE OPTIONS:
(Park Avenue) Luxury pkg. $1,821; Prestige pkg. $2,496. (Ultra) Luxury pkg. $730; Prestige pkg. $1,245. ETR AM/FM radio w/Cassette $50. Bose music syst $673-$723. ETR AM/FM radio w/CD player $244-$364. Astroroof $802-$918. Elect. heated driver's seat, (Park Avenue) $105; (Ultra) $60. P205/70R15 tires (Park Avenue) $76. Self-sealing tires $150. Leather/vinyl 55/45 seats w/armrest (Park Avenue) $600.

HISTORY: Buick rebounded, with fewer models offered, to score 6.1 percent of the total U.S. car market compared with 5.88 percent the year previous. Sales totaled 546,836 (including early-launch 1995 Riviera) compared to 500,691 automobiles in 1993.

1995

It was a year of returns and a year of change within the Buick Division of General Motors. Making an appearance after a one-year's absence were the Skylark Limited coupe, Century Limited sedan and the aforementioned Riviera. New for 1995 was the Roadmaster Estate Wagon Limited, which joined the now-base Estate Wagon. Other new items could be found under the hoods of Buicks. The 3800 Series II V-6 was an all-new design engine, rated at 205 horsepower, and standard in Park Avenue and Riviera. Also, Skylark's standard four-cylinder engine was revised as a dual overhead cam unit after previously being offered in single overhead cam configuration.

1995 Buick, Skylark Gran Sport coupe. (OCW)

1995 Buick, Skylark Custom coupe. (OCW)

1995 Buick, Skylark Limited sedan. (OCW)

1995 Buick, Skylark Gran Sport sedan. (OCW)

SKYLARK - SERIES 4N - FOUR/V-6 - With the return of the Limited coupe, Skylark again offered a six model lineup with coupe and sedan versions available in three trim levels: Custom, Limited and Gran Sport. The 2.3-liter four-cylinder engine standard on Custom and Limited Skylarks was upgraded from a single to a dual overhead cam unit, which boosted its horsepower rating from the previous 115 to 150. The DOHC four was fitted with two counter-rotating balance shafts, which resulted in smoother operation and less vibration. Cars employing this four were also fitted with larger mufflers to reduce exhaust noise. The GS models again used the 3.1-liter V-6 (optional for other Skylarks) coupled to the 4T60-E electronically controlled four-speed automatic transmission with overdrive. The three-speed automatic was standard with the four-cylinder engine, but the 4T60-E unit was designated the option transmission. All Skylarks benefited from a new tubular rear axle, which placed the rear springs and shocks along the wheel center line. This improved handling and smoothed the ride.

1995 Buick, Century Special sedan. (OCW)

1995 Buick, Century Custom sedan. (OCW)

CENTURY - SERIES 4A - FOUR/V-6 - After a year out of the lineup, the Limited sedan returned as a Century offering. It joined the Custom sedan and Special sedan and station wagon carried over from the year previous. Special models were pow-

ered by the 2.2-liter four-cylinder engine, now fitted with roller lifters to reduce valvetrain friction. Standard transmission for the Specials was the three-speed automatic, newly fitted with a reverse torque clutch that kept the torque converter clutch locked during closed throttle situations to reduce rpm surge as the throttle is reopened. Custom and Limited models used the 3.1-liter V-6 mated to the electronically controlled four-speed automatic transmission with overdrive. This setup was the option powertrain for Specials. Century's standard equipment included Soft-Ray tinted glass, adjustable steering column, automatic power door locks and air conditioning. New features included redesigned seats for more comfort and durability and an instrument cluster comprised of a full-arc speedometer, back-lit and with brighter warning lights. The Limited sedan featured remote keyless entry, six-way power driver's seat, leather seating and 14-inch wheel covers.

1995 Buick, Regal Limited sedan. (OCW)

1995 Buick, Regal Custom sedan. (OCW)

1995 Buick, Regal Gran Sport coupe. (OCW)

REGAL - SERIES 4W - V-6 - Regal's lineup remained intact from the year previous, but much else was new for 1995. A passenger side airbag was made standard equipment and joined a host of new features in Regal's revised interior. Inside, changes included new seats and door trim, an instrument panel with instrument cluster that sported easier-to-read gauges that were positioned in front of the driver. Cruise control and brake/transmission shift interlock were also added to the Regal's standard equipment list. Outside, new items included a revised grille, new fascias, taillamps and side moldings. Custom models were again powered by the 3.1-liter V-6 while Limited

and Gran Sport models used the 170 horsepower (not Series II) 3800 V-6 (optional on Customs). All Regals employed the 4T60-E electronically controlled four-speed automatic transmission with overdrive. Custom and Limited models also received new 15-inch bolt-on wheel covers.

1995 Buick, LeSabre Custom sedan. (OCW)

1995 Buick, LeSabre Llimited sedan. (OCW)

LESABRE - SERIES 4H - V-6 - LeSabre's lineup and makeup were unchanged from the year previous, but its interior received several updates to improve comfort and convenience of the driver and passengers. Among these updates were new climate control systems, larger controls that were backlit for easier night use, a more efficient air conditioning compressor and quieter blower motor. New optional equipment includes steering wheel controls for sound system and temperature control and an interactive traction control system that uses the anti-lock brakes and powertrain control computer to reduce wheelspin under slippery conditions. Again, LeSabre was powered by the 170 horsepower (not Series II) 3800 V-6 paired with the electronically controlled four-speed automatic transmission with overdrive.

1995 Buick, Roadmaster Limited sedan. (OCW)

1995 Buick, Roadmaster Limited Estate Wagon station wagon. (OCW)

ROADMASTER - SERIES 4B - V-8 - The Roadmaster lineup for 1995 included two sedans and two Estate Wagon station wagons in base and Limited trim levels. The new, upscale Limited wagon offering included automatic climate control, automatic programmable door locks, automatic power antenna, remote keyless entry and dual six-way power seats. The full-

frame, rear-wheel drive Roadmaster models continued using the 5.7-liter V-8 and electronically controlled four-speed automatic transmission with overdrive. New standard features included larger, fold-away exterior mirrors and, on wagons, a "vista" shade for the vista window in the roof and a security cover for the cargo area. Limited models received new seats that included electro-mechanical lumbar support for front seat occupants. Dual heated front seats with driver's seat memory were optional on Limited models.

1995 Buick, Park Avenue Ultra sedan. (OCW)

1995 Buick, Park Avenue sedan. (OCW)

PARK AVENUE - SERIES 4C - V-6 - The Park Avenue sedan received the new Series II 3800 V-6 as its standard powerplant, while the upscale Ultra sedan continued to use the supercharged 3800 V-6. The electronically controlled four-speed automatic transmission with overdrive was used with both engines. The Series II 3.8-liter V-6 was an all-new design. Its cast iron block had a lower deck height, which reduced the size and weight of the engine. Cross-bolted main caps stiffened the bottom end, reducing noise and improving durability. New cylinder heads with symmetrical combustion chambers provided a smoother idle and lower exhaust emissions. Larger valves and more efficient ports improved flow. Park Avenue's new exterior features included revised fascias, grille, side moldings and bumper guards. New optional items included an electrochromic rearview mirror—which included a compass—that automatically dimmed to reduce glare and interactive traction control to reduce wheel spin on slippery surfaces.

1995 Buick, Riviera coupe. (OCW)

RIVIERA - SERIES 4G - V-6 - Buick promoted its all-new Riviera as a "world-class personal luxury coupe." Launched in early 1994, the 1995 Riviera employed the Series II 3.8-liter V-6 as its standard engine while offering the supercharged 3.8-liter version as its optional power source. The 4T60-E electronically controlled four-speed automatic transmission was used with both engines. Riviera featured an all-new four-wheel independent suspension, with MacPherson struts in front and semi-trailing arms in back. Four-wheel anti-lock disc brakes were standard equipment. Interactive traction control was optional. Riviera's handling was enhanced by a new variable-effort steering gear that combined hydraulic, electronic and magnetic control to provide steering assist. The luxury coupe was also the first car to be equipped with Buick's new generation of orthopedically designed seats. Leather seating, a heated driver's seat and power lumbar control for the driver were optional. Standard equipment included power windows, automatic power door locks with a keyless remote, advanced Pass-Key II theft deterrent system, and dual automatic ComforTemp climate control.

I.D. DATA: The 1995 Buick Vehicle Identification Number (VIN) contains 17 characters. The first is the producing country: "1"—United States. The second character is "G" for General Motors. The third is "4" for Buick Division. The fourth and fifth characters identify the car line/series: "A/G"—Century Special & Wagon; "A/H"—Century Custom; "B/N"—Roadmaster; "B/R"—Roadmaster Estate Wagon; "B/T"—Roadmaster Limited; "C/U"—Park Avenue Ultra; "C/W"—Park Avenue; "G/D"—Riviera; "H/P"—LeSabre Custom; "H/R"—LeSabre Limited; "N/V"—Skylark Custom/Limited/GS; "W/B"—Regal Custom cpe/GS cpe; "W/D"—Regal Limited; and "W/F"—Regal GS sed. The sixth digit represents body style: "1"—coupe; "2"—two-door; "3"—convertible; "4"—2-dr station wagon; "5"—4-dr sedan; "6"—four-door and "8"—4-dr station wagon. The seventh character represents the restraint code: "1"—active (manual) belts; "2"—active (manual) belts w/dual airbags; "3"—active (manual) belts w/driver's side airbag; "4"—passive (automatic) belts; and "5"—passive (automatic) belts w/driver's side airbag; "6"—passive (automatic) belts w/dual airbags. The eighth digit is the engine code: "D"—LD2 2.3L L4; "K"—L36 3.8L V-6; "L"—L27 3.8L V-6; "M"—L82 3.1L V-6; "P"—LT1 5.7L V-8; "1"—L67 3.8L V-6; and "4"—LN2 2.2L L4. The ninth character is a check digit that verifies the accuracy of the VIN. The tenth character identifies the model year ("S" = 1995). The eleventh digit identifies the assembly plant. Characters twelve through seventeen are the production sequence number.

Skylark Custom (Four/V-6)

Model No.	Body/Style No.	Body Type & Seating	Factory Price	Shipping Weight	Prod. Total
V37	NV1	2-dr. Cpe.-5P	13700/14050	2888/2907	Note 1
V69	NV5	4-dr. Sed.-5P	13700/14050	2941/2960	Note 2

Skylark Limited (Four/V-6)

V37	NV5	2-dr. Cpe.-5P	14700/15050	2888/2907	Note 1
V69	NV5	4-dr. Sed.-5P	14700/15050	2941/2960	Note 2

Skylark Gran Sport (V-6)

V37	NV1	2-dr. Cpe.-5P	16400	3005	Note 1
V69	NV5	4-dr. Sed.-5P	16400	3058	Note 2

Note 1: Skylark coupe production totaled 9,725 with no further breakout available.

Note 2: Skylark sedan production totaled 43,707 with no further breakout available.

Century Special (Four/V-6)

G69	AG5	4-dr. Sed.-6P	15160/16160	2986/3004	Note 1
G35	AG8	4-dr. Sta. Wag.-6P	16160/17160	3130/3168	7,498

Century Custom (V-6)

H69	AH5	4-dr. Sed.-6P	17965	2993	Note 1

Century Limited (V-6)

G69	AG5	4-dr. Sed.-6P	18070	N/A	Note 1

Note 1: Century sedan production totaled 102,773 with no further breakout available.

Regal Custom (V-6)

B57	WB1	2-dr. Cpe.-6P	17960	3261	Note 1
B19	WB5	4-dr. Sed.-6P	18660	3335	Note 2

Regal Limited (V-6)

Model No.	Body/Style No.	Body Type & Seating	Factory Price	Shipping Weight	Prod. Total
D19	WD5	4-dr. Sed.-6P	21235	3463	Note 2

Regal Gran Sport (V-6)

Model No.	Body/Style No.	Body Type & Seating	Factory Price	Shipping Weight	Prod. Total
F57	WF1	2-dr. Cpe.-6P	19460	3328	Note 1
F19	WF5	4-dr. Sed.-6P	21870	3406	Note 2

Note 1: Regal coupe production totaled 18,106 with no further breakout available.

Note 2: Regal sedan production totaled 71,557 with no further breakout available.

LeSabre Custom (V-6)

Model No.	Body/Style No.	Body Type & Seating	Factory Price	Shipping Weight	Prod. Total
P69	HP5	4-dr. Sed.-6P	20410	3442	Note 1

LeSabre Limited (V-6)

Model No.	Body/Style No.	Body Type & Seating	Factory Price	Shipping Weight	Prod. Total
R69	HR5	4-dr. Sed.-6P	24110	3442	Note 1

Note 1: LeSabre sedan production totaled 163,524 with no further breakout available.

Roadmaster (V-8)

Model No.	Body/Style No.	Body Type & Seating	Factory Price	Shipping Weight	Prod. Total
N69	BN5	4-dr. Sed.-6P	24210	4211	Note 1

Roadmaster Limited (V-8)

Model No.	Body/Style No.	Body Type & Seating	Factory Price	Shipping Weight	Prod. Total
T69	BT5	4-dr. Sed-6P	27555	4244	Note 1

Roadmaster Estate Wagon (V-8)

Model No.	Body/Style No.	Body Type & Seating	Factory Price	Shipping Weight	Prod. Total
R35	BR8	4-dr. Sta. Wag.-8P	27070	4563	Note 2

Roadmaster Estate Wagon Limited (V-8)

Model No.	Body/Style No.	Body Type & Seating	Factory Price	Shipping Weight	Prod. Total
Z27	BR8	4-dr. Sta. Wag.-8P	29465	N/A	Note 2

Note 1: Roadmaster sedan production totaled 22,942 with no further breakout available.

Note 2: Roadmaster station wagon production totaled 5,522 with no further breakout available.

Park Avenue (V-6)

Model No.	Body/Style No.	Body Type & Seating	Factory Price	Shipping Weight	Prod. Total
W69	CW5	4-dr. Sed.-6P	26360	3532	Note 1

Park Avenue Ultra (V-6)

Model No.	Body/Style No.	Body Type & Seating	Factory Price	Shipping Weight	Prod. Total
U69	CU5	4-dr. Sed.-6P	33084	3642	Note 1

Note 1: Park Avenue sedan production totaled 62,994 with no further breakout available.

Riviera (V-6)

Model No.	Body/Style No.	Body Type & Seating	Factory Price	Shipping Weight	Prod. Total
D07	GD2	2-dr. Cpe.-6P	27632	3748	41,422

ENGINES: BASE FOUR (Century Special) Inline, overhead valve, four-cylinder. Cast iron block and aluminum head. Displacement: 133 cu. in. (2.2 liters). Bore & stroke: 3.50 in. x 3.46 in. Compression ratio: 9.0:1. Brake horsepower: 120 @ 5200 rpm. Torque: 130 lb.-ft. @ 4000 rpm. Multi-port fuel injection. BASE FOUR (Skylark Custom & Limited) Inline, dual overhead cam, four-cylinder. Cast iron block and aluminum head. Displacement: 138 cu. in. (2.3 liters). Bore & stroke: 3.63 in. x 3.35 in. Compression ratio: 9.5:1. Brake horsepower: 150 @ 6000 rpm. Torque: 145 lb.-ft. @ 4800 rpm. Multi-port fuel injection. BASE V-6 (Skylark GS, Century Custom & Limited, Regal Custom); OPTIONAL V-6 (Skylark Custom & Limited, Century Special) 60-degree overhead valve V-6. Cast iron block and aluminum head. Displacement: 191 cu. in. (3.1 liters). Bore & stroke: 3.50 in. x 3.31 in. Compression ratio: 9.6:1. Brake horsepower: 160 @ 5200 rpm (except Skylark - 155 @ 5200 rpm). Torque: 185 lb.-ft. @ 4000 rpm. Sequential Tuned Port fuel injection. BASE V-6 (Regal Limited & GS, LeSabre); OPTIONAL V-6 (Regal Custom) 90-degree overhead valve V-6 with balance shaft. Cast iron block and heads. Displacement: 231 cu. in. (3.8 liters). Bore & stroke: 3.80 in. x 3.40 in. Compression ratio: 9.0:1. Brake horsepower: 170 @ 4800 rpm. Torque: 225 lb.-ft. @ 3200 rpm. Sequential Tuned Port fuel injection. BASE V-6 (Park Avenue, Riviera) Series II 90-degree overhead valve V-6 with balance shaft. Cast iron block and heads. Displacement: 231 cu. in. (3.8 liters). Bore & stroke: 3.80 in. x 3.40 in. Compression ratio: 9.4:1. Brake horsepower: 205 @ 5200 rpm. Torque: 230 lb.-ft. @ 4000 rpm. Sequential Tuned Port fuel injection. BASE V-6 (Park Avenue Ultra); OPTIONAL V-6 (Riviera) supercharged 90-degree overhead valve V-6 with balance shaft. Cast iron block and heads. Displacement: 231 cu. in. (3.8 liters). Bore & stroke: 3.80 in. x 3.40 in. Compression ratio: 8.5:1. Brake horsepower: 225 @ 5000 rpm. Torque: 275 lb.-ft. @ 3200 rpm. Sequential Tuned Port fuel injection. BASE V-8 (Roadmaster) 90-degree overhead valve V-8. Cast iron block and aluminum heads. Displacement: 350 cu. in. (5.7 liters). Bore & stroke: 4.00 in. x 3.48 in. Compression ratio: 10.5:1. Brake horsepower: 260 @ 5000 rpm. Torque: 335 lb.-ft. @ 3200 rpm. Sequential Tuned Port fuel injection.

CHASSIS DATA: Wheelbase: (Skylark) 103.4 in.; (Century) 104.9 in.; (Regal) 107.5 in.; (LeSabre) 110.8 in.; (Roadmaster) 115.9 in.; (Park Avenue) 110.8 in.; (Riviera) 113.8 in. Overall length: (Skylark) 189.2 in.; (Century) 189.1 in.; (Century wagon) 190.9 in.; (Regal coupe) 193.9 in.; (Regal sedan) 193.7 in.; (LeSabre) 200.0 in.; (Roadmaster sedan) 215.8 in.; (Roadmaster Estate Wagon) 217.5 in.; (Park Avenue) 205.9 in.; (Riviera) 207.2 in. Height: (Skylark) 53.5 in.; (Century) 54.2 in.; (Regal coupe) 53.3 in.; (Regal sedan) 54.5 in.; (LeSabre) 55.7 in.; (Roadmaster) 55.9 in.; (Roadmaster Estate Wagon) 60.3 in.; (Park Avenue) 55.1 in.; (Riviera) 55.2 in. Width: (Skylark) 68.7 in.; (Century) 69.4 in.; (Regal) 72.5 in.; (LeSabre) 74.9 in.; (Roadmaster) 78.1 in.; (Roadmaster Estate Wagon) 79.9 in.; (Park Avenue) 74.1 in.; (Riviera) 75.0 in. Front Tread: (Skylark) 55.8 in.; (Century) 58.7 in.; (Regal) 59.5 in.; (LeSabre) 60.4 in.; (Roadmaster) 61.7 in.; (Roadmaster Estate Wagon) 62.1 in.; (Park Avenue) 60.4 in.; (Riviera) 62.5 in. Rear Tread: (Skylark) 55.3 in.; (Century) 56.7 in.; (Regal) 58.0 in.; (LeSabre) 60.4 in.; (Roadmaster) 60.7 in.; (Roadmaster Estate Wagon) 64.1 in.; (Park Avenue) 60.6 in.; (Riviera) 62.6 in. Standard Tires: (Skylark) P195/70R14; (Skylark GS) P205/55R16; (Century Special) P185/75R14; (Century Custom) P195/75R14; (Regal) P205/70R15; (Regal GS) P225/60R16; (LeSabre) P205/70R15; (Roadmaster) P235/70R15; (Roadmaster Estate Wagon) P225/75R15; (Park Avenue) P205/70R15; (Park Avenue Ultra) P215/70R15; (Riviera) P225/60R16.

TECHNICAL: Transmission: (Skylark, Century) Three-speed automatic; (Regal, LeSabre, Roadmaster, Park Avenue, Riviera) Electronically controlled four-speed automatic w/overdrive. Steering: (Skylark, Century, Regal, LeSabre, Park Avenue, Riviera) Rack and pinion; (Roadmaster) Integral. Front Suspension: (Skylark) MacPherson struts w/coil springs, hydraulic shock absorbers, stabilizer bar; (Century, Regal, LeSabre) MacPherson struts w/coil springs, deflected disc shock absorbers, stabilizer bar; (Roadmaster) Independent short/long arm w/coil springs, tube-gas charged shock absorbers, stabilizer bar; (Park Avenue) MacPherson struts w/coil springs, double acting hydraulic shock absorbers, stabilizer bar. (Riviera) MacPherson struts, twin tube shock absorbers, stabilizer bar. Rear Suspension: (Skylark) Trailing twist axle w/tubular control arm, double acting hydraulic shock absorbers, stabilizer bar; (Century) Trailing arm twist axle w/track bar, direct shock absorbers, stabilizer bar; (Regal) Tri-link independent w/transverse leaf spring, tubular deflected disc shock absorbers; (LeSabre) Chapman struts w/variable rate coil springs, deflected disc shock absorbers, stabilizer bar; (Roadmaster) Salisbury four link w/coil springs, tube gas-charged shock absorbers; (Park Avenue) Chapman struts, electronic level control w/air shock absorbers; (Riviera) Semi-trailing arm, electronic level control shock absorbers. Brakes: (Skylark, Century, LeSabre, Roadmaster, Park Avenue) Power front disc, rear drum w/anti-lock; (Regal, Riviera) Power four-wheel disc w/anti-lock. Body Construction: (Skylark, Century, Regal, Park Avenue, Riviera) Integral body/frame; (LeSabre) Integral body/frame w/isolated engine cradle; (Roadmaster) Welded body with full perimeter frame. Fuel Tank: (Skylark) 15.2 gal.; (Century) 16.5 gal.; (Regal) 17.1 gal.; (LeSabre) 18.0 gal.; (Roadmaster) 23.0 gal.; (Roadmaster Estate Wagon) 21.0 gal.; (Park Avenue) 18.0 gal.; (Riviera) 20.0 gal.

DRIVETRAIN OPTIONS: Engines: 3.1 liter V-6, (Skylark Custom & Limited) $350; (Century) $610. (Regal Custom) 3.8 liter V-6, $395. (Riviera) Supercharged 3800 V-6, $1,100. Transmission/Differential: electronically controlled four-speed automatic transmission with overdrive (w/V-6 only), (Skylark Custom

& Limited) $200; (Century) $200. FE2 Gran Touring suspension (Skylark Limited) $27. FX3 Adjustable Ride Control Suspension (Park Avenue) $380. G67 Auto Level Control Suspension (Roadmaster) $175. Y56 Gran Touring Suspension Package: (Regal) $745; (LeSabre) $419; (Park Avenue) $224-$399. NW9 Traction Control System (LeSabre Limited) $175; (Park Avenue) $175. V92 Trailer Towing Package: (LeSabre) $150-$325; (Roadmaster) $325; (Park Avenue) $150-$177. V92 Gran Touring/Trailer Towing Package: (Roadmaster) $225-$375. (Roadmaster) Limited slip differential $100.

SKYLARK CONVENIENCE/APPEARANCE OPTIONS: (Skylark Custom cpe/sed) Prestige pkg. $1,255/$1,255. Eng. block heater $18. Pwr windows: cpe $275; sed $340. Four-way adjust. driver's seat $35. ETR AM/FM radio w/CD player $256. ETR AM/FM radio w/Cassette player $165. Rear window grid antenna $22. Remote Keyless Entry $135. Lower accent paint $195. Cruise control $225. Astroroof $595. Front storage armrest $108. Custom headliner $24. Deluxe headliner $135. Analog instrument cluster $126. P195/75R14 tires (Custom) $72. P195/65R15 tires $131. Six-way pwr driver's seat $270-$305. Leather/cloth trim $345-$471. Bucket seats w/console $160. 15-inch styled whl covers $28. 16-inch alum whls (Limited) $575. 14-inch styled polycast whls (Custom) $115.

1995 Buick, Century Special station wagon with optional woodgrain appliqué and roof rack. (OCW)

CENTURY CONVENIENCE/APPEARANCE OPTIONS: (Special sed/wag) Premium pkg. $598/$638; Luxury pkg. $1,068/$1,126; Prestige pkg. $1,701/$1,525. (Custom sed) Luxury pkg. $748; Prestige pkg. $1,258. Century Special 4-cyl. Marketing Edition: sed $996; wag $1,375. Century Special 6-cyl. Marketing Edition: sed $1,946; wag $2,325. Limited Leather Marketing Pkg. $3,234. Remote keyless entry $135. Trunk convenience net $30. Carpet savers: frt $25; rear $20. H.D. cooling (V-6 only) $40. Deck lid luggage rack $115. Door edge moldings $25. Deluxe o/s mirrors $78. Eng. block heater $18. Cruise control (Custom sed) $225. ETR AM/FM radio w/Cassette player $140. ETR AM/FM radio w/CD player $276-$416. Pwr antenna $85. Six-way pwr driver's seat $305. Bodyside stripes (Special) $45. P185/75R14 tires $68. P195/75R14 $40-$108. Leather 55/45 seat w/armrest (Custom) $500. Remote trunk release $60. Locking wire whl covers $240. 14-inch styled steel whls $115. 14-inch alum whls $295. 14-inch chrome whls $35. Rear window wiper (wag only) $85. Woodgrain appliqué (wag only) $380.

1995 Buick, Regal Gran Sport sedan. (OCW)

REGAL CONVENIENCE/APPEARANCE OPTIONS: (Custom cpe/sed) Luxury pkg. $403/$403; Prestige pkg. $928/$928. (Limited sed) Luxury pkg. $473; Prestige pkg. $1,150. (Gran Sport cpe/sed) Luxury pkg. $473/$473; Prestige pkg. $1,150/$1,150. Custom Marketing Edition: cpe $928; sed

$1,323. GS Coupe Marketing Edition $928. 1SK Gran Sport pkg. $2,288. Carpet savers: frt $25; rear $20. H.D. cooling $150. Door edge guards $25. Engine block heater $18. Remote keyless entry (Limited, GS) $135. Decklid luggage rack $115. Lighted visor vanity mirror (Custom) $92. Dual six-way pwr seat (Limited, GS) $305. Six-way pwr driver's seat: (Custom) $305; (Limited, GS) $270. ETR AM/FM radio w/Cassette player $125-$195. ETR AM/FM radio w/CD player $100-$125. Steering whl mounted radio controls (Custom) $125. Pwr antenna (Custom) $85. Astroroof $695. P205/70R15 tires (Custom cpe) $76. Leather split bench seats (Limited) $550. Leather bucket seats w/console (Limited, GS) $550. 15-inch alum whls (Custom cpe) $325. 16-inch chrome whls (GS) $650.

LESABRE CONVENIENCE/APPEARANCE OPTIONS: (Custom sed) Luxury pkg. $1,161; Prestige pkg. $1,977. (Limited sed) Prestige pkg. $725. LeSabre Custom Marketing Package $1,824. LeSabre Limited Marketing Package $1,438. Leather trim (Custom) $995. Analog instrumentation $163. Elect. o/s rearview mirrors (Custom) $78. Pwr six-way driver's seat $305. Pwr six-way passenger seat $305. Remote trunk release $60. Remote keyless entry $135. ETR AM/FM radio w/cass $100-$250. ETR AM/FM radio w/CD player $100-$350. Pwr antenna $85. Leather split bench seats w/armrest (Limited) $550. P205/70R15 tires (Custom) $76. P205/70R15 self-sealing tires $150-$226. 15-inch alum whls (Custom) $325.

ROADMASTER CONVENIENCE/APPEARANCE OPTIONS: (Roadmaster) Luxury pkg. $768; Prestige pkg. $1,475. (Limited) Prestige pkg. $690. (Estate Wagon) Luxury pkg. $1,258; Prestige pkg. $1,935. Roadmaster Sedan Marketing Edition $1,773. Z27 Limited Estate Wagon pkg. $2,395. Programmable door locks $25. H.D. cooling: (Limited) $200; (Estate Wagon) $150. Lower accent paint (sed only) $150. ETR AM/FM radio w/CD & cassette player $200-$250. Remote keyless entry $135. Pwr six-way passenger seat $305. Memory driver's seat $290. Leather split bench seats $775 (exc. Limited Estate Wagon $685). Vinyl landau roof (N/A wag) $695. Cell phone prewiring $35. P225/75R15 self-sealing tires (wag only) $150. P235/70R15 self-sealing tires $150. Full-size spare $125. Locking wire whl covers (sed) $240. 15-inch alum whls (stnd on wag) $325.

PARK AVENUE CONVENIENCE/APPEARANCE OPTIONS: (Park Avenue) Luxury pkg. $1,846; Prestige pkg. $2,671. (Ultra) Luxury pkg. $730; Prestige pkg. $1,385. Park Avenue Marketing Edition $1,891. ETR AM/FM radio w/Cassette $150. ETR AM/FM radio w/CD player $100-$350. Astroroof $802-$918. Elect. heated driver & pass. seat $120. Leather split bench seat: (Park Avenue w/armrest) $650; (w/o armrest) $600. P205/70R15 self-sealing tires (Park Avenue) $150. P215/70R15 tires (Ultra) $226.

RIVIERA CONVENIENCE/APPEARANCE OPTIONS: Luxury pkg. $472; Prestige pkg. $992. ETR AM/FM radio w/CD player $244-$434. Leather split bench seat $600. Leather bucket seats w/console $650. Astroroof $995. Memory heated driver's seat $310. Eng. block heater $18.

HISTORY: Buick unveiled its 1997 Park Avenue luxury sedan in December of 1995. It was based on the Riviera's G platform. Buick sales slid totaling 471,819 compared with 546,836 the year previous. Total U.S. market share was 5.5 percent compared with 6.1 in 1994.

1996

1996 will be remembered as the final year of availability of the front-engine, rear-drive configuration as Buick discontinued its Roadmaster series at the end of the model year. All 1996 Road-

masters carried "Collector's Edition" hood ornaments to commemorate the occasion. Also, to commemorate the 100th birthday of the modern Olympic Games, Buick offered special Olympic Gold editions of the Skylark and Regal. The Olympic Gold Skylark featured gold USA/five-ring badging on fenders, gold accent trim, gold Skylark nameplates and gold accented wheel covers. The Olympic Gold Regal featured similar gold badging, trim and nameplate treatment as well as gold 15-inch aluminum wheels and bucket seats with the USA/five-ring design on the front headrests. All 1996 Buicks were delivered with long-life (five years/100,000 miles) engine coolant, platinum-tipped spark plugs (100,000 miles of service) and lifetime transmission fluid.

1996 Buick, Skylark Gran Sport sedan. (OCW)

1996 Buick, Skylark Custom sedan. (OCW)

1996 Buick, Skylark Gran Sport coupe. (OCW)

1996 Buick, Skylark Limited coupe. (OCW)

SKYLARK - SERIES 4N - FOUR/V-6 - The Skylark was restyled for 1996 receiving new fascia, grille, hood, parking lamps, headlamps and taillamps as well as revised bodyside moldings. The interior was also redesigned with dual airbags now standard. The instrument panel was all-new as were seats and door and trim panels. The previously standard 2.3-liter four-cylinder engine was discontinued, and replaced by a 2.4-liter Twin Cam four. The three-speed automatic transmission that was the previous standard unit was also dropped and replaced by the electronically controlled four-speed automatic with overdrive, which was now standard on all Skylarks. The Twin Cam engine featured a balance shaft system, mounted in the oil pan, that provided smoother idle. A new composite intake manifold was lighter than the previous aluminum unit and also improved noise control. Skylark again was offered in three trim levels: Custom, Limited and Gran Sport. GS models continued to use the 3100 V-6 as standard powerplant, which was again the option engine for Custom and Limited models. New standard equipment included OBD II on-board diagnostic system, an enhanced traction system, Passlock theft-deterrent system, Convenience Plus electrical features (including battery run-down protection and theater lighting), a single-key door locking system, air conditioning, tilt steering wheel, rear window defogger, carpet savers, delay windshield wipers and visor vanity mirrors.

1996 Buick, Century Custom sedan. (OCW)

1996 Buick, Century Special sedan. (OCW)

1996 Buick, Century Special station wagon with optional woodgrain appliqué and roof rack. (OCW)

CENTURY - SERIES 4A - FOUR/V-6 - The Century lineup carried over from the previous year with the Special station wagon and a sedan offered in three trim levels: Special, Custom and Limited. The 2.2-liter four-cylinder engine mated to a three-

speed automatic transmission continued as the standard powertrain for the Special sedan. An improved 3100 V-6 paired with the electronically controlled four-speed automatic with overdrive powered the remainder of the Century offerings. New standard features included Convenience Plus electrical features, power windows, stainless steel exhaust system, OBD II on-board diagnostics system and a rear window defogger. The Century's anti-lock brake control unit was also revised to make the ABS more durable and easier to service.

1996 Buick, Regal Custom coupe. (OCW)

1996 Buick, Regal Limited sedan. (OCW)

1996 Buick, Regal Gran Sport sedan. (OCW)

REGAL - SERIES 4W - V-6 - Changes to the 1996 Regal occurred mainly under the hood, as the lineup remained intact with the series comprised of a Custom coupe and sedan, Limited sedan and Gran Sport coupe and sedan. The Custom models received an updated 3100 V-6 as standard power source. The revised 3.1-liter engine, remaining rated at 160 horsepower, featured a low-friction valvetrain and improved engine management system. Newly standard on the Limited sedan and GS models (and optional on Custom models) was the Series II 3800 V-6. All Regals used the electronically controlled four-speed automatic transmission with overdrive. New features of the Regal included a low-torque-axis engine mount system that reduced noise and vibration at idle and a quieter starter motor. Also new were the OBD II on-board diagnostic system, Dual ComforTemp climate control and Convenience Plus electrical features. A new option for GS models were chrome 16-inch aluminum wheels.

1996 Buick, LeSabre Custom sedan. (OCW)

1996 Buick, LeSabre Limited sedan. (OCW)

LESABRE - SERIES 4H - V-6 - Both sedans comprising the LeSabre series, Custom and Limited, received the Series II 3800 V-6 as their standard engine in 1996. Both also again used the electronically controlled four-speed automatic transmission with overdrive. New standard features on the Custom sedan included vanity visor mirrors for driver and passenger, electric rear window defogger, front seat storage armrest and rear window antenna. For the Limited sedan, new standard equipment included automatic day/night inside rearview mirror, Twilight Sentinel (automatically turned headlamps on at dusk and off at dawn), rear window antenna, dual automatic ComforTemp climate control as well as rear seat ComforTemp. Also new to the Limited and optional for the Custom was the Personal Choice group of features whereby two different drivers could activate door locks and lighting set to their individual preferences with a touch of the remote keyless entry fob. OBD II on-board diagnostics and Convenience Plus electrical features were standard on all LeSabres, the latter including warning chimes for headlights left on or keys left in the ignition. LeSabre's optional Gran Touring suspension package featured a new magnetic variable-effort steering system.

1996 Buick, Roadmaster Limited Estate Wagon station wagon. (OCW)

ROADMASTER - SERIES 4B - V-8 - In its final year of production, all Roadmaster models came with a Collector's Edition designation in their stand-up hood ornaments. The lineup again consisted of base and Limited sedans and base and Limited station wagons. New standard items included the OBD II on-board diagnostics, clamshell-style armrest with storage for the 55/45 split-bench

front seat and Convenience Plus electrical features. All Roadmasters again used the LT1 5.7-liter V-8 mated to the 4T60-E electronically controlled four-speed automatic transmission with overdrive. When Roadmaster production ended, the GM plant in Arlington, Texas, where the full-size, rear-drive cars were assembled was converted to truck production.

1996 Buick, Park Avenue sedan. (OCW)

PARK AVENUE - SERIES 4C - V-6 - The potent, supercharged 3800 Series II V-6 powering the Park Avenue Ultra sedan was revised for 1996 and got a horsepower boost from its previous 225 to 240. The Park Avenue sedan continued using the normally aspirated version of the Series II 3800 V-6. Both Park Avenue sedans used the electronically controlled four-speed automatic transmission with overdrive. New standard features included OBD II on-board diagnostics, Convenience Plus electrical features, automatic power antenna (already standard on Ultra) and driver's visor vanity mirror (already standard on Ultra). The Ultra added magnetic variable-effort power steering (optional on Park Avenue) as well as Personal Choice features, such as memory door locks and perimeter lighting, activated by remote keyless entry for up to two drivers.

1996 Buick, Riviera coupe. (OCW)

RIVIERA - SERIES 4G - V-6 - One year after its re-launch as an all-new luxury coupe, the Riviera returned basically intact, fitted with the changes Buick offered for all its models in 1996. These new items included Personal Choice features activated via remote keyless entry and including battery run-down protection, theater dimming interior lights and memory mirrors (automatically adjusted); Convenience Plus electrical features and OBD II on-board diagnostics. Standard powertrain remained the Series II 3800 V-6 paired with the electronically controlled four-speed automatic transmission with overdrive. Optional was the revised supercharged Series II 3800 V-6, now rated at 240 horsepower (up from its previous 225). Riviera's instrument panel and console were also updated with real wood accents. New optional equipment included chrome-plated 16-inch aluminum wheels.

I.D. DATA: The 1996 Buick Vehicle Identification Number (VIN) contains 17 characters. The first is the producing country: "1"— United States. The second character is "G" for General Motors. The third is "4" for Buick Division. The fourth and fifth characters identify the car line/series: "A/G"—Century Special & Wagon; "A/H"—Century Custom; "B/N"—Roadmaster; "B/R"—Roadmaster Estate Wagon; "B/T"—Roadmaster Limited; "C/U"— Park Avenue Ultra; "C/W"—Park Avenue; "G/D"—Riviera;

"H/P"—LeSabre Custom; "H/R"—LeSabre Limited; "N/J"—Skylark; "W/B"—Regal Custom; "W/D"—Regal Limited; and "W/F"—Regal GS. The sixth digit represents body style: "1"— coupe; "2"—two-door; "3"—convertible; "4"—2-dr station wagon; "5"—4-dr sedan; "6"—four-door and "8"—4-dr station wagon. The seventh character represents the restraint code: "1"— active (manual) belts; "2"—active (manual) belts w/dual airbags; "3"—active (manual) belts w/driver's side airbag; "4"—passive (automatic) belts; "5"—passive (automatic) belts w/driver's side airbag; "6"—passive (automatic) belts w/dual airbags; and "7"— active (manual) belt driver and passive (automatic) belt passenger w/dual airbags. The eighth digit is the engine code: "K"— L36 3.8L V-6; "M"—L82 3.1L V-6; "P"—LT1 5.7L V-8; "T"—LD9 2.4L L4; "1"—L67 3.8L V-6; and "4"—LN2 2.2L L4. The ninth character is a check digit that verifies the accuracy of the VIN. The tenth character identifies the model year ("T" = 1996). The eleventh digit identifies the assembly plant. Characters twelve through seventeen are the production sequence number.

Skylark Custom (Four/V-6)

Model No.	Body/Style No.	Body Type & Seating	Factory Price	Shipping Weight	Prod. Total
J37	NJ1	2-dr. Cpe.-5P	15495/15890	2917/N/A	Note 1
J69	NJ5	4-dr. Sed.-5P	15495/15890	2948/N/A	Note 2

Skylark Limited (Four/V-6)

| J37 | NJ5 | 2-dr. Cpe.-5P | 16518/16913 | 2917/N/A | Note 1 |
| J69 | NJ5 | 4-dr. Sed.-5P | 16518/16913 | 2948/N/A | Note 2 |

Skylark Gran Sport (V-6)

| J37 | NJ1 | 2-dr. Cpe.-5P | 17701 | N/A | Note 1 |
| J69 | NJ5 | 4-dr. Sed.-5P | 17701 | N/A | Note 2 |

Note 1: Skylark coupe production totaled 6,783 with no further breakout available.

Note 2: Skylark sedan production totaled 35,089 with no further breakout available.

Century Special (Four/V-6)

| G69 | AG5 | 4-dr. Sed.-6P | 16720/17330 | 2951/N/A | Note 1 |
| G35 | AG8 | 4-dr. Sta. Wag.-6P | -----/18135 | ----/3118 | 6,843 |

Century Custom (V-6)

| G69 | AG5 | 4-dr. Sed.-6P | 18383 | N/A | Note 1 |

Century Limited (V-6)

| G69 | AG5 | 4-dr. Sed.-6P | 19406 | N/A | Note 1 |

Note 1: Century sedan production totaled 85,625 with no further breakout available.

Regal Custom (V-6)

| B57 | WB1 | 2-dr. Cpe.-6P | 19445 | 3232 | Note 1 |
| B19 | WB5 | 4-dr. Sed.-6P | 19740 | 3331 | Note 2 |

Regal Limited (V-6)

| D19 | WD5 | 4-dr. Sed.-6P | 21195 | N/A | Note 2 |

Regal Gran Sport (V-6)

| F57 | WF1 | 2-dr. Cpe.-6P | 21340 | N/A | Note 1 |
| F19 | WF5 | 4-dr. Sed.-6P | 21800 | N/A | Note 2 |

Note 1: Regal coupe production totaled 5,991 with no further breakout available.

Note 2: Regal sedan production totaled 107,056 with no further breakout available.

LeSabre Custom (V-6)

| P69 | HP5 | 4-dr. Sed.-6P | 21380 | 3430 | Note 1 |

LeSabre Limited (V-6)

| R69 | HR5 | 4-dr. Sed.-6P | 25385 | 3430 | Note 1 |

Note 1: LeSabre sedan production totaled 52,061 with no further breakout available.

Roadmaster (V-8)

| N69 | BN5 | 4-dr. Sed.-6P | 25560 | 4211 | Note 1 |

Roadmaster Limited (V-8)

| T69 | BT5 | 4-dr. Sed-6P | 27490 | 4244 | Note 1 |

Roadmaster Estate Wagon (V-8)

| R35 | BR8 | 4-dr. Sta. Wag.-8P | 27575 | 4563 | Note 2 |

Roadmaster Estate Wagon Limited (V-8)

| Z27 | BR8 | 4-dr. Sta. Wag.-8P | 29445 | N/A | Note 2 |

Note 1: Roadmaster sedan production totaled 12,581 with no further breakout available.

Note 2: Roadmaster station wagon production totaled 8,962 with no further breakout available.

Park Avenue (V-6)

Model No.	Body/Style No.	Body Type & Seating	Factory Price	Shipping Weight	Prod. Total
W69	CW5	4-dr. Sed.-6P	28205	3536	Note 1

Park Avenue Ultra (V-6)

Model No.	Body/Style No.	Body Type & Seating	Factory Price	Shipping Weight	Prod. Total
U69	CU5	4-dr. Sed.-6P	32820	3629	Note 1

Note 1: Park Avenue sedan production totaled 46,953 with no further breakout available.

Riviera (V-6)

Model No.	Body/Style No.	Body Type & Seating	Factory Price	Shipping Weight	Prod. Total
D07	GD2	2-dr. Cpe.-6P	29475	3690	17,389

ENGINES: BASE FOUR (Century Special sed) Inline, overhead valve, four-cylinder. Cast iron block and aluminum head. Displacement: 134 cu. in. (2.2 liters). Bore & stroke: 3.50 in. x 3.46 in. Compression ratio: 9.0:1. Brake horsepower: 120 @ 5200 rpm. Torque: 130 lb.-ft. @ 4000 rpm. Multi-port fuel injection. BASE FOUR (Skylark Custom & Limited) Inline, dual overhead cam, four-cylinder. Cast iron block and aluminum head. Displacement: 146 cu. in. (2.4 liters). Bore & stroke: 3.54 in. x 3.70 in. Compression ratio: 9.5:1. Brake horsepower: 150 @ 6000 rpm. Torque: 150 lb.-ft. @ 4400 rpm. Sequential Port fuel injection. BASE V-6 (Skylark GS, Century Special wag, Custom & Limited, Regal Custom); OPTIONAL V-6 (Skylark Custom & Limited, Century Special sed) 60-degree overhead valve V-6. Cast iron block and aluminum heads. Displacement: 191 cu. in. (3.1 liters). Bore & stroke: 3.51 in. x 3.31 in. Compression ratio: 9.6:1. Brake horsepower: 160 @ 5200 rpm (except Skylark - 155 @ 5200 rpm). Torque: 185 lb.-ft. @ 4000 rpm. Sequential Port fuel injection. BASE V-6 (Regal Limited & GS, LeSabre, Park Avenue, Riviera); OPTIONAL V-6 (Regal Custom) Series II 90-degree overhead valve V-6 with balance shaft. Cast iron block and heads. Displacement: 231 cu. in. (3.8 liters). Bore & stroke: 3.80 in. x 3.40 in. Compression ratio: 9.4:1. Brake horsepower: 205 @ 5200 rpm. Torque: 230 lb.-ft. @ 4000 rpm. Sequential Port fuel injection. BASE V-6 (Park Avenue Ultra); OPTIONAL V-6 (Riviera) supercharged 90-degree overhead valve V-6 with balance shaft. Cast iron block and heads. Displacement: 231 cu. in. (3.8 liters). Bore & stroke: 3.80 in. x 3.40 in. Compression ratio: 8.5:1. Brake horsepower: 240 @ 5200 rpm. Torque: 280 lb.-ft. @ 3200 rpm. Sequential Port fuel injection. BASE V-8 (Roadmaster) 90-degree overhead valve V-8. Cast iron block and aluminum heads. Displacement: 350 cu. in. (5.7 liters). Bore & stroke: 4.00 in. x 3.48 in. Compression ratio: 10.5:1. Brake horsepower: 260 @ 5000 rpm. Torque: 330 lb.-ft. @ 2400 rpm. Sequential Port fuel injection.

CHASSIS DATA: Wheelbase: (Skylark) 103.4 in.; (Century) 104.9 in.; (Regal) 107.5 in.; (LeSabre) 110.8 in.; (Roadmaster) 115.9 in.; (Park Avenue) 110.8 in.; (Riviera) 113.8 in. Overall length: (Skylark) 189.3 in.; (Century) 189.1 in.; (Century wagon) 190.9 in.; (Regal coupe) 193.9 in.; (Regal sedan) 193.7 in.; (LeSabre) 200.0 in.; (Roadmaster sedan) 215.8 in.; (Roadmaster Estate Wagon) 217.5 in.; (Park Avenue) 205.9 in.; (Riviera) 207.2 in. Height: (Skylark) 53.6 in.; (Century) 54.2 in.; (Regal coupe) 53.3 in.; (Regal sedan) 54.5 in.; (LeSabre) 55.7 in.; (Roadmaster) 55.9 in.; (Roadmaster Estate Wagon) 60.3 in.; (Park Avenue) 55.1 in.; (Riviera) 54.6 in. Width: (Skylark) 67.6 in.; (Century) 69.4 in.; (Regal) 72.5 in.; (LeSabre) 74.9 in.; (Roadmaster) 78.1 in.; (Roadmaster Estate Wagon) 79.9 in.; (Park Avenue) 74.1 in.; (Riviera) 75.0 in. Front Tread: (Skylark) 55.8 in.; (Century) 58.7 in.; (Regal) 59.5 in.; (LeSabre): 60.4 in.; (Roadmaster) 61.7 in.; (Roadmaster Estate Wagon) 62.1 in.; (Park Avenue) 60.4 in.; (Park Avenue Ultra) 60.6 in.; (Riviera) 62.5 in. Rear Tread: (Skylark) 55.3 in.; (Century) 56.7 in.; (Regal) 58.0 in.; (LeSabre) 60.4 in.; (Roadmaster) 60.7 in.; (Roadmaster Estate Wagon) 64.1 in.; (Park Avenue) 60.6 in.; (Park Avenue Ultra) 60.7 in.; (Riviera) 62.6 in. Standard Tires: (Skylark) P195/70R14; (Skylark GS) P205/55R16; (Century Special) P185/75R14; (Century Custom & Limited) P195/75R14; (Regal) P205/70R15; (Regal GS) P225/60R16; (LeSabre) P205/70R15; (Roadmaster) P235/70R15; (Roadmaster Estate Wagon) P225/75R15; (Park Avenue) P205/70R15; (Park Avenue Ultra) P215/70R15; (Riviera) P225/60R16.

TECHNICAL: Transmission: (Century Special sed) Three-speed automatic; (Skylark, Century Special wag, Century Custom, Century Limited, Regal, LeSabre, Roadmaster, Park Avenue, Riviera) Electronically controlled four-speed automatic w/overdrive. Steering: (Skylark, Century, Regal, LeSabre, Park Avenue, Riviera) Rack and pinion; (Roadmaster) Integral. Front Suspension: (Skylark) MacPherson struts w/coil springs, hydraulic shock absorbers, stabilizer bar; (Century, Regal, LeSabre) MacPherson struts w/coil springs, deflected disc shock absorbers, stabilizer bar; (Roadmaster) Independent short/long arm w/coil springs, twin tube-gas charged shock absorbers, stabilizer bar; (Park Avenue) MacPherson struts w/coil springs, double acting hydraulic shock absorbers, stabilizer bar. (Riviera) MacPherson struts, deflective disc strut shock absorbers, stabilizer bar. Rear Suspension: (Skylark) Trailing twist axle w/tubular control arm, double acting hydraulic shock absorbers, stabilizer bar; (Century) Trailing arm twist axle w/track bar, direct shock absorbers, stabilizer bar; (Regal) Tri-link independent w/transverse leaf spring, tubular deflected disc shock absorbers; (LeSabre) Chapman struts w/variable rate coil springs, deflected disc shock absorbers, stabilizer bar; (Roadmaster) Salisbury four link w/coil springs, twin tube gas-charged shock absorbers; (Park Avenue) Chapman struts, electronic level control w/air shock absorbers; (Riviera) Semi-trailing arm, twin tube w/electronic level control shock absorbers. Brakes: (Skylark, Century, LeSabre, Roadmaster, Park Avenue) Power front disc, rear drum w/anti-lock; (Regal, Riviera) Power four-wheel disc w/anti-lock. Body Construction: (Skylark, Century, Regal, Park Avenue, Riviera) Integral body/frame; (LeSabre) Integral body/frame w/isolated engine cradle; (Roadmaster) Welded body with full perimeter frame. Fuel Tank: (Skylark) 15.2 gal.; (Century) 16.5 gal.; (Regal) 17.1 gal.; (LeSabre) 18.0 gal.; (Roadmaster) 23.0 gal.; (Roadmaster Estate Wagon) 21.0 gal.; (Park Avenue) 18.0 gal.; (Riviera) 20.0 gal.

DRIVETRAIN OPTIONS: Engines: 3.1 liter V-6, (Skylark Custom & Limited) $395; (Century Special sed) $610. (Regal Custom) 3.8 liter V-6, $395. (Riviera) Supercharged 3800 V-6, $1,195. Transmission/Differential: electronically controlled four-speed automatic transmission with overdrive (Century Special sed w/V-6) $200. FX3 Adjustable Ride Control Suspension (Park Avenue) $473. G67 Auto Level Control Suspension (LeSabre, Roadmaster) $175. Y56 Gran Touring Suspension Package: (Regal) $745; (LeSabre) $337-$512; (Park Avenue) $261-$317. NW9 Traction Control System (LeSabre) $175; (Park Avenue) $175. V92 Trailer Towing Package: (Roadmaster) $325; (Park Avenue) $177. V92 Gran Touring/Trailer Towing Package: (Roadmaster) $225-$375. (Roadmaster) Limited slip differential $100.

SKYLARK CONVENIENCE/APPEARANCE OPTIONS: Custom pkg. NC. Limited pkg. $1,023. GS pkg. $2,206. Olympic Gold pkg. NC. Premium Gold pkg. $648. Luxury Gold pkg. $1,210. Eng. block heater $18. Pwr windows: cpe $290; sed $355. Four-way adjust. driver's seat $35. Deluxe o/s mirrors $78. ETR AM/FM radio w/CD player $225-$420. ETR AM/FM radio w/Cassette player $195-$220. Rear window grid antenna $22. Remote Keyless Entry $135. Steering whl mounted radio controls $125. Cruise control $225. Astroroof $595. Front storage armrest $108. Deluxe headliner $135. Analog instrument cluster $126. P195/75R14 tires (Custom) $72. P195/65R15 tires (Custom) $131. Six-way pwr driver's seat $270-$305. Leather/cloth trim $495-$620. Bucket seats w/console $160. Bucket seats w/lumbar control and console $175. 15-inch styled whl covers (Custom) $28. 14-inch styled polycast whls (Custom) $115.

CENTURY CONVENIENCE/APPEARANCE OPTIONS: Special pkg. NC. Custom pkg. $1,663. Limited pkg. $2,686. (Special wag) Premium pkg. $253. Remote keyless entry $135. Trunk convenience net $30. Carpet savers: frt $25; rear $20. H.D. cooling (V-6 only) $40. Roof luggage rack (wag only) $115. Cargo area security cover $69. Door edge moldings $25. Deluxe o/s mirrors $78. Eng. block heater $18. Cruise control $225. ETR AM/FM radio w/Cassette player $140. Pwr antenna $85. Six-way pwr driver's seat $305. Bodyside stripes $45. P185/75R14 tires $68. P195/75R14 $40-$108. Locking wire whl covers $205-$240. 14-inch styled steel whls $80-$115. 14-inch alum whls $55-$295. 14-inch chrome whl covers $35. Rear window wiper (wag only) $85. Woodgrain appliqué (wag only) $380. Vinyl third seat $215.

1996 Buick, Regal Gran Sport coupe. (OCW)

REGAL CONVENIENCE/APPEARANCE OPTIONS: (Custom cpe/sed) Luxury pkg. $185/$185; Prestige pkg. $655/$655. (Limited sed) Prestige pkg. $677. Gran Sport pkg. $1,895. Olympic Gold pkg. NC. Premium Gold pkg. $140. Luxury Gold pkg. $610. Trunk convenience net (Custom) $30. Carpet savers: frt $25; rear $20. Engine block heater $18. Remote keyless entry $135. Decklid luggage rack $115. Lighted visor vanity mirrors (Custom) $92. Dual six-way pwr seat (Limited, GS) $305. Six-way pwr driver's seat: (Custom) $305; (Limited, GS) $270. ETR AM/FM radio w/Cassette player $25. ETR AM/FM radio w/CD player $100-$125. ETR AM/FM radio w/Cassette & CD player $200-$225. Steering whl mounted radio controls $125. Pwr antenna (Custom) $85. Astroroof $695. P205/70R15 tires $76. Leather 55/45 seats w/armrest $550. Leather bucket seats w/console (Custom) $550. 15-inch alum whls (Custom) $325. 16-inch chrome whls $650.

LESABRE CONVENIENCE/APPEARANCE OPTIONS: (Custom sed) Luxury pkg. $941; Prestige pkg. $1,918. (Limited sed) Prestige pkg. $609. Leather trim (Custom) $995. Carpet savers: frt $25; rear $20. Memory door locks (Custom) $25. Cruise control (Custom) $225. Eng. block heater $18. Elect. o/s rearview mirrors (Custom) $78. Pwr six-way driver's seat (Custom) $305. Pwr six-way passenger seat (Custom) $305. Remote trunk release $60. Remote keyless entry $135. ETR AM/FM radio w/Cassette $150-$195. ETR AM/FM radio w/CD player $100-$250. ETR AM/FM radio w/Cassette and CD player $200-$350. Leather 55/45 seats w/armrest (Limited) $550. P205/70R15 tires (Custom) $76. P205/70R15 self-sealing tires $150-$226. 15-inch alum whls (Custom) $325. Twilight Sentinel headlamp control $60. Cornering lamps (Limited) $60. Theft deterrent system (Limited) $60.

1996 Buick, Roadmaster Limited sedan. (OCW)

ROADMASTER CONVENIENCE/APPEARANCE OPTIONS: (Roadmaster) Luxury pkg. $703; Prestige pkg. $1,340. (Limited) Prestige pkg. $945. (Estate Wagon) Luxury pkg. $613; Prestige pkg. $1,290. Z27 Limited Estate Wagon pkg. $1,870. Programmable door locks $25. H.D. cooling: (Limited) $200; (Estate Wagon) $150. ETR AM/FM radio w/CD & cassette player $200. Remote keyless entry $135. Pwr six-way passenger seat $305. Memory driver's seat $395. Leather split bench seats $775 (exc. Limited Estate Wagon $685). Vinyl landau roof (N/A wag) $695. P225/75R15 self-sealing tires (wag only) $150. P235/70R15 self-sealing tires $150. Full-size spare $125-$175. 15-inch locking wire whl covers (sed) $240. 15-inch alum whls (stnd on wag) $325.

1996 Buick, Park Avenue Ultra sedan. (OCW)

PARK AVENUE CONVENIENCE/APPEARANCE OPTIONS: (Park Avenue) Luxury pkg. $1,678; Prestige pkg. $2,503. (Ultra) Luxury pkg. $705; Prestige pkg. $1,465. ETR AM/FM radio w/Cassette $150. ETR AM/FM radio w/CD player $100-$350. Eng. block heater $18. Astroroof $802-$918. Lwr accent paint (Ultra) $195. Elect. heated driver & pass. seat $225. Leather 55/45 seats: (Park Avenue w/armrest) $650; (w/o armrest) $600. P205/70R15 self-sealing tires $150-$226. Rear seat ComforTemp $45. Automatic day/night rearview mirror: (Park Avenue) $150; (Ultra) $70.

RIVIERA CONVENIENCE/APPEARANCE OPTIONS: Prestige pkg. $1,150. Bright White Diamond Paint $395. Leather split bench seat $600. Leather bucket seats w/console $750. Astroroof $995. Memory heated driver's seat $310. Eng. block heater $18. Chrome whls $695.

HISTORY: Buick unveiled its 1997 Park Avenue luxury sedan in December of 1995. It was based on the Riviera's G platform. Buick 1996 sales plunged, totaling 427,316 compared with 471,819 the year previous. Total U.S. market share was 5.0 percent compared with 5.5 in 1995.

1997

It was a year of sweeping change at Buick Division of General Motors. The ranks were thinned not only by the discontinuation of the Roadmaster series, but also by the "gutting" of the Century and Regal lineups—now each offering only sedan models. Discontinued in those two series were the Century Special sedan and station wagon and the entire Regal coupe lineup from 1996. Regal, in 1997, was represented by Custom, Limited and Gran Sport sedans carried over from the 1996 model year on an extended run until late fall. At that time, the all-new 1997-1/2/1998 Regal was launched with the series comprised of an LS sedan and a more upscale GS sedan.

1997 Buick, Skylark Limited sedan. (OCW)

1997 Buick, Skylark Gran Sport sedan. (OCW)

1997 Buick, Skylark Gran Sport coupe. (OCW)

SKYLARK - SERIES 4N - FOUR/V-6 - While there would be a sedan produced for sale to fleet operations the following year, this was the final year of availability for the Skylark. A name that Buick originated in 1953, the Skylark's last stand was made with the same lineup offered the year previously. The 2.4-liter Twin Cam four-cylinder engine remained standard for Custom and Limited coupes and sedans, while the Gran Sport coupes and sedans again used the 3100 V-6 for power. The electronically controlled four-speed automatic transmission with overdrive was again used in all Skylarks. New features included improved powertrain isolation via throttle cable revisions and a new transmission mass damper and the deletion of the formerly offered engine oil level sensor. Two new exterior colors, Platinum Blue Pearl and Royal Orchid Pearl, and one new interior color, Pewter Gray (which replaced the previously available red), were offered. New standard equipment included a front storage armrest, four-way manual seat adjuster and, on Gran Sports, a deluxe headliner with passenger assist handles, lighted visor vanity mirrors, extendible sunshades and front/rear courtesy lights.

1997 Buick, Century Custom sedan. (OCW)

1997 Buick, Century Limited sedan. (OCW)

CENTURY - SERIES 4W - V-6 - It was an all-new Century that debuted in December 1996 as the 1997 offering. Now available as either a Custom sedan or Limited sedan, these Century models were longer (4.1 inches than the previous model), lower and wider than the decade-and-a-half-old sedan design they replaced. Gone were the Special sedan and station wagon available previously. Features of the redesigned Century included independent rear suspension and rubber-isolated rear crossmember, "theater-style" rear seating for better view and comfort, and triple door seals to eliminate wind noise. Standard equipment included anti-lock brakes, dual airbags, dynamic side impact protection, air filtration system, child security rear door locks, solar-control windshield, and daytime running lamps. Century's powertrain was comprised of the 160 horsepower 3100 V-6 mated to the electronically controlled four-speed automatic transmission with overdrive. The 2.2-liter four-cylinder engine and three-speed automatic that were standard previously were both discontinued. Optional equipment included steering wheel-mounted radio controls, Astroroof, dual ComforTemp climate control, and dual six-way power seats with metaphoric switches.

1997 Buick, Regal Limited sedan. (OCW)

1997 Buick, Regal Gran Sport sedan. (OCW)

Standard Catalog of Buick 1903-2000

REGAL - SERIES 4W - V-6 - The Regal was no longer offered in a coupe body style, and the Custom, Limited and Gran Sport sedans offered in 1996 were continued unchanged on an extended run until the launch in mid-1997 model year of the all-new 1997-1/2/1998 Regal (see 1998 Regal listing). New features included the availability of a Gold Package on the Custom sedan, which consisted of Jasper Green Pearl finish and specific trim. Also, the Gran Sport sedan received a new 16-inch wheel.

1997 Buick, LeSabre Custom sedan. (OCW)

1997 Buick, LeSabre Limited sedan. (OCW)

LESABRE - SERIES 4H - V-6 - The LeSabre, redesigned the previous year, returned with the same lineup with a "freshened" appearance for 1997. The revised look included a grille surround integrated with the hood and halogen headlamp assemblies that used fixed lenses to provide a tighter fit. Also, the taillamps and rear fascia received a diagonal cut line to provide easier access to the trunk. LeSabre now met the federal government's dynamic side impact safety standard. New standard equipment included daytime running lamps, electronically controlled converter clutch and the passive theft-deterrent system added to the Convenience Plus family of features. LeSabre again was powered by the Series II 3800 V-6 combined with the improved 4T60-E electronically controlled four-speed automatic transmission with overdrive. The 4T60-E received new electronic controls that modulated the energy during shifts for a smoother gear transition. Three new exterior colors were offered: Silvermist Metallic, Bordeaux Red Pearl and Santa Fe Red Pearl, which replaced Platinum Gray, Ruby Red and Dark Cherry.

1997 Buick, Park Avenue Ultra sedan. (OCW)

1997 Buick, Park Avenue sedan. (OCW)

PARK AVENUE - SERIES 4C - V-6 - The all-new 1997 Park Avenue debuted in the fall of 1996, again available in base sedan and Ultra sedan. The most significant change in the new Park Avenue was its use of refined architectural components—primarily body structure and chassis systems—that were previously debuted on the Riviera and its G platform. This refinement included safety-cage construction for improved crashworthiness. The 1997 Park Avenue featured a two-inch longer wheelbase than its predecessor. Gains were also achieved inside with enhanced headroom and hip room. A new innovation was, in the event of an airbag deployment, the Park Avenue's doors would automatically unlock in 15 seconds. The base sedan was again powered by the Series II 3800 V-6, while the Ultra used the supercharged Series II 3800 V-6. Both were matched with the new 4T65-E HD (heavy-duty) electronically controlled four-speed automatic transmission with overdrive. The 4T65-E featured a larger torque converter and more sophisticated electronic control than the 4T60-E unit it replaced. Other refinements of the Park Avenue included a higher-capacity four-wheel disc brake system, magnetic variable-effort power steering, aluminum suspension components, fixed-lens halogen headlamps, larger fold-away outside mirrors, and damage-resistant rear window radio antenna. Features standard on the Ultra and optional on the base sedan included moisture-sensing windshield wipers and a tire pressure monitoring system that alerted the driver to an under-inflated tire problem. Optional was Eye-Cue head-up display that provided speed, high-beam, turn signal and "check gauges" information on the inside surface of the windshield so the driver's eyes would not have to leave the road.

1997 Buick, Riviera coupe. (OCW)

RIVIERA - SERIES 4G - V-6 - The Riviera also gained the new 4T65-E electronically controlled four-speed automatic transmission with overdrive for use with the standard Series II 3800 V-6 or optional supercharged version of the Series II 3800 V-6. New standard equipment included flash-to-pass/Pass-Key II theft-deterrent system/daytime running lamps/retained accessory power/auxiliary power outlet all added to the Convenience Plus family of features; memory door locks joining the Personal Choice package; and Twilight Sentinel. Riviera's fully independent suspension was re-tuned for a tighter, more responsive ride. It featured revalved MacPherson struts up front and refined tuning of struts in back. Control arms, knuckles and related hardware were now all aluminum, resulting in a reduction in unsprung mass. Inside, a new Wyndham cloth was used for the Riviera's headliner and garnish trim application.

I.D. DATA: The 1997 Buick Vehicle Identification Number (VIN) contains 17 characters. The first is the producing country: "1"—United States. The second character is "G" for General Motors. The third is "4" for Buick Division. The fourth and fifth characters identify the car line/series: "C/U"—Park Avenue Ultra; "C/W"—Park Avenue; "G/D"—Riviera; "H/P"—LeSabre Custom; "H/R"—LeSabre Limited; "N/J"—Skylark; "W/B"—Regal LS; "W/F"—Regal GS; "W/S"—Century Custom and "W/Y"—Century Limited. The sixth digit represents body style: "1"—coupe; "2"—two-door; "3"—convertible; "5"—4-dr sedan; "6"—four-door and "8"—4-dr station wagon. The seventh character represents the restraint code: "2"—active (manual) belts w/dual frontal airbags; "4"— active (manual) belts w/dual frontal and side airbags. The eighth digit is the engine code: "K"—L36 3.8L V-6; "M"—L82 3.1L V-6; "T"—LD9 2.4L L4; and "1"—L67 3.8L V-6. The ninth character is a check digit that verifies the accuracy of the VIN. The tenth character identifies the model year ("V" = 1997). The eleventh digit identifies the assembly plant. Characters twelve through seventeen are the production sequence number.

Skylark Custom (Four/V-6)

Model No.	Body/Style No.	Body Type & Seating	Factory Price	Shipping Weight	Prod. Total
J37	NJ1	2-dr. Cpe.-5P	15970/16365	2945/N/A	Note 1
J69	NJ5	4-dr. Sed.-5P	15970/16365	2985/N/A	Note 2

Skylark Limited (Four/V-6)

Model No.	Body/Style No.	Body Type & Seating	Factory Price	Shipping Weight	Prod. Total
J37	NJ1	2-dr. Cpe.-5P	16958/17353	N/A/N/A	Note 1
J69	NJ5	4-dr. Sed.-5P	16958/17353	N/A/N/A	Note 2

Skylark Gran Sport (V-6)

Model No.	Body/Style No.	Body Type & Seating	Factory Price	Shipping Weight	Prod. Total
J37	NJ1	2-dr. Cpe.-5P	18276	N/A	Note 1
J69	NJ5	4-dr. Sed.-5P	18276	N/A	Note 2

Note 1: Skylark coupe production totaled 4,041 with no further breakout available.

Note 2: Skylark sedan production totaled 53,683 with no further breakout available.

Century Custom (V-6)

Model No.	Body/Style No.	Body Type & Seating	Factory Price	Shipping Weight	Prod. Total
S69	WS5	4-dr. Sed.-6P	17845	3364	Note 1

Century Limited (V-6)

Model No.	Body/Style No.	Body Type & Seating	Factory Price	Shipping Weight	Prod. Total
Y69	WY5	4-dr. Sed.-6P	19220	3378N	ote 1

Note 1: Century sedan production totaled 53,486 with no further breakout available.

Regal Custom (V-6)

Model No.	Body/Style No.	Body Type & Seating	Factory Price	Shipping Weight	Prod. Total
B19	WB5	4-dr. Sed.-6P	19740	3331	Note 1

Regal Limited (V-6)

Model No.	Body/Style No.	Body Type & Seating	Factory Price	Shipping Weight	Prod. Total
D19	WD5	4-dr. Sed.-6P	19740	3331	Note 1

Regal Gran Sport (V-6)

Model No.	Body/Style No.	Body Type & Seating	Factory Price	Shipping Weight	Prod. Total
F19	WF5	4-dr. Sed.-6P	21800	N/A	Note 1

Note 1: Regal sedan production totaled 29,239 with no further breakout available. These were carried-over 1996 models produced until the launch in mid-model year of the 1997-1/2/1998 Regal. All Regal sales for 1997 totaled 50,691 including 1996 and 1997-1/2 models.

LeSabre Custom (V-6)

Model No.	Body/Style No.	Body Type & Seating	Factory Price	Shipping Weight	Prod. Total
P69	HP5	4-dr. Sed.-6P	22015	3441	Note 1

LeSabre Limited (V-6)

Model No.	Body/Style No.	Body Type & Seating	Factory Price	Shipping Weight	Prod. Total
R69	HR5	4-dr. Sed.-6P	25565	3462	Note 1

Note 1: LeSabre sedan production totaled 211,651 with no further breakout available.

Park Avenue (V-6)

Model No.	Body/Style No.	Body Type & Seating	Factory Price	Shipping Weight	Prod. Total
W69	CW5	4-dr. Sed.-6P	29995	3788	Note 1

Park Avenue Ultra (V-6)

Model No.	Body/Style No.	Body Type & Seating	Factory Price	Shipping Weight	Prod. Total
U69	CU5	4-dr. Sed.-6P	34995	3879	Note 1

Note 1: Park Avenue sedan production totaled 59,637 with no further breakout available.

Riviera (V-6)

Model No.	Body/Style No.	Body Type & Seating	Factory Price	Shipping Weight	Prod. Total
D07	GD2	2-dr. Cpe.-6P	30110	3720	18,199

ENGINES: BASE FOUR (Skylark Custom & Limited) Inline, dual overhead cam, four-cylinder. Cast iron block and aluminum head. Displacement: 146 cu. in. (2.4 liters). Bore & stroke: 3.54 in. x 3.70 in. Compression ratio: 9.5:1. Brake horsepower: 150 @ 5600 rpm. Torque: 155 lb.-ft. @ 4400 rpm. Sequential Port fuel injection. BASE V-6 (Skylark GS, Century Custom & Limited, Regal Custom); OPTIONAL V-6 (Skylark Custom & Limited) 60-degree overhead valve V-6. Cast iron block and aluminum heads. Displacement: 191 cu. in. (3.1 liters). Bore & stroke: 3.51 in. x 3.31 in. Compression ratio: 9.6:1. Brake horsepower: 160 @ 5200 rpm (except Skylark - 155 @ 5200 rpm). Torque: 185 lb.-ft. @ 4000 rpm. Sequential Port fuel injection. BASE V-6 (Regal Limited & GS, LeSabre, Park Avenue, Riviera); OPTIONAL V-6 (Regal Custom) Series II 90-degree overhead valve V-6 with balance shaft. Cast iron block and heads. Displacement: 231 cu. in. (3.8 liters). Bore & stroke: 3.80 in. x 3.40 in. Compression ratio: 9.4:1. Brake horsepower: 205 @ 5200 rpm. Torque: 230 lb.-ft. @ 4000 rpm. Sequential Port fuel injection. BASE V-6 (Park Avenue Ultra); OPTIONAL V-6 (Riviera) supercharged 90-degree overhead valve V-6 with balance shaft. Cast iron block and heads. Displacement: 231 cu. in. (3.8 liters). Bore & stroke: 3.80 in. x 3.40 in. Compression ratio: 8.5:1. Brake horsepower: 240 @ 5200 rpm. Torque: 280 lb.-ft. @ 3200 rpm. Sequential Port fuel injection.

CHASSIS DATA: Wheelbase: (Skylark) 103.4 in.; (Century) 109.0 in.; (Regal) 107.5 in.; (LeSabre) 110.8 in.; (Park Avenue) 113.8 in.; (Riviera) 113.8 in. Overall length: (Skylark) 188.5 in.; (Century) 194.5 in.; (Regal) 194.1 in.; (LeSabre) 200.8 in.; (Park Avenue) 206.8 in.; (Riviera) 207.2 in. Height: (Skylark) 53.5 in.; (Century) 57.0 in.; (Regal) 56.3 in.; (LeSabre) 55.6 in.; (Park Avenue) 57.4 in.; (Riviera) 54.6 in. Width: (Skylark) 68.2 in.; (Century) 72.7 in.; (Regal) 72.9 in.; (LeSabre) 74.4 in.; (Park Avenue) 74.7 in.; (Riviera) 75.0 in. Front Tread: (Skylark) 55.8 in.; (Century) 62.0 in.; (Regal) 59.5 in.; (LeSabre): 60.4 in.; (Park Avenue) 62.7 in.; (Riviera) 62.5 in. Rear Tread: (Skylark) 55.3 in.; (Century) 61.5 in.; (Regal) 58.0 in.; (LeSabre) 60.4 in.; (Park Avenue) 62.3 in.; (Riviera) 62.6 in. Standard Tires: (Skylark) P195/70R14; (Skylark GS) P205/55R16; (Century) P205/70R15; (Regal) P205/70R15; (Regal GS) P225/60R16; (LeSabre) P205/70R15; (Park Avenue) P225/60R16; (Riviera) P225/60R16.

TECHNICAL: Transmission: (Skylark, Century, Regal, LeSabre) 4T60-E electronically controlled four-speed automatic w/overdrive. (Park Avenue, Riviera) 4T65-E electronically controlled four-speed automatic w/overdrive. Steering: (Skylark, Century, Regal, LeSabre, Park Avenue, Riviera) Rack and pinion; (Park Avenue Ultra) Magnetic variable-effort. Front Suspension: (Skylark) MacPherson struts w/coil springs, MacPherson strut shock absorbers, stabilizer bar; (Century) MacPherson strut w/L-shaped lower control arm and aluminum knuckle; (Regal, LeSabre) MacPherson struts w/coil springs, deflected disc shock absorbers, stabilizer bar; (Park Avenue) Independent DynaRide w/automatic level control; (Riviera) MacPherson struts, deflective disc strut shock absorbers, stabilizer bar. Rear Suspension: (Skylark) Trailing twist axle w/tubular control arm, double acting hydraulic shock absorbers, stabilizer bar; (Century) Isolated, independent coil over strut tri-link design, hybrid deflected disc shock absorbers w/blow-off shock valving, stabilizer bar; (Regal) Tri-link inde-

pendent w/transverse leaf spring, tubular deflected disc shock absorbers; (LeSabre) Chapman struts w/variable rate coil springs, deflected disc shock absorbers, stabilizer bar; (Park Avenue) Independent DynaRide w/automatic level control; (Riviera) Semi-trailing arm, twin tube shock absorbers w/electronic level control. Brakes: (Skylark, Century, LeSabre) Power front disc, rear drum w/anti-lock; (Regal, Park Avenue, Riviera) Power four-wheel disc w/anti-lock. Body Construction: (Skylark, Century, Regal, Park Avenue, Riviera) Integral body/frame; (LeSabre) Integral body/frame w/isolated engine cradle. Fuel Tank: (Skylark) 15.2 gal.; (Century) 17.0 gal.; (Regal) 17.1 gal.; (LeSabre) 18.0 gal.; (Park Avenue) 18.0 gal.; (Park Avenue Ultra) 19.0 gal.; (Riviera) 20.0 gal.

DRIVETRAIN OPTIONS: Engines: 3.1 liter V-6, (Skylark Custom & Limited) $395. (Regal Custom) 3.8 liter V-6, $395. (Riviera) Supercharged 3800 V-6, $1,195. G67 Auto Level Control Suspension (LeSabre) $175. Y56 Gran Touring Suspension Package: (Regal) $745; (LeSabre) $337-$512; (Park Avenue) $105-$240. NW9 Traction Control System (LeSabre) $175; (Park Avenue) $175.

SKYLARK CONVENIENCE/APPEARANCE OPTIONS: Limited pkg. $988. GS pkg. $2,306. Eng. block heater $18. Pwr windows: cpe $290; sed $355. Six-way pwr driver's seat $270. Deluxe o/s mirrors $78. ETR AM/FM radio w/CD player $420. ETR AM/FM radio w/Cassette player $195-$220. Rear window antenna $22. Remote Keyless Entry $135. Trunk convenience net $30. Steering whl mounted radio controls $125. Cruise control $225. Astroroof $595. Deluxe headliner $135. Analog instrument cluster $126. P195/70R14 tires (Custom) $72. P195/65R15 tires (Custom) $131. Leather/cloth trim $495-$620. Bucket seats w/lumbar control and console $175. 15-inch styled whl covers $28. 14-inch styled polycast whls $115.

CENTURY CONVENIENCE/APPEARANCE OPTIONS: (Custom) Popular pkg. $330; Premium pkg. $830. (Limited) Luxury pkg. $525; Prestige pkg. $1,620. Remote keyless entry $135. Leather int. trim (Limited) $550. Trunk convenience net $30. Carpet savers: frt $25; rear $20. Deluxe o/s mirrors (Custom) $98. Electrochromic rearview mirror (Custom) $80. Visor vanity mirror, lighted (Custom) $137. Eng. block heater $18. Cruise control $225. CD player prep pkg. $50. ETR AM/FM radio w/Cassette player $195. ETR AM/FM radio w/CD player $100-$320. ETR AM/FM radio w/Cassette & CD player $200-$420. Astroroof $695. Dual ComforTemp air cond. (Custom) $45. Rear window antenna $40. Steering whl mounted radio controls $125. Rear seat armrest (Limited) $45. Six-way pwr driver's seat $305. Child safety seat (Custom) $100. Bodyside stripes (Custom) $45. P205/70R15 tires $76. 15-inch alum whls (Custom) $325.

REGAL CONVENIENCE/APPEARANCE OPTIONS: (Custom) Luxury pkg. $185; Prestige pkg. $655. (Limited) Prestige pkg. $677. (Gran Sport) Prestige pkg. $677. Trunk convenience net (Custom) $30. Carpet savers: frt $25; rear $20. Engine block heater $18. Remote keyless entry $135. Decklid luggage rack $115. Lighted visor vanity mirrors (Custom) $92. Dual six-way pwr seat (Limited, GS) $305. Six-way pwr driver's seat: (Custom) $305; (Limited, GS) $270. ETR AM/FM radio w/Cassette player $25. ETR AM/FM radio w/CD player $100-$125. ETR AM/FM radio w/Cassette & CD player $200-$225. Steering whl mounted radio controls $125. Pwr antenna (Custom) $85. Astroroof $695. P205/70R15 tires $76. Leather 55/45 seats w/armrest $550. Leather bucket seats w/console (Custom) $550. 15-inch alum whls (Custom) $325. 16-inch chrome whls $650.

LESABRE CONVENIENCE/APPEARANCE OPTIONS: (Custom) Luxury pkg. $941; Prestige pkg. $1,918. (Limited) Prestige

pkg. $609. Leather trim (Custom) $995; (Limited) $550. Carpet savers: frt $25; rear $20. Memory door locks (Custom) $25. Cruise control (Custom) $225. Eng. block heater $18. Elect. o/s rearview mirrors (Custom) $78. Pwr six-way driver's seat (Custom) $305. Pwr six-way passenger seat (Custom) $305. Remote trunk release $60. Remote keyless entry $135. ETR AM/FM radio w/Cassette $150-$195. ETR AM/FM radio w/CD player $100-$250. ETR AM/FM radio w/Cassette and CD player $200-$350. Headliner lighting pkg. (Custom) $116. Theft deterrent syst. (Limited) $159. P205/70R15 tires (Custom) $76. P205/70R15 self-sealing tires $150-$226. 15-inch alum whls (Custom) $325. Cornering lamps (Limited) $60.

PARK AVENUE CONVENIENCE/APPEARANCE OPTIONS: (Park Avenue) Prestige pkg. $890. ETR AM/FM radio w/Cassette $150. ETR AM/FM radio w/CD player $100-$250. ETR AM/FM radio w/Cassette & CD player $100-$350. Trunk mounted CD changer (Ultra) $595. Cell phone readiness pkg. $75. 4-note horn (Park Avenue) $28. Eng. block heater $18. Astroroof $995. Eye Cue head-up display $275. Seating pkg. $380. 5-person leather seating pkg. $185. Rear seat pass-thru (Park Avenue) $50. Rear seat armrest (Park Avenue) $50. Air filtration syst. (Park Avenue) $50. Leather seats (Park Avenue) $600. P225/60R16 tires $85. P225/60R16 self-sealing tires $150. 16-inch chrome-plated whls $695. Electrochromic rearview mirror $70.

RIVIERA CONVENIENCE/APPEARANCE OPTIONS: Prestige pkg. $1,065. Bright White Diamond Paint $395. Leather split bench seat $600. Leather bucket seats w/console $750. Astroroof $995. Memory heated driver's seat $310. Eng. block heater $18. 16-inch chrome whls $695. Electrochromic rearview mirror $70.

HISTORY: Longtime Buick general manager Edward H. Mertz announced his retirement in February 1997. He was succeeded by Robert E. Coletta. The Roadmaster, while "officially" discontinued in 1997, was offered into the model year on an extended 1996 run. Total sales (breakdown by body style unavailable) reached 3,200. Buick 1997 sales totaled 438,064 compared with 427,316 the year previous. Total U.S. market share was 5.3 percent compared with 5.0 in 1996.

1998

Other than a fleet-only sedan, the Skylark was gone from the 1998 lineup. The all-new Regal, launched mid-model year in 1997, consisted of two sedans: LS and the more upscale GS, as well as a limited edition 25th Anniversary sedan. With the demise of the Skylark, the entire Buick lineup was now powered by V-6 engines.

1998 Buick, Century Custom sedan. (OCW)

1998 Buick, Century Limited sedan. (OCW)

CENTURY - SERIES 4W - V-6 - The two sedan lineup, Custom and Limited, returned as the Century offerings for 1998. Standard features included an acoustical package, air conditioning system fueled by non-CFC refrigerant, solar protection windshield and back glass and Soft-Ray tinted side glass, depowered dual airbags and a refueling vapor recovery system. Limited sedans added remote keyless entry and speed-sensitive variable-effort steering. The OnStar communications system was a new, dealer-installed option. Century's powertrain was again the 3100 V-6 mated to the electronically controlled four-speed automatic transmission with overdrive.

1998 Buick, Regal GS sedan. (OCW)

REGAL - SERIES 4W - V-6 - The Regal two-door hardtop was introduced in 1973 as a line extension of the Century. To commemorate the longevity of its availability, Buick offered a limited edition Regal 25th Anniversary Edition model, beginning in March of 1998. The remainder of the Regal lineup consisted of the LS and GS sedans, which were launched in mid-model year 1997. Standard features of the Regal included traction control, dual ComforTemp air conditioning with non-CFC refrigerant, solar protection windshield and back glass and Soft-Ray tinted side glass, remote keyless entry, rear theater seating, Tiltwheel

adjustable steering, speed-sensitive variable-effort steering, leather-wrapped steering wheel and power windows with driver's express down and passenger lockout feature. The more upscale GS model added six-way power driver's seat and leather bucket seats, leather-wrapped shifter knob and 16-inch aluminum wheels. The LS sedan was powered by the Series II 3800 V-6 while the GS used the supercharged Series II 3800 V-6. Both engines were paired with the 4T65-E electronically controlled four-speed automatic transmission with overdrive. The Regal 25th Anniversary Edition was based on the LS sedan and featured a color-keyed grille, black-accented body side cladding, and a distinctive 25th Anniversary medallion on the taillamp. It used the same powertrain as the regular LS sedan. The car was offered in four exterior colors: Black, Sante Fe Red, Jasper Green or White. It featured a leather interior as a standard feature, available in either taupe or gray. Also standard were the Gran Touring suspension and 16-inch cast aluminum wheels. Three Anniversary Edition content packages provided the flexibility of ordering 16-inch chrome wheels, power sunroof, or both.

1998 Buick, LeSabre Limited sedan. (OCW)

1998 Buick, LeSabre Custom sedan. (OCW)

LESABRE - SERIES 4H - V-6 - The "heavy-duty" 4T65-E electronically controlled four-speed automatic transmission with overdrive found its way into LeSabre in 1998, mated to the standard Series II 3800 V-6. Again offered as a sedan only in both Custom and Limited trim levels, LeSabre received numerous other upgrades in addition to its new transmission. To improve fuel economy, the LeSabre's final drive ratio was reduced. Depowered dual airbags and the onboard refueling vapor recovery

system were added as standard features. Cruise control was now made standard on Custom sedans. On Limited models, standard equipment included remote keyless entry with instant alarm perimeter lighting, security feedback and individually programmable transmitters. The dealer-installed OnStar communication system and electrochromic auto-dimming outside driver mirror were new options.

1998 Buick, Park Avenue sedan. (OCW)

1998 Buick, Park Avenue Ultra sedan. (OCW)

1998 Buick, Park Avenue Ultra sedan. (OCW)

PARK AVENUE - SERIES 4C - V-6 - The Park Avenue series was again comprised of a base sedan and Ultra sedan, both of which received several upgrades in 1998. As with other Buicks, the Park Avenue also was fitted with depowered dual airbags and the onboard refueling vapor recovery system. Other new features included outside folding power side mirrors and a programmable power window lock-out system that allowed front passenger switch to operate even when rear seat switches were off. Standard on the Ultra and optional on the base sedan was a parallel park feature that tilted passenger mirror for a better view of parking space. A new option was the OnStar communication system. Powertrain for the Park Avenue was again the Series II 3800 V-6 while the Ultra again used the supercharged Series II 3800 V-6. Both engines were paired with the 4T65-E electronically controlled four-speed automatic transmission with overdrive.

1998 Buick, Riviera coupe. (OCW)

RIVIERA - SERIES 4G - V-6 - The formerly optional supercharged Series II 3800 V-6 became Riviera's standard engine in 1998 replacing the previously used normally aspirated Series II 3800 V-6. The 4T65-E electronically controlled four-speed automatic transmission with overdrive that debuted the year previous returned for duty. Both Riviera's suspension and engine mounts were refined to reduce noise, vibration and ride harshness. The Riviera, too, received depowered dual airbags and the onboard refueling vapor recovery system. New standard features included leather upholstery and a full-length console. The OnStar communication system was a new option.

I.D. DATA: The 1998 Buick Vehicle Identification Number (VIN) contains 17 characters. The first is the producing country: "1"—United States. The second character is "G" for General Motors. The third is "4" for Buick Division. The fourth and fifth characters identify the car line/series: "C/U"—Park Avenue Ultra; "C/W"—Park Avenue; "G/D"—Riviera; "H/P"—LeSabre Custom; "H/R"—LeSabre Limited; "N/J"—Skylark (fleet sedan only); "W/B"—Regal LS; "W/F"—Regal GS; "W/S"—Century Custom and "W/Y"—Century Limited. The sixth digit represents body style: "1"—coupe; "2"—two-door; "3"—convertible; "5"—4-dr sedan; "6"—four-door and "8"—4-dr station wagon. The seventh character represents the restraint code: "2"—active (manual) belts w/dual frontal airbags; "4"— active (manual) belts w/dual frontal and side airbags. The eighth digit is the engine code: "K"—L36 3.8L V-6; "M"—L82 3.1L V-6; and "1"—L67 3.8L V-6. The ninth character is a check digit that verifies the accuracy of the VIN. The tenth character identifies the model year ("W" = 1998). The eleventh digit identifies the assembly plant. Characters twelve through seventeen are the production sequence number.

Century Custom (V-6)

Model No.	Body/Style No.	Body Type & Seating	Factory Price	Shipping Weight	Prod. Total
S69	WS5	4-dr. Sed.-6P	18215	3335	Note 1

Century Limited (V-6)

Model No.	Body/Style No.	Body Type & Seating	Factory Price	Shipping Weight	Prod. Total
Y69	WY5	4-dr. Sed.-6P	19575	3354	Note 1

Note 1: Century sedan production totaled 128,587 with no further breakout available.

Regal LS (V-6)

Model No.	Body/Style No.	Body Type & Seating	Factory Price	Shipping Weight	Prod. Total
B69	WF5	4-dr. Sed.-6P	20945	3447	Note 1

Regal GS (V-6)

Model No.	Body/Style No.	Body Type & Seating	Factory Price	Shipping Weight	Prod. Total
F69	WD5	4-dr. Sed.-6P	23690	3562	Note 1

Regal 25th Anniversary Edition (V-6)

Model No.	Body/Style No.	Body Type & Seating	Factory Price	Shipping Weight	Prod. Total
R9V	WF5	4-dr. Sed.-6P	23995	N/A	Note 1

Note 1: Regal sedan production totaled 70,257 with no further breakout available.

LeSabre Custom (V-6)

Model No.	Body/Style No.	Body Type & Seating	Factory Price	Shipping Weight	Prod. Total
P69	HP5	4-dr. Sed.-6P	22465	3443	Note 1

LeSabre Limited (V-6)

Model No.	Body/Style No.	Body Type & Seating	Factory Price	Shipping Weight	Prod. Total
R69	HR5	4-dr. Sed.-6P	25790	3465	Note 1

Note 1: LeSabre sedan production totaled 143,251 with no further breakout available.

Park Avenue (V-6)

Model No.	Body/Style No.	Body Type & Seating	Factory Price	Shipping Weight	Prod. Total
W69	CW5	4-dr. Sed.-6P	30675	3740	Note 1

Park Avenue Ultra (V-6)

Model No.	Body/Style No.	Body Type & Seating	Factory Price	Shipping Weight	Prod. Total
U69	CU5	4-dr. Sed.-6P	35550	3837	Note 1

Note 1: Park Avenue sedan production totaled 61,974 with no further breakout available.

Riviera (V-6)

Model No.	Body/Style No.	Body Type & Seating	Factory Price	Shipping Weight	Prod. Total
D07	GD2	2-dr. Cpe.-6P	32125	3699	10,613

ENGINES: BASE V-6 (Century Custom & Limited) 60-degree overhead valve V-6. Cast iron block and aluminum heads. Displacement: 191 cu. in. (3.1 liters). Bore & stroke: 3.51 in. x 3.31 in. Compression ratio: 9.6:1. Brake horsepower: 160 @ 5200 rpm. Torque: 185 lb.-ft. @ 4000 rpm. Sequential Port fuel injection. BASE V-6 (Regal LS, LeSabre, Park Avenue) Series II 90-degree overhead valve V-6 with balance shaft. Cast iron block and heads. Displacement: 231 cu. in. (3.8 liters). Bore & stroke: 3.80 in. x 3.40 in. Compression ratio: 9.4:1. Brake horsepower: 205 @ 5200 rpm (Regal LS - 195 @ 5200). Torque: 230 lb.-ft. @ 4000 rpm (Regal LS - 220 lb.-ft. @ 4000 rpm). Sequential Port fuel injection. BASE V-6 (Regal GS, Park Avenue Ultra, Riviera) Supercharged 90-degree overhead valve V-6 with balance shaft. Cast iron block and heads. Displacement: 231 cu. in. (3.8 liters). Bore & stroke: 3.80 in. x 3.40 in. Compression ratio: 8.5:1. Brake horsepower: 240 @ 5200 rpm. Torque: 280 lb.-ft. @ 3600 rpm. Sequential Port fuel injection.

CHASSIS DATA: Wheelbase: (Century) 109.0 in.; (Regal) 109.0 in.; (LeSabre) 110.8 in.; (Park Avenue) 113.8 in.; (Riviera) 113.8 in. Overall length: (Century) 194.5 in.; (Regal) 196.2 in.; (LeSabre) 200.8 in.; (Park Avenue) 206.8 in.; (Riviera) 207.2 in. Height: (Century) 57.0 in.; (Regal) 56.6 in.; (LeSabre) 55.6 in.; (Park Avenue) 55.1 in.; (Riviera) 54.6 in. Width: (Century) 72.7 in.; (Regal) 72.7 in.; (LeSabre) 74.4 in.; (Park Avenue) 74.1 in.; (Riviera) 75.0 in. Front Tread: (Century) 62.0 in.; (Regal) 62.0 in.; (LeSabre): 60.4 in.; (Park Avenue) 62.7 in.; (Riviera) 62.5 in. Rear Tread: (Century) 61.5 in.; (Regal) 61.3 in.; (LeSabre) 60.4 in.; (Park Avenue) 62.3 in.; (Riviera) 62.6 in. Standard Tires: (Century) P205/70R15; (Regal LS) P215/70R15; (Regal GS & 25th Anniversary Edition) P225/60R16; (LeSabre) P205/70R15; (Park Avenue) P225/60R16; (Riviera) P225/60R16.

TECHNICAL: Transmission: (Century) 4T60-E electronically controlled four-speed automatic w/overdrive. (Regal, LeSabre, Park Avenue, Riviera) 4T65-E electronically controlled four-speed automatic w/overdrive. Steering: (Century, LeSabre, Park Avenue, Riviera) Rack and pinion; (Regal, Park Avenue Ultra) Magnetic variable-effort. Front Suspension: (Century, Regal) MacPherson strut w/L-shaped lower control arm and aluminum knuckle, twin tube strut, stabilizer bar; (LeSabre, Park Avenue, Riviera) MacPherson struts w/coil springs, deflected disc strut shock absorbers, stabilizer bar. Rear Suspension: (Century) Isolated, independent coil over strut tri-link design, twin tube strut shock absorbers, stabilizer bar; (Regal) Tri-link independent w/coil spring over strut, twin tube strut shock absorbers; stabilizer bar; (LeSabre) Chapman struts w/variable rate coil springs, deflected disc shock absorbers, stabilizer bar; (Park Avenue) Semi-trailing w/lateral link, twin tube shock absorbers w/electronic control; (Riviera) Semi-trailing arm, twin tube shock absorbers w/electronic level control. Brakes: (Century, LeSabre) Power front disc, rear drum w/anti-lock; (Regal, Park Avenue, Riviera) Power four-wheel disc w/anti-lock. Body Construction: (Century, Regal, Park Avenue, Riviera) Integral body/frame; (LeSabre) Integral body/frame w/isolated engine cradle. Fuel Tank: (Century) 17.5 gal.; (Regal) 17.5 gal.; (LeSabre) 18.0 gal.; (Park Avenue) 18.5 gal.; (Riviera) 18.5 gal.

DRIVETRAIN OPTIONS: G67 Auto Level Control Suspension (LeSabre) $175. Y56 Gran Touring Suspension Package: (Regal) $552; (LeSabre) $337-$512; (Park Avenue) $105-$240.

NW9 Traction Control System (LeSabre) $175; (Park Avenue) $175.

CENTURY CONVENIENCE/APPEARANCE OPTIONS: (Custom) Popular pkg. $330; Premium pkg. $830. (Limited) Luxury pkg. $525; Prestige pkg. $1,620. Leather int. trim (Limited) $550. Trunk convenience net $30. Carpet savers: frt $25; rear $20. Dual pwr heated o/s mirrors (Custom) $58. Electrochromic rearview mirror $80-$217. Visor vanity mirror, lighted (Custom) $137. Eng. block heater $18. Cruise control $225. ETR AM/FM radio w/Cassette player $195. ETR AM/FM radio w/CD player $100-$320. ETR AM/FM radio w/Cassette & CD player $200-$420. Astroroof $695. Dual ComforTemp air cond. (Custom) $45. Rear window antenna $40. Rear seat armrest $45. Leather trim (Limited) $550. Six-way pwr driver's seat $305. Child safety seat (Custom) $100. Bodyside stripes (Custom) $75. P205/70R15 tires $150. 15-inch alum whls (Custom) $325.

1998 Buick, Regal 25th Anniversary Edition sedan. (OCW)

REGAL CONVENIENCE/APPEARANCE OPTIONS: (LS) Luxury pkg. $587; Prestige pkg. $887. R9V 25th Anniv. Ed. pkg. $2,500. R9W 25th Anniv. Ed. pkg. $2,500. R9Y 25th Anniv. Ed. pkg. $3,150. (GS) Luxury pkg. $330; Prestige pkg. $915. Cell phone prewire pkg. $75. Driver Info Center (LS) $75. Carpet savers: frt $25; rear $20. Engine block heater $18. Electrochromic rearview mirror $80. Driver's six-way pwr seat (LS) $305. Passenger's six-way pwr seat $305. ETR AM/FM radio w/Cassette player $95. ETR AM/FM radio w/Cassette & CD player $200-$295. CD player prep pkg. $50. Steering whl mounted radio controls $125. Leather seat trim (LS) $600. Heated bucket seats $225. Astroroof $695. Child safety seat $100. 15-inch alum whls (LS) $375. 16-inch chrome whls $650.

LESABRE CONVENIENCE/APPEARANCE OPTIONS: (Custom) Luxury pkg. $716; Prestige pkg. $1,668. (Limited) Prestige pkg. $659. Leather trim (Custom) $995; (Limited) $550. Carpet savers: frt $25; rear $20. Memory door locks (Custom) $25. Eng. block heater $18. Elect. o/s rearview mirrors (Custom) $78. Pwr six-way driver's seat (Custom) $305. Pwr six-way passenger seat (Custom) $305. Remote trunk release $60. Remote keyless entry $135. ETR AM/FM radio w/Cassette $150-$195. ETR AM/FM radio w/CD player $100-$250. ETR AM/FM radio w/Cassette and CD player $200-$350. Headliner lighting pkg. (Custom) $116. Theft deterrent syst. (Limited) $159. P205/70R15 tires (Custom) $76. P205/70R15 self-sealing tires

$150-$226. 15-inch alum whls (Custom) $325. Cornering lamps (Limited) $60. Bodyside paint stripe (Custom) $75.

PARK AVENUE CONVENIENCE/APPEARANCE OPTIONS: (Park Avenue) Prestige pkg. $890. ETR AM/FM radio w/Cassette $150. ETR AM/FM radio w/CD player $100-$250. ETR AM/FM radio w/Cassette & CD player $100-$350. Trunk mounted CD changer (Ultra) $595. Cell phone readiness pkg. $75. 4-note horn (Park Avenue) $28. Eng. block heater $18. Astroroof $995. Seating pkg. (Park Avenue) $380. 5-person leather seating pkg. $185. Rear seat armrest (Park Avenue) $50. Eye-Cue head-up display $275. Leather seats (Park Avenue) $600. P225/60R16 tires $85. 16-inch chrome-plated whls $695. Electrochromic rearview mirror $70.

RIVIERA CONVENIENCE/APPEARANCE OPTIONS: Prestige pkg. $1,145. Bright White Diamond Paint $395. Memory heated driver's & pass. seats $415. Astroroof $995. Eng. block heater $18. 16-inch chrome whls $695. Electrochromic rearview mirror $70.

HISTORY: The fleet-only Skylark Custom sedan was priced at $16,230 and weighed 2,985 pounds. It was powered by the 3100 V-6. During model year 1998, Buick produced 431,142 automobiles.

1999

Part of Buick's regular lineup since 1963, 1999 was the final year of production for the Riviera. This was Buick's 95th Anniversary as well as the 40th Anniversary of the LeSabre. On the heels of the previous year's Regal 25th Anniversary Edition sedan, Buick added two special Regals to its 1999 lineup: GSE and LSE sedans. Both were heavily contented with special pricing and aimed at buyers with families who still wanted performance.

1999 Buick, Century Custom sedan. (OCW)

1999 Buick, Century Limited sedan. (OCW)

CENTURY - SERIES 4W - V-6 - Century again was offered in sedan-only body style in two trim levels: Custom and Limited. New standard features included traction control, a more efficient anti-lock braking system and a tire inflation monitor to warn of a tire losing air. The traction control system operated at all forward speeds and in reverse, regulating engine output to enable traction in slippery road conditions. New options included electrochromic dimming outside rearview mirrors and diversity antenna system mounted in the windshield and back glass to improve radio reception. Century's suspension was also refined to improve ride and handling. Rear shock valving was increased and larger front and rear stabilizer bars were installed to reduce body roll. Under the hood again was the 3100 V-6 and 4T60-E electronically controlled four-speed automatic transmission with overdrive. The V-6 featured aluminum cylinder heads, sequential fuel injection, distributorless ignition, cross-bolted main bearings, a structural aluminum oil pan, roller hydraulic lifters and roller rocker arms.

1999 Buick, Regal LS sedan. (OCW)

REGAL - SERIES 4W - V-6 - The normally aspirated Series II 3800 V-6 that powered the Regal LS sedan was improved for 1999, receiving a boost in both horsepower (from the previous 195 to 200) and torque (from 220 to 225 pound-feet). The increased power was the result of a new low-reduction air cleaner and larger induction system. The more upscale GS sedan continued using the supercharged Series II 3800 V-6, and both engines were linked to the 4T65-E electronically controlled four-speed automatic transmission with overdrive. The LS sedan's transmission received a more efficient torque converter. Also, the accessory drive system of both engines available in Regals was revised and both were recalibrated to operate at a lower idle speed for better cold weather operation. In addition, a new steering intermediate shaft with concentric isolator, located between the steering gear assembly and steering column, provided all Regals with more precise steering. Regal LS sedans also received a quicker steering gear (from the previous 15.2:1 to 13.3:1), more rigid rubber components in engine cradle mounts, and increased shock absorber valving and more rigid chassis bushings. New optional equipment for the LS sedan included 15-inch aluminum wheels. Both the LS and GS sedans received DBC 7, which was a more efficient solenoid-based four-wheel anti-lock braking system. All 1999 Regals featured new programmable perimeter lighting for added night security. Previously standard on GS sedans, LS sedans now also had the tire inflation monitor. Two special edition Regal sedans were offered in 1999: the LSE and GSE. Regal LSE featured dual automatic ComforTemp climate control, leather-trimmed seating, Gran Touring suspension package, sunroof and/or 16-inch chrome-plated aluminum wheels, CD player with steering wheel controls and six-way power driver's seat. The GSE added a six-way power passenger's seat and a Monsoon audio system instead of the CD player. The LSE used the same powertrain

as the Regal LS sedan and the GSE mimicked the Regal GS sedan. Both were offered in four exterior colors: Bright White, Black, Santa Fe Red Pearl and Jasper Green. Each had a body-color grille.

1999 Buick, LeSabre Limited sedan. (OCW)

LESABRE - SERIES 4H - V-6 - In the 40 years since its introduction in 1959, more than six million LeSabres had been sold leading up to the 1999 version. LeSabre returned with its two trim level sedan lineup: Custom and Limited. Power was again supplied by the Series II 3800 V-6 mated with the 4T65-E electronically controlled four-speed automatic transmission with overdrive. The option list for LeSabre continued to offer the On-Star communications system (dealer-installed), which combined Global Positioning System satellite technology and a hands-free, voice-activated cellular telephone to link drivers with needed assistance. LeSabre sedans could also still be ordered with a Gran Touring package consisting of heavy-duty suspension, 16-inch aluminum wheels, magnetic variable-effort steering, 3.05 axle ratio, leather-wrapped steering wheel, automatic level control and Eagle GA 215/60R16 blackwall tires. Among the eleven exterior colors available on LeSabre, two were new: Sterling Silver Metallic and Dark Bronzemist Metallic.

1999 Buick, Park Avenue sedan. (OCW)

1999 Buick, Park Avenue Ultra sedan. (OCW)

PARK AVENUE - SERIES 4C - V-6 - Base and Ultra sedans were again the offerings from Buick's Park Avenue series. The normally aspirated Series II 3800 V-6 again powered the Park Avenue while the Ultra continued to use the supercharged Series II 3800 V-6. While both engines were paired with the 4T65-E electronically controlled four-speed automatic transmission with overdrive, the Ultra relied on the HD (heavy-duty) version of that unit. Refinements for 1999 included improved

taillamp appearance (to bring the Park Avenue more in line with the Ultra's look), Michelin tires becoming standard on Ultra and four new exterior colors: Sterling Silver Metallic, Titanium Blue Metallic, Gold Firemist and Dark Bronzemist Metallic. Bright White Diamond Metallic became available on Ultra late in the previous model year. Park Avenue's instrument panel and door plates also received a new Elite Walnut trim. A feature standard on Ultra and optional on the base sedan was the Driver Information Center, which provided buttons on the instrument panel to select information such as oil level and life, coolant level, calculations for fuel economy, tire pressure monitoring and two trip odometers.

1999 Buick, Riviera coupe. (OCW)

RIVIERA - SERIES 4G - V-6 - In its final model year of availability, the Riviera featured full-range traction control as standard equipment (formerly an option). Power was again supplied by the supercharged Series II 3800 V-6 matched with the 4T65-E HD (heavy-duty) electronically controlled four-speed automatic transmission with overdrive. Four new exterior colors were available: Sterling Silver Metallic, Titanium Blue Metallic, Gold Firemist Metallic and Dark Bronzemist Metallic. Since its introduction in its latest generation design in 1995, the "Riv" received numerous awards. One of the most interesting was the "Most Collectible Car of the Future" award from the National Automotive History Collection of the Detroit Public Library.

I.D. DATA: The 1999 Buick Vehicle Identification Number (VIN) contains 17 characters. The first is the producing country: "1"—United States. The second character is "G" for General Motors. The third is "4" for Buick Division. The fourth and fifth characters identify the car line/series: "C/U"—Park Avenue Ultra; "C/W"—Park Avenue; "G/D"—Riviera; "H/P"—LeSabre Custom; "H/R"—LeSabre Limited; "W/B"—Regal LS; "W/F"—Regal GS; "W/S"—Century Custom and "W/Y"—Century Limited. The sixth digit represents body style: "1"—coupe; "2"—two-door; "3"—convertible; "5"—4-dr sedan; "6"—four-door and "8"—4-dr station wagon. The seventh character represents the restraint code: "2"—active (manual) belts w/dual frontal airbags; "4"—active (manual) belts w/dual frontal and side airbags. The eighth digit is the engine code: "K"—L36 3.8L V-6; "M"—L82 3.1L V-6; and "1"—L67 3.8L V-6. The ninth character is a check digit that verifies the accuracy of the VIN. The tenth character identifies the model year ("X" = 1999). The eleventh digit identifies the assembly plant. Characters twelve through seventeen are the production sequence number.

*Note: Production figures for 1999 Buicks were not available when this book went to press.

Century Custom (V-6)

Model No.	Body/Style No.	Body Type & Seating	Factory Price	Shipping Weight	Prod. Total
S69	WS5	4-dr. Sed.-6P	18775	3353	*

Century Limited (V-6)

Model No.	Body/Style No.	Body Type & Seating	Factory Price	Shipping Weight	Prod. Total
Y69	WY5	4-dr. Sed.-6P	20145	3371	*

Regal LS (V-6)

Model No.	Body/Style No.	Body Type & Seating	Factory Price	Shipping Weight	Prod. Total
B69	WF5	4-dr. Sed.-6P	21695	3439	*

Regal GS (V-6)

F69	WD5	4-dr. Sed.-6P	24395	3543	*

Regal LSE (V-6)

B69	WF5	4-dr. Sed.-6P	24945	N/A	*

Regal GSE (V-6)

F69	WD5	4-dr. Sed.-6P	27145	N/A	*

LeSabre Custom (V-6)

P69	HP5	4-dr. Sed.-6P	22725	3443	*

LeSabre Limited (V-6)

R69	HR5	4-dr. Sed.-6P	25990	3468	*

Park Avenue (V-6)

W69	CW5	4-dr. Sed.-6P	31130	3778	*

Park Avenue Ultra (V-6)

U69	CU5	4-dr. Sed.-6P	36025	3884	*

Riviera (V-6)

D07	GD2	2-dr. Cpe.-6P	33820	3713	*

ENGINES: BASE V-6 (Century Custom & Limited) 60-degree overhead valve V-6. Cast iron block and aluminum heads. Displacement: 191 cu. in. (3.1 liters). Bore & stroke: 3.51 in. x 3.31 in. Compression ratio: 9.6:1. Brake horsepower: 160 @ 5200 rpm. Torque: 185 lb.-ft. @ 4000 rpm. Sequential Port fuel injection. BASE V-6 (Regal LS, Regal LSE, LeSabre, Park Avenue) Series II 90-degree overhead valve V-6 with balance shaft. Cast iron block and heads. Displacement: 231 cu. in. (3.8 liters). Bore & stroke: 3.80 in. x 3.40 in. Compression ratio: 9.4:1. Brake horsepower: 205 @ 5200 rpm (Regal LS/LSE - 200 @ 5200). Torque: 230 lb.-ft. @ 4000 rpm (Regal LS/LSE - 220 lb.-ft. @ 4000 rpm). Sequential Port fuel injection. BASE V-6 (Regal GS, Regal GSE, Park Avenue Ultra, Riviera) Supercharged 90-degree overhead valve V-6 with balance shaft. Cast iron block and heads. Displacement: 231 cu. in. (3.8 liters). Bore & stroke: 3.80 in. x 3.40 in. Compression ratio: 8.5:1. Brake horsepower: 240 @ 5200 rpm. Torque: 280 lb.-ft. @ 3600 rpm. Sequential Port fuel injection.

CHASSIS DATA: Wheelbase: (Century) 109.0 in.; (Regal) 109.0 in.; (LeSabre) 110.8 in.; (Park Avenue) 113.8 in.; (Riviera) 113.8 in. Overall length: (Century) 194.6 in.; (Regal) 196.2 in.; (LeSabre) 200.8 in.; (Park Avenue) 206.8 in.; (Riviera) 207.2 in. Height: (Century) 56.6 in.; (Regal) 56.6 in.; (LeSabre) 55.6 in.; (Park Avenue) 57.4 in.; (Riviera) 54.6 in. Width: (Century) 72.7 in.; (Regal) 72.7 in.; (LeSabre) 74.4 in.; (Park Avenue) 74.7 in.; (Riviera) 75.0 in. Front Tread: (Century) 62.0 in.; (Regal) 62.0 in.; (LeSabre) 60.4 in.; (Park Avenue) 62.7 in.; (Riviera) 62.5 in. Rear Tread: (Century) 61.1 in.; (Regal) 61.3 in.; (LeSabre) 60.4 in.; (Park Avenue) 62.3 in.; (Riviera) 62.6 in. Standard Tires: (Century) P205/70R15; (Regal LS) P215/70R15; (Regal GS/LSE/GSE) P225/60R16; (LeSabre) P205/70R15; (Park Avenue) P225/60R16; (Riviera) P225/60R16.

TECHNICAL: Transmission: (Century) 4T60-E electronically controlled four-speed automatic w/overdrive. (Regal, LeSabre, Park Avenue, Riviera) 4T65-E electronically controlled four-speed automatic w/overdrive. Steering: (Century, LeSabre, Park Avenue, Riviera) Rack and pinion; (Regal, Park Avenue Ultra) Magnetic variable-effort. Front Suspension: (Century, Regal) MacPherson strut w/L-shaped lower control arm and aluminum knuckle, twin tube strut, stabilizer bar; (LeSabre, Park Avenue, Riviera) MacPherson struts w/coil springs, deflected disc strut shock absorbers, stabilizer bar. Rear Suspension: (Century) Isolated, independent coil over strut tri-link design, twin tube strut shock absorbers, stabilizer bar; (Regal) Tri-link independent w/coil spring over strut, twin tube strut shock absorbers; stabilizer bar; (LeSabre) Chapman struts w/variable rate coil springs, deflected disc shock ab-

sorbers, stabilizer bar; (Park Avenue) Semi-trailing w/lateral link, twin tube shock absorbers w/electronic control; (Riviera) Semi-trailing arm, twin tube shock absorbers w/electronic level control. Brakes: (Century, LeSabre) Power front disc, rear drum w/anti-lock; (Regal, Park Avenue, Riviera) Power four-wheel disc w/anti-lock. Body Construction: (Century, Regal, Park Avenue, Riviera) Integral body/frame; (LeSabre) Integral body/frame w/isolated engine cradle. Fuel Tank: (Century) 17.5 gal.; (Regal) 17.5 gal.; (LeSabre) 18.0 gal.; (Park Avenue) 18.5 gal.; (Riviera) 18.5 gal.

DRIVETRAIN OPTIONS: G67 Auto Level Control Suspension (LeSabre) $175. Y56 Gran Touring Suspension Package: (Regal LS & GS) $600; (LeSabre) $337-$512; (Park Avenue) $200-$335. NW9 Traction Control System (LeSabre) $175; (Park Avenue) $175.

CENTURY CONVENIENCE/APPEARANCE OPTIONS: (Custom) Popular pkg. $300; Premium pkg. $885. (Limited) Luxury pkg. $495; Prestige pkg. $1,800. Trunk convenience net $30. Carpet savers: frt $25; rear $20. Electrochromic heated o/s mirrors $70. Electrochromic rearview mirror $120. Visor vanity mirror, lighted $137. Eng. block heater $18. Cruise control $225. ETR AM/FM radio w/Cassette player $195-$220. ETR AM/FM radio w/Cassette & CD player $200-$420. Astroroof $695. Dual automatic ComforTemp air cond. $175. Rear window antenna $40. Rear seat armrest $45. Leather seat trim $625. Six-way pwr driver's seat $305. Six-way pwr pass. seat $305. Bodyside stripes $75. P205/70R15 tires $150. 15-inch alum whls $375.

REGAL CONVENIENCE/APPEARANCE OPTIONS: (LS) Luxury pkg. $542; Prestige pkg. $1162. (GS) Luxury pkg. $950. Driver Info Center (LS) $75. Carpet savers: frt $25; rear $20. Engine block heater $18. Electrochromic o/s rearview mirrors $120. Driver's six-way pwr seat $330. Passenger's six-way pwr seat $330. ETR AM/FM radio w/Cassette & CD player $200. CD player prep pkg. $50. Monsoon audio system $295. Steering whl mounted radio controls $125. Leather bucket seats $650. Heated leather seats $225. Astroroof $695. 15-inch alum whls $350. 16-inch chrome alum whls $650.

LESABRE CONVENIENCE/APPEARANCE OPTIONS: (Custom) Luxury pkg. $716; Prestige pkg. $1,693. (Limited) Prestige pkg. $659. Leather seat trim (Custom) $995; (Limited) $695. Carpet savers: frt $25; rear $20. Memory door locks (Custom) $25. Eng. block heater $18. Elect. o/s rearview mirrors (Custom) $78. Rearview mirror w/compass (Limited) $80. Pwr six-way driver's seat (Custom) $330. Pwr six-way passenger seat (Custom) $330. Remote trunk release $60. Remote keyless entry (Custom) $135. ETR AM/FM radio w/Cassette $150. ETR AM/FM radio w/CD player $100-$250. ETR AM/FM radio w/Cassette and CD player $200-$350. Headliner lighting pkg. (Custom) $116. Theft deterrent system (Limited) $159. P205/70R15 tires (Custom) $226; (Limited) $150. 15-inch alum whls (Custom) $325. Cornering lamps (Limited) $60.

PARK AVENUE CONVENIENCE/APPEARANCE OPTIONS: (Park Avenue) Prestige pkg. $970. ETR AM/FM radio w/Cassette $150. ETR AM/FM radio w/CD player $100-$250. ETR AM/FM radio w/Cassette & CD player $100-$350. Trunk mounted CD changer (Ultra) $595. 4-note horn (Park Avenue) $28. Eng. block heater $18. Astroroof $1095. Seating pkg. (Park Avenue) $380. 5-person leather seating pkg. $185. Rear seat armrest (Park Avenue) $50. Eye-Cue head-up display $275. Leather seats (Park Avenue) $750. P225/60R16 tires $150. 16-inch chrome-plated whls $695. Bright white diamond paint (Ultra) $395.

RIVIERA CONVENIENCE/APPEARANCE OPTIONS: Prestige pkg. $1,340. Bright White Diamond Paint $395. Astroroof $1,095. Eng. block heater $18. 16-inch chrome whls $695.

HISTORY: Buick began work in the area of automated highways. Other future ideas were demonstrated on Buick concept vehicles named the XP2000 and Signia.

2000

The Riviera was no longer a part of the Buick lineup. Also gone were the Regal LSE and GSE sedans that were offered the year previously. New to the lineup was the Century 2000 Special Edition sedan, which was launched early in the summer of 1999 in base and uplevel trim versions.

2000 Buick, Century Custom sedan. (OCW)

2000 Buick, Century 2000 Special Edition sedan. (OCW)

CENTURY - SERIES 4W - V-6 - "A Luxury Car for Everyone" was Buick's slogan for the Century. In addition to the Custom and Limited sedans offered previously, the Century lineup gained a 2000 Special Edition sedan. Special Editions featured body-color mirrors, cruise control, six-way power driver's seat, trunk convenience net, AM/FM cassette player with steering wheel controls, rear window antenna, specific machined aluminum wheels, blacked-out grille, black door header moldings and body-color fascias and side molding. The Century 2000 sedan also had commemorative "2000" badging on its doors, taillamps and instrument panel and embroidered "Century 2000" lettering on its headrests and floor mats. An uplevel Special Edition added leather-trimmed seats that came with a side airbag for the driver as well as illuminated visor vanity mirrors, electrochromic automatic dimming inside and driver's side outside rearview mirrors, six-way power front passenger seat, split-folding pass-through rear seat, AM/FM compact disc player, Concert Sound III speaker system and windshield and rear window-mounted diversity antenna. The Century's Series 3100 V-6 underwent revision for 2000 and received a 15 horsepower increase (175 vs. 160 in 1999) and 10 pound-feet of torque increase (195 vs. 185 in 1999). These gains were achieved by revising cylinder head and engine calibration and by installing less restrictive air intake and exhaust manifolds. The V-6 is paired with an improved electronically controlled four-speed automatic transmission that featured a larger torque converter than the previous unit for smoother shifting. The Century lineup also received several refinements including a new-design Dual Zone Climate Control system that was standard equipment on all models. Electronic Dual Zone Climate Control, which replaced slide and knob controls with push buttons and LED and digital indicators, was standard on upper level Special Edition sedans and optional on Limited models. Standard on all Century models were remote keyless entry, automatic power door locks, daytime running lamps with Twilight Sentinel, door courtesy lights, battery rundown protection, anti-lock brakes, traction control, tire inflation monitor and Pass-Key II theft deterrent system. For 2000, Century Limited sedans received new chrome-plated wheel covers. Century's optional equipment included the three-button OnStar driver assistance system, which was dealer-installed. Century received two new exterior color choices for 2000, Gold Metallic and Sterling Silver Metallic while inside color choices were Taupe and Medium Gray. Century 2000 Special Edition sedans were available in nine colors: Black, Bordeaux Red Pearl, Bright White, Gold Metallic, Jasper Green Pearl, Light Sandrift Metallic, Midnight Blue Pearl, Twilight Blue Metallic, and Sterling Silver Metallic.

2000 Buick, Regal LS sedan with optional sunroof. (OCW)

REGAL - SERIES 4W - V-6 - The 2000 Regal lineup was half of what was offered the year previous, comprised of LS and GS sedans with the formerly available LSE and GSE sedans dropped. Regal LS sedans were again powered by the normally aspirated Series II 3800 V-6 while GS sedans used the supercharged Series II 3800 V-6. Both engines were again paired with the 4T65-E electronically controlled four-speed automatic transmission with overdrive, but the GS sedan used the heavy-duty version of that unit. New standard features found on Regals included a split-folding rear seat and two exterior color choices: Gold Metallic and Sterling Silver Metallic. A new option on Regals equipped with leather seats was a side-impact airbag for the driver. Regal GS sedans featured full-range traction control, which used the braking system and engine power controls to reduce loss of traction on slippery surfaces. Standard equipment on all Regal models included Dual ComforTemp Climate Control, electronic cruise control, power door locks with lockout protection, daytime running lamps with Twilight Sentinel, stainless steel dual exhaust, power dual remote outside mirrors with heated driver's side mirror, AM/FM cassette stereo with six-speaker Concert Sound II system, leather-wrapped steering wheel and shift knob, and Pass-Key theft deterrent system. The GS sedan added a six-way power driver's seat, bright dual exhaust outlets, full analog gauges and Driver Information Center (provided information such as fuel used, miles per gallon and tire pressure), dual illuminated visor mirrors, accent-colored lower body cladding, body-colored grille, trunk net, 16-inch aluminum wheels and Gran Touring suspension. The Gran Touring suspension package featured touring tires, stiffer front springs and front stabilizer bar, rear stabilizer bar, higher dampening load front struts and rear shock absorbers, magnetic variable-effort steering, and larger brake rotors. Optional on the GS was a Monsoon audio system with eight speakers while all Regal models could be ordered with the new three-button OnStar driver assistance system as a dealer-installed option.

2000 Buick, LeSabre Custom sedan. (OCW)

LESABRE - SERIES 4H - V-6 - The best-selling full-size sedan in America seven years in-a-row, LeSabre was all-new for 2000. Introduced early in 1999, LeSabre sedans were offered in two trim levels: Custom and Limited. Safety features of the new LeSabre included safety-cage construction, dual front and side airbags, balanced chassis design, energy absorbing sur-

faces and revised four-wheel anti-lock disc brakes. Also new were the "Catcher's Mitt" high-retention front seats that featured self-aligning head restraints for improved protection against whiplash injury in rear-impact collisions. In addition, front safety belts were now attached directly to the seat structure and shoulder and lap safety belts were provided for all three rear passengers. All LeSabres were again powered by the 3800 Series II V-6 paired with the 4T65-E electronically controlled four-speed automatic transmission with overdrive. Refinements to the 3.8-liter V-6 for 2000 included a new crankshaft damper and increased exhaust system volume for quieter operation. Special torque-axis powertrain mounts incorporated two fluid-filled rubber mounts to diminish noise and vibration transmitted to the engine compartment. The new LeSabre's exterior featured a blending of the front fascia up and around the top of the grille for a more unified appearance. Headlamps used clear lenses with parabolic reflectors. The 2000 LeSabre's wheels were moved out toward the four corners with a wheelbase of 112.2 inches (1.4 inches longer than the previous design) and wider front and rear track (increased 1.9 inches) for improved ride and handling. A "zoned" electrical system included smarter and more reliable circuits capable of managing extra comfort and convenience features while requiring fewer wires. A new cast magnesium beam located behind the instrument panel provided both a convenient means of pre-assembling the most complex part of the car plus eliminated squeaks and rattles in that area. This beam helped the LeSabre to achieve 27 percent more resistance to bending and a 62 percent gain in torsional rigidity over the previous design LeSabre. Standard features of the 2000 LeSabre included air conditioning, remote keyless entry, Pass-Key III theft-deterrent system, Solar-Ray tinted glass, automatic leveling suspension, AM/FM stereo radio, and Convenience Plus that featured battery rundown protection, lockout protection, delayed entry/exit lighting, Twilight Sentinel headlamp controls and retained accessory power. The Limited added automatic ComforTemp Dual Climate Controls, fresh air filtration system, Concert Sound II speaker system and aluminum wheels. LeSabre's optional equipment list included a sunroof, 12-disc CD changer mounted in the trunk, rain-sensing windshield wipers, three-channel garage door opener, convenience console with writing surface, and, on the Limited only, Driver Information Center. Other notable options included the three-button OnStar driver assistance system (dealer-installed), full-range traction control, Gran Touring Package, Driver Confidence Package, and, on the Limited only, heated front seats and heated outside rearview mirrors. The optional Gran Touring Package included a firmer suspension, rear anti-roll bar, 3.05:1 axle ratio, 16-inch aluminum wheels with P225/60R16 touring tires, magnetic variable-effort power steering, specific steering ratio and leather-wrapped steering wheel. The Driver Confidence Package was comprised of StabiliTrak driver control system, EyeCue head-up windshield display and self-sealing tires. Three new exterior color choices for LeSabres were: Dark Pearl Blue, Light Bronzemist Metallic and Medium Red Pearl.

2000 Buick, LeSabre Limited sedan with Gran Touring package. (OCW)

2000 Buick, Park Avenue sedan. (OCW)

2000 Buick, Park Avenue Ultra sedan. (OCW)

PARK AVENUE - SERIES 4C - V-6 - The Park Avenue series was again comprised of base and Ultra sedans. Park Avenue sedans were again powered by the normally aspirated Series II 3800 V-6 while the Ultra used the supercharged Series II 3800 V-6. While both engines were linked to the 4T65-E electronically controlled four-speed automatic transmission with overdrive, the Ultra relied on the heavy-duty version of that unit. For 2000, improvements to the all Park Avenue models included dual seat-mounted side airbags, rear seat child seat tether anchors, front seat map pocket and redesigned 16-inch aluminum wheels. Convenience Plus features were standard on all Park Avenue sedans and included battery rundown protection, lockout protection, delayed entry/exit lighting, Twilight Sentinel with daytime running lamps, retained accessory power and Pass-Key III theft-deterrent system. Standard equipment on Ultra models (optional on Park Avenue sedans) included full-range traction control; rain-sensing wipers; separate heated seats; trunk-mounted CD player; Personal Choice package that included numbered key fobs to allow two drivers to program separate settings for mirrors, seat adjustment and other features into "memory;" and StabiliTrak integrated vehicle stability control system. New exterior color choices were: Dark Blue Pearl, Medium Red Pearl and, optional on Park Avenue, Bright White Diamond Tri-Coat (standard on Ultra beginning mid-model year previous). Medici Red was a new interior color. Ultra sedans also sported new ebony instrument panel and door trim plates. Standard on all Park Avenues was automatic level control,

which adjusted rear air shocks to maintain proper vehicle height regardless of loading, and Dual ComforTemp Climate Control. Optional across-the-board was the new three-button OnStar driver assistance system (dealer-installed). Park Avenue's optional Gran Touring Package included a firmer suspension, rear anti-roll bar, touring tires, magnetic variable-effort power steering, and larger brake rotors.

I.D. DATA: The 2000 Buick Vehicle Identification Number (VIN) contains 17 characters. The first is the producing country: "1"—United States. The second character is "G" for General Motors. The third is "4" for Buick Division. The fourth and fifth characters identify the car line/series: "C/U"—Park Avenue Ultra; "C/W"—Park Avenue; "H/P"—LeSabre Custom; "H/R"—LeSabre Limited; "W/B"—Regal LS; "W/F"—Regal GS; "W/L"—Century 2000 Special Edition; "W/S"—Century Custom and "W/Y"—Century Limited. The sixth digit represents body style: "1"—coupe; "2"—two-door; "3"—convertible; "5"—4-dr sedan; "6"—four-door and "8"—4-dr station wagon. The seventh character represents the restraint code: "2"—active (manual) belts w/dual frontal airbags; "4"—active (manual) belts w/dual frontal and side airbags; "5"—active (manual) belts w/driver and passenger inflatable restraints, frontal and driver inflatable restraints - side; "6"—active (manual) belts w/driver and passenger inflatable restraints (frontal and side). Automatic occupant sensor (passenger); "7"—active (manual) belts w/driver and passenger inflatable restraints (frontal and side). Rear passenger inflatable restraints - side. The eighth digit is the engine code: "J"—LG8 3.1L V-6; "K"—L36 3.8L V-6; and "1"—L67 3.8L V-6. The ninth character is a check digit that verifies the accuracy of the VIN. The tenth character identifies the model year (Y = 2000). The eleventh digit identifies the assembly plant. Characters twelve through seventeen are the production sequence number.

*Note: Production totals for 2000 Buicks were not available when this book went to press.

Century Custom (V-6)

Model No.	Body/Style No.	Body Type & Seating	Factory Price	Shipping Weight	Prod. Total
S69	WS5	4-dr. Sed.-6P	20162	3368	*

Century Limited (V-6)

Y69	WY5	4-dr. Sed.-6P	22297	3371	*

Note: Century 2000 Special Edition price was $21,472.

Regal LS (V-6)

B69	WF5	4-dr. Sed.-6P	22708	3439	*

Regal GS (V-6)

F69	WD5	4-dr. Sed.-6P	25065	3543	*

LeSabre Custom (V-6)

P69	HP5	4-dr. Sed.-6P	23850	3567	*

LeSabre Limited (V-6)

R69	HR5	4-dr. Sed.-6P	27955	3591	*

Park Avenue (V-6)

W69	CW5	4-dr. Sed.-6P	32395	3778	*

Park Avenue Ultra (V-6)

U69	CU5	4-dr. Sed.-6P	37470	3884	*

ENGINES: BASE V-6 (Century Custom & Limited) 60-degree overhead valve V-6. Cast iron block and aluminum heads. Displacement: 191 cu. in. (3.1 liters). Bore & stroke: 3.51 in. x 3.31 in. Compression ratio: 9.6:1. Brake horsepower: 175 @ 5200 rpm. Torque: 195 lb.-ft. @ 4000 rpm. Sequential Port fuel injection. BASE V-6 (Regal LS, LeSabre, Park Avenue) Series II 90-degree overhead valve V-6 with balance shaft. Cast iron block and heads. Displacement: 231 cu. in. (3.8 liters). Bore & stroke: 3.80 in. x 3.40 in. Compression ratio: 9.4:1. Brake horsepower: 205 @ 5200 rpm (Regal LS - 200 @ 5200 rpm). Torque: 230 lb.-ft. @ 4000 rpm (Regal LS - 225 lb.-ft. @ 4000 rpm). Sequential Port fuel injection. BASE V-6 (Regal GS, Park Avenue Ultra) Supercharged 90-degree overhead valve V-6 with balance shaft. Cast iron block and heads. Displacement: 231 cu. in. (3.8 liters). Bore & stroke: 3.80 in. x 3.40 in. Compression ratio: 8.5:1.

Brake horsepower: 240 @ 5200 rpm. Torque: 280 lb.-ft. @ 3600 rpm. Sequential Port fuel injection.

2000 Buick, Regal GS sedan. (OCW)

CHASSIS DATA: Wheelbase: (Century) 109.0 in.; (Regal) 109.0 in.; (LeSabre) 112.2 in.; (Park Avenue) 113.8 in. Overall length: (Century) 194.6 in.; (Regal) 196.2 in.; (LeSabre) 200.0 in.; (Park Avenue) 206.8 in. Height: (Century) 56.6 in.; (Regal) 56.6 in.; (LeSabre) 57.0 in.; (Park Avenue) 57.4 in. Width: (Century) 72.7 in.; (Regal) 72.7 in.; (LeSabre) 73.5 in.; (Park Avenue) 74.7 in. Front Tread: (Century) 62.0 in.; (Regal) 62.0 in.; (LeSabre): 62.3 in.; (Park Avenue) 62.7 in. Rear Tread: (Century) 61.1 in.; (Regal) 61.3 in.; (LeSabre) 62.3 in.; (Park Avenue) 62.3 in. Standard Tires: (Century) P205/70R15; (Regal LS) P215/70R15; (Regal GS) P225/60R16; (LeSabre) P215/70R15; (Park Avenue) P225/60R16.

TECHNICAL: Transmission: (Century) 4T60-E electronically controlled four-speed automatic w/overdrive. (Regal LS, LeSabre, Park Avenue) 4T65-E electronically controlled four-speed automatic w/overdrive. (Regal GS, Park Avenue Ultra) Heavy-duty 4T65-E electronically controlled four-speed automatic w/overdrive. Steering: (Century, LeSabre, Park Avenue) Rack and pinion; (Regal, Park Avenue Ultra) Magnetic variable-effort. Front Suspension: (Century, Regal) MacPherson strut w/L-shaped lower control arm and aluminum knuckle, twin tube strut, stabilizer bar; (LeSabre) MacPherson struts w/coil springs and tubular stabilizer bar; (Park Avenue) MacPherson struts, deflected disc strut shock absorbers, stabilizer bar. Rear Suspension: (Century) Isolated, independent coil over strut tri-link design, twin tube strut shock absorbers, stabilizer bar; (Regal) Tri-link independent w/coil spring over strut, twin tube strut shock absorbers; stabilizer bar; (LeSabre) Semi-trailing arm w/coil springs and electronic level control and stabilizer bar; (Park Avenue) Semi-trailing w/lateral link, twin tube shock absorbers w/electronic control. Brakes: (Century) Power front disc, rear drum w/anti-lock; (Regal, LeSabre, Park Avenue) Power four-wheel disc w/anti-lock. Body Construction: (Century, Regal, Park Avenue) Integral body/frame; (LeSabre) Integral body/frame w/isolated engine cradle. Fuel Tank: (Century) 17.5 gal.; (Regal) 17.5 gal.; (LeSabre) 18.5 gal.; (Park Avenue) 18.5 gal.

DRIVETRAIN OPTIONS: Y56 Gran Touring Suspension Package: (Regal LS & GS) N/A; (LeSabre) $185; (Park Avenue) N/A. NW9 Traction Control System (LeSabre) $175; (Park Avenue) $175.

CENTURY CONVENIENCE/APPEARANCE OPTIONS: N/A at the time this book went to press.

REGAL CONVENIENCE/APPEARANCE OPTIONS: N/A at the time this book went to press.

2000 Buick, LeSabre Custom sedan with Gran Touring package. (OCW)

LESABRE CONVENIENCE/APPEARANCE OPTIONS: (Custom) Base pkg. $100; Premium pkg. $1088; Luxury pkg. $1593; Prestige pkg. $2298. (Limited) Base pkg. $100; Prestige pkg. $716. Y56 Gran Touring Pkg.: incl. Gran Touring susp., 16-in. alum. whls, P225/50R16 touring tires, 3.05:1 axle ratio, magnetic variable-assist pwr stng, leather-wrapped stng whl $185. T1U Driver Confidence Pkg.: incl. StabiliTrak, EyeCue head-up windshield display, self-sealing tires $800. Calif. emissions NC. Air filtration system (Custom) $50. Trunk convenience net (Custom) $30. Engine block heater $18. Leather seat trim (Custom) $695; (Limited) $735. Sunroof (Custom) $1045; (Limited) $995. Dual lighted visor mirrors (Custom) $92. Electrochromic rearview mirror $80. 6-way pwr driver's seat (Custom) $423. 6-way pwr pass. seat (Custom) $330. Memory driver's seat and outside mirrors (Limited) $145. Heated front seats and outside mirrors (Limited) $260. 5-Person Seating/Convenience Console Pkg.: incl. 45/45 bucket seats, console w/writing surface, phone/FAX provision (Limited) $70. 3-function universal transmitter (Limited) $100. (UL0) ETR AM/FM radio w/Cassette & stng whl controls (Custom) $150. (UN0) ETR AM/FM radio w/CD player & stng whl controls (Custom) $100-$250. (UN6) ETR AM/FM radio w/Pwr Load Cassette (Custom) $165. (UP0) ETR AM/FM radio w/Pwr Load Cassette and CD player & stng whl controls (Custom) $200-$350. (U1S) Trunk-mounted 12-disc CD changer $595. P215/70R15 WSW tires $70. 15-inch alum whls (Custom) $325. 16-inch Crosslace alum whls: (Custom) $375; (Limited) $50.

PARK AVENUE CONVENIENCE/APPEARANCE OPTIONS: N/A at the time this book went to press.

Buick Indianapolis 500 Pace Cars

May 30, 1939: 1939 Buick Roadmaster convertible sedan, in one photo pictured with race winner's Borg-Warner trophy. Note that in one photo the car has whitewall tires and in another blackwall tires,

May 30,1959: 1959 Buick Electra 225 convertible, in one photo pictured with speedway owner Tony Hulman at the wheel and in the other with race winner Roger Ward and his pooch behind the wheel. The gentlemen pictured with Hulman are Indianapolis-area Buick dealers. Note the second, identical Buick pace car parked behind Hulman's convertible. Ward was awarded the Buick pace car as a traditional gift presented to the winner of the Indy 500. (IMS)

May 25, 1975: 1975 Buick Century Custom T-top coupe, in one photo pictured on pit road and in the other with the four-cylinder-powered Buick Bug. The Bug, owned by the Sloan Transportation Museum of Flint, Michigan, set a record of 105 mph at Indianapolis in 1910, before the "official" Indianapolis 500 began. (IMS)

May 30, 1976: Buick returned for the second year in-in-a-row to pace the Indianapolis 500 with a turbocharged V-6-powered Century T-top coupe. (IMS)

May 24, 1981: 1981 Buick Regal Targa coupe, in one photo pictured on display at McCormick Place during the 1981 Chicago Auto Show and in the other on the famous yard of bricks that marks the finish line of the Indianapolis Motor Speedway. (IMS)

May 29, 1983: 1983 Buick Riviera XX (20th Anniversary Edition) convertible. (OCW)

VEHICLE CONDITION SCALE

Excellent

1) EXCELLENT: Restored to current maxiumum professional standards of quality in every area, or perfect original with components operating and appearing as new. A 95-plus point show vehicle that is not driven.

Fine

2) FINE: Well-restored, or a combination of superior restoration and excellent original. Also, an *extremely* well-maintained original showing very minimal wear.

Very Good

3) VERY GOOD: Completely operable original or "older restoration" showing wear. Also, a good amateur restoration, all presentable and serviceable inside and out. Plus, combinations of well-done restoration and good operable components or a partially restored vehicle with all parts necessary to complete and/or valuable NOS parts.

Good

4) GOOD: A driveable vehicle needing no or only minor work to be functional. Also, a deteriorated restoration or a very poor amateur restoration. All components may need restoration to be "excellent," but the vehicle is mostly useable "as is."

5) RESTORABLE: Needs *complete* restoration of body, chassis and interior. May or may not be running, but isn't weathered, wrecked or stripped to the point of being useful only for parts.

6) PARTS VEHICLE: May or may not be running, but is weathered, wrecked and/or stripped to the point of being useful primarily for parts.

A WORD ABOUT OLD BUICKS...

The market for cars more than 20 years old is strong. Some buyers of pre-1981 cars are collectors who invest in vehicles likely to increase in value the older they get. Other buyers prefer the looks, size, performance and reliability of yesterday's better-built automobiles.

With a typical 2000 model selling for $18,000 or more, some Americans find themselves priced out of the new-car market. Late-model used cars are pricy, too, although short on distinctive looks and roominess. The old cars may use a little more gas, but they cost a lot less.

New cars and late-model used cars rapidly depreciate in value. Many can't tow large trailers. Their high-tech engineering is expensive to maintain or repair. In contrast, well-kept old cars are mechanically simpler, but powerful. They appreciate in value as they grow more scarce and collectible. Insuring them is somewhat cheaper, too.

Selecting a car and paying the right price for it are two considerations old car buyers face. What models did Buick offer in 1958? Which 1963 Buick is worth the most today? What should someone pay for a 1968 Wildcat Custom convertible?

The *Standard Catalog of Buick 1903-2000* answers such questions. The "Price Guide" section shows most models made between 1903 and 1992. It helps to gauge what these models sell for in six different graded conditions. Models built since 1993 are generally considered "used cars" of which few, as yet, have achieved collectible status.

The price estimates contained in this book are current as of the publication date, January 2000. After that date, more current prices may be obtained by referring to *Old Cars Price Guide*, which is available from Krause Publications, 700 E. State St., Iola, WI 54990, telephone (715)445-2214.

HOW TO USE THE BUICK PRICE GUIDE

On the following pages is a **BUICK PRICE GUIDE.** The worth of an old car is a "ballpark" estimate at best. The estimates contained in this book are based upon national and regional data compiled by the editors of *Old Cars News & Marketplace* and *Old Cars Price Guide.* These data include actual bids and prices at collector car auctions and sales, classified and display advertising of such vehicles, verified reports of private sales and input from experts.

Price estimates are listed for cars in six different states of condition. These conditions (1-6) are illustrated and explained in the **VEHICLE CONDITION SCALE** on the following pages. Values are for complete vehicles — not parts cars — except as noted. Modified car values are not included, but can be estimated by figuring the cost of restoring the subject vehicle to original condition and adjusting the figures shown here accordingly.

Appearing below is a section of chart taken from the **BUICK PRICE GUIDE** to illustrate the following elements:

A. MAKE The make of car, or marque name, appears in large, boldface type at the beginning of each value section.

B. DESCRIPTION The extreme left-hand column indicates vehicle year, model name, body type, engine configuration and, in some cases, wheelbase.

C. CONDITION CODE The six columns to the right are headed by the numbers one through six (1-6) which correspond to the conditions described in the **VEHICLE CONDITION SCALE** on the following page.

D. PRICE. The price estimates, in dollars, appear below their respective condition code headings and across from the vehicle descriptions.

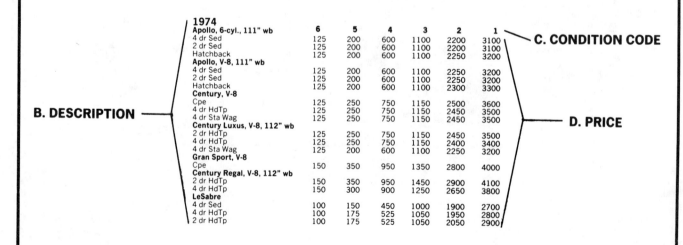

A. MAKE ——————— **BUICK**

1974	6	5	4	3	2	1	
Apollo, 6-cyl., 111" wb							← C. CONDITION CODE
4 dr Sed	125	200	600	1100	2200	3100	
2 dr Sed	125	200	600	1100	2200	3100	
Hatchback	125	200	600	1100	2250	3200	
Apollo, V-8, 111" wb							
4 dr Sed	125	200	600	1100	2250	3200	
2 dr Sed	125	200	600	1100	2250	3200	
Hatchback	125	200	600	1100	2300	3300	
Century, V-8							
Cpe	125	250	750	1150	2500	3600	
4 dr HdTp	125	250	750	1150	2450	3500	
4 dr Sta Wag	125	250	750	1150	2450	3500	
Century Luxus, V-8, 112" wb							← D. PRICE
2 dr HdTp	125	250	750	1150	2450	3500	
4 dr HdTp	125	250	750	1150	2400	3400	
4 dr Sta Wag	125	200	600	1100	2250	3200	
Gran Sport, V-8							
Cpe	150	350	950	1350	2800	4000	
Century Regal, V-8, 112" wb							
2 dr HdTp	150	350	950	1450	2900	4100	
4 dr HdTp	150	300	900	1250	2650	3800	
LeSabre							
4 dr Sed	100	150	450	1000	1900	2700	
4 dr HdTp	100	175	525	1050	1950	2800	
2 dr HdTp	100	175	525	1050	2050	2900	

B. DESCRIPTION

BUICK

	6	5	4	3	2	1
1904						
Model B, 2-cyl.						
Tr				value not estimable		
1905						
Model C, 2-cyl.						
Tr	1500	4800	8000	16,000	28,000	40,000
1906						
Model F & G, 2-cyl.						
Tr	1450	4700	7800	15,600	27,300	39,000
Rds	1450	4550	7600	15,200	26,600	38,000
1907						
Model F & G, 2-cyl.						
Tr	1450	4700	7800	15,600	27,300	39,000
Rds	1450	4550	7600	15,200	26,600	38,000
Model D, S, K & H, 4-cyl.						
Tr	1500	4800	8000	16,000	28,000	40,000
Rds	1450	4700	7800	15,600	27,300	39,000
1908						
Model F & G, 2-cyl.						
Tr	1700	5400	9000	18,000	31,500	45,000
Rds	1650	5300	8800	17,600	30,800	44,000
Model D & S, 4-cyl.						
Tr	1550	4900	8200	16,400	28,700	41,000
Rds	1600	5050	8400	16,800	29,400	42,000
Model 10, 4-cyl.						
Tr	1500	4800	8000	16,000	28,000	40,000
Model 5, 4-cyl.						
Tr	1700	5400	9000	18,000	31,500	45,000
1909						
Model G, (only 6 built in 1909).						
Rds	1750	5500	9200	18,400	32,200	46,000
Model F & G						
Tr	1650	5300	8800	17,600	30,800	44,000
Rds	1700	5400	9000	18,000	31,500	45,000
Model 10, 4-cyl.						
Tr	1600	5150	8600	17,200	30,100	43,000
Rds	1650	5300	8800	17,600	30,800	44,000
Model 16 & 17, 4-cyl.						
Rds	1700	5400	9000	18,000	31,500	45,000
Tr	1650	5300	8800	17,600	30,800	44,000
1910						
Model 6, 2-cyl.						
Tr	1500	4800	8000	16,000	28,000	40,000
Model F, 2-cyl.						
Tr	1450	4550	7600	15,200	26,600	38,000
Model 14, 2-cyl.						
Rds	1400	4450	7400	14,800	25,900	37,000
Model 10, 4-cyl.						
Tr	1300	4200	7000	14,000	24,500	35,000
Rds	1300	4200	7000	14,000	24,500	35,000
Model 19, 4-cyl.						
Tr	1550	4900	8200	16,400	28,700	41,000
Model 16 & 17, 4-cyl.						
Rds	1500	4800	8000	16,000	28,000	40,000
Tr	1450	4700	7800	15,600	27,300	39,000
Model 7, 4-cyl.						
Tr	1650	5300	8800	17,600	30,800	44,000
Model 41, 4-cyl.						
Limo	1450	4700	7800	15,600	27,300	39,000
1911						
Model 14, 2-cyl.						
Rds	1300	4100	6800	13,600	23,800	34,000
Model 21, 4-cyl.						
Tr	1300	4200	7000	14,000	24,500	35,000
Model 26 & 27, 4-cyl.						
Rds	1350	4300	7200	14,400	25,200	36,000
Tr	1300	4100	6800	13,600	23,800	34,000
Model 32 & 33						
Rds	1300	4200	7000	14,000	24,500	35,000
Tr	1300	4100	6800	13,600	23,800	34,000
Model 38 & 39, 4-cyl.						
Rds	1450	4550	7600	15,200	26,600	38,000
Tr	1450	4700	7800	15,600	27,300	39,000
Limo	2050	6600	11,000	22,000	38,500	55,000
1912						
Model 34, 35 & 36, 4-cyl.						
Rds	1250	3950	6600	13,200	23,100	33,000
Tr	1300	4100	6800	13,600	23,800	34,000
Model 28 & 29, 4-cyl.						
Rds	1300	4100	6800	13,600	23,800	34,000
Tr	1300	4200	7000	14,000	24,500	35,000
Model 43, 4-cyl.						
Tr	1350	4300	7200	14,400	25,200	36,000
1913						
Model 30 & 31, 4-cyl.						
Rds	1200	3850	6400	12,800	22,400	32,000
Tr	1250	3950	6600	13,200	23,100	33,000
Model 40, 4-cyl.						
Tr	1300	4200	7000	14,000	24,500	35,000

	6	5	4	3	2	1
Model 24 & 25, 4-cyl.						
Rds	1300	4200	7000	14,000	24,500	35,000
Tr	1350	4300	7200	14,400	25,200	36,000
1914						
Model B-24 & B-25, 4-cyl.						
Rds	1250	3950	6600	13,200	23,100	33,000
Tr	1300	4100	6800	13,600	23,800	34,000
Model B-36, B-37 & B-38, 4-cyl.						
Rds	1300	4100	6800	13,600	23,800	34,000
Tr	1300	4200	7000	14,000	24,500	35,000
Cpe	1200	3850	6400	12,800	22,400	32,000
Model B-55, 6-cyl.						
7P Tr	1350	4300	7200	14,400	25,200	36,000
1915						
Model C-24 & C-25, 4-cyl.						
Rds	1300	4100	6800	13,600	23,800	34,000
Tr	1300	4200	7000	14,000	24,500	35,000
Model C-36 & C-37, 4-cyl.						
Rds	1300	4200	7000	14,000	24,500	35,000
Tr	1350	4300	7200	14,400	25,200	36,000
Model C-54 & C-55, 6-cyl.						
Rds	1350	4300	7200	14,400	25,200	36,000
Tr	1400	4450	7400	14,800	25,900	37,000
1916						
Model D-54 & D-55, 6-cyl.						
Rds	1300	4100	6800	13,600	23,800	34,000
Tr	1300	4200	7000	14,000	24,500	35,000
1916-1917						
Model D-34 & D-35, 4-cyl.						
Rds	1200	3850	6400	12,800	22,400	32,000
Tr	1250	3950	6600	13,200	23,100	33,000
Model D-44 & D-45, 6-cyl.						
Rds	1250	3950	6600	13,200	23,100	33,000
Tr	1300	4100	6800	13,600	23,800	34,000
Model D-46 & D-47, 6-cyl.						
Conv Cpe	1150	3600	6000	12,000	21,000	30,000
Sed	850	2750	4600	9200	16,100	23,000
1918						
Model E-34 & E-35, 4-cyl.						
Rds	1100	3500	5800	11,600	20,300	29,000
Tr	1150	3600	6000	12,000	21,000	30,000
Model E-37, 4-cyl.						
Sed	850	2650	4400	8800	15,400	22,000
Model E-44, E-45 & E-49, 6-cyl.						
Rds	1150	3600	6000	12,000	21,000	30,000
Tr	1150	3700	6200	12,400	21,700	31,000
7P Tr	1200	3850	6400	12,800	22,400	32,000
Model E-46, E-47 & E-50, 6-cyl.						
Conv Cpe	1050	3350	5600	11,200	19,600	28,000
Sed	850	2750	4600	9200	16,100	23,000
7P Sed	900	2800	4700	9400	16,500	23,500
1919						
Model H-44, H-45 & H-49, 6-cyl.						
2d Rds	1100	3500	5800	11,600	20,300	29,000
4d Tr	1150	3600	6000	12,000	21,000	30,000
4d 7P Tr	1150	3700	6200	12,400	21,700	31,000
Model H-46, H-47 & H-50, 6-cyl.						
2d Cpe	900	2900	4800	9600	16,800	24,000
4d Sed	750	2400	4000	8000	14,000	20,000
4d 7P Sed	800	2500	4200	8400	14,700	21,000
1920						
Model K, 6-cyl.						
2d Cpe K-46	850	2650	4400	8800	15,400	22,000
4d Sed K-47	700	2150	3600	7200	12,600	18,000
2d Rds K-44	1100	3500	5800	11,600	20,300	29,000
4d Tr K-49	1050	3350	5600	11,200	19,600	28,000
4d Tr K-45	1000	3250	5400	10,800	18,900	27,000
4d 7P Sed K-50	700	2300	3800	7600	13,300	19,000
1921						
Series 40, 6-cyl.						
2d Rds	1100	3500	5800	11,600	20,300	29,000
4d Tr	1050	3350	5600	11,200	19,600	28,000
4d 7P Tr	1100	3500	5800	11,600	20,300	29,000
2d Cpe	600	1900	3200	6400	11,200	16,000
4d Sed	550	1800	3000	6000	10,500	15,000
2d Ewb Cpe	650	2050	3400	6800	11,900	17,000
4d 7P Sed	600	1900	3200	6400	11,200	16,000
1921-1922						
Series 30, 4-cyl.						
2d Rds	1000	3250	5400	10,800	18,900	27,000
4d Tr	1000	3100	5200	10,400	18,200	26,000
2d Cpe OS	550	1800	3000	6000	10,500	15,000
4d Sed	500	1550	2600	5200	9100	13,000
Series 40, 6-cyl.						
2d Rds	1100	3500	5800	11,600	20,300	29,000
4d Tr	1050	3350	5600	11,200	19,600	28,000
4d 7P Tr	1100	3500	5800	11,600	20,300	29,000
2d Cpe	600	1900	3200	6400	11,200	16,000
4d Sed	550	1700	2800	5600	9800	14,000
2d Cpe	700	2150	3600	7200	12,600	18,000
4d 7P Sed	650	2050	3400	6800	11,900	17,000
4d 50 7P Limo	700	2300	3800	7600	13,300	19,000

	6	5	4	3	2	1
1923						
Series 30, 4-cyl.						
2d Rds	900	2900	4800	9600	16,800	24,000
2d Spt Rds	950	3000	5000	10,000	17,500	25,000
4d Tr	900	2900	4800	9600	16,800	24,000
2d Cpe	600	1900	3200	6400	11,200	16,000
4d Sed	550	1700	2800	5600	9800	14,000
4d Tr Sed	550	1800	3000	6000	10,500	15,000
Series 40, 6-cyl.						
2d Rds	1000	3100	5200	10,400	18,200	26,000
4d Tr	950	3000	5000	10,000	17,500	25,000
4d 7P Tr	1000	3100	5200	10,400	18,200	26,000
2d Cpe	700	2150	3600	7200	12,600	18,000
4d Sed	600	1900	3200	6400	11,200	16,000
Master Series 50, 6-cyl.						
2d Spt Rds	1000	3250	5400	10,800	18,900	27,000
4d Spt Tr	1050	3350	5600	11,200	19,600	28,000
4d 7P Sed	700	2150	3600	7200	12,600	18,000
1924						
Standard Series 30, 4-cyl.						
2d Rds	1000	3100	5200	10,400	18,200	26,000
4d Tr	1000	3250	5400	10,800	18,900	27,000
2d Cpe	650	2050	3400	6800	11,900	17,000
4d Sed	550	1800	3000	6000	10,500	15,000
Master Series 40, 6-cyl.						
2d Rds	1000	3250	5400	10,800	18,900	27,000
4d Tr	1050	3350	5600	11,200	19,600	28,000
4d 7P Tr	1100	3500	5800	11,600	20,300	29,000
2d Cpe	700	2150	3600	7200	12,600	18,000
4d Sed	600	1900	3200	6400	11,200	16,000
4d Demi Sed	600	2000	3300	6600	11,600	16,500
Master Series 50, 6-cyl.						
2d Spt Rds	1050	3350	5600	11,200	19,600	28,000
4d Spt Tr	1100	3500	5800	11,600	20,300	29,000
2d Cabr Cpe	1000	3250	5400	10,800	18,900	27,000
4d Town Car	800	2500	4200	8400	14,700	21,000
4d 7P Sed	700	2300	3800	7600	13,300	19,000
4d Brgm Sed	750	2400	4000	8000	14,000	20,000
4d Limo	850	2650	4400	8800	15,400	22,000
1925						
Standard Series 20, 6-cyl.						
2d Rds	950	3000	5000	10,000	17,500	25,000
2d Spt Rds	1000	3100	5200	10,400	18,200	26,000
2d Encl Rds	1000	3250	5400	10,800	18,900	27,000
4d Tr	950	3000	5000	10,000	17,500	25,000
4d Encl Tr	1000	3100	5200	10,400	18,200	26,000
2d Bus Cpe	750	2400	4000	8000	14,000	20,000
2d Cpe	750	2450	4100	8200	14,400	20,500
4d Sed	700	2150	3600	7200	12,600	18,000
4d Demi Sed	700	2200	3700	7400	13,000	18,500
Master Series 40, 6-cyl.						
2d Rds	1000	3250	5400	10,800	18,900	27,000
2d Encl Rds	1050	3350	5600	11,200	19,600	28,000
4d Tr	1050	3350	5600	11,200	19,600	28,000
4d Encl Tr	1100	3500	5800	11,600	20,300	29,000
2d Cpe	800	2500	4200	8400	14,700	21,000
2d Sed	700	2150	3600	7200	12,600	18,000
4d Sed	700	2300	3800	7600	13,300	19,000
Master Series 50, 6-cyl.						
2d Spt Rds	1050	3350	5600	11,200	19,600	28,000
4d Spt Tr	1100	3500	5800	11,600	20,300	29,000
2d Cabr Cpe	1100	3500	5800	11,600	20,300	29,000
4d 7P Sed	800	2500	4200	8400	14,700	21,000
4d Limo	850	2650	4400	8800	15,400	22,000
4d Brgm Sed	850	2750	4600	9200	16,100	23,000
4d Town Car	950	3000	5000	10,000	17,500	25,000
1926						
Standard Series, 6-cyl.						
2d Rds	1000	3100	5200	10,400	18,200	26,000
4d Tr	1000	3250	5400	10,800	18,900	27,000
2d 2P Cpe	850	2750	4600	9200	16,100	23,000
2d 4P Cpe	850	2650	4400	8800	15,400	22,000
2d Sed	700	2300	3800	7600	13,300	19,000
4d Sed	750	2400	4000	8000	14,000	20,000
Master Series, 6-cyl.						
2d Rds	1000	3250	5400	10,800	18,900	27,000
4d Tr	1050	3350	5600	11,200	19,600	28,000
2d Spt Rds	1050	3350	5600	11,200	19,600	28,000
4d Spt Tr	1100	3500	5800	11,600	20,300	29,000
2d 4P Cpe	900	2900	4800	9600	16,800	24,000
2d Spt Cpe	950	3000	5000	10,000	17,500	25,000
2d Sed	850	2650	4400	8800	15,400	22,000
4d Sed	850	2750	4600	9200	16,100	23,000
4d Brgm	900	2900	4800	9600	16,800	24,000
4d 7P Sed	950	3000	5000	10,000	17,500	25,000
1927						
Series 115, 6-cyl.						
2d Rds	1000	3100	5200	10,400	18,200	26,000
4d Tr	1000	3250	5400	10,800	18,900	27,000
2d 2P Cpe	850	2650	4400	8800	15,400	22,000
2d 4P RS Cpe	850	2750	4600	9200	16,100	23,000
2d Spt Cpe	850	2650	4400	8800	15,400	22,000
2d Sed	700	2300	3800	7600	13,300	19,000
4d Sed	750	2400	4000	8000	14,000	20,000
4d Brgm	800	2500	4200	8400	14,700	21,000
Series 120, 6-cyl.						
2d 4P Cpe	850	2750	4600	9200	16,100	23,000
2d Sed	750	2400	4000	8000	14,000	20,000
4d Sed	800	2500	4200	8400	14,700	21,000
Series 128, 6-cyl.						
2d Spt Rds	1100	3500	5800	11,600	20,300	29,000
4d Spt Tr	1150	3600	6000	12,000	21,000	30,000
2d Conv	1000	3250	5400	10,800	18,900	27,000
2d 5P Cpe	900	2900	4800	9600	16,800	24,000
2d Spt Cpe RS	950	3000	5000	10,000	17,500	25,000
4d 7P Sed	850	2650	4400	8800	15,400	22,000
4d Brgm	850	2750	4600	9200	16,100	23,000
1928						
Series 115, 6-cyl.						
2d Rds	1000	3100	5200	10,400	18,200	26,000
4d Tr	1000	3250	5400	10,800	18,900	27,000
2d 2P Cpe	750	2400	4000	8000	14,000	20,000
2d Spt Cpe	800	2500	4200	8400	14,700	21,000
2d Sed	700	2150	3600	7200	12,600	18,000
4d Sed	700	2300	3800	7600	13,300	19,000
4d Brgm	750	2400	4000	8000	14,000	20,000
Series 120, 6-cyl.						
2d Cpe	800	2500	4200	8400	14,700	21,000
4d Sed	700	2300	3800	7600	13,300	19,000
4d Brgm	750	2400	4000	8000	14,000	20,000
Series 128, 6-cyl.						
2d Spt Rds	1150	3600	6000	12,000	21,000	30,000
4d Spt Tr	1150	3700	6200	12,400	21,700	31,000
2d 5P Cpe	800	2500	4200	8400	14,700	21,000
2d Spt Cpe	850	2650	4400	8800	15,400	22,000
4d 7P Sed	750	2400	4000	8000	14,000	20,000
4d Brgm	800	2500	4200	8400	14,700	21,000
1929						
Series 116, 6-cyl.						
4d Spt Tr	1150	3600	6000	12,000	21,000	30,000
2d Bus Cpe	700	2150	3600	7200	12,600	18,000
2d RS Cpe	750	2400	4000	8000	14,000	20,000
2d Sed	550	1800	3000	6000	10,500	15,000
4d Sed	600	1900	3200	6400	11,200	16,000
Series 121, 6-cyl.						
2d Spt Rds	1150	3700	6200	12,400	21,700	31,000
2d Bus Cpe	700	2300	3800	7600	13,300	19,000
2d RS Cpe	800	2500	4200	8400	14,700	21,000
2d 4P Cpe	750	2400	4000	8000	14,000	20,000
4d Sed	650	2050	3400	6800	11,900	17,000
4d CC Sed	650	2100	3500	7000	12,300	17,500
Series 129, 6-cyl.						
2d Conv	1200	3850	6400	12,800	22,400	32,000
4d Spt Tr	1250	3950	6600	13,200	23,100	33,000
4d 7P Tr	1150	3600	6000	12,000	21,000	30,000
2d 5P Cpe	850	2650	4400	8800	15,400	22,000
4d CC Sed	750	2400	4000	8000	14,000	20,000
4d 7P Sed	800	2500	4200	8400	14,700	21,000
4d Limo	850	2650	4400	8800	15,400	22,000
1930						
Series 40, 6-cyl.						
2d Rds	1250	3950	6600	13,200	23,100	33,000
4d Phae	1300	4100	6800	13,600	23,800	34,000
2d Bus Cpe	850	2650	4400	8800	15,400	22,000
2d RS Cpe	950	3000	5000	10,000	17,500	25,000
2d Sed	650	2100	3500	7000	12,300	17,500
4d Sed	700	2150	3600	7200	12,600	18,000
Series 50, 6-cyl.						
2d 4P Cpe	850	2750	4600	9200	16,100	23,000
4d Sed	700	2150	3600	7200	12,600	18,000
Series 60, 6-cyl.						
2d RS Rds	1300	4200	7000	14,000	24,500	35,000
4d 7P Tr	1350	4300	7200	14,400	25,200	36,000
2d RS Spt Cpe	1000	3250	5400	10,800	18,900	27,000
2d 5P Cpe	950	3000	5000	10,000	17,500	25,000
4d Sed	700	2300	3800	7600	13,300	19,000
4d 7P Sed	750	2400	4000	8000	14,000	20,000
4d Limo	800	2500	4200	8400	14,700	21,000
Marquette - Series 30, 6-cyl.						
2d Spt Rds	1050	3350	5600	11,200	19,600	28,000
4d Phae	1100	3500	5800	11,600	20,300	29,000
2d Bus Cpe	750	2400	4000	8000	14,000	20,000
2d RS Cpe	850	2650	4400	8800	15,400	22,000
2d Sed	550	1800	3000	6000	10,500	15,000
4d Sed	600	1850	3100	6200	10,900	15,500
1931						
Series 50, 8-cyl.						
2d Spt Rds	1300	4200	7000	14,000	24,500	35,000
4d Phae	1350	4300	7200	14,400	25,200	36,000
2d Bus Cpe	900	2900	4800	9600	16,800	24,000
2d RS Cpe	950	3000	5000	10,000	17,500	25,000
2d Sed	700	2150	3600	7200	12,600	18,000
4d Sed	700	2300	3800	7600	13,300	19,000
2d Conv	1350	4300	7200	14,400	25,200	36,000
Series 60, 8-cyl.						
2d Spt Rds	1400	4450	7400	14,800	25,900	37,000
4d Phae	1450	4550	7600	15,200	26,600	38,000
2d Bus Cpe	950	3000	5000	10,000	17,500	25,000
2d RS Cpe	1000	3100	5200	10,400	18,200	26,000
4d Sed	750	2400	4000	8000	14,000	20,000
Series 80, 8-cyl.						
2d Cpe	1000	3250	5400	10,800	18,900	27,000
4d Sed	850	2650	4400	8800	15,400	22,000
4d 7P Sed	850	2750	4600	9200	16,100	23,000
Series 90, 8-cyl.						
2d Spt Rds	1700	5400	9000	18,000	31,500	45,000
4d 7P Tr	1650	5300	8800	17,600	30,800	44,000
2d 5P Cpe	1150	3700	6200	12,400	21,700	31,000
2d RS Cpe	1150	3600	6000	12,000	21,000	30,000
2d Conv	1600	5150	8600	17,200	30,100	43,000
4d 5P Sed	950	3000	5000	10,000	17,500	25,000
4d 7P Sed	1000	3100	5200	10,400	18,200	26,000
4d Limo	1000	3250	5400	10,800	18,900	27,000
1932						
Series 50, 8-cyl						
4d Spt Phae	1450	4550	7600	15,200	26,600	38,000
2d Conv	1450	4700	7800	15,600	27,300	39,000
2d Phae	1500	4800	8000	16,000	28,000	40,000
2d Bus Cpe	850	2650	4400	8800	15,400	22,000
2d RS Cpe	850	2750	4600	9200	16,100	23,000
2d Vic Cpe	900	2900	4800	9600	16,800	24,000
4d Sed	700	2300	3800	7600	13,300	19,000
4d Spt Sed	750	2400	4000	8000	14,000	20,000
Series 60, 8-cyl.						
4d Spt Phae	1550	4900	8200	16,400	28,700	41,000
2d Conv	1600	5050	8400	16,800	29,400	42,000
2d Phae	1600	5150	8600	17,200	30,100	43,000
2d Bus Cpe	850	2750	4600	9200	16,100	23,000
2d RS Cpe	900	2900	4800	9600	16,800	24,000
2d Vic Cpe	950	3000	5000	10,000	17,500	25,000
4d Sed	800	2500	4200	8400	14,700	21,000
Series 80, 8-cyl.						
2d Vic Cpe	900	2900	4800	9600	16,800	24,000
4d Sed	850	2650	4400	8800	15,400	22,000
Series 90, 8-cyl.						
4d 7P Sed	1150	3600	6000	12,000	21,000	30,000

	6	5	4	3	2	1
4d Limo	1200	3850	6400	12,800	22,400	32,000
4d Clb Sed	1150	3700	6200	12,400	21,700	31,000
4d Spt Phae	1850	5900	9800	19,600	34,300	49,000
2d Phae	1800	5750	9600	19,200	33,600	48,000
2d Conv Cpe	1900	6000	10,000	20,000	35,000	50,000
2d RS Cpe	1250	3950	6600	13,200	23,100	33,000
2d Vic Cpe	1300	4100	6800	13,600	23,800	34,000
4d 5P Sed	1150	3600	6000	12,000	21,000	30,000

1933

	6	5	4	3	2	1
Series 50, 8-cyl.						
2d Conv	1200	3850	6400	12,800	22,400	32,000
2d Bus Cpe	750	2400	4000	8000	14,000	20,000
2d RS Spt Cpe	800	2500	4200	8400	14,700	21,000
2d Vic Cpe	850	2750	4600	9200	16,100	23,000
4d Sed	700	2300	3800	7600	13,300	19,000
Series 60, 8-cyl.						
2d Conv Cpe	1200	3850	6400	12,800	22,400	32,000
4d Phae	1250	3950	6600	13,200	23,100	33,000
2d Spt Cpe	850	2750	4600	9200	16,100	23,000
2d Vic Cpe	1000	3250	5400	10,800	18,900	27,000
4d Sed	850	2650	4400	8800	15,400	22,000
Series 80, 8-cyl.						
2d Conv	1400	4450	7400	14,800	25,900	37,000
4d Phae	1450	4700	7800	15,600	27,300	39,000
2d Spt Cpe	1100	3500	5800	11,600	20,300	29,000
2d Vic	1150	3600	6000	12,000	21,000	30,000
4d Sed	900	2900	4800	9600	16,800	24,000
Series 90, 8-cyl.						
2d Vic	1300	4100	6800	13,600	23,800	34,000
4d 5P Sed	1050	3350	5600	11,200	19,600	28,000
4d 7P Sed	1100	3500	5800	11,600	20,300	29,000
4d Clb Sed	1150	3600	6000	12,000	21,000	30,000
4d Limo	1250	3950	6600	13,200	23,100	33,000

1934

	6	5	4	3	2	1
Special Series 40, 8-cyl.						
2d Bus Cpe	800	2500	4200	8400	14,700	21,000
2d RS Cpe	850	2650	4400	8800	15,400	22,000
2d Tr Sed	700	2300	3800	7600	13,300	19,000
4d Tr Sed	800	2500	4200	8400	14,700	21,000
4d Sed	750	2400	4000	8000	14,000	20,000
Series 50, 8-cyl.						
2d Conv	1400	4450	7400	14,800	25,900	37,000
2d Bus Cpe	900	2900	4800	9600	16,800	24,000
2d Spt Cpe	1000	3100	5200	10,400	18,200	26,000
2d Vic Cpe	1000	3250	5400	10,800	18,900	27,000
4d Sed	800	2500	4200	8400	14,700	21,000
Series 60, 8-cyl.						
2d Conv	1450	4550	7600	15,200	26,600	38,000
4d Phae	1400	4450	7400	14,800	25,900	37,000
2d Spt Cpe	1000	3100	5200	10,400	18,200	26,000
2d Vic	1000	3250	5400	10,800	18,900	27,000
4d Sed	850	2650	4400	8800	15,400	22,000
4d Clb Sed	850	2750	4600	9200	16,100	23,000
Series 90, 8-cyl.						
2d Conv	1500	4800	8000	16,000	28,000	40,000
4d Phae	1450	4700	7800	15,600	27,300	39,000
4d Spt Cpe	1000	3250	5400	10,800	18,900	27,000
4d 5P Sed	950	3000	5000	10,000	17,500	25,000
4d 7P Sed	1000	3100	5200	10,400	18,200	26,000
4d Clb Sed	1000	3250	5400	10,800	18,900	27,000
4d Limo	1050	3350	5600	11,200	19,600	28,000
2d Vic	1150	3600	6000	12,000	21,000	30,000

1935

	6	5	4	3	2	1
Special Series 40, 8-cyl.						
2d Conv	1300	4100	6800	13,600	23,800	34,000
2d Bus Cpe	850	2650	4400	8800	15,400	22,000
2d RS Spt Cpe	900	2900	4800	9600	16,800	24,000
2d Sed	700	2300	3800	7600	13,300	19,000
2d Tr Sed	750	2400	4000	8000	14,000	20,000
4d Sed	750	2400	4000	8000	14,000	20,000
4d Tr Sed	800	2500	4200	8400	14,700	21,000
Series 50, 8-cyl.						
2d Conv	1300	4200	7000	14,000	24,500	35,000
2d Bus Cpe	850	2750	4600	9200	16,100	23,000
2d Spt Cpe	900	2900	4800	9600	16,800	24,000
2d Vic	950	3000	5000	10,000	17,500	25,000
4d Sed	800	2500	4200	8400	14,700	21,000
Series 60, 8-cyl.						
2d Conv	1300	4100	6800	13,600	23,800	34,000
4d Phae	1250	3950	6600	13,200	23,100	33,000
2d Vic	1050	3350	5600	11,200	19,600	28,000
4d Sed	850	2650	4400	8800	15,400	22,000
4d Clb Sed	850	2750	4600	9200	16,100	23,000
2d Spt Cpe	1000	3250	5400	10,800	18,900	27,000
Series 90, 8-cyl.						
2d Conv	1350	4300	7200	14,400	25,200	36,000
4d Phae	1300	4200	7000	14,000	24,500	35,000
2d Spt Cpe	1050	3350	5600	11,200	19,600	28,000
2d Vic	1100	3500	5800	11,600	20,300	29,000
4d 5P Sed	950	3000	5000	10,000	17,500	25,000
4d 7P Sed	1000	3100	5200	10,400	18,200	26,000
4d Limo	1050	3350	5600	11,200	19,600	28,000
4d Clb Sed	1000	3250	5400	10,800	18,900	27,000

1936

	6	5	4	3	2	1
Special Series 40, 8-cyl.						
2d Conv	1300	4100	6800	13,600	23,800	34,000
2d Bus Cpe	850	2650	4400	8800	15,400	22,000
2d RS Cpe	850	2750	4600	9200	16,100	23,000
2d Sed	750	2400	4000	8000	14,000	20,000
4d Sed	750	2400	4000	8000	14,000	20,000
Century Series 60, 8-cyl.						
2d Conv	1350	4300	7200	14,400	25,200	36,000
2d RS Cpe	1000	3100	5200	10,400	18,200	26,000
2d Sed	850	2650	4400	8800	15,400	22,000
4d Sed	900	2900	4800	9600	16,800	24,000
Roadmaster Series 80, 8-cyl.						
4d Phae	1300	4100	6800	13,600	23,800	34,000
4d Sed	950	3000	5000	10,000	17,500	25,000
Limited Series 90, 8-cyl.						
4d Sed	1000	3100	5200	10,400	18,200	26,000
4d 7P Sed	1000	3250	5400	10,800	18,900	27,000
4d Fml Sed	1050	3350	5600	11,200	19,600	28,000
4d 7P Limo	1150	3600	6000	12,000	21,000	30,000

1937

	6	5	4	3	2	1
Special Series 40, 8-cyl.						
2d Conv	1500	4800	8000	16,000	28,000	40,000
4d Phae	1450	4550	7600	15,200	26,600	38,000
2d Bus Cpe	800	2500	4200	8400	14,700	21,000
2d Spt Cpe	850	2650	4400	8800	15,400	22,000
2d FBk	750	2400	4000	8000	14,000	20,000
2d Sed	700	2300	3800	7600	13,300	19,000
4d FBk Sed	750	2400	4000	8000	14,000	20,000
4d Sed	750	2400	4000	8000	14,000	20,000
Century Series 60, 8-cyl.						
2d Conv	1600	5150	8600	17,200	30,100	43,000
4d Phae	1550	4900	8200	16,400	28,700	41,000
2d Spt Cpe	900	2900	4800	9600	16,800	24,000
2d FBk	800	2500	4200	8400	14,700	21,000
2d Sed	800	2500	4200	8400	14,700	21,000
4d FBk Sed	850	2650	4400	8800	15,400	22,000
4d Sed	850	2650	4400	8800	15,400	22,000
Roadmaster Series 80, 8-cyl.						
4d Sed	850	2750	4600	9200	16,100	23,000
4d Fml Sed	900	2900	4800	9600	16,800	24,000
4d Phae	1550	4900	8200	16,400	28,700	41,000
Limited Series 90, 8-cyl.						
4d Sed	900	2900	4800	9600	16,800	24,000
4d 7P Sed	950	3000	5000	10,000	17,500	25,000
4d Fml Sed	1000	3100	5200	10,400	18,200	26,000
4d Limo	1100	3500	5800	11,600	20,300	29,000

1938

	6	5	4	3	2	1
Special Series 40, 8-cyl.						
2d Conv	1600	5050	8400	16,800	29,400	42,000
4d Phae	1500	4800	8000	16,000	28,000	40,000
2d Bus Cpe	800	2500	4200	8400	14,700	21,000
2d Spt Cpe	850	2650	4400	8800	15,400	22,000
2d FBk	750	2400	4000	8000	14,000	20,000
2d Sed	750	2400	4000	8000	14,000	20,000
4d FBk Sed	800	2500	4200	8400	14,700	21,000
4d Sed	800	2500	4200	8400	14,700	21,000
Century Series 60, 8-cyl.						
2d Conv	1700	5400	9000	18,000	31,500	45,000
4d Phae	1600	5150	8600	17,200	30,100	43,000
2d Spt Cpe	900	2900	4800	9600	16,800	24,000
2d Sed	850	2650	4400	8800	15,400	22,000
4d FBk Sed	850	2650	4400	8800	15,400	22,000
4d Sed	850	2750	4600	9200	16,100	23,000
Roadmaster Series 80, 8-cyl.						
4d Phae	1700	5400	9000	18,000	31,500	45,000
4d FBk Sed	950	3000	5000	10,000	17,500	25,000
4d Sed	1000	3100	5200	10,400	18,200	26,000
4d Fml Sed	1000	3250	5400	10,800	18,900	27,000
Limited Series 90, 8-cyl.						
4d Sed	1050	3350	5600	11,200	19,600	28,000
4d 7P Sed	1100	3500	5800	11,600	20,300	29,000
4d Limo	1200	3850	6400	12,800	22,400	32,000

1939

	6	5	4	3	2	1
Special Series 40, 8-cyl.						
2d Conv	1650	5300	8800	17,600	30,800	44,000
4d Phae	1600	5050	8400	16,800	29,400	42,000
2d Bus Cpe	850	2750	4600	9200	16,100	23,000
2d Spt Cpe	900	2900	4800	9600	16,800	24,000
2d Sed	800	2500	4200	8400	14,700	21,000
4d Sed	800	2500	4200	8400	14,700	21,000
Century Series 60, 8-cyl.						
2d Conv	1750	5650	9400	18,800	32,900	47,000
4d Phae	1700	5400	9000	18,000	31,500	45,000
2d Spt Cpe	1000	3100	5200	10,400	18,200	26,000
2d Sed	850	2750	4600	9200	16,100	23,000
4d Sed	850	2750	4600	9200	16,100	23,000
Roadmaster Series 80, 8-cyl.						
4d Phae FBk	1800	5750	9600	19,200	33,600	48,000
4d Phae	1850	5900	9800	19,600	34,300	49,000
4d FBk Sed	1000	3100	5200	10,400	18,200	26,000
4d Sed	1000	3100	5200	10,400	18,200	26,000
4d Fml Sed	1050	3350	5600	11,200	19,600	28,000
Limited Series 90, 8-cyl.						
4d 8P Sed	1050	3350	5600	11,200	19,600	28,000
4d 4d Sed	1150	3600	6000	12,000	21,000	30,000
4d Limo	1000	3250	5400	10,800	18,900	27,000

1940

	6	5	4	3	2	1
Special Series 40, 8-cyl.						
2d Conv	1750	5500	9200	18,400	32,200	46,000
4d Phae	1650	5300	8800	17,600	30,800	44,000
2d Bus Cpe	850	2650	4400	8800	15,400	22,000
2d Spt Cpe	900	2900	4800	9600	16,800	24,000
2d Sed	800	2500	4200	8400	14,700	21,000
4d Sed	800	2500	4200	8400	14,700	21,000
Super Series 50, 8-cyl.						
2d Conv	1650	5300	8800	17,600	30,800	44,000
4d Phae	1600	5150	8600	17,200	30,100	43,000
2d Cpe	950	3000	5000	10,000	17,500	25,000
4d Sed	800	2500	4200	8400	14,700	21,000
4d Sta Wag	1200	3850	6400	12,800	22,400	32,000
Century Series 60, 8-cyl.						
2d Conv	1750	5650	9400	18,800	32,900	47,000
4d Phae	1700	5400	9000	18,000	31,500	45,000
2d Bus Cpe	1000	3100	5200	10,400	18,200	26,000
2d Spt Cpe	1000	3250	5400	10,800	18,900	27,000
4d Sed	850	2750	4600	9200	16,100	23,000
Roadmaster Series 70, 8-cyl.						
2d Conv	1800	5750	9600	19,200	33,600	48,000
4d Phae	1750	5500	9200	18,400	32,200	46,000
2d 2d Cpe	1050	3350	5600	11,200	19,600	28,000
4d Sed	950	3000	5000	10,000	17,500	25,000
Limited Series 80, 8-cyl.						
4d FBk Phae	1800	5750	9600	19,200	33,600	48,000
4d Phae	1850	5900	9800	19,600	34,300	49,000
4d FBk Sed	1050	3350	5600	11,200	19,600	28,000
4d Sed	1150	3600	6000	12,000	21,000	30,000
4d Fml Sed	1150	3700	6200	12,400	21,700	31,000
4d Fml FBk	1200	3850	6400	12,800	22,400	32,000
Limited Series 90, 8-cyl.						
4d 7P Sed	1150	3700	6200	12,400	21,700	31,000
4d Fml Sed	1200	3850	6400	12,800	22,400	32,000
4d Limo	1200	3850	6400	12,800	22,400	32,000

1941

	6	5	4	3	2	1
Special Series 40-A, 8-cyl.						
2d Conv	1600	5050	8400	16,800	29,400	42,000
2d Bus Cpe	800	2500	4200	8400	14,700	21,000
2d Spt Cpe	850	2650	4400	8800	15,400	22,000
4d Sed	750	2400	4000	8000	14,000	20,000
Special Series 40-B, 8-cyl.						
2d Bus Cpe	850	2750	4600	9200	16,100	23,000
2d S'net	900	2900	4800	9600	16,800	24,000
4d Sed	800	2500	4200	8400	14,700	21,000
4d Sta Wag	1200	3850	6400	12,800	22,400	32,000

NOTE: Add 5 percent for SSE.

	6	5	4	3	2	1
Super Series 50, 8-cyl.						
2d Conv	1750	5650	9400	18,800	32,900	47,000
4d Phae	1900	6100	10,200	20,400	35,700	51,000
2d Cpe	900	2950	4900	9800	17,200	24,500
4d Sed	850	2650	4400	8800	15,400	22,000
Century Series 60, 8-cyl.						
2d Bus Cpe	950	3000	5000	10,000	17,500	25,000
2d S'net	1000	3100	5200	10,400	18,200	26,000
4d Sed	900	2900	4800	9600	16,800	24,000
Roadmaster Series 70, 8-cyl.						
2d Conv	2000	6350	10,600	21,200	37,100	53,000
4d Phae	2050	6600	11,000	22,000	38,500	55,000
2d Cpe	1000	3250	5400	10,800	18,900	27,000
4d Sed	950	3000	5000	10,000	17,500	25,000
Limited Series 90, 8-cyl.						
4d 7P Sed	1300	4100	6800	13,600	23,800	34,000
4d Sed	1050	3350	5600	11,200	19,600	28,000
4d Fml Sed	1150	3700	6200	12,400	21,700	31,000
4d Limo	1300	4100	6800	13,600	23,800	34,000

1942

	6	5	4	3	2	1
Special Series 40-A, 8-cyl.						
2d Bus Cpe	700	2150	3600	7200	12,600	18,000
2d S'net	750	2350	3900	7800	13,700	19,500
2d 3P S'net	700	2200	3700	7400	13,000	18,500
2d Conv	1200	3850	6400	12,800	22,400	32,000
4d Sed	700	2150	3600	7200	12,600	18,000
Special Series 40-B, 8-cyl.						
2d 3P S'net	750	2400	4000	8000	14,000	20,000
2d S'net	800	2500	4200	8400	14,700	21,000
4d Sed	700	2150	3600	7200	12,600	18,000
4d Sta Wag	1150	3700	6200	12,400	21,700	31,000
Super Series 50, 8-cyl.						
2d Conv	1300	4100	6800	13,600	23,800	34,000
2d S'net	850	2650	4400	8800	15,400	22,000
4d Sed	700	2200	3700	7400	13,000	18,500
Century Series 60, 8-cyl.						
2d S'net	850	2750	4600	9200	16,100	23,000
4d Sed	750	2350	3900	7800	13,700	19,500
Roadmaster Series 70, 8-cyl.						
2d Conv	1550	4900	8200	16,400	28,700	41,000
2d S'net	900	2900	4800	9600	16,800	24,000
4d Sed	850	2650	4400	8800	15,400	22,000
Limited Series 90, 8-cyl.						
4d 8P Sed	850	2750	4600	9200	16,100	23,000
4d Sed	850	2650	4400	8800	15,400	22,000
4d Fml Sed	900	2900	4800	9600	16,800	24,000
4d Limo	950	3000	5000	10,000	17,500	25,000

1946-1948

	6	5	4	3	2	1
Special Series 40, 8-cyl.						
2d S'net	750	2400	4000	8000	14,000	20,000
4d Sed	650	2050	3400	6800	11,900	17,000
Super Series 50, 8-cyl.						
2d Conv	1500	4800	8000	16,000	28,000	40,000
2d S'net	800	2500	4200	8400	14,700	21,000
4d Sed	700	2200	3700	7400	13,000	18,500
4d Sta Wag	1200	3850	6400	12,800	22,400	32,000
Roadmaster Series 70, 8-cyl.						
2d Conv	1750	5500	9200	18,400	32,200	46,000
2d S'net	900	2900	4800	9600	16,800	24,000
4d Sed	850	2650	4400	8800	15,400	22,000
4d Sta Wag	1300	4200	7000	14,000	24,500	35,000

1949

	6	5	4	3	2	1
Special Series 40, 8-cyl.						
2d S'net	800	2500	4200	8400	14,700	21,000
4d Sed	700	2150	3600	7200	12,600	18,000
Super Series 50, 8-cyl.						
2d Conv	1450	4700	7800	15,600	27,300	39,000
2d S'net	800	2500	4200	8400	14,700	21,000
4d Sed	750	2400	4000	8000	14,000	20,000
4d Sta Wag	1150	3700	6200	12,400	21,700	31,000
Roadmaster Series 70, 8-cyl.						
2d Conv	1700	5400	9000	18,000	31,500	45,000
2d Riv HT	1150	3600	6000	12,000	21,000	30,000
2d S'net	900	2900	4800	9600	16,800	24,000
4d Sed	850	2750	4600	9200	16,100	23,000
4d Sta Wag	1300	4100	6800	13,600	23,800	34,000

NOTE: Add 10 percent for sweap spear side trim on late 1949 Road master models.

1950

	6	5	4	3	2	1
Special Series 40, 8-cyl., 121 1/2" wb						
2d Bus Cpe	550	1700	2800	5600	9800	14,000
2d S'net	600	1900	3200	6400	11,200	16,000
4d S'net	550	1800	3000	6000	10,500	15,000
4d Tr Sed	550	1700	2800	5600	9800	14,000
Special DeLuxe Series 40, 8-cyl., 121 1/2" wb						
2d S'net	650	2050	3400	6800	11,900	17,000
4d S'net	600	1900	3200	6400	11,200	16,000
4d Tr Sed	550	1800	3000	6000	10,500	15,000
Super Series 50, 8-cyl.						
2d Conv	1100	3500	5800	11,600	20,300	29,000
2d Riv HT	800	2500	4200	8400	14,700	21,000
2d S'net	700	2150	3600	7200	12,600	18,000
4d Sed	600	1900	3200	6400	11,200	16,000
4d Sta Wag	1150	3700	6200	12,400	21,700	31,000
Roadmaster Series 70, 8-cyl.						
2d Conv	1300	4200	7000	14,000	24,500	35,000
2d Riv HT	1050	3350	5600	11,200	19,600	28,000
2d S'net	800	2500	4200	8400	14,700	21,000
4d Sed 71	650	2050	3400	6800	11,900	17,000
4d Sed 72	700	2150	3600	7200	12,600	18,000
4d Sta Wag	1250	3950	6600	13,200	23,100	33,000
4d Riv Sed DeL	700	2150	3600	7200	12,600	18,000

1951-1952

	6	5	4	3	2	1
Special Series 40, 8-cyl., 121 1/2" wb						
2d Bus Cpe (1951 only)	550	1700	2800	5600	9800	14,000
2d Sed (1951 only)	500	1550	2600	5200	9100	13,000
4d Sed	500	1550	2600	5200	9100	13,000
2d Spt Cpe	550	1700	2800	5600	9800	14,000
Special DeLuxe Series 40, 8-cyl., 121 1/2" wb						
4d Sed	550	1700	2800	5600	9800	14,000
2d Sed	550	1700	2800	5600	9800	14,000
2d Riv HT	800	2500	4200	8400	14,700	21,000
2d Conv	1000	3250	5400	10,800	18,900	27,000
Super Series 50, 8-cyl.						
2d Conv	1050	3350	5600	11,200	19,600	28,000
2d Riv HT	900	2900	4800	9600	16,800	24,000
4d Sta Wag	1150	3700	6200	12,400	21,700	31,000
2d S'net (1951 only)	700	2150	3600	7200	12,600	18,000
4d Sed	600	1900	3200	6400	11,200	16,000
Roadmaster Series 70, 8-cyl.						
2d Conv	1150	3600	6000	12,000	21,000	30,000
2d Riv HT	1050	3350	5600	11,200	19,600	28,000
4d Sta Wag	1200	3850	6400	12,800	22,400	32,000
4d Riv Sed	700	2150	3600	7200	12,600	18,000

1953

	6	5	4	3	2	1
Special Series 40, 8-cyl.						
4d Sed	550	1800	3000	6000	10,500	15,000
2d Sed	550	1800	3050	6100	10,600	15,200
2d Riv HT	800	2500	4200	8400	14,700	21,000
2d Conv	1150	3700	6200	12,400	21,700	31,000
Super Series 50, V-8						
2d Riv HT	950	3000	5000	10,000	17,500	25,000
2d Conv	1200	3850	6400	12,800	22,400	32,000
4d Sta Wag	1200	3850	6400	12,800	22,400	32,000
4d Riv Sed	600	1900	3200	6400	11,200	16,000
Roadmaster Series 70, V-8						
2d Riv HT	1100	3500	5800	11,600	20,300	29,000
2d Skylark	2150	6850	11,400	22,800	39,900	57,000
2d Conv	1300	4100	6800	13,600	23,800	34,000
4d DeL Sta Wag	1250	3950	6600	13,200	23,100	33,000
4d Riv Sed	700	2150	3600	7200	12,600	18,000

1954

	6	5	4	3	2	1
Special Series 40, V-8						
4d Sed	500	1550	2600	5200	9100	13,000
2d Sed	500	1550	2600	5200	9100	13,000
2d Riv HT	850	2750	4600	9200	16,100	23,000
2d Conv	1200	3850	6400	12,800	22,400	32,000
4d Sta Wag	550	1800	3000	6000	10,500	15,000
Century Series 60, V-8						
4d DeL	550	1700	2800	5600	9800	14,000
2d Riv HT	1000	3100	5200	10,400	18,200	26,000
2d Conv	1450	4550	7600	15,200	26,600	38,000
4d Sta Wag	600	1900	3200	6400	11,200	16,000
Super Series 50, V-8						
4d Sed	500	1550	2600	5200	9100	13,000
2d Riv HT	900	2900	4800	9600	16,800	24,000
2d Conv	1250	3950	6600	13,200	23,100	33,000
Roadmaster Series 70, V-8						
4d Sed	550	1700	2800	5600	9800	14,000
2d Riv HT	1100	3500	5800	11,600	20,300	29,000
2d Conv	1450	4550	7600	15,200	26,600	38,000
Skylark Series, V-8						
2d Spt Conv	2050	6500	10,800	21,600	37,800	54,000

1955

	6	5	4	3	2	1
Special Series 40, V-8						
4d Sed	500	1550	2600	5200	9100	13,000
4d Riv HT	600	1900	3200	6400	11,200	16,000
2d Sed	500	1550	2600	5200	9100	13,000
2d Riv HT	950	3000	5000	10,000	17,500	25,000
2d Conv	1450	4700	7800	15,600	27,300	39,000
4d Sta Wag	600	1900	3200	6400	11,200	16,000
Century Series 60, V-8						
4d Sed	550	1700	2800	5600	9800	14,000
4d Riv HT	650	2050	3400	6800	11,900	17,000
2d Riv HT	1000	3250	5400	10,800	18,900	27,000
2d Conv	1550	4900	8200	16,400	28,700	41,000
4d Sta Wag	650	2050	3400	6800	11,900	17,000
Super Series 50, V-8						
4d Sed	550	1700	2800	5600	9800	14,000
2d Riv HT	1000	3100	5200	10,400	18,200	26,000
2d Conv	1450	4700	7800	15,600	27,300	39,000
Roadmaster Series 70, V-8						
4d Sed	600	1900	3200	6400	11,200	16,000
2d Riv HT	1100	3500	5800	11,600	20,300	29,000
2d Conv	1650	5300	8800	17,600	30,800	44,000

1956

	6	5	4	3	2	1
Special Series 40, V-8						
4d Sed	500	1550	2600	5200	9100	13,000
4d Riv HT	650	2050	3400	6800	11,900	17,000
2d Sed	500	1550	2600	5200	9100	13,000
2d Riv HT	950	3000	5000	10,000	17,500	25,000
2d Conv	1500	4800	8000	16,000	28,000	40,000
4d Sta Wag	600	1900	3200	6400	11,200	16,000
Century Series 60, V-8						
4d Sed	550	1700	2800	5600	9800	14,000
4d Riv HT	700	2300	3800	7600	13,300	19,000
2d Riv HT	1000	3250	5400	10,800	18,900	27,000
2d Conv	1600	5050	8400	16,800	29,400	42,000
4d Sta Wag	650	2050	3400	6800	11,900	17,000
Super Series 50						
4d Sed	550	1700	2800	5600	9800	14,000
4d Riv HT	800	2500	4200	8400	14,700	21,000
2d Riv HT	1000	3100	5200	10,400	18,200	26,000
2d Conv	1450	4700	7800	15,600	27,300	39,000
Roadmaster Series 70, V-8						
4d Sed	550	1800	3000	6000	10,500	15,000
4d Riv HT	850	2750	4600	9200	16,100	23,000
2d Riv HT	1050	3350	5600	11,200	19,600	28,000
2d Conv	1600	5150	8600	17,200	30,100	43,000

1957

	6	5	4	3	2	1
Special Series 40, V-8						
4d Sed	450	1450	2400	4800	8400	12,000
4d Riv HT	650	2050	3400	6800	11,900	17,000
2d Sed	450	1450	2400	4800	8400	12,000
2d Riv HT	900	2900	4800	9600	16,800	24,000
2d Conv	1400	4450	7400	14,800	25,900	37,000
4d Sta Wag	700	2150	3600	7200	12,600	18,000
4d HT Wag	850	2750	4600	9200	16,100	23,000
Century Series 60, V-8						
4d Sed	500	1550	2600	5200	9100	13,000
4d Riv HT	700	2150	3600	7200	12,600	18,000
2d Riv HT	1000	3250	5400	10,800	18,900	27,000
2d Conv	1450	4700	7800	15,600	27,300	39,000
4d HT Wag	950	3000	5000	10,000	17,500	25,000
Super Series 50, V-8						
4d Riv HT	700	2300	3800	7600	13,300	19,000
2d Riv HT	1000	3250	5400	10,800	18,900	27,000
2d Conv	1450	4550	7600	15,200	26,600	38,000
Roadmaster Series 70, V-8						
4d Riv HT	750	2400	4000	8000	14,000	20,000
2d Riv HT	1100	3500	5800	11,600	20,300	29,000
2d Conv	1500	4800	8000	16,000	28,000	40,000

NOTE: Add 5 percent for 75 Series.

1958

	6	5	4	3	2	1
Special Series 40, V-8						
4d Sed	400	1300	2200	4400	7700	11,000
4d Riv HT	550	1700	2800	5600	9800	14,000
2d Sed	400	1300	2200	4400	7700	11,000
2d Riv HT	750	2400	4000	8000	14,000	20,000
2d Conv	950	3000	5000	10,000	17,500	25,000
4d Sta Wag	450	1450	2400	4800	8400	12,000
4d HT Wag	650	2050	3400	6800	11,900	17,000
Century Series 60, V-8						
4d Sed	450	1450	2400	4800	8400	12,000
4d Riv HT	550	1800	3000	6000	10,500	15,000
2d Riv HT	850	2750	4600	9200	16,100	23,000
2d Conv	1000	3250	5400	10,800	18,900	27,000
4d HT Wag	700	2300	3800	7600	13,300	19,000
Super Series 50, V-8						
4d Riv HT	600	1900	3200	6400	11,200	16,000
2d Riv HT	900	2900	4800	9600	16,800	24,000
Roadmaster Series 75, V-8						
4d Riv HT	650	2050	3400	6800	11,900	17,000
2d Riv HT	950	3000	5000	10,000	17,500	25,000
2d Conv	1150	3700	6200	12,400	21,700	31,000
Limited Series 700, V-8						
4d Riv HT	700	2300	3800	7600	13,300	19,000
2d Riv HT	1050	3350	5600	11,200	19,600	28,000
2d Conv	1600	5050	8400	16,800	29,400	42,000

1959

	6	5	4	3	2	1
LeSabre Series 4400, V-8						
4d Sed	400	1300	2200	4400	7700	11,000
4d HT	500	1550	2600	5200	9100	13,000
2d Sed	400	1350	2250	4500	7800	11,200
2d HT	600	1900	3200	6400	11,200	16,000
2d Conv	950	3000	5000	10,000	17,500	25,000
4d Sta Wag	500	1550	2600	5200	9100	13,000
Invicta Series 4600, V-8						
4d Sed	450	1450	2400	4800	8400	12,000
4d HT	550	1700	2800	5600	9800	14,000
2d HT	650	2050	3400	6800	11,900	17,000
2d Conv	1050	3350	5600	11,200	19,600	28,000
4d Sta Wag	550	1700	2800	5600	9800	14,000
Electra Series 4700, V-8						
4d Sed	500	1550	2600	5200	9100	13,000
4d HT	550	1800	3000	6000	10,500	15,000
2d HT	700	2300	3800	7600	13,300	19,000
Electra 225 Series 4800, V-8						
4d Riv HT 6W	550	1700	2800	5600	9800	14,000
4d HT 4W	550	1800	3000	6000	10,500	15,000
2d Conv	1150	3700	6200	12,400	21,700	31,000

1960

	6	5	4	3	2	1
LeSabre Series 4400, V-8						
4d Sed	400	1300	2200	4400	7700	11,000
4d HT	500	1550	2600	5200	9100	13,000
2d Sed	400	1350	2250	4500	7800	11,200
2d HT	650	2050	3400	6800	11,900	17,000
2d Conv	1000	3100	5200	10,400	18,200	26,000
4d Sta Wag	450	1450	2400	4800	8400	12,000
Invicta Series 4600, V-8						
4d Sed	450	1450	2400	4800	8400	12,000
4d HT	550	1700	2800	5600	9800	14,000
2d HT	700	2150	3600	7200	12,600	18,000
2d Conv	1100	3500	5800	11,600	20,300	29,000
4d Sta Wag	500	1550	2600	5200	9100	13,000
Electra Series 4700, V-8						
4d Riv HT 6W	550	1800	3000	6000	10,500	15,000
4d HT 4W	600	1900	3200	6400	11,200	16,000
2d HT	700	2300	3800	7600	13,300	19,000
Electra 225 Series 4800, V-8						
4d Riv HT 6W	600	1900	3200	6400	11,200	16,000
4d HT 4W	650	2050	3400	6800	11,900	17,000
2d Conv	1150	3700	6200	12,400	21,700	31,000

NOTE: Add 5 percent for bucket seat option.

1961

	6	5	4	3	2	1
Special Series 4000, V-8, 112" wb						
4d Sed	400	1200	2000	4000	7000	10,000
2d Cpe	400	1300	2200	4400	7700	11,000
4d Sta Wag	400	1300	2200	4400	7700	11,000
Special DeLuxe Series 4100, V-8, 112" wb						
4d Sed	400	1250	2100	4200	7400	10,500
2d Skylark Cpe	450	1450	2400	4800	8400	12,000
4d Sta Wag	450	1450	2400	4800	8400	12,000

NOTE: Deduct 5 percent for V-6.

	6	5	4	3	2	1
LeSabre Series 4400, V-8						
4d Sed	400	1300	2200	4400	7700	11,000
4d HT	450	1450	2400	4800	8400	12,000
2d Sed	400	1300	2200	4400	7700	11,000
2d HT	500	1550	2600	5200	9100	13,000
2d Conv	850	2650	4400	8800	15,400	22,000
4d Sta Wag	450	1450	2400	4800	8400	12,000
Invicta Series 4600, V-8						
4d HT	450	1450	2400	4800	8400	12,000
2d HT	550	1700	2800	5600	9800	14,000
2d Conv	900	2900	4800	9600	16,800	24,000
Electra Series 4700, V-8						
4d Sed	450	1400	2300	4600	8100	11,500
4d HT	450	1450	2400	4800	8400	12,000
2d HT	500	1550	2600	5200	9100	13,000
Electra 225 Series 4800, V-8						
4d Riv HT 6W	450	1450	2400	4800	8400	12,000
4d Riv HT 4W	450	1500	2500	5000	8800	12,500
2d Conv	1050	3350	5600	11,200	19,600	28,000

1962

	6	5	4	3	2	1
Special Series 4000, V-6, 112.1" wb						
4d Sed	400	1250	2100	4200	7400	10,600
2d Cpe	450	1400	2300	4600	8100	11,500
2d Conv	650	2050	3400	6800	11,900	17,000
4d Sta Wag	400	1300	2200	4400	7700	11,000
Special DeLuxe Series 4100, V-8, 112.1" wb						
4d Sed	400	1300	2200	4400	7700	11,000
2d Conv	700	2300	3800	7600	13,300	19,000
4d Sta Wag	450	1450	2400	4800	8400	12,000
Special Skylark Series 4300, V-8, 112.1" wb						
2d HT	450	1400	2300	4600	8100	11,500
2d Conv	750	2400	4000	8000	14,000	20,000
LeSabre Series 4400, V-8						
4d Sed	400	1300	2200	4400	7700	11,000
4d HT	450	1450	2400	4800	8400	12,000
2d Sed	400	1300	2200	4400	7700	11,000
2d HT	550	1700	2800	5600	9800	14,000
Invicta Series 4600, V-8						
4d HT	450	1450	2400	4800	8400	12,000
2d HT	550	1800	3000	6000	10,500	15,000
2d HT Wildcat	600	1900	3200	6400	11,200	16,000
2d Conv	900	2900	4800	9600	16,800	24,000
4d Sta Wag*	450	1450	2400	4800	8400	12,000

NOTE: Add 10 percent for bucket seat option where offered.

	6	5	4	3	2	1
Electra 225 Series 4800, V-8						
4d Sed	400	1300	2200	4400	7700	11,000
4d Riv HT 6W	500	1550	2600	5200	9100	13,000
4d HT 4W	550	1700	2800	5600	9800	14,000
2d HT	650	2050	3400	6800	11,900	17,000
2d Conv	1050	3350	5600	11,200	19,600	28,000

1963

	6	5	4	3	2	1
Special Series 4000, V-6, 112" wb						
4d Sed	400	1250	2100	4200	7400	10,600
2d Cpe	400	1300	2150	4300	7500	10,700
2d Conv	550	1800	3000	6000	10,500	15,000
4d Sta Wag	400	1300	2200	4400	7700	11,000
Special DeLuxe Series 4100, V-6, 112" wb						
4d Sed	400	1300	2150	4300	7500	10,700
4d Sta Wag	450	1400	2300	4600	8100	11,500
Special DeLuxe Series 4100, V-8, 112" wb						
4d Sed	400	1300	2150	4300	7600	10,800
4d Sta Wag	450	1400	2350	4700	8300	11,800
Special Skylark Series 4300, V-8, 112" wb						
2d HT	450	1500	2500	5000	8800	12,500
2d Conv	600	1900	3200	6400	11,200	16,000
LeSabre Series 4400, V-8						
4d Sed	400	1300	2150	4300	7500	10,700
4d HT	450	1450	2400	4800	8400	12,000
2d Sed	400	1250	2100	4200	7400	10,500
2d HT	550	1700	2800	5600	9800	14,000
4d Sta Wag	400	1300	2200	4400	7700	11,000
2d Conv	700	2300	3800	7600	13,300	19,000
Invicta Series 4600, V-8						
4d Sta Wag	450	1500	2500	5000	8800	12,500
Wildcat Series 4600, V-8						
4d HT	450	1500	2500	5000	8800	12,500
2d HT	550	1800	3000	6000	10,500	15,000
2d Conv	850	2650	4400	8800	15,400	22,000
Electra 225 Series 4800, V-8						
4d Sed	400	1250	2100	4200	7400	10,500
4d HT 6W	450	1450	2400	4800	8400	12,000
4d HT 4W	450	1500	2500	5000	8800	12,500
2d HT	600	1900	3200	6400	11,200	16,000
2d Conv	900	2900	4800	9600	16,800	24,000
Riviera Series 4700, V-8						
2d HT	700	2150	3600	7200	12,600	18,000

1964

	6	5	4	3	2	1
Special Series 4000, V-6, 115" wb						
4d Sed	450	1080	1800	3600	6300	9000
2d Cpe	950	1100	1850	3700	6450	9200
2d Conv	550	1800	3000	6000	10,500	15,000
4d Sta Wag	450	1140	1900	3800	6650	9500
Special Deluxe Series 4100, V-6, 115" wb						
4d Sed	450	1120	1875	3750	6500	9300
2d Cpe	450	1140	1900	3800	6650	9500
4d Sta Wag	400	1200	2000	4000	7000	10,000
Special Skylark Series 4300, V-6, 115" wb						
4d Sed	450	1140	1900	3800	6650	9500
2d HT	400	1200	2000	4000	7000	10,000
2d Conv	650	2050	3400	6800	11,900	17,000
Special Series 4000, V-8, 115" wb						
4d Sed	450	1140	1900	3800	6650	9500
2d Cpe	450	1150	1900	3850	6700	9600
2d Conv	650	2050	3400	6800	11,900	17,000
4d Sta Wag	400	1200	2050	4100	7100	10,200
Special DeLuxe Series 4100, V-8, 115" wb						
4d Sed	450	1160	1950	3900	6800	9700
2d Cpe	450	1170	1975	3900	6850	9800
4d Sta Wag	400	1250	2100	4200	7400	10,500
Skylark Series 4300, V-8, 115" wb						
4d Sed	400	1200	2000	4000	7000	10,000
2d HT	400	1300	2200	4400	7700	11,000
2d Conv	750	2400	4000	8000	14,000	20,000
Skylark Series 4200, V-8, 120" wb						
4d Spt Wag	400	1200	2000	4000	7000	10,000
4d Cus Spt Wag	400	1200	2050	4100	7100	10,200
LeSabre Series 4400, V-8						
4d Sed	400	1200	2050	4100	7100	10,200
4d HT	400	1250	2100	4200	7400	10,500

	6	5	4	3	2	1
2d HT	550	1700	2800	5600	9800	14,000
2d Conv	750	2400	4000	8000	14,000	20,000
4d Spt Wag	400	1350	2250	4500	7900	11,300
Wildcat Series 4600, V-8						
4d Sed	400	1250	2050	4100	7200	10,300
4d HT	450	1500	2500	5000	8800	12,500
2d HT	600	1900	3200	6400	11,200	16,000
2d Conv	800	2500	4200	8400	14,700	21,000
Electra 225 Series 4800, V-8						
4d Sed	400	1250	2100	4200	7300	10,400
4d HT 6W	450	1400	2300	4600	8100	11,500
4d HT 4W	450	1450	2400	4800	8400	12,000
2d HT	550	1800	3000	6000	10,500	15,000
2d Conv	850	2650	4400	8800	15,400	22,000
Riviera Series 4700, V-8						
2d HT	700	2150	3600	7200	12,600	18,000

1965

	6	5	4	3	2	1
Special, V-6, 115" wb						
4d Sed	350	900	1500	3000	5250	7500
2d Cpe	350	950	1500	3050	5300	7600
2d Conv	550	1700	2800	5600	9800	14,000
4d Sta Wag	350	1020	1700	3400	5950	8500
Special DeLuxe, V-6, 115" wb						
4d Sed	350	1040	1750	3500	6100	8700
4d Sta Wag	450	1050	1800	3600	6200	8900
Skylark, V-6, 115" wb						
4d Sed	450	1080	1800	3600	6300	9000
2d Cpe	450	1120	1875	3750	6500	9300
2d HT	400	1250	2050	4100	7200	10,300
2d Conv	650	2050	3400	6800	11,900	17,000
Special, V-8, 115" wb						
4d Sed	350	1040	1750	3500	6100	8700
2d Cpe	450	1050	1750	3550	6150	8800
2d Conv	700	2150	3600	7200	12,600	18,000
4d Sta Wag	350	1040	1750	3500	6100	8700
Special DeLuxe, V-8, 115" wb						
4d Sed	450	1050	1800	3600	6200	8900
4d Sta Wag	450	1080	1800	3600	6300	9000
Skylark, V-8, 115" wb						
4d Sed	450	1120	1875	3750	6500	9300
2d Cpe	450	1140	1900	3800	6650	9500
2d HT	400	1300	2150	4300	7600	10,800
2d Conv	700	2300	3800	7600	13,300	19,000

NOTE: Add 20 percent for Skylark Gran Sport Series (400 CID/325hp V-8). Deduct 5 percent for V-6.

	6	5	4	3	2	1
Sport Wagon, V-8, 120" wb						
4d 2S Sta Wag	450	1150	1900	3850	6700	9600
4d 3S Sta Wag	450	1160	1950	3900	6800	9700
Custom Sport Wagon, V-8, 120" wb						
4d 2S Sta Wag	450	1170	1975	3900	6850	9800
4d 3S Sta Wag	450	1190	2000	3950	6900	9900
LeSabre, V-8, 123" wb						
4d Sed	350	975	1600	3250	5700	8100
4d HT	350	1000	1650	3350	5800	8300
2d HT	450	1120	1875	3750	6500	9300
LeSabre Custom, V-8, 123" wb						
4d Sed	350	1000	1650	3350	5800	8300
4d HT	450	1050	1800	3600	6200	8900
2d HT	400	1300	2200	4400	7700	11,000
2d Conv	550	1800	3000	6000	10,500	15,000
Wildcat, V-8, 126" wb						
4d Sed	450	1050	1750	3550	6150	8800
4d HT	450	1120	1875	3750	6500	9300
2d HT	500	1550	2600	5200	9100	13,000
Wildcat DeLuxe, V-8, 126" wb						
4d Sed	450	1080	1800	3600	6300	9000
4d HT	450	1140	1900	3800	6650	9500
2d HT	500	1600	2700	5400	9500	13,500
2d Conv	600	1900	3200	6400	11,200	16,000
Wildcat Custom, V-8, 126" wb						
4d HT	450	1170	1975	3900	6850	9800
2d HT	550	1700	2800	5600	9800	14,000
2d Conv	650	2050	3400	6800	11,900	17,000
Electra 225, V-8, 126" wb						
4d Sed	450	1120	1875	3750	6500	9300
4d HT	400	1250	2050	4100	7200	10,300
2d HT	500	1600	2700	5400	9500	13,500
Electra 225 Custom, V-8, 126" wb						
4d Sed	450	1140	1900	3800	6650	9500
4d HT	400	1250	2100	4200	7400	10,600
2d HT	450	1400	2350	4700	8200	11,700
2d Conv	650	2050	3400	6800	11,900	17,000
Riviera, V-8, 117" wb						
2d HT	550	1800	3000	6000	10,500	15,000
2d HT GS	600	1900	3200	6400	11,200	16,000

NOTE: Add 20 percent for 400.

1966

	6	5	4	3	2	1
Special, V-6, 115" wb						
4d Sed	350	840	1400	2800	4900	7000
2d Cpe	350	850	1450	2850	4970	7100
2d Conv	550	1800	3000	6000	10,500	15,000
4d Sta Wag	350	840	1400	2800	4900	7000
Special DeLuxe, V-6, 115" wb						
4d Sed	350	850	1450	2850	4970	7100
2d Cpe	350	860	1450	2900	5050	7200
2d HT	350	1000	1650	3350	5800	8300
4d Sta Wag	350	850	1450	2850	4970	7100
Skylark, V-6, 115" wb						
4d HT	350	880	1500	2950	5180	7400
2d Cpe	350	900	1500	3000	5250	7500
2d HT	450	1050	1750	3550	6150	8800
2d Conv	600	1900	3200	6400	11,200	16,000
Special, V-8, 115" wb						
4d Sed	350	870	1450	2900	5100	7300
2d Cpe	350	880	1500	2950	5180	7400
2d Conv	550	1800	3000	6000	10,500	15,000
4d Sta Wag	350	870	1450	2900	5100	7300
Special DeLuxe, V-8						
4d Sed	350	900	1500	3000	5250	7500
2d Cpe	350	950	1550	3150	5450	7800
2d HT	450	1050	1750	3550	6150	8800
4d Sta Wag	350	900	1500	3000	5250	7500

	6	5	4	3	2	1
Skylark, V-8						
4d HT	350	975	1600	3200	5600	8000
2d Cpe	350	975	1600	3250	5700	8100
2d HT	450	1120	1875	3750	6500	9300
2d Conv	650	2050	3400	6800	11,900	17,000
Skylark Gran Sport, V-8, 115" wb						
2d Cpe	700	2150	3600	7200	12,600	18,000
2d HT	450	1450	2400	4800	8400	12,000
2d Conv	700	2300	3800	7600	13,300	19,000
Sport Wagon, V-8, 120" wb						
4d 2S Sta Wag	350	1020	1700	3400	5900	8400
4d 3S Sta Wag	350	1020	1700	3400	5950	8500
4d 2S Cus Sta Wag	350	1040	1700	3450	6000	8600
4d 3S Cus Sta Wag	450	1050	1750	3550	6150	8800
LeSabre, V-8, 123" wb						
4d Sed	350	870	1450	2900	5100	7300
4d HT	350	1000	1650	3350	5800	8300
2d HT	400	1200	2000	4000	7000	10,000
LeSabre Custom, V-8, 123" wb						
4d Sed	350	950	1550	3100	5400	7700
4d HT	350	1000	1650	3350	5800	8300
2d H p	400	1250	2100	4200	7400	10,500
2d Conv	650	2050	3400	6800	11,900	17,000
Wildcat, V-8, 126" wb						
4d Sed	350	950	1550	3150	5450	7800
4d HT	450	1050	1750	3550	6150	8800
2d HT	400	1300	2200	4400	7700	11,000
2d Conv	700	2150	3600	7200	12,600	18,000
Wildcat Custom, V-8, 126" wb						
4d Sed	350	975	1600	3200	5500	7900
4d HT	350	1000	1650	3300	5750	8200
2d HT	450	1400	2300	4600	8100	11,500
2d Conv	700	2300	3800	7600	13,300	19,000

NOTE: Add 20 percent for Wildcat Gran Sport Series.

	6	5	4	3	2	1
Electra 225, V-8, 126" wb						
4d Sed	450	1050	1750	3550	6150	8800
4d HT	450	1120	1875	3750	6500	9300
2d HT	450	1450	2400	4800	8400	12,000
Electra 225 Custom, V-8						
4d Sed	450	1050	1750	3550	6150	8800
4d HT	450	1170	1975	3900	6850	9800
2d HT	450	1500	2500	5000	8800	12,500
2d Conv	750	2400	4000	8000	14,000	20,000
Riviera, V-8						
2d HT GS	500	1550	2600	5200	9100	13,000
2d HT	450	1450	2400	4800	8400	12,000

NOTE: Add 20 percent for 400. Not available in Riviera.

1967

	6	5	4	3	2	1
Special, V-6, 115" wb						
4d Sed	350	830	1400	2950	4830	6900
2d Cpe	350	840	1400	2800	4900	7000
4d Sta Wag	350	820	1400	2700	4760	6800
Special DeLuxe, V-6, 115" wb						
4d Sed	350	840	1400	2800	4900	7000
2d HT	350	975	1600	3200	5600	8000
Skylark, V-6, 115" wb						
2d Cpe	350	950	1550	3150	5450	7800
Special, V-8, 115" wb						
4d Sed	350	850	1450	2850	4970	7100
2d Cpe	350	900	1500	3000	5250	7500
4d Sta Wag	350	860	1450	2900	5050	7200
Special DeLuxe, V-8, 115" wb						
4d Sed	350	860	1450	2900	5050	7200
2d HT	350	1020	1700	3400	5950	8500
4d Sta Wag	350	870	1450	2900	5100	7300
Skylark, V-8, 115" wb						
4d Sed	350	870	1450	2900	5100	7300
4d HT	350	900	1500	3000	5250	7500
2d Cpe	350	975	1600	3200	5600	8000
2d HT	450	1080	1800	3600	6300	9000
2d Conv	600	1900	3200	6400	11,200	16,000
Sport Wagon, V-8, 120" wb						
4d 2S Sta Wag	350	850	1450	2850	4970	7100
4d 3S Sta Wag	350	860	1450	2900	5050	7200
Gran Sport 340, V-8, 115" wb						
2d HT	450	1450	2400	4800	8400	12,000
Gran Sport 400, V-8, 115" wb						
2d Cpe	400	1200	2000	4000	7000	10,000
2d HT	450	1500	2500	5000	8800	12,500
2d Conv	650	2050	3400	6800	11,900	17,000
LeSabre, V-8, 123" wb						
4d Sed	350	880	1500	2950	5180	7400
4d HT	350	950	1500	3050	5300	7600
2d HT	450	1080	1800	3600	6300	9000
LeSabre Custom, V-8, 123" wb						
4d Sed	350	950	1500	3050	5300	7600
4d HT	350	950	1550	3150	5450	7800
2d HT	450	1140	1900	3800	6650	9500
2d Conv	550	1800	3000	6000	10,500	15,000
Wildcat, V-8, 126" wb						
4d Sed	350	950	1550	3150	5450	7800
4d HT	350	975	1600	3200	5600	8000
2d HT	400	1200	2000	4000	7000	10,000
2d Conv	600	1900	3200	6400	11,200	16,000
Wildcat Custom, V-8, 126" wb						
4d HT	350	950	1550	3150	5450	7800
2d HT	400	1250	2100	4200	7400	10,500
2d Conv	700	2150	3600	7200	12,600	18,000
Electra 225, V-8, 126" wb						
4d Sed	350	950	1550	3100	5400	7700
4d HT	350	975	1600	3200	5500	7900
2d HT	400	1300	2200	4400	7700	11,000
Electra 225 Custom, V-8, 126" wb						
4d Sed	350	975	1600	3250	5700	8100
4d HT	350	1020	1700	3400	5900	8400
2d HT	450	1400	2300	4600	8100	11,500
2d Conv	750	2400	4000	8000	14,000	20,000
Riviera Series, V-8						
2d HT GS	450	1500	2500	5000	8800	12,500
2d HT	450	1450	2400	4800	8400	12,000

NOTE: Add 20 percent for 400. Not available in Riviera.

	6	5	4	3	2	1
1968						
Special DeLuxe, V-6, 116" wb, 2 dr 112" wb						
4d Sed	350	800	1350	2700	4700	6700
2d Sed	350	820	1400	2700	4760	6800
Skylark, V-6, 116" wb, 2 dr 112" wb						
4d Sed	350	820	1400	2700	4760	6800
2d HT	350	900	1500	3000	5250	7500
Special DeLuxe, V-8, 116" wb, 2 dr 112" wb						
4d Sed	350	820	1400	2700	4760	6800
2d Sed	350	830	1400	2950	4830	6900
4d Sta Wag	350	830	1400	2950	4830	6900
Skylark, V-8, 116" wb, 2 dr 112" wb						
4d Sed	350	830	1400	2950	4830	6900
4d HT	350	840	1400	2800	4900	7000
Skylark Custom, V-8, 116" wb, 2 dr 112" wb						
4d Sed	350	840	1400	2800	4900	7000
4d HT	350	870	1450	2900	5100	7300
2d HT	350	975	1600	3200	5600	8000
2d Conv	550	1800	3000	6000	10,500	15,000
Sport Wagon, V-8, 121" wb						
4d 2S Sta Wag	350	870	1450	2900	5100	7300
4d 3S Sta Wag	350	880	1500	2950	5180	7400
Gran Sport GS 350, V-8, 112" wb						
	450	1500	2500	5000	8800	12,500
Gran Sport GS 400, V-8, 112" wb						
2d HT	500	1550	2600	5200	9100	13,000
2d Conv	600	1900	3200	6400	11,200	16,000
NOTE: Add 15 percent for Skylark GS Calif. Spl.						
LeSabre, V-8, 123" wb						
4d Sed	350	870	1450	2900	5100	7300
4d HT	350	950	1500	3050	5300	7600
2d HT	450	1140	1900	3800	6650	9500
LeSabre Custom, V-8, 123" wb						
4d Sed	350	880	1500	2950	5180	7400
4d HT	350	950	1550	3100	5400	7700
2d HT	400	1200	2000	4000	7000	10,000
2d Conv	600	1900	3200	6400	11,200	16,000
Wildcat, V-8, 126" wb						
4d Sed	350	900	1500	3000	5250	7500
4d HT	350	950	1550	3150	5450	7800
2d HT	400	1250	2100	4200	7400	10,500
Wildcat Custom, V-8, 126" wb						
4d HT	350	975	1600	3250	5700	8100
2d HT	400	1300	2200	4400	7700	11,000
2d Conv	700	2150	3600	7200	12,600	18,000
Electra 225, V-8, 126" wb						
4d Sed	350	975	1600	3200	5600	8000
4d HT	350	1020	1700	3400	5900	8400
2d HT	450	1400	2300	4600	8100	11,500
Electra 225 Custom, V-8, 126" wb						
4d Sed	350	975	1600	3250	5700	8100
4d HT	350	1020	1700	3400	5950	8500
2d HT	450	1450	2400	4800	8400	12,000
2d Conv	750	2400	4000	8000	14,000	20,000
Riviera Series, V-8						
2d HT GS	450	1500	2500	5000	8800	12,500
2d HT	450	1450	2400	4800	8400	12,000
NOTE: Add 20 percent for 400. Not available in Riviera.						
1969						
Special DeLuxe, V-6, 116" wb, 2 dr 112" wb						
4d Sed	350	800	1350	2700	4700	6700
2d Sed	350	790	1350	2650	4620	6600
Skylark, V-6, 116" wb, 2 dr 112" wb						
4d Sed	350	820	1400	2700	4760	6800
2d HT	350	840	1400	2800	4900	7000
Special DeLuxe, V-8, 116" wb, 2 dr 112" wb						
4d Sed	350	820	1400	2700	4760	6800
2d Sed	350	800	1350	2700	4700	6700
4d Sta Wag	350	820	1400	2700	4760	6800
Skylark, V-8, 116" wb, 2 dr 112" wb						
4d Sed	350	830	1400	2950	4830	6900
2d HT	350	975	1600	3200	5600	8000
Skylark Custom, V-8, 116" wb, 2 dr 112" wb						
4d Sed	350	840	1400	2800	4900	7000
4d HT	350	850	1450	2850	4970	7100
2d HT	450	1080	1800	3600	6300	9000
2d Conv	550	1700	2800	5600	9800	14,000
Gran Sport GS 350, V-8, 112" wb						
2d Calif GS	450	1450	2400	4800	8400	12,000
2d HT	500	1550	2600	5200	9100	13,000
Gran Sport GS 400, V-8, 112" wb						
2d HT	550	1700	2800	5600	9800	14,000
2d Conv	700	2150	3600	7200	12,600	18,000
NOTE: Add 30 percent for Stage I option.						
Sport Wagon, V-8, 121" wb						
4d 2S Sta Wag	350	850	1450	2850	4970	7100
4d 3S Sta Wag	350	860	1450	2900	5050	7200
LeSabre, V-8, 123.2" wb						
4d Sed	350	860	1450	2900	5050	7200
4d HT	350	870	1450	2900	5100	7300
2d HT	350	1020	1700	3400	5950	8500
LeSabre Custom, V-8, 123.2" wb						
4d Sed	350	870	1450	2900	5100	7300
4d HT	350	880	1500	2950	5180	7400
2d HT	450	1080	1800	3600	6300	9000
2d Conv	550	1700	2800	5600	9800	14,000
Wildcat, V-8, 123.2" wb						
4d Sed	350	900	1500	3000	5250	7500
4d HT	350	950	1550	3100	5400	7700
2d HT	450	1140	1900	3800	6650	9500
Wildcat Custom, V-8, 123.2" wb						
4d HT	350	975	1600	3200	5500	7900
2d HT	400	1200	2000	4000	7000	10,000
2d Conv	550	1800	3000	6000	10,500	15,000
Electra 225, V-8, 126.2" wb						
4d Sed	350	950	1500	3050	5300	7600
4d HT	350	950	1550	3100	5400	7700
2d HT	400	1250	2100	4200	7400	10,500
Electra 225 Custom, V-8, 126.2" wb						
4d Sed	350	950	1550	3150	5450	7800
4d HT	350	975	1600	3250	5700	8100

	6	5	4	3	2	1
2d HT	400	1300	2200	4400	7700	11,000
2d Conv	700	2150	3600	7200	12,600	18,000
Riviera Series, V-8						
2d GS HT	450	1500	2500	5000	8800	12,500
2d HT	450	1450	2400	4800	8400	12,000
NOTE: Add 20 percent for 400. Not available in Riviera.						
1970						
Skylark, V-6, 116" wb, 2 dr 112" wb						
4d Sed	350	820	1400	2700	4760	6800
2d Sed	350	800	1350	2700	4700	6700
Skylark 350, V-6, 116" wb, 2 dr 112" wb						
4d Sed	350	830	1400	2950	4830	6900
2d HT	350	900	1500	3000	5250	7500
Skylark, V-8, 116" wb, 2 dr 112" wb						
4d Sed	350	830	1400	2950	4830	6900
2d Sed	350	820	1400	2700	4760	6800
Skylark 350, V-8, 116" wb, 2 dr 112.2" wb						
4d Sed	350	840	1400	2800	4900	7000
2d HT	350	1020	1700	3400	5950	8500
Skylark Custom, V-8, 116" wb, 2 dr 112" wb						
4d Sed	350	850	1450	2850	4970	7100
4d HT	350	860	1450	2900	5050	7200
2d HT	450	1140	1900	3800	6650	9500
2d Conv	700	2150	3600	7200	12,600	18,000
Gran Sport GS, V-8, 112" wb						
2d HT	500	1550	2600	5200	9100	13,000
Gran Sport GS 455, V-8, 112" wb						
2d HT	550	1700	2800	5600	9800	14,000
2d Conv	700	2300	3800	7600	13,300	19,000
NOTE: Add 40 percent for Stage I 455.						
GSX, V-8, 455, 112" wb						
2d HT	750	2400	4000	8000	14,000	20,000
Sport Wagon, V-8, 116" wb						
2S Sta Wag	350	860	1450	2900	5050	7200
LeSabre, V-8, 124" wb						
4d Sed	350	880	1500	2950	5180	7400
4d HT	350	950	1500	3050	5300	7600
2d HT	450	1080	1800	3600	6300	9000
LeSabre Custom, V-8, 124" wb						
4d Sed	350	900	1500	3000	5250	7500
4d HT	350	950	1550	3100	5400	7700
2d HT	450	1140	1900	3800	6650	9500
2d Conv	550	1700	2800	5600	9800	14,000
LeSabre Custom 455, V-8, 124" wb						
4d Sed	350	950	1550	3100	5400	7700
4d HT	350	975	1600	3200	5600	8000
2d HT	450	1170	1975	3900	6850	9800
Estate Wagon, V-8, 124" wb						
4d 2S Sta Wag	350	900	1500	3000	5250	7500
4d 3S Sta Wag	350	950	1550	3150	5450	7800
Wildcat Custom, V-8, 124" wb						
4d HT	350	975	1600	3200	5500	7900
2d HT	400	1200	2000	4000	7000	10,000
2d Conv	550	1800	3000	6000	10,500	15,000
Electra 225, V-8, 127" wb						
4d Sed	350	950	1550	3150	5450	7800
4d HT	350	1000	1650	3300	5750	8200
2d HT	400	1250	2100	4200	7400	10,500
Electra Custom 225, V-8, 127" wb						
4d Sed	350	975	1600	3200	5500	7900
4d HT	350	1020	1700	3400	5900	8400
2d HT	400	1300	2200	4400	7700	11,000
2d Conv	700	2300	3800	7600	13,300	19,000
Riviera Series, V-8						
2d GS Cpe	450	1450	2400	4800	8400	12,000
2d HT Cpe	450	1400	2300	4600	8100	11,500
NOTE: Add 40 percent for 455, except in Riviera.						
1971-1972						
Skylark, V-8, 116" wb, 2 dr 112" wb						
4d Sed	200	745	1250	2500	4340	6200
2d Sed	200	730	1250	2450	4270	6100
2d HT	350	840	1400	2800	4900	7000
Skylark 350, V-8, 116" wb, 2 dr 112" wb						
4d Sed	350	770	1300	2550	4480	6400
2d HT	350	975	1600	3200	5600	8000
Skylark Custom, V-8						
4d Sed	200	750	1275	2500	4400	6300
4d HT	350	780	1300	2600	4550	6500
2d HT	450	1080	1800	3600	6300	9000
2d Conv	550	1700	2800	5600	9800	14,000
Gran Sport, 350, V-8						
2d HT	500	1550	2600	5200	9100	13,000
2d Conv	700	2150	3600	7200	12,600	18,000
2d HT GSX	750	2400	4000	8000	14,000	20,000
NOTE: Add 40 percent for Stage I & 20 percent for GS-455 options.						
Add 15 percent for folding sun roof.						
Sport Wagon, V-8, 116" wb						
4d 2S Sta Wag	200	650	1100	2150	3780	5400
LeSabre						
4d Sed	200	670	1200	2300	4060	5800
4d HT	200	720	1200	2400	4200	6000
2d HT	200	745	1250	2500	4340	6200
LeSabre Custom, V-8						
4d Sed	200	700	1200	2350	4130	5900
4d HT	200	730	1250	2450	4270	6100
2d HT	350	770	1300	2550	4480	6400
2d Conv	500	1550	2600	5200	9100	13,000
Centurion, V-8						
4d HT	200	750	1275	2500	4400	6300
2d HT	350	790	1350	2650	4620	6600
2d Conv	550	1700	2800	5600	9800	14,000
Estate Wagon, V-8, 124" wb						
4d 2S Sta Wag	200	720	1200	2400	4200	6000
4d 3S Sta Wag	200	730	1250	2450	4270	6100
Electra 225, V-8, 127" wb						
4d HT	350	770	1300	2550	4480	6400
2d HT	350	800	1350	2700	4700	6700
Electra Custom 225, V-8						
4d HT	350	780	1300	2600	4550	6500
2d HT	350	840	1400	2800	4900	7000

	6	5	4	3	2	1
Riviera, V-8						
2d HT GS	350	1020	1700	3400	5950	8500
2d HT	350	900	1500	3000	5250	7500
Wagons						
4d 2S Wag	200	750	1275	2500	4400	6300
4d 4S Wag	350	770	1300	2550	4480	6400

NOTE: Add 40 percent for 455.

1973
	6	5	4	3	2	1
Apollo, 6-cyl., 111" wb						
4d Sed	200	700	1050	2100	3650	5200
2d Sed	200	650	1100	2150	3780	5400
2d HBk	200	670	1150	2250	3920	5600
Apollo, V-8						
4d Sed	200	700	1075	2150	3700	5300
2d Sed	200	660	1100	2200	3850	5500
2d HBk	200	685	1150	2300	3990	5700
Century, V-8, 116" wb, 2 dr 112" wb						
2d Cpe	200	670	1150	2250	3920	5600
4d Sed	200	660	1100	2200	3850	5500
4d 3S Sta Wag	200	650	1100	2150	3780	5400
Century Luxus, V-8						
4d Sed	200	670	1150	2250	3920	5600
2d Cpe	200	685	1150	2300	3990	5700
4d 3S Wag	200	660	1100	2200	3850	5500
Century Regal, V-8						
2d HT	350	780	1300	2600	4550	6500

NOTE: Add 30 percent for Gran Sport pkg. Add 70 percent for GS Stage I, 455 option.

	6	5	4	3	2	1
LeSabre, V-8, 124" wb						
4d Sed	200	700	1050	2050	3600	5100
4d HT	200	700	1050	2100	3650	5200
2d HT	200	660	1100	2200	3850	5500
LeSabre Custom, V-8						
4d Sed	200	685	1150	2300	3990	5700
4d HT	200	670	1200	2300	4060	5800
2d HT	200	750	1275	2500	4400	6300
4d 3S Est Wag	200	685	1150	2300	3990	5700
Centurion, V-8						
4d HT	200	700	1200	2350	4130	5900
2d HT	350	770	1300	2550	4480	6400
2d Conv	400	1250	2100	4200	7400	10,500
Electra 225, V-8, 127" wb						
4d HT	200	720	1200	2400	4200	6000
2d HT	350	800	1350	2700	4700	6700
Electra Custom 225, V-8						
4d HT	200	730	1250	2450	4270	6100
2d HT	350	820	1400	2700	4760	6800
Riviera, V-8						
2d HT GS	350	975	1600	3200	5600	8000
2d HT	350	840	1400	2800	4900	7000

1974
	6	5	4	3	2	1
Apollo, 6-cyl., 111" wb						
4d Sed	200	700	1050	2050	3600	5100
2d Sed	200	700	1050	2050	3600	5100
2d HBk	200	700	1050	2100	3650	5200
Apollo, V-8, 111" wb						
4d Sed	200	745	1250	2500	4340	6200
2d Sed	200	745	1250	2500	4340	6200
2d HBk	200	750	1275	2500	4400	6300
Century, V-8						
2d Cpe	200	670	1150	2250	3920	5600
4d Sed	200	660	1100	2200	3850	5500
4d Sta Wag	200	660	1100	2200	3850	5500
Century Luxus, V-8, 112" wb						
2d HT	200	660	1100	2200	3850	5500
4d HT	200	650	1100	2150	3780	5400
4d Sta Wag	200	650	1100	2150	3780	5400
Gran Sport, V-8						
2d Cpe	200	720	1200	2400	4200	6000
Century Regal, V-8, 112" wb						
2d HT	200	730	1250	2450	4270	6100
4d HT	200	670	1200	2300	4060	5800
LeSabre						
4d Sed	200	685	1150	2300	3990	5700
4d HT	200	670	1200	2300	4060	5800
2d HT	200	700	1200	2350	4130	5900
LeSabre, V-8, 123" wb						
4d Sed	350	790	1350	2650	4620	6600
4d HT	350	800	1350	2700	4700	6700
2d HT	350	830	1400	2950	4830	6900
LeSabre Luxus, V-8, 123" wb						
4d Sed	350	800	1350	2700	4700	6700
4d HT	350	820	1400	2700	4760	6800
2d HT	350	840	1400	2800	4900	7000
2d Conv	400	1200	2000	4000	7000	10,000
Estate Wagon, V-8						
4d Sta Wag	350	820	1400	2700	4760	6800
Electra 225, V-8						
2d HT	350	860	1450	2900	5050	7200
4d HT	350	800	1350	2700	4700	6700
Electra 225 Custom, V-8						
2d HT	350	880	1500	2950	5180	7400
4d HT	350	830	1400	2950	4830	6900
Electra Limited, V-8						
2d HT	350	950	1500	3050	5300	7600
4d HT	350	850	1450	2850	4970	7100
Riviera, V-8						
2d HT	350	900	1500	3000	5250	7500

NOTES: Add 10 percent for Apollo GSX.
  Add 10 percent for Century Grand Sport.
  Add 15 percent for Century GS-455.
  Add 20 percent for GS-455 Stage I.
  Add 5 percent for sunroof.
  Add 15 percent for Riviera GS or Stage I.

1975
	6	5	4	3	2	1
Skyhawk, V-6						
2d 'S'HBk	200	700	1075	2150	3700	5300
2d HBk	200	700	1075	2150	3700	5300
Apollo, V-8						
4d Sed	200	700	1050	2100	3650	5200

	6	5	4	3	2	1
4d 'SR' Sed	200	700	1075	2150	3700	5300
Skylark, V-8						
2d Cpe	200	650	1100	2150	3780	5400
2d HBk	200	660	1100	2200	3850	5500
2d 'SR' Cpe	200	660	1100	2200	3850	5500
2d 'SR' HBk	200	670	1150	2250	3920	5600
Century, V-8						
4d Sed	200	700	1050	2050	3600	5100
2d Cpe	200	700	1050	2050	3600	5100
4d Cus Sed	200	650	1100	2150	3780	5400
2d Cus Cpe	200	660	1100	2200	3850	5500
4d 2S Sta Wag	200	700	1050	2050	3600	5100
4d 3S Sta Wag	200	700	1050	2100	3650	5200
Regal, V-8						
4d Sed	200	700	1075	2150	3700	5300
2d Cpe	200	700	1075	2150	3700	5300
LeSabre, V-8						
4d Sed	200	650	1100	2150	3780	5400
4d HT	200	670	1150	2250	3920	5600
2d Cpe	200	660	1100	2200	3850	5500
LeSabre Custom, V-8						
4d Sed	200	670	1150	2250	3920	5600
4d HT	200	700	1200	2350	4130	5900
2d Cpe	200	700	1200	2350	4130	5900
2d Conv	400	1200	2000	4000	7000	10,000
Estate Wagon, V-8						
4d 2S Sta Wag	200	685	1150	2300	3990	5700
4d 3S Sta Wag	200	700	1200	2350	4130	5900
Electra 225 Custom, V-8						
4d HT	200	720	1200	2400	4200	6000
2d Cpe	200	745	1250	2500	4340	6200
Electra 225 Limited, V-8						
4d HT	200	730	1250	2450	4270	6100
2d Cpe	350	770	1300	2550	4480	6400
Riviera, V-8						
2d HT	350	780	1300	2600	4550	6500

NOTE: Add 15 percent for Park Avenue DeLuxe.
  Add 5 percent for Park Avenue, Century, GS or Riviera GS options.

1976
	6	5	4	3	2	1
Skyhawk, V-6						
2d HBk	150	575	900	1750	3100	4400
Skylark S, V-8						
2d Cpe	150	600	950	1850	3200	4600
Skylark, V-8						
4d Sed	150	600	950	1850	3200	4600
2d Cpe	150	650	950	1900	3300	4700
2d HBk	150	650	975	1950	3350	4800
Skylark SR, V-8						
4d Sed	150	650	950	1900	3300	4700
2d Cpe	150	650	975	1950	3350	4800
2d HBk	200	675	1000	1950	3400	4900
Century Special, V-6						
2d Cpe	150	600	900	1800	3150	4500
Century, V-8						
4d Sed	200	675	1000	2000	3500	5000
2d Cpe	150	650	950	1900	3300	4700
Century Custom, V-8						
4d Sed	200	700	1050	2100	3650	5200
2d Cpe	150	650	975	1950	3350	4800
4d 2S Sta Wag	150	600	950	1850	3200	4600
4d 3S Sta Wag	150	650	950	1900	3300	4700
Regal, V-8						
4d Sed	200	700	1075	2150	3700	5300
2d Cpe	200	675	1000	1950	3400	4900
LeSabre, V-6						
4d Sed	200	650	1100	2150	3780	5400
4d HT	200	675	1000	2000	3500	5000
2d Cpe	200	700	1050	2050	3600	5100
LeSabre Custom, V-8						
4d Sed	200	660	1100	2200	3850	5500
4d HT	200	700	1050	2100	3650	5200
2d Cpe	200	700	1075	2150	3700	5300
Estate, V-8						
4d 2S Sta Wag	200	660	1100	2200	3850	5500
4d 3S Sta Wag	200	670	1150	2250	3920	5600
Electra 225, V-8						
4d HT	200	685	1150	2300	3990	5700
2d Cpe	200	660	1100	2200	3850	5500
Electra 225 Custom, V-8						
4d HT	200	700	1200	2350	4130	5900
2d Cpe	200	685	1150	2300	3990	5700
Riviera, V-8						
2d Spt Cpe	200	720	1200	2400	4200	6000

NOTE: Deduct 5 percent for 6 cylinder.

1977
	6	5	4	3	2	1
Skyhawk, V-6						
2d HBk	100	360	600	1200	2100	3000
Skylark S, V-8						
2d Cpe	125	380	650	1300	2250	3200
Skylark, V-8						
4d Sed	125	380	650	1300	2250	3200
2d Cpe	125	400	675	1350	2300	3300
2d HBk	125	400	700	1375	2400	3400
Skylark SR, V-8						
4d Sed	125	400	675	1350	2300	3300
2d Cpe	125	400	700	1375	2400	3400
2d HBk	125	450	700	1400	2450	3500
Century, V-8						
4d Sed	150	500	800	1600	2800	4000
2d Cpe	150	550	850	1650	2900	4100
Century Special, V-6						
2d Cpe	150	550	850	1675	2950	4200
Century Custom, V-8						
4d Sed	150	550	850	1650	2900	4100
2d Cpe	150	550	850	1675	2950	4200
4d 2S Sta Wag	150	500	800	1550	2700	3900
4d 3S Sta Wag	150	500	800	1600	2800	4000
Regal, V-8						
4d Sed	150	575	875	1700	3000	4300
2d Cpe	150	575	900	1750	3100	4400

	6	5	4	3	2	1
LeSabre, V-8						
4d Sed	150	550	850	1650	2900	4100
2d Cpe	150	550	850	1675	2950	4200
LeSabre Custom, V-8						
4d Sed	150	550	850	1675	2950	4200
2d Cpe	150	575	875	1700	3000	4300
2d Spt Cpe	150	575	900	1750	3100	4400
Electra 225, V-8						
4d Sed	150	575	900	1750	3100	4400
2d Cpe	150	600	900	1800	3150	4500
Electra 225 Limited, V-8						
4d Sed	150	600	950	1850	3200	4600
2d Cpe	150	650	975	1950	3350	4800
Riviera, V-8						
2d Cpe	200	675	1000	1950	3400	4900

NOTE: Deduct 5 percent for V-6.

1978

	6	5	4	3	2	1
Skyhawk						
2d 'S' HBk	125	380	650	1300	2250	3200
2d HBk	125	400	700	1375	2400	3400
Skylark						
2d 'S' Cpe	125	400	675	1350	2300	3300
4d Sed	125	400	700	1375	2400	3400
2d Cpe	125	400	700	1375	2400	3400
2d HBk	125	450	700	1400	2450	3500
Skylark Custom						
4d Sed	125	400	700	1375	2400	3400
2d Cpe	125	450	700	1400	2450	3500
2d HBk	125	450	750	1450	2500	3600
Century Special						
4d Sed	125	450	700	1400	2450	3500
2d Cpe	125	450	750	1450	2500	3600
Sta Wag	125	400	700	1375	2400	3400
Century Custom						
4d Sed	125	450	750	1450	2500	3600
2d Cpe	150	475	750	1475	2600	3700
Sta Wag	125	450	700	1400	2450	3500
Century Sport						
2d Cpe	150	500	800	1550	2700	3900
Century Limited						
4d Sed	150	475	775	1500	2650	3800
2d Cpe	150	500	800	1550	2700	3900
Regal						
2d Cpe	150	475	750	1475	2600	3700
Spt Cpe	150	475	775	1500	2650	3800
Regal Limited						
2d Cpe	150	500	800	1600	2800	4000
LeSabre						
4d Sed	150	475	750	1475	2600	3700
2d Cpe	150	475	775	1500	2650	3800
2d Spt Turbo Cpe	150	550	850	1650	2900	4100
LeSabre Custom						
4d Sed	150	475	775	1500	2650	3800
2d Cpe	150	500	800	1550	2700	3900
Estate Wagon						
4d Sta Wag	150	475	750	1475	2600	3700
Electra 225						
4d Sed	150	500	800	1550	2700	3900
2d Cpe	150	550	850	1675	2950	4200
Electra Limited						
4d Sed	150	500	800	1600	2800	4000
2d Cpe	150	600	900	1800	3150	4500
Electra Park Avenue						
4d Sed	150	550	850	1675	2950	4200
2d Cpe	150	650	975	1950	3350	4800
Riviera						
2d Cpe	200	660	1100	2200	3850	5500

NOTE: Deduct 5 percent for 6 cyl.

1979

	6	5	4	3	2	1
Skyhawk, V-6						
2d HBk	125	450	700	1400	2450	3500
2d 'S' HBk	125	400	700	1375	2400	3400
Skylark 'S', V-8						
2d 'S' Cpe	125	400	675	1350	2300	3300
Skylark, V-8						
4d Sed	125	450	700	1400	2450	3500
2d Cpe	125	450	700	1400	2450	3500
2d HBk	125	450	750	1450	2500	3600
Skylark Custom, V-8						
4d Sed	125	450	750	1450	2500	3600
2d Cpe	125	450	750	1450	2500	3600
Century Special, V-8						
4d Sed	125	450	750	1450	2500	3600
2d Cpe	125	450	700	1400	2450	3500
4d Sta Wag	125	450	750	1450	2500	3600
Century Custom, V-8						
4d Sed	150	475	750	1475	2600	3700
2d Cpe	125	450	750	1450	2500	3600
4d Sta Wag	150	475	750	1475	2600	3700
Century Sport, V-8						
2d Cpe	150	500	800	1600	2800	4000
Century Limited, V-8						
4d Sed	150	500	800	1550	2700	3900

NOTE: Deduct 7 percent for 6-cyl.

	6	5	4	3	2	1
Regal, V-6						
2d Cpe	150	500	800	1550	2700	3900
Regal Sport Turbo, V-6						
2d Cpe	150	575	900	1750	3100	4400
Regal, V-8						
2d Cpe	150	500	800	1600	2800	4000
Regal Limited, V-8 & V-6						
2d Cpe V-6	150	500	800	1550	2700	3900
2d Cpe V-8	150	550	850	1675	2950	4200
LeSabre, V-8						
4d Sed	150	500	800	1550	2700	3900
2d Cpe	150	475	775	1500	2650	3800
LeSabre Limited, V-8						
4d Sed	150	500	800	1600	2800	4000
2d Cpe	150	500	800	1550	2700	3900

NOTE: Deduct 7 percent for V-6.

	6	5	4	3	2	1
LeSabre Sport Turbo, V-6						
2d Cpe	150	600	900	1800	3150	4500
LeSabre Estate Wagon						
4d Sta Wag	150	500	800	1600	2800	4000
Electra 225, V-8						
4d Sed	150	550	850	1650	2900	4100
2d Cpe	150	575	875	1700	3000	4300
Electra Limited, V-8						
4d Sed	150	575	875	1700	3000	4300
2d Cpe	150	600	950	1850	3200	4600
Electra Park Avenue, V-8						
4d Sed	150	600	950	1850	3200	4600
2d Cpe	200	675	1000	1950	3400	4900
Riviera, V-8						
2d 'S' Cpe	350	975	1600	3200	5600	8000

NOTE: Deduct 10 percent for V-6.

1980

	6	5	4	3	2	1
Skyhawk, V-6						
2d HBk S	150	475	750	1475	2600	3700
2d HBk	150	475	775	1500	2650	3800
Skylark, V-6						
4d Sed	150	475	775	1500	2650	3800
2d Cpe	150	500	800	1550	2700	3900
4d Sed Ltd	150	500	800	1550	2700	3900
2d Cpe Ltd	150	500	800	1600	2800	4000
4d Sed Spt	150	550	850	1650	2900	4100
2d Cpe Spt	150	550	850	1675	2950	4200

NOTE: Deduct 10 percent for 4-cyl.

	6	5	4	3	2	1
Century, V-8						
4d Sed	125	450	750	1450	2500	3600
2d Cpe	150	475	775	1500	2650	3800
4d Sta Wag Est	150	475	750	1475	2600	3700
2d Cpe Spt	150	500	800	1550	2700	3900

NOTE: Deduct 12 percent for V-6.

	6	5	4	3	2	1
Regal, V-8						
2d Cpe	150	500	800	1550	2700	3900
2d Cpe Ltd	150	500	800	1600	2800	4000

NOTE: Deduct 12 percent for V-6.

	6	5	4	3	2	1
Regal Turbo, V-6						
2d Cpe	200	660	1100	2200	3850	5500
LeSabre, V-8						
4d Sed	150	550	850	1650	2900	4100
2d Cpe	150	550	850	1675	2950	4200
4d Sed Ltd	150	575	875	1700	3000	4300
2d Cpe Ltd	150	575	900	1750	3100	4400
4d Sta Wag Est	150	575	875	1700	3000	4300
LeSabre Turbo, V-6						
2d Cpe Spt	200	675	1000	1950	3400	4900
Electra, V-8						
4d Sed Ltd	150	600	950	1850	3200	4600
2d Cpe Ltd	150	650	950	1900	3300	4700
4d Sed Park Ave	150	650	950	1900	3300	4700
2d Cpe Park Ave	150	650	975	1950	3350	4800
4d Sta Wag Est	200	675	1000	1950	3400	4900
Riviera S Turbo, V-6						
2d Cpe	200	745	1250	2500	4340	6200
Riviera, V-8						
2d Cpe	350	975	1600	3200	5600	8000

1981

	6	5	4	3	2	1
Skylark, V-6						
4d Sed Spt	150	550	850	1675	2950	4200
2d Cpe Spt	150	575	875	1700	3000	4300

NOTE: Deduct 10 percent for 4-cyl.
   Deduct 5 percent for lesser model.

	6	5	4	3	2	1
Century, V-8						
4d Sed Ltd	150	475	775	1500	2650	3800
4d Sta Wag Est	150	500	800	1550	2700	3900

NOTE: Deduct 12 percent for V-6.
   Deduct 5 percent for lesser model.

	6	5	4	3	2	1
Regal, V-8						
2d Cpe	150	500	800	1550	2700	3900
2d Cpe Ltd	150	500	800	1600	2800	4000

NOTE: Deduct 12 percent for V-6.

	6	5	4	3	2	1
Regal Turbo, V-6						
2d Cpe Spt	200	670	1150	2250	3920	5600
LeSabre, V-8						
4d Sed Ltd	150	575	875	1700	3000	4300
2d Cpe Ltd	150	575	900	1750	3100	4400
4d Sta Wag Est	150	600	900	1800	3150	4500

NOTE: Deduct 12 percent for V-6 except Estate Wag.
   Deduct 5 percent for lesser models.

	6	5	4	3	2	1
Electra, V-8						
4d Sed Ltd	150	575	900	1750	3100	4400
2d Cpe Ltd	150	600	900	1800	3150	4500
4d Sed Park Ave	150	600	950	1850	3200	4600
2d Cpe Park Ave	150	650	950	1900	3300	4700
4d Sta Wag Est	150	650	950	1900	3300	4700

NOTE: Deduct 15 percent for V-6 except Estate Wag.

	6	5	4	3	2	1
Riviera, V-8						
2d Cpe	350	975	1600	3200	5600	8000
Riviera, V-6						
2d Cpe	350	900	1500	3000	5250	7500
2d Cpe Turbo T Type	350	950	1550	3100	5400	7700

1982

	6	5	4	3	2	1
Skyhawk, 4-cyl.						
4d Sed Ltd	150	500	800	1550	2700	3900
2d Cpe Ltd	150	500	800	1600	2800	4000

NOTE: Deduct 5 percent for lesser models.

	6	5	4	3	2	1
Skylark, V-6						
4d Sed Spt	150	575	900	1750	3100	4400
2d Cpe Spt	150	600	900	1800	3150	4500

NOTE: Deduct 10 percent for 4-cyl.
   Deduct 5 percent for lesser models.

	6	5	4	3	2	1
Regal, V-6						
4d Sed	150	575	900	1750	3100	4400
2d Cpe	150	600	900	1800	3150	4500
2d Cpe Turbo	200	660	1100	2200	3850	5500
2d Grand National	850	2650	4400	8800	15,400	22,000
4d Sed Ltd	150	650	950	1900	3300	4700

	6	5	4	3	2	1
2d Cpe Ltd	150	650	975	1950	3350	4800
4d Sta Wag	150	650	975	1950	3350	4800
NOTE: Add 10 percent for T-top option.						
Century, V-6						
4d Sed Ltd	200	675	1000	1950	3400	4900
2d Cpe Ltd	200	675	1000	2000	3500	5000
NOTE: Deduct 10 percent for 4-cyl. Deduct 5 percent for lesser models.						
LeSabre, V-8						
4d Sed Ltd	200	675	1000	1950	3400	4900
2d Cpe Ltd	200	675	1000	2000	3500	5000
4d Sta Wag Est	200	675	1000	2000	3500	5000
NOTE: Deduct 12 percent for V-6 except Estate Wag. Deduct 5 percent for lesser models.						
Electra, V-8						
4d Sed Ltd	200	675	1000	1950	3400	4900
2d Cpe Ltd	200	700	1050	2050	3600	5100
4d Sed Park Ave	200	700	1050	2100	3650	5200
2d Cpe Park Ave	200	650	1100	2150	3780	5400
4d Sta Wag Est	200	650	1100	2150	3780	5400
NOTE: Deduct 15 percent for V-6 except Estate Wag.						
Riviera, V-6						
2d Cpe	350	900	1500	3000	5250	7500
2d Cpe T Type	350	950	1550	3150	5450	7800
2d Conv	650	2050	3400	6800	11,900	17,000
Riviera, V-8						
2d Cpe	350	975	1600	3200	5600	8000
2d Conv	700	2150	3600	7200	12,600	18,000
1983						
Skyhawk, 4-cyl.						
4d Sed Ltd	150	550	850	1675	2950	4200
2d Cpe Ltd	150	575	875	1700	3000	4300
4d Sta Wag Ltd	150	575	875	1700	3000	4300
2d Cpe T Type	200	675	1000	1950	3400	4900
NOTE: Deduct 5 percent for lesser models.						
Skylark, V-6						
4d Sed Ltd	150	550	850	1675	2950	4200
2d Cpe Ltd	150	575	875	1700	3000	4300
2d Cpe T Type	200	700	1050	2050	3600	5100
NOTE: Deduct 10 percent for 4-cyl. except T Type. Deduct 5 percent for lesser models.						
Century, V-6						
4d Sed T Type	200	675	1000	2000	3500	5000
2d Cpe T Type	200	660	1100	2200	3850	5500
NOTE: Deduct 12 percent for 4-cyl. except T Type. Deduct 5 percent for lesser models.						
Regal, V-6						
4d Sed T Type	200	670	1200	2300	4060	5800
2d Cpe T Type	200	745	1250	2500	4340	6200
4d Sta Wag	150	650	950	1900	3300	4700
NOTE: Add 10 percent for T-top option. Deduct 5 percent for lesser models.						
LeSabre, V-8						
4d Sed Ltd	200	700	1050	2100	3650	5200
2d Cpe Ltd	200	700	1075	2150	3700	5300
4d Sta Wag	200	700	1075	2150	3700	5300
NOTE: Deduct 12 percent for V-6 except Estate. Deduct 5 percent for lesser models.						
Electra, V-8						
4d Sed Ltd	200	700	1050	2100	3650	5200
2d Cpe Ltd	200	700	1075	2150	3700	5300
4d Sed Park Ave	200	650	1100	2150	3780	5400
2d Cpe Park Ave	200	660	1100	2200	3850	5500
4d Sta Wag Est	200	660	1100	2200	3850	5500
NOTE: Deduct 15 percent for V-6.						
Riviera, V-6						
2d Cpe	350	900	1500	3000	5250	7500
2d Conv	650	2050	3400	6800	11,900	17,000
2d T Type	350	1020	1700	3400	5950	8500
NOTE: Add 20 percent for XX option.						
Riviera, V-8						
2d Cpe	350	1040	1700	3450	6000	8600
2d Conv	700	2150	3600	7200	12,600	18,000
1984						
Skyhawk Limited, 4-cyl.						
4d Sed	150	575	875	1700	3000	4300
2d Sed	150	575	875	1700	3000	4300
4d Sta Wag	150	575	875	1700	3000	4300
NOTE: Deduct 5 percent for lesser models.						
Skyhawk T Type, 4-cyl.						
2d Sed	200	675	1000	2000	3500	5000
Skylark Limited, V-6						
4d Sed	150	575	900	1750	3100	4400
2d Sed	150	600	900	1800	3150	4500
NOTE: Deduct 5 percent for lesser models. Deduct 8 percent for 4-cyl.						
Skylark T Type, V-6						
2d Sed	200	700	1050	2100	3650	5200
Century Limited, 4-cyl.						
NOTE: Deduct 5 percent for lesser models. Deduct 8 percent for 4-cyl.						
Century Limited, V-6						
4d Sed	150	600	900	1800	3150	4500
2d Sed	150	600	950	1850	3200	4600
4d Sta Wag Est	150	600	950	1850	3200	4600
Century T Type, V-6						
4d Sed	200	700	1050	2050	3600	5100
2d Sed	200	670	1150	2250	3920	5600
Regal, V-6						
4d Sed	150	575	900	1750	3100	4400
2d Sed	150	600	900	1800	3150	4500
2d Grand Natl	550	1700	2800	5600	9800	14,000
Regal Limited, V-6						
4d Sed	150	600	900	1800	3150	4500
2d Sed	150	600	950	1850	3200	4600
Regal T Type, V-6						
2d Sed	200	720	1200	2400	4200	6000

	6	5	4	3	2	1
LeSabre Custom, V-8						
4d Sed	200	700	1050	2100	3650	5200
2d Sed	200	700	1050	2100	3650	5200
LeSabre Limited, V-8						
4d Sed	200	700	1075	2150	3700	5300
2d Sed	200	700	1075	2150	3700	5300
NOTE: Deduct 10 percent for V-6 cyl.						
Electra Limited, V-8						
4d Sed	200	670	1150	2250	3920	5600
2d Sed	200	685	1150	2300	3990	5700
4d Est Wag	200	685	1150	2300	3990	5700
Electra Park Avenue, V-8						
4d Sed	200	670	1150	2250	3920	5600
2d Sed	200	685	1150	2300	3990	5700
NOTE: Deduct 10 percent for V-6 cyl.						
Riviera, V-6						
2d Cpe	350	950	1500	3050	5300	7600
2d Conv	650	2100	3500	7000	12,300	17,500
Riviera, V-8						
2d Cpe	350	975	1600	3200	5600	8000
2d Conv	700	2200	3700	7400	13,000	18,500
Riviera T Type, V-6 Turbo						
2d Cpe	350	975	1600	3200	5500	7900
1985						
Skyhawk, 4-cyl.						
4d Sed Ltd	150	575	900	1750	3100	4400
2d Ltd	150	575	900	1750	3100	4400
4d Sta Wag Ltd	150	575	900	1750	3100	4400
2d T Type	200	700	1050	2050	3600	5100
NOTE: Deduct 5 percent for lesser models.						
Skylark, V-6						
4d Cus Sed	150	575	900	1750	3100	4400
4d Sed Ltd	150	600	900	1800	3150	4500
NOTE: Deduct 10 percent for 4-cyl.						
Century, V-6						
4d Sed Ltd	150	600	950	1850	3200	4600
2d Ltd	150	600	950	1850	3200	4600
4d Sta Wag Est	150	650	975	1950	3350	4800
4d Sed T Type	200	660	1100	2200	3850	5500
2d T Type	200	685	1150	2300	3990	5700
NOTE: Deduct 10 percent for 4-cyl. where available. Deduct 5 percent for lesser models.						
Somerset Regal, V-6						
2d Cus	150	650	950	1900	3300	4700
2d Ltd	150	650	975	1950	3350	4800
NOTE: Deduct 10 percent for 4-cyl.						
Regal, V-6						
2d	150	600	950	1850	3200	4600
2d Ltd	150	650	950	1900	3300	4700
2d T Type	200	720	1200	2400	4200	6000
2d T Type Grand Natl	450	1450	2400	4800	8400	12,000
LeSabre, V-8						
4d Sed Ltd	200	650	1100	2150	3780	5400
2d Ltd	200	650	1100	2150	3780	5400
4d Sta Wag Est	200	685	1150	2300	3990	5700
4d Electra Sta Wag Est	200	670	1200	2300	4060	5800
NOTE: Deduct 20 percent for V-6. Deduct 5 percent for lesser models.						
Electra, V-6						
4d Sed	200	660	1100	2200	3850	5500
2d	200	670	1150	2250	3920	5600
Electra Park Avenue, V-6						
4d Sed	200	670	1150	2250	3920	5600
2d Sed	200	685	1150	2300	3990	5700
Electra T Type, V-6						
4d Sed	200	670	1200	2300	4060	5800
2d	200	700	1200	2350	4130	5900
Riviera T Type, V-6						
2d Turbo	350	975	1600	3200	5500	7900
Riviera, V-8						
2d	350	975	1600	3200	5600	8000
Conv	700	2300	3800	7600	13,300	19,000
NOTE: Deduct 30 percent for diesel where available.						
1986						
Skyhawk, 4-cyl.						
4d Cus Sed	150	575	900	1750	3100	4400
2d Cus Cpe	150	575	875	1700	3000	4300
4d Cus Sta Wag	150	600	900	1800	3150	4500
4d Ltd Sed	150	600	900	1800	3150	4500
2d Cpe Ltd	150	575	900	1750	3100	4400
4d Sta Wag Ltd	150	600	950	1850	3200	4600
2d Spt HBk	150	650	950	1900	3300	4700
2d T-Type HBk	150	650	975	1950	3350	4800
2d T-Type Cpe	150	650	950	1900	3300	4700
Skylark, V-6						
2d Cus Cpe	150	575	900	1750	3100	4400
4d Sed Ltd	150	600	900	1800	3150	4500
Somerset, V-6						
2d Cus Cpe	150	650	975	1950	3350	4800
2d Cpe T Type	200	700	1050	2100	3650	5200
Century Custom						
2d Cpe	200	675	1000	1950	3400	4900
4d Sed	150	650	975	1950	3350	4800
4d Sta Wag	200	675	1000	2000	3500	5000
Century Limited, V-6						
2d Cpe	200	675	1000	2000	3500	5000
4d Sed	200	675	1000	1950	3400	4900
4d Sta Wag	200	700	1050	2050	3600	5100
4d Sed T Type	200	650	1100	2150	3780	5400
Regal, V-6						
2d Cpe, V-8	150	650	950	1900	3300	4700
2d Cpe Ltd, V-8	200	675	1000	1950	3400	4900
2d Cpe T Type	350	975	1600	3200	5600	8000
2d T Type Grand Natl	550	1800	3000	6000	10,500	15,000
LeSabre Custom, V-6						
2d Cpe	200	660	1100	2200	3850	5500
4d Sed	200	650	1100	2150	3780	5400
LeSabre Limited						
2d Cpe Grand Natl	450	1450	2400	4800	8400	12,000

	6	5	4	3	2	1
2d Cpe	200	670	1150	2250	3920	5600
4d Sed	200	660	1100	2200	3850	5500
4d Sta Wag Est, V-8	200	720	1200	2400	4200	6000
Electra, V-6						
2d Cpe	200	670	1150	2250	3920	5600
4d Sed	200	670	1150	2250	3920	5600
Electra Park Avenue, V-6						
2d Cpe	200	685	1150	2300	3990	5700
4d Sed	200	685	1150	2300	3990	5700
4d Sed T Type	200	700	1200	2350	4130	5900
4d Sta Wag Est	200	745	1250	2500	4340	6200
Riviera, V-6						
2d Cpe	350	950	1550	3150	5450	7800
2d Cpe T Type	350	975	1600	3200	5600	8000

NOTES: Add 10 percent for deluxe models.
Deduct 5 percent for smaller engines where available.

1987

	6	5	4	3	2	1
Skyhawk, 4-cyl.						
4d Cus Sed	150	575	900	1750	3100	4400
2d Cus Cpe	150	575	875	1700	3000	4300
4d Cus Sta Wag	150	600	900	1800	3150	4500
4d Sed Ltd	150	600	900	1800	3150	4500
2d Cpe Ltd	150	575	900	1750	3100	4400
4d Sta Wag Ltd	150	600	950	1850	3200	4600
Spt HBk	150	650	950	1900	3300	4700

NOTE: Add 5 percent for Turbo.

	6	5	4	3	2	1
Somerset, 4-cyl.						
2d Cus Cpe	200	675	1000	1950	3400	4900
2d Cpe Ltd	200	675	1000	2000	3500	5000

NOTE: Add 10 percent for V-6.

	6	5	4	3	2	1
Skylark						
4d Cus Sed	150	650	950	1900	3300	4700
4d Sed Ltd	150	650	975	1950	3350	4800

NOTE: Add 10 percent for V-6.

	6	5	4	3	2	1
Century, 4-cyl.						
4d Cus Sed	200	675	1000	1950	3400	4900
2d Cus Cpe	150	650	975	1950	3350	4800
4d Cus Sta Wag	200	675	1000	2000	3500	5000
4d Sed Ltd	200	675	1000	2000	3500	5000
2d Cpe Ltd	200	675	1000	1950	3400	4900
4d Sta Wag Est	200	700	1050	2050	3600	5100

NOTE: Add 10 percent for V-6.

	6	5	4	3	2	1
Regal, V-6						
2d Cpe	200	675	1000	2000	3500	5000
2d Cpe Ltd	200	700	1050	2050	3600	5100
2d Cpe Turbo T	550	1800	3000	6000	10,500	15,000
2d Cpe Turbo T Ltd	600	1900	3200	6400	11,200	16,000
2d Cpe Turbo Grand Natl	750	2400	4000	8000	14,000	20,000
2d Cpe GNX	1250	3950	6600	13,200	23,100	33,000
Regal, V-8						
2d Cpe	200	670	1200	2300	4060	5800
2d Cpe Ltd	200	700	1200	2350	4130	5900
LeSabre, V-6						
4d Sed	200	660	1100	2200	3850	5500
4d Cus Sed	200	670	1150	2250	3920	5600
2d Cus Cpe	200	660	1100	2200	3850	5500
2d Cpe T Type	200	685	1150	2300	3990	5700
LeSabre, V-8						
4d Sta Wag	200	730	1250	2450	4270	6100
Electra, V-6						
4d Sed Ltd	200	670	1200	2300	4060	5800
4d Sed Park Ave	200	720	1200	2400	4200	6000
2d Cpe Park Ave	200	700	1200	2350	4130	5900
4d Sed T Type	200	720	1200	2400	4200	6000
Electra, V-8						
4d Sta Wag Est	200	745	1250	2500	4340	6200
Riviera, V-6						
2d Cpe	350	975	1600	3200	5600	8000
2d Cpe T Type	350	1000	1650	3300	5750	8200

1988

	6	5	4	3	2	1
Skyhawk, 4-cyl.						
4d Sed	150	600	950	1850	3200	4600
2d Cpe	150	600	900	1800	3150	4500
2d Cpe SE	150	650	975	1950	3350	4800
4d Sta Wag	150	650	950	1900	3300	4700
Skylark, 4-cyl.						
4d Cus Sed	150	650	950	1900	3300	4700
2d Cus Cpe	150	650	975	1950	3350	4800
4d Sed Ltd	150	650	975	1950	3350	4800
2d Cpe Ltd	200	675	1000	1950	3400	4900

NOTE: Add 10 percent for V-6.

	6	5	4	3	2	1
Century, 4-cyl.						
4d Cus Sed	150	650	950	1900	3300	4700
2d Cus Cpe	150	650	975	1950	3350	4800
4d Cus Sta Wag	200	675	1000	1950	3400	4900
4d Sed Ltd	150	650	975	1950	3350	4800
2d Cpe Ltd	200	675	1000	1950	3400	4900
4d Sta Wag Ltd	200	675	1000	2000	3500	5000

NOTE: Add 10 percent for V-6.

	6	5	4	3	2	1
Regal, V-6						
2d Cus Cpe	200	720	1200	2400	4200	6000
2d Cpe Ltd	350	780	1300	2600	4550	6500
LeSabre, V-6						
2d Cpe	200	660	1100	2200	3850	5500
4d Cus Sed	200	720	1200	2400	4200	6000
2d Cpe Ltd	200	750	1275	2500	4400	6300
4d Sed Ltd	200	745	1250	2500	4340	6200
2d Cpe T Type	350	770	1300	2550	4480	6400
4d Sta Wag, V-8	350	790	1350	2650	4620	6600
Electra, V-6						
4d Sed Ltd	350	780	1300	2600	4550	6500
4d Sed Park Ave	350	860	1450	2900	5050	7200
4d Sed T Type	350	840	1400	2800	4900	7000
4d Sta Wag, V-8	350	950	1550	3100	5400	7700
Riviera, V-6						
2d Cpe	350	880	1500	2950	5180	7400
2d Cpe T Type	350	1000	1650	3300	5750	8200
Reatta, V-6						
2d Cpe	400	1300	2200	4400	7700	11,000

1989

	6	5	4	3	2	1
Skyhawk, 4-cyl.						
4d Sed	150	650	975	1950	3350	4800
2d Cpe	150	650	950	1900	3300	4700
2d SE Cpe	200	700	1050	2100	3650	5200
4d Sta Wag	200	675	1000	2000	3500	5000
Skylark, 4-cyl.						
2d Cus Cpe	200	675	1000	2000	3500	5000
2d Cpe Ltd	200	700	1050	2100	3650	5200
4d Cus Sed	200	650	1100	2150	3780	5400
4d Sed Ltd	200	670	1150	2250	3920	5600
Skylark, V-6						
2d Cus Cpe	200	700	1050	2050	3600	5100
2d Cpe Ltd	200	700	1075	2150	3700	5300
4d Cus Sed	200	660	1100	2200	3850	5500
4d Sed Ltd	200	685	1150	2300	3990	5700
Century, 4-cyl.						
4d Cus Sed	200	700	1050	2100	3650	5200
4d Sed Ltd	200	650	1100	2150	3780	5400
2d Cus	200	700	1075	2150	3700	5300
4d Cus Sta Wag	200	670	1150	2250	3920	5600
4d Sta Wag Ltd	200	685	1150	2300	3990	5700
Century, V-6						
4d Cus Sed	200	700	1075	2150	3700	5300
4d Sed Ltd	200	660	1100	2200	3850	5500
2d Cus	200	650	1100	2150	3780	5400
4d Cus Sta Wag	200	685	1150	2300	3990	5700
4d Sta Wag Ltd	200	670	1200	2300	4060	5800
Regal, V-6						
2d Cus	350	820	1400	2700	4760	6800
2d Ltd	350	830	1400	2950	4830	6900
LeSabre, V-6						
2d	350	820	1400	2700	4760	6800
2d Ltd	350	830	1400	2950	4830	6900
2d T Type	350	900	1500	3000	5250	7500
4d Cus	350	800	1350	2700	4700	6700
4d Ltd	350	820	1400	2700	4760	6800
4d Sta Wag, V-8	350	860	1450	2900	5050	7200
Electra, V-6						
4d Sed Ltd	350	975	1600	3200	5500	7900
4d Park Ave	450	1050	1800	3600	6200	8900
4d Park Ave Ultra	400	1300	2200	4400	7700	11,000
4d T Type	350	1020	1700	3400	5950	8500
4d Sta Wag, V-8	450	1140	1900	3800	6650	9500
Riviera, V-6						
2d Cpe	450	1080	1800	3600	6300	9000
Reatta, V-6						
2d Cpe	400	1300	2200	4400	7700	11,000

1990

	6	5	4	3	2	1
Skylark, 4-cyl.						
2d Cpe	200	660	1100	2200	3850	5500
4d Sed	200	670	1150	2250	3920	5600
2d Cus Cpe	200	685	1150	2300	3990	5700
4d Cus Sed	200	670	1200	2300	4060	5800
2d Gran Spt Cpe	200	720	1200	2400	4200	6000
4d LE Sed	200	720	1200	2400	4200	6000

NOTE: Add 10 percent for V-6 where available.

	6	5	4	3	2	1
Century, 4-cyl.						
2d Cus	350	780	1300	2600	4550	6500
4d Cus	350	790	1350	2650	4620	6600
4d Cus Sta Wag	350	820	1400	2700	4760	6800
4d Ltd Sed	350	820	1400	2700	4760	6800
4d Ltd Sta Wag	350	840	1400	2800	4900	7000

NOTE: Add 10 percent for V-6 where available.

	6	5	4	3	2	1
Regal, V-6						
2d Cus Cpe	350	900	1500	3000	5250	7500
2d Ltd Cpe	350	975	1600	3200	5600	8000
LeSabre, V-6						
2d Cpe	350	975	1600	3200	5600	8000
4d Cus Sed	350	975	1600	3250	5700	8100
2d Ltd Cpe	350	1020	1700	3400	5950	8500
4d Ltd Sed	350	1040	1700	3450	6000	8600
Estate, V-8						
4d Sta Wag	450	1080	1800	3600	6300	9000
Electra, V-6						
4d Ltd Sed	450	1080	1800	3600	6300	9000
4d Park Ave	450	1140	1900	3800	6650	9500
4d Ultra Sed	450	1450	2400	4800	8400	12,000
4d T Type Sed	450	1140	1900	3800	6650	9500
Riviera, V-6						
2d Cpe	450	1140	1900	3800	6650	9500
Reatta, V-6						
2d Cpe	400	1300	2200	4400	7700	11,000
2d Conv	600	1900	3200	6400	11,200	16,000

1991

	6	5	4	3	2	1
Skylark, 4-cyl.						
2d Cpe	200	675	1000	2000	3500	5000
4d Sed	200	700	1050	2050	3600	5100
2d Cus Cpe	200	700	1050	2050	3600	5100
4d Cus Sed	200	700	1050	2100	3650	5200
2d Gran Spt Cpe	200	660	1100	2200	3850	5500
4d LE Sed	200	670	1150	2250	3920	5600

NOTE: Add 10 percent for V-6 where available.

	6	5	4	3	2	1
Century, 4-cyl.						
4d Spl Sed	200	700	1050	2050	3600	5100
4d Cus Sed	200	700	1050	2100	3650	5200
2d Cus Cpe	200	700	1050	2050	3600	5100
4d Cus Sta Wag	200	650	1100	2150	3780	5400
4d Ltd Sed	200	700	1075	2150	3700	5300
4d Ltd Sta Wag	200	670	1150	2250	3920	5600

NOTE: Add 10 percent for V-6 where available.

	6	5	4	3	2	1
Regal, V-6						
4d Cus Sed	350	770	1300	2550	4480	6400
2d Cus Cpe	200	750	1275	2500	4400	6300
4d Ltd Sed	350	790	1350	2650	4620	6600
2d Ltd Cpe	350	780	1300	2600	4550	6500
LeSabre, V-6						
2d Cpe	350	820	1400	2700	4760	6800
4d Cus Sed	350	830	1400	2950	4830	6900
4d Ltd Sed	350	880	1500	2950	5180	7400
2d Ltd Cpe	350	870	1450	2900	5100	7300

Model	6	5	4	3	2	1
Roadmaster, V-8						
4d Est Sta Wag	450	1140	1900	3800	6650	9500
Park Avenue, V-6						
4d Sed	350	1020	1700	3400	5950	8500
4d Ultra Sed	450	1080	1800	3600	6300	9000
Riviera, V-6						
2d Cpe	450	1140	1900	3800	6650	9500
Reatta, V-6						
2d Cpe	500	1550	2600	5200	9100	13,000
2d Conv	650	2050	3400	6800	11,900	17,000
1992						
Skylark, 4-cyl.						
2d Quad 4 Cpe	200	660	1100	2200	3850	5500
4d Quad 4 Sed	200	660	1100	2200	3850	5500
2d Cpe	200	720	1200	2400	4200	6000
4d Sed	200	720	1200	2400	4200	6000
2d Gran Spt Cpe	350	780	1300	2600	4550	6500
4d Gran Spt Sed	350	780	1300	2600	4550	6500

NOTE: Add 10 percent for V-6 where available.

Model	6	5	4	3	2	1
Century, 4-cyl.						
4d Spl Sed	200	720	1200	2400	4200	6000
4d Cus Sed	200	745	1250	2500	4340	6200

Model	6	5	4	3	2	1
2d Cus Cpe	350	780	1300	2600	4550	6500
4d Sed Ltd	350	840	1400	2800	4900	7000
4d Cus Sta Wag	350	860	1450	2900	5050	7200
4d Ltd Sta Wag	350	900	1500	3000	5250	7500

NOTE: Add 10 percent for V-6 where available.

Model	6	5	4	3	2	1
Regal, V-6						
4d Cus Sed	350	840	1400	2800	4900	7000
2d Cus Cpe	350	840	1400	2800	4900	7000
4d Ltd Sed	350	900	1500	3000	5250	7500
2d Ltd Cpe	350	900	1500	3000	5250	7500
4d Gran Spt Sed	350	975	1600	3200	5600	8000
2d Gran Spt Cpe	350	975	1600	3200	5600	8000
LeSabre, V-6						
4d Cus Sed	350	975	1600	3200	5600	8000
4d Ltd Sed	350	1020	1700	3400	5950	8500
Roadmaster, V-8						
4d Sed	450	1080	1800	3600	6300	9000
4d Ltd Sed	450	1140	1900	3800	6650	9500
4d Est Sta Wag	400	1200	2000	4000	7000	10,000
Park Avenue, V-6						
4d Sed	450	1140	1900	3800	6650	9500
4d Ultra Sed	400	1200	2000	4000	7000	10,000
Riviera, V-6						
2d Cpe	400	1300	2200	4400	7700	11,000

The celebration for the 23-millionth Buick, a Regal, built on March 18, 1981. (L-to-R) Edward DuCharme, Buick's general manufacturing manager; Edna Cunningham, the Regal's new owner; Leland Furse Jr., car assembly plant manager.

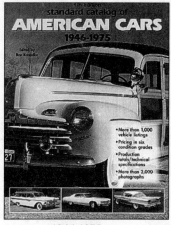
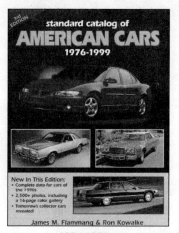

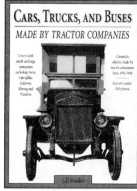

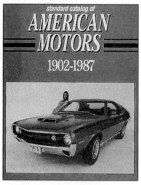
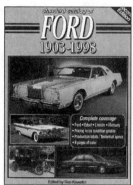
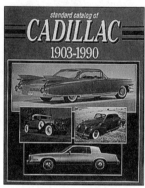
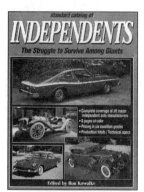
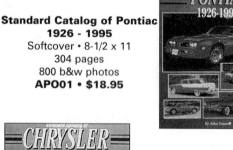

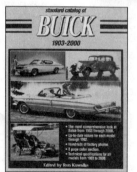
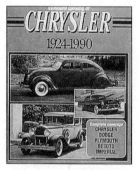
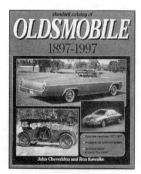